THE
CARAVAN
& CAMPING
GUIDE
2017

AA Lifestyle Guides

Published by AA Publishing, a trading name of AA Media Limited, whose registered office is Fanum House, Basing View, Basingstoke RG21 4EA. Registered number 06112600

49th edition November 2016
© AA Media Limited 2016

Assessments of the AA campsites are based on the experience of the AA Caravan & Camping Inspectors on the occasion(s) of their visit(s) and therefore descriptions given in this guide necessarily contain an element of subjective opinion which may not reflect or dictate a reader's own opinion on another occasion. See pages 10-11 for a clear explanation of how, based on our Inspectors' inspection experiences, campsites are graded.

AA Media Limited strives to ensure accuracy of the information in this guide at the time of printing. Nevertheless, the Publisher cannot be held responsible for any errors or omissions, or for changes in the details given in this guide, or for the consequences of any reliance on the information provided by the same. This does not affect your statutory rights. Due to the constantly evolving nature of the subject matter the information is subject to change. AA Media Limited gratefully receives advice from readers regarding any necessary update.

Please contact:
Advertising Sales Department: advertisingsales@theAA.com
Editorial Department: lifestyleguides@theAA.com

Photographs in the gazetteer are provided by the establishments.

Typeset/Repro by Servis Filmsetting Ltd, Stockport
Printed and bound by Printer Trento SRL, Trento

Directory compiled by the AA Lifestyle Guides Department and managed in the Librios Information Management System.

Country and county opening pages: Nick Channer

Campsite Cooking feature: by courtesy and under the copyright of The Camping and Caravanning Club.

Maps prepared by the Mapping Services Department of AA Publishing.

Maps © AA Media Limited 2016

Contains Ordnance Survey data © Crown copyright and database right 2016

Information on National Parks in England provided by the Countryside Agency (Natural England).

Information on National Parks in Scotland provided by Scottish Natural Heritage.

Information on National Parks in Wales provided by The Countryside Council for Wales.

A CIP catalogue for this book is available from the British Library.

ISBN: 978-0-7495-7832-9

A05443

Contents

Welcome to the AA Caravan & Camping Guide 2017

Welcome to the 49th edition of the AA's bestselling Caravan & Camping Guide featuring over 830 fully inspected and independently graded camping parks across England, Scotland, Wales, Northern Ireland and the Republic of Ireland.

Who's in the guide?

Within these pages you'll find simple rural campsites, beautifully landscaped parks with top quality toilet facilities and excellent customer care, and self-contained Holiday Centres that offer a wide range of sport, leisure and entertainment facilities. We also include Holiday Home Parks offering holiday caravans, chalets and lodges for hire and glamping sites with different types of 'outdoor' accommodation. The sites pay an annual fee for the inspection, recognition and rating.

AA Pennant classification

Campsites apply for AA recognition and they receive an unannounced visit each year by one of the AA's qualified Campsite inspectors. Touring pitches, facilities and hospitality are fully checked and campsites are graded from 1 to 5 Pennants, or rated as a Holiday Centre or Holiday Home Park, using fixed criteria for each Pennant rating. A qualitative assessment score is also given to each campsite. Gold Pennants identify the top quality parks that score 90% and above within the 2 to 5 Pennant ratings and Green Pennants signify glamping-only sites.

AA Campsites of the Year

Following nominations by our inspectors we award an overall winner from three national finalists; five regional winners and a Holiday Centre winner – all are selected for their outstanding overall quality and high levels of customer care. Our two special awards recognise the best small campsite, and the most improved campsite.

Vale of Pickering Caravan Park, Allerston, North Yorkshire is the worthy overall winner for 2017 (see page 14 for details). We have introduced a new award for 2017 – AA Glamping Site of the Year. The first winner of this award is Durrell Wildlife Camp, Trinty, Jersey (see page 19).

An in-depth look

This year we're including a story by one of our campsite inspectors, Mike Ellis, who took on the task of refurbishing an old Autosleeper Rhapsody and giving it a 21st-century makeover. Rosie, as the vehicle became known, now takes Mike to campsites for his AA work and also provides many happy holidays for himself, his wife, Heather and their dog.

In our second feature, Ali Ray, freelance food and travel writer, offers some handy hints and ideas on campsite cooking and how to get the best results from the ingredients you have at hand. There are also useful checklists that she has found invaluable over the years.

The best sites for...

Our quick reference list (pages 34-35) details the AA inspectors' favourite campsites for stunning views, waterside pitches, on-site fishing, great places to stay with your children, good restaurants on site, those that are eco-friendly and even where the toilets are really top-notch.

How to use the AA Caravan & Camping Guide

1.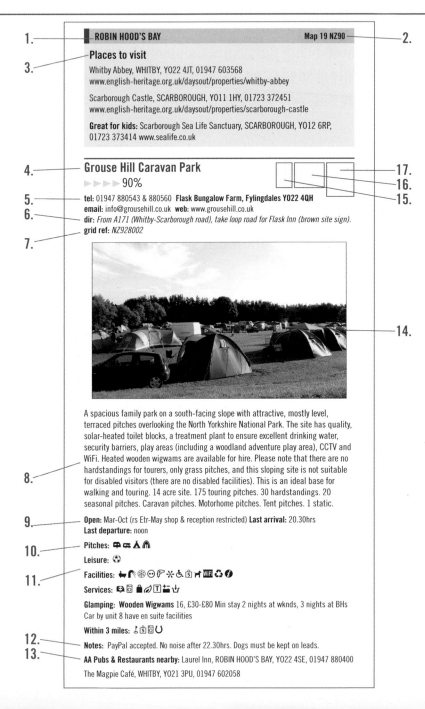

ROBIN HOOD'S BAY   Map 19 NZ90

Places to visit

Whitby Abbey, WHITBY, YO22 4JT, 01947 603568
www.english-heritage.org.uk/daysout/properties/whitby-abbey

Scarborough Castle, SCARBOROUGH, YO11 1HY, 01723 372451
www.english-heritage.org.uk/daysout/properties/scarborough-castle

Great for kids: Scarborough Sea Life Sanctuary, SCARBOROUGH, YO12 6RP, 01723 373414 www.sealife.co.uk

Grouse Hill Caravan Park
▶ ▶ ▶ ▶ 90%

tel: 01947 880543 & 880560 **Flask Bungalow Farm, Fylingdales YO22 4QH**
email: info@grousehill.co.uk **web:** www.grousehill.co.uk
dir: *From A171 (Whitby-Scarborough road), take loop road for Flask Inn (brown site sign).*
grid ref: *NZ928002*

A spacious family park on a south-facing slope with attractive, mostly level, terraced pitches overlooking the North Yorkshire National Park. The site has quality, solar-heated toilet blocks, a treatment plant to ensure excellent drinking water, security barriers, play areas (including a woodland adventure play area), CCTV and WiFi. Heated wooden wigwams are available for hire. Please note that there are no hardstandings for tourers, only grass pitches, and this sloping site is not suitable for disabled visitors (there are no disabled facilities). This is an ideal base for walking and touring. 14 acre site. 175 touring pitches. 30 hardstandings. 20 seasonal pitches. Caravan pitches. Motorhome pitches. Tent pitches. 1 static.

Open: Mar-Oct (rs Etr-May shop & reception restricted) **Last arrival:** 20.30hrs
Last departure: noon
Pitches: 🚐 🚗 ⛺ 🏕
Leisure: ⚽
Facilities: 🚿📻❄️☺️🅿️🍴✂️♿️🛒🔧📶♻️ℹ️
Services: 🔌🚽🛢️🧹Ⓣ🚰🚮
Glamping: **Wooden Wigwams** 16, £30-£80 Min stay 2 nights at wknds, 3 nights at BHs Car by unit 8 have en suite facilities
Within 3 miles: 🎣⛳🛒🎡↺
Notes: PayPal accepted. No noise after 22.30hrs. Dogs must be kept on leads.
AA Pubs & Restaurants nearby: Laurel Inn, ROBIN HOOD'S BAY, YO22 4SE, 01947 880400
The Magpie Café, WHITBY, YO21 3PU, 01947 602058

1.
2.
3.
4.
5.
6.
7.
8.
9.
10.
11.
12.
13.
14.
15.
16.
17.

1. Location
Place names are listed alphabetically within each county.

2. Map reference
Each site is given a map reference for use in conjunction with the atlas section at the back of the guide. The map reference comprises the guide map page number, the National Grid location square and a two-figure map location reference.
For example: **Map 19 NZ90**.
19 refers to the page number of the map section at the back of the guide.
NZ is the National Grid lettered square (representing 100,000sq metres) in which the location will be found.
9 is the figure reading across the top or bottom of the map page.
0 is the figure reading down each side of the map page.

3. Places to visit
Suggestions of nearby places to visit for adults and children.

4. Site name and rating
▶ Campsites are listed in descending order of their Pennant rating. Sites are rated from 1 to 5 Pennants and are also awarded a score ranging from 50–100% according to how they compare with other parks within the same Pennant rating. Some sites are given a HOLIDAY CENTRE grading. For a fuller explanation see pages 10-11.
RV indicates a category of park catering only for recreational vehicles (no toilet facilities are provided at these sites).

Where the name of the site appears in italic type, the information that follows has not been confirmed by the campsite for the 2017 edition.

NEW indicates that the site is new in the guide this year.

5. Contact details

6. Directions
Brief directions from a recognisable point, such as a main road, are included in each entry. Please contact the individual site for more detailed directions or use the AA Route Planner at **theAA.com**, and enter the site's postcode.

7. Grid reference
Each entry includes a six-figure National Grid reference as many sites are in remote locations. Use the reference alongside the relevant Ordnance Survey map and in conjunction with the atlas at the back of this guide to help you find the precise location.

8. Description
Descriptions are based on information supplied by the AA inspector at the time of the last visit.
Please note: The AA Pennant classification is based on the touring pitches and the facilities only. AA inspectors do not visit or report on statics or chalets for hire under the AA Caravan & Camping quality standards scheme. However, the AA has a category of HOLIDAY HOME PARK and these static caravan, chalet or lodge-only parks are inspected.
For sites other than those listed as HOLIDAY HOME PARK we only include the number of static caravan pitches in order to give an indication of the nature and size of the site.

9. Opening, arrival and departure times
Parks are not necessarily open all year and while most sites permit arrivals at any time, checking beforehand is advised (see page 12).

10. Pitches
Rates given after each appropriate symbol ⌖ (caravan), ⌗ (motorhome), Å (tent) are the overnight cost for one unit. The prices can vary according to the number of people in the party, but some parks have a fixed fee per pitch regardless of the number of people. Please note that some sites charge separately for certain facilities, including showers; and some sites charge a different rate for pitches with or without electricity. Prices are supplied to us in good faith by the site operators and are as accurate as possible. They are, however, only a guide and are subject to change during the currency of this publication. ⋒ indicates that the campsite offers one or more types of glamping accommodation (see point 15). * If this symbol appears before the prices, it indicates that the site has not advised us of the prices for 2017; they relate to 2016.

11. Symbols and abbreviations
These are divided into Pitches, Leisure, Facilities, Services and Within 3 miles sections. A guide to abbreviations and symbols can be found on page 9 and on pages throughout the guide.

12. Notes
This includes information about additional facilities and any restrictions the site would like their visitors to be aware of. (☻) As most sites now accept credit and debit cards, we have only indicated those that don't accept cards.

13. AA pubs and restaurants
An entry may include suggestions for nearby pubs and/or restaurants recognised by the AA. Some of these establishments will have been awarded AA Rosettes for food excellence. To find out the distance by road between the campsite and the pub or restaurant, enter both postcodes into a Sat Nav or the AA Route Planner at **theAA.com**.

14. Photograph
Optional photograph/s supplied by the campsite.

15. Glamping
⋒ The campsite offers one or more types of 'glamorous camping' accommodation, i.e. wooden pods, tipis, yurts, bell tents, safari tents, shepherd's huts, Airstream caravans, vintage caravans etc.

16. Best of British
 A group of over 50 parks, both large and small, which focus on high quality facilities and amenities. www.bob.org.uk

17. David Bellamy Awards
Many AA recognised sites are also recipients of a David Bellamy Award for Conservation. The awards are graded Gold, Silver and Bronze. The symbols we show indicate the 2015/16 winners as this was the most up-to-date information at the time of going to press. For the 2016/17 winners please see www.bellamyparks.co.uk

Facilities for disabled guests
The Equality Act 2010 provides legal rights for disabled people including access to goods, services and facilities, and means that service providers may have to consider making adjustments to their premises. For more information about the Act see: www.gov.uk/definition-of-disability-under-equality-act-2010

If a site has told us that they provide facilities for disabled visitors their entry in the guide will include the following symbol: ♿. The sites in this guide should be aware of their responsibilities under the Act. However, we recommend that you always phone in advance to ensure the site you have chosen has facilities to suit your needs.

Haven touring +camping

Look forward to days away

Save up to
50%*
on 2017 holidays

Find your perfect coastal escape with Haven

- 22 UK touring and camping holiday parks dotted around the coast
- Choice of 6 pitch types – from basic grass to fully serviced hard-standing
- Modern shower blocks and amenities
- Pets welcome for only £1† a night
- Splash around in our heated pools - some with flumes and slides

- Be adventurous - try out our many activities from Aerial Adventure to learning archery and fencing skills
- Family friendly entertainment and fun packed kids' clubs
- There's plenty of tasty food and drink on the menu at all our parks
- Most of our parks are right beside the sea - so don't forget your buckets and spades

To find out more, order a brochure and to book
haventouring.com/toaa

Alternatively, give us a call on **0333 202 1658** Quoting: **TO_AA**

Calls to 0333 numbers are charged at standard UK rates and will be included in any inclusive minute bundles.

Symbols and abbreviations

Pitches

Caravan

Motorhome

Tent

Glamping accommodation

Leisure

Indoor swimming pool

Outdoor swimming pool

Tennis court

Games room

Children's playground

Kid's club

Stables & horse riding

Golf course (on site or within 3 miles)

Boat hire

Cycle hire

Cinema

Entertainment

Fishing

Mini golf

Watersports

Gym

Sports field

Pitch n putt

Facilities

Bath

Shower

Private washing cubicles

Electric shaver

Hairdryer

Ice packs

Disabled facilities

Shop on site or within 200yds

Mobile shop (calling at least 5 days per week)

BBQ area

Picnic area

WiFi access

Internet access

Recycling facilities

Tourist information

Dog exercise area

Car hire can be arranged

Services

Toilet fluid

Café or restaurant

Fast food/Takeaway

Baby care

Electric hook up

Motorvan service point

Launderette

Licensed bar

Calor Gas

Camping Gaz

Battery charging

Other

No dogs

No credit or debit cards

Abbreviations

BH/BHs   Bank Holiday/s

Etr   Easter

Spring BH
   Spring Bank Holiday (late May)

fr   from

hrs   hours

m   mile

mdnt   midnight

rdbt   roundabout

rs   restricted service

RV   Recreational vehicles

U   rating not confirmed

wk   week

wknd   weekend

The AA classification scheme

AA parks are classified on a 5-point scale according to their style and the range of facilities they offer. As the number of Pennants increases, so the quality and variety of facilities is generally greater.

What can you expect at an AA-rated park?

All AA parks must meet a minimum standard: they should be clean, well maintained and welcoming. In addition they must have a local authority site licence (unless specially exempt), and satisfy local authority fire regulations.

The AA inspection

Each campsite that applies for AA recognition receives an unannounced visit each year by one of the AA's highly qualified team of inspectors. They make a thorough check of the site's touring pitches, facilities and hospitality. The sites pay an annual fee for the inspection, recognition and rating, and receive a text entry in the *AA Caravan & Camping Guide*.

   AA inspectors pay when they stay overnight on a site. The criteria used by the inspectors in awarding the AA Pennant rating is shown on this and the opposite page.

AA Quality percentage score

AA rated Campsites, Caravan Parks, Holiday Centres Holiday Home Parks and Glamping sites are awarded a percentage score alongside their Pennant rating, Holiday Centre or Holiday Home Park status. This is a qualitative assessment of various factors including customer care and hospitality, toilet facilities and park landscaping. The % score runs from 50% to 100% and indicates the relative quality of parks with the same number of Pennants. For example, one 3-Pennant park may score 70%, while another 3-Pennant park may achieve 90%.
Holiday Centres and Holiday Home Parks also receive a percentage score between 50% and 100% to differentiate between quality levels within this grading. Like the Pennant rating, the percentage is reassessed annually.

The Pennant Criteria

AA One Pennant Parks

These parks offer a fairly simple standard of facilities including:
- No more than 30 pitches per acre
- At least 5% of the total pitches allocated to touring caravans
- An adequate drinking water supply and reasonable drainage
- Washroom with flush toilets and toilet paper provided, unless no sanitary facilities are provided in which case this should be clearly stated
- Chemical disposal arrangements, ideally with running water, unless tents only
- Adequate refuse disposal that is clearly signed
- Well-drained ground and some level pitches
- Entrance and access roads of adequate width and surface
- Location of emergency phone clearly signed
- Emergency phone numbers fully displayed

AA Two Pennant Parks

Parks in this category should meet all of the above requirements, but offer an increased level of facilities, services, customer care, security and ground maintenance. They should include the following:
- Separate washrooms, including at least two male and two female WCs and washbasins per 30 pitches
- Hot and cold water direct to each basin
- Externally lit toilet blocks
- Warden available during day, times to be indicated
- Whereabouts of shop/chemist is clearly signed
- Dish-washing facilities, covered and lit
- Basic security (i.e. lockable gate and/or CCTV)
- Reception area

AA Three Pennant Parks

Many parks come within this rating and the range of facilities is wide. All parks will be of a very good standard and will meet the following minimum criteria:
- Facilities, services and park grounds are clean and well maintained, with buildings in good repair and attention paid to customer care and park security
- Evenly surfaced roads and paths

- Clean modern toilet blocks with all-night lighting and containing toilet seats in good condition, soap and hand dryers or paper towels, mirrors, shelves and hooks, shaver and hairdryer points, and lidded waste bins in female toilets
- Modern shower cubicles with sufficient hot water and attached, private changing space
- Electric hook-ups
- Some hardstanding/wheel runs/firm, level ground
- Laundry with automatic washing and drying facilities, separate from toilets
- Children's playground with safe equipment
- 24-hour public phone on site or nearby where mobile reception is poor
- Warden availability and 24-hour contact number clearly signed

AA Four Pennant Parks

These parks have achieved an excellent standard in all areas, including landscaping of grounds, natural screening and attractive park buildings, and customer care and park security. Toilets are smart, modern and immaculately maintained, and generally offer the following facilities:

- Spacious vanitory-style washbasins, at least two male and two female per 25 pitches
- Fully-tiled shower cubicles with doors, dry areas, shelves and hooks, at least one male and one female per 30 pitches
- Availability of washbasins in lockable cubicles, or combined toilet/washing cubicles, or a private/family room with shower/toilet/washbasin

Other requirements are:
- Baby changing facilities
- A shop on site, or within reasonable distance
- Warden available 24 hours
- Reception area open during the day, with tourist information available
- Internal roads, paths and toilet blocks lit at night
- Maximum 25 pitches per campable acre
- Toilet blocks heated October to Easter
- Approximately 50% of pitches with electric hook-ups
- Approximately 10% of pitches have hardstandings
- Late arrivals enclosure
- Security barrier and/or CCTV

AA Five Pennant Premier Parks

Premier parks are of an extremely high standard, set in attractive surroundings with superb mature landscaping. Facilities, security and customer care are of an exceptional quality. As well as the above they will also offer:
- First-class toilet facilities including several designated self-contained cubicles, ideally with WC, washbasin and shower

- Ideally electric hook-ups to 75% of pitches
- Approximately 20% of pitches have hardstandings
- Some fully-serviced 'super' pitches: of larger size, with water and electricity supplies connected
- A motorhome service point
- Toilet block/s should be heated
- Excellent security – coded barrier or number plate recognition and CCTV

Many Premier Parks will also provide:
- Heated swimming pool
- Well-equipped shop
- Café or restaurant and bar
- A designated walking area for dogs (if accepted)

Gold Pennants ▶ ▶ ▶ ▶ ▶

AA Gold Pennants are awarded to the very best camping parks scoring 90% and above within the 2, 3, 4 and 5 Pennant ratings.

Green Pennants ▶ ▶ ▶ ▶ ▶

AA Green Pennants (3, 4 and 5 Pennants) are awarded to sites that specialise in glamping-style accommodation.

Holiday Centres and Holiday Home Parks

There are separate categories for Holiday Centres and Holiday Home Parks. The AA inspects these sites and awards an appropriate quality percentage score.

HOLIDAY CENTRES

In this category we distinguish parks that cater for all holiday needs including cooked meals and entertainment. They provide:
- A wide range of on-site sports, leisure and recreational facilities
- Supervision and security at a very high level
- A choice of eating outlets
- Facilities for touring caravans that equal those available to rented holiday accommodation
- A maximum density of 25 pitches per acre
- Clubhouse with entertainment
- Laundry with automatic washing machines

HOLIDAY HOME PARKS

Parks in this category are static – only parks offering holiday caravans, chalets or lodges for hire and catering for all holiday needs. They provide:
- Quality holiday hire caravans and chalets or luxurious lodges
- A wide range of on-site sports, leisure and recreational facilities
- Supervision and security at a very high level
- A choice of eating outlets
- Clubhouse with entertainment

Useful information

Booking information

It is advisable to book in advance during peak holiday seasons and in school or public holidays. It is also wise to check whether or not a reservation entitles you to a particular pitch. It does not necessarily follow that an early booking will secure the best pitch; you may simply have the choice of what is available at the time you check in.

Some parks may require a deposit on booking which may be non-returnable if you have to cancel your holiday. If you do have to cancel, notify the proprietor at once because you may be held legally responsible for partial or full payment unless the pitch can be re-let. Consider taking out insurance such as AA Travel Insurance, tel: 0800 912 5002 or visit theAA.com for details to cover a lost deposit or compensation. Some parks will not accept overnight bookings unless payment for the full minimum period (e.g. two or three days) is made.

Last arrival Unless otherwise stated, parks will usually accept arrivals at any time of the day or night, but some have a special 'late arrivals' enclosure where you have to make temporary camp to avoid disturbing other people on the park. Please note that on some parks access to the toilet block is by key or pass card only, so if you know you will be late, do check what arrangements can be made.

Last departure Most parks will specify their overnight period e.g. noon to noon. If you overstay the departure time you can be charged for an extra day.

Chemical closet disposal point

You will usually find one on every park, except those catering only for tents. It must be a specially constructed unit, or a WC permanently set aside for the purpose of chemical disposal and with adjacent rinsing and soak-away facilities. However, some local authorities are concerned about the effect of chemicals on bacteria in cesspools etc, and may prohibit or restrict provision of chemical closet disposal points in their areas.

Complaints

If you have any complaints speak to the park proprietor or supervisor immediately, so that the matter can be sorted out on the spot. If this personal approach fails you may decide, if the matter is serious, to approach the local authority or tourist board. AA guide users may also write to:

The Editor, AA Caravan & Camping Guide,
AA Lifestyle Guides, 8th floor, Fanum House,
Basing View, Basingstoke, RG21 4EA

The AA may at its sole discretion investigate any complaints received from guide users for the purpose of making any necessary amendments to the guide. The AA will not in any circumstances act as representative or negotiator or undertake to obtain compensation or enter into further correspondence or deal with the matter in any other way whatsoever. The AA will not guarantee to take any specific action.

Dogs

Dogs may or may not be accepted at parks; this is entirely at the owner's or warden's discretion (assistance dogs should be accepted). Even when the park states that they accept dogs, it is still discretionary, and certain breeds may not be considered as suitable, so we strongly advise that you check when you book. Some sites have told us they do not accept dangerous breeds. (The following breeds are covered under the Dangerous Dogs Act 1991 – Pit Bull Terrier, Japanese Tosa, Dogo Argentino and Fila Brazilerio). Dogs should always be kept on a lead and under control, and letting them sleep in cars is not encouraged.

Electric hook-up

Many parks now have electric hook-ups available on some of their pitches, however if you need electric you should request it when making your booking. Generally the voltage is 240v AC, 50 cycles, although this can vary slightly according to the location. The supply however can vary considerably from 5 amps to 16 amps although 16 amps is becoming the norm – again you should check with the campsite if this is important to you. Remember, if your consumption is greater than the supply the electricity will trip out and need resetting.

Electric hook-up connections are now standardised in the UK with the blue coloured safety connectors. However, it is good practice to always connect your cable to your caravan, motorhome or tent electric distribution unit **before** connecting to the hook-up supply.

It is also important that tents or trailer tents have a Residual Circuit Device (RCD) for safety reasons and to avoid overloading the circuit. Caravans and motorhomes have RCDs built in. You should remember that if your RCD trips out at 16 amps and the campsite supply is say 10 amps you can easily overload the supply and cause the hook-up to trip out.

It is quite easy to check what demands your appliances can place on the supply at any one time. Details are normally available in the caravan or motorhome handbooks which show the wattage of appliances fitted.

The amperage used is based on the wattage of appliance divided by the supply voltage.

The following table is a quick check of electrical consumption, depending what is switched on.

Average amperage (based on a 240v supply)

Caravan fridge (125 watts)	0.5 amps
Caravan heater set at (500 watts)	2.1 amps
Caravan heater set at (1000 watts)	4.2 amps
Caravan heater set at (2000 watts)	8.4 amps
Caravan water heater (850 watts)	3.5 amps
Kettle (domestic type) (1500 watts)	6.3 amps
Kettle (low wattage type) (750 watts)	3.1 amps
Hairdryer (2100 watts)	8.8 amps
Microwave (750 watts)	3.1 amps
Colour TV (flat-screen LED type) (30 watts)	0.13 amps
Battery charger (built-in type) (200 watts)	0.8 amps

Motorhomes

At some parks motorhomes are only accepted if they remain static throughout the stay. Also check that there are suitable level pitches at the parks where you plan to stay.

Overflow pitches

Campsites are legally entitled to use an overflow field which is not a normal part of their camping area for up to 28 days in any one year as an emergency method of coping with additional numbers at busy periods. When this 28-day rule is being invoked site owners should increase the numbers of sanitary facilities accordingly. In these circumstances the extra facilities are sometimes no more than temporary portacabins.

Parking

Some park operators insist that cars are left in a parking area separate from the pitches; others will not allow more than one car to be parked beside each caravan, tent or glamping unit.

Park restrictions

Many parks in our guide are selective about the categories of people they will accept on their parks. In the caravan and camping world there are many restrictions and some categories of visitor are banned altogether. Where a park has told us of a restriction/s this is included in the notes in their entry.

On many parks in this guide, unaccompanied young people, single-sex groups, single adults, and motorcycle groups will not be accepted. The AA takes no stance in this matter, basing its Pennant classification on facilities, quality and maintenance. On the other hand, some parks cater well for teenagers and offer magnificent sporting and leisure facilities as well as discos; others have only very simple amenities. A small number of parks in our guide exclude all children in order to create an environment aimed at holiday makers in search of total peace and quiet (see page 45).

Pets

The importation of animals into the UK is subject to strict controls. Penalties for trying to avoid these controls are severe. However, the Pet Travel Scheme (PETS) allows cats, dogs, ferrets and certain other pets coming from the EU and certain other countries to enter the UK without quarantine provided the appropriate conditions are met.
For more details: www.gov.uk/take-pet-abroad/overview
PETS Helpline: 0370 241 1710

Pets resident in the British Isles (UK, Republic of Ireland, Isle of Man and Channel Islands) are not subject to any quarantine or PETS rules when travelling within the British Isles.

Seasonal touring pitches

Some park operators allocate a number of their hardstanding pitches for long-term seasonal caravans. These pitches can be reserved for the whole period the campsite is open, generally between Easter and September, and a fixed fee is charged for keeping the caravan on the park for the season. These pitches are in great demand, especially in popular tourist areas, so enquire well in advance if you wish to book one.

Shops

The range of provisions in shops is usually in proportion to the park's size. As far as AA Pennant requirements are concerned, a mobile shop calling several times a week, or a general store within easy walking distance of the park is acceptable.

AA Campsites of the Year

VALE OF PICKERING CARAVAN PARK ▷▷▷▷▷ 94%
ALLERSTON, NORTH YORKSHIRE page 333

Since winning an AA regional award in 2013, hands-on owners Tony and Dianne Stockdale have continued to invest each year at their beautifully maintained and spacious family park. This year our inspector was stunned by the quality and design of the new state-of-the-art facilities block which has six fully-equipped wet rooms (one with bath; five with showers) and a very smart dishwashing room. With underfloor heating, quality marble walls and floor-to-ceiling photographs in each (beach, woodland, polar bear, poppies) they certainly have the wow factor. Elsewhere, the lush grass touring areas are beautifully landscaped with mature trees, shrubs and seasonal flowers; many of the generously sized pitches are hedge-screened to ensure optimum privacy. New electric posts and a dog wash, with shower, were also added for 2016. The woodland walk is an additional bonus and children of all ages have a choice of a fabulous play area (with rubberised surface) and a ball games field. Customer care is a real strength here and all the team are genuinely pleased to help. The park is peacefully located in open countryside close to the North York Moors National Park, and also Scarborough and its many attractions. The Vale of Pickering Caravan Park is a worthy winner indeed.

SCOTLAND

BLAIR CASTLE CARAVAN PARK ▷▷▷▷ 91%
BLAIR ATHOLL, PERTH & KINROSS, page 398

An attractive and secluded site set within the historic Atholl Estate, surrounded by mature woodland and the River Tilt. Although a large park, the various groups of pitches are located throughout the extensive parkland, and each has its own sanitary block with all-cubicle facilities of a very high standard. It is a very popular park with a good variety of static vans, both owner-occupied and for hire, and there's an excellent choice of grass pitches, hardstanding and fully serviced pitches; it is particularly suitable for the larger type of motorhome. Two wooden pods have been carefully placed in a semi-secluded location by the river, and while only providing a sofa-type bed, with no cooking or washing facilities, are proving to be a popular addition to the park. One of the main attractions here is the central 9-acre open grass area which provides a safe environment for children to play whilst also offering stunning views from all the pitches to the nearby hills. There are resident Highland cows and ducks, and native red squirrels can be spotted throughout the park. Walkers and cyclists can access a 50-mile network of off-road trials directly from the park, and there are opportunities for fishing, pony trekking and a Land Rover safari into the hills.

Following nominations by our inspectors, we award an overall winner from three national finalists, five regional winners, a holiday centre winner and a glamping site winner – all are selected for their outstanding overall quality and high levels of customer care. Our two special awards recognise the best small campsite and the most improved campsite.

WALES

FFOREST FIELDS CARAVAN & CAMPING PARK
▶▶▶▶▶ **85%** BUILTH WELLS, POWYS page 437

A long established hillside farm is the location for this superb holiday destination, located a few miles from Builth Wells and the Royal Welsh Showground. The meandering tree-lined drive creates a happy feeling of anticipation, and on clearing the outer forest, the gentle slope stops at the level touring areas. The excellent pitch density results in optimum privacy, and the surrounding densely planted hills are home to a wide range of indigenous wildlife. This is a walkers' paradise as there's lakes, woodland and moorland all within the park's boundaries. The site has a conveniently located, spacious eco-friendly amenities block, fuelled by a bio-mass boiler and solar panels, which provides excellent facilities for adults and families, including drying rooms and a commercial laundry. In addition to the excellent reception, there's a stylish café that serves local and home-reared produce and, for a glamping holiday, there's two bell tents, 'Betty' and 'Harry', each with a kitchen. In recent years, new members of the Barstow family have brought individual and specialised talents to the team equation; the park is very popular with outdoor adventure groups and the Barstow family are to be commended for their partnership with local youth groups who certainly enjoy time spent at the park.

SOUTH WEST ENGLAND

PADSTOW TOURING PARK ▶▶▶▶ **97%**
PADSTOW, CORNWALL page 94

Family owned and run by a dedicated team, Padstow Touring Park is a top quality park set in open countryside above the quaint fishing town. Padstow can be approached via a footpath directly from the park, and guests can savour panoramic views across the north Cornwall countryside from many of the pitches. This site is divided into well-landscaped paddocks by stone walls and maturing bushes and hedges that create a peaceful and relaxing holiday atmosphere. The main facility blocks, both now extended and upgraded to include superb unisex facilities, have been designed and decorated to a very high standard, with underfloor heating and hotel-grade fixtures and fittings. There is an excellent children's play area with 'Lifeboat Station' play equipment, and a spacious reception area with a well-stocked shop and an excellent coffee lounge that has a decked terrace offering country views. A campers' kitchen is the most recent addition to the park, and due to customer demand, 2017 will see the development of more hardstanding pitches, underlining the high levels of customer care and the commitment to improving the park year-on-year. The park fully deserves the 97% Quality Score and the Campsite of the Year Award for the South West – this is a stunning site.

AA Campsites of the Year *continued*

SOUTH EAST ENGLAND

SUMNERS PONDS FISHERY & CAMPSITE ►►►► 88%
BARNS GREEN, WEST SUSSEX page 315

Dedication by the Smith family to provide high quality camping continues apace at this working farm set in attractive surroundings on the edge of the quiet village of Barns Green. There are three well-laid out touring areas; the original field has a mix of neat grass and spacious hardstanding pitches, and a small, newly refurbished toilet and shower block; the middle field continues to develop and includes camping pods and extra hardstandings; the lakeside area, which has a stunning modern toilet block, has excellent pitches on the banks of one of the well-stocked fishing lakes. Here you will also find perfectly located camping pods, a fully equipped safari tent, and four new shepherd's huts, all enjoying private lakeside views. There are many cycle paths on site and the woodland bluebell walk has direct access to miles of footpaths. The brilliant Café by the Lake has proved so popular that it now has extensive lakeside seating, a posh safari tent with sofas and extra seating, and outside is a new barbecue hut. It's licensed, and serves meals from breakfast onwards. Customer care takes high priority at Sumners Ponds – nothing is too much trouble for the Smith family. Horsham and Brighton are within easy reach.

HEART OF ENGLAND

THE OLD BRICK KILNS ►►►►► 93%
BARNEY, NORFOLK page 256

Located between Fakenham and Holt and just eight miles from the beautiful sandy beaches on the north Norfolk coast, Old Brick Kilns is a secluded and tranquil park approached via a quiet, leafy country lane off the A148. The 13-acre park, set on three levels, is surrounded by many mature trees and divided into shady wooded glades and sunny open areas, plus there are glorious landscaped garden areas and a wildlife pond. Excellent, well-planned toilet facilities can be found in two beautifully appointed blocks – one is due for refurbishment in time for the 2017 season. There are 60 spacious, all-weather hardstanding pitches, and several are suitable for larger motorhomes. Kate Dyas and David Moore bought the park in 2014 and have made significant improvements, including refurbishing Barney's Restaurant and Bar, upgrading many of the hardstandings, improving the drainage across the park, and developing the on-site shop, which now offers freshly baked bread and croissants. Children have a giant chess set, an excellent fenced play area and a TV and games room to keep them amused. Both Sandringham House and Holkham Hall are just a short drive away. This is a top class park, well deserving of the 93% Quality Score and this coveted regional award.

NORTH WEST ENGLAND

CASTLERIGG HALL CARAVAN & CAMPING PARK
▶▶▶▶▶ **90%** KESWICK, CUMBRIA page 136

Spectacular views over Derwent Water to the mountains beyond are among the many attractions at this lovely Lakeland park. Owned by the Jackson family since 1938, successive generations have invested in the park to ensure a memorable holiday experience for both campers and tourers. The pitches have been carefully levelled to create stunning terraces on the undulating land, which leads towards Derwent Water; each pitch enjoys wonderful views of the lake or surrounding fells. With its lush grass, colourful shrubs and a range of mature trees of an arboretum standard, this peaceful and relaxing site is a magnet for wildlife. The excellent on-site facilities include a large shop at the entrance which offers a wide range of items, many locally sourced, and the stylish Jiggers Bistro that serves breakfasts, lunches and teas. A campers' kitchen with electrical appliances, seating and a sun terrace is also available and, in addition to the main, superbly-equipped amenities block at the top end of the park, a new top notch facility, adjacent to the pod village, was opened for 2016. Situated two miles from Keswick town centre, Castlerigg Hall is an ideal base for walking; electric bikes and cars are also available for hire. Above all, a warm welcome is assured.

NORTH EAST ENGLAND

COTE GHYLL CARAVAN & CAMPING PARK ▶▶▶▶▶ 89%
OSMOTHERLEY, NORTH YORKSHIRE page 348

A quiet, peaceful site secluded in a pleasant valley within walking distance of pretty Osmotherley village and just minutes from the glorious North Yorkshire Moors. It is the perfect base for active people, with pony trekking, mountain biking and excellent moorland walking (Cleveland Way, Coast-to-Coast Path, Lyke Wake Walk) on the doorstep. It is also a great place to relax – the park is south facing, well landscaped and divided into terraces bordered by woodland, and offers a good mix of grass and hardstanding pitches, including 12 very spacious, fully serviced pitches for larger units. The well-appointed amenity block is a welcome addition to this attractive park – it has underfloor heating, good privacy cubicles and a well-equipped family bathroom. Children can let off steam on the two excellent play areas, and Cod Beck, which flows through the park, is a great and safe place for children to paddle and just have fun. Mature trees, shrubs and an abundance of seasonal floral displays create a relaxing and peaceful atmosphere, and the whole park is immaculately maintained. There are holiday statics for hire, a café and well-stocked shop (with bakery), and good pubs in Osmotherley. This is an impressive park run by dedicated family owners.

AA Campsites of the Year *continued*

HOLIDAY CENTRE OF THE YEAR

ROCKLEY PARK 94%
POOLE, DORSET page 199

Rockley Park is the complete holiday centre for all the family, offering plenty of sports and leisure activities to keep all ages entertained regardless of the weather. Youngsters will appreciate the two swimming pools, especially the splash zone and exciting water slides in the impressive indoor pool area. Children can also get active with mini-golf, climbing, Segway riding and archery, or enjoy the range of indoor events such as face painting and the various kids clubs, or they can explore the nature trail, where they can listen to nature talks and make campfires. Unique to Rockley Park are the water sport activities, which include sailing, kayaking and boat and jet-ski hire, all with tuition available. Adults also have a quality spa and health retreat. There is a wide choice of restaurants and takeaways, including a quality fish and chip restaurant, and the main restaurant and bars have been refurbished. The full daytime and evening entertainment programme offers something for all ages, including an excellent children's entertainment programme. The holiday homes are modern, very well appointed and provide a comfortable place to stay on this beautifully laid out park. Its location near Poole and Bournemouth and some great beaches, make Rockley Park a great holiday base.

MOST IMPROVED CAMPSITE

HAW WOOD FARM CARAVAN PARK ▶▶▶▶ 91%
DUNWICH, SUFFOLK page 304

'What a difference a year makes' stated our inspector following his visit to this massively improved family-orientated park, which occupies two large fields in a peaceful rural location close to Saxmundham, RSPB Minsmere and the glorious Suffolk coast. Since 2015 the forward-thinking owners have invested in the park, transforming it from a simple farm site into a top Four Gold Pennant park. They have completely redeveloped the amenity block to a very high standard, replete with underfloor heating, hotel-grade fixtures and three family wet rooms, as well as creating an excellent reception area, a popular new play area, a great farm shop and Café@Hawwood that offers breakfast, lunches, afternoon teas plus fish and chips on Friday nights. For 2016, they resurfaced the roads, added a new motorhome service point, a recycling area and created several newly planted areas to encourage wildlife. They have plans to increase the number of hardstandings and electric hook-ups, and add more fully serviced pitches for the 2017 season. Guests can expect excellent levels of customer service (welly boots, cots, pushchairs and baby toys are all available on loan) during their stay from friendly, hands-on managers, Georgina and Dan.

SMALL CAMPSITE OF THE YEAR

DRUMROAMIN FARM CAMPING & TOURING SITE
▶▶▶ **90%** WIGTOWN, DUMFRIES & GALLOWAY page 385

Drumroamin Farm is tucked away down a mile-long single-track road in a particularly quiet and rural farmland location near Wigtown, and enjoys beautiful views across Wigtown Bay and the Galloway Hills. It's an open, spacious and peaceful site with excellent, modern facilities that are maintained in an exemplary manner by the dedicated owners; the site is ideal for all customers who wish to enjoy staying on a high quality site, whether they bring a caravan, a motorhome or a tent. There is a large, and separate, tent field with a well-equipped day room, while the touring pitches can easily accommodate rally events, and there is a secure storage area for bikes and boats. The recent addition of a sheltered camp kitchen has proved very popular especially in adverse weather, and a drive-through motorhome service point has also just been added. The RSPB's Crook of Baldoon Reserve is located a 10-minute walk away and the area is renowned for its dark skies, making it the perfect spot for stargazing. Owners Lesley and Ralph Shell take great pride in making their customers' experience the best it can be, so you can be assured of a warm welcome. There is a good bus service at the top of the road, which goes to Newton Stewart, Wigtown and Whithorn.

GLAMPING SITE OF THE YEAR

DURRELL WILDLIFE CAMP ▶▶▶▶▶ 93%
TRINITY, JERSEY page 366

Part of the Durrell Wildlife Park, the camp consists of 12 canvas geo domes set in a beautifully landscaped area. Each unit, named after different Lemur species, is sited in its own separate area offering good privacy. Inside is a king-size bed, two singles, a wood-burning stove and clothing storage space. Set on wooden decking, they have their own additional pod with high quality toilet, wash basin and shower plus a spacious fully-equipped kitchen. Smaller tipis are available for extra children or friends. Guests have complimentary access to the Durrell Wildlife Zoo and have use of the zoo's excellent Café Firefly, which serves breakfasts, lunches and early evening meals, plus takeaway pizzas and Thai food. They can also expect a remarkable level of customer service from a dedicated team, who go out of their way to ensure guests enjoy a complete holiday experience. Lemur Lodge, a large safari tent, serves as reception, meeting place and function area, and has a decked area right next to the zoo – you can see lemurs in the trees. Durrell Wildlife Camp offers quality accommodation, excellent customer service and a unique holiday experience and is a worthy winner of the AA's first Glamping Award.

Updating Rosie

The New Lady in My Life

A couple of years ago AA campsite inspector, Mike Ellis, decided to refurbish an old campervan to use while inspecting. Here he tells us how he transformed a neglected Talbot into a valued family member.

At my time of life, (let's just call me a Seenager) and as an AA campsite inspector, I could never have imagined another female in my life, but on one summer day in 2014, our eyes met across an empty parking space and my heart skipped a beat!

Introducing a real beauty

At the time, I didn't tell my wife Heather, but this sleek 25-year-old beauty had a body that was somewhat abused. Her eyes had lost their shine and her general demeanor was that of being somewhat 'unloved', but nevertheless I fell for her! She purred on tick-over and even more exciting, she ran on dual fuel. After an hour of tenderly looking over her, taking her on a short run, a little negotiating and an exchange of my hard-earned cash, 'Rosie' the *Autosleeper Rhapsody* was all mine. With only a small budget, my wife and I had been seeking a small camper for a year, and the old saying of 'patience is a virtue' had finally paid off.

I had retired as a campsite manager some four years earlier and after touring Europe in our 28ft motorhome I had become all 'toured out'. Heather and I decided to settle down and sell our much-loved *Autotrail*, but retirement was not meant to be. Within a few months I found myself as an AA campsite inspector so therefore in need of a small camper in which to drive from site to site and carry out my inspections. After a year of trawling through classified advertisements, and nearly giving up completely, I finally found my treasure in Rosie.

To most, she must have looked like a campervan that had 'been around the block a few times', but at a mere 25 years old and with only 43,000 miles on her clock, I could see that my Rosie had potential, and I was sure that with our tender care, repair and renovation, the future with Rosie on the UK roads was indeed going to be rosy!

Getting things going

Where to start though? Well, firstly her rust had to be tackled because UK weather can be unrelenting as we all know. Her skottles, around the windscreen, were rusted and the water running down the leaking windscreen was forming in puddles under her bonnet. Her rusty rear wheel arches also had to be rust-free, either by being repaired or replaced.

Now, engineering is no problem to me, but repairing bodywork is somewhat of a mystery, so I located an excellent body repair guy and after a full week of rubbing down and cutting out, Rosie was soon cosmetically perfect on the outside. Next came that windscreen … I had to contact a specialist company and after two visits Rosie was leak-free and happily still sporting her original screen.

The cleaning-up of the engine was tackled next. After removing straw and even a very old bird's nest from the engine compartment and cleaning everything up, oil and water was added. Heather requested that I remove all external light clusters next. With moss growing in the indicators and weeds in the headlights, I could see her point, and after removing all the external fittings, including the front grill, she then proceeded to wash everything and I must admit they really shone when she had finished, with one exception. The headlights were held in place with cable-ties and the chrome reflectors had rusted. I sourced a good supplier, and within two days Rosie's eyes were shining bright again with two new headlights. I then set about attacking all the grey plastic external fittings such as the grill and bumpers with a heat gun, for which internet research proved invaluable. What a difference – Rosie looked years younger!

By this time our energy levels had started to drop, not to mention that our bank manager was suffering from high blood pressure, but we carried on regardless as we had to have Rosie ready for the 2015 AA inspection season. Next on the list of jobs to do was the Ascot water heater. This was located in the wardrobe, and on first ignition…woosh, an AA inspector was minus his eyebrows! After much deliberation we both decided that it was too dangerous for me to continue. Considering the heater was located in a wooden wardrobe, the decision was made to remove it completely, manage without it and utilise the space for clothes storage (or Heather's idea, for extra shoes and bottles of wine). I decided to try my luck selling the Ascot heater on an auction website, and low and behold, such was the response, I could have sold hundreds more.

◁ Mike, Heather and Tilly with Rosie

> # "she looked absolutely perfect with upholstery in blue and gold to match the carpet and curtains"

Looks on the inside

Rosie's internal appearance was nothing that a female touch couldn't put right. With much scrubbing, cleaning, and bleaching she really shone. The curtains – very nice in their day I'm sure, but now daylight shone through the moth-eaten blue velvet. Out came Heather's treasured Singer sewing machine, and within a week she had produced a full set of curtains in a much lighter fabric which co-ordinated with the newly scrubbed-up original carpet. However, the original flowery Dralon upholstery was rotting in places, but at least the foam insides were still in good condition. Colourful throws had to suffice until six months down the line when funds were raised, we all (the family dog, Tilly, included) set out for Derbyshire where a professional upholsterer took just a day to make all the difference to our Rosie's interior. She looked absolutely perfect with upholstery in blue and gold to match the carpet and curtains.

I found that all the internal electrics and lighting were dodgy to say the least, so after an extensive internet search for instructions, I completely rewired her and fitted new LED lighting in addition to external awning lights. I installed two new batteries, replaced the two battery chargers, and at great expense – four new tyres. So now Rosie was well-lit, safe and watertight. I did seal up the original sliding windows as the original window catches fell short of today's required security levels. Then it was time to tackle the engine again.

Although she fired up fine and started first time, she had a very bad cough and a fuel starvation problem.....in other words she kept conking out! A phone call to my mate, HGV mechanic Dave, and the problem was soon identified – Rosie's water cooling system was not functioning! So, in addition to removing the mechanical fuel pump and replacing it with an electric one,

plus replacing the obligatory fuel pipes and jubilee clips, we took a trip down to the New Forest where a new precision-engineered part to the water cooling system was fitted.

Taking her out for a spin

Heather is a keen driver too, and was just as eager to drive Rosie as I was, but without power steering she decided otherwise. This problem was easily solved. A chap based in Stratford-upon-Avon had perfected a power-steering system for old ladies such as Rosie (not Heather!).

So, in just three days we had driven Rosie from our home in Lincolnshire to the New Forest and back, then from Lincolnshire to Stratford and back. All without a hitch and her new power steering was proving a real bonus.

By this time Heather was as much in love with Rosie as I was, but did not relish everyone seeing her with fading *Autosleeper* livery. You can guess the next move I'm sure. My wife quickly sourced a local firm that renewed exterior paintwork, and within a week, Rosie's graphics had changed from turquoise stripes to sea blue. Rosie's fridge/freezer, water system, heating system and cooker were all original and worked perfectly. I installed a microwave, TV and aerial, additional electrical sockets, on-board dashboard camera and video, Sat Nav and even a brand new portable loo – so who needs a £50K motorhome?

Off to work we go

After a thorough external wash and a showroom polish, I set off in March 2015 for my first site inspections with Rosie, and I must admit it was with some trepidation as the sites I had to visit were as far apart as Berwick-upon-Tweed and Land's End. Poor old Rosie was really going to be put to the test. However, I needn't have worried – she negotiated motorways, hills, rough tracks and even the narrow roads of Cornwall. She took hills slower than everyone else, but on motorways she cruised at a steady 70mph with no bother, (she even overtook a Jaguar XJ6, and no, it wasn't standing still). It was so much easier inspecting sites in our little camper for at the end of each day, I simply stayed on a pitch on the last site and moved off the next morning – simple!

We completed inspections in record time in 2015 thanks to Rosie. She proved that she can be parked easily and she is of a good size for cooking a good meal and for providing a great night's sleep. The only hiccup on her maiden trip was the loss of her LPG fuel cap and a wheel trim, which vibrated themselves loose.

Her interior has proved extremely comfortable, and even on very cold evenings we are really warm and toasty. Satisfaction

knows no bounds now that this successful renovation is complete, and even though it came in slightly over budget I am extremely proud of my (sorry, our) Rosie. She has raised a considerable amount of interest wherever we've gone (and maybe a few sniggers), but once fellow campers are introduced to her, they are amazed at her superb condition both inside and out. I would seriously recommend to anyone who is contemplating buying a camper that they consider 'doing up' an old lady….take it from me, it is extremely satisfying, and there are some real beauties out there just waiting to be discovered.

Why the name Rosie you might wonder? Well, after an attempted amateur repair to a graphic on her bonnet, the word 'Rosie', which just sprang to mind, was just the right length to cover up the resulting scratches.

So, after some hard graft our Rosie was born and she's become a very much loved member of our family.

Campsite Cooking

by Ali Ray, The Camping & Caravanning Club's food guru

Cooking on a campsite is surely the best form of meal-making. None of the usual kitchen rules apply: schedules, timings, whizzing gizmos are left behind at home. In fact, outdoor cooking is a pretty relaxed affair. Being alfresco lets you watch the world go by: you can listen to birdsong and the kids yelling while enjoying a glass of something cold. A bit of freeform creativity and ingenuity may be called for on occasion – but that's all part of the fun.

Cooking on gas stoves

Think of campsite cooking and most people immediately think of barbecues. But, from my observations, many campers actually tend to favour the gas stove. From the single pocket-sized glorified Bunsen burner with one small collapsible pan, to the dual ring stove with added grill, gas is probably going to feature somewhere in your cooking kit.

If you have a double gas burner I'd recommend getting a suitable cast-iron griddle or hot plate that will sit on top of it; this will give you ultimate versatility in your cooking. Alternatively you can use a heavy-bottomed griddle pan. Obviously, if you are in a caravan, campervan or a motorhome then you will probably have a gas stove as part of your kitchen.

Barbecuing

Sizzle, spit and smoke – a barbecue should feature at least once in any camping weekend. Cooking on barbecues can be done in two ways.

- **Direct heat method:** the food is put directly over the main heat source. This method is perfect for grilling items that will cook quickly like steaks, burgers and pieces of fish.
- **Indirect heat method:** is best used for larger pieces or joints of meat, where you would otherwise use an oven at home. It involves moving the glowing charcoals to either side of the barbecue and leaving a cooler area in the middle. Once the barbecue lid is down, the heat circulates and cooks the food evenly. Gas barbecues sometimes have heat deflection attachments or you can turn the burners off on one side to achieve the same effect.

Charcoal barbecues

These are seen as the genuine article by many. After all, real fire is involved! The upside is that you get great barbecue flavours in your food, and you can take the grill off after cooking and chuck on some more charcoal or wood and feel like you are sitting around a camp fire. For me, the only disadvantage is the time it takes to heat up to the right temperature when you have hungry children.

Tips on lighting a charcoal barbecue:

- Open the vents on the side of your barbecue. Add a single layer of coals/briquettes on the grate, then pile them into a pyramid with about 3-4 firelighters. Try to use the waxy firelighters made specifically for barbecues. The ones for domestic fires or liquid lighters are more likely to taint the taste of the food. Light with a long match!
- If your barbecue is big enough, pile some coals higher on one side. That way, if you need a high heat to sear your meat first, you use this area, where the heat will be more intense, before moving it to a cooler area.
- Natural charcoal tends to start more quickly than briquettes and burns with about twice the level of heat. It smells cleaner, too.
- Generally it will take about 30 minutes or so for your barbecue to get to cooking heat. It is ready when the coals are covered in a layer of white ash, and you can't hold your hand 15cm above for more than three seconds.

Gas barbecues

You don't get the lovely smoky flavours with gas, but you do get more control over your cooking temperatures, and of course you are ready to cook immediately. Marinating your meat is even more important if cooking on gas in order to add those extra flavours.

If you haven't been able to get all of the residue off your barbecue from its last use, turn the gas on, let the bars get hot to burn off the residue, then give them a brisk brush with a wire brush.

It is also worth taking all the fat trays, grates and burners out now and again to give them a really good clean to get rid of the gunk. It helps to prevent the flare-ups and too much smoking – which can affect the flavour of your food.

Lightly brush the bars with some oil before cooking to prevent the meat sticking.

Disposable barbecues

My advice is just don't – unless you like the taste of lighter fuel in your food. You can buy reusable 'bucket barbecues' using charcoal that cost next to nothing

Campfires

Sitting around a campfire has been a vital part of human ritual since one lucky soul discovered the spark. Even now it fulfils the basic need for warmth and cooking in many cultures. Our need might no longer exist, but the desire to sit around a fire is still as strong as ever. The crackle of burning logs and glowing embers draws people in like moths. A fire encourages good old-fashioned late-night storytelling and singsongs with guitars. And, there is satisfaction to be had from cooking a meal over a fire that is hard to beat. The best way of cooking on a campfire is to use old pans or aluminium trays set on a low metal trivet or triangle of bricks over the glowing embers around the edge. Potatoes and bananas wrapped in foil are also great nestled in the embers. If you are a regular campfire cook, I'd recommend investing in a steel tripod from which to hang your cooking pot.

Barbecuing tips

- **Be prepared.** Barbecuing is so much easier if you do all your prep before you start cooking. I don't always listen to my own advice here, but a successful barbecue usually requires constant prodding and basting – which won't happen if you are still busy cutting veg.
- **Let the meat get up to ambient temperature.** If you put meat straight from the cool box on to the barbecue the outside is likely to burn before the inside begins to cook. The closer you can get the middle temperature to the outside temperature the less likely you are to suffer from barbecuer's curse – black on the outside and raw in the middle.
- **Keep watching.** The best piece of advice is to stay with your barbecue and watch what you are cooking. I have learnt to my peril that getting distracted chatting to friends and family has too often ended up in over-cooked food.
- **Don't turn the food too often.** Just turn once if you can get away with it. It will be easier to turn and gets those lovely grill marks across it if you leave it alone for longer. Use tongs, not a fork, so that the meat doesn't pierce and start to lose its juices.
- **The perfect steak.** If grilling meat, sear it briefly over the hottest part of the coals, then move it further away from the coals to cook it more evenly and slowly. Putting a lid on will help it cook through.

> *"Sitting around a campfire has been a vital part of human ritual since one lucky soul discovered the spark."*

- **Cooking a large joint.** Wrap it in foil before you cook it as this will keep it juicy. You will need a lidded barbecue for this, which will cook the meat like an oven. When the meat is almost cooked, take it out of the foil and finish it off directly over the heat on the barbecue to colour up and soak up the smoky flavours.
- **Talking of smoky flavours...** if you don't have a smoking box but still want an extra smoky flavour, throw some twigs of rosemary or thyme or untreated woodchips on to some of the cooler coals. The smoke will slowly infuse the flavours into the meat.
- **Rest up.** ALWAYS rest your meat once it has cooked. A piece of meat hot off the barbecue will be tough, but letting it rest for 5-10 minutes (covered in foil so it doesn't go cold) will allow the meat to relax, soften and re-absorb all the lovely juices.

Food safety and hygiene

It goes without saying but always use separate utensils, plates and chopping boards for raw and cooked food.

Never pour any leftover marinade from the raw meat on to the cooked meat at the end.

The only way to make sure those sausages and chicken pieces are cooked through is to cut one in half to check. If there are any pink juices when pressed, it's not cooked and not safe to eat! Put it back on the grill.

General campsite cooking safety

NEVER EVER use a barbecue or any other cooking appliance in your tent or awning – it can cause carbon monoxide poisoning, which can be fatal.

Check the coals are fully extinguished or the gas is turned off properly before leaving your barbecue unattended. It's worth having a fire extinguisher or bucket to hand. Keep children and pets well away.

Tricks of the trade

Here are a few campsite cooking techniques I have developed over the years that make life a little easier.

- **Marinating.** This is the perfect way to add flavour and also makes the meat tender. Marinate for as long as you can for best results.
- Don't add salt to your marinade! It will draw all the moisture out of your meat and it will end up dry.
- Also, if your marinade contains sugar, don't put the meat over a high temperature otherwise the sugar will burn too quickly.

Store cupboard kit

Salt

Pepper

Mustard

Worcestershire sauce

Sweet chilli sauce

Sugar

Plastic bottle of lemon juice

Olive or rapeseed oil

Balsamic vinegar

Runny honey

Garlic

Soy sauce

Stock cubes

Dried herbs: mixed herbs, oregano, mint

Spices: smoked paprika, chilli powder, cumin, coriander, cinnamon

Curry powder

Ketchup

Mayonnaise

Rice

Pasta

Couscous

Plain flour

Harissa paste

Tinned chickpeas, kidney beans & cannellini beans

Tinned tomatoes

White wine vinegar

Soft tortilla wraps

Butter, Milk & Eggs – bought on arrival, or in a cool box from home

- Most meats benefit from marinating. The easiest way to do it is in a large, resealable freezer bag. Put the empty, open bag into a bowl so that you can fold back the opening of the bag around the rim of the bowl. This holds the bag steady and open for you while you put your marinade ingredients in, then your meat. Seal the bag, squish it all around to coat the meat, then pop it into the cool box. It saves on space in your fridge and there is no washing-up or mess.
- **Foil Parcels.** This is a nifty way to make a meal. The trick for foil-parcel food is to make sure you have at least a double layer of foil. Even better, place three large rectangles of foil on top of each other, put your food (be it fish or vegetables) in and fold it over like a padded envelope.
- **Smoking.** Smoking food on the barbecue is fun, tasty and really easy. You can buy a 'smoking box' from camp shops or online, or you can easily make your own. Use a small aluminium tray, the kind you get takeaway food in. In a separate bowl soak a couple of handfuls of natural (untreated) wood chips in water for 30 minutes to stop the chips burning too quickly. You can buy smoking chips in garden centres and hardware stores. Drain the soaked chips then put them into the aluminium tray, cover the top with tin foil and make lots of holes across the top to allow the smoke to come out. Put the 'box' in between the elements of your gas barbecue or nestled down in the charcoal. Heat your barbecue up with the lid on until you notice the wonderful smoky smells coming out. Quickly open the lid and put your meat or fish on the grill and put the lid down. Cook it as normal, allowing it to 'soak up the smoke'.

A word on ingredients

It's simply not realistic to suggest that all of your cooking ingredients need to be sourced from the field next door. Eating local certainly isn't about setting rules on where you must buy all your food. It is about enjoying the process of buying some of your ingredients from interesting places and people who are passionate about their products, farm shops and markets.

To be called a farmers' market, stalls have to be certified under the rules and regulations set out by FARMA (the National Farmers and Retail Association, www.farma.org.uk). All the produce on sale at a farmers' market should have been grown, reared, caught, brewed, pickled, baked, smoked or processed by the stallholder. There are also about 300 weekly Country Markets (www.country-markets.co.uk) held in village halls and town squares across England and Wales. They tend to run for an

hour or two and sell home-baked goods, preserves and garden-grown vegetables and fruit. Check markets are running before you travel.

Making an effort to locally source key ingredients like meat, vegetables, quirky local cheese or freshly caught fish can make a huge difference to your meal. It will taste better simply for not having been freighted halfway across the world. It will also taste better because you will cook it differently. When you meet the person who produced that food, or know a bit about its provenance and the way it was produced, you are bound to care more about it and get more pleasure from eating it than if it came wrapped in clingfilm and polystyrene from the supermarket.

The camping store cupboard

Every camper should have one – a pre-packed bag or box of store cupboard basics to take with you on every trip. Get this bit right and you'll find campsite cooking a delight and a doddle.

Having all the basics to hand, such as rice, pasta, herbs and oil, leaves you the flexibility a buy a couple of steaks or fresh fish from the local market knowing you've got everything you need to transform it into a great meal back at the site.

No-one wants to buy a whole pot of honey each time they need one teaspoon of it for a recipe, so stock up on the basics and keep them all in a neat lightweight box and it will save you money and make you smug. Trust me!

On the opposite page is a list of what I have in my transportable store cupboard – it's the kind of thing you can add to whenever you come across handy travel-size or mini versions of things.

Find out more about what to eat and how to cook it in *Pitch Up Eat Local* written by Ali Ray.

Cooking gear checklist

It's a good Idea to keep two large plastic storage boxes ready packed with all the camping cooking gear.

- ✔ Good quality re-sealable freezer bags of varying sizes
- ✔ Aluminium foil
- ✔ Chopping boards — green for veg, red for raw meat and blue for fish.
- ✔ Grater
- ✔ Three sharp knives — one for cutting raw meat, one for veg and a thin-bladed one for fish
- ✔ Pans — two saucepans with lids. One quite large
- ✔ Frying pans — one small, one large
- ✔ Skewers
- ✔ Camping kettle
- ✔ Nest of plastic bowls
- ✔ Serving plates, bowls and cutlery
- ✔ Wooden spoons
- ✔ Gas lighter and matches
- ✔ Plastic measuring jug/cup
- ✔ Washing-up bowl, liquid and loads of tea towels
- ✔ Aluminium trays
- ✔ Barbecue tongs
- ✔ Spatula
- ✔ Bottle opener
- ✔ Tin opener
- ✔ Kitchen roll
- ✔ Water carrier
- ✔ Cool box with freezer blocks
- ✔ Bin bags
- ✔ Tupperware pots with lids
- ✔ Cooking appliances: campfire grill, gas stove, ideally with two burners and a bottle of gas

SAUSAGE AND ALE SUPPER

This is a simple and rustic big pan feast that can be plonked on the table to serve a group of hungry campers. The addition of the ale provides an extra depth of flavour to the dish.

You'll need a two-ring gas stove, a large frying pan and a saucepan for the rice.

Serves 4

300g short-grain rice

salt

1 tbsp olive oil

8 fine butchers' sausages (pork and apple, or pork and chilli would be good)

4 rashers smoked bacon

1 onion, sliced

1 red pepper, deseeded and sliced

2 garlic cloves, crushed

1 tbsp harissa paste

250ml Shepherd Neame ale – something slightly citrussy and malty like Goldings Ale

1 x 400g tin chopped tomatoes

1 x 400g tin cannellini beans, drained and rinsed

a small bunch of parsley, chopped (optional)

- Put the rice on to cook in salted water before you get going on the rest of the meal. It will need about 12 minutes.

- Heat the oil in a frying pan. Snip each sausage and each bacon rasher into three pieces using scissors and fry in the oil for 5 minutes.

- Add the onion and pepper and continue to cook until browned.

- Add the garlic, harissa paste and ale and simmer for 2-3 minutes before adding the tomatoes and cannellini beans. Heat through for 5 minutes.

- Once the rice has cooked, drain it well, rinse it in hot water, and let it steam for a couple of minutes, with a tea-towel over the top of the pan.

- Stir the cooked rice into the contents of the frying pan, making sure it is combined well.

- Take off the heat, season well and sprinkle with some fresh parsley if you have it. If not, just plonk the pan on the table and serve in bowls along with a few bottles of the same fine ale!

There's many more easy and delicious recipes in *Pitch Up Eat Local*

First-time campers: a checklist of Dos, and a couple of Don'ts

Key: C = caravans M = motorhomes T = tents

Before you leave home or the site (hitching)

▶ Before you go away for the first time practise putting up your tent; hitching and unhitching your caravan; reversing your motorhome or towed van into an enclosed space. **(CMT)**

▶ Make a list of all the essentials you need to take with you. Mains lead, gas cylinder, levelling ramps and/or chocks... all the way through to small essentials like a box of matches, spare fuses, and a torch (check batteries). **(CMT)**

▶ Check all interior items are safely stored, cupboards closed, all interior electrics are set correctly, turn off gas bottles, make sure roof lights and windows are closed and the external door is locked. **(CM)**

▶ Empty fresh and waste water containers and toilet cassettes. **(CM)**

▶ Check that corner steadies are raised tightly, and chocks and steps stowed. **(C)**

▶ Connect tow bracket electric plugs, check that the breakaway safety cable is connected and, if used, that the anti-snake device is fitted correctly. **(C)**

▶ Check the caravan's noseweight. **(C)**

▶ Adjust the hitch height – i.e. above the car's towball. **(C)**

▶ Secure the hitch on the towball. **(C)**

▶ Use the jockey wheel to raise the car about 2.5cm to ensure the caravan and car are properly coupled. If fitted, also check the tow hitch indicator (green = correctly coupled). **(C)**

▶ Raise the jockey wheel and lock in position. **(C)**

▶ Check that the caravan number plate is secure (and that it replicates the towing vehicle's number plate). **(C)**

▶ Ask another person to stand behind the caravan or motorhome to check all the lights and indicators work. **(CM)**

▶ On leaving a site disconnect the hook-ups and make that final check of the empty pitch. **(CM)**

Arriving at your destination (unhitching)

▶ Tell the site this is your first time. They're more likely to go out of their way to help. **(CMT)**

▶ Listen to what the site staff tell you when you arrive (if you're a family, it's a good idea for you all to step into reception – that way you all understand the same message). **(CMT)**

▶ Check caravan handbrake is on, chocks are in place and corner steadies are lowered. **(C)**

▶ Lower jockey wheel and level the caravan and then lock in place. **(C)**

▶ Give everyone in the family designated tasks when you arrive on site (finding the way to the toilet block, locating the nearest fresh water point etc). **(CMT)**

▶ Get to know your surroundings. An early-evening stroll around any campsite is a great opportunity to check out the facilities. **(CMT)**

▶ Say hello to your neighbours. They might just come in handy, and who knows you might a make a lot of new friends. **(CMT)**

DON'T churn up the grass. You're only ruining things for subsequent visitors. If you have a bit of a mishap, let the staff know so they can rectify things as soon as possible.

And finally **DON'T** be afraid to ask. All the campsites in this guide are adept at helping first-timers – most will happily guide you to your pitch if you ask. Although you'll soon find your fellow campers are happy to chip in and help out, too.

There's even more useful information on www.theaa.com/motoring_advice/general-advice/towing-advice-what-you-need-to-know.html

The best sites for…

…WATERSIDE PITCHES

ENGLAND

South End Caravan Park,
Barrow-in-Furness, Cumbria
River Dart Country Park,
Ashburton, Devon
Riverside C&C Park,
South Molton, Devon
Sleningford Watermill CC Park,
North Stainley, North Yorkshire

SCOTLAND

Banff Links Caravan Park,
Banff, Aberdeenshire
Inver Mill Farm Caravan Park,
Dunkeld, Perth & Kinross
Skye C&C Club Site,
Edinbane, Isle of Skye

WALES

Riverside Camping,
Caernarfon, Gwynedd

NORTHERN IRELAND

Drumaheglis Marina & Caravan Park,
Ballymoney, County Antrim

…STUNNING VIEWS

ENGLAND

Tristram C&C Park,
Polzeath, Cornwall
Sykeside Camping Park,
Patterdale, Cumbria
Warcombe Farm C&C Park,
Woolacombe, Devon
Highlands End Holiday Park,
Bridport, Dorset
Sea Barn Farm,
Weymouth, Dorset
New Hall Farm Touring Park,
Southwell, Nottinghamshire
Wimbleball Lake,
Dulverton, Somerset
Howgill Lodge,
Bolton Abbey, North Yorkshire
Wolds Way Caravan and Camping,
West Knapton, North Yorkshire

CHANNEL ISLANDS

Rozel Camping Park,
St Martin, Jersey

SCOTLAND

Oban C&C Park,
Oban, Argyll & Bute
Linnhe Lochside Holidays,
Corpach, Highland
Invercoe C&C Park,
Glencoe, Highland
John O'Groats Caravan Site,
John O'Groats, Highland
Strathfillan Wigwam Village,
Tyndrum, Stirling

WALES

St David's Park,
Red Wharf Bay, Isle of Anglesey
Bron-Y-Wendon Caravan Park,
Llanddulas, Conwy
Bodnant Caravan Park,
Llanwrst, Conwy
Beach View Caravan Park,
Abersoch, Gwynedd
Tyn-y-Mur Touring & Camping,
Abersoch, Gwynedd
Trawsdir Touring C&C Park,
Barmouth, Gwynedd
Eisteddfa,
Criccieth, Gwynedd
Fishguard Bay Resort,
Fishguard, Pembrokeshire
Carreglwyd C&C Park,
Port Eynon, Swansea

…GOOD ON-SITE RESTAURANTS

ENGLAND

Stroud Hill Park,
St Ives, Cambridgeshire
Tristram C&C Park,
Polzeath, Cornwall
Cofton Country Holidays,
Dawlish, Devon
Bingham Grange T&C Park,
Bridport, Dorset
Highlands End Holiday Park,
Bridport, Dorset

Bay View Holiday Park,
Bolton-le-Sands, Lancashire
The Old Brick Kilns,
Barney, Norfolk
Beaconsfield Farm Caravan Park,
Shrewsbury, Shropshire

CHANNEL ISLANDS

Beuvelande Camp Site,
St Martin, Jersey

SCOTLAND

Glen Nevis C&C Park,
Fort William, Highland

WALES

St David's Park,
Red Wharf Bay, Isle of Anglesey

…TOP TOILETS

ENGLAND

Carnon Downs C&C Park,
Truro, Cornwall
Beech Croft Farm,
Buxton, Derbyshire
Crealy Meadows C&C Park,
Clyst St Mary, Devon
Riverside C&C Park,
South Molton, Devon
Meadowbank Holidays,
Christchurch, Dorset
Shamba Holidays,
St Leonards, Dorset
Teversal C&C Club Site,
Teversal, Nottinghamshire
Dell Touring Park,
Bury St Edmunds, Suffolk
Moon & Sixpence,
Woodbridge, Suffolk
Riverside Caravan Park,
High Bentham, North Yorkshire
Wayside Holiday Park,
Pickering, North Yorkshire
Moor Lodge Park,
Leeds, West Yorkshire

SCOTLAND

Beecraigs C&C Site,
  Linlithgow, West Lothian
Skye C&C Club Site,
  Edinbane, Isle of Skye

...ON-SITE FISHING

ENGLAND

Fields End Water CP & Fishery,
  Doddington, Cambridgeshire
Upper Tamar Lake,
  Kilkhampton, Cornwall
Back of Beyond Touring Park,
  St Leonards, Dorset
Blackmore Vale C&C Park,
  Shaftesbury, Dorset
Woodland Waters,
  Ancaster, Lincolnshire
Lakeside Caravan Park & Fisheries,
  Downham Market, Norfolk
Northam Farm Caravan & Touring Park,
  Brean, Somerset
Thorney Lakes Caravan Park,
  Langport, Somerset
Carlton Meres Country Park,
  Saxmundham, Suffolk
Marsh Farm Caravan Site,
  Saxmundham, Suffolk
Sumners Ponds Fishery & Campsite,
  Barns Green, West Sussex

SCOTLAND

Hoddom Castle Caravan Park,
  Ecclefechan, Dumfries & Galloway
Milton of Fonab Caravan Park,
  Pitlochry, Perth & Kinross
Gart Caravan Park,
  Callander, Stirling

WALES

Afon Teifi C&C Park,
  Newcastle Emlyn, Carmarthenshire
Ynysymaengwyn Caravan Park,
  Tywyn, Gwynedd

...THE KIDS

ENGLAND

Trevornick,
  Holywell Bay, Cornwall
Eden Valley Holiday Park,
  Lostwithiel, Cornwall
Golden Valley C&C Park,
  Ripley, Derbyshire
Freshwater Beach Holiday Park,
  Bridport, Dorset
Sandy Balls Holiday Village,
  Fordingbridge, Hampshire
Heathland Beach Caravan Park,
  Kessingland, Suffolk
Golden Square C&C Park,
  Helmsley, North Yorkshire
Riverside Caravan Park,
  High Bentham, North Yorkshire
Goosewood Holiday Park,
  Sutton-on-the-Forest, North Yorkshire

SCOTLAND

Blair Castle Caravan Park,
  Blair Atholl, Perth & Kinross
Beecraigs C&C Site,
  Linlithgow, West Lothian

WALES

Home Farm Caravan Park,
  Marian-Glas, Isle of Anglesey
Hendre Mynach Touring C&C Park,
  Barmouth, Gwynedd
Trawsdir Touring C&C Park,
  Barmouth, Gwynedd

...BEING ECO-FRIENDLY

ENGLAND

South Penquite Farm,
  Blisland, Cornwall
Lowarth Glamping,
  Wadebridge, Cornwall
River Dart Country Park,
  Ashburton, Devon
Brook Lodge Farm C&C Park (Bristol),
  Cowslip Green, Somerset

SCOTLAND

Carradale Bay Caravan Park,
  Carradale, Argyll & Bute
Shieling Holidays,
  Craignure, Isle of Mull

WALES

Caerfai Bay Caravan & Tent Park,
  St Davids, Pembrokeshire

▶▶▶▶▶ Premier Parks

5 GOLD PENNANTS
▷▷ ▷▷ ▷

ENGLAND

CAMBRIDGESHIRE
DODDINGTON
Fields End Water Caravan Park & Fishery

ST IVES
Stroud Hill Park

CHESHIRE
CODDINGTON
Manor Wood Country Caravan Park

WHITEGATE
Lamb Cottage Caravan Park

CORNWALL
BUDE
Wooda Farm Holiday Park

CARLYON BAY
Carlyon Bay Caravan & Camping Park

CRANTOCK (NEAR NEWQUAY)
Trevella Park

HOLYWELL BAY
Trevornick

MEVAGISSEY
Seaview International Holiday Park

NEWQUAY
Hendra Holiday Park

PADSTOW
Padstow Touring Park

REDRUTH
Globe Vale Holiday Park

REJERRAH
Newperran Holiday Park

ST IVES
Polmanter Touring Park

ST JUST-IN-ROSELAND
Trethem Mill Touring Park

TRURO
Carnon Downs Caravan & Camping Park

CUMBRIA
AMBLESIDE
Skelwith Fold Caravan Park

KESWICK
Castlerigg Hall Caravan & Camping Park

WINDERMERE
Park Cliffe Camping & Caravan Estate

DEVON
BRAUNTON
Hidden Valley Park

DARTMOUTH
Woodlands Grove Caravan
    & Camping Park

DAWLISH
Cofton Country Holidays

DREWSTEIGNTON
Woodland Springs Adult Touring Park

NEWTON ABBOT
Dornafield
Ross Park

SIDMOUTH
Oakdown Country Holiday Park

TAVISTOCK
Woodovis Park

DORSET
BRIDPORT
Bingham Grange Touring
    & Camping Park
Highlands End Holiday Park

CHARMOUTH
Wood Farm Caravan & Camping Park

POOLE
South Lytchett Manor Caravan
    & Camping Park

WAREHAM
Wareham Forest Tourist Park

WEYMOUTH
East Fleet Farm Touring Park

HAMPSHIRE
FORDINGBRIDGE
Sandy Balls Holiday Village

ISLE OF WIGHT
NEWBRIDGE
The Orchards Holiday Caravan Park

RYDE
Whitefield Forest Touring Park

WROXALL
Appuldurcombe Gardens Holiday Park

LANCASHIRE
SILVERDALE
Silverdale Caravan Park

LINCOLNSHIRE
WOODHALL SPA
Woodhall Country Park

NORFOLK
BARNEY
The Old Brick Kilns

CLIPPESBY
Clippesby Hall

NORTHUMBERLAND
BELFORD
South Meadows Caravan Park

BELLINGHAM
Bellingham Camping & Caravanning
    Club Site

HALTWHISTLE
Herding Hill Farm

NOTTINGHAMSHIRE
TEVERSAL
Teversal Camping & Caravanning
    Club Site

OXFORDSHIRE
HENLEY-ON-THAMES
Swiss Farm Touring & Camping

STANDLAKE
Lincoln Farm Park Oxfordshire

SHROPSHIRE
SHREWSBURY
Beaconsfield Farm Caravan Park

SOMERSET
BISHOP SUTTON
Bath Chew Valley Caravan Park

GLASTONBURY
The Old Oaks Touring Park

WELLS
Wells Touring Park

STAFFORDSHIRE
LONGNOR
Longnor Wood Holiday Park

SUFFOLK
LEISTON
Cakes & Ale

WOODBRIDGE
Moon & Sixpence

SUSSEX, WEST
CHICHESTER
Concierge Camping

YORKSHIRE, NORTH
ALLERSTON
Vale of Pickering Caravan Park

HIGH BENTHAM
Riverside Caravan Park

SCOTLAND

ABERDEENSHIRE
HUNTLY
Huntly Castle Caravan Park

FIFE
ST ANDREWS
Cairnsmill Holiday Park
Craigtoun Meadows Holiday Park

LOTHIAN, EAST
DUNBAR
Thurston Manor Leisure Park

PERTH & KINROSS

BLAIR ATHOLL
Blair Castle Caravan Park

STIRLING

ABERFOYLE
Trossachs Holiday Park

SCOTTISH ISLANDS

ISLE OF ARRAN

KILMORY
Runach Arainn

WALES

ANGLESEY, ISLE OF

DULAS
Tyddyn Isaf Caravan Park

MARIAN-GLAS
Home Farm Caravan Park

GWYNEDD

BARMOUTH
Trawsdir Touring Caravans
 & Camping Park

TAL-Y-BONT
Islawrffordd Caravan Park

PEMBROKESHIRE

ST DAVIDS
Caerfai Bay Caravan & Tent Park

POWYS

BRECON
Pencelli Castle Caravan & Camping Park

WREXHAM

EYTON
Plassey Holiday Park

NORTHERN IRELAND

COUNTY ANTRIM

BUSHMILLS
Ballyness Caravan Park

5 BLACK PENNANTS
►►►►►

ENGLAND

BERKSHIRE

HURLEY
Hurley Riverside Park

CORNWALL

GOONHAVERN
Silverbow Park

LANDRAKE
Dolbeare Park Caravan and Camping

LEEDSTOWN
Calloose Caravan & Camping Park

LOOE
Camping Caradon Touring
 Park
Tregoad Park

LOSTWITHIEL
Eden Valley Holiday Park

PENTEWAN
Sun Valley Resort

ST AUSTELL
River Valley Holiday Park

ST IVES
Ayr Holiday Park
Trevalgan Touring Park

ST MERRYN
Atlantic Bays Holiday Park

ST MINVER
Gunvenna Holiday Park

TRURO
Cosawes Park
Truro Caravan and Camping Park

WATERGATE BAY
Watergate Bay Touring Park

CUMBRIA

APPLEBY-IN-WESTMORLAND
Wild Rose Park

BOOT
Eskdale Camping & Caravanning
 Club Site

KIRKBY LONSDALE
Woodclose Caravan Park

PENRITH
Lowther Holiday Park

ULVERSTON
Bardsea Leisure Park

WATERMILLOCK
The Quiet Site

WINDERMERE
Hill of Oaks & Blakeholme

DERBYSHIRE

BIRCHOVER
Barn Farm Campsite

DEVON

CLYST ST MARY
Crealy Meadows Caravan
 and Camping Park

COMBE MARTIN
Newberry Valley Park

DAWLISH
Lady's Mile Holiday Park

KINGSBRIDGE
Island Lodge Caravan & Camping Site
Parkland Caravan and Camping Site

PAIGNTON
Beverley Parks Caravan & Camping Park

SAMPFORD PEVERELL
Minnows Touring Park

SIDMOUTH
Kings Down Tail Caravan
 & Camping Park

TAVISTOCK
Langstone Manor C&C Park

WOOLACOMBE
Warcombe Farm Caravan
 & Camping Park

DORSET

ALDERHOLT
Hill Cottage Farm Camping
 and Caravan Park

CHARMOUTH
Newlands Caravan & Camping Park

CHIDEOCK
Golden Cap Holiday Park

CHRISTCHURCH
Meadowbank Holidays

ST LEONARDS
Shamba Holidays

SWANAGE
Ulwell Cottage Caravan Park

WIMBORNE MINSTER
Wilksworth Farm Caravan Park

HAMPSHIRE

ROMSEY
Hill Farm Caravan Park

KENT

ASHFORD
Broadhembury Caravan & Camping Park

MARDEN
Tanner Farm Touring Caravan
 & Camping Park

LANCASHIRE

CAPERNWRAY
Old Hall Caravan Park

FAR ARNSIDE
Hollins Farm Camping & Caravanning

THORNTON
Kneps Farm Holiday Park

▶▶▶▶▶ **Premier Parks** *continued*

NORFOLK
BELTON
Rose Farm Touring & Camping Park

KING'S LYNN
King's Lynn Caravan and Camping Park

NORTH WALSHAM
Two Mills Touring Park

NORTHUMBERLAND
BERWICK-UPON-TWEED
Ord House Country Park

RUTLAND
GREETHAM
Rutland Caravan & Camping

SHROPSHIRE
BRIDGNORTH
Stanmore Hall Touring Park

SHREWSBURY
Oxon Hall Touring Park

TELFORD
Severn Gorge Park

WHEATHILL
Wheathill Touring Park

SOMERSET
BRIDGETOWN
Exe Valley Caravan Site

CROWCOMBE
Quantock Orchard Caravan Park

PORLOCK
Porlock Caravan Park

WIVELISCOMBE
Waterrow Touring Park

WARWICKSHIRE
HARBURY
Harbury Fields

WILTSHIRE
LANDFORD
Greenhill Farm Caravan & Camping Park

WORCESTERSHIRE
HONEYBOURNE
Ranch Caravan Park

YORKSHIRE, NORTH
ALNE
Alders Caravan Park

HARROGATE
Ripley Caravan Park
Rudding Holiday Park

HELMSLEY
Golden Square Caravan & Camping Park

OSMOTHERLEY
Cote Ghyll Caravan & Camping Park

RIPON
Riverside Meadows Country Caravan Park

SCARBOROUGH
Jacobs Mount Caravan Park

SNAINTON
Jasmine Caravan Park

SUTTON-ON-THE-FOREST
Goosewood Caravan Park

WYKEHAM
St Helens Caravan Park

CHANNEL ISLANDS
GUERNSEY
CASTEL
Fauxquets Valley Campsite

JERSEY
ST MARTIN
Beuvelande Camp Site
Rozel Camping Park

SCOTLAND
DUMFRIES & GALLOWAY
BRIGHOUSE BAY
Brighouse Bay Holiday Park

ECCLEFECHAN
Hoddom Castle Caravan Park

KIRKCUDBRIGHT
Seaward Caravan Park

DUNBARTONSHIRE, WEST
BALLOCH
Lomond Woods Holiday Park

HIGHLAND
CORPACH
Linnhe Lochside Holidays

MORAY
LOSSIEMOUTH
Silver Sands Holiday Park

PERTH & KINROSS
BLAIR ATHOLL
River Tilt Caravan Park

WALES
CARMARTHENSHIRE
LLANDOVERY
Erwlon Caravan & Camping Park

NEWCASTLE EMLYN
Cenarth Falls Holiday Park

CONWY
LLANDDULAS
Bron-Y-Wendon Caravan Park

LLANRWST
Bron Derw Touring Caravan Park

GWYNEDD
BARMOUTH
Hendre Mynach Touring Caravan
  & Camping Park

DINAS DINLLE
Dinlle Caravan Park

MONMOUTHSHIRE
USK
Pont Kemys Caravan & Camping Park

POWYS
BUILTH WELLS
Fforest Fields Caravan & Camping Park

CHURCHSTOKE
Daisy Bank Caravan Park

LLANIDLOES
Red Kite Touring Park

SWANSEA
PONTARDDULAIS
River View Touring Park

NORTHERN IRELAND
COUNTY ANTRIM
BALLYMONEY
Drumaheglis Marina & Caravan Park

COUNTY FERMANAGH
BELCOO
Rushin House Caravan Park

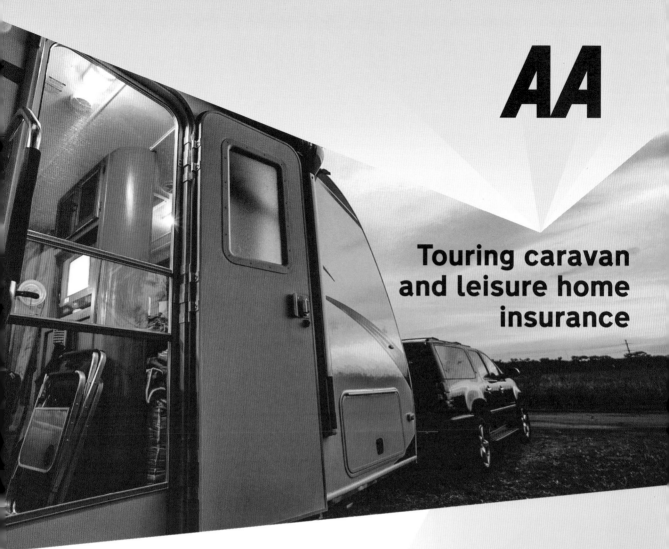

AA

Touring caravan and leisure home insurance

Understanding your pursuits on and off the road, you can sit in comfort knowing you're in safe hands. Quote 'AA 20' to receive £20 off when you take out a new policy.

Call us for a quote on:
0344 346 0162

£20 off
AA Touring caravan and leisure home insurance

Gold Pennant parks

ENGLAND

CAMBRIDGESHIRE

COMBERTON
▷ ▷ ▷ ▷ Highfield Farm Touring Park

DODDINGTON
▷ ▷ ▷ ▷ ▷ Fields End Water Caravan
Park & Fishery

ST IVES
▷ ▷ ▷ ▷ Stroud Hill Park

CHESHIRE

CODDINGTON
▷ ▷ ▷ ▷ Manor Wood Country
Caravan Park

WHITEGATE
▷ ▷ ▷ ▷ Lamb Cottage Caravan Park

CORNWALL

BUDE
▷ ▷ ▷ ▷ Budemeadows Touring Park
▷ ▷ ▷ ▷ Wooda Farm Holiday Park

CARLYON BAY
▷ ▷ ▷ ▷ Carlyon Bay Caravan
& Camping Park

CRANTOCK (NEAR NEWQUAY)
▷ ▷ ▷ ▷ Trevella Park

GWITHIAN
▷ ▷ ▷ ▷ Gwithian Farm Campsite

HOLYWELL BAY
▷ ▷ ▷ ▷ Trevornick

KENNACK SANDS
▷ ▷ ▷ ▷ Chy Carne Holiday Park

MARAZION
▷ ▷ ▷ ▷ Wayfarers Caravan
& Camping Park

MEVAGISSEY
▷ ▷ ▷ ▷ ▷ Seaview International
Holiday Park

NEWQUAY
▷ ▷ ▷ ▷ Hendra Holiday Park
▷ ▷ ▷ ▷ Treloy Touring Park

PADSTOW
▷ ▷ ▷ ▷ Padstow Touring Park

PORTHTOWAN
▷ ▷ ▷ ▷ Porthtowan Tourist Park

REDRUTH
▷ ▷ ▷ ▷ Globe Vale Holiday Park

REJERRAH
▷ ▷ ▷ ▷ ▷ Newperran Holiday Park

ROSUDGEON
▷ ▷ ▷ ▷ Kenneggy Cove Holiday Park

ST IVES
▷ ▷ ▷ ▷ ▷ Polmanter Touring Park

ST JUST-IN-ROSELAND
▷ ▷ ▷ ▷ ▷ Trethem Mill Touring Park

SUMMERCOURT
▷ ▷ ▷ Carvynick Country Club

TRURO
▷ ▷ ▷ ▷ ▷ Carnon Downs Caravan
& Camping Park

WADEBRIDGE
▷ ▷ ▷ ▷ The Laurels Holiday Park
▷ ▷ ▷ ▷ St Mabyn Holiday Park

CUMBRIA

AMBLESIDE
▷ ▷ ▷ ▷ Skelwith Fold Caravan Park

KESWICK
▷ ▷ ▷ ▷ Castlerigg Hall Caravan
& Camping Park

WINDERMERE
▷ ▷ ▷ ▷ Park Cliffe Camping
& Caravan Estate

DERBYSHIRE

BUXTON
▷ ▷ ▷ Clover Fields Touring
Caravan Park
▷ ▷ ▷ ▷ Lime Tree Park

MATLOCK
▷ ▷ ▷ ▷ Lickpenny Caravan Site

DEVON

BRAUNTON
▷ ▷ ▷ ▷ ▷ Hidden Valley Park

BUCKFASTLEIGH
▷ ▷ Churchill Farm Campsite

COMBE MARTIN
▷ ▷ ▷ Stowford Farm Meadows

DARTMOUTH
▷ ▷ ▷ ▷ Woodlands Grove Caravan
& Camping Park

DAWLISH
▷ ▷ ▷ ▷ Cofton Country Holidays

DREWSTEIGNTON
▷ ▷ ▷ ▷ Woodland Springs Adult
Touring Park

NEWTON ABBOT
▷ ▷ ▷ ▷ Dornafield
▷ ▷ ▷ ▷ Ross Park

SIDMOUTH
▷ ▷ ▷ ▷ Oakdown Country
Holiday Park

SOUTH MOLTON
▷ ▷ ▷ Riverside Caravan
& Camping Park

TAVISTOCK
▷ ▷ ▷ ▷ Woodovis Park

DORSET

BRIDPORT
▷ ▷ ▷ ▷ Bingham Grange Touring
& Camping Park
▷ ▷ ▷ ▷ Highlands End Holiday Park

CHARMOUTH
▷ ▷ ▷ ▷ ▷ Wood Farm Caravan
& Camping Park

CORFE CASTLE
▷ ▷ ▷ ▷ Corfe Castle Camping &
Caravanning Club Site

POOLE
▷ ▷ ▷ ▷ South Lytchett Manor
Caravan & Camping Park

ST LEONARDS
▷ ▷ ▷ ▷ Back of Beyond Touring Park

WAREHAM
▷ ▷ ▷ ▷ Wareham Forest Tourist Park

WEYMOUTH
▷ ▷ ▷ ▷ East Fleet Farm Touring Park
▷ ▷ ▷ West Fleet Holiday Farm

GLOUCESTERSHIRE

CHELTENHAM
▷ ▷ ▷ ▷ Briarfields Motel & Touring Park

HAMPSHIRE

FORDINGBRIDGE
▷ ▷ ▷ ▷ Sandy Balls Holiday Village

ISLE OF WIGHT

NEWBRIDGE
▷ ▷ ▷ ▷ The Orchards Holiday
Caravan Park

RYDE
▷ ▷ ▷ ▷ Whitefield Forest
Touring Park

WROXALL
▷ ▷ ▷ ▷ Appuldurcombe Gardens
Holiday Park

LANCASHIRE

SILVERDALE
▷ ▷ ▷ ▷ Silverdale Caravan Park

LINCOLNSHIRE

BOSTON
▷ ▷ ▷ Long Acres Touring Park

MARSTON
▷ ▷ ▷ Wagtail Country Park

WOODHALL SPA
▷ ▷ ▷ ▷ Woodhall Country Park

NORFOLK

BARNEY
▷ ▷ ▷ ▷ The Old Brick Kilns

CLIPPESBY
▷ ▷ ▷ ▷ Clippesby Hall

NORTHUMBERLAND

BELFORD
►►►►► South Meadows
Caravan Park

BELLINGHAM
►►►►► Bellingham Camping
& Caravanning Club Site

HALTWHISTLE
►►►► Herding Hill Farm

NOTTINGHAMSHIRE

TEVERSAL
►►►►► Teversal Camping
& Caravanning Club Site

OXFORDSHIRE

BLETCHINGDON
►►►► Greenhill Leisure Park

HENLEY-ON-THAMES
►►►►► Swiss Farm Touring
& Camping

STANDLAKE
►►►►► Lincoln Farm Park
Oxfordshire

SHROPSHIRE

SHREWSBURY
►►►► Beaconsfield Farm
Caravan Park

SOMERSET

BISHOP SUTTON
►►►►► Bath Chew Valley
Caravan Park

BREAN
►►►► Northam Farm Caravan
& Touring Park

GLASTONBURY
►►►►► The Old Oaks Touring Park

PORLOCK
►►► Burrowhayes Farm Caravan
& Camping Site

SHEPTON MALLET
►► Greenacres Camping

WELLS
►►►► Wells Touring Park

STAFFORDSHIRE

LONGNOR
►►►►► Longnor Wood Holiday Park

SUFFOLK

DUNWICH
►►►► Haw Wood Farm Caravan Park

KESSINGLAND
►►►► Heathland Beach Caravan Park

LEISTON
►►►► Cakes & Ale

SAXMUNDHAM
►► Marsh Farm Caravan Site

WOODBRIDGE
►►►► Moon & Sixpence

SUSSEX, WEST

CHICHESTER
►►►► Concierge Camping

WEST MIDLANDS

MERIDEN
►►►► Somers Wood Caravan Park

WILTSHIRE

SALISBURY
►►►► Coombe Touring Park

YORKSHIRE, EAST RIDING OF

BRANDESBURTON
►►►► Blue Rose Caravan
Country Park

SPROATLEY
►►►► Burton Constable Holiday Park
& Arboretum

YORKSHIRE, NORTH

ALLERSTON
►►►►► Vale of Pickering
Caravan Park

FILEY
►►► Crows Nest Caravan Park
►►► Lebberston Touring Park

HARROGATE
►► Harrogate Caravan Park

HIGH BENTHAM
►►►►► Riverside Caravan Park

NABURN
►►►► Naburn Lock Caravan Park

ROBIN HOOD'S BAY
►►►► Grouse Hill Caravan Park
►►► Middlewood Farm Holiday Park

SCARBOROUGH
►►►► Cayton Village Caravan Park

STAINFORTH
►►►► Knight Stainforth Hall Caravan
& Campsite

WHITBY
►►►► Ladycross Plantation
Caravan Park

CHANNEL ISLANDS

GUERNSEY

ST SAMPSON
►►► Le Vaugrat Camp Site

SCOTLAND

ABERDEENSHIRE

HUNTLY
►►►► Huntly Castle Caravan Park

ARGYLL & BUTE

CARRADALE
►►► Carradale Bay Caravan Park

DUMFRIES & GALLOWAY

WIGTOWN
►►► Drumroamin Farm Camping
& Touring Site

FIFE

ST ANDREWS
►►►► Cairnsmill Holiday Park
►►►► Craigtoun Meadows
Holiday Park

FORT WILLIAM
►►► Glen Nevis Caravan
& Camping Park

LOTHIAN, EAST

DUNBAR
►►►► Thurston Manor Leisure Park

LOTHIAN, WEST

LINLITHGOW
►►►► Beecraigs Caravan
& Camping Site

PERTH & KINROSS

BLAIR ATHOLL
►►►► Blair Castle Caravan Park

PITLOCHRY
►►►► Milton of Fonab Caravan Park

STIRLING

ABERFOYLE
►►►► Trossachs Holiday Park

BLAIRLOGIE
►►►► Witches Craig Caravan
& Camping Park

SCOTTISH ISLANDS

SKYE, ISLE OF

EDINBANE
►►► Skye Camping & Caravanning
Club Site

WALES

ANGLESEY, ISLE OF

DULAS
►►►►► Tyddyn Isaf Caravan Park

MARIAN-GLAS
►►►►► Home Farm Caravan Park

CARMARTHENSHIRE

LLANGENNECH
►►► South Wales Touring Park

CEREDIGION

ABERAERON
►►► Aeron Coast Caravan Park

DENBIGHSHIRE

RHUALLT
►►►► Penisar Mynydd Caravan Park

GWYNEDD

BARMOUTH
►►►► Trawsdir Touring Caravans
& Camping Park

TAL-Y-BONT
►►►►► Islawrffordd Caravan Park

PEMBROKESHIRE

FISHGUARD
►►► Fishguard Bay Resort

ST DAVIDS
►►►► Caerfai Bay Caravan &
Tent Park

POWYS

BRECON
►►►►► Pencelli Castle Caravan
& Camping Park

SWANSEA

RHOSSILI
►►► Pitton Cross Caravan
& Camping Park

WREXHAM

EYTON
►►►►► Plassey Holiday Park

NORTHERN IRELAND

COUNTY ANTRIM

BUSHMILLS
►►►►► Ballyness Caravan Park

AA Holiday Centres

These parks cater for all holiday needs. See page 11 for further information.

ENGLAND

CORNWALL

HAYLE
St Ives Bay Holiday Park

LOOE
Tencreek Holiday Park

PERRANPORTH
Perran Sands Holiday Park

WIDEMOUTH BAY
Widemouth Bay Caravan Park

CUMBRIA

FLOOKBURGH
Lakeland Leisure Park

POOLEY BRIDGE
Park Foot Caravan & Camping Park

SILLOTH
Stanwix Park Holiday Centre

DEVON

EXMOUTH
Devon Cliffs Holiday Park

WOOLACOMBE
Golden Coast Holiday Park
Twitchen House Holiday Park
Woolacombe Bay Holiday Park

DORSET

BRIDPORT
Freshwater Beach Holiday Park

WEYMOUTH
Littlesea Holiday Park
Seaview Holiday Park

ESSEX

MERSEA ISLAND
Waldegraves Holiday Park

ST OSYTH
The Orchards Holiday Park

ISLE OF WIGHT

WHITECLIFF BAY
Whitecliff Bay Holiday Park

LANCASHIRE

BLACKPOOL
Marton Mere Holiday Village

LONGRIDGE
Beacon Fell View Holiday Park

LINCOLNSHIRE

CLEETHORPES
Thorpe Park Holiday Centre

MABLETHORPE
Golden Sands Holiday Park

MERSEYSIDE

SOUTHPORT
Riverside Holiday Park

NORFOLK

BELTON
Wild Duck Holiday Park

CAISTER-ON-SEA
Caister-on-Sea Holiday Park

GREAT YARMOUTH
Vauxhall Holiday Park

HUNSTANTON
Searles Leisure Resort

NORTHUMBERLAND

BERWICK-UPON-TWEED
Haggerston Castle Holiday Park

SOMERSET

BREAN
Holiday Resort Unity
Warren Farm Holiday Centre

BRIDGWATER
Mill Farm Caravan & Camping Park

BURNHAM-ON-SEA
Burnham-on-Sea Holiday Village

SUSSEX, WEST

SELSEY
Warner Farm

YORKSHIRE, EAST RIDING OF

SKIPSEA
Skirlington Leisure Park

TUNSTALL
Sand le Mere Holiday Village

YORKSHIRE, NORTH

FILEY
Blue Dolphin Holiday Park
Flower of May Holiday Park
Primrose Valley Holiday Park
Reighton Sands Holiday Park

Poole, Dorset

SCOTLAND

AYRSHIRE, SOUTH

AYR
Craig Tara Holiday Park

DUMFRIES & GALLOWAY

GATEHOUSE OF FLEET
Auchenlarie Holiday Park

LOTHIAN, EAST

LONGNIDDRY
Seton Sands Holiday Village

WALES

DENBIGHSHIRE

PRESTATYN
Presthaven Sands Holiday Park

GWYNEDD

PORTHMADOG
Greenacres Holiday Park

PWLLHELI
Hafan y Môr Holiday Park

PEMBROKESHIRE

TENBY
Kiln Park Holiday Centre

SWANSEA

SWANSEA
Riverside Caravan Park

Green Pennant parks

ENGLAND

CORNWALL
WADEBRIDGE
▶▶▶▶ Lowarth Glamping

DEVON
OTTERY ST MARY
▶▶▶▶ Cuckoo Down Farm Glamping

WELCOMBE
▶▶▶ Koa Tree Camp

DORSET
HOLDITCH
▶▶▶▶▶ Crafty Camping

SHAFTESBURY
▶▶▶▶▶ Dorset Country Holidays

ISLE OF WIGHT
NEWPORT
▶▶▶▶▶ Wight Glamping Holidays

KENT
AYLESFORD
▶▶▶▶▶ Kits Coty Glamping

NORFOLK
BELTON
▶▶▶▶ Swallow Park Leisure

NORTHUMBERLAND
HALTWHISTLE
▶▶▶▶▶ Herding Hill Farm,
Glamping Site

SOMERSET
GLASTONBURY
▶▶▶▶▶ Middlewick Farm

SUSSEX, WEST
CHICHESTER
▶▶▶▶▶ Concierge Glamping
▶▶▶▶ Plush Tents Glamping

YORKSHIRE, NORTH
KIRKLINGTON
▶▶▶▶ Camp Kátur

CHANNEL ISLANDS

JERSEY
TRINITY
▶▶▶▶▶ Durrell Wildlife Camp

SCOTLAND

HIGHLAND
AVIEMORE
▶▶▶▶ Aviemore Glamping

LAIRG
▶▶▶▶▶ Loch Shin Wigwams

MORAY
ELGIN
▶▶▶▶ Woodlands Rest

STIRLING
TYNDRUM
▶▶▶▶▶ Strathfillan Wigwam Village

SCOTTISH ISLANDS

ISLE OF ARRAN
KILMORY
▶▶▶▶▶ Runach Arainn

WALES

MONMOUTHSHIRE
LLANVAIR DISCOED
▶▶▶▶▶ Penhein Glamping

SWANSEA
OLDWALLS
▶▶▶▶ Oldwalls Gower Glamping

WREXHAM
BRONINGTON
▶▶▶▶ The Little Yurt Meadow

Adults only – no children parks

ENGLAND

CAMBRIDGESHIRE

BURWELL
Stanford Park

DODDINGTON
Fields End Water Caravan Park & Fishery

ST IVES
Stroud Hill Park

CHESHIRE

WETTENHALL
New Farm Caravan Park

WHITEGATE
Lamb Cottage Caravan Park

CORNWALL

CHACEWATER
Killiwerris Touring Park

MARAZION
Wayfarers Caravan & Camping Park

ROSE
Higher Hendra Park

CUMBRIA

CARLISLE
Green Acres Caravan Park

MEALSGATE
Larches Caravan Park

DERBYSHIRE

BUXTON
Clover Fields Touring Caravan Park

DEVON

DREWSTEIGNTON
Woodland Springs Adult Touring Park

TORQUAY
Widdicombe Farm Touring Park

DORSET

BRIDPORT
Bingham Grange Touring
 & Camping Park

HOLDITCH
Crafty Camping

HURN
Fillybrook Farm Touring Park

ST LEONARDS
Back of Beyond Touring Park

GLOUCESTERSHIRE

CHELTENHAM
Briarfields Motel & Touring Park

LANCASHIRE

BLACKPOOL
Manor House Caravan Park

LINCOLNSHIRE

BOSTON
Long Acres Touring Park
Orchard Park

CAISTOR
Wolds View Touring Park

NORFOLK

NORTH WALSHAM
Two Mills Touring Park

STANHOE
The Rickels Caravan & Camping Park

SWAFFHAM
Breckland Meadows Touring Park

NORTHAMPTONSHIRE

DULWICK
New Lodge Farm Caravan
 & Camping Site

NORTHUMBERLAND

SEAHOUSES
Westfield Paddock

NOTTINGHAMSHIRE

SOUTHWELL
New Hall Farm Touring Park

OXFORDSHIRE

BURFORD
Wysdom Touring Park

SHROPSHIRE

CRAVEN ARMS
Wayside Camping and Caravan Park

SHREWSBURY
Beaconsfield Farm Caravan Park

TELFORD
Severn Gorge Park

WHEATHILL
Wheathill Touring Park

SOMERSET

BISHOP SUTTON
Bath Chew Valley Caravan Park

BRIDGETOWN
Exe Valley Caravan Site

GLASTONBURY
The Old Oaks Touring Park

HIGHBRIDGE
Greenacre Place Touring Caravan Park

SPARKFORD
Long Hazel Park

WELLINGTON
Greenacres Touring Park

WELLS
Homestead Park
Wells Touring Park

WIVELISCOMBE
Waterrow Touring Park

STAFFORDSHIRE

LONGNOR
Longnor Wood Holiday Park

SUFFOLK

THEBERTON
Sycamore Park

WOODBRIDGE
Moat Barn Touring Caravan Park

WEST MIDLANDS

MERIDEN
Somers Wood Caravan Park

YORKSHIRE, EAST RIDING OF

BRANDESBURTON
Blue Rose Caravan Country Park

YORKSHIRE, NORTH

HARROGATE
Shaws Trailer Park

HELMSLEY
Foxholme Caravan Park

YORK
Rawcliffe Manor Caravan Park

YORKSHIRE, WEST

LEEDS
Moor Lodge Park
St Helena's Caravan Park

WALES

CARMARTHENSHIRE

LLANGENNECH
South Wales Touring Park

MONMOUTHSHIRE

ABERGAVENNY
Wernddu Caravan Park

POWYS

CHURCHSTOKE
Daisy Bank Caravan Park

CRICKHOWELL
Riverside Caravan & Camping Park

LLANDRINDOD WELLS
Dalmore Camping & Caravanning Park

LLANIDLOES
Red Kite Touring Park

WREXHAM

OVERTON
The Trotting Mare Caravan Park

Island camping

Channel Islands

Tight controls are operated because of the narrow width of the mainly rural roads. On all of the islands tents can be hired on recognised campsites and some sites offer luxury glamping units. Early booking is strongly recommended during July and August.

Alderney

Neither caravans nor motorhomes are allowed, and campers must have a confirmed booking on the one official campsite before they arrive on the island.

Guernsey

Only islanders may own and use towed caravans, but a limited number of motorhomes are permitted on the island. The motorhome, used for overnight accommodation, must be not more than 6.9mtrs long and 2.3mtrs wide, must be booked into an authorised site (Fauxquets Valley Campsite, La Bailloterie or Le Vaugrat Camp Site) and a permit must be obtained from the site operator before embarking on a ferry for Guernsey – Condor Ferries will not accept motorhomes without this permit. The permit must be displayed in the window at all times, motorhomes must return to the site each night, and permits are valid for a maximum of one month. Permission is not required to bring a trailer tent to the island. (See www.visitguernsey.com).

Herm and Sark

These two small islands are traffic free. Herm has a small campsite for tents, and these can also be hired. Sark has two campsites. New arrivals are met from the boat by a tractor which carries people and luggage up the steep hill from the harbour. All travel is on foot, by bike, or by horse and cart.

Jersey

Visiting caravans and motorhomes (size restrictions apply) require a permit (maximum one month) that must be displayed at all times and they are restricted to one journey to, and one journey from, the campsite and the port. Caravans must remain on the designated campsites for the period of the permit. Motorhomes can travel around the island on a daily basis but must return to the designated campsite each night. Many roads on the island are narrow and may have limited access (see www.jersey.com).

Bookings should be made through the chosen campsite and they will also arrange a permit.

Isle of Man

A permit maybe required, and obtained in advance. For details see www.gov.im/catergories/leisure-and-entertainment/camping/

Isles of Scilly

Caravans and motorhomes are not allowed on the islands, and campers must stay at official sites. Booking is advisable on all sites, especially during school holidays.

Scotland

For advice on wild camping in Scotland see the Scottish Outdoor Access Code website (http://outdooraccess-scotland.com/practical-guide/public/camping)

Inner Hebrides

Arran, Coll, Islay & Mull – all have official campsites and welcome caravans, motorhomes and tents; wild camping is also permitted but access rights apply (check each island's website for details). **Colonsay and Cumbrae** – prior arrangements must be made if you wish to camp with a motor vehicle or go wild camping (see www.colonsay.org.uk). **Great Cumbrae** – caravanning or camping is not permitted. **Iona** – a backpackers' paradise and non-residents' vehicles are not permitted; tents are only permitted on the campsite. **Isle of Bute** – camping is only permitted on the official site. **Jura and Gigha** – both have small, designated areas. Prior arrangements are required. **Lismore** – caravans and motorhomes are banned but tents are permitted (there are no official sites and few suitable places). **Rùm and Eigg** – the ferries only take foot passengers and there are no campsites. **Skye** – caravans, motorhomes and tents are permitted and there are official campsites. **Tiree** – caravans, motorhomes and tents are permitted. Wild camping is permitted but check the island's website for details (www.isleoftiree.com).

Orkney

There are no camping and caravanning restrictions, and there are plenty of beauty spots where you can pitch camp.

Shetland Islands

There are official campsites on some of the Shetland Islands, and wild camping is possible with landowner's permission. Caravans and motorhomes must keep to the main roads. Camping 'böds' offer basic accommodation for campers with their own bed rolls and sleeping bags. **Fetlar** – there is no longer a dedicated campsite but wild camping is permitted with the landowner's permission (see www.fetlar.org). **Noss**, **Bressay and Fair Isle** – camping and caravanning is not permitted.

Western Isles (Outer Hebrides)

Harris, **Lewis**, **North & South Uist** – there are official campsites on these islands, and wild camping is allowed with the landowner's prior permission.

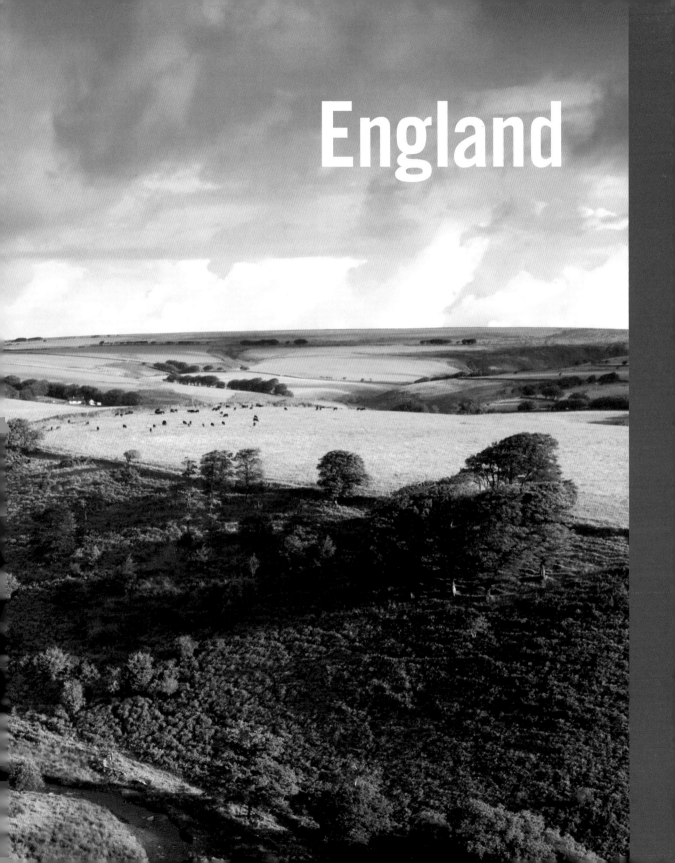

England

BERKSHIRE

FINCHAMPSTEAD
Map 5 SU76

Places to visit

West Green House Gardens, HARTLEY WINTNEY, RG27 8JB, 01252 844611 www.westgreenhouse.co.uk

Museum of English Rural Life, READING, RG1 5EX, 0118 378 8660 www.merl.org.uk

Great for kids: The Look Out Discovery Centre, BRACKNELL, RG12 7QW, 01344 354400 www.bracknell-forest.gov.uk/be

California Chalet & Touring Park
▶▶▶80%

tel: 0118 973 3928 & 07447 475833 **Nine Mile Ride RG40 4HU**
email: enquiries@californiapark.co.uk
dir: From A321 (S of Wokingham), right onto B3016 to Finchampstead. Follow Country Park signs on Nine Mile Ride. **grid ref:** SU788651

A simple, peaceful and well located woodland site with secluded pitches among the trees, adjacent to the country park. Several pitches occupy a prime position beside the lake with their own fishing area. The site has large hardstandings and the toilet block has quality vanity units and fully tiled showers. The sparsely planted trees allow sunshine onto pitches. Future investment plans remain very positive for this well located park. 5.5 acre site. 44 touring pitches. 44 hardstandings. Caravan pitches. Motorhome pitches. Tent pitches.

Open: all year **Last arrival:** flexible **Last departure:** noon

Pitches: 🚐 🚖 ⛺ 🏕

Leisure: 🎡 ✑

Facilities: 🐾 ☺ ✒ 🚽 🖊 🖊 WiFi ♻ ✿

Services: 🚐 🗑 🛒 T 🚿 🖊

Glamping: **Wooden Pods** 2, £38 Min stay 3 nights Car by unit

Within 3 miles: 🖊 🎪 ✑ ◎ 🛒 🗑 U

Notes: No ground fires, no washing of caravans. Dogs must be kept on leads.

AA Pubs & Restaurants nearby: The Broad Street Tavern, WOKINGHAM, RG40 1AU, 0118 977 3706

L'Ortolan, SHINFIELD, RG2 9BY, 0118 988 8500

HURLEY

Places to visit

Cliveden, CLIVEDEN, SL6 0JA, 01628 605069 www.nationaltrust.org.uk/cliveden

The Hell-Fire Caves, WEST WYCOMBE, HP14 3AJ, 01494 524411 (office) www.hellfirecaves.co.uk

Great for kids: Bekonscot Model Village and Railway, BEACONSFIELD, HP9 2PL, 01494 672919 www.bekonscot.co.uk

HURLEY
Map 5 SU88

PREMIER PARK

Hurley Riverside Park
▶▶▶▶▶85%

GOLD

tel: 01628 824493 & 823501 **Park Office SL6 5NE**
email: info@hurleyriversidepark.co.uk **web:** www.hurleyriversidepark.co.uk
dir: Signed on A4130 (Henley to Maidenhead rd), just W of Hurley. **grid ref:** SU826839

A large Thames-side site with a good touring area close to the river. A quality park with three beautifully appointed toilet blocks, one of which houses excellent, fully serviced unisex facilities. Level grassy pitches are sited in small, sectioned areas, and this is a generally peaceful setting. There are furnished tents for hire. 15 acre site. 200 touring pitches. 41 hardstandings. Caravan pitches. Motorhome pitches. Tent pitches. 290 statics.

Open: Mar-Oct **Last arrival:** 20.00hrs **Last departure:** noon

Pitches: * 🚐 £15-£32 🚖 £15-£32 ⛺ £13-£28 **Leisure:** ✪

Facilities: ☺ ✒ ✳ 🚽 🖊 🖊 WiFi ♻ ✿

Services: 🚐 🗑 🛒 ⊘ T 🖊

Within 3 miles: 🖊 🚤 🎪 ✑ 🛒 🗑

Notes: No unsupervised groups of young people, no commercial vehicles, no fires or fire pits, quiet-park policy applies, max 2 dogs per pitch. Dogs must be kept on leads. Fishing in season, slipway, nature trail, riverside picnic grounds.

AA Pubs & Restaurants nearby: The Olde Bell Inn, HURLEY, SL6 5LX, 01628 825881

Hotel du Vin Henley-on-Thames, HENLEY-ON-THAMES, RG9 2BP, 01491 848400

See advert on opposite page

LEISURE: 🏊 Indoor pool 🏊 Outdoor pool 🎡 Children's playground 👦 Kid's club 🎾 Tennis court 🎱 Games room ⛳ Golf course 🚣 Boat hire 🚲 Cycle hire
🎭 Cinema 🎵 Entertainment ✑ Fishing ◎ Mini golf ⛳ Pitch n putt 🏄 Watersports 🏋 Gym ✪ Sports field U Stables **FACILITIES:** 🛁 Bath 🚿 Shower
P🗒 Private washing cubicles ☺ Electric shaver ✂ Hairdryer ✳ Ice Packs 🚽 Disabled facilities 🛒 Shop on site 🖊 Mobile shop 🍴 BBQ area 🖊 Picnic area
WiFi Wi-fi 🖥 Internet access ♻ Recycling ✿ Tourist info 🖊 Dog exercise area 🚗 Car hire can be arranged

NEWBURY
Map 5 SU46

Places to visit

Highclere Castle & Gardens, HIGHCLERE, RG20 9RN, 01635 253210
www.highclerecastle.co.uk

Great for kids: The Living Rainforest, HAMPSTEAD NORREYS, RG18 0TN,
01635 202444 www.livingrainforest.org

Bishops Green Farm Camp Site
▶▶▶82%

tel: 01635 268365 **Bishops Green RG20 4JP**
dir: *Exit A339 (opposite New Greenham Park) towards Bishops Green & Ecchinswell. Site on left, approx 0.5m by barn.* **grid ref:** *SU502630*

A sheltered and secluded meadowland park close to the Hampshire-Berkshire border, offering very clean and well-maintained facilities, including a toilet block with a disabled/family room. There are woodland and riverside walks to be enjoyed around the farm, and coarse fishing is also available. The site is very convenient for visiting the nearby market town of Newbury with an attractive canal in the town centre. 1.5 acre site. 30 touring pitches. 6 hardstandings. Caravan pitches. Motorhome pitches. Tent pitches.

Open: Apr-Oct **Last arrival:** 21.30hrs

Pitches: 🚐 🚐 Å

Leisure: 🎣

Facilities: 🍴 ✳ 🛒

Services: 🔌 🖲 🖤

Within 3 miles: 🛁 🎣 💲

Notes: 🚫 Dogs must be kept on leads.

AA Pubs & Restaurants nearby: The Newbury, NEWBURY, RG14 5HB, 01635 49000
The Wellington Arms, BAUGHURST, RG26 5LP, 0118 982 0110

RISELEY
Map 5 SU76

Places to visit

Basildon Park, LOWER BASILDON, RG8 9NR, 01491 672382
www.nationaltrust.org.uk/basildonpark

Mapledurham House, MAPLEDURHAM, RG4 7TR, 0118 972 3350
www.mapledurham.co.uk

Great for kids: Beale Park, LOWER BASILDON, RG8 9NH, 0118 976 7480
www.bealepark.co.uk

Wellington Country Park
▶▶▶86%

tel: 0118 932 6444 **Odiham Rd RG7 1SP**
email: info@wellington-country-park.co.uk **web:** www.wellington-country-park.co.uk
dir: *M4 junct 11, A33 S towards Basingstoke. Or M3 junct 5, B3349 N towards Reading.* **grid ref:** *SU728628*

A peaceful woodland site, popular with families, set within an extensive country park, which comes complete with lakes and nature trails, accessible to campers after the country park closes. The park offers good facilities that include a laundry

continued

PITCHES: 🚐 Caravans 🚐 Motorhomes Å Tents 🏕 Glamping accommodation **SERVICES:** 🔌 Electric hook up 🖲 Launderette 🍺 Licensed bar
🔥 Calor Gas 🔥 Camping Gaz Ⓣ Toilet fluid 🍽 Café/Restaurant 🍔 Fast Food/Takeaway 🔋 Battery charging 🍼 Baby care 🚐 Motorvan service point
ABBREVIATIONS: BHs – bank holidays Etr – Easter Spring BH – Spring Bank Holiday fr – from hrs – hours m – mile mdnt – midnight
rdbt – roundabout rs – restricted service wk – week wknd – weekend x-roads – crossroads 🚫 No credit or debit cards 🚫 No dogs

RISELEY *continued*

and a good motorhome service point. There's also a herd of Red and Fallow deer that roam the meadow area. This site is ideal for those travelling on the M4 but it is advised not to follow Sat Nav as it takes you to a central point of the post code, which is not the entrance. 80 acre site. 87 touring pitches. 18 hardstandings. Caravan pitches. Motorhome pitches. Tent pitches.

Open: Mar-Nov **Last arrival:** 17.30hrs (last arrival 16.30hrs in low season) **Last departure:** noon

Pitches: 🚐 🚚 🅰

Leisure: 🎵

Facilities: 🍴 ☉ 🗝 ⚹ ⚗ ⓢ 🎋 WiFi ▦ ♻ 🛈

Services: 🔌 ⓢ 🚻 ⓣ⊙ 🖴

Within 3 miles: ⚓ ◎ ⚓ ⓢ ⓢ U

Notes: No open fires. Dogs must be kept on leads. Miniature railway, crazy golf, animal farm, access to Wellington Country Park.

L'Ortolan, SHINFIELD, RG2 9BY, 0118 988 8500

BRISTOL

See Cowslip Green (Somerset)

CAMBRIDGESHIRE

Stanford Park
▶▶▶81%

tel: 01638 741547 & 07802 439997 **Weirs Drove CB25 0BP**
email: enquiries@stanfordcaravanpark.co.uk
dir: *A14 junct 37, A142, left signed Burwell. Or from A14 junct 35, B1102 to Burwell (site approx 4m from Newmarket; 8m from Cambridge).* **grid ref:** *TL580665*

Set on the edge of the fens and within walking distance of the historic village of Burwell, this park is an attractive tranquil adults-only site. It is ideally placed for visiting the Wicken Fen National Nature Reserve, Ely Cathedral, Newmarket races and Cambridge. The park is expertly maintained with clean, modern facilities and four open paddocks sheltered by mature deciduous trees. There is an exclusive area for seasonal pitches where winter storage is also available. It is advisable to book for Bank Holidays (minimum three nights stay) and for peak periods. 20 acre site. 103 touring pitches. 20 hardstandings. Caravan pitches. Motorhome pitches. Tent pitches.

Open: all year **Last arrival:** 21.00hrs **Last departure:** 11.00hrs

Pitches: 🚐 🚚 🅰

Facilities: ☉ 🗝 ⚹ 🐎 🛈

Services: 🔌 ⓢ 🚻 ⊘ 🖴

Within 3 miles: ⚓ ⚓ 🗝 ⚓ ⓢ ⓢ U

Notes: Adults only. 🐕 Dogs must be kept on leads.

Highfield Farm Touring Park
▶▶▶▶ 92%

tel: 01223 262308 **Long Rd CB23 7DG**
email: enquiries@highfieldfarmtouringpark.co.uk
web: www.highfieldfarmtouringpark.co.uk
dir: *M11 junct 12, A603 (Sandy). 0.5m, right onto B1046 to Comberton.*
grid ref: *TL389572*

Run by a very efficient and friendly family, the park is on a well-sheltered hilltop, with spacious pitches including a cosy backpackers' and cyclists' area, and separate sections for couples and families. Around the family farm there is a one and a half mile marked walk that has stunning views. 8 acre site. 120 touring pitches. 52 hardstandings. Caravan pitches. Motorhome pitches. Tent pitches.

Open: Apr-Oct **Last arrival:** 20.00hrs **Last departure:** 14.00hrs

Pitches: 🚐 £17-£22 🚚 £17-£22 🅰 £15-£22

Facilities: ☉ 🗝 ⚹ ⓢ 🐎 WiFi 🛈

Services: 🔌 ⓢ 🚻 ⊘ ⓣ 🖴 🛒

Within 3 miles: ⚓ 🗝 ⓢ ⓢ U

Notes: Max 2 dogs per pitch. Dogs must be kept on leads. Postbox.

AA Pubs & Restaurants nearby: The Three Horseshoes, MADINGLEY, CB23 8AB, 01954 210221

Restaurant 22, CAMBRIDGE, CB4 3AX, 01223 351880

LEISURE: 🏊 Indoor pool 🏊 Outdoor pool 🎢 Children's playground 🙌 Kid's club 🎾 Tennis court 🎯 Games room ⛳ Golf course 🚣 Boat hire 🚲 Cycle hire 🎬 Cinema 🎵 Entertainment 🎣 Fishing ◎ Mini golf 🏏 Pitch n putt 🏄 Watersports 🏋 Gym 🏟 Sports field U Stables **FACILITIES:** 🛁 Bath 🚿 Shower 📷 Private washing cubicles ☉ Electric shaver 🗝 Hairdryer ⚹ Ice Packs ♿ Disabled facilities ⓢ Shop on site 🏪 Mobile shop 🍴 BBQ area 🎋 Picnic area WiFi Wi-fi ▦ Internet access ♻ Recycling 🛈 Tourist info 🐎 Dog exercise area 🚗 Car hire can be arranged

DODDINGTON
Map 12 TL49

Places to visit

WWT Welney Wetland Centre, WELNEY, PE14 9TN, 01353 860711
www.wwt.org.uk/welney

Flag Fen Archaeology Park, PETERBOROUGH, PE6 7QJ, 01733 313414
www.vivacity-peterborough.com/museums-and-heritage/flag-fen

PREMIER PARK

Fields End Water Caravan Park & Fishery

▶▶▶▶▶ 90%

tel: 01354 740199 **Benwick Rd PE15 0TY**
email: info@fieldsendfishing.co.uk
dir: Exit A141, follow signs to Doddington. At clock tower in Doddington turn right into Benwick Rd. Site 1.5m on right after sharp bends. **grid ref:** TL378908

This meticulously planned and executed park makes excellent use of its slightly elevated position in The Fens. The 33 fully serviced pitches, all with very generous hardstandings, are on smart terraces with sweeping views of the countryside. The two newly upgraded toilet blocks contain several combined cubicle spaces, and there are shady walks through mature deciduous woodland adjacent to two large and appealing landscaped fishing lakes. High quality pine lodges are available as holiday lets. 20 acre site. 52 touring pitches. 23 hardstandings. Caravan pitches. Motorhome pitches. Tent pitches.

Open: all year **Last arrival:** 20.30hrs **Last departure:** noon

Pitches: 🚐 £16-£23 🚙 £16-£23 ⛺ £16-£21 ⛺ prices shown below

Leisure: 🎣

Facilities: 🏪🅿️⊙🌂❄️🔥👶 WiFi ♻️ 🐾

Services: 🔌🔅🔋🍽️

Glamping: Cabins 6, £70-£166 Changeover day Mon, Fri Min stay 3 nights (Fri-Mon), 4 nights (Mon-Fri) Own kitchen Car by unit

Within 3 miles: 🚶🎣◉🏧🛒

Notes: Adults only. No large groups. Dogs must be kept on leads.

AA Pubs & Restaurants nearby: The Old Bridge Hotel, HUNTINGDON, PE29 3TQ, 01480 424300

GUYHIRN

Places to visit

Peckover House & Garden, WISBECH, PE13 1JR, 01945 583463
www.nationaltrust.org.uk/peckover

Great for kids: WWT Welney Wetland Centre, WELNEY, PE14 9TN, 01353 860711
www.wwt.org.uk/welney

GUYHIRN
Map 12 TF40

Tall Trees Leisure Park
▶▶▶ 87%

tel: 01945 450952 & 450131 **Gull Rd PE13 4ER**
email: enquiries@talltreesleisurepark.co.uk
dir: A47 from Peterborough towards Wisbech. Left onto B1187 signed Guyhirn.
grid ref: TF393035

Tall Trees Leisure Park is a family-run caravan site set in 35 acres of a former commercial fruit farm. There are 59 electric pitches, each with its own water tap, set out in two perfectly level and maturely landscaped fields. There is also a separate, large rally field. Toilets are provided in well-maintained raised buildings, and the reception also houses a small shop and café. Security is given high priority with an entrance barrier and CCTV. 35 acre site. 94 touring pitches. 6 seasonal pitches. Caravan pitches. Motorhome pitches.

Open: all year **Last arrival:** 17.00hrs **Last departure:** noon

Pitches: 🚐🚙

Facilities: ♿🔅🏧🐾

Services: 🔌🔋🚿🔋

Within 3 miles: 🚶🎣🏧

Notes: Dogs must be kept on leads.

HEMINGFORD ABBOTS
Map 12 TL27

Quiet Waters Caravan Park
▶▶▶ 80%

tel: 01480 463405 **PE28 9AJ**
email: quietwaters.park@btopenworld.com
dir: From A14 junct 25 (E of Huntingdon) follow Hemingford Abbots signs. Site in village centre. **grid ref:** TL283712

This is an attractive little site on the banks of the Great Ouse that has been in the same family ownership for over 80 years. It is found in a really charming village just a mile from the A14, making an ideal centre from which to tour the Cambridgeshire area. There are fishing opportunities, rowing boats for hire and many walks and cycling routes directly from the park. There are holiday statics for hire. 1 acre site. 20 touring pitches. 18 hardstandings. Caravan pitches. Motorhome pitches. Tent pitches. 40 statics.

Open: Apr-Oct **Last arrival:** 20.00hrs **Last departure:** noon

Pitches: * 🚐 £19-£23 🚙 £19-£23 ⛺ £19-£23

Leisure: 🎣

Facilities: 🏪⊙🌂❄️♿ WiFi 🐾

Services: 🔌🔅🔋🚿

Within 3 miles: 🚶🎣🏊🍽️🏧🛒⛳

Notes: Dogs must be kept on leads. Boat mooring.

AA Pubs & Restaurants nearby: The Cock Pub and Restaurant, HEMINGFORD GREY, PE28 9BJ, 01480 463609

The Old Bridge Hotel, HUNTINGDON, PE29 3TQ, 01480 424300

PITCHES: 🚐 Caravans 🚙 Motorhomes ⛺ Tents ⛺ Glamping accommodation **SERVICES:** 🔌 Electric hook up 🔅 Launderette 🍺 Licensed bar 🔋 Calor Gas 🔥 Camping Gaz 🔋 Toilet fluid 🍽️ Café/Restaurant 🍔 Fast Food/Takeaway 🔋 Battery charging 👶 Baby care 🚐 Motorvan service point
ABBREVIATIONS: BHs – bank holidays Etr – Easter Spring BH – Spring Bank Holiday fr – from hrs – hours m – mile mdnt – midnight rdbt – roundabout rs – restricted service wk – week wknd – weekend x-roads – crossroads 🚫 No credit or debit cards 🚫 No dogs

HUNTINGDON
Map 12 TL27

Places to visit

Ramsey Abbey Gatehouse, RAMSEY, PE26 1DG, 01480 301494
www.nationaltrust.org.uk

WWT Welney Wetland Centre, WELNEY, PE14 9TN, 01353 860711
www.wwt.org.uk/welney

Great for kids: The Raptor Foundation, WOODHURST, PE28 3BT, 01487 741140
www.raptorfoundation.org.uk

The Willows Caravan Park
►►► 82%

tel: 01480 437566 **Bromholme Ln, Brampton PE28 4NE**
email: thewillowscaravanpark@gmail.com
dir: A1 junct 21 onto A14 (signed Cambridge). Follow Brampton & Huntingdon signs onto B1514. Straight on at 2 rdbts. Right into Bromholme Ln. Site on right (near Brampton Mill pub). **grid ref:** TL224708

A small, friendly site in a pleasant setting beside the River Ouse, on the Ouse Valley Walk. Bay areas have been provided for caravans and motorhomes, and planting for screening is gradually maturing. There are launching facilities and free river fishing. 4 acre site. 50 touring pitches. 10 hardstandings. 10 seasonal pitches. Caravan pitches. Motorhome pitches. Tent pitches.

Open: all year **Last arrival:** 20.00hrs **Last departure:** noon
Pitches: * ⊞ £19-£21 ⊞ £19-£21 ▲ £10-£21
Leisure: ⚠ ⊛
Facilities: ↖ ⊙ ✳ ⚼ WiFi ❼
Services: ⊞ ⊚ ⬛
Within 3 miles: ↓ ≟ ⊟ 🌣 ≝ ⑤
Notes: ⊜ No cars by tents. 5mph one-way system, no generators, no groundsheets, ball games permitted on field only. Dogs must be kept on leads. Free book lending & exchange.
AA Pubs & Restaurants nearby: The Old Bridge Hotel, HUNTINGDON, PE29 3TQ, 01480 424300

Huntingdon Boathaven & Caravan Park
►►► 80%

tel: 01480 411977 **The Avenue, Godmanchester PE29 2AF**
email: boathaven.hunts@virgin.net
dir: A14 junct 24, follow Godmanchester & Huntington signs onto B1044. Under A14, at mini rdbt 2nd exit into Post St. Just before A14 flyover bridge, left into site.
grid ref: TL249706

A small, well laid out site overlooking a boat marina and the River Ouse, set close to the A14 and within walking distance of Huntingdon town centre. The toilets are clean and well kept. A pretty area has been created for tents beside the marina, with wide views across the Ouse Valley. Weekend family activities are organised throughout the season. 2 acre site. 24 touring pitches. 18 hardstandings. Caravan pitches. Motorhome pitches. Tent pitches.

Open: all year (rs Winter - open subject to weather conditions) **Last arrival:** 21.00hrs
Last departure: variable
Pitches: ⊞ ⊞ ▲
Leisure: ✐
Facilities: ↖ ℙ ⊙ ℱ ✳ ⚼ ⊟ ⋈ WiFi ❼
Services: ⊞ ⬛ ⊘ ⬚
Within 3 miles: ↓ ≟ ⊟ 🌣 ≝ ⑤
Notes: No cars by tents. Dogs must be kept on leads. Boat mooring.
AA Pubs & Restaurants nearby: The Old Bridge Hotel, HUNTINGDON, PE29 3TQ, 01480 424300

King William IV, FENSTANTON, PE28 9JF, 01480 462467

ST IVES

Places to visit

The Farmland Museum and Denny Abbey, WATERBEACH, CB25 9PQ, 01223 860988 www.english-heritage.org.uk/daysout/properties/denny-abbey-and-the-farmland-museum

Oliver Cromwell's House, ELY, CB7 4HF, 01353 662062 www.visitely.org.uk

Stroud Hill Park
Touring Caravans & Camping

Stroud Hill Park is a privately owned, exclusively adult, touring caravan site in Pidley, Cambridgeshire. Caravans, motorhomes & tents and well behaved dogs are all welcome. The quiet, stunning, rural Park provides a central Cambridgeshire location for touring caravans and campers. This premier site has been awarded many industry accolades in recognition of the high standard of the on-site facilities. At the heart of the site is a green oak framed building which houses reception and a restaurant, along with the excellent toilets and showers. The facilities are built to be accessible to all. There are 60 pitches (44 hard standing and 16 grass pitches), all with 16 amp electric hook up, fresh water connection and grey water disposal. Pitches approx 8m x 8m. Larger motorhomes can also be accommodated.

*** One night bookings accepted ***
*** ARRIVAL CAN BE ANYTIME AFTER 9 AM. ***
*** DEPARTURE CAN BE ANYTIME UP TO LATE AFTERNOON. ***
*** FREE WIFI AVAILABLE ON MOST PITCHES ***

AA Caravan & Camping 2016 Gold Award

AA CAMPSITE OF THE YEAR 2008

enjoyEngland.com TOURING & CAMPING PARK

TRANQUIL TOURING PARKS

TOP 100 SITES 2016

The Best of British quality touring and holiday parks

LEISURE: ⬗ Indoor pool ⬗ Outdoor pool ⚠ Children's playground ⬇ Kid's club ⬗ Tennis court ⬗ Games room ⬗ Golf course ⬗ Boat hire ⬗ Cycle hire ⊟ Cinema ⬗ Entertainment ✐ Fishing ◎ Mini golf ⬗ Pitch n putt ≝ Watersports ⬗ Gym ⬗ Sports field ⊍ Stables **FACILITIES:** ⬗ Bath ↖ Shower ℙ Private washing cubicles ⊙ Electric shaver ℱ Hairdryer ✳ Ice Packs ⚼ Disabled facilities ⑤ Shop on site ⬗ Mobile shop ⬗ BBQ area ⋈ Picnic area WiFi Wi-fi ⬛ Internet access ⊘ Recycling ❼ Tourist info ⋈ Dog exercise area ⬚ Car hire can be arranged

ST IVES	Map 12 TL37

Stroud Hill Park

▶▶▶▶▶ 93%

Best of British

tel: 01487 741333 & 07831 119302 **Fen Rd, Pidley PE28 3DE**
email: stroudhillpark@gmail.com **web:** www.stroudhillpark.co.uk
dir: *Exit B1040 in Pidley follow signs for Lakeside Lodge Complex, into Fen Rd, site on right.* **grid ref:** *TL335787*

A superb adults-only caravan park designed to a very high specification in a secluded and sheltered spot not far from St Ives. A modern timber-framed barn houses the exceptional facilities. These include the beautifully tiled toilets with spacious cubicles, each containing a shower, washbasin and toilet. A bar and café, and restaurant (The Barn), small licensed shop, tennis court and coarse fishing are among the attractions. There are three pay-as-you-go golf courses plus ten-pin bowling nearby. 6 acre site. 60 touring pitches. 44 hardstandings. 10 seasonal pitches. Caravan pitches. Motorhome pitches. Tent pitches.

Open: all year **Last arrival:** 22.00hrs (arrivals from 09.00hrs)
Last departure: 17.00hrs

Pitches: 🚐 🚗 🏕 **Leisure:** 🏊 ✎
Facilities: 🐾 🄿 ⊙ 🄿 ❄ ⚬ 🚿 WiFi 🗑 ♻ 🄸 🔋 ☎
Services: 🄴 🄻 🍴 🛢 🔲 🍴 **Within 3 miles:** ♨ 🍴 🌳 ♨ ⊚ ♨ 🏪 🔺
Notes: Adults only. No large motorhomes. Dogs must be kept on leads.
AA Pubs & Restaurants nearby: The Lazy Otter, STRETHAM, CB6 3LU, 01353 649780

See advert on opposite page

WISBECH	Map 12 TF40

Places to visit
Peckover House & Garden, WISBECH, PE13 1JR, 01945 583463
www.nationaltrust.org.uk/peckover

Great for kids: WWT Welney Wetland Centre, WELNEY, PE14 9TN, 01353 860711
www.wwt.org.uk/welney

Little Ranch Leisure

▶▶▶ 85%

tel: 01945 860066 **Begdale, Elm PE14 0AZ**
email: littleranchleisure@begdalecambs.wanadoo.co.uk
web: www.littleranchleisure.co.uk
dir: *From rdbt on A47 (SW of Wisbech), take Redmoor Lane to Begdale.* **grid ref:** *TF456062*

A friendly family site set in an apple orchard, with 25 fully serviced pitches and a beautifully designed, spacious toilet block. The site overlooks two fishing lakes and pitches are available by the water; the famous horticultural auctions at Wisbech are nearby. 10 acre site. 40 touring pitches. 40 hardstandings. Caravan pitches. Motorhome pitches. Tent pitches.

Open: all year
Pitches: * 🚐 £12-£17 🚗 £12-£17 🏕 £12-£17
Facilities: ⊙ 🄿 ❄ ⚬ 🚿 ♻ 🄸
Services: 🄴 🄻 🔲
Within 3 miles: 🍴 🏪
Notes: 🐕 Dogs must be kept on leads.
AA Pubs & Restaurants nearby: Crown Lodge Hotel, WISBECH, PE14 8SE, 01945 773391
The Hare Arms, STOW BARDOLPH, PE34 3HT, 01366 382229

CHESHIRE

CODDINGTON
Map 15 SJ45

Places to visit

Cholmondeley Castle Gardens, CHOLMONDELEY, SY14 8AH, 01829 720383
www.cholmondeleycastle.com

Hack Green Secret Nuclear Bunker, NANTWICH, CW5 8AP, 01270 629219
www.hackgreen.co.uk

Great for kids: Dewa Roman Experience, CHESTER, CH1 1NL, 01244 343407
www.dewaromanexperience.co.uk

Chester Zoo, CHESTER, CH2 1LH, 01244 380280 www.chesterzoo.org

PREMIER PARK

Manor Wood Country Caravan Park
▶▶▶▶▶ 90%

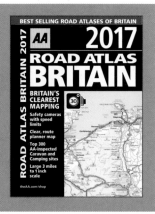

tel: 01829 782990 & 07762 817827 **Manor Wood CH3 9EN**
email: info@manorwoodcaravans.co.uk **web:** www.cheshire-caravan-sites.co.uk
dir: *From A534 at Barton, turn opposite Cock O'Barton pub signed Coddington. Left in 100yds. Site 0.5m on left.* **grid ref:** *SJ453553*

A secluded landscaped park in a tranquil country setting with extensive views towards the Welsh Hills across the Cheshire Plain. The park offers fully serviced pitches, a heated outdoor swimming pool and all-weather tennis courts. The generous pitch density provides optimum privacy and the superb amenities block has excellent decor, underfloor heating and smart modern facilities with very good privacy options. Wildlife is encouraged and there is a fishing lake; country walks and nearby pubs are added attractions. 8 acre site. 45 touring pitches. 30 hardstandings. 30 seasonal pitches. Caravan pitches. Motorhome pitches. Tent pitches. 21 statics.

Open: all year (rs Oct-Mar swimming pool closed) **Last arrival:** 19.00hrs **Last departure:** 11.00hrs

Pitches: * ⊞ £19-£27 ⊞ £19-£27 Å £19-£27 **Leisure:** ⚞ ⚬ ⊙ ⚜

Facilities: ⚟ ⚟ ⊙ ⚟ ☀ ⚟ ⚟ ⚟ ⚟ ⚟ ⚟ ⚟ **Services:** ⚟ ⚟ ⚟

Within 3 miles: ⚟ ⚟ ⚟ ⚟

Notes: No cars by caravans. No noise after 23.00hrs. Dogs must be kept on leads.

AA Pubs & Restaurants nearby: The Calveley Arms, HANDLEY, CH3 9DT, 01829 770619

1851 Restaurant at Peckforton Castle, PECKFORTON, CW6 9TN, 01829 260930

DELAMERE
Map 15 SJ56

Places to visit

Jodrell Bank Discovery Centre, JODRELL BANK, SK11 9DL, 01477 571766
www.jodrellbank.net

Little Moreton Hall, CONGLETON, CW12 4SD, 01260 272018
www.nationaltrust.org.uk

Great for kids: Chester Zoo, CHESTER, CH2 1LH, 01244 380280
www.chesterzoo.org

Fishpool Farm Caravan Park
▶▶▶▶ 85%

tel: 01606 883970 & 07501 506583 **Fishpool Rd CW8 2HP**
email: enquiries@fishpoolfarmcaravanpark.co.uk
dir: *From A49 (Tarporley to Cuddington road), onto A54 signed Chester. At Fishpool Inn left onto B5152 (Fishpool Rd). Site on right.* **grid ref:** *SJ567672*

The staff at this site are friendly, helpful and really know the area well so you can get the most out of your visit. If you would like to do your own research there is an internet café where home baking and local produce are also available. This is a lovely site with hardstanding touring pitches (with electric hook-up) and 20 tent pitches plus static vans, two smaller Shieling vans and lodges for hire. There are several good walks nearby. 5.5 acre site. 50 touring pitches. 14 hardstandings. Caravan pitches. Motorhome pitches. Tent pitches. 1 static.

Open: 15 Feb-15 Jan **Last arrival:** 19.00hrs **Last departure:** noon

Pitches: ⊞ ⊞ Å

Leisure: ⊙ ⚜

Facilities: ⊙ ⚟ ☀ ⚟ ⚟ ⚟ ⚟ ⚟ ⚟ ⚟ ⚟

Services: ⚟ ⚟ ⚟

Within 3 miles: ⚟ ⚟ ⊙ ⚟ ⚟ ⚟ ⚟

Notes: No noise after 23.00hrs. Dogs must be kept on leads. Dog walks. Fresh eggs from own hens.

AA Pubs & Restaurants nearby: The Fishpool Inn, DELAMERE, CW8 2HP, 01606 883277

Alvanley Arms Inn, TARPORLEY, CW6 9DS, 01829 760200

LEISURE: ⚞ Indoor pool ⚞ Outdoor pool Ⓐ Children's playground ⚞ Kid's club ⚞ Tennis court ⚞ Games room ⚞ Golf course ⚞ Boat hire ⚞ Cycle hire ⚞ Cinema ⚞ Entertainment ⚞ Fishing ⊙ Mini golf ⚞ Pitch n putt ⚞ Watersports ⚞ Gym ⚞ Sports field ⚞ Stables **FACILITIES:** ⚞ Bath ⚞ Shower ⚟ Private washing cubicles ⊙ Electric shaver ⚟ Hairdryer ☀ Ice Packs ⚞ Disabled facilities ⚟ Shop on site ⚟ Mobile shop ⚞ BBQ area ⚞ Picnic area ⚞ Wi-fi ⚞ Internet access ⚞ Recycling ⚞ Tourist info ⚞ Dog exercise area ⚞ Car hire can be arranged

KNUTSFORD
Map 15 SJ77

Places to visit

The Tabley House Collection, KNUTSFORD, WA16 0HB, 01565 750151
www.tableyhouse.co.uk

Great for kids: Jodrell Bank Discovery Centre, JODRELL BANK, SK11 9DL,
01477 571766 www.jodrellbank.net

Woodlands Park
►►►78%

tel: 01565 723429 & 01332 810818 **Wash Ln, Allostock WA16 9LG**
dir: *M6 junct 18, A50 N towards Holmes Chapel. 3m, into Wash Ln by Boundary Water
Park. Site 0.25m on left.* **grid ref:** *SJ743710*

A very tranquil and attractive park in the heart of rural Cheshire, and set in 16
acres of mature woodland where in spring the rhododendrons look stunning. Tourers
are located in three separate wooded areas that teem with wildlife and you will
wake up to the sound of birdsong. This park is just five miles from Jodrell Bank. 16
acre site. 40 touring pitches. Caravan pitches. Motorhome pitches. Tent pitches.
140 statics.

Open: Mar-6 Jan **Last arrival:** 21.00hrs **Last departure:** 11.00hrs

Pitches: * ⬛ fr £15 ⬛ fr £15 ⬛ fr £13

Facilities: ☉ ⬛

Services: ⬛ ⬛

Within 3 miles: ⬛ ⬛ ⬛ ⬛

Notes: ⊗ No skateboards or rollerblades. Dogs must be kept on leads.

AA Pubs & Restaurants nearby: The Three Greyhounds Inn, ALLOSTOCK, WA16 9JY,
01565 723455

The Dog Inn, KNUTSFORD, WA16 8UP, 01625 861421

SIDDINGTON

Places to visit

Capesthorne Hall, CAPESTHORNE, SK11 9JY, 01625 861221
www.capesthorne.com

Gawsworth Hall, GAWSWORTH, SK11 9RN, 01260 223456
www.gawsworthhall.com

Great for kids: Jodrell Bank Discovery Centre, JODRELL BANK, SK11 9DL,
01477 571766 www.jodrellbank.net

SIDDINGTON
Map 15 SJ87

Capesthorne Hall
►►►►88%

tel: 01625 861221 **Congleton Rd SK11 9JY**
email: info@capesthorne.com
dir: *Access to site from A34 between Congleton to Wilmslow. Phone for detailed directions.*
grid ref: *SJ841727*

Located within the grounds of the notable Jacobean Capesthorne Hall, this lush, all
level site provides generously sized pitches, all with electricity and most with
hardstandings. The Scandanavian-style amenities block has a smart, quality,
modern interior and very good privacy levels. Guests also have the opportunity to
visit the award-winning gardens on certain days and there are many extensive
walking opportunities directly from the camping areas. 5 acre site. 50 touring
pitches. 30 hardstandings. Caravan pitches. Motorhome pitches.

Open: Mar-Oct **Last arrival:** 22.00hrs **Last departure:** noon

Pitches: ⬛ ⬛ **Facilities:** ⬛ ⬛ ⬛ ⬛ ⬛ ⬛ ⬛

Services: ⬛ ⬛ ⬛

Within 3 miles: ⬛ ⬛ ⬛

Notes: Minimum 3 night stay on BH wknds. No motorised scooters or skateboards. Gas
BBQs only. Touring area may close if large events take place (contact site for details).
Dogs must be kept on leads. Access to Capesthorne Hall & Gardens – additional cost for
hall only.

AA Pubs & Restaurants nearby: The Davenport Arms, MARTON, SK11 9HF, 01260 224269

Egerton Arms, CHELFORD, SK11 9BB, 01625 861366

WETTENHALL
Map 15 SJ66

New Farm Caravan Park
►►►87%

tel: 01270 528213 & 07970 221112 **Long Ln CW7 4DW**
email: info@newfarmcheshire.com
dir: *M6 junct 16, A500 towards Nantwich, right onto Nantwich bypass A51. At lights turn
right, follow A51 Caster & Tarporely signs. After Calveley right into Long Ln, follow site
sign. Site in 2m.* **grid ref:** *SJ613608*

Diversification at New Farm led to the development of four fishing lakes and the
creation of a peaceful small touring park. The proprietors provide a very welcome
touring destination within this peaceful part of Cheshire. Expect good landscaping,
generous hardstanding pitches, a spotless toilet block, and good attention to detail
throughout. Nearly all pitches are very spacious and fully serviced. Please note,
there is no laundry. 40 acre site. 26 touring pitches. 23 hardstandings. 10 seasonal
pitches. Caravan pitches. Motorhome pitches.

Open: all year **Last arrival:** 20.00hrs **Last departure:** 11.30hrs

Pitches: * ⬛ £22-£25 ⬛ £22-£25

Leisure: ⬛

Facilities: ⬛ ⬛ ⬛ ⬛ ⬛ ⬛ ⬛ ⬛ ⬛ ⬛

Services: ⬛ ⬛ ⬛

Within 3 miles: ⬛ ⬛ ⬛ ⬛ ⬛

Notes: Adults only. Arrivals from 13.30hrs. Dogs must be kept on leads.

AA Pubs & Restaurants nearby: The Badger Inn, CHURCH MINSHULL, CW5 6DY,
01270 522348

The Nags Head, HAUGHTON MOSS, CW6 9RN, 01829 260265

PITCHES: ⬛ Caravans ⬛ Motorhomes ⬛ Tents ⬛ Glamping accommodation **SERVICES:** ⬛ Electric hook up ⬛ Launderette ⬛ Licensed bar
⬛ Calor Gas ⬛ Camping Gaz ⬛ Toilet fluid ⬛ Café/Restaurant ⬛ Fast Food/Takeaway ⬛ Battery charging ⬛ Baby care ⬛ Motorvan service point
ABBREVIATIONS: BHs – bank holidays Etr – Easter Spring BH – Spring Bank Holiday fr – from hrs – hours m – mile mdnt – midnight
rdbt – roundabout rs – restricted service wk – week wknd – weekend x-roads – crossroads ⊗ No credit or debit cards ⊗ No dogs

WHITEGATE
Map 15 SJ66

Places to visit

Beeston Castle, BEESTON, CW6 9TX, 01829 260464 www.english-heritage.org.uk/daysout/properties/beeston-castle-and-woodland-park

Chester Cathedral, CHESTER, CH1 2HU, 01244 500958 www.chestercathedral.com

PREMIER PARK

Lamb Cottage Caravan Park
▶▶▶▶▶ 92%

tel: 01606 882302 **Dalefords Ln CW8 2BN**
email: info@lambcottage.co.uk
dir: *From A556 turn at Sandiway lights into Dalefords Ln, signed Winsford. Site 1m on right.* **grid ref:** *SJ613692*

A secluded and attractively landscaped adults-only park in a glorious location where the emphasis is on peace and relaxation. The serviced pitches are spacious with wide grass borders for sitting out and the high quality toilet block is spotlessly clean and immaculately maintained. A good central base for exploring this area, with access to nearby woodland walks and cycle trails. 6 acre site. 45 touring pitches. 45 hardstandings. 14 seasonal pitches. Caravan pitches. Motorhome pitches. 26 statics.

Open: Mar-Oct **Last arrival:** 20.00hrs **Last departure:** noon

Pitches: * 🚐 £24-£30 🚎 £22-£28

Facilities: 🏕🅿⊙𝄞♿🚾WiFi♻𝒊

Services: 🔌🔋🛒🚽

Within 3 miles: ⌯🎣🏪∪

Notes: Adults only. No tents (except trailer tents), no commercial vehicles. Dogs must be kept on leads.

AA Pubs & Restaurants nearby: The Fishpool Inn, DELAMERE, CW8 2HP, 01606 883277

Fox & Barrel, COTEBROOK, CW6 9DZ, 01829 760529

LEISURE: 🏊 Indoor pool 🏊 Outdoor pool 🛝 Children's playground 🧒 Kid's club 🎾 Tennis court 🎱 Games room ⛳ Golf course 🚣 Boat hire 🚴 Cycle hire 🎬 Cinema 🎵 Entertainment 🎣 Fishing ⛳ Mini golf ⛳ Pitch n putt 🏄 Watersports 🏋 Gym 🏟 Sports field ∪ Stables **FACILITIES:** 🛁 Bath 🚿 Shower 🅿 Private washing cubicles ⊙ Electric shaver 🗲 Hairdryer ❄ Ice Packs ♿ Disabled facilities 🏪 Shop on site 🏬 Mobile shop 🍖 BBQ area 🪑 Picnic area WiFi Wi-fi 💻 Internet access ♻ Recycling 𝒊 Tourist info 🐕 Dog exercise area 🚗 Car hire can be arranged

PITCHES: 🚐 Caravans 🚍 Motorhomes ▲ Tents ⛺ Glamping accommodation **SERVICES:** 🔌 Electric hook up 🔲 Launderette 🍷 Licensed bar
🔋 Calor Gas 🔥 Camping Gaz ⊤ Toilet fluid 🍽 Café/Restaurant 🍔 Fast Food/Takeaway 🔋 Battery charging 🛒 Baby care 🚐 Motorvan service point
ABBREVIATIONS: BHs – bank holidays Etr – Easter Spring BH – Spring Bank Holiday fr – from hrs – hours m – mile mdnt – midnight
rdbt – roundabout rs – restricted service wk – week wknd – weekend x-roads – crossroads 🚫 No credit or debit cards 🚫 No dogs

Cornwall

It's not hard to see why thousands of tourists and holidaymakers flock to Cornwall every year. It has just about everything — wild moorland landscapes, glorious river valley scenery, picturesque villages and miles of breathtaking coastline. It has long been acknowledged as one of Britain's top holiday destinations.

Cornwall's southerly latitude and the influence of the Gulf Stream make the county the mildest and sunniest climate in Britain. It's not surprising therefore that one of its greatest and most popular pursuits is surfing. With more than 80 surfing spots, and plenty of sporting enthusiasts who make their way here to enjoy other similar coastal activities, such as wave-surfing, kite surfing and blokarting, the county is an internationally famous surfing hot spot. Blessed with wonderful surf beaches, Newquay is Cornwall's surfing capital. Nearby Watergate Bay is renowned for its glassy waves and Sennen, near Land's End, is where you might even get to surf with dolphins. Certainly the sea is strikingly blue here and the sands dazzlingly white.

A long-running TV series, filmed in a scenic location, is often a guaranteed way to boost tourism and that is certainly the case at Port Isaac on the north Cornwall coast. The village doubles as Portwenn in the drama *Doc Martin*, starring Martin Clunes as the irascible local GP. Much of Port Isaac has been used for location shooting over the years and it's quite common to bump into actors from the series at different points in the village when filming is taking place. Many films and TV series have been shot in Cornwall – including productions of Daphne du Maurier's *Jamaica Inn* and *Rebecca*, though the original version of the latter, made in 1940, was Alfred Hitchcock's first film in Hollywood and shot entirely in California.

In the book, the setting is a large house on the Cornish coast where the atmosphere is decidedly gothic. Daphne du Maurier modelled the house – which she called Manderley – and its location on the Menabilly estate, near Fowey. *Rebecca* was published in 1938 and five years later the writer made Menabilly her home. The house is not open to the public, but it is possible to explore the setting for the story on foot, following a leafy path from the car park at Menabilly Barton Farm to Polridmouth Bay where there are two secluded and remote coves. A bird's eye view of the entire area is possible from the path to Gribben Head, though Menabilly, at the heart of the story, is hidden by trees, thus preserving the mystery of the book.

The Cornish coastline offers breathtakingly beautiful scenery. The north coast is open and exposed; the 735-ft High Cliff, between Boscastle and St Gennys, represents the highest sheer drop cliff in the county. The Lizard, at Cornwall's most southerly point, is a geological masterpiece of awesome cliffs, stacks and arches.

In recent years new or restored visitor attractions have helped to increase tourism in the region – Tim Smit has been the inspiration and driving force behind two of the county's most visited attractions. The Eden Project is famous for its giant geodesic domes housing exotic plants from different parts of the globe, while nearby the Lost Gardens of Heligan at Pentewan has impressive kitchen gardens and a wildlife hide.

Perhaps the last word on this magical corner of Britain should go to Daphne du Maurier. In her book *Vanishing Cornwall*, published in 1967, she wrote: 'A county known and loved in all its moods becomes woven into the pattern of life, something to be shared. As one who sought to know it long ago…in a quest for freedom, and later put down roots and found content, I have come a small way up the path. The beauty and the mystery beckon still.'

◁ Talland Bay

CORNWALL & ISLES OF SCILLY

ASHTON
Map 2 SW62

Places to visit

Godolphin House, GODOLPHIN CROSS, TR13 9RE, 01736 763194
www.nationaltrust.org.uk/godolphin

Poldark Mine and Heritage Complex, WENDRON, TR13 0ER, 01326 573173
www.poldark-mine.co.uk

Great for kids: The Flambards Theme Park, HELSTON, TR13 0QA, 01326 573404
www.flambards.co.uk

Boscrege Caravan & Camping Park
►►►79%

tel: 01736 762231 **TR13 9TG**
email: enquiries@caravanparkcornwall.com
dir: A394 from Helston signed Penzance. In Ashton (Lion & Lamb pub on right) right into
Higher Lane, approx 1.5m (thatched cottage on right) left at site sign. (NB for
recommended towing route contact the park). **grid ref:** SW595305

A quiet and bright little touring park divided into small paddocks with hedges, that
offers plenty of open spaces for children to play in. This family-owned park has
clean, well-painted toilet facilities and neatly trimmed grass. By an Area of
Outstanding Natural Beauty at the foot of Tregonning Hill, this site makes an ideal
base for touring the southern tip of Cornwall; Penzance, Land's End, St Ives and the
beaches in between are all within easy reach. 14 acre site. 50 touring pitches. 10
seasonal pitches. Caravan pitches. Motorhome pitches. Tent pitches. 38 statics.

Open: all year (rs Oct-Mar no camping) **Last arrival:** 22.00hrs **Last departure:** 11.00hrs

Pitches: 🚐 🚙 ▲

Leisure: 🎠 ⚽

Facilities: 🅿️ 📷 ⊙ ℱ ✳ 🛏 🚿 📶 ♻️ ❶ ☎

Services: 🔌 🗑 💧 ⊘ Ⓣ 🛒

Within 3 miles: 🎣 ⛳ 🏌 ◎ ☆ 🛒 🏇 🛢 Ü

Notes: PayPal accepted. No fires, no noise after 23.00hrs, no groups. Dogs must be kept
on leads. Microwave & freezer available, fresh eggs.

AA Pubs & Restaurants nearby: The Victoria Inn, PERRANUTHNOE, TR20 9NP,
01736 710309

New Yard Restaurant, HELSTON, TR12 6AF, 01326 221595

BLACKWATER

Places to visit

Royal Cornwall Museum, TRURO, TR1 2SJ, 01872 272205
www.royalcornwallmuseum.org.uk

East Pool Mine, POOL, TR15 3NP, 01209 315027 www.nationaltrust.org.uk

Great for kids: National Maritime Museum Cornwall, FALMOUTH, TR11 3QY,
01326 313388 www.nmmc.co.uk

BLACKWATER
Map 2 SW74

Trevarth Holiday Park
►►►►84%

tel: 01872 560266 **TR4 8HR**
email: trevarth@btconnect.com **web:** www.trevarth.co.uk
dir: Exit A30 at Chiverton rdbt onto B3277 signed St Agnes. At next rdbt take road signed
Blackwater. Site on right in 200mtrs. **grid ref:** SW744468

A neat and compact park with touring pitches laid out on attractive, well-screened
high ground adjacent to the A30 and A39 junction. This pleasant little park is
centrally located for touring, and is maintained to a very good standard. There is a
large grassed area for children to play on which is away from all tents. 4 acre site.
30 touring pitches. 14 hardstandings. 6 seasonal pitches. Caravan pitches.
Motorhome pitches. Tent pitches. 20 statics.

Open: Apr-Oct **Last arrival:** 21.30hrs **Last departure:** 11.30hrs

Pitches: * 🚐 £13.50-£21 🚙 £13.50-£21 ▲ £13.50-£21

Leisure: 🎱

Facilities: 🅿️ ⊙ ℱ ✳ 📶 ♻️ ❶

Services: 🔌 🗑 💧 ⊘ 🛒 ⅄

Within 3 miles: ⛳ 🛒 🏇 Ü

Notes: No gazebos, no noise after 22.30hrs. Dogs must be kept on leads.

AA Pubs & Restaurants nearby: Driftwood Spars, ST AGNES, TR5 0RT, 01872 552428

BLISLAND — Map 2 SX17

Places to visit

Lanhydrock, LANHYDROCK, PL30 5AD, 01208 265950 www.nationaltrust.org.uk

Tintagel Old Post Office, TINTAGEL, PL34 0DB, 01840 770024 www.nationaltrust.org.uk/main/w-tintageloldpostoffice

South Penquite Farm
▶▶▶ 86%

tel: 01208 850491 **South Penquite PL30 4LH**
email: thefarm@bodminmoor.co.uk
dir: *From Exeter on A30 exit at 1st sign to St Breward on right, (from Bodmin 2nd sign on left). Follow narrow road across Bodmin Moor. Ignore left & right turns until South Penquite Farm Lane on right in 2m.* **grid ref:** *SX108751*

This genuine 'back to nature' site is situated high on Bodmin Moor on a farm committed to organic agriculture. As well as camping there are facilities for adults and children to learn about conservation, organic farming and the local environment, including a fascinating and informative farm trail (pick up a leaflet); there is also a Geocaching trail. Toilet facilities are enhanced by a timber building with quality showers and a good disabled facility. The site has designated areas where fires may be lit. Organic home-reared lamb burgers and sausages are for sale, and one field contains four Mongolian yurts, available for holiday let. In addition, there is bunkhouse accommodation and one wooden pod adjoining. 4 acre site. 40 touring pitches. Motorhome pitches. Tent pitches.

Open: Apr-Oct **Last arrival:** dusk **Last departure:** 14.30hrs

Pitches: ⌂ ▲ £20 ⋔ prices shown below

Leisure: ⋔ ⬧ ✐

Facilities: ⌂ ☺ ⌖ ✳ ⏁ ♻ ❂

Services: ⌷

Glamping: Wooden Pods 1, £30-£40 Min stay 1 night **Yurts** 4, £60-£85 Min stay 1 night Own kitchen Car by unit

Within 3 miles: ⌁ ✐ ≽ ⌷ ⌷ ∪

Notes: ⊗ No caravans, no pets.

AA Pubs & Restaurants nearby: St Tudy Inn, ST TUDY, PL30 3NN, 01208 850656

Who has won England Campsite of the Year? See page 14

BODMIN — Map 2 SX06

Places to visit

Restormel Castle, RESTORMEL, PL22 0EE, 01208 872687 www.english-heritage.org.uk/daysout/properties/restormel-castle

Great for kids: Eden Project, ST AUSTELL, PL24 2SG, 01726 811911 www.edenproject.com

Mena Caravan & Camping Park
▶▶▶▶ 80%

tel: 01208 831845 **PL30 5HW**
email: mena@campsitesincornwall.co.uk **web:** www.campsitesincornwall.co.uk
dir: *Exit A30 onto A389 N signed Lanivet & Wadebridge. In 0.5m 1st right & pass under A30. 1st left signed Lostwithiel & Fowey. In 0.25m right at top of hill. 0.5m then 1st right. Entrance 100yds on right.* **grid ref:** *SW041626*

This grassy site is about four miles from the Eden Project and midway between the north and south Cornish coasts. Set in a secluded, elevated position with high hedges for shelter, it offers plenty of peace and quiet. There is a small coarse fishing lake on site, hardstanding pitches, a shop and a café, with an alfresco decking area, where breakfasts, cream teas and takeaway food can be purchased. The site is on the Saint's Way, and nearby is the neolithic hill fort of Helman Tor, the highest point on Bodmin Moor. There is a fish and chip restaurant in Lanivet (approximately one mile) – from here there is a bus service to Bodmin. 15 acre site. 25 touring pitches. 4 hardstandings. Caravan pitches. Motorhome pitches. Tent pitches. 2 statics.

Open: all year **Last arrival:** 22.00hrs **Last departure:** noon

Pitches: ⌂ ⌂ ▲

Leisure: ⬧ ✐ ⚇

Facilities: ⌂ ☺ ⌖ ✳ ⚄ ⌷ ⏁ ⚐ WiFi ♻ ❂

Services: ⚄ ⌷ ⌷ ⚇ ⏁ ⌷ ⌷

Within 3 miles: ⌁ ✐ ≽ ⌷ ⌷ ∪

Notes: Snooker, table tennis.

AA Pubs & Restaurants nearby: Trehellas House Hotel & Restaurant, BODMIN, PL30 3AD, 01208 72700

The Crown Inn, LANLIVERY, PL30 5BT, 01208 872707

PITCHES: ⌂ Caravans ⌂ Motorhomes ▲ Tents ⋔ Glamping accommodation **SERVICES:** ⚄ Electric hook up ⌷ Launderette ⚑ Licensed bar ⚐ Calor Gas ⚋ Camping Gaz ⏁ Toilet fluid ⌷ Café/Restaurant ⚇ Fast Food/Takeaway ⚄ Battery charging ⚇ Baby care ∪ Motorvan service point **ABBREVIATIONS:** BHs – bank holidays Etr – Easter Spring BH – Spring Bank Holiday fr – from hrs – hours m – mile mdnt – midnight rdbt – roundabout rs – restricted service wk – week wknd – weekend x-roads – crossroads ⊗ No credit or debit cards ⊗ No dogs

BRYHER (ISLES OF SCILLY)　　　Map 2 SV81

Bryher Camp Site
►►►82%

tel: 01720 422068 **TR23 0PR**
email: relax@bryhercampsite.co.uk
dir: *Accessed from the mainland by ferry or plane or by boat from main island of St Mary's.* **grid ref:** *SV880155*

Set on the smallest inhabited Scilly Isle with spectacular scenery and white beaches, this tent-only site is in a sheltered valley surrounded by hedges. Pitches are located in paddocks at the northern end of the island which is only a short walk from the quay. There is a good, modern toilet block, and plenty of peace and quiet. Although located in a very quiet area, the Fraggle Rock Bar and Restaurant and a well-equipped shop are within easy reach. There is easy boat access to all the other islands. 2.25 acre site. 38 touring pitches. Tent pitches.

Open: Apr-Oct
Pitches: * ⛺ fr £20.50
Leisure: ⚽
Facilities: 🚿⊙🗜✳ WiFi ♻🛈
Services: 🗑🔋🚮🛄
Within 3 miles: 🎣🏇⛳◎🛶🏄🎣🛶∪
Notes: No cars by tents. No pets.
AA Pubs & Restaurants nearby: Hell Bay, BRYHER, TR23 0PR, 01720 422947

BUDE　　　Map 2 SS20

See also Kilkhampton, Bridgerule (Devon) & Holsworthy (Devon)

PREMIER PARK

Wooda Farm Holiday Park
►►►►► 94%

Best of British GOLD

tel: 01288 352069 **Poughill EX23 9HJ**
email: stay@wooda.co.uk **web:** www.wooda.co.uk
dir: *From A39 at Stratton follow Poughill & brown site signs into Stamford Hill. Approx 1m to site on right.* **grid ref:** *SS229080*

An attractive park set on raised ground overlooking Bude Bay, with lovely sea views. The park is divided into paddocks by hedges and mature trees, and offers high quality facilities in extensive colourful gardens. A variety of activities is provided by way of the large sports hall and hard tennis court, and there's a super children's playground. There are holiday static caravans for hire. An

LEISURE: 🏊 Indoor pool 🏊 Outdoor pool 🛝 Children's playground 🪁 Kid's club 🎾 Tennis court 🎱 Games room ⛳ Golf course 🚣 Boat hire 🚲 Cycle hire 🎬 Cinema 🎵 Entertainment 🎣 Fishing ◎ Mini golf ⛳ Pitch n putt 🏄 Watersports 💪 Gym ⚽ Sports field ∪ Stables **FACILITIES:** 🛁 Bath 🚿 Shower 🅿 Private washing cubicles ⊙ Electric shaver 🗜 Hairdryer ✳ Ice Packs ♿ Disabled facilities 🅂 Shop on site 🏪 Mobile shop 🍖 BBQ area 🪑 Picnic area WiFi Wi-fi 💻 Internet access ♻ Recycling 🛈 Tourist info 🐕 Dog exercise area 🚗 Car hire can be arranged

interactive information screen in the reception area is for customer use. 50 acre site. 200 touring pitches. 80 hardstandings. 10 seasonal pitches. Caravan pitches. Motorhome pitches. Tent pitches. 55 statics.

Wooda Farm Holiday Park

Open: Apr-Oct (rs Apr-May & mid Sep-Oct shop hours limited, bar & takeaway) **Last arrival:** 20.00hrs **Last departure:** 10.30hrs

Pitches: * ⮔ £20-£36 ⮔ £14-£36 ⮔ £14-£31

Leisure: ♈ ⛰ ⚾ ⚽ ⛳ ⛵ ⚲ ♪ ⚮

Facilities: ⮔ ⮔ P̄ ⊙ ⍟ ☼ ⭑ ⑤ ⟲ ⭡ WiFi ♺ ❶

Services: ⮔ ⑤ 🍴 ⮔ ⚳ Ⓣ ⑩ ⭲ ⭷ ⮔

Within 3 miles: ⬇ ⭤ ⛳ ⛵ ⊙ ⭥ ⑤ ⑤ ♺ ◡

Notes: Restrictions on certain dog breeds, no skateboards, rollerblades or scooters. Dogs must be kept on leads. Coarse fishing, woodland walks, farmyard animals.

AA Pubs & Restaurants nearby: Bay View Inn, WIDEMOUTH BAY, EX23 0AW, 01288 361273

See advert on opposite page

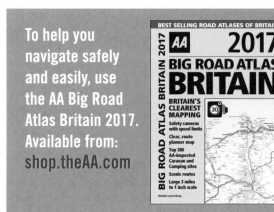
Budemeadows Touring Park

▶ ▶ ▶ ▶ 90%

tel: 01288 361646 **Widemouth Bay EX23 0NA**
email: holiday@budemeadows.com **web:** www.budemeadows.com
dir: *3m S of Bude on A39. Follow signs after turn to Widemouth Bay. Site accessed via layby from A39.* **grid ref:** *SS215012*

This is a very well-kept site of distinction, with good quality facilities, hardstandings and eight fully serviced pitches. Budemeadows is set on a gentle sheltered slope in nine acres of naturally landscaped parkland, surrounded by mature hedges. The internal doors in the facility block have all been painted in pastel colours to resemble beach huts. The site is just one mile from Widemouth Bay, and three miles from the unspoilt resort of Bude. 9 acre site. 145 touring pitches. 34 hardstandings. 4 seasonal pitches. Caravan pitches. Motorhome pitches. Tent pitches.

Open: all year (rs Sep-late May shop, bar & pool closed, takeaway summer only) **Last arrival:** 21.00hrs **Last departure:** 11.00hrs

Pitches: * ⮔ £18-£31.50 ⮔ £18-£31.50 ⮔ £13.50-£30.50

Leisure: ⮔ ⚲

Facilities: ⮔ ⮔ P̄ ⊙ ⍟ ☼ ⭑ ⑤ ⭡ WiFi ⮔ ♺ ❶

Services: ⮔ ⑤ 🍴 ⚳ ⚳ Ⓣ ⭲ ⭷ ⮔

Within 3 miles: ⬇ ⭤ ⛳ ⛵ ⊙ ⭥ ⑤ ⑤ ♺ ◡

Notes: No noise after 23.00hrs, breathable groundsheets only, no open fires or firepits. Dogs must be kept on leads. Table tennis, giant chess, baby changing facility.

AA Pubs & Restaurants nearby: Bay View Inn, WIDEMOUTH BAY, EX23 0AW, 01288 361273

PITCHES: ⮔ Caravans ⮔ Motorhomes ⮔ Tents ⮔ Glamping accommodation **SERVICES:** ⮔ Electric hook up ⑤ Launderette 🍴 Licensed bar
⮔ Calor Gas ⚳ Camping Gaz Ⓣ Toilet fluid ⑩ Café/Restaurant ⭲ Fast Food/Takeaway ⭷ Battery charging ⮔ Baby care ⮔ Motorvan service point
ABBREVIATIONS: BHs – bank holidays Etr – Easter Spring BH – Spring Bank Holiday fr – from hrs – hours m – mile mdnt – midnight
rdbt – roundabout rs – restricted service wk – week wknd – weekend x-roads – crossroads ⊗ No credit or debit cards ⊗ No dogs

BUDE *continued*

Pentire Haven Holiday Park
►►►►89%

tel: 01288 321601 **Stibb Rd, Kilkhampton EX23 9QY**
email: holidays@pentirehaven.co.uk **web:** www.pentirehaven.co.uk
dir: *A39 from Bude towards Bideford, in 3m turn left signed Sandymouth Bay.*
grid ref: *SS246111*

A very open grass site handy for many beautiful beaches, but in particular the surfing beach of Bude only four miles away. The management and enthusiastic staff continue to make a real impression on this improving park. There are excellent toilet facilities in addition to a very good children's playground and a small swimming pool, which is open during the busy season. There is a rally field and holiday static caravans are available for hire or to buy. 23 acre site. 120 touring pitches. 46 hardstandings. 40 seasonal pitches. Caravan pitches. Motorhome pitches. Tent pitches. 18 statics.

Open: all year **Last arrival:** 23.30hrs **Last departure:** 10.30hrs
Pitches: * 🚐 £9.95-£23 🚐 £9.95-£23 ▲ £9.95-£23
Leisure: 🏊🏄🎾🎿🎣🏐🎱🎵
Facilities: 🔥☉☕✂♿🅂🔥📶🔌ℹ
Services: 🔌🔋🚽🚿🚰🅣🍽🛒🏪🛗
Within 3 miles: 🎣🏇🐎🏌⛵🎿🛒🅂U
Notes: PayPal accepted. No fires. Dogs must be kept on leads.
AA Pubs & Restaurants nearby: Bay View Inn, WIDEMOUTH BAY, EX23 0AW, 01288 361273
See advert on opposite page

Widemouth Fields Caravan & Camping Park
►►►►87%

tel: 01288 361351 **Park Farm, Poundstock EX23 0NA**
email: reception@widemouthfields.co.uk
dir: *M5 junct 27 (signed Barnstaple). A361 to rdbt before Barnstaple. Take A39 signed Bideford & Bude. (NB do not exit A39 at Stratton). S for 3m, follow sign just past x-roads to Widemouth Bay. Into layby, entrance on left.* **grid ref:** *SS215010*

In a quiet location with far reaching views over rolling countryside, this site is only one mile from the golden beach at Widemouth Bay, and just three miles from the resort of Bude. The park has a well-stocked shop, many hardstanding pitches and a cosy bar that offers takeaway breakfasts. The toilets are of outstanding quality with many combined fully serviced cubicles. All the buildings resemble log cabins which certainly adds to the appeal of the site. There is a courtesy shuttle bus into Bude and to the Widemouth Bay Holiday Village (Spring Bank Holiday to August only), where the facilities can be used by the touring campers. Wooden pods are available for hire. 15 acre site. 156 touring pitches. 156 hardstandings. 40 seasonal pitches. Caravan pitches. Motorhome pitches. Tent pitches. 5 statics.

Open: Apr-Sep **Last arrival:** 21.00hrs **Last departure:** noon
Pitches: * 🚐 £16-£44 🚐 £22-£54 ▲ £19-£54 🏠 prices shown below
Leisure: 🏐
Facilities: ☉☕✂♿🅂🔥📶🔌ℹ
Services: 🔌🔋🚽🚿🚰🅣🍽🛒🛗
Glamping: Wooden Pods 5, £25-£110 Changeover day Any day Min stay 1 night Car by unit
Within 3 miles: 🎣🏇🐎🏌◎⛵🎿🛒🅂U
Notes: Entry to site by swipecard only, deposit taken at time of check-in.
AA Pubs & Restaurants nearby: Bay View Inn, WIDEMOUTH BAY, EX23 0AW, 01288 361273

Upper Lynstone Caravan Park
►►►►84%

tel: 01288 352017 **Lynstone EX23 0LP**
email: reception@upperlynstone.co.uk
dir: *0.75m S of Bude on coastal road to Widemouth Bay.* **grid ref:** *SS205053*

There are extensive views over Bude to be enjoyed from this quiet, sheltered family-run park, a terraced grass site suitable for all units. There's a spotlessly clean and top quality toilet block, plus a children's playground and a reception with a shop that sells basic food supplies and camping spares. Static caravans are available for holiday hire. A path leads directly to the coastal footpath with its stunning sea views, and the old Bude Canal is just a stroll away. 6 acre site. 65 touring pitches. Caravan pitches. Motorhome pitches. Tent pitches. 41 statics.

Open: Apr-Oct **Last arrival:** 22.00hrs **Last departure:** 10.00hrs
Pitches: * 🚐 £17.50-£24 🚐 £17.50-£24 ▲ £15-£22
Leisure: 🎿
Facilities: 🔥☉☕✂♿🅂🔥📶🔌ℹ
Services: 🔌🔋🚽🚰🅣🛒
Within 3 miles: 🎣🏇🐎🏌◎⛵🎿🛒🅂U
Notes: No groups. Dogs must be kept on leads. Baby changing room.
AA Pubs & Restaurants nearby: Bay View Inn, WIDEMOUTH BAY, EX23 0AW, 01288 361273

LEISURE: 🏊 Indoor pool 🏊 Outdoor pool 🎢 Children's playground 🚣 Kid's club 🎾 Tennis court 🎱 Games room ⛳ Golf course 🚣 Boat hire 🚲 Cycle hire 🎬 Cinema 🎵 Entertainment 🎣 Fishing ◎ Mini golf ⛳ Pitch n putt 🏄 Watersports 🏋 Gym 🏟 Sports field U Stables **FACILITIES:** 🛁 Bath 🚿 Shower 🅿 Private washing cubicles ☉ Electric shaver 🪒 Hairdryer ❄ Ice Packs ♿ Disabled facilities 🅂 Shop on site 🚐 Mobile shop 🍖 BBQ area 🌲 Picnic area 📶 Wi-fi 💻 Internet access 🔌 Recycling ℹ Tourist info 🐕 Dog exercise area 🚗 Car hire can be arranged

Willow Valley Holiday Park
►►►► 84%

tel: 01288 353104 **Bush EX23 9LB**
email: willowvalley@talk21.com
dir: *On A39, 0.5m N of junct with A3072 at Stratton.* **grid ref:** *SS236078*

A small sheltered park in the Strat Valley with level grassy pitches and a stream running through it. The friendly family owners have improved all areas of this attractive park, including a smart toilet block and an excellent reception and shop. The park has direct access from the A39, and is only two miles from the sandy beaches at Bude. There are four pine lodges for holiday hire. 4 acre site. 41 touring pitches. 8 hardstandings. Caravan pitches. Motorhome pitches. Tent pitches. 4 statics.

Open: Mar-end Oct **Last arrival:** 21.00hrs **Last departure:** 11.00hrs

Pitches: ⊑ £14-£19 ⊑ £14-£19 ▲ £14-£19

Leisure: ⋀

Facilities: 🅿 ⊙ 🅿 ✳ ₺ 🔥 ⊞ ⊞ 🐕 ♻ 🛈

Services: 🔌 🔥 🍺 🧼 ⊤ 🔋

Within 3 miles: ↨ ⟲ ♨ ◎ 🌊 🍴 🔥 ⛳

Notes: 🐕 Dogs must be kept on leads.

Juliot's Well Holiday Park
►►►► 89%

SILVER

tel: 01840 213302 **PL32 9RF**
email: holidays@juliotswell.com
dir: *From A39 (SW of Camelford) at Valley Truckle follow B3266 & Boscastle signs. 1st left signed Lanteglos, site 300yds on right.* **grid ref:** *SX095829*

Set in the wooded grounds of an old manor house, this quiet site enjoys lovely and extensive views across the countryside. A rustic inn on site occasionally offers entertainment, and there is plenty to do, both on the park and in the vicinity. The superb, fully serviced toilet facilities are very impressive. There are also self-catering pine lodges, static caravans and five cottages for hire. 33 acre site. 39 touring pitches. Caravan pitches. Motorhome pitches. Tent pitches. 82 statics.

Open: all year **Last arrival:** 20.00hrs **Last departure:** 11.00hrs

Pitches: * ⊑ £10-£25 ⊑ £10-£25 ▲ £10-£25

Leisure: 🏊 ⋀ 🔍 **Facilities:** 🛁 🐾 🅿 ⊙ 🅿 ₺ 🔥 ⊞ 🐕 WiFi ▦ ♻ 🛈

Services: 🔌 🔥 🍺 🍴 🛒 🔋 **Within 3 miles:** ↨ ⟲ 🍴 🔥 ⛳

Notes: Complimentary use of cots & high chairs.

AA Pubs & Restaurants nearby: The Mill House Inn, TREBARWITH, PL34 0HD, 01840 770200

PITCHES: ⊑ Caravans ⊑ Motorhomes ▲ Tents ⋀ Glamping accommodation **SERVICES:** 🔌 Electric hook up 🍺 Launderette 🍺 Licensed bar 🔥 Calor Gas ⊘ Camping Gaz ⊤ Toilet fluid 🍴 Café/Restaurant 🍟 Fast Food/Takeaway 🔋 Battery charging 🛒 Baby care 🚐 Motorvan service point
ABBREVIATIONS: BHs – bank holidays Etr – Easter Spring BH – Spring Bank Holiday fr – from hrs – hours m – mile mdnt – midnight rdbt – roundabout rs – restricted service wk – week wknd – weekend x-roads – crossroads 🚫 No credit or debit cards 🚫 No dogs

CAMELFORD *continued*

Lakefield Caravan Park

81%

tel: 01840 213279 **Lower Pendavey Farm PL32 9TX**
email: lakefieldcaravanpark@btconnect.com
dir: *From A39 in Camelford onto B3266, right at T-junct, site 1.5m on left.*
grid ref: *SX095853*

Set in a rural location, this friendly park is part of a specialist equestrian centre, and offers good quality services. All the facilities are immaculate and spotlessly clean. Riding lessons and hacks are always available, with a BHS qualified instructor. Newquay, Padstow and Bude are all easily accessed from this site. 5 acre site. 40 touring pitches. Caravan pitches. Motorhome pitches. Tent pitches.

Open: Etr or Apr-Oct **Last arrival:** 22.00hrs **Last departure:** 11.00hrs

Pitches: * £15.50-£18.50 £15.50-£18.50 £15.50-£18.50

Leisure:

Facilities:

Services:

Within 3 miles:

Notes: Dogs must be kept on leads. On-site lake.

AA Pubs & Restaurants nearby: The Port William, TREBARWITH, PL34 0HB, 01840 770230

CARLYON BAY

Places to visit

Charlestown Shipwreck & Heritage Centre, ST AUSTELL, PL25 3NJ, 01726 69897 www.shipwreckcharlestown.com

The Lost Gardens of Heligan, PENTEWAN, PL26 6EN, 01726 845100 www.heligan.com

Great for kids: Wheal Martyn, ST AUSTELL, PL26 8XG, 01726 850362 www.wheal-martyn.com

Eden Project, ST AUSTELL, PL24 2SG, 01726 811911 www.edenproject.com

CARLYON BAY — Map 2 SX05

PREMIER PARK

Carlyon Bay Caravan & Camping Park

92%

tel: 01726 812735 **Bethesda, Cypress Av PL25 3RE**
email: holidays@carlyonbay.net **web:** www.carlyonbay.net
dir: *Exit A390 W of St Blazey, left onto A3092 for Par, right in 0.5m. Cypress Ave to Carlyon Bay.* **grid ref:** *SX052526*

An attractive, secluded site set amongst a belt of trees with background woodland. The spacious grassy park is beautifully landscaped and offers quality toilet and shower facilities and plenty of on-site attractions, including a well-equipped games room, TV room, café, an inviting swimming pool, and occasional family entertainment. It is less than half a mile from a sandy beach and the Eden Project is only two miles away. 35 acre site. 180 touring pitches. 12 hardstandings. Caravan pitches. Motorhome pitches. Tent pitches.

Open: Etr-28 Sep (rs Etr-mid May & mid-end Sep swimming pool, takeaway & shop closed) **Last arrival:** 21.00hrs **Last departure:** 11.00hrs

Pitches: * £14-£36 £14-£36 £14-£35 **Leisure:**

Facilities: **Services:**

Within 3 miles:

Notes: No noise after 23.00hrs, no hoverboards or motorised scooters (except invalid mobility scooters). Dogs must be kept on leads. Crazy golf. Children's entertainment Jul-Aug only.

AA Pubs & Restaurants nearby: Austell's, ST AUSTELL, PL25 3PH, 01726 813888

The Britannia Inn & Restaurant, PAR, PL24 2SL, 01726 812889

See advert on opposite page

East Crinnis Camping & Caravan Park
▶▶▶▶84%

tel: 01726 813023 & 07435 974961 **Lantyan, East Crinnis PL24 2SQ**
email: info@eastcrinnis.com
dir: *From A390 (Lostwithiel to St Austell), take A3082 signed Fowey at rdbt by Britannia Inn, site on left.* **grid ref:** *SX062528*

A small rural park with spacious pitches set in individual bays, about one mile from the beaches at Carlyon Bay, and just two miles from the Eden Project. The friendly owners keep the site very clean and well maintained, and also offer three self-catering holiday lodges, two yurts and one geo dome for hire. The park offers a takeaway food facility but it's only a short walk to Par where restaurants can be found. 2 acre site. 38 touring pitches. 9 hardstandings. 18 seasonal pitches. Caravan pitches. Motorhome pitches. Tent pitches.

Open: Etr-Oct **Last arrival:** 21.00hrs **Last departure:** 11.00hrs

Pitches: ⌑ ⌑ Å ⌂

Leisure: ⊙

Facilities: ⊙ ⌂ ⌘ ⌘ ⌂ ⌐ ⌐ WiFi ⌐ ⌂ ⌘

Services: ⌑ ⌂

Glamping: Yurts 2 Geo domes 1

Within 3 miles: ⌄ ⌄ ⌂ ⌐ ⌐ ◎ ⌐ ⌂ ⌐ ∪

Notes: No noise after 23.00hrs. Dogs must be kept on leads. Coarse fishing, wildlife & pond area with dog walk.

AA Pubs & Restaurants nearby: The Britannia Inn & Restaurant, PAR, PL24 2SL, 01726 812889

The Rashleigh Inn, POLKERRIS, PL24 2TL, 01726 813991

Austell's, ST AUSTELL, PL25 3PH, 01726 813888

CARNHELL GREEN | **Map 2 SW63**

Lavender Fields Touring Park
NEW ▶▶▶▶83%

tel: 01209 832188 & 07855 227773 **Penhale Rd TR14 0LU**
email: info@lavenderfieldstouring.co.uk
dir: *Exit A30 at Camborne W junct. At top of slip road left at rdbt, 2nd exit through Roseworthy, left after Roseworthy signed Carnhell Green, over level crossing to T-junct, turn left. Site 750yds on right.* **grid ref:** *SW623377*

A family owned and run park in the heart of the Cornish countryside on the outskirts of the idyllic village of Carnhell Green, yet only a short car or bus ride to towns and glorious golden beaches. Developed on an old mine waste site, the park is maturing well, with lush grass and neat and tidy pitches, and has a smart new toilet block and some good hardstandings for larger units. There are wonderful countryside views to the south which gives this site a pleasant open feel. A kettle in the dishwash area is provided for campers' use. Dogs are very welcome to accompany their owners and can stay free of charge. 6 acre site. 45 touring pitches. 21 hardstandings. 5 seasonal pitches. Caravan pitches. Motorhome pitches. Tent pitches. 6 statics.

Open: all year **Last arrival:** 20.00hrs **Last departure:** 10.00hrs

Pitches: ⌑ £12.50-£17 ⌑ £12.50-£17 Å £8-£22.50

Leisure: ⌂

Facilities: ⌐ ⌐ ⊙ ⌂ ⌘ ⌐ ⌘ ⌂

Services: ⌑ ⌂ ⌂ ⌐

Within 3 miles: ⌄ ⌄ ⌂ ⌐ ◎ ⌐ ⌂ ⌐ ∪

Notes: Dogs must be kept on leads.

PITCHES: ⌑ Caravans ⌑ Motorhomes Å Tents ⌂ Glamping accommodation **SERVICES:** ⌑ Electric hook up ⌂ Launderette ⌐ Licensed bar ⌂ Calor Gas ⌀ Camping Gaz Ⓣ Toilet fluid ⌐ Café/Restaurant ⌂ Fast Food/Takeaway ⌂ Battery charging ⌑ Baby care ⌐ Motorvan service point **ABBREVIATIONS:** BHs – bank holidays Etr – Easter Spring BH – Spring Bank Holiday fr – from hrs – hours m – mile mdnt – midnight rdbt – roundabout rs – restricted service wk – week wknd – weekend x-roads – crossroads Ⓒ No credit or debit cards Ⓝ No dogs

CHACEWATER
Map 2 SW74

Places to visit

Royal Cornwall Museum, TRURO, TR1 2SJ, 01872 272205
www.royalcornwallmuseum.org.uk

Trelissick, TRELISSICK, TR3 6QL, 01872 862090
www.nationaltrust.org.uk/trelissick

Killiwerris Touring Park
▶▶▶▶ 81%

tel: 01872 561356 & 07734 053593 **Penstraze TR4 8PF**
email: killiwerris@aol.com
dir: *Take A30 towards Penzance, at Chiverton Cross rdbt take 3rd exit signed St Agnes. At next mini rdbt take Blackwater exit, in 500yds left into Kea Downs Rd, park 1m on right.*
grid ref: *SW753454*

A small, adults-only, family-run touring park, just five miles from Truro and four miles from the coastal village of St Agnes, making it an ideal base for exploring west Cornwall. The site has a sunny aspect yet is sheltered by mature trees giving it a very private feel. The facilities are of an exceptionally high standard and include a modern and smart amenities block. It is a peaceful spot in which to relax and get away from the crowds. 2.2 acre site. 17 touring pitches. 17 hardstandings. 3 seasonal pitches. Caravan pitches. Motorhome pitches.

Open: all year **Last arrival:** 21.00hrs **Last departure:** 11.00hrs

---

Pitches: 🚐 🚌
Facilities: 🐾 📶 ☺ 🅿 ⚡ 🚿 ⚿ 🚾 💻 ♻ ⚘ ⓘ ☎
Services: 🛢 🖎
Within 3 miles: ⚓ 🎣 🏌 🛒 🖎 ⛹
Notes: Adults only. Dogs must be kept on leads.

COVERACK
Map 2 SW71

Places to visit

Cornish Seal Sanctuary, GWEEK, TR12 6UG, 01326 221361
www.sealsanctuaries.com

The Flambards Theme Park, HELSTON, TR13 0QA, 01326 573404
www.flambards.co.uk

Little Trevothan Caravan & Camping Park
▶▶▶ 80%

tel: 01326 280260 **Trevothan TR12 6SD**
email: sales@littletrevothan.co.uk
dir: *A3083 onto B3293 signed Coverack, approx 2m after Goonhilly Earth Station, right at petrol station onto unclassified road. Approx 1m, 3rd left. Site 0.5m on left.*
grid ref: *SW772179*

A secluded site, with excellent facilities, near the unspoilt fishing village of Coverack, with a large recreation area and good play equipment for children. The

---

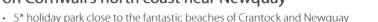

nearby sandy beach has lots of rock pools for children to play in, and the many walks both from the park and the village offer stunning scenery. 10.5 acre site. 70 touring pitches. 10 hardstandings. 10 seasonal pitches. Caravan pitches. Motorhome pitches. Tent pitches. 22 statics.

Open: Mar-Oct **Last arrival:** 21.00hrs **Last departure:** noon

Pitches: 🚐 🚎 🅰

Leisure: 🕌 ♻ 🔍

Facilities: 🏪 ☉ ℙ ☀ 🔋 🛒 ♻ ❶

Services: 🔌 🔋 🔋 🛢 🖊 T 🔋

Within 3 miles: 🚲 🛶 🔋 🔋

Notes: 🚫 No noise between 22.00hrs-08.30hrs. Dogs must be kept on leads.

AA Pubs & Restaurants nearby: Cadgwith Cove Inn, CADGWITH, TR12 7JX, 01326 290513

CRANTOCK (NEAR NEWQUAY) — Map 2 SW76

Places to visit

Trerice, TRERICE, TR8 4PG, 01637 875404 www.nationaltrust.org.uk/trerice/

PREMIER PARK

Trevella Park

▶▶▶▶▶ 94%

GOLD

tel: 01637 830308 **TR8 5EW**
email: holidays@trevella.co.uk **web:** www.trevella.co.uk
dir: *Between Crantock & A3075.* **grid ref:** *SW801599*

A well-established and very well-run family site, with outstanding floral displays. Set in a rural area close to Newquay, this stunning park boasts three teeming fishing lakes for both the experienced and novice angler, and a superb outdoor swimming pool and paddling area. The spotlessly clean toilet facilities include excellent en suite wet rooms. All areas are neat and clean and the whole park looks stunning. Canvas geo-domes, fully equipped ready-erected tents and safari tents are available for hire. 15 acre site. 165 touring pitches. 54 hardstandings. 16 seasonal pitches. Caravan pitches. Motorhome pitches. Tent pitches. 104 statics.

Trevella Park

Open: Etr-Oct (rs Etr-mid May & mid Sep-Oct pool closed) **Last arrival:** 21.00hrs **Last departure:** 10.00hrs

Pitches: 🚐 🚎 🅰 🏕 **Leisure:** 🏊 🕌 🔍 🔋

Facilities: ☉ ℙ ☀ 🔋 🔋 🛒 WiFi ♻ ❶ **Services:** 🔌 🔋 🛢 🖊 T 🍴 🔋 🚜 🛒 🔋

Glamping: Safari tents 9, £70.33-£114.43 Changeover day Fri/Sat Min stay 3 nights Own kitchen Car by unit **Erected Tents** 9, £56.67-£81.86 Changeover day Fri/Sat Min stay 3 nights Own kitchen Car by unit **Geo domes** 3, £84.34-£132.43 Changeover day Fri/Sat Min stay 3 nights Own kitchen Car by unit

Within 3 miles: 🔋 🔋 🔋 🔋 🔋 ◎ 🔋 🔋 🔋 U

Notes: Families & couples only. Dogs must be kept on leads. Crazy golf, children's ranger activities, games room, fresh croissants & pasties.

AA Pubs & Restaurants nearby: The Smugglers' Den Inn, CUBERT, TR8 5PY, 01637 830209

The Lewinnick Lodge Bar & Restaurant, NEWQUAY, TR7 1NX, 01637 878117

See advert on opposite page

Treago Farm Caravan Site

▶▶▶▶ 86%

tel: 01637 830277 **TR8 5QS**
email: info@treagofarm.co.uk
dir: *From A3075 (W of Newquay), turn right for Crantock. Site signed beyond village.*
grid ref: *SW782601*

A grass site in open farmland in a south-facing sheltered valley with a fishing lake. This friendly family park has spotless toilet facilities, which include three excellent heated family rooms, a good shop and bar with takeaway food, and it has direct access to Crantock and Polly Joke beaches, National Trust land and many natural beauty spots. 5 acre site. 90 touring pitches. Caravan pitches. Motorhome pitches. Tent pitches. 10 statics.

Open: mid May-mid Sep (rs Mid May, mid Sep-Oct restricted services in shop & bar) **Last arrival:** 22.00hrs **Last departure:** 18.00hrs

Pitches: * 🚐 £15.50-£21 🚎 £15.50-£21 🅰 £15.50-£21 **Leisure:** 🔍

Facilities: 🏪 ℙ ☉ ℙ ☀ 🔋 🔋 🛒 ♻ ❶ **Services:** 🔌 🔋 🍴 🛢 🖊 T 🔋

Within 3 miles: 🔋 🔋 🔋 ◎ 🔋 🔋 🔋 U

Notes: Dogs must be kept on leads.

AA Pubs & Restaurants nearby: The Smugglers' Den Inn, CUBERT, TR8 5PY, 01637 830209

The Lewinnick Lodge Bar & Restaurant, NEWQUAY, TR7 1NX, 01637 878117

PITCHES: 🚐 Caravans 🚎 Motorhomes 🅰 Tents 🏕 Glamping accommodation **SERVICES:** 🔌 Electric hook up 🔋 Launderette 🍴 Licensed bar 🛢 Calor Gas 🖊 Camping Gaz T Toilet fluid 🍴 Café/Restaurant 🚜 Fast Food/Takeaway 🔋 Battery charging 🛒 Baby care 🔋 Motorvan service point
ABBREVIATIONS: BHs – bank holidays Etr – Easter Spring BH – Spring Bank Holiday fr – from hrs – hours m – mile mdnt – midnight rdbt – roundabout rs – restricted service wk – week wknd – weekend x-roads – crossroads 🚫 No credit or debit cards 🚫 No dogs

CRANTOCK (NEAR NEWQUAY) *continued*

Quarryfield Holiday Park
▶▶▶83%

tel: 01637 872792 & 830338 **TR8 5RJ**
email: quarryfield@crantockcaravans.orangehome.co.uk **web:** www.quarryfield.co.uk
dir: *From A3075 Newquay-Redruth road follow Crantock signs. Site signed.*
grid ref: *SW793608*

This park has a private path down to the dunes and golden sands of Crantock Beach, about 10 minutes away, and it is within easy reach of all that Newquay has to offer, particularly for families. The park has very modern facilities, and provides plenty of amenities including a great swimming pool. 10 acre site. 145 touring pitches. 12 seasonal pitches. Caravan pitches. Motorhome pitches. Tent pitches. 43 statics.

Open: Etr-Oct **Last arrival:** 23.00hrs **Last departure:** 10.00hrs

Pitches: * 🚐 fr £20 🚍 fr £20 ▲ fr £20

Leisure: 🏊 🅰 🎱

Facilities: 🌣👁🄿☀🕭🅂🎋🚻🆆🖥♳

Services: 🔌🗑🍴🔧🪣🍳🍽🛒🚮🕳

Within 3 miles: 🎣🎠🎲🀄◎🅂🎱U

Notes: No campfires, quiet after 22.30hrs. Dogs must be kept on leads.

AA Pubs & Restaurants nearby: The Smugglers' Den Inn, CUBERT, TR8 5PY, 01637 830209

The Lewinnick Lodge Bar & Restaurant, NEWQUAY, TR7 1NX, 01637 878117

Crantock Plains Touring Park
▶▶▶81%

GOLD

tel: 01637 830955 & 07837 534964 **TR8 5PH**
email: crantockp@btconnect.com
dir: *Exit Newquay on A3075, 2nd right signed to park & Crantock. Site on left in 0.75m on narrow road.* **grid ref:** *SW805589*

A small rural park with pitches on either side of a narrow lane, surrounded by mature trees for shelter. This spacious, family-run park has good modern toilet facilities and is ideal for campers who appreciate peace and quiet; it is situated approximately 1.2 miles from pretty Crantock, and Newquay is within easy reach. 6 acre site. 60 touring pitches. 20 seasonal pitches. Caravan pitches. Motorhome pitches. Tent pitches.

Open: mid Apr-end Sep **Last arrival:** 22.00hrs **Last departure:** noon

Pitches: 🚐🚍▲

Leisure: 🎱

Facilities: 👁🅿☀🕭🅂🎋🚻🆗🗑

Services: 🔌🗑🛒

Within 3 miles: 🎣🎠🀄🎲◎🛒🅂🎱U

Notes: No skateboards. Dogs must be kept on leads.

AA Pubs & Restaurants nearby: The Smugglers' Den Inn, CUBERT, TR8 5PY, 01637 830209

The Lewinnick Lodge Bar & Restaurant, NEWQUAY, TR7 1NX, 01637 878117

CUBERT — Map 2 SW75

Places to visit

Trerice, TRERICE, TR8 4PG, 01637 875404 www.nationaltrust.org.uk/trerice/

Great for kids: Dairy Land Farm World, NEWQUAY, TR8 5AA, 01872 510246 www.dairylandfarmworld.com

---

Cottage Farm Touring Park
▶▶▶83%

tel: 01637 831083 Treworgans **TR8 5HH**
email: info@cottagefarmpark.co.uk
dir: *From A392 towards Newquay, left onto A3075 towards Redruth. In 2m right signed Cubert, right again in 1.5m signed Crantock, left in 0.5m.* **grid ref:** *SW786589*

A small grassy touring park situated in the tiny hamlet of Treworgans, in sheltered open countryside close to a lovely beach at Holywell Bay. This quiet family-run park boasts very good quality facilities including a fenced playground for children, with a climbing frame, swings, slides etc. 2 acre site. 45 touring pitches. 2 hardstandings. Caravan pitches. Motorhome pitches. Tent pitches. 1 static.

Open: Apr-Sep **Last arrival:** 22.30hrs **Last departure:** noon

Pitches: 🚐🚍▲

Leisure: 🅰

Facilities: 🌣🅿👁🅿☀♳🕭

Services: 🔌🗑🛒

Within 3 miles: 🎣🎠🀄🎲◎🛒🅂🎱U

Notes: PayPal accepted. No noise after 23.00hrs. Dogs must be kept on leads.

AA Pubs & Restaurants nearby: The Smugglers' Den Inn, CUBERT, TR8 5PY, 01637 830209

The Plume of Feathers, MITCHELL, TR8 5AX, 01872 510387

EDGCUMBE

Places to visit

Poldark Mine and Heritage Complex, WENDRON, TR13 0ER, 01326 573173 www.poldark-mine.co.uk

Great for kids: Cornish Seal Sanctuary, GWEEK, TR12 6UG, 01326 221361 www.sealsanctuaries.com

The Flambards Theme Park, HELSTON, TR13 0QA, 01326 573404 www.flambards.co.uk

---

EDGCUMBE   Map 2 SW73

Retanna Holiday Park
▶▶▶81%

tel: 01326 340643 **TR13 0EJ**
email: retannaholpark@btconnect.com
dir: On A394 towards Helston, site signed on right. Site in 100mtrs. **grid ref:** SW711327

A small family-owned and run park in a rural location midway between Falmouth and Helston, and only about eight miles from Redruth. Its well-sheltered grassy pitches make this an ideal location for visiting the lovely beaches and towns nearby. For a fun day out the Flambards Theme Park is only a short drive away, and for sailing enthusiasts, Stithians Lake is on the doorstep. 8 acre site. 24 touring pitches. Caravan pitches. Tent pitches. 23 statics.

Open: Apr-Oct **Last arrival:** 21.00hrs **Last departure:** noon

Pitches: * ⬛ £16.50-£22.50 ▲ £16.50-£22.50

Leisure: 🅰 ✪ ⚲

Facilities: 🔦 ☉ ✳ 🅱 📷 🚻 WiFi 🖥 ♻ 🛈

Services: 🔌 🔲 🔋 ⏚ T 🔋 🚼

Within 3 miles: ⬇ ⚞ 🦮 ◎ 🥾 🛍 🔲 ↺

Notes: PayPal accepted. No pets, no disposable BBQs, no open fires, no noise between 22.30-08.30hrs. Free use of fridge-freezer in laundry room, free air bed inflation, free mobile phone charging.

AA Pubs & Restaurants nearby: Trengilly Wartha Inn, CONSTANTINE, TR11 5RP, 01326 340332

FALMOUTH   Map 2 SW83

Places to visit

Pendennis Castle, FALMOUTH, TR11 4LP, 01326 316594
www.english-heritage.org.uk/daysout/properties/pendennis-castle

Trebah Garden, MAWNAN SMITH, TR11 5JZ, 01326 252200
www.trebah-garden.co.uk

Great for kids: National Maritime Museum Cornwall, FALMOUTH, TR11 3QY, 01326 313388 www.nmmc.co.uk

Tregedna Farm Touring Caravan & Tent Park
▶▶▶80%

tel: 01326 250529 **Maenporth TR11 5HL**
email: enquiries@tregednafarmholidays.co.uk
dir: Take A39 from Truro to Falmouth. Turn right at Hill Head rdbt. Site 2.5m on right. **grid ref:** SW785305

Set in the picturesque Maen Valley, this gently-sloping, south-facing park is part of a 100-acre farm. It is surrounded by beautiful wooded countryside just minutes from the beach, with spacious pitches and well-kept facilities. 12 acre site. 40 touring pitches. 6 hardstandings. Caravan pitches. Motorhome pitches. Tent pitches.

Open: Apr-Sep **Last arrival:** 22.00hrs **Last departure:** 13.00hrs

Pitches: ⬛ ⬛ ▲

Leisure: 🅰

Facilities: 🔦 🅿 ☉ ✳ 🐾 ♻ 🛈

Services: 🔌 🔲
Within 3 miles: ⬇ 🅱 🦮 ◎ 🥾 🛍 🔲

Notes: 🚫 1 dog only per pitch. Dogs must be kept on leads. Boat storage.

AA Pubs & Restaurants nearby: Trengilly Wartha Inn, CONSTANTINE, TR11 5RP, 01326 340332

Budock Vean - The Hotel on the River, MAWNAN SMITH, TR11 5LG, 01326 250288

FOWEY   Map 2 SX15

Places to visit

St Catherine's Castle, FOWEY, 0370 333 1181
www.english-heritage.org.uk/daysout/properties/st-catherines-castle

Restormel Castle, RESTORMEL, PL22 0EE, 01208 872687
www.english-heritage.org.uk/daysout/properties/restormel-castle

Great for kids: Wheal Martyn, ST AUSTELL, PL26 8XG, 01726 850362
www.wheal-martyn.com

Eden Project, ST AUSTELL, PL24 2SG, 01726 811911 www.edenproject.com

Penmarlam Caravan & Camping Park
▶▶▶86%

tel: 01726 870088 **Bodinnick PL23 1LZ**
email: info@penmarlampark.co.uk
dir: From A390 at East Taphouse take B3359 signed Looe & Polperro. Follow signs for Bodinnick & Fowey, via ferry. Site on right at entrance to Bodinnick. **grid ref:** SX134526

This continually improving, tranquil park (with access to the water) is set above the Fowey estuary in an Area of Outstanding Natural Beauty. The pitches are level and sheltered by trees and bushes in two paddocks, and the toilets are spotlessly clean and well maintained. The shop is licensed and sells local and other Cornish produce. Online booking is available and there is good CCTV security around the park. Good walks surrounding the site include one to the Polruan passenger ferry, and one to the Bodinnick car ferry which offers easy access to Fowey. 4 acre site. 63 touring pitches. 20 seasonal pitches. Caravan pitches. Motorhome pitches. Tent pitches.

Open: Apr-Oct **Last arrival:** 20.00hrs **Last departure:** noon

Pitches: * ⬛ £18-£30 ⬛ £18-£30 ▲ £18-£30

Leisure: 🦮

Facilities: 🔦 🅿 ☉ 🦮 ✳ 🅱 📷 🚻 🛒 WiFi ♻ 🛈

Services: 🔌 🔲 🔋 ⏚ T 🔋

Within 3 miles: ⬇ ⚞ 🅱 🦮 🥾 🛍 🔲 ↺

Notes: No noise after 22.00hrs. Dogs must be kept on leads. Private slipway, small boat storage.

AA Pubs & Restaurants nearby: The Ship Inn, FOWEY, PL23 1AZ, 01726 832230

The Fowey Hotel, FOWEY, PL23 1HX, 01726 832551

PITCHES: ⬛ Caravans ⬛ Motorhomes ▲ Tents 🏕 Glamping accommodation **SERVICES:** 🔌 Electric hook up 🔲 Launderette 🍺 Licensed bar
🔋 Calor Gas ⏚ Camping Gaz T Toilet fluid 🍽 Café/Restaurant 🍔 Fast Food/Takeaway 🔋 Battery charging 🚼 Baby care ↻ Motorvan service point
ABBREVIATIONS: BHs – bank holidays Etr – Easter Spring BH – Spring Bank Holiday fr – from hrs – hours m – mile mdnt – midnight
rdbt – roundabout rs – restricted service wk – week wknd – weekend x-roads – crossroads 🚫 No credit or debit cards 🚫 No dogs

Silverbow Park

GOONHAVERN
Map 2 SW75

See also Rejerrah

Places to visit

Trerice, TRERICE, TR8 4PG, 01637 875404 www.nationaltrust.org.uk/trerice/

Blue Reef Aquarium, NEWQUAY, TR7 1DU, 01637 878134 www.bluereefaquarium.co.uk

Great for kids: Dairy Land Farm World, NEWQUAY, TR8 5AA, 01872 510246 www.dairylandfarmworld.com

Newquay Zoo, NEWQUAY, TR7 2LZ, 01637 873342 www.newquayzoo.org.uk

PREMIER PARK

Silverbow Park
►►►►► 84%

GOLD

tel: 01872 572347 **Perranwell TR4 9NX**
email: silverbowhols@btconnect.com **web:** www.silverbowpark.co.uk
dir: *Adjacent to A3075, 0.5m S of village.* **grid ref:** *SW782531*

This park, on the main road to Newquay, has a quiet garden atmosphere and appeals to families with young children. The superb landscaped grounds and good quality toilet facilities (with four family rooms) that are housed in an attractive chalet-style building, are maintained to a very high standard. Leisure facilities include two inviting swimming pools (outdoor and indoor), a bowling green, a nature walk around small lakes, and a summer house where children can take part in a number of nature activities. Top quality eco-lodges are available for hire. 14 acre site. 90 touring pitches. 2 hardstandings. 30 seasonal pitches. Caravan pitches. Motorhome pitches. Tent pitches. 15 statics.

Open: all year (rs end Sep-Apr – no caravans, motohomes or tents; only eco lodges) **Last arrival:** 22.00hrs **Last departure:** 10.30hrs

Pitches: ⊞ ⇌ Å **Leisure:** ⚐ ⚐ ⚐ ⚐ ⚐ ⚐

Facilities: ⊙ ℙ ⚒ ⚑ ⚑ ⚑ ⚑ ⚑ ⚑ WiFi ⚑ ⚑

Services: ⚑ ⚑ ⚑ ⚑ T ⚑

Within 3 miles: ⚑ ⚑ ℘ ◎ ⚑ ⚑ ⚑ ⚑ ∪

Notes: No cycling, no skateboards, no noise after 21.00hrs. Short mat bowls rink, conservation & information area, indoor & outdoor table tennis, all weather tennis courts.

AA Pubs & Restaurants nearby: The Smugglers' Den Inn, CUBERT, TR8 5PY, 01637 830209

The Plume of Feathers, MITCHELL, TR8 5AX, 01872 510387

See advert on opposite page

Penrose Holiday Park
►►►► 86%

tel: 01872 573185 **TR4 9QF**
email: info@penroseholidaypark.com
dir: *From Exeter take A30, past Bodmin & Indian Queens. Just after Wind Farm take B3285 towards Perranporth, site on left on entering Goonhavern.* **grid ref:** *SW795534*

A quiet sheltered park set in five paddocks divided by hedges and shrubs, only a short walk from the village. Lovely floral displays enhance the park's appearance, and the grass and hedges are neatly trimmed. The four cubicle family rooms prove very popular, and there is a good laundry, a smart reception building and an internet café. Static caravans are available for hire. 9 acre site. 110 touring pitches. 48 hardstandings. 34 seasonal pitches. Caravan pitches. Motorhome pitches. Tent pitches. 24 statics.

Open: Apr-Oct **Last arrival:** 21.30hrs **Last departure:** 10.00hrs

Pitches: ⊞ ⇌ Å **Facilities:** ⚑ ℙ ⊙ ℙ ⚒ ⚑ ⚑ ⚑ ⚑ WiFi ⚑ ⚑ ⚑

Services: ⚑ ⚑ ⚑ ⚑ T ⚑ ⚑ ⚑ ⚑

Within 3 miles: ⚑ ⚑ ℘ ◎ ⚑ ⚑ ⚑ ⚑ ∪

Notes: Families & couples only. Dogs must be kept on leads. Campers' kitchen, fridge freezer & microwave available, coffee & breakfast mobile unit, fish & chips mobile unit (summer only).

AA Pubs & Restaurants nearby: The Smugglers' Den Inn, CUBERT, TR8 5PY, 01637 830209

The Plume of Feathers, MITCHELL, TR8 5AX, 01872 510387

LEISURE: 🏊 Indoor pool 🏊 Outdoor pool 🎢 Children's playground 👦 Kid's club 🎾 Tennis court 🎯 Games room ⛳ Golf course 🚤 Boat hire 🚲 Cycle hire 🎬 Cinema 🎵 Entertainment 🎣 Fishing ◎ Mini golf ⛳ Pitch n putt 🏄 Watersports 🏋 Gym ⚽ Sports field ∪ Stables **FACILITIES:** 🛁 Bath 🚿 Shower 🅿 Private washing cubicles ⊙ Electric shaver 🪮 Hairdryer ❄ Ice Packs ♿ Disabled facilities 🛒 Shop on site 🚐 Mobile shop 🍖 BBQ area 🪑 Picnic area WiFi Wi-fi 💻 Internet access ♻ Recycling 🛈 Tourist info 🐕 Dog exercise area 🚗 Car hire can be arranged

Little Treamble Farm Touring Park
▶▶▶83%

tel: 01872 573823 & 07971 070760 **Rose TR4 9PR**
email: info@treamble.co.uk
dir: *A30 onto B3285 signed Perranporth. Approx 0.5m right into Scotland Rd signed Newquay. Approx 2m to T-junct, right onto A3075 signed Newquay. 0.25m left at Rejerrah sign. Site signed 0.75m on right.* **grid ref:** *SW785560*

This site, within easy reach of Padstow, Newquay and St Ives, is set in a quiet rural location with extensive countryside views across an undulating valley. There is a small toilet block with a disabled facility and a well-stocked shop. This working farm is adjacent to a Caravan Club site. 1.5 acre site. 20 touring pitches. Caravan pitches. Motorhome pitches. Tent pitches.

Open: all year **Last departure:** noon

Pitches: 🚐 🚐 Å

Facilities: 🏳 ✳ 🖥 ♻ 🛈

Services: 🔌 🖥 Ⓣ 🔋

Within 3 miles: ⚓ 🎣 ◎ 🖥 ∪

AA Pubs & Restaurants nearby: The Smugglers' Den Inn, CUBERT, TR8 5PY, 01637 830209

The Plume of Feathers, MITCHELL, TR8 5AX, 01872 510387

GORRAN

Places to visit

Caerhays Castle Gardens, GORRAN, PL26 6LY, 01872 501310
www.caerhays.co.uk

The Lost Gardens of Heligan, PENTEWAN, PL26 6EN, 01726 845100
www.heligan.com

Great for kids: Wheal Martyn, ST AUSTELL, PL26 8XG, 01726 850362
www.wheal-martyn.com

GORRAN Map 2 SW94

Treveor Farm Campsite
▶▶▶84%

tel: 01726 842387 **PL26 6LW**
email: info@treveorfarm.co.uk **web:** www.treveorfarm.co.uk
dir: *From St Austell bypass left onto B3273 for Mevagissey. On hilltop before descent to village turn right onto unclassified road for Gorran. Right in 5m, site on right.* **grid ref:** *SW988418*

A small family-run camping park set on a working farm, with grassy pitches backing onto mature hedging. This quiet site, with good facilities, is close to beaches and offers a large coarse fishing lake. 4 acre site. 47 touring pitches. Caravan pitches. Motorhome pitches. Tent pitches.

Open: Apr-Oct **Last arrival:** 21.00hrs **Last departure:** 11.00hrs

Pitches: * 🚐 £6-£23 🚐 £6-£23 Å £6-£23 **Leisure:** 🅰

Facilities: 🏳 🅿 ☉ 🏳 ✳ 📶 ♻ 🛈 **Services:** 🔌 🖥 **Within 3 miles:** 🔋 🖥

Notes: Dogs must be kept on leads.

AA Pubs & Restaurants nearby: The Ship Inn, MEVAGISSEY, PL26 6UQ, 01726 843324

The Crown Inn, ST EWE, PL26 6EY, 01726 843322

PITCHES: 🚐 Caravans 🚐 Motorhomes Å Tents 🏠 Glamping accommodation **SERVICES:** 🔌 Electric hook up 🖥 Launderette 🍺 Licensed bar 🔥 Calor Gas 🔥 Camping Gaz Ⓣ Toilet fluid 🍽 Café/Restaurant 🍟 Fast Food/Takeaway 🔋 Battery charging 🍼 Baby care 🚐 Motorvan service point
ABBREVIATIONS: BHs – bank holidays Etr – Easter Spring BH – Spring Bank Holiday fr – from hrs – hours m – mile mdnt – midnight rdbt – roundabout rs – restricted service wk – week wknd – weekend x-roads – crossroads 🈲 No credit or debit cards 🚫 No dogs

GORRAN *continued*

Treveague Farm Caravan & Camping Site
▶▶▶ 82%

tel: 01726 842295 **PL26 6NY**
email: treveague@btconnect.com
dir: *B3273 from St Austell towards Mevagissey, pass Pentewan at top of hill, right signed Gorran. Past Heligan Gardens towards Gorran Churchtown. Follow brown tourist signs from fork in road. (NB roads to site are single lane & very narrow. It is advisable to follow these directions & not Sat Nav).* **grid ref:** *SX002410*

Spectacular panoramic coastal views can be enjoyed from this rural park, which is set on an organic farm and well equipped with modern facilities. A stone-faced toilet block with a Cornish slate roof is an attractive feature, as is the building that houses the smart reception, café and shop, which sells meat produced on the farm. There is an aviary with exotic birds, and also chinchillas. A footpath leads to the fishing village of Gorran Haven in one direction, and the secluded sandy Vault Beach in the other. The site is close to a bus route. 4 acre site. 46 touring pitches. Caravan pitches. Motorhome pitches. Tent pitches.

Open: Apr-Sep **Last arrival:** 21.00hrs **Last departure:** noon
Pitches: * 🚐 £10-£28 🚙 £10-£28 ⚊ £8-£24
Leisure: 🄰 ✪
Facilities: 🌢 P⌂ ⊙ ℱ ✳ 🅚 🚿 📷 🅟 WiFi 🛒 ♻ ✪
Services: 🖂 🖸 🚽 T 🍴 🍺 👜 🛒
Within 3 miles: 🛶 🎣 🏊 🅟 🖸
Notes: No fires. Dogs must be kept on leads. Bird & animal hide, weekly story teller.
AA Pubs & Restaurants nearby: The Ship Inn, MEVAGISSEY, PL26 6UQ, 01726 843324
The Crown Inn, ST EWE, PL26 6EY, 01726 843322

GORRAN HAVEN Map 2 SX04

Places to visit
Caerhays Castle Gardens, GORRAN, PL26 6LY, 01872 501310 www.caerhays.co.uk

The Lost Gardens of Heligan, PENTEWAN, PL26 6EN, 01726 845100 www.heligan.com

Great for kids: Wheal Martyn, ST AUSTELL, PL26 8XG, 01726 850362 www.wheal-martyn.com

---

Trelispen Caravan & Camping Park
▶ 74%

tel: 01726 843501 **PL26 6NT**
email: trelispen@care4free.net
dir: *B3273 from St Austell towards Mevagissey, on hilltop at x-roads before descent into Mevagissey turn right on unclassified road to Gorran. Through village, 2nd right towards Gorran Haven, site signed on left in 250mtrs. (NB it is advisable to follow these directions not Sat Nav).* **grid ref:** *SX008421*

A quiet rural site set in three paddocks, and sheltered by mature trees and hedges. The simple toilets have plenty of hot water, and there is a small laundry. Sandy beaches, pubs and shops are nearby, and Mevagissey is two miles away. There is a bus stop 100yds from the site with a regular service to Mevagissey and St Austell. 2 acre site. 40 touring pitches. Caravan pitches. Motorhome pitches. Tent pitches.

Open: Etr & Apr-Oct **Last arrival:** 22.00hrs **Last departure:** noon

Pitches: * 🚐 £20-£30 🚙 £20-£30 ⚊ £15-£25
Facilities: 🌢 ⊙ ✳ ♻ ✪
Services: 🖂 🖸
Within 3 miles: 🛶 🎣 🏊 🅟 🖸
Notes: 🐕 30-acre nature reserve.
AA Pubs & Restaurants nearby: The Ship Inn, MEVAGISSEY, PL26 6UQ, 01726 843324
The Crown Inn, ST EWE, PL26 6EY, 01726 843322

GWITHIAN Map 2 SW54

Places to visit
East Pool Mine, POOL, TR15 3NP, 01209 315027 www.nationaltrust.org.uk

---

Gwithian Farm Campsite
▶▶▶▶ 92%

tel: 01736 753127 **Gwithian Farm TR27 5BX**
email: camping@gwithianfarm.co.uk
dir: *Exit A30 at Hayle rdbt, 4th exit signed Hayle, 100mtrs. At 1st mini-rdbt right onto B3301 signed Portreath. Site 2m on left on entering village.* **grid ref:** *SW586412*

An unspoilt site located behind the sand dunes of Gwithian's golden beach, which can be reached by footpath directly from the site, making this an ideal location for surfers. The site boasts stunning floral displays, a superb toilet block with excellent facilities, including a bathroom and baby-changing unit, and first-class hardstanding pitches. Each attractive pitch has been screened by hedge planting. 7.5 acre site. 87 touring pitches. 32 hardstandings. Caravan pitches. Motorhome pitches. Tent pitches.

Open: 31 Mar-1 Oct **Last arrival:** 21.00hrs **Last departure:** 17.00hrs
Pitches: * 🚐 £16-£31 🚙 £16-£31 ⚊ £16-£31
Leisure: ✪
Facilities: ⊙ ℱ ✳ 🅚 📷 🅟 🚿 WiFi ♻ ✪
Services: 🖂 🖸 🛢 ⌀ T 👜 🛒 ⚒
Within 3 miles: 🛶 🎣 ◉ 🏊 🅟 🖸 U
Notes: No ball games after 21.00hrs, no noise after 22.30hrs. Debit cards accepted (no credit cards). Dogs must be kept on leads. Surf board & wet suit hire, table tennis.
AA Pubs & Restaurants nearby: Basset Arms, PORTREATH, TR16 4NG, 01209 842077
Porthminster Beach Restaurant, ST IVES, TR26 2EB, 01736 795352

HAYLE

Places to visit
Tate St Ives, ST IVES, TR26 1TG, 01736 796226 www.tate.org.uk/stives

Barbara Hepworth Museum & Sculpture Garden, ST IVES, TR26 1AD, 01736 796226 www.tate.org.uk/stives

---

LEISURE: 🏊 Indoor pool 🏊 Outdoor pool 🄰 Children's playground 🧒 Kid's club 🎾 Tennis court ♟ Games room ⛳ Golf course 🚣 Boat hire 🚲 Cycle hire 🎬 Cinema 🎵 Entertainment 🎣 Fishing ◉ Mini golf ⛳ Pitch n putt 🏄 Watersports 🏋 Gym ♻ Sports field U Stables **FACILITIES:** 🛁 Bath 🌢 Shower P Private washing cubicles ⊙ Electric shaver ℱ Hairdryer ✳ Ice Packs 🅚 Disabled facilities 🆂 Shop on site 📷 Mobile shop BBQ area 🅟 Picnic area WiFi Wi-fi 🖥 Internet access ♻ Recycling 🛈 Tourist info 🐕 Dog exercise area 🚗 Car hire can be arranged

HAYLE
Map 2 SW53

St Ives Bay Holiday Park
HOLIDAY CENTRE 91%

tel: 01736 752274 **73 Loggans Rd, Upton Towans TR27 5BH**
email: enquiries@stivesbay.co.uk **web:** www.stivesbay.co.uk
dir: *Exit A30 at Hayle then immediate right onto B3301 at mini-rdbts. Site entrance 0.5m on left.* **grid ref:** *SW577398*

St Ives Bay Holiday Park

An extremely well-maintained holiday park with a relaxed atmosphere situated adjacent to a three mile beach. The various camping fields are set in hollows amongst the sand dunes and are very tastefully laid out, with the high camping fields enjoying stunning views over St Ives Bay. The touring sections are in a number of separate locations around the extensive site. The park is specially geared for families and couples, and as well as the large indoor swimming pool there are two pubs with seasonal entertainment. There are 17 camping pods for hire. 90 acre site. 240 touring pitches. Caravan pitches. Motorhome pitches. Tent pitches. 250 statics.

Open: Etr-30 Oct **Last arrival:** 21.00hrs **Last departure:** 09.00hrs

Pitches: 🚐 🚐 🛆 🏕

Leisure: 🏊 🎱 🎣 🎵

Facilities: 🔥 ⊙ 🌳 ✳ ♿ 🖎 🚻 📶 🛒 ♻ ⓘ

Services: 🔌 🗄 🍴 🛢 🚽 🍽 🔋 👶 🛠

Glamping: Wooden Pods 17, £22.71-£69.85 Changeover day Sat Min stay 7 nights Car by unit

Within 3 miles: 🚣 🎣 ⊚ 🎿 🏌 🚴 ∪

Notes: No pets. Crazy golf.

AA Pubs & Restaurants nearby: The Red River Inn, GWITHIAN, TR27 5BW, 01736 753223
Porthminster Beach Restaurant, ST IVES, TR26 2EB, 01736 795352

See advert below

PITCHES: 🚐 Caravans 🚐 Motorhomes 🛆 Tents 🏕 Glamping accommodation **SERVICES:** 🔌 Electric hook up 🗄 Launderette 🍴 Licensed bar 🛢 Calor Gas 🚿 Camping Gaz 🚽 Toilet fluid 🍽 Café/Restaurant 🏪 Fast Food/Takeaway 🔋 Battery charging 👶 Baby care 🛠 Motorvan service point

ABBREVIATIONS: BHs – bank holidays Etr – Easter Spring BH – Spring Bank Holiday fr – from hrs – hours m – mile mdnt – midnight rdbt – roundabout rs – restricted service wk – week wknd – weekend x-roads – crossroads 🚫 No credit or debit cards 🚫 No dogs

HAYLE *continued*

Atlantic Coast Holiday Park

►►►►82%

tel: 01736 752071 **53 Upton Towans, Gwithian TR27 5BL**
email: enquiries@atlanticcoastpark.co.uk
dir: *From A30 into Hayle, right at double rdbt. Site 1.5m on left.* **grid ref:** *NW580400*

Fringed by the sand dunes of St Ives Bay and close to the golden sands of Gwithian Beach, the small, friendly touring area continues to improve year on year and offers fully serviced pitches. There's freshly baked bread, a takeaway and a bar next door. This park is ideally situated for visitors to enjoy the natural coastal beauty and attractions of south-west Cornwall. There is superb landscaping and planting, and campers have the use of facilities such as a kettle and microwave for campers. Static caravans are available for holiday hire. 4.5 acre site. 15 touring pitches. 2 hardstandings. 5 seasonal pitches. Caravan pitches. Motorhome pitches. Tent pitches. 50 statics.

Open: Mar-early Jan **Last arrival:** 20.00hrs **Last departure:** 11.00hrs
Pitches: 🚐 🚏 Å
Facilities: 🏕 P⊙ 🌡 ✳ 🛁 🚿 📶 ♻ ❼
Services: 🔌🔲 T 🍽 🍺
Within 3 miles: ↡ 🎣 ◎ 🚣 🛒🔲 ∪
Notes: No commercial vehicles, gazebos or day tents. Dogs must be kept on leads. Freshly baked bread, croissants, pasties, newspapers.
AA Pubs & Restaurants nearby: The Red River Inn, GWITHIAN, TR27 5BW, 01736 753223
Porthminster Beach Restaurant, ST IVES, TR26 2EB, 01736 795352

Higher Trevaskis Caravan & Camping Park

►►►84%

tel: 01209 831736 **Gwinear Rd, Connor Downs TR27 5JQ**
email: forward@highertrevaskiscaravanpark.co.uk
web: www.highertrevaskiscaravanpark.co.uk
dir: *On A30 at Hayle rdbt take exit signed Connor Downs, in 1m right signed Carnhell Green. Site 0.75m just after level crossing.* **grid ref:** *SW611381*

An attractive paddocked and terraced park in a sheltered rural position on a valley side with views towards St Ives. The terrace areas are divided by hedges. This secluded park is personally run by owners who keep it quiet and welcoming. Fluent German is spoken. 6.5 acre site. 82 touring pitches. 4 hardstandings. Caravan pitches. Motorhome pitches. Tent pitches.

Open: mid Apr-Sep **Last arrival:** 20.00hrs **Last departure:** 10.30hrs

Pitches: * 🚐 £14-£22 🚏 £14-£22 Å £14-£22
Leisure: ⊛
Facilities: 🏕⊙🌡✳🛁♻❼
Services: 🔌🔲 🛢 T 🔋 🍺
Within 3 miles: ↡🎣◎🚣🛒🔲
Notes: ⊛ 5mph speed limit on site, ball games permitted on designated field only. max 2 dogs per pitch, certain dog breeds not accepted (contact site for details). Dogs must be kept on leads.
AA Pubs & Restaurants nearby: The Red River Inn, GWITHIAN, TR27 5BW, 01736 753223
Porthminster Beach Restaurant, ST IVES, TR26 2EB, 01736 795352

Treglisson Touring Park

►►►81%

tel: 01736 753141 **Wheal Alfred Rd TR27 5JT**
email: treglisson@hotmail.co.uk
dir: *From A30 (Camborne towards Penzance) take 4th exit at rdbt signed Hayle. Left at next mini rdbt, follow site signs. Approx 1.5m past golf course, site sign on left.* **grid ref:** *SW581367*

A small secluded site in a peaceful wooded meadow and a former apple and pear orchard. This quiet rural site has level grass pitches and a well-planned modern toilet block, and is just two miles from the glorious beach at Hayle with its vast stretch of golden sand. 3 acre site. 26 touring pitches. 6 hardstandings. Caravan pitches. Motorhome pitches. Tent pitches.

Open: Etr-Sep **Last arrival:** 20.00hrs **Last departure:** 11.00hrs
Pitches: * 🚐 £11-£19 🚏 £11-£19 Å £11-£19
Leisure: 🎠
Facilities: 🏕⊙🌡✳🛁🐕📶♻❼
Services: 🔌🔲 🍺
Within 3 miles: ↡🎣🚣🛒🔲
Notes: Max 6 people per pitch, max tent size of 7mtrs. Dogs must be kept on leads.
AA Pubs & Restaurants nearby: The Red River Inn, GWITHIAN, TR27 5BW, 01736 753223
Porthminster Beach Restaurant, ST IVES, TR26 2EB, 01736 795352

Riviere Sands Holiday Park
HOLIDAY HOME PARK 86%

tel: 01736 752132 **Riviere Towans TR27 5AX**
email: rivieresands@haven.com **web:** www.haven.com/rivieresands
dir: *A30 towards Redruth. Follow signs into Hayle, cross double mini rdbt. Turn right opposite petrol station signed Towans & beaches. Park 1m on right.* **grid ref:** *SW556386*

Close to St Ives and with direct access to a safe, white-sand beach, Riviere Sands is an exciting holiday park with much to offer families. Children can enjoy the crazy golf, amusements, swimming pool complex, and the beach of course; the evening entertainment for adults is extensive and lively. There is a good range of holiday caravans and apartments.

Open: Mar-Oct
Changeover day: Mon, Fri, Sat
Arrival and departure times: Please contact the site
Statics: 295 Sleeps 6-8 Bedrms 2-3 Bathrms 1-2 Toilets 1-2 Microwave Freezer TV Sky/FTV Elec inc Gas inc Grass area
Children: 👣 Cots Highchair **Leisure:** 🏊 🏖 Cycle hire 🖐 🎠

LEISURE: 🏊 Indoor pool 🏖 Outdoor pool 🎠 Children's playground 🖐 Kid's club ⚲ Tennis court ⚽ Games room ↡ Golf course 🚣 Boat hire 🚲 Cycle hire 🎬 Cinema 🎵 Entertainment 🎣 Fishing ◎ Mini golf ⚑ Pitch n putt 🚤 Watersports 💪 Gym ⊛ Sports field ∪ Stables **FACILITIES:** 🛁 Bath 🚿 Shower P🔲 Private washing cubicles ⊙ Electric shaver 🌡 Hairdryer ✳ Ice Packs 🛁 Disabled facilities 🛒 Shop on site 🛍 Mobile shop 🍖 BBQ area 🌲 Picnic area 📶 Wi-fi 🖥 Internet access ♻ Recycling ❼ Tourist info 🐕 Dog exercise area 🚗 Car hire can be arranged

HELSTON
Map 2 SW62

See also Ashton

Places to visit
Great for kids: The Flambards Theme Park, HELSTON, TR13 0QA, 01326 573404
www.flambards.co.uk

Cornish Seal Sanctuary, GWEEK, TR12 6UG, 01326 221361
www.sealsanctuaries.com

Lower Polladras Touring Park
▶▶▶▶ 87%

tel: 01736 762220 **Carleen, Breage TR13 9NX**
email: lowerpolladras@btinternet.com
dir: *From Helston take A394 then B3302 (Hayle road) at Ward Garage, 2nd left to Carleen, site 2m on right.* **grid ref:** *SW617308*

An attractive rural park with extensive views of surrounding fields, appealing to families who enjoy the countryside. The planted trees and shrubs are maturing, and help to divide the area into paddocks with spacious grassy pitches. The site has a dish-washing area, a games room, a dog and nature walk, two fully serviced family rooms and WiFi. 4 acre site. 39 touring pitches. 23 hardstandings. Caravan pitches. Motorhome pitches. Tent pitches. 3 statics.

Open: Apr-Jan **Last arrival:** 22.00hrs **Last departure:** noon **Pitches:** 🚐 🚍 ⛺
Leisure: ✎ **Facilities:** ☉ 🌮 ☀ ⅃ 🚻 🚶 🚿 WiFi **Services:** 🔌 🔄 🔋 ⚙ 🝙 🚽 ⬇
Within 3 miles: ⅃ ♨ 🎱 🛒 ◎ ⚓ 🏕 🗑 🎣 ∪

Notes: ☺ Caravan storage.

AA Pubs & Restaurants nearby: The Ship Inn, PORTHLEVEN, TR13 9JS, 01326 564204
Kota Restaurant with Rooms, PORTHLEVEN, TR13 9JA, 01326 562407
New Yard Restaurant, HELSTON, TR12 6AF, 01326 221595

Skyburriowe Farm
▶▶▶ 82%

tel: 01326 221646 **Garras TR12 6LR**
email: bkbenney@hotmail.co.uk **web:** www.skyburriowefarm.co.uk
dir: *From Helston take A3083 to The Lizard. After Culdrose Naval Airbase continue straight on at rdbt, in 1m left at Skyburriowe Ln sign. In 0.5m right at Skyburriowe B&B/Campsite sign. Pass bungalow to farmhouse. Site on left.* **grid ref:** *SW698227*

A leafy no-through road leads to this picturesque farm park in a rural location on the Lizard Peninsula. The toilet block offers excellent quality facilities, and most

---

pitches have electric hook-ups. There are some beautiful coves and beaches nearby, and for a great day out Flambards Theme Park is also close by. Under the supervision of the owner, children are permitted to watch his herd of Friesian cows being milked. 4 acre site. 30 touring pitches. 4 hardstandings. Caravan pitches. Motorhome pitches. Tent pitches.

Open: Apr-Oct **Last arrival:** 22.00hrs **Last departure:** 11.00hrs
Pitches: 🚐 £15-£21 🚍 £15-£21 ⛺ £15-£21
Facilities: 🌮 ☉ ☀ ⅃ & 🚶 🚻 WiFi 🔋 🗑 🎯
Services: 🔌 🍼
Within 3 miles: ⅃ 🎱 ♨ ◎ ⚓ 🏕 🗑 ∪

Notes: Quiet after 23.00hrs. Dogs must be kept on leads. Fresh vegetables in season.
AA Pubs & Restaurants nearby: The Ship Inn, PORTHLEVEN, TR13 9JS, 01326 564204
Kota Restaurant with Rooms, PORTHLEVEN, TR13 9JA, 01326 562407
New Yard Restaurant, HELSTON, TR12 6AF, 01326 221595

Poldown Caravan Park
▶▶▶ 79%

tel: 01326 574560 **Poldown, Carleen TR13 9NN**
email: stay@poldown.co.uk
dir: *From Helston follow Penzance signs for 1m, right onto B3302 to Hayle, 2nd left to Carleen, 0.5m to site.* **grid ref:** *SW629298*

Ideally located for visiting the towns of Helston, Penzance and St Ives, this small, quiet site is set in attractive countryside. The park is sheltered by mature trees and shrubs. All the level grass pitches have electricity, and there are toilet facilities. Two safari tents are available for hire. 2 acre site. 13 touring pitches. 2 hardstandings. Caravan pitches. Motorhome pitches. Tent pitches. 7 statics.

Open: Apr-Sep **Last arrival:** 21.00hrs **Last departure:** noon
Pitches: * 🚐 £17.50-£21.50 🚍 £17.50-£21.50 ⛺ £13.50-£17.50 🏠 prices shown below
Facilities: ☉ 🌮 ☀ & 🚶 🚻 WiFi 🔋 🗑 🎯
Services: 🔌 🔄 🍼 ⬇
Glamping: **Safari tents** 2, £39-£59 Min stay 3 nights Own kitchen Car by unit
Within 3 miles: ⅃ 🎱 ♨ ◎ ⚓ 🏕 🗑 ∪

Notes: PayPal & debit cards accepted (no credit cards). Dogs must be kept on leads. Table tennis.
AA Pubs & Restaurants nearby: The Ship Inn, PORTHLEVEN, TR13 9JS, 01326 564204
Kota Restaurant with Rooms, PORTHLEVEN, TR13 9JA, 01326 562407
New Yard Restaurant, HELSTON, TR12 6AF, 01326 221595

New to camping?
See page 33 for a helpful check list

PITCHES: 🚐 Caravans 🚍 Motorhomes ⛺ Tents 🏠 Glamping accommodation **SERVICES:** 🔌 Electric hook up 🔄 Launderette 🍺 Licensed bar 🔋 Calor Gas ⚙ Camping Gaz 🚽 Toilet fluid 🍽 Café/Restaurant 🍔 Fast Food/Takeaway 🔋 Battery charging 🍼 Baby care ⬇ Motorvan service point
ABBREVIATIONS: BHs – bank holidays Etr – Easter Spring BH – Spring Bank Holiday fr – from hrs – hours m – mile mdnt – midnight rdbt – roundabout rs – restricted service wk – week wknd – weekend x-roads – crossroads ⊛ No credit or debit cards ⊗ No dogs

HOLYWELL BAY
Map 2 SW75

Places to visit
Trerice, TRERICE, TR8 4PG, 01637 875404 www.nationaltrust.org.uk/trerice/

Blue Reef Aquarium, NEWQUAY, TR7 1DU, 01637 878134
www.bluereefaquarium.co.uk

Great for kids: Newquay Zoo, NEWQUAY, TR7 2LZ, 01637 873342
www.newquayzoo.org.uk

PREMIER PARK

Trevornick
▶▶▶▶▶ 90%

 Best of British

tel: 01637 830531 & 832905 **TR8 5PW**
email: bookings@trevornick.co.uk
dir: *3m from Newquay exit A3075 towards Redruth. Follow Cubert & Holywell Bay signs.* **grid ref:** *SW776586*

A large seaside holiday complex with excellent facilities and amenities. There is plenty of entertainment including a children's club and an evening cabaret, adding up to a full holiday experience for all the family. A sandy beach is just a 15-minute footpath walk away. The park has 55 Euro tents for hire. 20 acre site. 688 touring pitches. 53 hardstandings. 8 seasonal pitches. Caravan pitches. Motorhome pitches. Tent pitches.

Open: Etr & mid May-mid Sep **Last arrival:** 21.00hrs **Last departure:** 10.00hrs

Pitches: 🚐 🚍 Å 🏕

Leisure: 🏊 ⛲ 👦 🎾 🎵 Spa

Facilities: 🚿 🅿 ⊙ 🏷 ☀ 🔌 ♿ 🛒 🚻 📶 ♻ ❔

Services: 🔌 🛢 🍴 🛢 🔒 🗑 T 🍴 🛒 🏧

Glamping: Erected Tents 55

Within 3 miles: ⌚ 🎣 🛢 🌐 ⛳ 🛢 🛒 🛢 ⛵ ⛳

Notes: Families & couples only. Dogs must be kept on leads. Fishing, golf course, entertainment, fun park, nature trail, segways.

AA Pubs & Restaurants nearby: The Smugglers' Den Inn, CUBERT, TR8 5PY, 01637 830209

INDIAN QUEENS
Map 2 SW95

Places to visit
Wheal Martyn, ST AUSTELL, PL26 8XG, 01726 850362 www.wheal-martyn.com

Trerice, TRERICE, TR8 4PG, 01637 875404 www.nationaltrust.org.uk/trerice/

Gnome World Caravan & Camping Park
▶▶▶ 80%

tel: 01726 860812 & 860101 **Moorland Rd TR9 6HN**
email: gnomesworld@btconnect.com
dir: *Signed from slip road at A30 & A39 rdbt in village of Indian Queens – site on old A30, now unclassified road.* **grid ref:** *SW890599*

Set in open countryside, this spacious park is set on level grassy land only half a mile from the A30 (Cornwall's main arterial route) and in a central holiday location for touring the county, and accessing the sandy beaches on the north Cornwall coast. Ablaze with summer flowering plants, it offers spotless facilities, an exciting children's playgound and a shop. Please note, there are no narrow lanes to negotiate. 4.5 acre site. 50 touring pitches. 25 hardstandings. Caravan pitches. Motorhome pitches. Tent pitches. 60 statics.

Open: Mar-Dec **Last arrival:** 22.00hrs **Last departure:** noon

Pitches: 🚐 🚍 Å **Facilities:** ⊙ ☀ 🔌 ♿ 🚻 🛒

Services: 🔌 🛢 🔒 **Within 3 miles:** ⌚ 🛢 🛒 ⛵

Notes: Dogs must be kept on leads. Nature trail.

AA Pubs & Restaurants nearby: The Plume of Feathers, MITCHELL, TR8 5AX, 01872 510387

See advert on opposite page

ISLES OF SCILLY

See Bryher and St Mary's

JACOBSTOW
Map 2 SX19

Places to visit

Launceston Castle, LAUNCESTON, PL15 7DR, 01566 772365
www.english-heritage.org.uk/daysout/properties/launceston-castle

Tamar Otter & Wildlife Centre, LAUNCESTON, PL15 8GW, 01566 785646
www.tamarotters.co.uk

Great for kids: Launceston Steam Railway, LAUNCESTON, PL15 8DA,
01566 775665 www.launcestonsr.co.uk

Edmore Tourist Park
▶▶▶81%

tel: 01840 230467 **Edgar Rd, Wainhouse Corner EX23 0BJ**
email: enquiries@cornwallvisited.co.uk
dir: Exit A39 at Wainhouse Corner onto Edgar Rd, site signed on right in 200yds.
grid ref: SX184955

A quiet family-owned site in a rural location with extensive views, set close to the sandy surfing beaches of Bude, and the unspoilt sandy beach and rock pools at Crackington Haven. The friendly owners keep all facilities in a very good condition including the lovely grounds, and the site has hardstanding pitches and gravel access roads. There is an excellent children's play area. The site is handy for bus routes as it is close to the A39. 3 acre site. 24 touring pitches. 5 hardstandings. 2 seasonal pitches. Caravan pitches. Motorhome pitches. Tent pitches. 3 statics.

Open: 1 wk before Etr-Oct **Last arrival:** 21.00hrs **Last departure:** noon

Pitches: * 🚐 £16-£19.50 🚍 £16-£19.50 ▲ £16-£19.50

Leisure: ⚠ **Facilities:** 🅿☉🅿✳♻️ℹ️ **Services:** 🔌🗑 🔋🛒

Within 3 miles: 🆂

Notes: 🐾 Dogs must be kept on leads.

AA Pubs & Restaurants nearby: Bay View Inn, WIDEMOUTH BAY, EX23 0AW, 01288 361273

KENNACK SANDS
Map 2 SW71

Places to visit

Cornish Seal Sanctuary, GWEEK, TR12 6UG, 01326 221361
www.sealsanctuaries.com

Great for kids: The Flambards Theme Park, HELSTON, TR13 0QA, 01326 573404
www.flambards.co.uk

Chy Carne Holiday Park
▶▶▶▶ 90%

tel: 01326 290200 & 291161 **Kuggar, Ruan Minor TR12 7LX**
email: enquiries@chycarne.co.uk
dir: From A3083 onto B3293 after Culdrose Naval Air Station. At Goonhilly ESS right onto unclassified road signed Kennack Sands. Left in 3m at junct. **grid ref:** SW725164

This spacious, beautifully maintained, 12-acre park is in a quiet rural location and has excellent family facilities and a stunning toilet block. There are extensive sea and coastal views over the sand at Kennack Sands, less than half a mile away. Food is available from the site's takeaway, and the local hostelry is not far away in the village. 12 acre site. 30 touring pitches. 7 hardstandings. Caravan pitches. Motorhome pitches. Tent pitches. 30 statics.

Open: Etr-Oct **Last arrival:** dusk

Pitches: 🚐🚍▲

Leisure: 🎣⚠♨️

Facilities: 🅿☉🅿✳♿🅂🔩♻️ℹ️🖥 WiFi

Services: 🔌🗑🍴🔋⊘ T 🍴🛒 🖨

Within 3 miles: 🚴🛶🅿◎🆂🗑∪

Notes: Table tennis, football table, pool table.

AA Pubs & Restaurants nearby: Cadgwith Cove Inn, CADGWITH, TR12 7JX, 01326 290513

PITCHES: 🚐 Caravans 🚍 Motorhomes ▲ Tents 🏕 Glamping accommodation **SERVICES:** 🔌 Electric hook up 🗑 Launderette 🍴 Licensed bar 🔋 Calor Gas ⊘ Camping Gaz T Toilet fluid 🍴 Café/Restaurant 🖨 Fast Food/Takeaway 🛒 Battery charging 🛒 Baby care ∪ Motorvan service point
ABBREVIATIONS: BHs – bank holidays Etr – Easter Spring BH – Spring Bank Holiday fr – from hrs – hours m – mile mdnt – midnight rdbt – roundabout rs – restricted service wk – week wknd – weekend x-roads – crossroads 🐾 No credit or debit cards ⊗ No dogs

KENNACK SANDS *continued*

Silver Sands Holiday Park
►►► 86%

tel: 01326 290631 **Gwendreath TR12 7LZ**
email: info@silversandsholidaypark.co.uk
dir: *From Helston follow signs to St Keverne. After BT Goonhilly Station turn right at x-roads signed Kennack Sands, 1.5m, left at Gwendreath sign, site 1m. (NB it is recommended that these directions are followed not Sat Nav).* **grid ref:** *SW727166*

A small, family-owned park in a remote location, with individually screened pitches providing sheltered suntraps. The owners continue to upgrade the park, improving the landscaping, access roads and toilets; lovely floral displays greet you on arrival. A footpath through the woods leads to the beach and the local pub. One of the nearby beaches is the historic Mullion Cove, and for the children a short car ride will ensure a great day out at the Flambards Theme Park. 9 acre site. 35 touring pitches. Caravan pitches. Motorhome pitches. Tent pitches. 16 statics.

Open: 21 Mar-2 Nov **Last arrival:** 21.00hrs **Last departure:** 11.00hrs
Pitches: * 🚐 £15.50-£24 🚃 £16-£24 ▲ £15-£23
Leisure: /⚽ ⚙
Facilities: 🏈🅿⊙🌡☀📷🚿 WiFi ♻❶⛟
Services: 🔌🗑🔒🪓
Within 3 miles: ↓🎣⛵🛍↺

Notes: No noise after 23.00hrs. Dogs must be kept on leads.
AA Pubs & Restaurants nearby: Cadgwith Cove Inn, CADGWITH, TR12 7JX, 01326 290513

Upper Tamar Lake
►► 75%

tel: 01288 321712 **Upper Tamar Lake EX23 9SB**
email: info@swlakestrust.org.uk
dir: *From A39 at Kilkhampton onto B3254, left in 0.5m onto unclassified road, follow signs approx 4m to site.* **grid ref:** *SS288118*

A well-trimmed, slightly sloping site overlooking the lake and surrounding countryside, with several signed walks. The site benefits from the excellent facilities provided for the watersports centre and coarse anglers, with a rescue launch on the lake when the flags are flying. A good family site, with Bude's beaches and the surfing waves only eight miles away. 1 acre site. 28 touring pitches. 2 hardstandings. Caravan pitches. Motorhome pitches. Tent pitches.

Open: Apr-Oct **Last departure:** 11.00hrs
Pitches: 🚐 🚃 ▲ 🏠
Leisure: /⚽🎣 **Facilities:** 🏈🅿☀♿🚿♻❶⛟
Services: 🔌🍴🏪 **Glamping:** Wooden Pods 1, £35 Car by unit
Within 3 miles: ↓🎣⛵🛍↺

Notes: No open fires, off-ground BBQs only, no swimming in lake. Dogs must be kept on leads. Canoeing, sailing, windsurfing, cycle hire.

PREMIER PARK

Dolbeare Park Caravan and Camping
▶▶▶▶▶ 88%

tel: 01752 851332 **St Ive Rd PL12 5AF**
email: reception@dolbeare.co.uk **web:** www.dolbeare.co.uk
dir: A38 to Landrake, 4m W of Saltash. At footbridge over A38 turn right, follow signs to site (0.75m from A38). **grid ref:** SX363616

Set in meadowland close to the A38 and the Devon-Cornwall border, this attractive touring park is run by innovative, forward-thinking owners who have adopted a very 'green' approach to running the park. The smart toilet block is very eco-friendly – electronic sensor showers, an on-demand boiler system, flow control valves on the taps, and low-energy lighting, as well as an impressive family room. The park is extremely well presented, with excellent hardstanding pitches, a good tenting field that offers spacious pitches, and good provision for children with a separate ball games paddock and nature trail. Expect high levels of customer care and cleanliness. The on-site shop sells fresh bread and local produce. One pre-erected, fully-equipped Eurotent and two Lotus belle tents are available for hire. 9 acre site. 60 touring pitches. 54 hardstandings. 12 seasonal pitches. Caravan pitches. Motorhome pitches. Tent pitches.

Open: all year **Last arrival:** 18.00hrs **Last departure:** 11.00hrs
Pitches: 🚐 £19-£25 🚍 £19-£25 ⛺ fr £16.50 🎪 prices shown below
Leisure: ⚠ ✪
Facilities: 🏕 🅿 ⊙ ℉ ✳ ⅋ 🔥 ⌷ 📶 💻 ♻ 𝟬
Services: 🔌 🔲 🔋 ⌀ 🅃 🔋 🚮 ♨

Glamping: Lotus Belle tents 2, £80 (seasonally variable) Changeover day Fri Min stay 3 nights Own kitchen Car by unit **Erected Tents** 1, £238-£350 Changeover day Sat Min stay 7 nights Own kitchen Car by unit

Within 3 miles: ⅃ ⅌ ℘ 🔲 🔲 ∪

Notes: No cycling, no kite flying, fee payable for arrivals after 18.00hrs. Dogs must be kept on leads. Off licence, free use of fridge & freezer, freshly baked bread & croissants.

AA Pubs & Restaurants nearby: The Crooked Inn, SALTASH, PL12 4RZ, 01752 848177

See advert on opposite page

Places to visit

East Pool Mine, POOL, TR15 3NP, 01209 315027 www.nationaltrust.org.uk

Godolphin House, GODOLPHIN CROSS, TR13 9RE, 01736 763194 www.nationaltrust.org.uk/godolphin

PREMIER PARK

Calloose Caravan & Camping Park
▶▶▶▶▶ 85%

tel: 01736 850431 & 0800 328 7589 **TR27 5ET**
email: calloose@hotmail.com
dir: From Hayle take B3302 to Leedstown, turn left opposite village hall before entering village. Site 0.5m on left at bottom of hill. **grid ref:** SW597352

A comprehensively equipped leisure park in a remote rural setting in a small river valley. This very good park is busy and bustling, and offers bright, clean toilet facilities, an excellent games room, an inviting pool, a good children's play area, and log cabins and static caravans for holiday hire. 12.5 acre site. 109 touring pitches. 29 hardstandings. Caravan pitches. Motorhome pitches. Tent pitches. 25 statics.

Open: all year **Last arrival:** 22.00hrs **Last departure:** 11.00hrs
Pitches: 🚐 🚍 ⛺
Leisure: ⚽ ♨ ✎
Facilities: ⊙ ℉ ✳ ⅋ 🔲 🚿
Services: 🔌 🔲 🔋 🔋 ⌀ 🅃 🍽 🔋 ♨
Within 3 miles: ℘ 🔲 🔲

Notes: No noise after mdnt, no pets in statics or log cabins. Crazy golf, skittle alley.

AA Pubs & Restaurants nearby: Mount Haven Hotel & Restaurant, MARAZION, TR17 0DQ, 01736 710249

PITCHES: 🚐 Caravans 🚍 Motorhomes ⛺ Tents 🎪 Glamping accommodation **SERVICES:** 🔌 Electric hook up 🔲 Launderette 🍸 Licensed bar 🔋 Calor Gas ⌀ Camping Gaz 🅃 Toilet fluid 🍽 Café/Restaurant 🔋 Fast Food/Takeaway 🔋 Battery charging 🚼 Baby care ♨ Motorvan service point
ABBREVIATIONS: BHs – bank holidays Etr – Easter Spring BH – Spring Bank Holiday fr – from hrs – hours m – mile mdnt – midnight rdbt – roundabout rs – restricted service wk – week wknd – weekend x-roads – crossroads ⊗ No credit or debit cards ⊗ No dogs

LOOE Map 2 SX25

Places to visit

Antony House, TORPOINT, PL11 2QA, 01752 812191
www.nationaltrust.org.uk/antony

Mount Edgcumbe House & Country Park, TORPOINT, PL10 1HZ, 01752 822236
www.mountedgcumbe.gov.uk

Great for kids: Wild Futures Monkey Sanctuary, LOOE, PL13 1NZ, 01503 262532
www.monkeysanctuary.org

Tencreek Holiday Park

HOLIDAY CENTRE 82%

tel: 01503 262447 **Polperro Rd PL13 2JR**
email: reception@tencreek.co.uk **web:** www.dolphinholidays.co.uk
dir: *Take A387 1.25m from Looe. Site on left.* **grid ref:** *SX233525*

Occupying a lovely position with extensive countryside and sea views, this holiday centre is in a rural spot but close to Looe and Polperro. There is a full family entertainment programme, with indoor and outdoor swimming pools, an adventure playground and an exciting children's club. The superb amenities blocks include several private family shower rooms with toilet and washbasin. 24 acre site. 254 touring pitches. 12 hardstandings. 120 seasonal pitches. Caravan pitches. Motorhome pitches. Tent pitches. 101 statics.

Open: all year **Last arrival:** 22.00hrs **Last departure:** 10.00hrs

Pitches: * 🚐 £14-£26 🚌 £14-£26 ⛺ £10-£20

Leisure: 🏊 🛝 ✋ 🎾 ⚽ 🎱 🎵

Facilities: 🚿 [P] ⊙ 💨 ❄ ♿ [S] 🐕 [WiFi] 💻 ♻ ℹ

Services: 🚐 🧺 🍺 🔒 🍃 [T] 🍴 🧊 🛒 🚜 ⛛

Within 3 miles: ⛳ ⛵ 🎬 🎣 ◎ 🌊 [S] 🧺 🐴

Notes: Families & couples only. Dogs must be kept on leads. Multi-sports pitch.

AA Pubs & Restaurants nearby: Trelaske Hotel & Restaurant, LOOE, PL13 2JS, 01503 262159

See advert on opposite page

PREMIER PARK

Camping Caradon Touring Park

►►►►► 80%

tel: 01503 272388 **Trelawne PL13 2NA**
email: enquiries@campingcaradon.co.uk
dir: *Site signed from junct of A387 & B3359, between Looe & Polperro. Take B3359 towards Pelynt then 1st right. Site 250mtrs on the left.* **grid ref:** *SX218539*

Set in a quiet rural location between the popular coastal resorts of Looe and Polperro, this family-run and developing eco-friendly park is just one and half miles from the beach at Talland Bay. The site caters for both families and couples. The owners take great pride in the site and offer some quality facilities and service to their campers throughout their stay; their constant aim is to provide a carefree and relaxing holiday. The local bus stops inside the park entrance. 3.5 acre site. 75 touring pitches. 23 hardstandings. Caravan pitches. Motorhome pitches. Tent pitches.

Open: all year (rs Nov-Mar prior booking only) **Last arrival:** 20.00hrs
Last departure: 11.00hrs

Pitches: 🚐 🚌 ⛺

Leisure: 🛝 🎱

Facilities: 🚿 ⊙ 💨 ❄ ♿ [S] 🧺 [WiFi] ♻ ℹ

Services: 🚐 🧺 🍺 🔒 🍃 [T] 🍴 🧊 ⛛

Within 3 miles: ⛵ 🎣 ◎ 🌊 [S] 🧺

Notes: Quiet from 23.00hrs-07.00hrs & barrier not operational. Dogs must be kept on leads. Family room with TV, undercover washing-up area, RCD lead hire, rallies welcome.

AA Pubs & Restaurants nearby: The Ship Inn, LOOE, PL13 1AD, 01503 263124

Who are the AA's award-winning campsites this year? See pages 14-19

LEISURE: 🏊 Indoor pool 🏊 Outdoor pool 🛝 Children's playground ✋ Kid's club 🎾 Tennis court 🎱 Games room ⛳ Golf course ⛵ Boat hire 🚲 Cycle hire 🎬 Cinema 🎵 Entertainment 🎣 Fishing ◎ Mini golf ⛳ Pitch n putt 🌊 Watersports 🏋 Gym ⚽ Sports field 🐴 Stables **FACILITIES:** 🛁 Bath 🚿 Shower [P] Private washing cubicles ⊙ Electric shaver 💨 Hairdryer ❄ Ice Packs ♿ Disabled facilities [S] Shop on site 🚚 Mobile shop 🍖 BBQ area 🧺 Picnic area [WiFi] Wi-fi 💻 Internet access ♻ Recycling ℹ Tourist info 🐕 Dog exercise area 🚗 Car hire can be arranged

Tregoad Park
►►►►► 80%

tel: 01503 262718 **St Martin PL13 1PB**
email: info@tregoadpark.co.uk
dir: *Signed with direct access from B3253, or from E on A387 follow B3253 for 1.75m towards Looe. Site on left at bottom of cliff.* **grid ref:** SX272560

Investment continues at this smart, terraced park with extensive sea and rural views, about a mile and a half from Looe. All pitches are level. The facilities are well maintained and spotlessly clean, and there is a swimming pool with adjacent jacuzzi and sun patio, and a licensed bar where bar meals are served in the conservatory. The site has fishing lakes stocked with carp, tench and roach. There is a bus stop at the bottom of the drive for the Plymouth and Truro routes. Static caravans, holiday cottages and camping pods are available for holiday hire. 55 acre site. 200 touring pitches. 60 hardstandings. Caravan pitches. Motorhome pitches. Tent pitches. 7 statics.

Open: all year (rs Low season bistro closed) **Last arrival:** 20.00hrs
Last departure: 11.00hrs
Pitches: 🚐 £12-£38 🚐 £12-£38 ▲ £12-£38 🏕 prices shown below
Leisure: 🏊 ⚠ 🐎 🎣 🎱 Spa
Facilities: 🚿 ⚙ 🅿 ☕ ✳ ♿ 🛁 🚻 📶 💻 ♻ ⓘ
Services: 🔌 🚿 🍴 🔋 🚽 🍽 🏪 🚮 ⛽
Glamping: Wooden Pods 10, £25-£60 Min stay 1 night Car by unit
Within 3 miles: 🎣 🚴 ♿ 🏊 ⛽ U
Notes: Dogs must be kept on leads. Crazy golf, ball sports area.
AA Pubs & Restaurants nearby: Trelaske Hotel & Restaurant, LOOE, PL13 2JS, 01503 262159

Looe Country Park
►►►► 83%

tel: 01503 240265 **Bucklawren Rd, St Martin PL13 1QS**
email: info@looecountrypark.co.uk
dir: *Follow A38 to Trerulefoot rdbt, turn left at A374 signed Looe & Torpoint, then A387 towards Looe. Through Hessenford & onto Widegates, then stay left onto the B3253 turning left for No Mans Land after 1m. At the top of lane turn left into Bucklawren Rd. Site entrance on right.* **grid ref:** SX283557

This is a very neat and well-kept small grassy site on high ground above Looe in a peaceful rural setting. The friendly and enthusiastic owners continue to invest in the park. The toilet facilities have upmarket fittings (note the infra-red operated taps and underfloor heating). A bus stops at the bottom of the lane, but you must flag down the driver. A coastal walk runs by the site, and it is a 20-minute walk to the beach at Looe. 3.3 acre site. 31 touring pitches. 19 hardstandings. Caravan pitches. Motorhome pitches. Tent pitches. 5 statics.

Open: all year **Last arrival:** 22.00hrs **Last departure:** 11.00hrs
Pitches: * 🚐 £11-£23.50 🚐 £11-£23.50 ▲ £11-£23.50 🏕 prices shown below
Leisure: ⚠
Facilities: 🚿 ⚙ 🅿 ☕ ✳ 🛁 🚻 📶 ♻ ⓘ
Services: 🔌 🚿 🔋 🚽 🚮
Glamping: Wooden Pods 2, £35-£50 Min stay 1 night Car by unit
Within 3 miles: 🎣 🚴 ♿ 🏊 ⛽ U
Notes: Dogs must be kept on leads.
AA Pubs & Restaurants nearby: Trelaske Hotel & Restaurant, LOOE, PL13 2JS, 01503 262159

PITCHES: 🚐 Caravans 🚐 Motorhomes ▲ Tents 🏕 Glamping accommodation **SERVICES:** 🔌 Electric hook up 🚿 Launderette 🍴 Licensed bar 🔋 Calor Gas 🔥 Camping Gaz 🚽 Toilet fluid 🍽 Café/Restaurant 🏪 Fast Food/Takeaway 🔋 Battery charging 🚮 Baby care ⛽ Motorvan service point
ABBREVIATIONS: BHs – bank holidays Etr – Easter Spring BH – Spring Bank Holiday fr – from hrs – hours m – mile mdnt – midnight rdbt – roundabout rs – restricted service wk – week wknd – weekend x-roads – crossroads ⊘ No credit or debit cards ⊗ No dogs

LOSTWITHIEL
Map 2 SX15

Places to visit

Restormel Castle, RESTORMEL, PL22 0EE, 01208 872687
www.english-heritage.org.uk/daysout/properties/restormel-castle

Lanhydrock, LANHYDROCK, PL30 5AD, 01208 265950 www.nationaltrust.org.uk

Great for kids: Eden Project, ST AUSTELL, PL24 2SG, 01726 811911
www.edenproject.com

PREMIER PARK

Eden Valley Holiday Park
▶▶▶▶▶85%

GOLD

tel: 01208 872277 **PL30 5BU**
email: edenvalleyholidaypark@btconnect.com **web:** www.edenvalleyholidaypark.co.uk
dir: 1.5m SW of Lostwithiel on A390 turn right at brown/white sign in 400mtrs. (NB it
is advisable to follow these directions not Sat Nav). **grid ref:** SX083593

A grassy park set in attractive paddocks with mature trees. A gradual upgrading
of facilities continues, and both buildings and grounds are carefully maintained
and contain an impressive children's play area. This park is ideally located for
visiting the Eden Project, the nearby golden beaches and sailing at Fowey. There
are also two self-catering lodges. 12 acre site. 56 touring pitches. 40
hardstandings. 25 seasonal pitches. Caravan pitches. Motorhome pitches. Tent
pitches. 38 statics.

Open: Etr or Apr-Oct **Last arrival:** 22.00hrs **Last departure:** 11.30hrs

Pitches: ⌖ ⌖ Å

Leisure: ⋔ ⊙ ⚲

Facilities: ⌖ ⌖ ⊙ ⌖ ⌖ ⌖ ⌖ ⌖ ⌖ WiFi ♻ ⓲

Services: ⌖ ⌖ ⌖ ⌖ ⌖ ⌖

Within 3 miles: ⌖ ⌖ ⌖ ⌖ ⌖ ⌖ U

Notes: No large dogs. Dogs must be kept on leads. Table football, pool, table tennis,
football. Walks, wildlife & wildlife conservation information room.

AA Pubs & Restaurants nearby: The Crown Inn, LANLIVERY, PL30 5BT, 01208 872707

LUXULYAN
Map 2 SX05

Places to visit

Restormel Castle, RESTORMEL, PL22 0EE, 01208 872687
www.english-heritage.org.uk/daysout/properties/restormel-castle

Eden Project, ST AUSTELL, PL24 2SG, 01726 811911 www.edenproject.com

Great for kids: Wheal Martyn, ST AUSTELL, PL26 8XG, 01726 850362
www.wheal-martyn.com

Croft Farm Holiday Park
▶▶▶80%

tel: 01726 850228 **PL30 5EQ**
email: enquiries@croftfarm.co.uk
dir: Exit A30 at Bodmin onto A391 towards St Austell. In 7m left at double rdbt onto
unclassified road towards Luxulyan/Eden Project, continue to rdbt at Eden, left signed
Luxulyan. Site 1m on left. (NB do not approach any other way as roads are very narrow).
grid ref: SX044568

A peaceful, picturesque setting at the edge of a wooded valley, and only one mile
from The Eden Project. Facilities include a well-maintained toilet block, a well-
equipped dishwashing area, replete with freezer and microwave, and a revamped
children's play area reached via an attractive woodland trail. There is a good bus
service to St Austell and Luxulyan (the bus stop is at the site's entrance) and trains
run to Newquay. 10.5 acre site. 22 touring pitches. 18 hardstandings. 10 seasonal
pitches. Caravan pitches. Motorhome pitches. Tent pitches. 63 statics.

Open: 21 Mar-21 Jan **Last arrival:** 18.00hrs **Last departure:** 11.00hrs

Pitches: ⌖ ⌖ Å

Leisure: ⚲

Facilities: ⌖ ⊙ ⌖ ⌖ ⌖ ⌖ ⌖ WiFi ♻ ⓲

Services: ⌖ ⌖ ⌖ ⌖ ⌖ ⌖

Within 3 miles: ⌖ ⌖ ⌖ ⌖ ⌖ ⌖ ⌖

Notes: PayPal accepted. No skateboarding, ball games only in playing field, quiet
between 23.00hrs-07.00hrs. Dogs must be kept on leads. Woodland walk, information
room.

AA Pubs & Restaurants nearby: The Crown Inn, LANLIVERY, PL30 5BT, 01208 872707

MARAZION

See also St Hilary

Places to visit

St Michael's Mount, MARAZION, TR17 0HT, 01736 710507
www.stmichaelsmount.co.uk

Trengwainton Garden, PENZANCE, TR20 8RZ, 01736 363148
www.nationaltrust.org.uk/trengwainton

MARAZION
Map 2 SW53

Wayfarers Caravan & Camping Park
►►►► 90%

tel: 01736 763326 **Relubbus Ln, St Hilary TR20 9EF**
email: elaine@wayfarerspark.co.uk
dir: *Exit A30 onto A394 signed Helston. 2m, left at rdbt onto B3280 signed Goldsithney. Through Goldsithney. Site 1m on left on bend (NB slow down at 1st brown sign; it is advisable to ignore Sat Nav as directions not suitable if towing a caravan).*
grid ref: *SW558314*

Located in the centre of St Hilary, two and half miles from St Michael's Mount, this is a quiet, sheltered park in a peaceful rural setting. It offers spacious, well-drained pitches and very well maintained facilities, including a new chill-out barbecue area. It has a separate car park for campers which makes their area a safer environment. 4.8 acre site. 32 touring pitches. 25 hardstandings. Caravan pitches. Motorhome pitches. Tent pitches. 3 statics.

Open: May-Sep **Last arrival:** 18.00hrs **Last departure:** 11.00hrs

Pitches: 🚐 🚙 ▲

Facilities: 🕪 🅿 ☉ ⌐ ✻ 🕭 🗟 🛒 ♻ 🚻 ❦

Services: 🔌 🗟 🔋 🗑 🚽 🔌 ↯

Within 3 miles: ↧ ✦ ⌐ ◎ ≛ 🗟 🗟 ∪

Notes: Adults only. ⊗ No pets.

AA Pubs & Restaurants nearby: The Victoria Inn, PERRANUTHNOE, TR20 9NP, 01736 710309

Wheal Rodney Holiday Park
►►► 82%

tel: 01736 710605 **Gwallon Ln TR17 0HL**
email: reception@whealrodney.co.uk
dir: *Exit A30 at Crowlas, signed Rospeath. Site 1.5m on right. From Marazion centre turn opposite Fire Engine Inn, site 500mtrs on left.* **grid ref:** *SW525315*

Set in a quiet rural location surrounded by farmland, with level grass pitches and well-kept facilities. Within half a mile are the beach at Marazion and the causeway or ferry to St Michael's Mount. A cycle route is within 400 yards; Penzance is only a short car or cycle ride away. 2.5 acre site. 30 touring pitches. Caravan pitches. Motorhome pitches. Tent pitches.

Open: Etr-Oct **Last arrival:** 20.00hrs **Last departure:** 11.00hrs

Pitches: * 🚐 £16-£24 🚙 £16 £24 ▲ £14-£20

Leisure: ⌣

Facilities: 🕪 🅿 ☉ ⌐ ✻ 🗟 WiFi ♻ ❦

Services: 🔌 🗟 🔋

Within 3 miles: ↧ ⌐ ◎ ≛ 🗟 🗟 ∪

Notes: Quiet after 22.00hrs. Dogs must be kept on leads.

AA Pubs & Restaurants nearby: The Victoria Inn, PERRANUTHNOE, TR20 9NP, 01736 710309

Mount Haven Hotel & Restaurant, MARAZION, TR17 0DQ, 01736 710249

MAWGAN PORTH
Map 2 SW86

Sun Haven Valley Country Holiday Park
►►►► 84%

tel: 01637 860373 & 0800 634 6744 **TR8 4BQ**
email: sunhaven@sunhavenvalley.com **web:** www.sunhavenvalley.com
dir: *Exit A30 at Highgate Hill junct for Newquay; follow signs for airport. At T-junct turn right. At beach level in Mawgan Porth take only road inland, then 0.25m. Site 0.5m beyond 'S' bend.* **grid ref:** *SW861669*

An attractive site with level pitches on the side of a river valley; being just off the B3276 this makes an ideal base for touring the Padstow and Newquay areas. The very high quality facilities include a TV lounge and a games room in a Swedish-style chalet, and a well-kept adventure playground. Trees and hedges fringe the park, and the ground is well drained. 5 acre site. 109 touring pitches. 11 hardstandings. Caravan pitches. Motorhome pitches. Tent pitches. 38 statics.

Open: Etr-Oct **Last arrival:** 22.00hrs **Last departure:** 10.30hrs

Pitches: 🚐 🚙 ▲

Leisure: ⚷ ☜

Facilities: ☉ ⌐ ✻ 🕭 🗟 🛒 WiFi 🖥 ♻ ❦

Services: 🔌 🗟 🔋 🗑 🚽

Within 3 miles: ↧ ⌐ ◎ ≛ 🗟 🗟

Notes: Families & couples only, no noise after 22.30hrs. Dogs must be kept on leads. Microwave available, pizza ovens.

AA Pubs & Restaurants nearby: The Falcon Inn, ST MAWGAN, TR8 4EP, 01637 860225

The Scarlet Hotel, MAWGAN PORTH, TR8 4DQ, 01637 861800

See advert on page 88

PITCHES: 🚐 Caravans 🚙 Motorhomes ▲ Tents 🏕 Glamping accommodation **SERVICES:** 🔌 Electric hook up 🗟 Launderette 🍺 Licensed bar 🔋 Calor Gas ⊘ Camping Gaz 🗍 Toilet fluid 🍽 Café/Restaurant 🍔 Fast Food/Takeaway 🔋 Battery charging 🛒 Baby care ↯ Motorvan service point
ABBREVIATIONS: BHs – bank holidays Etr – Easter Spring BH – Spring Bank Holiday fr – from hrs – hours m – mile mdnt – midnight rdbt – roundabout rs – restricted service wk – week wknd – weekend x-roads – crossroads ⊗ No credit or debit cards ⊗ No dogs

MAWGAN PORTH *continued*

Trevarrian Holiday Park

►►► 83%

tel: 01637 860381 & 0845 225 5910 *(Calls cost 7p per minute plus your phone company's access charge)* **TR8 4AQ**
email: holiday@trevarrian.co.uk
dir: *From A39 at St Columb rdbt turn right onto A3059 towards Newquay. Fork right in approx 2m for St Mawgan onto B3276. Turn right, site on left.* **grid ref:** *SW853661*

A well-established and well-run holiday park overlooking Mawgan Porth beach. This park has a wide range of attractions including a free entertainment programme in peak season and a 10-pin bowling alley with licensed bar. It is only a short drive to Newquay and approximately 20 minutes to Padstow. 7 acre site. 185 touring pitches. 10 hardstandings. Caravan pitches. Motorhome pitches. Tent pitches.

Open: all year **Last arrival:** 22.00hrs **Last departure:** 11.00hrs

Pitches: 🚐 🚌 ⛺

Leisure: 🏊 ⚽ 🏓 🎵

Facilities: 🪒 💨 ❄ ♿ 🛒 🐕 [WiFi] ♻ ℹ

Services: 🔌 🧺 🍷 🔒 🌿 [T] 🍴 🍔 🛍 ⛽

Within 3 miles: ⛳ ⛵ 🎬 🎣 ◎ 🛒 🧺 🐎

Notes: No noise after mdnt. Dogs must be kept on leads. Crazy golf.

AA Pubs & Restaurants nearby: The Falcon Inn, ST MAWGAN, TR8 4EP, 01637 860225

MEVAGISSEY Map 2 SX04

See also Gorran & Pentewan

PREMIER PARK

Seaview International Holiday Park

►►►►► 93%

DAVID BELLAMY CONSERVATION AWARD GOLD

tel: 01726 843425 **Boswinger PL26 6LL**
email: seaview@swholidayparks.co.uk **web:** www.seaviewinternational.com
dir: *From St Austell take B3273 signed Mevagissey. Turn right before entering village. Follow brown tourist signs to site. (NB very narrow lanes to this site; it is advisable to follow these directions not Sat Nav).* **grid ref:** *SW990412*

An attractive holiday park set in a beautiful environment overlooking Veryan Bay, with colourful landscaping, including attractive flowers and shrubs. It continues to offer an outstanding holiday experience, with its luxury family pitches, super toilet facilities, takeaway, shop and an alfresco eating area complete with a TV screen. The beach is just half a mile away. There is also an 'off the lead' dog walk, and a 'ring and ride' bus service to Truro, St Austell and Plymouth stops at the park gate. Static caravans are available for holiday hire. 28 acre site. 201

touring pitches. 29 hardstandings. 15 seasonal pitches. Caravan pitches. Motorhome pitches. Tent pitches. 39 statics.

Seaview International Holiday Park

Open: Mar-end Sep (rs Mar-end May & mid Sep-end Sep swimming pool closed) **Last arrival:** 20.00hrs **Last departure:** 10.00hrs

Pitches: 🚐 🚐 🛆

Leisure: 🏊 ⚽ 🎯

Facilities: ⊙ 🍴 ⚒ ♿ 🛁 📷 ⚡ WiFi 🖥 ♻ ❶

Services: 🔌 🗑 🛢 ⚗ T 🍴 🛒 ↯

Within 3 miles: 🚴 ⚲ ◎ 🛒 🏇 🗑

Notes: Restrictions on certain dog breeds. Dogs must be kept on leads. Crazy golf, volleyball, badminton, scuba diving, boules, tennis.

AA Pubs & Restaurants nearby: The Ship Inn, MEVAGISSEY, PL26 6UQ, 01726 843324

See advert below

MULLION	Map 2 SW61

Places to visit

Great for kids: Cornish Seal Sanctuary, GWEEK, TR12 6UG, 01326 221361 www.sealsanctuaries.com

The Flambards Theme Park, HELSTON, TR13 0QA, 01326 573404 www.flambards.co.uk

Franchis Holiday Park
►►► 78%

tel: 01326 240301 **Cury Cross Lanes TR12 7AZ**
email: enquiries@franchis.co.uk **web:** www.franchis.co.uk
dir: *Exit A3083 on left 0.5m past Wheel Inn PH, between Helston & The Lizard.*
grid ref: *SW698203*

A mainly grassy site surrounded by hedges and trees, located on Goonhilly Downs and in an ideal position for exploring the Lizard Peninsula. The site is divided into two paddocks for tourers, and the pitches are a mix of level and slightly sloping.

continued

PITCHES: 🚐 Caravans 🚐 Motorhomes 🛆 Tents 🏕 Glamping accommodation **SERVICES:** 🔌 Electric hook up 🗑 Launderette 🍴 Licensed bar 🛢 Calor Gas ⊘ Camping Gaz T Toilet fluid 🍴 Café/Restaurant 🛒 Fast Food/Takeaway 🔋 Battery charging 🚼 Baby care ↯ Motorvan service point **ABBREVIATIONS:** BHs – bank holidays Etr – Easter Spring BH – Spring Bank Holiday fr – from hrs – hours m – mile mdnt – midnight rdbt – roundabout rs – restricted service wk – week wknd – weekend x-roads – crossroads ⊘ No credit or debit cards ⊗ No dogs

MULLION *continued*

There are good facilities for families, and for a fun-filled family day out Flambards Theme Park is less than 20 minutes' drive away in Helston. 16 acre site. 57 touring pitches. 14 seasonal pitches. Caravan pitches. Motorhome pitches. Tent pitches. 12 statics.

Franchis Holiday Park

Open: 7 Apr-14 Oct **Last arrival:** 20.00hrs **Last departure:** 10.30hrs

Pitches: 🚐 🚍 ▲

Facilities: ⬛☉✳🖐 📶♻🔧

Services: 🔌⬛ T 🍴

Within 3 miles: ⬛ 🏊 🎣 🛒🍴∪

Notes: Dogs must be kept on leads.

AA Pubs & Restaurants nearby: The Halzephron Inn, GUNWALLOE, TR12 7QB, 01326 240406

NEWQUAY

See also Rejerrah

Places to visit

Blue Reef Aquarium, NEWQUAY, TR7 1DU, 01637 878134 www.bluereefaquarium.co.uk

Trerice, TRERICE, TR8 4PG, 01637 875404 www.nationaltrust.org.uk/trerice/

Great for kids: Dairy Land Farm World, NEWQUAY, TR8 5AA, 01872 510246 www.dairylandfarmworld.com

Newquay Zoo, NEWQUAY, TR7 2LZ, 01637 873342 www.newquayzoo.org.uk

PREMIER PARK

Hendra Holiday Park
▶▶▶▶▶ **90%** Best of British

tel: 01637 875778 **TR8 4NY**
email: enquiries@hendra-holidays.com **web:** www.hendra-holidays.com
dir: *A30 onto A392 signed Newquay. At Quintrell Downs over rdbt, signed Lane, site 0.5m on left.* **grid ref:** *SW833601*

A large complex with holiday statics and superb facilities including an indoor fun pool and an outdoor pool. There is a children's club for the over 6s, evening entertainment during high season, a skateboard park, fish and chip shop and a fantastic coffee shop. The touring pitches, occupying 12 fields, are set amid mature trees and shrubs, and some have fully serviced facilities. All amenities are open to the public. This site generates most of its own electricity from a 1.5 megawatt solar farm. The Hendra Pod Village area has 10 smart wooden pods for hire. This park offers the complete holiday package for all, including children of all ages. As well as the beaches at Newquay, there are plenty of attractions in the area. 80 acre site. 548 touring pitches. 28 hardstandings. Caravan pitches. Motorhome pitches. Tent pitches. 307 statics.

Open: 25 Mar-4 Nov (rs Apr-Spring BH & Sep-Oct outdoor pool closed) **Last arrival:** dusk **Last departure:** 10.00hrs

Pitches: 🚐 🚍 ▲ 🏠

Leisure: 🏊🏊🎾🎢⚽♟🎱🎣🎮🎵

Facilities: ☉📺✳🖐🛒🖐📶💻♻🔧

Services: 🔌⬛🍴🛢🚿T🍴🍴♻🚗

Glamping: Wooden Pods 10, £40-£57.50 Min stay 1 night Car by unit

Within 3 miles: ↕ ⚘ ☰ ♿ ✎ ◎ ⚓ 🛒 🔄 ∪

Notes: Families & couples only. Dogs must be kept on leads. Land train rides, skate & scooter park.

AA Pubs & Restaurants nearby: The Lewinnick Lodge Bar & Restaurant, NEWQUAY, TR7 1NX, 01637 878117

See advert on page 95

Treloy Touring Park

▶ ▶ ▶ ▶ 92%

tel: 01637 872063 **TR8 4JN**
email: stay@treloy.co.uk **web:** www.treloy.co.uk
dir: On A3059 (St Columb Major to Newquay road). **grid ref:** SW858625

An attractive site with fine countryside views, that is within easy reach of resorts and beaches. The pitches are set in four paddocks with mainly level but some slightly sloping grassy areas. Maintenance and cleanliness are very high. There is a heated swimming pool and separate paddling pool surrounded by a paved patio area with tables, an excellent reception, shop and first aid room. Three dedicated family shower rooms are available. 23 acre site. 223 touring pitches. 30 hardstandings. 15 seasonal pitches. Caravan pitches. Motorhome pitches. Tent pitches.

Treloy Touring Park

Open: 28 May-4 Jun, Jul-3 Sep **Last arrival:** 20.00hrs **Last departure:** 10.00hrs

Pitches: * 🚐 £17.50-£19.50 🚌 £17.50-£19.50 ⛺ £17.50-£19.50

Leisure: ⛱ ⚲ ♻ ♠ 🎵

Facilities: 🚿 🌂 ☉ ⚲ ✳ ♿ 🛁 🔌 🐕 🚿 📶 ☀ ❶ ☕

Services: 🔌 🗑 🍴 🛢 ⚲ T ☕ 🍴 🔋 🍼 🛒 ↯

Within 3 miles: ↕ ⚘ ☰ ♿ ✎ ◎ ⚓ 🛒 🔄 ∪

Notes: Dogs must be kept on leads. Concessionary green fees at Treloy Golf Club.

AA Pubs & Restaurants nearby: The Lewinnick Lodge Bar & Restaurant, NEWQUAY, TR7 1NX, 01637 878117

See advert below

PITCHES: 🚐 Caravans 🚌 Motorhomes ⛺ Tents 🏠 Glamping accommodation **SERVICES:** 🔌 Electric hook up 🗑 Launderette 🍴 Licensed bar
🛢 Calor Gas ⊘ Camping Gaz T Toilet fluid ☕ Café/Restaurant 🍴 Fast Food/Takeaway 🔋 Battery charging 🍼 Baby care ↯ Motorvan service point
ABBREVIATIONS: BHs – bank holidays Etr – Easter Spring BH – Spring Bank Holiday fr – from hrs – hours m – mile mdnt – midnight
rdbt – roundabout rs – restricted service wk – week wknd – weekend x-roads – crossroads ⊗ No credit or debit cards ⊗ No dogs

NEWQUAY *continued*

Trencreek Holiday Park
► ► ► ► 87%

tel: 01637 874210 **Hillcrest, Higher Trencreek TR8 4NS**
email: trencreek@btconnect.com
dir: *A392 to Quintrell Downs, right towards Newquay, left at 2 mini-rdbts into Trevenson Rd to site.* **grid ref:** *SW828609*

An attractively landscaped park in the village of Trencreek, with modern toilet facilities of a very high standard. Two well-stocked fishing lakes, and evening entertainment in the licensed clubhouse, are extra draws. Located about two miles from Newquay with its beaches and surfing opportunities. 10 acre site. 194 touring pitches. 8 hardstandings. Caravan pitches. Motorhome pitches. Tent pitches. 6 statics.

Open: Spring BH–mid Sep **Last arrival:** 22.00hrs **Last departure:** noon

Pitches: 🚐 🚲 ⛺

Leisure: 🏊 🎣 ✐

Facilities: 🚿 🅿️ ⊙ 🌀 ✳ ♿ 🛒 ⛱ 📶 🖥 ♻ ⓘ

Services: 🔌 🛢 🍳 🛁 🚿 ⊤ 🍴 🍱 🏪 ⟱

Within 3 miles: ⅃ ⚓ ⊟ ✐ ◎ 🛥 🏊 🛒 ♻ ∪

Notes: ⊗ Families & couples only.

AA Pubs & Restaurants nearby: The Lewinnick Lodge Bar & Restaurant, NEWQUAY, TR7 1NX, 01637 878117

Porth Beach Holiday Park
► ► ► ► 82%

tel: 01637 876531 **Porth TR7 3NH**
email: info@porthbeach.co.uk **web:** www.porthbeach.co.uk
dir: *From Newquay take A3058 towards St Columb Major. At rdbt left onto B3276 signed Padstow. Site on right.* **grid ref:** *SW834629*

This attractive, popular park offers level, grassy pitches in neat and tidy surroundings. It is a well-run site set in meadowland in a glorious location adjacent to excellent sands of Porth Beach. The site offers two fully-equipped camping pods positioned on a raised terrace. 6 acre site. 185 touring pitches. 19 hardstandings. Caravan pitches. Motorhome pitches. Tent pitches. 30 statics.

Porth Beach Holiday Park

Open: Mar–Nov **Last arrival:** 18.00hrs **Last departure:** 10.00hrs

Pitches: 🚐 £22–£41 🚲 £22–£41 ⛺ £19–£46 🏠 prices shown below

Facilities: 🚿 🅿️ ⊙ ♿ 📶 ♻ ⓘ

Services: 🔌 🛢 🛁 🚿 🍴 ⟱

Glamping: **Wooden Pods** 2, £45–£65 Changeover day Any day Min stay 1 night

Within 3 miles: ⅃ ⚓ ⊟ ✐ ◎ 🛥 🏊 🛒 ♻ ∪

Notes: Families & couples only. Dogs must be kept on leads.

AA Pubs & Restaurants nearby: The Lewinnick Lodge Bar & Restaurant, NEWQUAY, TR7 1NX, 01637 878117

See advert on page 95

Trethiggey Holiday Park
► ► ► ► 82%

tel: 01637 877672 **Quintrell Downs TR8 4QR**
email: enquiries@trethiggey.co.uk **web:** www.trethiggey.co.uk
dir: *A30 onto A392 signed Newquay at Quintrell Downs rdbt, left onto A3058, pass Newquay Pearl centre. Site 0.5m on left.* **grid ref:** *SW846596*

A family-owned park in a rural setting that is ideal for touring this part of Cornwall. It is pleasantly divided into paddocks with maturing trees and shrubs, and offers coarse fishing and tackle hire. This site has a car park for campers as the camping fields are set in a car-free zone for children's safety. 15 acre site. 200 touring pitches. 35 hardstandings. 12 seasonal pitches. Caravan pitches. Motorhome pitches. Tent pitches. 12 statics.

Trethiggey Holiday Park

Open: Mar-Dec **Last arrival:** 22.00hrs **Last departure:** 10.30hrs

Pitches: 🚐 🚙 🏕 **Leisure:** ⚲ 🔍 ✐

Facilities: 🖍 📶 ⊙ 🅿 ✳ ⅋ 🅢 🎋 📶 🖥 ♻ ❶

Services: 🔌 🔆 🍸 🔋 ⌀ 🅣 🍴 🔌 🚽 ⅏ **Within 3 miles:** ⅃ 🎣 🎠 🎢 🏊 🅢 🅢 U

Notes: PayPal accepted. No noise after mdnt. Dogs must be kept on leads. Off licence, recreation field.

AA Pubs & Restaurants nearby: The Lewinnick Lodge Bar & Restaurant, NEWQUAY, TR7 1NX, 01637 878117

See advert below

Trenance Holiday Park
▶▶▶▶ 81%

tel: 01637 873447 **Edgcumbe Av TR7 2JY**
email: enquiries@trenanceholidaypark.co.uk
dir: *Exit A3075 near viaduct. Site by boating lake rdbt, turn right then 1st right.*
grid ref: *SW818612*

A mainly static park popular with tenters, close to Newquay's vibrant nightlife, and with café serving excellent breakfasts and takeaways. Set on high ground in an urban area of town, with cheerful owners and clean facilities; the site offers a motorhome service point. The local bus stops at the site entrance. 12 acre site. 50 touring pitches. Caravan pitches. Motorhome pitches. Tent pitches. 190 statics.

Open: 21 Apr-22 Sep (rs 21 Apr-mid May no shop) **Last arrival:** 22.00hrs **Last departure:** 10.00hrs

Pitches: * 🚐 £16-£19 🚙 £16-£19 🏕 £16-£19 **Leisure:** 🔍

Facilities: 🖍 ⊙ 🅿 ✳ ⅋ 🅢 📶 🖥 ♻ ❶

Services: 🔌 🔆 🍸 🔋 ⌀ 🅣 🍴 🔌 ⅏ **Within 3 miles:** ⅃ 🎣 🎠 🎢 🏊 🅢 🅢 U

Notes: No pets, no noise after mdnt.

AA Pubs & Restaurants nearby: The Lewinnick Lodge Bar & Restaurant, NEWQUAY, TR7 1NX, 01637 878117

Trebellan Park
▶▶▶ 84%

tel: 01637 830522 **Cubert TR8 5PY**
email: enquiries@trebellan.co.uk
dir: *S of Newquay from A392 onto A3075 towards Rejerrah. In approx. 4m, turn right signed Cubert. Left in 0.75m onto unclassified road.* **grid ref:** *SW790571*

A terraced grassy rural park within a picturesque valley with views of Cubert Common, and adjacent to the Smuggler's Den, a 16th-century thatched inn. This park has a very inviting swimming pool and three well-stocked coarse fishing lakes. 8 acre site. 150 touring pitches. Caravan pitches. Motorhome pitches. Tent pitches. 7 statics.

Open: May-Oct **Last arrival:** 21.00hrs **Last departure:** 10.00hrs

Pitches: * 🚐 £20.50-£26 🚙 £20.50-£26 🏕 £15.50-£21

Leisure: ≈ ✐ **Facilities:** 🖍 ⊙ 🅿 ✳ ⅋ 🎋 📶 🖥 ❶

Services: 🔌 🔆 🔌 **Within 3 miles:** ⅃ ✐ 🎠 🏊 🅢 🅢 U

Notes: Families & couples only. Dogs must be kept on leads.

AA Pubs & Restaurants nearby: The Smugglers' Den Inn, CUBERT, TR8 5PY, 01637 830209

The Lewinnick Lodge Bar & Restaurant, NEWQUAY, TR7 1NX, 01637 878117

PITCHES: 🚐 Caravans 🚙 Motorhomes 🏕 Tents ⚲ Glamping accommodation **SERVICES:** 🔌 Electric hook up 🔆 Launderette 🍸 Licensed bar 🔋 Calor Gas ⌀ Camping Gaz 🅣 Toilet fluid 🍴 Café/Restaurant 🔌 Fast Food/Takeaway 🔋 Battery charging 🚼 Baby care ⅏ Motorvan service point
ABBREVIATIONS: BHs – bank holidays Etr – Easter Spring BH – Spring Bank Holiday fr – from hrs – hours m – mile mdnt – midnight rdbt – roundabout rs – restricted service wk – week wknd – weekend x-roads – crossroads 🅢 No credit or debit cards ⊗ No dogs

NEWQUAY *continued*

Riverside Holiday Park
►►► 80%

tel: 01637 873617 **Gwills Ln TR8 4PE**
email: info@riversideholidaypark.co.uk **web:** www.riversideholidaypark.co.uk
dir: *A30 onto A392 signed Newquay. At Quintrell Downs cross rdbt signed Lane. 2nd left in 0.5m onto unclassified road signed Gwills. Site in 400yds.* **grid ref:** *SW829592*

A sheltered valley beside a river in a quiet location is the idyllic setting for this lightly wooded park that caters for families and couples only; the site is well placed for exploring Newquay and Padstow. There is a lovely swimming pool. The site is close to the wide variety of attractions offered by this major resort. Self-catering lodges, cabins and static vans are for hire. 11 acre site. 65 touring pitches. Caravan pitches. Motorhome pitches. Tent pitches. 65 statics.

Open: Mar-Oct **Last arrival:** 22.00hrs **Last departure:** 10.00hrs

Pitches: * ♛ £15-£20 ♛ £15-£20 ▲ £15-£20

Leisure: 🏊 ⅍ 🎯

Facilities: 🅿️ ⊙ ⧉ ✳ 🔥 🔒 WiFi 🌀 ❓

Services: 🔌 🛢 📲 💧 ⌷ T 🚮 🏚

Within 3 miles: ↨ ⅟ ☷ 🎣 ◎ 🔥 📆 🔥 ∪

Notes: Families & couples only. Dogs must be kept on leads.

AA Pubs & Restaurants nearby: The Lewinnick Lodge Bar & Restaurant, NEWQUAY, TR7 1NX, 01637 878117

PADSTOW

See also Rumford

Places to visit

Prideaux Place, PADSTOW, PL28 8RP, 01841 532411 www.prideauxplace.co.uk

Great for kids: Devon's Crealy Great Adventure Park, CLYST ST MARY, EX5 1DR, 01395 233200 www.crealy.co.uk

---

PADSTOW | Map 2 SW97

REGIONAL WINNER – SOUTH WEST ENGLAND AA CAMPSITE OF THE YEAR 2017

PREMIER PARK

Padstow Touring Park
►►►►► 97%

tel: 01841 532061 **PL28 8LE**
email: bookings@padstowtouringpark.co.uk
dir: *1m S of Padstow, on E side of A389 (Padstow to Wadebridge road).*
grid ref: *SW913738*

Improvements continue at this top quality park set in open countryside above the quaint fishing town of Padstow, which can be approached via a footpath directly from the park. This site is divided into paddocks by maturing bushes and hedges that create a peaceful and relaxing holiday atmosphere. The main facility blocks have been designed and decorated to a very high standard, plus there is a good children's play area, a well-stocked shop and an excellent coffee lounge with a decked terrace offering country views. 13.5 acre site. 150 touring pitches. 45 hardstandings. Caravan pitches. Motorhome pitches. Tent pitches. 12 statics.

Open: all year **Last arrival:** 21.00hrs **Last departure:** 11.00hrs

Pitches: * ♛ £18.50-£36 ♛ £17.50-£36 ▲ £12.50-£36 **Leisure:** ⅍

Facilities: 🅿️ 🅿️ ⊙ ⧉ ✳ 🔥 🔒 📆 🏚 WiFi 🌀 ❓

Services: 🔌 🛢 🛢 💧 ⌷ T 🚮 🏚 ⅃ **Within 3 miles:** ↨ ⅟ 🎣 ◎ 🔥 📆 🔥 ∪

Notes: No groups, no noise after 22.00hrs. Dogs must be kept on leads. Freshly baked bread, coffee lounge.

AA Pubs & Restaurants nearby: The Seafood Restaurant, PADSTOW, PL28 8BY, 01841 532700

Paul Ainsworth at No. 6, PADSTOW, PL28 8AP, 01841 532093

Padstow Holiday Park
HOLIDAY HOME PARK 78%

tel: 01841 532289 **Cliffdowne PL28 8LB**
email: mail@padstowholidaypark.co.uk
dir: *Exit A39 onto either A389 or B3274 to Padstow. Site signed 1.5m before Padstow.*
grid ref: *SW009073*

In an Area of Outstanding Natural Beauty and within a mile of the historic fishing village of Padstow, which can be reached via a footpath, this static-only park with 12 well-equipped units for hire aims to provide comfortable relaxing accommodation in a quiet and peaceful atmosphere. With no clubhouse or pool on site, it is ideal for families and couples who want a quiet base that is convenient for all the attractions Cornwall has to offer.

Open: 6 Feb-6 Jan

Statics: 12 Sleeps 4 Bedrms 2 Bathrms 1 (ien suite) Toilets 2 Microwave Freezer TV Sky/FTV DVD Modem/Wi-fi Elec inc Gas inc Grass area Garden/patio furniture
Low season £200-£220 High season £520-£690

Children: 🍼 Cots Highchair Child gate

Leisure: ⅍ **Within 3 miles:** 🌳 ∪ 🎣

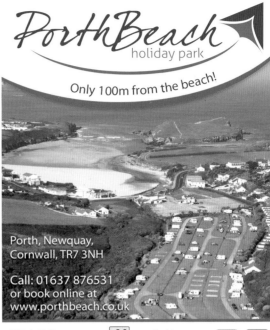

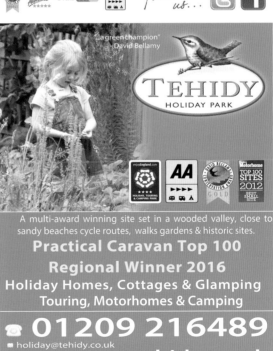

PENTEWAN
Map 2 SX04

Places to visit

The Lost Gardens of Heligan, PENTEWAN, PL26 6EN, 01726 845100
www.heligan.com

Charlestown Shipwreck & Heritage Centre, ST AUSTELL, PL25 3NJ, 01726 69897
www.shipwreckcharlestown.com

Great for kids: Eden Project, ST AUSTELL, PL24 2SG, 01726 811911
www.edenproject.com

PREMIER PARK

Sun Valley Resort
▶▶▶▶▶ 85%

tel: 01726 843266 & 844393 **Pentewan Rd PL26 6DJ**
email: hello@sunvalleyresort.co.uk
dir: From St Austell take B3273 towards Mevagissey. Site 2m on right.
grid ref: SX005486

In a picturesque wooded valley, this neat park has experienced owners who maintain high standards throughout. The extensive amenities include tennis courts, indoor swimming pool, takeaway, licensed clubhouse and restaurant. The sea is just a mile away, and can be accessed via a footpath and cycle path along the river bank. Bicycles can be hired on site. A public bus stops at the site entrance. 20 acre site. 29 touring pitches. 13 hardstandings. Caravan pitches. Motorhome pitches. Tent pitches. 75 statics.

Open: all year (rs Winter — pool, restaurant & touring field) **Last arrival:** 22.00hrs **Last departure:** 10.30hrs

Pitches: * ⬛ £12-£35 ⬛ £12-£35 ▲ £12-£35

Leisure: 🏊 🏊 🎱 🎵 ⛳

Facilities: ⊙ 🖋 ✳ ♿ 🛁 🏪 🐕 WiFi ♻ ⓘ

Services: 🔌 🔋 🍽 🚰 ⌀ 🍴 🛒 ⚓ ⬇

Within 3 miles: 🎣 🏖 🍴 ⛳ 🚣 🏪 🎮 🐎 ⛲

Notes: No motorised scooters, skateboards or bikes at night, certain pet restrictions apply (contact site for details). Dogs must be kept on leads. Pets' corner, outdoor & indoor play areas.

AA Pubs & Restaurants nearby: The Crown Inn, ST EWE, PL26 6EY, 01726 843322

Heligan Woods
▶▶▶▶ 82%

tel: 01726 842714 & 844414 **PL26 6BT**
email: info@pentewan.co.uk
dir: From A390 take B3273 for Mevagissey at x-roads signed 'No caravans beyond this point'. Right onto unclassified road towards Gorran, site 0.75m on left.
grid ref: SW998470

A pleasant peaceful park adjacent to the Lost Gardens of Heligan, with views over St Austell Bay and well-maintained facilities, including a smart disabled/family room. Guests can also use the extensive amenities at the sister park, Pentewan Sands, and there's a footpath with direct access to Heligan Gardens. 12 acre site. 89 touring pitches. 24 hardstandings. 12 seasonal pitches. Caravan pitches. Motorhome pitches. Tent pitches. 17 statics.

Open: 16 Jan-26 Nov (reception open 09.00hrs-11.00hrs & 17.00hrs-18.00hrs)

Last arrival: 22.00hrs **Last departure:** 10.30hrs

Pitches: ⬛ ⬛ ▲

Facilities: ⬛ 🅿 ⊙ 🖋 ✳ ♿ 🛁 🏪 🐕 WiFi ♻ ⓘ

Services: 🔌 🔋 🚰 ⌀ ⚓ ⬇

Within 3 miles: 🎣 🏖 🍴 ⛳ 🚣 🏪 🎮 🐎 ⛲

Notes: Dogs must be kept on leads.

AA Pubs & Restaurants nearby: Austell's, ST AUSTELL, PL25 3PH, 01726 813888

Little Winnick Touring Park
▶▶▶▶ 81%

tel: 01726 843687 **PL26 6DL**
email: mail@littlewinnick.co.uk **web:** www.littlewinnick.co.uk
dir: A390 to St Austell, then B3273 towards Mevagissey, site in 3m on left.
grid ref: SX007482

A small, well maintained rural site within walking distance of Pentewan and its beautiful beach. It has neat level pitches, including some hardstanding pitches, an excellent children's play area, and an ultra-modern toilet block. It borders the River Winnick and also the Pentewan cycle trail from St Austell to Pentewan, and The Lost Gardens of Heligan and Mevagissey are nearby. There is a bus stop outside the park to Mevagissey and Gorran Haven or St Austell (Asda), Charlestown and Fowey. 14 acre site. 90 touring pitches. 28 hardstandings. 6 seasonal pitches. Caravan pitches. Motorhome pitches. Tent pitches.

Open: Etr-early Oct **Last arrival:** 20.00hrs **Last departure:** 11.00hrs

Pitches: * ⬛ £10-£28 ⬛ £10-£28 ▲ £10-£28

Leisure: 🛝 ⛲

Facilities: ⬛ 🅿 ⊙ 🖋 ✳ ♿ 🛁 🏪 🐕 WiFi 🛒 ♻ ⓘ

Services: 🔌 🔋 ⚓ ⬇

Within 3 miles: 🎣 🏖 🍴 ⛳ 🚣 🏪 🎮

Notes: No noise 22.00hrs-07.00hrs. Dogs must be kept on leads.

AA Pubs & Restaurants nearby: The Ship Inn, MEVAGISSEY, PL26 6UQ, 01726 843324
The Crown Inn, ST EWE, PL26 6EY, 01726 843322

LEISURE: 🏊 Indoor pool 🏊 Outdoor pool 🛝 Children's playground 🧒 Kid's club 🎾 Tennis court 🎱 Games room ⛳ Golf course 🚣 Boat hire 🚲 Cycle hire 🎬 Cinema 🎵 Entertainment 🎣 Fishing ⛳ Mini golf ⛳ Pitch n putt 🏄 Watersports 🏋 Gym ⛲ Sports field 🐎 Stables **FACILITIES:** 🛁 Bath 🚿 Shower 🅿 Private washing cubicles ⊙ Electric shaver 🖋 Hairdryer ✳ Ice Packs ♿ Disabled facilities 🏪 Shop on site 🏬 Mobile shop 🍴 BBQ area 🍴 Picnic area WiFi Wi-fi ⌨ Internet access ♻ Recycling ⓘ Tourist info 🐕 Dog exercise area 🚗 Car hire can be arranged

PENZANCE
Map 2 SW43

See also Rosudgeon

Places to visit
Trengwainton Garden, PENZANCE, TR20 8RZ, 01736 363148
www.nationaltrust.org.uk/trengwainton

St Michael's Mount, MARAZION, TR17 0HT, 01736 710507
www.stmichaelsmount.co.uk

Bone Valley Caravan & Camping Park
►►►80%

tel: 01736 360313 **Heamoor TR20 8UJ**
email: wardmandie@yahoo.co.uk
dir: *Exit A30 at Heamoor/Madron rdbt. 4th on right into Josephs Ln. 800yds left into Bone Valley. Entrance 200yds on left.* grid ref: SW472316

A compact grassy park on the outskirts of Penzance with well-maintained facilities. It is divided into paddocks by mature hedges, and a small stream runs alongside. 1 acre site. 17 touring pitches. 6 hardstandings. Caravan pitches. Motorhome pitches. Tent pitches. 3 statics.

Open: all year **Last arrival:** 22.00hrs **Last departure:** 10.00hrs

Pitches: 🚐 🚌 ⛺

Facilities: 🍴 🅿️ ⊙ ℘ ☀ 🖵 📶 🗑 ♻ ✆

Services: 🔌 🗄

Within 3 miles: ⛴ 🎇 🗄 🗄 ∪

Notes: No noise after mdnt. Dogs must be kept on leads. Campers' lounge, kitchen & laundry room.

AA Pubs & Restaurants nearby: Dolphin Tavern, PENZANCE, TR18 4BD, 01736 364106

Harris's Restaurant, PENZANCE, TR18 2LZ, 01736 364408

PERRANPORTH

See also Rejerrah

Places to visit
Royal Cornwall Museum, TRURO, TR1 2SJ, 01872 272205
www.royalcornwallmuseum.org.uk

Trerice, TRERICE, TR8 4PG, 01637 875404 www.nationaltrust.org.uk/trerice/

Great for kids: Blue Reef Aquarium, NEWQUAY, TR7 1DU, 01637 878134
www.bluereefaquarium.co.uk

PERRANPORTH
Map 2 SW75

Perran Sands Holiday Park
HOLIDAY CENTRE 90%

tel: 01872 573551 **TR6 0AQ**
email: perransands@haven.com web: www.haven.com/perransands
dir: *A30 onto B3285 towards Perranporth. Site on right before descent on hill into Perranporth.* grid ref: SW767554

Situated amid 500 acres of protected dune grassland, and with a footpath through to the surf and three miles of golden sandy beach, this lively park is set in a large village-style complex. It offers a complete range of on-site facilities and entertainment for all the family, which makes it an extremely popular park. There are two top-of-the-range facility blocks. Safari tents, ready-erected tents, geo domes and yurts are available for hire. 550 acre site. 341 touring pitches. 28 hardstandings. Caravan pitches. Motorhome pitches. Tent pitches. 600 statics.

Open: mid Mar-end Oct (rs mid Mar-May & Sep-Oct some facilities may be reduced) **Last arrival:** 22.00hrs **Last departure:** 10.00hrs

Pitches: 🚐 🚌 ⛺ 🏠 **Leisure:** 🏊 ⚡ 🎱 🎾 🎵 **Facilities:** 🍴 ℘ ☀ 🅿️ 🗄 📶 ♻ ✆

Services: 🔌 🗄 🍴 🧴 ∅ 🍽 🛒

Glamping: Safari tents 10 **Erected Tents** 49 **Yurts** 4 **Geo domes** 8

Within 3 miles: ⛴ ℘ ⊙ 🎇 🗄 🗄 ∪

Notes: No commercial vehicles, no bookings by persons under 21yrs unless a family booking, max 2 dogs per booking, certain dog breeds banned. Dogs must be kept on leads.

AA Pubs & Restaurants nearby: Driftwood Spars, ST AGNES, TR5 0RT, 01872 552428

See advert on page 99

PERRANPORTH *continued*

Tollgate Farm Caravan & Camping Park

▶▶▶▶ 82%

tel: 01872 572130 **Budnick Hill TR6 0AD**
email: enquiries@tollgatefarm.co.uk **web:** www.tollgatefarm.co.uk
dir: *Exit A30 onto B3285 to Perranporth. Site on right 1.5m after Goonhavern.*
grid ref: *SW768547*

Tollgate Farm Caravan & Camping Park

A quiet site in a rural location with spectacular coastal views. Pitches are divided into four paddocks sheltered and screened by mature hedges, and there's a fully-equipped campers' kitchen. Children will like the play equipment and pets' corner. The three miles of sand at Perran Bay are just a walk away through the sand dunes, or by car it is a three-quarter mile drive. There are five camping pods for hire. 10 acre site. 102 touring pitches. 10 hardstandings. 12 seasonal pitches. Caravan pitches. Motorhome pitches. Tent pitches.

Open: Etr-Sep **Last arrival:** 20.00hrs **Last departure:** 10.30hrs

Pitches: * 🚐 £16-£27 �'s £16-£27 ▲ £16-£27 🛖 prices shown below

Leisure: ⋀ ✿

Facilities: 🌂 🅿 ⊙ 🖋 ✳ ⅙ 🚿 🛏 WIFI ♻ 🛈 ⟲

Services: 🔌 🗑 🛢 🧺 Ⓣ 🛒 🐕 ⚓

Glamping: Wooden Pods 5, £50-£60 Min stay 2 nights Car by unit

Within 3 miles: ⅙ ≋ 🗓 🖉 ◎ ≋ 🗓 🗓 ∪

Notes: No large groups. Dogs must be kept on leads.

AA Pubs & Restaurants nearby: Driftwood Spars, ST AGNES, TR5 0RT, 01872 5524280

See advert below

Higher Golla Touring & Caravan Park

►►►82%

tel: 01872 573963 & 07800 558407 **Penhallow TR4 9LZ**
email: trevor.knibb@gmail.com **web:** www.caravanparkincornwall.com
dir: *A30 onto B3284 towards Perranporth (straight on at junct with A3075). Approx 2m. Site signed on right.* **grid ref:** *SW756514*

This peacefully located park is just two miles from Perranporth and its stunning beach, and extensive country views can be enjoyed from all pitches. It has high quality and immaculate toilet facilities, and every pitch has electricity and a water tap. 3 acre site. 30 touring pitches. 2 hardstandings. 4 seasonal pitches. Caravan pitches. Motorhome pitches. Tent pitches. 2 statics.

Open: 10 May-20 Sep (Spring BH wk & peak season shop open) **Last arrival:** 20.00hrs
Last departure: 10.30hrs

Pitches: 🚐 £14-£21 🚙 £14-£21 ⛺ £14-£21

Leisure: 🎣

Facilities: 📶 ⊙ ⚡ ❄ ⓢ ⊓ 🔌 📶 ♻ ❀ ❓
Services: ⚡ 🔋 🍴 Ⓣ ⚓
Within 3 miles: ⚓ 🏌 ◎ ⛷ ⚓ 🔋 ⛵

Notes: No kite flying, quiet between 21.00hrs-08.00hrs. Dogs must be kept on leads.

AA Pubs & Restaurants nearby: Driftwood Spars, ST AGNES, TR5 0RT, 01872 552428

Perranporth Camping & Touring Park

►►►71%

tel: 01872 572174 **Budnick Rd TR6 0DB**
email: info@perranporth-camping.co.uk **web:** www.perranporth-camping.co.uk
dir: *At mini rdbt in Perranporth take B3285 towards Newquay. 0.5m to site.*
grid ref: *SW768542*

A pleasant site, great for families and just a five-minute, easy walk to Perranporth's beautiful beach and less than 10 minutes to the shops and restaurants in the town centre. There is a clubhouse/bar and heated swimming pool for the sole use of those staying on the site. There is also a takeaway food outlet and small shop. Nine

continued

PITCHES: 🚐 Caravans 🚙 Motorhomes ⛺ Tents 🏕 Glamping accommodation **SERVICES:** ⚡ Electric hook up 🔋 Launderette 🍷 Licensed bar 🔥 Calor Gas ⚗ Camping Gaz Ⓣ Toilet fluid 🍴 Café/Restaurant 🍟 Fast Food/Takeaway 🔋 Battery charging 🍼 Baby care ⚓ Motorvan service point
ABBREVIATIONS: BHs – bank holidays Etr – Easter Spring BH – Spring Bank Holiday fr – from hrs – hours m – mile mdnt – midnight rdbt – roundabout rs – restricted service wk – week wknd – weekend x-roads – crossroads 🚫 No credit or debit cards 🚫 No dogs

PERRANPORTH *continued*

static caravans are available for holiday hire. 6 acre site. 120 touring pitches. 4 hardstandings. Caravan pitches. Motorhome pitches. Tent pitches. 9 statics.

Perranporth Camping & Touring Park

Open: Spring BH-Sep (rs End Sep - shop, swimming pool & club facilities closed) **Last arrival:** 23.00hrs **Last departure:** noon

Pitches: 🚐 🚍 Å

Leisure: ⚎ ⋀ ⚲

Facilities: ⛟ 🌣 ⊙ 🌣 ✲ 🕹 🖪 🎋 WiFi 🟊

Services: 🖳 🔄 🍽 🗄 🛢 T 🔥 🛒

Within 3 miles: ⚘ ⚘ 🖉 ◎ ⚓ 🖪 U

Notes: No noise after 23.00hrs. Dogs must be kept on leads.

AA Pubs & Restaurants nearby: Driftwood Spars, ST AGNES, TR5 0RT, 01872 552428

POLPERRO | Map 2 SX25

Places to visit

Restormel Castle, RESTORMEL, PL22 0EE, 01208 872687 www.english-heritage.org.uk/daysout/properties/restormel-castle

Great for kids: Wild Futures Monkey Sanctuary, LOOE, PL13 1NZ, 01503 262532 www.monkeysanctuary.org

---

Great Kellow Farm Caravan & Camping Site
▶▶ 79%

tel: 01503 272387 **Lansallos PL13 2QL**

email: enquiries@greatkellowfarm.co.uk

dir: *From Looe to Pelynt. In Pelynt left at church follow Lansallos sign. Left at x-roads, 0.75m. At staggered x-roads left, follow site signs. (NB access is via single track lanes. It is advisable to follow these directions not Sat Nav).* **grid ref:** *SX201522*

Set on a high level grassy paddock with extensive views of Polperro Bay, this attractive site is on a working dairy and beef farm, and close to National Trust properties and gardens. It is situated in a very peaceful location close to the fishing

village of Polperro. 3 acre site. 30 touring pitches. 20 seasonal pitches. Caravan pitches. Motorhome pitches. Tent pitches. 10 statics.

Open: Mar-3 Jan **Last arrival:** 22.00hrs **Last departure:** noon

Pitches: 🚐 🚍 Å

Facilities: ⛟ ⊙ 🌣 🎋 🟊 🔄 🟊

Services: 🖳

Within 3 miles: ⚘ 🖉 🖪

Notes: No noise after 23.00hrs. Debit cards accepted (no credit cards). Dogs must be kept on leads.

AA Pubs & Restaurants nearby: Talland Bay Hotel, TALLAND BAY, PL13 2JB, 01503 272667

POLRUAN | Map 2 SX15

Places to visit

Restormel Castle, RESTORMEL, PL22 0EE, 01208 872687 www.english-heritage.org.uk/daysout/properties/restormel-castle

Great for kids: Wild Futures Monkey Sanctuary, LOOE, PL13 1NZ, 01503 262532 www.monkeysanctuary.org

---

Polruan Holidays-Camping & Caravanning
▶▶▶▶ 82%

tel: 01726 870263 **Polruan-by-Fowey PL23 1QH**

email: polholiday@aol.com

dir: *A38 to Dobwalls, left onto A390 to East Taphouse. Left onto B3359. Right in 4.5m signed Polruan.* **grid ref:** *SX133509*

A very rural and quiet site in a lovely elevated position above the village, with immaculate pitches and stunning views of the sea. The River Fowey passenger ferry is close by, and the site has a good shop, a spacious reception area, and barbecues are available to borrow. The bus for Polperro and Looe stops outside the gate, and the foot ferry to Fowey, which runs until 11pm, is only a 10-minute walk away. 3 acre site. 35 touring pitches. 7 hardstandings. Caravan pitches. Motorhome pitches. Tent pitches. 10 statics.

Open: Etr-Oct **Last arrival:** 21.00hrs **Last departure:** 11.00hrs

Pitches: 🚐 🚍 Å

Leisure: ⋀

Facilities: ⛟ ⊙ 🌣 🌣 🎋 WiFi 🖪 🔄 🟊 🟊 🚗

Services: 🖳 🔄 🍽 🛢 T 🛒 🛒

Within 3 miles: ⚘ 🖉 ⚓ 🖪 U

Notes: No skateboards, rollerskates, bikes, water pistols or water bombs. Dogs must be kept on leads.

AA Pubs & Restaurants nearby: The Ship Inn, FOWEY, PL23 1AZ, 01726 832230

The Fowey Hotel, FOWEY, PL23 1HX, 01726 832551

POLZEATH
Map 2 SW97

South Winds Caravan & Camping Park
►►►87%

tel: 01208 863267 & 862215 **Polzeath Rd PL27 6QU**
email: info@southwindscamping.co.uk **web:** www.polzeathcamping.co.uk
dir: *Exit B3314 onto unclassified road signed Polzeath, site on right just past turn to New Polzeath.* **grid ref:** *SW948790*

A peaceful site with beautiful sea and panoramic rural views, within walking distance of a golf complex, and just three quarters of a mile from beach and village. There are three spacious fields that offer plenty of room for cars to be parked by tents or caravans. There's an impressive reception building, replete with tourist information, TV, settees and a range of camping spares. Dogs are welcome. 16 acre site. 165 touring pitches. Caravan pitches. Motorhome pitches. Tent pitches.

Open: May-mid Sep **Last arrival:** 21.00hrs **Last departure:** 10.30hrs

Pitches: * 🚐 £16-£35 🚍 £16-£35 ▲ £14-£35

Facilities: ☺ 🏊 ⚒ ♿ 🚿 🛒 📶 ♻ 🛈

Services: 🔌 🧺 🍺 🚰 🔋 📺 🛁 ⚓

Within 3 miles: 🎣 ⛳ 🏇 🎯 🌊 🛥 🎿 ⚓

Notes: Families & couples only, no disposable BBQs, no noise 23.00hrs-07.00hrs. Dogs must be kept on leads. Restaurant & farm shop adjacent, Stepper Field open mid Jul-Aug.

AA Pubs & Restaurants nearby: The Maltsters Arms, CHAPEL AMBLE, PL27 6EU, 01208 812473

See advert below

PITCHES: 🚐 Caravans 🚍 Motorhomes ▲ Tents 🏠 Glamping accommodation **SERVICES:** 🔌 Electric hook up 🧺 Launderette 🍺 Licensed bar 🔥 Calor Gas 🔥 Camping Gaz 🔲 Toilet fluid 🍽 Café/Restaurant 🍟 Fast Food/Takeaway 🔋 Battery charging 🍼 Baby care ⚓ Motorvan service point **ABBREVIATIONS:** BHs – bank holidays Etr – Easter Spring BH – Spring Bank Holiday fr – from hrs – hours m – mile mdnt – midnight rdbt – roundabout rs – restricted service wk – week wknd – weekend x-roads – crossroads 🚫 No credit or debit cards 🚫 No dogs

POLZEATH *continued*

Tristram Caravan & Camping Park

►►► 87%

tel: 01208 862215 **PL27 6TP**
email: info@tristramcampsite.co.uk **web:** www.polzeathcamping.co.uk
dir: *From B3314 onto unclassified road signed Polzeath. Through village, up hill, site 2nd right.* **grid ref:** *SW936790*

An ideal family site, positioned on a gently sloping cliff with grassy pitches and glorious sea views, which are best enjoyed from the terraced premier pitches, or over lunch or dinner at Café India adjacent to the reception overlooking the beach. There is direct, gated access to the beach, where surfing is very popular, and the park has a holiday bungalow for rent. The local amenities of the village are only a few hundred yards away. 10 acre site. 100 touring pitches. Caravan pitches. Motorhome pitches. Tent pitches.

Open: Mar-Nov (rs mid Sep reseeding the site) **Last arrival:** 21.00hrs
Last departure: 10.00hrs

Pitches: * 🚐 £24-£70 🚌 £24-£70 ⛺ £20-£70

Facilities: 🚿 Electric shaver Hairdryer Ice Packs ♿ Shop on site Wi-fi ♻ ℹ **Services:** 🔧 ▣ 🔒 ⌀ [T] 🍴 🛏

Within 3 miles: Golf course Boat hire 🎬 Fishing Mini golf 🌊 Shop on site ▣ Stables

Notes: No ball games, no disposable BBQs, no noise between 23.00hrs-07.00hrs. Dogs must be kept on leads. Surf equipment hire.

AA Pubs & Restaurants nearby: The Maltsters Arms, CHAPEL AMBLE, PL27 6EU, 01208 812473

See advert on page 101

PORTHTOWAN Map 2 SW64

Porthtowan Tourist Park

►►►► 96%

DAVID BELLAMY CONSERVATION AWARD SILVER

tel: 01209 890256 **Mile Hill TR4 8TY**
email: admin@porthtowantouristpark.co.uk **web:** www.porthtowantouristpark.co.uk
dir: *Exit A30 at Avers Junct signed Redruth & Porthtowan. At rdbt follow Portreath, B3300 & brown camping signs. Approx 2m, right at T-junct, follow site sign. Site on left at top of hill.* **grid ref:** *SW693473*

A neat, level grassy site on high ground above Porthtowan, with plenty of shelter from mature trees and shrubs. The superb toilet facilities considerably enhance the appeal of this peaceful rural park, which is almost midway between the small seaside resorts of Portreath and Porthtowan, with their beaches and surfing. There is a purpose-built games and meeting room with a good library where tourist information leaflets are available. A tearoom adjacent to the campsite serves takeaway meals during the peak season (limited opening hours at other times of

LEISURE: Indoor pool · Outdoor pool · Children's playground · Kid's club · Tennis court · Games room · Golf course · Boat hire · Cycle hire · 🎬 Cinema · 🎵 Entertainment · Fishing · Mini golf · Pitch n putt · 🌊 Watersports · Gym · Sports field · Stables **FACILITIES:** 🛁 Bath · 🚿 Shower · [P] Private washing cubicles · Electric shaver · Hairdryer · Ice Packs · ♿ Disabled facilities · Shop on site · Mobile shop · BBQ area · Picnic area · Wi-fi Wi-fi · 💻 Internet access · ♻ Recycling · ℹ Tourist info · Dog exercise area · Car hire can be arranged

the year). 5 acre site. 80 touring pitches. 11 hardstandings. 8 seasonal pitches. Caravan pitches. Motorhome pitches. Tent pitches.

Porthtowan Tourist Park

Open: Apr-Sep **Last arrival:** 21.30hrs **Last departure:** 11.00hrs

Pitches: * ⊞ £12-£20 ⊞ £12-£20 ▲ £12-£20 **Leisure:** ⚠️⚽🔍

Facilities: 🅿️🅿️☉🅿️✳️⚠️🗑️🖨️📶🔌♻️🛈 **Services:** 🔌🔄🔋📋🛒🔧

Within 3 miles: ⚓🕊️🅟♨️🛥️🔄🛒🕄

Notes: No bikes or skateboards in Jul & Aug. Dogs must be kept on leads. Table tennis.

AA Pubs & Restaurants nearby: Driftwood Spars, ST AGNES, TR5 0RT, 01872 552428

See advert on opposite page

Wheal Rose Caravan & Camping Park
▶▶▶▶75%

tel: 01209 891496 **Wheal Rose TR16 5DD**
email: whealrose@aol.com
dir: *Exit A30 at Scorrier sign, follow signs to Wheal Rose. Site 0.5m on left on the Wheal Rose to Porthtowan road.* **grid ref:** SW717449

A quiet, peaceful park in a secluded valley setting, which is well placed for visiting both the lovely countryside and the surfing beaches of Porthtowan (two miles away). The friendly owner works hard to keep this park in immaculate condition, with a bright toilet block and well-trimmed pitches. There is a swimming pool and a games room. 6 acre site. 50 touring pitches. 6 hardstandings. Caravan pitches. Motorhome pitches. Tent pitches. 3 statics.

Open: Mar-Dec **Last arrival:** 21.00hrs **Last departure:** 11.00hrs

Pitches: ⊞ ⊞ ▲

Leisure: ♨️⚽🔍

Facilities: ☉🅿️✳️⚠️🗑️🖨️📶🔌♻️🛈

Services: 🔌🔄🔋📋📋🛒

Within 3 miles: ⚓🕊️🅟♨️🛥️🔄🛒🕄

Notes: 5mph speed limit, minimum noise after 23.00hrs, gates locked 23.00hrs. Dogs must be kept on leads.

AA Pubs & Restaurants nearby: Basset Arms, PORTREATH, TR16 4NG, 01209 842077

PORTREATH

Places to visit
East Pool Mine, POOL, TR15 3NP, 01209 315027 www.nationaltrust.org.uk

---

PORTREATH
Map 2 SW64

Tehidy Holiday Park
▶▶▶▶88%

tel: 01209 216489 **Harris Mill, Illogan TR16 4JQ**
email: holiday@tehidy.co.uk **web:** www.tehidy.co.uk
dir: *Exit A30 at Redruth/Portreath junct onto A3047 to 1st rdbt. Left onto B3300. At junct straight over signed Tehidy Holiday Park. Past Cornish Arms pub, site 800yds at bottom of hill on left.* **grid ref:** SW682432

An attractive wooded location in a quiet rural area only two and a half miles from popular beaches. Mostly level pitches on tiered ground, and the toilet facilities are bright and modern. Holiday static caravans and wooden wigwams are available for hire. 4.5 acre site. 18 touring pitches. 11 hardstandings. 4 seasonal pitches. Caravan pitches. Motorhome pitches. Tent pitches. 32 statics.

Open: all year (rs Nov-Mar part of shower block & shop closed) **Last arrival:** 20.00hrs **Last departure:** 10.00hrs

Pitches: ⊞ £16-£23 ⊞ £16-£23 ▲ £16-£23 🏠 prices shown below

Leisure: ⚠️⚽🔍 **Facilities:** 🅿️🅿️☉🅿️✳️⚠️🗑️🖨️📶🔌♻️🛈

Services: 🔌🔄♻️📋🛒🔧

Glamping: Wooden Wigwams 2, £50-£65 Changeover day Any day Min stay 2 nights Own kitchen Car by unit

Within 3 miles: ⚓🕊️🕊️🅟♨️◎🛥️🔄🛒🕄

Notes: No pets, no noise after 23.00hrs. Pre-booking required for large motorhomes & caravans. Off licence, cooking shelter, trampoline.

AA Pubs & Restaurants nearby: Basset Arms, PORTREATH, TR16 4NG, 01209 842077

See advert on page 95

PITCHES: ⊞ Caravans ⊞ Motorhomes ▲ Tents 🏠 Glamping accommodation **SERVICES:** 🔌 Electric hook up 🔄 Launderette 🍺 Licensed bar 🔋 Calor Gas 🔋 Camping Gaz 📋 Toilet fluid 🍴 Café/Restaurant 🍔 Fast Food/Takeaway 🔋 Battery charging 🛒 Baby care 🔧 Motorvan service point
ABBREVIATIONS: BHs – bank holidays Etr – Easter Spring BH – Spring Bank Holiday fr – from hrs – hours m – mile mdnt – midnight rdbt – roundabout rs – restricted service wk – week wknd – weekend x-roads – crossroads 🚫 No credit or debit cards 🚫 No dogs

PORTSCATHO — Map 2 SW83

Places to visit

St Mawes Castle, ST MAWES, TR2 3AA, 01326 270526
www.english-heritage.org.uk/daysout/properties/st-mawes-castle

Trelissick, TRELISSICK, TR3 6QL, 01872 862090
www.nationaltrust.org.uk/trelissick

Trewince Farm Touring Park

►►► 80%

tel: 01872 580430 **TR2 5ET**
email: info@trewincefarm.co.uk
dir: *From St Austell take A390 towards Truro. Left on B3287 to Tregony, following signs to St Mawes. At Trewithian, turn left to St Anthony. Site 0.75m past church.*
grid ref: *SW868339*

A site on a working farm with spectacular sea views from its elevated position. There are many quiet golden sandy beaches close by, and boat launching facilities and mooring can be arranged at the nearby Percuil River Boatyard. The village of Portscatho with shops and pubs and attractive harbour is approximately one mile away. 3 acre site. 25 touring pitches. Caravan pitches. Motorhome pitches. Tent pitches.

Open: May-Sep **Last arrival:** 23.00hrs **Last departure:** 11.00hrs

Pitches: 🚃 🚐 ⛺

Facilities: 🚿 ⊙ 💨 ❄ 🧺 🐕 ♻ ℹ

Services: 🛋 [▫] 🧳

Within 3 miles: ⛵ 🎣 🌊 [$]

Notes: 🚫 Dogs must be kept on leads.

AA Pubs & Restaurants nearby: The New Inn, VERYAN, TR2 5QA, 01872 501362
The Victory Inn, ST MAWES, TR2 5DQ, 01326 270324

Find out about the AA's Pennant rating scheme on pages 10-11

REDRUTH

Places to visit

East Pool Mine, POOL, TR15 3NP, 01209 315027 www.nationaltrust.org.uk

Pendennis Castle, FALMOUTH, TR11 4LP, 01326 316594
www.english-heritage.org.uk/daysout/properties/pendennis-castle

Great for kids: National Maritime Museum Cornwall, FALMOUTH, TR11 3QY, 01326 313388 www.nmmc.co.uk

REDRUTH — Map 2 SW64

PREMIER PARK

Globe Vale Holiday Park

►►►►► 92%

tel: 01209 891183 **Radnor TR16 4BH**
email: info@globevale.co.uk **web:** www.globevale.co.uk
dir: *From A30 at rdbt (NE of Redruth) follow Porthreath & B3300 signs. At next x-roads right into Radnor Rd, follow brown site signs. 0.5m turn left at site sign, 0.5m on left.*
grid ref: *SW708447*

A family owned and run park set in a quiet rural location yet close to some stunning beaches and coastline. The park's touring area has a number of full facility hardstanding pitches, a high quality toilet block, a comfortable lounge bar serving bar meals, and holiday static caravans. 18 acre site. 138 touring pitches. 25 hardstandings. 6 seasonal pitches. Caravan pitches. Motorhome pitches. Tent pitches. 57 statics.

Open: all year **Last arrival:** 20.00hrs **Last departure:** 10.00hrs

Pitches: 🚃 🚐 ⛺

Leisure: 🛝 ⚽ 🎱

Facilities: 🚿 [P] ❄ ♿ [$] 🐕 [WiFi] ♻ ℹ

Services: 🛋 [▫] 🍷 🔒 🌿 [T] 🍽 🧳 🍴

Within 3 miles: ⛳ 🎬 🌊 [$] [▫]

Notes: Dogs must be kept on leads. Shower block heated in winter.

AA Pubs & Restaurants nearby: Basset Arms, PORTREATH, TR16 4NG, 01209 842077

See advert on opposite page

LEISURE: 🏊 Indoor pool 🏖 Outdoor pool 🛝 Children's playground ✋ Kid's club 🎾 Tennis court 🎱 Games room ⛳ Golf course ⛵ Boat hire 🚲 Cycle hire 🎬 Cinema 🎵 Entertainment 🎣 Fishing ◎ Mini golf 🏌 Pitch n putt 🌊 Watersports 🏋 Gym ⚽ Sports field 🐴 Stables **FACILITIES:** 🛁 Bath 🚿 Shower [P] Private washing cubicles ⊙ Electric shaver 💨 Hairdryer ❄ Ice Packs ♿ Disabled facilities [$] Shop on site 🚚 Mobile shop 🔥 BBQ area 🧺 Picnic area [WiFi] Wi-fi 💻 Internet access ♻ Recycling ℹ Tourist info 🐕 Dog exercise area 🚗 Car hire can be arranged

Lanyon Holiday Park
►►►► 87%

tel: 01209 313474 **Loscombe Ln, Four Lanes TR16 6LP**
email: info@lanyonholidaypark.co.uk **web:** www.lanyonholidaypark.co.uk
dir: *Exit A30 signed Camborne & Pool onto A3047. Straight on at next two lights. Pass Tesco Extra on left. Right signed Four Lanes, over rail bridge. In Four Lanes right at staggered x-roads onto B2397, 2nd right at Pencoys Hall into Loscombe Ln. Site on left in approx 400mtrs.* **grid ref:** *SW684387*

Lanyon Holiday Park

Open: Mar-Oct (rs Mar-Spring BH bar/restaurant closed weekdays (except school summer hols), pool closed Mar & Oct) **Last arrival:** 21.00hrs **Last departure:** 11.00hrs

Pitches: * ⊞ £19-£27 ⊞ £19-£27 Å £15-£23

Leisure: 🏊 ⚑ ⚓ ♫

Facilities: ➟ ⓡ P 🅿 ⊙ 🎣 ☀ ⌁ 🛒 ⌨ WiFi 🖥 ♻ ❶

Services: 🔌 🅾 🍺 🍴 🔋 🛒

Within 3 miles: ↓ ⇅ 🎣 🎠 ◎ 🛒 🔋 🛡 ∪

Notes: Families only, no commercial vehicles. Dogs must be kept on leads. Breakfast catering van during peak season school hols.

AA Pubs & Restaurants nearby: Basset Arms, PORTREATH, TR16 4NG, 01209 842077
See advert on page 106

A small, friendly rural park in an elevated position with fine views to distant St Ives Bay. This family owned and run park continues to be upgraded in all areas; there is a smart toilet block and two family rooms.The park has a well-stocked bar and a very inviting swimming pool. Stithians Reservoir for fishing, sailing and windsurfing is two miles away, and the site is close to a cycling trail. Two holiday cottages are available for hire. 14 acre site. 25 touring pitches. 5 seasonal pitches. Caravan pitches. Motorhome pitches. Tent pitches. 49 statics.

PITCHES: ⊞ Caravans ⊞ Motorhomes Å Tents ⋒ Glamping accommodation **SERVICES:** 🔌 Electric hook up 🅾 Launderette 🍺 Licensed bar 🔋 Calor Gas ⚗ Camping Gaz T Toilet fluid 🍴 Café/Restaurant 🛒 Fast Food/Takeaway 🔋 Battery charging 🍼 Baby care ⌁ Motorvan service point
ABBREVIATIONS: BHs – bank holidays Etr – Easter Spring BH – Spring Bank Holiday fr – from hrs – hours m – mile mdnt – midnight rdbt – roundabout rs – restricted service wk – week wknd – weekend x-roads – crossroads ⊘ No credit or debit cards ⊗ No dogs

REDRUTH *continued*

St Day Tourist Park
NEW ►►► 82%

tel: 01209 820459 **Church Hill, St Day TR16 5LE**
email: holidays@stday.co.uk
dir: *On A30 from Bodmin towards Redruth. 2m after Chiverton rdbt, left onto A3047 to Scorrier. Site signed. 2m, left at Crossroads Motel onto B3298. Follow campsite signs, site on right.* **grid ref:** *SW731422*

This rurally located park, run by keen friendly owners, is situated in a quiet area between Falmouth and Newquay and within close walking distance of the attractive village of St Day. It provides a very good touring area with modern, centrally positioned toilet facilities. The touring pitches are divided by hedging plants to create some privacy. There is a separate small field for tents. 5 acre site. 81 touring pitches. Caravan pitches. Motorhome pitches. Tent pitches. 3 statics.

Open: Etr-Oct **Last arrival:** phone site if arriving after 18:00hrs **Last departure:** 11.00hrs

Pitches: * 🚐 £16-£20 �caravan £16-£20 ▲ £16-£20

Cambrose Touring Park
►►► 79%

tel: 01209 890747 **Portreath Rd TR16 4HT**
email: cambrosetouringpark@gmail.com
dir: *A30 onto B3300 towards Portreath. Approx 0.75m at 1st rdbt right onto B3300. Take unclassified road on right signed Porthtowan. Site 200yds on left.* **grid ref:** *SW684453*

Situated in a rural setting surrounded by trees and shrubs, this park is divided into grassy paddocks. It is about two miles from the harbour village of Portreath. The site has an excellent swimming pool with a sunbathing area. 6 acre site. 60 touring pitches. 6 seasonal pitches. Caravan pitches. Motorhome pitches. Tent pitches.

Open: Apr-Oct **Last arrival:** 22.00hrs **Last departure:** 11.30hrs

Pitches: 🚐 �caravan ▲

Leisure: 🚣 ⚽ 🔍
Facilities: 🚿 ☉ 🌊 ✳ ⚕ Ⓢ 🚲 🌐 📺 ♻ ℹ
Services: 🔌 🗄 💧 🚽 🛒 🍴
Within 3 miles: ⚓ 🎬 ℗ ◎ Ⓢ 🛒 U

Notes: No noise after 23.30hrs. Dogs must be kept on leads. Mini football pitch.

AA Pubs & Restaurants nearby: Basset Arms, PORTREATH, TR16 4NG, 01209 842077

Stithians Lake Country Park
►►► 72%

tel: 01209 860301 **Stithians Lake, Menherion TR16 6NW**
email: stithianswatersports@swlakestrust.org.uk
dir: *From Redruth take B3297 towards Helston. Follow brown tourist signs to Stithians Lake, entrance by Golden Lion Inn.* **grid ref:** *SW705369*

This simple campsite is a two-acre field situated adjacent to the Watersports Centre, which forms part of a large activity complex beside Stithians Lake. Campers are required to use the functional toilet and shower facilities at the centre, and there is an excellent waterside café that also serves breakfasts. This is the perfect campsite for watersport enthusiasts. 2.1 acre site. 40 touring pitches. Caravan pitches. Motorhome pitches. Tent pitches.

Open: 3 Apr-Oct **Last arrival:** 17.30hrs **Last departure:** noon

Pitches: 🚐 �caravan ▲

Leisure: 🛝 ✎
Facilities: ✳ ⚕ 🌐 ♻ ℹ
Services: 🔌 🗄 🍴
Within 3 miles: 🎣 🎬 ℗ 🚣 Ⓢ 🛒 U

Notes: No noise after mdnt, no swimming in lake, charges apply to use equipment on lake. Dogs must be kept on leads.

AA Pubs & Restaurants nearby: Basset Arms, PORTREATH, TR16 4NG, 01209 842077

LEISURE: 🏊 Indoor pool 🏊 Outdoor pool 🛝 Children's playground 👦 Kid's club 🎾 Tennis court 🎱 Games room ⛳ Golf course 🚣 Boat hire 🚲 Cycle hire 🎬 Cinema 🎵 Entertainment 🎣 Fishing ⛳ Mini golf 🏌 Pitch n putt 🏄 Watersports 💪 Gym ⚽ Sports field U Stables **FACILITIES:** 🛁 Bath 🚿 Shower 🅿 Private washing cubicles ☉ Electric shaver 💇 Hairdryer ✳ Ice Packs ⚕ Disabled facilities Ⓢ Shop on site 🏪 Mobile shop 🍴 BBQ area 🏕 Picnic area 🌐 Wi-fi 💻 Internet access ♻ Recycling ℹ Tourist info 🐕 Dog exercise area 🚗 Car hire can be arranged

REJERRAH · Map 2 SW75

Places to visit

Trerice, TRERICE, TR8 4PG, 01637 875404 www.nationaltrust.org.uk/trerice/

Blue Reef Aquarium, NEWQUAY, TR7 1DU, 01637 878134 www.bluereefaquarium.co.uk

Great for kids: Newquay Zoo, NEWQUAY, TR7 2LZ, 01637 873342 www.newquayzoo.org.uk

PREMIER PARK

Newperran Holiday Park

▶▶▶▶▶ 90%

tel: 01872 572407 **TR8 5QJ**
email: holidays@newperran.co.uk **web:** www.newperran.co.uk
dir: 4m SE of Newquay & 1m S of Rejerrah on A3075. Or A30 (Redruth), exit B3275 Perranporth, at 1st T-junct right onto A3075 towards Newquay, site 300mtrs on left.
grid ref: SW801555

A family site in a lovely rural position near several beaches and bays. This airy park offers screening on some pitches, which are set in paddocks on level ground. High season entertainment is available in the park's top quality country inn, and the café has an extensive menu. There is also a swimming pool with a separate toddlers' paddling area, and a skateboard park has now been created. 25 acre site. 357 touring pitches. 34 hardstandings. 15 seasonal pitches. Caravan pitches. Motorhome pitches. Tent pitches. 30 statics.

Open: Etr-Oct **Last arrival:** 21.00hrs **Last departure:** 10.00hrs
Pitches: 🚐 🚍 ▲

Leisure: 🏊 ⚲ ⚽ 🎣 🎵
Facilities: 🚿 🅿 ⊙ 🅿 ❄ & 🔥 🛗 📶 🖥 ♻ 🛈 🕹
Services: 🔌 🖥 🍴 🔋 🐾 T 🍴 🍴 🚮 🛒 🚮 ⚡
Within 3 miles: 🚶 🚴 ⛳ 🏇 ◎ 🎣 🎿 ⛵ 🎯 ↻

Notes: Families & couples only. Dogs must be kept on leads.

AA Pubs & Restaurants nearby: The Smugglers' Den Inn, CUBERT, TR8 5PY, 01637 830209

See advert on page 95

ROSE · Map 2 SW75

Places to visit

St Agnes and Chapel Porth (NT), ST AGNES, TR5 0NS, 01872 552412 http://www.nationaltrust.org.uk/st-agnes-and-chapel-porth/

Higher Hendra Park
NEW ⓤ

tel: 01872 571496 **Higher Hendra, Treamble TR4 9PS**
email: cowe43@btinternet.com
dir: W of A3075, N of Goonhavern. **grid ref:** SW790553

Currently the rating for this site is not confirmed. This may be due to a change of ownership or because it has only recently joined the AA rating scheme. 2 acre site. 10 touring pitches. 8 hardstandings. Caravan pitches. Motorhome pitches.

Open: all year **Last departure:** 10.00hrs
Pitches: * 🚐 £18 🚍 £18
Facilities: 🚿 🅿 & 🖥 🛈
Services: 🔌
Within 3 miles: 🚶 ⛳ 🎯 ↻

Notes: Adults only. 🚫 Dogs must be kept on leads.

AA Pubs & Restaurants nearby: The Smugglers' Den Inn, CUBERT, TR8 5PY, 01637 830209

Bolingey Inn, BOLINGEY, TR6 0DH, 01872 571626

PITCHES: 🚐 Caravans 🚍 Motorhomes ▲ Tents 🏕 Glamping accommodation **SERVICES:** 🔌 Electric hook up 🖥 Launderette 🍴 Licensed bar 🔥 Calor Gas 🝙 Camping Gaz T Toilet fluid 🍴 Café/Restaurant 🚮 Fast Food/Takeaway 🔋 Battery charging 🚮 Baby care ⚡ Motorvan service point
ABBREVIATIONS: BHs – bank holidays Etr – Easter Spring BH – Spring Bank Holiday fr – from hrs – hours m – mile mdnt – midnight rdbt – roundabout rs – restricted service wk – week wknd – weekend x-roads – crossroads 🚫 No credit or debit cards 🚫 No dogs

ROSUDGEON	Map 2 SW52

Places to visit

Trengwainton Garden, PENZANCE, TR20 8RZ, 01736 363148
www.nationaltrust.org.uk/trengwainton

Great for kids: The Flambards Theme Park, HELSTON, TR13 0QA, 01326 573404
www.flambards.co.uk

Kenneggy Cove Holiday Park
►►►► 90%

tel: 01736 763453 **Higher Kenneggy TR20 9AU**
email: enquiries@kenneggycove.co.uk **web:** www.kenneggycove.co.uk
dir: *On A394 between Penzance & Helston, turn S into signed lane to site & Higher Kenneggy.* **grid ref:** *SW562287*

Set in an Area of Outstanding Natural Beauty with spectacular sea views, this family-owned park is quiet and well kept. There is a well-equipped children's play area, superb toilets, and, in addition to a variety of meals available in the excellent site café, takeaway pizzas are baked on site. A short walk along a country footpath leads to the Cornish Coastal Path, and onto the golden sandy beach at Kenneggy Cove. It's a half mile walk to the main road to pick up the local bus which goes to Penzance or Helston, with many pretty Cornish coves en route. There is also a fish and chip shop and Chinese restaurant with takeaway a short drive away. 4 acre site. 40 touring pitches. Caravan pitches. Motorhome pitches. Tent pitches. 7 statics.

Open: mid May-Sep **Last arrival:** 21.00hrs **Last departure:** 11.00hrs

Pitches: * 🚐 £19-£29 🚍 £19-£29 ⛺ £12-£19

Leisure: 🅰 ⚽

Facilities: 🅿 📵 ⊙ 🏷 ✳ WiFi 🆓 ♻ 🅰

Services: 🔌 📶 🛢 🍴 🚿 🍽 ♨

Within 3 miles: ⚘ 🚴 🎣 🏄 🛒 🔟 ♨

Notes: 🚫 No large groups, no noise after 22.00hrs. Dogs must be kept on leads. Fresh bakery items, breakfasts, home-made evening meals.

AA Pubs & Restaurants nearby: The Victoria Inn, PERRANUTHNOE, TR20 9NP, 01736 710309

The Ship Inn, PORTHLEVEN, TR13 9JS, 01326 564204

RUMFORD	Map 2 SW87

Places to visit

Prideaux Place, PADSTOW, PL28 8RP, 01841 532411 www.prideauxplace.co.uk

Great for kids: Devon's Crealy Great Adventure Park, CLYST ST MARY, EX5 1DR, 01395 233200 www.crealy.co.uk

Music Water Touring Park
►►► 81%

tel: 01841 540257 **PL27 7SJ**
email: info@musicwatertouringpark.co.uk
dir: *From A39 at Winnards Perch rdbt take B3274 signed Padstow. Left in 2m onto unclassified road signed Rumford & St Eval. Site 500mtrs on right.* **grid ref:** *SW906685*

Set in a peaceful location yet only a short drive to the pretty fishing town of Padstow, and many sandy beaches and coves. This family owned and run park has grassy paddocks, and there is a quiet lounge bar and a separate children's games room. 8 acre site. 55 touring pitches. 2 hardstandings. Caravan pitches. Motorhome pitches. Tent pitches. 2 statics.

Open: Apr-Oct **Last arrival:** 23.00hrs **Last departure:** 10.30hrs

Pitches: 🚐 🚍 ⛺

Leisure: 🏊 🔍

Facilities: ⊙ 🏷 ✳ 🏷 🐾 ♻ 🅰

Services: 🔌 📶 🛢 🍴 🍽 ♨

Within 3 miles: 🎣 🏄 🛒 🔟 ♨

Notes: 🚫 One tent per pitch, max 2 dogs per pitch (no Pit Bull Terriers). Dogs must be kept on leads. Pets' corner (ponies, chickens).

AA Pubs & Restaurants nearby: The Seafood Restaurant, PADSTOW, PL28 8BY, 01841 532700

St Petroc's & Bistro, PADSTOW, PL28 8EA, 01841 532700

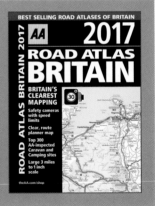
LEISURE: 🏊 Indoor pool 🏊 Outdoor pool 🅰 Children's playground 👶 Kid's club 🎾 Tennis court 🎱 Games room ⛳ Golf course 🚣 Boat hire 🚲 Cycle hire 🎬 Cinema 🎵 Entertainment 🎣 Fishing ⛳ Mini golf 🏌 Pitch n putt 🏄 Watersports 🏋 Gym 🏟 Sports field ♨ Stables **FACILITIES:** 🛁 Bath 🚿 Shower 🅿 Private washing cubicles ⊙ Electric shaver 🏷 Hairdryer ✳ Ice Packs ♿ Disabled facilities 🛒 Shop on site 🚐 Mobile shop 🍴 BBQ area 🍽 Picnic area 📶 Wi-fi 💻 Internet access ♻ Recycling ⓘ Tourist info 🐾 Dog exercise area 🚗 Car hire can be arranged

RUTHERNBRIDGE — Map 2 SX06

Places to visit

Prideaux Place, PADSTOW, PL28 8RP, 01841 532411 www.prideauxplace.co.uk

Cornwall's Regimental Museum, BODMIN, PL31 1EG, 01208 72810

Great for kids: Pencarrow, BODMIN, PL30 3AG, 01208 841369 www.pencarrow.co.uk

Devon's Crealy Great Adventure Park, CLYST ST MARY, EX5 1DR, 01395 233200 www.crealy.co.uk

Ruthern Valley Holidays
►►►81%

tel: 01208 831395 **PL30 5LU**
email: camping@ruthernvalley.com **web:** www.ruthernvalley.com
dir: A389 through Bodmin, follow St Austell signs, then Lanivet signs. At top of hill right onto unclassified road signed Ruthernbridge. Follow signs. **grid ref:** SX014665

An attractive woodland site peacefully located in a small river valley west of Bodmin Moor. This away-from-it-all park is ideal for those wanting a quiet holiday, and the informal pitches are spread in four natural areas, with plenty of sheltered space. There are also 12 lodges, heated wooden wigwams, wooden pods, 'mega' pods and static holiday vans for hire. 7.5 acre site. 26 touring pitches. 2 hardstandings. Caravan pitches. Motorhome pitches. Tent pitches. 3 statics.

Open: all year **Last arrival:** 20.30hrs **Last departure:** noon
Pitches: ⌂ £16-£25 ⌂ £16-£25 Å £12.50-£20 ⌂ prices shown below
Leisure: ☆
Facilities: ☉ ✳ ⓢ ☴ WiFi ▬ ⓕ
Services: ⌂ ⓢ ⓐ ⌀ ⓣ ⓽

Glamping: Wooden Pods 3, £27.50-£45 Car by unit Wooden Wigwams 4, £35-£65 Min stay 2 nights Own kitchen Car by unit Mega pods 2, £45-£75 Min stay 2 nights En suite Own kitchen Car by unit

Within 3 miles: ⌂ ⌀ ⓢ ⓢ ∪

Notes: ⊗ No noise 22.30hrs-07.00hrs, no fires. Farm animals, freshly baked bread & croissants.

AA Pubs & Restaurants nearby: Trehellas House Hotel & Restaurant, BODMIN, PL30 3AD, 01208 72700

ST AGNES — Map 2 SW75

Places to visit

Royal Cornwall Museum, TRURO, TR1 2SJ, 01872 272205 www.royalcornwallmuseum.org.uk

Trerice, TRERICE, TR8 4PG, 01637 875404 www.nationaltrust.org.uk/trerice/

Beacon Cottage Farm Touring Park
►►►►82%

tel: 01872 552347 & 07879 413862 **Beacon Dr TR5 0NU**
email: jane@beaconcottagefarmholidays.co.uk
dir: From A30 at Threeburrows rdbt take B3277 to St Agnes, left into Goonvrea Rd, right into Beacon Drive, follow brown sign to site. **grid ref:** SW705502

A neat and compact site on a working farm, utilising a cottage and outhouses, an old orchard and adjoining walled paddock. The location on a headland looking north-east along the coast has stunning views towards St Ives, and the keen friendly family owners keep all areas of their site very well maintained. 5 acre site. 70 touring pitches. 5 hardstandings. 4 seasonal pitches. Caravan pitches. Motorhome pitches. Tent pitches.

Open: Apr-Oct **Last arrival:** 20.00hrs **Last departure:** noon
Pitches: ⌂ ⌂ Å
Leisure: ✦
Facilities: ℝ ⓟ ☉ ℗ ✳ ⓢ ☴ ⓝ WiFi ▬ ♻ ⓕ
Services: ⌂ ⓢ ⓐ ⌀ ⓽ ⓩ
Within 3 miles: ⌂ ✦ ⌀ ◎ ⓢ ⓢ ⓢ ∪

Notes: No large groups, no noise after 22.00hrs. Dogs must be kept on leads. Secure year-round caravan storage.

AA Pubs & Restaurants nearby: Driftwood Spars, ST AGNES, TR5 0RT, 01872 552428

Presingoll Farm Caravan & Camping Park
►►►84%

tel: 01872 552333 **TR5 0PB**
email: pam@presingollfarm.co.uk
dir: From A30 Chiverton rdbt take B3277 towards St Agnes. Site 3m on right. **grid ref:** SW721494

An attractive rural park adjoining farmland, with extensive views of the coast beyond. Family owned and run, with level grass pitches, and a modernised toilet block in smart converted farm buildings. There is also a campers' room with microwave, freezer, kettle and free coffee and tea, and a children's play area. This is an ideal base for touring the Newquay and St Ives areas. 5 acre site. 90 touring pitches. 6 hardstandings. Caravan pitches. Motorhome pitches. Tent pitches.

Open: Etr & Apr-Oct **Last departure:** 10.00hrs
Pitches: * ⌂ fr £15 ⌂ fr £15 Å fr £15
Leisure: ⚠
Facilities: ℝ ☉ ℗ ✳ ⓢ ⓢ ☴ ⓝ ♻ ⓕ ☆
Services: ⌂ ⓢ ⓽
Within 3 miles: ⌀ ⓢ ∪

Notes: No large groups. Dogs must be kept on leads.

AA Pubs & Restaurants nearby: Driftwood Spars, ST AGNES, TR5 0RT, 01872 552428

PITCHES: ⌂ Caravans ⌂ Motorhomes Å Tents ⌂ Glamping accommodation **SERVICES:** ⌂ Electric hook up ⓢ Launderette ⓡ Licensed bar ⓐ Calor Gas ⌀ Camping Gaz ⓣ Toilet fluid ⓘ⌐ Café/Restaurant ⓽ Fast Food/Takeaway ⓩ Battery charging ⌐ Baby care ⓽ Motorvan service point **ABBREVIATIONS:** BHs — bank holidays Etr — Easter Spring BH — Spring Bank Holiday fr — from hrs — hours m — mile mdnt — midnight rdbt — roundabout rs — restricted service wk — week wknd — weekend x-roads — crossroads ⊗ No credit or debit cards ⊗ No dogs

ST AGNES *continued*

Blue Hills Touring Park
▶▶▶ 80%

tel: 01872 552999 **Cross Combe, Trevellas TR5 0XP**
email: camping@blue-hills.co.uk
dir: *From A30 at Boxheater junct take B3285 signed Perranporth & St Agnes. In Trevellas, right, follow Cross Coombe & site signs. (NB it is advisable not to use Sat Nav; do not arrive via Wheal Kitty or Mithian School as roads are very narrow).* **grid ref:** *SW732521*

In an Area of Outstanding Natural Beauty, this small and tranquil campsite enjoys superb views over the Cornish countryside. Located on the rugged north Cornish coast, just a short walk away from the dog-friendly Trevellas Porth cove, the site is split into three attractive, slightly sloping areas, offering mainly level pitches and 28 with electric hook-ups. The facilities are good and include a laundry and utility room, and the reception stocks a limited number of essential items; there are fridges and freezers for campers' use. At busy periods, a breakfast van visits the site in the mornings. Small club rallies can be catered for. 2.5 acre site. 30 touring pitches. Caravan pitches. Motorhome pitches. Tent pitches.

Open: Mar-Oct **Last arrival:** 22.00hrs (phone site if arrival expected after 19.00hrs)
Last departure: 11.00hrs

Pitches: 🚐 🚍 ⛺

Leisure: ⚽

Facilities: ⊙ 🌁 ⚙ ⚡ ♿ 🔥 🚿 WiFi ♻ ⓘ

Services: 🔌 🔋 🛒 🚮

Within 3 miles: ⛳ 🎣 ⏰ 🌊 ⚓ 🔥 ⛵ 🛒 U

Notes: Dogs must be kept on leads. Breakfast coffee van, fish & chip van.

AA Pubs & Restaurants nearby: Driftwood Spars, ST AGNES, TR5 0RT, 01872 552428

Who has won England Campsite of the Year? See page 14

ST AUSTELL

See also Carlyon Bay

Places to visit

Charlestown Shipwreck & Heritage Centre, ST AUSTELL, PL25 3NJ, 01726 69897
www.shipwreckcharlestown.com

Eden Project, ST AUSTELL, PL24 2SG, 01726 811911 www.edenproject.com

Great for kids: Wheal Martyn, ST AUSTELL, PL26 8XG, 01726 850362
www.wheal-martyn.com

ST AUSTELL Map 2 SX05

PREMIER PARK

River Valley Holiday Park
▶▶▶▶▶ 87%

tel: 01726 73533 **London Apprentice PL26 7AP**
email: mail@rivervalleyholidaypark.co.uk **web:** www.rivervalleyholidaypark.co.uk
dir: *Take B3273 from St Austell to London Apprentice. Site signed, direct access to site from B3273.* **grid ref:** *SX010503*

A neat, well-maintained family-run park set in a pleasant river valley. The quality toilet block and attractively landscaped grounds make this a delightful base for a holiday. All pitches are hardstanding, mostly divided by low fencing and neatly trimmed hedges, and the park offers a good range of leisure facilities, including an inviting swimming pool, a games room, an internet room, and an excellent children's play area. There is direct access to river walks and an off-road cycle trail to the beach at Pentewan. The site is on the bus route to St Austell. 2 acre site. 45 touring pitches. 45 hardstandings. Caravan pitches. Motorhome pitches. Tent pitches. 40 statics.

Open: Apr-end Sep **Last arrival:** 21.00hrs **Last departure:** 11.00hrs
Pitches: * 🚐 £16.50-£35 🚍 £16.50-£35 ⛺ £16.50-£35 **Leisure:** 🏊 🎱 ⚽
Facilities: 🔥 📻 ⊙ 🌁 ⚙ ⚡ ♿ 🔥 WiFi ♻ ⓘ
Services: 🔌 🔋 🛒
Within 3 miles: ⛳ 🎣 ⏰ 🌊 ⛵ 🛒 U
Notes: Dogs must be kept on leads.
AA Pubs & Restaurants nearby: Austell's, ST AUSTELL, PL25 3PH, 01726 813888

LEISURE: 🏊 Indoor pool 🏊 Outdoor pool 🎢 Children's playground 👦 Kid's club 🎾 Tennis court 🎱 Games room ⛳ Golf course ⛵ Boat hire 🚲 Cycle hire 🎬 Cinema 🎵 Entertainment 🎣 Fishing ⛳ Mini golf ⛳ Pitch n putt 🌊 Watersports 💪 Gym ⚽ Sports field U Stables **FACILITIES:** 🛁 Bath 🚿 Shower 📻 Private washing cubicles ⊙ Electric shaver 🌁 Hairdryer ❄ Ice Packs ♿ Disabled facilities 🛒 Shop on site 📱 Mobile shop 🔥 BBQ area 🔥 Picnic area WiFi Wi-fi 💻 Internet access ♻ Recycling ⓘ Tourist info 🐕 Dog exercise area 🚗 Car hire can be arranged

Meadow Lakes Holiday Park

►►►► 84%

tel: 01726 882540 & & 01934 823288 **Hewas Water PL26 7JG**
email: info@meadow-lakes.co.uk **web:** www.meadow-lakes.co.uk
dir: *From A390 4m SW of St Austell onto B3287, Tregony. 1m, site on left.*
grid ref: *SW966485*

Set in a quiet rural area, this extensive park is divided into paddocks with mature hedges and trees, and has its own coarse fishing lakes. This friendly, family park has enthusiastic and hands-on owners – all facilities are immaculate and spotlessly clean. The park offers organised indoor and outdoor activities for children in the summer holidays (there is a play barn for when the weather is unsuitable for using the two outdoor play areas), and at other times caters for adult breaks. There are animals in pens which children can enter. Self-catering lodges, static caravans, wooden pods and smaller cabins are available for hire. The bus to Truro and St Austell stops within half a mile of the site. 56 acre site. 200 touring pitches.

11 hardstandings. 30 seasonal pitches. Caravan pitches. Motorhome pitches. Tent pitches. 35 statics.

Meadow Lakes Holiday Park

Open: mid Mar-end Oct **Last arrival:** 20.00hrs **Last departure:** 11.00hrs

Pitches: 🚐 🚐 ⛺ ⋒   **Leisure:** ⩓ ⩕ ⌽ ⚽ ♦ ✐

Facilities: ⛽ ⌂ 🅿 📷 ⚶ ⚵ 🖐 ⚶ 🛏 ⚶ WiFi 🖳 ⚙ ♻ ⊘

Services: 🔌 📷 🔒 ⏲ 🍴 🚰

Glamping: **Wooden Pods** 4, £38-£53 Car by unit **Cosy cabins:** (4 persons) 3, £46-£59 Min stay 2 nights Car by unit

Within 3 miles: ⚶ ⚶ ⤢ 🎯 ⚶ 🎣 🐴 ∪

Notes: No commercial vehicles, no noise after 23.00hrs. Dogs must be kept on leads. Table tennis, tots' TV room, zip wire, skittles, hot tub hire.

AA Pubs & Restaurants nearby: Austell's, ST AUSTELL, PL25 3PH, 01726 813888

See advert below

PITCHES: 🚐 Caravans 🚐 Motorhomes ⛺ Tents ⋒ Glamping accommodation **SERVICES:** 🔌 Electric hook up 📷 Launderette 🍺 Licensed bar 🛢 Calor Gas ⚗ Camping Gaz 🚽 Toilet fluid 🍴 Café/Restaurant 🍟 Fast Food/Takeaway ⚡ Battery charging 🍼 Baby care 🚐 Motorvan service point
ABBREVIATIONS: BHs – bank holidays Etr – Easter Spring BH – Spring Bank Holiday fr – from hrs – hours m – mile mdnt – midnight rdbt – roundabout rs – restricted service wk – week wknd – weekend x-roads – crossroads ⊘ No credit or debit cards ⊗ No dogs

ST AUSTELL *continued*

Court Farm Holidays
►►►81%

tel: 01726 823684 & 07973 773681 **St Stephen PL26 7LE**
email: info@courtfarmcornwall.co.uk
dir: *Take A3058 towards St Austell, through St Stephen (pass Peugeot garage), right at St Stephen/Coombe Hay/Langreth/Industrial site sign. Site 400yds on right.*
grid ref: *SW953524*

Set in a peaceful rural location, this large camping field offers plenty of space, and is handy for the Eden Project and the Lost Gardens of Heligan. Coarse fishing, and star-gazing facilities at the Roseland Observatory (including astronomy lectures) are among the on-site attractions. It is a five-minute walk to a Co-op store, and also to the bus stop on the Newquay to St Austell route. 4 acre site. 50 touring pitches. 5 hardstandings. Caravan pitches. Motorhome pitches. Tent pitches.

Open: Apr-Sep **Last arrival:** by dark **Last departure:** 11.00hrs

Pitches: ⊞ ⌷ Å

Facilities: ⊙ ✳ ⤶ ⤙ WiFi ❶

Services: 🔌 🗑 🚮

Within 3 miles: ↥ ☶ ✎ 🗵 🗵 ∪

Notes: No noise after dark. Dogs must be kept on leads.

AA Pubs & Restaurants nearby: Austell's, ST AUSTELL, PL25 3PH, 01726 813888

ST BLAZEY GATE Map 2 SX05

Places to visit
Eden Project, ST AUSTELL, PL24 2SG, 01726 811911 www.edenproject.com

St Catherine's Castle, FOWEY, 0370 333 1181
www.english-heritage.org.uk/daysout/properties/st-catherines-castle

Great for kids: Wheal Martyn, ST AUSTELL, PL26 8XG, 01726 850362 www.wheal-martyn.com

Doubletrees Farm
►►►►80%

tel: 01726 812266 **Luxulyan Rd PL24 2EH**
email: doubletreesfarm@gmail.com
dir: *On A390 at Blazey Gate. Turn by Leek Seed Chapel, almost opposite petrol station. After approx 300yds turn right by public bench into site.* **grid ref:** *SX060540*

A popular park with terraced pitches that offers superb sea and coastal views. It is close to beaches, and the Eden Project is only a 20-minute walk away. This site is very well maintained by the friendly owners and the facilities are spotlessly clean. There is a Chinese restaurant and a fish and chip shop just 300 yards away. 1.57 acre site. 32 touring pitches. 6 hardstandings. Caravan pitches. Motorhome pitches. Tent pitches.

Open: all year **Last arrival:** 22.30hrs **Last departure:** 11.30hrs

Pitches: ⊞ ⌷ Å

Facilities: ⌔ ⊙ ✳ ⅙ ⤶ ⤙ WiFi

Services: 🔌 🗑 ⬓ 🚮

Within 3 miles: ↥ ☶ ✎ ◎ 🗵 🗵 ∪

Notes: ☻ No noise after mdnt. Dogs must be kept on leads.

AA Pubs & Restaurants nearby: Austell's, ST AUSTELL, PL25 3PH, 01726 813888

ST COLUMB MAJOR Map 2 SW96

Places to visit
Prideaux Place, PADSTOW, PL28 8RP, 01841 532411 www.prideauxplace.co.uk

Cornwall's Regimental Museum, BODMIN, PL31 1EG, 01208 72810

Great for kids: Pencarrow, BODMIN, PL30 3AG, 01208 841369 www.pencarrow.co.uk

Devon's Crealy Great Adventure Park, CLYST ST MARY, EX5 1DR, 01395 233200 www.crealy.co.uk

Trewan Hall
►►►►83%

tel: 01637 880261 & 07900 677397 **TR9 6DB**
email: enquiries@trewan-hall.co.uk
dir: *From A39 N of St Columb Major (do not enter town) turn left signed Talskiddy & St Eval. Site 1m on left.* **grid ref:** *SW911646*

Trewan Hall lies at the centre of a Cornish estate amid 36 acres of wooded grounds. The site's extensive amenities include good toilet facilities, hook-ups and good security, plus a 25-metre swimming pool, and a free, live theatre in a stone barn throughout July and August. The campsite shop stocks everything from groceries to camping equipment. The site also has fine gardens, four acres of woodland for dog walking and a field available for ball games. St Columb is just a short walk away. 14.27 acre site. 200 touring pitches. Caravan pitches. Motorhome pitches. Tent pitches.

Open: 13 May-12 Sep (rs Low season - shop opens for shorter hours) **Last arrival:** 20.00hrs **Last departure:** noon

Pitches: * ⊞ £19-£27 ⌷ £19-£27 Å £14-£22

Leisure: ⥿ ⩘ ⅍ ⚽ 🎵

Facilities: ⤶ ⌔ P ⊙ ⌒ ✳ ⅙ 🗵 ⤶ ⤙ WiFi ♺ ❶

Services: 🔌 🗑 ⬓ T 🚮 🏷

Within 3 miles: ↥ ☶ ◎ ⅙ 🗵 🗵 ∪

Notes: Families & couples only, no cycling, no driving on fields from mdnt-08.00hrs, no noise after mdnt. Dogs must be kept on leads. Library, billiard room, table tennis, pool table.

AA Pubs & Restaurants nearby: The Falcon Inn, ST MAWGAN, TR8 4EP, 01637 860225

Southleigh Manor Naturist Park
►►►87%

tel: 01637 880938 **TR9 6HY**
email: enquiries@southleigh-manor.com
dir: *Exit A30 at junct with A39 signed Wadebridge. At Highgate Hill rdbt take A39. At Halloon rdbt take A39. At Trekenning rdbt take 4th exit signed RSPCA & Springfield Centre. Site 500mtrs on right.* **grid ref:** *SW918623*

A very well maintained, naturist park in the heart of the Cornish countryside, catering for families and couples only. Seclusion and security are very well planned, and the lovely gardens provide a calm setting. There are two lodges and static caravans for holiday hire. A bus stop at the entrance gate gives easy access to Newquay, Padstow or St Ives. 4 acre site. 50 touring pitches. Caravan pitches. Motorhome pitches. Tent pitches.

Open: Etr-Oct **Last arrival:** 20.00hrs **Last departure:** 10.30hrs

Pitches: ⊞ ⌷ Å

LEISURE: 🏊 Indoor pool 🏊 Outdoor pool ⅍ Children's playground 🧒 Kid's club 🎾 Tennis court 🎱 Games room ⛳ Golf course 🚣 Boat hire 🚲 Cycle hire 🎬 Cinema 🎵 Entertainment 🎣 Fishing ◎ Mini golf ⛳ Pitch n putt 🤽 Watersports 🏋 Gym 🏟 Sports field ∪ Stables **FACILITIES:** 🛁 Bath ⌔ Shower P Private washing cubicles ⊙ Electric shaver 🪮 Hairdryer ✳ Ice Packs ⅙ Disabled facilities 🗵 Shop on site 🏪 Mobile shop 🍖 BBQ area 🏕 Picnic area WiFi Wi-fi 💻 Internet access ♺ Recycling ❶ Tourist info ⤙ Dog exercise area 🏷 Car hire can be arranged

Leisure: ⛲

Facilities: ⊙ 🅿 ✳ 🎋 📶 ♻ ❓

Services: 🔌 🔄 🍴 🛢 🕳 T 🍽 🔋

Within 3 miles: 🎣 🥾 ⛳ 🎡 U

Notes: 🐕 Dogs must remain on tent, motorhome or caravan pitch except when exercised off site. Sauna, spa bath, pool table, putting green.

AA Pubs & Restaurants nearby: The Falcon Inn, ST MAWGAN, TR8 4EP, 01637 860225

ST HILARY Map 2 SW53

Places to visit

Godolphin House, GODOLPHIN CROSS, TR13 9RE, 01736 763194
www.nationaltrust.org.uk/godolphin

St Michael's Mount, MARAZION, TR17 0HT, 01736 710507
www.stmichaelsmount.co.uk

Great for kids: The Flambards Theme Park, HELSTON, TR13 0QA, 01326 573404
www.flambards.co.uk

Trevair Touring Park
▶▶▶ 79%

tel: 01736 740647 **South Treveneague TR20 9BY**
email: luxford623@btinternet.com
dir: *A30 onto A394 signed Helston. 2m to rdbt, left onto B3280. Through Goldsithney. Left at brown site sign. Through 20mph zone to site, 1m on right.* **grid ref:** *SW548326*

Set in a rural location adjacent to woodland, this park is level and secluded, with grassy pitches. Marazion's beaches and the famous St Michael's Mount are just three miles away. The friendly owners live at the farmhouse on the park. 3.5 acre site. 40 touring pitches. Caravan pitches. Motorhome pitches. Tent pitches. 2 statics.

Open: Etr-Nov **Last arrival:** 22.00hrs **Last departure:** 11.00hrs

Pitches: 🚐 🚎 ▲

Facilities: 🅿 ⊙ ✳ ♻ ❓

Services: 🔌 🔄 🔋

Within 3 miles: 🎣 ⛳ 🏊 🎡 U

Notes: 🐕 PayPal accepted. No noise after 23.00hrs. Dogs must be kept on leads.

AA Pubs & Restaurants nearby: The Victoria Inn, PERRANUTHNOE, TR20 9NP, 01736 710309

ST IVES

Places to visit

Barbara Hepworth Museum & Sculpture Garden, ST IVES, TR26 1AD, 01736 796226 www.tate.org.uk/stives

Tate St Ives, ST IVES, TR26 1TG, 01736 796226 www.tate.org.uk/stives

---

ST IVES Map 2 SW54

PREMIER PARK

Polmanter Touring Park
▶▶▶▶▶ 97%

Best of British

tel: 01736 795640 **Halsetown TR26 3LX**
email: reception@polmanter.co.uk **web:** www.polmanter.co.uk
dir: *Signed from B3311 at Halsetown.* **grid ref:** *SW510388*

A well-developed touring park on high ground, Polmanter is an excellent choice for family holidays and offers high quality in all areas, from the immaculate modern toilet blocks to the outdoor swimming pool and hard tennis courts. Pitches are individually marked and sited in meadows, and the tastefully landscaped park offers a field with full-facility hardstanding pitches to accommodate larger caravans and motorhomes. The fishing port and beaches of St Ives are just a mile and a half away, and there is a bus service in high season. 20 acre site. 270 touring pitches. 60 hardstandings. Caravan pitches. Motorhome pitches. Tent pitches.

Open: Spring BH-10 Sep (rs Spring BH – shop, pool & bar closed; takeaway food unavailable; bus unavailable) **Last arrival:** 21.00hrs **Last departure:** 10.00hrs

Pitches: 🚐 🚎 ▲ **Leisure:** ⛲ 🏊 ⚽ 🎱

Facilities: ⊙ 🅿 ✳ ♿ 🛁 🎋 📶 ♻ ❓ **Services:** 🔌 🔄 🍴 🛢 🕳 T 🍽 🔋 🚚 🔧

Within 3 miles: 🎣 🏇 🎋 ⛳ ◎ 🏊 🎡 U

Notes: Family camping only, no skateboards, rollerblades or heelys. Dogs must be kept on leads. Putting green.

AA Pubs & Restaurants nearby: The Tinners Arms, ZENNOR, TR26 3BY, 01736 796927

See advert on page 115

PITCHES: 🚐 Caravans 🚎 Motorhomes ▲ Tents 🛖 Glamping accommodation **SERVICES:** 🔌 Electric hook up 🔄 Launderette 🍴 Licensed bar 🛢 Calor Gas 🕳 Camping Gaz T Toilet fluid 🍽 Café/Restaurant 🚚 Fast Food/Takeaway 🔋 Battery charging 🚼 Baby care 🔧 Motorvan service point

ABBREVIATIONS: BHs – bank holidays Etr – Easter Spring BH – Spring Bank Holiday fr – from hrs – hours m – mile mdnt – midnight rdbt – roundabout rs – restricted service wk – week wknd – weekend x-roads – crossroads ⊗ No credit or debit cards ⊗ No dogs

ST IVES *continued*

PREMIER PARK

Ayr Holiday Park
►►►►►87%

tel: 01736 795855 **TR26 1EJ**
email: recept@ayrholidaypark.co.uk **web:** www.ayrholidaypark.co.uk
dir: *From A30 follow St Ives 'large vehicles' route via B3311 through Halsetown onto B3306. Site signed towards St Ives town centre. (NB that it is advisable not to follow Sat Nav; use these directions & avoid the town centre)* **grid ref:** *SW509408*

A well-established park on a cliff side overlooking St Ives Bay, with a heated toilet block that makes winter holidaying more attractive. There are stunning views from most pitches, and the town centre, harbour and beach are only half a mile away, with direct access to the coastal footpath. This makes an excellent base for surfing enthusiasts. 4 acre site. 40 touring pitches. 20 hardstandings. Caravan pitches. Motorhome pitches. Tent pitches.

Open: all year **Last arrival:** 22.00hrs **Last departure:** 11.00hrs

Pitches: * ⊞ £19-£39 ⊟ £19-£39 ▲ £19-£39

Leisure: 🐦 🔍

Facilities: ⯪ ⯮ Ⓟ ⦿ ℱ ✳ ⅃ ℸ WiFi ▤ ♻ ⓘ

Services: ⊟ 🔋 🛢 ⬚ Ⓣ 🍴 ☕ 🖙 ⅃

Within 3 miles: ↧ ⅃ 🎣 ℰ ⦿ ≋ 🖫 ⓖ U

Notes: No disposable BBQs. Dogs must be kept on leads.

AA Pubs & Restaurants nearby: The Sloop Inn, ST IVES, TR26 1LP, 01736 796584
The Queens, ST IVES, TR26 1RR, 01736 796468

Campsite cooking
See pages 24-31
for handy tips

Trevalgan Touring Park
►►►►►85%

Best of British

tel: 01736 791892 **Trevalgan TR26 3BJ**
email: reception@trevalgantouringpark.co.uk **web:** www.trevalgantouringpark.co.uk
dir: *From A30 follow holiday route to St Ives. B3311 through Halsetown to B3306. Left towards Land's End. Site signed 0.5m on right.* **grid ref:** *SW490402*

Serious investment by the hands-on owners has taken place over the last few years at this welcoming park, which is set in a rural area on the coastal road from St Ives to Zennor. The park is surrounded by mature hedges but there are still extensive views over the sea. There is a smart wood-clad reception and shop (daily-baked bread and pastries are available), excellent upmarket toilet facilities which have family rooms and underfloor heating, and extensive landscaping across the park that has resulted in more spacious pitches which offer both privacy and shelter. A regular bus service connects the park with St Ives from late May to September. A good base for motorhomes. 9 acre site. 135 touring pitches. 13 hardstandings. Caravan pitches. Motorhome pitches. Tent pitches.

Open: Etr-Sep **Last arrival:** 22.00hrs **Last departure:** 11.00hrs

Pitches: ⊞ ⊟ ▲ **Leisure:** ⚽ ☺ 🔍

Facilities: ⯮ Ⓟ ⦿ ℱ ✳ ⅃ 🆂 WiFi ▤ ♻ ⓘ

Services: ⊟ 🔋 🛢 ⬚ Ⓣ ⅃

Within 3 miles: ↧ ⅃ 🎣 ℰ ⦿ ≋ 🖫 ⓖ U

Notes: Dogs must be kept on leads. Fresh bread, pastries, coffee, local produce.

AA Pubs & Restaurants nearby: The Queens, ST IVES, TR26 1RR, 01736 796468
The Sloop Inn, ST IVES, TR26 1LP, 01736 796584

LEISURE: 🏊 Indoor pool ⛱ Outdoor pool ⛰ Children's playground ✋ Kid's club ⚲ Tennis court 🔍 Games room ⅃ Golf course ⛵ Boat hire 🚲 Cycle hire 🎬 Cinema 🎵 Entertainment 🎣 Fishing ⦿ Mini golf ⛳ Pitch n putt ≋ Watersports 🏋 Gym ♣ Sports field U Stables **FACILITIES:** 🛁 Bath 🚿 Shower Ⓟ Private washing cubicles ☺ Electric shaver ℱ Hairdryer ✳ Ice Packs ⅃ Disabled facilities 🆂 Shop on site 🛒 Mobile shop 🍴 BBQ area 🪑 Picnic area WiFi Wi-fi ▤ Internet access ♻ Recycling ⓘ Tourist info 🐕 Dog exercise area 🚗 Car hire can be arranged

Higher Penderleath Caravan & Camping Park
►►►►81%

tel: 01736 798403 & 07840 208542 **Towednack TR26 3AF**
email: holidays@penderleath.co.uk **web:** www.penderleath.co.uk
dir: *From A30 take A3074 towards St Ives. Left at 2nd mini-rdbt, approx 3m to T-junct. Left then immediately right. Next left.* **grid ref:** *SW496375*

Set in a rugged rural location, this tranquil park has extensive views towards St Ives Bay and the north coast. Facilities are all housed in modernised granite barns, and include spotless toilets with fully serviced shower rooms, and there's a quiet licensed bar with beer garden, a food takeaway, breakfast room and bar meals. The owners are welcoming and helpful. There is a bus service to St Ives available in high season. 10 acre site. 75 touring pitches. Caravan pitches. Motorhome pitches. Tent pitches.

Open: Etr-Oct **Last arrival:** 21.30hrs **Last departure:** 10.30hrs

Pitches: ⌂ ⌂ Å

Leisure: ✎

Facilities: ⊙ ☞ ✳ ♿ ⒮ ↻ ♨ ❻
Services: ⊞ ⒮ ❣ ⬛ ⌀ Ⓣ ⦿ ⌂ 🔋
Within 3 miles: ⌣ ♣ ☷ ♬ ◎ ⩭ ⒮ ⒮ U

Notes: No campfires, no noise after 23.00hrs. Dogs must be well behaved & kept on leads.

AA Pubs & Restaurants nearby: The Watermill, ST IVES, TR27 6LQ, 01736 757912

Balnoon Camping Site
►►88%

tel: 01736 795431 & 07751 600555 **Halsetown TR26 3JA**
email: nat@balnoon.fsnet.co.uk
dir: *From A30 take A3074, at 2nd mini-rdbt 1st left signed Tate/St Ives. In 3m turn right after The Lodge at Balnoon.* **grid ref:** *SW509382*

Small, quiet and friendly, this sheltered site offers superb views of the adjacent rolling hills. The two paddocks are surrounded by mature hedges, and the toilet facilities are kept spotlessly clean. The beaches of Carbis Bay and St Ives are about two miles away. 1 acre site. 23 touring pitches. Caravan pitches. Motorhome pitches. Tent pitches.

Open: Etr-Oct **Last arrival:** 20.00hrs **Last departure:** 11.00hrs

Pitches: * ⌂ £13-£17 ⌂ £13-£17 Å £13-£17

Facilities: ♨ ⊙ ☞ ✳ ↻ ❻
Services: ⊞ ⌀ Ⓣ 🔋
Within 3 miles: ⌣ ♣ ☷ ♬ ◎ ⩭ ⒮ ⒮ U

Notes: ⊘ No noise between 23.00hrs-07.30hrs. Dogs must be kept on leads. Milk & eggs for sale (peak season).

AA Pubs & Restaurants nearby: The Watermill, ST IVES, TR27 6LQ, 01736 757912

PITCHES: ⌂ Caravans ⌂ Motorhomes Å Tents ⌂ Glamping accommodation **SERVICES:** ⊞ Electric hook up ⒮ Launderette ❣ Licensed bar ⬛ Calor Gas ⌀ Camping Gaz Ⓣ Toilet fluid ⦿ Café/Restaurant ⊞ Fast Food/Takeaway 🔋 Battery charging ⌂ Baby care ⌂ Motorvan service point
ABBREVIATIONS: BHs – bank holidays Etr – Easter Spring BH – Spring Bank Holiday fr – from hrs – hours m – mile mdnt – midnight rdbt – roundabout rs – restricted service wk – week wknd – weekend x-roads – crossroads ⊘ No credit or debit cards ⊗ No dogs

ST JUST (NEAR LAND'S END)
Map 2 SW33

Places to visit

Geevor Tin Mine, PENDEEN, TR19 7EW, 01736 788662 www.geevor.com

Carn Euny Ancient Village, SANCREED, 0370 333 1181
www.english-heritage.org.uk/daysout/properties/carn-euny-ancient-village

Roselands Caravan and Camping Park
►►►87%

tel: 01736 788571 & 07718 745065 **Dowran TR19 7RS**
email: info@roselands.co.uk
dir: *From A30 Penzance bypass onto A3071 for St Just. 5m, left at sign after tin mine chimney, follow signs to site.* **grid ref:** *SW387305*

A small, friendly park in a sheltered rural setting, an ideal location for a quiet family holiday. The owners continue to upgrade the park, and in addition to the attractive little bar there is an indoor games room, children's playground and good toilet facilities. 4 acre site. 25 touring pitches. Caravan pitches. Motorhome pitches. Tent pitches. 19 statics.

Open: Mar-Oct **Last arrival:** 21.00hrs **Last departure:** 11.00hrs
Pitches: * ⊡ £13.50-£19.50 ⊡ £13.50-£19.50 ▲ £12-£16
Leisure: ⋔ ♣
Facilities: ↾ ⊙ ℱ ✳ ⑤ ♒ ⼊ WiFi ▭ ♻ ❼
Services: ⊡ ⑤ ⊞ ⚫ ⬧ ⊤
Within 3 miles: ⌇ ⌁ ⥩ ⑤ ⑤ ∪
Notes: Dogs must be kept on leads.
AA Pubs & Restaurants nearby: Harris's Restaurant, PENZANCE, TR18 2LZ, 01736 364408

The Tinners Arms, ZENNOR, TR26 3BY, 01736 796927

Trevaylor Caravan & Camping Park
►►►84%

tel: 01736 787016 & 07816 992519 **Botallack TR19 7PU**
email: trevaylor@cornishcamping.co.uk **web:** www.cornishcamping.co.uk
dir: *On B3306 (St Just to St Ives road), site on right 0.75m from St Just.*
grid ref: *SW368222*

A sheltered grassy site located off the beaten track in a peaceful location at the western tip of Cornwall; it makes an ideal base for discovering Penzance and Land's End. The dramatic coastline and the pretty villages nearby are truly unspoilt. Clean, well-maintained facilities including a good shop are offered along with a bar serving meals. The enthusiastic owners offer pitches with electric hook-ups and a shower block with heating. An open-top bus stops at the entrance to the site. 6 acre site. 50 touring pitches. 11 hardstandings. Caravan pitches. Motorhome pitches. Tent pitches. 6 statics.

Open: all year **Last arrival:** 21.00hrs **Last departure:** 11.00hrs
Pitches: ⊡ ⊡ ▲
Leisure: ⋔ ♣
Facilities: ↾ ℱ ✳ ⑤ WiFi ♻ ❼
Services: ⊡ ⑤ ⊞ ⚫ ⬧ ⊤ ⚭ ▬ ⬦ ⬧
Within 3 miles: ⌇ ⌁ ⥩ ⑤ ⑤ ∪
Notes: Quiet after 22.00hrs. Dogs must be kept on leads.
AA Pubs & Restaurants nearby: Harris's Restaurant, PENZANCE, TR18 2LZ, 01736 364408

The Tinners Arms, ZENNOR, TR26 3BY, 01736 796927

Kelynack Caravan & Camping Park
►►►81%

tel: 01736 787633 **Kelynack TR19 7RE**
email: enquiries@kelynackholidays.co.uk **web:** www.kelynackholidays.co.uk
dir: *1m S of St Just, 5m N of Land's End on B3306.* **grid ref:** *SW374301*

A small secluded park that sits alongside a stream in an unspoilt rural location. The level grass pitches are in two areas. The park is within reach of Land's End, Sennen Cove, Minack Theatre and Penzance. 3 acre site. 28 touring pitches. 3 hardstandings. Caravan pitches. Motorhome pitches. Tent pitches. 13 statics.

Open: all year **Last arrival:** 22.00hrs **Last departure:** 10.00hrs
Pitches: ⊡ ⊡ ▲
Leisure: ⋔ ♣
Facilities: ↾ ⊙ ℱ ✳ ⓺ ⑤ ♒ WiFi ♻ ❼ ⚘
Services: ⊡ ⑤ ⚫ ⬧ ⊤ ▬ ⬧
Within 3 miles: ⌇ ⌁ ⥩ ⑤ ⑤ ∪
Notes: Dogs must be kept on leads. Cooking & dining shelter.
AA Pubs & Restaurants nearby: Harris's Restaurant, PENZANCE, TR18 2LZ, 01736 364408

The Tinners Arms, ZENNOR, TR26 3BY, 01736 796927

LEISURE: 🏊 Indoor pool 🏊 Outdoor pool ⋔ Children's playground 🖐 Kid's club 🎾 Tennis court ♣ Games room ⛳ Golf course ⛵ Boat hire 🚲 Cycle hire 🎦 Cinema 🎵 Entertainment 🎣 Fishing ⛳ Mini golf ⛳ Pitch n putt 🏄 Watersports 🏋 Gym ⚽ Sports field ∪ Stables **FACILITIES:** 🛁 Bath ↾ Shower ℙ Private washing cubicles ⊙ Electric shaver ℱ Hairdryer ✳ Ice Packs ♿ Disabled facilities ⑤ Shop on site ⛟ Mobile shop ▬ BBQ area ⼊ Picnic area WiFi Wi-fi ▭ Internet access ♻ Recycling ❼ Tourist info 🐕 Dog exercise area ⚘ Car hire can be arranged

Secret Garden Caravan & Camping Park

▶▶▶ 79%

tel: 01736 788301 **Bosavern House TR19 7RD**
email: mail@bosavern.com
dir: *Exit A3071 near St Just onto B3306 (Land's End road). Site 0.5m on left.*
grid ref: SW370305

A neat little site in a walled garden behind a guest house, where visitors can enjoy breakfast, and snacks in the bar in the evening. This site is in a fairly sheltered location with all grassy pitches. Please note that there is no children's playground. 1.5 acre site. 12 touring pitches. Caravan pitches. Motorhome pitches. Tent pitches.

Open: Mar-Oct **Last arrival:** 22.00hrs **Last departure:** noon

Pitches: * 🚐 fr £19 �🚌 fr £19 ⛺ fr £19

Facilities: 🅿️ ⊙ ✳ WiFi ♻ ⚙ ❼

Services: 🔌 🗑 🍽 ⛽ 🛒 ↯

Within 3 miles: ↨ 🎣 ⛸ 🏤 🗑

Notes: No pets, no open fires or fire pits.

AA Pubs & Restaurants nearby: Harris's Restaurant, PENZANCE, TR18 2LZ, 01736 364408

The Tinners Arms, ZENNOR, TR26 3BY, 01736 796927

ST JUST-IN-ROSELAND   Map 2 SW83

Places to visit

St Mawes Castle, ST MAWES, TR2 3AA, 01326 270526
www.english-heritage.org.uk/daysout/properties/st-mawes-castle

Trelissick, TRELISSICK, TR3 6QL, 01872 862090
www.nationaltrust.org.uk/trelissick

PREMIER PARK

Trethem Mill Touring Park

▶▶▶▶▶ 95%

Best of British
GOLD

tel: 01872 580504 **TR2 5JF**
email: reception@trethem.com **web:** www.trethem.com
dir: *From Tregony on A3078 to St Mawes. 2m after Trewithian, follow signs to site.*
grid ref: SW860365

A quality park in all areas, with good amenities including a reception, shop, laundry, and disabled/family room. This carefully-tended and sheltered park is

in a lovely rural setting, with spacious pitches separated by young trees and shrubs. The very keen family who own the site are continually looking for ways to enhance its facilities. A pizza van serving excellent wood-fired pizzas visits the site once a week. 11 acre site. 84 touring pitches. 67 hardstandings. Caravan pitches. Motorhome pitches. Tent pitches.

Open: Apr-mid Oct **Last arrival:** 20.00hrs **Last departure:** 11.00hrs

Pitches: * 🚐 £20-£28 🚌 £20-£28 ⛺ £20-£28

Leisure: 🎱 ⚽

Facilities: 🅿️ 🅿 ⊙ ℗ ✳ & 🔓 🚽 WiFi ♻ ⚙ ❼ 🎪

Services: 🔌 🗑 🔋 🗑 🛒 ↯

Within 3 miles: ↨ 🎣 ⛸ 🏤 🗑

Notes: No bikes, skateboards or rollerblades. Dogs must be kept on leads. Information centre.

AA Pubs & Restaurants nearby: The Victory Inn, ST MAWES, TR2 5DQ, 01326 270324

Hotel Tresanton, ST MAWES, TR2 5DR, 01326 270055

Driftwood, PORTSCATHO, TR2 5EW, 01872 580644

ST MARY'S (ISLES OF SCILLY)   Map 2 SV91

Places to visit

Isles of Scilly Museum, ST MARY'S, TR21 0JT, 01720 422337
www.iosmuseum.org

Garrison Campsite

▶▶▶ 82%

tel: 01720 422670 **Tower Cottage, The Garrison TR21 0LS**
email: info@garrisonholidays.com
dir: *10 mins' walk from quay to site.* **grid ref:** SV897104

Set on the top of an old fort with superb views, this park offers tent-only pitches in a choice of well-sheltered paddocks, including fully-equipped ready-erected tents which are available for hire. There are modern toilet facilities (with powerful showers), a superb children's play area and a good shop at this attractive site, which is only 10 minutes from the town, the quay and the nearest beaches. There is easy access to the other islands via the direct boat service from the Hugh Town quay; the campsite owners will transport all luggage, camping equipment etc to and from the quay. Good food is available in the many hostelries in the main town. 9.5 acre site. 120 touring pitches. Tent pitches.

Open: Etr-Oct **Last arrival:** 20.00hrs **Last departure:** 19.00hrs

Pitches: * ⛺ £18.40-£22.90 🎪 prices shown below

Facilities: 🅿️ ⊙ ℗ ✳ 🔓 WiFi ♻ ❼

Services: 🔌 🗑 🔋 🗑 🛒

Glamping: Erected Tents 6, £28-£83.50 Min stay 3 nights

Within 3 miles: ↨ ↨ 🎣 ⛸ 🏤 🗑 ↻

Notes: No cars on site, no open fires, dogs by prior arrangement only. Dogs must be kept on leads.

PITCHES: 🚐 Caravans 🚌 Motorhomes ⛺ Tents 🎪 Glamping accommodation **SERVICES:** 🔌 Electric hook up 🗑 Launderette 🍽 Licensed bar 🔋 Calor Gas ⊘ Camping Gaz 🔲 Toilet fluid 🍽 Café/Restaurant 🏭 Fast Food/Takeaway 🔋 Battery charging 🚼 Baby care ↯ Motorvan service point **ABBREVIATIONS:** BHs – bank holidays Etr – Easter Spring BH – Spring Bank Holiday fr – from hrs – hours m – mile mdnt – midnight rdbt – roundabout rs – restricted service wk – week wknd – weekend x-roads – crossroads 🚫 No credit or debit cards 🚫 No dogs

ST MERRYN (NEAR PADSTOW) Map 2 SW87

Places to visit

Prideaux Place, PADSTOW, PL28 8RP, 01841 532411 www.prideauxplace.co.uk

Great for kids: Devon's Crealy Great Adventure Park, CLYST ST MARY, EX5 1DR, 01395 233200 www.crealy.co.uk

PREMIER PARK

Atlantic Bays Holiday Park

►►►►► 88%

tel: 01841 520855 **St Merryn PL28 8PY**
email: info@atlanticbaysholidaypark.co.uk **web:** www.atlanticbaysholidaypark.co.uk
dir: *From A30 SW of Bodmin take exit signed Victoria & Roche, 1st exit at rdbt. At Trekenning rdbt 4th exit signed A39 & Wadebridge. At Winnards Perch rdbt left B3274 signed Padstow. Left in 3m, follow signs.* **grid ref:** *SW890717*

Atlantic Bays has a mix of hardstanding and grass pitches, a high quality toilet and shower block and a comfortable bar and restaurant. The park is set in a rural area yet only two miles from the coast and beautiful sandy beaches, and within easy reach of the quaint fishing village of Padstow, and Newquay for fantastic surfing. 27 acre site. 70 touring pitches. 50 hardstandings. 6 seasonal pitches. Caravan pitches. Motorhome pitches. Tent pitches. 171 statics.

Open: Mar-2 Jan **Last arrival:** 21.00hrs **Last departure:** noon

Pitches: 🚐 🚌 ⛺ **Leisure:** 🛝 ⚽ 🎱

Facilities: 🪒 💨 ❄ ♿ 🏪 🚚 🧺 🐕 📶 💻 ♻ ℹ

Services: 🧼 ▣ 🍺 [T] 🛒 🍴 ⚓ **Within 3 miles:** ⛳ ⛵ 🎬 🎣 ◎ 🏄 🏪 ▣ 🐎

Notes: Dogs must be kept on leads.

AA Pubs & Restaurants nearby: The Cornish Arms, ST MERRYN, PL28 8ND, 01841 532700

The Seafood Restaurant, PADSTOW, PL28 8BY, 01841 532700

See advert on opposite page

Carnevas Holiday Park

►►►► 84%

tel: 01841 520230 & 521209 **Carnevas Farm PL28 8PN**
email: carnevascampsite@aol.com **web:** www.carnevasholidaypark.com
dir: *From St Merryn on B3276 towards Porthcothan Bay. Approx 2m turn right at site sign onto unclassified road opposite Tredrea Inn. Site 0.25m on right.* **grid ref:** *SW862728*

A family-run park on a working farm, divided into four paddocks on slightly sloping grass. The toilets are central to all areas, and there is a small licensed bar serving bar meals. An ideal base for exploring the fishing town of Padstow or the surfing beach at Newquay. 8 acre site. 195 touring pitches. Caravan pitches. Motorhome pitches. Tent pitches. 14 statics.

Open: Apr-Oct (rs Apr-Spring BH & mid Sep-Oct shop, bar & restaurant closed)

Pitches: * 🚐 £12-£19.50 🚌 £12-£19.50 ⛺ £12-£19.50

Leisure: 🛝 🎱 **Facilities:** 🚿 🪒 💨 ❄ ♿ 🏪 📶 ♻ ℹ

Services: 🧼 ▣ 🍺 🛍 🍃 [T] 🍴 🍳 ⚓ **Within 3 miles:** ⛳ 🎣 🏄 🏪 ▣ 🐎

Notes: No skateboards, no supermarket deliveries. Dogs must be kept on leads.

AA Pubs & Restaurants nearby: The Cornish Arms, ST MERRYN, PL28 8ND, 01841 532700

The Seafood Restaurant, PADSTOW, PL28 8BY, 01841 532700

See advert on opposite page

Atlantic Bays Holiday Park

St Merryn, Padstow, Cornwall PL28 8PY

The Touring Park comprises 20 fully serviced hard standing pitches, 50 electric only hard standing pitches and we also have grassed pitches available. The spacious pitches are designed to allow us to accommodate and cater for all sizes of tents, caravans and motor-homes, for a peaceful and relaxing stay. The coded facilities ensure exclusive use and have been built to the highest of standards recently winning us 5 Pennant rating and status as an AA recognised park. We also cater for Rallies.

✓ Free Showers
✓ Hairdryers
✓ Electric Shaver Points
✓ Ironing Equipment

✓ Indoor and Outdoor Wash up area
✓ Chemical Disposal Units
✓ Electric Hook-ups
✓ Full Service Pitches

Tel: 01841 520855 **Website:** www.atlanticbaysholidaypark.co.uk
Email: info@atlanticbaysholidaypark.co.uk

CARNEVAS

HOLIDAY PARK

Situated in the unspoilt country of the North Cornish Coast, our park is ideal for touring Cornwall; *Newquay - 10 miles & Padstow - 4 miles.*

We are pleased to offer: Modern 6+ Caravans - Holiday Bungalows - Sites for Touring Caravans & Tents - Electric Hook-Ups - Residential Licensed Bar & restaurant - Children's Play Area - Toilet Block & Showers - Laundry Facilities •Modern Shop

For our brochure please write:
CARNEVAS HOLIDAY PARK,
ST. MERRYN, Nr PADSTOW,
CORNWALL

TEL: 01841 520230
www.carnevasholidaypark.com
carnevascampsite@aol.com

GUNVENNA HOLIDAY PARK [Wi Fi]

www.gunvenna.com

tripadvisor
2013 and 2016 WINNER
CERTIFICATE OF EXCELLENCE

Street food available on site in the school holidays

Touring, Motorhomes, Camping, Glamping, RV's
St. Minver, Wadebridge, Cornwall PL27 6QN   Tel 01208 862405

PITCHES: 🚐 Caravans 🚍 Motorhomes 🅰 Tents 🏕 Glamping accommodation **SERVICES:** 🔌 Electric hook up 🧺 Launderette 🍺 Licensed bar
🔋 Calor Gas ⊘ Camping Gaz Ⓣ Toilet fluid 🍽 Café/Restaurant 🍔 Fast Food/Takeaway 🔋 Battery charging 🍼 Baby care ⛽ Motorvan service point
ABBREVIATIONS: BHs – bank holidays Etr – Easter Spring BH – Spring Bank Holiday fr – from hrs – hours m – mile mdnt – midnight
rdbt – roundabout rs – restricted service wk – week wknd – weekend x-roads – crossroads 🚫 No credit or debit cards 🚫 No dogs

ST MERRYN (NEAR PADSTOW) *continued*

Tregavone Touring Park

▶▶▶ 77%

tel: 01841 520148 **Tregavone Farm PL28 8JZ**
email: info@tregavone.co.uk
dir: *From A389 towards Padstow, right after Little Petherick. In 1m just beyond Padstow Holiday Park turn left onto unclassified road signed Tregavone. Site on left, approx 1m.*
grid ref: *SW898732*

Situated on a working farm with unspoilt country views, this spacious grassy park, run by friendly family owners, makes an ideal base for exploring the north Cornish coast and the seven local golden beaches with surfing areas, or for enjoying quiet country walks from the park. 3 acre site. 40 touring pitches. Caravan pitches. Motorhome pitches. Tent pitches. 1 static.

Open: Mar-Oct

Pitches: ⌂ ⌂ ▲

Facilities: ⌂ ⊙ ℙ ✳ ⌂

Services: ⌂ ⌂ ⌂

Within 3 miles: ⌂ ✈ ℘ ⊚ ⌂ ⌂ ⌂ U

Notes: ⌂ Dogs must be kept on leads.

AA Pubs & Restaurants nearby: The Cornish Arms, ST MERRYN, PL28 8ND, 01841 532700

The Seafood Restaurant, PADSTOW, PL28 8BY, 01841 532700

ST MINVER	Map 2 SW97

PREMIER PARK

Gunvenna Holiday Park

▶▶▶▶▶ 87%

tel: 01208 862405 **PL27 6QN**
email: gunvenna.bookings@gmail.com **web:** www.gunvenna.com
dir: *From A39 N of Wadebridge take B3314 (Port Isaac road), site 4m on right.*
grid ref: *SW969782*

An attractive park with extensive rural views in a quiet country location, yet within three miles of Polzeath. This popular park is family owned and run, and

provides good facilities in an ideal position for touring north Cornwall. The park has excellent hardstanding pitches, maturing landscaping and a beautiful indoor swimming pool with a glass roof. A mini wooden glamping cabin, a railway carriage, a holiday cottage and static caravans are for hire. The beach at Polzeath is very popular with the surfers. 10 acre site. 75 touring pitches. 24 hardstandings. 15 seasonal pitches. Caravan pitches. Motorhome pitches. Tent pitches. 44 statics.

Gunvenna Holiday Park

Open: Etr-Oct **Last arrival:** 20.30hrs **Last departure:** 11.00hrs

Pitches: ⌂ ⌂ ▲ ⌂

Leisure: ⌂ ⌂ ⌂

Facilities: ⌂ ⌂ ℙ ⊙ ℘ ✳ ⌂ ⌂ ⌂ ⌂ WiFi ⌂ ♻ ⌂

Services: ⌂ ⌂ ⌂ ⌂ T ⌂ ⌂ ⌂

Glamping: Cabins 1, £55-£60 Changeover day Any day Car by unit
Railway Carriages 1, £55-£60 Changeover day Any day Car by unit

Within 3 miles: ⌂ ✈ ⌂ ℘ ⌂ ⌂ ⌂

Notes: Children under 16yrs must be accompanied by an adult in pool, owners must clear up after their dogs. Dogs must be kept on leads.

AA Pubs & Restaurants nearby: The Maltsters Arms, CHAPEL AMBLE, PL27 6EU, 01208 812473

Restaurant Nathan Outlaw, PORT ISAAC, PL29 3SB, 01208 880896

See advert on page 119

SENNEN

Places to visit

Carn Euny Ancient Village, SANCREED, 0370 333 1181
www.english-heritage.org.uk/daysout/properties/carn-euny-ancient-village

Chysauster Ancient Village, CHYSAUSTER ANCIENT VILLAGE, TR20 8XA, 07831 757934
www.english-heritage.org.uk/daysout/properties/chysauster-ancient-village

Great for kids: Geevor Tin Mine, PENDEEN, TR19 7EW, 01736 788662
www.geevor.com

LEISURE: ⌂ Indoor pool ⌂ Outdoor pool ⌂ Children's playground ⌂ Kid's club ⌂ Tennis court ⌂ Games room ⌂ Golf course ⌂ Boat hire ⌂ Cycle hire ⌂ Cinema ⌂ Entertainment ℘ Fishing ⊚ Mini golf ⌂ Pitch n putt ⌂ Watersports ⌂ Gym ⌂ Sports field U Stables **FACILITIES:** ⌂ Bath ⌂ Shower ℙ Private washing cubicles ⊙ Electric shaver ℘ Hairdryer ✳ Ice Packs ⌂ Disabled facilities ⌂ Shop on site ⌂ Mobile shop ⌂ BBQ area ⌂ Picnic area WiFi Wi-fi ⌂ Internet access ♻ Recycling ⌂ Tourist info ⌂ Dog exercise area ⌂ Car hire can be arranged

SENNEN
Map 2 SW32

Trevedra Farm Caravan & Camping Site
►►►88%

tel: 01736 871818 & 871835 **TR19 7BE**
email: trevedra@btconnect.com
dir: *Take A30 towards Land's End. After junct with B3306 turn right into farm lane. (NB Sat Nav directs beyond site entrance to next lane which is unsuitable for caravans).*
grid ref: *SW368276*

A working farm with dramatic sea views over to the Scilly Isles, just a mile from Land's End. This popular campsite offers well-appointed toilets, a well-stocked shop, and a cooked breakfast or evening meal from the food bar. There is direct access to the coastal footpath, and two beautiful beaches are a short walk away. 8 acre site. 100 touring pitches. Caravan pitches. Motorhome pitches. Tent pitches.

Open: Etr or Apr-Oct **Last arrival:** 19.00hrs **Last departure:** 10.30hrs

Pitches: * ⊞ £17.50-£23 ⇔ £17.50-£23 ▲ £14.50-£21

Facilities: ⬚⊙🅟✳⟲🅢WiFi🖳♻🛈
Services: 🔌🅢🔋🗑🚽🍴🔌♨🛒🛠

Within 3 miles: 🛶🏊🅢🅢

Notes: No open fires, no noise 22.00hrs-08.00hrs. Dogs must be kept on leads. Fresh produce, newspapers.

AA Pubs & Restaurants nearby: The Tinners Arms, ZENNOR, TR26 3BY, 01736 796927

SUMMERCOURT
Map 2 SW85

Places to visit
Trerice, TRERICE, TR8 4PG, 01637 875404 www.nationaltrust.org.uk/trerice/

Blue Reef Aquarium, NEWQUAY, TR7 1DU, 01637 878134 www.bluereefaquarium.co.uk

Great for kids: Dairy Land Farm World, NEWQUAY, TR8 5AA, 01872 510246 www.dairylandfarmworld.com

Carvynick Country Club
RV ►►►► 93%

tel: 01872 510716 **TR8 5AF**
email: info@carvynick.co.uk
dir: *Accessed from A3058.* grid ref: *SW878564*

Set within the gardens of an attractive country estate and under new ownership, this spacious, dedicated American RV Park provides full facility pitches on hardstandings. The extensive on-site amenities, shared by the high-quality time share village, include an indoor leisure area with swimming pool, fitness suite, badminton court and a bar and restaurant serving good food. 47 touring pitches. 47 hardstandings. Caravan pitches. Motorhome pitches.

Open: all year **Pitches:** ⊞ ⇔
Leisure: 🏊🎯🎱 **Facilities:** ⊙🅟WiFi♻🛈
Services: 🔌🅢🔌🍴🛠

Within 3 miles: 🛶🅢🅢

Notes: Dogs must be kept on leads & exercised off site. 5-hole golf course, sauna.

AA Pubs & Restaurants nearby: The Plume of Feathers, MITCHELL, TR8 5AX, 01872 510387

TINTAGEL
Map 2 SX08

See also Camelford

Places to visit
Tintagel Castle, TINTAGEL, PL34 0HE, 01840 770328 www.english-heritage.org.uk/daysout/properties/tintagel-castle

Tintagel Old Post Office, TINTAGEL, PL34 0DB, 01840 770024 www.nationaltrust.org.uk/main/w-tintageloldpostoffice

Great for kids: Tamar Otter & Wildlife Centre, LAUNCESTON, PL15 8GW, 01566 785646 www.tamarotters.co.uk

Headland Caravan & Camping Park
►►►77%

tel: 01840 770239 **Atlantic Rd PL34 0DE**
email: headland.caravan@btconnect.com **web:** www.headlandcaravanpark.co.uk
dir: *From B3263 follow brown tourist signs through village to Headland.*
grid ref: *SX056887*

A peaceful family-run site in the mystical village of Tintagel, close to the ruins of King Arthur's Castle. There are two well-terraced camping areas with sea and countryside views, immaculately clean toilet facilities, and good, colourful planting across the park. The Cornish coastal path and the spectacular scenery are just two of the attractions here, and there are safe bathing beaches nearby. There are holiday statics for hire. 5 acre site. 62 touring pitches. Caravan pitches. Motorhome pitches. Tent pitches. 28 statics.

Open: Etr-Oct **Last arrival:** 21.00hrs

Pitches: * ⊞ £15-£18 ⇔ £14-£17 ▲ £15-£18

Leisure: 🎢

Facilities: ⬚⊙🅟✳🅢WiFi🛈
Services: 🔌🅢🔋🗑🚽♨🛠

Within 3 miles: 🎯🏊🅢🅢↻

Notes: Quiet after 23.00hrs. Dogs must be exercised off site. Dogs must be kept on leads.

AA Pubs & Restaurants nearby: The Port William, TREBARWITH, PL34 0HB, 01840 770230

PITCHES: ⊞ Caravans ⇔ Motorhomes ▲ Tents 🎪 Glamping accommodation **SERVICES:** 🔌 Electric hook up 🅢 Launderette 🍺 Licensed bar
🔋 Calor Gas ⊘ Camping Gaz 🅣 Toilet fluid 🍴 Café/Restaurant 🍟 Fast Food/Takeaway 🔋 Battery charging 🛒 Baby care 🛠 Motorvan service point
ABBREVIATIONS: BHs – bank holidays Etr – Easter Spring BH – Spring Bank Holiday fr – from hrs – hours m – mile mdnt – midnight
rdbt – roundabout rs – restricted service wk – week wknd – weekend x-roads – crossroads 🈯 No credit or debit cards ⊗ No dogs

TORPOINT
Map 3 SX45

Places to visit

Antony House, TORPOINT, PL11 2QA, 01752 812191
www.nationaltrust.org.uk/antony

Mount Edgcumbe House & Country Park, TORPOINT, PL10 1HZ, 01752 822236
www.mountedgcumbe.gov.uk

Great for kids: Wild Futures Monkey Sanctuary, LOOE, PL13 1NZ, 01503 262532
www.monkeysanctuary.org

Whitsand Bay Lodge & Touring Park
►►►► 82%

tel: 01752 822597 **Millbrook PL10 1JZ**
email: enquiries@whitsandbayholidays.co.uk
dir: From Torpoint take A374, left at Anthony onto B3247 for 1.25m to T-junct. Turn left, 0.25m, right into Cliff Rd. Site 2m on left. **grid ref:** SX410515

A very well-equipped park with panoramic coastal, sea and countryside views from its terraced pitches. A quality park with upmarket toilet facilities and other amenities. There is a guided historic walk around The Battery most Sundays, and a bus stop close by. 27 acre site. 49 touring pitches. 30 hardstandings. 15 seasonal pitches. Caravan pitches. Motorhome pitches. Tent pitches. 5 statics.

Open: all year (rs Sep-Mar opening hours at bar restricted) **Last arrival:** 19.00hrs **Last departure:** 10.00hrs

Pitches: 🚐 🚌 Å

Leisure: 🏊 🅰 ⛳ 🎣 🎵

Facilities: 🎣 🅿 ⊙ ✳ ⚲ 🛁 🔥 ☕ WiFi 💻 ♻ ❶ 🏕

Services: 🔌 🗑 🛒 🍴 🚿 ⚱ ✉ ⬇

Within 3 miles: ⚓ 🎣 🏌 ◎ ⛳ 💲 🏪 🔄 ⛵ U

Notes: Families & couples only. Dogs must be kept on leads. Chapel, library, heritage centre.

AA Pubs & Restaurants nearby: The Finnygook Inn, CRAFTHOLE, PL11 3BQ, 01503 230338

TRURO

See also Portscatho

Places to visit

Royal Cornwall Museum, TRURO, TR1 2SJ, 01872 272205
www.royalcornwallmuseum.org.uk

Trelissick, TRELISSICK, TR3 6QL, 01872 862090
www.nationaltrust.org.uk/trelissick

TRURO
Map 2 SW84

PREMIER PARK

Carnon Downs Caravan & Camping Park

►►►►► 96%

tel: 01872 862283 **Carnon Downs TR3 6JJ**
email: info@carnon-downs-caravanpark.co.uk
dir: Take A39 from Truro towards Falmouth. 1st left at Carnon Downs rdbt, site signed. **grid ref:** SW805406

A beautifully mature park set in meadowland and woodland close to the village amenities of Carnon Downs. The four toilet blocks provide exceptional facilities in bright modern surroundings. An extensive landscaping programme has been carried out to give more spacious pitch sizes, and there is an exciting children's playground with modern equipment, plus a football pitch. 33 acre site. 150 touring pitches. 80 hardstandings. Caravan pitches. Motorhome pitches. Tent pitches. 2 statics.

Open: all year **Last arrival:** 22.00hrs **Last departure:** 11.00hrs

Pitches: * 🚐 £24-£33 🚌 £24-£33 Å £24-£33

Leisure: 🅰

Facilities: 🚿 🎣 🅿 ⊙ 🔥 ✳ ⚲ 🛁 🔥 WiFi ♻ ❶ 🏕

Services: 🔌 🗑 🛒 ⚱ T ✉ ⬇

Within 3 miles: ⚓ 🎣 🏌 🏳 ⛳ 💲 🏪 🔄 U

Notes: No children's bikes in Jul & Aug. Babies' & children's bathroom.

AA Pubs & Restaurants nearby: The Pandora Inn, MYLOR BRIDGE, TR11 5ST, 01326 372678

Tabb's, TRURO, TR1 3BZ, 01872 262110

PREMIER PARK

Cosawes Park

►►►►► 84%

tel: 01872 863724 **Perranarworthal TR3 7QS**
email: info@cosawes.com
dir: Exit A39 midway between Truro & Falmouth. Direct access at site sign after Perranarworthal. **grid ref:** SW768376

A small touring park, close to Perranarworthal, in a peaceful wooded valley, midway between Truro and Falmouth, with a two-acre touring area. There are spotless toilet facilities (with underfloor heating) that include two smart family rooms. Its stunning location is ideal for visiting the many nearby hamlets and villages close to the Carrick Roads, a stretch of tidal water, which is a centre for sailing and other boats. 2 acre site. 59 touring pitches. 30 hardstandings. 15 seasonal pitches. Caravan pitches. Motorhome pitches. Tent pitches.

Open: all year **Last arrival:** 21.00hrs **Last departure:** 10.00hrs

Pitches: * 🚐 £17.50-£23.50 🚌 £17.50-£23.50 Å £13.50-£19.50

Facilities: 🎣 🅿 ⊙ 🔥 ✳ ⚲ 🛁 🔥 WiFi ♻ ❶ 🏕

Services: 🔌 🗑 🛒 T ✉ ⬇

Within 3 miles: ⚓ 🎣 🗓 🏳 ◎ ⛳ 💲 🏪 🔄 U

Notes: Dogs must be kept on leads.

AA Pubs & Restaurants nearby: The Pandora Inn, MYLOR BRIDGE, TR11 5ST, 01326 372678

LEISURE: 🏊 Indoor pool 🏊 Outdoor pool 🅰 Children's playground 🪁 Kid's club 🎾 Tennis court 🎱 Games room ⛳ Golf course ⛵ Boat hire 🚲 Cycle hire 🎬 Cinema 🎵 Entertainment 🎣 Fishing ⛳ Mini golf ⛳ Pitch n putt 🏄 Watersports 🏋 Gym 🏟 Sports field U Stables **FACILITIES:** 🛁 Bath 🚿 Shower 🅿 Private washing cubicles ⊙ Electric shaver 🔥 Hairdryer ✳ Ice Packs ♿ Disabled facilities 💲 Shop on site 🚐 Mobile shop 🔥 BBQ area 🔄 Picnic area WiFi Wi-fi 💻 Internet access ♻ Recycling ❶ Tourist info 🐕 Dog exercise area 🏕 Car hire can be arranged

Truro Caravan and Camping Park

►►►►►82%

tel: 01872 560274 **TR4 8QN**
email: info@trurocaravanandcampingpark.co.uk
dir: *Exit A390 at Threemilestone rdbt onto unclassified road towards Chacewater. Site signed on right in 0.5m.* **grid ref:** *SW772452*

An attractive south-facing and well-laid out park with spacious pitches, including good hardstandings, and quality modern toilets that are kept spotlessly clean. It is situated on the edge of Truro yet close to many beaches, with St Agnes just 10 minutes away by car. It is equidistant from both the rugged north coast and the calmer south coastal areas. There is a good bus service from the gate of the park to Truro. 8.5 acre site. 51 touring pitches. 26 hardstandings. Caravan pitches. Motorhome pitches. Tent pitches. 49 statics.

Open: all year **Last arrival:** 18.00hrs **Last departure:** 10.30hrs

Pitches: ⚏ ⚏ Å

Facilities: ☉ ℙ ⚓ ✳ ⚐ ㎡ WiFi 🖥 ♻ ❼

Services: ⚡🗑 🗑 ⬟ ⌀ Ⓣ ▦ �

Within 3 miles: ↓ 🎯 ℙ ◎ 🏧 🗑 ∪

Notes: Dogs must be kept on leads.

AA Pubs & Restaurants nearby: Old Ale House, TRURO, TR1 2HD, 01872 271122

Summer Valley

►►►82%

tel: 01872 277878 **Shortlanesend TR4 9DW**
email: sv@summervalley.co.uk
dir: *From Truro take B3284 to Shortlanesend (approx 3m). Through village, site on left.*
grid ref: *SW800479*

A very attractive and secluded site in a rural setting midway between the A30 and the cathedral city of Truro. The keen owners maintain the facilities to a good standard. 3 acre site. 60 touring pitches. Caravan pitches. Motorhome pitches. Tent pitches.

Open: Apr-Oct **Last arrival:** 20.00hrs **Last departure:** 11.00hrs

Pitches: * ⚏ £13.50-£18.50 ⚏ £13.50-£18.50 Å £13.50-£18.50

Leisure: 🎱 **Facilities:** ⚹ ☉ ℙ ✳ 🏧 ㎡ WiFi ♻ ❼

Services: ⚡🗑 ⬟ ⌀ Ⓣ ▦ **Within 3 miles:** ↓ 🎯 ℙ ◎ 🏧 🗑 ∪

Notes: No noise after 22.30hrs. Dogs must be kept on leads. Campers' lounge.

AA Pubs & Restaurants nearby: Old Ale House, TRURO, TR1 2HD, 01872 271122

WADEBRIDGE

Places to visit

Prideaux Place, PADSTOW, PL28 8RP, 01841 532411 www.prideauxplace.co.uk

Cornwall's Regimental Museum, BODMIN, PL31 1EG, 01208 72810

Great for kids: Pencarrow, BODMIN, PL30 3AG, 01208 841369
www.pencarrow.co.uk

Devon's Crealy Great Adventure Park, CLYST ST MARY, EX5 1DR, 01395 233200
www.crealy.co.uk

WADEBRIDGE Map 2 SW97

The Laurels Holiday Park

►►►►91%

tel: 01209 313474 **Padstow Rd, Whitecross PL27 7JQ**
email: info@thelaurelsholidaypark.co.uk **web:** www.thelaurelsholidaypark.co.uk
dir: *A39 onto A389 signed Padstow, follow signs. Site entrance 1st right.*
grid ref: *SW957715*

A very smart and well-equipped park with individual pitches screened by hedges and young shrubs. The enclosed dog walk is of great benefit to pet owners, and the Camel (cycle) Trail and Padstow are not far away. An excellent base if visiting the Royal Cornwall Showground. Four holiday cottages are also available. 2.2 acre site. 30 touring pitches. 4 hardstandings. 5 seasonal pitches. Caravan pitches. Motorhome pitches. Tent pitches.

Open: Etr or Apr-Oct **Last arrival:** 20.00hrs **Last departure:** 11.00hrs

Pitches: * ⚏ £19-£27 ⚏ £19-£27 Å £15-£23

Leisure: 🎱

Facilities: ⚹ ☉ ℙ ✳ 🏧 ㎡ WiFi 🖥 ♻ ❼

Services: ⚡🗑 ▦ **Within 3 miles:** ↓ 🎯 🎯 ℙ ≋ 🏧 🗑 ∪

Notes: Family park, no group bookings, no commercial vehicles. Dogs must be kept on leads. Wet suit dunking bath & drying area.

AA Pubs & Restaurants nearby: The Quarryman Inn, WADEBRIDGE, PL27 7JA, 01208 816444

See advert on page 124

WADEBRIDGE *continued*

St Mabyn Holiday Park

►►►► 90%

GOLD

tel: 01208 841677 **Longstone Rd, St Mabyn PL30 3BY**
email: info@stmabyn.co.uk
dir: *S of Camelford on A39, left after BP garage onto B3266 to Bodmin, 6m to Longstone, right at x-roads to St Mabyn, site approx 400mtrs on right.* **grid ref:** *SX055733*

A family-run site situated close to the picturesque market town of Wadebridge and within easy reach of Bodmin; it is centrally located for exploring both the north and south coasts of Cornwall. The park offers peace and tranquillity in a country setting and at the same time provides plenty of on-site activities including a swimming pool and children's play areas. Holiday chalets, fully-equipped holiday homes and a wooden pod (a 'camping snug') are available to rent, along with a choice of pitches. 12 acre site. 120 touring pitches. 49 hardstandings. Caravan pitches. Motorhome pitches. Tent pitches. 28 statics.

Open: Mar-Oct (rs 15 Mar-Spring BH & mid Sep-Oct swimming pool may be closed) **Last arrival:** 21.00hrs **Last departure:** 11.00hrs

Pitches: 🚐 🚍 ⛺ 🛖

Leisure: 🏊 🛝 🏓

Facilities: 🚿 [P] ⊙ 💨 ❄ ♿ [$] 🪑 🐕 [WiFi] 💻 ♻ ℹ

Services: 🚰 🧺 🛢 ⌀ [T] **Glamping:** **Wooden Pods** 1, £25-£35 Car by unit

Within 3 miles: ⛳ 🎣 [$] 🧺 🐎

Notes: Quiet from 23.00hrs-07.00hrs. Dogs must be kept on leads. Information book on arrival, freshly baked croissants & bread, small animal area with goats.

AA Pubs & Restaurants nearby: Trehellas House Hotel & Restaurant, BODMIN, PL30 3AD, 01208 72700

Lowarth Glamping

►►►► 84%

tel: 01208 812011 & 07733 272148 **Chapel Farm, Edmonton PL27 7JA**
email: avrilrea@gmail.com
dir: *A39 from Wadebridge towards Truro. After rdbt take 1st right signed Edmonton, pass Quarryman pub on right & cottages, 1st right, 300yds, 1st right at Lowarth sign.*
grid ref: *SW964727*

This site is in a secluded paddock in a peaceful location just outside Wadebridge and enjoys stunning panoramic views across rolling countryside towards Bodmin Moor. Avril Rea is the very proud owner and she does everything to ensure that a stay here will be a glamping holiday with a difference; high levels of customer care are assured. The six comfortable Lotus Belle tents, set in their own little garden ('lowarth' means garden in Cornish), are beautifully furnished in an understated, contemporary style, with comfortable double beds with duvets, soft rugs, a wood-burning stove plus a fully equipped kitchen annexe. There is a separate wooden cabin housing spotless unisex toilets and showers, a dish washing room and laundry, and a Shiatsu treatment cabin (with views across the Camel Estuary). A fire pit with seating proves popular for evening get togethers. 0.5 acre site.

Open: Apr-Sep **Last arrival:** 22.00hrs **Last departure:** 11.00hrs

Facilities: 🚿 [P] ⊙ ❄ [WiFi] ♻ ℹ

Services: 🧺 🛢 🛏

Glamping: **Lotus Belle tents** 6, £35-£77 (discount for 3 nights if Fri-Sun) Changeover day Sat Min stay 2 nights (Mon-Tue, Wed-Thu, Fri-Sat) Own kitchen

Within 3 miles: 🎬 🎣 [$] 🧺

Notes: 🚫🐕 No pets.

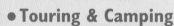

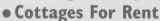

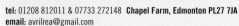

LEISURE: 🏊 Indoor pool 🏊 Outdoor pool 🛝 Children's playground 👋 Kid's club 🎾 Tennis court 🏓 Games room ⛳ Golf course ⛵ Boat hire 🚲 Cycle hire 🎬 Cinema 🎭 Entertainment 🎣 Fishing ◎ Mini golf ⛳ Pitch n putt 🌊 Watersports 🏋 Gym ⚽ Sports field 🐎 Stables **FACILITIES:** 🛁 Bath 🚿 Shower [P] Private washing cubicles ⊙ Electric shaver 💨 Hairdryer ❄ Ice Packs ♿ Disabled facilities [$] Shop on site 🚚 Mobile shop 🔥 BBQ area 🪑 Picnic area [WiFi] Wi-fi 💻 Internet access ♻ Recycling ℹ Tourist info 🐕 Dog exercise area 🚗 Car hire can be arranged

Little Bodieve Holiday Park
▶▶▶ 84%

tel: 01208 812323 **Bodieve Rd PL27 6EG**
email: info@littlebodieve.co.uk
dir: *From A39 rdbt on Wadebridge by-pass take B3314 signed Rock & Port Isaac, site 0.25m on right.* **grid ref:** *SW995734*

Rurally located with pitches in three large grassy paddocks, this family park is close to the Camel Estuary. The licensed clubhouse provides bar meals, with an entertainment programme in high season, and there is a swimming pool with sun terrace plus a separate waterslide and splash pool. This makes a good base from which to visit the Royal Cornwall Showground. 22 acre site. 195 touring pitches. Caravan pitches. Motorhome pitches. Tent pitches. 75 statics.

Open: Apr-Oct (rs Early & late season pool, shop & clubhouse closed)
Last arrival: 21.00hrs **Last departure:** 11.00hrs

Pitches: 🚐 🚎 ⛺

Leisure: 🏊 🎱 🎵

Facilities: ☉ 🅿 ⚒ ♿ ⑤ 🚿 🚽 WiFi 🖥 ♻ ❶

Services: 🔌 🅾 🚻 ♨ ⊘ T ⑩ 🍔 ⚡ 🚰

Within 3 miles: ♨ ☕ 🚴 ⚓ 🌊 ⑤ ⑤ ⛳

Notes: Families & couples only. Dogs must be kept on leads. Crazy golf.

AA Pubs & Restaurants nearby: The Quarryman Inn, WADEBRIDGE, PL27 7JA, 01208 816444

WATERGATE BAY	Map 2 SW86

PREMIER PARK

Watergate Bay Touring Park
▶▶▶▶▶ 89%

tel: 01637 860387 **TR8 4AD**
email: email@watergatebaytouringpark.co.uk
web: www.watergatebaytouringpark.co.uk
dir: *From Bodmin on A30 follow Newquay airport signs. Continue past airport, left at T-junct, site 0.5m on right. (NB for Sat Nav use TR8 4AE).* **grid ref:** *SW850653*

A well-established park above Watergate Bay, where acres of golden sand, rock pools and surf are all contribute to making this a holidaymakers' paradise. The toilet facilities are appointed to a high standard and include top quality family/disabled rooms; there is a well-stocked shop and café, an inviting swimming pool, and a wide range of activities including tennis. There is regular entertainment in the clubhouse and outdoor facilities are tailored for all ages.

continued

PITCHES: 🚐 Caravans 🚎 Motorhomes ⛺ Tents 🏕 Glamping accommodation **SERVICES:** 🔌 Electric hook up 🅾 Launderette 🍸 Licensed bar 🅰 Calor Gas ⊘ Camping Gaz T Toilet fluid ⑩ Café/Restaurant 🍔 Fast Food/Takeaway ⚡ Battery charging 🚼 Baby care ⛟ Motorvan service point **ABBREVIATIONS:** BHs – bank holidays Etr – Easter Spring BH – Spring Bank Holiday fr – from hrs – hours m – mile mdnt – midnight rdbt – roundabout rs – restricted service wk – week wknd – weekend x-roads – crossroads 🚫 No credit or debit cards 🚫 No dogs

WATERGATE BAY *continued*

30 acre site. 171 touring pitches. 14 hardstandings. Caravan pitches. Motorhome pitches. Tent pitches. 2 statics.

Watergate Bay Touring Park

Open: Mar-Nov (rs Mar-Spring BH & Sep-Oct restricted bar, café, shop & pool)
Last arrival: 22.00hrs **Last departure:** noon

Pitches: 🚐 🚏 ▲

Leisure: 🏊 🏄 ⚽ 🎯 🎵

Facilities: ⊙ 📷 ⚒ ♿ 🛗 🐕 WiFi 💻 ♻ ✪

Services: 🔌 🗑 🔧 💧 ⬭ T 🍴 ⬛ ⬆ ⬇

Within 3 miles: ♨ ⌖ ◎ ⛵ 🛒 🛒

Notes: Dogs must be kept on leads. Free mini bus to beach during main school holidays.

AA Pubs & Restaurants nearby: Fifteen Cornwall, WATERGATE BAY, TR8 4AA, 01637 861000

See advert on page 125

Piran Meadows Resort and Spa
HOLIDAY HOME PARK 94%

tel: 01726 860415 **TR8 4LW**
email: enquiries@piranmeadows.co.uk
dir: *From A30 take A392 toward Newquay. At x-roads in White Cross left, under rail bridge, site on right.* **grid ref:** SW889597

A stunning development that provides excellent standards and facilities for couples and families. Generously spaced, superbly equipped lodges and static holiday homes are equipped with both practical and thoughtful extras and have unrivalled countryside views. The stylish main building with a welcoming reception is decorated and furnished with quality and comfort, and the many facilities include a modern swimming pool, special areas and attractions for children, and the excellent Serenity Spa offering a wide range of treatments. The 'Go Active' sports programme has its own instructors and the restaurant with bar has a spacious exterior area for alfresco dining.

Open: 9 Feb-9 Jan

Changeover day: Mon, Fri & Sat

Arrival and departure times: Please contact the site

Statics: 104 Sleeps 6 Bedrms 2-3 Bathrms 1-2 (inc en suite) Toilets 1-2 Dishwasher Microwave Freezer TV Sky/FTV DVD Modem/Wi-fi Linen inc Towels inc Elec inc Gas inc Grass area Garden/patio furniture BBQ

Lodges: 11 Sleeps 8 Bedrms 3-4 Bathrms 2-3 (inc en suite) Toilets 2-3 Dishwasher Wash Machine T/drier Freezer TV Sky/FTV DVD Modem/Wi-fi Linen inc Towels inc Elec inc Gas inc Grass area Garden/patio furniture BBQ

Children: 🧒 Cots Highchair **Dogs:** 1 on leads

Leisure: 🏊 Spa 🏋 ⚽ ⚁

Within 3 miles: 🏊 Spa 🏋 ∪ ⌖

WIDEMOUTH BAY
Map 2 SS20

Widemouth Bay Caravan Park
HOLIDAY CENTRE 72%

tel: 01271 866766 **EX23 0DF**
email: bookings@jfhols.co.uk
dir: *From A39 take Widemouth Bay coastal road, turn left. Site on left.* **grid ref:** *SS199008*

A partly sloping rural site set in countryside overlooking the sea and one of Cornwall's finest beaches. There's nightly entertainment in the high season with an emphasis on children's and family club programmes. This park is located less than half a mile from the sandy beaches of Widemouth Bay. A superb base for surfing. One wooden pod and three safari tents are available for hire. 58 acre site. 220 touring pitches. 90 hardstandings. 4 seasonal pitches. Caravan pitches. Motorhome pitches. Tent pitches. 200 statics.

Open: Etr-Oct (rs Etr week pools & clubhouse closed) **Last arrival:** dusk
Last departure: 10.00hrs

Pitches: 🚐 🚗 🛖

Leisure: 🏊 ⚽ 🎱 🎵

Facilities: 🌳 📷 ⊙ 🅟 ✳ 🛒 🖐 ⑤ 🏧 🛒 WiFi 🖥 ♻ ❶

Services: 🔌 🗄 🍺 🍽 🕳 🚼

Within 3 miles: ⚓ ⛳ 🎣 🏕 🐎 ⊙ 🚣 🎱 ⛳ ∪

Notes: No noise after 23.00hrs. Dogs must be kept on leads. Crazy golf.

AA Pubs & Restaurants nearby: Bay View Inn, WIDEMOUTH BAY, EX23 0AW, 01288 361273

Cornish Coasts Caravan & Camping Park
►►►83%

tel: 01288 361380 **Middle Penlean, Poundstock, Bude EX23 0EE**
email: admin@cornishcoasts.co.uk
dir: *From Bude take A39 towards Wadebridge. Approx 5m to site on right (0.5m S of Rebel Cinema on left).* **grid ref:** *SS202981*

Situated on the A39 midway between Padstow and the beautiful surfing beaches of Bude and Widemouth Bay, this is a quiet park with lovely terraced pitches that make the most of the stunning views over the countryside to the sea. The reception is in a 13th-century cottage, and the park is well equipped and tidy, with the well maintained and quirky toilet facilities (note the mosaic vanity units) housed in a freshly painted older-style building. 3.5 acre site. 46 touring pitches. 8 hardstandings. Caravan pitches. Motorhome pitches. Tent pitches. 4 statics.

Open: Apr-Oct **Last arrival:** 22.00hrs **Last departure:** 10.30hrs

Pitches: 🚐 🚗 🛖

Facilities: ⊙ 🅟 ✳ 🛒 ⑤ WiFi ♻ ❶

Services: 🔌 🗄 🔋 🖊 T 🕳 🚼

Within 3 miles: ⚓ ⛳ 🎣 🏕 🐎 ⊙ 🚣 🎱 ⛳ ∪

Notes: Quiet after 22.00hrs. Dogs must be kept on leads. Post office.

AA Pubs & Restaurants nearby: Bay View Inn, WIDEMOUTH BAY, EX23 0AW, 01288 361273

Penhalt Farm Holiday Park
►►►75%

tel: 01288 361210 **EX23 0DG**
email: info@penhaltfarm.co.uk **web:** www.penhaltfarm.co.uk
dir: *From Bude on A39 take 2nd right to Widemouth Bay road, left at end by Widemouth Manor signed Millook onto coastal road. Site 0.75m on left.* **grid ref:** *SS194003*

Splendid views of the sea and coast can be enjoyed from all pitches on this sloping but partly level site, set in a lovely rural area on a working farm. About one mile away is one of Cornwall's finest beaches which proves popular with all the family as well as surfers. 8 acre site. 100 touring pitches. 12 hardstandings. Caravan pitches. Motorhome pitches. Tent pitches. 1 static.

Open: Etr-Oct

Pitches: 🚐 🚗 🛖

Leisure: 🎱

Facilities: 🌳 ⊙ 🅟 ✳ 🛒 ⑤ 🏧

Services: 🔌 🗄 🔋 🖊 🚼

Within 3 miles: ⚓ ⛳ 🎣 🅿 🚣 ⑤ ∪

Notes: No rollerblades, no noise after mdnt. Dogs must be kept on leads. Pool table, netball, air hockey & table tennis.

AA Pubs & Restaurants nearby: Bay View Inn, WIDEMOUTH BAY, EX23 0AW, 01288 361273

Prefer a child-free site?
See our list on page 45

PITCHES: 🚐 Caravans 🚗 Motorhomes 🛖 Tents 🏠 Glamping accommodation **SERVICES:** 🔌 Electric hook up 🗄 Launderette 🍺 Licensed bar 🔋 Calor Gas 🖊 Camping Gaz T Toilet fluid 🍽 Café/Restaurant 🕳 Fast Food/Takeaway 🔋 Battery charging 🚼 Baby care ⚡ Motorvan service point
ABBREVIATIONS: BHs – bank holidays Etr – Easter Spring BH – Spring Bank Holiday fr – from hrs – hours m – mile mdnt – midnight rdbt – roundabout rs – restricted service wk – week wknd – weekend x-roads – crossroads ⊘ No credit or debit cards ⊗ No dogs

Cumbria

Cumbria means the Lake District really – a rumpled, rugged landscape that is hard to beat for sheer natural beauty and grandeur. It is almost certainly England's best known and most scenic national park, famous for Lake Windermere, the country's largest lake, and Derwentwater, described as the 'Queen of the English Lakes.'

The Lake District is a region of Britain that leaves some visitors relaxed, others completely exhausted. The list of activities and places to visit is endless. The old adage 'always leave something to come back for' is certainly apt in this remote corner of the country.

This region has long been inextricably associated with poets, artists and writers. Not surprisingly, it was this beautiful countryside that inspired William Wordsworth, Samuel Taylor Coleridge, Arthur Ransome and Robert Southey. Born in the Cumbrian town of Cockermouth, Wordsworth and his sister Dorothy moved to Dove Cottage in Grasmere in 1799. Their annual rent was £5. The poet later moved to Rydal Mount in Ambleside, a family home with a 4-acre garden and a charming setting on the banks of Rydal Water. Today, both Dove Cottage and Rydal Mount are among the most visited of all the Lake District attractions. Another house with strong literary links is Hill Top, the 17th-century farmhouse home of Beatrix Potter who moved here in 1905. Located near Windermere, Hill Top and its surroundings sparked Potter's imagination and she painstakingly reproduced much of what she saw and cherished in her charming book illustrations. Tom Kitten, Samuel Whiskers and Jemima Puddleduck were all created here and the outstanding success of the recent film about Potter's life has introduced her extraordinary work to new audiences.

Walkers are spoilt for choice in Cumbria and the Lake District. The 70-mile Cumbria Way follows the valley floors rather than the mountain summits, while the 190-mile Coast to Coast has just about every kind of landscape and terrain imaginable. The route, pioneered by the well-known fell walker and writer Alfred Wainwright, cuts across the Lake District, the Yorkshire Dales and the North York Moors, spanning the width of England between St Bees on the Cumbrian west coast, and Robin Hood's Bay on the North Yorkshire and Cleveland Heritage Coast. The region is also popular with cyclists and there are a great many cycle hire outlets and plenty of routes available.

As with any popular scenic region of the country, the Lake District has an abundance of attractions but there are plenty of places within its boundaries and outside them where you can experience peace, tranquillity and a true sense of solitude. The southern half of Cumbria is often overlooked in favour of the more obvious attractions of the region. The Lune Valley, for example, remains as lovely as it was when Turner came here to paint. In the 19th century, writer John Ruskin described the view from 'The Brow', a walk running behind Kirkby Lonsdale's parish church, as 'one of the loveliest scenes in England.'

The Cumbrian coast is also one of the county's secret gems. Overlooking the Solway Firth and noted in the area for its wide cobbled streets and spacious green, the town of Silloth is one of the finest examples of a Victorian seaside resort in the north of England and yet outside Cumbria few people know its name. There are other historic towns along this coastline, including Whitehaven, Workington and Maryport. The Roman defences at Ravenglass are a reminder of the occupation, as is the Cumbrian section of Hadrian's Wall where it follows the county's northern coast. Well worth a visit is the ancient and historic city of Carlisle. Once a Roman camp – its wall still runs north of the city – it was captured during the Jacobean rising of 1745. The cathedral dates back to the early 12th century.

Lake Windermere ▷

CUMBRIA

AMBLESIDE

Map 18 NY30

Places to visit

The Armitt Museum & Library, AMBLESIDE, LA22 9BL, 015394 31212
www.armitt.com

Beatrix Potter Gallery, HAWKSHEAD, LA22 0NS, 015394 36269
www.nationaltrust.org.uk

PREMIER PARK

Skelwith Fold Caravan Park
▶▶▶▶▶ 91%

GOLD

tel: 015394 32277 **LA22 0HX**
email: info@skelwith.com
dir: From Ambleside on A593 towards Coniston, left at Clappersgate onto B5286 (Hawkshead road). Site 1m on right. **grid ref:** NY355029

In the grounds of a former mansion, this park is in a beautiful setting close to Lake Windermere. Touring areas are dotted in paddocks around the extensively wooded grounds, and the all-weather pitches are set close to the many facility buildings. The premium pitches are quite superb. There is a five-acre family recreation area, which has spectacular views of Loughrigg Fell. 130 acre site. 150 touring pitches. 130 hardstandings. 30 seasonal pitches. Caravan pitches. Motorhome pitches. 320 statics.

Open: Mar-15 Nov **Last arrival:** dusk **Last departure:** noon

Pitches: ⊞ ⊟

Leisure: ⊆ ⊕

Facilities: ⊙ ⌕ ☼ ⅙ ⑤ ⊞ ⟑ WIFI ▤ ♻

Services: ⊡⑤ ⬙ ⊘ T 🍖 ⬇

Within 3 miles: ⅃ ⧖ ⊞ ⌕ ◎ ⇙ ⑤⑤ ∪

Notes: Dogs must be kept on leads.

AA Pubs & Restaurants nearby: Wateredge Inn, AMBLESIDE, LA22 0EP, 015394 32332

Drunken Duck Inn, AMBLESIDE, LA22 0NG, 015394 36347

The Croft Caravan & Campsite
▶▶▶ 80%

GOLD

tel: 015394 36374 **North Lonsdale Rd, Hawkshead LA22 0NX**
email: enquiries@hawkshead-croft.com
dir: From B5285 in Hawkshead turn into site opposite main public car & coach park. **grid ref:** SD352981

In the historic village of Hawkshead, which is now a popular destination for Beatrix Potter fans, this former working farm has a large tent and touring field, bordering a beck and the sound of running water and birdsong are welcome distractions. Most pitches are fully serviced with water, electricity, TV hook-up and waste water disposal. The smart amenities block provides family bathrooms. In an adjoining field there are stylish wood-clad lodges. 5 acre site. 54 touring pitches. 26 hardstandings. Caravan pitches. Motorhome pitches. Tent pitches. 20 statics.

Open: Mar-Jan **Last arrival:** 20.30hrs **Last departure:** noon

Pitches: ⊞ ⊟ Å

Leisure: ◉

Facilities: ⬅ ⌕ PS ⊙ ⌕ ☼ ⅙ ⑥ WIFI ♻ ✪

Services: ⊡⑤ ⬇

Within 3 miles: ⌕ ⑤⑤

Notes: No noise 23.00hrs-07.00hrs. Dogs must be kept on leads.

AA Pubs & Restaurants nearby: The Queen's Head Inn & Restaurant, HAWKSHEAD, LA22 0NS, 015394 36271

Kings Arms, HAWKSHEAD, LA22 0NZ, 015394 36372

Hawkshead Hall Farm
▶▶▶ 80%

tel: 015394 36221 **Hawkshead LA22 0NN**
email: enquiries@hawksheadhall-campsite.com
dir: From Ambleside take A593 signed Coniston, then B5286 signed Hawkshead. Site signed on left just before Hawkshead. Or from Coniston take B5285 to T-junct. Left, then 1st right into site. **grid ref:** SD349988

A mainly camping site a few minutes' walk from village centre in a landscape of gentle rolling hills. The pitch sizes are generous and there's a very well-equipped, purpose-built amenities block, and a large comfortable TV and WiFi lounge with dining tables for campers during wet weather. Surrounded by unspoiled countryside, the adjoining fields are a delight for families, especially during the lambing season. 3 acre site. 55 touring pitches. Caravan pitches. Motorhome pitches. Tent pitches.

Open: Mar-Oct **Last arrival:** 21.00hrs **Last departure:** noon

Pitches: ⊞ ⊟ Å

Facilities: ⊙ ⌕ ☼ ⑥ ♻ ✪

Services: ⊡⑤

Within 3 miles: ⧖ ⌕ ⇙ ⑤⑤ ∪

Notes: No noise 23.00hrs-07.00hrs. Dogs must be kept on leads.

AA Pubs & Restaurants nearby: The Queen's Head Inn & Restaurant, HAWKSHEAD, LA22 0NS, 015394 36271

Kings Arms, HAWKSHEAD, LA22 0NZ, 015394 36372

Low Wray National Trust Campsite
▶▶▶ 80%

tel: 015394 32733 & 32039 **Low Wray LA22 0JA**
email: campsite.bookings@nationaltrust.org.uk
dir: 3m SW of Ambleside on A593 to Clappersgate, then B5286. Approx 1m left at Wray sign. Site approx 1m on left. **grid ref:** NY372013

Picturesquely set on the wooded shores of Lake Windermere, this site is a favourite with tenters and watersport enthusiasts. The toilet facilities are housed in wooden cabins, and tents can be pitched in wooded glades with lake views or open grassland; here there are wooden camping pods and a mini-reservation of tipis and solar-heated bell tents. In partnership with Quest 4 Adventure, many outdoor activities are available for families (bookable during school holidays). Fresh bread is now baked daily on site, and opposite the reception there is a rustic covered area with a pizza oven. 10 acre site. 140 touring pitches. Motorhome pitches. Tent pitches.

Open: wk before Etr-Oct **Last arrival:** variable **Last departure:** 11.00hrs

Pitches: ⊟ Å ⛺

Leisure: ⇙

Facilities: ⊙ ⌕ ☼ ⅙ ⑥ ⊞ ♻ ✪

LEISURE: ⚹ Indoor pool ⚹ Outdoor pool ⚁ Children's playground ⚓ Kid's club ⚏ Tennis court ◉ Games room ⚐ Golf course ⧖ Boat hire ⚟ Cycle hire ⊞ Cinema ♫ Entertainment ⌕ Fishing ◎ Mini golf ⚑ Pitch n putt ⇙ Watersports ⚐ Gym ⚘ Sports field ∪ Stables **FACILITIES:** ⬅ Bath ⌕ Shower PS Private washing cubicles ⊙ Electric shaver ⌕ Hairdryer ☼ Ice Packs ⅙ Disabled facilities ⑤ Shop on site ⚏ Mobile shop 🍖 BBQ area 🔲 Picnic area WIFI Wi-fi ▤ Internet access ♻ Recycling ✪ Tourist info ⟑ Dog exercise area ⛟ Car hire can be arranged

Services: ▣ 🗑⌀

Glamping: Bell tents 3 **Wooden Pods** 10 **Tipis** 12 **Gypsy Vardos** 2 **Berber tents:** 2

Within 3 miles: ⚓️Ⓗ⌀◎♨️🛁▣

Notes: No cars by tents. No groups larger than 4 unless a family group with children, no noise between 23.00hrs-07.00hrs. Dogs must be kept on leads. Launching area for sailing craft, orienteering course.

AA Pubs & Restaurants nearby: Wateredge Inn, AMBLESIDE, LA22 0EP, 015394 32332

Drunken Duck Inn, AMBLESIDE, LA22 0NG, 015394 36347

Kings Arms, HAWKSHEAD, LA22 0NZ, 015394 36372

Places to visit

Acorn Bank Garden and Watermill, TEMPLE SOWERBY, CA10 1SP, 017683 61893
www.nationaltrust.org.uk

Great for kids: Wetheriggs Animal Rescue & Conservation Centre, BARNARD CASTLE, DL12 9TY, 01833 627444 www.wetheriggsanimalrescue.co.uk

---

PREMIER PARK

Wild Rose Park
▶▶▶▶▶ 89%

tel: 017683 51077 **Ormside CA16 6EJ**
email: reception@wildrose.co.uk
dir: In Burrells on B6260 (between Appleby & Hoff) follow site signs. Left, site signed. **grid ref:** NY698165

Situated in the Eden Valley, this large leisure group-run park has been carefully landscaped and offers superb facilities maintained to an extremely high standard, including four wooden wigwams for hire. There are several individual pitches, and extensive views from most areas of the park. Traditional stone walls and the planting of lots of indigenous trees help the site to blend into the environment; wildlife is actively encouraged. There is a stylish reception with adjacent internet café, the Pennine View bar with slate floor and pub games (and where dogs are welcome) and a choice of adults-only and family entertainment rooms have all been added. Please note, tents are not accepted. 85 acre site. 226 touring pitches. 140 hardstandings. Caravan pitches. Motorhome pitches. 273 statics.

Open: all year (rs Nov-Mar shop closed, restaurant restricted hours, pool closed 6 Sep-27 May) **Last arrival:** 22.00hrs **Last departure:** 11.00hrs

Pitches: * 🚐 £25-£35 🚍 £25-£35 🏠 prices shown below

Leisure: 🏊👫🎱🎵

Facilities: 🏠🅿️⊙⌀✳️🔥🔥📶🖥️♻️⚙️

Services: 🔌🗑️🍴🍺🛢⌀🔋🍴🔋♿️🚼↻

Glamping: **Wooden Wigwams** 4, £35-£45 Changeover day Fri Own kitchen

Within 3 miles: 🚣⌀▣🛁

Notes: No unaccompanied teenagers, no group bookings, no noise after 22.30hrs, no dangerous dogs. Dogs must be kept on leads.

AA Pubs & Restaurants nearby: Tufton Arms Hotel, APPLEBY-IN-WESTMORLAND, CA16 6XA, 017683 51593

Appleby Manor Country House Hotel, APPLEBY-IN-WESTMORLAND, CA16 6JB, 017683 51571

Places to visit

The Dock Museum, BARROW-IN-FURNESS, LA14 2PW, 01229 876400
www.dockmuseum.org.uk

Furness Abbey, BARROW-IN-FURNESS, LA13 0PJ, 01229 823420
www.english-heritage.org.uk/daysout/properties/furness-abbey

Great for kids: South Lakes Safari Zoo, DALTON-IN-FURNESS, LA15 8JR, 01229 466086 www.safarizoo.co.uk

---

South End Caravan Park
▶▶▶ 86%

tel: 01229 472823 & 471556 **Walney Island LA14 3YQ**
email: enquiries@secp.co.uk **web:** www.walneyislandcaravanpark.co.uk
dir: M6 junct 36, A590 to Barrow, follow signs for Walney Island. Cross bridge, turn left. Site 6m south. **grid ref:** SD208628

A friendly family-owned and run park next to the sea and close to a nature reserve, on the southern end of Walney Island. It offers an extensive range of quality amenities including an adult lounge, and high standards of cleanliness and maintenance. 7 acre site. 50 touring pitches. 15 hardstandings. 34 seasonal pitches. Caravan pitches. Motorhome pitches. 250 statics.

Open: Mar-Oct (rs Mar-Etr & Oct pool closed) **Last arrival:** 22.00hrs **Last departure:** noon
Pitches: 🚐🚍 **Leisure:** 🏊👫🎱 **Facilities:** 🏠⊙✳️🔥🔥📶🖥️♻️
Services: 🔌🗑️🍴🍺🛢⌀🔋🍴 **Within 3 miles:** 🚣⌀▣🛁↻
Notes: Dogs must be kept on leads. Bowling green, snooker table.
AA Pubs & Restaurants nearby: The Stan Laurel Inn, ULVERSTON, LA12 0AB, 01229 582814

PITCHES: 🚐 Caravans 🚍 Motorhomes 🛖 Tents 🏠 Glamping accommodation **SERVICES:** 🔌 Electric hook up 🗑 Launderette 🍺 Licensed bar 🛢 Calor Gas ⌀ Camping Gaz 🔲 Toilet fluid 🍴 Café/Restaurant 🍴 Fast Food/Takeaway 🔋 Battery charging 🚼 Baby care ↻ Motorvan service point **ABBREVIATIONS:** BHs – bank holidays Etr – Easter Spring BH – Spring Bank Holiday fr – from hrs – hours m – mile mdnt – midnight rdbt – roundabout rs – restricted service wk – week wknd – weekend x-roads – crossroads 🚫 No credit or debit cards 🚫 No dogs

BOOT
Map 18 NY10

Places to visit

Hardknott Roman Fort, BOOT
http://www.english-heritage.org.uk/daysout/properties/hardknott-roman-fort

Great for kids: Ravenglass & Eskdale Railway, RAVENGLASS, CA18 1SW, 01229 717171 www.ravenglass-railway.co.uk

PREMIER PARK

Eskdale Camping & Caravanning Club Site
▶▶▶▶▶ 85%

tel: 019467 23253 & 0845 130 7633 *(Calls cost 7p per minute plus your phone company's access charge)* **CA19 1TH**
email: eskdale.site@thefriendlyclub.co.uk
dir: *Exit A595 at Gosforth or Holmrook to Eskdale Green, then signs for Boot. Site on left towards Hardknott Pass after railway, 150mtrs after Brook House Inn.*
grid ref: *NY179011*

Stunningly located in Eskdale, a feeling of peace and tranquillity prevails at this top quality campsite, with the sounds of running water and birdsong the only welcome distractions. Although mainly geared to campers, the facilities here are very impressive, with a smart amenities block, equipped with efficient modern facilities including an excellent fully serviced wet room-style, family room with power shower. The surrounding mountains, and the mature trees and shrubs create a wonderful 'back to nature' feeling. There's a nest of camping pods under the trees, with gravel paths and barbecues, a super backpackers' field and a self-catering camping barn for up to 8 people. Expect great attention to detail and a high level of customer care. The park is only a quarter of a mile from Boot station on the Ravenglass/Eskdale railway (La'al Ratty). 8 acre site. 100 touring pitches. Motorhome pitches. Tent pitches.

Open: Mar-14 Jan **Last arrival:** 20.00hrs **Last departure:** noon

Pitches: ⚐ Å ⛺

Leisure: ⚽

Facilities: ⚐ 🅿 ⊙ 🍴 ✳ ⅁ 🅂 🚻 📶 ♻ ❶ ☕

Services: ⚐ 🖾 🛢 🧺 🚽 🛒 ⚓

Glamping: Wooden Pods 10, £45.50 Car by unit

Within 3 miles: ⅃ ⌔ 🅂 🖾 ↻

Notes: Site gates closed & no noise 23.00hrs-07.00hrs, no open fires. Dogs must be kept on leads. Free drying room, hot & cold drinks station, toast & hot snacks.

AA Pubs & Restaurants nearby: Brook House Inn, BOOT, CA19 1TG, 019467 23288

BOWNESS-ON-WINDERMERE

Sites are listed under Windermere

CARLISLE
Map 18 NY35

Places to visit

Lanercost Priory, BRAMPTON, CA8 2HQ, 01697 73030
www.english-heritage.org.uk/daysout/properties/lanercost-priory

Tullie House Museum & Art Gallery Trust, CARLISLE, CA3 8TP, 01228 618718
www.tulliehouse.co.uk

Great for kids: Carlisle Castle, CARLISLE, CA3 8UR, 01228 591922
www.english-heritage.org.uk/daysout/properties/carlisle-castle

Green Acres Caravan Park
▶▶▶▶ 87%

tel: 01228 675418 & 07720 343820 **High Knells, Houghton CA6 4JW**
email: info@caravanpark-cumbria.com
dir: *M6 junct 44, A689 E towards Brampton for 1m. Left at Scaleby sign. Site 1m on left.*
grid ref: *NY416614*

A small, adults-only touring park in rural surroundings close to the M6 with distant views of the fells. A convenient stopover, this pretty park is run by keen, friendly owners who maintain high standards throughout. The site has a caravan and motorhome pressure-washer area, a field and woodland dog walk and two superb unisex shower rooms which include toilet and wash basin. 3 acre site. 35 touring pitches. 35 hardstandings. 17 seasonal pitches. Caravan pitches. Motorhome pitches. Tent pitches.

Open: Apr-Oct **Last arrival:** 21.00hrs **Last departure:** noon

Pitches: * ⚐ £17-£19 ⚐ £17-£19 Å £12-£16

Leisure: ⚽

Facilities: ⚐ 🅿 ⊙ 🍴 ✳ 🚻 📶 🖾 ♻ ❶

Services: ⚐ 🖾

Within 3 miles: ⅃ 🅂

Notes: Adults only. 🐕 Dogs must be kept on leads.

AA Pubs & Restaurants nearby: The Golden Fleece, IRTHINGTON, CA6 4NF, 01228 573686

Dandy Dinmont Caravan & Camping Park
▶▶▶ 88%

tel: 01228 674611 **Blackford CA6 4EA**
email: dandydinmont@btopenworld.com
dir: *M6 junct 44, A7 N. Site 1.5m on right after Blackford sign.* **grid ref:** *NY399620*

A sheltered, rural site, screened on two sides by hedgerows and only one mile from the M6 and Carlisle. The grass pitches are immaculately kept, and there are some larger hardstandings for motorhomes. This park attracts mainly adults; please note that cycling and ball games are not allowed. Touring customers are invited to view the private award-winning garden. 4.5 acre site. 47 touring pitches. 14 hardstandings. Caravan pitches. Motorhome pitches. Tent pitches. 15 statics.

Open: Mar-Oct **Last arrival:** 21.00hrs **Last departure:** noon

Pitches: ⚐ ⚐ Å

Facilities: ⊙ 🍴 ✳ 🚻 📶 ♻ ❶

Services: ⚐ 🖾 🛢 **Within 3 miles:** ⅃ ⌔ ◎ 🅂 🖾 ↻

Notes: Children's activities are restricted. Dogs must be kept on leads & exercised off site. Covered dishwashing area.

AA Pubs & Restaurants nearby: The Golden Fleece, IRTHINGTON, CA6 4NF, 01228 573686

CARTMEL
Map 18 SD37

Places to visit

Holker Hall & Gardens, HOLKER, LA11 7PL, 015395 58328 www.holker.co.uk

Hill Top, NEAR SAWREY, LA22 0LF, 015394 36269 www.nationaltrust.org.uk/hilltop

Great for kids: Lakes Aquarium, LAKESIDE, LA12 8AS, 015395 30153 www.lakesaquarium.co.uk

---

Greaves Farm Caravan Park
►►►82%

tel: 015395 36587 **Field Broughton LA11 6HR**
email: info@greavesfarmcaravanpark.co.uk
dir: *M6 junct 36, A590 signed Barrow. Approx 1m before Newby Bridge, turn left at end of dual carriageway signed Cartmel & Holker. Site 2m on left just before church.*
grid ref: SD391823

A small family-owned park close to a working farm in a peaceful rural area. Motorhomes are parked in a paddock which has spacious hardstandings, and there is a large field for tents and caravans. This simple park is carefully maintained, offers electric pitches (6amp), and there is always a sparkle to the toilet facilities. Static holiday caravans for hire. 3 acre site. 20 touring pitches. 9 hardstandings. Caravan pitches. Motorhome pitches. Tent pitches. 20 statics.

Open: Mar-Oct **Last arrival:** 21.00hrs **Last departure:** noon

Pitches: ⌖ ⌖ Å

Facilities: ☉ ℗ ⌗ ⌖ ♻ ❶

Services: ⌖ ⌖

Within 3 miles: ⌖ ⌖ ℗ ⌖ ↻

Notes: ⌖ Couples & families only. No open fires, no noise after 22.30hrs. Dogs must be kept on leads. Separate chalet for dishwashing, small freezer & fridge available.

AA Pubs & Restaurants nearby: Rogan & Company Restaurant, CARTMEL, LA11 6QD, 015395 35917

The Masons Arms, CARTMEL, LA11 6NW, 015395 68486

CROOKLANDS

Places to visit

Levens Hall, LEVENS, LA8 0PD, 015395 60321 www.levenshall.co.uk

RSPB Leighton Moss & Morecambe Bay Nature Reserve, SILVERDALE, LA5 0SW, 01524 701601 www.rspb.org.uk/leightonmoss

---

CROOKLANDS
Map 18 SD58

Waters Edge Caravan Park
►►►►82%

tel: 015395 67708 & 67527 **LA7 7NN**
email: stay@watersedgecaravanpark.co.uk
dir: *M6 junct 36, A65 towards Kirkby Lonsdale, at 2nd rdbt follow signs for Crooklands & Endmoor. Site 1m on right at Crooklands garage, just beyond 40mph limit.*
grid ref: SD533838

A peaceful, well-run park close to the M6, pleasantly bordered by streams and woodland. A Lakeland-style building houses a shop and bar, and the attractive toilet block is clean and modern. This is ideal either as a stopover or for longer stays. 3 acre site. 26 touring pitches. 26 hardstandings. 8 seasonal pitches. Caravan pitches. Motorhome pitches. Tent pitches. 21 statics.

Open: Mar-14 Nov (rs Low season - bar not always open on weekdays)
Last arrival: 22.00hrs **Last departure:** noon

Pitches: * ⌖ £17.90-£26.90 ⌖ £17.90-£26.90 Å £10-£27.50

Leisure: ⌖

Facilities: ⌖ ⌖ ☉ ℗ ⌗ ⌖ ⌖ ⌖ ⌖ WiFi ⌖ ❶

Services: ⌖ ⌖ ⌖ ⌖ ⌖ ⌖ T

Within 3 miles: ℗ ⌖ ↻

Notes: No cars by tents. No noise after mdnt. Dogs must be kept on leads.

AA Pubs & Restaurants nearby: Plough Inn, LUPTON, LA6 1PJ, 015395 67700

CUMWHITTON
Map 18 NY55

Places to visit

Lanercost Priory, BRAMPTON, CA8 2HQ, 01697 73030 www.english-heritage.org.uk/daysout/properties/lanercost-priory

---

Cairndale Caravan Park
►►►69%

tel: 01768 896280 **CA8 9BZ**
dir: *Exit A69 at Warwick Bridge on unclassified road through Great Corby to Cumwhitton, left at village sign, site 1m.* **grid ref:** NY518523

Lovely grass site set in the tranquil Eden Valley with good views to distant hills. The all-weather touring pitches have electricity, and are located close to the immaculately maintained toilet facilities. Static holiday caravans for hire. 2 acre site. 5 touring pitches. 5 hardstandings. Caravan pitches. Motorhome pitches. 15 statics.

Open: Mar-Oct **Last arrival:** 22.00hrs

Pitches: ⌖ ⌖

Facilities: ⌖ ☉ ⌗ ♻

Services: ⌖ ⌖ ⌖

Within 3 miles: ⌖ ⌖ ℗ ⌖

Notes: ⌖

AA Pubs & Restaurants nearby: The String of Horses Inn, FAUGH, CA8 9EG, 01228 670297

PITCHES: ⌖ Caravans ⌖ Motorhomes Å Tents ⌖ Glamping accommodation **SERVICES:** ⌖ Electric hook up ⌖ Launderette ⌖ Licensed bar ⌖ Calor Gas ⌖ Camping Gaz T Toilet fluid ⌖ Café/Restaurant ⌖ Fast Food/Takeaway ⌖ Battery charging ⌖ Baby care ⌖ Motorvan service point
ABBREVIATIONS: BHs – bank holidays Etr – Easter Spring BH – Spring Bank Holiday fr – from hrs – hours m – mile mdnt – midnight
rdbt – roundabout rs – restricted service wk – week wknd – weekend x-roads – crossroads ⌖ No credit or debit cards ⌖ No dogs

FLOOKBURGH
Map 18 SD37

Places to visit
Holker Hall & Gardens, HOLKER, LA11 7PL, 015395 58328 www.holker.co.uk

Lakeland Leisure Park
HOLIDAY CENTRE 87%
GOLD

tel: 01539 558556 **Moor Ln LA11 7LT**
email: lakeland@haven.com **web:** www.haven.com/lakeland
dir: *On B5277 through Grange-over-Sands to Flookburgh. Left at village square, site 1m.*
grid ref: *SD372743*

A complete leisure park with full range of activities and entertainment, making this flat, grassy site ideal for families. The touring area, which includes 24 fully-serviced pitches, is quietly situated away from the main amenities, but the swimming pools and evening entertainment are just a short stroll away. There is a lake offering water sporting opportunities. 105 acre site. 177 touring pitches. 24 hardstandings. Caravan pitches. Motorhome pitches. Tent pitches. 800 statics.

Open: mid Mar-end Oct (rs mid Mar-May & Sep-Oct reduced activities, outdoor pool closed) **Last arrival:** anytime **Last departure:** 10.00hrs

Pitches: 🚐 🚙 ▲
Leisure: 🏊 🏊 🖐 🎾 ⚽ 🎵 ♪🎯
Facilities: ♠ ⊙ 🚿 ⚿ 🛒 🚽 ♨ 🅿 📺 ♻ ❶

Services: 🔌 🔋 🔧 🛢 T 🍴 ♨
Within 3 miles: ⅃ 🎣 ◎ ⛸ 🛒 🅿 ♻ ⛵

Notes: No cars by caravans or tents. No commercial vehicles, no bookings by persons under 21yrs unless a family booking. Max 2 dogs per booking, certain dog breeds banned. Dogs must be kept on leads.

AA Pubs & Restaurants nearby: Rogan & Company Restaurant, CARTMEL, LA11 6QD, 015395 35917

The Masons Arms, CARTMEL, LA11 6NW, 015395 68486

See advert on opposite page

GRANGE-OVER-SANDS
Map 18 SD47

See also Cartmel

Oak Head Caravan Park
▶▶▶ 80%

tel: 015395 31475 **Ayside LA11 6JA**
email: oakheadcaravanpark@btconnect.com
dir: *M6 junct 36, A590 towards Newby Bridge, 14m. From A590 bypass follow signs for Ayside.* **grid ref:** *SD389839*

Three miles from Grange-over-Sands and with direct access from A590 south of Newby Bridge, this is a pleasant terraced site with two separate areas – grass for tents and all gravel pitches for caravans and motorhomes. The site is enclosed within mature woodland and surrounded by hills; it is located in a less busy area but convenient for all the Lake District attractions. 10 acre site. 60 touring pitches. 30 hardstandings. Caravan pitches. Motorhome pitches. Tent pitches. 71 statics.

Open: Mar-Oct **Last arrival:** 20.00hrs **Last departure:** noon

Pitches: 🚐 🚙 ▲
Leisure: ⚽
Facilities: ♠ 🅿 ⊙ 🚿 ⚿ ♨ 🚽
Services: 🔌 🔋 🛒 ♨ ❷
Within 3 miles: ⅃ ⅄ 🎣 ⛸ 🅿 ⛵

Notes: No open fires, no noise after 23.00hrs. Dogs must be kept on leads.

AA Pubs & Restaurants nearby: The Cavendish Arms, CARTMEL, LA11 6QA, 015395 36240

The Masons Arms, CARTMEL, LA11 6NW, 015395 68486

Rogan & Company Restaurant, CARTMEL, LA11 6QD, 015395 35917

LEISURE: 🏊 Indoor pool 🏊 Outdoor pool 🎢 Children's playground 🖐 Kid's club 🎾 Tennis court 🎱 Games room 🏌 Golf course ⛵ Boat hire 🚲 Cycle hire 🎬 Cinema 🎵 Entertainment 🎣 Fishing ◎ Mini golf ⛳ Pitch n putt 🏄 Watersports 🏋 Gym ♻ Sports field ⛵ Stables **FACILITIES:** 🛁 Bath 🚿 Shower 🅿 Private washing cubicles ⊙ Electric shaver 🪮 Hairdryer ❄ Ice Packs ♿ Disabled facilities 🛒 Shop on site 📷 Mobile shop 🍖 BBQ area 🪑 Picnic area 📶 Wi-fi 💻 Internet access ♻ Recycling ❶ Tourist info 🐕 Dog exercise area 🚗 Car hire can be arranged

GREAT LANGDALE
Map 18 NY20

Great Langdale National Trust Campsite
►►►77%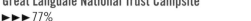

tel: 015394 63862 & 32733 **LA22 9JU**
email: campsite.bookings@nationaltrust.org.uk
dir: From Ambleside, A593 to Skelwith Bridge, right onto B5343, approx 5m to New Dungeon Ghyll Hotel. Site on left 500mtrs after hotel. **grid ref:** NY286059

Situated in a green valley, sheltered by mature trees and surrounded by stunning fell views, this site is an ideal base for campers, climbers and fell walkers. The large grass tent area has some gravel parking for cars, and there is a separate area for groups, and one for families that has a children's play area. Attractive wooden cabins house the toilets, the reception and shop (selling fresh baked bread and pastries), and drying rooms, and there are wooden camping pods, three yurts and three tipis for hire. It is a gentle 10-minute walk to The Sticklebarn Tavern, the only National Trust run pub. 9 acre site. 220 touring pitches. Motorhome pitches. Tent pitches.

Open: all year **Last departure:** 11.00hrs

Pitches: ⌖ 🅰 🏕

Facilities: ☉ ⚙ ⅙ 🖪 ♻

Services: 🖥 🔋 ⌀

Glamping: Wooden Pods 9, £35-£57.50 Min stay 2 nights **Tipis** 3 **Yurts** 3

Within 3 miles: 🖉 🖪

Notes: No cars by tents. No noise between 23.00hrs-07.00hrs, no groups of 4 or more unless a family with children. Dogs must be kept on leads.

AA Pubs & Restaurants nearby: The Britannia Inn, ELTERWATER, LA22 9HP, 015394 37210

HOLMROOK
Map 18 SD09

Places to visit
Great for kids: Ravenglass & Eskdale Railway, RAVENGLASS, CA18 1SW, 01229 717171 www.ravenglass-railway.co.uk

Seven Acres Caravan Park
►►►78%

tel: 01946 822777 **CA19 1YD**
email: reception@seacote.com
dir: Site signed on A595 between Holmrook & Gosforth. **grid ref:** NY078014

This sheltered park is close to quiet west Cumbrian coastal villages and beaches, and also handy for Eskdale and Wasdale. There is a good choice of pitches, some with hedged bays for privacy and some with coastal views. The park has a heated toilet block. 7 acre site. 37 touring pitches. 20 hardstandings. Caravan pitches. Motorhome pitches. Tent pitches. 16 statics.

Open: Mar-15 Jan **Last arrival:** 21.00hrs **Last departure:** 10.30hrs

Pitches: ⌺ ⌖ 🅰

Facilities: ☉ 🅿 ⚙ 🗂 ⌁ ♻ 🛈

Services: 🔌🖥 ⌀

Within 3 miles: ⌁ 🖉 ◎ 🖥 ∪

Notes: Dogs must be kept on leads.

AA Pubs & Restaurants nearby: Brook House Inn, BOOT, CA19 1TG, 019467 23288
Bridge Inn, SANTON BRIDGE, CA19 1UX, 019467 26221

KESWICK

Map 18 NY22

Places to visit

The Pencil Museum, KESWICK, CA12 5NG, 017687 73626
www.pencilmuseum.co.uk

Honister Slate Mine, BORROWDALE, CA12 5XN, 01768 777230
www.honister-slate-mine.co.uk

Great for kids: Mirehouse, KESWICK, CA12 4QE, 017687 72287
www.mirehouse.com

REGIONAL WINNER – NORTH WEST ENGLAND
AA CAMPSITE OF THE YEAR 2017

PREMIER PARK

Castlerigg Hall Caravan & Camping Park
▶▶▶▶▶90%

GOLD

tel: 017687 74499 **Castlerigg Hall CA12 4TE**
email: info@castlerigg.co.uk web: www.castlerigg.co.uk
dir: *1.5m SE of Keswick on A591, turn right at sign. Site 200mtrs on right past Heights Hotel.* **grid ref:** *NY282227*

Spectacular views over Derwent Water to the mountains beyond are among the many attractions at this lovely Lakeland park. Old farm buildings have been tastefully converted into excellent toilets with private washing cubicles and a family bathroom, reception and a well-equipped shop, and there is a kitchen/dining area for campers, and a restaurant/takeaway. There is a superb toilet block, and wooden camping pods and a further ten all-weather pitches are located in the tent field. 8 acre site. 68 touring pitches. 68 hardstandings. Caravan pitches. Motorhome pitches. Tent pitches. 30 statics.

Castlerigg Hall Caravan & Camping Park

Open: mid Mar-7 Nov **Last arrival:** 21.00hrs **Last departure:** 11.30hrs

Pitches: 🚐 £20-£37 🚚 £20-£37 ▲ £19-£29 🏠 prices shown below

Leisure: ⚽ 🎯

Facilities: 🛁 🚿 🅿 ⊙ 🗝 ✳ ♿ ⑤ 🖅 WiFi ♻ ❶ 🚗

Services: 🚽 🔌 🛢 🚮 🇹 🍴 🖼 ♨ ⚒

Glamping: **Wooden Pods** 7, £45-£68 Car by unit

Within 3 miles: 🎣 ⛳ 🏇 ◉ 🚲 🚤 U

Notes: Dogs must not be left unattended, no noise after 22.30hrs. Dogs must be kept on leads. Campers' kitchen, sitting room, gallery.

AA Pubs & Restaurants nearby: The Kings Head, KESWICK, CA12 4TN, 017687 72393

See advert below

LEISURE: 🏊 Indoor pool 🏊 Outdoor pool 🅰 Children's playground 🧒 Kid's club 🎾 Tennis court ♟ Games room ⛳ Golf course 🚣 Boat hire 🚲 Cycle hire 🎬 Cinema 🎵 Entertainment 🎣 Fishing ◉ Mini golf 🏌 Pitch n putt 🏄 Watersports 💪 Gym 🏟 Sports field U Stables **FACILITIES:** 🛁 Bath 🚿 Shower 🅿 Private washing cubicles ⊙ Electric shaver 🗝 Hairdryer ✳ Ice Packs ♿ Disabled facilities ⑤ Shop on site 🏪 Mobile shop 🍖 BBQ area 🪑 Picnic area 📶 Wi-fi 🖥 Internet access ♻ Recycling ❶ Tourist info 🐕 Dog exercise area 🚗 Car hire can be arranged

Burns Farm Caravan Park
▶▶▶ 77%

tel: 017687 79225 & 79112 **St Johns in the Vale CA12 4RR**
email: linda@burns-farm.co.uk **web:** www.burns-farm.co.uk
dir: *Exit A66 signed Castlerigg Stone Circle, Youth Centre & Burns Farm. Site on right in 0.5m.* **grid ref:** NY307244

Lovely views of Blencathra and Skiddaw can be enjoyed from this secluded park, set on a working farm which extends a warm welcome to families. This is a good choice for exploring the beautiful and interesting countryside. Pub food available in Threlkeld. 2.5 acre site. 32 touring pitches. Caravan pitches. Motorhome pitches. Tent pitches.

Open: Mar-4 Nov **Last departure:** noon (peak season)

Pitches: ⌂ ⌂ ⅄

Facilities: ⌂ ⌂ ⊙ ✳ ⅄ ⅢⅢ ⌂

Services: ⌂ ⌂ ⌂ ⌂

Within 3 miles: ⅄ ⅄ ⅄ ⅄ ⊚ ⅄ ⅄ ⅄ ∪

Notes: ⊚ No noise after mdnt. Dogs must be kept on leads.

AA Pubs & Restaurants nearby: The Horse & Farrier Inn, KESWICK, CA12 4SQ, 017687 79688

PREMIER PARK

Woodclose Caravan Park
▶▶▶▶▶ 87%

tel: 015242 71597 **High Casterton LA6 2SE**
email: info@woodclosepark.com **web:** www.woodclosepark.com
dir: *On A65, 0.25m after Kirkby Lonsdale towards Skipton, park on left.*
grid ref: SD618786

A peaceful, well-managed park set in idyllic countryside within the beautiful Lune Valley, and centrally located for exploring the Lakes and Dales. Ideal for that 'back to nature' experience, with riverside walks, on-site woodland walks for both families and dogs, and top notch amenities blocks with fully serviced cubicles with one allocated for the wigwam pod village and camping field. The generous pitches are surrounded by mature trees and seasonal planting. Parts of the site are havens for wildlife. 9 acre site. 22 touring pitches. 20 hardstandings. 22 seasonal pitches. Caravan pitches. Motorhome pitches. Tent pitches. 85 statics.

Open: Mar-Oct **Last arrival:** 21.00hrs (no arrivals before 13.00hrs)
Last departure: noon

Pitches: ⌂ ⌂ ⅄ ⋔

Leisure: ⌂ ⌂

Facilities: ⌂ ⌂ ⊙ ⌂ ✳ ⅄ ⌂ ⌂ ⌂ ⅢⅢ ⌂ ⌂ ⌂ ⌂ ⌂

Services: ⌂ ⌂ ⌂ ⌂ ⅄

Glamping: **Wooden Wigwams** 10, Min stay 1 night (3 nights in peak season & BHs) Own kitchen

Within 3 miles: ⅄ ⌂ ⌂ ⌂ ∪

Notes: No cars by tents. Tents only permitted on certain dates Apr-Sep (contact site for details). Dogs must be kept on leads. Crock boxes for hire.

AA Pubs & Restaurants nearby: The Sun Inn, KIRKBY LONSDALE, LA6 2AU, 01524 271965

The Pheasant Inn, KIRKBY LONSDALE, LA6 2RX, 01524 271230

KIRKBY LONSDALE *continued*

New House Caravan Park
►►►► 82%

tel: 015242 71590 **LA6 2HR**
email: colinpreece9@aol.com
dir: *1m SE of Kirkby Lonsdale on A65, turn right into site entrance 300yds past Whoop Hall Inn.* **grid ref:** *SD628774*

Colourful floral displays greet new arrivals, creating an excellent first impression at this former farm, which has been carefully changed to provide well-spaced pitches, with hardstandings sheltered by surrounding mature trees and shrubs. An ideal base for exploring the Yorkshire Dales and the Lake District. 3 acre site. 50 touring pitches. 50 hardstandings. Caravan pitches. Motorhome pitches.

Open: Mar-Oct **Last arrival:** 21.00hrs **Last departure:** noon

Pitches: * ⊞ £18 ⊞ £18

Facilities: ⬤⬤⬤⬤⬤⬤⬤⬤⬤ 🚐⬤⬤

Services: ⬤⬤⬤⬤⬤⬤⬤⬤

Within 3 miles: ⬤⬤⬤⬤

Notes: ⬤ No cycling. Dogs must be kept on leads.

AA Pubs & Restaurants nearby: The Sun Inn, KIRKBY LONSDALE, LA6 2AU, 01524 271965

The Pheasant Inn, KIRKBY LONSDALE, LA6 2RX, 01524 271230

MEALSGATE   Map 18 NY24

Places to visit

Jennings Brewery Tour and Shop, COCKERMOUTH, CA13 9NE, 01900 820362 www.jenningsbrewery.co.uk

Wordsworth House and Garden, COCKERMOUTH, CA13 9RX, 01900 824805 www.nationaltrust.org.uk/wordsworthhouse

---

Larches Caravan Park
►►► 84%

tel: 016973 71379 **CA7 1LQ**
dir: *On A595 (Carlisle to Cockermouth road).* **grid ref:** *NY205415*

This over 18s-only park is set in wooded rural surroundings on the fringe of the Lake District National Park. Touring units are spread out over two sections. The friendly family-run park offers constantly improving facilities, including a well-stocked shop that also provides a very good range of camping and caravanning spares. 20 acre site. 35 touring pitches. 30 hardstandings. Caravan pitches. Motorhome pitches. Tent pitches.

Open: Mar-Oct (rs Early & late season) **Last arrival:** 21.30hrs **Last departure:** noon

Pitches: ⊞⊞ Å

Facilities: ⬤⬤⬤⬤⬤⬤⬤⬤🚐⬤

Services: ⬤⬤⬤⬤⬤⬤⬤

Within 3 miles: ⬤⬤⬤⬤

Notes: Adults only. ⬤ Dogs must be kept on leads.

AA Pubs & Restaurants nearby: The Pheasant, BASSENTHWAITE LAKE, CA13 9YE, 017687 76234

MILNTHORPE   Map 18 SD48

Places to visit

RSPB Leighton Moss & Morecambe Bay Nature Reserve, SILVERDALE, LA5 0SW, 01524 701601 www.rspb.org.uk/leightonmoss

Levens Hall, LEVENS, LA8 0PD, 015395 60321 www.levenshall.co.uk

Hall More Caravan Park
►►►► 77%

tel: 01524 781453 & 784221 **Hale LA7 7BP**
email: enquiries@pureleisure-holidays.co.uk
dir: *M6 junct 35, A6 towards Milnthorpe for 4m. Left at Lakeland Wildlife Oasis, follow brown signs.* **grid ref:** *SD502771*

Major investment has increased facilities and standards on this long-established holiday destination. Set on former meadowland and surrounded by mature trees, this constantly improving rural park provides neat, well-spaced pitches with colourful hedged areas enhanced by pretty seasonal flowers. The site is adjacent to a fishery where fly-fishing for trout is possible, and a farm with stables that offers pony trekking is nearby. There are seven wooden camping pods for hire. 4 acre site. 44 touring pitches. 7 hardstandings. Caravan pitches. Motorhome pitches. Tent pitches. 60 statics.

Open: Mar-Jan **Last arrival:** 22.00hrs **Last departure:** 10.00hrs

Pitches: ⊞⊞ Å ⋔

Leisure: ⬤ ⬤

Facilities: ⬤⬤⬤⬤⬤

Services: ⬤⬤⬤⬤⬤⬤⬤

Glamping: Wooden Pods 7

Within 3 miles: ⬤⬤⬤⬤⬤

AA Pubs & Restaurants nearby: The Wheatsheaf at Beetham, BEETHAM, LA7 7AL, 015395 62123

NETHER WASDALE   Map 18 NY10

Places to visit

Ravenglass & Eskdale Railway, RAVENGLASS, CA18 1SW, 01229 717171 www.ravenglass-railway.co.uk

Hardknott Roman Fort, BOOT http://www.english-heritage.org.uk/daysout/properties/hardknott-roman-fort

Church Stile Farm & Holiday Park
►►►► 80%

tel: 01946 726252 & 726028 **Church Stile CA20 1ET**
email: info@churchstile.com
dir: *M6 junct 36, (follow signs for Western Lakes) A590, A5092, A595 (towards Whitehaven). In Gosforth follow Nether Wasdale signs. Pass 2 pubs. Site immediately after church.* **grid ref:** *NY125040*

A superb secluded park surrounded by mature trees, hedging and Lakeland stone walling in a peaceful valley setting. The combination of indigenous trees, flora and fauna creates stunning displays to complement the beauty of the surrounding hills. A renowned farm shop with a wide range of local produce is situated within the stylish reception and café. The site now offers two shepherd's huts for hire. 10 acre

---

LEISURE: ⬤ Indoor pool ⬤ Outdoor pool ⬤ Children's playground ⬤ Kid's club ⬤ Tennis court ⬤ Games room ⬤ Golf course ⬤ Boat hire ⬤ Cycle hire ⬤ Cinema ⬤ Entertainment ⬤ Fishing ⬤ Mini golf ⬤ Pitch n putt ⬤ Watersports ⬤ Gym ⬤ Sports field ⬤ Stables **FACILITIES:** ⬤ Bath ⬤ Shower ⬤ Private washing cubicles ⬤ Electric shaver ⬤ Hairdryer ⬤ Ice Packs ⬤ Disabled facilities ⬤ Shop on site ⬤ Mobile shop ⬤ BBQ area ⬤ Picnic area ⬤ Wi-fi ⬤ Internet access ⬤ Recycling ⬤ Tourist info ⬤ Dog exercise area ⬤ Car hire can be arranged

site. 50 touring pitches. 13 hardstandings. Motorhome pitches. Tent pitches. 47 statics.

Open: Mar-15 Nov **Last arrival:** 21.00hrs **Last departure:** 11.00hrs

Pitches: * 🚌 £17-£20.50 ⛺ £17-£24.50 🛖 prices shown below

Leisure: 🛝 ⚽

Facilities: 🚿 ⊙ 💨 ✲ ♿ [S] 🪑 🐕 [WiFi] 💻 ♻ ℹ

Services: 🔌 🧺 🔥 🍴 🍼

Glamping: **Shepherd's Huts** 2, £37.50-£50 Changeover day Fri, Sat, Mon Min stay 3 nights Car by unit

Within 3 miles: 🎣 ≋ [S] 🧺 U

Notes: No noise after 23.30hrs. Dogs must be kept on leads. Picnic tables, table tennis.

AA Pubs & Restaurants nearby: Wasdale Head Inn, WASDALE HEAD, CA20 1EX, 019467 26229

Bridge Inn, SANTON BRIDGE, CA19 1UX, 019467 26221

PATTERDALE — Map 18 NY31

Sykeside Camping Park

►►► 80%

tel: 017684 82239 **Brotherswater CA11 0NZ**
email: info@sykeside.co.uk
dir: *Direct access from A592 (Windermere to Ullswater road) at foot of Kirkstone Pass.* **grid ref:** *NY403119*

A camper's delight, this family-run park is sited at the foot of Kirkstone Pass, under the 2,000ft Hartsop Dodd in a spectacular area with breathtaking views. The park has mainly grass pitches with a few hardstandings and for those campers without a tent there is bunkhouse accommodation. There's a small campers' kitchen and the bar serves breakfast and bar meals. There is abundant wildlife. 10 acre site. 86 touring pitches. 25 hardstandings. Caravan pitches. Motorhome pitches. Tent pitches.

Open: all year **Last arrival:** 22.30hrs **Last departure:** 14.00hrs

Pitches: * 🚐 £18-£24 🚌 £18-£24 ⛺ £14-£22

Facilities: 🚿 ⊙ 💨 ✲ [S] 🪑 🐕 [WiFi] 💻 ♻ ℹ

Services: 🔌 🧺 🍷 🛢 🔥 [T] 🍴 🔋 🍟

Within 3 miles: ⛵ 🎣 ≋ [S] 🧺

Notes: No noise after 23.00hrs. Laundry & drying room.

PENRITH

Places to visit

Dalemain Mansion & Historic Gardens, DALEMAIN, CA11 0HB, 017684 86450 www.dalemain.com

Shap Abbey, SHAP, CA10 3NB, 0370 333 1181 www.english-heritage.org.uk/daysout/properties/shap-abbey

Great for kids: The Rheged Centre, PENRITH, CA11 0DQ, 01768 868000 penruddockwww.rheged.com

PENRITH — Map 18 NY53

PREMIER PARK

Lowther Holiday Park

►►►►► 86%

DAVID BELLAMY CONSERVATION AWARD GOLD

tel: 01768 863631 **Eamont Bridge CA10 2JB**
email: alan@lowther-holidaypark.co.uk **web:** www.lowther-holidaypark.co.uk
dir: *3m S of Penrith on A6.* **grid ref:** *NY527265*

A secluded natural woodland site with lovely riverside walks and glorious countryside all around. The park is home to a rare colony of red squirrels, and trout fishing is available on the two-mile stretch of the River Lowther which runs through it. A birdwatch scheme, with a coloured brochure, has been introduced, that invites guests to spot some of the 30 different species that can be seen on the park. Fully-serviced pitches are available. 50 acre site. 180 touring pitches. 50 hardstandings. 80 seasonal pitches. Caravan pitches. Motorhome pitches. Tent pitches. 447 statics.

Open: early Mar-mid Nov **Last arrival:** 22.00hrs **Last departure:** 22.00hrs

Pitches: * 🚐 £26-£35 🚌 £26-£35 ⛺ £26-£35 🛖 prices shown below

Leisure: 🛝 ⚽ 🏓 ♫ 🎣 **Facilities:** 🛁 🚿 [P] ⊙ 💨 ✲ ♿ [S] 🪑 🐕 [WiFi] 💻 ♻ ℹ

Services: 🔌 🧺 🍷 🛢 🔥 [T] 🍴 🔋 🍟 🍼 🚰 **Glamping:** **Wooden Pods** 2, £38-£50 Car by unit **Within 3 miles:** ⛳ H 🎣 ◎ ≋ [S] 🧺 U

Notes: Families only, no commercial vehicles, rollerblades or skateboards, no cats. Dogs must be kept on leads.

AA Pubs & Restaurants nearby: The Yanwath Gate Inn, YANWATH, CA10 2LF, 01768 862386

Cross Keys Inn, PENRITH, CA11 8TP, 01768 865588

PITCHES: 🚐 Caravans 🚌 Motorhomes ⛺ Tents 🛖 Glamping accommodation **SERVICES:** 🔌 Electric hook up 🧺 Launderette 🍷 Licensed bar 🛢 Calor Gas 🔥 Camping Gaz [T] Toilet fluid 🍴 Café/Restaurant 🍟 Fast Food/Takeaway 🔋 Battery charging 🍼 Baby care 🚰 Motorvan service point
ABBREVIATIONS: BHs – bank holidays Etr – Easter Spring BH – Spring Bank Holiday fr – from hrs – hours m – mile mdnt – midnight rdbt – roundabout rs – restricted service wk – week wknd – weekend x-roads – crossroads 💳 No credit or debit cards 🚫🐕 No dogs

PENRITH *continued*

Flusco Wood

►►►► 87%

GOLD

tel: 017684 80020 & 07818 552931 **Flusco CA11 0JB**
email: info@fluscowood.co.uk
dir: *From Penrith to Keswick on A66 turn right signed Flusco. Approx 800mtrs, up short incline to right. Site on left.* **grid ref:** *NY345529*

Flusco Wood is set in mixed woodland with outstanding views towards Blencathra and the fells around Keswick. It combines two distinct areas, one of which has been designed specifically for touring caravans in neat glades with hardstandings, all within close proximity of the excellent log cabin-style toilet facilities. 24 acre site. 36 touring pitches. 36 hardstandings. 20 seasonal pitches. Caravan pitches. Motorhome pitches.

Open: 22 Mar-Oct **Last arrival:** 20.00hrs **Last departure:** noon

Pitches: 🚐 🚌

Facilities: 🪒 💨 ❄ ♿ [$] 🧺 🐕 💻 ♻ ℹ

Services: 🔧 🫧 👜 [T]

Within 3 miles: 🎬

Notes: Quiet site, not suitable for large groups. Dogs must be kept on leads.

AA Pubs & Restaurants nearby: The Yanwath Gate Inn, YANWATH, CA10 2LF, 01768 862386

Cross Keys Inn, PENRITH, CA11 8TP, 01768 865588

PENRUDDOCK — Map 18 NY42

Beckses Caravan Park

►►► 81%

tel: 01768 483224 **CA11 0RX**
email: contact@beckses caravanpark.co.uk
dir: *M6 junct 40, A66 towards Keswick. Approx 6m, at caravan park sign turn right onto B5288. Site on right in 0.25m.* **grid ref:** *NY419278*

A small, pleasant site on sloping ground with level pitches and views of distant fells, on the edge of the National Park. This sheltered park is in a good location for touring the north lakes. The park is adjacent to a car sales and maintenance garage, which also services caravans and motorhomes. 4 acre site. 25 touring pitches. 25 hardstandings. Caravan pitches. Motorhome pitches. Tent pitches. 18 statics.

Open: Etr-Oct **Last arrival:** 20.00hrs **Last departure:** 11.00hrs

Pitches: 🚐 🚌 ⛺

Leisure: 🛝

Facilities: 🚿 🪒 💨 🐕 ♻

Services: 🔧 👜 ⛽ 🍔

Within 3 miles: 🎣 🐎

Notes: No noise after 22.00hrs. Dogs must be kept on leads.

AA Pubs & Restaurants nearby: Rampsbeck Country House Hotel, WATERMILLOCK, CA11 0LP, 017684 86442

Macdonald Leeming House, WATERMILLOCK, CA11 0JJ, 01768 486674

PENTON — Map 21 NY47

Twin Willows

🛖

►►► 79%

tel: 01228 577313 & 07850 713958 **The Beeches CA6 5QD**
email: davidson_b@btconnect.com
dir: *M6 junct 44, A7 signed Longtown, right into Netherby St, 6m to Bridge Inn pub. Right then 1st left, site 300yds on right.* **grid ref:** *NY449771*

Located close to Longtown, Twin Willows is a spacious park in a rural location on a ridge overlooking the Scottish border. All facilities, including all-weather pitches, are of a high quality. The park is suited to those who enjoy being away-from-it-all yet at the same time like to explore the area's rich history. A seasonal marquee is erected to hold regular barbecue and hog roast parties. 3 acre site. 16 touring pitches. 16 hardstandings. 10 seasonal pitches. Caravan pitches. Motorhome pitches. Tent pitches. 1 static.

Open: all year **Last arrival:** 22.00hrs **Last departure:** 10.00hrs

Pitches: * 🚐 £20-£25 🚌 £20-£28 ⛺ £10-£60 🛖

Leisure: 🏋 ⚽ **Facilities:** 🚿 🪒 💨 ❄ ♿ 🧺 🐕 [WiFi] 💻 ♻ ℹ

Services: 🔧 🫧 👜 ⛽ [T] 🍴 🍔 🔌

Glamping: **Wooden Pods** 1, Changeover day Sat Min stay 1 night Car by unit

Within 3 miles: 🎣 [$] 🫧 🐎

Notes: PayPal accepted. Dogs must be kept on leads.

AA Pubs & Restaurants nearby: Liddesdale, NEWCASTLETON, TD9 0QD, 01387 375255

POOLEY BRIDGE — Map 18 NY42

Park Foot Caravan & Camping Park

HOLIDAY CENTRE 88%

tel: 017684 86309 **Howtown Rd CA10 2NA**
email: holidays@parkfootullswater.co.uk **web:** www.parkfootullswater.co.uk
dir: *M6 junct 40, A66 towards Keswick, then A592 to Ullswater. Turn left for Pooley Bridge, right at church, right at x-rds signed Howtown.* **grid ref:** *NY469235*

A lively park with good outdoor sports facilities, and boats can be launched directly onto Lake Ullswater. The attractive, mainly tenting, park has many mature trees, lovely views across the lake, and a superb amenities block in the family-only field. The Country Club bar and restaurant provides good meals, as well as discos, live music and entertainment in a glorious location. There are lodges and static caravans for holiday hire. 40 acre site. 323 touring pitches. 32 hardstandings. Caravan pitches. Motorhome pitches. Tent pitches. 131 statics.

LEISURE: 🏊 Indoor pool 🏊 Outdoor pool 🛝 Children's playground 👋 Kid's club 🎾 Tennis court 🎱 Games room ⛳ Golf course 🚤 Boat hire 🚲 Cycle hire 🎬 Cinema 🎵 Entertainment 🎣 Fishing ◎ Mini golf 🏌 Pitch n putt 🌊 Watersports 🏋 Gym ⚽ Sports field 🐎 Stables **FACILITIES:** 🛁 Bath 🚿 Shower [P] Private washing cubicles 🪒 Electric shaver 💨 Hairdryer ❄ Ice Packs ♿ Disabled facilities [$] Shop on site 🚚 Mobile shop 🍖 BBQ area 🧺 Picnic area [WiFi] Wi-fi 💻 Internet access ♻ Recycling ℹ Tourist info 🐕 Dog exercise area 🚗 Car hire can be arranged

Open: Mar-Oct (rs Mar-Apr & mid Sep-Oct clubhouse open wknds only)
Last arrival: 22.00hrs **Last departure:** noon

Pitches: 🚐 🚐 ⛺

Leisure: 🎣 ♨ ⚽ 🎱 ♫ 🎿 🎯

Facilities: 🔫 🅿 ⊙ 🍴 ✳ ♿ 🖄 🖵 🔥 WiFi 🖵 ♻ 🛈

Services: 🔌 🔄 🍺 🔋 🛢 ⊘ T 🍴 🚼 🎪 🛒 ♨

Within 3 miles: 🎣 🖉 ⛳ 🎿 🔄 🔄 ↺

Notes: Families & couples only. Dogs must be kept on leads. Boat launch, pony trekking, pool table, table tennis, bike hire, kids' club in summer holidays.

AA Pubs & Restaurants nearby: The Yanwath Gate Inn, YANWATH, CA10 2LF, 01768 862386

Waterfoot Caravan Park
▶▶▶▶ 84%

GOLD

tel: 017684 86302 **CA11 0JF**
email: bookings@waterfootpark.co.uk **web:** www.waterfootpark.co.uk
dir: M6 junct 40, A66 for 1m, A592 for 4m, site on right before lake. (NB do not leave A592 until site entrance; Sat Nav not compatible). **grid ref:** NY462246

A quality touring park with neat, hardstanding pitches (most are fully serviced) in a grassy glade within the wooded grounds of an elegant Georgian mansion. The toilet facilities are clean and well maintained, and the lounge bar, with a separate family room, enjoys lake views. A path leads to Ullswater, and Aira Force waterfall, Dalemain House and Gardens and Pooley Bridge are all close by. Wooden wigwam pods for two adults and two children are available for hire. Please note that there is no access via Dacre. 22 acre site. 34 touring pitches. 32 hardstandings. Caravan pitches. Motorhome pitches. 146 statics.

Open: Mar-14 Nov **Last arrival:** 21.30hrs **Last departure:** noon

Pitches: 🚐 🚐 🏠

Leisure: 🎱 ♨ ⚽ ♫

Facilities: 🔫 ⊙ 🍴 ✳ ♿ 🖄 🖵 🔥 WiFi 🖵 ♻ 🛈 🎯

Services: 🔌 🔄 🍺 🔋 🛢 ⊘ T 🎪 ♨

Glamping: Wooden Wigwams 4, Min stay 1 night (3 nights in peak season & BHs) En suite Own kitchen Car by unit

Within 3 miles: 🎣 🎿 日 🖉 ◎ 🔄 🔄 🔄 ↺

Notes: No tents. Dogs must be kept on leads. Coffee lounge. Fish & chips mobile unit (peak season only).

AA Pubs & Restaurants nearby: The Yanwath Gate Inn, YANWATH, CA10 2LF, 01768 862386

SILLOTH Map 18 NY15

Stanwix Park Holiday Centre
HOLIDAY CENTRE 91%

tel: 016973 32666 **Greenrow CA7 4HH**
email: enquiries@stanwix.com **web:** www.stanwix.com
dir: 1m SW on B5300. From A596 (Wigton bypass), follow signs to Silloth on B5302. In Silloth follow signs to site, approx 1m on B5300. **grid ref:** NY108527

A large well-run family park within easy reach of the Lake District. Attractively laid out, with lots of amenities to ensure a lively holiday, including a 4-lane automatic, 10-pin bowling alley. Excellent touring areas with hardstandings, one in a peaceful glade well away from the main leisure complex, and there's a campers' kitchen and clean, well-maintained toilet facilities. Four camping pods are now available to hire in Skiddaw touring field. 4 acre site. 121 touring pitches. 100 hardstandings. Caravan pitches. Motorhome pitches. Tent pitches. 212 statics.

Open: all year except 25-26 Dec (rs Nov-Feb (ex New Year) - no entertainment, shop closed) **Last arrival:** 21.00hrs **Last departure:** 11.00hrs

Pitches: 🚐 🚐 ⛺ 🏠

Leisure: ♨ ⛵ ♣ ♨ ♨ ⚽ ♫ Spa

Facilities: ⊙ 🍴 ✳ ♿ 🖄 WiFi ♻ 🛈

Services: 🔌 🔄 🍺 🛢 T 🍴 🎪 ♨

Glamping: Wooden Pods 4

Within 3 miles: 🎣 🖉 ◎ 🔄 🔄

Notes: Families only. Dogs must be kept on leads. Amusement arcade.

See advert on page 142

PITCHES: 🚐 Caravans 🚐 Motorhomes ⛺ Tents 🏠 Glamping accommodation **SERVICES:** 🔌 Electric hook up 🔄 Launderette 🍺 Licensed bar 🛢 Calor Gas ⊘ Camping Gaz T Toilet fluid 🍴 Café/Restaurant 🎪 Fast Food/Takeaway 🔋 Battery charging 🛒 Baby care ♨ Motorvan service point
ABBREVIATIONS: BHs – bank holidays Etr – Easter Spring BH – Spring Bank Holiday fr – from hrs – hours m – mile mdnt – midnight rdbt – roundabout rs – restricted service wk – week wknd – weekend x-roads – crossroads 🚫 No credit or debit cards 🚫 No dogs

SILLOTH *continued*

Hylton Caravan Park
►►►► 88%

tel: 016973 31707 & 32666 **Eden St CA7 4AY**
email: enquiries@stanwix.com **web:** www.stanwix.com
dir: *On entering Silloth on B5302 follow signs for site, approx 0.5m on left, at end of Eden St.* **grid ref:** NY113533

A smart, modern touring park with excellent toilet facilities including several bathrooms. This high quality park is a sister site to Stanwix Park, which is just a mile away and offers all the amenities of a holiday centre, which are available to Hylton tourers. 18 acre site. 90 touring pitches. Caravan pitches. Motorhome pitches. Tent pitches. 213 statics.

Open: Mar-15 Nov **Last arrival:** 21.00hrs **Last departure:** 11.00hrs

Pitches: 🚐 🚙 ⛺

Facilities: ☺ 🅿 🚻 ♿

Services: 🔌 🗑 🔒 🛒

Within 3 miles: 🐴 ⚓ ◎ 🏪 🛍

Notes: Families only. Dogs must be kept on leads. Use of facilities at Stanwix Park Holiday Centre.

Tebay Services Caravan Site
►►► 79%

GOLD

tel: 01539 711322 **Orton CA10 3SB**
email: caravans@westmorland.com **web:** www.westmorland.com/caravan
dir: *Exit M6 at Westmorland Services, 1m from junct 38. Site accessed through service area from either N'bound or S'bound carriageways. Follow site signs.* **grid ref:** NY609060

An ideal stopover site adjacent to the Tebay service station on the M6, and handy for touring the Lake District. The park is screened by high grass banks, bushes and trees, and is within walking distance of the excellent farm shop and restaurant within the services complex, where caravan park customers enjoy a 10% discount. 4 acre site. 80 touring pitches. 80 hardstandings. 43 seasonal pitches. Caravan pitches. Motorhome pitches. 7 statics.

Open: Mar-Nov **Last arrival:** anytime **Last departure:** noon

Pitches: * 🚐 £21-£23 🚙 £21-£23 **Facilities:** 🔥 ☺ 🅿 🚿 ✳ ♿ 🛢 🏪 🚻 WiFi 💻 ♻ 🅸

Services: 🔌 🗑 🍳 🔒 📵 T 🍴 🛒 🛍 **Within 3 miles:** ⚓ 🛍 🛒

Notes: Dogs must be kept on leads.

AA Pubs & Restaurants nearby: The Fat Lamb Country Inn, RAVENSTONEDALE, CA17 4LL, 015396 23242

The Black Swan, RAVENSTONEDALE, CA17 4NG, 015396 23204

LEISURE: 🏊 Indoor pool 🏊 Outdoor pool 🛝 Children's playground 🎣 Kid's club 🎾 Tennis court 🎱 Games room ⛳ Golf course 🚣 Boat hire 🚲 Cycle hire 🎬 Cinema 🎵 Entertainment 🎣 Fishing ◎ Mini golf ⛳ Pitch n putt 🏄 Watersports 💪 Gym ⚽ Sports field ♘ Stables **FACILITIES:** 🛁 Bath 🚿 Shower
🅿 Private washing cubicles 🔌 Electric shaver 💨 Hairdryer ❄ Ice Packs ♿ Disabled facilities 🅂 Shop on site 🚐 Mobile shop 🍖 BBQ area 🪑 Picnic area
WiFi Wi-fi 💻 Internet access ♻ Recycling 🅸 Tourist info 🐕 Dog exercise area 🚗 Car hire can be arranged

ULVERSTON   Map 18 SD27

Places to visit

The Dock Museum, BARROW-IN-FURNESS, LA14 2PW, 01229 876400
www.dockmuseum.org.uk

Furness Abbey, BARROW-IN-FURNESS, LA13 0PJ, 01229 823420
www.english-heritage.org.uk/daysout/properties/furness-abbey

Great for kids: South Lakes Safari Zoo, DALTON-IN-FURNESS, LA15 8JR,
01229 466086 www.safarizoo.co.uk

PREMIER PARK

Bardsea Leisure Park

►►►►►88%

tel: 01229 584712 & 484363 **Priory Rd LA12 9QE**
email: reception@bardsealeisure.co.uk
dir: M6 junct 36, A590 towards Barrow. At Ulverston take A5087, site 1m on right.
grid ref: SD292765

This attractively landscaped former quarry creates a quiet and very sheltered
site; set on the southern edge of the town, it is convenient for both the coast and
the Lake District. Many of the generously-sized pitches offer all-weather full
facilities. The refurbished and superb amenities blocks that provide excellent
privacy opened for the 2016 season. The site has an excellent caravan
accessories shop. Please note, this site does not accept tents. 5 acre site. 83
touring pitches. 83 hardstandings. 50 seasonal pitches. Caravan pitches.
Motorhome pitches. 88 statics.

Open: all year **Last arrival:** 22.00hrs **Last departure:** noon

Pitches: 🚐 🚎

Leisure: ⚽

Facilities: ☉ ℘ ☀ ⛨ ♿ ⑤ 🚻 🛖 WiFi 🖥

Services: 🔌 ⑤ 🛢 🖉 T 🍴 ♨ 🚐

Within 3 miles: ♨ 🍽 ℘ ⑤ ♨ U

Notes: No noise after 22.30hrs. Dogs must be kept on leads.

AA Pubs & Restaurants nearby: The Farmers, ULVERSTON, LA12 7BA, 01229 584469

WASDALE HEAD   Map 18 NY10

Wasdale Head National Trust Campsite

►►► 79%

tel: 015394 63862 & 32733 **CA20 1EX**
email: campsite.bookings@nationaltrust.org.uk
dir: From A595 N towards Whitehaven turn left at Gosforth; from Whitehaven S on A595
right at Holmrook for Santon Bridge, follow signs to Wasdale Head. **grid ref:** NY183076

This site is set in a remote and beautiful spot at Wasdale Head, under the stunning
Scafell peaks at the head of the deepest lake in England. The clean, well-kept
facilities are set centrally amongst open grass pitches and trees, where seven
camping pods (including four family pods) and two Nordic-style tipis are also
located. There are eight hardstandings for motorhomes and eight electric hook-ups
for tents. A hot food van operates at weekends during the summer months. The
renowned Wasdale Head Inn is close by. 5 acre site. 120 touring pitches. 10
hardstandings. Motorhome pitches. Tent pitches.

Open: all year (rs Nov-Feb - shop open for reduced hours at wknds) **Last arrival:** 21.00hrs
Last departure: 11.00hrs

Pitches: * 🚎 £18.50-£23 🅰 £14.50-£19 🛖 prices shown below

Facilities: ℘ ☉ ℘ ☀ ♿ ⑤ ♨ 🔧

Services: 🔌 ⑤ 🛢 🖉 🚐

Glamping: Wooden Pods 7, £37.50-£57.50 Min stay 2 nights (1 night in low season on
request) **Tipis** 2, £35-£60 Min stay 2 nights (1 night in low season on request)

Within 3 miles: ⑤

Notes: No cars by tents. No groups of more than 4 unless a family with children. Dogs
must be kept on leads. Pop-up café at wknds. 3rd party outdoor activities by West Lake
Adventure Ltd.

AA Pubs & Restaurants nearby: Wasdale Head Inn, WASDALE HEAD, CA20 1EX,
019467 26229

WATERMILLOCK   Map 18 NY42

PREMIER PARK

The Quiet Site

►►►►► 85%

tel: 07768 727016 **Ullswater CA11 0LS**
email: info@thequietsite.co.uk
dir: M6 junct 40, A592 towards Ullswater. Right at lake junct, then right at
Brackenrigg Hotel. Site 1.5m on right. **grid ref:** NY431236

A well-maintained site in a lovely, peaceful location, with good terraced pitches
that offer great fell views; the very good toilet facilities include family
bathrooms, and there's a charming 'olde-worlde' bar. Their policy of green
sustainability is commendable, with solar panels and a biomass boiler
delivering heat and hot water to the amenity blocks, even when the site is busy.
There are wooden camping pods, seasonal bell tents and 10 superb heated
'Hobbit Holes' (underground accommodation for six people), each with an en
suite toilet and wash basin. 10 acre site. 100 touring pitches. 60 hardstandings.
15 seasonal pitches. Caravan pitches. Motorhome pitches. Tent pitches. 23
statics.

Open: all year (rs Low season - bar closed certain weekdays) **Last arrival:** 21.00hrs
Last departure: noon (11.00hrs for pods)

Pitches: * 🚐 £15-£37 🚎 £15-£37 🅰 £15-£37 🛖 prices shown below

Leisure: ⚽ 🎱 🛝

Facilities: ☉ ℘ ☀ ♿ ⑤ 🚻 🛖 WiFi 🖥 ♨ 🔧 🎡

Services: 🔌 ⑤ 🍴 🛢 🖉 T 🚐 ♨ 🔧

Glamping: Bell tents 4, £50-£60 Min stay 2 nights at wknds & school hols Car by unit
No dogs **Wooden Pods** 14, £35-£60 Min stay 2 nights at wknds & school hols Car by
unit No dogs **Hobbit Houses** 10, £65-£90 Min stay 2 nights at wknds & school hols
En suite Car by unit

Within 3 miles: 🚣 ℘ ♨ ⑤ ⑤

Notes: Quiet from 22.00hrs. Pool table, soft play area for toddlers, caravan storage.

AA Pubs & Restaurants nearby: Macdonald Leeming House, WATERMILLOCK,
CA11 0JJ, 01768 486674

Rampsbeck Country House Hotel, WATERMILLOCK, CA11 0LP, 017684 86442

PITCHES: 🚐 Caravans 🚎 Motorhomes 🅰 Tents 🛖 Glamping accommodation **SERVICES:** 🔌 Electric hook up ⑤ Launderette 🍴 Licensed bar
🛢 Calor Gas 🖉 Camping Gaz T Toilet fluid 🍴 Café/Restaurant ♨ Fast Food/Takeaway 🔋 Battery charging 🚼 Baby care 🔧 Motorvan service point
ABBREVIATIONS: BHs – bank holidays Etr – Easter Spring BH – Spring Bank Holiday fr – from hrs – hours m – mile mdnt – midnight
rdbt – roundabout rs – restricted service wk – week wknd – weekend x-roads – crossroads Ⓝ No credit or debit cards Ⓧ No dogs

WATERMILLOCK *continued*

Ullswater Holiday Park
▶▶▶▶84%

tel: 017684 86666 **High Longthwaite CA11 0LR**
email: info@ullswaterholidaypark.co.uk
dir: *M6 junct 40, A592, W towards Ullswater for 5m. Right, alongside Ullswater for 2m, right at phone box. Site 0.5m on right.* **grid ref:** *NY438232*

A pleasant rural site with its own nearby boat launching and marine storage facility, making it ideal for sailors. The family-owned and run park enjoys fell and lake views, and there is a bar, a stylish café, a splendid undercover area for campers, and a shop on site. Many of the pitches are fully serviced and there are wooden cabins with barbecues. Please note that the Marine Park is one mile from the camping area. 12 acre site. 160 touring pitches. 58 hardstandings. Caravan pitches. Motorhome pitches. Tent pitches. 55 statics.

Open: Mar-Nov (rs Low season bar open wknds only) **Last arrival:** 21.00hrs
Last departure: noon

Pitches: * 🚐 £15.25-£28.25 🚌 £15.25-£28.25 ▲ £15.25-£28.25 🏠 prices shown below

Leisure: 🛝 🔍

Facilities: 🦮⊙🅿✳⚲🛁🚻🐾 WiFi 🖥♻ ❼

Services: 🔌🔅 🍴🛒🔥⊘ T 🛒

Glamping: Cabins 4, £33.50-£38.50 Min stay 1 night Car by unit

Within 3 miles: ⦿🎣⛵🛥🚲🐎∪

Notes: No open fires, no noise after 23.30hrs. Dogs must be kept on leads. Boat launching & moorings 1m.

AA Pubs & Restaurants nearby: Macdonald Leeming House, WATERMILLOCK, CA11 0JJ, 01768 486674

Rampsbeck Country House Hotel, WATERMILLOCK, CA11 0LP, 017684 86442

Cove Caravan & Camping Park
▶▶▶▶83%

tel: 017684 86549 **Ullswater CA11 0LS**
email: info@cove-park.co.uk
dir: *M6 junct 40, A592 for Ullswater. Right at lake junct, then right at Brackenrigg Inn. Site 1.5m on left.* **grid ref:** *NY431236*

A peaceful family site in an attractive and elevated position with extensive fell views and glimpses of Ullswater Lake. Extensive ground works have been carried out in order to provide spacious, mostly level pitches. Pretty, seasonal flowers are planted amid the wide variety of mature trees and shrubs. 3 acre site. 50 touring pitches. 27 hardstandings. 10 seasonal pitches. Caravan pitches. Motorhome pitches. Tent pitches. 39 statics.

Open: Mar-Oct **Last arrival:** 21.00hrs **Last departure:** noon

Pitches: * 🚐 £20-£34 🚌 £20-£34 ▲ £15-£30

Leisure: 🛝 **Facilities:** 🦮🅿⊙🅿✳⚲🛁🚻♻❼

Services: 🔌🔅 🔥⊘

Within 3 miles: ⦿🎣⛵🛥🚲🐎∪

Notes: No open fires, no noise after 22.30hrs. Dogs must be kept on leads.

AA Pubs & Restaurants nearby: Macdonald Leeming House, WATERMILLOCK, CA11 0JJ, 01768 486674

Rampsbeck Country House Hotel, WATERMILLOCK, CA11 0LP, 017684 86442

WINDERMERE
Map 18 SD49

Places to visit
Holehird Gardens, WINDERMERE, LA23 1NP, 015394 46008
www.holehirdgardens.org.uk

Blackwell The Arts & Crafts House, BOWNESS-ON-WINDERMERE, LA23 3JT, 015394 46139 www.blackwell.org.uk

Great for kids: Brockhole on Windermere, WINDERMERE, LA23 1LJ, 015394 46601 www.brockhole.co.uk

---

PREMIER PARK

Park Cliffe Camping & Caravan Estate
▶▶▶▶▶91%

GOLD

tel: 015395 31344 **Birks Rd, Tower Wood LA23 3PG**
email: info@parkcliffe.co.uk **web:** www.parkcliffe.co.uk
dir: *M6 junct 36, A590. Right at Newby Bridge onto A592. 3.6m right into site. (NB due to difficult access from main road this is the only advised direction for approaching the site).* **grid ref:** *SD391912*

A lovely hillside park set in 25 secluded acres of fell land. The camping area is sloping and uneven in places, but well drained and sheltered; some pitches have spectacular views of Lake Windermere and the Langdales. The park offers a high level of customer care and is very well equipped for families (family bathrooms), and there is an attractive bar and brasserie restaurant serving quality food; 10 wooden pods and three static holiday caravans are for hire. 25 acre site. 60 touring pitches. 60 hardstandings. 25 seasonal pitches. Caravan pitches. Motorhome pitches. Tent pitches. 56 statics.

Open: Mar-mid Nov (wknds & school hols facilities fully open)
Last arrival: 22.00hrs **Last departure:** noon

Pitches: * 🚐 £27-£34 🚌 £27-£34 ▲ £21-£33 🏠 prices shown below

Leisure: 🛝 🔍 **Facilities:** ⊙🅿✳⚲🛁🚻🐾 WiFi ♻❼

Services: 🔌🔅 🍴🔥⊘T🍴🛒🚐🔽

Glamping: Wooden Pods 10, £44-£52 Min stay 2 nights at wknds, 3 nights at BHs Car by unit

Within 3 miles: ⛵⦿🎣🅿◎🚲🐎∪

Notes: No noise 23.00hrs-07.30hrs. Dogs must be kept on leads. Off licence.

AA Pubs & Restaurants nearby: Eagle & Child Inn, WINDERMERE, LA8 9LP, 01539 821320

Beech Hill Hotel & Spa, WINDERMERE, LA23 3LR, 015394 42137

LEISURE: 🏊 Indoor pool 🏊 Outdoor pool 🛝 Children's playground 🛝 Kid's club 🎾 Tennis court 🔍 Games room ⛳ Golf course ⛵ Boat hire 🚲 Cycle hire 🎦 Cinema 🎵 Entertainment 🎣 Fishing ◎ Mini golf ⛳ Pitch n putt 🏄 Watersports 🏋 Gym ⚽ Sports field ∪ Stables **FACILITIES:** 🛁 Bath 🚿 Shower 🅿 Private washing cubicles 🔌 Electric shaver ✳ Hairdryer ✳ Ice Packs ⚲ Disabled facilities 🛒 Shop on site 🛒 Mobile shop 🍴 BBQ area 🧺 Picnic area WiFi Wi-fi 🖥 Internet access ♻ Recycling ❼ Tourist info 🐾 Dog exercise area 🚗 Car hire can be arranged

Hill of Oaks & Blakeholme
▶▶▶▶▶ 84%

GOLD

tel: 015395 31578 **LA12 8NR**
email: enquiries@hillofoaks.co.uk web: www.hillofoaks.co.uk
dir: *M6 junct 36, A590 towards Barrow. At rdbt signed Bowness turn right onto A592. Site approx 3m on left.* grid ref: *SD386899*

A secluded, heavily wooded park on the shores of Lake Windermere. Pretty lakeside picnic areas, woodland walks and a play area make this a delightful park for families; there are excellent serviced pitches, a licensed shop and a heated toilet block. Both the ladies and gents amenities have quality fittings and very good privacy options. Watersports include sailing and canoeing, with private jetties for boat launching. The private pier was upgraded in 2016 to provide a regular ferry service to Bowness. 31 acre site. 43 touring pitches. 46 hardstandings. Caravan pitches. Motorhome pitches. 220 statics.

Open: Mar–14 Nov **Last departure:** noon

Pitches: 🚐 �"

Leisure: 🎠 ⊙ ✐

Facilities: 🖍 🅿 ⊙ ℱ ✳ 🕭 🏧 🚻 WiFi 🖥 ♻ 🐾 ♨

Services: 🔌 🛢 🍺 T ↯

Within 3 miles: ⬆ 🚲 ▥ ℱ ◎ ⊰ 🛥 ⛳ ↺

Notes: No tents (except trailer tents), no groups. Dogs must be kept on leads. Daily lake cruise connections in peak season.

AA Pubs & Restaurants nearby: Eagle & Child Inn, WINDERMERE, LA8 9LP, 01539 821320

ASHBOURNE
Map 10 SK14

Places to visit
Kedleston Hall, KEDLESTON HALL, DE22 5JH, 01332 842191
www.nationaltrust.org.uk/kedleston-hall

Carsington Fields Caravan Park
▶▶▶ 84%

tel: 01335 372872 **Millfields Ln, Nr Carsington Water DE6 3JS**
email: bookings@carsingtoncaravaning.co.uk
dir: *From Belper towards Ashbourne on A517, right approx 0.25m past Hulland Ward into Dog Ln. 0.75m right at x-rds signed Carsington. Site on right approx 0.75m.* grid ref: *SK251493*

A very well-presented and spacious park with a good toilet block, open views and a large fenced pond that attracts plenty of wildlife. The popular tourist attraction of Carsington Water is a short stroll away, with its variety of leisure facilities including fishing, sailing, windsurfing and children's play area. The park is also a good base for walkers. 6 acre site. 58 touring pitches. 14 hardstandings. 18 seasonal pitches. Caravan pitches. Motorhome pitches. Tent pitches.

Open: Mar–Sep **Last arrival:** 21.00hrs **Last departure:** 13.00hrs

Pitches: * 🚐 £24–£29 �" £24–£29 🛖 £20–£29

Facilities: 🖍 ⊙ ℱ ✳ 🕭 🗄 🚻 WiFi ♻ 🐾 **Services:** 🔌 T 🛒

Within 3 miles: 🚲 ℱ 🛥 🛒 ⛳ ↺

Notes: No large groups or group bookings, no noise after 22.30hrs. Dogs must be kept on leads. Indian takeaway free delivery to site.

AA Pubs & Restaurants nearby: The Coach and Horses Inn, FENNY BENTLEY, DE6 1LB, 01335 350246

BAKEWELL
Map 16 SK26

Places to visit
Chatsworth, CHATSWORTH, DE45 1PP, 01246 565300 www.chatsworth.org

Greenhills Holiday Park
▶▶▶▶ 80%

tel: 01629 813052 & 813467 **Crowhill Ln DE45 1PX**
email: info@greenhillsholidaypark.co.uk
dir: *1m NW of Bakewell on A6. Signed before Ashford-in-the-Water, onto unclassified road on right.* grid ref: *SK202693*

A well-established park set in lovely countryside within the Peak District National Park. Many pitches enjoy uninterrupted views, and there is easy accessibility to all facilities, including the spotlessly clean amenity blocks. The clubhouse, shop and children's playground are popular features. 8 acre site. 172 touring pitches. 70 hardstandings. 50 seasonal pitches. Caravan pitches. Motorhome pitches. Tent pitches. 73 statics.

Open: Feb–Nov (rs Feb–Apr & Oct–Nov bar & shop closed) **Last arrival:** 22.00hrs **Last departure:** noon

Pitches: 🚐 �" 🛖 **Leisure:** ⊙ 🎵 **Facilities:** ⊙ ℱ ✳ 🕭 🗄 🚻 WiFi 🖥 🐾 ♻

Services: 🔌 🛢 🍺 ⊘ T 🍴 🛒 ↯ **Within 3 miles:** 🚲 ℱ ◎ 🛒 ⛳ ↺

AA Pubs & Restaurants nearby: Piedaniel's, BAKEWELL, DE45 1BX, 01629 812687

PITCHES: 🚐 Caravans �" Motorhomes 🛖 Tents 🏠 Glamping accommodation **SERVICES:** 🔌 Electric hook up 🛢 Launderette 🍺 Licensed bar
🛢 Calor Gas ⊘ Camping Gaz T Toilet fluid 🍴 Café/Restaurant 🛒 Fast Food/Takeaway 🔋 Battery charging 🚼 Baby care ↯ Motorvan service point
ABBREVIATIONS: BHs – bank holidays Etr – Easter Spring BH – Spring Bank Holiday fr – from hrs – hours m – mile mdnt – midnight
rdbt – roundabout rs – restricted service wk – week wknd – weekend x-roads – crossroads Ⓢ No credit or debit cards Ⓝ No dogs

Places to visit

Haddon Hall, HADDON HALL, DE45 1LA, 01629 812855 www.haddonhall.co.uk

The Heights of Abraham Cable Cars, Caverns & Hilltop Park, MATLOCK BATH, DE4 3PD, 01629 582365 www.heightsofabraham.com

PREMIER PARK

Barn Farm Campsite

▶▶▶▶▶ 82%

tel: 01629 650245 **Barn Farm DE4 2BL**
email: gilberthh@msn.com
dir: *From A6 take B5056 towards Ashbourne. Follow brown signs to site.*
grid ref: *SK238621*

An interesting park on a former dairy farm with the many and varied facilities housed in high quality conversions of old farm buildings. The three large and well-maintained touring fields offer sweeping views across the Peak District National Park. There is an excellent choice of privacy cubicles, including shower and washbasin cubicles, a fully serviced family room, and even a shower and sauna. There are five stylish, self-catering camping barns for hire. 15 acre site. 62 touring pitches. 13 hardstandings. Caravan pitches. Motorhome pitches. Tent pitches.

Open: Apr-Oct **Last arrival:** 21.00hrs **Last departure:** 11.00hrs

Pitches: * 🚐 £17-£22 🚍 £17-£22 Å £6-£10

Leisure: 🅰 ⚙ 🔍

Facilities: 🏕 P⃝ ⊙ ⨍ ✳ & 🚿 🖂 🛏 ♻ 🛈

Services: 🔌🔁 🛢 🖉 🆃

Within 3 miles: ♨ ♉ ⚲ ◎ ⛴ ⓢ🔲 ∪

Notes: No music after 22.30hrs, minimum noise 22.30hrs-07.00hrs. Dogs must be kept on leads. Vending machines, sauna, sunbed.

AA Pubs & Restaurants nearby: The Druid Inn, BIRCHOVER, DE4 2BL, 01629 653836

The Peacock at Rowsley, ROWSLEY, DE4 2EB, 01629 733518

Places to visit

Poole's Cavern (Buxton Country Park), BUXTON, SK17 9DH, 01298 26978 www.poolescavern.co.uk

Great for kids: Go Ape Buxton, BUXTON, SK17 9DH, 0845 643 9215 *(Calls cost 7p per minute plus your phone company's access charge)* www.goape.co.uk/buxton

Lime Tree Park

▶▶▶▶ 90%

tel: 01298 22988 **Dukes Dr SK17 9RP**
email: info@limetreeparkbuxton.com
dir: *1m S of Buxton, between A515 & A6.* **grid ref:** *SK070725*

A most attractive and well-designed site, set on the side of a narrow valley in an elevated location, with separate, neatly landscaped areas for statics, tents, touring caravans and motorhomes. There's good attention to detail throughout including

the clean toilets and showers, and WiFi is free of charge. Its backdrop of a magnificent old railway viaduct and views over Buxton and the surrounding hills, make this a sought-after destination. There are eight static caravans, a pine lodge and two apartments available for holiday lets. 10.5 acre site. 106 touring pitches. 22 hardstandings. Caravan pitches. Motorhome pitches. Tent pitches. 43 statics.

Open: Mar-Oct **Last arrival:** 18.00hrs **Last departure:** noon

Pitches: 🚐 🚍 Å

Leisure: 🔍

Facilities: 🏕 P⃝ ⊙ ⨍ ✳ & 🚿 🖂 🛏 WiFi 🖥 ♻ 🛈

Services: 🔌🔁 🛢 🖉 🆃 🍴 ⟱

Within 3 miles: ♨ ◎ ⛴ ⓢ🔲 ∪

Notes: No noise after 22.00hrs, no fires. Dogs must be kept on leads.

AA Pubs & Restaurants nearby: The Queen Anne Inn, GREAT HUCKLOW, SK17 8RF, 01298 871246

Beech Croft Farm

▶▶▶▶ 87%

tel: 01298 85330 **Beech Croft, Blackwell in the Peak SK17 9TQ**
email: mail@beechcroftfarm.co.uk **web:** www.beechcroftfarm.co.uk
dir: *Exit A6 midway between Buxton & Bakewell. Site signed.* **grid ref:** *SK122720*

A small terraced farm site with lovely Peak District views. There's a fine stone-built toilet block with ultra-modern fittings, underfloor heating and additional unisex facilities, fully-serviced hardstanding pitches, gravel roads, a campers' shelter, and a super tarmac pathway leading from the camping field to the toilet block. All the tent pitches now have hook-up via a card paying system. This makes an ideal site for those touring or walking in the Peak District. 3 acre site. 30 touring pitches. 30 hardstandings. Caravan pitches. Motorhome pitches. Tent pitches.

Open: all year (rs Nov-Feb - tents not accepted) **Last arrival:** 20.00hrs **Last departure:** noon

Pitches: * 🚐 £22.00-£24.50 🚍 £22.00-£24.50 Å £15-£18

Leisure: 🅰 ⚙ **Facilities:** 🏕 P⃝ ⊙ ✳ & 🚿 🖂 🛏 WiFi ♻ 🛈

Services: 🔌🔁 🛢 🖉 🆃 ⟱

Within 3 miles: ⓢ

Notes: No noise after 22.00hrs. Dogs must be kept on leads. Snack van & wood-fired pizza (high season only).

AA Pubs & Restaurants nearby: The Queen Anne Inn, GREAT HUCKLOW, SK17 8RF, 01298 871246

LEISURE: 🏊 Indoor pool ⚊ Outdoor pool 🅰 Children's playground 👟 Kid's club ♉ Tennis court 🔍 Games room ♨ Golf course ⛴ Boat hire 🚲 Cycle hire 🎭 Cinema 🎵 Entertainment ⚲ Fishing ◎ Mini golf ⛳ Pitch n putt ⚓ Watersports 🏋 Gym ⚙ Sports field ∪ Stables **FACILITIES:** 🛁 Bath 🏕 Shower P⃝ Private washing cubicles ⊙ Electric shaver ⨍ Hairdryer ✳ Ice Packs & Disabled facilities ⓢ Shop on site 🏪 Mobile shop 🛏 BBQ area 🖂 Picnic area WiFi Wi-fi 🖥 Internet access ♻ Recycling 🛈 Tourist info 🐕 Dog exercise area 🚗 Car hire can be arranged

Clover Fields Touring Caravan Park

▶▶▶ 96%

tel: 01298 78731 & 212474 **1 Heath View, Harpur Hill SK17 9PU**
email: reservations@cloverfieldstouringpark.co.uk
dir: *A515, B5053, then immediately right. Site 0.5m on left.* **grid ref:** *SK075704*

A developing and spacious adults-only park, just over a mile from the attractions of Buxton, with very good facilities, including an upmarket, timber chalet-style toilet block. All pitches are fully serviced and have individual barbecues, and are set out on terraces, each with extensive views over the countryside. Swathes of natural meadow grasses and flowers cloak the terraces and surrounding fields. The Teapot Café serves a good range of meals. 12 acre site. 45 touring pitches. 39 hardstandings. 6 seasonal pitches. Caravan pitches. Motorhome pitches. Tent pitches.

Open: all year **Last arrival:** 19.00hrs **Last departure:** noon

Pitches: ⊕ ⊡ Å

Facilities: ☺ ✳ ⅙ ⑤ ✿ ♻ ❂ ❻

Services: ⊕ ⑤ 🛢 ⊘ T ⑩ ⬆

Within 3 miles: ⌁ ℓ ⑤ ⑤ ∪

Notes: Adults only. No commercial vehicles. Dogs must be kept on leads.

AA Pubs & Restaurants nearby: The Queen Anne Inn, GREAT HUCKLOW, SK17 8RF, 01298 871246

HOPE
Map 16 SK18

Places to visit
Peveril Castle, CASTLETON, S33 8WQ, 01433 620613
www.english-heritage.org.uk/daysout/properties/peveril-castle

Speedwell Cavern, CASTLETON, S33 8WA, 01433 620512
www.speedwellcavern.co.uk

Pindale Farm Outdoor Centre

▶▶▶ 79%

tel: 01433 620111 **Pindale Rd S33 6RN**
email: pindalefarm@btconnect.com
dir: *From A6187 in Hope follow Pindale sign between church & Woodroffe Arms. Site 1m on left.* **grid ref:** *SK163825*

Set around a 13th-century farmhouse and a former lead mine pump house (now converted to a self-contained bunkhouse for up to 60 people), this simple, off-the-beaten-track site is an ideal base for walking, climbing, caving and various outdoor pursuits. Around the farm are several deeply wooded areas available for tents, and old stone buildings that have been converted to house modern toilet facilities. 4 acre site. 60 touring pitches. Tent pitches.

Open: Mar-Oct

Pitches: Å

Facilities: ☺ ✳ ⅙ WiFi **Services:** ⊕ ⑤ **Within 3 miles:** ⑤ ∪

Notes: No anti-social behaviour, noise must be kept to minimum after 21.00hrs, no fires. Dogs must be kept on leads. Charge for WiFi.

AA Pubs & Restaurants nearby: The Old Hall Hotel, HOPE, S33 6RH, 01433 620160

Ye Olde Nags Head, CASTLETON, S33 8WH, 01433 620248

The Yorkshire Bridge Inn, BAMFORD, S33 0AZ, 01433 651361

MATLOCK
Map 16 SK35

Places to visit
Peak District Mining Museum, MATLOCK BATH, DE4 3NR, 01629 583834
www.peakmines.co.uk

Haddon Hall, HADDON HALL, DE45 1LA, 01629 812855 www.haddonhall.co.uk

Great for kids: The Heights of Abraham Cable Cars, Caverns & Hilltop Park, MATLOCK BATH, DE4 3PD, 01629 582365 www.heightsofabraham.com

---

Lickpenny Caravan Site

▶▶▶▶ 90%

tel: 01629 583040 **Lickpenny Ln, Tansley DE4 5GF**
email: enquiries@lickpennycaravanpark.co.uk
dir: *From Matlock take A615 towards Alfreton for 3m. Site signed to left, into Lickpenny Ln, right into site near end of road.* **grid ref:** *SK339597*

A picturesque site in the grounds of an old plant nursery with areas broken up and screened by a variety of shrubs, and with spectacular views, which are best enjoyed from the upper terraced areas. The pitches, several fully serviced, are spacious, well screened and well marked, and facilities are kept to a very good standard. The bistro/coffee shop is popular with visitors. 16 acre site. 80 touring pitches. 80 hardstandings. 20 seasonal pitches. Caravan pitches. Motorhome pitches.

Open: all year **Last arrival:** 20.00hrs **Last departure:** noon (late departures until 17.00hrs - charge applies)

Pitches: ⊕ ⊡

Leisure: ⋀

Facilities: ⭐ P ☺ P ⅙ ⑤ A ⅙ WiFi ▦ ♻ ❻ ☕

Services: ⊕ ⑤ 🛢 T ⬆ ⬆

Within 3 miles: ⌁ ⅏ ℓ ⑩ ⑤ ⑤ ∪

Notes: No noise after 23.00hrs, 1 car per pitch. Dogs must be kept on leads. Child's bath available.

AA Pubs & Restaurants nearby: The Red Lion, MATLOCK, DE4 3BT, 01629 584888

Stones Restaurant, MATLOCK, DE4 3LT, 01629 56061

PITCHES: ⊕ Caravans ⊡ Motorhomes Å Tents ⋒ Glamping accommodation **SERVICES:** ⊕ Electric hook up ⑤ Launderette 🍺 Licensed bar 🛢 Calor Gas ⊘ Camping Gaz T Toilet fluid ⑩ Café/Restaurant ▦ Fast Food/Takeaway ⬆ Battery charging ⬆ Baby care ⬆ Motorvan service point
ABBREVIATIONS: BHs – bank holidays Etr – Easter Spring BH – Spring Bank Holiday fr – from hrs – hours m – mile mdnt – midnight rdbt – roundabout rs – restricted service wk – week wknd – weekend x-roads – crossroads Ⓝ No credit or debit cards Ⓧ No dogs

NEWHAVEN   Map 16 SK16

Places to visit

Middleton Top Engine House, MIDDLETON, DE4 4LS, 01629 823204 www.derby-shire.gov.uk/countryside/countryside_sites/visitor_centres/middlton_top

Peak District Mining Museum, MATLOCK BATH, DE4 3NR, 01629 583834 www.peakmines.co.uk

---

Newhaven Caravan & Camping Park
►►►►83%

tel: 01298 84300 **SK17 0DT**
email: newhavencaravanpark@btconnect.com
dir: *Between Ashbourne & Buxton at A515 & A5012 junct.* **grid ref:** *SK167602*

Pleasantly situated within the Peak District National Park, this park has mature trees screening the three touring areas. Very good toilet facilities cater for touring vans and a large tent field, and there's a restaurant adjacent to the site. The static caravans on the site are privately owned. 30 acre site. 125 touring pitches. 95 hardstandings. 40 seasonal pitches. Caravan pitches. Motorhome pitches. Tent pitches. 73 statics.

Open: Mar-Oct **Last arrival:** 20.00hrs **Last departure:** 13.00hrs

Pitches: * ⌂ £16.25-£21.25 ⌂ £16.25-£21.25 ▲ £12.50-£17.50

Leisure: 🎱 🔍

Facilities: 📶 ⊙ 🚿 ※ 🖙 🚽 🎋 🛒 ♻ ✱

Services: 🚐 🔋 🔒 ⌷ 🏧 ⊤ 🍽

Within 3 miles: 🖙 ⛵ ⛟ 🛒 🔋 ♨

Notes: No noise after 23.00hrs. Dogs must be kept on leads.

AA Pubs & Restaurants nearby: Red Lion Inn, BIRCHOVER, DE4 2BN, 01629 650363

The Druid Inn, BIRCHOVER, DE4 2BL, 01629 653836

RIDDINGS   Map 16 SK45

Riddings Wood Caravan and Camping Park
►►►►85%

tel: 01773 605160 **Bullock Ln DE55 4BP**
email: info@riddingswoodcaravanandcampingpark.co.uk
dir: *M1 junct 27, A608 signed Heanor. Right onto B600 signed Alfreton & Selston. Left onto B6016 signed Jacksdale. Through Jacksdale towards Ridding. Site on right.*
grid ref: *SK430524*

Located close to both Derby and Nottingham, this site can be described as a sloping amphitheatre in layout. It is surrounded by the mature trees of Riddings Wood on all sides and has a fabulous panoramic view looking down towards Jacksdale. Beyond the sweeping driveway and security barrier, you'll find a smart chalet-style reception, neat gravel hardstandings, manicured grass tent pitches, and a modern and stylish amenity block with quality shower and toilet facilities. Picnic benches are scattered around the park for campers to use, and fully serviced pitches are available. A local bus service runs every nine minutes from the site entrance to both Derby and Nottingham. 11.5 acre site. 75 touring pitches. 26 hardstandings. Caravan pitches. Motorhome pitches. Tent pitches.

Open: Mar-Dec **Last arrival:** 22.00hrs **Last departure:** 11.30hrs

Pitches: ⌂ £17-£26 ⌂ £17-£26 ▲ £13-£23

Leisure: 🎱 ⚽ **Facilities:** 📶 ⊙ 🚿 ※ 🛁 🎋 🛒 WiFi ✱

Services: 🚐 🔋 🔒 ⌷   **Within 3 miles:** 🖙 ⛵ 🛒 🔋 ♨

Notes: Children must be accompanied by an adult at all times. Rubbish must be placed in designated areas. No noise after 23.00hrs. Dogs must be kept on leads.

RIPLEY   Map 16 SK35

Places to visit

Midland Railway Butterley, RIPLEY, DE5 3QZ, 01773 747674 www.midlandrailwaycentre.co.uk

Denby Pottery Visitor Centre, DENBY, DE5 8NX, 01773 740799 www.denbyvisitorcentre.co.uk

---

Golden Valley Caravan & Camping Park
►►►►84%

GOLD

tel: 01773 513881 & 746786 **Coach Rd DE55 4ES**
email: enquiries@goldenvalleycaravanpark.co.uk
web: www.goldenvalleycaravanpark.co.uk
dir: *M1 junct 26, A610 to Codnor. Right at lights. Right into Alfreton Rd. In 1m left into Coach Rd, park on left. (NB it is advisable to ignore Sat Nav for last few miles & these directions are followed).* **grid ref:** *SK408513*

This superbly landscaped park is set within 30 acres of woodland in the Amber Valley. The fully serviced pitches are set out in informal groups in clearings amongst the trees. The park has a cosy bar and bistro with outside patio, a fully stocked fishing lake, an innovative and well-equipped play area, an on-site jacuzzi and fully equipped fitness suite. There is also a wildlife pond and a nature trail, plus a camping pod for hire. 30 acre site. 45 touring pitches. 45 hardstandings. 12 seasonal pitches. Caravan pitches. Motorhome pitches. Tent pitches. 1 static.

Open: all year (rs Low season at wknds only - bar & café open & children's activities available) **Last arrival:** 21.00hrs **Last departure:** noon

Pitches: ⌂ £22-£32 ⌂ £22-£32 ▲ £15-£30 🏠 prices shown below

Leisure: 🎯 🎱 ♿ 🔍   **Facilities:** ⊙ 🚿 ※ 🛁 🖙 🚽 🎋 🛒 WiFi ▤ ♻ ✱

Services: 🚐 🔋 🍽 ⌷ ⊘ ⊤ 🍽 🏧 🛒 🔋 ⌷

Glamping: Wooden Pods 1, £25-£45 Own kitchen

Within 3 miles: 🖙 ⛟ 🎋 ⛵ 🛒 🔋 ♨

Notes: No vehicles on grass, no open fires or disposable BBQs, no noise after 22.30hrs. Dogs must be kept on leads. Zip slide, tractor train, log flume ride, battery boats, quad bikes.

AA Pubs & Restaurants nearby: Santo's Higham Farm Hotel, HIGHAM, DE55 6EH, 01773 833812

LEISURE: 🏊 Indoor pool 🏊 Outdoor pool 🎱 Children's playground 🪁 Kid's club 🎾 Tennis court 🔍 Games room 🏌 Golf course ⛵ Boat hire 🚲 Cycle hire 🎬 Cinema 🎵 Entertainment 🎣 Fishing ⛳ Mini golf ⛳ Pitch n putt 🏄 Watersports 🏋 Gym 🎯 Sports field ♨ Stables **FACILITIES:** 🛁 Bath 📶 Shower 🚿 Private washing cubicles ⊙ Electric shaver 🖙 Hairdryer ※ Ice Packs ♿ Disabled facilities 🛒 Shop on site 🚚 Mobile shop 🍖 BBQ area 🎋 Picnic area WiFi Wi-fi 🖥 Internet access ♻ Recycling 🌐 Tourist info 🐕 Dog exercise area 🚗 Car hire can be arranged

Places to visit

Ashby-de-la-Zouch Castle, ASHBY-DE-LA-ZOUCH, LE65 1BR, 01530 413343
www.english-heritage.org.uk/daysout/properties/ashby-de-la-zouch-castle

Great for kids: Conkers, MOIRA, DE12 6GA, 01283 216633
www.visitconkers.com

Beehive Woodland Lakes
▶▶▶▶85%

tel: 01283 763981 **DE12 8HZ**
email: info@beehivefarm-woodlandlakes.co.uk
dir: *From A444 in Castle Gresley into Mount Pleasant Rd, follow Rosliston signs for 3.5m through Linton to T-junct. Left signed Beehive Farms.* **grid ref:** *SK249161*

A small, informal and continually developing caravan area secluded from an extensive woodland park in the heart of the National Forest National Park. Toilet facilities include four family rooms. Young children will enjoy the on-site animal farm and playground, whilst anglers can pass many a happy hour fishing at the park's three lakes. There is an adults-only area and camping pods are available for hire. The Honey Pot tearoom provides snacks and is open most days. 2.5 acre site. 46 touring pitches. 46 hardstandings. Caravan pitches. Motorhome pitches. Tent pitches.

Open: all year **Last arrival:** 20.00hrs (18.00hrs low season) **Last departure:** noon

Pitches: 🚐 🚐 ▲ 🏠

Leisure: 🎣 🎣

Facilities: 🔦 🅿 ⊙ 🚰 ✳ ⚸ 🚿 🛁 WiFi 🛒 ❶

Services: 🔌 🖥 🛢 🚽 🍴 🚌

Glamping: Wooden Pods 4, £40–£60 Min stay 2 nights Car by unit

Within 3 miles: 🎣 🛁 🎣 ◎ 🅿

Notes: Dogs must be kept on leads. Takeaway food delivered to site.

AA Pubs & Restaurants nearby: The Waterfront, BARTON-UNDER-NEEDWOOD, DE13 8DZ, 01283 711500

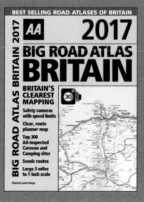
Places to visit

Temple Mine, MATLOCK BATH, DE4 3NR, 01629 583834 www.peakmines.co.uk

Great for kids: The Heights of Abraham Cable Cars, Caverns & Hilltop Park, MATLOCK BATH, DE4 3PD, 01629 582365 www.heightsofabraham.com

Grouse & Claret
▶▶▶80%

tel: 01629 733233 **Station Rd DE4 2EB**
email: grouseandclaret.matlock@marstons.co.uk
dir: *M1 junct 29. Site on A6, 5m from Matlock & 3m from Bakewell.* **grid ref:** *SK258660*

A well-designed, purpose-built park at the rear of an eating house on the A6 between Bakewell and Chatsworth, and adjacent to the New Peak Shopping Village. The park comprises a level grassy area running down to the river, and all pitches have hardstandings and electric hook-ups. TV sockets are installed around site for improved reception. 2.5 acre site. 28 touring pitches. 28 hardstandings. Caravan pitches. Motorhome pitches.

Open: all year **Last arrival:** 22.00hrs **Last departure:** 11.00hrs

Pitches: * 🚐 £20–£27 🚐 £20–£27

Facilities: ⊙ 🚰 WiFi **Services:** 🔌 🍴 🛢 🍴 🚌 ⚓

Within 3 miles: 🛁 🎣 🚶 ◎ ∪ **Notes:** Dogs must be kept on leads.

AA Pubs & Restaurants nearby: The Grouse & Claret, ROWSLEY, DE4 2EB, 01629 733233

The Peacock at Rowsley, ROWSLEY, DE4 2EB, 01629 733518

Places to visit

Melbourne Hall & Gardens, MELBOURNE, DE73 8EN, 01332 862502
www.melbournehall.com

Shardlow Marina Caravan Park
▶▶▶72%

tel: 01332 792832 **London Rd DE72 2GL**
email: admin@shardlowmarina.co.uk
dir: *M1 junct 24a, A50 signed Derby. Exit from A50 junct 1 at rdbt signed Shardlow. Site 1m on right.* **grid ref:** *SK444303*

A large marina site with restaurant facilities, situated on the Trent and Merseyside Canal. Pitches are on grass surrounded by mature trees, and for the keen angler, the site offers fishing within the marina. The attractive grass touring area overlooks the marina. 25 acre site. 35 touring pitches. 26 hardstandings. 10 seasonal pitches. Caravan pitches. Motorhome pitches. Tent pitches. 73 statics.

Open: Mar–Jan **Last arrival:** 17.00hrs **Last departure:** noon

Pitches: * 🚐 £18–£28 🚐 £18–£28 ▲ £18–£28

Leisure: 🎣 **Facilities:** 🔦 🅿 ⊙ ✳ ⚸ 🚿 ❸ ❶

Services: 🔌 🖥 🍴 🛢 🚽 🍴 🚌 **Within 3 miles:** 🛁 🚶 🎣 ◎ 🅿 🛁 ∪

Notes: Office closed between 13.00hrs–14.00hrs. Max 2 dogs per unit. Dogs must be kept on leads & not left unattended or tied up outside camping unit.

AA Pubs & Restaurants nearby: The Old Crown Inn, SHARDLOW, DE72 2HL, 01332 792392

PITCHES: 🚐 Caravans 🚐 Motorhomes ▲ Tents 🏠 Glamping accommodation **SERVICES:** 🔌 Electric hook up 🖥 Launderette 🍴 Licensed bar
🛢 Calor Gas 🚱 Camping Gaz 🚽 Toilet fluid 🍴 Café/Restaurant 🍴 Fast Food/Takeaway 🚌 Battery charging ⚓ Baby care ⚓ Motorvan service point
ABBREVIATIONS: BHs – bank holidays Etr – Easter Spring BH – Spring Bank Holiday fr – from hrs – hours m – mile mdnt – midnight
rdbt – roundabout rs – restricted service wk – week wknd – weekend x-roads – crossroads 🚫 No credit or debit cards 🚫 No dogs

Devon

With magnificent coastlines, two historic cities and the world-famous Dartmoor National Park, Devon sums up all that is best about the British landscape. For centuries it has been a fashionable and much loved holiday destination – especially south Devon's glorious English Riviera.

When the crime writer Agatha Christie was born in Torquay on Devon's glorious south coast, the town was a popular seaside resort. It was 1890, the start of Queen Victoria's last decade as monarch, and Torquay was a fashionable destination for all sorts of people; those looking for a permanent home by the sea as well as holidaymakers in search of long hours of sunshine and a mild climate. In many ways, Torquay remains much the same today and its impressive setting still evokes a sense of its Victorian heyday. A local steam train attraction adds to the atmosphere; you can travel from Paignton to Dartmouth, alighting on the way at the small station at Churston, just as Hercule Poirot does in Christie's 1930s detective novel *The ABC Murders*. The Queen of Crime herself used this station when she had a summer home nearby. The house, Greenway, overlooks a glorious sweep of the River Dart and is now managed as a popular visitor attraction by the National Trust.

Close to the English Riviera lies Dartmoor, one of the south-west's most spectacular landscapes. The contrast between the traditional attractions of the coast and this expanse of bleak, brooding moorland could not be greater. The National Park, which contains Dartmoor, covers 365 square miles and includes many fascinating geological features – isolated granite tors and two summits exceeding 2,000 feet among them. Dartmoor's waterfalls, including the tumbling Whitelady Waterfall at Lydford Gorge, can be seen in full spate even in the depths of winter. Everywhere you venture on Dartmoor, there are stone circles, burial chambers and mysterious clues to the distant past. The place oozes antiquity. Sir Arthur Conan Doyle set his classic Sherlock Holmes story *The Hound of the Baskervilles* on Dartmoor, and Agatha Christie stayed at a local hotel for two weeks at the height of the First World War in order to finish writing her first detective novel *The Mysterious Affair at Styles*, first published in 1920.

Not surprisingly, Dartmoor equates with walking and the opportunities are enormous. For something really adventurous, try the Two Moors Way. This long-distance route begins at Ivybridge and crosses the National Park to enter neighbouring Exmoor, which straddles the Devon/Somerset border. At Lynton and Lynmouth the trail connects with the South West Coast Path, which takes walkers on a breathtaking journey to explore north Devon's gloriously rugged coastline, renowned for its extraordinary collection of peaks and outcrops. Cycling in the two National Parks is also extremely popular and there is a good choice of off-road routes taking you to the heart of Dartmoor and Exmoor.

Devon's towns and cities offer a pleasing but stimulating alternative to the rigours of the countryside. There are scores of small market towns in the region – for example there is Tavistock with its popular farmers' market, one of many in the county. Plymouth lies in Devon's south-west corner and is a striking city and naval port. Much of its transformation over the years is a reminder of the devastation it suffered, together with Exeter, during the Second World War. The city places particular emphasis, of course, on the Spanish Armada and the voyage of the Pilgrim Fathers to America.

On the theme of sailing, Devon is synonymous with this most invigorating of boating activities. Salcombe, on the county's south coast, is a sailing playground. Situated on a tree-fringed estuary beneath lush rolling hills, the town thrives on boats – it hosts the week-long Salcombe Regatta in August. It's even suitable for swimming, with several sandy beaches and sheltered bays.

◁ Valley of Rocks, Exmoor National Park

DEVON

ASHBURTON — Map 3 SX77

Places to visit

Compton Castle, COMPTON, TQ3 1TA, 01803 842382
www.nationaltrust.org.uk/comptoncastle

Tuckers Maltings, NEWTON ABBOT, TQ12 4AA, 01626 334734
www.tuckersmaltings.com

Great for kids: Prickly Ball Farm and Hedgehog Hospital, NEWTON ABBOT, TQ12 6BZ, 01626 362319 www.pricklyballfarm.com

Parkers Farm Holiday Park

►►►► 86%

tel: 01364 654869 **Higher Mead Farm TQ13 7LJ**
email: parkersfarm@btconnect.com
dir: *From Exeter on A38, 2nd left after Plymouth (29m) sign, signed Woodland & Denbury. From Plymouth on A38 take A383 Newton Abbot exit, turn right across bridge, rejoin A38, then as above.* **grid ref:** *SX779713*

A well-developed site terraced into rising ground with stunning views across rolling countryside to the Dartmoor tors. Part of a working farm, this park offers excellent fully serviced hardstanding pitches, which make the most of the fine views; it is beautifully maintained and has good quality toilet facilities, a popular games room and a bar/restaurant that serves excellent meals. Large family rooms with two shower cubicles, a large sink and a toilet are especially appreciated by families with small children. There are regular farm walks when all the family can meet and feed the various animals. 25 acre site. 100 touring pitches. 20 hardstandings. Caravan pitches. Motorhome pitches. Tent pitches. 18 statics.

Open: Etr-end Oct (rs Low season bar & restaurant open wknds only)
Last arrival: 22.00hrs **Last departure:** 10.00hrs

Pitches: 🚐 🚌 ⛺

Leisure: 🛝 ✋ ⚽ ♟ 🎵

Facilities: 🚿 🪒 💨 ❄ ♿ [S] 🧺 🐕 [WiFi] ♻ ℹ

Services: 🔧 🫧 🍷 🛢 🔥 [T] 🍴 🥡 👶 🔋

Within 3 miles: 🎣 [S] 🫧

Notes: Dogs must be kept on leads. Large field for dog walking.

AA Pubs & Restaurants nearby: The Rising Sun, ASHBURTON, TQ13 7JT, 01364 652544

River Dart Country Park

►►►► 86%

tel: 01364 652511 **Holne Park TQ13 7NP**
email: info@riverdart.co.uk
dir: *M5 junct 31, A38 towards Plymouth. In Ashburton at Peartree junct follow brown site signs. Site 1m on left. (NB Peartree junct is 2nd exit at Ashburton; do not exit at Linhay junct as narrow roads are unsuitable for caravans).* **grid ref:** *SX734700*

Set in 90 acres of magnificent parkland that was once part of a Victorian estate, with many specimen and exotic trees, this peaceful, hidden-away touring park occupies several camping areas, all served with good quality toilet facilities. In spring the park is a blaze of colour from the many azaleas and rhododendrons. There are numerous outdoor activities for all ages including abseiling, caving and canoeing, plus high quality, well-maintained facilities. The open moorland of Dartmoor is only a few minutes away. 90 acre site. 170 touring pitches. 34 hardstandings. Caravan pitches. Motorhome pitches. Tent pitches.

Open: Apr-Sep (rs Low/mid season - shop & café bar restricted opening hours)
Last arrival: 21.00hrs **Last departure:** 11.00hrs

Pitches: * 🚐 £15-£34 🚌 £15-£34 ⛺ £15-£34

Leisure: 🛝 🎾 ♟ 🎣 🚲

Facilities: 🛁 🚿 [P] 🪒 💨 ❄ ♿ [S] 🧺 🐕 [WiFi] 💻 ♻ ℹ

Services: 🔧 🫧 🍷 🛢 🔥 [T] 🍴 🥡 👶 🔋

Within 3 miles: ⛳ 🎣 [S] 🫧 🐴

Notes: Dogs must be kept on leads. Adventure playground.

AA Pubs & Restaurants nearby: The Rising Sun, ASHBURTON, TQ13 7JT, 01364 652544

AXMINSTER — Map 4 SY29

Places to visit

Branscombe - The Old Bakery, Manor Mill and Forge, BRANSCOMBE, EX12 3DB, 01752 346585 www.nationaltrust.org.uk

Allhallows Museum, HONITON, EX14 1PG, 01404 44966
www.honitonmuseum.co.uk

Great for kids: Pecorama Pleasure Gardens, BEER, EX12 3NA, 01297 21542
www.pecorama.co.uk

Andrewshayes Holiday Park

►►►► 87%

tel: 01404 831225 **Dalwood EX13 7DY**
email: info@andrewshayes.co.uk **web:** www.andrewshayes.co.uk
dir: *3m from Axminster (towards Honiton) on A35, right at Taunton Cross signed Dalwood & Stockland. Site 150mtrs on right.* **grid ref:** *ST248088*

An attractive family park within easy reach of Lyme Regis, Seaton, Branscombe and Sidmouth in an ideal touring location. This popular park offers modern toilet facilities, a quiet, cosy bar and takeaway service, and an excellent play area for children, set beside the swimming pool, bar and restaurant area. 12 acre site. 150 touring pitches. 105 hardstandings. 100 seasonal pitches. Caravan pitches. Motorhome pitches. Tent pitches. 80 statics.

Open: Apr-Nov (rs Off-peak season - shop & bar reduced hours & takeaway availability limited) **Last arrival:** 22.00hrs **Last departure:** 11.00hrs

Pitches: 🚐 £17-£25 🚌 £17-£25 ⛺ £17-£25

Leisure: 🏊 🛝 ⚽ ♟

LEISURE: 🏊 Indoor pool 🌊 Outdoor pool 🛝 Children's playground ✋ Kid's club 🎾 Tennis court ♟ Games room ⛳ Golf course ⛵ Boat hire 🚲 Cycle hire 🎬 Cinema 🎵 Entertainment 🎣 Fishing ◎ Mini golf 🏌 Pitch n putt 🏄 Watersports 🏋 Gym ⚽ Sports field 🐴 Stables **FACILITIES:** 🛁 Bath 🚿 Shower [P] Private washing cubicles 🪒 Electric shaver 💨 Hairdryer ❄ Ice Packs ♿ Disabled facilities [S] Shop on site 🚚 Mobile shop 🍖 BBQ area 🧺 Picnic area [WiFi] Wi-fi 💻 Internet access ♻ Recycling ℹ Tourist info 🐕 Dog exercise area 🚗 Car hire can be arranged

Facilities: 🐾 🅿 ☉ 🅵 ※ ♿ 🚿 🚽 📶 ♻ ❶

Services: ⊕🗟 🍴 🛢 🥤🔌🛒 🐛

Within 3 miles: 🎣 🏧🛒

Notes: Children under 12 must be supervised by an adult in pool. Dogs must be kept on leads. Table tennis.

AA Pubs & Restaurants nearby: The Old Inn, KILMINGTON, EX13 7RB, 01297 32096

Hawkchurch Resort & Spa
NEW HOLIDAY HOME PARK 93%

tel: 01297 678402 **Hawkchurch EX13 5UL**
email: reception@hawkchurchresort.co.uk
dir: *From A35 between Axminster & Charmouth take B3165 signed Crewkerne. Left signed Hawkchurch.* **grid ref:** *SY345986*

This superb park is located in lovely countryside near Axminster and the Jurassic Coast and enjoys views over the Axe Valley. The luxury lodges are fully equipped and have en suite facilities. There are excellent leisure facilities – the Ezina Spa offering a wide range of luxury treatments, plus a spa pool and gym. In addition, there is a good restaurant, The Beeches, as well as an alfresco eating and drinking area.

Open: all year
Lodges: 120 Sleeps 8 Elec inc Gas inc
Children: 🛏 Cots (cot linen charged) Highchair **Dogs:** 2 on leads
Leisure: 🏊 Spa 🏌

Mill Park Touring Caravan & Camping Park
NEW ►►►86%

tel: 01271 882647 **Mill Ln EX34 9SH**
email: enquiries@millparklimited.com
dir: *M5 junct 27, A361 towards Barnstaple. Right onto A399 towards Combe Martin. At Sawmills Inn take turn opposite Berrynarbor sign.* **grid ref:** *SS559471*

Under new enthusiastic ownership, this well managed park is set in an attractive wooded valley with a stream that runs into a lake where coarse fishing is available. There is a quiet bar and restaurant with a family room, a very pleasant camping meadow, an excellent children's play area, clean and tidy toilet facilities. The park has lakeside wooden pods (cocoons) suitable for two adults and two children, and a wooden tent, with a lockable patio door, for hire. The site is located two miles from Combe Martin and Ilfracombe and just a stroll across the road from the small harbour at Watermouth. 30 acre site. 155 touring pitches. Caravan pitches. Motorhome pitches. Tent pitches.

Open: Mar-Oct **Last arrival:** 21.00hrs **Last departure:** 10.00hrs
Pitches: ✱ 🚐 £10-£26.50 🚙 £10-£26.50 🅰 £8-£26.50 🏕 prices shown below
Leisure: 🎣
Facilities: ☉🅵※♿🅸🚿🚽📶🖥♻❶
Services: ⊕🗟 🍴🛢🥤T🍴🛒
Glamping: Wooden Pods 5, £18-£50
Within 3 miles: ⏷🚴♿🎣🎣◎🏊🏧🛒U

AA Pubs & Restaurants nearby: Sandy Cove Hotel, ILFRACOMBE, EX34 9SR, 01271 882243

The Quay Restaurant, ILFRACOMBE, EX34 9EQ, 01271 868090

Places to visit
Bradley Manor, NEWTON ABBOT, TQ12 6BN, 01803 843235
www.nationaltrust.org.uk/devoncornwall

Lemonford Caravan Park
►►►►83%

tel: 01626 821242 **TQ12 6JR**
email: info@lemonford.co.uk web: www.lemonford.co.uk
dir: *From Exeter on A38 take A382, 3rd exit at rdbt, follow Bickington signs.*
grid ref: *SX793723*

Small, secluded and well-maintained park with a good mixture of attractively laid out pitches. The friendly owners pay a great deal of attention to the little details, and the toilets in particular are kept spotlessly clean. This good touring base is only one mile from Dartmoor and 10 miles from the seaside at Torbay. The bus to Exeter, Plymouth and Torbay stops outside the park. 7 acre site. 82 touring pitches. 55 hardstandings. Caravan pitches. Motorhome pitches. Tent pitches. 44 statics.

Open: all year **Last arrival:** 22.00hrs **Last departure:** 11.00hrs
Pitches: 🚐 £14-£21.50 🚙 £16-£23.50 🅰 £14-£21.50
Facilities: 🛁🐾☉🅵※♿🅸🚿📶🖥♻❶
Services: ⊕🗟🛢🥤T🛒🐛 **Within 3 miles:** ♿🚴🏧🛒U

Notes: No noise after 23.00hrs. Dogs must be kept on leads. Clothes drying area.

AA Pubs & Restaurants nearby: The Wild Goose Inn, NEWTON ABBOT, TQ12 4RA, 01626 872241

Agaric, ASHBURTON, TQ13 7QD, 01364 654478

See advert on page 154

PITCHES: 🚐 Caravans 🚙 Motorhomes 🅰 Tents 🏕 Glamping accommodation SERVICES: ⊕ Electric hook up 🗟 Launderette 🍴 Licensed bar 🛢 Calor Gas 🥤 Camping Gaz T Toilet fluid 🍴 Café/Restaurant 🛒 Fast Food/Takeaway 🥤 Battery charging 🐛 Baby care 🏌 Motorvan service point
ABBREVIATIONS: BHs – bank holidays Etr – Easter Spring BH – Spring Bank Holiday fr – from hrs – hours m – mile mdnt – midnight
rdbt – roundabout rs – restricted service wk – week wknd – weekend x-roads – crossroads ⊛ No credit or debit cards ⊗ No dogs

BRAUNTON
Map 3 SS43

Places to visit

Marwood Hill Gardens, BARNSTAPLE, EX31 4EB, 01271 342528
www.marwoodhillgarden.co.uk

Great for kids: Combe Martin Wildlife Park & Dinosaur Park, COMBE MARTIN, EX34 0NG, 01271 882486 www.wildlifedinosaurpark.co.uk

PREMIER PARK

Hidden Valley Park
▶▶▶▶▶ 90%

Best of British

tel: 01271 813837 **West Down EX34 8NU**
email: info@hiddenvalleypark.com
dir: Direct access from A361, 8m from Barnstaple & 2m from Mullacott Cross.
grid ref: SS499408

A delightful, well-appointed family site set in a wooded valley, with superb toilet facilities and a café. The park is set in a very rural, natural location not far from the beautiful coast around Ilfracombe. The woodland is home to nesting buzzards and woodpeckers, and otters have taken up residence by the lake. WiFi is available. There are three fully equipped timber cabins for hire, and the Lakeside Restaurant and Bar serves good home-cooked meals. 32 acre site. 100 touring pitches. 50 hardstandings. 15 seasonal pitches. Caravan pitches. Motorhome pitches. Tent pitches. 3 statics.

Open: all year **Last arrival:** 21.00hrs **Last departure:** 10.30hrs

Pitches: * ♉ £11-£23 ⛺ £11-£23 ▲ £11-£25

Leisure: ⚠

Facilities: 🛁🚿📶🅿️💈⚡✳️👶🚾🏧🚮📶🖥️♻️ℹ️

Services: 🔌🚽🛒💧⚫🚰🍴♿

Within 3 miles: 🔱🎣⚓🚴🏇🏊🛒🏧🎿⛳

Notes: PayPal accepted.

AA Pubs & Restaurants nearby: The Rock Inn, GEORGEHAM, EX33 1JW, 01271 890322

Lobb Fields Caravan & Camping Park
▶▶▶ 83%

tel: 01271 812090 **Saunton Rd EX33 1HG**
email: info@lobbfields.com **web:** www.lobbfields.com
dir: At x-roads in Braunton take B3231 towards Croyde. Site signed on right.
grid ref: SS475378

A bright, tree-lined park with gently-sloping grass pitches divided into two open areas, plus a camping field in August. Braunton is an easy walk away, and a bus service from the entrance makes the golden beaches of Saunton and Croyde, or the market town of Barnstaple, easily accessible. 14 acre site. 180 touring pitches. 11 hardstandings. 12 seasonal pitches. Caravan pitches. Motorhome pitches. Tent pitches.

Open: 18 Mar-Oct **Last arrival:** 22.00hrs **Last departure:** 10.30hrs

Pitches: * ♉ £15-£32 ⛺ £15-£32 ▲ £11-£32

Leisure: ⚠ **Facilities:** 📶🅿️⚡✳️👶🚾📶♻️ℹ️

Services: 🔌🚽🛒💧⚫🏧⛟ **Within 3 miles:** 🔱🚴🏊🛒🏧⛳

Notes: No under 18s unless accompanied by an adult, no fires, no noise after 23.00hrs. Dogs must be kept on leads. Surfing, boards & wet suits for hire, wet suit washing areas.

AA Pubs & Restaurants nearby: The Rock Inn, GEORGEHAM, EX33 1JW, 01271 890322

LEISURE: 🏊 Indoor pool 🏊 Outdoor pool ⚠ Children's playground 🪁 Kid's club 🎾 Tennis court 🎱 Games room ⛳ Golf course 🚣 Boat hire 🚴 Cycle hire 🎬 Cinema 🎵 Entertainment 🎣 Fishing ⛳ Mini golf 🏌️ Pitch n putt 🏄 Watersports 🏋️ Gym 🏟️ Sports field ⛵ Stables **FACILITIES:** 🛁 Bath 🚿 Shower 🅿️ Private washing cubicles ⊙ Electric shaver 🪒 Hairdryer ✳️ Ice Packs ♿ Disabled facilities 🛒 Shop on site 🚐 Mobile shop 🍖 BBQ area 🧺 Picnic area 📶 Wi-fi 🖥️ Internet access ♻️ Recycling ℹ️ Tourist info 🐕 Dog exercise area 🚗 Car hire can be arranged

Places to visit

Lydford Castle and Saxon Town, LYDFORD, EX20 4BH, 0370 333 1181
www.english-heritage.org.uk/daysout/properties/lydford-castle-and-saxon-town

Museum of Dartmoor Life, OKEHAMPTON, EX20 1HQ, 01837 52295
www.museumofdartmoorlife.org.uk

Bridestowe Caravan Park
▶▶▶76%

tel: 01837 861261 **EX20 4ER**
email: ali.young53@btinternet.com
dir: *Exit A30 at A386 & Sourton Cross junct, follow B3278 signed Bridestowe, left in 3m. In village centre, left onto unclassified road for 0.5m.* **grid ref:** *SX519893*

A small, well-established park in a rural setting close to Dartmoor National Park. This mainly static park has a small, peaceful touring space, and there are many activities to enjoy in the area including fishing and riding. Part of the National Cycle Route 27 (the Devon Coast to Coast) passes close to this park. 1 acre site. 13 touring pitches. 3 hardstandings. Caravan pitches. Motorhome pitches. Tent pitches. 40 statics.

Open: Mar-Dec **Last arrival:** 22.30hrs **Last departure:** noon
Pitches: 🚐 🚍 Å **Leisure:** 🔍 **Facilities:** 🏪 ⊙ ✻ 🛐 ♻ ❶
Services: 🔌 🖭 🛢 ⊘ T ➡ **Within 3 miles:** 🛐
Notes: 🐾 Dogs must be kept on leads.
AA Pubs & Restaurants nearby: The Arundell Arms, LIFTON, PL16 0AA, 01566 784666

Hedley Wood Caravan & Camping Park
▶▶▶87%

tel: 01288 381404 **EX22 7ED**
email: alan@hedleywood.co.uk **web:** www.hedleywood.co.uk
dir: *From Exeter, A30 to Launceston, B3254 towards Bude. Left into Tackbear Rd signed Marhamchurch & Widemouth (at Devon-Cornwall border). Site on right.* **grid ref:** *SS262013*

Set in a very rural location about four miles from Bude, this relaxed family-owned site has a peaceful, easy-going atmosphere. Pitches are in separate paddocks, some with extensive views, and this wooded park is quite sheltered in the lower areas. The restaurant/club house is a popular place to relax. 16.5 acre site. 120

touring pitches. 30 hardstandings. 27 seasonal pitches. Caravan pitches. Motorhome pitches. Tent pitches. 18 statics.

Open: all year (rs Except main holidays shop, bar & restaurant may be closed)
Last arrival: anytime **Last departure:** anytime
Pitches: * 🚐 £14-£24 🚍 £14-£24 Å £14-£24
Leisure: 🅰 🔍
Facilities: 🏪 P ⊙ 🖭 ✻ 🛐 🚻 WiFi 🖥 ♻ ❶
Services: 🔌 🖭 🛢 ⊘ T 🍴 ➡ 🚌 👶 ⛟
Within 3 miles: 🎣 🏌 🛐 🖭 ♺

Notes: PayPal accepted. Dogs must be kept on leads. Dog kennels, dog walk, nature trail & caravan storage.

AA Pubs & Restaurants nearby: Bay View Inn, WIDEMOUTH BAY, EX23 0AW, 01288 361273

Places to visit

Lydford Gorge, LYDFORD, EX20 4BH, 01822 820320
www.nationaltrust.org.uk/lydford-gorge

Launceston Steam Railway, LAUNCESTON, PL15 8DA, 01566 775665
www.launcestonsr.co.uk

Great for kids: Tamar Otter & Wildlife Centre, LAUNCESTON, PL15 8GW, 01566 785646 www.tamarotters.co.uk

Roadford Lake
▶▶▶81%

tel: 01409 211507 **Lower Goodacre PL16 0JL**
email: info@swlaketrust.org.uk
dir: *Exit A30 between Okehampton & Launceston at Roadford Lake signs, cross dam wall, site 0.25m on right.* **grid ref:** *SX421900*

Located right at the edge of Devon's largest inland water, this popular rural park is well screened by mature trees and shrubs. There is an excellent watersports school for sailing, windsurfing, rowing and kayaking, with hire and day launch facilities. This is an ideal location for brown trout fly fishing. 3 acre site. 49 touring pitches. 13 hardstandings. Caravan pitches. Motorhome pitches. Tent pitches.

Open: all year **Arrival:** late arrivals by prior arrangement. **Last departure:** 11.00hrs
Pitches: 🚐 🚍 Å
Leisure: 🏌
Facilities: 🏪 ⊙ 🖭 ✻ 🛐 🚻 WiFi ♻ ❶
Services: 🔌 🖭 🍴
Within 3 miles: 🎣 🏌 ♺ 🛐

Notes: Off-ground BBQs only, no open fires. Dogs must be kept on leads. Climbing wall, archery, high ropes, watersports.

AA Pubs & Restaurants nearby: Arundell Arms, LIFTON, PL16 0AA, 01566 784666

PITCHES: 🚐 Caravans 🚍 Motorhomes Å Tents 🏠 Glamping accommodation **SERVICES:** 🔌 Electric hook up 🖭 Launderette 🍷 Licensed bar
🛢 Calor Gas ⊘ Camping Gaz T Toilet fluid 🍴 Café/Restaurant 🚚 Fast Food/Takeaway 🔋 Battery charging 👶 Baby care ⛟ Motorvan service point
ABBREVIATIONS: BHs – bank holidays Etr – Easter Spring BH – Spring Bank Holiday fr – from hrs – hours m – mile mdnt – midnight
rdbt – roundabout rs – restricted service wk – week wknd – weekend x-roads – crossroads 🐾 No credit or debit cards 🚫 No dogs

BUCKFASTLEIGH
Map 3 SX76

Places to visit

Buckfast Abbey, BUCKFASTLEIGH, TQ11 0EE, 01364 645500
www.buckfast.org.uk

Great for kids: Buckfast Butterfly Farm & Dartmoor Otter Sanctuary,
BUCKFASTLEIGH, TQ11 0DZ, 01364 642916 www.ottersandbutterflies.co.uk

Churchill Farm Campsite
▶▶ 90%

tel: 01364 642844 & 07977 113175 **TQ11 0EZ**
email: apedrick@btinternet.com
dir: From A38 follow Buckfast Abbey signs. Pass Abbey entrance on right, At top of hill left into no-through road. Pass Abbey entrance, up hill, left at x-roads to site entrance opposite Holy Trinity Church. **grid ref:** SX743664

A working family farm in a relaxed and peaceful setting, with keen, friendly owners. Set on the hills above Buckfast Abbey, this attractive park is maintained to a good standard. The spacious pitches in the neatly trimmed paddock enjoy extensive country views towards Dartmoor, and the clean, simple toilet facilities include smart showers and a family room. This is a hidden gem for those who love traditional camping. Close to a local bus service and within walking distance of Buckfastleigh, the Abbey and the South Devon Steam Railway. This site is within a Site of Special Scientific Interest (SSSI). 3 acre site. 25 touring pitches. Caravan pitches. Motorhome pitches. Tent pitches.

Open: May-Sep **Last arrival:** 22.00hrs

Pitches: 🚐 £12-£15 🚃 £12-£15 ▲ £12-£15

Facilities: 🌳 🅿 ⊙ ✳ ⅊ ♻ 𝟢

Services: 🔌 🛒

Within 3 miles: 🏪

Notes: 🚫 No ball games. Dogs must be kept on leads.

AA Pubs & Restaurants nearby: Church House Inn, RATTERY, TQ10 9LD, 01364 642220
Sea Trout Inn, STAVERTON, TQ9 6PA, 01803 762274

Beara Farm Caravan & Camping Site
▶ 84%

tel: 01364 642234 **Colston Rd TQ11 0LW**
dir: From Exeter take Buckfastleigh exit at Dart Bridge, follow South Devon Steam Railway & Butterfly Farm signs. 200mtrs past entrance to South Devon Steam Railway 1st left into Old Totnes Rd, 0.5m right at red brick cottages signed Beara Farm. Approx 1m to site.
grid ref: SX751645

A very good farm park, with clean unisex facilities, run by very keen and friendly owners. A well-trimmed camping field offers peace and quiet. Close to the River Dart and the Dart Valley Steam Railway line, within easy reach of the sea and moors. Please note that the approach to the site is narrow, with passing places, and care needs to be taken. 3.63 acre site. 30 touring pitches. 1 hardstanding. Caravan pitches. Motorhome pitches. Tent pitches.

Open: all year **Last arrival:** 21.00hrs **Last departure:** anytime

Pitches: * 🚐 fr £11 🚃 fr £11 ▲ fr £11

Facilities: 🌳 ⊙ ✳ 𝔸 𝒉 ♻ 𝟢

Services: 🛒

Within 3 miles: 𝒫 🏪

Notes: 🚫 No noise after 22.30hrs. Dogs must be kept on leads. Access to River Dart.

AA Pubs & Restaurants nearby: Church House Inn, RATTERY, TQ10 9LD, 01364 642220
Sea Trout Inn, STAVERTON, TQ9 6PA, 01803 762274

BUDLEIGH SALTERTON
Map 3 SY08

Places to visit

Otterton Mill, OTTERTON, EX9 7HG, 01395 568521 www.ottertonmill.com

Great for kids: Bicton Park Botanical Gardens, BICTON, EX9 7BJ, 01395 568465
www.bictongardens.co.uk

Pooh Cottage Holiday Park
▶▶▶▶ 83%

tel: 01395 442354 & 07875 685595 **Bear Ln EX9 7AQ**
email: bookings@poohcottage.co.uk
dir: M5 junct 30, A376 towards Exmouth. Left onto B3179 towards Woodbury & Budleigh Salterton. Left into Knowle onto B3178. Through village, at brow of hill take sharp left into Bear Lane. Site 200yds. **grid ref:** SY053831

A rural park with wide views of the sea and surrounding peaceful countryside. Expect a friendly welcome to this attractive site that has a lovely play area, and a new toilet and shower block with a disabled unit and baby changing facilities. From the site there is easy access to plenty of walks, as well as the Buzzard Cycle Way. Cycle hire is available on site and there's also a bus stop within walking distance. 8 acre site. 10 touring pitches. 45 seasonal pitches. Caravan pitches. Motorhome pitches. Tent pitches. 3 statics.

Open: 15 Mar-Oct **Last arrival:** 21.00hrs **Last departure:** 11.30hrs

Pitches: 🚐 🚃 ▲

Leisure: 𝔸 🎠

Facilities: 🛁 🌳 🅿 ⊙ ℙ ✳ ⅊ 🏪 𝔸 📶 💻 ♻ 𝟢

Services: 🔌 🛒 🧺 ⊘ 🛒 🚚

Within 3 miles: ⅃ ⅊ 🎣 𝒫 ◎ ⅊ 🏪 🏪 ∪

Notes: PayPal accepted. No gazebos, no open fires, 5mph speed limit. Dogs must be kept on leads.

AA Pubs & Restaurants nearby: Blue Ball Inn, SIDMOUTH, EX10 9QL, 01395 514062
The Salty Monk, SIDMOUTH, EX10 9QP, 01395 513174

CHUDLEIGH

Places to visit

Canonteign Falls, CHUDLEIGH, EX6 7NT, 01647 252434
www.canonteignfalls.co.uk

Exeter's Underground Passages, EXETER, EX1 1GA, 01392 665887
www.exeter.gov.uk/passages

Great for kids: Prickly Ball Farm and Hedgehog Hospital, NEWTON ABBOT,
TQ12 6BZ, 01626 362319 www.pricklyballfarm.com

CHUDLEIGH   Map 3 SX87

Holmans Wood Holiday Park
►►►►85%

tel: 01626 853785 **Harcombe Cross TQ13 0DZ**
email: enquiries@holmanswood.co.uk
dir: *M5 junct 31, A38. After racecourse at top of Haldon Hill left at BP petrol station signed Chudleigh, site entrance on left of slip road.* **grid ref:** *SX881812*

A delightful small park set back from the A38 in a secluded wooded area, handy for touring Dartmoor National Park, and the lanes and beaches of south Devon. The facilities are bright and clean, and the grounds are attractively landscaped. 12 acre site. 73 touring pitches. 71 hardstandings. Caravan pitches. Motorhome pitches. Tent pitches. 34 statics.

Open: mid Mar-end Oct **Last arrival:** 22.00hrs **Last departure:** 11.00hrs

Pitches: * ⬜ £19-£29 ⬜ £19-£29 ⬟ £12-£18

Facilities: 🐾⊙🅿☀️♿🚻🌳📶🖥️❶

Services: 🔌🔲🔋🧺

Within 3 miles: 🛒🔲↺

Notes: No cycling or skateboards, pets only permitted at management's discretion. Dogs must be kept on leads.

AA Pubs & Restaurants nearby: Cridford Inn, TRUSHAM, TQ13 0NR, 01626 853694

CLYST ST MARY   Map 3 SX99

Places to visit
Exeter Cathedral, EXETER, EX1 1HS, 01392 285983 www.exeter-cathedral.org.uk

Exeter's Underground Passages, EXETER, EX1 1GA, 01392 665887 www.exeter.gov.uk/passages

Great for kids: The World of Country Life, EXMOUTH, EX8 5BU, 01395 274533 www.worldofcountrylife.co.uk

PREMIER PARK

Crealy Meadows Caravan and Camping Park
►►►►►87%

tel: 01395 234888 **Sidmouth Rd EX5 1DR**
email: stay@crealymeadows.co.uk
dir: *M5 junct 30, A3052 signed Exmouth. At rdbt take A3052 signed Seaton. Follow brown Crealy Great Adventure Park signs. Turn right.* **grid ref:** *SY001906*

A quality park with excellent toilet facilities, spacious, fully serviced pitches and good security, adjacent to the popular Crealy Adventure Park, with free or discounted entry available for all campers. The park is within a short drive of Exeter and the seaside attractions at Sidmouth. Free WiFi is available and free kennels can be used on request. Pre-erected luxury safari tents and safari cabins are for hire, and also in the Camelot Village there are medieval-style pavillion tents for a real glamping holiday. For children there is a unique 'own pony' experience. 14.65 acre site. 120 touring pitches. 21 hardstandings. Caravan pitches. Motorhome pitches. Tent pitches.

Open: Mar-Oct **Last arrival:** 20.00hrs **Last departure:** 10.00hrs

Pitches: ⬜ ⬜ ⬟ ⛺

Leisure: ⚽ 🎵

Facilities: 🅿☀️♿🚻🌳📶🖥️❶

Services: 🔌🔲🗣️🔒🧺▣🍴🛒

Glamping: Safari tents, Safari cabins, Pavillion tents

Within 3 miles: 🛶🎣🛒🔲

Notes: Dogs must be kept on leads.

AA Pubs & Restaurants nearby: Bridge Inn, TOPSHAM, EX3 0QQ, 01392 873862

COMBE MARTIN   Map 3 SS54

Places to visit
Arlington Court, ARLINGTON, EX31 4LP, 01271 850296 www.nationaltrust.org.uk/arlington-court

Great for kids: Combe Martin Wildlife Park & Dinosaur Park, COMBE MARTIN, EX34 0NG, 01271 882486 www.wildlifedinosaurpark.co.uk

PREMIER PARK

Newberry Valley Park
►►►►►87%

tel: 01271 882334 **Woodlands EX34 0AT**
email: relax@newberryvalleypark.co.uk
dir: *M5 junct 27, A361 towards Barnstaple. Right at North Aller rdbt onto A399, through Combe Martin to sea. Left into site.* **grid ref:** *SS576473*

A family owned and run touring park on the edge of Combe Martin, with all its amenities just a five-minute walk away. The park is set in a wooded valley with its own coarse fishing lake and has a stunning toilet block with underfloor heating and excellent unisex privacy cubicles. There is a wooden pod named Lily, and a shepherd's hut called Rose, located in a quite spot and available to hire. The safe beaches of Newberry and Combe Martin are reached by a short footpath opposite the park entrance, where the South West Coastal Path is located. 20 acre site. 110 touring pitches. 32 hardstandings. 20 seasonal pitches. Caravan pitches. Motorhome pitches. Tent pitches.

Open: 15 Mar-Oct (rs Low season - limited office hours) **Last arrival:** variable (dusk in winter) **Last departure:** 11.00hrs

Pitches: ⬜ ⬜ ⬟ ⛺

Leisure: ⚿ 🎣

Facilities: 🛏️🐾🅿⊙🅿☀️♿🚻🌳📶 ❶🌴

Services: 🔌🔲 T🛒↯

Glamping: Wooden Pods 1, £40-£65 Changeover day Any day Min stay 3 nights Car by unit **Shepherd's Huts** 1, £65-£95 Changeover day Any day Min stay 3 nights Own kitchen Car by unit

Within 3 miles: 🛶🎣🏊🛒🔲↺

Notes: No camp fires. Dogs must be kept on leads. Kitchen prep area, fridge & microwave available.

AA Pubs & Restaurants nearby: The Quay Restaurant, ILFRACOMBE, EX34 9EQ, 01271 868090

PITCHES: ⬜ Caravans ⬜ Motorhomes ⬟ Tents ⛺ Glamping accommodation **SERVICES:** 🔌 Electric hook up 🔲 Launderette 🗣️ Licensed bar 🔒 Calor Gas ⌀ Camping Gaz T Toilet fluid 🍴 Café/Restaurant ▣ Fast Food/Takeaway 🔋 Battery charging 👶 Baby care ↯ Motorvan service point
ABBREVIATIONS: BHs – bank holidays Etr – Easter Spring BH – Spring Bank Holiday fr – from hrs – hours m – mile mdnt – midnight rdbt – roundabout rs – restricted service wk – week wknd – weekend x-roads – crossroads ⊘ No credit or debit cards Ⓧ No dogs

COMBE MARTIN *continued*

Stowford Farm Meadows
▶▶▶▶ 92%

tel: 01271 882476 **Berry Down EX34 0PW**
email: enquiries@stowford.co.uk
dir: *M5 junct 27, A361 to Barnstaple. Take A39 from town centre towards Lynton, in 1m left onto B3230. Right at garage at Lynton Cross onto A3123, site 1.5m on right.*
grid ref: *SS560427*

A very gently sloping, grassy, sheltered and south-facing site approached down a wide, well-kept driveway. This family friendly site is set in 500 acres of rolling countryside. It offers many quality amenities including a large swimming pool and horse riding. A woodland walk is an added attraction, as is the 'petorama' with its stock of friendly animals. There's also a new and used caravan sales centre and a comprehensive caravan accessory shop. 100 acre site. 700 touring pitches. 130 hardstandings. 348 seasonal pitches. Caravan pitches. Motorhome pitches. Tent pitches.

Open: all year (rs Winter at certain times - bars closed & catering not available)
Last arrival: 20.00hrs **Last departure:** 10.00hrs

Pitches: 🚐 🚚 ⛺

Leisure: 🏊 ☀ ⛳ 🎱 🎵 ♪

Facilities: ☀ 🖋 ❄ ⚕ 🚿 🎒 📶 ♻ ❶

Services: 🔌 🔵 🍴 🐕 📮 🛒 🛒 ⛽

Within 3 miles: ⚓ 🖋 ◎ 🛍 🛒 ∪

Notes: No noise after 23.00hrs, 10mph speed limit on site. Max 3 dogs. Dogs must be kept on leads. Caravan accessory shop, storage, workshop & sales.

AA Pubs & Restaurants nearby: The Quay Restaurant, ILFRACOMBE, EX34 9EQ, 01271 868090

CROYDE   Map 3 SS43

Places to visit

Marwood Hill Gardens, BARNSTAPLE, EX31 4EB, 01271 342528 www.marwoodhillgarden.co.uk

Great for kids: Watermouth Castle & Family Theme Park, ILFRACOMBE, EX34 9SL, 01271 863879 www.watermouthcastle.com

---

Bay View Farm Caravan & Camping Park
▶▶▶▶ 81%

tel: 01271 890501 **EX33 1PN**
email: info@bayviewfarm.co.uk
dir: *M5 junct 27, A361, through Barnstaple to Braunton, left onto B3231. Site at entrance to Croyde.* **grid ref:** *SS443388*

A very busy and popular park close to surfing beaches and rock pools, with a public footpath leading directly to the sea. Set in a stunning location with views out over the Atlantic to Lundy Island, it is just a short stroll from Croyde. The facilities are clean and well maintained; a family bathroom is available. There is a fish and chip shop on site. Please note that dogs are not permitted. 10 acre site. 70 touring pitches. 40 hardstandings. 15 seasonal pitches. Caravan pitches. Motorhome pitches. Tent pitches. 3 statics.

Open: Mar-Oct **Last arrival:** 21.30hrs **Last departure:** 11.00hrs

Pitches: 🚐 🚚 ⛺ 🏠

Leisure: 🎢

Facilities: ☀ 🖋 🅿 ◎ 🖋 ❄ ⚕ 🎒 📶 ♻ ❶

Services: 🔌 🔵 🛢 🐕 📮 🛒 🛒

Glamping: **Wooden Pods** 2, Changeover day Mon, Fri Min stay 3 nights (in high season only Mon-Fri, Fri-Mon or weekly bookings) Car by unit

Within 3 miles: ⚓ 🏇 🖋 ◎ 🛍 🛒 ∪

Notes: ⊗ No noise after mdnt. Fresh produce available in high season.

AA Pubs & Restaurants nearby: The Rock Inn, GEORGEHAM, EX33 1JW, 01271 890322

The Quay Restaurant, ILFRACOMBE, EX34 9EQ, 01271 868090

CULLOMPTON

See Kentisbeare

DARTMOUTH   Map 3 SX85

Places to visit

Dartmouth Castle, DARTMOUTH, TQ6 0JN, 01803 833588 www.english-heritage.org.uk/daysout/properties/dartmouth-castle

PREMIER PARK

Woodlands Grove Caravan & Camping Park
▶▶▶▶▶ 90%

Best of British

tel: 01803 712598 **Blackawton TQ9 7DQ**
email: holiday@woodlandsgrove.com **web:** www.woodlands-caravanpark.com
dir: *From Dartmouth take A3122, 4m. Or from A38 take A385 to Totnes. Then A381 towards Salcombe, after Halwell take A3122 towards Dartmouth, site signed (brown tourist signs).* **grid ref:** *SX813522*

A quality caravan and tent park with smart toilet facilities (including excellent family rooms), spacious pitches, including decent hardstandings and good attention to detail throughout, all set in an extensive woodland environment with a terraced grass camping area. Free entry to the adjoining Woodlands Theme Park makes an excellent package holiday for families, but also good for adults travelling without children who are perhaps seeking a low season break. Please check with the site with reference to their minimum stay policy. There is a bus stop at the entrance. 16 acre site. 350 touring pitches. 129 hardstandings. Caravan pitches. Motorhome pitches. Tent pitches.

Woodlands Grove Caravan & Camping Park

Open: 24 Mar-29 Oct **Last arrival:** 21.30hrs **Last departure:** 11.00hrs

Pitches: * 🚐 £15.50-£34 🚐 £15.50-£34 ⛺ £15.50-£34

Leisure: ⚙ 🎯 🎱 ♪

Facilities: 🚿 🔗 📳 ⊙ ℘ ✳ ㋛ 🔥 🛒 💶 ♻ ❗

Services: 🔌 🔄 🔋 🚿 Ⓣ 🍽 ⛽ 🚽 ↯

Within 3 miles: ⤓ ⊙ 📶 📶

Notes: No open fires, fire pits or chimeneas, quiet 22.30hrs-08.00hrs. Dogs must be kept on leads. Falconry centre, woodland walk, mini golf, zoo, farm, dog kennels.

AA Pubs & Restaurants nearby: The George Inn, BLACKAWTON, TQ9 7BG, 01803 712342

The Seahorse, DARTMOUTH, TQ6 9BH, 01803 835147

PREMIER PARK

Cofton Country Holidays
▶ ▶ ▶ ▶ ▶ 90%

GOLD

tel: 01626 890111 & 0800 085 8649 **Starcross EX6 8RP**
email: info@coftonholidays.co.uk **web:** www.coftonholidays.co.uk
dir: *On A379 (Exeter to Dawlish road), 3m from Dawlish.* **grid ref:** *SX967801*

This park is set in a rural location surrounded by spacious open grassland, with plenty of well-kept flowerbeds throughout. Most pitches overlook either the swimming pool complex or the coarse fishing lakes and woodlands. All the refurbished purpose-built toilet blocks offer smart modern facilities and the on-site pub serves drinks, meals and snacks for all the family, and a mini-market caters for most shopping needs. 45 acre site. 450 touring pitches. 60 hardstandings. 110 seasonal pitches. Caravan pitches. Motorhome pitches. Tent pitches. 82 statics.

Open: all year **Last arrival:** 20.00hrs **Last departure:** 11.00hrs

Pitches: * 🚐 £17.50-£34 🚐 £17.50-£34 ⛺ £17.50-£34

Leisure: 🏊 🎣 🎾 ⚙ ❋ 🎯 🎱 ♪ ℘

Facilities: 🚿 🔗 📳 ⊙ ℘ ✳ ㋛ 🔥 🛒 💶 ♻ ❗

Services: 🔌 🔄 🍺 🔋 🚿 Ⓣ 🍽 ⛽ 🚽 ↯

Within 3 miles: ⤓ 🚴 🏇 ℘ ⊙ 🚣 📶 📶

Notes: Dogs must be kept on leads. Soft play area, sauna & steam room, bowlingo.

See advert on page 160

DAWLISH *continued*

Lady's Mile Holiday Park
►►►►► 86%

tel: 01626 863411 **EX7 0LX**
email: info@ladysmile.co.uk
dir: *1m N of Dawlish on A379.* **grid ref:** *SX968784*

A family owned and run touring park with a wide variety of pitches, including some that are fully serviced. There are plenty of activities for everyone, including two swimming pools with waterslides, a children's splash pool, a well-equipped gym, a sauna in the main season, a large adventure playground, extensive restaurant facilities, and a bar with entertainment in high season. Facilities are kept very clean, and the surrounding beaches are easily accessed. Holiday homes and two, high quality glamping pods are also available. 18 acre site. 570 touring pitches. 67 hardstandings. 200 seasonal pitches. Caravan pitches. Motorhome pitches. Tent pitches. 120 statics.

Open: all year (23 Mar-Oct facilities fully open) **Last arrival:** 20.00hrs **Last departure:** 11.00hrs

Pitches: 🚐 🚌 ▲ 🏠 prices shown below

Leisure: ⬆️ ⬆️ ⚡ ᛉ ↓ ⊙ ♦ ♫ Spa

Facilities: 🚿 🏠 ⊙ 🍴 ⚡ ⬆ 🔋 📷 ♿ 🕴 WIFI ♻ 🛈

Services: 🔌 🔋 ♨ 🍴 🧺 🚽 🍴 🛒 ⬆ ⬇

Glamping: Wooden Pods 2, £35-£50 Changeover day Any day Min stay 1 night Car by unit

Within 3 miles: ↓ ⚡ 🎣 📷 ◎ ⬆ 🛒 🔋 U

Notes: No noise after mdnt. Dogs must be kept on leads. Bowling alley.

AA Pubs & Restaurants nearby: The Elizabethan, LUTON (NEAR CHUDLEIGH), TQ13 0BL, 01626 775425

The Anchor Inn, COCKWOOD, EX6 8RA, 01626 890203

Leadstone Camping
►►► 84%

tel: 01626 864411 **Warren Rd EX7 0NG**
email: info@leadstonecamping.co.uk **web:** www.leadstonecamping.co.uk
dir: *M5 junct 30, A379 to Dawlish. Before village turn left on brow of hill, signed Dawlish Warren. Site 0.5m on right.* **grid ref:** *SX974782*

A traditional, mainly level, grassy camping park approximately a half-mile walk from the sands and dunes at Dawlish Warren — a nature reserve and Blue Flag beach. This mainly tented park has been run by the same friendly family for many years, and is an ideal base for touring south Devon. A regular bus service from outside the gate takes in a wide area. The smart, well-equipped timber cabin toilet facility includes some privacy cubicles. There is a pub a short walk away. 8 acre site. 137 touring pitches. 14 seasonal pitches. Caravan pitches. Motorhome pitches. Tent pitches.

Open: 26 May-4 Sep **Last arrival:** 22.00hrs **Last departure:** noon

Pitches: * 🚐 £20-£28 🚌 £16-£24 ▲ £16-£24

Leisure: 🛝

Facilities: 🏠 🅿 ⊙ 📷 ✳ ♿ 🕴 WIFI ♻ 🛈

LEISURE: 🏊 Indoor pool 🏊 Outdoor pool 🛝 Children's playground 🤚 Kid's club 🎾 Tennis court ♦ Games room ⛳ Golf course 🚣 Boat hire 🚴 Cycle hire 🎬 Cinema 🎵 Entertainment 🎣 Fishing ◎ Mini golf ⛳ Pitch n putt 🏄 Watersports 🏋 Gym ⚽ Sports field U Stables **FACILITIES:** 🛁 Bath 🚿 Shower 🅿 Private washing cubicles ⊙ Electric shaver 🪮 Hairdryer ✳ Ice Packs ♿ Disabled facilities 🛒 Shop on site 🏪 Mobile shop 🍴 BBQ area 🌳 Picnic area WIFI Wi-fi 💻 Internet access ♻ Recycling 🛈 Tourist info 🐕 Dog exercise area 🚗 Car hire can be arranged

Services: 🔌🗐🔋⌀Ⓣ🔋⛽

Within 3 miles: ⚓🎣◎🛒🗐

Notes: No noise after 23.00hrs, only portable & disposable BBQs permitted. Dogs must be kept on leads.

AA Pubs & Restaurants nearby: The Elizabethan, LUTON (NEAR CHUDLEIGH), TQ13 0BL, 01626 775425

The Anchor Inn, COCKWOOD, EX6 8RA, 01626 890203

DREWSTEIGNTON   Map 3 SX79

Places to visit

Castle Drogo, DREWSTEIGNTON, EX6 6PB, 01647 433306
www.nationaltrust.org.uk/castle-drogo

Finch Foundry, STICKLEPATH, EX20 2NW, 01837 840046
www.nationaltrust.org.uk

PREMIER PARK

Woodland Springs Adult Touring Park
►►►►► 90%

tel: 01647 231695 Venton EX6 6PG
email: enquiries@woodlandsprings.co.uk
dir: Exit A30 at Whiddon Down junct onto A382 towards Moretonhampstead. Site 1.5m on left. grid ref: SX695912

An attractive and very well managed park in a rural area within Dartmoor National Park. This site is surrounded by woodland and farmland, and is very peaceful. The toilet block offers superb facilities, including four fully serviced cubicles, some sutiable for disabled visitors. Guests can expect high levels of customer care. Please note, children are not accepted. 4 acre site. 81 touring pitches. 48 hardstandings. 20 seasonal pitches. Caravan pitches. Motorhome pitches. Tent pitches.

Open: all year Last arrival: 20.00hrs Last departure: 11.00hrs

Pitches: 🚐🚍⛺

Facilities: 🏪🅿🗐☉🌊🔥♿🗐🔥WiFi♻🛈

Services: 🔌🗐🔋⌀Ⓣ🔋⛽

Within 3 miles: 🎣🗐

Notes: Adults only. No fires, no noise 23.00hrs-08.00hrs. Dogs must be kept on leads. Day kennels, freezer, coffee vending machine.

AA Pubs & Restaurants nearby: The Old Inn, DREWSTEIGNTON, EX6 6QR, 01647 281276

EAST ALLINGTON

Places to visit

Kingsbridge Cookworthy Museum, KINGSBRIDGE, TQ7 1AW, 01548 853235
www.kingsbridgemuseum.org.uk

Great for kids: Woodlands Family Theme Park, DARTMOUTH, TQ9 7DQ, 01803 712598 www.woodlandspark.com

---

EAST ALLINGTON   Map 3 SX74

Mounts Farm Touring Park
►►► 78%

tel: 01548 521591 The Mounts TQ9 7QJ
email: mounts.farm@lineone.net
dir: A381 from Totnes towards Kingsbridge (NB ignore signs for East Allington). At 'Mounts', site 0.5m on left. grid ref: SX757488

A neat, grassy park divided into four paddocks by mature natural hedges. Three of the paddocks are for the tourers and campers, and the fourth is a children's play area. The laundry, toilets and well-stocked little shop are in converted farm buildings. There's an on-site snack bar and calor gas retailer. 7 acre site. 50 touring pitches. 10 seasonal pitches. Caravan pitches. Motorhome pitches. Tent pitches.

Open: Mar-Nov Last arrival: 22.00hrs Last departure: 16.00hrs

Pitches: 🚐🚍⛺

Leisure: ⚽

Facilities: ☉🌊☀🗐♻🛈

Services: 🔌🗐🔋⌀Ⓣ🔋

Within 3 miles: ⚓🎣♿🗐🗐↻

Notes: Dogs must be kept on leads. Camping accessories shop on site.

AA Pubs & Restaurants nearby: The Fortescue Arms, EAST ALLINGTON, TQ9 7RA, 01548 521215

EAST WORLINGTON   Map 3 SS71

Yeatheridge Farm Caravan Park
►►►► 85%

tel: 01884 860330 EX17 4TN
email: yeatheridge@talk21.com
dir: M5 junct 27, A361, at 1st rdbt at Tiverton take B3137 for 9m towards Witheridge. Fork left 1m past Nomansland onto B3042. Site on left in 3.5m. (NB do not enter East Worlington). grid ref: SS768110

A well-kept park in a remote woodland setting on the edge of the Tamar Valley. It is peacefully located at the end of a private, half-mile, tree-lined drive; it offers superb on-site facilities, including an excellent restaurant and bar area with outside seating, a large children's play area, and high levels of customer care from the hands-on owners. The toilets are immaculate and well maintained, plus there is an indoor swimming pool, sauna and a good information and games room – all have a friendly atmosphere. Two fishing lakes are also available. 12 acre site. 103 touring pitches. 8 hardstandings. Caravan pitches. Motorhome pitches. Tent pitches. 19 statics.

Open: 15 Mar-end Sep Last arrival: 22.00hrs Last departure: 10.00hrs

Pitches: 🚐🚍⛺

Leisure: 🏊⚽❓

Facilities: ☉🌊☀♿🗐🔥WiFi♻🛈

Services: 🔌🗐🔋⌀Ⓣ🍴🔋🏧🛒⛽

Within 3 miles: 🎣🗐🗐↻

Notes: Dogs must be kept on leads.

AA Pubs & Restaurants nearby: The Grove Inn, KINGS NYMPTON, EX37 9ST, 01769 580406

PITCHES: 🚐 Caravans 🚍 Motorhomes ⛺ Tents 🏕 Glamping accommodation   SERVICES: 🔌 Electric hook up 🗐 Launderette 🔋 Licensed bar 🔋 Calor Gas ⌀ Camping Gaz Ⓣ Toilet fluid 🍴 Café/Restaurant 🏧 Fast Food/Takeaway 🔋 Battery charging 🛒 Baby care ⛽ Motorvan service point
ABBREVIATIONS: BHs – bank holidays   Etr – Easter   Spring BH – Spring Bank Holiday   fr – from   hrs – hours   m – mile   mdnt – midnight
rdbt – roundabout   rs – restricted service   wk – week   wknd – weekend   x-roads – crossroads   🚫 No credit or debit cards   🚫 No dogs

EXETER

See Kennford

EXMOUTH
Map 3 SY08

Places to visit

A la Ronde, EXMOUTH, EX8 5BD, 01395 265514
www.nationaltrust.org.uk/alaronde

Bicton Park Botanical Gardens, BICTON, EX9 7BJ, 01395 568465
www.bictongardens.co.uk

Great for kids: The World of Country Life, EXMOUTH, EX8 5BU, 01395 274533
www.worldofcountrylife.co.uk

Devon Cliffs Holiday Park
HOLIDAY CENTRE 91%

tel: 01395 226226 & 0871 230 2760
(Calls cost 10p per minute plus your phone company's access charge)
Sandy Bay EX8 5BT
email: devoncliffs@haven.com
dir: *M5 junct 30, A376 towards Exmouth, follow brown signs to Sandy Bay.*
grid ref: SY036807

A large and exciting holiday park on a hillside setting close to Exmouth, with spectacular views across Sandy Bay. This all-action park offers a superb entertainment programme for all ages throughout the day, with very modern sports and leisure facilities available for everyone. An internet café is just one of the quality amenities, and though some visitors may enjoy relaxing and watching others play, the temptation to join in is overwhelming. South Beach Café, which overlooks the sea, is well worth a visit. Please note, that from 2017 this park will not accept any tourers or tents. 163 acre site. 1800 statics.

Open: mid Mar-end Oct (rs mid Mar-May & Sep-Oct some facilities may be reduced) **Last arrival:** anytime **Last departure:** 10.00hrs

Leisure: 🏊‍♂️ 🏊 🎾 ✋ 🎣 🎵
Facilities: ☉ 🪒 🚿 🛗 🔥 WiFi 🖥️ ♻️ ❶
Services: 🔌 🔲 🍴 🍽️ 🍺
Within 3 miles: 🚴 🎣 🎮 ◎ 🚤 🛒 🛍️ ⛵

Notes: No commercial vehicles, no bookings by persons under 21yrs unless a family booking, max 2 dogs per booking, certain dog breeds banned, no dogs on beach May-Sep. Dogs must be kept on leads. Crazy golf, fencing, archery, bungee trampoline, aqua jets.

AA Pubs & Restaurants nearby: Les Saveurs, EXMOUTH, EX8 1NT, 01395 269459

HOLSWORTHY
Map 3 SS30

Places to visit

Dartington Crystal, GREAT TORRINGTON, EX38 7AN, 01805 626242
www.dartington.co.uk

RHS Garden Rosemoor, GREAT TORRINGTON, EX38 8PH, 0845 265 8072 *(Calls cost 7p per minute plus your phone company's access charge)* www.rhs.org.uk/rosemoor

Great for kids: The Milky Way Adventure Park, CLOVELLY, EX39 5RY, 01237 431255 www.themilkyway.co.uk

---

Headon Farm Caravan Site
▶▶▶ 83%

tel: 01409 254477 **Headon Farm, Hollacombe EX22 6NN**
email: reader@headonfarm.co.uk
dir: *From Holsworthy A388 signed Launceston. 0.5m, at hill brow left into Staddon Rd. 1m (follow site signs) right signed Ashwater. 0.5m, left at hill brow. Site 25yds.*
grid ref: SS367023

Set on a working farm in a quiet rural location. All pitches have extensive views of the Devon countryside, yet the park is only two and a half miles from the market town of Holsworthy, and within easy reach of roads to the coast and beaches of north Cornwall. 2 acre site. 19 touring pitches. 11 hardstandings. Caravan pitches. Motorhome pitches. Tent pitches.

Open: all year **Last arrival:** 19.00hrs **Last departure:** noon

Pitches: 🚐 🚍 ⛺
Leisure: ⊕
Facilities: 🏊 🅿️ ☉ 🚿 🛗 🔥 ♻️ ❶ 🎱
Services: 🔌 🍽️
Within 3 miles: 🚴 🎣 🛒 🛍️ ⛵

Notes: PayPal accepted. Breathable groundsheets only. Dogs must be kept on leads. Caravan & motorhome storage (outside or undercover).

AA Pubs & Restaurants nearby: The Devil's Stone Inn, SHEBBEAR, EX21 5RU, 01409 281210

Noteworthy Farm Caravan and Campsite
▶▶ 78%

tel: 01409 253731 & 07811 000071 **Noteworthy, Bude Rd EX22 7JB**
email: enquiries@noteworthy-devon.co.uk
dir: *On A3072 between Holsworthy & Bude. 3m from Holsworthy on right.*
grid ref: SS303052

This campsite is owned by a friendly young couple with their own children. There are good views from the quiet rural location, and simple toilet facilities. The local bus stops outside the gate on request. 5 acre site. 5 touring pitches. 3 hardstandings. Caravan pitches. Motorhome pitches. Tent pitches. 5 statics.

Open: all year **Last departure:** 11.00hrs

Pitches: * 🚐 £12-£15 🚍 £12-£15 ⛺ £12-£15
Leisure: 🎣 **Facilities:** 🏊 ☉ 🚿 🔥 ♻️ ❶
Services: 🔌 **Within 3 miles:** 🚴 🎣 🛍️ ⛵

Notes: 🐾 PayPal accepted. No open fires, no noise after 22.30hrs. Dogs must be kept on leads. Dog grooming available.

AA Pubs & Restaurants nearby: Bay View Inn, WIDEMOUTH BAY, EX23 0AW, 01288 361273

LEISURE: 🏊 Indoor pool 🏊 Outdoor pool 🎠 Children's playground ✋ Kid's club 🎾 Tennis court 🎱 Games room 🏌 Golf course 🚤 Boat hire 🚲 Cycle hire 🎬 Cinema 🎵 Entertainment 🎣 Fishing ◎ Mini golf ⛳ Pitch n putt 🏊 Watersports 🏋 Gym Sports field ⛵ Stables **FACILITIES:** 🛁 Bath 🚿 Shower 🅿️ Private washing cubicles ☉ Electric shaver 🪒 Hairdryer ❄ Ice Packs 🛗 Disabled facilities 🛒 Shop on site 🛍️ Mobile shop 🔥 BBQ area 🎋 Picnic area WiFi Wi-fi 🖥️ Internet access ♻️ Recycling ❶ Tourist info 🐾 Dog exercise area 🎱 Car hire can be arranged

ILFRACOMBE
Map 3 SS54

Places to visit

Arlington Court, ARLINGTON, EX31 4LP, 01271 850296
www.nationaltrust.org.uk/arlington-court

Exmoor Zoological Park, BLACKMOOR GATE, EX31 4SG, 01598 763352
www.exmoorzoo.co.uk

Great for kids: Watermouth Castle & Family Theme Park, ILFRACOMBE,
EX34 9SL, 01271 863879 www.watermouthcastle.com

Hele Valley Holiday Park
►►►►88%

tel: 01271 862460 **Hele Bay EX34 9RD**
email: holidays@helevalley.co.uk **web:** www.helevalley.co.uk
dir: *M5 junct 27, A361, through Barnstaple & Braunton to Ilfracombe. Take A399 towards
Combe Martin. Follow brown Hele Valley signs. In 400mtrs sharp right to T-junct. Park on
left.* **grid ref:** *SS533472*

A deceptively spacious park set in a picturesque valley with glorious tree-lined hilly
views from most pitches. High quality toilet facilities are provided, and the park is
within walking distance of a lovely beach and on a regular bus route. Camping
pods are available to hire. The harbour and other attractions of Ilfracombe are just
a mile away. 17 acre site. 50 touring pitches. 15 hardstandings. Caravan pitches.
Motorhome pitches. Tent pitches. 80 statics.

Open: Etr-Oct **Last arrival:** 18.00hrs **Last departure:** 11.00hrs
Pitches: * ▣ £24-£38 ▣ £19-£38 Å £19-£38 ⋔ prices shown below
Leisure: Spa
Facilities: ⚒ ▣ ⊙ ℘ ✳ ⅋ ♿ ⊞ ⊞ 🐕 WiFi 🖥 ♻ ❂
Services: ▣ ▣ 🛢 ⊘ 🚽 ➡ ⅃
Glamping: **Wooden Pods** 3, £43-£76 Changeover day Sat Min stay 1 night
Within 3 miles: ⅃ ⅌ ⅃ ℘ ◎ ⅀ 🛢 ⅃ ∪

Notes: Groups, motorhomes & tourers by arrangement only. Dogs must be kept on leads.
Nature trail, postal collection.

AA Pubs & Restaurants nearby: The Quay Restaurant, ILFRACOMBE, EX34 9EQ,
01271 868090

Sunnymead Farm Camping & Touring Site
NEW ►►► 80%

tel: 01271 879845 & 07826 184874 **Morthoe Rd EX34 8NZ**
email: info@sunnymead-farm.co.uk
dir: *From A361 between Ilfracombe & Braunton, at Mulacott Cross rdbt, take B3343
signed Woolacombe. Site approx 1m on right, just after Veterinary Hospital; opposite
Highways Guest House.* **grid ref:** *SS500441*

Peace and tranquillity abound at this small farm site that's set in the beautiful
north Devon countryside with easy reach to Ilfracombe and Woolacombe. 30 grass
pitches are set around a well mown and tended paddock, most have electric
hook-up and some enjoy superb sea views. Expect spotlessly clean toilet facilities
and a traditional camping atmosphere. 3 acre site. 30 touring pitches. 12
hardstandings. 7 seasonal pitches. Caravan pitches. Motorhome pitches.
Tent pitches. 2 statics.

Open: Etr-Oct (rs Low season - reduced hours at reception/shop)
Last departure: 10.30hrs
Pitches: * ▣ £14-£27 ▣ £14-£27 Å £14-£27 **Leisure:** ⅍
Facilities: ⚒ ▣ ⊙ ✳ 🛢 🐕 ♻ ❂ **Services:** ▣ 🛒
Within 3 miles: ⅃ ⅃ ℘ ◎ ⅀ 🛢 ⅃ ∪

Notes: Booking advisable during school hols. Dogs must be kept on leads. Storage
facilities.

KENNFORD
Map 3 SX98

Places to visit

St Nicholas Priory, EXETER, EX4 3BL, 01392 665858 www.exeter.gov.uk/priory

Custom House Visitor Centre, EXETER, EX2 4AN, 01392 271611
www.exeter.gov.uk/customhouse

Great for kids: Devon's Crealy Great Adventure Park, CLYST ST MARY, EX5 1DR,
01395 233200 www.crealy.co.uk

Kennford International Caravan Park
►►►►83%

tel: 01392 833046 **EX6 7YN**
email: ian@kennfordinternational.com
dir: *At end of M5 take A38, site signed at Kennford slip road.* **grid ref:** *SX912857*

Screened from the A38 by trees and shrubs, this park offers pitches divided by
hedging for privacy. A high quality toilet block complements the park's facilities.
A good, centrally-located base for exploring the coast and touring the countryside of
Devon, and Exeter is easily accessible via buses that stop nearby. 15 acre site.
22 touring pitches. 4 hardstandings. Caravan pitches. Motorhome pitches. Tent
pitches. 65 statics.

Open: all year **Last arrival:** 21.00hrs (winter - check with site for arrival times)
Last departure: 11.00hrs
Pitches: * ▣ £16-£19 ▣ £16-£19 Å £16-£19
Leisure: ⅍ **Facilities:** ⚒ ▣ ⊙ ♿ 🐕 WiFi ♻ ❂
Services: ▣ 🛢 🛢 ⊤ ➡ ⅃
Within 3 miles: ⅃ ⅌ ⅃ ℘ 🛢 ⅃ ∪

Notes: PayPal accepted. Dogs must be kept on leads.

AA Pubs & Restaurants nearby: Bridge Inn, TOPSHAM, EX3 0QQ, 01392 873862

PITCHES: ▣ Caravans ▣ Motorhomes Å Tents ⋔ Glamping accommodation **SERVICES:** ▣ Electric hook up 🛢 Launderette 🍺 Licensed bar
🛢 Calor Gas ⊘ Camping Gaz ⊤ Toilet fluid 🍽 Café/Restaurant 🍟 Fast Food/Takeaway ➡ Battery charging 👶 Baby care ⅃ Motorvan service point
ABBREVIATIONS: BHs – bank holidays Etr – Easter Spring BH – Spring Bank Holiday fr – from hrs – hours m – mile mdnt – midnight
rdbt – roundabout rs – restricted service wk – week wknd – weekend x-roads – crossroads ⊗ No credit or debit cards ⊗ No dogs

KENTISBEARE
Map 3 ST00

Places to visit

Killerton House & Garden, KILLERTON, EX5 3LE, 01392 881345
www.nationaltrust.org.uk

Allhallows Museum, HONITON, EX14 1PG, 01404 44966
www.honitonmuseum.co.uk

Great for kids: Diggerland, CULLOMPTON, EX15 2PE, 0871 227 7007 *(Calls cost 10p per minute plus your phone company's access charge)* www.diggerland.com

Forest Glade Holiday Park
▶▶▶▶ 82%

GOLD

tel: 01404 841381 **EX15 2DT**
email: enquiries@forest-glade.co.uk
dir: *Tent traffic: from A373 turn left past Keepers Cottage Inn (2.5m E of M5 junct 28). (NB due to narrow roads, touring caravans & larger motorhomes must approach from Honiton direction. Please phone park for access details).* **grid ref:** *ST101073*

A quiet, attractive park in a forest clearing with well-kept gardens and beech hedge screening. One of the main attractions is the site's immediate proximity to the forest which offers magnificent hillside walks with surprising views over the valleys. There's an undercover heated swimming pool, a good children's play area and large games room; camping pods are available for hire. Please note, that because the roads are narrow around the site, it is best to phone the site for suitable route details. 26 acre site. 80 touring pitches. 40 hardstandings. 28 seasonal pitches. Caravan pitches. Motorhome pitches. Tent pitches. 42 statics.

Open: mid Mar-end Oct (rs Low season limited shop hours) **Last arrival:** 21.00hrs
Last departure: noon

Pitches: 🚐 £15.50-£23.50 🚌 £15.50-£23.50 ▲ £15.50-£22.50 🏠 prices shown below

Leisure: 🏊 ⚲ ⚽ ♨ 🎱

Facilities: 🏦 P️ ☉ ⚡ ✻ ⚱ 🔆 🎋 ⛱ WiFi ♻ ❶

Services: 🚌 🖥 💧 🛒 T️ 🛏 🖤 ⛽

Glamping: Wooden Pods 2, £30-£45 Changeover day Any day Min stay 2 nights
Car by unit

Within 3 miles: ⚲ 🔆 ∪

Notes: PayPal accepted. Families & couples only. Dogs must be kept on leads. Adventure & soft play areas, wildlife information room, paddling pool.

AA Pubs & Restaurants nearby: The Blacksmiths Arms, PLYMTREE, EX15 2JU, 01884 277474

KINGSBRIDGE

Places to visit

Kingsbridge Cookworthy Museum, KINGSBRIDGE, TQ7 1AW, 01548 853235
www.kingsbridgemuseum.org.uk

Overbeck's, SALCOMBE, TQ8 8LW, 01548 842893 www.nationaltrust.org.uk

KINGSBRIDGE
Map 3 SX74

PREMIER PARK

Parkland Caravan and Camping Site
▶▶▶▶▶ 82%

tel: 01548 852723 & 07968 222008 **Sorley Green Cross TQ7 4AF**
email: enquiries@parklandsite.co.uk **web:** www.parklandsite.co.uk
dir: *A384 to Totnes, A381 towards Kingsbridge. 12m, at Stumpy Post Cross rdbt turn right, 1m. Site 200yds on left after Sorley Green Cross.* **grid ref:** *SX728462*

Expect a high level of customer care at this family-run park set in the glorious South Hams countryside; it has panoramic views over Salcombe and the rolling countryside towards Dartmoor. The immaculately maintained grounds offer generous grass pitches, hardstandings and super pitches (RVs can be accommodated), and a new dedicated touring field with 10 fully-serviced pitches. The on-site shop sells seasonal produce, everyday provisions, pre-ordered hampers and camping supplies; the toilet facilities feature quality cubicles, family washrooms, a bathroom and a fully-fitted disabled suite. Babysitting is available by arrangement. A bus stops close to the site entrance, which is handy for exploring the local towns and villages. 3 acre site. 50 touring pitches. 30 hardstandings. 25 seasonal pitches. Caravan pitches. Motorhome pitches. Tent pitches.

Open: all year **Last arrival:** 21.30hrs **Last departure:** 11.30hrs

Pitches: * 🚐 £10-£40 🚌 £10-£40 ▲ £10-£40

Leisure: ♨ 🎱

Facilities: 🚿 🏦 P️ ☉ ⚡ ✻ ⚱ 🔆 🎋 WiFi 🖥 ♻ ❶ 🚗

Services: 🚌 🖥 💧 🛒 T️ 🛏 🖤 ⛽

Within 3 miles: ⚓ ⚲ 🎣 ◎ 🔆 🔆 ∪

Notes: ⊗ PayPal accepted. No camp fires, no noise after 23.00hrs, children must be accompanied by an adult when using facilities, site gates closed 22.00hrs-07.00hrs. Use of fridge freezers, campers' kitchen, coffee shop, freshly baked croissants, short term caravan storage facility, electric car charging point.

AA Pubs & Restaurants nearby: The Fortescue Arms, EAST ALLINGTON, TQ9 7RA, 01548 521215

The Crabshell Inn, KINGSBRIDGE, TQ7 1JZ, 01548 852345

LEISURE: 🏊 Indoor pool 🏊 Outdoor pool ⛰ Children's playground 🏌 Kid's club ⚲ Tennis court 🎱 Games room ⛳ Golf course ⚓ Boat hire 🚲 Cycle hire 🎬 Cinema 🎵 Entertainment 🎣 Fishing ◎ Mini golf ⛳ Pitch n putt 🏄 Watersports 🏋 Gym ⚽ Sports field ∪ Stables **FACILITIES:** 🛁 Bath 🚿 Shower P️ Private washing cubicles ☉ Electric shaver ⚡ Hairdryer ✻ Ice Packs 🔆 Disabled facilities 🖥 Shop on site 🚐 Mobile shop 🛒 BBQ area 🎋 Picnic area WiFi Wi-fi 🖥 Internet access ♻ Recycling ❶ Tourist info 🎋 Dog exercise area 🚗 Car hire can be arranged

Island Lodge Caravan & Camping Site
►►►►►80%

tel: 01548 852956 & 07968 222007 **Stumpy Post Cross TQ7 4BL**
email: enquiries@islandlodgesite.co.uk **web:** www.islandlodgesite.co.uk
dir: Take A381 from Totnes towards Kingsbridge. In 12m, at rdbt (Stumpy Post Cross) right, 300mtrs left into lane, site signed. 200mtrs on left. **grid ref:** SX738470

A small, peaceful and well-established park, with extensive views over the South Hams, which has been run by the same family for many years. The site has a security barrier, low-level lighting around the park, good hardstanding pitches, and a motorhome service point. There are immaculate toilet facilities. A scenic 35-minute walk will take you to Kingsbridge, or the Kingsbridge bus stops close to the site. There are several dog-friendly beaches nearby. 2 acre site. 30 touring pitches. 2 hardstandings. 20 seasonal pitches. Caravan pitches. Motorhome pitches. Tent pitches.

Open: all year (rs Nov-Mar shop closed) **Last arrival:** 20.30hrs **Last departure:** 11.30hrs

Pitches: * ♙ £22-£30 ♙ £22-£30 ♙ £22-£30

Leisure: ♙

Facilities: ♙♙♙♙♙♙♙♙♙♙♙♙♙

Services: ♙♙♙♙♙♙♙♙♙♙

Within 3 miles: ♙♙♙♙♙♙♙♙♙♙

Notes: ♙ No generators. Play area open 09.00hrs-21.00hrs. 24hr CCTV. Electronic security barrier closed overnight. Restrictions on certain dog breeds. Dogs must be kept on leads. Secure caravan storage yard, boat park.

AA Pubs & Restaurants nearby: The Fortescue Arms, EAST ALLINGTON, TQ9 7RA, 01548 521215

The Crabshell Inn, KINGSBRIDGE, TQ7 1JZ, 01548 852345

LYNTON

Places to visit
Arlington Court, ARLINGTON, EX31 4LP, 01271 850296 www.nationaltrust.org.uk/arlington-court

Great for kids: Exmoor Zoological Park, BLACKMOOR GATE, EX31 4SG, 01598 763352 www.exmoorzoo.co.uk

LYNTON Map 3 SS74

Channel View Caravan and Camping Park
►►►►72%

tel: 01598 753349 **Manor Farm EX35 6LD**
email: relax@channel-view.co.uk
dir: On A39 from Barbrook towards Hillsford Bridge. Approx 0.5m to site on left. **grid ref:** SS724482

On the top of the cliffs overlooking the Bristol Channel, this is a well-maintained park on the edge of Exmoor, and close to both Lynton and Lynmouth. Pitches can be selected from either those in a hidden hedged area or those with panoramic views over the coast. 6 acre site. 76 touring pitches. 15 hardstandings. Caravan pitches. Motorhome pitches. Tent pitches. 31 statics.

Open: 15 Mar-15 Nov **Last arrival:** 22.00hrs **Last departure:** noon

Pitches: * ♙ £13-£21 ♙ £13-£21 ♙ £13-£21

Facilities: ♙♙♙♙♙♙♙♙♙♙♙♙♙

Services: ♙♙♙♙♙♙♙♙ **Within 3 miles:** ♙♙♙♙♙♙♙♙

Notes: Groups by prior arrangement only. Dogs must be kept on leads. Parent & baby room.

AA Pubs & Restaurants nearby: Rising Sun Hotel, LYNMOUTH, EX35 6EG, 01598 753223

Rockford Inn, BRENDON, EX35 6PT, 01598 741214

Sunny Lyn Holiday Park
►►►78%

tel: 01598 753384 **Lynbridge EX35 6NS**
email: info@caravandevon.co.uk **web:** www.caravandevon.co.uk
dir: M5 junct 27, A361 to South Molton. Right onto A399 to Blackmoor Gate, right onto A39, left onto B3234 towards Lynmouth. Site 1m on right. **grid ref:** SS719486

Set in a sheltered riverside location in a wooded combe within a mile of the sea, in Exmoor National Park. This family-run park offers good facilities including an excellent café. 4.5 acre site. 9 touring pitches. 5 hardstandings. Caravan pitches. Motorhome pitches. Tent pitches. 7 statics.

Open: Mar-Oct **Last arrival:** 20.00hrs **Last departure:** 11.00hrs

Pitches: * ♙ £15.50-£18 ♙ £15.50-£18 ♙ £13-£15.50 **Leisure:** ♙

Facilities: ♙♙♙♙♙♙♙♙♙♙♙ **Services:** ♙♙♙♙♙♙♙♙

Within 3 miles: ♙♙♙♙♙♙♙

Notes: No cars by tents. No wood fires, quiet after 22.30hrs. Dogs must be kept on leads.

AA Pubs & Restaurants nearby: Rising Sun Hotel, LYNMOUTH, EX35 6EG, 01598 753223

Rockford Inn, BRENDON, EX35 6PT, 01598 741214

PITCHES: ♙ Caravans **♙** Motorhomes **♙** Tents **♙** Glamping accommodation **SERVICES: ♙** Electric hook up **♙** Launderette **♙** Licensed bar **♙** Calor Gas **♙** Camping Gaz **♙** Toilet fluid **♙** Café/Restaurant **♙** Fast Food/Takeaway **♙** Battery charging **♙** Baby care **♙** Motorvan service point **ABBREVIATIONS:** BHs – bank holidays Etr – Easter Spring BH – Spring Bank Holiday fr – from hrs – hours m – mile mdnt – midnight rdbt – roundabout rs – restricted service wk – week wknd – weekend x-roads – crossroads ♙ No credit or debit cards ♙ No dogs

MODBURY | Map 3 SX65

Places to visit

Kingsbridge Cookworthy Museum, KINGSBRIDGE, TQ7 1AW, 01548 853235
www.kingsbridgemuseum.org.uk

Overbeck's, SALCOMBE, TQ8 8LW, 01548 842893 www.nationaltrust.org.uk

Great for kids: National Marine Aquarium, PLYMOUTH, PL4 0LF, 01752 275200
www.national-aquarium.co.uk

Pennymoor Camping & Caravan Park
►►► 84%

tel: 01548 830542 **PL21 0SB**
email: enquiries@pennymoor-camping.co.uk **web:** www.pennymoor-camping.co.uk
dir: *Exit A38 at Wrangaton Cross. Left & then right at x-roads. After by-passing Ermington, turn left onto A379, pass through Modbury, turn left at Harraton Cross. Site on left.* **grid ref:** *SX685516*

Owned and run by the same family since 1935, this well-established, rural and lovingly tended park is tucked away in South Hams; it is close to glorious beaches and has good views over rolling countryside to Dartmoor in the distance. On part level, part gently sloping grass, Pennymoor is an ideal base for exploring south Devon and offers everything for relaxing and peaceful family stay, with spotless, well-maintained toilets, a fully-equipped children's play area, a well-stocked shop, site-wide WiFi and a relaxing atmosphere. 12.5 acre site. 119 touring pitches. 3 hardstandings. Caravan pitches. Motorhome pitches. Tent pitches. 76 statics.

Open: 15 Mar-15 Nov (rs 15 Mar-mid May only one toilet & shower block open)
Last arrival: 20.00hrs (later arrival time possible by prior arrangement)
Last departure: 11.00hrs

Pitches: * ⊞ £14-£24 ⊟ £14-£24 ▲ £14-£24

Leisure: ⁄Å

Facilities: ⌂ ⊙ ⌐ ✳ & Ⓢ ⋔ WiFi ♻ ❶

Services: ⊞ Ⓢ ▐ ⊘ Ⓣ ⛟ ⛟

Within 3 miles: & Ⓢ

Notes: No skateboards or scooters, no noise after 22.00hrs. Dogs must be kept on leads. Emergency phone, table tennis.

AA Pubs & Restaurants nearby: California Country Inn, MODBURY, PL21 0SG, 01548 821449

Rose & Crown, YEALMPTON, PL8 2EB, 01752 880223

MORTEHOE | Map 3 SS44

See also Woolacombe

Places to visit

Marwood Hill Gardens, BARNSTAPLE, EX31 4EB, 01271 342528
www.marwoodhillgarden.co.uk

Great for kids: Watermouth Castle & Family Theme Park, ILFRACOMBE, EX34 9SL, 01271 863879 www.watermouthcastle.com

North Morte Farm Caravan & Camping Park
►►►► 88%

tel: 01271 870381 **North Morte Rd EX34 7EG**
email: info@northmortefarm.co.uk **web:** www.northmortefarm.co.uk
dir: *From B3343 into Mortehoe, right at post office. Site 500yds on left.*
grid ref: *SS462455*

Set in spectacular coastal countryside close to National Trust land and 500 yards from Rockham Beach. This attractive park is very well run and maintained by friendly family owners, and the quaint village of Mortehoe with its cafés, shops and pubs, is just a five-minute walk away. 22 acre site. 180 touring pitches. 25 hardstandings. 13 seasonal pitches. Caravan pitches. Motorhome pitches. Tent pitches. 73 statics.

Open: Apr-Oct **Last arrival:** 22.00hrs **Last departure:** noon

Pitches: * ⊞ £15.50-£24 ⊟ £13-£24 ▲ £13-£19.50

Leisure: ⁄Å

Facilities: ⌂ ⌐ ⊙ ⌐ ✳ & Ⓢ ⋔ WiFi ♻ ❶

Services: ⊞ Ⓢ ▐ ⊘ Ⓣ ⛟ ⛟

Within 3 miles: & ⌐ ◎ Ⓢ Ⓢ ∪

Notes: No large groups. Dogs must be kept on leads.

AA Pubs & Restaurants nearby: Watersmeet Hotel, WOOLACOMBE, EX34 7EB, 01271 870333

The Quay Restaurant, ILFRACOMBE, EX34 9EQ, 01271 868090

NEWTON ABBOT

Map 3 SX87

See also Bickington

Places to visit

Tuckers Maltings, NEWTON ABBOT, TQ12 4AA, 01626 334734
www.tuckersmaltings.com

Bradley Manor, NEWTON ABBOT, TQ12 6BN, 01803 843235
www.nationaltrust.org.uk/devoncornwall

Great for kids: Prickly Ball Farm and Hedgehog Hospital, NEWTON ABBOT, TQ12 6BZ, 01626 362319 www.pricklyballfarm.com

PREMIER PARK

Ross Park

▶▶▶▶▶ 98%

tel: 01803 812983 **Park Hill Farm, Ipplepen TQ12 5TT**
email: enquiries@rossparkcaravanpark.co.uk web: www.rossparkcaravanpark.co.uk
dir: *N of Ipplepen on A381 follow brown site signs & sign for Woodland opposite Texaco garage.* grid ref: SX845671

A top-class park in every way, with large secluded pitches, high quality toilet facilities (which include excellent family rooms) and colourful flower displays throughout – note the wonderful floral walk to the toilets. The beautiful tropical conservatory also offers a breathtaking show of colour. There's a conservation walk through glorious wild flower meadows, replete with nature trail, a dog shower/grooming area, and six fully serviced pitches. This very rural park enjoys superb views of Dartmoor, and good quality meals to suit all tastes and pockets are served in the restaurant. Expect high levels of customer care – this park gets better each year. Home-grown produce and honey are sold in the shop. A bus, which stops close to the entrance, runs to Totnes and Newton Abbot. 32 acre site. 110 touring pitches. 110 hardstandings. Caravan pitches. Motorhome pitches. Tent pitches.

Open: Mar-2 Jan (rs 1st 3 wks Mar & Nov & Dec (except Xmas & New Year) - restaurant/bar closed) **Last arrival:** 21.00hrs **Last departure:** 11.00hrs

Pitches: * ⬛ £16.75-£29.50 ⬛ £16.75-£29.50 ⬛ £15.75-£29.50

Leisure: 🅰♿🎣 **Facilities:** 🅿🅿⊙🅿✳♿🖰🔯🖰 🚾♻🛈

Services: 🔌🅖🍽🛢⊘🇹🍴🔋♿🚻 **Within 3 miles:** ⬇🏇🅿🛒🔯🛒∪

Notes: Bikes, skateboards & scooters only permitted on leisure field. Dogs must be kept on leads. Snooker, table tennis, badminton.

AA Pubs & Restaurants nearby: The Church House Inn, MARLDON, TQ3 1SL, 01803 558279

PREMIER PARK

Dornafield

▶▶▶▶▶ 96%

tel: 01803 812732 **Dornafield Farm, Two Mile Oak TQ12 6DD**
email: enquiries@dornafield.com web: www.dornafield.com
dir: *From Newton Abbot take A381 signed Totnes for 2m. At Two Mile Oak Inn right, left at x-roads in 0.5m. Site on right.* grid ref: SX838683

An immaculately kept park in a tranquil wooded valley between Dartmoor and Torbay, divided into three areas. At the heart of the 30-acre site is Dornafield, a 14th-century farmhouse, adapted for campers' to use but still retaining much charm. The friendly family owners are always available for help or to give advice. The site has superb facilities in two ultra modern toilet blocks. On-site there is the Quarry Café which provides takeaway fish and chips or jacket potatoes. This is a quiet and peaceful location convenient for Torbay, Dartmoor and the charming coastal villages of the South Hams. A bus service to Totnes or Newton Abbot runs nearby. 30 acre site. 135 touring pitches. 119 hardstandings. 26 seasonal pitches. Caravan pitches. Motorhome pitches. Tent pitches.

Open: 16 Mar-7 Nov **Last arrival:** 22.00hrs **Last departure:** 11.00hrs

Pitches: * ⬛ £18.50-£34.50 ⬛ £18.50-£34.50 ⬛ £16.50-£20.50

Leisure: 🅰♿🎣 **Facilities:** 🅿🅿⊙🅿✳♿🖰 🚾🖥♻🛈

Services: 🔌🅖🛢⊘🇹🔋♿🚻

Within 3 miles: ⬇🅿🔯🛒

Notes: No commercial vehicles; no sign-written vehicles. Dogs must be kept on leads. Table tennis, secure caravan storage (all year), freshly baked bread.

AA Pubs & Restaurants nearby: The Church House Inn, MARLDON, TQ3 1SL, 01803 558279

PITCHES: ⬛ Caravans ⬛ Motorhomes ⬛ Tents ⬛ Glamping accommodation **SERVICES:** 🔌 Electric hook up 🅖 Launderette 🍽 Licensed bar 🛢 Calor Gas ⊘ Camping Gaz 🇹 Toilet fluid 🍴 Café/Restaurant 🍴 Fast Food/Takeaway 🔋 Battery charging ♿ Baby care 🚻 Motorvan service point

ABBREVIATIONS: BHs – bank holidays Etr – Easter Spring BH – Spring Bank Holiday fr – from hrs – hours m – mile mdnt – midnight rdbt – roundabout rs – restricted service wk – week wknd – weekend x-roads – crossroads Ⓔ No credit or debit cards Ⓧ No dogs

NEWTON ABBOT *continued*

Twelve Oaks Farm Caravan Park
▶▶▶▶ 81%

tel: 01626 335015 & 07976 440456 **Teigngrace TQ12 6QT**
email: info@twelveoaksfarm.co.uk **web:** www.twelveoaksfarm.co.uk
dir: *A38 from Exeter left signed Teigngrace (only), 0.25m before Drumbridges rdbt. 1.5m, through village, site on left. Or from Plymouth pass Drumbridges rdbt, take slip road for Chudleigh Knighton. Right over bridge, rejoin A38 towards Plymouth. Left for Teigngrace (only), then as above.* **grid ref:** SX852737

An attractive small park on a working farm close to Dartmoor National Park, and bordered by the River Teign. The tidy pitches are located amongst trees and shrubs, and the modern facilities are very well maintained. There are two well-stocked fishing lakes and children will enjoy visiting all the farm animals. Close by is Stover Country Park and also the popular Templar Way walking route. 2 acre site. 50 touring pitches. 25 hardstandings. 15 seasonal pitches. Caravan pitches. Motorhome pitches. Tent pitches.

Open: all year **Last arrival:** 21.00hrs **Last departure:** 10.30hrs

Pitches: * 🚐 £15.50-£24 🚐 £15.50-£24 🛖 £15.50-£24

Leisure: 🏊 ⚘ 🎣

Facilities: 🚿 🔥 ☉ 🗭 ✳ ⚒ Ⓢ 🎯 WiFi ♻ ℹ

Services: 🔌 🗑 🚽 Ⓣ ⚙

Within 3 miles: ♨ 🎠 🎣 ☉ ⛷ Ⓢ Ⓢ ♺

Notes: No noise after 23.00hrs. Dogs must be kept on leads.

AA Pubs & Restaurants nearby: The Elizabethan, LUTON (NEAR CHUDLEIGH), TQ13 0BL, 01626 775425

The Union Inn, DENBURY, TQ12 6DQ, 01803 812595

OTTERY ST MARY Map 3 SY19

Places to visit

Cadhay, OTTERY ST MARY, EX11 1QT, 01404 813511 www.cadhay.org.uk

Cuckoo Down Farm Glamping
▶▶▶▶ 80%

tel: 01271 27743 **Lower Broad Oak Rd, West Hill EX11 1UE**
email: enquiries@cuckoodownfarm.co.uk **web:** luxurydevonyurts.co.uk
dir: *M5, A30 signed Honiton, after airport on left, left signed Daisymount & Ottery St Mary. At mini rdbt, last exit (under bridge). At next mini rdbt follow West Hill sign. 0.5m, left into Bendarroch Rd. 3rd right into School Ln, right at end, immediately left into Elsdon Ln. At end straight over onto track. 0.5m, fork right to site (bumpy road).* **grid ref:** SY075938

On arrival at Cuckoo Down Farm the first thing that strikes you is the peace and tranquillity and the far-reaching views from the very spacious, 6-acre glamping meadow. There are two safari tents (Daisy & Poppy) sleeping six and three yurts (Clover, Bluebell & Buttercup) sleeping four; all units are kitted out with style. Each has a wood-burning stove, rugs and scatter cushions to make them cosy and comfortable, and down duvets and quilts on the beds. Each unit has a decked outside area, a fully-equipped kitchen cabin and a compost toilet; showers, fridges, freezers, washing machine and tumble drier are located in a nearby barn, which also has a small 'honesty' shop of essentials.

Open: all year

Glamping: Safari tents 2 **Yurts** 3, En suite Own kitchen

AA Pubs & Restaurants nearby: The Talaton Inn, OTTERY ST MARY, EX5 2RQ, 01404 822214

LEISURE: 🏊 Indoor pool 🏊 Outdoor pool 🎠 Children's playground ✋ Kid's club 🎾 Tennis court 🎱 Games room ⛳ Golf course ⛵ Boat hire 🚲 Cycle hire 🎬 Cinema 🎵 Entertainment 🎣 Fishing ⛳ Mini golf 🚩 Pitch n putt 🏄 Watersports 🏋 Gym ⚽ Sports field ♘ Stables **FACILITIES:** 🛁 Bath 🚿 Shower 🅿 Private washing cubicles ⊙ Electric shaver 🗭 Hairdryer ✳ Ice Packs ♿ Disabled facilities Ⓢ Shop on site 🏪 Mobile shop 🍖 BBQ area ⛱ Picnic area WiFi Wi-fi 💻 Internet access ♻ Recycling ℹ Tourist info 🐕 Dog exercise area 🚗 Car hire can be arranged

PAIGNTON

Map 3 SX86

Places to visit

Dartmouth Steam Railway & River Boat Company, PAIGNTON, TQ4 6AF, 01803 555872 www.dartmouthrailriver.co.uk

Kents Cavern, TORQUAY, TQ1 2JF, 01803 215136 www.kents-cavern.co.uk

Great for kids: Paignton Zoo Environmental Park, PAIGNTON, TQ4 7EU, 01803 697500 www.paigntonzoo.org.uk

PREMIER PARK

Beverley Parks Caravan & Camping Park
►►►►►87%

tel: 01803 661961 **Goodrington Rd TQ4 7JE**
email: info@beverley-holidays.co.uk
dir: *On A380, A3022, 2m S of Paignton left into Goodrington Rd. Beverley Park on right.* **grid ref:** *SX886582*

A high quality family-run park with extensive views of the bay and plenty of on-site amenities. The park boasts indoor and outdoor heated swimming pools, plus good bars and restaurants. The toilet facilities are modern and very clean and include excellent fully serviced family rooms. The park complex is attractively laid out with the touring areas divided into nicely screened areas. 12 acre site. 172 touring pitches. 49 hardstandings. Caravan pitches. Motorhome pitches. Tent pitches.

Open: all year **Last arrival:** 21.00hrs **Last departure:** 10.00hrs

Pitches: ⌑ ⌑ ▲

Leisure: ≋ ≋ ⚡ ⊰ 🎱 🎵 Spa

Facilities: ⊯ ⋔ ⊙ ⊮ ⋇ ⏦ 🔅 ⊓ WiFi ⬛ ♻ ✪

Services: 🔌 🔲 🔋 🛢 ⌀ T ⏍ 🍴 ⏚ ⇥ ⛟

Within 3 miles: ⌿ ⊱ 🗓 ⊘ ◎ ⊱ 🏢 🗗 ∪

Notes: No pets. Table tennis, sauna, crazy golf, letter box trail.

AA Pubs & Restaurants nearby: The Church House Inn, MARLDON, TQ3 1SL, 01803 558279

Cary Arms, TORQUAY, TQ1 3LX, 01803 327110

The Elephant Restaurant and Brasserie, TORQUAY, TQ1 2BH, 01803 200044

Whitehill Country Park
►►►►81%

tel: 01803 782338 **Stoke Rd TQ4 7PF**
email: info@whitehill-park.co.uk **web:** www.whitehill-park.co.uk
dir: *A385 through Totnes towards Paignton. Turn right by Parkers Arms into Stoke Rd towards Stoke Gabriel. Site on left after approx 1.5m.* **grid ref:** *SX857588*

A family-owned and run park set in rolling countryside, with many scenic beaches just a short drive away. This extensive country park covers 40 acres with woodland walks, plenty of flora and fauna and an excellent outdoor swimming pool, a café, plus a bar/restaurant with summer entertainment. It offers ideal facilities, including luxury lodges and camping pods, for an excellent holiday. 40 acre site. 260 touring pitches. Caravan pitches. Motorhome pitches. Tent pitches. 60 statics.

Open: Etr-Sep **Last arrival:** 21.00hrs **Last departure:** 10.00hrs

Pitches: ⌑ ⌑ ▲ ⌂

Leisure: ≋ 🎱

Facilities: ⊯ ⋔ ⊮ ⋇ ⏦ 🔅 ⊓ WiFi ⬛ ♻ ✪

Services: 🔌 🔲 🔋 🛢 ⌀ 🍴 ⏚ ⛟

Glamping: Wooden Pods 5

Within 3 miles: ⌿ ⊱ 🗓 ⊘ ◎ ⊱ 🏢 🗗 ∪

Notes: Dogs must be kept on leads. Walking & cycling trails, letter box trail, craft room, table tennis.

AA Pubs & Restaurants nearby: The Church House Inn, MARLDON, TQ3 1SL, 01803 558279

Cary Arms, TORQUAY, TQ1 3LX, 01803 327110

The Elephant Restaurant and Brasserie, TORQUAY, TQ1 2BH, 01803 200044

PITCHES: ⌑ Caravans ⌑ Motorhomes ▲ Tents ⌂ Glamping accommodation **SERVICES:** 🔌 Electric hook up 🔲 Launderette 🔋 Licensed bar 🛢 Calor Gas ⌀ Camping Gaz T Toilet fluid 🍴 Café/Restaurant ⏚ Fast Food/Takeaway 🔋 Battery charging 👶 Baby care ⛟ Motorvan service point
ABBREVIATIONS: BHs – bank holidays Etr – Easter Spring BH – Spring Bank Holiday fr – from hrs – hours m – mile mdnt – midnight rdbt – roundabout rs – restricted service wk – week wknd – weekend x-roads – crossroads 🚫 No credit or debit cards 🚫 No dogs

PLYMOUTH Map 3 SX45

Places to visit

Plymouth City Museum & Art Gallery, PLYMOUTH, PL4 8AJ, 01752 304774 www.plymouthmuseum.gov.uk

The Elizabethan House, PLYMOUTH, PL1 2NA, 01752 304774 www.plymouth.gov.uk/museums

Great for kids: National Marine Aquarium, PLYMOUTH, PL4 0LF, 01752 275200 www.national-aquarium.co.uk

Riverside Caravan Park

►►►► 85%

tel: 01752 344122 **Leigham Manor Dr PL6 8LL**
email: office@riversidecaravanpark.com **web:** www.riversidecaravanpark.com
dir: *From A38 at Marsh Mills rdbt, follow signs for Plympton (B3416) & brown 'Riverside' signs. At lights left into Riverside Rd signed 'Riverside'. 400mtrs, right into Leighham Manor Drive (River Plym on right) to site on right.* **grid ref:** *SX515575*

A well-groomed site on the outskirts of Plymouth on the banks of the River Plym, in a surprisingly peaceful location surrounded by woodland. The toilet facilities are appointed to a very good standard, and include private cubicles, plus there's a good games room and bar/restaurant serving food. This park is an ideal stopover for the ferries to France and Spain, and makes an excellent base for touring Dartmoor and the coast. The local bus stop is just a 10-minute walk from the site. 11 acre site. 259 touring pitches. 63 hardstandings. Caravan pitches. Motorhome pitches. Tent pitches. 22 statics.

Open: all year (rs Oct-Etr bar, restaurant, takeaway & pool closed) **Last arrival:** 22.00hrs **Last departure:** 11.00hrs

Pitches:

Leisure:

Facilities:

Services:

Within 3 miles:

Notes: Dogs must be kept on leads.

AA Pubs & Restaurants nearby: Artillery Tower Restaurant, PLYMOUTH, PL1 3QR, 01752 257610

The Greedy Goose, PLYMOUTH, PL1 2AE, 01752 252001

PRINCETOWN Map 3 SX57

The Plume of Feathers Inn

NEW ►► 78%

tel: 01822 890240 **Plymouth Hill PL20 6QQ**
email: contact@theplumeoffeathersdartmoor.co.uk
dir: *Site accessed from B3212 rdbt (by Plume of Feathers Inn) in centre of Princetown.* **grid ref:** *SX588733*

Set amidst the rugged beauty of Dartmoor, and behind the village pub, this campsite boasts good toilet facilities and all the amenities of the inn. The Plume of Feathers is Princetown's oldest building, and serves all day food in an atmospheric setting – try the 'camp and breakfast' deal that's on offer. This campsite is mainly for tents. 5 acre site. 80 touring pitches. Motorhome pitches. Tent pitches.

Open: all year **Last arrival:** 23.00hrs **Last departure:** noon

Pitches: * £13.90 £13.90 **Services:**

SALCOMBE Map 3 SX73

Places to visit

Overbeck's, SALCOMBE, TQ8 8LW, 01548 842893 www.nationaltrust.org.uk

Kingsbridge Cookworthy Museum, KINGSBRIDGE, TQ7 1AW, 01548 853235 www.kingsbridgemuseum.org.uk

Karrageen Caravan & Camping Park

►►►► 82%

tel: 01548 561230 **Bolberry, Malborough TQ7 3EN**
email: phil@karrageen.co.uk
dir: *At Malborough on A381, sharp right through village, in 0.6m right again, 0.9m, site on right.* **grid ref:** *SX686395*

A small friendly, family-run park with secluded hidden dells for tents and terraced grass pitches giving extensive sea and country views. There is a well-stocked shop and an excellent toilet block that has two cubicled units – one suitable for families and for less able visitors. This park is just one mile from the beach and pretty hamlet of Hope Cove and is a really peaceful park from which to explore the South Hams coast. 7.5 acre site. 70 touring pitches. Caravan pitches. Motorhome pitches. Tent pitches. 25 statics.

Open: Etr-Sep **Last arrival:** 21.00hrs **Last departure:** 11.30hrs

Pitches: * £15-£28 £15-£28 £15-£33

Facilities:

Services:

Within 3 miles:

Notes: ⊛ Noise to be kept to a minimum after 22.00hrs. BACS payment accepted. Dogs must be kept on leads. Freshly baked bread & croissants.

AA Pubs & Restaurants nearby: The Victoria Inn, SALCOMBE, TQ8 8BU, 01548 842604

Soar Mill Cove Hotel, SALCOMBE, TQ7 3DS, 01548 561566

Bolberry House Farm Caravan & Camping Park
►►► 82%

tel: 01548 561251 **Bolberry TQ7 3DY**
email: enquiries@bolberryparks.co.uk
dir: *At Malborough on A381 turn right signed Hope Cove & Bolberry. Take left fork after village signed Soar & Bolberry. Right in 0.6m. Site signed in 0.5m.* **grid ref:** *SX687395*

A very popular park in a peaceful setting on a coastal farm with sea views, fine cliff walks and nearby beaches. Customers are assured of a warm welcome and the nicely tucked-away portaloo facilities are smart and beautifully maintained. Ten hardstandings are available. A mobile fish and chip van calls weekly in high season. There's a super dog-walking area. 6 acre site. 70 touring pitches. 7 hardstandings. Caravan pitches. Motorhome pitches. Tent pitches. 10 statics.

Open: Etr-Oct **Last arrival:** 20.00hrs **Last departure:** 11.30hrs

Pitches: 🚐 🚐 🅰

Facilities: ⊙ 🏴 ✳ ⑤ 🖬 📶 ♻ 𝒊

Services: 🔌 ⑤ 🔋

Within 3 miles: ↧ 🎣 🗓 🏌 ◎ ⛷ 🐴 🛒

Notes: ⊛ All noise to a minimum 22.00hrs-08.30hrs. Dogs must be kept on leads & not left unattended. Shop on site (high season only).

AA Pubs & Restaurants nearby: The Victoria Inn, SALCOMBE, TQ8 8BU, 01548 842604

Soar Mill Cove Hotel, SALCOMBE, TQ7 3DS, 01548 561566

Higher Rew Caravan & Camping Park
►►► 81%

tel: 01548 842681 **Higher Rew, Malborough TQ7 3BW**
email: enquiries@higherrew.co.uk
dir: *A381 to Malborough. Right at Townsend Cross, follow signs to Soar for 1m. Left at Rew Cross for 0.5m, site is on the right.* **grid ref:** *SX714383*

A long-established park in a remote location within sight of the sea. The spacious, open touring field has some tiered pitches in the sloping grass, and there are lovely countryside or sea views from every pitch. The friendly family owners are continually improving the facilities. 5 acre site. 90 touring pitches. Caravan pitches. Motorhome pitches. Tent pitches.

Open: Etr-Oct **Last arrival:** 22.00hrs **Last departure:** noon

Pitches: * 🚐 £15-£22 🚐 £15-£22 🅰 £14-£21

Leisure: 🎱 ♨ 🎣

Facilities: ⊙ 🏴 ✳ ⑤ 🖬 🛒 ♻ 𝒊

Services: 🔌 ⑤ 🔋 ⊘ 🅣 🔋

Within 3 miles: ⅃ 🎣 ⛷ 🐴 🛒

Notes: ⊛ Minimum noise after 23.00hrs. Dogs must be kept on leads. Play barn with table tennis. Freshly baked bread & croissants available in high season.

AA Pubs & Restaurants nearby: The Victoria Inn, SALCOMBE, TQ8 8BU, 01548 842604

Soar Mill Cove Hotel, SALCOMBE, TQ7 3DS, 01548 561566

Alston Camping and Caravan Site
►► 69%

tel: 01548 561260 & 0780 803 0921 **Malborough, Kingsbridge TQ7 3BJ**
email: info@alstoncampsite.co.uk
dir: *From Salcombe on A381 towards Kingsbridge, through Malborough, site signed on right.* **grid ref:** *SX716406*

An established farm site in a rural location adjacent to the Kingsbridge-Salcombe estuary. The site is well sheltered and screened, and approached down a long, well-surfaced narrow farm lane with passing places. The toilet facilities are basic. 16 acre site. 90 touring pitches. Caravan pitches. Motorhome pitches. Tent pitches. 58 statics.

Open: 15 Mar-Oct

Pitches: 🚐 🚐 🅰

Facilities: ⊙ 🏴 ✳ ♿ ⑤ 🖬 📶 ♻ 𝒊

Services: 🔌 ⑤ 🔋 ⊘ 🅣 🔋

Within 3 miles: ⅃ 🎣 🗓 🏌 ⛷ 🐴 🛒

Notes: Dogs must be kept on leads.

AA Pubs & Restaurants nearby: The Victoria Inn, SALCOMBE, TQ8 8BU, 01548 842604

Soar Mill Cove Hotel, SALCOMBE, TQ7 3DS, 01548 561566

PITCHES: 🚐 Caravans 🚐 Motorhomes 🅰 Tents 🏕 Glamping accommodation **SERVICES:** 🔌 Electric hook up ⑤ Launderette 🍷 Licensed bar
🔋 Calor Gas ⊘ Camping Gaz 🅣 Toilet fluid 🍽 Café/Restaurant 🍟 Fast Food/Takeaway 🔋 Battery charging 🍼 Baby care ⛟ Motorvan service point
ABBREVIATIONS: BHs – bank holidays **Etr** – Easter **Spring BH** – Spring Bank Holiday **fr** – from **hrs** – hours **m** – mile **mdnt** – midnight
rdbt – roundabout **rs** – restricted service **wk** – week **wknd** – weekend **x-roads** – crossroads ⊛ No credit or debit cards ⊗ No dogs

SAMPFORD PEVERELL Map 3 ST01

Places to visit

Tiverton Castle, TIVERTON, EX16 6RP, 01884 253200 www.tivertoncastle.com

Tiverton Museum of Mid Devon Life, TIVERTON, EX16 6PJ, 01884 256295 www.tivertonmuseum.org.uk

Great for kids: Diggerland, CULLOMPTON, EX15 2PE, 0871 227 7007 *(Calls cost 10p per minute plus your phone company's access charge)* www.diggerland.com

PREMIER PARK

Minnows Touring Park

►►►►► 85%

tel: 01884 821770 **Holbrook Ln EX16 7EN**
email: admin@minnowstouringpark.co.uk **web:** www.minnowstouringpark.co.uk
dir: *M5 junct 27, A361 signed Tiverton & Barnstaple. In 600yds take 1st slip road, right over bridge, site ahead.* **grid ref:** *SS042148*

A small, well-sheltered park, peacefully located amidst fields and mature trees. The toilet facilities are of a high quality in keeping with the rest of the park, and there is a good laundry. The park has direct gated access to the canal towpath; a brisk 20-minute walk leads to a choice of pubs and a farm shop, and the bus stop is 15 minutes away. All pitches are hardstanding with some large enough for American RVs; fully serviced pitches are also available. The park has WiFi. 5.5 acre site. 59 touring pitches. 59 hardstandings. Caravan pitches. Motorhome pitches. Tent pitches. 1 static.

Open: 6 Mar-30 Oct **Last arrival:** 20.00hrs (earliest arrival time 13.00hrs)
Last departure: noon

Pitches: 🚐 🚙 ⛺

Leisure: 🛝

Facilities: 🚿 [P] 🪒 💨 ❄ ♿ [$] 🧺 [WiFi] ♻ ℹ

Services: 🔧 🧼 🔒 🍃 [T] 🍳 🚰

Within 3 miles: ⛳ 🎣 🏄 [$]

Notes: No cycling, no groundsheets on grass. Dogs must be kept on leads. Caravan storage.

AA Pubs & Restaurants nearby: The Butterleigh Inn, BUTTERLEIGH, EX15 1PN, 01884 855433

SHALDON Map 3 SX97

Places to visit

'Bygones', TORQUAY, TQ1 4PR, 01803 326108 www.bygones.co.uk

Great for kids: Babbacombe Model Village, TORQUAY, TQ1 3LA, 01803 315315 www.model-village.co.uk

Coast View Holiday Park

HOLIDAY HOME PARK 82%

tel: 01626 818350 **Torquay Rd TQ14 0BG**
email: holidays@coastview.co.uk
dir: *M5 junct 31, A38 then A380 towards Torquay. A381 towards Teignmouth. Right in 4m at lights, over Shaldon Bridge. 0.75m, up hill, site on right.* **grid ref:** *SX935716*

Set high on the cliffs above Shaldon and with spectacular views across Teignmouth Bay and the Jurassic Coast, this popular holiday home park makes the most of the stunning location, with quality park homes spaciously laid out on neat terraces, each with a glass sheltered decked area from which to soak up the glorious sea views. Serious investment across the park has seen significant improvements to the layout and landscaping; plus refurbishment of the reception area and the traditional wooden chalets, the addition of new, fully equipped statics and luxury lodges and, for 2016, the opening of an impressive and very smart new complex featuring a restaurant and bar and indoor swimming pool.

Open: mid Mar-end Oct

Leisure: 🏊 🛝

Within 3 miles: 🎣

SIDMOUTH

Places to visit

Branscombe - The Old Bakery, Manor Mill and Forge, BRANSCOMBE, EX12 3DB, 01752 346585 www.nationaltrust.org.uk

Otterton Mill, OTTERTON, EX9 7HG, 01395 568521 www.ottertonmill.com

Great for kids: Pecorama Pleasure Gardens, BEER, EX12 3NA, 01297 21542 www.pecorama.co.uk

SIDMOUTH | Map 3 SY18

PREMIER PARK

Oakdown Country Holiday Park

▶ ▶ ▶ ▶ 96%

tel: 01297 680387 **Gatedown Ln, Weston EX10 0PT**
email: enquiries@oakdown.co.uk **web:** www.oakdown.co.uk
dir: *Exit A3052, 2.5m E of junct with A375.* **grid ref:** *SY167902*

A quality, friendly, well-maintained park with good landscaping and plenty of maturing trees that make it well screened from the A3052. Pitches are grouped in groves surrounded by shrubs, with a 50-pitch development replete with an upmarket toilet block. The park has excellent facilities including a 9-hole par 3 golf course and a good shop and café. There are four-berth wooden pods and a toilet cabin for the pods. The park's conservation areas, with their natural flora and fauna, offer attractive walks, and there is a hide by the Victorian reed bed for both casual and dedicated birdwatchers. 16 acre site. 150 touring pitches. 90 hardstandings. 35 seasonal pitches. Caravan pitches. Motorhome pitches. Tent pitches. 15 statics.

Open: Apr-Oct **Last arrival:** 22.00hrs **Last departure:** 10.30hrs
Pitches: * ▦ £12.85-£31.60 ▥ £12.85-£31.60 ⅄ £12.85-£25.30 ⋔ prices shown below
Leisure: ⋀ ☌ ☏ ♒ **Facilities:** ⬱ ⋔ ℙ☉ ☌ ⚘ ⛶ ⬥ ⬚ ⊕ 📶 ▦ ♻ ✪
Services: ⊞ ⬚ ⬛ ⬧ ⊤ ◉ ⬱ ⬿
Glamping: Wooden Pods 5, £40-£55 Changeover day Any day Min stay 1 night Car by unit
Within 3 miles: ⬆ ⬇ ⊟ ✎ ◎ ⬚ ⬚ ⬚ ↻

Notes: No bikes, skateboards or kite flying. Dogs must be kept on leads. Microwave available, field trail to donkey sanctuary.
AA Pubs & Restaurants nearby: Blue Ball Inn, SIDMOUTH, EX10 9QL, 01395 514062
The Salty Monk, SIDMOUTH, EX10 9QP, 01395 513174
See advert on page 174

PREMIER PARK

Kings Down Tail Caravan & Camping Park

▶ ▶ ▶ ▶ 82%

tel: 01297 680313 & 07796 618668 **Salcombe Regis EX10 0PD**
email: info@kingsdowntail.co.uk
dir: *M5 junct 30, A3052 towards Sidmouth. Through Sidford, up hill for 2m, turn left just before Branscombe Cross.* **grid ref:** *SY173907*

This well managed, family-run park is well located near Sidmouth. There are excellent facilities, including a stunning reception building and well-appointed family rooms. There is also a play area for children including a pirate ship and den. Four upmarket glamping pods were added for the 2016 season. The park is perfect for visiting south-east Devon, including Sidmouth, Beer, and Lyme Regis in Dorset. 5 acre site. 80 touring pitches. 68 hardstandings. 50 seasonal pitches. Caravan pitches. Motorhome pitches. Tent pitches.

Open: 15 Mar-15 Nov **Last departure:** 11.00hrs **Pitches:** ▦ ▥ ⅄ ⋔
Leisure: ⋀ ☌ **Facilities:** ⬱ ⋔ ℙ☉ ☌ ⚘ ⛶ ⬥ ⬚ ⊕ 📶 ▦ ♻ ✪
Services: ⊞ ⬚ ⬛ ⬧ ⊤ ◉ ⬱ ⬿
Glamping: Wooden Pods 4, £40-£45 Min stay 2 nights Car by unit
Within 3 miles: ⬆ ⬇ ⊟ ✎ ◎ ⬚ ⬚ ⬚ ↻
Notes: Dogs must be kept on leads. Bakery, newspapers available.
AA Pubs & Restaurants nearby: Blue Ball Inn, SIDMOUTH, EX10 9QL, 01395 514062
The Salty Monk, SIDMOUTH, EX10 9QP, 01395 513174

Salcombe Regis Caravan & Camping Park

▶ ▶ ▶ ▶ 82%

tel: 01395 514303 **Salcombe Regis EX10 0JH**
email: contact@salcombe-regis.co.uk
dir: *Exit A3052 1m E of junct with A375. From opposite direction turn left past Donkey Sanctuary. (NB it is advisable to follow brown tourist signs not Sat Nav).* **grid ref:** *SY153892*

Set in quiet countryside with glorious views, this spacious park has well-maintained facilities, and a good mix of grass and hardstanding pitches. A footpath runs from the park to the coastal path and the beach. There is a self-catering holiday cottage and static caravans for hire. This is a perfect location for visiting Sidmouth, Lyme Regis and the coastal area of south-east Devon. 16 acre site. 100 touring pitches. 40 hardstandings. 26 seasonal pitches. Caravan pitches. Motorhome pitches. Tent pitches. 10 statics.

Open: Etr-end Oct **Last arrival:** 20.15hrs **Last departure:** noon
Pitches: ▦ £14.50-£26.50 ▥ £14.50-£26.50 ⅄ £14.50-£26.50 **Leisure:** ⋀ ☌
Facilities: ⬱ ⋔ ℙ☉ ☌ ⚘ ⬚ ⬚ ⊕ 📶 ▦ ♻ ✪ ⬚
Services: ⊞ ⬚ ⬛ ⬧ ⊤ ⬱ ⬿ **Within 3 miles:** ⬆ ⬇ ⊟ ✎ ◎ ⬚ ⬚ ⬚ ↻
Notes: Quiet at 22.00hrs, no noise from 23.00hrs. Dogs must be kept on leads. Putting green, table tennis, goal posts, badminton, croissants baked to order.
AA Pubs & Restaurants nearby: Blue Ball Inn, SIDMOUTH, EX10 9QL, 01395 514062
The Salty Monk, SIDMOUTH, EX10 9QP, 01395 513174

PITCHES: ▦ Caravans ▥ Motorhomes ⅄ Tents ⋔ Glamping accommodation **SERVICES:** ⊞ Electric hook up ⬚ Launderette ⬚ Licensed bar
⬛ Calor Gas ⬧ Camping Gaz ⊤ Toilet fluid ◉ Café/Restaurant ⬱ Fast Food/Takeaway ⬚ Battery charging ⬱ Baby care ⬿ Motorvan service point
ABBREVIATIONS: BHs – bank holidays Etr – Easter Spring BH – Spring Bank Holiday fr – from hrs – hours m – mile mdnt – midnight
rdbt – roundabout rs – restricted service wk – week wknd – weekend x-roads – crossroads ⊗ No credit or debit cards ⊗ No dogs

SOURTON CROSS — Map 3 SX59

Places to visit

Lydford Gorge, LYDFORD, EX20 4BH, 01822 820320
www.nationaltrust.org.uk/lydford-gorge

Okehampton Castle, OKEHAMPTON, EX20 1JB, 01837 52844
www.english-heritage.org.uk/daysout/properties/okehampton-castle

Bundu Camping & Caravan Park

►►► 82%

tel: 01837 861747 **EX20 4HT**
email: bundu@btconnect.com
dir: From A30, W of Okehampton towards Launceston, left onto A386 signed Tavistock. 1st left & left again. **grid ref:** SX546916

The welcoming, friendly owners set the tone for this well-maintained site, ideally positioned on the border of the Dartmoor National Park. Along with fine views, well-maintained toilet facilities, level grassy pitches and two new bell tents for hire, the Granite Way cycle track (from Lydford to Okehampton) that runs along the old railway line passes the edge of the park. There is a bus stop, cycle hire and a good pub a few minutes' walk away. Dogs are accepted. 4.5 acre site. 38 touring pitches. 16 hardstandings. Caravan pitches. Motorhome pitches. Tent pitches.

Open: all year **Last arrival:** 21.00hrs **Last departure:** noon

Pitches: * 🚐 £14-£20 🚐 £14-£20 ▲ £10-£12 🏠 prices shown below

Leisure: 🚴

Facilities: 🪻🅿️☉🍴🌡️♿🛅🚰 WiFi ▦♻️ℹ️

Services: 🔌🚿🔒🌱🚽🚮

Glamping: Bell tents 2, £35-£40 Min stay 2 nights Car by unit

Within 3 miles: 🎣🏇⚓️🛒🏪

Notes: Dogs must be kept on leads.

SOUTH MOLTON — Map 3 SS72

Places to visit

Quince Honey Farm, SOUTH MOLTON, EX36 3AZ, 01769 572401
www.quincehoneyfarm.com

Cobbaton Combat Collection, CHITTLEHAMPTON, EX37 9RZ, 01769 540740
www.cobbatoncombat.co.uk

Great for kids: Exmoor Zoological Park, BLACKMOOR GATE, EX31 4SG, 01598 763352 www.exmoorzoo.co.uk

Riverside Caravan & Camping Park

►►►► 92%

tel: 01769 579269 **Marsh Ln, North Molton Rd EX36 3HQ**
email: relax@exmoorriverside.co.uk **web:** www.exmoorriverside.co.uk
dir: M5 junct 27, A361 towards Barnstaple. Site signed 1m before South Molton on right. **grid ref:** SS723274

A family-run park set alongside the River Mole and in 70 acres of landscaped parkland with 10 acres of woodland trails. This is an ideal base for exploring Exmoor, as well as north Devon's golden beaches. The site offers 58 premium,

LEISURE: 🏊 Indoor pool 🏊 Outdoor pool 🎠 Children's playground ✋ Kid's club 🎾 Tennis court 🎱 Games room ⛳ Golf course ⛵ Boat hire 🚲 Cycle hire 🎦 Cinema 🎵 Entertainment 🎣 Fishing ⛳ Mini golf ⛳ Pitch n putt 🏄 Watersports 💪 Gym 🏐 Sports field ⛺ Stables **FACILITIES:** 🛁 Bath 🚿 Shower 🅿️ Private washing cubicles 🔌 Electric shaver 💈 Hairdryer ❄️ Ice Packs ♿ Disabled facilities 🛒 Shop on site 🚐 Mobile shop 🍖 BBQ area 🍴 Picnic area WiFi Wi-fi 💻 Internet access ♻️ Recycling ℹ️ Tourist info 🐕 Dog exercise area 🚗 Car hire can be arranged

fully-serviced pitches for RVs, motorhomes, caravans and campervans, 40 jumbo grass pitches with electricity for tents, a large camping field and rally field, an award-winning shower block, the Country Club restaurant and bar, family entertainment, caravan storage and a collection service. There is a public footpath linking the park to South Molton and the local bus stops at park entrance. 70 acre site. 58 touring pitches. 54 hardstandings. Caravan pitches. Motorhome pitches. Tent pitches. 3 statics.

Riverside Caravan & Camping Park

Open: all year **Last arrival:** 22.00hrs **Last departure:** 11.00hrs

Pitches: 🚃 🚐 ⛺

Leisure: ⚽ ♫ 🎣

Facilities: 🚿 [P] ☺ ⚡ ❄ ♿ [S] ⛩ 🐕 [WiFi] 💻 ♻ ⓘ

Services: 🔌 🧺 🍷 🔥 ⛽ [T] 🍴 🔋 🍔 ⬇

Within 3 miles: ⛳ ⛨ 🎣 ≋ [S] 🧺 Ս

Notes: Quiet after 23.00hrs. Dogs must be kept on leads.

See advert below

STARCROSS

See Dawlish

STOKE GABRIEL

Map 3 SX85

Places to visit

Berry Pomeroy Castle, TOTNES, TQ9 6NJ, 01803 866618 www.english-heritage.org.uk/daysout/properties/berry-pomeroy-castle

Totnes Elizabethan House Museum, TOTNES, TQ9 5RU, 01803 863821 www.devonmuseums.net/totnes

Great for kids: Paignton Zoo Environmental Park, PAIGNTON, TQ4 7EU, 01803 697500 www.paigntonzoo.org.uk

Higher Well Farm Holiday Park

►►► 85%

tel: 01803 782289 **Waddeton Rd TQ9 6RN**
email: higherwell@talk21.com
dir: *From Exeter A380 to Paignton, turn right onto A385 for Totnes, in 0.5m left for Stoke Gabriel, follow signs.* **grid ref:** *SX857577*

Set on a quiet farm yet only four miles from Paignton, this rural holiday park is on the outskirts of the picturesque village of Stoke Gabriel. A toilet block, with some en suite facilities, is an excellent amenity, and tourers are housed in an open field with very good views. 10 acre site. 80 touring pitches. 3 hardstandings. Caravan pitches. Motorhome pitches. Tent pitches. 19 statics.

Open: 8 Apr-Oct **Last arrival:** 22.00hrs **Last departure:** 10.00hrs

Pitches: 🚃 £13.50-£21 🚐 £13.50-£21 ⛺ £13.50-£21

Facilities: 🚿 [P] ☺ ⚡ ❄ ♿ [S] 🐕 ♻ ⓘ

Services: 🔌 🧺 🔥 ⛽ [T] 🔋 ⬇

Within 3 miles: ⛳ 🎣 [S] 🧺

Notes: No commercial vehicles, pets must not be left unattended in caravans, motorhomes or tents. Dogs must be kept on leads.

AA Pubs & Restaurants nearby: The Durant Arms, TOTNES, TQ9 7UP, 01803 732240

Steam Packet Inn, TOTNES, TQ9 5EW, 01803 863880

The White Hart Bar & Restaurant, TOTNES, TQ9 6EL, 01803 847111

STOKE GABRIEL *continued*

Broadleigh Farm Park
▶▶▶ 81%

tel: 01803 782110 **Coombe House Ln, Aish TQ9 6PU**
email: enquiries@broadleighfarm.co.uk
dir: *From Exeter on A38 then A380 towards Torbay. Right onto A385 for Totnes. In 0.5m right at Whitehill Country Park. Site approx 0.75m on left.* **grid ref:** SX851587

Set in a very rural location on a working farm bordering Paignton and Stoke Gabriel. The large sloping field with a timber-clad toilet block in the centre is sheltered and peaceful, surrounded by rolling countryside but handy for the beaches. There is also an excellent rally field with good toilets and showers. 7 acre site. 80 touring pitches. Caravan pitches. Motorhome pitches. Tent pitches.

Open: Mar-Oct **Last arrival:** 21.00hrs **Last departure:** 11.00hrs

Pitches: 🚐 🚚 ▲

Facilities: 🏳 🅿 ⊙ 🇫 ✳ 🖑 🛱 🛒 🚮 WiFi 🖥 ♻ ❶

Services: 🚽 🗑 🛒

Within 3 miles: ↧ ❅ 🗄 🖉 ◎ 🛶 🛍 🛒

Notes: Dogs must be kept on leads. Fish & chip van Saturdays in high season, basic essentials shop.

AA Pubs & Restaurants nearby: Royal Seven Stars Hotel, TOTNES, TQ9 5DD, 01803 862125

TAVISTOCK Map 3 SX47

Places to visit

Morwellham Quay, MORWELLHAM, PL19 8JL, 01822 832766
www.morwellhamquay.co.uk

Woodovis Park
▶▶▶▶▶ 90%

tel: 01822 832968 **Gulworthy PL19 8NY**
email: info@woodovis.com
dir: *A390 from Tavistock signed Callington & Gunnislake. At hill top right at rdbt signed Lamerton & Chipshop. Site 1m on left.* **grid ref:** SX431745

A well-kept park in a remote woodland setting on the edge of the Tamar Valley. Peacefully located at the end of a private, half-mile, tree-lined drive, it offers superb on-site facilities and high levels of customer care from hands-on owners. The toilets are immaculate and well maintained, plus there is an indoor swimming pool, sauna and a good information and games room, all creating a friendly atmosphere. Facilities include electric bike hire and a charging point for electric cars. 2-berth and 4-berth wooden pods are available for hire. 14.5 acre site. 50 touring pitches. 33 hardstandings. 8 seasonal pitches. Caravan pitches. Motorhome pitches. Tent pitches. 35 statics.

Open: 24 Mar-28 Oct **Last arrival:** 20.00hrs **Last departure:** 11.00hrs

Pitches: * 🚐 £20-£42 🚚 £20-£42 ▲ £20-£42 🏠 prices shown below

Leisure: 🏊 🄰 ♣ ❅ **Facilities:** 🛁 🏳 🅿 ⊙ 🇫 ✳ 🖑 🛱 🚮 WiFi 🖥 ♻ ❶

Services: 🚽 🗑 🛒 🖉 🗄 🛒 🛒 ↧

Glamping: Wooden Pods 4, £49-£84 Changeover day Any day Min stay 1 night Car by unit

---

Within 3 miles: ↧ 🗄 🖉 ◎ 🛶 🛍 🛒 U

Notes: No open fires. Dogs must be kept on leads. Pétanque court, outdoor table tennis, archery, water-walking, infrared therapy cabin, hot tub, circus skills workshops & story telling (in school hols).

AA Pubs & Restaurants nearby: The Cornish Arms, TAVISTOCK, PL19 8AN, 01822 612145

Langstone Manor Camping & Caravan Park
▶▶▶▶▶ 82%

tel: 01822 613371 **Moortown PL19 9JZ**
email: jane@langstone-manor.co.uk **web:** www.langstone-manor.co.uk
dir: *Take B3357 from Tavistock to Princetown. Approx 1.5m turn right at x-roads, follow signs. Over bridge, cattle grid, up hill, left at sign, left again to park.* **grid ref:** SX524738

A secluded and very peaceful site set in the well-maintained grounds of a manor house in Dartmoor National Park. Many attractive mature trees provide screening within the park, yet the west-facing terraced pitches on the main park enjoy the superb summer sunsets. There are excellent toilet facilities plus a popular lounge bar offering a very good menu of reasonably priced evening meals. Plenty of activities and places of interest can be found within the surrounding moorland. Dogs are accepted. Wooden pods in a wooded setting are available for hire. 6.5 acre site. 40 touring pitches. 18 hardstandings. 3 seasonal pitches. Caravan pitches. Motorhome pitches. Tent pitches. 25 statics.

Open: 15 Mar-15 Nov (rs Weekdays - bar & restaurant closed except BHs & school hols) **Last arrival:** 21.00hrs **Last departure:** 11.00hrs

Pitches: * 🚐 £14.50-£20 🚚 £14.50-£20 ▲ £14.50-£20 🏠 prices shown below

Leisure: 🄰 ♣ ❅

Facilities: 🛁 🏳 🅿 ⊙ 🇫 ✳ 🖑 🛒 WiFi ♻ ❶ 🛎

Services: 🚽 🗑 🛒 🖉 🗄 T 🍴 🛒 ↧ ↧

Glamping: Wooden Pods 11, £40-£60 Changeover day Any day Min stay 1 night Car by unit

Within 3 miles: ↧ 🗄 🖉 ◎ 🛶 🛍 🛒 U

Notes: Dogs must be kept on leads. Cycle shed. Baguettes, croissants etc available.

AA Pubs & Restaurants nearby: The Cornish Arms, TAVISTOCK, PL19 8AN, 01822 612145

LEISURE: 🏊 Indoor pool 🏊 Outdoor pool 🄰 Children's playground 🖑 Kid's club ⊙ Tennis court 🔍 Games room ⛳ Golf course 🚣 Boat hire 🚲 Cycle hire 🎬 Cinema 🎵 Entertainment 🎣 Fishing ◎ Mini golf 🏌 Pitch n putt 🏄 Watersports 💪 Gym 🏐 Sports field U Stables **FACILITIES:** 🛁 Bath 🚿 Shower 🅿 Private washing cubicles ⊙ Electric shaver 🇫 Hairdryer ✳ Ice Packs 🖑 Disabled facilities 🛍 Shop on site 🚚 Mobile shop 🍖 BBQ area 🛒 Picnic area WiFi Wi-fi 🖥 Internet access ♻ Recycling ❶ Tourist info 🐕 Dog exercise area 🚗 Car hire can be arranged

Harford Bridge Holiday Park
▶▶▶▶ 84%

tel: 01822 810349 & 07773 251457 **Peter Tavy PL19 9LS**
email: stay@harfordbridge.co.uk **web:** www.harfordbridge.co.uk
dir: A386 from Tavistock towards Okehampton, 2m, right signed Peter Tavy, site 200yds on right. **grid ref:** SX504767

This beautiful spacious park is set beside the River Tavy in the Dartmoor National Park. Pitches are located beside the river and around the copses, and the park is very well equipped for holidaymakers. An adventure playground and games room keep children entertained, and there is fly-fishing and a free tennis court. A lovely, authentic shepherd's hut complete with fridge and woodburner, and two S-pods are available to let. 16 acre site. 125 touring pitches. 20 hardstandings. 5 seasonal pitches. Caravan pitches. Motorhome pitches. Tent pitches. 70 statics.

Open: all year (rs 14 Nov-15 Mar - no camping or touring pitches; holiday caravans, lodges & studio lodges only) **Last arrival:** 21.00hrs **Last departure:** noon

Pitches: * ⊞ £16-£25.75 ⊞ £16-£25.75 ▲ £16-£25.75 ⋒ prices shown below

Leisure: ⋔ ♨ ☺ ⚲ ⸗

Facilities: ⚡ �ℙ ⊙ ⸗ ☀ ⸋ ⛝ ⓢ ⤨ ⤙ WiFi ▆ ♻ ❻

Services: ⊡ ⑤ ⬛ ⊘ ⊤ ⛟ ⬇

Glamping: **Shepherd's Huts** 1, £36-£40 Changeover day Sat Min stay 1 night Car by unit **Studio Lodges (S-Pods):** 2, £40-£46 Changeover day Sat Min stay 1 night En suite Own kitchen Car by unit

Within 3 miles: ↧ ⌿ ⸗ ⤙ ⓢ ⑤ ∪

Notes: Expedition groups & rallies welcome by prior arrangement. Dogs must be kept on leads. Baguettes, croissants, snacks, sweets, cold drinks, ices & grocery basics available.

AA Pubs & Restaurants nearby: Peter Tavy Inn, TAVISTOCK, PL19 9NN, 01822 810348

TEDBURN ST MARY

Places to visit
Finch Foundry, STICKLEPATH, EX20 2NW, 01837 840046
www.nationaltrust.org.uk

Castle Drogo, DREWSTEIGNTON, EX6 6PB, 01647 433306
www.nationaltrust.org.uk/castle-drogo

TEDBURN ST MARY Map 3 SX89

Springfield Holiday Park
▶▶▶▶ 84%

tel: 01647 24242 **EX6 6EW**
email: info@springfield-park.co.uk
dir: M5 junct 31, A30 towards Okehampton, exit at junct, signed to Cheriton Bishop. Follow brown tourist signs to site. (NB for Sat Nav use EX6 6JN). **grid ref:** SX788935

Set in a quiet rural location with countryside views, this park continues to be upgraded to a smart standard. It has the advantage of being close to Dartmoor National Park, with village pubs and stores less than a mile away. There is a very inviting heated outdoor swimming pool. 9 acre site. 48 touring pitches. 38 hardstandings. 25 seasonal pitches. Caravan pitches. Motorhome pitches. Tent pitches. 49 statics.

Open: 15 Mar-30 Oct **Last arrival:** 21.00hrs **Last departure:** noon **Pitches:** ⊞ ⊞ ▲

Leisure: ≈ ⋔ ⚲ **Facilities:** ⚡ ℙ ☀ ⤨ ⤙ WiFi ▆ ♻ ❻

Services: ⊡ ⑤ ⬛ ⊘ ⬇ **Within 3 miles:** ↧ ⌿ ⓢ ⑤ ∪

Notes: Dogs must be kept on leads.

AA Pubs & Restaurants nearby: The Old Inn, DREWSTEIGNTON, EX6 6QR, 01647 281276

TIVERTON

See East Worlington

TORQUAY Map 3 SX96

See also Newton Abbot

Places to visit
Torre Abbey Historic House & Gallery, TORQUAY, TQ2 5JE, 01803 293593
www.torre-abbey.org.uk

'Bygones', TORQUAY, TQ1 4PR, 01803 326108 www.bygones.co.uk

Widdicombe Farm Touring Park
▶▶▶▶ 87%

tel: 01803 558325 **Marldon TQ3 1ST**
email: info@widdicombefarm.co.uk
dir: On A380, midway between Torquay & Paignton ring road. **grid ref:** SX876643

A friendly family-run park on a working farm with good quality facilities, extensive views and easy access as there are no narrow roads. The level pitches are terraced to take advantage of the views towards the coast and Dartmoor. This is the only adult touring park within Torquay, and is also handy for Paignton and Brixham. There's a bus service from the park to the local shopping centre and Torquay's harbour. It has a small shop, a restaurant and a bar with entertainment from Easter to the end of September. Club WiFi is available throughout the park and The Nippy Chippy van calls regularly. 8 acre site. 180 touring pitches. 180 hardstandings. 20 seasonal pitches. Caravan pitches. Motorhome pitches. Tent pitches. 3 statics.

Open: mid Mar-end Oct **Last arrival:** 20.00hrs **Last departure:** 11.00hrs

Pitches: ⊞ ⊞ ▲

Leisure: ♫

Facilities: ⊙ ⸗ ☀ ⸋ ⓢ ⤙ WiFi ♻ ❻

PITCHES: ⊞ Caravans ⊞ Motorhomes ▲ Tents ⋒ Glamping accommodation **SERVICES:** ⊡ Electric hook up ⑤ Launderette ⬛ Licensed bar ⬛ Calor Gas ⊘ Camping Gaz ⊤ Toilet fluid ⎢○⎢ Café/Restaurant ⬛ Fast Food/Takeaway ⬛ Battery charging ⬛ Baby care ⬇ Motorvan service point
ABBREVIATIONS: BHs – bank holidays Etr – Easter Spring BH – Spring Bank Holiday fr – from hrs – hours m – mile mdnt – midnight rdbt – roundabout rs – restricted service wk – week wknd – weekend x-roads – crossroads ⊗ No credit or debit cards ⊗ No dogs

TORQUAY continued

Services: 🅿️🖥️ 🔌🔥⚗️🚰⏱️🍴🛒🏛️⚒️

Within 3 miles: 🎣⛷️🎠🎯◎🏊⛵🚲📷

Notes: Adults only. No groups. Most dog breeds accepted (contact site for details). Dogs must be kept on leads.

AA Pubs & Restaurants nearby: The Church House Inn, MARLDON, TQ3 1SL, 01803 558279

Cary Arms, TORQUAY, TQ1 3LX, 01803 327110

The Elephant Restaurant and Brasserie, TORQUAY, TQ1 2BH, 01803 200044

WELCOMBE　　　　　　　　　　　　Map 2 SS21

Koa Tree Camp
NEW ▶ ▶ ▶ 80%

tel: 07492 750861 **EX39 6HE**
email: info@koatreecamp.com
dir: At x-roads on A39 (between Bude & Higher Clovelly) follow Welcombe signs. Site at 2nd property on left after Little Hollacombe Farm. grid ref: SS248181

A unique, back-to-nature glamping site on a farm site set in the rolling Devon countryside. It offers three different types of stylish accommodation – Mongolian yurts for two-six people, a bell tent for up to three, and turf-roofed Norwegian-style log cabins for four. Each type of accommodation has a private wooden platform with seating plus a BBQ and/or a fire pit; inside they all have log-burners and an ample supply of logs. There is a community-run shop on site. The Rainy Day Room and Kitchens, a converted barn, makes an ideal place to socialise; six private bathrooms are adjoining. Lots of interesting activities are on offer including surfing and paddle-boarding lessons and art classes; regular guest events and entertainment are provided too. The site is easily accessed from the A39. 3.5 acre site.

Open: Apr-30 Oct Last arrival: 21.00hrs Last departure: 10.30hrs

Glamping: Bell tents 1, £40-£100 Changeover day Mon, Fri Min stay 3 nights Yurts 5, £60-£140 Changeover day Mon, Fri Min stay 3 nights Cabins 4, £45-£130 Changeover day Mon, Fri Min stay 3 nights

WHIDDON DOWN　　　　　　　　　　Map 3 SX69

Places to visit
Castle Drogo, DREWSTEIGNTON, EX6 6PB, 01647 433306
www.nationaltrust.org.uk/castle-drogo

Dartmoor View Holiday Park
▶ ▶ ▶ 82%

tel: 01647 231545 & 07585 301613 **EX20 2QL**
email: dartmoorviewtouring@haulfryn.co.uk web: www.dartmoorviewtouring.co.uk
dir: From M5 junct 31, take A30 to Okehampton. At Whiddon Down take left junct through village. Turn right at small rdbt. Park is 400mtrs on the right. grid ref: SX685925

Located just off the A30 near Okehampton, on the northern edge of Dartmoor, this immaculate 20-acre park certainly lives up to its name, and more. Although predominantly a static park, the 27 designated super pitches (hardstandings with electric, water and waste drainage) for touring caravans and motorhomes are secluded in a separate, well-landscaped field, replete with a spotlessly clean and well-equipped amenities block. Dogs and children are very welcome and there's an extensive children's play area and a heated outdoor swimming pool, which has a sun-deck area. Dartmoor View is the ideal base for those keen to explore Dartmoor on foot or by bike. 20 acre site. 26 touring pitches. 26 hardstandings. 26 seasonal pitches. Caravan pitches. Motorhome pitches.

Open: Mar-Oct Last arrival: 18.00hrs Last departure: 11.00hrs

Pitches: * 🚐 £18-£30 ⊟ £18-£30 Leisure: ≈♠🔍✐ Facilities: 🏕️🅿️👶👨‍🦽🛏️
📶🗑️♻️🌐 Services: 🅿️🖥️ Within 3 miles: ⚓🛒📷

Notes: 10mph speed limit. Dogs must be kept on leads.

AA Pubs & Restaurants nearby: The Chagford Inn, CHAGFORD, TQ13 8AW, 01647 433109

See advert on opposite page

PITCHES: 🚐 Caravans 🚌 Motorhomes 🅰 Tents 🏠 Glamping accommodation **SERVICES:** 🔌 Electric hook up 🧺 Launderette 🍷 Licensed bar 🔋 Calor Gas 🔥 Camping Gaz 🚾 Toilet fluid 🍽 Café/Restaurant 🍔 Fast Food/Takeaway 🔋 Battery charging 🍼 Baby care 🚐 Motorvan service point
ABBREVIATIONS: BHs – bank holidays Etr – Easter Spring BH – Spring Bank Holiday fr – from hrs – hours m – mile mdnt – midnight rdbt – roundabout rs – restricted service wk – week wknd – weekend x-roads – crossroads No credit or debit cards No dogs

WOOLACOMBE
Map 3 SS44

See also Mortehoe

Twitchen House Holiday Park

HOLIDAY CENTRE 87%

tel: 01271 872302 **Mortehoe Station Rd, Mortehoe EX34 7ES**
email: goodtimes@woolacombe.com **web:** www.woolacombe.co.uk
dir: *M5 junct 27, A361 to Ilfracombe. From Mullacott Cross rdbt take B3343 (Woolacombe road) to Turnpike Cross junct. Take right fork, site 1.5m on left.* **grid ref:** *SS465447*

A very attractive, seaside park with excellent leisure facilities, all-weather activities and entertainment; visitors can use the amenities at all three of the group's holiday parks and a bus service connects them all with the beach. There's a show room, indoor soft play area, a 2D and 3D cinema and craft centre. The touring area features many fully serviced pitches and 80 that are available for tents; they have either sea views or a woodland countryside outlook. 45 acre site. 333 touring pitches. 110 hardstandings. Caravan pitches. Motorhome pitches. Tent pitches. 236 statics.

Open: mid Mar-end Oct (rs mid Mar-end May & mid Sep-end Oct outdoor pool closed)
Last arrival: mdnt **Last departure:** 10.00hrs

Pitches: 🚐 🚏 👤

Leisure: 🏊 🏊 🎠 ✋ 🎱 🎵

Facilities: 🚿 P 📷 ☀ ✳ ⚐ 🛒 🎪 🚽 WiFi 🔲 ♻

Services: 🔌 🗑 🍴 💧 T 🍽 🛒 🏪 🛒 ⛽

Within 3 miles: ⚴ ⛳ 🎣 ✏ 🏌 ◎ 🏄 🛒 ⛵ ♨

Notes: Dogs must be kept on leads. Table tennis, sauna, swimming & surfing lessons, climbing wall, bungee trampoline, kiddy karts, cinema, flumes & splash pads.

AA Pubs & Restaurants nearby: Watersmeet Hotel, WOOLACOMBE, EX34 7EB, 01271 870333

See advert on opposite page

Woolacombe Bay Holiday Park

HOLIDAY CENTRE 87%

tel: 01271 872302 **Sandy Ln EX34 7AH**
email: goodtimes@woolacombe.com **web:** www.woolacombe.co.uk
dir: *M5 junct 27, A361 to Ilfracombe. At Mullacott rdbt take 1st exit to Woolacombe. Follow Mortehoe signs.* **grid ref:** *SS465442*

There's a well-developed touring section at this seaside holiday complex that offers a full entertainment and leisure programme. There are super pitches with TV aerial, water, drainage, electricity and a night light. The park has excellent amenities including a steam room and sauna, and an outdoor sports area with a circular Ocean Bar. For a small charge, a bus takes holidaymakers to the other Woolacombe Bay holiday centres where they can take part in any of the many activities offered, and there is also a bus to the beach. The sports complex features a surfing simulator, high ropes course and a climbing wall. 8.5 acre site. 119 touring pitches. Motorhome pitches. Tent pitches. 236 statics.

Open: mid Mar-end Oct (rs mid Mar-end May & mid Sep-end Oct outdoor pool closed)
Last arrival: mdnt **Last departure:** 10.00hrs

Pitches: 🚐 👤

Leisure: 🏊 🏊 🎠 🎪 ✋ 🎱 ◎ 🌸 🎣 🎱 🎵 Spa ♪

Facilities: 🚿 P 📷 ☀ ✳ ⚐ 🛒 🎪 🚽 WiFi 🔲 ♻

Services: 🔌 🗑 🍴 💧 T 🍽 🛒 🏪 ⛽

Within 3 miles: ⛳ ⚴ 🎣 ✏ ◎ 🏄 🛒 ⛵ ♨

Notes: Max 21ft motorhomes, site not ideal for guests with mobility problems due to hills & stairs. Dogs must be kept on leads. Bungee trampoline, climbing wall, cinema, sun terrace, pottery painting, kiddy karts, pirate ship toddler fun pool.

AA Pubs & Restaurants nearby: Watersmeet Hotel, WOOLACOMBE, EX34 7EB, 01271 870333

See advert on opposite page

PITCHES: 🚐 Caravans 🚐 Motorhomes ⛺ Tents 🏕 Glamping accommodation SERVICES: ⚡ Electric hook up 🔲 Launderette 🍺 Licensed bar
🔋 Calor Gas ⛽ Camping Gaz Ⓣ Toilet fluid 🍽 Café/Restaurant 🍟 Fast Food/Takeaway 🔌 Battery charging 👶 Baby care 🚐 Motorvan service point
ABBREVIATIONS: BHs – bank holidays Etr – Easter Spring BH – Spring Bank Holiday fr – from hrs – hours m – mile mdnt – midnight
rdbt – roundabout rs – restricted service wk – week wknd – weekend x-roads – crossroads Ⓩ No credit or debit cards Ⓧ No dogs

WOOLACOMBE *continued*

Golden Coast Holiday Park
HOLIDAY CENTRE 86%

tel: 01271 872302 **Station Rd EX34 7HW**
email: goodtimes@woolacombe.com **web:** www.woolacombe.co.uk
dir: *M5 junct 27, A361 to Ilfracombe. At Mullacott rdbt 1st exit to Woolacombe.*
grid ref: *SS482436*

A seaside holiday village, set beside a three mile sandy beach, that offers excellent leisure facilities together with the amenities available at the other Woolacombe Bay holiday parks. There is a neat touring area with a unisex toilet block that has underfloor heating and individual cubicles – all maintained to a high standard; the super pitches have water, drainage, electricity, TV aerial and night light. The sports complex features ten-pin bowling, high ropes course, climbing wall, surfing simulator and adventure golf and much more; there are over 40 free activities available to try. 10 acre site. 89 touring pitches. 89 hardstandings. Caravan pitches. Motorhome pitches. Tent pitches. 342 statics.

Open: Feb-Nov (rs Feb-May & mid Sep-Nov outdoor pool closed) **Last arrival:** mdnt
Last departure: 10.00hrs

Pitches: 🚐 🚏 Å

Leisure: 🏊 🏊 ⅍ 👋 🎾 🏐 🎯 🐎 🎣 🎵 Spa ℘

Facilities: 🏨 🅿️ ⊙ 🔗 ✳️ ♿ 🗲 🪑 🚻 WiFi 💻 ♻️ 🛈

Services: 🔌 🗄 🗯 🖉 T 🍴 🧺 🏪 🚲 ⅃

Within 3 miles: ⅃ 🛶 🏇 ℘ ◎ ⅍ 🛒 🗄 🛒 ∪

Notes: No pets on caravan, motorhome or tent pitches. Dogs must be kept on leads. Sauna, fishing, snooker, cinema, bungee trampoline, playzone, sports complex, outdoor gym, swimming & surfing lessons.

AA Pubs & Restaurants nearby: Watersmeet Hotel, WOOLACOMBE, EX34 7EB, 01271 870333

See advert on page 181

Warcombe Farm Caravan & Camping Park
►►►►► 87%

tel: 01271 870690 **Station Rd, Mortehoe EX34 7EJ**
email: info@warcombefarm.co.uk
dir: *On B3343 towards Woolacombe turn right towards Mortehoe. Site less than 1m on right.* **grid ref:** *SS478445*

Extensive views over the Bristol Channel can be enjoyed from the open areas of this attractive park, while other pitches are sheltered in paddocks with maturing trees. The site has 14 excellent super pitches with hardstandings. The superb sandy, Blue Flag beach at Woolacombe Bay is only a mile and a half away, and there is a fishing lake with direct access from some pitches. The local bus stops outside the park entrance. 35 acre site. 250 touring pitches. 82 hardstandings. 12 seasonal pitches. Caravan pitches. Motorhome pitches. Tent pitches.

Open: 15 Mar-Oct **Last arrival:** 21.00hrs **Last departure:** 11.00hrs

Pitches: * 🚐 £15-£31 🚏 £15-£31 Å £15-£31 ℘

Leisure: ⅍ ☺ ℘

Facilities: 🏨 🏨 ⊙ 🔗 ✳️ ♿ 🗲 🪑 🚻 WiFi ♻️ 🛈 🚗

Services: 🔌 🗄 🛡 🖉 T 🍴 🧺 🏪 ⅃

Within 3 miles: ⅃ 🛶 🏇 ℘ ◎ ⅍ 🗄 🛒 ∪

Notes: No noise after 22.30hrs. Dogs must be kept on leads.

AA Pubs & Restaurants nearby: Watersmeet Hotel, WOOLACOMBE, EX34 7EB, 01271 870333

The Quay Restaurant, ILFRACOMBE, EX34 9EQ, 01271 868090

Easewell Farm Holiday Park
►►►85%

tel: 01271 872302 **Mortehoe Station Rd, Mortehoe EX34 7EH**
email: goodtimes@woolacombe.com **web:** www.woolacombe.co.uk
dir: *M5 junct 27, A361 to Ilfracombe. At Mullacott rdbt 1st exit to Woolacombe. Follow Mortehoe signs.* **grid ref:** *SS465455*

A peaceful cliff-top park with superb views that offers full facility pitches for caravans and motorhomes. The shower rooms have underfloor heating and individual cubicles, plus there's a sauna, steam room, launderette, washing up area and chemical disposal facilities. The sports complex has a surfing simulator, high ropes course and climbing wall; the 40 activities available include indoor bowling, snooker and a 9-hole par 33 golf course. All the facilities at the three other nearby holiday centres within this group are open to everyone. 17 acre site. 318 touring pitches. 186 hardstandings. Caravan pitches. Motorhome pitches. Tent pitches. 3 statics.

Open: Mar-end Oct (rs Etr) **Last arrival:** 22.00hrs **Last departure:** 10.00hrs

Pitches: 🚐 🚐 ▲

Leisure: 🏊 ⚒ 👐 🎣 🎵 ♪

Facilities: 🐾 📷 ☺ 🅿 ✳ ♿ 📷 🚻 🐕 Wifi ♻ 🄹

Services: 🔌 🅾 🍴 📷 🅃 🍽 🎃 🍼 🚲

Within 3 miles: 👣 🎯 🏇 🅿 ◎ 🎿 📷 🅾 ↻

Notes: Dogs must be kept on leads.

AA Pubs & Restaurants nearby: Watersmeet Hotel, WOOLACOMBE, EX34 7EB, 01271 870333

See advert on page 181

PITCHES: 🚐 Caravans 🚐 Motorhomes ▲ Tents ⛺ Glamping accommodation **SERVICES:** 🔌 Electric hook up 🅾 Launderette 🍸 Licensed bar 🔋 Calor Gas ⚗ Camping Gaz 🅃 Toilet fluid 🍽 Café/Restaurant 🍴 Fast Food/Takeaway 🔋 Battery charging 🍼 Baby care 🚲 Motorvan service point **ABBREVIATIONS:** BHs – bank holidays Etr – Easter Spring BH – Spring Bank Holiday fr – from hrs – hours m – mile mdnt – midnight rdbt – roundabout rs – restricted service wk – week wknd – weekend x-roads – crossroads 🚫 No credit or debit cards 🚫 No dogs

Dorset

Dorset means rugged varied coastlines and high chalk downlands with more than a hint of Thomas Hardy, its most famous son. Squeezed in among the cliffs and set amid some of Britain's most beautiful scenery is a chain of picturesque villages and seaside towns.

Along the coast you'll find the Lulworth Ranges, which run from Kimmeridge Bay in the east to Lulworth Cove in the west. Walking is the most obvious and rewarding recreational activity here, but the British Army firing ranges mean that access to this glorious landscape is restricted. This is Britain's Jurassic Coast, a UNESCO World Heritage Site and Area of Outstanding Natural Beauty, noted for its layers of shale and numerous fossils embedded in the rock. Among the best-known natural landmarks on this stretch of the Dorset coast is Durdle Door, a rocky arch that has been shaped and sculpted to perfection by the elements. The whole area has the unmistakable stamp of prehistory. The landscape and coastal views may be spectacular but the up-and-down nature of the walking here is often physically demanding.

This designated coastline stretches from Swanage and the Isle of Purbeck to east Devon, offering miles of breathtaking scenery. Beyond the seaside town of Weymouth is Chesil Beach, a long shingle reef running for 10 miles between Portland and Abbotsbury. The beach is covered by a vast wall of shingle left by centuries of dramatic weather-induced activity along the Devon and Dorset coast. Beyond Bridport and West Bay, where the hugely successful TV series *Broadchurch* is filmed, lies quaint Lyme Regis, with its sturdy breakwater, known as The Cobb. It's the sort of place where Georgian houses and pretty cottages jostle with historic pubs and independently run shops. With its blend of architectural styles and old world charm, Lyme Regis looks very much like a film set. Perhaps that is why film producers chose this setting as a location for the making of *The French Lieutenant's Woman* in 1981. Jeremy Irons and Meryl Streep starred in the film, based on the novel by John Fowles.

Away from Dorset's magical coastline lies a landscape with a very different character and atmosphere, but one that is no less appealing. Here, winding, hedge-lined country lanes lead beneath lush, green hilltops to snug, sleepy villages hidden from view and the wider world. The main roads lead to the country towns of Sherborne, Blandford Forum, Wareham and Shaftesbury and in September these routes fill with even more traffic as the county prepares to host the annual Dorset Steam Fair. This famous event draws many visitors who come to admire the various vintage and classic vehicles on display. The same month is also set aside for the two-day County Show, an eagerly anticipated annual fixture.

Inland there are further links with literature. Dorset is justifiably proud of the achievements of Thomas Hardy, and much of the county is immortalized in his writing. He was born at Higher Bockhampton, near Dorchester, and this quaint old cob-and-thatch cottage was where the writer lived until he was 34. As a child, Hardy spent much of his time here reading and writing poems about the countryside. The cottage contains the desk where he wrote *Far from the Madding Crowd*. In later years Hardy lived at Max Gate on the edge of Dorchester and here he was visited by many distinguished writers of the day, including Rudyard Kipling and Virginia Woolf. Even the Prince of Wales called on him one day in 1923. Both homes are now in the care of the National Trust.

One of Thomas Hardy's great friends was T. E. (Thomas Edward) Lawrence, better known as Lawrence of Arabia, who lived nearby in a modest cottage known as Clouds Hill. The cottage, also managed by the National Trust, was Lawrence's secluded retreat from the world, where he could read and play music.

◁ Durdle Door

DORSET

ALDERHOLT
Map 5 SU11

Places to visit

Breamore House & Countryside Museum, BREAMORE, SP6 2DF, 01725 512468
www.breamorehouse.com

Great for kids: Rockbourne Roman Villa, ROCKBOURNE, SP6 3PG, 01725 518541
www.hants.gov.uk/rockbourne-roman-villa

PREMIER PARK

Hill Cottage Farm Camping and Caravan Park
▶▶▶▶▶82%

tel: 01425 650513 & 07714 648690 **Sandleheath Rd SP6 3EG**
email: hillcottagefarmcaravansite@supanet.com
dir: Take B3078 W of Fordingbridge. Exit at Alderholt, site 0.25m on left after railway bridge. **grid ref:** SU119133

Set within extensive grounds, this rural and beautifully landscaped park offers fully serviced pitches set in individual hardstanding bays with mature dividing hedges to give adequate pitch privacy. The modern toilet block is kept immaculately clean, and there's a good range of leisure facilities. In high season there is an area available for tents; rallies are very welcome. A function room with skittle alley is available, and there is a fully-equipped shepherd's hut for hire. The park is well situated for exploring the New Forest. 40 acre site. 95 touring pitches. 35 hardstandings. Caravan pitches. Motorhome pitches. Tent pitches.

Open: Mar-Nov **Last arrival:** 20.00hrs **Last departure:** 11.00hrs

Pitches: * 🚐 £21-£30 🚚 £21-£30 ▲ £19-£26 🏠

Leisure: 🎱 🔍 ✐

Facilities: 🐾 🅿️ ⊙ 🗲 ⚒ ⚙ 🛁 🚻 🐕 WiFi ▦ ♻ ➋ ☎

Services: 🔌 🔲 🛢 ⌀ T ⅄

Glamping: Shepherd's Huts 1

Within 3 miles: ↓ ✐ 🏊 🛍 🛒 ♺

Notes: PayPal accepted. No noise after 22.30hrs. Dogs must be kept on leads.

AA Pubs & Restaurants nearby: The Augustus John, FORDINGBRIDGE, SP6 1DG, 01425 652098

Who has won England Campsite of the Year?
See page 14

BERE REGIS
Map 4 SY89

Places to visit

Kingston Lacy, WIMBORNE, BH21 4EA, 01202 883402 (Mon-Fri)
www.nationaltrust.org.uk/kingston-lacy

Priest's House Museum and Garden, WIMBORNE, BH21 1HR, 01202 882533
www.priest-house.co.uk

Great for kids: Monkey World-Ape Rescue Centre, WOOL, BH20 6HH,
01929 462537 www.monkeyworld.org

Rowlands Wait Touring Park
▶▶▶88%

tel: 01929 472727 **Rye Hill BH20 7LP**
email: enquiries@rowlandswait.co.uk **web:** www.rowlandswait.co.uk
dir: From A35 or A31 to Bere Regis, follow Bovington Tank Museum signs. 0.75m, at top of Rye Hill turn right. 200yds to site. **grid ref:** SY842933

This park lies in a really attractive setting overlooking Bere Regis and the Dorset countryside, and is set amongst undulating areas of trees and shrubs. It is located within a few miles of The Tank Museum (Bovingdon Camp) with its mock battles, and is also very convenient for visiting the Dorchester, Poole and Swanage areas. The toilet facilities include two family rooms. The park has six fully-equipped bell tents (a pop-up Glampotel as they call them) each with a shower, toilet and wash basin, as well as a wood-burning stove. 8 acre site. 71 touring pitches. 2 hardstandings. 23 seasonal pitches. Caravan pitches. Motorhome pitches. Tent pitches.

Open: mid Mar-Oct (winter by arrangement) (rs Nov-Feb own facilities required)
Last arrival: 21.00hrs **Last departure:** noon

Pitches: 🚐 🚚 ▲ 🏠

Leisure: 🔍

Facilities: ⊙ 🗲 ⚒ ⚙ 🛁 🚻 🐕 WiFi ♻ ➋

Services: 🔌 🔲 🛢 ⌀ T 🛒 ⅄

Glamping: Bell tents 6

Within 3 miles: ↓ ✐ ⊚ 🛍 🛒 ♺

Notes: No open fires. Dogs must be kept on leads.

AA Pubs & Restaurants nearby: The Cock & Bottle, EAST MORDEN, BH20 7DL, 01929 459238

BLANDFORD FORUM — Map 4 ST80

Places to visit

Kingston Lacy, WIMBORNE, BH21 4EA, 01202 883402 (Mon-Fri) www.nationaltrust.org.uk/kingston-lacy

Old Wardour Castle, TISBURY, SP3 6RR, 01747 870487 www.english-heritage.org.uk/daysout/properties/old-wardour-castle

Great for kids: Monkey World-Ape Rescue Centre, WOOL, BH20 6HH, 01929 462537 www.monkeyworld.org

---

The Inside Park

►►►► 86%

tel: 01258 453719 **Down House Estate DT11 9AD**
email: mail@theinsidepark.co.uk
dir: *From Blandford Forum follow Winterborne Stickland signs. Site in 1.5m.*
grid ref: *ST869046*

An attractive, well-sheltered and quiet park, half a mile along a country lane in a wooded valley, yet close to Blandford Forum. The spacious pitches are divided by mature trees and shrubs, and the amenities are housed in an 18th-century coach house and stables. There are some lovely woodland walks within the park, an excellent fenced play area for children and a dog-free area; four dog kennels are available for daily hire. This site makes the perfect base for anyone visiting the Blandford Steam Fair in August, and there are over six miles of private waymarked farm walks for guests to use. 12 acre site. 125 touring pitches. Caravan pitches. Motorhome pitches. Tent pitches.

Open: Etr-Oct **Last arrival:** 22.00hrs **Last departure:** noon

Pitches: 🚐 🚎 ⅄

Leisure: ⚙ 🎣

Facilities: ⊙ 🐾 ⚒ ⚑ 🔥 ⓢ 🔦 WIFI ♻ ❼

Services: 🔌 🗑 🔋 🚿 T ⛽ ⬇

Within 3 miles: ⅃ ⌁ 🛒 🗑 ∪

Notes: Dogs must be kept on leads. Kennels (charges apply).

AA Pubs & Restaurants nearby: The Hambro Arms, MILTON ABBAS, DT11 0BP, 01258 880233

The Anchor Inn, SHAPWICK, DT11 9LB, 01258 857269

BRIDPORT — Map 4 SY49

Places to visit

Dorset County Museum, DORCHESTER, DT1 1XA, 01305 262735 www.dorsetcountymuseum.org

Great for kids: Abbotsbury Swannery, ABBOTSBURY, DT3 4JG, 01305 871858 www.abbotsbury-tourism.co.uk

---

BRIDPORT — Map 4 SY49

Freshwater Beach Holiday Park

HOLIDAY CENTRE 92%

tel: 01308 897317 **Burton Bradstock DT6 4PT**
email: office@freshwaterbeach.co.uk **web:** www.freshwaterbeach.co.uk
dir: *Take B3157 from Bridport towards Burton Bradstock. Site 1.5m from Crown rdbt on right.* **grid ref:** *SY493892*

A family holiday centre sheltered by a sand bank and enjoying its own private beach. The park offers a wide variety of leisure and entertainment programmes for all the family, plus the Jurassic Fun Centre with indoor pool, gym, 6-lane bowling alley, restaurant and bar is excellent. There is an adults-only Sunset Lounge Bar and Cellar function room. The park is well placed at one end of the Weymouth to Bridport coastal area with spectacular views of Chesil Beach. There are three immaculate toilet blocks with excellent private rooms. 40 acre site. 500 touring pitches. 25 hardstandings. Caravan pitches. Motorhome pitches. Tent pitches. 250 statics.

Open: mid Mar-mid Nov **Last arrival:** 22.00hrs **Last departure:** 10.00hrs

Pitches: 🚐 🚎 ⅄ **Leisure:** 🏊 🏊 🎾 ⚙ ❄ 🎣 🎵 Spa

Facilities: 🔥 📶 ⊙ 🐾 ⚒ ⓢ 🔦 WIFI 🖥 ❼

Services: 🔌 🗑 🍴 🔋 🚿 T ⚙ ⬆ 🚾 ⬇ **Within 3 miles:** ⅃ ❄ 🗑 ⌁ ◎ ⓢ 🗑

Notes: Families & couples only. Dogs must be kept on leads. Large TV, kids' club in high season & BHs.

AA Pubs & Restaurants nearby: The Shave Cross Inn, BRIDPORT, DT6 6HW, 01308 868358

Riverside Restaurant, BRIDPORT, DT6 4EZ, 01308 422011

The Anchor Inn, CHIDEOCK, DT6 6JU, 01297 489215

See advert on page 189

PITCHES: 🚐 Caravans 🚎 Motorhomes ⅄ Tents ⋒ Glamping accommodation SERVICES: 🔌 Electric hook up 🗑 Launderette 🍴 Licensed bar
🔋 Calor Gas ⚙ Camping Gaz T Toilet fluid 🍴 Café/Restaurant 🍟 Fast Food/Takeaway 🔋 Battery charging 🚾 Baby care ⬇ Motorvan service point
ABBREVIATIONS: BHs — bank holidays Etr — Easter Spring BH — Spring Bank Holiday fr — from hrs — hours m — mile mdnt — midnight
rdbt — roundabout rs — restricted service wk — week wknd — weekend x-roads — crossroads ⊛ No credit or debit cards ⊗ No dogs

BRIDPORT *continued*

PREMIER PARK

Highlands End Holiday Park

▶▶▶▶▶ 93%

Best of British / GOLD

tel: 01308 422139 & 426947 **Eype DT6 6AR**
email: holidays@wdlh.co.uk
dir: *1m W of Bridport on A35, follow signs for Eype. Site signed.* **grid ref:** *SY454913*

A well-screened site with magnificent cliff-top views over the Channel and the Dorset coast, adjacent to National Trust land and overlooking Lyme Bay. The pitches are mostly sheltered by hedging and well spaced on hardstandings. The excellent facilities include a tasteful bar and restaurant, indoor pool, leisure centre and The Cowshed Café, a very good coffee shop. There is a mixture of statics and tourers, but the tourers enjoy the best cliff-top positions, including gravel hardstanding pitches overlooking Lyme Bay. Six luxury lodges and wooden pods, that sleep four, are available for hire. 9 acre site. 195 touring pitches. 45 hardstandings. Caravan pitches. Motorhome pitches. Tent pitches. 160 statics.

Open: Mar-Nov **Last arrival:** 22.00hrs **Last departure:** 11.00hrs

Pitches: * 🚐 £17.25-£40 🚐 £17.25-£40 ▲ £17.25-£35.50 🏠 prices shown below

Leisure: 🏊‍♂️🎾⛰️🎱☺️♟️🎯♫

Facilities: 🔦ᴘ⊙🚿✳️♿🛁🆂🏕️🚻 📶 ♻️ ℹ️

Services: 🔌🚽🍴🔒🧺🚰🅣🍽️🛒🛗♨️

Glamping: Wooden Pods 2, £45-£65 Changeover day Mon, Fri, Sat (Sat only in peak season) Min stay 3 nights Car by unit

Within 3 miles: ⚓🛶🎋🎣🏊‍♀️🅂🛍️

Notes: Dogs must be kept on leads. Steam room, sauna, pitch & putt.

AA Pubs & Restaurants nearby: The Shave Cross Inn, BRIDPORT, DT6 6HW, 01308 868358

Riverside Restaurant, BRIDPORT, DT6 4EZ, 01308 422011

The Anchor Inn, CHIDEOCK, DT6 6JU, 01297 489215

PREMIER PARK

Bingham Grange Touring & Camping Park

▶▶▶▶▶ 92%

tel: 01308 488234 **Melplash DT6 3TT**
email: enquiries@binghamgrange.co.uk
dir: *From A35 at Bridport take A3066 N towards Beaminster. Site on left in 3m.* **grid ref:** *SY478963*

Set in a quiet rural location but only five miles from the Jurassic Coast, this adults-only park enjoys views over the west Dorset countryside. The mostly level pitches are attractively set amongst shrub beds and ornamental trees. There is an excellent restaurant with lounge bar and takeaway, and all facilities are of a high quality. This is a very dog-friendly site. 20 acre site. 150 touring pitches. 85 hardstandings. 50 seasonal pitches. Caravan pitches. Motorhome pitches. Tent pitches.

Open: 16 Mar-end Oct (contact site for exact date) (rs Tue & Wed restaurant & bar closed)
Last arrival: 19.00hrs (21.00hrs in high season by prior arrangement)
Last departure: 11.00hrs

Pitches: 🚐 🚐 ▲

Facilities: 🔦ᴘ⊙🚿✳️♿🛁🆂🏕️ 📶 ♻️ ℹ️

Services: 🔌🚽🍴🔒🧺🅣🍽️🛗♨️

Within 3 miles: ⚓🎋🎣🛍️🅂🛍️🛶

Notes: Adults only. No children under 18yrs may stay or visit, no noise after 23.00hrs, Dogs must be kept on leads. Woodland walks.

AA Pubs & Restaurants nearby: The Shave Cross Inn, BRIDPORT, DT6 6HW, 01308 868358

Riverside Restaurant, BRIDPORT, DT6 4EZ, 01308 422011

Graston Copse Holiday Park

▶▶▶ 88%

GOLD

tel: 01308 426912 & 422139 **Annings Ln, Burton Bradstock DT6 4QP**
email: holidays@wdlh.co.uk
dir: *From Dorchester take A35 to Bridport. In Bridport follow 'Westbound through traffic' sign at mini rdbt. At next rdbt left onto B3157 to Burton Bradstock. In village, left at Anchor Inn, 2nd right into Annings Ln. 1m to site.* **grid ref:** *SY491893*

This small, peaceful site offering good facilities for families, is located near the village of Burton Bradstock making it a perfect base for visiting the stunning cliffs and beaches along the Jurassic coastline. The facilities are modern and spotlessly clean. Wooden pods that sleep four are available to hire. Please note, care is needed if driving through Burton Bradstock to the site. 9 acre site. 26 touring pitches. Caravan pitches. Motorhome pitches. Tent pitches. 90 statics.

Open: 28 Apr-25 Sep **Last arrival:** 22.00hrs **Last departure:** 11.00hrs

Pitches: * 🚐 £16.25-£27 🚐 £16.25-£27 ▲ £13.50-£24.50 🏠 prices shown below

Facilities: 🔦⊙🚿✳️🏕️🚻 📶 ♻️ ℹ️

Services: 🔌🚽

Glamping: Wooden Pods 2, £45-£65 Changeover day Mon, Fri, Sat (Sat only in peak season) Min stay 3 nights Car by unit

Within 3 miles: ⚓🎋🎣🎣◎🏊‍♀️🛍️🅂🛶

Notes: Dogs must be kept on leads.

AA Pubs & Restaurants nearby: Riverside Restaurant, BRIDPORT, DT6 4EZ, 01308 422011

The Crown Inn, PUNCKNOWLE, DT2 9BN, 01308 897711

LEISURE: 🏊 Indoor pool 🏊 Outdoor pool ⛰️ Children's playground 🖐️ Kid's club 🎾 Tennis court 🎱 Games room ⛳ Golf course 🚣 Boat hire 🚲 Cycle hire 🎭 Cinema 🎪 Entertainment 🎣 Fishing ◎ Mini golf ⛳ Pitch n putt 🏄 Watersports 🏋️ Gym ♻️ Sports field ♨️ Stables **FACILITIES:** 🛁 Bath 🚿 Shower ᴘ Private washing cubicles ⊙ Electric shaver 🪒 Hairdryer ❄️ Ice Packs ♿ Disabled facilities 🆂 Shop on site 🏪 Mobile shop 🍖 BBQ area 🪵 Picnic area 📶 Wi-fi 💻 Internet access ♻️ Recycling ℹ️ Tourist info 🐕 Dog exercise area 🚗 Car hire can be arranged

FreshwaterBeach
HOLIDAY PARK

Featuring...

As seen on TV!

A film location for
BROADCHURCH

CAMPING • TOURING • HOLIDAY HOME HIRE

Great family holidays on Dorset's World Heritage Coast.

Previous Holiday Centre of the Year   **AA**

Call 01308 897317

www.freshwaterbeach.co.uk

CERNE ABBAS — Map 4 ST60

Places to visit

Athelhampton House & Gardens, ATHELHAMPTON, DT2 7LG, 01305 848363
www.athelhampton.co.uk

Hardy's Cottage, DORCHESTER, DT2 8QJ, 01305 262366
www.nationaltrust.org.uk

Great for kids: Maiden Castle, DORCHESTER, DT2 9PP, 0370 333 1181
www.english-heritage.org.uk/daysout/properties/maiden-castle

Lyons Gate Caravan and Camping Park
►►►► 79%

tel: 01300 345260 Lyons Gate DT2 7AZ
email: info@lyons-gate.co.uk
dir: *Direct access from A352, 3m N of Cerne Abbas, site signed.* **grid ref:** *ST660062*

A peaceful park with pitches set out around the four attractive coarse fishing lakes. It is surrounded by mature woodland, with many footpaths and bridleways. Other easily accessible attractions include the Cerne Giant carved into the hills, the old market town of Dorchester, and the superb sandy beach at Weymouth. 10 acre site. 90 touring pitches. 24 hardstandings. Caravan pitches. Motorhome pitches. Tent pitches. 14 statics.

Open: all year **Last arrival:** 20.00hrs **Last departure:** 11.30hrs
Pitches: 🚐 🚌 ▲ **Leisure:** 🎣 **Facilities:** ☉ 🖗 ⚒ ⚐ 🛒 🎋 WiFi ⓘ

Services: 🔌 🗑 🔒 🚿 **Within 3 miles:** 🎣 🚴 🛒 ∪

Notes: Dogs must be kept on leads.

AA Pubs & Restaurants nearby: The New Inn, CERNE ABBAS, DT2 7JF, 01300 341274
The Poachers Inn, PIDDLETRENTHIDE, DT2 7QX, 01300 348358

Giants Head Caravan & Camping Park
►►► 78%

tel: 01300 341242 Giants Head Farm, Old Sherborne Rd DT2 7TR
email: holidays@giantshead.co.uk
dir: *From Dorchester into town avoiding by-pass, at Top O'Town rdbt take A352 (Sherborne road), in 500yds right fork at BP (Loder's) garage & Lidl store.* **grid ref:** *ST675029*

A pleasant, though rather basic, park set in Dorset downland near the Cerne Giant (the famous landmark figure cut into the chalk) and with stunning views. There is a smart toilet block which is kept very clean. This is a good stopover site especially for tenters and backpackers on The Ridgeway National Trail. The site also offers 'Treasure Trail' routes for Dorset. Holiday chalets are available to let. 4 acre site. 50 touring pitches. Caravan pitches. Motorhome pitches. Tent pitches.

Open: Etr-Oct (rs Etr shop & bar closed) **Last arrival:** anytime **Last departure:** 13.00hrs
Pitches: 🚐 🚌 ▲ **Facilities:** 🖗 ☉ 🖗 ⚒ 🛒 🎋 ♻ ⓘ
Services: 🔌 🗑 🔒 🚿 🛒 **Within 3 miles:** 🚴 🛒 🗑

Notes: Dogs must be kept on leads.

AA Pubs & Restaurants nearby: The Greyhound Inn, SYDLING ST NICHOLAS, DT2 9PD, 01300 341303

LEISURE: 🏊 Indoor pool 🏊 Outdoor pool 🛝 Children's playground 🧒 Kid's club 🎾 Tennis court 🎱 Games room ⛳ Golf course 🚣 Boat hire 🚲 Cycle hire 🎬 Cinema 🎵 Entertainment 🎣 Fishing ⛳ Mini golf 🏌 Pitch n putt 🏄 Watersports 💪 Gym ♻ Sports field ∪ Stables **FACILITIES:** 🛁 Bath 🚿 Shower 🅿 Private washing cubicles ☉ Electric shaver 🖗 Hairdryer ❄ Ice Packs ♿ Disabled facilities 🛒 Shop on site 📱 Mobile shop 🍖 BBQ area 🎋 Picnic area WiFi Wi-fi 💻 Internet access ♻ Recycling ⓘ Tourist info 🐕 Dog exercise area 🚗 Car hire can be arranged

CHARMOUTH — Map 4 SY39

Places to visit

Forde Abbey, THORNCOMBE, TA20 4LU, 01460 221290 www.fordeabbey.co.uk

Great for kids: Abbotsbury Swannery, ABBOTSBURY, DT3 4JG, 01305 871858 www.abbotsbury-tourism.co.uk

---

PREMIER PARK

Wood Farm Caravan & Camping Park

►►►►► 93%

Best of British

tel: 01297 560697 **Axminster Rd DT6 6BT**
email: reception@woodfarm.co.uk **web:** www.woodfarm.co.uk
dir: *Accessed directly from A35 rdbt, on Axminster side of Charmouth.*
grid ref: *SY356940*

This top quality park, the perfect place to relax, is set amongst mature native trees with the various levels of the ground falling away into a beautiful valley below. The park offers excellent facilities including family rooms and fully serviced pitches. Everything throughout the park is spotless. At the bottom end of the park there is an indoor swimming pool and leisure complex, plus the licensed, conservatory-style Offshore Café. There's a very good children's play room and excellent play area, in addition to tennis courts and a well-stocked, coarse-fishing lake. The park is well positioned on the Heritage Coast near Lyme Regis. Static holiday homes are also available for hire. 13 acre site. 175 touring pitches. 175 hardstandings. 20 seasonal pitches. Caravan pitches. Motorhome pitches. Tent pitches. 92 statics.

Open: Etr-Oct **Last arrival:** 19.00hrs **Last departure:** noon

---

Pitches: 🚐 🚍 ⛺ **Leisure:** 🏊 ⚽ 🎣 🎱 ✏
Facilities: 🚿 ♿ 🅿 ⊙ ℱ ✶ & 🚽 ♨ 🚶 Wifi 🖥 ♻ 🛈
Services: 🚐 🗑 🔋 ⊘ 🚽 🍴 🌭 ⚡
Within 3 miles: 🎿 ☇ 🎯 ℱ ◎ 🏊 🐶 🎱 ∪

Notes: No bikes, skateboards, scooters or roller skates. Dogs must be kept on leads.

AA Pubs & Restaurants nearby: The Mariners, LYME REGIS, DT7 3HS, 01297 442753
See advert on opposite page

PREMIER PARK

Newlands Holidays

►►►►► 85%

tel: 01297 560259 **DT6 6RB**
email: enq@newlandsholidays.co.uk **web:** www.newlandsholidays.co.uk
dir: *4m W of Bridport on A35.* **grid ref:** *SY374935*

A very smart site with excellent touring facilities, set on gently sloping ground in hilly countryside near the sea. During the high season, the park offers a full entertainment programme, and boasts an indoor swimming pool and an outdoor pool with water slide. New level and very spacious pitches have been added for 2016 and the clubhouse was upgraded. Lodges, apartments and motel rooms are available, plus there are four camping pods for hire. 23 acre site. 240 touring pitches. 72 hardstandings. 40 seasonal pitches. Caravan pitches. Motorhome pitches. Tent pitches. 86 statics.

Open: 10 Mar-4 Nov **Last arrival:** 21.00hrs **Last departure:** 10.00hrs
Pitches: * 🚐 £14-£46 🚍 £14-£46 ⛺ £14-£46 🏠 prices shown below

continued

PITCHES: 🚐 Caravans 🚍 Motorhomes ⛺ Tents 🏠 Glamping accommodation **SERVICES:** 🚐 Electric hook up 🗑 Launderette 🍸 Licensed bar 🔋 Calor Gas ⊘ Camping Gaz 🚽 Toilet fluid 🍴 Café/Restaurant 🌭 Fast Food/Takeaway ⚡ Battery charging 🍼 Baby care ♨ Motorvan service point
ABBREVIATIONS: BHs – bank holidays Etr – Easter Spring BH – Spring Bank Holiday fr – from hrs – hours m – mile mdnt – midnight rdbt – roundabout rs – restricted service wk – week wknd – weekend x-roads – crossroads Ⓢ No credit or debit cards Ⓝ No dogs

CHARMOUTH *continued*

Leisure: 🏊🏖️⛰️🎿🎱🎵

Facilities: 🔥🅿️💈🔌📷✳️♿🚻🚽📶🔲♻️🅾️ℹ️

Services: 🔌🛢️🍴🎒🧺🧼🚰🚻🛒🗑️🚐

Glamping: Wooden Pods 4, £55-£65 Min stay 2 nights Car by unit

Within 3 miles: 🎣⛰️🎪⛳◎🏇🚴🛶🎱🎯⛵

Notes: Dogs must be kept on leads. Kids' club during school holidays, freshly baked bread available.

AA Pubs & Restaurants nearby: The Mariners, LYME REGIS, DT7 3HS, 01297 442753

See advert below

Manor Farm Holiday Centre
▶▶▶▶85%

tel: 01297 560226 **DT6 6QL**
email: enquiries@manorfarmholidaycentre.co.uk
dir: *From E: A35 into Charmouth, site 0.75m on right.* **grid ref:** *SY368937*

Set just a short walk from the safe sand and shingle beach at Charmouth, this popular family park offers a good range of facilities. There is an indoor-outdoor swimming pool plus café, a fully-equipped gym and sauna. Children certainly enjoy the activity area and the park also offers a lively programme in the extensive bar and entertainment complex. In addition there are 16 luxury cottages available for hire and smart lodges for sale. 30 acre site. 400 touring pitches. 80 hardstandings. 100 seasonal pitches. Caravan pitches. Motorhome pitches. Tent pitches. 29 statics.

Open: all year (rs mid Mar-end Oct statics only) **Last arrival:** 20.00hrs
Last departure: 10.00hrs

Pitches: * 🚐 £15-£38 🚎 £15-£38 ⛺ £15-£32

Leisure: 🏊🏖️🎿⛰️🎱🎵 Spa

Facilities: 🔥🅿️💈🔌📷✳️♿🚻📶♻️ℹ️

Services: 🔌🛢️🍴🎒🧼🚰🚻🛒🗑️🚐🛶

Within 3 miles: 🎣⛰️🎪⛳◎🏇🚴🛶🎱🎯⛵

Notes: No skateboards. Dogs must be kept on leads.

AA Pubs & Restaurants nearby: The Mariners, LYME REGIS, DT7 3HS, 01297 442753

LEISURE: 🏊 Indoor pool 🏖️ Outdoor pool ⛰️ Children's playground 🎿 Kid's club 🎱 Tennis court 🎱 Games room ⛳ Golf course 🏄 Boat hire 🚴 Cycle hire 🎪 Cinema 🎵 Entertainment 🎣 Fishing ◎ Mini golf ⛳ Pitch n putt 🏄 Watersports 🎽 Gym 🎯 Sports field ⛵ Stables **FACILITIES:** 🛁 Bath 🚿 Shower 🅿️ Private washing cubicles ⊙ Electric shaver ✂️ Hairdryer ✳️ Ice Packs ♿ Disabled facilities 🛢️ Shop on site 🚐 Mobile shop 🍴 BBQ area 🧺 Picnic area 📶 Wi-fi 📧 Internet access ♻️ Recycling ℹ️ Tourist info 🐕 Dog exercise area 🚗 Car hire can be arranged

CHIDEOCK
Map 4 SY49

Places to visit
Mapperton, BEAMINSTER, DT8 3NR, 01308 862645 www.mapperton.com

Golden Cap Holiday Park
▶▶▶▶▶ 84%

tel: 01308 422139 & 426947 **Seatown DT6 6JX**
email: holidays@wdlh.co.uk
dir: *On A35, in Chideock follow Seatown signs, site signed.* **grid ref:** *SY422919*

A grassy site, overlooking the sea and beach and surrounded by National Trust parkland. This uniquely placed park slopes down to the sea, although pitches are generally level. A slight dip hides the view of the beach from the back of the park, but this area benefits from having trees, scrub and meadows, unlike the barer areas closer to the sea which do have a spectacular outlook. The toilet and shower block was refurbished for the 2016 season, plus there's a new reception, shop and café and takeaway. Three luxury lodges, with outstanding views, and wooden pods that sleep four are available to hire. This makes an ideal base for touring Dorset and Devon. Lake fishing is possible (a licence can be obtained locally). 11 acre site. 108 touring pitches. 24 hardstandings. Caravan pitches. Motorhome pitches. Tent pitches. 234 statics.

Open: Mar-Nov **Last arrival:** 22.00hrs **Last departure:** 11.00hrs

Pitches: * 🚐 £17.25-£40 🚐 £17.25-£40 🛖 £17.25-£35.50 🏠 prices shown below

Leisure: 🎱 ✏

Facilities: 🚿⊙♿✳⚲🔥♨🚻 WIFI ♻ ✪

Services: 🔌🔖 🗑⊘T♨

Glamping: Wooden Pods 3, £45-£65 Changeover day Mon, Fri, Sat (Sat only in peak) Min stay 3 nights Car by unit

Within 3 miles: 🎱✏🔖🔖

Notes: Dogs must be kept on leads.

AA Pubs & Restaurants nearby: Riverside Restaurant, BRIDPORT, DT6 4EZ, 01308 422011

CHRISTCHURCH
Map 5 SZ19

Places to visit
Red House Museum & Gardens, CHRISTCHURCH, BH23 1BU, 01202 482860 www3.hants.gov.uk/redhouse

Great for kids: Oceanarium, BOURNEMOUTH, BH2 5AA, 01202 311993 www.oceanarium.co.uk

Meadowbank Holidays
▶▶▶▶▶ 86%

tel: 01202 483597 **Stour Way BH23 2PQ**
email: enquiries@meadowbank-holidays.co.uk
web: www.meadowbank-holidays.co.uk
dir: *A31 onto A338 towards Bournemouth. 5m, left towards Christchurch on B3073. Right at 1st rdbt into St Catherine's Way, becomes River Way. 3rd right into Stour Way to site.* **grid ref:** *SZ136946*

A very smart park on the banks of the River Stour, with a colourful display of hanging baskets and flower-filled tubs placed around the superb reception area. The toilet block is excellent, with modern, stylish facilities. Visitors can choose between the different pitch sizes, including luxury, fully serviced ones. There is also an excellent play area, a good shop on site and coarse fishing. Statics are available for hire. The park is well located in a peaceful area and very convenient for visiting nearby Christchurch, the south coast and the New Forest. 2 acre site. 41 touring pitches. 22 hardstandings. Caravan pitches. Motorhome pitches. 180 statics.

Open: Mar-Oct **Last arrival:** 21.00hrs **Last departure:** noon

Pitches: 🚐 🚐

Leisure: 🎣

Facilities: ⊙♿♿🔥♨🚻 WIFI 🖥 ♻✪

Services: 🔌🔖 🗑⊘T♨🔧

Within 3 miles: 🎱✏🚻✏◎🔖🔖U

Notes: No pets.

PITCHES: 🚐 Caravans 🚐 Motorhomes 🛖 Tents 🏠 Glamping accommodation **SERVICES:** 🔌 Electric hook up 🔖 Launderette 🍺 Licensed bar
🔋 Calor Gas ⊘ Camping Gaz T Toilet fluid 🍽 Café/Restaurant 🍔 Fast Food/Takeaway ♨ Battery charging 🍼 Baby care 🔧 Motorvan service point
ABBREVIATIONS: BHs – bank holidays Etr – Easter Spring BH – Spring Bank Holiday fr – from hrs – hours m – mile mdnt – midnight
rdbt – roundabout rs – restricted service wk – week wknd – weekend x-roads – crossroads ⊛ No credit or debit cards ⊗ No dogs

CORFE CASTLE
Map 4 SY98

Places to visit

Brownsea Island, BROWNSEA ISLAND, BH13 7EE, 01202 707744
www.nationaltrust.org.uk/brownsea-island

Great for kids: Swanage Railway, SWANAGE, BH19 1HB, 01929 425800
www.swanagerailway.co.uk

Corfe Castle Camping & Caravanning Club Site
▶▶▶▶ 92%

tel: 01929 480280 & 02476 475426 **Bucknowle BH20 5PQ**
dir: A351 from Wareham towards Swanage for 4m. Right at foot of Corfe Castle signed Church Knowle. 0.75m, right at Corfe Castle C&CC Site sign. **grid ref:** SY950819

This lovely campsite, where non-members are also very welcome, is set in woodland near the famous Corfe Castle at the foot of the Purbeck Hills. It has a stone reception building, which has a really comfortable information lounge, on-site shop and modern toilet and shower facilities, which are spotless. Although the site is sloping, pitches are level and include spacious hardstandings. The site is perfect for anyone visiting the many attractions of the Purbeck area, including the award-winning beaches at Studland and Swanage, and the seaside towns of Poole, Bournemouth and Weymouth. There is also a station at Corfe for the Swanage Steam Railway. The site is pet friendly. 6 acre site. 80 touring pitches. 35 hardstandings. Caravan pitches. Motorhome pitches. Tent pitches.

Open: Mar-Oct **Last arrival:** 20.00hrs (later arrivals by prior arrangement only) **Last departure:** noon

Pitches: * 🚐 £15.80-£26.60 🚍 £15.80-£26.60 ▲ £15.80-£26.60

Leisure: 🅰

Facilities: 🏠 🅿 ⊙ 🗗 ☀ ♿ 🔯 ♻ 🛈

Services: 🔌 🔋 🔒 🗑 🅣 🎍 ⚲

Within 3 miles: 🎣 ⛄ 🍽 ◎ 🚣 🔯 🛶 ♨

Notes: Site gates closed 23.00hrs-07.00hrs. Dogs must be kept on leads. Bread & newspapers can be ordered. Local sausages, bacon, ice cream & free-range eggs available.

AA Pubs & Restaurants nearby: The New Inn, CHURCH KNOWLE, BH20 5NQ, 01929 480357

Woodyhyde Camp Site
▶▶▶ 81%

tel: 01929 480274 **Valley Rd BH20 5HT**
email: camp@woodyhyde.co.uk **web:** www.woodyhyde.co.uk
dir: From Corfe Castle towards Swanage on A351, site approx 1m on right.
grid ref: SY974804

A large grassy campsite in a sheltered location for tents and motorhomes only, divided into three paddocks — one is dog free. There is a well-stocked shop on site, a modern toilet and shower block, a new shepherd's hut for hire, and a regular bus service that stops near the site entrance. Electric hook-ups and some hardstandings are available. This site offers traditional camping in a great location between Corfe Castle and Swanage. 13 acre site. 150 touring pitches. 25 hardstandings. Motorhome pitches. Tent pitches.

Open: Mar-Oct **Last departure:** noon

Pitches: 🚍 ▲ 🏠

Facilities: ⊙ 🗗 ☀ ♿ 🔯 ♻ 🛈

Services: 🔌 🔒 🗑 🅣 🎍 🛒 ⚲

Glamping: Shepherd's Huts 1

Within 3 miles: 🎣 ⛄ 🍽 🚲 ◎ 🚣 🔯 🛶 ♨

Notes: No noise after 23.00hrs, no open fires. Dogs must be kept on leads.

AA Pubs & Restaurants nearby: The New Inn, CHURCH KNOWLE, BH20 5NQ, 01929 480357

LEISURE: 🏊 Indoor pool 🏊 Outdoor pool 🛝 Children's playground 🧒 Kid's club 🎾 Tennis court 🎱 Games room ⛳ Golf course 🚣 Boat hire 🚲 Cycle hire 🎬 Cinema 🎵 Entertainment 🎣 Fishing ⛳ Mini golf ⛳ Pitch n putt 🏄 Watersports 🏋 Gym ⚽ Sports field ♨ Stables **FACILITIES:** 🛁 Bath 🚿 Shower 🅿 Private washing cubicles ⊙ Electric shaver 💇 Hairdryer ☀ Ice Packs ♿ Disabled facilities 🔯 Shop on site 🛒 Mobile shop 🍖 BBQ area 🌲 Picnic area 📶 Wi-fi 💻 Internet access ♻ Recycling 🛈 Tourist info 🐕 Dog exercise area 🚗 Car hire can be arranged

DORCHESTER

See Cerne Abbas

DRIMPTON
Map 4 ST40

Places to visit

Forde Abbey, THORNCOMBE, TA20 4LU, 01460 221290 www.fordeabbey.co.uk

Mapperton, BEAMINSTER, DT8 3NR, 01308 862645 www.mapperton.com

Oathill Farm Touring and Camping Site
►►►► 84%

tel: 01460 30234 **Oathill TA18 8PZ**
email: oathillfarm@btconnect.com
dir: *From Crewkerne take B3165. Site on left just after Clapton.* **grid ref:** *ST404055*

This small peaceful park borders Somerset and Devon, with the Jurassic Coast at Lyme Regis, Charmouth and Bridport only a short drive away. The modern facilities are spotless and there are hardstandings and fully serviced pitches available. There is also a very pleasant camping area which has two additional hardstandings. Lucy's Tea Room serves breakfast and meals. The well-stocked, landscaped fishing ponds prove a hit with anglers. Three luxury lodges are available for hire. 10 acre site. 13 touring pitches. 18 hardstandings. 8 seasonal pitches. Caravan pitches. Motorhome pitches. Tent pitches. 3 statics.

Open: all year (rs Winter - shop not fully stocked) **Last arrival:** 20.00hrs
Last departure: noon

Pitches: 🚐 🚍 Å

Leisure: ⚽

Facilities: ⊙ 𝒫 ✳ 🗑 🎏 🚾 ♻ 𝟎

Services: 🔌 🖸 🍽 🛢 ⊘ Ⓣ 🍴 🎂 🧺 ⚱

Within 3 miles: ↓ 🎣 🛒 📕 🖸 ↺

Notes: No washing lines, no quad bikes, no noise after 23.00hrs. Separate recreational areas.

AA Pubs & Restaurants nearby: The George Inn, CREWKERNE, TA18 7LP, 01460 73650

FERNDOWN

Places to visit

Kingston Lacy, WIMBORNE, BH21 4EA, 01202 883402 (Mon-Fri) www.nationaltrust.org.uk/kingston-lacy

Great for kids: Oceanarium, BOURNEMOUTH, BH2 5AA, 01202 311993 www.oceanarium.co.uk

FERNDOWN
Map 5 SU00

St Leonards Farm Caravan & Camping Park
►►► 87%

tel: 01202 872637 **Ringwood Rd, West Moors BH22 0AQ**
email: enquiries_stleonards@yahoo.co.uk **web:** www.stleonardsfarmpark.com
dir: *From Ringwood on A31 (dual carriageway) towards Ferndown, exit left into slip road at site sign. From Wimborne Minster on A31 at rdbt (junct of A31 & A347) follow signs for Ringwood (A31)(pass Texaco garage on left) to next rdbt. 3rd exit (ie double back towards Ferndown) exit at slip road for site.* **grid ref:** *SU093014*

A private road accessed from the A31 leads to this well-screened park divided into paddocks that have spacious pitches; the site has an excellent secure children's play area, and is well located for visiting nearby Bournemouth and the New Forest National Park. A new toilet and shower block with excellent family/disabled rooms, and a new late arrival point, with electricity and water, were added in 2016. A shepherd's hut is available for hire, complete with a fully-equipped utility cabin. 12 acre site. 151 touring pitches. 30 seasonal pitches. Caravan pitches. Motorhome pitches. Tent pitches. 6 statics.

Open: 7 Feb-6 Jan (rs 31 Oct-6 Jan; 7 Feb-31 Mar - only open Fri-Sun)
Arrivals: late arrivals by prior arrangement **Last departure:** 14.30hrs
Pitches: * 🚐 £12-£27 🚍 £12-£27 Å £12-£27 🏕 prices shown below
Leisure: 🛝 ♲ **Facilities:** 🏕 📷 ⊙ 𝒫 ✳ 🚿 🎏 🎢 ♻ 𝟎 **Services:** 🔌 🖸 🛢 ⊘ 🧺
Glamping: Shepherd's Huts 1, £40 Changeover day Mon Own kitchen Car by unit
Within 3 miles: ↓ 🎣 🖸 🖸 ↺

Notes: No large groups, no noise after 23.00hrs, no disposable BBQs, no gazebos, no dogs Jul-Aug. Dogs must be kept on leads.

AA Pubs & Restaurants nearby: Les Bouviers Restaurant with Rooms, WIMBORNE MINSTER, BH21 3BD, 01202 889555

PITCHES: 🚐 Caravans 🚍 Motorhomes Å Tents 🏕 Glamping accommodation **SERVICES:** 🔌 Electric hook up 🖸 Launderette 🍽 Licensed bar 🛢 Calor Gas ⊘ Camping Gaz Ⓣ Toilet fluid 🍴 Café/Restaurant 🎂 Fast Food/Takeaway 🔋 Battery charging 🛒 Baby care ⚱ Motorvan service point **ABBREVIATIONS:** BHs – bank holidays Etr – Easter Spring BH – Spring Bank Holiday fr – from hrs – hours m – mile mdnt – midnight rdbt – roundabout rs – restricted service wk – week wknd – weekend x-roads – crossroads 🚫 No credit or debit cards 🚫 No dogs

HOLDITCH — Map 4 ST30

Places to visit

Forde Abbey, THORNCOMBE, TA20 4LU, 01460 221290 www.fordeabbey.co.uk

Crafty Camping

NEW ▶ ▶ ▶ ▶ ▶ 85%

tel: 01460 221102 **Woodland Workshop, Yonder Hill TA20 4NL**
email: enquiries@mallinson.co.uk
dir: *From A358 between Axminster & Chard, in Tytherleigh into Broom Ln signed Holditch (becomes Holditch Ln). Through Holditch, after Manor Farm, after sharp left bend, car park on left in 200yds. NB it is advisable not to use Sat Nav.*
grid ref: ST347030

Crafty Camping offers a unique holiday adventure in peaceful and beautiful surroundings. If you have a desire to experience a different type of holiday, then this adults-only site could fit the bill. Choose from fully-equipped yurts or a shepherd's hut, each with their own toilet and shower facilities, or bell tents and a tipi, which share excellent communal facilities, or book 'the jewel in the crown', a spectacular tree house. Here there's a double bed, toilet and shower facilities, including a copper bath, a wood-burning stove, and a decked area with table and chairs, hammock, pizza oven and even an open-air shower. There is a spiral staircase to an upper level, which has a sauna and a hot tub – you can even get to the forest floor via a slide! There is also a communal kitchen and eating area, and woodland craft courses are also available. Although hidden away in the hamlet of Holditch, it is close to Axminster, Lyme Regis and the Jurassic Coast. 14 acre site.

Open: all year **Last arrival:** anytime **Last departure:** 11.00hrs

Leisure: 🎣 ✎

Facilities: 🔥 🄿 ⊠ ✳ 🚞 📶 ♻ ❶

Services: 🍴

Glamping: Bell tents 3, £88–£113 Changeover day Mon, Wed, Fri Min stay 2 nights (Mon-Tue or Wed-Thu), 3 nights (Fri-Sun) **Tipis** 1, £126–£158 Changeover day Mon, Wed, Fri Min stay 2 nights (Mon-Tue or Wed-Thu), 3 nights (Fri-Sun) En suite **Yurts** 2, £126–£158 Changeover day Mon, Wed, Fri Min stay 2 nights (Mon-Tue or Wed-Thu), 3 nights (Fri-Sun) En suite **Shepherd's Huts** 1, £126–£158 Changeover day Mon, Wed, Fri Min stay 2 nights (Mon-Tue or Wed-Thu), 3 nights (Fri-Sun) En suite **Tree Houses** 1, £276–£330 Changeover day Mon, Wed, Fri Min stay 2 nights (Mon-Tue or Wed-Thu), 3 nights (Fri-Sun)

Within 3 miles: ↨ ✎ 🅂 🖥

Notes: Adults only. PayPal accepted. 🚫

HURN — Map 5 SZ19

Places to visit

Red House Museum & Gardens, CHRISTCHURCH, BH23 1BU, 01202 482860 www3.hants.gov.uk/redhouse

Oceanarium, BOURNEMOUTH, BH2 5AA, 01202 311993 www.oceanarium.co.uk

Fillybrook Farm Touring Park
▶ ▶ 85%

tel: 01202 478266 **Matchams Ln BH23 6AW**
email: enquiries@fillybrookfarm.co.uk
dir: *M27 junct 1, A31 to Ringwood, then Poole, left immediately after Texaco Garage signed Verwood & B3081, left into Hurn Ln signed Matchams. Site on right in 4m.*
grid ref: SZ128997

A small adults-only and very dog-friendly park that's well located on the edge of Hurn Forest, with Bournemouth, Christchurch, Poole and the New Forest within easy reach. Fillybrook provides a pleasant, peaceful camping environment, and the facilities are both modern and very clean. A dry-ski slope, with an adjoining restaurant and small bar, is a short walk from the site. There is also a separate rally field. 1 acre site. 18 touring pitches. Caravan pitches. Motorhome pitches. Tent pitches.

Open: Etr-Oct **Last arrival:** 20.00hrs **Last departure:** 11.00hrs

Pitches: 🚐 🚏 ▲

Facilities: 🔥 ⊙ 🄿 ✳ 🚞 ♻ ❶

Services: 🚰 🛁 ⚇

Within 3 miles: ↨ ✎ 🅂 🖥 ∪

Notes: Adults only. 🚫 No large groups, no commercial vehicles, no campfires. Dogs must be kept on leads.

AA Pubs & Restaurants nearby: The Three Tuns, BRANSGORE, BH23 8JH, 01425 672232

LYME REGIS

See also Charmouth

Places to visit

Pecorama Pleasure Gardens, BEER, EX12 3NA, 01297 21542 www.pecorama.co.uk

---

LEISURE: 🏊 Indoor pool 🏊 Outdoor pool ⛰ Children's playground ✋ Kid's club ⚲ Tennis court 🎱 Games room ⛳ Golf course ⛵ Boat hire 🚲 Cycle hire 🎬 Cinema 🎵 Entertainment 🎣 Fishing ⊙ Mini golf ⛳ Pitch n putt 🏄 Watersports ⚥ Gym ⊛ Sports field ∪ Stables **FACILITIES:** 🛁 Bath 🔥 Shower 🄿 Private washing cubicles ⊙ Electric shaver 🄿 Hairdryer ✳ Ice Packs ♿ Disabled facilities 🅂 Shop on site 🖥 Mobile shop 🍖 BBQ area 🚞 Picnic area 📶 Wi-fi 🖥 Internet access ♻ Recycling ❶ Tourist info 🐕 Dog exercise area 🚗 Car hire can be arranged

LYME REGIS
Map 4 SY39

Shrubbery Touring Park

►►►► 87%

tel: 01297 442227 **Rousdon DT7 3XW**
email: info4shrubberypark@yahoo.co.uk **web:** www.shrubberypark.co.uk
dir: *3m W of Lyme Regis on A3052 (coast road).* **grid ref:** SY300914

Mature trees enclose this peaceful park, which has distant views of the lovely countryside. The modern facilities are well kept, the hardstanding pitches are spacious, and there is plenty of space for children to play in the grounds. There is a small area set aside for adults only and there are two new camping pods for hire. Well located for visiting Lyme Regis, Sidmouth and Seaton, the park is right on the Jurassic Coast bus route, which is popular with visitors to this area. 10 acre site. 120 touring pitches. 28 hardstandings. Caravan pitches. Motorhome pitches. Tent pitches.

Open: Apr-1 Nov **Last arrival:** 21.00hrs **Last departure:** 11.00hrs

Pitches: 🚐 🚍 ▲ 🏕

Facilities: ☉ 🏳 ☼ ⅏ 🔥 🙌 ♻ ❸

Services: 🔌 🗑 🛢 ∅ T 🖤

Glamping: Wooden Pods 2

Within 3 miles: ↥ ⅃ Η ✐ ◎ ≟ 🗐 🗐 ∪

Notes: No groups (except rallies), no motor scooters, roller skates or skateboards. Dogs must be kept on leads. Crazy golf.

AA Pubs & Restaurants nearby: The Mariners, LYME REGIS, DT7 3HS, 01297 442753

Hook Farm Caravan & Camping Park
►►► 85%

tel: 01297 442801 **Gore Ln, Uplyme DT7 3UU**
email: information@hookfarm-uplyme.co.uk
dir: *A35 onto B3165 towards Lyme Regis & Uplyme at Hunters Lodge pub. In 2m right into Gore Ln, site 400yds on right.* **grid ref:** SY323930

Set in a peaceful and very rural location, this popular farm site enjoys lovely views of Lym Valley and is just a mile from the seaside at Lyme Regis. There are modern toilet facilities at the top and bottom of the site, and good on-site amenities. Most pitches are level due to excellent terracing – it is a great site for tents but also suited to motorhomes and caravans. Please note, it is advised that if arriving in a motorhome or if towing a caravan that Sat Nav is not used; there are many narrow roads that only have a few passing places. 5.5 acre site. 100 touring pitches. 4 hardstandings. Caravan pitches. Motorhome pitches. Tent pitches. 17 statics.

Open: Mar-Oct **Last arrival:** 20.00hrs **Last departure:** 11.00hrs

Pitches: * 🚐 £12-£29 🚍 £12-£29 ▲ £10-£31

Leisure: 🅰

Facilities: 🔥 ☉ 🏳 ☼ ⅏ 🔥 🙌 🌐 ♻ ❸ 🍵

Services: 🔌 🗑 🛢 ∅ 🖤 🖤

Within 3 miles: ↥ ⅃ Η ✐ ◎ ≟ 🗐 🗐 ∪

Notes: 🐾 No groups of 5 adults or more, no dangerous dog breeds. Dogs must be kept on leads. Cycle storage.

AA Pubs & Restaurants nearby: The Mariners, LYME REGIS, DT7 3HS, 01297 442753

LYTCHETT MATRAVERS
Map 4 SY99

Places to visit
Brownsea Island, BROWNSEA ISLAND, BH13 7EE, 01202 707744
www.nationaltrust.org.uk/brownsea-island

Poole Museum, POOLE, BH15 1BW, 01202 262600
www.boroughofpoole.com/museums

Great for kids: Swanage Railway, SWANAGE, BH19 1HB, 01929 425800
www.swanagerailway.co.uk

Huntick Farm Caravan Park
►►► 84%

tel: 01202 622222 **Huntick Rd BH16 6BB**
email: huntickcaravans@btconnect.com
dir: *Site between Lytchett Minster & Lytchett Matravers. From A31 take A350 towards Poole. Follow Lytchett Minster signs, then Lytchett Matravers signs. Into Huntick Rd by Rose & Crown pub.* **grid ref:** SY955947

A really attractive little park situated in rural surroundings edged by woodland, a mile from the village amenities of Lytchett Matravers. This neat grassy park is divided into three, peaceful paddocks, yet it is close to the attractions that both Poole and Bournemouth have to offer. There are excellent toilet facilities. 4 acre site. 30 touring pitches. 13 seasonal pitches. Caravan pitches. Motorhome pitches. Tent pitches.

Open: Apr-Oct **Last arrival:** 21.00hrs **Last departure:** noon

Pitches: 🚐 £16-£26 🚍 £16-£26 ▲ £16-£26

Leisure: ⚽

Facilities: 🔥 ☉ ☼ 🙌 🌐 ♻ ❸

Services: 🔌 🛢

Within 3 miles: ↥ 🗐 🗐 ∪

Notes: Ball games permitted only on games field, no noise 22.00hrs-08.00hrs, no gazebos. Dogs must be kept on leads.

AA Pubs & Restaurants nearby: The Cock & Bottle, EAST MORDEN, BH20 7DL, 01929 459238

PITCHES: 🚐 Caravans 🚍 Motorhomes ▲ Tents 🏕 Glamping accommodation **SERVICES:** 🔌 Electric hook up 🗑 Launderette 🖤 Licensed bar 🛢 Calor Gas ∅ Camping Gaz T Toilet fluid 🍽 Café/Restaurant 🍔 Fast Food/Takeaway 🖤 Battery charging 🖤 Baby care 🖤 Motorvan service point **ABBREVIATIONS:** BHs – bank holidays Etr – Easter Spring BH – Spring Bank Holiday fr – from hrs – hours m – mile mdnt – midnight rdbt – roundabout rs – restricted service wk – week wknd – weekend x-roads – crossroads 🐾 No credit or debit cards 🐾 No dogs

OWERMOIGNE
Map 4 SY78

Places to visit

RSPB Nature Reserve Radipole Lake and Wild Weymouth Discovery Centre, WEYMOUTH, DT4 7TZ, 01305 778313 www.rspb.org.uk

Clouds Hill, BOVINGTON CAMP, BH20 7NQ, 01929 405616 www.nationaltrust.org.uk

Great for kids: Weymouth Sea Life Adventure Park & Marine Sanctuary, WEYMOUTH, DT4 7SX, 0871 423 2110 *(Calls cost 10p per minute plus your phone company's access charge)* www.sealifeweymouth.com

Sandyholme Holiday Park
►►► 84%

GOLD

tel: 01308 422139 & 426947 **Moreton Rd DT2 8HZ**
email: holidays@wdlh.co.uk
dir: *From A352 (Wareham to Dorchester road) turn towards Owermoigne. Site on left after 1m.* **grid ref:** *SY768863*

A pleasant quiet site surrounded by trees and within easy reach of the coast at Lulworth Cove, and handy for several seaside resorts, including Weymouth, Portland, Purbeck and Swanage. The facilities are good, including a children's play area, small football pitch, a shop and tourist information. 6 acre site. 46 touring pitches. 20 seasonal pitches. Caravan pitches. Motorhome pitches. Tent pitches. 52 statics.

Open: 18 Mar-6 Nov (rs Etr) **Last arrival:** 22.00hrs **Last departure:** 11.00hrs

Pitches: * 🚐 £14.75-£23 🚐 £14.75-£23 ▲ £12.50-£22

Leisure: ⊙ ⚽ 🎱

Facilities: 🅿️ ⊙ 🌡️ ✳ 🗲 🛢️ 🏺 WiFi ♻ 🛈

Services: 🔌 🔋 🛢️ 🚽 🛒 ⬆

Within 3 miles: 🚲 🛢️ 🔋

Notes: Dogs must be kept on leads. Table tennis, wildlife lake, football pitch.

AA Pubs & Restaurants nearby: Lulworth Cove Inn, WEST LULWORTH, BH20 5RQ, 01929 400333

POOLE

See also Wimborne Minster

Places to visit

Brownsea Island, BROWNSEA ISLAND, BH13 7EE, 01202 707744 www.nationaltrust.org.uk/brownsea-island

Poole Museum, POOLE, BH15 1BW, 01202 262600 www.boroughofpoole.com/museums

Great for kids: Oceanarium, BOURNEMOUTH, BH2 5AA, 01202 311993 www.oceanarium.co.uk

POOLE
Map 4 SZ09

PREMIER PARK

South Lytchett Manor Caravan & Camping Park
►►►►► 96%

Best of British

tel: 01202 622577 Dorchester Rd, Lytchett Minster BH16 6JB
email: info@southlytchettmanor.co.uk **web:** www.southlytchettmanor.co.uk
dir: *Exit A35 onto B3067, 1m E of Lytchett Minster, 600yds on right after village.*
grid ref: *SY954926*

Every year this site improves. Situated in the grounds of a historic manor house, it has modern facilities that are spotless and well maintained. There's a TV hook-up on every pitch and there's free WiFi across the park. A warm and friendly welcome awaits at this lovely park which is well located for visiting Poole and Bournemouth; the Jurassic X53 bus route (Exeter to Poole) has a stop just outside the park. Four stylishly furnished and well-equipped Romany caravans, replete with double bed and two singles plus kitchen and fridge, are available for hire. 22 acre site. 150 touring pitches. 90 hardstandings. 4 seasonal pitches. Caravan pitches. Motorhome pitches. Tent pitches.

Open: Mar-2 Jan **Last arrival:** 21.00hrs **Last departure:** 11.00hrs

Pitches: * 🚐 fr £17.50 🚐 fr £17.50 ▲ fr £14.50 🏚 prices shown below

Leisure: 🎪 ⊙ 🎱 🚗

Facilities: ⊙ 🌡️ ✳ 🗲 🛢️ 🏺 WiFi 🖥️ ♻ 🛈 🚗

Services: 🔌 🔋 🛢️ 🚽 🛒 ⬆

Glamping: **Gypsy Caravans** 4, £70-£130 Min stay 3 nights at wknds Own kitchen Car by unit

---

LEISURE: 🏊 Indoor pool 🏊 Outdoor pool 🎪 Children's playground 🎈 Kid's club 🎾 Tennis court 🎱 Games room ⛳ Golf course ⛵ Boat hire 🚲 Cycle hire 🎬 Cinema 🎭 Entertainment 🎣 Fishing ⊙ Mini golf ⛳ Pitch n putt 🌊 Watersports 🏋 Gym 🏟 Sports field ⛺ Stables **FACILITIES:** 🛁 Bath 🚿 Shower 🅿 Private washing cubicles ⊙ Electric shaver 🗲 Hairdryer ✳ Ice Packs 🗲 Disabled facilities 🛢 Shop on site 🏪 Mobile shop 🍖 BBQ area 🏺 Picnic area WiFi Wi-fi 🖥 Internet access ♻ Recycling 🛈 Tourist info 🐕 Dog exercise area 🚗 Car hire can be arranged

Within 3 miles: 🚴🅷🖊🏊💰🛒↺

Notes: No camp fires or Chinese lanterns, no noise after 22.30hrs. Dogs must be kept on leads. Table tennis, football nets. Bread & croissants available in high season.

AA Pubs & Restaurants nearby: The Plantation, POOLE, BH13 7JF, 01202 701531

The Cock & Bottle, EAST MORDEN, BH20 7DL, 01929 459238

See advert below

AA HOLIDAY CENTRE OF THE YEAR 2017

Rockley Park
HOLIDAY HOME PARK 94%

tel: 0800 197 2075 **Hamworthy BH15 4LZ**
email: rockleypark@haven.com **web:** www.haven.com/rockleypark
dir: *M27 junct 1, A31 to Poole centre, then follow signs to site.* **grid ref:** *SY982909*

A complete holiday experience, including a wide range of day and night entertainment, and plenty of sports and leisure activities, notably watersports. There is also mooring and launching from the park. A great base for all the family, set in a good location for exploring Poole and Bournemouth, offering something for all ages, and there are a wide choice of quality eating outlets.

Open: mid Mar-end Oct (rs mid Mar-May & Sep-Oct)

Statics: 250

Dogs: must be kept on leads

Leisure: 🏊 🏊 Spa 🎣 🖊

PITCHES: 🚐 Caravans 🚐 Motorhomes ⛺ Tents 🏕 Glamping accommodation **SERVICES:** 🔌 Electric hook up 🅾 Launderette 🍺 Licensed bar 🔥 Calor Gas 🔥 Camping Gaz Ⓣ Toilet fluid 🍽 Café/Restaurant 🍟 Fast Food/Takeaway 🔋 Battery charging 👶 Baby care 🚽 Motorvan service point **ABBREVIATIONS:** BHs – bank holidays Etr – Easter Spring BH – Spring Bank Holiday fr – from hrs – hours m – mile mdnt – midnight rdbt – roundabout rs – restricted service wk – week wknd – weekend x-roads – crossroads ⊗ No credit or debit cards ⊗ No dogs

PORTESHAM — Map 4 SY68

Places to visit

Tutankhamun Exhibition, DORCHESTER, DT1 1UW, 01305 269571
www.tutankhamun-exhibition.co.uk

Maiden Castle, DORCHESTER, DT2 9PP, 0370 333 1181
www.english-heritage.org.uk/daysout/properties/maiden-castle

Great for kids: Teddy Bear Museum, DORCHESTER, DT1 1JU, 01305 266040
www.teddybearmuseum.co.uk

Portesham Dairy Farm Campsite

▶▶▶▶81%

tel: 01305 871297 **Weymouth DT3 4HG**
email: info@porteshamdairyfarm.co.uk
dir: From Dorchester take A35 towards Bridport. In 5m left at Winterbourne Abbas, follow Portesham signs. Through village, left at Kings Arms pub, site 350yds on right.
grid ref: SY602854

Located at the edge of the picturesque village of Portesham close to the Dorset coast. This family-run, level park is part of a small working farm in a quiet rural location. Fully serviced and seasonal pitches are available. There is an excellent pub just a short walk from the site. This quiet park is close to Abbotsbury Swannery and well postioned for visiting many areas of the West Dorset coast. 8 acre site. 90 touring pitches. 61 hardstandings. 60 seasonal pitches. Caravan pitches. Motorhome pitches. Tent pitches.

Open: Apr-Oct **Last arrival:** 18.00hrs **Last departure:** 11.00hrs
Pitches: * 🚐 £16-£26 🚐 £16-£26 ▲ £13-£22
Leisure: 🎪
Facilities: 🌳 🅿 ⊙ ℱ ☀ 🛁 ᵂⁱᶠⁱ ❶
Services: 🔌 ⓢ 🔒
Within 3 miles: 🥾 ⓢ

Notes: No commercial vehicles, no groups, no camp fires, minimum noise after 22.00hrs. Dogs must be kept on leads. Caravan storage.
AA Pubs & Restaurants nearby: The Crown Inn, PUNCKNOWLE, DT2 9BN, 01308 897711

PUNCKNOWLE

Places to visit

Dinosaur Museum, DORCHESTER, DT1 1EW, 01305 269880
www.thedinosaurmuseum.com

Hardy's Cottage, DORCHESTER, DT2 8QJ, 01305 262366
www.nationaltrust.org.uk

Great for kids: Abbotsbury Swannery, ABBOTSBURY, DT3 4JG, 01305 871858
www.abbotsbury-tourism.co.uk

PUNCKNOWLE — Map 4 SY58

Home Farm Caravan and Campsite

▶▶▶80%

tel: 01308 897258 **Home Farm, Rectory Ln DT2 9BW**
dir: From Dorchester towards Bridport on A35, left at start of dual carriageway, at hill bottom right to Litton Cheney. Through village, 2nd left to Puncknowle (Hazel Ln). Left at T-junct, left at phone box. Site 150mtrs on right. Caravan route: approach via A35 Bridport, then Swyre on B3157, continue to Swyre Ln & Rectory Ln. **grid ref:** SY535887

This quiet site, hidden away on the edge of a little hamlet, has good facilities and is an excellent place to camp; hardstanding pitches are available. It offers sweeping views of the Dorset countryside from most pitches, and is just five miles from Abbotsbury, and one and a half miles from the South West Coast Path. This is a really good base from which to tour this attractive area. There is an excellent pub and shop in the village, just a short walk from the campsite. 6.5 acre site. 47 touring pitches. 14 seasonal pitches. Caravan pitches. Motorhome pitches. Tent pitches.

Open: Apr-6 Oct **Last arrival:** 20.00hrs (21.00hrs by prior arrangement only)
Last departure: noon
Pitches: 🚐 🚐 ▲
Facilities: 🌳 ⊙ ℱ ☀ 🛁 ᵂⁱᶠⁱ ♻ ❶
Services: 🔌 🔒 🧹 📮 🛒
Within 3 miles: 🥾 ⓢ

Notes: 🐕 No cats. No wood-burning fires, skateboards, rollerblades, motorised toys or loud music. Dogs must be kept on leads. Calor gas exchange. Nearby pub offers freshly baked bread, takeaway & meals.

AA Pubs & Restaurants nearby: The Crown Inn, PUNCKNOWLE, DT2 9BN, 01308 897711
The Manor Hotel, WEST BEXINGTON, DT2 9DF, 01308 897660

ST LEONARDS — Map 5 SU10

Places to visit

Rockbourne Roman Villa, ROCKBOURNE, SP6 3PG, 01725 518541
www.hants.gov.uk/rockbourne-roman-villa

Red House Museum & Gardens, CHRISTCHURCH, BH23 1BU, 01202 482860
www3.hants.gov.uk/redhouse

Great for kids: Moors Valley Country Park and Forest, RINGWOOD, BH24 2ET, 01425 470721 www.moors-valley.co.uk

PREMIER PARK

Shamba Holidays

▶▶▶▶▶86%

Best of British
GOLD

tel: 01202 873302 **Ringwood Rd, East Moors Ln BH24 2SB**
email: enquiries@shambaholidays.co.uk
dir: From Poole on A31, pass Woodman Pub on left, straight on at rdbt (keep in left lane), immediately left into East Moors Ln. Site 1m on right. **grid ref:** SU105029

This top quality park is situated in a popular location near the south coast and is handy for visiting Bournemouth, Poole or Christchurch, as well as the New Forest. The toilet and shower block is excellent and offers some of the best facilities you will find in the country. There is a lovely indoor-outdoor swimming pool as well as a very tasteful clubhouse which serves food, and has

LEISURE: 🏊 Indoor pool ⛱ Outdoor pool 🎪 Children's playground 🙌 Kid's club 🎾 Tennis court 🎱 Games room ⛳ Golf course ⛵ Boat hire 🚲 Cycle hire
🎬 Cinema 🎵 Entertainment 🎣 Fishing ⊙ Mini golf ⛳ Pitch n putt 🏄 Watersports 🏋 Gym ⚽ Sports field ♘ Stables **FACILITIES:** 🛁 Bath 🚿 Shower
🅿 Private washing cubicles ⊙ Electric shaver ℱ Hairdryer ☀ Ice Packs ♿ Disabled facilities ⓢ Shop on site 📱 Mobile shop 🍖 BBQ area 🌲 Picnic area
ᵂⁱᶠⁱ Wi-fi 💻 Internet access ♻ Recycling ❶ Tourist info 🐕 Dog exercise area 🚗 Car hire can be arranged

entertainment in the main season. You can always be assured of a warm welcome. 7 acre site. 150 touring pitches. 40 seasonal pitches. Caravan pitches. Motorhome pitches. Tent pitches.

Open: Mar-Oct (rs Low & mid season some facilities open only at wknds)
Last arrival: 20.00hrs (later arrivals by prior arrangement only)
Last departure: 11.00hrs

Pitches: 🚐 🚌 ⛺

Leisure: 🏊 ⚽ 🎱 🎣

Facilities: ☉ 🅿 ✳ 👶 🖰 🔧 WiFi ♻ ❶

Services: 🔌 🗄 🍽 🛢 🔩 T 🍴 🔋 🗑 ⚓

Within 3 miles: ↕ 🏌 💲🗄 ∪

Notes: No large groups or commercial vehicles, no noise after 23.00hrs. Dogs must be kept on leads.

AA Pubs & Restaurants nearby: The Kings Arms, FERNDOWN, BH22 9AA, 01202 577490

Back of Beyond Touring Park
▶ ▶ ▶ ▶ 90%

tel: 01202 876968 **234 Ringwood Rd BH24 2SB**
email: info@backofbeyondtouringpark.co.uk
dir: From E: on A31 over Little Chef rdbt, pass St Leonard's Hotel, at next rdbt U-turn into lane immediately left. Site at end of lane. From W: on A31 pass Texaco garage & Woodman Inn, immediately left to site. **grid ref:** SU103034

This lovely adults-only park, a member of the Tranquil Parks group, is set in 30 acres of woodland and offers plenty of pleasant walks. Visitors are sure to receive a warm welcome from the owners and their team. In addition to good caravan and motorhome pitches there are some excellent areas for tents. The site has a fishing lake and a picnic area, and the whole area is a haven for wildlife. The facilities are well appointed and very clean. There are fish and chip and pizza nights as well as BBQ evenings. Three fully-equipped bell tents are available for hire. 30 acre site. 80 touring pitches. 40 seasonal pitches. Caravan pitches. Motorhome pitches. Tent pitches.

Open: Mar-Oct **Last arrival:** 18.30hrs **Last departure:** 11.00hrs

Pitches: * 🚐 £26-£31 🚌 £26-£31 ⛺ £21-£26 🏠 prices shown below

Leisure: 🪁 🎣 🏌 🎣

Facilities: 🐾 🅿 ☉ 🅿 ✳ 👶 🖰 🔧 WiFi ♻ ❶ 🎣

Services: 🔌 🗄 🛢 🔩 T 🔋 ⚓

Glamping: Bell tents 3, £70-£90 Changeover day Any day Min stay 2 nights Own kitchen Car by unit No dogs

Within 3 miles: ↕ 🎣 🏌 ◎ 🚣 💲 🗄 ∪

Notes: Adults only. PayPal accepted. No commercial vehicles, no groups, no noise after 22.30hrs. Visiting food vans, coffee & tea available, morning bakery.

AA Pubs & Restaurants nearby: The Kings Arms, FERNDOWN, BH22 9AA, 01202 577490

SHAFTESBURY

Places to visit
Shaftesbury Abbey Museum & Garden, SHAFTESBURY, SP7 8JR, 01747 852910
www.shaftesburyabbey.org.uk

SHAFTESBURY   **Map 4 ST82**

Dorset Country Holidays
▶ ▶ ▶ ▶ ▶ 88%

tel: 01747 851523 & 01225 290924 **Sherborne Causeway SP7 9PX**
email: info@dche.co.uk
dir: From Shaftesbury's Ivy Cross rdbt take A30 signed Sherborne. Site 2m on right.
grid ref: ST835233

Blackmore Vale Caravan & Camping Park (see next entry) has a separate glamping area which is well screened from the main park and is run by its own 24/7, dedicated team. Two luxury yurts, of British design and manufacture offer excellent insulation, heating and lighting; they have king-size double beds, two singles, a fridge, a TV and are fully carpeted. Set on wooden decking, each comes with picnic benches and a BBQ and guests receive a welcome breakfast pack and towelling gowns. In addition there are three bell tents, including one large family bell tent, a geo-dome and a vintage caravan plus a 'country kabin' – all are fully equipped to a high standard. There's a modern and well-appointed toilet and shower room block. Customer service here is excellent and guests can be collected from the local railway station. 1 acre site.

Open: all year **Last arrival:** 21.00hrs **Last departure:** noon

Glamping: Bell tents 3, £65-£105 Yurts 2, £65-£105 Cabins 1
Geo domes 1, £65-£105 Vintage Caravans 1, £65-£105

AA Pubs & Restaurants nearby: The Kings Arms Inn, GILLINGHAM, SP8 5NB, 01747 838325

The Coppleridge Inn, MOTCOMBE, SP7 9HW, 01747 851980

Blackmore Vale Caravan & Camping Park
▶ ▶ ▶ ▶ 86%

tel: 01747 851523 & 01225 290924 **Sherborne Causeway SP7 9PX**
email: info@dche.co.uk
dir: From Shaftesbury's Ivy Cross rdbt take A30 signed Sherborne. Site 2m on right.
grid ref: ST835233

This small park set in open countryside just outside Shaftesbury (famous for the steep, cobbled street known as Gold Hill) offers a wide range of camping opportunities, including touring pitches (some with large hardstandings), and an area for four luxury lodges. The facilities are modern and very clean, and a fully equipped gym is available to all customers. There is a separate glamping area with a dedicated team to look after guests (see previous entry). 3 acre site. 13 touring pitches. 7 hardstandings. Caravan pitches. Motorhome pitches. Tent pitches.

Open: all year **Last arrival:** 21.00hrs

Pitches: 🚐 🚌 ⛺

Leisure: 🎣

Facilities: ☉ 🅿 ✳ 👶 🖰 🔧 ♻ ❶

Services: 🔌 🗄 🛢 🔩 T 🔋

Within 3 miles: 🏌 💲 🗄

Notes: No noise after 23.00hrs. Dogs must be kept on leads. Caravan sales & accessories.

AA Pubs & Restaurants nearby: The Kings Arms Inn, GILLINGHAM, SP8 5NB, 01747 838325

The Coppleridge Inn, MOTCOMBE, SP7 9HW, 01747 851980

PITCHES: 🚐 Caravans 🚌 Motorhomes ⛺ Tents 🏠 Glamping accommodation **SERVICES:** 🔌 Electric hook up 🗄 Launderette 🍽 Licensed bar 🛢 Calor Gas 🔩 Camping Gaz T Toilet fluid 🍴 Café/Restaurant 🔋 Fast Food/Takeaway 🔋 Battery charging 👶 Baby care ⚓ Motorvan service point **ABBREVIATIONS:** BHs – bank holidays Etr – Easter Spring BH – Spring Bank Holiday fr – from hrs – hours m – mile mdnt – midnight rdbt – roundabout rs – restricted service wk – week wknd – weekend x-roads – crossroads 🚫 No credit or debit cards 🚫 No dogs

SIXPENNY HANDLEY   Map 4 ST91

Places to visit

Larmer Tree Gardens, TOLLARD ROYAL, SP5 5PT, 01725 516971
www.larmertree.co.uk

Shaftesbury Abbey Museum & Garden, SHAFTESBURY, SP7 8JR, 01747 852910
www.shaftesburyabbey.org.uk

Great for kids: Moors Valley Country Park and Forest, RINGWOOD, BH24 2ET,
01425 470721 www.moors-valley.co.uk

Church Farm Caravan & Camping Park
►►►► 85%

tel: 01725 552563 & 07766 677525 **The Bungalow, Church Farm, High St SP5 5ND**
email: churchfarmcandcpark@hotmail.co.uk **web:** www.churchfarmcandcpark.co.uk
dir: 1m S of Handley Hill rdbt. Exit for Sixpenny Handley, right by school, site 300yds by
church. **grid ref:** ST994173

A spacious park located within the Cranborne Chase Area of Outstanding Natural
Beauty; the site is split into several camping areas including one for adults only.
There is a first-class facility block with good private facilities, an excellent café and
restaurant, and a new function room, Hanlega's. The pretty village of Sixpenny
Handley, with all its amenities, is just 200 yards away, and the site is well
positioned for visiting the Great Dorset Steam Fair, the New Forest National Park,
Bournemouth, Poole and Stonehenge. 10 acre site. 35 touring pitches. 4
hardstandings. 5 seasonal pitches. Caravan pitches. Motorhome pitches. Tent
pitches. 2 statics.

Open: all year (rs Nov-Mar maximum of 10 vans accepted) **Last arrival:** 21.00hrs
Last departure: 11.00hrs

Pitches: 🚐 🚅 ▲

Facilities: ⊙ ❄ ⅊ ⌂ ⌐ WiFi 🖳 ♻ 𝒊

Services: 🗨 🗑 🍴 🛢 T ⁙⌕ 🍴 ⊞ 📤 🛒

Within 3 miles: ⅃ ⑤

Notes: Quiet after 23.00hrs. Dogs must be kept on leads. Use of fridge freezer
& microwave.

AA Pubs & Restaurants nearby: The Museum Inn, FARNHAM, DT11 8DE, 01725 516261

SWANAGE   Map 5 SZ07

Places to visit

Corfe Castle, CORFE CASTLE, BH20 5EZ, 01929 481294
www.nationaltrust.org.uk/corfecastle

Brownsea Island, BROWNSEA ISLAND, BH13 7EE, 01202 707744
www.nationaltrust.org.uk/brownsea-island

Great for kids: Swanage Railway, SWANAGE, BH19 1HB, 01929 425800
www.swanagerailway.co.uk

PREMIER PARK

Ulwell Cottage Caravan Park
►►►►► 84%

tel: 01929 422823 **Ulwell Cottage, Ulwell BH19 3DG**
email: enq@ulwellcottagepark.co.uk **web:** www.ulwellcottagepark.co.uk
dir: From Swanage N for 2m on unclassified road towards Studland.
grid ref: SZ019809

Sitting under the Purbeck Hills and surrounded by scenic walks, this park is only
two miles from the beach. It is a family-run and caters well for families and
couples, and offers a toilet and shower block complete with good family rooms,
all appointed to a high standard. There are fully serviced pitches, a good indoor
swimming pool and the village inn offers a good range of meals. There is a
camping pod for hire plus a new and stylish self-contained unit, with a decking
area, suitable for a couple. 13 acre site. 77 touring pitches. 23 hardstandings.
Caravan pitches. Motorhome pitches. Tent pitches. 140 statics.

Open: Mar-7 Jan (rs Mar-Spring BH & mid Sep-early Jan takeaway closed, shop open
variable hours) **Last arrival:** 22.00hrs **Last departure:** 11.00hrs

Pitches: 🚐 🚅 ▲ ⋒

Leisure: 🏊 ⋒ ♨

Facilities: 🐾 ⊙ ⌇ ❄ ⅊ 🖒 ⑤ ⌐ WiFi 🖳 ♻ 𝒊

Services: 🗨 🗑 🍴 🛢 ⌀ ⁙⌕ 📤

Glamping: Wooden Pods 1 Cabins 1, Car by unit

Within 3 miles: ⅃ ⅄ 🏇 🅟 ◎ 🛶 ⑤ ⑤ ∪

Notes: No bonfires or fireworks. Dogs must be kept on leads.

AA Pubs & Restaurants nearby: The Bankes Arms Hotel, STUDLAND, BH19 3AU,
01929 450225

The Square and Compass, WORTH MATRAVERS, BH19 3LF, 01929 439229

LEISURE: 🏊 Indoor pool 🏊 Outdoor pool ⋀ Children's playground 🖐 Kid's club 🎾 Tennis court ⚫ Games room ⅃ Golf course ⚓ Boat hire 🚲 Cycle hire
🎬 Cinema 🎵 Entertainment ⅊ Fishing ◎ Mini golf 🚩 Pitch n putt 🏄 Watersports 💪 Gym ◎ Sports field ∪ Stables **FACILITIES:** 🛁 Bath 🚿 Shower
🅟 Private washing cubicles ⊙ Electric shaver ⅊ Hairdryer ❄ Ice Packs 🖒 Disabled facilities ⑤ Shop on site ⑤ Mobile shop 🍴 BBQ area 🌲 Picnic area
WiFi Wi-fi 🖳 Internet access ♻ Recycling 𝒊 Tourist info 🐕 Dog exercise area 🚗 Car hire can be arranged

Herston Caravan & Camping Park 🛖

►►► 83%

tel: 01929 422932 **Washpond Ln BH19 3DJ**
email: office@herstonleisure.co.uk
dir: *From Wareham on A351 towards Swanage. Washpond Ln on left just after 'Welcome to Swanage' sign.* **grid ref:** *SZ018785*

Set in a rural area, with extensive views of the Purbecks, this tree-lined park has fully serviced pitches plus large camping areas. A new toilet and shower block with excellent family rooms opened in 2016. There is also a bar and restaurant, takeaway and barbecue food, and entertainment in the high season. Herston Halt, a stop for the famous Swanage Steam Railway between the town centre and Corfe Castle, is within walking distance. There are also Mongolian yurts and lodges available for hire. 10 acre site. 100 touring pitches. 17 hardstandings. Caravan pitches. Motorhome pitches. Tent pitches. 3 statics.

Open: all year

Pitches: * 🚐 £18-£45 🚌 ⛺ £12-£37 🛖

Facilities: 🚿 [P] ⊙ ✲ ♿ [$] ⛩ 🐕 [WiFi] ♻ ⓘ

Services: 🔌 [◻] 🍷 [T] 🍴 🔋 🍟 ⬇

Glamping: Yurts 6

Within 3 miles: ⛳ 🏇 ⛵ 🎾 ◎ 🏊 [$] [◻] ∪

Notes: No noise after 23.00hrs. Dogs must be kept on leads.

AA Pubs & Restaurants nearby: The Bankes Arms Hotel, STUDLAND, BH19 3AU, 01929 450225

The Square and Compass, WORTH MATRAVERS, BH19 3LF, 01929 439229

Acton Field Camping Site

►► 78%

tel: 01929 424184 & 439424 **Acton Field, Langton Matravers BH19 3HS**
email: enquiries@actonfieldcampsite.co.uk **web:** www.actonfieldcampsite.co.uk
dir: *From A351 right after Corfe Castle onto B3069 to Langton Matravers, 2nd right after village (bridleway sign).* **grid ref:** *SY991785*

This informal campsite, bordered by farmland on the outskirts of Langton Matravers, offers good toilet facilities. There are superb views of the Purbeck Hills and towards the Isle of Wight, and a footpath leads to the coastal path. The site occupies what was once a stone quarry so rock pegs may be required. Its location and views make it a wonderful place to camp. 7 acre site. 80 touring pitches. Caravan pitches. Motorhome pitches. Tent pitches.

Open: early May BH wknd, Spring BH week, 8 Jul-end Aug (open for organised groups from Etr-end Oct) **Last arrival:** 22.00hrs **Last departure:** noon

Pitches: 🚐 🚌 ⛺

Facilities: ⊙ ✲ [$] ♻

Services: 🔋

Within 3 miles: ⛳ 🏇 🎾 ◎ 🏊 [$] [◻] ∪

Notes: 💳 No open fires, no noise after 23.00hrs. Dogs must be kept on leads.

AA Pubs & Restaurants nearby: The Bankes Arms Hotel, STUDLAND, BH19 3AU, 01929 450225

The Square and Compass, WORTH MATRAVERS, BH19 3LF, 01929 439229

PITCHES: 🚐 Caravans 🚌 Motorhomes ⛺ Tents 🛖 Glamping accommodation **SERVICES:** 🔌 Electric hook up [◻] Launderette 🍷 Licensed bar 🔒 Calor Gas 🎾 Camping Gaz [T] Toilet fluid 🍴 Café/Restaurant 🍟 Fast Food/Takeaway 🔋 Battery charging 👶 Baby care ⬇ Motorvan service point
ABBREVIATIONS: BHs – bank holidays Etr – Easter Spring BH – Spring Bank Holiday fr – from hrs – hours m – mile mdnt – midnight rdbt – roundabout rs – restricted service wk – week wknd – weekend x-roads – crossroads 💳 No credit or debit cards 🚫 No dogs

THREE LEGGED CROSS

Map 5 SU00

Places to visit

Moors Valley Country Park and Forest, RINGWOOD, BH24 2ET, 01425 470721
www.moors-valley.co.uk

Woolsbridge Manor Farm Caravan Park

►►►► 84%

tel: 01202 826369 **BH21 6RA**
email: woolsbridge@btconnect.com **web:** www.woolsbridgemanorcaravanpark.co.uk
dir: *From Ringwood take A31 towards Ferndown. Approx 1m, follow signs for Three Legged Cross & Horton. Site 2m on right.* **grid ref:** *SU099052*

A small farm site with spacious pitches on a level field. This quiet site is an excellent central base for touring the New Forest National Park, Salisbury and the south coast, and is close to Moors Valley Country Park for outdoor family activities. The facilities are good and very clean and there are excellent family rooms

available. A camping pod is available for hire. 6.75 acre site. 60 touring pitches. Caravan pitches. Motorhome pitches. Tent pitches.

Woolsbridge Manor Farm Caravan Park

Open: Mar-Oct **Last arrival:** 20.00hrs **Last departure:** 10.30hrs

Pitches: 🚐 🚏 ▲ ⛺

Leisure: ⚠ ✎

Facilities: ♠ 🅿 ⊙ 🌡 ✳ ⚳ ⑤ 🎋 🛒 📶 ♻ 🛈 🌡

Services: 🚐 ⑤ 🛢 ✐ ⓣ 🧺

Glamping: Wooden Pods 1

Within 3 miles: ⚓ ✎ ⑤ ⑤ ∪

Notes: Dogs must be kept on leads.

AA Pubs & Restaurants nearby: The Augustus John, FORDINGBRIDGE, SP6 1DG, 01425 652098

See advert below

LEISURE: 🏊 Indoor pool 🏊 Outdoor pool ⚠ Children's playground 🖐 Kid's club 🎾 Tennis court 🎱 Games room ⛳ Golf course ⛵ Boat hire 🚲 Cycle hire 🎬 Cinema 🎵 Entertainment 🎣 Fishing ◎ Mini golf ⛳ Pitch n putt 🏄 Watersports 🏋 Gym 🏅 Sports field ∪ Stables **FACILITIES:** 🛁 Bath 🚿 Shower 🅿 Private washing cubicles ⊙ Electric shaver 💨 Hairdryer ❄ Ice Packs ♿ Disabled facilities ⑤ Shop on site 🛒 Mobile shop 🍖 BBQ area ⛱ Picnic area 📶 Wi-fi 💻 Internet access ♻ Recycling 🛈 Tourist info 🐕 Dog exercise area 🚗 Car hire can be arranged

WAREHAM

Map 4 SY98

Places to visit

Brownsea Island, BROWNSEA ISLAND, BH13 7EE, 01202 707744
www.nationaltrust.org.uk/brownsea-island

PREMIER PARK

Wareham Forest Tourist Park

►►►►► 96%

Best of British GOLD

tel: 01929 551393 **North Trigon BH20 7NZ**
email: holiday@warehamforest.co.uk **web:** www.warehamforest.co.uk
dir: *From A35 between Bere Regis & Lytchett Minster follow Wareham sign into Sugar Hill. Site on left.* **grid ref:** *SY894912*

A woodland park within the tranquil Wareham Forest, with its many walks and proximity to Poole, Dorchester and the Purbeck coast. Two luxury blocks, with combined washbasin and toilets for total privacy, are maintained to a high standard of cleanliness. A heated outdoor swimming pool, off licence, shop and games room add to the enjoyment of a stay on this top quality park. There is a bike wash and a separate dog wash with hot water. 55 acre site. 200 touring pitches. 70 hardstandings. 70 seasonal pitches. Caravan pitches. Motorhome pitches. Tent pitches.

Open: all year (rs Off-peak season limited services) **Last arrival:** 21.00hrs **Last departure:** 11.00hrs

Pitches: * 🚐 £18-£38.40 🚚 £18-£38.40 ⛺ £14.80-£30.60

Leisure: 🏊 🛝 🎱

Facilities: 🚿 [P] ⊙ 🚽 ❄ ♿ [S] 🪑 🐕 WiFi ♻ ℹ

Services: 🔌 🧺 🔒 🧯 [T] 🔋 ⤓

Within 3 miles: ⛳ 🐟 🎬 🌿 [S] 🧺 ∪

Notes: Families & couples only, no group bookings. Dogs must be kept on leads. Fresh bread & croissants (high season), table tennis.

AA Pubs & Restaurants nearby: The New Inn, CHURCH KNOWLE, BH20 5NQ, 01929 480357

Birchwood Tourist Park

►►►► 84%

tel: 01929 554763 **Bere Rd, Coldharbour BH20 7PA**
email: birchwoodtouristpark@hotmail.com **web:** www.birchwoodtouristpark.co.uk
dir: *From Poole (A351) or Dorchester (A352) on N side of railway line at Wareham, follow Bere Regis signs. 2nd park after 2.25m.* **grid ref:** *SY896905*

Set in 50 acres of parkland located within Wareham Forest, this site offers direct access to areas that are ideal for walking, mountain biking and horse and pony riding. This is a spacious open park, ideal for families, with plenty of room for young people to play games, including football, and there is a small pool for children and a new games room. The modern facilities are in two central locations and are very clean. The site has a good security barrier system. The park is only a short drive from Bournemouth and Swanage. 25 acre site. 175 touring pitches. 25 hardstandings. 50 seasonal pitches. Caravan pitches. Motorhome pitches. Tent pitches.

Open: all year **Last arrival:** 21.00hrs **Last departure:** 11.30hrs

Pitches: * 🚐 £14-£32.50 🚚 £14-£32.50 ⛺ £11-£29.50

Leisure: ⚽ 🛝 🎱

Facilities: 🚿 ⊙ 🚽 ❄ [S] 🪑 🐕 WiFi ♻ ℹ

Services: 🔌 🧺 🔒 🧯 [T] 🔋 ⤓

Within 3 miles: ⛳ 🐟 🎬 🌿 [S]

Notes: No groups on BH, no generators or camp fires. Dogs must be kept on leads. Paddling pool, table tennis.

AA Pubs & Restaurants nearby: The New Inn, CHURCH KNOWLE, BH20 5NQ, 01929 480357

See advert on page 206

WAREHAM *continued*

Norden Farm Touring Caravan and Camping Site
►►►► 81%

tel: 01929 480098 **Norden Farm, Corfe Castle BH20 5DS**
email: campsite@nordenfarm.com
dir: *On A351 from Wareham towards Swanage, 3.5m to site on right.* **grid ref:** *SY950828*

This delightful farm site offers traditional camping but with excellent toilet and shower facilities. It is a very dog-friendly site and is ideally suited for those who enjoy country pursuits. Its location is very close to Corfe Castle so it's very convenient for visiting the Isle of Purbeck and Swanage (maybe by using the park and ride at Norden railway station and taking the train). There is a holiday cottage for hire. 10 acre site. 140 touring pitches. Variable seasonal pitches. Caravan pitches. Motorhome pitches. Tent pitches.

Open: Mar-Oct (weather depending) (rs Early Mar or late Oct – 1 shower block may be closed) **Last arrival:** 22.00hrs **Last departure:** 11.00hrs (flexible times in low season)

Pitches: * 🚐 £8.50-£21 🚕 £8.50-£21 ▲ £5.50-£17
Facilities: 🛁 🏕 P🛏 ⊙ P ✳ 🔥 🖈 🗟 🛒 WiFi ♻ ❶
Services: 🚐🖾 🔒 🚽 ⬆ **Within 3 miles:** ↓ 🛶 🗄 ℘ 🖸🗟

Notes: Strict 5mph speed limit on site, no noise after 23.00hrs. Dogs must be kept on leads. Hot shower washroom for dogs.

AA Pubs & Restaurants nearby: The New Inn, CHURCH KNOWLE, BH20 5NQ, 01929 480357

East Creech Farm Campsite
►►► 83%

tel: 01929 480519 & 481312 **East Creech Farm, East Creech BH20 5AP**
email: farmhouse@eastcreechfarm.co.uk
dir: *From Wareham on A351 S towards Swanage. On bypass at 3rd rdbt take Furzebrook/ Blue Pool Rd exit, site approx 2m on right.* **grid ref:** *SY928827*

This grassy park set in a peaceful location beneath the Purbeck Hills, with extensive views towards Poole and Brownsea Island. The park boasts a woodland play area, bright, clean toilet facilities and a farm shop selling milk, eggs and bread. There

are also four coarse fishing lakes teeming with fish, and a good little tearoom, The Cake Room, adjacent to the site, is open in the main season. The park is close to Norden Station on the Swanage to Norden steam railway line, and is well located for visiting Corfe Castle, Swanage and the Purbeck coast. 4 acre site. 80 touring pitches. Caravan pitches. Motorhome pitches. Tent pitches.

Open: Apr-Oct **Last arrival:** 20.00hrs **Last departure:** noon
Pitches: 🚐 £13-£16 🚕 £13-£16 ▲ £13-£16 **Leisure:** ℘
Facilities: 🛏 ⊙ P ✳ ♻ ❶ **Services:** 🚐🖾 🍴
Within 3 miles: ↓ 🛶 🗄 ℘ 🖸🗟

Notes: No camp fires, no loud noise. Dogs must be kept on leads.

AA Pubs & Restaurants nearby: The New Inn, CHURCH KNOWLE, BH20 5NQ, 01929 480357

Ridge Farm Camping & Caravan Park
►►► 78%

tel: 01929 556444 & 07970 964672 **Barnhill Rd, Ridge BH20 5BG**
email: info@ridgefarm.co.uk
dir: *From Wareham take B3075 towards Corfe Castle, cross river, into Stoborough, left to Ridge. Follow site signs for 1.5m.* **grid ref:** *SY939868*

A quiet rural park, adjacent to a working farm and surrounded by trees and bushes. This away-from-it-all park is ideally located for touring this part of Dorset, and especially for birdwatchers, or those who enjoy walking and cycling. This site is perfect for visiting the Arne Nature Reserve, the Blue Pool and Corfe Castle. There are good supermarkets and shops in nearby Wareham. 3.47 acre site. 60 touring pitches. 2 hardstandings. Caravan pitches. Motorhome pitches. Tent pitches.

Open: Etr-Sep **Last arrival:** 21.00hrs **Last departure:** noon
Pitches: 🚐 🚕 ▲ **Facilities:** ⊙ P ✳ 🖸 ♻ ❶
Services: 🚐🖾 ⬆ **Within 3 miles:** ↓ 🛶 🗄 ℘ 🖸🗟 ∪

Notes: 🚫 No dogs Jul-Aug. Dogs must be kept on leads.

AA Pubs & Restaurants nearby: The New Inn, CHURCH KNOWLE, BH20 5NQ, 01929 480357

LEISURE: 🏊 Indoor pool 🏊 Outdoor pool 🎠 Children's playground 👋 Kid's club 🎾 Tennis court 🎱 Games room ⛳ Golf course 🚣 Boat hire 🚲 Cycle hire 🎬 Cinema 🎵 Entertainment 🎣 Fishing ◎ Mini golf ⛳ Pitch n putt 🏄 Watersports 🏋 Gym 🎯 Sports field ∪ Stables **FACILITIES:** 🛁 Bath 🚿 Shower P🛏 Private washing cubicles ⊙ Electric shaver P Hairdryer ✳ Ice Packs 🔥 Disabled facilities 🗟 Shop on site 🛒 Mobile shop 🍴 BBQ area 🏕 Picnic area WiFi Wi-fi 🖥 Internet access ♻ Recycling ❶ Tourist info 🐕 Dog exercise area 🚗 Car hire can be arranged

WEYMOUTH
Map 4 SY67

Places to visit

RSPB Nature Reserve Radipole Lake and Wild Weymouth Discovery Centre, WEYMOUTH, DT4 7TZ, 01305 778313 www.rspb.org.uk

Portland Castle, PORTLAND, DT5 1AZ, 01305 820539 www.english-heritage.org.uk/daysout/properties/portland-castle

Great for kids: Weymouth Sea Life Adventure Park & Marine Sanctuary, WEYMOUTH, DT4 7SX, 0871 423 2110 *(Calls cost 10p per minute plus your phone company's access charge)* www.sealifeweymouth.com

Littlesea Holiday Park
HOLIDAY CENTRE 88%

tel: 01305 774414 **Lynch Ln DT4 9DT**
email: littlesea@haven.com **web:** www.haven.com/littlesea
dir: *A35 onto A354 signed Weymouth. Right at 1st rdbt, 3rd exit at 2nd rdbt towards Chickerell. Left into Lynch Lane after lights. Site at far end of road.* **grid ref:** *SY654783*

Just three miles from Weymouth with its lovely beaches and many attractions, Littlesea has a cheerful family atmosphere and fantastic facilities. Indoor and outdoor entertainment and activities are on offer for all the family, and the toilet facilities on the touring park are modern and spotlessly clean as well as being nice and warm. The touring section of this holiday complex is at the far end of the site adjacent to the South West Coast Path in a perfect location. An excellent base for visiting the many attractions close to Weymouth and Portland. 100 acre site. 141 touring pitches. Caravan pitches. Motorhome pitches. Tent pitches. 720 statics.

Open: end Mar-end Oct (rs end Mar-May & Sep-Oct facilities may be reduced)
Last arrival: mdnt **Last departure:** 10.00hrs

Pitches: 🚐 🚍 ▲ **Leisure:** 🏊 ⬧ 🎯 👋 💆 ⚽ 🎣 🎵
Facilities: 🏧 ⊙ 🍴 ☀ ⬧ 🛁 🚻 📶 ♨ 🔌
Services: 🔌 🏧 🍴 🍺 🔋 🚿 T 🍽 ⬧ 🚮 **Within 3 miles:** ⬧ 🚴 🎯 🚶 ⊙ ⬧ 🚤 ⛳ U

Notes: No commercial vehicles, no bookings by persons under 21yrs unless a family booking, no boats, max 2 dogs per booking, certain dog breeds banned. Dogs must be kept on leads.

AA Pubs & Restaurants nearby: The Old Ship Inn, WEYMOUTH, DT3 5QQ, 01305 812522
See advert on page 209

Seaview Holiday Park
HOLIDAY CENTRE 86%

tel: 01305 832271 **Preston DT3 6DZ**
email: seaview@haven.com **web:** www.haven.com/seaview
dir: *A354 to Weymouth, follow signs for Preston & Wareham onto A353. Site 3m on right just after Weymouth Bay Holiday Park.* **grid ref:** *SY707830*

A fun-packed holiday centre especially suited to families and for all ages, with plenty of activities and entertainment during the day or evening. Guests can use the facilities offered at the sister park, Weymouth Bay Holiday Park, which can be reached via a walkway from Seaview Holiday Park. There is a touring section for caravans, motorhomes and tents, the upper area having all fully serviced pitches, whilst the lower section is mainly for tents. There are also six fully-equipped safari tents in this area for anyone wishing to try a glamping experience. 20 acre site. 82 touring pitches. 35 hardstandings. Caravan pitches. Motorhome pitches. Tent pitches. 259 statics.

Open: mid Mar-end Oct (rs mid Mar-May & Sep-Oct facilities may be reduced)
Last arrival: mdnt **Last departure:** 10.00hrs

PITCHES: 🚐 Caravans 🚍 Motorhomes ▲ Tents 🏕 Glamping accommodation **SERVICES:** 🔌 Electric hook up 🏧 Launderette 🍺 Licensed bar
🔥 Calor Gas 🔥 Camping Gaz T Toilet fluid 🍽 Café/Restaurant 🚮 Fast Food/Takeaway 🔋 Battery charging 🍼 Baby care 🔧 Motorvan service point
ABBREVIATIONS: BHs – bank holidays Etr – Easter Spring BH – Spring Bank Holiday fr – from hrs – hours m – mile mdnt – midnight
rdbt – roundabout rs – restricted service wk – week wknd – weekend x-roads – crossroads Ⓔ No credit or debit cards Ⓧ No dogs

WEYMOUTH *continued*

Pitches: 🚐 🚙 ▲ 🛖 **Leisure:** 🌊 ⚽ 🎾 🎮 🎵 **Facilities:** ⊙ 🅿 & 🖅 🚿 🏧 WIFI ♻ 🛈

Services: 🔌 🔗 🍴 🗑 🍲 ⛲ **Within 3 miles:** ⅃ ⚓ 🎣 ◎ ⅃ 🏪 🐕 ∪

Glamping: Safari tents 6

Notes: No commercial vehicles, no bookings by persons under 21yrs unless a family booking, max 2 dogs per booking, certain dog breeds banned. Dogs must be kept on leads.

AA Pubs & Restaurants nearby: The Old Ship Inn, WEYMOUTH, DT3 5QQ, 01305 812522

See advert below

East Fleet Farm Touring Park

▶ ▶ ▶ ▶ ▶ 91%

Best of British / GOLD

tel: 01305 785768 **Chickerell DT3 4DW**
email: enquiries@eastfleet.co.uk
dir: *On B3157 (Weymouth to Bridport road), 3m from Weymouth.* **grid ref:** SY640797

Set on a working organic farm and in a unique location on the shores of the Fleet Lagoon, overlooking Chesil Beach and the sea, with direct access to the South West Coast Path. There is a wide variety of pitches, including hardstandings and fully serviced pitches, and the largest family tents can be accommodated. This park offers excellent toilet and shower facilities with family rooms. There are good play facilities for children, including a fenced play area for younger ones and a separate play barn with table tennis and other activities. The Old Barn has a tasteful bar and lovely patio area, where customers are welcome to take their own food, or order locally and have the food delivered to the bar. In addition, there is 'Festival Food', an area for pizzas and fish and chips, which is very popular with guests. The park is well positioned for visiting Weymouth and Portland, as well as other local attractions, such as the Abbotsbury Swannery and the Abbotsbury Subtropical Gardens. There is a fine drive along the coast road from East Fleet to Bridport with spectacular views of Chesil Beach. 21 acre site. 400 touring pitches. 90 hardstandings. 40 seasonal pitches. Caravan pitches. Motorhome pitches. Tent pitches.

Open: 16 Mar-Oct **Last arrival:** 22.00hrs **Last departure:** 10.30hrs

Pitches: * 🚐 £20-£32.50 🚙 £20-£32.50 ▲ £20-£32.50

Leisure: ♦ ⚛

Facilities: 🏕 🅿 ⊙ 🖅 ❄ & 🖅 🚿 🐕 WIFI 💻 ♻ 🛈 ⚡

Services: 🔌 🔗 🍴 🗑 🚰 T 🛒 ⛲ 🚮 ↓

Within 3 miles: ⅃ ⚓ 🎣 ◎ ⅃ 🏪 🐕 ∪

Notes: Dogs must be kept on leads. Camping & caravan accessories shop.

AA Pubs & Restaurants nearby: The Old Ship Inn, WEYMOUTH, DT3 5QQ, 01305 812522

Bagwell Farm Touring Park

▶ ▶ ▶ ▶ 88%

SILVER

tel: 01305 782575 **Knights in the Bottom, Chickerell DT3 4EA**
email: aa@bagwellfarm.co.uk **web:** www.bagwellfarm.co.uk
dir: *From A354 follow signs for Weymouth town centre, then B3157 to Chickerell & Abbotsbury, 1m past Chickerell left into site 500yds after Victoria Inn.* **grid ref:** SY627816

This well located park is set in a small valley with access to the South West Coast Path and is very convenient for visiting Weymouth and Portland. It has excellent

---

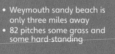

LEISURE: 🌊 Indoor pool 🌊 Outdoor pool ▲ Children's playground 🖐 Kid's club 🎾 Tennis court 🎮 Games room ⅃ Golf course ⚓ Boat hire 🚲 Cycle hire 🎬 Cinema 🎵 Entertainment 🎣 Fishing ◎ Mini golf ⛳ Pitch n putt 🌊 Watersports 🏋 Gym ♻ Sports field ∪ Stables **FACILITIES:** 🛁 Bath 🚿 Shower 🅿 Private washing cubicles ⊙ Electric shaver 🖅 Hairdryer ❄ Ice Packs & Disabled facilities 🏪 Shop on site 🏬 Mobile shop 🍖 BBQ area 🚿 Picnic area WIFI Wi-fi 💻 Internet access ♻ Recycling 🛈 Tourist info 🐕 Dog exercise area ⚡ Car hire can be arranged

facilities including a good shop, pets' corner, children's play area plus the Red Barn bar and restaurant. A good range of hardstandings is available, including 25 super pitches, which are very spacious and can take the longest units. This is an excellent place to stay at any time of the year. 14 acre site. 320 touring pitches. 35 hardstandings. 70 seasonal pitches. Caravan pitches. Motorhome pitches. Tent pitches.

Bagwell Farm Touring Park

Open: all year (rs Winter - bar closed) **Last arrival:** 21.00hrs **Last departure:** 11.00hrs

Pitches: * ⊕ £16.50-£30.50 ⊕ £16.50-£30.50 Ⓐ £13-£28

Leisure: ⋀ ⚐

Facilities: ⬥ 🛈 🅿 ⊙ ⌀ ☼ ♿ 🛈 🚿 ⊣ 📶 ⊟ ♻ 🛈 🔧 ⚲

Services: ⊞ 🗍 🍽 🛢 ⊘ Ⓣ 🍴 🎣 ♨ ⛟ ⬇

Within 3 miles: 🎣 ♨ ↻

Notes: Families & couples only, no noise after 23.00hrs. Dogs must be kept on leads. Wet suit shower, campers' shelter.

AA Pubs & Restaurants nearby: The Old Ship Inn, WEYMOUTH, DT3 5QQ, 01305 812522

Pebble Bank Caravan Park

► ► ► ► 81%

tel: 01305 774844 **Camp Rd, Wyke Regis DT4 9HF**
email: info@pebblebank.co.uk
dir: *From Weymouth take Portland road. At last rdbt turn right, then 1st left to Army Tent Camp. Site opposite.* **grid ref:** *SY659775*

This site, although only one and a half miles from Weymouth, is in a peaceful location overlooking Chesil Beach and The Fleet, and is an excellent place to stay. There is a friendly little bar, which offers even better views. The toilet and shower block is very modern and spotlessly clean and there are now 12 hardstandings available. The park is adjacent to the South West Coast Path making it a good base for walkers. 4 acre site. 40 touring pitches. Caravan pitches. Motorhome pitches. Tent pitches. 80 statics.

Open: Etr-mid Oct (High season & wknds only - bar open) **Last arrival:** 18.00hrs **Last departure:** 11.00hrs

Pitches: ⊕ ⊕ Ⓐ

Leisure: ⋀

Facilities: 🛈 ⊙ 🅿 ☼ ♿ 📶 🛈

Services: ⊞ 🗍 🍽 🛢 ♨

Within 3 miles: ♨ ⚓ Ⓗ ⌀ ◎ ♒ 🎣 🛢 ↻

Notes: Dogs must be kept on leads.

AA Pubs & Restaurants nearby: The Old Ship Inn, WEYMOUTH, DT3 5QQ, 01305 812522

PITCHES: ⊕ Caravans ⊕ Motorhomes Ⓐ Tents 🏕 Glamping accommodation **SERVICES:** ⊞ Electric hook up 🗍 Launderette 🍽 Licensed bar 🛢 Calor Gas ⌀ Camping Gaz Ⓣ Toilet fluid 🍴 Café/Restaurant ⬛ Fast Food/Takeaway 🔋 Battery charging ♨ Baby care ⬇ Motorvan service point
ABBREVIATIONS: BHs – bank holidays Etr – Easter Spring BH – Spring Bank Holiday fr – from hrs – hours m – mile mdnt – midnight rdbt – roundabout rs – restricted service wk – week wknd – weekend x-roads – crossroads ⊘ No credit or debit cards ⊗ No dogs

WEYMOUTH *continued*

West Fleet Holiday Farm
▶ ▶ ▶ 90%

tel: 01305 782218 **Fleet DT3 4EF**
email: aa@westfleetholidays.co.uk **web:** www.westfleetholidays.co.uk
dir: *From Weymouth take B3157 towards Abbotsbury for 3m. Past Chickerell turn left at mini-rdbt to Fleet, site 1m on right.* **grid ref:** SY625811

A spacious farm site with both level and sloping pitches divided into paddocks and screened by hedges. This site has good views of the Dorset countryside, and is a relaxing place for a family holiday, particularly suited to tents, especially family-sized tents, and small motorhomes or campervans. The Barn Clubhouse has a bar, restaurant and entertainment area. There is an excellent and very popular outdoor swimming pool, which is great for families. WiFi is also available. 12 acre site. 250 touring pitches. Caravan pitches. Motorhome pitches. Tent pitches.

Open: Etr-Sep (rs Etr-May clubhouse & pool closed) **Last arrival:** 21.00hrs **Last departure:** 11.00hrs

Pitches: * ⛺ £14-£28 ⛺ £14-£28 ▲ £14-£28

Leisure: ⚓ 瓜 ⊕ 🎵

Facilities: 🛁 📷 🅿 ⊙ 🖍 ✳ ⚕ 🛓 WiFi ♻ ❶

Services: 🖼 🖫 🗌 🝙 ⊘ 🗌 🍴 🛒 🝤

Within 3 miles: 🛓 🛍

Notes: Non-family groups by arrangement only. Dogs restricted to certain areas & must be kept on leads.

AA Pubs & Restaurants nearby: The Old Ship Inn, WEYMOUTH, DT3 5QQ, 01305 812522

Rosewall Camping
▶ ▶ ▶ 87%

tel: 01305 832248 **East Farm Dairy, Osmington Mills DT3 6HA**
email: holidays@weymouthcamping.com
dir: *Take A353 towards Weymouth. At Osmington Mills sign (opposite garage) turn left, 0.25m, site on 1st right.* **grid ref:** SY736820

This well positioned sloping tent site is adjacent to the South West Coast Path and affords great sea views from virtually every pitch. There are excellent toilet and shower facilities including a newly refurbished block at the bottom of the campsite. There is a well-stocked shop and for those that like horseriding or learning how to ride, there is 'Rosewall Equestrian' near the site entrance. The location at Osmington is just a few miles to the east of Weymouth. 13 acre site. 225 touring pitches. Motorhome pitches. Tent pitches.

Open: Etr-Oct (rs Apr-May & Oct shop opening times vary) **Last arrival:** 22.00hrs **Last departure:** 10.00hrs

Pitches: ⛺ ▲

Leisure: 瓜 ✎

Facilities: 📷 ⊙ ✳ ⚕ 🛓 ♻ ❶

Services: 🖫 🝙 ⊘ 🝤

Within 3 miles: 🗓 ✎ ⚓ 🛓 🛍 ∪

Notes: Families & couples only, no noise after 23.00hrs. Dogs must be kept on leads. Riding stables & coarse fishing.

AA Pubs & Restaurants nearby: The Old Ship Inn, WEYMOUTH, DT3 5QQ, 01305 812522

Sea Barn Farm
▶ ▶ ▶ 82%

tel: 01305 782218 **Fleet DT3 4ED**
email: aa@seabarnfarm.co.uk **web:** www.seabarnfarm.co.uk
dir: *From Weymouth take B3157 towards Abbotsbury for 3m. Past Chickerell turn left at mini-rdbt into Fleet Rd, site 1m on left.* **grid ref:** SY625807

This site is set high on the Dorset coast and has spectacular views over Chesil Beach, The Fleet and Lyme Bay, and it is also on the South West Coast Path. Optional use of the clubhouse and swimming pool (in high seaon) at West Fleet Holiday Farm is available. The pitches are sheltered by hedging, and there is an excellent toilet facility block, and plenty of space for outdoor games. This site is suitable mainly for tents, especially large family tents, and small motorhomes or campervans. 12 acre site. 250 touring pitches. Caravan pitches. Motorhome pitches. Tent pitches. 1 static.

Open: 15 Mar-Oct **Last arrival:** 21.00hrs **Last departure:** 11.00hrs

Pitches: * ⛺ £14-£28 ⛺ £14-£28 ▲ £14-£28

Facilities: 🛁 📷 🅿 ⊙ 🖍 ✳ ⚕ 🛓 🝰 WiFi ♻ ❶

Services: 🖼 🖫 🝙 ⊘ 🗌

Within 3 miles: 🛓 🛍 ∪

Notes: Non-family groups by prior arrangement only. Dogs must be kept on leads. Use of West Fleet facilities including outdoor pool, motorhome service point, bar & restaurant Mar-Jun & Sep-Oct.

AA Pubs & Restaurants nearby: The Old Ship Inn, WEYMOUTH, DT3 5QQ, 01305 812522

Weymouth Bay Holiday Park
HOLIDAY HOME PARK 93%

tel: 01305 832271 **Preston DT3 6BQ**
email: weymouthbay@haven.com **web:** www.haven.com/weymouthbay
dir: *From A35 towards Dorchester take A354 signed Weymouth. Follow towards Preston signs onto A353. At Chalbury rdbt 1st left into Preston Rd. Park on right.*
grid ref: *SY705830*

This well-located holiday park, just a short drive away from Weymouth beach, offers the complete holiday experience for the whole family. It has excellent indoor and outdoor pools complete with a 'Lazy River' attraction. There is an excellent choice of eating outlets as well as a full entertainment programme for all. The holiday homes are well appointed throughout. The park is conveniently placed for visiting Portland Bill, Lulworth Cove and Chesil Beach.

Open: Mar-Oct

Changeover day: Mon, Fri, Sat

Arrival and departure times: Please contact the site

Statics: 83 Sleeps 6-8 Bedrms 2-3 Bathrms 1-2 Toilets 1-2 Microwave Freezer TV Sky/FTV Elec inc Gas inc Grass area

Children: Cots Highchair **Dogs:** 2 on leads No dangerous dogs

Leisure:

WIMBORNE MINSTER   Map 5 SZ09

Places to visit

Kingston Lacy, WIMBORNE, BH21 4EA, 01202 883402 (Mon-Fri)
www.nationaltrust.org.uk/kingston-lacy

Priest's House Museum and Garden, WIMBORNE, BH21 1HR, 01202 882533
www.priest-house.co.uk

PREMIER PARK

Wilksworth Farm Caravan Park
▶▶▶▶▶ 89%

tel: 01202 885467 **Cranborne Rd BH21 4HW**
email: info@wilksworthfarmcaravanpark.co.uk
dir: *1m N of Wimborne on B3078,* **grid ref:** *SU004018*

A popular and attractive park peacefully set in the grounds of a listed house in the heart of rural Dorset. This spacious site has much to offer visitors, including an excellent heated swimming pool, tennis courts, takeaway and café, a bar and restaurant plus a games room and an excellent Tiny Town play area for young children. The modern toilet facilities contain en suite rooms and good family rooms. 11 acre site. 85 touring pitches. 20 hardstandings. Caravan pitches. Motorhome pitches. Tent pitches. 77 statics.

Open: Apr-Oct (rs Oct no shop) **Last arrival:** 20.00hrs **Last departure:** 11.00hrs

Pitches: * £16-£33 £16-£33 £16-£33

Leisure: **Facilities:**

Services: **Within 3 miles:**

Notes: No cars by tents. No noise 23.00hrs-07.00 hrs. Max 2 dogs per pitch. Dogs must be kept on leads. Paddling pool, volley ball, mini football pitch.

AA Pubs & Restaurants nearby: Les Bouviers Restaurant with Rooms, WIMBORNE MINSTER, BH21 3BD, 01202 889555

Charris Camping & Caravan Park
▶▶▶▶ 86%

tel: 01202 885970 **Candy's Ln, Corfe Mullen BH21 3EF**
email: bookings@charris.co.uk
dir: *From E, exit Wimborne bypass (A31) W end. 300yds after Caravan Sales, follow brown sign. From W on A31, over A350 rdbt, take next turn after B3074, follow brown signs.*
grid ref: *SY992988*

A sheltered park of grassland lined with trees on the edge of the Stour Valley, with Poole and the south coast resorts only a short drive away. Customers can be assured of a warm welcome at this well located park. The facilities are very clean, some hardstandings are available, and social get-togethers are held for customers including barbecues which prove very popular. A new top quality toilet and shower block was added in 2016. 3.5 acre site. 45 touring pitches. 12 hardstandings. 10 seasonal pitches. Caravan pitches. Motorhome pitches. Tent pitches.

Open: all year **Last arrival:** 21.00hrs (earliest arrival 11.00hrs) **Last departure:** 11.00hrs

Pitches: * £19.50-£21.50 £19.50-£21.50 £15.50-£21.50 prices shown below

Leisure:

Facilities:

Services:

Glamping: Shepherd's Huts 1, £40-£45 Car by unit

Within 3 miles:

Notes: No noise after 23.00hrs. Dogs must be kept on leads.

AA Pubs & Restaurants nearby: Les Bouviers Restaurant with Rooms, WIMBORNE MINSTER, BH21 3BD, 01202 889555

Springfield Touring Park
▶▶▶ 84%

tel: 01202 881719 **Candys Ln, Corfe Mullen BH21 3EF**
email: john.clark18@btconnect.com
dir: *From Wimborne on Wimborne by-pass (A31) at W end turn left after Caravan Sales, follow brown sign.* **grid ref:** *SY987989*

A small touring park with extensive views over the Stour Valley and a quiet and friendly atmosphere. It is well positioned for visiting Poole, Bournemouth or the really lovely town of Wimborne. The park is maintained immaculately, has a well-stocked shop, and is a great place to stay. 3.5 acre site. 45 touring pitches. 38 hardstandings. Caravan pitches. Motorhome pitches. Tent pitches.

Open: Apr-14 Oct **Last arrival:** 21.00hrs **Last departure:** 11.00hrs

Pitches:

Leisure:

Facilities:

Services:

Within 3 miles:

Notes: No skateboards. Dogs must be kept on leads.

AA Pubs & Restaurants nearby: Les Bouviers Restaurant with Rooms, WIMBORNE MINSTER, BH21 3BD, 01202 889555

PITCHES: Caravans Motorhomes Tents Glamping accommodation **SERVICES:** Electric hook up Launderette Licensed bar Calor Gas Camping Gaz Toilet fluid Café/Restaurant Fast Food/Takeaway Battery charging Baby care Motorvan service point
ABBREVIATIONS: BHs – bank holidays   Etr – Easter   Spring BH – Spring Bank Holiday   fr – from   hrs – hours   m – mile   mdnt – midnight
rdbt – roundabout   rs – restricted service   wk – week   wknd – weekend   x-roads – crossroads   No credit or debit cards   No dogs

COUNTY DURHAM

BARNARD CASTLE
Map 19 NZ01

Places to visit

Barnard Castle, BARNARD CASTLE, DL12 8PR, 01833 638212
www.english-heritage.org.uk/daysout/properties/barnard-castle

The Bowes Museum, BARNARD CASTLE, DL12 8NP, 01833 690606
www.thebowesmuseum.org.uk

Great for kids: Raby Castle, STAINDROP, DL2 3AH, 01833 660202
www.rabycastle.com

Pecknell Farm Caravan Park
►►► 81%

tel: 01833 638357 **Lartington DL12 9DF**
dir: 1.5m from Barnard Castle. From A66 take B6277. Site on right 1.5m from junct with A67. **grid ref:** NZ028178

A small well laid out site on a working farm in beautiful rural meadowland, with spacious marked pitches on level ground. There are many walking opportunities that start directly from this friendly site. 1.5 acre site. 20 touring pitches. 5 hardstandings. Caravan pitches. Motorhome pitches.

Open: Apr-Oct **Last arrival:** 20.00hrs **Last departure:** noon

Pitches: 🚐 🚍

Facilities: 🌂 ⊙ 🅿 ♻ 🛈

Services: 🔌 🗻

Within 3 miles: ↨ 🎱 🏌 ⊙ 🔯 U

Notes: 🐕 No noise after 22.30hrs. Max 2 dogs per pitch. Dogs must be kept on leads.

AA Pubs & Restaurants nearby: The Fox and Hounds, COTHERSTONE, DL12 9PF, 01833 650241

The Morritt Hotel, BARNARD CASTLE, DL12 9SE, 01833 627232

The Rose & Crown, ROMALDKIRK, DL12 9EB, 01833 650213

Follow the AA
on twitter
@TheAA_Lifestyle

ESSEX

MERSEA ISLAND
Map 7 TM01

Places to visit

Layer Marney Tower, LAYER MARNEY, CO5 9US, 01206 330784
www.layermarneytower.co.uk

Waldegraves Holiday Park
HOLIDAY CENTRE 82%

GOLD

tel: 01206 382898 & 381195 **CO5 8SE**
email: holidays@waldegraves.co.uk **web:** www.waldegraves.co.uk
dir: A12 junct 26, B1025 to Mersea Island across The Strood. Left to East Mersea, 2nd right, follow tourist signs to site. **grid ref:** TM033133

A spacious and pleasant site located between farmland and its own private beach on the Blackwater Estuary. There are well-maintained standard grass pitches or a limited selection of hardstanding and serviced pitches – some have hedges to offer a greater level of privacy; the pitches are flat and spacious. There are excellent facilities including the restaurant, bar, shop, coarse fishing lakes, entertainment and heated outdoor swimming pool. 25 acre site. 30 seasonal pitches. Caravan pitches. Motorhome pitches. Tent pitches.

Open: Mar-Nov (rs Mar-Jun & Sep-Nov (excl BH & school half terms) pool, shop & clubhouse reduced opening hours; pool open May-Sep weather permitting)
Last arrival: 22.00hrs **Last departure:** 13.00hrs

Pitches: * 🚐 £20-£32 🚍 £20-£32 ▲ £20-£32

Leisure: ⌇ 🎢 🛝 ⚓ 🎾 🔍 🎵 🎣 🚲

Facilities: 🌂 ⊙ 🅿 ✳ ♿ 🛁 🚿 🔯 WiFi ♻ 🛈 🚲

Services: 🔌 🗻 🍽 🛒 🛢 ⊘ T 🍽 📷 🛒 🗻

Within 3 miles: ↨ 🏌 ⊙ 🎣 🗻 🛒

Notes: No groups of under 21s. Dogs must be kept on leads. Boating lake, slipway, pitch & putt, driving range, crazy golf, foot golf, family games room, family entertainment.

AA Pubs & Restaurants nearby: The Peldon Rose, PELDON, CO5 7QJ, 01206 735248

Fen Farm Caravan Site
►►►►84%

GOLD

tel: 01206 383275 **Moore Ln, East Mersea CO5 8FE**
email: havefun@fenfarm.co.uk **web:** www.fenfarm.co.uk
dir: *B1025 from Colchester to Mersea Island, left signed East Mersea. 1st right after Dog & Pheasant pub into Moore Lane. (NB road is tidal, please check tide times).*
grid ref: *TM059143*

The first tents were pitched at Fen Farm in 1923 and over the years the farm gave way entirely to becoming a caravan park. Enjoying an enviable location beside the Blackwater Estuary, it has unique atmosphere with a mixture of meadow, woodland and marine shore, and varied wildlife to match each environment. There are two excellent solar-heated toilet blocks, which include three family rooms and privacy cubicles, with the newest block constructed in the local style of black clapboard and a red tile roof. There is a woodland dog walk and two well-equipped play areas, while crabbing in the beach pools is also a popular pastime. 90 touring pitches. 3 hardstandings. 65 seasonal pitches. Caravan pitches. Motorhome pitches. Tent pitches. 90 statics.

Open: Mar-Oct **Last arrival:** dusk

Pitches: ⛺ 🚐 Å

Leisure: 🎪 ✪

Facilities: 🏕 🅿 ⅌ ✳ ⚘ ⓢ 🚻 📶 ♻ 𝒊

Services: 🔌 ⓢ 🛢 ⊘ 🅣 ⛟

Within 3 miles: ⅌ ◉ ⓢ ⓢ

Notes: No open fires, no noise after 23.00hrs. Dogs must be kept on leads.

AA Pubs & Restaurants nearby: The Peldon Rose, PELDON, CO5 7QJ, 01206 735248

Seaview Holiday Park
►►►80%

tel: 01206 382534 **Seaview Av, West Mersea CO5 8DA**
email: seaviewholidaypark@googlemail.com
dir: *From A12 (Colchester) onto B1025 (Mersea Island), cross causeway, left towards East Mersea, 1st right, follow signs.* **grid ref:** *TM025125*

With sweeping views across the Blackwater Estuary, this interesting, well-established park has its own private beach, complete with boat slipway and attractive beach cabins, a modern shop, café and a stylish clubhouse which offers evening meals and drinks in a quiet family atmosphere. The touring area is well maintained and has 40 fully serviced pitches. 30 acre site. 106 touring pitches. 40 hardstandings. 30 seasonal pitches. Caravan pitches. Motorhome pitches. 240 statics.

Open: Apr-Oct **Last arrival:** 18.00hrs (phone site if late arrival expected)
Last departure: noon

Pitches: ⛺ 🚐

Facilities: ♿ ⓢ 🚻 𝒊

Services: 🔌 ⓢ 🍸 🍽 🍟 ⛟

Within 3 miles: ⅌ ⚓ ⓢ ⓢ ∪

Notes: No noise after mdnt, no boats or jet skis. Dogs must be kept on leads. Private beach.

AA Pubs & Restaurants nearby: The Peldon Rose, PELDON, CO5 7QJ, 01206 735248

ROCHFORD | Map 7 TQ89

Riverside Village Holiday Park
►►►82%

tel: 01702 258297 **Creeksea Ferry Rd, Wallasea Island, Canewdon SS4 2EY**
email: riversidevillage@tiscali.co.uk
dir: *M25 junct 29, A127 towards Southend-on-Sea. Take B1013 towards Rochford. Follow signs for Wallasea Island & Baltic Wharf.* **grid ref:** *TQ929951*

Situated adjacent to a nature reserve beside the River Crouch, this holiday park is surrounded by wetlands but only eight miles from Southend. A modern toilet block, with disabled facilities, is provided for tourers and there's a smart reception area. The park has several fishing lakes for site guests (permits available at reception). Several restaurants and pubs are within a short distance. 25 acre site. 60 touring pitches. Caravan pitches. Motorhome pitches. Tent pitches. 159 statics.

Open: Mar-Oct

Pitches: ⛺ 🚐 Å

Leisure: ⅌

Facilities: 🏕 🅿 ☉ ⅌ ✳ ♿ ⓢ 🪑 🚻 📶 ♻ 𝒊

Services: 🔌 ⓢ 🛢 ⊘ 🅣

Within 3 miles: ⅌ ⅌ ⓢ ⓢ

Notes: No dogs in tents, no vans or commercial vehicles. Dogs must be kept on leads.

PITCHES: ⛺ Caravans 🚐 Motorhomes Å Tents 🎪 Glamping accommodation **SERVICES:** 🔌 Electric hook up ⓢ Launderette 🍸 Licensed bar 🛢 Calor Gas ⊘ Camping Gaz 🅣 Toilet fluid 🍽 Café/Restaurant 🍟 Fast Food/Takeaway 🔋 Battery charging 👶 Baby care ⛟ Motorvan service point **ABBREVIATIONS:** BHs – bank holidays Etr – Easter Spring BH – Spring Bank Holiday fr – from hrs – hours m – mile mdnt – midnight rdbt – roundabout rs – restricted service wk – week wknd – weekend x-roads – crossroads ⊗ No credit or debit cards ⊗ No dogs

ST OSYTH

Map 7 TM11

Places to visit

Colchester, St Botolph's Priory, COLCHESTER http://www.english-heritage.org.uk/daysout/properties/colchester-st-botolphs-priory

Colchester Castle Museum, COLCHESTER, CO1 1TJ, 01206 282939 www.colchestermuseums.org.uk

Great for kids: Colchester Zoo, COLCHESTER, CO3 0SL, 01206 331292 www.colchesterzoo.org

The Orchards Holiday Park

HOLIDAY CENTRE 83%

GOLD

tel: 01255 820651 **CO16 8LJ**
email: theorchards@haven.com **web:** www.haven.com/theorchards
dir: From Clacton-on-Sea take B1027 towards Colchester. Left after petrol station, straight on at x-roads in St Osyth. Follow signs to Point Clear. Park in 3m.
grid ref: TM125155

The Orchards offers good touring facilities with a quality toilet block which includes a laundry, play area and two very spacious family rooms. The touring pitches are generously sized. There's also direct access to all the leisure, entertainment and dining outlets available on this large popular holiday park on the Essex coast. 140 acre site. 63 touring pitches. Caravan pitches. Tent pitches. 1000 statics.

The Orchards Holiday Park

Open: end Mar-end Oct (rs end Mar-May & Sep-end Oct some facilities may be reduced) **Last arrival:** anytime **Last departure:** 10.00hrs

Pitches: 🚐 ⛺ **Leisure:** 🏊 ⚽ ♠ ♫ ♪ 🎣

Facilities: 🏪 ⊙ 🅿 ♿ 🖪 🛜 🖳 ♻ ❓

Services: 🚽 🖪 ♨ 🏧 🍴 🛒

Within 3 miles: ♪ 🐾 ◎ ⛳ 🐴 🛒 U

Notes: No cars by tents. No commercial vehicles, no bookings by persons under 21yrs unless a family booking, max 2 dogs per booking, certain dog breeds banned.

AA Pubs & Restaurants nearby: The Rose & Crown Hotel, COLCHESTER, CO1 2TZ, 01206 866677

The Whalebone, FINGRINGHOE, CO5 7BG, 01206 729307

See advert below

GLOUCESTERSHIRE

BERKELEY — Map 4 ST69

Places to visit

Dr Jenner's House, Museum and Garden, BERKELEY, GL13 9BN, 01453 810631 www.jennermuseum.com

WWT Slimbridge Wetland Centre, SLIMBRIDGE, GL2 7BT, 01453 891900 www.wwt.org.uk/slimbridge

Great for kids: Berkeley Castle & Butterfly House, BERKELEY, GL13 9BQ, 01453 810303 www.berkeley-castle.com

Hogsdown Farm Caravan & Camping Park

►►► 81%

tel: 01453 810224 **Hogsdown Farm, Lower Wick GL11 6DD**
web: www.hogsdownfarm.co.uk
dir: *M5 junct 14 (Falfield), A38 towards Gloucester. Through Stone & Woodford. After Newport turn right signed Lower Wick.* **grid ref:** *ST710974*

A pleasant site with good toilet facilities, located between Bristol and Gloucester. It is well positioned for visiting Berkeley Castle and the Cotswolds, and makes an excellent overnight stop when travelling to or from the West Country. 5 acre site. 45 touring pitches. 12 hardstandings. Caravan pitches. Motorhome pitches. Tent pitches.

Open: all year **Last arrival:** 21.00hrs **Last departure:** 16.00hrs

Pitches: 🚐 🚌 ⛺

Leisure: 🛝

Facilities: 🚿 ⊙ ✱ ♻ ℹ

Services: 🔌 🧺 🛢 🔋

Within 3 miles: ⛳ 🎣 [S] 🧺 ∪

Notes: No skateboards or bikes. Dogs must be kept on leads.

AA Pubs & Restaurants nearby: The Malt House, BERKELEY, GL13 9BA, 01453 511177

The Anchor Inn, OLDBURY-ON-SEVERN, BS35 1QA, 01454 413331

CHELTENHAM — Map 10 SO92

Places to visit

Holst Birthplace Museum, CHELTENHAM, GL52 2AY, 01242 524846 www.holstmuseum.org.uk

Sudeley Castle, Gardens & Exhibitions, WINCHCOMBE, GL54 5JD, 01242 609485 www.sudeleycastle.co.uk

Briarfields Motel & Touring Park

►►►► 90%

DAVID BELLAMY CONSERVATION AWARD GOLD

tel: 01242 235324 **Gloucester Rd GL51 0SX**
email: briarfields@hotmail.co.uk
dir: *M5 junct 11, A40 towards Cheltenham. At rdbt left onto B4063, site 200mtrs on left.*
grid ref: *SO909218*

This is a well-designed, level, adults-only park, with a motel, where the facilities are modern and very clean. It is well-positioned between Cheltenham and Gloucester, with easy access to the Cotswolds. And, being close to the M5, it makes a perfect overnight stopping point. 5 acre site. 72 touring pitches. 72 hardstandings. Caravan pitches. Motorhome pitches. Tent pitches.

Open: all year **Last arrival:** 21.00hrs **Last departure:** noon

Pitches: * 🚐 £17-£21 🚌 £17-£21 ⛺ £13-£21

Facilities: 🚿 [P] ⊙ 🚰 ✱ ♿ [WiFi] ♻ ℹ 🏧

Services: 🔌 🧺 ⬇ **Within 3 miles:** ⛳ 🏊 🎬 🎣 [S] 🧺 ∪

Notes: Adults only. No noise after 22.00hrs. Dogs must be kept on leads.

AA Pubs & Restaurants nearby: The Gloucester Old Spot, CHELTENHAM, GL51 9SY, 01242 680321

The Royal Oak Inn, CHELTENHAM, GL52 3DL, 01242 522344

CIRENCESTER — Map 5 SP00

Places to visit

New Brewery Arts, CIRENCESTER, GL7 1JH, 01285 657181 www.newbreweryarts.org.uk

Mayfield Park

NEW ►►►► 87%

tel: 01285 831301 & 07483 327535 **Cheltenham Rd GL7 7BH**
email: enquiries@mayfieldpark.co.uk
dir: *In Cirencester at rdbt junct of A429 & A417, take A417 signed Cheltenham & A435. Right onto A435 signed Cheltenham, follow brown camping signs, pass golf course, site on left.* **grid ref:** *SP020052*

A much improved and gently sloping park on the edge of the Cotswolds that offers level pitches and a warm welcome. Popular with couples and families, it has a newly refurbished reception area, a small shop selling essentials and offers 43 fully serviced hardstanding pitches and caravans for hire. This lovely park makes an ideal base for exploring the Cotswolds and its many attractions, and for walking the nearby Monarch's Way and the Cotswold Way long-distance paths. 13 acre site. 105 touring pitches. 22 hardstandings. 21 seasonal pitches. Caravan pitches. Motorhome pitches. Tent pitches.

Open: all year **Pitches:** * 🚐 £16-£24 🚌 £16-£24 ⛺ £16-£24 **Leisure:** 🛝

Facilities: 🚿 [P] ⊙ 🚰 ✱ ♿ [S] 🪑 🐕 [WiFi] 💻 ♻ ℹ

Services: 🔌 🧺 🛢 ⊘ [T] 🔋 ⬇ **Within 3 miles:** ⛳ [S]

Notes: No bikes, scooters or skateboards, no noise after 23.00hrs, min 3 nights booking for BHs. Dogs must be kept on leads.

PITCHES: 🚐 Caravans 🚌 Motorhomes ⛺ Tents 🛖 Glamping accommodation **SERVICES:** 🔌 Electric hook up 🧺 Launderette 🍷 Licensed bar 🛢 Calor Gas ⊘ Camping Gaz [T] Toilet fluid 🍴 Café/Restaurant 🍔 Fast Food/Takeaway 🔋 Battery charging 🍼 Baby care ⬇ Motorvan service point
ABBREVIATIONS: BHs – bank holidays Etr – Easter Spring BH – Spring Bank Holiday fr – from hrs – hours m – mile mdnt – midnight rdbt – roundabout rs – restricted service wk – week wknd – weekend x-roads – crossroads 💳 No credit or debit cards 🚫 No dogs

GLOUCESTER | Map 10 SO81

Places to visit

Gloucester Folk Museum, GLOUCESTER, GL1 2PG, 01452 396868
www.gloucester.gov.uk/folkmuseum

Nature in Art, GLOUCESTER, GL2 9PA, 01452 731422 www.natureinart.org.uk

Great for kids: National Waterways Museum Gloucester, GLOUCESTER, GL1 2EH, 01452 318200 www.canalrivertrust.org.uk/gloucester-waterways-museum

Red Lion Caravan & Camping Park

▶▶▶ 77%

tel: 01452 731810 & 01299 400787 **Wainlode Hill, Norton GL2 9LW**
email: redlion.loveri@btconnect.com
dir: *Exit A38 at Norton, follow road to river.* **grid ref:** *SO849258*

An attractive meadowland park, adjacent to a traditional pub, with the River Severn just across a country lane. There is a private lake for freshwater fishing. This makes an ideal touring base. 24 acre site. 60 touring pitches. 10 hardstandings. 60 seasonal pitches. Caravan pitches. Motorhome pitches. Tent pitches. 85 statics.

Open: all year **Last arrival:** 21.30hrs **Last departure:** 11.00hrs

Pitches: 🚐 🚏 Å **Facilities:** 🌣⊙🛱☀️🕙🗠🎡🛈

Services: 🔌🖥 🗐🛒🐾🚰🚻🍽

Within 3 miles: 🎣🗠🛒

Notes: 🐾 No noise after 22.00hrs, no open fires. Dogs must be kept on leads.

AA Pubs & Restaurants nearby: Queens Head, GLOUCESTER, GL2 9EJ, 01452 301882

The Queens Arms, ASHLEWORTH, GL19 4HT, 01452 700395

NEWENT | Map 10 SO72

Places to visit

Odda's Chapel, DEERHURST, 0370 333 1181
www.english-heritage.org.uk/daysout/properties/oddas-chapel

Westbury Court Garden, WESTBURY-ON-SEVERN, GL14 1PD, 01452 760461
www.nationaltrust.org.uk

Great for kids: International Centre for Birds of Prey, NEWENT, GL18 1JJ, 01531 820286 www.icbp.org

Pelerine Caravan and Camping

▶▶▶ 85%

tel: 01531 822761 & 07909 914262 **Ford House Rd GL18 1LQ**
email: pelerine@hotmail.com
dir: *1m from Newent.* **grid ref:** *SO645183*

A pleasant, French-themed site divided into separate areas (Rue de Pelerine and Avenue des Families), plus one for adults-only; there are some hardstandings and electric hook-ups in each area. Facilities are very good, especially for families. It is close to several vineyards, and well positioned in the north of the Forest of Dean with Tewkesbury, Cheltenham and Ross-on-Wye within easy reach. 5 acre site. 35 touring pitches. 2 hardstandings. Caravan pitches. Motorhome pitches. Tent pitches.

Open: Mar-Nov **Last arrival:** 22.00hrs **Last departure:** 16.00hrs

Pitches: 🚐 £20-£22 🚏 £20-£22 Å £15-£22

Facilities: 🌣⊙🛱☀️🕙🗠🎡🛈

Services: 🔌🖥 🗐🛒 **Within 3 miles:** 🎣🗠🛒🛒🛒⛵

Notes: 🐾 PayPal accepted. Dogs must be kept on leads. Woodburners, chimneas, burning pits available.

AA Pubs & Restaurants nearby: The Yew Tree, CLIFFORD'S MESNE, GL18 1JS, 01531 820719

Three Choirs Vineyards, NEWENT, GL18 1LS, 01531 890223

SLIMBRIDGE | Map 4 SO70

Places to visit

Berkeley Castle & Butterfly House, BERKELEY, GL13 9BQ, 01453 810303
www.berkeley-castle.com

Great for kids: WWT Slimbridge Wetland Centre, SLIMBRIDGE, GL2 7BT, 01453 891900 www.wwt.org.uk/slimbridge

Tudor Caravan & Camping

▶▶▶▶ 88%

tel: 01453 890483 **Shepherds Patch GL2 7BP**
email: aa@tudorcaravanpark.co.uk **web:** www.tudorcaravanpark.com
dir: *M5 juncts 13 & 14, follow WWT Wetlands Wildlife Centre-Slimbridge signs. Site at rear of Tudor Arms pub.* **grid ref:** *SO728040*

This park benefits from one of the best locations in the county, situated right alongside the Sharpness to Gloucester canal and just a short walk from the famous Wildfowl & Wetlands Trust at Slimbridge. The site has two areas, one for adults only, and a more open area with a facility block. There are both grass and gravel pitches complete with electric hook-ups. Being beside the canal, there are excellent walks plus the National Cycle Network route 41 can be accessed from the site. There is a pub and restaurant adjacent to the site. 8 acre site. 75 touring pitches. 48 hardstandings. 4 seasonal pitches. Caravan pitches. Motorhome pitches. Tent pitches.

Open: all year **Last arrival:** 20.00hrs **Last departure:** 11.00hrs

Pitches: * 🚐 £13-£24 🚏 £13-£24 Å £8-£24

Leisure: 🗠

Facilities: 🌣🅿⊙☀️🕙🗠🎡🛈

Services: 🔌🖥 🛒🐾🚰🚻🍽🛒🛒

Within 3 miles: 🚴🗠🛒🛒⛵

Notes: Debit cards accepted (no credit cards). Dogs must be kept on leads.

STONEHOUSE Map 4 SO80

Places to visit

Painswick Rococo Garden, PAINSWICK, GL6 6TH, 01452 813204 www.rococogarden.org.uk

WWT Slimbridge Wetland Centre, SLIMBRIDGE, GL2 7BT, 01453 891900 www.wwt.org.uk/slimbridge

Apple Tree Park Caravan and Camping Site

►►►► 88%

tel: 01452 742362 & 07708 221457 **A38, Claypits GL10 3AL**
email: appletreepark@hotmail.co.uk
dir: *M5 junct 13, A38. Take 1st exit at rdbt. Site 0.7m on left, 400mtrs beyond filling station.* **grid ref:** *SO766063*

This is a family-owned park conveniently located on the A38, not far from the M5. A peaceful site with glorious views of the Cotswolds, it offers modern and spotlessly clean toilet facilities with underfloor heating. The park is well located for visiting Slimbridge Wildfowl & Wetlands Trust and makes an excellent stopover for M5 travellers. There is a bus stop directly outside the park which is handy for those with motorhomes who wish to visit nearby Gloucester and Cheltenham. 6.5 acre site. 65 touring pitches. 14 hardstandings. 10 seasonal pitches. Caravan pitches. Motorhome pitches. Tent pitches.

Open: all year **Last arrival:** 21.00hrs **Last departure:** noon

Pitches: 🚐 🚌 ⛺

Leisure: ⚽

Facilities: 🚿 [P] ⊙ 🚿 ✲ ♿ [$] 🐕 [WiFi] 💻 ♻ ℹ

Services: 🔌 🛢 ⛽ [T] ⚓

Within 3 miles: 🏌 🎣 🏊 [$]

Notes: Minimum noise after 22.30hrs. Dogs must be kept on leads.

AA Pubs & Restaurants nearby: The Old Passage Inn, ARLINGHAM, GL2 7JR, 01452 740547

GREATER MANCHESTER

LITTLEBOROUGH Map 16 SD91

Hollingworth Lake Caravan Park

►►► 89%

tel: 01706 378661 & 373919 **Round House Farm, Rakewood Rd, Rakewood OL15 0AT**
email: info@hollingworthlakecaravanpark.com
dir: *From Littleborough or Milnrow (M62 junct 21), follow Hollingworth Lake Country Park signs to Fishermans Inn & The Wine Press. Take 'No Through Road' to Rakewood, then 2nd right.* **grid ref:** *SD943146*

A popular park adjacent to Hollingworth Lake, at the foot of the Pennines, within easy reach of many local attractions. Backpackers walking the Pennine Way are welcome at this family-run park, and there are also large rally fields. 5 acre site. 50 touring pitches. 25 hardstandings. Caravan pitches. Motorhome pitches. Tent pitches. 53 statics.

Open: all year **Last arrival:** 20.00hrs **Last departure:** noon

Pitches: * 🚐 £15-£20 🚌 £15-£20 ⛺ £10-£20 **Leisure:** ⚽

Facilities: 🚿 [P] ⊙ ✲ ♿ [$] ♻ ℹ

Services: 🔌 🧺 🛢 ⛽ [T] 🔋 ⚓

Within 3 miles: 🏌 🏊 🎣 🏊 [$] 🧺 🐎

Notes: 💳 Family groups only. Max 1 dog per pitch. Dogs must be kept on leads. Pony trekking.

AA Pubs & Restaurants nearby: The White House, LITTLEBOROUGH, OL15 0LG, 01706 378456

HAMPSHIRE

BRANSGORE Map 5 SZ19

Places to visit

Sammy Miller Motorcycle Museum, NEW MILTON, BH25 5SZ, 01425 620777 www.sammymiller.co.uk

Red House Museum & Gardens, CHRISTCHURCH, BH23 1BU, 01202 482860 www3.hants.gov.uk/redhouse

Great for kids: Moors Valley Country Park and Forest, RINGWOOD, BH24 2ET, 01425 470721 www.moors-valley.co.uk

Harrow Wood Farm Caravan Park

►►► 86%

SILVER

tel: 01425 672487 **Harrow Wood Farm, Poplar Ln BH23 8JE**
email: harrowwood@caravan-sites.co.uk **web:** www.caravan-sites.co.uk
dir: *From Ringwood take B3347 towards Christchurch. At Sopley, left for Bransgore, to T-junct. Turn right. Straight on at x-roads. Left in 400yds (just after garage) into Poplar Lane.* **grid ref:** *SZ194978*

A well laid-out, well-drained and spacious site in a pleasant rural position adjoining woodland and fields. Free on-site coarse fishing is available at this peaceful park. Well located for visiting Christchurch, the New Forest National Park and the south coast. 6 acre site. 60 touring pitches. 60 hardstandings. Caravan pitches. Motorhome pitches. Tent pitches.

Open: Mar-6 Jan **Last arrival:** 22.00hrs **Last departure:** noon

Pitches: 🚐 🚌 ⛺ **Leisure:** 🎣

Facilities: 🚿 ⊙ 🚿 ✲ ♿ [WiFi] ℹ

Services: 🔌 🧺 🛢 🔋 ⚓

Within 3 miles: 🎣 [$]

Notes: 🚫🐕 No open fires.

AA Pubs & Restaurants nearby: The Three Tuns, BRANSGORE, BH23 8JH, 01425 672232

FORDINGBRIDGE — Map 5 SU11

Places to visit

Rockbourne Roman Villa, ROCKBOURNE, SP6 3PG, 01725 518541
www.hants.gov.uk/rockbourne-roman-villa

Breamore House & Countryside Museum, BREAMORE, SP6 2DF, 01725 512468
www.breamorehouse.com

Great for kids: Moors Valley Country Park and Forest, RINGWOOD, BH24 2ET,
01425 470721 www.moors-valley.co.uk

PREMIER PARK

Sandy Balls Holiday Village
▶▶▶▶▶90%

GOLD

tel: 0844 693 1336 *(Calls cost 7p per minute plus your phone company's access charge)*
Sandy Balls Estate Ltd, Godshill SP6 2JZ
email: post@sandyballs.co.uk
dir: *M27 junct 1, B3078, B3079, 8m to Godshill. Site 0.25m after cattle grid.*
grid ref: *SU167148*

A large, mostly wooded New Forest holiday complex with good provision of touring facilities on terraced, well laid-out fields. Pitches are fully serviced with shingle bases, and groups can be sited beside the river and away from the main site. There are excellent sporting, leisure and entertainment facilities for the whole family including a jacuzzi, sauna, beauty therapy, horse riding and children's activities. There's also a bistro, information centre and ready-erected tents, lodges and camping pods for hire. This a large holiday village with something for all ages — children and teenagers love it here as there is so much to keep them occupied. 120 acre site. 225 touring pitches. 225 hardstandings. Caravan pitches. Motorhome pitches. Tent pitches. 37 statics.

Open: all year (rs Nov-Feb number of pitches reduced, activities limited but swimming pool & leisure centre open) **Last arrival:** 21.00hrs **Last departure:** 11.00hrs

Pitches: * ☐ £10-£60 ☐ £10-£60 ▲ £10-£60 ⛺ prices shown below

Leisure: 🏊‍♀️🏊🚴🎣🏐⚽🎣🎵🎶 Spa 🎣🚲

Facilities: 🛁📷🅿️☉🍴✂️🚿👶📷🛒🚻 WiFi ♻️ℹ️

Services: 🔌📷🍴📷🚿🔥🚽🍴🛒🚮🚽

Glamping: Safari tents 8, £93-£214 Changeover day Fri Min stay 3 nights at wknds, 4 nights mid wk Own kitchen Car by unit **Wooden Pods** 8, £40-£100 Changeover day Fri Min stay 3 nights at wknds, 4 nights mid wk Car by unit

Within 3 miles: 🎣🏊🛒🛒U

Notes: Groups by prior arrangement only, no gazebos, no noise after 23.00hrs. Dogs must be kept on leads. Freshly baked bread available.

AA Pubs & Restaurants nearby: The Augustus John, FORDINGBRIDGE, SP6 1DG, 01425 652098

HAMBLE-LE-RICE — Map 5 SU40

Riverside Holidays
▶▶▶▶83%

tel: 023 8045 3220 **Satchell Ln SO31 4HR**
email: enquiries@riversideholidays.co.uk
dir: *M27 junct 8, follow signs to Hamble on B3397. Left into Satchell Lane, site in 1m.*
grid ref: *SU481081*

A small, peaceful park beside the marina, and close to the pretty village of Hamble. The park is neatly kept, and there are two toilet and shower blocks, with the central facilities block having excellent private rooms. A pub and restaurant are very close by and there are good river walks alongside the Hamble. 6 acre site. 60 touring pitches. Caravan pitches. Motorhome pitches. Tent pitches. 15 statics.

Open: Mar-Oct **Last arrival:** 22.00hrs **Last departure:** 11.00hrs

Pitches: * ☐ £17-£46 ☐ £17-£46 ▲ £15-£30

Facilities: 🛁📷🅿️☉🍴✂️🚿👶ℹ️

Services: 🔌📷🛒🚮

Within 3 miles: 🎣🏊🎣🛒🛒U

Notes: Dogs must be kept on leads. Baby changing facilities.

LINWOOD — Map 5 SU10

Places to visit

The New Forest Centre, LYNDHURST, SO43 7NY, 023 8028 3444
www.newforestcentre.org.uk

Furzey Gardens, MINSTEAD, SO43 7GL, 023 8081 2464 www.furzey-gardens.org

Great for kids: Paultons Park, OWER, SO51 6AL, 023 8081 4442
www.paultonspark.co.uk

Red Shoot Camping Park
▶▶▶86%

tel: 01425 473789 **BH24 3QT**
email: enquiries@redshoot-campingpark.com
dir: *A31 onto A338 towards Fordingbridge & Salisbury. Right at brown signs for caravan park towards Linwood on unclassified roads, site signed.* **grid ref:** *SU187094*

Located behind the Red Shoot Inn in one of the most attractive parts of the New Forest, this park is in an ideal spot for nature lovers and walkers. It is personally supervised by friendly owners, and offers many amenities including a children's play area. There are modern and spotless facilities plus a smart reception and shop selling fresh bread and croissants and local farm produce. 3.5 acre site. 110 touring pitches. Caravan pitches. Motorhome pitches. Tent pitches.

Open: Mar-Oct **Last arrival:** 19.00hrs **Last departure:** 13.00hrs

Pitches: * ☐ £23.50-£34.50 ☐ £17-£34.50 ▲ £17-£34.50

Leisure: ⛺

Facilities: 📷☉🍴✂️🚿👶🛒♻️ℹ️🚗

Services: 🔌📷🍴📷🚿🚽🍴🛒🚽

Within 3 miles: 🎣🏊🛒🛒U

Notes: Quiet after 22.30hrs. Dogs must be kept on leads.

LEISURE: 🏊 Indoor pool 🏊 Outdoor pool ⛺ Children's playground 🖐 Kid's club 🎾 Tennis court 🎱 Games room ⛳ Golf course 🛶 Boat hire 🚲 Cycle hire 🎬 Cinema 🎵 Entertainment 🎣 Fishing ⛳ Mini golf 🏏 Pitch n putt 🏄 Watersports 🏋 Gym 🏐 Sports field U Stables **FACILITIES:** 🛁 Bath 🚿 Shower 🅿️ Private washing cubicles ☉ Electric shaver 🍴 Hairdryer ✂️ Ice Packs 🚻 Disabled facilities 🛒 Shop on site 📷 Mobile shop 🔥 BBQ area 🍴 Picnic area WiFi Wi-fi 💻 Internet access ♻️ Recycling ℹ️ Tourist info 🐕 Dog exercise area 🚗 Car hire can be arranged

RINGWOOD

See St Leonards (Dorset)

ROMSEY	Map 5 SU32

Places to visit

Sir Harold Hillier Gardens, AMPFIELD, SO51 0QA, 01794 369318
www.hilliergardens.org.uk

Mottisfont, MOTTISFONT, SO51 0LP, 01794 340757
www.nationaltrust.org.uk/mottisfont

Great for kids: Longdown Activity Farm, ASHURST, SO40 7EH, 023 8029 2837
www.longdownfarm.co.uk

Paultons Park, OWER, SO51 6AL, 023 8081 4442
www.paultonspark.co.uk

PREMIER PARK

Hill Farm Caravan Park
►►►►► 88%

tel: 01794 340402 **Branches Ln, Sherfield English SO51 6FH**
email: gjb@hillfarmpark.com
dir: *Signed from A27 (Salisbury to Romsey road) in Sherfield English. 4m NW of Romsey & M27 junct 2.* **grid ref:** *SU287238*

A small, well-sheltered park peacefully located amidst mature trees and meadows. The two toilet blocks offer smart unisex showers as well as a fully en suite family and disabled room, and plenty of privacy in the washrooms. The Garden Room, a good café and restaurant, with an outside patio, serves a wide range of snacks and meals, and there is an excellent village shop incorporated into the reception area. This attractive park is well placed for visiting Salisbury and the New Forest National Park, and the south coast is only a short drive away, making it an appealing holiday location. There is a separate caravan sales and full repair centre – South Coast Caravans. 10.5 acre site. 100 touring pitches. 60 hardstandings. Caravan pitches. Motorhome pitches. Tent pitches. 6 statics.

Open: Mar-Oct **Last arrival:** 20.00hrs **Last departure:** noon
Pitches: 🚐 🚍 🅰
Leisure: 🎱 ⚙
Facilities: ⊙ 𝒫 ⁂ ♿ 🖆 🕮 🖾 ⿴ 🍴 WIFI 🖳 ♻ 𝒊
Services: 🔌 🖻 🔋 ⊘ 🅣 🍴 🛒 ⚓
Within 3 miles: ⫯ ⑁ 𝒫 ◎ 🖻 🖻 ∪
Notes: Minimum noise at all times & no noise after 23.00hrs, one unit per pitch, site unsuitable for teenagers.
AA Pubs & Restaurants nearby: The Three Tuns, ROMSEY, SO51 8HL, 01794 512639

Green Pastures Farm Camping & Touring Park
►►► 84%
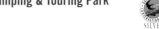

tel: 023 8081 4444 **Ower SO51 6AJ**
email: enquiries@greenpasturesfarm.com
dir: *M27 junct 2. Follow Salisbury signs for 0.5m, then brown tourist signs for Green Pastures. Also signed from A36 & A3090 at Ower.* **grid ref:** *SU321158*

This pleasant site offers a variety of easily accessed pitches, including those with electric hook-up. There is a code access security barrier to the site. Green Pastures is well located for visiting Paultons Theme Park, Southampton and the New Forest National Park, and being close to the M27 it is convenient for overnight stops. There are kennels where dogs can be left while you visit the theme park or go shopping. 6 acre site. 60 touring pitches. 6 hardstandings. Caravan pitches. Motorhome pitches. Tent pitches.

Open: 13 Mar-Oct **Last arrival:** 20.00hrs **Last departure:** 11.00hrs
Pitches: * 🚐 £20-£25 🚍 £20-£25 🅰 £15-£31 **Facilities:** 𝒫 ⁂ ♿ 🖻 ♻ 𝒊
Services: 🔌 🖻 🔋 ⊘ 🅣 🛒 ⚓ **Within 3 miles:** ⫯ 𝒫 🖻 🖻
Notes: No water games, only off-ground BBQs permitted. Dogs must be kept on leads. Fish & chip van Friday nights.
AA Pubs & Restaurants nearby: Sir John Barleycorn, CADNAM, SO40 2NP, 023 8081 2236

WARSASH	Map 5 SU40

Places to visit

Explosion Museum of Naval Firepower, GOSPORT, PO12 4LE, 023 9250 5600
www.explosion.org.uk

Portchester Castle, PORTCHESTER, PO16 9QW, 023 9237 8291
www.english-heritage.org.uk/daysout/properties/portchester-castle

Great for kids: Blue Reef Aquarium, PORTSMOUTH, PO5 3PB, 023 9287 5222
www.bluereefaquarium.co.uk

Dibles Park
►►►► 85%

tel: 01489 575232 **Dibles Rd SO31 9SA**
email: dibles.park@btconnect.com
dir: *M27 junct 9, at rdbt 5th exit (Parkgate A27), 3rd rdbt 1st exit, 4th rdbt 2nd exit. Site 500yds on left. Or M27 junct 8, at rdbt 1st exit (Parkgate), next rdbt 3rd exit (Brook Ln), 4th rdbt 2nd exit. Site 500yds on left.* **grid ref:** *SU505060*

A small peaceful touring park adjacent to a private residential park. The facilities are excellent and spotlessly clean, and the spacious pitches are all hardstanding with electric and can take the largest RVs. A warm welcome awaits visitors to this well-managed park, which is very convenient for the Hamble, the Solent and very well positioned for an overnight stay if heading for the cross-channel ferry port at Portsmouth, which is about 14 miles away. WiFi is available. The park also offers free leaflets of the many excellent walks around the area. 0.75 acre site. 14 touring pitches. 14 hardstandings. Caravan pitches. Motorhome pitches. Tent pitches. 46 statics.

Open: all year **Last arrival:** 20.30hrs **Last departure:** 11.00hrs
Pitches: * 🚐 £20-£23 🚍 £20-£23 🅰 £20-£23 **Facilities:** 𝒫 Ⓟ ⊙ 𝒫 ⁂ WIFI ♻ 𝒊
Services: 🔌 🖻 🔋 ⚓ **Within 3 miles:** ⚐ ⑁ 𝒫 ⚐ 🖻 🖻 ∪
Notes: No noise after 23.00 hrs, no children's ball games, no cycling, no scooters. Dogs must be kept on leads.
AA Pubs & Restaurants nearby: Solent Hotel & Spa, FAREHAM, PO15 7AJ, 01489 880000
The Bun Penny, LEE-ON-THE-SOLENT, PO13 9JH, 023 9255 0214

PITCHES: 🚐 Caravans 🚍 Motorhomes 🅰 Tents 🏕 Glamping accommodation **SERVICES:** 🔌 Electric hook up 🖻 Launderette 🍸 Licensed bar 🔋 Calor Gas ⊘ Camping Gaz 🅣 Toilet fluid 🍴 Café/Restaurant 🍟 Fast Food/Takeaway 🔋 Battery charging 🛒 Baby care ⚓ Motorvan service point **ABBREVIATIONS:** BHs – bank holidays Etr – Easter Spring BH – Spring Bank Holiday fr – from hrs – hours m – mile mdnt – midnight rdbt – roundabout rs – restricted service wk – week wknd – weekend x-roads – crossroads 🈵 No credit or debit cards 🈲 No dogs

HEREFORDSHIRE

SYMONDS YAT (WEST)   Map 10 SO51

Places to visit

The Nelson Museum & Local History Centre, MONMOUTH, NP25 3XA, 01600 710630

Great for kids: Goodrich Castle, GOODRICH, HR9 6HY, 01600 890538 www.english-heritage.org.uk/daysout/properties/goodrich-castle

---

Doward Park Camp Site
►►► 86%

tel: 01600 890438 **Great Doward HR9 6BP**
email: enquiries@dowardpark.co.uk
dir: *A40 from Monmouth towards Ross-on-Wye. In 2m left signed Crockers Ash, Ganarew & The Doward. Cross over A40, 1st left at T-junct, in 0.5m 1st right signed The Doward. Follow park signs up hill. NB it is advised that Sat Nav is not used for end of journey.*
grid ref: SO539167

This delightful little park is set in peaceful woodlands on the hillside above the Wye Valley. It is ideal for campers and motorhomes but not caravans due to the narrow, twisting approach roads. A warm welcome awaits and the facilities are kept spotless. The Bluebell Wood children's play area is a great place for imaginative games. 1.5 acre site. 28 touring pitches. 6 seasonal pitches. Motorhome pitches. Tent pitches.

Open: Mar-Oct **Last arrival:** 20.00hrs **Last departure:** 11.30hrs

Pitches: ⊞ ▲

Leisure: ⚠

Facilities: ⌐⊙☞✳&⑤ WiFi ♻ ❶

Services: ⊕⑤ ⬛⬀☲

Within 3 miles: ⌳⫯☞◎⥯⑤⊡

Notes: No cars by tents. No fires, quiet after 22.00hrs. Dogs must be kept on leads.

AA Pubs & Restaurants nearby: The Mill Race, WALFORD, HR9 5QS, 01989 562891

HERTFORDSHIRE

HODDESDON   Map 6 TL30

Lee Valley Caravan Park Dobbs Weir
►►►► 80%

tel: 03000 030 619 **Charlton Meadows, Essex Rd EN11 0AS**
email: dobbsweircampsite@vibrantpartnerships.co.uk
web: www.visitleevalley.org.uk/en/content/cms/where-to-stay-and-short-breaks
dir: *From A10 follow Hoddesdon signs, at 2nd rdbt left signed Dobbs Weir. At next rdbt take 3rd exit. 1m to site on right.* **grid ref:** TL382080

This site provides much needed camping facilities close to London. Situated on level ground beside the River Lee, the park has a modernised toilet block with good facilities, a large timber chalet housing the reception and shop, an extremely innovative motorhome service point, plus 12 wooden wigwams and pre-pitched tents for hire. On-site fishing is available. Free WiFi on site. 11 acre site. 70 touring pitches. 26 hardstandings. Caravan pitches. Motorhome pitches. Tent pitches. 24 statics.

Open: Mar-Jan **Last arrival:** 21.00hrs **Last departure:** noon

Pitches: * ⊞ £14.50-£22.50 ⊞ £14.50-£22.50 ▲ £14.50-£22.50 ⋒

Leisure: ⚠ ☞ 🎣

Facilities: ⌐⊙✳&⑤☲⫯ WiFi ♻ ❶

Services: ⊕⑤ ⬛⬀Ⓣ⥯

Glamping: **Bell tents** 5, Min stay 2 Car by unit **Wooden Wigwams** 12, Min stay 2 Car by unit

Within 3 miles: ⫯☞⥯⑤⊡

Notes: No commercial vehicles. Dogs must be kept on leads. Fire pit area.

AA Pubs & Restaurants nearby: The Fox and Hounds, HUNSDON, SG12 8NH, 01279 843999

LEISURE: 🏊 Indoor pool 🏊 Outdoor pool ⚠ Children's playground ✋ Kid's club 🎾 Tennis court 🎱 Games room ⛳ Golf course 🚣 Boat hire 🚴 Cycle hire
🎬 Cinema 🎵 Entertainment 🎣 Fishing ◎ Mini golf Pitch n putt 🏄 Watersports 💪 Gym Sports field Stables **FACILITIES:** 🛁 Bath ⌐ Shower
Ⓟ Private washing cubicles ⊙ Electric shaver ☞ Hairdryer ✳ Ice Packs & Disabled facilities ⑤ Shop on site Mobile shop BBQ area Picnic area
WiFi Wi-fi 💻 Internet access ♻ Recycling ❶ Tourist info Dog exercise area Car hire can be arranged

PITCHES: 🚐 Caravans 🚍 Motorhomes ⛺ Tents ⛺ Glamping accommodation **SERVICES:** ⚡ Electric hook up 🔘 Launderette 🍷 Licensed bar
🔲 Calor Gas 🔗 Camping Gaz 🔲T Toilet fluid 🍽 Café/Restaurant 🎪 Fast Food/Takeaway ⚡ Battery charging 🛒 Baby care 🔧 Motorvan service point
ABBREVIATIONS: BHs – bank holidays Etr – Easter Spring BH – Spring Bank Holiday fr – from hrs – hours m – mile mdnt – midnight
rdbt – roundabout rs – restricted service wk – week wknd – weekend x-roads – crossroads 🚫 No credit or debit cards 🚫 No dogs

Isle of Wight

There is a timeless quality to the Isle of Wight. For many it embodies the spirit and atmosphere of English seaside holidays over the years, and being an island, it has a unique and highly distinctive identity. Small and intimate – it's just 23 miles by 13 miles – it's a great place to get away-from-it-all, and with its mild climate, long hours of sunshine and colourful architecture, it has something of a continental flavour.

The Isle of Wight is probably most famous for the world's premier sailing regatta. Cowes Week, which takes place at the height of summer, is a key annual fixture in the country's sporting calendar, with the regatta drawing more than 1,000 boats and around 100,000 spectators. It is a hugely colourful event attracting Olympic veterans, weekend sailors and top names from the worlds of sport and the media. Various spectator boats offer good views of the action, but for something less hectic and more sedate, take to the island's 65-mile Coast Path, which offers a continual, unfolding backdrop of magnificent coastal scenery and natural beauty. The sea is seen at numerous points along the route and during Cowes Week, you get constant views of the energetic sailing activity. The regatta is held in the first week of August.

The Isle of Wight Coast Path is a good way to explore the island's varied coastline at any time of the year. Even in the depths of winter, the weather conditions are often favourable for walking. Much of the trail in the southern half of the island represents a relatively undemanding walk over majestic chalk downs. Beyond Freshwater Bay the coast is largely uninhabited with a palpable air of isolation. It is on this stretch that walkers can appreciate how the elements have shaped and weathered the island over many centuries. Away from the coast an intricate network of paths offers the chance to discover a rich assortment of charming villages, hidden valleys and country houses. In all, the Isle of Wight has more than 500 miles of public rights of way and over half the island is acknowledged as an Area of Outstanding Natural Beauty. There is an annual walking festival in May and a weekend walking festival in October. Cycling is also extremely popular here, with the Round the Island Cycle Route attracting many enthusiasts. The route runs for 49 miles and there are starting points at Yarmouth, Cowes and Ryde.

Away from walking and cycling, the Isle of Wight offers numerous attractions and activities. You could plan a week's itinerary on the island and not set foot on the beach. The island's history is a fascinating and crucial aspect of its story. It was long considered as a convenient stepping stone for the French in their plan to invade the mainland, and various fortifications – including Fort Victoria and Yarmouth Castle – reflect its key strategic role in the defence of our coastline. Carisbrooke Castle at Newport – the island's capital – is where Charles I was held before his execution in 1649.

The Isle of Wight has been a fashionable destination for the rich and famous over the years, and members of royalty made their home here. Queen Victoria and Prince Albert boosted tourism hugely when they chose the island as the setting for their summer home, Osborne House, which is now open to the public. Elsewhere, there are echoes of the Isle of Wight's fascinating literary links. Charles Dickens is said to have written six chapters of *David Copperfield* in the village of Bonchurch, near Ventnor, and the Victorian Poet Laureate Alfred Lord Tennyson lived at Faringford House, near Freshwater Bay. He claimed that the air on the coast here was worth 'sixpence a pint.'

The Needles ▷

ISLE OF WIGHT

BEMBRIDGE

See Whitecliff Bay

BRIGHSTONE
Map 5 SZ48

Places to visit
Mottistone Gardens, MOTTISTONE, PO30 4ED, 01983 741302
www.nationaltrust.org.uk/isleofwight

Grange Farm
► ► ► ► 79%

tel: 01983 740296 Grange Chine PO30 4DA
email: grangefarmholidays@gmail.com web: www.grangefarmholidays.com
dir: From Freshwater Bay take A3055 towards Ventnor, 5m (pass Isle of Wight Pearl). Site approx 0.5m on right. grid ref: SZ421820

This family-run site is set in a stunning location on the south-west coast of the island in Brighstone Bay. The facilities are very good. For children there is an imaginative play area and a wide range of animals to see including llamas and water buffalo. This site is right on the coastal path and ideally located for those who like walking and cycling. There are camping pods for hire plus static homes on a lower level by the beach. 8 acre site. 60 touring pitches. 8 hardstandings. Caravan pitches. Motorhome pitches. Tent pitches. 12 statics.

Open: Mar-Oct Last arrival: noon Last departure: noon

Pitches: ⌂ ⌂ Å ⌂

Facilities: ☺ ℱ ⚹ 🛇 ⌀ ⊞ WIFI ♻ ❶

Services: 🔧 🔲 🗑 ⌀ Ⓣ 🛒 ⌄

Glamping: Wooden Pods 8

Within 3 miles: ⌀ ≋ 🛇 🔲

Notes: No fires. Dogs must be kept on leads. Bakery.

AA Pubs & Restaurants nearby: The Crown Inn, SHORWELL, PO30 3JZ, 01983 740293

FRESHWATER
Map 5 SZ38

Places to visit
Yarmouth Castle, YARMOUTH, PO41 0PB, 01983 760678
www.english-heritage.org.uk/daysout/properties/yarmouth-castle

Dimbola Lodge Museum, FRESHWATER, PO40 9QE, 01983 756814
www.dimbola.co.uk

Great for kids: The Needles Park, ALUM BAY, PO39 0JD, 0871 720 0022 *(Calls cost 13p per minute plus your phone company's access charge)* www.theneedles.co.uk

Heathfield Farm Camping
► ► ► ► 88%

tel: 01983 407822 Heathfield Rd PO40 9SH
email: web@heathfieldcamping.co.uk web: www.heathfieldcamping.co.uk
dir: 2m W from Yarmouth ferry port on A3054, left to Heathfield Rd, entrance 200yds on right. grid ref: SZ335879

A well located park in the far west of the island, perfect for visiting the Needles, Freshwater, Totland and Tennyson Down. There are large grass pitches (many over 200 square metres) giving plenty of space, and the facilities are modern, well appointed and very clean. There is also a good backpackers' area for camping with picnic tables. The local town of Freshwater has an excellent supermarket and good range of shops. The closest ferry point is at Yarmouth but the site is easily reached from all ferry ports. 10 acre site. 75 touring pitches. Caravan pitches. Motorhome pitches. Tent pitches.

Open: May-Sep Last arrival: 20.00hrs Last departure: 11.00hrs

Pitches: ⌂ ⌂ Å

Leisure: ⚡

Facilities: ⌀ ☺ ℱ ⚹ ⌀ ⊞ WIFI ♻ ❶ 🚗

Services: 🔧 🔲 ⌀ ⌄

Within 3 miles: ⌀ ⚡ ⌀ ◎ ≋ 🛇 🔲 U

Notes: Dogs must be kept on leads.

AA Pubs & Restaurants nearby: The Red Lion, FRESHWATER, PO40 9BP, 01983 754925

LEISURE: 🏊 Indoor pool ⚡ Outdoor pool 🎠 Children's playground 👶 Kid's club 🎾 Tennis court 🎱 Games room ⛳ Golf course 🚣 Boat hire 🚲 Cycle hire 🎬 Cinema 🎵 Entertainment 🎣 Fishing ◎ Mini golf ⛳ Pitch n putt 🏄 Watersports 🏋 Gym 🏟 Sports field U Stables FACILITIES: 🛁 Bath 🚿 Shower 🅿 Private washing cubicles ☺ Electric shaver ✂ Hairdryer ❄ Ice Packs ♿ Disabled facilities 🛒 Shop on site 🚐 Mobile shop 🍖 BBQ area 🍴 Picnic area 📶 Wi-fi 💻 Internet access ♻ Recycling ❶ Tourist info 🐕 Dog exercise area 🚗 Car hire can be arranged

NEWBRIDGE
Map 5 SZ48

Places to visit
Newtown Old Town Hall, NEWTOWN, PO30 4PA, 01983 531785
www.nationaltrust.org.uk/isleofwight

Great for kids: Yarmouth Castle, YARMOUTH, PO41 0PB, 01983 760678
www.english-heritage.org.uk/daysout/properties/yarmouth-castle

PREMIER PARK

The Orchards Holiday Caravan Park
▶▶▶▶▶ 95%

tel: 01983 531331 & 531350 **Main Rd PO41 0TS**
email: info@orchards-holiday-park.co.uk **web:** www.orchards-holiday-park.co.uk
dir: A3054 from Yarmouth, right in 3m at Horse & Groom Inn. Follow signs to
Newbridge. Entrance opposite post office. Or from Newport, 6m, via B3401.
grid ref: SZ411881

A really excellent, well-managed park set in a peaceful village location amid
downs and meadowland, with glorious downland views. The pitches are terraced
and offer a good provision of hardstandings, including those that are water
serviced. There is a high quality facility centre offering excellent, spacious
showers and family rooms, plus there is access for less able visitors to all site
facilities and disabled toilets. The park has indoor and outdoor swimming pools,
a takeaway and licensed shop. Static homes are available for hire and 'ferry
plus stay' packages are on offer. The site is just 10 minutes from the Wightlink
ferry terminal in Yarmouth and there are buses that stop at the entrance every
hour. 15 acre site. 160 touring pitches. 52 hardstandings. Caravan pitches.
Motorhome pitches. Tent pitches. 65 statics.

Open: 28 Mar-3 Nov (rs Mar-late May & mid/late-Sep-Nov outdoor pool
closed) **Last arrival:** 23.00hrs **Last departure:** 11.00hrs
Pitches: ⚲ ⚲ Å **Leisure:** 🏊 ⚲ ⚽ ◉
Facilities: 🔧 🅿 ◉ ⚲ ✕ ⚲ 🚿 🚻 WiFi ♻ ⓞ 🔧
Services: ⚲ 🗑 🏪 🍽 🚚 🚮 ⚲ **Within 3 miles:** ⚲ 🗑 🗑

Notes: No cycling, no noise after mdnt. Dogs must be kept on leads. Table tennis
room, poolside coffee shop.

AA Pubs & Restaurants nearby: The New Inn, SHALFLEET, PO30 4NS, 01983 531314

NEWPORT
Map 5 SZ48

Wight Glamping Holidays
▶▶▶▶▶ 85%

tel: 01983 532507 **Everland, Long Ln PO30 2NW**
email: info@wightglampingholidays.co.uk
dir: From Cowes to Newport on A3020. In Newport follow Sandown A3054 signs. Take
middle lane at lights (signed Sandown & A3054). At rdbt 1st exit into Fairlee Rd
(A3054) signed Ryde. Right into Staples Rd. Left into Long Ln signed Sandown &
Brading. **grid ref:** SZ519886

Situated in the heart of the island with open countryside views over a valley, this
site (Everlands Camping) comprises four Lotus Belle Tents. Standing on their
individual decking areas each of the carpeted tents is very well equipped with a
king-size bed, plus a sofa which can be converted to either another king-size
bed or two singles. The bed linen and covers are of the highest quality and each
tent is also equipped with a table and four chairs, plus good storage space for
clothes. The heating and lighting is electric. Adjoining at the rear is a separate
utility tent with a fridge and cooking unit. Externally, each tent has a picnic
table and easy chairs as well as the use of a BBQ. There is a separate high
quality toilet and shower block with two shower rooms plus two toilet and wash
basin rooms – a dishwashing area is behind this small block. Cars are parked
adjacent to the glamping area but do not spoil the views or the setting. 1 acre
site.

Open: Apr-Sep **Last arrival:** 22.00hrs **Last departure:** 11.00hrs
Facilities: 🔧 🅿 ◉ ⚲ ♻ ⓞ
Services: ⚲ 🏪
Glamping: Lotus Belle tents 4
Within 3 miles: ⚲ 🗑 ⚲ ⚲ 🗑 🗑 ⚲
Notes: ⊗ ⊗

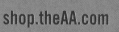

PITCHES: ⚲ Caravans ⚲ Motorhomes Å Tents 🏠 Glamping accommodation **SERVICES:** ⚲ Electric hook up 🗑 Launderette 🍺 Licensed bar
🔋 Calor Gas ⚲ Camping Gaz T Toilet fluid 🍽 Café/Restaurant 🚚 Fast Food/Takeaway 🔋 Battery charging 🚼 Baby care ⚲ Motorvan service point
ABBREVIATIONS: BHs – bank holidays Etr – Easter Spring BH – Spring Bank Holiday fr – from hrs – hours m – mile mdnt – midnight
rdbt – roundabout rs – restricted service wk – week wknd – weekend x-roads – crossroads ⊗ No credit or debit cards ⊗ No dogs

RYDE
Map 5 SZ59

Places to visit

Nunwell House & Gardens, BRADING, PO36 0JQ, 01983 407240

Bembridge Windmill, BEMBRIDGE, PO35 5SQ, 01983 873945
www.nationaltrust.org.uk/isleofwight

Great for kids: Robin Hill Country Park, ARRETON, PO30 2NU, 01983 527352
www.robin-hill.com

PREMIER PARK

Whitefield Forest Touring Park

▶▶▶▶▶ 95%

Best of British
GOLD

tel: 01983 617069 **Brading Rd PO33 1QL**
email: pat&louise@whitefieldforest.co.uk
dir: From Ryde follow A3055 towards Brading, after Tesco rdbt site 0.5m on left.
grid ref: SZ604893

This park is beautifully laid out in the Whitefield Forest, and offers a wide variety of pitches, including 21 that are fully serviced; it is conveniently located on a bus route. It offers excellent modern facilities which are kept spotlessly clean. The park takes great care to retain the natural beauty of the forest, and is a haven for wildlife; red squirrels can be spotted throughout the park, including along the nature walk. Activities such as foraging, bushcraft and cycle rides for children and adults are available at certain times of the year. 23 acre site. 90 touring pitches. 38 hardstandings. Caravan pitches. Motorhome pitches. Tent pitches.

Open: 18 Mar-3 Oct **Last arrival:** 21.00hrs **Last departure:** 11.00hrs
Pitches: * ➝ £17.50-£26 ➝ £17.50-£26 ▲ £17.50-£26
Leisure: ⚲
Facilities: ⚲⚲⚲⚲⚲⚲⚲⚲⚲⚲
Services: ⚲⚲⚲⚲⚲⚲⚲
Within 3 miles: ⚲⚲⚲⚲⚲⚲⚲⚲
Notes: Dogs must be kept on leads.
AA Pubs & Restaurants nearby: The Boathouse, SEAVIEW, PO34 5AW, 01983 810616
Seaview Hotel, SEAVIEW, PO34 5EX, 01983 612711

Roebeck Country Park

▶▶▶ 84%

tel: 01983 562505 & 07768 491187 **Gatehouse Rd, Upton PO33 4BP**
email: info@roebeckcountrypark.co.uk
dir: From Fishbourne ferry turn right, at T-junct left at lights onto A3054 towards Ryde. At lights into right lane, straight on into Pellhurst Rd (follow Sandown (A3055) signs). At T-junct right into Upton Rd. At mini rdbt straight on into Gatehouse Rd (site signed).
grid ref: SZ458902

Roebeck Country Park is located approximately two miles south of Ryde on the north-east side of the island and just five minutes from the beach. It offers a peaceful camping environment for families and couples and the facilities are very clean. Pitches with hook-ups are available and there is a small kitchen with fridge, kettle and microwave. There is a second road that large units can use by prior arrangement with the warden. There's a well-stocked fishing lake. There are also three Sioux-style tipis situated around the well-stocked fishing lake; each sleeps a maximum of four. 13.8 acre site. 140 touring pitches. 4 hardstandings. Caravan pitches. Motorhome pitches. Tent pitches.

Open: all year **Last arrival:** by prior arrangement **Last departure:** by prior arrangement
Pitches: ➝➝▲⚲
Leisure: ⚲
Facilities: ⚲⚲⚲⚲⚲⚲⚲
Services: ⚲⚲⚲⚲⚲⚲⚲⚲
Glamping: **Tipis** 3, Changeover day Fri, Mon Min stay 2 nights (Fri-Sat), 3 nights (Fri-Mon), 4 nights (Mon-Fri), 7 nights (Fri-Fri)
Within 3 miles: ⚲⚲⚲⚲⚲⚲⚲⚲
Notes: Dogs must be kept on leads.

SANDOWN
Map 5 SZ58

Places to visit

Nunwell House & Gardens, BRADING, PO36 0JQ, 01983 407240

Bembridge Windmill, BEMBRIDGE, PO35 5SQ, 01983 873945
www.nationaltrust.org.uk/isleofwight

Great for kids: Dinosaur Isle, SANDOWN, PO36 8QA, 01983 404344
www.dinosaurisle.com

Old Barn Touring Park

▶▶▶▶ 79%

tel: 01983 866414 **Cheverton Farm, Newport Rd, Apse Heath PO36 9PJ**
email: mail@oldbarntouring.co.uk
dir: On A3056 from Newport, site on left after Apse Heath rdbt. **grid ref:** SZ571833

A terraced site with several secluded camping areas that are divided by hedges. This site is well positioned for visiting the eastern side of the island, and customers can be sure of a warm welcome from the friendly staff. Rallies are very welcome. 5 acre site. 60 touring pitches. 9 hardstandings. 6 seasonal pitches. Caravan pitches. Motorhome pitches. Tent pitches.

Open: May-Sep **Last arrival:** 21.00hrs **Last departure:** noon
Pitches: ➝➝▲
Leisure: ⚲
Facilities: ⚲⚲⚲⚲⚲⚲⚲⚲⚲⚲⚲
Services: ⚲⚲⚲⚲⚲⚲⚲
Within 3 miles: ⚲⚲⚲⚲⚲⚲⚲⚲
Notes: Dogs must be kept on leads.
AA Pubs & Restaurants nearby: The Crab & Lobster Inn, BEMBRIDGE, PO35 5TR, 01983 872244

LEISURE: 🏊 Indoor pool 🏊 Outdoor pool ⚲ Children's playground ⚲ Kid's club ⚲ Tennis court ⚲ Games room ⚲ Golf course ⚲ Boat hire ⚲ Cycle hire ⚲ Cinema ⚲ Entertainment ⚲ Fishing ⚲ Mini golf ⚲ Pitch n putt ⚲ Watersports ⚲ Gym ⚲ Sports field ⚲ Stables **FACILITIES:** ⚲ Bath ⚲ Shower ⚲ Private washing cubicles ⚲ Electric shaver ⚲ Hairdryer ⚲ Ice Packs ⚲ Disabled facilities ⚲ Shop on site ⚲ Mobile shop ⚲ BBQ area ⚲ Picnic area ⚲ Wi-fi ⚲ Internet access ⚲ Recycling ⚲ Tourist info ⚲ Dog exercise area ⚲ Car hire can be arranged

SHANKLIN

Map 5 SZ58

Places to visit

Shanklin Chine, SHANKLIN, PO37 6PF, 01983 866432 www.shanklinchine.co.uk

Ventnor Botanic Garden, VENTNOR, PO38 1UL, 01983 855397 www.botanic.co.uk

Great for kids: Dinosaur Isle, SANDOWN, PO36 8QA, 01983 404344 www.dinosaurisle.com

Ninham Country Holidays

▶▶▶▶ 86%

tel: 01983 864243 **Ninham PO37 7PL**
email: office@ninham-holidays.co.uk **web:** www.ninham-holidays.co.uk
dir: *Signed from A3056 Newport to Sandown road.* **grid ref:** *SZ573825*

Enjoying a lofty rural location with fine country views, this delightful, spacious park occupies two separate, well-maintained areas in a country park setting near the sea and beach. It has an excellent toilet and shower block in The Orchards that has a good layout of pitches; there is also a good outdoor pool, a games room and an excellent children's play area. Willow Bank is a separate camping area that

provides more basic, but adequate, facilities, which is used for rallies, events or as an overflow area when very busy. There are also static holiday homes for hire. 12 acre site. 135 touring pitches. Caravan pitches. Motorhome pitches. Tent pitches. 6 statics.

Ninham Country Holidays

Open: May-Sep **Last arrival:** 20.00hrs (late night arrival area available)
Last departure: 10.00hrs

Pitches: 🚐 🚌 ▲

Leisure: 🏊 /⚲\ 🎱 🎣 ✎

Facilities: 🐾 🅿 ⊙ 🍴 ❅ 占 🛒 WiFi ♻ 🛈 🎁

Services: 🔌 🅾 🫗 ⊘ 🍴 🛒 ⬆

Within 3 miles: 占 🚤 ✎ ◎ 🏊 🅢 🅾 ∪

Notes: PayPal accepted. Swimming pool & coarse fishing rules apply. Dogs must be kept on leads.

AA Pubs & Restaurants nearby: The Bonchurch Inn, BONCHURCH, PO38 1NU, 01983 852611

The Taverners, GODSHILL, PO38 3HZ, 01983 840707

See advert below

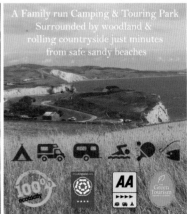
PITCHES: 🚐 Caravans 🚌 Motorhomes ▲ Tents 🏠 Glamping accommodation **SERVICES:** 🔌 Electric hook up 🅾 Launderette 🍴 Licensed bar 🔋 Calor Gas ⊘ Camping Gaz ⊤ Toilet fluid 🍴 Café/Restaurant 🛒 Fast Food/Takeaway ⬆ Battery charging 🍼 Baby care ⬆ Motorvan service point
ABBREVIATIONS: BHs – bank holidays Etr – Easter Spring BH – Spring Bank Holiday fr – from hrs – hours m – mile mdnt – midnight
rdbt – roundabout rs – restricted service wk – week wknd – weekend x-roads – crossroads 🚫 No credit or debit cards 🚫 No dogs

TOTLAND BAY — Map 5 SZ38

Places to visit

Dimbola Lodge Museum, FRESHWATER, PO40 9QE, 01983 756814 www.dimbola.co.uk

Mottistone Gardens, MOTTISTONE, PO30 4ED, 01983 741302 www.nationaltrust.org.uk/isleofwight

Great for kids: Yarmouth Castle, YARMOUTH, PO41 0PB, 01983 760678 www.english-heritage.org.uk/daysout/properties/yarmouth-castle

Stoats Farm Caravan & Camping

►►►78%

tel: 01983 755258 & 753416 **PO39 0HE**
email: bookings@stoats-farm.co.uk
dir: *0.75m S of Totland. NB It is advisable for caravans & motorhomes to approach via Moons Hill (do not approach via Weston Ln which is narrow).* **grid ref:** *SZ324865*

A friendly, personally run site in a quiet country setting close to Alum Bay, Tennyson Down and The Needles. It has good laundry and shower facilities, and the shop, although small, is well stocked. Popular with families, walkers and cyclists, it makes the perfect base for campers wishing to explore this part of the island. 10 acre site. 100 touring pitches. Caravan pitches. Motorhome pitches. Tent pitches.

Open: Apr-Oct

Pitches: 🚐 🚌 ⛺

Facilities: 🚿 ⊙ 💨 ❄ ♿ [S] 🐕 ℹ

Services: 🔌 🧺 🌿 🛏 🗑

Within 3 miles: ⛳ ⛵ 🎣 ◎ 🏄 [S] 🧺 🐴

Notes: No loud noise after 23.00hrs, no camp fires. Dogs must be kept on leads. Campers' fridge available.

AA Pubs & Restaurants nearby: The Red Lion, FRESHWATER, PO40 9BP, 01983 754925

WHITECLIFF BAY — Map 5 SZ68

Places to visit

Bembridge Windmill, BEMBRIDGE, PO35 5SQ, 01983 873945 www.nationaltrust.org.uk/isleofwight

Nunwell House & Gardens, BRADING, PO36 0JQ, 01983 407240

Great for kids: Lilliput Antique Doll & Toy Museum, BRADING, PO36 0DJ, 01983 407231 www.lilliputmuseum.co.uk

Whitecliff Bay Holiday Park

HOLIDAY CENTRE 89%

DAVID BELLAMY CONSERVATION AWARD GOLD

tel: 01983 872671 **Hillway Rd, Bembridge PO35 5PL**
email: holiday.sales@away-resorts.com
dir: *1m S of Bembridge, signed from B3395 in village.* **grid ref:** *SZ637862*

This is a large seaside complex on two sites, with camping on one and self-catering chalets and statics on the other. There is an indoor pool with flume and spa pool, and an outdoor pool with a kiddies' pool, a family entertainment club, and plenty of traditional on-site activities including crazy golf and table tennis, plus an indoor soft play area, a restaurant and a choice of bars. Activities include a My Active programme for all the family in partnership with Fit4Life. There is access to a secluded beach from the park. The glamping area offers fully-equipped Canvas Cottages for up to eight people (with heating and TV; two have a cedar barrel hot tub); 12 equipped bell tents and three vintage caravans. 49 acre site. 400 touring pitches. 50 hardstandings. 400 seasonal pitches. Caravan pitches. Motorhome pitches. Tent pitches. 227 statics.

Open: all year (rs Off-peak season facilities reduced) **Last arrival:** flexible
Last departure: 10.00hrs

Pitches: 🚐 🚌 ⛺ 🏕

Leisure: 🏊 🌊 🛝 👋 ⚽ 🏌 🎱 🎵 🚲

Facilities: 🚿 [P] ⊙ 💨 ❄ ♿ [S] 🧺 🐕 [WiFi] 💻 ♻ ℹ

Services: 🔌 🧺 🍷 🔒 🌿 [T] 🍴 🛏 🛒 🗑

Glamping: Bell tents 12, Changeover day Mon, Fri, Sat Min stay 3 nights Car by unit **Vintage Caravans** 3, Changeover day Mon, Fri, Sat Min stay 3 nights Own kitchen Car by unit **Canvas cottages:** 11, Changeover day Mon, Fri, Sat Min stay 3 nights Car by unit

Within 3 miles: ⛳ ⛵ 🎣 ◎ 🏄 [S] 🧺 🐴

Notes: Adults & families only. Dogs must be kept on leads. Sauna, sports TV lounge, outdoor cinema.

AA Pubs & Restaurants nearby: The Crab & Lobster Inn, BEMBRIDGE, PO35 5TR, 01983 872244

LEISURE: 🏊 Indoor pool 🌊 Outdoor pool 🛝 Children's playground 👋 Kid's club 🎾 Tennis court 🎱 Games room ⛳ Golf course ⛵ Boat hire 🚲 Cycle hire 🎬 Cinema 🎵 Entertainment 🎣 Fishing ◎ Mini golf 🏌 Pitch n putt 🏄 Watersports 🏋 Gym ⚽ Sports field 🐴 Stables **FACILITIES:** 🛁 Bath 🚿 Shower [P] Private washing cubicles ⊙ Electric shaver 💨 Hairdryer ❄ Ice Packs ♿ Disabled facilities [S] Shop on site 🚚 Mobile shop 🍖 BBQ area 🧺 Picnic area [WiFi] Wi-fi 💻 Internet access ♻ Recycling ℹ Tourist info 🐕 Dog exercise area 🚗 Car hire can be arranged

WOOTTON BRIDGE
Map 5 SZ59

Places to visit

Osborne House, OSBORNE HOUSE, PO32 6JX, 01983 200022
www.english-heritage.org.uk/daysout/properties/osborne

Carisbrooke Castle, CARISBROOKE, PO30 1XY, 01983 522107
www.english-heritage.org.uk/daysout/properties/carisbrooke-castle

Great for kids: Robin Hill Country Park, ARRETON, PO30 2NU, 01983 527352
www.robin-hill.com

Kite Hill Farm Caravan & Camping Park
▶▶▶87%

tel: 01983 883261 **Firestone Copse Rd PO33 4LE**
email: welcome@kitehillfarm.co.uk **web:** www.kitehillfarm.co.uk
dir: *Signed from A3054 at Wootton Bridge, between Ryde & Newport.* **grid ref:** *SZ549906*

The park, on a gently sloping field, is tucked away behind the owners' farm, just a short walk from the village and attractive river estuary. The facilities are excellent and very clean, and even include a defibrulator at reception. This park provides a pleasant relaxing atmosphere for a stay on the island and is well located for visiting Cowes. Rallies are welcome. 12.5 acre site. 50 touring pitches. Caravan pitches. Motorhome pitches. Tent pitches.

Open: all year **Last arrival:** anytime **Last departure:** noon

Pitches: 🚐 £15-£18.50 🚎 £15-£18.50 ▲ £15-£18.50

Leisure: ⚑

Facilities: ♠☉❉❉ ⛟ ✿ ❂ ❢

Services: 🚐🔲 ⊘ 🔋

Within 3 miles: 🏂 ⚓ 🎡 ✎ ◎ ⬆️ 🛝 🟦 ⛴ ∪

Notes: Owners must clean up after their pets. Dogs must be kept on leads.

AA Pubs & Restaurants nearby: The Folly, WHIPPINGHAM, PO32 6NB, 01983 297171

Duke of York Inn, COWES, PO31 7BT, 01983 295171

WROXALL
Map 5 SZ57

Places to visit

Appuldurcombe House, WROXALL, PO38 3EW, 01983 852484
www.english-heritage.org.uk/daysout/properties/appuldurcombe-house

Great for kids: Blackgang Chine - Land of Imagination, BLACKGANG, PO38 2HN, 01983 730330 www.blackgangchine.com

PREMIER PARK

Appuldurcombe Gardens Holiday Park
▶▶▶▶▶ 92%

tel: 01983 852597 **Appuldurcombe Rd PO38 3EP**
email: info@appuldurcombegardens.co.uk **web:** www.appuldurcombegardens.co.uk
dir: *From Newport take A3020 towards Shanklin & Ventnor. Through Rookley & Godshill. Right at Whiteley Bank rdbt towards Wroxall village, then follow brown signs.*
grid ref: *SZ546804*

This well-appointed park is set in a unique setting fairly close to the town of Ventnor. It has modern and smart facilities including a spotless toilet and shower block, and a very tasteful lounge bar and function room. There is an excellent, screened outdoor pool and paddling pool (completely upgraded for 2016), and this area, replete with café and shop, is the focal point of the park. It has the added advantage of being away from the camping areas making it a fun area without impacting on the peaceful camping areas. All pitches have electric hook-up. The site is close to cycle routes and is only 150 yards from the bus stop, making it perfect for those with a motorhome or those not wanting to use their car. There is secure cycle storage plus a free-standing cycle work station, great for pumping tyres up or making adjustments to your bike. Static caravans and apartments are also available for hire. 14 acre site. 130 touring pitches. 40 hardstandings. Caravan pitches. Motorhome pitches. Tent pitches. 40 statics.

Open: Mar-Nov **Last arrival:** 21.00hrs **Last departure:** 11.00hrs

Pitches: * 🚐 £17.95-£33.95 🚎 £17.95-£33.95 ▲ £17.95-£33.95

Leisure: ⇌ ⚑ ❋ Facilities: ⛟ ♠☉⅌❉❉⛟🔆🔲 ₩ⁱᶠⁱ ❂ ❢ 🎄

Services: 🚐🔲 🐟⊘ T 🍴 🔋 👶 ⬆️ **Within 3 miles:** 🏂 ⚓ 🎡 ✎ ◎ ⬆️ 🛝 🟦 ⛴ ∪

Notes: No skateboards. Dogs must be kept on leads. Entertainment in high season only.

YARMOUTH

See Newbridge

KENT

ASHFORD
Map 7 TR04

Places to visit
Kent & East Sussex Railway, TENTERDEN, TN30 6HE, 01580 765155
www.kesr.org.uk

Great for kids: Port Lympne Wild Animal Park, LYMPNE, CT21 4LR,
0844 842 4647 *(Calls cost 7p per minute plus your phone company's access charge)*
www.aspinallfoundation.org/portlympne

PREMIER PARK

Broadhembury Caravan & Camping Park
▶▶▶▶▶ 88%

Best of British

tel: 01233 620859 **Steeds Ln, Kingsnorth TN26 1NQ**
email: holidaypark@broadhembury.co.uk **web:** www.broadhembury.co.uk
dir: *M20 junct 10, A2070 towards Brenzett. Straight on at 1st rdbt. Left at 2nd rdbt
(avoid fork left). Straight on at next rdbt. Left at 2nd x-roads in village.*
grid ref: TR009387

A well-run and well-maintained small family park surrounded by open pasture;
it is neatly landscaped with pitches sheltered by mature hedges. There is a well-
equipped campers' kitchen adjacent to the spotless toilet facilities and children
will love the play areas, games room and football pitch. The adults-only area,
close to the excellent reception building, includes popular fully serviced
hardstanding pitches; this area has its own first-class, solar heated toilet block.
10 acre site. 110 touring pitches. 20 hardstandings. Caravan pitches.
Motorhome pitches. Tent pitches. 25 statics.

Open: all year **Last arrival:** 21.00hrs (late arrivals to use designated area)
Last departure: noon

Pitches: * 🚐 £20-£32 🚌 £20-£32 ▲ £16-£20

Leisure: 🅰 ☺ 🎱

Facilities: 🚿 🏠 Ⓟ ⊙ ☂ ✳ ⚿ ᔥ ⌕ WIFI 🖥 ♻ 🛈 🚲

Services: 🚐 🔋 🔒 🧺 ⌖ T 🛒 ⌄

Within 3 miles: ↨ 🎏 ✎ ⓪ ᔥ 🕳 Ụ

Notes: No noise after 22.00hrs. Dogs must be kept on leads.

AYLESFORD
Map 6

Places to visit
Aylesford Priory, AYLESFORD, ME20 7BX, 01622 717272 www.thefriars.org.uk

Kits Coty Glamping
NEW ▶▶▶▶▶ 86%

tel: 01634 685862 **84 Collingwood Rd, Kits Coty Estate ME20 7ER**
email: info@kitscotyglamping.co.uk
dir: *M2 junct 3, A229 towards Maidstone, follow Eccles & Burham signs. Under
motorway bridge, 1st right signed Kits Coty Estate. 1st left into Salisbury Rd (before
joining M2). 2nd left into Beresford Rd. Right at T-junct to site at end.*
grid ref: TQ743613

Established in a lush paddock opposite the owners house, Kits Coty Glamping is
located in glorious countryside between Maidstone and Chatham, with far-
reaching views. The well landscaped paddock is home to a shepherd's hut
(traditionally decorated and with a double bed and log-burning stove) and three
spacious bell tents. Careful thought has been given to the space between the
units and the attention to detail is excellent, as is the customer care from
hands-on owners Ami and Mark, who are passionate about their unique
glamping patch. The spacious bell tents (Festival & Marrakesh; plus Marmadou
that sleeps just two) have quality mattresses, chest of drawers, electric lighting
and stove, Egyptian cotton sheets, cosy duvets, throws and blankets. Each unit
has a decked area outside, with chairs, a picnic bench and rustic log seats
around a brazier. The facility cabin houses a well-equipped washing up area
that also contains every conceivable cooking utensil plus a fridge and freezer,
kettle, microwave and toaster. There are also two spacious fully serviced wet
rooms with big showers, posh toiletries, underfloor heating and quirky decor, and
two extra toilet and washbasin cubicles. There's a great outdoor space for ball
games in a separate paddock, which also contains the communal eating area,
chill-out room and a large fire pit. 1 acre site.

Open: Apr-Sep **Last arrival:** 22.00hrs **Last departure:** 10.30hrs

Glamping: Bell tents 3, £85-£180 Min stay 1 night **Shepherd's Huts** 1, £85-£180
Min stay 4 nights

DETLING
Map 7 TQ75

Scragged Oak Caravan Park
▶▶▶ 84%

tel: 01622 631298 **Scragged Oak Rd ME14 3HB**
email: bookings@scraggedoak.co.uk
dir: *From M20 junct 7, A429 towards Ramsgate. After Detling left signed Bredhurst into
Scragged Oak Rd.* **grid ref:** TQ806578

Situated on top of the North Downs, adjacent to the Kent Showground, this peaceful
park has a smart toilet block and provides a handy overnight stop for the ferries
and Channel Tunnel. The experienced and enthusiastic wardens have positive plans
to gradually improve the park. 6 acre site. 80 touring pitches. 14 hardstandings.
Caravan pitches. Motorhome pitches. Tent pitches.

Open: Mar-Oct **Last arrival:** 22.00hrs **Last departure:** noon

Pitches: 🚐 🚌 ▲

Facilities: 🏠 Ⓟ ⊙ ☂ ✳ ⚿ ᔥ ⌕ WIFI ♻ 🛈

Services: 🚐 🔋 🔒 🧺 T 🛒 ⌄

Within 3 miles: ✎ ᔥ

Notes: No unaccompanied children in toilet block, no noise after 22.30hrs, no gazebos, no wood burning. Dogs must be kept on leads. Freshly baked bread, croissants & sausage rolls available.

FOLKESTONE
Map 7 TR23

Places to visit

Dymchurch Martello Tower, DYMCHURCH, CT16 1HU, 01304 211067
www.english-heritage.org.uk/daysout/properties/dymchurch-martello-tower

Dover Castle & Secret Wartime Tunnels, DOVER, CT16 1HU, 01304 211067
www.english-heritage.org.uk/daysout/properties/dover-castle

Great for kids: Port Lympne Wild Animal Park, LYMPNE, CT21 4LR, 0844 842 4647 (Calls cost 7p per minute plus your phone company's access charge) www.aspinallfoundation.org/portlympne

Little Switzerland Camping & Caravan Site
►►77%

tel: 01303 252168 **Wear Bay Rd CT19 6PS**
email: btony328@aol.com
dir: M20 junct 13, A259 (Folkestone Harbour). At 2nd rdbt follow brown Country Park sign (A260). Right at next rdbt (Country Park). 8th left into Swiss Way, site signed.
grid ref: TR248380

Set on a narrow plateau below the White Cliffs and above The Warren, this unique site offers sheltered, traditional camping in secluded dells and enjoys fine views across the English Channel to the French coast — probably best enjoyed from the grassy alfresco area at the popular café. The toilet facilities are basic and unsuitable for disabled visitors. 3 acre site. 32 touring pitches. Caravan pitches. Motorhome pitches. Tent pitches. 13 statics.

Open: Mar-Oct **Last arrival:** mdnt **Last departure:** noon

Pitches: 🚐 🚍 ⛺

Facilities: ⊙ ✳ 🛒 WiFi 🖥 ♻ ✪

Services: 🔌 🗑 🚽 🔒 ⊘ T 🍽 🔋 🎕 ♨

Within 3 miles: 🔆 🚣 🎿 ♒ 🏧 ♨ 🛍 🗑 ∪

Notes: 🐾 No open fires, no noise after 22.30hrs. Dogs must be kept on leads.

AA Pubs & Restaurants nearby: Rocksalt Rooms, FOLKESTONE, CT19 6NN, 01303 212070

LEYSDOWN-ON-SEA
Map 7 TR07

Priory Hill
►►►71%

tel: 01795 510267 **Wing Rd ME12 4QT**
email: touringpark@prioryhill.co.uk
dir: M2 junct 5, A249 signed Sheerness, then A2500 to Eastchurch, then B2231 to Leysdown, follow brown tourist signs. **grid ref:** TR038704

A small well-maintained touring area on an established family-run holiday park close to the sea, with views of the north Kent coast. Amenities include a clubhouse and a swimming pool. The pitch price includes membership of the clubhouse with live entertainment, and use of the indoor swimming pool. 1.5 acre site. 34 touring pitches. Caravan pitches. Motorhome pitches. Tent pitches.

Open: Mar-Oct (rs Low season - shorter opening times for pool & club)
Last arrival: 18.00hrs **Last departure:** noon

Pitches: 🚐 🚍 ⛺

Leisure: 🏊 ⚽ 🎱

Facilities: ⊙ 🛒 ✳ ♿ 🔆 🛒 WiFi ♻ ✪

Services: 🔌 🗑 🚽 🔒 🍽 ♨

Within 3 miles: ♒ ◎ 🛍 🗑

Notes: Dogs must be kept on leads.

AA Pubs & Restaurants nearby: The Ferry House Inn, LEYSDOWN-ON-SEA, ME12 4BQ, 01795 510214

MARDEN
Map 6 TQ74

Places to visit

Finchcocks Musical Museum, GOUDHURST, TN17 1HH, 01580 211702
www.finchcocks.co.uk

Scotney Castle, LAMBERHURST, TN3 8JN, 01892 893868
www.nationaltrust.org.uk/scotneycastle

PREMIER PARK

Tanner Farm Touring Caravan & Camping Park
►►►►►89%

tel: 01622 832399 **Tanner Farm, Goudhurst Rd TN12 9ND**
email: enquiries@tannerfarmpark.co.uk
dir: From A21 or A229 onto B2079. Midway between Marden & Goudhurst.
grid ref: TQ732415

At the heart of a 150-acre Wealden farm, this extensive, long-established touring park is peacefully tucked away down a quiet farm drive deep in unspoilt Kent countryside, yet close to Sissinghurst Castle and within easy reach of London (Marden station is three miles away). Perfect for families, as it has farm animals, two excellent play areas and a recreation/wet weather room (with TV); it offers quality toilet blocks with privacy cubicles, a good shop, spacious hardstandings (12 fully serviced), and high levels of security and customer care. Two camping pods are available. 15 acre site. 120 touring pitches. 34 hardstandings. 11 seasonal pitches. Caravan pitches. Motorhome pitches. Tent pitches.

Open: all year **Last arrival:** 20.00hrs **Last departure:** noon

Pitches: * 🚐 £15.90-£29.95 🚍 £15.90-£29.95 ⛺ £21.40-£29.95 🏕 prices shown below

Leisure: 🎠 ⚽ 🎱

Facilities: 🐕 🅿 ⊙ 🛒 ✳ ♿ 🔆 🛒 WiFi ♻ ✪

Services: 🔌 🗑 🔒 ⊘ T ♨

Glamping: Wooden Pods 2, £27.50-£40 Min stay 2 nights at wknds (Fri, Sat & Sun) Car by unit

Within 3 miles: ♒ 🛍 🗑

Notes: No groups, 1 car per pitch, no commercial vehicles. Dogs must be kept on leads.

AA Pubs & Restaurants nearby: The Bull Inn, LINTON, ME17 4AW, 01622 743612

The Star & Eagle, GOUDHURST, TN17 1AL, 01580 211512

Green Cross Inn, GOUDHURST, TN17 1HA, 01580 211200

PITCHES: 🚐 Caravans 🚍 Motorhomes ⛺ Tents 🏕 Glamping accommodation **SERVICES:** 🔌 Electric hook up 🗑 Launderette 🚽 Licensed bar 🔒 Calor Gas ⊘ Camping Gaz T Toilet fluid 🍽 Café/Restaurant 🎕 Fast Food/Takeaway 🔋 Battery charging ♨ Baby care ♨ Motorvan service point
ABBREVIATIONS: BHs – bank holidays Etr – Easter Spring BH – Spring Bank Holiday fr – from hrs – hours m – mile mdnt – midnight rdbt – roundabout rs – restricted service wk – week wknd – weekend x-roads – crossroads ♨ No credit or debit cards 🐾 No dogs

ROCHESTER
Map 6 TQ76

Places to visit

Guildhall Museum, ROCHESTER, ME1 1PY, 01634 332900
www.guildhallmuseumrochester.co.uk

Upnor Castle, UPNOR, ME2 4XG, 01634 718742
www.english-heritage.org.uk/daysout/properties/upnor-castle

Great for kids: Diggerland, STROOD, ME2 2NU, 0871 227 7007 *(Calls cost 10p per minute plus your phone company's access charge)* www.diggerland.com

Allhallows Holiday Park
HOLIDAY HOME PARK 82%

GOLD

tel: 01634 270385 **Allhallows-on-Sea ME3 9QD**
email: allhallows@haven.com **web:** www.haven.com/allhallows
dir: *M25 junct 2, A2 signed Rochester, A289 signed Gillingham. A228 signed Grain. Follow site signs.* **grid ref:** *TQ841784*

Located in a peaceful country park setting close to Rochester, Allhallows is a static-only holiday park offering a wide range of sporting and leisure activities for all the family, including swimming pools, tennis courts, coarse fishing, a 9-hole golf course and fencing. Children will love the kids' club and play area, while there is a restaurant and bar with evening entertainment for adults.

Open: Mar-Oct

Changeover day: Mon, Fri, Sat

Arrival and departure times: Please contact the site

Statics: 93 Sleeps 6-8 Bedrms 2-3 Bathrms 1-2 Toilets 1-2 Dishwasher Microwave Freezer TV Sky/FTV Elec inc Gas inc Grass area

Children: ⚑ Cots inc Highchair **Dogs:** 2 on leads No dangerous dogs

Leisure: ≋ ≋ ⚲ ∪ ℘ Cycle hire 🖐 ⚠

ST NICHOLAS AT WADE
Map 7 TR26

Places to visit

Reculver Towers & Roman Fort, RECULVER, CT6 6SU, 01227 740676
www.english-heritage.org.uk/daysout/properties/reculver-towers-and-roman-fort

Great for kids: Richborough Roman Fort & Amphitheatre, RICHBOROUGH, CT13 9JW, 01304 612013 www.english-heritage.org.uk/daysout/properties/richborough-roman-fort-and-amphitheatre

St Nicholas Camping Site
►►78%

tel: 01843 847245 **Court Rd CT7 0NH**
web: www.stnicholascampingsite.co.uk
dir: *Signed from A299 & A28, site at W end of village near church.* **grid ref:** *TR254672*

A gently-sloping field with mature hedging, on the edge of the village close to the shop. This pretty site offers good facilities, including a family/disabled room, and is conveniently located close to primary routes and the north Kent coast. 3 acre site. 75 touring pitches. 6 seasonal pitches. Caravan pitches. Motorhome pitches. Tent pitches.

Open: Etr-Oct **Last arrival:** 22.00hrs **Last departure:** 14.00hrs

Pitches: * ⊞ £21-£25 ⊞ £20-£23 ▲ £20-£25

Leisure: ⚠

Facilities: 🛁 ⊙ ℘ ✳ & 🐕 ❶

Services: 🔌 🛢 ⌀ Ⓣ

Within 3 miles: ℘ 🛒 ∪

Notes: 🔇 No music after 22.30hrs. Dogs must be kept on leads. Baby changing area.

WHITSTABLE
Map 7 TR16

Places to visit

Canterbury Westgate Towers Museum, CANTERBURY, CT1 2BZ, 01227 458629
www.onepoundlane.co.uk

The Canterbury Tales, CANTERBURY, CT1 2TG, 01227 479227
www.canterburytales.org.uk

Great for kids: Druidstone Park, CANTERBURY, CT2 9JR, 01227 765168
www.druidstone.net

Homing Park
▶▶▶▶84%

tel: 01227 771777 **Church Ln, Seasalter CT5 4BU**
email: info@homingpark.co.uk
dir: Exit A299 for Whitstable & Canterbury, left at brown camping-caravan sign into Church Ln. Site entrance has 2 large flag poles. **grid ref:** TR095645

A small touring park close to Seasalter Beach and Whitstable, which is famous for its oysters. All pitches are generously sized and fully serviced, and most are separated by hedging and shrubs. A clubhouse and swimming pool are available on site with a small cost for the use of the swimming pool. Wooden camping pods, for four or six people, are available for hire; their outwardly sloping walls adds to the internal space. 12.6 acre site. 43 touring pitches. Caravan pitches. Motorhome pitches. Tent pitches. 195 statics.

Open: Etr-Oct **Last arrival:** 20.00hrs **Last departure:** 11.00hrs

Pitches: * 🚐 £21-£33 🚍 £21-£33 ⛺ £21-£33 🛖 prices shown below

Leisure: 🏊 🎱 ♨

Facilities: 🔦 🅿 ⊙ ℐ ✳ ♿ 📶 ♻ ❓

Services: 🔌 🔲 🍴 🛢 🗑 🍽

Glamping: Wooden Pods 3, £38-£52 Changeover day Any day Min stay 2 nights
Car by unit

Within 3 miles: 🎣 🍴 ℐ 🏊 🛒 🗑 ∪

Notes: No commercial vehicles, no tents larger than 8 berths or 5mtrs wide, no unaccompanied minors, no cycles or scooters. Dogs must be kept on leads.

AA Pubs & Restaurants nearby: The Sportsman, WHITSTABLE, CT5 4BP, 01227 273370

Prefer a child-free site?
See our list on page 45

WROTHAM HEATH

Places to visit

Ightham Mote, IGHTHAM, TN15 0NT, 01732 810378 www.nationaltrust.org.uk

St Leonard's Tower, WEST MALLING, ME19 6PE, 01732 870872
www.english-heritage.org.uk/daysout/properties/st-leonards-tower

Great for kids: Kent Life, MAIDSTONE, ME14 3AU, 01622 763936
www.kentlife.org.uk

Gate House Wood Touring Park
▶▶▶80%

tel: 01732 843062 **Ford Ln TN15 7SD**
email: contact@gatehousewoodtouringpark.com
web: www.gatehousewoodtouringpark.com
dir: M26 junct 2a, A20 S towards Maidstone, through lights at Wrotham Heath. 1st left signed Trottiscliffe, left at next junct into Ford Ln. Site 100yds on left. **grid ref:** TQ635585

A well-sheltered and mature site in a former quarry surrounded by tall deciduous trees and gorse banks. The well-designed facilities include a reception, shop and smart toilets, 11 hardstandings, and there is good entrance security and high levels of customer care. The colourful flower beds and hanging baskets are impressive and give a positive first impression. Conveniently placed for the M20 and M25 and a fast rail link to central London. 3.5 acre site. 55 touring pitches. Caravan pitches. Motorhome pitches. Tent pitches.

Open: Mar-Oct **Last arrival:** 21.00hrs **Last departure:** noon

Pitches: 🚐 🚍 ⛺

Leisure: ⅍

Facilities: 🔦 ⊙ ℐ ✳ ♿ 🅂 📶 ♻ ❓

Services: 🔌 🔲 🛢 🗑 Ⓣ 🔧

Within 3 miles: 🎣 🍴 ℐ 🏊 🛒 ∪

Notes: No commercial vehicles, no noise after 23.00hrs, no camp fires, soft balls only. Dogs must be kept on leads. Fresh bread & newspapers to order at peak times only.

AA Pubs & Restaurants nearby: The Bull, WROTHAM, TN15 7RF, 01732 789800

LANCASHIRE

See also sites under Greater Manchester & Merseyside

BLACKPOOL
Map 18 SD33

See also Lytham St Annes & Thornton

Places to visit

Blackpool Zoo, BLACKPOOL, FY3 8PP, 01253 830830 www.blackpoolzoo.org.uk

Marton Mere Holiday Village
HOLIDAY CENTRE 88%

GOLD

tel: 01253 767544 **Mythop Rd FY4 4XN**
email: martonmere@haven.com **web:** www.haven.com/martonmere
dir: M55 junct 4, A583 towards Blackpool. Right at Clifton Arms lights into Mythop Rd. Site 150yds on left. **grid ref:** SD347349

A very attractive holiday centre in an unusual setting on the edge of the mere, with plenty of birdlife to be spotted. The site has a stylish Mediterranean seaside-themed Boathouse Restaurant and the on-site entertainment is tailored for all ages, and includes a superb show bar. There's a regular bus service into Blackpool for those who want to explore further afield. The separate touring area is well equipped with hardstandings and electric pitches, and there are good quality facilities, including a superb amenities block. 30 acre site. 82 touring pitches. 82 hardstandings. Caravan pitches. Motorhome pitches. 700 statics.

Open: mid Mar-end Oct (rs Mar-end May & Sep-Oct reduced facilities, splash zone closed) **Last arrival:** 22.00hrs **Last departure:** 10.00hrs

Pitches: 🚐 🚑

Leisure: 🏊 ⚴ 🤚 🎵
Facilities: ☉ 🌡 ✳ ♿ 🚿 🚽 🛒 ♻ ❶
Services: 🚐 🗑 🍴 💧 🍽 🏪
Within 3 miles: 🎣 ♿ 🗓 ⛳ 🎡 🛶 🎿 🎱 🎢 ♨

Notes: No commercial vehicles, no bookings by persons under 21yrs unless a family booking, max 2 dogs per booking, certain dog breeds banned. Dogs must be kept on leads.

See advert on opposite page

Manor House Caravan Park
►►►► 82%

tel: 01253 764723 **Kitty Ln, Marton Moss FY4 5EG**
email: info@manorhousecaravanpark.co.uk
dir: At rdbt at end of M55 junct 4, take A5230 signed Sq Gate. At next rdbt take 3rd exit (Blackpool/Sq Gate/A5230). In 0.5m left at lights into Midgeland Rd. 500yds, straight on at x-roads. 250yds, right into Kitty Ln. 250yds site on right. (NB it is advisable not to follow Sat Nav). **grid ref:** SD336318

A sympathetically converted former small holding close to both Lytham St Annes and Blackpool, this peacefully located adults-only park is surrounded by high neat hedges and generous sized hardstanding pitches ensure optimum privacy. A warm welcome is assured by the resident owners and although there is no shop or launderette, both services are within a 10-minute drive. There are caravan pitches and motorhome pitches. Please note that tents are not accepted. 1 acre site. 10 touring pitches. 10 hardstandings. Caravan pitches. Motorhome pitches.

Open: Feb-Nov **Last arrival:** 20.00 (or dusk) **Last departure:** 11.30hrs

Pitches: 🚐 £21-£30 🚑 £21-£30

Facilities: 🚿 🚽 ♻ ❶
Services: 🚐 🖕
Within 3 miles: 🎣 🗓 ⛳ 🎡 🎿 🎱 🎢 ♨

Notes: Adults only. No ball games or loud music, pets accepted by prior arrangement only. Dogs must be kept on leads.

BOLTON-LE-SANDS

Places to visit

Lancaster Maritime Museum, LANCASTER, LA1 1RB, 01524 382264 www.lancashire.gov.uk/museums

Lancaster City Museum, LANCASTER, LA1 1HT, 01524 64637 www.lancashire.gov.uk/museums

Great for kids: Lancaster Castle, LANCASTER, LA1 1YJ, 01524 64998 www.lancastercastle.com

---

LEISURE: 🏊 Indoor pool 🏊 Outdoor pool 🛝 Children's playground 🤚 Kid's club 🎾 Tennis court 🎱 Games room ⛳ Golf course 🛶 Boat hire 🚲 Cycle hire 🎬 Cinema 🎵 Entertainment 🎣 Fishing 🏌 Mini golf 🏏 Pitch n putt 🎿 Watersports 💪 Gym ⚽ Sports field ♨ Stables **FACILITIES:** 🛁 Bath 🚿 Shower 🅿 Private washing cubicles ⚡ Electric shaver 🌡 Hairdryer ✳ Ice Packs ♿ Disabled facilities 🅂 Shop on site 🏪 Mobile shop 🍖 BBQ area 🪑 Picnic area 📶 Wi-fi 💻 Internet access ♻ Recycling ❶ Tourist info 🐾 Dog exercise area 🚗 Car hire can be arranged

BOLTON-LE-SANDS

Map 18 SD46

Bay View Holiday Park
►►►► 86%

tel: 01524 732854 & 701508 **LA5 9TN**
email: info@holgatesleisureparks.co.uk **web:** www.holgates.co.uk
dir: *M6 junct 25, A6 through Carnforth to Bolton-le-Sands. Site on right.*
grid ref: *SD478683*

A high quality, family-oriented seaside destination with fully serviced all-weather pitches, many of which have views of Morecambe Bay and the Cumbrian hills. A stylish bar/restaurant is just one of the park's amenities, and there is a wide range of activities and attractions on offer within a few miles. This makes a good choice for a family holiday by the sea; two family pods are available to hire. 10 acre site. 100 touring pitches. 50 hardstandings. 127 seasonal pitches. Caravan pitches. Motorhome pitches. Tent pitches. 100 statics.

Open: all year (rs Quiet periods – restaurant & bar reduced hours) **Last arrival:** 20.00hrs **Last departure:** noon

Pitches: * 🚐 £22.50-£28.50 🚐 £22.50-£28.50 ▲ £18-£21 🏕 prices shown below

Leisure: 🅰 ❄ 🎣

Facilities: 🏸 🅿 ⊙ ☼ ♿ 🖲 🚻 ⊣ 🐾 WiFi 🖥 ♻ 🛈 🎯

Services: 🔌 🖲 🍽 🧴 🚽 🍴 ♨ 🔋 🚼 ⚓

Glamping: Wooden Pods 2, £35-£45 Changeover day Sat Min stay 2 nights Car by unit No dogs

Within 3 miles: 🕹 🛶 🎯 🌊 🦮 🎱 ⛳ 🎮 ♻

Notes: No noise after 23.00hrs. Dogs must be kept on leads.

AA Pubs & Restaurants nearby: The Longlands Inn and Restaurant, CARNFORTH, LA6 1JH, 01524 781256

Hest Bank Inn, HEST BANK, LA2 6DN, 01524 824339

See advert on page 241

Red Bank Farm
►►► 80%

tel: 01524 823196 **LA5 8JR**
email: mark.archer@hotmail.co.uk
dir: *From Morecambe take A5015 towards Carnforth. After Hest Bank left into Pastures Ln (follow brown site sign). Over rail bridge, right (follow site sign). At T-junct left into The Shore to site at end.* grid ref: *SD472681*

A gently sloping grassy field with mature hedges, close to the sea shore and a RSPB reserve. This farm site has smart toilet facilities, a superb view across Morecambe Bay to the distant Lake District hills, and is popular with tenters. Archers Café serves a good range of cooked food, including home-reared marsh lamb dishes. 3 acre site. 60 touring pitches. Motorhome pitches. Tent pitches.

Open: Mar-Oct

Pitches: 🚐 ▲

Facilities: 🏸 ⊙ 🎯 ☼ ♻ 🛈

Services: 🔌 🖲 🍽

Within 3 miles: 🕹 🛶 🎯 🌊 ◎ ⛳ 🎱 ♻

Notes: No noise after 22.30hrs. Dogs must be kept on leads. Pets' corner.

AA Pubs & Restaurants nearby: The Longlands Inn and Restaurant, CARNFORTH, LA6 1JH, 01524 781256

Hest Bank Inn, HEST BANK, LA2 6DN, 01524 824339

PITCHES: 🚐 Caravans 🚐 Motorhomes ▲ Tents 🏕 Glamping accommodation **SERVICES:** 🔌 Electric hook up 🖲 Launderette 🍽 Licensed bar 🗋 Calor Gas 🔥 Camping Gaz T Toilet fluid 🍴 Café/Restaurant 🍟 Fast Food/Takeaway 🔋 Battery charging 🚼 Baby care ⚓ Motorvan service point
ABBREVIATIONS: BHs – bank holidays Etr – Easter Spring BH – Spring Bank Holiday fr – from hrs – hours m – mile mdnt – midnight rdbt – roundabout rs – restricted service wk – week wknd – weekend x-roads – crossroads ⊗ No credit or debit cards ⊗ No dogs

CAPERNWRAY · Map 18 SD57

Places to visit

Leighton Hall, CARNFORTH, LA5 9ST, 01524 734474 www.leightonhall.co.uk

RSPB Leighton Moss & Morecambe Bay Nature Reserve, SILVERDALE, LA5 0SW, 01524 701601 www.rspb.org.uk/leightonmoss

PREMIER PARK

Old Hall Caravan Park

▶▶▶▶▶ 85%

tel: 01524 733276 **LA6 1AD**
email: info@oldhallcaravanpark.co.uk
dir: *M6 junct 35, A601(M) follow signs for Over Kellet, at T-junct left onto B6254. In Over Kellet left at village green signed Capernwray. Site 1.5m on right.*
grid ref: *SD533716*

A lovely secluded park set in a clearing amongst trees at the end of a half-mile long drive. This peaceful park is home to a wide variety of wildlife, and there are marked walks in the woods. A pathway over a meandering brook through woodland separates the reception from the touring area. All pitches are fully serviced and a smart amenities block includes unisex showers with toilet and washbasin. The facilities are well maintained by the friendly owners, and booking is advisable. Please note, on Bank Holidays a minimum stay of three nights is required. 3 acre site. 38 touring pitches. 38 hardstandings. 30 seasonal pitches. Caravan pitches. Motorhome pitches. 260 statics.

Open: Mar-Oct (Nov-Jan seasonal tourers can stay longer by arrangement)
Last departure: noon

Pitches: * 🚐 fr £21 🚏 fr £21

Leisure: ⚞

Facilities: 🖌 🅿 ⊙ 🍴 👪 🚻 🌭 📶 🖳 ♻ ❼

Services: 🔌🗑 🛢 ⚗ ♨ ⚐

Within 3 miles: ⚓ 🎣 🎿 ⛷ 🏕 🛍 🔁 ♨

Notes: No skateboards, rollerblades or roller boots. Dogs must be kept on leads.
AA Pubs & Restaurants nearby: The Highwayman, BURROW, LA6 2RJ, 01524 273338

COCKERHAM

Places to visit

Lancaster Maritime Museum, LANCASTER, LA1 1RB, 01524 382264 www.lancashire.gov.uk/museums

Lancaster City Museum, LANCASTER, LA1 1HT, 01524 64637 www.lancashire.gov.uk/museums

Great for kids: Blackpool Zoo, BLACKPOOL, FY3 8PP, 01253 830830 www.blackpoolzoo.org.uk

COCKERHAM · Map 18 SD45

Moss Wood Caravan Park

▶▶▶▶ 87%

tel: 01524 791041 **Crimbles Ln LA2 0ES**
email: info@mosswood.co.uk
dir: *M6 junct 33, A6, approx 4m to site. From Cockerham take W A588. Left into Crimbles Lane to site.* grid ref: *SD456497*

A tree-lined grassy park with sheltered, level pitches, located on peaceful Cockerham Moss. A spacious air-conditioned licensed shop at the entrance stocks a variety of local produce including cheeses, smoked bacon and ales. The modern toilet block is attractively clad in stained wood, and the facilities include cubicle washing units and a launderette. 25 acre site. 25 touring pitches. 25 hardstandings. Caravan pitches. Motorhome pitches. Tent pitches. 143 statics.

Open: Mar-Oct **Last arrival:** 20.00hrs **Last departure:** 16.00hrs

Pitches: 🚐 🚏 🏕

Leisure: ⚽

Facilities: 🖌 🅿 ⊙ 🍴 👪 🌭 🚻 📶

Services: 🔌🗑 🛢 ⚗ ⚐

Within 3 miles: ⚓ 🎣 🛍 ♨

Notes: Dogs must be kept on leads. Woodland walks.

AA Pubs & Restaurants nearby: The Bay Horse Inn, FORTON, LA2 0HR, 01524 791204

CROSTON · Map 15 SD41

Places to visit

Harris Museum & Art Gallery, PRESTON, PR1 2PP, 01772 258248 www.harrismuseum.org.uk

Rufford Old Hall, RUFFORD, L40 1SG, 01704 821254 www.nationaltrust.org.uk/ruffordoldhall

Royal Umpire Caravan Park

▶▶▶ 85%

tel: 01772 600257 **Southport Rd PR26 9JB**
email: info@royalumpire.co.uk
dir: *From N: M6 junct 28 (from S: M6 junct 27), onto B5209, right onto B5250.*
grid ref: *SD504190*

A large park with tree- or hedge-lined bays for touring caravans and motorhomes, plus a large camping field in open countryside. There are many areas for children's activities and several pubs and restaurants within walking distance. Four camping pods are available for hire. 60 acre site. 195 touring pitches. 180 hardstandings. Caravan pitches. Motorhome pitches. Tent pitches.

Open: all year **Last arrival:** 20.00hrs **Last departure:** 16.00hrs

Pitches: * 🚐 £17-£35 🚏 £17-£35 🏕 £15-£25 🛖 prices shown below

Leisure: ⚞ ⚽

Facilities: 🖌 🅿 ⊙ 🍴 ❄ 👪 🌭 🚻 📶 ♻ ❼

Services: 🔌🗑 🛢 ⚗ ⚐

Glamping: Wooden Pods 4, £30-£45 Min stay 1 night Own kitchen Car by unit

Within 3 miles: ⚓ ⚓ 🎣 ⛷ 🛍 🔁 ♨

Notes: Dogs must be kept on leads.

LEISURE: 🏊 Indoor pool 🏊 Outdoor pool ⚞ Children's playground 🙋 Kid's club 🎾 Tennis court ♟ Games room ⛳ Golf course 🚣 Boat hire 🚲 Cycle hire 🎬 Cinema 🎵 Entertainment 🎣 Fishing ⛳ Mini golf 🏌 Pitch n putt 🏄 Watersports 🏋 Gym ⚽ Sports field ♨ Stables **FACILITIES:** 🛁 Bath 🖌 Shower 🅿 Private washing cubicles ⊙ Electric shaver 🍴 Hairdryer ❄ Ice Packs 👪 Disabled facilities 🛍 Shop on site 🚐 Mobile shop 🌭 BBQ area 🚻 Picnic area 📶 Wi-fi 🖳 Internet access ♻ Recycling ❼ Tourist info 🐕 Dog exercise area 🚗 Car hire can be arranged

FAR ARNSIDE   Map 18 SD47

Places to visit

Rufford Old Hall, RUFFORD, L40 1SG, 01704 821254
www.nationaltrust.org.uk/ruffordoldhall

RSPB Leighton Moss & Morecambe Bay Nature Reserve, SILVERDALE, LA5 0SW, 01524 701601 www.rspb.org.uk/leightonmoss

PREMIER PARK

Hollins Farm Camping & Caravanning
► ► ► ► 86%

GOLD

tel: 01524 701767 & 701508 **LA5 0SL**
email: reception@holgates.co.uk **web:** www.holgates.co.uk
dir: M6 junct 35, A601 (Carnforth). Left in 1m at rdbt to Carnforth. Right in 1m at lights signed Silverdale. Left in 1m into Sands Ln, signed Silverdale. 2.4m over auto-crossing, 0.3m to T-junct. Right, follow signs to site, in approx 3m take 2nd left after passing Holgates. **grid ref:** SD450764

Hollins Farm is a long established park that continues to be upgraded by the owners. There are 50 fully serviced hardstanding pitches for tourers and 25 fully serviced tent pitches; the excellent amenities block provides very good facilities and privacy options. It has a traditional family camping feel and offers high standard facilities; most pitches offer views towards Morecambe Bay. Two family pods (Daisy and Buttercup) are available for hire. The leisure and recreation facilities of the nearby, much larger, sister park (Silverdale Caravan Park) can be accessed by guests here. 30 acre site. 12 touring pitches. 12 hardstandings. 38 seasonal pitches. Caravan pitches. Motorhome pitches. Tent pitches.

Open: 14 Mar-7 Nov **Last arrival:** 20.00hrs **Last departure:** noon
Pitches: * 🚐 £33.50 🚍 £33.50 🅰 £33.50 🏕 prices shown below
Leisure: 🎠 🔍
Facilities: 🐾 Ⓟ ☺ ✳ ♿ ❼
Services: 🔌 🔾 🛢 🚿 ♿
Glamping: Wooden Pods 2, £40-£50 Changeover day Sat Min stay 4 nights
Within 3 miles: ⤵ 🏌 ◎ ⛵ 🛒 🎦 🔾 ∪
Notes: No unaccompanied children. Dogs must be kept on leads.

FLEETWOOD   Map 18 SD34

Places to visit

Blackpool Zoo, BLACKPOOL, FY3 8PP, 01253 830830 www.blackpoolzoo.org.uk

Cala Gran Holiday Park
HOLIDAY HOME PARK 85%

GOLD

tel: 01253 872555 **Fleetwood Rd FY7 8JY**
email: calagran@haven.com **web:** www.haven.com/calagran
dir: M55 junct 3, A585 signed Fleetwood. At 4th rdbt (Nautical College on left) take 3rd exit. Park 250yds on left. **grid ref:** SD330451

Cala Gran is a lively holiday park close to Blackpool with a range of quality holiday caravans and apartments. The park is all about fun, and the entertainment includes live music, comedy shows and resident DJs, while for children there are swimming pools and SplashZone, and a Pic 'n' Paint room.

Open: Mar-Oct **Changeover day:** Mon, Fri, Sat
Arrival and departure times: Please contact the site
Statics: 226 Sleeps 6-8 Bedrms 2-3 Bathrms 1-2 Toilets 1-2 Microwave Freezer TV Sky/FTV Elec inc Gas inc Grass area
Children: ⛹ Cots Highchair **Dogs:** 2 on leads No dangerous dogs
Leisure: 🚲 Cycle hire 🖐 🎠

GARSTANG   Map 18 SD44

Places to visit

Lancaster Maritime Museum, LANCASTER, LA1 1RB, 01524 382264 www.lancashire.gov.uk/museums

Lancaster City Museum, LANCASTER, LA1 1HT, 01524 64637 www.lancashire.gov.uk/museums

Great for kids: Lancaster Castle, LANCASTER, LA1 1YJ, 01524 64998 www.lancastercastle.com

Claylands Caravan Park
► ► ► ► 85%

tel: 01524 791242 **Cabus PR3 1AJ**
email: alan@claylands.com
dir: M6 junct 33, A6 towards Garstang, approx 6m, past Thorpy's chipshop, left into Weavers Lane. **grid ref:** SD496485

Colourful seasonal floral displays create an excellent first impression. A well-maintained site with lovely river and woodland walks and good views over the River Wyre towards the village of Scorton. This friendly park is set in delightful countryside where guests can enjoy fishing, the Stepping Stones Bar & Bisto, and the atmosphere is very relaxed. The quality facilities and amenities are of a high standard, and everything is immaculately maintained. 14 acre site. 30 touring pitches. 30 hardstandings. Caravan pitches. Motorhome pitches. Tent pitches. 68 statics.

Open: Mar-Jan **Last arrival:** 23.00hrs **Last departure:** noon **Pitches:** 🚐 🚍 🅰
Leisure: 🎵 **Facilities:** ☺ ✳ ♿ Ⓢ 🖐 🌳 📶 ♻ ❼
Services: 🔌 🔾 🍴 🚿 🅣 🍽 🚌 🔋 **Within 3 miles:** ⤵ 🎣 🏌 🛒 🎦 ∪
Notes: No rollerblades or skateboards. Dogs must be kept on leads.
AA Pubs & Restaurants nearby: Owd Nell's Tavern, BILSBORROW, PR3 0RS, 01995 640010

PITCHES: 🚐 Caravans 🚍 Motorhomes 🅰 Tents 🏕 Glamping accommodation **SERVICES:** 🔌 Electric hook up 🔾 Launderette 🍴 Licensed bar 🛢 Calor Gas 🚿 Camping Gaz 🅣 Toilet fluid 🍽 Café/Restaurant 🚌 Fast Food/Takeaway 🔋 Battery charging 👶 Baby care ♿ Motorvan service point **ABBREVIATIONS:** BHs – bank holidays Etr – Easter Spring BH – Spring Bank Holiday fr – from hrs – hours m – mile mdnt – midnight rdbt – roundabout rs – restricted service wk – week wknd – weekend x-roads – crossroads ⊗ No credit or debit cards ⊗ No dogs

GARSTANG *continued*

Bridge House Marina & Caravan Park
►►► 80%

tel: 01995 603207 **Nateby Crossing Ln, Nateby PR3 0JJ**
email: edwin@bridgehousemarina.co.uk
dir: *Exit A6 at pub & Knott End sign, immediately right into Nateby Crossing Ln, over canal bridge to site on left.* **grid ref:** *SD483457*

A well-maintained site in attractive countryside by the Lancaster Canal, with good views towards the Trough of Bowland. The boatyard atmosphere is interesting, and there is a good children's playground. 4 acre site. 50 touring pitches. 50 hardstandings. Caravan pitches. Motorhome pitches. 40 statics.

Open: Feb-Jan **Last arrival:** 22.00hrs **Last departure:** 13.00hrs

Pitches: 🚐 🚲

Facilities: ⊙ 🥄 🌳 ⚅ 🛁 Ⓢ 📶 ❶

Services: 🔌 🔋 🗑 ⊘ Ⓣ 🚮

Within 3 miles: ⚓ 🚣 ⚲ Ⓢ 🗒

Notes: Dogs must be kept on leads.

AA Pubs & Restaurants nearby: Owd Nell's Tavern, BILSBORROW, PR3 0RS, 01995 640010

LANCASTER

Places to visit

Lancaster Maritime Museum, LANCASTER, LA1 1RB, 01524 382264
www.lancashire.gov.uk/museums

Lancaster City Museum, LANCASTER, LA1 1HT, 01524 64637
www.lancashire.gov.uk/museums

Great for kids: Lancaster Castle, LANCASTER, LA1 1YJ, 01524 64998
www.lancastercastle.com

LANCASTER
Map 18 SD46

New Parkside Farm Caravan Park
►►► 83%

tel: 015247 70723 **Denny Beck, Caton Rd LA2 9HH**
email: enquiries@newparksidefarm.co.uk
dir: *M6 junct 34, A683 towards Caton & Kirkby Lonsdale. Site 1m on right.* **grid ref:** *SD507633*

A peaceful, friendly, grassy park on a working farm convenient for exploring the historic City of Lancaster and the delights of the Lune Valley. 4 acre site. 40 touring pitches. 40 hardstandings. Caravan pitches. Motorhome pitches. Tent pitches. 16 statics.

Open: Mar-Oct **Last arrival:** 20.00hrs **Last departure:** 16.00hrs

Pitches: * 🚐 £16-£18 🚲 £16-£18 ▲ £13-£15

Facilities: 🌳 ⊙ 🥄 ⚅ ♻ ❶

Services: 🔌 🛁 **Within 3 miles:** ⚓ 🎂 ⚲ Ⓢ 🗒

Notes: ⊘ No football. Dogs must be kept on leads.

AA Pubs & Restaurants nearby: The Sun Hotel and Bar, LANCASTER, LA1 1ET, 01524 66006

The White Cross, LANCASTER, LA1 4XT, 01524 33999

LONGRIDGE
Map 18 SD63

Places to visit

Brockholes Nature Reserve, SAMLESBURY, PR5 0AG, 01772 872000
www.brockholes.org

Beacon Fell View Holiday Park
HOLIDAY CENTRE 80%

tel: 01772 783233 **110 Higher Rd PR3 2TF**
email: beacon@hagansleisure.co.uk
dir: *At junct of Dilworth Rd (B6243) & King St in Longridge into Higher Rd. Site on right.* **grid ref:** *SD616380*

Located on the outskirts of Longridge with fine views of the surrounding fells, this long-established family holiday destination has a good range of all-weather attractions for both adults and children. In addition to holiday homes, the touring areas have good hardstanding pitches for caravans or motorhomes with electric hook-ups to all. 32 acre site. 79 touring pitches. 79 hardstandings. 25 seasonal pitches. Caravan pitches. Motorhome pitches. Tent pitches. 300 statics.

Open: Mar-11 Nov **Last arrival:** 22.00hrs **Last departure:** 11.00hrs

Pitches: 🚐 🚲 ▲

Leisure: 🏊 🎾 ⚆ 🖐 🎱 🎵

Facilities: 🌳 ⚅ Ⓢ 🔥 🛋 📶 🖥 ♻ ❶

Services: 🔌 🔋 🗑 🛁 🚮 🚿

Within 3 miles: ◎ Ⓢ 🗒

Notes: No cars by caravans or tents. Dogs must be kept on leads.

AA Pubs & Restaurants nearby: Derby Arms, LONGRIDGE, PR3 2NB, 01772 782370

LEISURE: 🏊 Indoor pool 🏊 Outdoor pool 🎢 Children's playground 👶 Kid's club 🎾 Tennis court 🎱 Games room ⛳ Golf course 🚣 Boat hire 🚲 Cycle hire 🎬 Cinema 🎵 Entertainment 🎣 Fishing ◎ Mini golf 🏌 Pitch n putt 🏄 Watersports 🏋 Gym 🏟 Sports field ♘ Stables **FACILITIES:** 🛁 Bath 🚿 Shower P Private washing cubicles ⊙ Electric shaver 🥄 Hairdryer ❄ Ice Packs ⚅ Disabled facilities Ⓢ Shop on site 🏪 Mobile shop 🔥 BBQ area 🪑 Picnic area 📶 Wi-fi 🖥 Internet access ♻ Recycling ❶ Tourist info 🐕 Dog exercise area 🚗 Car hire can be arranged

LYTHAM ST ANNES

Places to visit

Blackpool Zoo, BLACKPOOL, FY3 8PP, 01253 830830 www.blackpoolzoo.org.uk

LYTHAM ST ANNES Map 18 SD32

Eastham Hall Caravan Park

►►►► 82%

GOLD

tel: 01253 737907 **Saltcotes Rd FY8 4LS**
email: info@easthamhall.co.uk **web:** www.easthamhall.co.uk
dir: *M55 junct 3. Straight over 3 rdbts onto B5259. Through Wrea Green & Moss Side, site 1m after level crossing.* **grid ref:** *SD379291*

A large family-run park in a tranquil rural setting, surrounded by trees and mature shrubs. The pitch density is very good and some are fully serviced, plus the amenities blocks have been appointed to a high standard. Please note, this site does not accept tents. 30 acre site. 114 touring pitches. 114 hardstandings. 81 seasonal pitches. Caravan pitches. Motorhome pitches. 160 statics.

Eastham Hall Caravan Park

Open: Mar-Nov **Last arrival:** 20.00hrs **Last departure:** noon

Pitches: 🚐 🚌

Leisure: ⛹ ⚽

Facilities: 🚿 [P] ⊙ ⚙ ✲ ♿ [S] 🐕 [WiFi] ♻ ⓘ

Services: 🔌 [Ō] ⛽ ⛺ [T]

Within 3 miles: ⛳ ⚓ 🎾 ◎ ≋ [S] [Ō] U

Notes: No tents. Only breathable groundsheets permitted in awnings, 10mph speed limit. Dogs must be kept on leads. Football field. Local produce available.

AA Pubs & Restaurants nearby: Greens Bistro, LYTHAM ST ANNES, FY8 1SX, 01253 789990

See advert below

MORECAMBE
Map 18 SD46

Places to visit

Leighton Hall, CARNFORTH, LA5 9ST, 01524 734474 www.leightonhall.co.uk

Lancaster City Museum, LANCASTER, LA1 1HT, 01524 64637
www.lancashire.gov.uk/museums

Venture Caravan Park
► ► ► 81%

tel: 01524 412986 **Langridge Way, Westgate LA4 4TQ**
email: mark@venturecaravanpark.co.uk
dir: M6 junct 34, A683, follow Morecambe signs. At 2nd rdbt 1st exit, into Westgate. 1st right after fire station (site signed). **grid ref:** SD436633

A large family park close to the town centre, with good modern facilities, including a small indoor heated pool, a licensed clubhouse and a family room with children's entertainment. The site has many statics, some of which are for holiday hire. 17.5 acre site. 56 touring pitches. 40 hardstandings. 25 seasonal pitches. Caravan pitches. Motorhome pitches. Tent pitches. 304 statics.

Open: all year (rs Winter - only one toilet block open) **Last arrival:** 22.00hrs
Last departure: noon

Pitches: * 🚐 £17-£24 🚃 £17-£24 ▲ £17-£21

Leisure: 🏊 🎢 🎪 ⚽ 🔍

Facilities: 🛁 🚿 🅿 ⊙ 🍴 ✳ ♿ 🛒 WiFi ♻ 🔧

Services: 🔌 🚽 🧺 📶 T ⛟ 🚮 🛢

Within 3 miles: 🛶 🏇 🎣 🛒 🛍

Notes: Dogs must be kept on leads. Amusement arcade, off licence, seasonal entertainment.

AA Pubs & Restaurants nearby: Hest Bank Inn, HEST BANK, LA2 6DN, 01524 824339

SILVERDALE

Places to visit

Leighton Hall, CARNFORTH, LA5 9ST, 01524 734474 www.leightonhall.co.uk

Great for kids: RSPB Leighton Moss & Morecambe Bay Nature Reserve, SILVERDALE, LA5 0SW, 01524 701601 www.rspb.org.uk/leightonmoss

SILVERDALE
Map 18 SD47

PREMIER PARK

Silverdale Caravan Park

► ► ► ► ► 95%

tel: 01524 701508 **Middlebarrow Plain, Cove Rd LA5 0SH**
email: caravan@holgates.co.uk **web:** www.holgates.co.uk
dir: M6 junct 35, A601(M) follow Kirkby Lonsdale (B6254) signs. At T-junct right to Carnforth. In Carnforth centre at x-roads, straight on (Silverdale). 1m, left into Sands Ln (Silverdale). 2.4m, over automatic level crossing. Right at T-junct, follow Holgates sign. 1m left, 0.5m right into Cove Rd, 0.7m to site. **grid ref:** SD455762

A superb family holiday destination set in extensive wooded countryside overlooking the sea. All areas of the park are maintained in excellent condition with mature trees, shrubs and pretty, seasonal flowers creating a peaceful and relaxing atmosphere. The pitch density is generous and the spotlessly clean amenities blocks are conveniently located. There's an indoor swimming pool, well-stocked licensed mini-market, smart bar and bistro, an internet room, bowling alley with amusements and a toddlers' soft ball area. Family camping pods are available for hire. 100 acre site. 80 touring pitches. 80 hardstandings. 2 seasonal pitches. Caravan pitches. Motorhome pitches. Tent pitches. 339 statics.

Open: all year **Last arrival:** 20.00hrs **Last departure:** noon
Pitches: * 🚐 £36 🚃 £36 ▲ £36 🏠 prices shown below
Leisure: 🏊 🎾 🎢 ⚽ 🏌 🎱 🎣 🚗
Facilities: 🅿 ⊙ 🍴 ✳ ♿ 🛒 🚿 🔌 WiFi 🛢 ♻ 🔧 🚗
Services: 🔌 🚽 🧺 🛢 🚿 T 🍴 🚮 🛢 🛢

Glamping: Wooden Pods 8, £45-£55 Changeover day Sat Min stay 4 nights

---

Within 3 miles: ↕ ✐ ◎ ≋ 🖫 🖫 ℧

Notes: No unaccompanied children. Dogs must be kept on leads. Sauna, spa pool, steam room.

AA Pubs & Restaurants nearby: The Longlands Inn and Restaurant, CARNFORTH, LA6 1JH, 01524 781256

The Wheatsheaf at Beetham, BEETHAM, LA7 7AL, 015395 62123

See advert below

THORNTON
Map 18 SD34

Places to visit

Blackpool Zoo, BLACKPOOL, FY3 8PP, 01253 830830 www.blackpoolzoo.org.uk

---

PREMIER PARK

Kneps Farm Holiday Park

►►►►► 82%

tel: 01253 823632 **River Rd, Stanah FY5 5LR**
email: enquiries@knepsfarm.co.uk
dir: *Exit A585 at rdbt onto B5412 to Little Thornton. Right at mini-rdbt after school into Stanah Rd, over 2nd mini rdbt, leading to River Rd.* **grid ref:** SD353429

A quality park, quietly located, adjacent to the River Wyre and the Wyre Estuary Country Park, handily placed for the attractions of Blackpool and the Fylde coast. This family-run park offers an excellent toilet block with immaculate facilities, and a mixture of hard and grass pitches (no tents are accepted), plus there are 4-berth and 6-berth wooden pods for hire. 10 acre site. 40 touring pitches. 40 hardstandings. 5 seasonal pitches. Caravan pitches. Motorhome pitches. 40 statics.

Open: Mar-mid Nov (rs Mar & early Nov shop closed) **Last arrival:** 20.00hrs
Last departure: noon

Pitches: * 🚐 £21.50-£26.50 🚐 £21.50-£26.50 🏠 prices shown below

Leisure: ⚠

Facilities: 🚿 🖿 🅿 ⊙ 🗗 ✻ 🕭 🖫 📶 ♻ ❼

Services: 🔌 🖸 🛢 ⊘ 🖸 ⛟ ⛟

Glamping: Wooden Pods 6, £35-£45 Min stay 2 nights (Fri-Sat) Car by unit

Within 3 miles: ↕ 🖫 ✐ ◎ ≋ 🖫 🖫

Notes: No commercial vehicles, max 2 dogs (chargeable) per unit. Dogs must be kept on leads.

AA Pubs & Restaurants nearby: Twelve Restaurant and Lounge Bar, THORNTON, FY5 4JZ, 01253 821212

PITCHES: 🚐 Caravans 🚐 Motorhomes ⛺ Tents 🏠 Glamping accommodation **SERVICES:** 🔌 Electric hook up 🖸 Launderette 🍷 Licensed bar 🛢 Calor Gas ⊘ Camping Gaz 🅃 Toilet fluid 🍽 Café/Restaurant 🏬 Fast Food/Takeaway ⚡ Battery charging 🍼 Baby care ⛟ Motorvan service point **ABBREVIATIONS:** BHs – bank holidays Etr – Easter Spring BH – Spring Bank Holiday fr – from hrs – hours m – mile mdnt – midnight rdbt – roundabout rs – restricted service wk – week wknd – weekend x-roads – crossroads 🚫 No credit or debit cards 🚫 No dogs

LEICESTERSHIRE

See also Wolvey (Warwickshire)

CASTLE DONINGTON
Map 11 SK42

Places to visit

Calke Abbey, CALKE, DE73 7LE, 01332 863822 www.nationaltrust.org.uk

Ashby-de-la-Zouch Castle, ASHBY-DE-LA-ZOUCH, LE65 1BR, 01530 413343 www.english-heritage.org.uk/daysout/properties/ashby-de-la-zouch-castle

Great for kids: Snibston Discovery Museum, COALVILLE, LE67 3LN, 01530 278444 www.snibston.com

---

Donington Park Farmhouse
►►► 75%

tel: 01332 862409 **Melbourne Rd, Isley Walton DE74 2RN**
email: info@parkfarmhouse.co.uk
dir: *M1 junct 24, pass airport to Isley Walton, right towards Melbourne. Site 0.5m on right.*
grid ref: *SK414254*

A secluded touring site, at the rear of a hotel beside Donington Park Racing Circuit, which is very popular on race days so booking is essential. Reception for the campsite is at the hotel. Please note that both day and night flights from nearby East Midlands Airport may cause disturbance. 10 acre site. 90 touring pitches. 50 hardstandings. Caravan pitches. Motorhome pitches. Tent pitches.

Open: Jan-23 Dec (rs Winter - hardstandings only) **Last arrival:** 21.00hrs
Last departure: noon

Pitches: * 🚐 £17-£40 🚐 £17-£40 ▲ £15-£38

Facilities: 🏕 🅿️ ⊙ ❅ 🚿 ♿ 🛒 ♻️ 🚾

Services: 🚽 🖥 🍴 🔌 🛢 🇹 🍴 🖐

Within 3 miles: ⌃ 🎣 🛥 🏇 ⛹ ⛳ ∪

Notes: PayPal accepted. Dogs must be kept on leads. Bread & milk available, on-site hotel with bar.

Discover a great day out
at theaa.com/event-and-days-out

LINCOLNSHIRE

ANCASTER
Map 11 SK94

Places to visit

Belton House Park & Gardens, BELTON, NG32 2LS, 01476 566116 www.nationaltrust.org.uk/belton-house

---

Woodland Waters
►►►► 78%

tel: 01400 230888 **Willoughby Rd NG32 3RT**
email: info@woodlandwaters.co.uk
dir: *On A153 W of junct with B6403.* **grid ref:** *SK979435*

Peacefully set around five impressive fishing lakes, with a few log cabins in a separate area, this is a pleasant open park. The access road is through mature woodland, and there is an excellent heated toilet block, and a pub and clubhouse with restaurant. 72 acre site. 128 touring pitches. 5 hardstandings. Caravan pitches. Motorhome pitches. Tent pitches.

Open: all year **Last arrival:** 20.00hrs **Last departure:** noon

Pitches: 🚐 🚐 ▲

Leisure: 🎡 🎣 🚲

Facilities: ⊙ 🅿️ ♿ 🚽 🛒 🚾 🚾 ⊘

Services: 🚽 🖥 🍴 🛢 🌀 🍴 � 🌐

Within 3 miles: ⌃ 🎣 🏇 🛒 ∪

Notes: No noise after 23.00hrs. Dogs must be kept on leads.

AA Pubs & Restaurants nearby: The Bustard Inn & Restaurant, SLEAFORD, NG34 8QG, 01529 488250

The Brownlow Arms, HOUGH-ON-THE-HILL, NG32 2AZ, 01400 250234

BOSTON
Map 12 TF34

Places to visit

Battle of Britain Memorial Flight Visitor Centre, CONINGSBY, LN4 4SY, 01522 782040 www.lincolnshire.gov.uk/bbmf

Tattershall Castle, TATTERSHALL, LN4 4LR, 01526 342543 www.nationaltrust.org.uk/tatterhall-castle

---

Long Acres Touring Park
▷▷▷▷▷ 91%

Best of British
GOLD

tel: 01205 871555 **Station Rd, Old Leake PE22 9RF**
email: info@long-acres.co.uk
dir: *From A16 take B1184 at Sibsey (by church); approx 1m at T-junct turn left. 1.5m, after level crossing take next right into Station Rd. Park entrance approx 0.5m on left.*
grid ref: *TF384531*

A small rural adults-only park in an attractive setting within easy reach of Boston, Spalding and Skegness. The park has a smart toilet block, which is very clean and has an appealing interior, with modern, upmarket fittings. Excellent shelter is provided by the high, mature boundary hedging. A holiday cottage is available to let. Now a member of Tranquil Parks group. 3 acre site. 40 touring pitches. 40 hardstandings. Caravan pitches. Motorhome pitches. Tent pitches.

Open: Mar-8 Jan **Last arrival:** 20.00hrs **Last departure:** 11.00hrs

Pitches: * ⛟ £18-£22 ⛍ £18-£22 Ⰰ £18-£22

Facilities: 🅝⊙🄿✳🄮🐾 🆆🄸🄵🏵🄸

Services: 🔌🛒👶⚒

Within 3 miles: 🌀🛒

Notes: Adults only. Dogs must be kept on leads.

Orchard Park
▶▶▶▶ 85%

GOLD

tel: 01205 290328 **Frampton Ln, Hubbert's Bridge PE20 3QU**
email: info@orchardpark.co.uk **web:** www.orchardpark.co.uk
dir: *On B1192 between A52 (Boston to Grantham road) & A1121 (Boston to Sleaford road).* **grid ref:** *TF274432*

Ideally located for exploring the unique fenlands, this continually improving park has two lakes – one for fishing and the other set aside for conservation. The very attractive restaurant and bar prove popular with visitors, and Sandy's Café offers a delivery service to those fishing at the lake. 51 acre site. 87 touring pitches. 15 hardstandings. Caravan pitches. Motorhome pitches. Tent pitches. 164 statics.

Open: all year (rs Dec-Feb - bar, shop & café closed) **Last arrival:** 22.30hrs **Last departure:** 16.00hrs

Pitches: ⛟ ⛍ Ⰰ

Leisure: 🏊🎣🎱🎮

Facilities: 🚿🅝🄿⊙🄿✳🄮🄿🐾🆆🄼🏵🄸

Services: 🔌🛒🍸👶⚒🄣🍴🔋🚚⚒

Within 3 miles: 🌀🍴🄮🛒🅂🏌

Notes: Adults only. 🚫 No washing lines. Dogs must be kept on leads.

Pilgrims Way Caravan & Camping Park
▶▶▶▶ 81%

tel: 01205 366646 & 07973 941955 **Church Green Rd, Fishtoft PE21 0QY**
email: holidays@pilgrimswaycaravanandcamping.co.uk
dir: *E from Boston on A52. In 1m, after junct with A16, at Ball House pub turn right. Follow tourist signs to site.* **grid ref:** *TF358434*

A beautifully maintained and peaceful park within easy walking distance of the town centre that has many attractions. All pitches, named after birds species, are screened by well trimmed hedges to create optimum privacy; a lush tent field is also available. Regular barbecue evenings with entertainment are held during the warmer months. 2.5 acre site. 22 touring pitches. 15 hardstandings. Caravan pitches. Motorhome pitches. Tent pitches.

Open: all year **Last arrival:** 22.00hrs **Last departure:** noon

Pitches: * ⛟ £15-£25 ⛍ £15-£25 Ⰰ £5-£30

Leisure: 🎱🎵

Facilities: 🅝⊙🄿✳🄮🄿🏵🄸

Services: 🔌🛒👶✂🔋

Within 3 miles: 🌀🍴🄹🌀🄮🛒🅂🏌

Notes: 🅟 PayPal accepted. Tea house & sun terrace, dogs' day kennels. Dogs must be kept on leads.

CAISTOR
Map 17 TA10

Wolds View Touring Park
NEW ▶▶▶▶ 87%

tel: 01472 851099 **115 Brigg Rd LN7 6RX**
email: phil@wvtp.co.uk
dir: *From A46, at Caistor, follow Brigg & A1084 signs. 1st left signed Brigg & Caistor. Through Caistor, continue on A1084. Approx 1m, site on left.* **grid ref:** *TA113021*

Set in the Lincolnshire Wolds with spectacular views, Wolds View is extremely welcoming, really modern and tidy, with good wide access, newly stoned roads, and good shrubbery and hedging throughout. The facilities block is a beautiful, purpose-designed, wooden building, painted cornflower blue – at one end is a fabulous café and coffee shop serving a variety of drinks, breakfasts and home-made cakes, and at the other end are light, modern and spotless toilet and shower facilities, and a professionally managed reception. 4.5 acre site. 60 touring pitches. 20 hardstandings. Caravan pitches. Motorhome pitches. Tent pitches.

Open: all year **Last arrival:** 20.00hrs **Last departure:** 13.00hrs

Pitches: ⛟ £20-£23 ⛍ £20-£23 Ⰰ £20-£23

Facilities: 🅝🄿⊙🄿✳🄮🄿🐾🆆🄸🏵🄸

Services: 🔌🛒👶🄣🍴⚒

Within 3 miles: 🌀🅂🛒🏌

Notes: Adults only. No noise after 23.00hrs, no groups. Dogs must be kept on leads.

CLEETHORPES
Map 17 TA30

Places to visit
Fishing Heritage Centre, GRIMSBY, DN31 1UZ, 01472 323345
www.thefishingheritagecentre.com

Great for kids: Pleasure Island Family Theme Park, CLEETHORPES, DN35 0PL, 01472 211511 www.pleasure-island.co.uk

Thorpe Park Holiday Centre
HOLIDAY CENTRE 84%

GOLD

tel: 01472 813395 **DN35 0PW**
email: thorpepark@haven.com **web:** www.haven.com/thorpepark
dir: *From A180 at Cleethorpes take unclassified road signed Humberstone & Holiday Park.*
grid ref: *TA321035*

A large static site, adjacent to the beach, with touring facilities, including fully serviced pitches and pitches with hardstandings. This holiday centre offers excellent recreational and leisure activities including an indoor pool with bar, bowling greens, crazy golf, 9-hole golf course, lake coarse fishing, tennis courts and a games area. Parts of the site overlook the sea. 300 acre site. 134 touring pitches. 81 hardstandings. Caravan pitches. Motorhome pitches. Tent pitches. 1357 statics.

Thorpe Park Holiday Centre

Open: mid Mar-end Oct (rs mid Mar-May & Sep-Oct some facilities may be reduced) **Last arrival:** anytime **Last departure:** 10.00hrs

Pitches: 🚐 🚙 ▲

Leisure: 🏊 🏊 ⛰ 👋 ⛳ 🎵 🎣 ✏

Facilities: 🔫 ⊙ 🅿 👤 🖐 🗒 🚿 📶 💻 ♻ 🛈

Services: 🔌 🗑 🍴 🍷 💼 🧺 🍴 🔟 🛒

Within 3 miles: 👣 🏇 ⚓ ◎ 🎣 🏊 🔟 🔟 🗽

Notes: No commercial vehicles, no bookings by persons under 21yrs unless a family booking, max 2 dogs per booking, certain dog breeds banned. Dogs must be kept on leads.

AA Pubs & Restaurants nearby: The Ship Inn, BARNOLDBY LE BECK, DN37 0BG, 01472 822308

See advert below

GREAT CARLTON
Map 17 TF48

Places to visit

Cadwell Park Circuit, LOUTH, LN11 9SE, 0843 453 9000 *(Calls cost 7p per minute plus your phone company's access charge)* www.cadwellpark.co.uk

West End Farm
▶▶▶87%

tel: 01507 450949 & 07766 278740 **Salters Way LN11 8BF**
email: info@westendfarm.co.uk
dir: *From A157 follow Great Carlton signs at Gayton Top. Follow brown sign for West End Farm in 0.5m, right into site.* **grid ref:** *TF418842*

A neat and well-maintained four-acre touring park situated on the edge of the Lincolnshire Wolds. Surrounded by mature trees and bushes and well away from the busy main roads, yet connected by walking and cycling paths, it offers enjoyable peace and quiet close to the popular holiday resort of Mablethorpe. The site has good, clean facilities throughout and there's a passionate approach to everything 'green', with a reed bed sewage system, wild areas, bird and bat boxes and wildlife identification charts. 4 acre site. 35 touring pitches. 4 seasonal pitches. Caravan pitches. Motorhome pitches. Tent pitches.

Open: 28 Mar-2 Oct **Last arrival:** 20.30hrs **Last departure:** 14.00hrs

Pitches: 🚐 🚍 ⅄

Facilities: 🅟 ✳ 🛆 🖥 𝟶

Services: 🔌 🔄 🔋 🔌

Within 3 miles: ↓ 🏌 ◎ 🛉 ∪

Notes: No fires, quiet after 22.30hrs. Dogs must be kept on leads. Fridge available.

AA Pubs & Restaurants nearby: Kings Head Inn, THEDDLETHORPE ALL SAINTS, LN12 1PB, 01507 339798

LANGWORTH
Map 17 TF07

Places to visit

The Collection: Art & Archaeology in Lincolnshire, LINCOLN, LN2 1LP, 01522 550990 www.thecollectionmuseum.com

Lincoln Castle, LINCOLN, LN1 3AA, 01522 554559 www.lincolncastle.com

Barlings Country Holiday Park
▶▶▶▶85%
BRONZE

tel: 01522 753200 **Barlings Ln LN3 5DF**
email: sean@barlingscountrypark.co.uk
dir: *From Lincoln take A158 towards Horncastle. In Langham right into Barlings Ln signed Barlings & Reepham.* **grid ref:** *TF065762*

Set in rural Lincolnshire and only a short car journey from Lincoln, this idyllic 26-acre site offers both seasonal and touring pitches positioned around four lakes. With wildlife in abundance, the park is well landscaped, with beautifully mown grass and trimmed shrubs, a wooden reception chalet, spotlessly clean, older-style toilet facilities, including family rooms, and fishing from purpose-built jetties on two of the lakes. A glamping cabin with hot tub is available for hire. 26 acre site. 84 touring pitches. 43 hardstandings. 40 seasonal pitches. Caravan pitches. Motorhome pitches. Tent pitches. 29 statics.

Open: all year **Last arrival:** 18.00hrs (later arrivals can be arranged) **Last departure:** noon

Pitches: 🚐 🚍 ⅄ 🏠

Leisure: ⚽

Facilities: ☉ ♿ 🛆 🖥 📶 ✿ 𝟶

Services: 🔌 🔄 🔋 🔄 ↺

Glamping: Cabins 1

Within 3 miles: 🏌 🛉 🛒

Notes: No music after 22.00hrs, quiet 23.00hrs-08.00hrs. Dogs must be kept on leads. Mobile shop Fri 11-11.30hrs only, ice cream van (summer).

AA Pubs & Restaurants nearby: The Victoria, LINCOLN, LN1 3BJ, 01522 541000

Wig & Mitre, LINCOLN, LN2 1LU, 01522 535190

PITCHES: 🚐 Caravans 🚍 Motorhomes ⅄ Tents 🏠 Glamping accommodation **SERVICES:** 🔌 Electric hook up 🔄 Launderette 🍺 Licensed bar 🔋 Calor Gas 🔥 Camping Gaz 🇹 Toilet fluid 🍴 Café/Restaurant 🍔 Fast Food/Takeaway 🔌 Battery charging 🍼 Baby care ↺ Motorvan service point

ABBREVIATIONS: BHs – bank holidays Etr – Easter Spring BH – Spring Bank Holiday fr – from hrs – hours m – mile mdnt – midnight rdbt – roundabout rs – restricted service wk – week wknd – weekend x-roads – crossroads 🚫 No credit or debit cards 🚫 No dogs

MABLETHORPE Map 17 TF58

Places to visit

Great for kids: Skegness Natureland Seal Sanctuary, SKEGNESS, PE25 1DB, 01754 764345 www.skegnessnatureland.co.uk

Golden Sands Holiday Park

HOLIDAY CENTRE 88%

GOLD

tel: 01507 477871 **Quebec Rd LN12 1QJ**
email: goldensands@haven.com **web:** www.haven.com/goldensands
dir: *From centre of Mablethorpe turn left into Quebec Rd (seafront road). Site on left.* **grid ref:** *TF501861*

A large, well-equipped seaside holiday park with many all-weather attractions and a good choice of entertainment and eating options. The large touring area is serviced by two amenities blocks and is close to the mini market and laundry. 23 acre site. 172 touring pitches. 20 hardstandings. Caravan pitches. Motorhome pitches. Tent pitches. 1500 statics.

Open: mid Mar-end Oct **Last arrival:** anytime **Last departure:** 10.00hrs

Pitches: **Leisure:**

Facilities: **Services:**

Within 3 miles:

Notes: No commercial vehicles, no bookings by persons under 21yrs unless a family booking, max 2 dogs per booking, certain dog breeds banned. Dogs must be kept on leads. Mini bowling alley, snooker & pool, amusement arcade.

AA Pubs & Restaurants nearby: Red Lion Inn, PARTNEY, PE23 4PG, 01790 752271

See advert on opposite page

Kirkstead Holiday Park

►►► 83%

tel: 01507 441483 **North Rd, Trusthorpe LN12 2QD**
email: mark@kirkstead.co.uk
dir: *From Mablethorpe town centre take A52 S towards Sutton-on-Sea. 1m, sharp right by phone box into North Rd. Site signed in 300yds.* **grid ref:** *TF509835*

A well-established family-run park catering for all age groups, just a few minutes' walk from Trusthorpe and the sandy beaches of Mablethorpe. The main touring area, which is serviced by good quality toilet facilities, has 37 fully serviced pitches on what was once the football pitch, and here toilets have been installed. The site is particularly well maintained. 12 acre site. 60 touring pitches. 3 hardstandings. 30 seasonal pitches. Caravan pitches. Motorhome pitches. Tent pitches. 70 statics.

Open: Mar-Nov **Last arrival:** 22.00hrs **Last departure:** 14.00hrs

Pitches: * £12-£18 £12-£18 £10-£22

Leisure:

Facilities:

Services:

Within 3 miles:

Notes: No dogs in tents. Dogs must be kept on leads.

AA Pubs & Restaurants nearby: Kings Head Inn, THEDDLETHORPE ALL SAINTS, LN12 1PB, 01507 339798

MARSTON Map 11 SK84

Places to visit

Belton House Park & Gardens, BELTON, NG32 2LS, 01476 566116 www.nationaltrust.org.uk/belton-house

Newark Air Museum, NEWARK-ON-TRENT, NG24 2NY, 01636 707170 www.newarkairmuseum.org

Wagtail Country Park

►►►► 91%

tel: 01400 251955 & 07814 481088 (bookings) **Cliff Ln NG32 2HU**
email: info@wagtailcountrypark.co.uk
dir: *From A1 exit at petrol station signed Barkston & Marston, right signed Barkston into Green Ln, follow park signs.* **grid ref:** *SK897412*

A peaceful site near the village of Marston, surrounded by trees and where birdsong is the only welcome distraction. The touring areas are neatly laid out and enhanced by mature shrubs and pretty seasonal flowers. There is a stunning facilities block that includes four family rooms. There is a separate adults-only area, and coarse fishing is also available. 20 acre site. 76 touring pitches. 76 hardstandings. 10 seasonal pitches. Caravan pitches. Motorhome pitches.

Open: all year **Last arrival:** 17.00hrs **Last departure:** 11.00hrs

Pitches: **Leisure:**

Facilities:

Services: **Within 3 miles:**

Notes: No noise after 23.00hrs. Dogs must be kept on leads. Fishing bait, milk & ice creams available.

AA Pubs & Restaurants nearby: The Brownlow Arms, HOUGH-ON-THE-HILL, NG32 2AZ, 01400 250234

SKEGNESS
Map 17 TF56

Places to visit

Skegness Natureland Seal Sanctuary, SKEGNESS, PE25 1DB, 01754 764345
www.skegnessnatureland.co.uk

The Village-Church Farm Museum, SKEGNESS, PE25 2HF, 01754 766658
www.churchfarmvillage.org.uk

Eastview Caravan Park
►►►►80%

tel: 01754 875324 & 07710 336145 **Trunch Ln, Chapel St Leonards PE24 5UA**
email: enquiries@eastviewcaravans.co.uk
dir: A52 from Skegness to Chapel St Leonards. Turn left into Trunch Ln. 2nd caravan park
on left. **grid ref:** TF555778

Set in 15 acres and only a short walk from one of Lincolnshire's finest beaches,
Eastview Caravan Park is neat and tidy and a good all-round campsite. It has
beautifully mown grass, well-trimmed shrubbery and spotlessly clean and modern
toilet facilities. There is a children's playground and a shop. It is well placed for
exploring both the coast and the countryside, especially the beautiful Lincolnshire
Wolds. 15 acre site. 53 touring pitches. 56 hardstandings. 112 seasonal pitches.
Caravan pitches. Motorhome pitches. Tent pitches. 9 statics.

Open: Mar-Oct **Last arrival:** 20.00hrs **Last departure:** 10.30hrs (late departures until
17.00hrs - fee applies)

Pitches: * 🚐 £18-£25 🚍 £18-£25 ▲ £16.50-£18.50

Facilities: ⊙✳⚲♿🏃🚻 WiFi 🖥 ♻ 🛈

Services: 🔌🔠 🛢T ↯

Within 3 miles: ↨🎡🖩🖊◎⛴🏧🛒⛳U

Notes: No motorised scooters, BB guns or kites. Maximum 2 dogs per pitch. Dogs must
be kept on leads. BBQs to be at least 1ft off ground, quiet after 22.30hrs.

TATTERSHALL
Map 17 TF25

Places to visit

Tattershall Castle, TATTERSHALL, LN4 4LR, 01526 342543
www.nationaltrust.org.uk/tattershall-castle

Tattershall Lakes Country Park
►►►►88%

tel: 01526 348800 **Sleaford Rd LN4 4LR**
email: tattershall.holidays@away-resorts.com
dir: Access from A153 in Tattershall. **grid ref:** TF234587

Set amongst woodlands, lakes and parkland on the edge of Tattershall in the heart
of the Lincolnshire Fens, this mature country park has been created from old gravel
pits and the flat, well-drained and maintained touring area offers plenty of space
for campers. There's a lot to entertain the youngsters as well as the grown-ups,
with good fishing on excellent lakes, an 18-hole golf course, water-ski and jet-ski
lakes and an indoor heated pool with spa facilities. There is a separate adults-only
field, three fully-equipped bell tents (sleeping 2-4) and a new canvas cottage
(sleeping 2-8) for hire. 365 acre site. 186 touring pitches. 20 hardstandings. 25
seasonal pitches. Caravan pitches. Motorhome pitches. Tent pitches. 500 statics.

Open: end Mar-end Oct (rs Off-peak season reduced services) **Last arrival:** 19.00hrs
Last departure: 10.00hrs

Pitches: 🚐 🚍 ▲ 🏕

Leisure: 🏊 🎾 🎣♿🎯 Spa

Facilities: ⊙🅿♿🔠🏃🚻 WiFi 🖥 ♻ 🛈

Services: 🔌🔠 🍽🛢🍴🎂

Glamping: Bell tents 3 **Canvas cottage:** 1

Within 3 miles: ↨🎣🖩🖊⛴🏧

Notes: No excessive noise after mdnt. Dogs must be kept on leads.

AA Pubs & Restaurants nearby: The Lea Gate Inn, CONINGSBY, LN4 4RS, 01526 342370

PITCHES: 🚐 Caravans 🚍 Motorhomes ▲ Tents 🏕 Glamping accommodation **SERVICES:** 🔌 Electric hook up 🔠 Launderette 🍽 Licensed bar
🛢 Calor Gas ⊘ Camping Gaz T Toilet fluid 🍴 Café/Restaurant 🎂 Fast Food/Takeaway 🔋 Battery charging 👶 Baby care ↯ Motorvan service point
ABBREVIATIONS: BHs – bank holidays Etr – Easter Spring BH – Spring Bank Holiday fr – from hrs – hours m – mile mdnt – midnight
rdbt – roundabout rs – restricted service wk – week wknd – weekend x-roads – crossroads No credit or debit cards No dogs

WADDINGHAM Map 17 SK99

Places to visit

Gainsborough Old Hall, GAINSBOROUGH, DN21 2NB, 01427 612669
www.english-heritage.org.uk/daysout/properties/gainsborough-old-hall

Brandy Wharf Leisure Park

►►► 75%

tel: 01673 818010 **Brandy Wharf DN21 4RT**
email: brandywharflp@freenetname.co.uk **web:** www.brandywharfleisurepark.co.uk
dir: *From A15 onto B1205 through Waddingham. Site in 3m.* **grid ref:** *TF014968*

A delightful site in a very rural area on the banks of the River Ancholme, where fishing is available. The toilet block has unisex rooms with combined facilities as well as a more conventional ladies and gents with washbasins and toilets. All the grassy pitches have electricity, and there's a play and picnic area. This site will appeal to bikers, groups, music lovers, and also cider aficionados as there is a renowned cider hostelry next door. Advance booking is necessary for weekend pitches. 5 acre site. 50 touring pitches. Caravan pitches. Motorhome pitches. Tent pitches.

Open: all year (rs Nov-Etr no tents) **Last arrival:** dusk **Last departure:** 17.00hrs

Pitches:

Leisure:

Facilities:

Services:

Within 3 miles:

Notes: No disposable BBQs on grass, no music after 23.00hrs. Boat mooring & slipway, canoe hire, pedalos, pets' corner.

AA Pubs & Restaurants nearby: The George, KIRTON IN LINDSEY, DN21 4LX, 01652 640600

WOODHALL SPA

Places to visit

Tattershall Castle, TATTERSHALL, LN4 4LR, 01526 342543
www.nationaltrust.org.uk/tatterhall-castle

Battle of Britain Memorial Flight Visitor Centre, CONINGSBY, LN4 4SY, 01522 782040 www.lincolnshire.gov.uk/bbmf

WOODHALL SPA Map 17 TF16

PREMIER PARK

Woodhall Country Park

91%

tel: 01526 353710 **Stixwold Rd LN10 6UJ**
email: info@woodhallcountrypark.co.uk **web:** www.woodhallcountrypark.co.uk
dir: *In Woodhall Spa at rdbt in High St take Stixwold Rd. 1m, site on right, just before Village Limits pub.* **grid ref:** *TF189643*

A peaceful and attractive touring park situated just a short walk from Woodhall Spa. The owners transformed part of the woodland area into a countryside retreat for campers who wish to escape from a hectic lifestyle. Well organised and well laid out, the park offers fishing lakes, three log cabin amenity blocks, fully serviced pitches and high levels of customer care. There's a strong ethos towards sustainability and a bio-mass boiler provides all the heating and hot water to the three superb amenities blocks, plus there are bird hides around the park. Two and four-berth camping pods and four luxury lodges are available for hire. 80 acre site. 115 touring pitches. 88 hardstandings. Caravan pitches. Motorhome pitches. Tent pitches.

Open: Mar-Nov **Last arrival:** 20.00hrs **Last departure:** noon

Pitches: * £20-£29 £20-£29 £16-£26 prices shown below

Leisure:

Facilities:

Services:

LEISURE: Indoor pool Outdoor pool Children's playground Kid's club Tennis court Games room Golf course Boat hire Cycle hire Cinema Entertainment Fishing Mini golf Pitch n putt Watersports Gym Sports field Stables **FACILITIES:** Bath Shower Private washing cubicles Electric shaver Hairdryer Ice Packs Disabled facilities Shop on site Mobile shop BBQ area Picnic area Wi-fi Internet access Recycling Tourist info Dog exercise area Car hire can be arranged

Glamping: Wooden Pods 12, £35-£40 Min stay 2 nights at wknds, 3 nights at BHs

Within 3 miles: ⚓🏃🎨🐾🛒🎠♻

Notes: No cars by tents. No fires, Chinese lanterns or fireworks, no noise between 23.00hrs-07.00hrs, BBQs must be off ground. Dogs must be kept on leads. Food prep room, worktops, freezer, kettle, grill & microwave available.

AA Pubs & Restaurants nearby: Village Limits Country Pub, Restaurant & Motel, WOODHALL SPA, LN10 6UJ, 01526 353312

See advert below

Petwood Caravan Park
▶▶▶▶ 89%

tel: 01526 354799 **Off Stixwould Rd LN10 6QH**

email: info@petwoodcaravanpark.co.uk

dir: *From Lincoln take A15 towards Sleaford. Left onto B1188 signed Woodhall Spa. Approx 7.5m at Metheringham left onto B1189 (signed Billinghay). 3.7m left onto B1191 (Woodhall Spa). Approx 6m at rdbt in Woodhall Spa, 1st exit into Stixwould Rd. In 0.3m left into Jubilee Park, follow site signs.* **grid ref:** *TF191633*

Covering seven immaculate acres of beautifully manicured grounds, Petwood Caravan Park is a hidden gem of a touring park located behind a much larger static park in the heart of Woodhall Spa. There are 98 pitches, all with electric hook-ups; 18 have spacious hardstandings suitable for caravans and motorhomes. There is a modern reception and shop, and two excellent heated toilet blocks, each containing a spotlessly maintained family room. Dogs are welcome at no extra charge. 7 acre site. 98 touring pitches. 8 hardstandings. 20 seasonal pitches. Caravan pitches. Motorhome pitches. Tent pitches.

Open: 18 Mar-16 Oct **Last arrival:** 21.00hrs **Last departure:** noon

Pitches: ⚓ 🚐 Å

Facilities: 📻⊙🅿☀♿🅂🚮 WiFi ♻🄌

Services: ⚓🄍↯

Within 3 miles: ⚓🏃🎨◎🛒🎠

Notes: No rollerblades, no noise after 23.00hrs. Dogs must be kept on leads.

AA Pubs & Restaurants nearby: Village Limits Country Pub, Restaurant & Motel, WOODHALL SPA, LN10 6UJ, 01526 353312

PITCHES: ⚓ Caravans 🚐 Motorhomes Å Tents 🏠 Glamping accommodation **SERVICES:** ⚓ Electric hook up 🄍 Launderette 🍷 Licensed bar 🔋 Calor Gas 🛢 Camping Gaz 🅃 Toilet fluid 🍽 Café/Restaurant 🏭 Fast Food/Takeaway 🔋 Battery charging 🍼 Baby care ↯ Motorvan service point

ABBREVIATIONS: BHs – bank holidays Etr – Easter Spring BH – Spring Bank Holiday fr – from hrs – hours m – mile mdnt – midnight rdbt – roundabout rs – restricted service wk – week wknd – weekend x-roads – crossroads 🅒 No credit or debit cards ⊗ No dogs

LONDON

E4 CHINGFORD
Map 6 TQ39

Places to visit

Waltham Abbey Gatehouse, Bridge & Entrance to Cloisters, WALTHAM ABBEY, 01992 702200
www.english-heritage.org.uk/daysout/properties/waltham-abbey-gatehouse-and-bridge

Lee Valley Campsite
▶▶▶▶ 85%

tel: 020 8529 5689 **Sewardstone Rd, Chingford E4 7RA**
email: sewardstonecampsite@vibrantpartnerships.co.uk
web: www.visitleevalley.org.uk/wheretostay
dir: *M25 junct 26, A112. Site signed.* **grid ref:** *TQ381970*

Overlooking King George's Reservoir and close to Epping Forest, this popular and very peaceful park features very good modern facilities and excellent hardstanding pitches including nine that are able to accommodate larger motorhomes. This impressive park is maintained to a high standard and there is glamping accommodation (2-berth cocoons and 4-berth small cabins) in a separate shady glade. A bus calls at the site hourly to take passengers to the nearest tube station, and Enfield is easily accessible. 12 acre site. 81 touring pitches. 65 hardstandings. Caravan pitches. Motorhome pitches. Tent pitches.

Open: Mar-Jan **Last arrival:** 21.00hrs **Last departure:** noon

Pitches: * 🚐 £14.50-£22.50 🚄 £14.50-£22.50 ▲ £14.50-£22.50 🏠 prices shown below

Leisure: 🅰

Facilities: 🅿 ⊙ 🍴 ☼ ⅙ ⑤ ♨ 🚽 📶 ♻ ❶

Services: 🔌 🗑 🖳 ⊘ ⊤ 🚰 ↓

Glamping: Wooden Pods 8, £30-£45 Min stay 1 night Car by unit **Cabins** 9, £35-£45 Min stay 1 night En suite

Within 3 miles: ↓ ☷ 🎣 ⅙ ⑤ ⑤ ∪

Notes: Under 18s must be accompanied by an adult, no commercial vehicles. Dogs must be kept on leads.

See advert below

Campsite cooking
See pages 24-31 for handy tips

LEISURE: 🏊 Indoor pool 🏊 Outdoor pool 🅰 Children's playground 🙋 Kid's club 🎾 Tennis court 🎱 Games room ⛳ Golf course 🚣 Boat hire 🚲 Cycle hire 🎬 Cinema 🎵 Entertainment 🎣 Fishing ⛳ Mini golf ⛳ Pitch n putt 🏄 Watersports 🏋 Gym 🏟 Sports field ∪ Stables **FACILITIES:** 🛁 Bath 🚿 Shower 🅿 Private washing cubicles ⊙ Electric shaver 🖐 Hairdryer ❄ Ice Packs 🦽 Disabled facilities ⑤ Shop on site 📱 Mobile shop 🍖 BBQ area 🪑 Picnic area 📶 Wi-fi 🖥 Internet access ♻ Recycling ❶ Tourist info 🐕 Dog exercise area 🚗 Car hire can be arranged

N9 EDMONTON
Map 6 TQ39

Lee Valley Camping & Caravan Park

►►►►84%

tel: 020 8803 6900 **Meridian Way N9 0AR**
email: edmontoncampsite@vibrantpartnerships.
co.uk **web:** www.visitleevalley.org.uk/wheretostay
dir: *M25 junct 25, A10 S, 1st left onto A1055, approx 5m to Leisure Complex. From A406 (North Circular), N on A1010, left after 0.25m, right into Pickets Lock Ln.*
grid ref: TQ360945

A pleasant, open site within easy reach of London yet peacefully located close to two large reservoirs. There are excellent gravel access roads to the camping field, good signage and lighting, and smartly refurbished toilets. The site has the advantage of being next to an 18-hole golf course and a multi-screen cinema. There are also camping pods and timber cabins for hire. A convenient bus stop provides a direct service to central London. 7 acre site. 100 touring pitches. 54 hardstandings. Caravan pitches. Motorhome pitches. Tent pitches.

Open: all year **Last arrival:** 20.00hrs **Last departure:** noon
Pitches: * ⊞ £14.50-£22.50 ⊞ £14.50-£22.50 Å £14.50-£22.50
ⓜ prices shown below
Leisure: ⋀ ♨
Facilities: ⬤⊙℗✳♿⑤⌹ WiFi ♻ ❶
Services: ⬤⑤ ⬛Ⓣ⑩⬛⬍
Glamping: Wooden Pods 12, £35-£45 Min stay 1 night Car by unit
Within 3 miles: ⬇⊟

Notes: Under 18s must be accompanied by an adult. Dogs must be kept on leads. Foot golf.

MERSEYSIDE

SOUTHPORT
Map 15 SD31

Places to visit

The British Lawnmower Museum, SOUTHPORT, PR8 5AJ, 01704 501336
www.lawnmowerworld.com

Great for kids: Dunes Splash World, SOUTHPORT, PR8 1RX, 01704 537160
www.splashworldsouthport.com

Riverside Holiday Park

HOLIDAY CENTRE 86%

tel: 01704 228886 **Southport New Rd PR9 8DF**
email: reception@harrisonleisureuk.com
dir: *M6 junct 27, A5209 towards Parbold/Burscough, right onto A59. Left onto A565 at lights in Tarleton. Continue to dual carriageway. At rdbt straight across, site 1m on left.*
grid ref: SD405192

A family friendly park north of Southport, with many indoor attractions, including a swimming pool, sauna, steam room and jacuzzi, and a new clubhouse in 2016. The generously sized pitches are located on carefully landscaped grounds and served by two well-equipped, modern amenities blocks. Free WiFi is provided in an attractive café. 80 acre site. 260 touring pitches. 130 hardstandings. Caravan pitches. Motorhome pitches. 355 statics.

Open: 14 Feb-Jan **Last arrival:** 17.00hrs **Last departure:** 11.00hrs
Pitches: ⊞ ⊞
Leisure: ♨♨♙ ♫
Facilities: ℗♿⑤ WiFi⬛❶
Services: ⬤⑤ ⬛Ⓣ⑩⬛
Within 3 miles: ⬇⬇♨⑤⬛U

Notes: One car per pitch. Dogs must be kept on leads.

AA Pubs & Restaurants nearby: Bistrot Vérité, SOUTHPORT, PR8 4AR, 01704 564199

Gusto Trattoria, SOUTHPORT, PR8 1QB, 01704 544255

Vincent Hotel, SOUTHPORT, PR8 1JR, 01704 883800

SOUTHPORT *continued*

Willowbank Holiday Home & Touring Park
►►►►87%

GOLD

tel: 01704 571566 **Coastal Rd, Ainsdale PR8 3ST**
email: info@willowbankcp.co.uk **web:** www.willowbankcp.co.uk
dir: *From A565 between Formby & Ainsdale exit at Woodvale lights onto coast road, site 150mtrs on left. From N: M6 junct 31, A59 towards Preston, A565, through Southport & Ainsdale, right at Woodvale lights.* **grid ref:** SD305110

Set in woodland on a nature reserve next to sand dunes, this constantly improving park is a peaceful and relaxing holiday destination with mature trees, shrubs and colourful seasonal flowers surrounding neat pitches and modern amenities blocks. 8 acre site. 87 touring pitches. 61 hardstandings. Caravan pitches. Motorhome pitches. 228 statics.

Open: 14 Feb-Jan **Last arrival:** 21.00hrs **Last departure:** noon

Pitches: * 🚐 £16-£21.20 🚐 £16-£21.20

Leisure: ✪

Facilities: 🏕⊙🅿✳🕭☕🚻 WiFi ♻ ❶

Services: 🔧🔲🛢◔↥

Within 3 miles: ↓⛵🎯🏌◎⛵🛒🛍🛍∪

Notes: Cannot accommodate continental door entry units, no commercial vehicles, no dangerous dog breeds. Dogs must be kept on leads. Baby changing facility.

AA Pubs & Restaurants nearby: Gusto Trattoria, SOUTHPORT, PR8 1QB, 01704 544255

Bistrot Vérité, SOUTHPORT, PR8 4AR, 01704 564199

Vincent Hotel, SOUTHPORT, PR8 1JR, 01704 883800

LEISURE: 🏊 Indoor pool 🏊 Outdoor pool 🎢 Children's playground ✋ Kid's club 🎾 Tennis court 🎱 Games room ⛳ Golf course ⛵ Boat hire 🚲 Cycle hire 🎬 Cinema 🎵 Entertainment 🎣 Fishing ◎ Mini golf 🏌 Pitch n putt 🏄 Watersports 🏋 Gym ⚽ Sports field ∪ Stables **FACILITIES:** 🛁 Bath 🚿 Shower 🅿 Private washing cubicles ⊙ Electric shaver 🅿 Hairdryer ✳ Ice Packs ♿ Disabled facilities 🛒 Shop on site 🛍 Mobile shop 🍖 BBQ area 🍴 Picnic area WiFi Wi-fi 💻 Internet access ♻ Recycling ❶ Tourist info 🐕 Dog exercise area 🚗 Car hire can be arranged

Hurlston Hall Country Caravan Park
►►►►80%

tel: 01704 840400 & 842829 **Southport Rd L40 8HB**
email: enquiries@hurlstonhallcaravanpark.co.uk
dir: *On A570, 3m from Ormskirk towards Southport.* **grid ref:** *SD398107*

A peaceful tree-lined touring park next to a static site in attractive countryside about 10 minutes' drive from Southport. The park is maturing well, with growing trees and a coarse fishing lake, and the excellent on-site facilities include golf, a bistro (refurbished for 2016), a well-equipped health centre, a bowling green and model boat lake. Please note, neither tents nor dogs are accepted at this site.
5 acre site. 60 touring pitches. Caravan pitches. Motorhome pitches. 68 statics.

Open: Etr-Oct **Last arrival:** 20.30hrs (18.30hrs at wknds & BHs) **Last departure:** 17.00hrs

Pitches: 🚐 🚐

Leisure: ≋ ⚑ Spa ♪

Facilities: ☉ 🖢 ♿ ■ ♻

Services: 🔌 🔲 🍴 🔒 ♨ 🍽

Within 3 miles: 🚶 🎣 🛒🔲

Notes: 🚫

AA Pubs & Restaurants nearby: Gusto Trattoria, SOUTHPORT, PR8 1QB, 01704 544255

Bistrot Vérité, SOUTHPORT, PR8 4AR, 01704 564199

Vincent Hotel, SOUTHPORT, PR8 1JR, 01704 883800

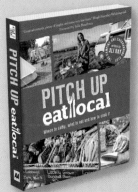

PITCHES: 🚐 Caravans 🚐 Motorhomes 🅰 Tents 🏠 Glamping accommodation **SERVICES:** 🔌 Electric hook up 🔲 Launderette 🍸 Licensed bar
🔒 Calor Gas ⌀ Camping Gaz 🅣 Toilet fluid 🍽 Café/Restaurant ⊞ Fast Food/Takeaway ⚡ Battery charging 🚼 Baby care 🚐 Motorvan service point
ABBREVIATIONS: BHs – bank holidays Etr – Easter Spring BH – Spring Bank Holiday fr – from hrs – hours m – mile mdnt – midnight
rdbt – roundabout rs – restricted service wk – week wknd – weekend x-roads – crossroads 🚫 No credit or debit cards 🚫 No dogs

Norfolk

Think of Norfolk, and the theme of water – in particular the Norfolk Broads, a complex network of mostly navigable rivers and man-made waterways – usually springs to mind. This delightfully unspoiled region attracts thousands of visitors every year, as does the North Norfolk Coast, designated an Area of Outstanding Natural Beauty and probably the finest of its kind in Europe.

'A long way from anywhere' and 'a remote corner of England that has been able to hold on to its traditions and ancient secrets,' are two of the apt descriptions that apply to this spacious corner of the country that still seems a separate entity, as if it is strangely detached from the rest of the country.

The coastline here represents a world of lonely beaches, vast salt marshes and extensive sand dunes stretching to the far horizon. It remains essentially unchanged, a stark reminder of how this area has long been vulnerable to attack and enemy invasion.

The highly successful thriller writer Jack Higgins chose this theme as the subject of his hugely popular adventure yarn *The Eagle has Landed*, published in 1975. The book, about a wartime Nazi plot to kidnap and assassinate Winston Churchill while he is spending the weekend at a country house near the sea in this part of East Anglia, vividly conveys the strange, unsettling atmosphere of the North Norfolk Coast.

Walking is the best way to gain a flavour of that atmosphere and visit the story's memorable setting. The 93-mile Peddars Way and North Norfolk Coast Path is one of Britain's most popular national trails. Made up of two paths strung together to form one continuous route, the trail begins near Thetford on the Suffolk/Norfolk border and follows ancient tracks and sections of Roman road before reaching the coast near Hunstanton. Cycling is another popular pastime in this region and in places you can combine it with a local train ride. One option, for example, is to cycle beside the Bure Valley Railway on a 9-mile trail running from Aylsham to Wroxham, returning to the start by train. There is also the North Norfolk Coast Cycleway between King's Lynn and Cromer, among other routes.

Norfolk prides itself on its wealth of historic houses, the most famous being Sandringham, where Her Majesty the Queen and her family spend Christmas. The Grade II-listed house, which is surrounded by 20,000 acres, has been the private home of four generations of monarchs since 1862. 'Dear old Sandringham, the place I love better than anywhere in the world,' wrote King George V. The house and gardens are open to visitors. Among the other great houses in the region are Holkham Hall – the magnificent Palladian home of the Earls of Leicester – and the National Trust properties of Blickling Hall and Felbrigg Hall.

Many of Norfolk's towns have a particular charm and a strong sense of community. The quiet market towns of Fakenham and Swaffham are prime examples, and there is also Thetford, with its popular museum focusing on the iconic TV comedy series *Dad's Army*. Much of the filming for this cherished BBC production took place in the town and in nearby Thetford Forest. On the coast, you'll find a string of quaint villages and small towns. Wells-next-the-Sea is a popular destination for many visitors to Norfolk, as is Blakeney, renowned for its mudflats and medieval parish church, dedicated to the patron saint of seafarers, standing guard over the village and the estuary of the River Glaven. With its iconic pier, a key feature of coastal towns, Cromer is a classic example of a good old fashioned seaside resort where rather grand Victorian hotels look out to sea. Together with Sheringham, Cromer hosts a Crab and Lobster Festival in May.

◁ A windmill near the River Thurne

NORFOLK

BARNEY
Map 13 TF93

Places to visit

Holkham Hall, HOLKHAM, NR23 1AB, 01328 710227 www.holkham.co.uk

Great for kids: Dinosaur Adventure Park, LENWADE, NR9 5JW, 01603 876310 www.dinosauradventure.co.uk

REGIONAL WINNER – HEART OF ENGLAND
AA CAMPSITE OF THE YEAR 2017

PREMIER PARK

The Old Brick Kilns
▶▶▶▶▶ 93%

Best of British
GOLD

tel: 01328 878305 **Little Barney Ln NR21 0NL**
email: enquiries@old-brick-kilns.co.uk **web:** www.old-brick-kilns.co.uk
dir: *From A148 (Fakenham to Cromer road) follow brown tourist signs to Barney, left into Little Barney Ln. Site at end of lane.* **grid ref:** TG007328

This secluded and peaceful park is approached via a quiet, leafy country lane. The park is on two levels with its own boating and fishing pool and many mature trees. Excellent, well-planned toilet facilities can be found in two beautifully appointed blocks, and there is a short dog walk. In Barney's Restaurant bar food and takeaways are available on selected nights of the week (except in the low season) and there is also a midweek fish and chips night. Please note due to a narrow access road, no arrivals are accepted until after 1pm. There are four self-catering holiday cottages. 12.73 acre site. 65 touring pitches. 65 hardstandings. 7 seasonal pitches. Caravan pitches. Motorhome pitches. Tent pitches.

Open: 15 Mar-2 Jan (rs Etr-Sep bar food & takeaway available on selected nights only; not available in low season) **Last arrival:** 21.00hrs (no arrivals until 13:00) **Last departure:** 11.00hrs

Pitches: * 🚐 £17-£32 🚏 £17-£32 ⛺ £15-£27

Leisure: ⚗ 🎣 🚴

Facilities: 🐕🅿️⊙☂️🔥❄️♿🔼🚻 WiFi 💻♻️ℹ️

Services: 🔌📡🍽️🏪✉️🚰🅃🍴🚮🚾♻️

Within 3 miles: 🏌️🛒📮

Notes: No gazebos. Dogs must be kept on leads. Outdoor draughts, chess, family games, freshly baked bread.

BELTON
Map 13 TG40

Places to visit

Burgh Castle, BURGH CASTLE, NR31 9PZ, 0370 333 1181 www.english-heritage.org.uk/daysout/properties/burgh-castle

Wild Duck Holiday Park
HOLIDAY CENTRE 76%

GOLD

tel: 01493 780268 **Howards Common NR31 9NE**
email: wildduck@haven.com **web:** www.haven.com/wildduck
dir: *A47 to Great Yarmouth, 3rd exit at Asda rdbt, straight on at next 2 rdbts. Left onto A143 signed Beccles. Right at lights, 2m to dual carriageway, right signed Belton. Straight on at mini rdbt. Right at T-junct, left at next T-junct. Park 200yds on right.* **grid ref:** TG475028

This a large holiday complex with plenty to do for all ages both indoors and out. This level grassy site has well laid-out facilities and is set in a forest with small, cleared areas for tourers. Clubs for children and teenagers, sporting activities and evening shows all add to the fun of a stay here. There are six new fully equipped safari tents for hire, each with their own stone-built barbecue and facility block. 97 acre site. 108 touring pitches. Caravan pitches. Motorhome pitches. Tent pitches. 560 statics.

Open: 16 Mar-5 Nov (rs mid Mar-May & Sep-early Nov some facilities may be reduced) **Last arrival:** 21.00hrs **Last departure:** 10.00hrs

Pitches: 🚐 🚏 ⛺ 🏠 **Facilities:** 🐕⊙♿🔼🚻 WiFi ♻️ℹ️

Services: 🔌📡🍽️🏪🍴♻️ **Glamping:** Safari tents 6

Within 3 miles: 🎿🚴🏌️◎🛒📮

Notes: No commercial vehicles, no bookings by persons under 21yrs unless a family booking. Max 2 dogs per booking, certain dog breeds banned. Dogs must be kept on leads.

AA Pubs & Restaurants nearby: Andover House, GREAT YARMOUTH, NR30 3JB, 01493 843490

See advert below

Rose Farm Touring & Camping Park
▶▶▶▶▶ 85%

tel: 01493 780896 **Stepshort NR31 9JS**
email: myhra@rosefarmtouringpark.fsnet.co.uk
dir: *From A143 follow signs to Belton. In Belton, from mini rdbt on New Rd into Stepshort, site on right.* **grid ref:** *TG488033*

A former railway line is the setting for this very peaceful, beautifully presented site which enjoys rural views. It is brightened with many flower and herb beds. The toilet facilities are smart, spotlessly clean, inviting to use and include family rooms. The customer care here is truly exceptional and the quality café (open in peak season only) is very popular. Wooden cabins ('summerhouses') are now available for hire. 10 acre site. 145 touring pitches. 20 hardstandings. Caravan pitches. Motorhome pitches. Tent pitches.

Open: all year **Pitches:** 🚐 🚙 ⛺ 🏠
Leisure: 🎱 ♣ **Facilities:** 🔌 🅿 ⊙ 🍴 ✳ 🚿 ♿ 🎯 WiFi ▬ ♻ 🅸
Services: 🔌 🔵 🧺 🔋 ⊘

Glamping: Cabins 2, £30–£40 Car by unit (1 cabin for daily or weekly hire, 1 for seasonal hire)

Within 3 miles: 🎣 ⛳ 🎬 ◎ 🅿 🛒 🛍 ↻

Notes: No dog fouling. Dogs must be kept on leads.

AA Pubs & Restaurants nearby: Andover House, GREAT YARMOUTH, NR30 3JB, 01493 843490

Swallow Park Leisure
▶▶▶▶ 74%

tel: 01493 601180 **Lawns Ln, Beccles Rd NR31 9JQ**
email: coll.colby@icloud.com
dir: *From A143 from Beccles towards Great Yarmouth, 0.5m after Cherry Lane Garden Centre left into Beccles Rd. In 400yds right into Lawns Ln.* **grid ref:** *TG486023*

This leisure park is located close to the village of Belton, only three miles from the beautiful beach at Gorleston, two miles from the Norfolk Broads and a short distance from Fritton Lake Outdoor Centre. This family owned park is a pleasant, quiet site and offers both fully-equipped safari tents with their own cooking, shower and toilet facilities, and bell tents with external cooking huts. These either have a wooden porch or decking areas, very good quality furnishings, and dining and cooking equipment. Heating in all glamping units is provided by log-burning stoves, and free fuel is provided. There are also five camping pitches. 3 acre site. 5 touring pitches. Caravan pitches. Motorhome pitches.

Open: Apr-Oct **Last arrival:** 22.00hrs **Last departure:** 10.30hrs
Pitches: 🚐 🚙 🏠
Leisure: ♣
Facilities: 🔌 🅿 ✳ 🎯 ♻ 🅸
Services: 🔌 ⊘

Glamping: Bell tents 3, £60–£99 Min stay 1 night Own kitchen Car by unit
Safari tents 3, £87–£199 Changeover day Mon, Fri Min stay 3 nights En suite Own kitchen Car by unit

Within 3 miles: 🎣 ⛳ 🎬 ◎ 🅿 🛒 🛍 ↻

Notes: 🚫 No noise after mdnt. Dogs must be kept on leads.

PITCHES: 🚐 Caravans 🚙 Motorhomes ⛺ Tents 🏠 Glamping accommodation **SERVICES:** 🔌 Electric hook up 🔵 Launderette 🍺 Licensed bar 🔋 Calor Gas 🛢 Camping Gaz 🚽 Toilet fluid 🍴 Café/Restaurant 🍟 Fast Food/Takeaway 🔋 Battery charging 👶 Baby care ↺ Motorvan service point
ABBREVIATIONS: BHs – bank holidays Etr – Easter Spring BH – Spring Bank Holiday fr – from hrs – hours m – mile mdnt – midnight rdbt – roundabout rs – restricted service wk – week wknd – weekend x-roads – crossroads 🚫 No credit or debit cards 🚫 No dogs

CAISTER-ON-SEA | Map 13 TG51

Places to visit

Caister Roman Fort, CAISTER-ON-SEA, 0370 333 1181
www.english-heritage.org.uk/daysout/properties/caister-roman-fort

Thrigby Hall Wildlife Gardens, FILBY, NR29 3DR, 01493 369477
www.thrigbyhall.co.uk

Caister-on-Sea Holiday Park
HOLIDAY CENTRE 88%

GOLD

tel: 01493 728931 **Ormesby Rd NR30 5NH**
email: caister@haven.com **web:** www.haven.com/caister
dir: *A1064 signed Caister-on-Sea. At rdbt 2nd exit onto A149, at next rdbt 1st exit onto Caister by-pass, at 3rd rdbt 3rd exit to Caister-on-Sea. Park on left.* **grid ref:** *TG519132*

An all-action holiday park located beside the beach north of the resort of Great Yarmouth, yet close to the attractions of the Norfolk Broads. The touring area offers 46 fully serviced pitches and a modern purpose-built toilet block, which was beautifully refurbished for 2016. Customer care is of an extremely high standard with a full time, experienced and caring warden. Please note, this park does not accept tents. 138 acre site. 49 touring pitches. 49 seasonal pitches. Caravan pitches. Motorhome pitches. 900 statics.

Open: mid Mar-end Oct **Last arrival:** anytime **Last departure:** 10.00hrs
Pitches: 🏕 🚐
Leisure: 🎣 🏊 🛝 ⚽ 🎱 🎵 ⛳
Facilities: 🚿 🝑 🐕 🛒 WiFi ♻ 🛈
Services: 🔌 🛢 🧺 🚽 🍴 🛒 ⛺ 🚮

Within 3 miles: 🚣 ⛳ 🎣 🎱 🚤 🛝

Notes: No tents, no commercial vehicles, no bookings by persons under 21yrs unless a family booking, no sleeping in awnings, max 2 dogs per booking, certain dog breeds not accepted. Dogs must be kept on leads.

AA Pubs & Restaurants nearby: Fishermans Return, WINTERTON-ON-SEA, NR29 4BN, 01493 393305

See advert on opposite page

CLIPPESBY | Map 13 TG41

Places to visit

Fairhaven Woodland & Water Garden, SOUTH WALSHAM, NR13 6DZ, 01603 270449 www.fairhavengarden.co.uk

Great for kids: Caister Roman Fort, CAISTER-ON-SEA, 0370 333 1181
www.english-heritage.org.uk/daysout/properties/caister-roman-fort

PREMIER PARK

Clippesby Hall
▶▶▶▶▶ 93%

GOLD

tel: 01493 367800 **Hall Ln NR29 3BL**
email: holidays@clippesby.com **web:** www.clippesby.com
dir: *From A47 follow tourist signs for The Broads. At Acle rdbt take A1064, in 2m left onto B1152, 0.5m left opposite village sign, site 400yds on right.* **grid ref:** *TG423147*

A lovely country house estate with secluded pitches hidden among the trees or in sheltered sunny glades. The toilet facilities, appointed to a very good standard, provide a wide choice of cubicles. Amenities include a coffee shop with both WiFi and wired internet access, a family bar and restaurant and family golf. Excellent hardstanding pitches are available as the park is open all year. There are pine lodges and cottages for holiday lets. 30 acre site. 120 touring pitches. 41 hardstandings. Caravan pitches. Motorhome pitches. Tent pitches.

Open: all year (rs Nov-Mar coffee shop, bar & restaurant closed) **Last arrival:** 17.30hrs
Last departure: 11.00hrs

Pitches: * 🏕 £16.50-£41 🚐 £16.50-£41 ⛺ £12.50-£37
Leisure: 🎣 🛝 🏊 ⚽ 🎱 🏌 ⛳
Facilities: 🚿 🝑 🖨 📷 ✂ 🐕 🛒 WiFi 🖥 ♻ 🛈
Services: 🔌 🛢 🧺 🛢 🚽 🍴 🛒 🚮
Within 3 miles: 🚣 ⛳ 🎣 🎱 🚤 🛝 ⛺

Notes: No groups, no noise after 23.00hrs, no camp fires. Dogs must be kept on leads. Table tennis, cycle trail.

AA Pubs & Restaurants nearby: Fishermans Return, WINTERTON-ON-SEA, NR29 4BN, 01493 393305

The Fur & Feather Inn, WOODBASTWICK, NR13 6HQ, 01603 720003

CROMER	Map 13 TG24

Places to visit

RNLI Henry Blogg Museum, CROMER, NR27 9ET, 01263 511294
www.rnli.org/henryblogg

Felbrigg Hall, FELBRIGG, NR11 8PR, 01263 837444
www.nationaltrust.org.uk/felbrigg-hall

Manor Farm Caravan & Camping Site
►►►► 83%

tel: 01263 512858 **East Runton NR27 9PR**
email: stay@manorfarmcampsite.co.uk
dir: *1m W of Cromer, exit A148 or A149 (recommended towing route) at Manor Farm sign.* **grid ref:** *TG198416*

A well-established family-run site on a working farm enjoying panoramic sea views. There are good modern facilities across the site, including three smart toilet blocks that include two quality family rooms and privacy cubicles, two good play areas and a large expanse of grass for games – the park is very popular with families. Care must be taken on approaching the site, which is along a 0.5 mile long farm track; if required, please ask for directions from reception. 17 acre site. 250 touring pitches. Caravan pitches. Motorhome pitches. Tent pitches.

Open: Etr-Sep **Last arrival:** 20.30hrs **Last departure:** noon

Pitches: ⊞ ⊞ ⋏

Leisure: ⚽ ♨

Facilities: ☞ P ⊙ ⚒ ⚓ ♺ ☺ ⓘ

Services: ⚡ ⓢ ⓵ ⊘ ☲

Within 3 miles: ⛵ ⋕ ⚑ ◎ ⚘ ⓢ ⓢ

Notes: ⊗ No groups, no noise after 23.00hrs. Dogs must be kept on leads. 2 dog-free fields available.

AA Pubs & Restaurants nearby: The Red Lion Food and Rooms, CROMER, NR27 9HD, 01263 514964

The White Horse Overstrand, CROMER, NR27 0AB, 01263 579237

Sea Marge Hotel, CROMER, NR27 0AB, 01263 579579

Forest Park
►►►► 82%

tel: 01263 513290 **Northrepps Rd NR27 0JR**
email: info@forest-park.co.uk
dir: *A140 from Norwich, left at T-junct signed Cromer, right signed Northrepps, right then immediately left, left at T-junct, site on right.* **grid ref:** *TG233405*

Surrounded by forest, this gently sloping park offers a wide choice of pitches. Visitors have the use of a heated indoor swimming pool, and a large clubhouse with entertainment. 100 acre site. 262 touring pitches. Caravan pitches. Motorhome pitches. Tent pitches. 420 statics.

Open: 15 Mar-15 Jan **Last arrival:** 21.00hrs **Last departure:** 11.00hrs

Pitches: ⊞ ⊞ ⋏

Leisure: ⌂ ⚲

Facilities: ⊙ ⓟ ⚒ ⚓ ⓢ ⏂ WiFi

Services: ⚡ ⓢ ⓵ ⓵ ⊘ T ⓞ ☲ ♨

Within 3 miles: ⛵ ⚶ ⋕ ⚑ ◎ ⚘ ⓢ ⓢ ∪

AA Pubs & Restaurants nearby: The Red Lion Food and Rooms, CROMER, NR27 9HD, 01263 514964

The White Horse Overstrand, CROMER, NR27 0AB, 01263 579237

Sea Marge Hotel, CROMER, NR27 0AB, 01263 579579

PITCHES: ⊞ Caravans ⊞ Motorhomes ⋏ Tents ⌂ Glamping accommodation **SERVICES:** ⚡ Electric hook up ⓢ Launderette ⓵ Licensed bar ⓵ Calor Gas ⊘ Camping Gaz T Toilet fluid ⓞ Café/Restaurant ⏬ Fast Food/Takeaway ☲ Battery charging ♨ Baby care ⚡ Motorvan service point **ABBREVIATIONS:** BHs – bank holidays Etr – Easter Spring BH – Spring Bank Holiday fr – from hrs – hours m – mile mdnt – midnight rdbt – roundabout rs – restricted service wk – week wknd – weekend x-roads – crossroads ⊗ No credit or debit cards ⊗ No dogs

DOWNHAM MARKET Map 12 TF60

Lakeside Caravan Park & Fisheries

►►►► 82%

tel: 01366 383491 & 387074 (out of hrs) **Sluice Rd, Denver PE38 0DZ**
email: richesflorido@aol.com **web:** www.westhallfarmholidays.co.uk
dir: *Exit A10 towards Denver, follow signs to Denver Windmill, site on right.*
grid ref: *TF608013*

A peaceful, rapidly improving park set around five pretty fishing lakes. There are several grassy touring areas which are sheltered by mature hedging and trees, a function room for social get togethers, shop, laundry and children's play area. Electric hook-up pitches are available and rallies are welcome. New toilet and shower facilities were added for 2016. 30 acre site. 100 touring pitches. Caravan pitches. Motorhome pitches. Tent pitches. 1 static.

Open: all year (rs Oct-Mar) **Last arrival:** 21.00hrs **Last departure:** 10.30hrs

Pitches: 🚃 🚐 ⛺

Leisure: 🎣

Facilities: 🚿 ⊙ 💨 ❄ ♿ 🛒 🧺 🐕 [WiFi]

Services: 🔌 🌀 🧯 🍃 [T] 🔋

Within 3 miles: 🏌 ⛵ 🎬 🎣 🏄 🛒 🌀

Notes: No noise after 23.00hrs. Dogs must be kept on leads. Pool table, fishing tackle & bait, caravan accessories, caravan storage, newspapers, bread & milk.

AA Pubs & Restaurants nearby: The Hare Arms, STOW BARDOLPH, PE34 3HT, 01366 382229

FAKENHAM

Places to visit

Houghton Hall & Gardens, HOUGHTON, PE31 6UE, 01485 528569 www.houghtonhall.com

Great for kids: Pensthorpe Nature Reserve & Gardens, FAKENHAM, NR21 0LN, 01328 851465 www.pensthorpe.co.uk

FAKENHAM Map 13 TF92

Fakenham Fairways Campsite

►►► 87%

tel: 01328 856614 **Burnham Market Rd, Sculthorpe NR21 9SA**
email: hello@fakenhamfairways.uk
dir: *From Fakenham take A148 towards King's Lynn then right onto B1355 towards Burnham Market. Site on right in 400yds.* **grid ref:** *TF907310*

Enthusiastic owners run this peaceful site that is surrounded by tranquil countryside and which is part of a 9-hole, par 3 golf complex and driving range. The toilet facilities are of good quality, and there is a golf shop. Please note, there is no laundry. 4 acre site. 50 touring pitches. 13 hardstandings. Caravan pitches. Motorhome pitches. Tent pitches.

Open: all year **Last arrival:** 20.00hrs **Last departure:** noon

Pitches: 🚃 🚐 ⛺

Leisure: 🛝 ⛳

Facilities: 🚿 [P] ❄ 🐕 [WiFi] 💻 ♻ ℹ

Services: 🔌 🍃

Within 3 miles: 🏌 🎬 🎣 🛒

Notes: No noise after 22.30hrs. Dogs must be kept on leads.

AA Pubs & Restaurants nearby: The Blue Boar Inn, GREAT RYBURGH, NR21 0DX, 01328 829212

The Wensum Lodge Hotel, FAKENHAM, NR21 9AY, 01328 862100

Caravan Club M.V.C. Site

►►► 83%

tel: 01328 862388 **Fakenham Racecourse NR21 7NY**
email: caravan@fakenhamracecourse.co.uk
dir: *From B1146, S of Fakenham follow brown Racecourse signs (with tent & caravan symbols) leads to site entrance.* **grid ref:** *TF926288*

A very well laid-out site set around the racecourse, with a grandstand offering smart, modern toilet facilities. Tourers move to the centre of the course on race days, and enjoy free racing, and there's a wide range of sporting activities in the club house. 11.4 acre site. 120 touring pitches. 25 hardstandings. 22 seasonal pitches. Caravan pitches. Motorhome pitches. Tent pitches.

Open: all year **Last arrival:** 21.00hrs **Last departure:** noon

Pitches: 🚃 🚐 ⛺

Leisure: 🎾 🏌

Facilities: ⊙ 💨 ❄ ♿ 🛒 🐕 [WiFi] ♻ ℹ

Services: 🔌 🌀 🍷 🧯 🍃 [T] 🍴 🥡

Within 3 miles: 🏌 🎬 🎣 ◎ 🛒 🌀 🐎

Notes: Max 2 dogs per pitch. Dogs must be kept on leads. TV aerial hook-ups.

AA Pubs & Restaurants nearby: The Blue Boar Inn, GREAT RYBURGH, NR21 0DX, 01328 829212

The Wensum Lodge Hotel, FAKENHAM, NR21 9AY, 01328 862100

GREAT YARMOUTH

Map 13 TG50

Places to visit

Yesterday's World Great Yarmouth, GREAT YARMOUTH, NR30 2EN, 01493 331148 www.yesterdaysworld.co.uk

Great for kids: Time and Tide Museum of Great Yarmouth Life, GREAT YARMOUTH, NR30 3BX, 01493 743930 www.museums.norfolk.gov.uk

Vauxhall Holiday Park

HOLIDAY CENTRE 90%

tel: 01493 857231 **Acle New Rd NR30 1TB**
email: info@vauxhallholidays.co.uk **web:** www.vauxhallholidaypark.co.uk
dir: On A47 towards Great Yarmouth. **grid ref:** TG520083

A very large holiday complex with plenty of entertainment and access to beach, river, estuary, lake and the A47. The touring pitches are laid out in four separate areas, each with its own amenity block (refurbished in 2016), and all arranged around the main entertainment. Fully serviced pitches and a new children's play

area were added for the 2016 season. Four-person wooden pods are also available for hire. 40 acre site. 180 touring pitches. Caravan pitches. Motorhome pitches. Tent pitches. 434 statics.

Vauxhall Holiday Park

Open: Etr, mid May-Sep & Oct half term **Last arrival:** 21.00hrs **Last departure:** 10.00hrs

Pitches: * 🚐 £21-£66 🚙 £21-£66 ▲ £21-£66 🏠 prices shown below

Leisure: 🏊‍♂️ ⛳ 🎣 🎡 ⬇ 🏇 ⚽ 🎱 🎵 🎯

Facilities: 🔌 ⊙ 🚿 ☀ 🚻 💲 📶 ♻ ❶

Services: 🔌 🗑 🍴 🍽 🛒 🚼

Glamping: Wooden Pods 5, £52.50-£75.50 Min stay 2 nights En suite Own kitchen Car by unit

Within 3 miles: 🚴 ♨ 🎯 🎣 ⊙ 🛥 📍 📮 ⛵

Notes: No pets. Children's pool, sauna, solarium.

AA Pubs & Restaurants nearby: Andover House, GREAT YARMOUTH, NR30 3JB, 01493 843490

See advert below

PITCHES: 🚐 Caravans 🚙 Motorhomes ▲ Tents 🏠 Glamping accommodation **SERVICES:** 🔌 Electric hook up 🗑 Launderette 🍴 Licensed bar
🔋 Calor Gas 🔵 Camping Gaz 🅣 Toilet fluid 🍽 Café/Restaurant 🛒 Fast Food/Takeaway 🔋 Battery charging 🚼 Baby care ⛟ Motorvan service point
ABBREVIATIONS: BHs – bank holidays Etr – Easter Spring BH – Spring Bank Holiday fr – from hrs – hours m – mile mdnt – midnight
rdbt – roundabout rs – restricted service wk – week wknd – weekend x-roads – crossroads 🚫 No credit or debit cards 🚫 No dogs

GREAT YARMOUTH *continued*

The Grange Touring Park
►►►► 82%

tel: 01493 730306 & 730023 **Yarmouth Rd, Ormesby St Margaret NR29 3QG**
email: info@grangetouring.co.uk
dir: *From A149, 3m N of Great Yarmouth. Site at junct of A149 & B1159, signed.*
grid ref: TG510142

A mature, ever improving park with plenty of trees, located just one mile from the sea, within easy reach of both coastal attractions and the Norfolk Broads. The level pitches have electric hook-ups and include 13 hardstanding pitches, and there are clean, modern toilets including three spacious family rooms. All pitches have WiFi. 3.5 acre site. 70 touring pitches. 7 hardstandings. Caravan pitches. Motorhome pitches. Tent pitches.

Open: Etr-Oct **Last arrival:** 21.00hrs **Last departure:** 14.00hrs

Pitches: * ⊞ £14-£26 ⊞ £14-£26 ▲ £13-£15

Leisure: /A\

Facilities: ↑ P ⊙ P ✳ ⅃ WiFi ▆ ⊘

Services: ⊟ ⅍ ⎚ ⬛ ⬥ ⬛ ⋃

Within 3 miles: ⅃ ⌀ ⊙ ⑤ ⑤ ∪

Notes: No football, no open fires. Dogs must be kept on leads.

AA Pubs & Restaurants nearby: Andover House, GREAT YARMOUTH, NR30 3JB, 01493 843490

Seashore Holiday Park
HOLIDAY HOME PARK 87%

tel: 01493 851131 **North Denes NR30 4HG**
email: seashore@haven.com **web:** www.haven.com/seashore
dir: *A149 from Great Yarmouth to Caister. Right at 2nd lights signed seafront & racecourse. Continue to sea, turn left. Park on left.* **grid ref:** TG653103

Bordered by sand dunes and with direct access to a sandy beach, Seashore Holiday Park is located in Great Yarmouth yet is close enough for day trips to the peaceful Norfolk Broads. Facilities include excellent water activities and bike hire for children and lively evening entertainment for adults. There is a good range of holiday caravans and apartments.

Open: Mar-Oct

Changeover day: Mon, Fri, Sat

Arrival and departure times: Please contact the site

Statics: 285 Sleeps 6-8 Bedrms 2-3 Bathrms 1-2 Toilets 1-2 Microwave Freezer TV Sky/FTV Elec inc Gas inc

Children: ⅃ Cots Highchair **Dogs:** 2 on leads No dangerous dogs

Leisure: ⌀ Cycle hire ⅃ /A\

| HOPTON ON SEA | Map 13 TM59 |

Places to visit

St Olave's Priory, ST OLAVES, 0370 333 1181
www.english-heritage.org.uk/daysout/properties/st-olaves-priory

Hopton Holiday Park
HOLIDAY HOME PARK 94%

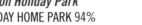

tel: 01502 730214 **NR31 9BW**
email: hopton@haven.com **web:** www.haven.com/hopton
dir: *Site signed from A12 between Great Yarmouth & Lowestoft.* **grid ref:** TG531002

Located between Lowestoft and Great Yarmouth, close to beaches and the town attractions, this lively holiday park offers excellent sport activities, including golf on the 9-hole course and tennis coaching, plus popular evening entertainment in the form of shows, music and dancing. There is a good range of holiday caravans and apartments.

Open: Mar-Oct

Changeover day: Mon, Fri, Sat

Arrival and departure times: Please contact the site

Statics: 216 Sleeps 6-8 Bedrms 2-3 Bathrms 1-2 Toilets 1-2 Microwave Freezer TV Sky/FTV Elec inc Gas inc Grass area

Children: ⅃ Cots Highchair **Dogs:** 2 on leads No dangerous dogs

Leisure: ⌀ ⌀ ⊙ Cycle hire ⅃ /A\

| HUNSTANTON | Map 12 TF64 |

Places to visit

Lynn Museum, KING'S LYNN, PE30 1NL, 01553 775001
www.museums.norfolk.gov.uk

Norfolk Lavender, HEACHAM, PE31 7JE, 01485 570384
www.norfolk-lavender.co.uk

Great for kids: Hunstanton Sea Life Sanctuary, HUNSTANTON, PE36 5BH, 01485 533576 www.sealife.co.uk

Searles Leisure Resort
HOLIDAY CENTRE 90%

tel: 01485 534211 **South Beach Rd PE36 5BB**
email: bookings@searles.co.uk
dir: *A149 from King's Lynn to Hunstanton. At rdbt follow signs for South Beach. Straight on at 2nd rdbt. Site on left.* **grid ref:** TF671400

A large seaside holiday complex with well managed facilities, adjacent to sea and beach. The tourers have their own areas, including two excellent toilet blocks, and pitches are individually marked by small maturing shrubs for privacy. The bars and entertainment, restaurant, bistro and takeaway, heated indoor and outdoor pools, golf, fishing and bowling green make this park popular throughout the year. 50 acre site. 255 touring pitches. 91 hardstandings. Caravan pitches. Motorhome pitches. Tent pitches. 158 statics.

Open: all year (rs Dec-Mar (except Feb half term) limited facilities. Outdoor pool open May-Sep only)

LEISURE: ⌀ Indoor pool ⌀ Outdoor pool /A\ Children's playground ⅃ Kid's club ⊙ Tennis court ⬤ Games room ⅃ Golf course ⌀ Boat hire ⌀ Cycle hire ⬛ Cinema ♫ Entertainment ⌀ Fishing ⊙ Mini golf ⌀ Pitch n putt ⌀ Watersports ⌀ Gym ⬤ Sports field ∪ Stables **FACILITIES:** ⬤ Bath ↑ Shower P Private washing cubicles ⊙ Electric shaver P Hairdryer ✳ Ice Packs ⅃ Disabled facilities ⑤ Shop on site ⌀ Mobile shop ⬛ BBQ area ⌀ Picnic area WiFi Wi-fi ⬛ Internet access ♻ Recycling ⊙ Tourist info ⌀ Dog exercise area ⌀ Car hire can be arranged

Pitches: 🚐 🚌 ⛺ 🛖

Leisure: 🏊 🏊 🎾 ✋ 🎳 ⚽ 🔍 🎵 ⛳

Facilities: ✲ ♿ [S] ⛩ 🐕 [WiFi] 💻 ♻ ℹ

Services: 🔌 🧺 🍷 🛢 💧 [T] 🍽 🔋 🍔 👶 🚰

Glamping: Wooden pods

Within 3 miles: ⛳ 🎣 🏊 [S] 🧺 ∪

Notes: Restrictions on certain dog breeds (contact site for details). Dogs must be kept on leads.

AA Pubs & Restaurants nearby: The King William IV Country Inn & Restaurant, HUNSTANTON, PE36 5LU, 01485 571765

The Neptune Restaurant with Rooms, HUNSTANTON, PE36 6HZ, 01485 532122

KING'S LYNN — Map 12 TF62

See also Stanhoe

Places to visit

Bircham Windmill, GREAT BIRCHAM, PE31 6SJ, 01485 578393
www.birchamwindmill.co.uk

Castle Rising Castle, CASTLE RISING, PE31 6AH, 01553 631330
www.english-heritage.org.uk/daysout/properties/castle-rising-castle

PREMIER PARK

King's Lynn Caravan and Camping Park 🛖

►►►►► 84%

tel: 01553 840004 **New Rd, North Runcton PE33 0RA**
email: klcc@btconnect.com
dir: *From King's Lynn take A47 signed Swaffham & Norwich, in 1.5m turn right signed North Runcton. Site 100yds on left.* **grid ref:** *TF645160*

Set in approximately 10 acres of parkland, this developing camping park is situated on the edge of North Runcton, just a few miles south of the historic town of King's Lynn. The three very extensive touring fields are equipped with 150 electric hook-ups and one field is reserved for rallies. There is an eco-friendly toilet block which is powered by solar panels and an air-sourced heat pump which also recycles rainwater – this in itself proves a source of great interest to visitors. There are eight high quality camping pods and four new pine lodges for hire. 9 acre site. 150 touring pitches. 2 hardstandings. 54 seasonal pitches. Caravan pitches. Motorhome pitches. Tent pitches. 8 statics.

Open: all year **Last arrival:** flexible **Last departure:** flexible

Pitches: 🚐 £15-£20 🚌 £15-£20 ⛺ £8-£12 🛖 prices shown below

Leisure: ⛩

Facilities: 🛁 🚿 [P] ⊙ 🔫 ✲ ♿ [S] 🐕 [WiFi] ♻ ℹ

Services: 🔌 🧺 🛢 💧 [T] 🔋 🚰

Glamping: **Wooden Pods** 8, £30-£45 Own kitchen **Cabins** 4, £75-£125 Min stay 3 nights En suite Own kitchen Car by unit

Within 3 miles: ⛳ 🏨 🎣 🏊 [S] 🧺 ∪

Notes: PayPal accepted. No skateboards or fires. Dogs must be kept on leads.

AA Pubs & Restaurants nearby: The Stuart House Hotel, Bar & Restaurant, KING'S LYNN, PE30 5QX, 01553 772169

Bank House, KING'S LYNN, PE30 1RD, 01553 660492

NORTH WALSHAM — Map 13 TG23

Places to visit

Blickling Estate, BLICKLING, NR11 6NF, 01263 738030
www.nationaltrust.org.uk/blickling

Mannington Gardens, ERPINGHAM, NR11 7BB, 01263 584175
www.manningtongardens.co.uk

PREMIER PARK

Two Mills Touring Park

►►►►► 87%

tel: 01692 405829 **Yarmouth Rd NR28 9NA**
email: enquiries@twomills.co.uk
dir: *1m S of North Walsham on Old Yarmouth road past police station & hospital on left.* **grid ref:** *TG291286*

An intimate, beautifully presented park set in superb countryside in a peaceful, rural spot, which is also convenient for touring. The 'Top Acre' section is maturing and features fully serviced pitches, offering panoramic views over the site, an immaculate toilet block and good planting, plus the layout of pitches and facilities are excellent. A new cabin-style building housing a fully-equipped disabled room and a dishwashing area was added for 2016. The very friendly and helpful owners keep the park in immaculate condition. Please note, this park is for adults only. 7 acre site. 81 touring pitches. 81 hardstandings. 30 seasonal pitches. Caravan pitches. Motorhome pitches. Tent pitches.

Open: Mar-3 Jan **Last arrival:** 20.30hrs **Last departure:** noon

Pitches: * 🚐 £17.95-£29.50 🚌 ⛺

Facilities: 🚿 [P] ⊙ 🔫 ✲ ♿ [S] ⛩ 🐕 [WiFi] 💻 ♻ ℹ

Services: 🔌 🧺 🛢 💧 [T] 🔋 🚰

Within 3 miles: 🎣 [S] 🧺

Notes: Adults only. Max 2 dogs per pitch. Dogs must be kept on leads. Library, DVDs, tea & coffee facilities.

AA Pubs & Restaurants nearby: Beechwood Hotel, NORTH WALSHAM, NR28 0HD, 01692 403231

PITCHES: 🚐 Caravans 🚌 Motorhomes ⛺ Tents 🛖 Glamping accommodation **SERVICES:** 🔌 Electric hook up 🧺 Launderette 🍷 Licensed bar 🛢 Calor Gas 💧 Camping Gaz [T] Toilet fluid 🍽 Café/Restaurant 🍔 Fast Food/Takeaway 🔋 Battery charging 👶 Baby care 🚰 Motorvan service point
ABBREVIATIONS: BHs – bank holidays Etr – Easter Spring BH – Spring Bank Holiday fr – from hrs – hours m – mile mdnt – midnight rdbt – roundabout rs – restricted service wk – week wknd – weekend x-roads – crossroads 💳 No credit or debit cards 🐕 No dogs

SCRATBY Map 13 TG51

Places to visit

Time and Tide Museum of Great Yarmouth Life, GREAT YARMOUTH, NR30 3BX, 01493 743930 www.museums.norfolk.gov.uk

Great for kids: Caister Roman Fort, CAISTER-ON-SEA, 0370 333 1181 www.english-heritage.org.uk/daysout/properties/caister-roman-fort

Scratby Hall Caravan Park

►►► 87%

tel: 01493 730283 **NR29 3SR**
email: scratbyhall@aol.com **web:** www.scratbyhall.co.uk
dir: *5m N of Great Yarmouth. Exit A149 onto B1159, site signed.* **grid ref:** *TG501155*

A neatly-maintained site with a popular children's play area, well-equipped shop and outdoor swimming pool with sun terrace. The toilets are kept very clean. The beach and the Norfolk Broads are close by. 5 acre site. 85 touring pitches. Caravan pitches. Motorhome pitches. Tent pitches.

Open: Etr-end Sep (rs Etr-3rd wk Jul & Sep pool closed) **Last arrival:** 21.00hrs
Last departure: noon

Pitches: 🚐 🚌 ⛺

Leisure: 🏊

Facilities: 🚿 [P] ⊙ 💇 ❄ ♿ [S] [WiFi] ♻ ⓘ

Services: 🧺 ▣ 🔒 🌿 [T] 🍴

Within 3 miles: ⛳ ⛵ 🎣 [S] ▣ 🐴

Notes: No commercial vehicles, no noise after 23.00hrs. Dogs must be kept on leads. Food preparation room.

AA Pubs & Restaurants nearby: Fishermans Return, WINTERTON-ON-SEA, NR29 4BN, 01493 393305

STANHOE Map 13 TF83

Places to visit

Norfolk Lavender, HEACHAM, PE31 7JE, 01485 570384 www.norfolk-lavender.co.uk

Walsingham Abbey Grounds & Shirehall Museum, LITTLE WALSINGHAM, NR22 6BP, 01328 820510 www.walsinghamabbey.com

The Rickels Caravan & Camping Park

►►► 85%

tel: 01485 518671 **Bircham Rd PE31 8PU**
email: therickelscaravanandcampingpark@hotmail.co.uk
dir: *Take A149 (S of King's Lynn) signed Cromer (& A148). Right at rdbt onto A148 signed Fakenham & Cromer. Left on B1153 signed Flitcham & Great Bircham. In Great Bircham right onto B115 signed Stanhoe. At x-roads (junct with B1454) straight across (Stanhoe). Site on left.* **grid ref:** *TF794355*

Set in three acres of grassland, with sweeping country views and a pleasant, relaxing atmosphere fostered by being for adults only. The meticulously maintained grounds and facilities are part of the attraction, and the slightly sloping land has some level areas and sheltering for tents. A field is available to hire for rallies. 3 acre site. 30 touring pitches. Caravan pitches. Motorhome pitches. Tent pitches.

Open: all year **Last arrival:** 21.00hrs **Last departure:** 11.00hrs

Pitches: * 🚐 £11-£16 🚌 £11-£16 ⛺ £11-£16

Facilities: 🚿 [P] ⊙ ❄ 🐕 [WiFi] ♻ ⓘ

Services: 🧺 ▣ 🔒 🌿 🍴

Within 3 miles: 🎣 [S]

Notes: Adults only. 🚫 No groundsheets. Dogs must be kept on leads.

AA Pubs & Restaurants nearby: The Lord Nelson, BURNHAM THORPE, PE31 8HN, 01328 738241

SWAFFHAM — Map 13 TF80

Places to visit

Gressenhall Farm and Workhouse, GRESSENHALL, NR20 4DR, 01362 860563 www.museums.norfolk.gov.uk/Gressenhall

Castle Acre Priory and Castle, CASTLE ACRE, PE32 2XD, 01760 755394 www.english-heritage.org.uk/daysout/properties/castle-acre-castle-acre-priory

Breckland Meadows Touring Park

►►►► 82%

tel: 01760 721246 **Lynn Rd PE37 7PT**
email: info@brecklandmeadows.co.uk
dir: *1m W of Swaffham on old A47.* **grid ref:** *TF809094*

An immaculate, well-landscaped little park on the edge of Swaffham. The toilet block is a very impressive facility, replete with quality fixtures and fittings, spacious cubicles, including a family/disabled room, a large, well-equipped laundry, and a high tech, and very efficient, hot water system. There are hardstandings with electricity, and the plentiful planting makes attractive screening. 3 acre site. 45 touring pitches. 35 hardstandings. 5 seasonal pitches. Caravan pitches. Motorhome pitches. Tent pitches.

Open: all year **Last arrival:** 21.00hrs **Last departure:** noon

Pitches: 🚐 🚌 ⛺

Facilities: ⊙ ✻ ♿ [S] 🪑 🐕 [WiFi] 💻 ♻ ℹ

Services: 🔌 🧺 🛢 🔥 [T] 🔋

Within 3 miles: ⛳ 🎣 [S] 🧺

Notes: Adults only. Dogs must be kept on leads. Newspaper deliveries.

AA Pubs & Restaurants nearby: The Ostrich Inn, CASTLE ACRE, PE32 2AE, 01760 755398

SYDERSTONE — Map 13 TF83

Places to visit

Creake Abbey, NORTH CREAKE, NR21 9LF, 0370 333 1181 www.english-heritage.org.uk/daysout/properties/creake-abbey

The Garden Caravan Site

►►► 80%

tel: 01485 578220 **Barmer Hall Farm PE31 8SR**
email: nlmason@tiscali.co.uk
dir: *Signed from B1454 at Barmer between A148 & Docking, 1m N of Syderstone.*
grid ref: *TF812337*

In the tranquil setting of a former walled garden beside a large farmhouse, with mature trees and shrubs, a secluded site surrounded by woodland. The site is run mainly on trust, with a daily notice indicating which pitches are available, and an honesty box for basic foods. An ideal site for the discerning camper, and well placed for touring north Norfolk. 3.5 acre site. 30 touring pitches. Caravan pitches. Motorhome pitches. Tent pitches.

Open: Mar-Nov **Last arrival:** 21.00hrs **Last departure:** noon

Pitches: 🚐 🚌 ⛺

Facilities: 🚿 ⊙ 💨 ✻ ♿ 🐕 ♻ ℹ

Services: 🔌 🛢 🔋 🚰

Within 3 miles: ⛳ H ◎ [S]

Notes: 💳 Max 2 dogs per pitch, max tent width 5mtrs. Dogs must be kept on leads. Cold drinks, ice creams & eggs available.

AA Pubs & Restaurants nearby: The Lord Nelson, BURNHAM THORPE, PE31 8HN, 01328 738241

WORTWELL — Map 13 TM28

Places to visit

Bressingham Steam Museum & Gardens, BRESSINGHAM, IP22 2AB, 01379 686900 www.bressingham.co.uk

Little Lakeland Caravan Park

►►►► 84%

tel: 01986 788646 **IP20 0EL**
email: info@littlelakeland.co.uk
dir: *From W: exit A143 at sign for Wortwell. In village turn right 300yds past garage. From E: on A143, left onto B1062, then right. After 800yds turn left.* **grid ref:** *TM279849*

A well-kept and pretty site built round a fishing lake, and accessed by a lake-lined drive. The individual pitches are sited in hedged enclosures for complete privacy, and the purpose-built toilet facilities are excellent. 4.5 acre site. 34 touring pitches. 6 hardstandings. 17 seasonal pitches. Caravan pitches. Motorhome pitches. Tent pitches. 24 statics.

Open: all year **Last arrival:** 20.00hrs **Last departure:** noon

Pitches: * 🚐 £19-£26 🚌 £19-£26 ⛺ £19-£26

Leisure: 🛝 🎣

Facilities: 🚿 [P] ⊙ 💨 ✻ ♿ [S] [WiFi] ♻ ℹ

Services: 🔌 🧺 🛢 🔥 [T] 🔋

Within 3 miles: ⛳ 🏇 🎣 [S]

Notes: No noise after 22.30hrs. Dogs must be kept on leads. Library.

AA Pubs & Restaurants nearby: The Dove Restaurant with Rooms, ALBURGH, IP20 0EP, 01986 788315

Fox & Goose Inn, FRESSINGFIELD, IP21 5PD, 01379 586247

PITCHES: 🚐 Caravans 🚌 Motorhomes ⛺ Tents 🛖 Glamping accommodation **SERVICES:** 🔌 Electric hook up 🧺 Launderette 🍷 Licensed bar 🛢 Calor Gas 🔥 Camping Gaz [T] Toilet fluid 🍴 Café/Restaurant 🍔 Fast Food/Takeaway 🔋 Battery charging 🍼 Baby care 🚰 Motorvan service point
ABBREVIATIONS: BHs – bank holidays Etr – Easter Spring BH – Spring Bank Holiday fr – from hrs – hours m – mile mdnt – midnight rdbt – roundabout rs – restricted service wk – week wknd – weekend x-roads – crossroads 💳 No credit or debit cards 🚫 No dogs

NORTHAMPTONSHIRE

BULWICK
Map 11 SP99

Places to visit

Lyveden New Bield, LYVEDEN NEW BIELD, PE8 5AT, 01832 205158
www.nationaltrust.org.uk/lyveden

New Lodge Farm Caravan & Camping Site
►►►► 87%

tel: 01780 450493 **New Lodge Farm NN17 3DU**
email: shop@newlodgefarm.com
dir: *On A43 between Corby (5m) & Stamford (8m) turn right at Laxton & Harringworth junct. Site signed.* **grid ref:** *SP959951*

Simon and Sarah Singlehurst have worked hard to create this beautiful adults-only site on their working farm in rural Northamptonshire. The result is impressive – large, fully serviced and level pitches (25 with hardstandings), all with views over the farm and rolling countryside. The heated toilet and amenity block is located in a beautifully restored stone barn, as is the site reception. There's an award-winning farm shop that sells home-reared meats, bread, cakes and locally grown fruit and vegetables. Attached to the shop is a cosy licensed café with a patio area overlooking the site – here breakfasts, lunches and afternoon teas are served. The site is situated in the heart of Rockingham Forest, making it a good base for visiting Stamford, Oundle and Uppingham. 4 acre site. 72 touring pitches. 25 hardstandings. Caravan pitches. Motorhome pitches. Tent pitches.

Open: 3 Apr-Oct **Last arrival:** 20.00hrs **Last departure:** noon

Pitches: 🚐 �♿ 🏕

Facilities: 🏨 🅿 ☉ ℱ ☀ ♿ ⓢ 🚿 WiFi 🖥 ♻ ❶ ⓔ 🎦

Services: 🔌 🖃 🍴 🧺 🔧 Ⓣ 🍽 🛒 🏧 ⬇

Within 3 miles: ⌕ ℱ ⓢ ⓢ ↻

Notes: Adults only. No noise after 23.00hrs. Dogs must be kept on leads. Farm shop & butchery.

NORTHUMBERLAND

BAMBURGH
Map 21 NU13

Places to visit

Chillingham Wild Cattle Park, CHILLINGHAM, NE66 5NP, 01668 215250
www.chillinghamwildcattle.com

Great for kids: Bamburgh Castle, BAMBURGH, NE69 7DF, 01668 214515
www.bamburghcastle.com

Waren Caravan & Camping Park
►►►► 87%

tel: 01668 214366 & 214224 **Waren Mill NE70 7EE**
email: waren@meadowhead.co.uk
dir: *2m E of town. From A1 onto B1342 signed Bamburgh. Take unclassified road past Waren Mill, signed Budle.* **grid ref:** *NU155343*

An attractive seaside site with footpath access to the beach, surrounded by a slightly sloping grassy embankment giving shelter to caravans. The park offers excellent facilities, including smartened up toilet/shower blocks, which have several family bathrooms, fully serviced pitches, and the on-site restaurant serves a good breakfast. There are also wooden wigwam pods for hire. 4 acre site. 150 touring pitches. 41 hardstandings. Caravan pitches. Motorhome pitches. Tent pitches. 300 statics.

Open: Mar-Oct (rs Mar-Spring BH & Oct splash pool closed) **Last arrival:** 20.00hrs **Last departure:** noon

Pitches: * 🚐 £12.50-£28 �♿ £12.50-£28 🏕 £12.50-£25 🏠 prices shown below

Leisure: ⚊ 🎢 🎣 🎵

Facilities: 🛁 🏨 🅿 ☉ ℱ ☀ ♿ ⓢ 🚿 WiFi 🖥 ♻ ❶ ⓔ

Services: 🔌 🖃 🍴 🧺 🔧 Ⓣ 🍽 🛒 🏧 ⬇

Glamping: Wooden Wigwams 8, £31-£58 Changeover day Any day Min stay 2 nights Own kitchen Car by unit

Within 3 miles: ⌕ ℱ ☉ ⓢ ↻

Notes: No noise after 23.00hrs. Dogs must be kept on leads. 100 acres of private heathland. Fire pits for hire, BBQ hut for hire, freshly baked bread available.

AA Pubs & Restaurants nearby: The Olde Ship Inn, SEAHOUSES, NE68 7RD, 01665 720200

Waren House Hotel, BAMBURGH, NE70 7EE, 01668 214581

Glororum Caravan Park
►►►► 81%

tel: 01670 860256 **Glororum Farm NE69 7AW**
email: enquiries@northumbrianleisure.co.uk
dir: *Exit A1 at junct with B1341 (Purdy's Lodge). In 3.5m left onto unclassified road. Site 300yds on left.* **grid ref:** *NU166334*

A pleasantly situated site in an open countryside setting with good views of Bamburgh Castle. A popular holiday destination where tourers have their own separate area – 43 excellent, well-spaced, fully serviced pitches have a lush grass area in addition to the hardstanding. This field also has an excellent purpose-built amenities block with a smartly clad interior and modern, efficient fittings. 6 acre site. 43 touring pitches. 43 hardstandings. 30 seasonal pitches. Caravan pitches. Motorhome pitches. 170 statics.

Open: Mar-end Nov **Last arrival:** 18.00hrs **Last departure:** noon

Pitches: 🚐 🚍

Leisure: ⚽

Facilities: ⊙ 🅿 ✳ ♿ 🚿 🚾 🐕 ❶

Services: 🔌 🔄 🖉 T

Within 3 miles: ⬇ 🚴 🎣 ♨ 🏠 🏌 ↻

Notes: No commercial vehicles, no noise after 23.00hrs. Dogs must be kept on leads.

AA Pubs & Restaurants nearby: The Olde Ship Inn, SEAHOUSES, NE68 7RD, 01665 720200

The Bamburgh Castle Inn, SEAHOUSES, NE68 7SQ, 01665 720283

BELFORD　　　　　　　　　　Map 21 NU13

Places to visit

Bamburgh Castle, BAMBURGH, NE69 7DF, 01668 214515
www.bamburghcastle.com

Lindisfarne Castle, HOLY ISLAND [LINDISFARNE], TD15 2SH, 01289 389244
www.nationaltrust.org.uk

PREMIER PARK

South Meadows Caravan Park

▶ ▶ ▶ ▶ ▶ 93%

tel: 01668 213326 **South Rd NE70 7DP**
email: info@southmeadows.co.uk **web:** www.southmeadows.co.uk
dir: From A1 between Alnwick & Berwick-upon-Tweed take B6349 towards Belford, at right bend site signed, turn left, site on right. **grid ref:** NU115331

South Meadows has become a top quality touring and holiday park. Set in open countryside, it is extremely spacious and no expense has been spared in its landscaping and redevelopment. Tree planting on a grand scale has been carried out, grassy areas are expertly mown and all pitches are fully serviced. The solar heated amenity block is ultra modern, with quality fittings and smart family rooms; everywhere is spotlessly clean and fresh. There's an adventure playground complete with a zip-wire and even dogs have two walking areas, one in a bluebell wood. 50 acre site. 83 touring pitches. 46 hardstandings. 63 seasonal pitches. Caravan pitches. Motorhome pitches. Tent pitches. 103 statics.

Open: all year **Last departure:** 16.00hrs

Pitches: 🚐 🚍 🛖

Leisure: ⚑ ⚽

Facilities: 🚾 🅿 ⊙ 🅿 ✳ ♿ 🖉 🚿 🐕 🚾 ♻ ❶

Services: 🔌 🔄 🔋 🖉 T 🔋 🍼 ↯

Within 3 miles: ⬇ 🏠 🏌 ↻

Notes: Minimum noise after 23.00hrs, under 12s must be supervised in toilet blocks. Dogs must be kept on leads. Baby changing facilities.

AA Pubs & Restaurants nearby: The Apple Inn, LUCKER, NE70 7JL, 01668 213824

BELLINGHAM　　　　　　　　Map 21 NY88

Places to visit

Wallington, CAMBO, NE61 4AR, 01670 773600
www.nationaltrust.org.uk/wallington

PREMIER PARK

Bellingham Camping & Caravanning Club Site

▶ ▶ ▶ ▶ 90%

tel: 01434 220175 & 0845 130 7633 *(Calls cost 7p per minute plus your phone company's access charge)*
Brown Rigg NE48 2JY
dir: From A69 take A6079 N to Chollerford & B6320 to Bellingham. Pass Forestry Commission land, site 0.5m S of Bellingham. **grid ref:** NY835826

A beautiful and peaceful campsite set in the glorious Northumberland National Park. It is exceptionally well managed by the enthusiastic owners who offer high levels of customer care, maintenance and cleanliness. The excellent toilet facilities are spotlessly clean, and there are family washrooms, a recreation room, a campers' kitchen, a drying room, and star-gazing equipment for customers to use. There are four camping pods for hire. This is a perfect base for exploring an undiscovered part of England, and it is handily placed for visiting the beautiful Northumberland coast. 5 acre site. 64 touring pitches. 42 hardstandings. Caravan pitches. Motorhome pitches. Tent pitches.

Open: Mar-4 Jan **Last arrival:** 20.00hrs **Last departure:** noon

Pitches: 🚐 🚍 🛖 🏕

Leisure: 🔍

Facilities: ⊙ 🅿 ✳ ♿ 🖉 🐕 🚾 🖥 ♻ ❶

Services: 🔌 🔄 🔋 🖉 T 🍼 ↯

Glamping: Wooden Pods 4, Min stay 2 nights (3 on BHs)

Within 3 miles: ⬇ 🎣 🏠 🏌

Notes: Site gates closed & quiet time 23.00hrs-07.00hrs. Dogs must be kept on leads.

AA Pubs & Restaurants nearby: The Pheasant Inn, FALSTONE, NE48 1DD, 01434 240382

PITCHES: 🚐 Caravans 🚍 Motorhomes 🛖 Tents 🏕 Glamping accommodation **SERVICES:** 🔌 Electric hook up 🔄 Launderette 🍺 Licensed bar 🔋 Calor Gas 🖉 Camping Gaz T Toilet fluid 🍽 Café/Restaurant 🍔 Fast Food/Takeaway 🔋 Battery charging 🍼 Baby care ↯ Motorvan service point **ABBREVIATIONS:** BHs – bank holidays Etr – Easter Spring BH – Spring Bank Holiday fr – from hrs – hours m – mile mdnt – midnight rdbt – roundabout rs – restricted service wk – week wknd – weekend x-roads – crossroads 🚫 No credit or debit cards 🚫 No dogs

BERWICK-UPON-TWEED
Map 21 NT95

Places to visit

Berwick-upon-Tweed Barracks, BERWICK-UPON-TWEED, TD15 1DF,
01289 304493 www.english-heritage.org.uk/daysout/properties/
berwick-upon-tweed-barracks-and-main-guard

Paxton House, Gallery & Country Park, BERWICK-UPON-TWEED, TD15 1SZ,
01289 386291 www.paxtonhouse.com

Great for kids: Norham Castle, NORHAM, TD15 2JY, 01289 382329
www.english-heritage.org.uk/daysout/properties/norham-castle

Haggerston Castle Holiday Park
HOLIDAY CENTRE 81%

tel: 01289 381333 **Beal TD15 2PA**
email: haggerstoncastle@haven.com **web:** www.haven.com/haggerstoncastle
dir: *On A1, 7m S of Berwick-upon-Tweed, site signed.* **grid ref:** *NU041435*

A large holiday centre with a very well equipped touring park, offering
comprehensive holiday activities. The entertainment complex contains amusements
for the whole family, and there are several bars, an adventure playground, boating
on the lake, a children's club, a 9-hole golf course, tennis courts, and various
eating outlets. Please note that this site does not accept tents. 100 acre site. 140
touring pitches. 140 hardstandings. Caravan pitches. Motorhome pitches. 1200
statics.

Haggerston Castle Holiday Park

Open: mid Mar-end Oct (rs mid Mar-May & Sep-Oct some facilities may be
reduced) **Last arrival:** anytime **Last departure:** 10.00hrs

Pitches: 🚐 🚗

Leisure: 🏊 🎿 🖐 🏕 🎵 Spa 🎣

Facilities: 🛒 ⊙ ✳ ⚷ 🖊 ⑤ 🛒 ⤴ 📶 🖥 ♻ 𝒊

Services: 🚽 🗑 🔧 🏪 🛢 🍴 🍺

Within 3 miles: ⚓ ⊹ ◎ ⑤ 🛢 ↻

Notes: No commercial vehicles, no bookings by persons under 21yrs unless a family
booking. Max 2 dogs per booking, certain dog breeds banned. Dogs must be kept on
leads.

See advert below

LEISURE: 🏊 Indoor pool 🏊 Outdoor pool 🎢 Children's playground 🖐 Kid's club 🎾 Tennis court 🎯 Games room ⛳ Golf course ⚓ Boat hire 🚲 Cycle hire 🎬 Cinema 🎵 Entertainment 🎣 Fishing ◎ Mini golf 🚩 Pitch n putt 🏄 Watersports 🏋 Gym 🏟 Sports field ↻ Stables **FACILITIES:** 🛁 Bath 🚿 Shower 🅿 Private washing cubicles ⊙ Electric shaver 🖊 Hairdryer ✳ Ice Packs ⚷ Disabled facilities ⑤ Shop on site 🛒 Mobile shop 🍖 BBQ area 🏔 Picnic area 📶 Wi-fi 🖥 Internet access ♻ Recycling 𝒊 Tourist info 🐕 Dog exercise area 🚗 Car hire can be arranged

PREMIER PARK

Ord House Country Park
►►►►►86%

tel: 01289 305288 East Ord TD15 2NS
email: enquiries@ordhouse.co.uk
dir: *At rdbt junct of A1 (Berwick bypass) & A698 take exit signed East Ord, follow brown camping signs.* grid ref: *NT982515*

Set within the grounds of 18th-century Ord House, this very well run park takes great pride in the quality of its landscaping and in the siting and spacing of touring pitches, some of which are fully serviced. Young people are well catered for with a fantastic adventure playground, miniature golf and a football field. A broad range of meals are available in Maguires Bar & Restaurant where there is also a soft toy play area for children. Wooden wigwams, each sleeping four, are available for hire. 42 acre site. 79 touring pitches. 46 hardstandings. 30 seasonal pitches. Caravan pitches. Motorhome pitches. Tent pitches. 255 statics.

Open: all year **Last arrival:** 23.00hrs **Last departure:** noon

Pitches: ⊕ ⊕ Å ⋒

Leisure: ✪

Facilities: ⛟ ⋔ ☉ ⌾ ⁂ ⅙ ⓢ ♉ ⼓ ᵂᴵᶠ ✿ 𝟬

Services: ⊕ ⓢ ⓣ ⌂ ∅ ⼂ ⓣ ⓞⅼ ⼓ ⼗

Glamping: Wooden Wigwams 10, £42-£47 Min stay 1 night Car by unit

Within 3 miles: ↧ ⅞ ⊟ ⌇ ☺ ⓢ ⓢ

Notes: No noise after mdnt. Dogs must be kept on leads. Crazy golf, table tennis.

AA Pubs & Restaurants nearby: The Wheatsheaf at Swinton, SWINTON, TD11 3JJ, 01890 860257

Old Mill Caravan Site
►►80%

tel: 01289 381295 & 07791 976535 West Kyloe Farm, Fenwick TD15 2PF
email: leyland@westkyloe.fsnet.co.uk
dir: *A1 onto B6353 (9m S of Berwick-upon-Tweed) signed Lowick & Fenwick. Site 1.5m signed on left.* grid ref: *NU055401*

Small, secluded site accessed through a farm complex, and overlooking a mill pond complete with resident ducks. Some pitches are in a walled garden, and the amenity block is simple but well kept. Delightful walks can be enjoyed on the 600-acre farm. A holiday cottage is also available. 2.5 acre site. 12 touring pitches. Caravan pitches. Motorhome pitches. Tent pitches.

Open: Apr-Oct **Last arrival:** 19.00hrs **Last departure:** 11.00hrs

Pitches: ⊕ ⊕ Å

Facilities: ⋔ ☉ ⅙ ⼓ ✿ 𝟬

Services: ⊕ ⼗

Within 3 miles: ⓢ

Notes: ⊗ No gazebos or open fires. Dogs must be kept on leads. Wet room.

Berwick Holiday Park
HOLIDAY HOME PARK 86%

tel: 01289 307113 Magdalene Fields TD15 1NE
email: berwick@haven.com web: www.haven.com/berwick
dir: *From A1 follow Berwick-upon-Tweed signs. At Morrisons/McDonalds rdbt take 2nd exit. At mini rdbt straight on, into North Rd (pass Shell garage on left). At next mini rdbt 1st exit into Northumberland Ave. Park at end.* grid ref: *NT998535*

This all-happening, static-only holiday park has direct access to a beach on the edge of Berwick, and offers exciting family activities and entertainment including the FunWorks Amusement Centre and a multisports court.

Open: Mar-Oct

Changeover day: Mon, Fri, Sat

Arrival and departure times: Please contact the site

Statics: 204 Sleeps 6-8 Bedrms 2-3 Bathrms 1-2 Toilets 1-2 Microwave Freezer TV Sky/FTV Elec inc Gas inc Grass area

Children: ⋔⋔ Cots Highchair **Dogs:** 2 on leads No dangerous dogs

Leisure: ☁ ☁ Cycle hire ✋ ⼓

PITCHES: ⊕ Caravans ⊕ Motorhomes Å Tents ⋒ Glamping accommodation **SERVICES:** ⊕ Electric hook up ⓢ Launderette ⓣ Licensed bar ⌂ Calor Gas ∅ Camping Gaz ⓣ Toilet fluid ⓞⅼ Café/Restaurant ⼓ Fast Food/Takeaway ⼂ Battery charging ⼓ Baby care ⼗ Motorvan service point
ABBREVIATIONS: BHs – bank holidays Etr – Easter Spring BH – Spring Bank Holiday fr – from hrs – hours m – mile mdnt – midnight rdbt – roundabout rs – restricted service wk – week wknd – weekend x-roads – crossroads ⊗ No credit or debit cards ⊗ No dogs

HALTWHISTLE　　　　　　　　　　　Map 21 NY76

Places to visit

Corbridge Roman Site and Museum, CORBRIDGE, NE45 5NT, 01434 632349 www.english-heritage.org.uk/daysout/properties/corbridge-roman-town-hadrians-wall

Chesters Roman Fort, WALWICK, NE46 4EP, 01434 681379 www.english-heritage.org.uk/daysout/properties/chesters-roman-fort-and-museum-hadrians-wall

PREMIER PARK

Herding Hill Farm
▶▶▶▶▶ 90%

tel: 01434 320175 **Shield Hill NE49 9NW**
email: bookings@herdinghillfarm.co.uk **web:** www.herdinghillfarm.co.uk
dir: *From W: exit A69 at Greenhead onto B6318 towards Chollerford. Follow brown campsite signs. From E: exit A69 at Corbridge onto A68 N, left onto B6318 towards Greenhead. Approx 12m, follow campsite signs.* **grid ref:** NY712649

In an idyllic moorland location above Haltwhistle, close to Hadrian's Wall, this beautifully developed working farm site is geared to families and offers a mix of accommodation — excellent tent pitches, quality hardstandings, a bunkhouse sleeping 28, a 6-berth lodge, and a glamping area (see next entry). The upmarket amenity block is really ultra-modern — the internal red and grey partitioning really sets off the very high standard of fixtures and fittings, and the underfloor heating is very welcoming. A drying room, barbecues and fire baskets, a playground and petting farm, an excellent shop and café, and activities such as star-gazing, geo-caching, and walking along Hadrian's Wall complete the package. This is a top-class site developed over the last few years by the hands-on owners. 4.86 acre site. 22 touring pitches. 13 hardstandings. Caravan pitches. Motorhome pitches. Tent pitches.

Open: Feb-3 Jan **Last arrival:** 20.00hrs (later arrivals by prior arrangement) **Last departure:** 11.00hrs

Pitches: ⚐ £24-£28 ⚑ £24-£28 Å £24-£32

Facilities: ⬢🏠Ⓟ⊙☛✳⚲🅰🛒📶♻❶

Services: ⚐🔟🅱🖊Ⓣ🛒⚱🖤↯

Within 3 miles: ↧🖊🅢🔟∪

Notes: No noise after 23.00hrs. Dogs must be kept on leads. Unisex sauna, takeaway pizza Fri-Sat in season. Only basic essentials sold.

Herding Hill Farm, Glamping Site
NEW ▶▶▶▶▶ 88%　　　　　　　　　　　　🏛

tel: 01434 320175 **Shied Hill NE49 9NW**
email: bookings@herdinghillfarm.co.uk **web:** www.herdinghillfarm.co.uk
dir: *From W: exit A69 at Greenhead onto B6318 towards Chollerford. Follow brown campsite signs. From E: exit A69 at Corbridge onto A68 N, left onto B6318 towards Greenhead. Approx 12m, follow campsite signs.*

Located above the town of Haltwhistle and very close to Hadrian's Wall, this developing glamping site is ideally suited for walkers, ramblers and historians alike. Separate from the touring area at the bottom of the site on a rolling hillside, the units enjoy panoramic views. Owners Steve and Ann have created diversity by mixing wooden wigwams with tipis and Lotus Belle tents. Each unit has electric heating and seven of the wigwams have their own toilet and washbasin; all units have full use of the modern amenity block located between the glamping and touring areas. Bedding is provided in the Lotus Belle tents only. BBQs and fire pits can be hired, and there is a sauna too. 4 acre site.

Open: 3 Feb-Jan **Last arrival:** 20.00hrs **Last departure:** 10.00hrs

Glamping: Lotus Belle tents 4, £60-£88 Changeover day Any day Min stay 2 nights Own kitchen **Wooden Wigwams** 17, £60-£88 Changeover day Any day Min stay 2 nights En suite Own kitchen Car by unit **Tipis** 3, £60-£88 Changeover day Any day Min stay 2 nights

HEXHAM　　　　　　　　　　　　　　Map 21 NY96

Places to visit

Vindolanda (Chesterholm), BARDON MILL, NE47 7JN, 01434 344277 www.vindolanda.com

Temple of Mithras (Hadrian's Wall), CARRAWBROUGH, 0370 333 1181 www.english-heritage.org.uk/daysout/properties/temple-of-mithras-carrawburgh-hadrians-wall

Great for kids: Housesteads Roman Fort, HOUSESTEADS, NE47 6NN, 01434 344363 www.english-heritage.org.uk/daysout/properties/housesteads-roman-fort-hadrians-wall

Hexham Racecourse Caravan Site
▶▶▶ 74%

tel: 01434 606847 & 606881 **Hexham Racecourse NE46 2JP**
email: hexrace.caravan@btconnect.com
dir: *From Hexham take B6305 signed Allendale & Alston. Left in 3m signed to racecourse. Site 1.5m on right.* **grid ref:** NY919623

A part-level and part-sloping grassy site situated on a racecourse overlooking Hexhamshire Moors. The facilities, although clean, are of an older but functional type. 4 acre site. 50 touring pitches. 20 seasonal pitches. Caravan pitches. Motorhome pitches. Tent pitches.

Open: May-Sep **Last arrival:** 20.00hrs **Last departure:** noon

Pitches: * ⚐ £15-£18 ⚑ £15-£18 Å fr £11

Leisure: 🅐🎣

Facilities: 🏠⊙Ⓟ✳🅰🛒📶❶

Services: ⚐🔟🅱🖊🖤

Within 3 miles: ↧☕🎣🖊◎🅢🔟

Notes: No noise after 23.00hrs. Dogs must be kept on leads.

AA Pubs & Restaurants nearby: Miners Arms Inn, HEXHAM, NE46 4PW, 01434 603909

Dipton Mill Inn, HEXHAM, NE46 1YA, 01434 606577

Rat Inn, HEXHAM, NE46 4LN, 01434 602814

SEAHOUSES
Map 21 NU23

Places to visit

Bamburgh Castle, BAMBURGH, NE69 7DF, 01668 214515
www.bamburghcastle.com

Lindisfarne Castle, HOLY ISLAND (LINDISFARNE), TD15 2SH, 01289 389244
www.nationaltrust.org.uk

Westfield Paddock
► 71%

tel: 01665 478988 & 721380 **Westfield Farmhouse NE68 7UR**
email: info@westfieldpaddock.co.uk
dir: From A1 (15m N of Alnwick) take B1341 to Bamburgh. Right to Seahouses on B1340. In 2m right signed Elford. Site 1.5m at x-roads. **grid ref:** NU203318

A peaceful, adults-only site set in a lush grassy paddock beside the owners' house; it's a 20-minute walk to Seahouses and a 15-minute walk to Bamburgh beach. The site is popular with self-sufficient motorhome and caravan owners (tents are not permitted), each of the 10 pitches has its own water and electricity. The site does not have toilets and showers, and therefore own facilities are essential; there is a chemical waste disposal point. The site has a totally enclosed dog run. Fresh eggs can be bought from the owners. 2 acre site. 10 touring pitches. 2 hardstandings. Caravan pitches. Motorhome pitches.

Open: Mar-2 Jan **Last arrival:** 21.00hrs **Last departure:** 11.00hrs

Pitches: * ⊞ £15-£18 ⊞ £15-£18

Facilities: ✳ ⌁ WiFi 🖵 ♻ ❶

Services: ⊞ T ≟

Within 3 miles: ≟ ≑ ⊞ ⌁ ◎ ≋ 🖩 🖩 ∪

Notes: Adults only. PayPal accepted. Dogs must be kept on leads.

AA Pubs & Restaurants nearby: The Bamburgh Castle Inn, SEAHOUSES, NE68 7SQ, 01665 720283

WOOLER

Places to visit

Chillingham Castle, CHILLINGHAM, NE66 5NJ, 01668 215359
www.chillingham-castle.com

Great for kids: Chillingham Wild Cattle Park, CHILLINGHAM, NE66 5NP, 01668 215250 www.chillinghamwildcattle.com

WOOLER
Map 21 NT92

Riverside Leisure Park
►►►85%

tel: 01668 281447 **South Rd NE71 6NJ**
email: reception@riverside-wooler.co.uk
dir: From S: A1 to Morpeth, A697 signed Wooler & Coldstream. In Wooler, park on left. From N: From Berwick-upon-Tweed on A1, 1st right signed Wooler (B6525). Through Wooler on A697. Park on right. **grid ref:** NT993279

This is the sister park to Thurston Manor Leisure Park at Dunbar in East Lothian. It is set in the heart of stunning Northumberland countryside on the edge of Wooler Water. Very much family orientated, the park offers excellent leisure facilities including swimming pools, a bar and a restaurant, weekend entertainment and riverside and woodland walks. Fly fishing for rainbow trout is possible at the site's own lake. Please note, tents are not accepted. Wooden pods are available for hire. 90 acre site. 50 touring pitches. 50 hardstandings. 35 seasonal pitches. Caravan pitches. Motorhome pitches. 350 statics.

Open: all year (rs Nov-Mar swimming pool closed) **Last departure:** noon

Pitches: ⊞ ⊞ 🅰 **Leisure:** ≋ ⌁ ◉ ❀ 🎵

Facilities: ⊙ ℐ ✳ ⅊ 🖩 🖩 ⌁ WiFi ♻ ❶

Services: ⊞ ⊟ 🍽 🔋 ⌀ T 🍴 ≟

Glamping: Wooden Pods 4

Within 3 miles: ≟ ⌁ 🖩 🖩 ∪

Notes: No noise after 22.00hrs. Dogs must be kept on leads.

AA Pubs & Restaurants nearby: The Red Lion Inn, MILFIELD, NE71 6JD, 01668 216224

NOTTINGHAMSHIRE

CHURCH LANEHAM
Map 17 SK87

Places to visit

Newark Air Museum, NEWARK-ON-TRENT, NG24 2NY, 01636 707170
www.newarkairmuseum.org

Trentfield Farm
►►►81%

tel: 01777 228651 **DN22 0NJ**
email: post@trentfield.co.uk
dir: A1 onto A57 towards Lincoln for 6m. Left signed Laneham, 1.5m, through Laneham & Church Laneham (pass Ferryboat pub on left) Site 300yds on right. **grid ref:** SK815774

A delightfully rural and level grass park tucked away on the banks of the River Trent. The park has its own river frontage with free coarse fishing available to park residents. The cosy local pub, which serves food, is under the same ownership. 34 acre site. 45 touring pitches. 20 seasonal pitches. Caravan pitches. Motorhome pitches. Tent pitches.

Open: Etr-Nov **Last arrival:** 20.00hrs **Last departure:** noon

Pitches: ⊞ £18-£23.50 ⊞ £18-£23.50 🅰 £10-£23.50

Facilities: ⋔ 🅿 ⊙ ⅊ ✳ 🖩 🖩 ⌁ WiFi ♻ ❶

Services: ⊞ ⊟ ≟ ⌁ **Within 3 miles:** ≟ ⌁ 🖩 🖩 ∪

Notes: Dogs must be kept on leads. 24hr mini shop.

PITCHES: ⊞ Caravans ⊞ Motorhomes 🅰 Tents 🅜 Glamping accommodation **SERVICES:** ⊞ Electric hook up ⊟ Launderette 🍽 Licensed bar 🔋 Calor Gas ⌀ Camping Gaz T Toilet fluid 🍴 Café/Restaurant ⊞ Fast Food/Takeaway ≟ Battery charging ≋ Baby care ⌁ Motorvan service point

ABBREVIATIONS: BHs – bank holidays Etr – Easter Spring BH – Spring Bank Holiday fr – from hrs – hours m – mile mdnt – midnight rdbt – roundabout rs – restricted service wk – week wknd – weekend x-roads – crossroads 🚫 No credit or debit cards 🚫 No dogs

MANSLEY
MANSFIELD
Map 16 SK56

Places to visit

Sherwood Forest Country Park & Visitor Centre, EDWINSTOWE, NG21 9HN, 01623 823202 www.nottinghamshire.gov.uk/sherwoodforestcp

Tall Trees Touring Park
▶▶▶86%

BRONZE

tel: 01623 626503 & 07770 661957 **Old Mill Ln, Forest Town NG19 0JP**
email: info@talltreestouringpark.co.uk web: www.talltreestouringpark.co.uk
dir: *A60 from Mansfield towards Worksop. After 1m turn right at lights into Old Mill Lane. Site approx 0.5m on left.* grid ref: *SK551626*

A very pleasant park situated just on the outskirts of Mansfield and within easy walking distance of shops and restaurants. It is surrounded on three sides by trees and shrubs, and securely set at the back of the residential park. This site has a modern amenities block, a fishing lake to the rear of the site and an extra grassed area to give more space for caravans and tents. 10 acre site. 37 touring pitches. 10 hardstandings. 5 seasonal pitches. Caravan pitches. Motorhome pitches. Tent pitches.

Open: all year **Last arrival:** anytime **Last departure:** anytime
Pitches: * ⊞ £15-£27 ⊞ £15-£27 ▲ £15-£27
Leisure: ⋒ ⊕ ⅃ ✎
Facilities: ⋔ ⊙ ℙ & ⊟ ⇌ 📶 ♲ ❼
Services: 🔌 ⑤
Within 3 miles: ⅃ ⊟ ✎ ⑤ ⑤ ∪

Notes: No noise after mdnt. Dogs must be kept on leads.
AA Pubs & Restaurants nearby: Forest Lodge, EDWINSTOWE, NG21 9QA, 01623 824443
Fox & Hounds, BLIDWORTH, NG21 0NW, 01623 792383

NEWARK

See Southwell

RADCLIFFE ON TRENT
Map 11 SK63

Places to visit

Nottingham Castle Museum & Art Gallery, NOTTINGHAM, NG1 6EL, 0115 876 1400 www.nottinghamcity.gov.uk/Castle

Wollaton Hall, Gardens & Deer Park, NOTTINGHAM, NG8 2AE, 0115 915 3900 www.nottingham.gov.uk/wollatonhall

Thornton's Holt Camping Park
▶▶▶83%

tel: 0115 933 2125 & 933 4204 **Stragglethorpe Rd, Stragglethorpe NG12 2JZ**
email: camping@thorntons-holt.co.uk
dir: *Take A52, 3m E of Nottingham. Turn S at lights towards Cropwell Bishop. Site 0.5m on left. Or A46 SE of Nottingham (Stragglethorpe junct) site 2.5m on right.*
grid ref: *SK638377*

A well-run family site in former meadowland, with pitches located among young trees and bushes for a rural atmosphere and outlook. The toilets are housed in converted farm buildings, and an indoor swimming pool is a popular attraction. 13 acre site. 155 touring pitches. 35 hardstandings. 20 seasonal pitches. Caravan pitches. Motorhome pitches. Tent pitches.

Open: all year (rs Nov-Mar swimming pool & shop closed) **Last arrival:** 20.00hrs
Last departure: noon
Pitches: * ⊞ £19.50-£24 ⊞ £19.50-£24 ▲ £16-£24
Leisure: ⇔ ⋒
Facilities: ⋔ ⊙ ℙ ✲ & ⑤ ⇌ 📶 ▭ ♲ ❼
Services: 🔌 ⑤ 🛢 ⊘ ⊤ ⊠ ⅄
Within 3 miles: ⅃ ✦ ⊟ ✎ ⇔ ⑤ ⑤ ∪

Notes: No noise after 22.00hrs. Dogs must be kept on leads.
AA Pubs & Restaurants nearby: Ye Olde Trip to Jerusalem, NOTTINGHAM, NG1 6AD, 0115 947 3171
World Service, NOTTINGHAM, NG1 6AF, 0115 847 5587

SOUTHWELL
Map 17 SK65

Places to visit

The Workhouse, SOUTHWELL, NG25 0PT, 01636 817260
www.nationaltrust.org.uk/theworkhouse

New Hall Farm Touring Park
▶▶▶82%

tel: 01623 883041 **New Hall Farm, New Hall Ln NG22 8BS**
email: enquiries@newhallfarm.co.uk
dir: *From A614 at White Post Modern Farm Centre follow Southwell signs. Immediately after Edingley into New Hall Ln to site.* grid ref: *SK660550*

A park on a working stock farm with the elevated pitching area enjoying outstanding panoramic views. It is within a short drive of medieval Newark and

LEISURE: ⇔ Indoor pool ⇔ Outdoor pool ⋒ Children's playground ⅃ Kid's club ⅃ Tennis court ⚲ Games room ⅃ Golf course ✦ Boat hire ⚙ Cycle hire ⊟ Cinema ♫ Entertainment ✎ Fishing ⊙ Mini golf ⚲ Pitch n putt ⇔ Watersports ⅄ Gym ⊛ Sports field ∪ Stables **FACILITIES:** ⛉ Bath ⋔ Shower ℙ Private washing cubicles ⊙ Electric shaver ℙ Hairdryer ✲ Ice Packs & Disabled facilities ⑤ Shop on site ⚏ Mobile shop ▭ BBQ area ⇌ Picnic area 📶 Wi-fi ▭ Internet access ♲ Recycling ❼ Tourist info ⇌ Dog exercise area ⚐ Car hire can be arranged

Sherwood Forest. A log cabin viewing gantry offers a place to relax and take in the spectacular scenery. 2.5 acre site. 25 touring pitches. 10 hardstandings. 7 seasonal pitches. Caravan pitches. Motorhome pitches. Tent pitches.

Open: Mar-Oct **Last arrival:** 21.00hrs **Last departure:** 13.00hrs

Pitches: ⚐ £10-£22 ⛟ £10-£22 ⚑ £10-£22

Facilities: ☉ ✻ ⌓ ⚞ ♺ ❼

Services: ⚐⊠ ▤

Within 3 miles: ⚓ ⋰ ᐧ⌂⊠⊙

Notes: Adults only. ⊗ Quiet after 22.00hrs. Dogs must be kept on leads.

AA Pubs & Restaurants nearby: Tom Browns Brasserie, GUNTHORPE, NG14 7FB, 0115 966 3642

TEVERSAL	Map 16 SK46

Places to visit

Hardwick Hall, HARDWICK HALL, S44 5QJ, 01246 850430
www.nationaltrust.org.uk/hardwick

PREMIER PARK

Teversal Camping & Caravanning Club Site
▶▶▶▶▶ 92%

tel: 01623 551838 Silverhill Ln NG17 3JJ
dir: *M1 junct 28, A38 towards Mansfield. Left at lights onto B6027. At top of hill straight over at lights, left at Tesco Express. Right onto B6014, left at Carnarvon Arms, site on left.* **grid ref:** *SK472615*

A top notch park with excellent purpose-built facilities and innovative, hands-on owners. Each pitch is spacious, the excellent toilet facilities are state-of-the-art, and there are views of, and access to, the countryside and nearby Silverhill Community Woods. Both the attention to detail and the all-round quality are truly exceptional – guests can even hire a car for a day and there is a special area for washing dogs and bikes. The site has a shop. Buses for Sutton Ashfield and Chesterfield stop just a five-minute walk from the site. A six-berth holiday caravan, luxury ready-erected safari tents and a log cabin are available for hire. Good pub food can be found only a few minutes' walk from the site. 6 acre site. 126 touring pitches. 92 hardstandings. Caravan pitches. Motorhome pitches. Tent pitches. 7 statics.

Open: all year **Last arrival:** 20.00hrs **Last departure:** noon

Pitches: ⚐ ⛟ ⚑ ⋔

Leisure: ✿

Facilities: ☉ ⌱ ✻ ⅃ ❶ ⚞ WiFi ♺ ❼ ⚒

Services: ⚐⊠ ⚿⌀ T ᐧ⌂

Glamping: Safari tents 2, £44-£66 Changeover day Any day Min stay 3 nights Own kitchen Car by unit **Cabins** 1, £50-£80 Changeover day Mon, Fri Min stay 3 nights (Fri-Sun), 4 nights (Mon-Fri) Own kitchen Car by unit

Within 3 miles: ⚓ ⋰ ⌂⊙

Notes: Site gates closed 23.00hrs-07.00hrs. Dogs must be kept on leads.

OXFORDSHIRE

BANBURY	Map 11 SP44

Places to visit

Banbury Museum, BANBURY, OX16 2PQ, 01295 753752
www.banburymuseum.org

Great for kids: Deddington Castle, DEDDINGTON, OX15 0TE, 0370 333 1181
www.english-heritage.org.uk/daysout/properties/deddington-castle

Barnstones Caravan & Camping Site
▶▶▶▶ 84%

tel: 01295 750289 Great Bourton OX17 1QU
dir: *Take A423 from Banbury signed Southam. In 3m turn right signed Great Bourton & Cropredy, site 100yds on right.* **grid ref:** *SP455454*

A popular, neatly laid-out site with plenty of hardstandings, some fully serviced pitches, a smart up-to-date toilet block, and excellent rally facilities. Well run by a very personable owner, this is an excellent value park. The site is well positioned for stopovers or for visiting nearby Banbury. 3 acre site. 49 touring pitches. 44 hardstandings. Caravan pitches. Motorhome pitches. Tent pitches.

Open: all year

Pitches: ⚐ £14-£16 ⛟ £14-£16 ⚑ £10-£14

Leisure: ✿

Facilities: ☉ ✻ ⅃ ⌓ ⚞ WiFi ♺ ❼

Services: ⚐⊠ ⚿⌀ ▤ ⊞ ᐧ⌂

Within 3 miles: ⚓ ⋰ ᐧ⊟⌱ ◎ ⋰⌂⊠⊙

Notes: ⊗ Dogs must be kept on leads.

AA Pubs & Restaurants nearby: Ye Olde Reindeer Inn, BANBURY, OX16 5NA, 01295 270972

The Wykham Arms, BANBURY, OX15 5RX, 01295 788808

Saye and Sele Arms, BROUGHTON, OX15 5ED, 01295 263348

PITCHES: ⚐ Caravans ⛟ Motorhomes ⚑ Tents ⋔ Glamping accommodation **SERVICES:** ⚐ Electric hook up ⊠ Launderette ⚑ Licensed bar ⚿ Calor Gas ⌀ Camping Gaz T Toilet fluid ⽏ Café/Restaurant ⊞ Fast Food/Takeaway ▤ Battery charging ⚒ Baby care ᐧ⌂ Motorvan service point **ABBREVIATIONS:** BHs – bank holidays Etr – Easter Spring BH – Spring Bank Holiday fr – from hrs – hours m – mile mdnt – midnight rdbt – roundabout rs – restricted service wk – week wknd – weekend x-roads – crossroads ⊗ No credit or debit cards ⊗ No dogs

BLETCHINGDON   Map 11 SP51

Places to visit

Rousham House, ROUSHAM, OX25 4QX, 01869 347110 www.rousham.org

Museum of the History of Science, OXFORD, OX1 3AZ, 01865 277280 www.mhs.ox.ac.uk

Great for kids: Oxford University Museum of Natural History, OXFORD, OX1 3PW, 01865 272950 www.oum.ox.ac.uk

Greenhill Leisure Park
▶▶▶▶ 91%

tel: 01869 351600 **Greenhill Farm, Station Rd OX5 3BQ**
email: info@greenhill-leisure-park.co.uk **web:** www.greenhill-leisure-park.co.uk
dir: M40 junct 9, A34 S for 3m. Take B4027 to Bletchingdon. Site 0.5m after village on left. **grid ref:** SP488178

An all-year round park with spacious pitches, set in open countryside near the village of Bletchingdon and well placed for visiting Oxford and the Cotswolds. Fishing is available at the park's two well-stocked lakes and nearby river. This is a family-friendly park and certainly maintains the owner's 'where fun meets the countryside' philosophy. The facilities are very good and include an excellent reception, shop and café-bar, and 12 fully serviced pitches. 7 acre site. 92 touring pitches. 44 hardstandings. 20 seasonal pitches. Caravan pitches. Motorhome pitches. Tent pitches.

Open: all year (rs Oct-Mar no dogs, games room closed) **Last arrival:** 21.00hrs (20.00hrs in winter) **Last departure:** noon

Pitches: ⛟ £16-£22 ⛺ £16-£22 ▲ £16-£22

Leisure: ◣ ✐

Facilities: ⌂ Ⓟ ⊙ ☞ ✳ ⚙ ⓢ ⌸ ⊞ ⅷ ▤ ♺ ❻

Services: ⚑ ⓢ ⌁ ⎖ ⌔ Ⓣ ❘❙ ⚞

Within 3 miles: ⌿ ✐ ⓢ ⓢ

Notes: PayPal accepted. No camp fires or fire pits. Dogs must be kept on leads.

AA Pubs & Restaurants nearby: The Oxford Arms, KIRTLINGTON, OX5 3HA, 01869 350208

The Feathers Hotel, WOODSTOCK, OX20 1SX, 01993 812291

Diamond Farm Caravan & Camping Park
▶▶▶▶ 85%

tel: 01869 350909 **Islip Rd OX5 3DR**
email: warden@diamondpark.co.uk
dir: M40 junct 9, A34 S for 3m, B4027 to Bletchingdon. Site 1m on left.
grid ref: SP513170

A well-run, quiet rural site in good level surroundings, and ideal for touring the Cotswolds, situated seven miles north of Oxford in the heart of the Thames Valley. This popular park has excellent facilities, and offers a heated outdoor swimming pool, a games room for children and a small bar. 3 acre site. 37 touring pitches. 20 hardstandings. Caravan pitches. Motorhome pitches. Tent pitches.

Open: all year (rs Sep-May bar & swimming pool closed) **Last arrival:** dusk **Last departure:** 11.00hrs

Pitches: * ⛟ £19-£22 ⛺ £19-£22 ▲ £19-£22

Leisure: ◣ ◢ ◥ **Facilities:** ⌂ ⌐ Ⓟ ⊙ ☞ ✳ ⓢ ⅷ ▤ ♺ ❻

Services: ⚑ ⓢ ⌁ ⎖ ⌔ Ⓣ ⚞ ⌄

Within 3 miles: ⌿ ✐ ⓢ

Notes: ⊙ PayPal accepted. No gazebos or campfires, no groups occupying more than 3 pitches, no noise after 22.30hrs. Dogs must be kept on leads.

AA Pubs & Restaurants nearby: The Oxford Arms, KIRTLINGTON, OX5 3HA, 01869 350208

The Feathers Hotel, WOODSTOCK, OX20 1SX, 01993 812291

BURFORD   Map 5 SP21

Places to visit

Minster Lovell Hall & Dovecote, MINSTER LOVELL, OX29 0RR, 0370 333 1181 www.english-heritage.org.uk/daysout/properties/ minster-lovell-hall-and-dovecote

Cotswold Wildlife Park and Gardens, BURFORD, OX18 4JP, 01993 823006 www.cotswoldwildlifepark.co.uk

Wysdom Touring Park
▶▶ 85%

tel: 01993 823207 **Cheltenham Rd OX18 4PL**
dir: From rdbt on A40 in Burford take A361 towards Lechdale-on-Thames. Turn right signed Burford School. 100yds to site. **grid ref:** SP248117

Owned by Burford School, this small adults-only park is very much a hidden gem being just a five-minute walk from Burford, one of prettiest towns in the Cotswolds. The pitches have good privacy; all have electricity and there are many hardstandings for caravans and motorhomes. The unisex toilet facilities are very clean. This makes a good base from which to explore the Cotswolds. 25 touring pitches. 14 hardstandings. Caravan pitches. Motorhome pitches.

Open: all year **Last arrival:** 21.00hrs **Last departure:** noon

Pitches: * ⛟ £15-£17 ⛺ £15-£17

Facilities: ⌂ Ⓟ ⊙ ❻

Services: ⚑ **Within 3 miles:** ⌿ ⓢ ⓢ

Notes: Adults only. Dogs must be kept on leads.

AA Pubs & Restaurants nearby: The Lamb Inn, BURFORD, OX18 4LR, 01993 823155

The Highway Inn, BURFORD, OX18 4RG, 01993 823661

The Angel at Burford, BURFORD, OX18 4SN, 01993 822714

LEISURE: ◣ Indoor pool ◢ Outdoor pool ◿ Children's playground ⛹ Kid's club ◔ Tennis court ◣ Games room ⌿ Golf course ◥ Boat hire ◉ Cycle hire
◰ Cinema ♫ Entertainment ✐ Fishing ◉ Mini golf ⚑ Pitch n putt ◿ Watersports ⚐ Gym ◉ Sports field ◡ Stables **FACILITIES:** ⌸ Bath ⌂ Shower
Ⓟ Private washing cubicles ⊙ Electric shaver ☞ Hairdryer ✳ Ice Packs ⅷ Disabled facilities ⓢ Shop on site ⌨ Mobile shop ▤ BBQ area ⌷ Picnic area
ⅷ Wi-fi ▤ Internet access ♺ Recycling ❻ Tourist info ⌀ Dog exercise area ⌇ Car hire can be arranged

FRINGFORD

Map 11 SP62

Places to visit

Rousham House, ROUSHAM, OX25 4QX, 01869 347110 www.rousham.org

Buckinghamshire Railway Centre, QUAINTON, HP22 4BY, 01296 655720 www.bucksrailcentre.org

Glebe Leisure
►►► 79%

tel: 01869 277800 & 277410 **Stratton Ln OX27 8RJ**
email: ann.herring@btinternet.com
dir: *M40 junct 10, A43 (signed Northampton). At next rdbt take B4100 signed Bicester. 2nd right onto unclassified road signed Hethe & Stoke Lyne. Follow brown site signs.*
grid ref: *SP589273*

Glebe Leisure is a peaceful small park in a good countryside location just a few miles from Bicester and the M40, making it an ideal overnight stopover site. It is also very popular with fishing enthusiasts due to the well-stocked lake, and with keen shoppers wishing to spend time at the Bicester Village shopping outlet, three miles away. The park comprises two well-tended fields — one with hardstandings and three camping pods, the other with neat grassy pitches. The main toilet block offers clean, well maintained facilities and there's a good motorhome service point. 5 acre site. 39 touring pitches. 15 hardstandings. Caravan pitches. Motorhome pitches. Tent pitches.

Open: all year **Last arrival:** anytime **Last departure:** anytime

Pitches: * ☐ £18-£26 ☐ £18-£26 ▲ £18-£22 ☐ prices shown below

Leisure: ✐

Facilities: ☐ & ☐ ☐ WiFi ☐ ☐ ☐

Services: ☐ ☐ ☐ ☐

Glamping: **Wooden Pods** 3, £30-£40 Changeover day Any day Min stay 1 day Car by unit

Within 3 miles: ☐ ☐ ✐ ☐ ☐ ∪

Notes: No noise or taxis after 23.00hrs, no unaccompanied children in toilet block or around lakes. Dogs must be kept on leads. Dog walks.

AA Pubs & Restaurants nearby: The Butchers Arms, FRINGFORD, OX27 8EB, 01869 277363

The Muddy Duck, HETHE, OX27 8ES, 01869 278099

HENLEY-ON-THAMES
Map 5 SU78

Places to visit

Greys Court, HENLEY-ON-THAMES, RG9 4PG, 01491 628529
www.nationaltrust.org.uk

River & Rowing Museum, HENLEY-ON-THAMES, RG9 1BF, 01491 415600
www.rrm.co.uk

PREMIER PARK

Swiss Farm Touring & Camping

▶▶▶▶▶ 93%

Best of British

tel: 01491 573419 **Marlow Rd RG9 2HY**
email: info@swissfarmhenley.co.uk **web:** www.swissfarmcamping.co.uk
dir: *From Henley-on-Thames take A4155, towards Marlow. 1st left after rugby club.*
grid ref: *SU759837*

This park enjoys an excellent location within easy walking distance of the town
and is perfect for those visiting the Henley Regatta (but booking is essential at
that time). Pitches are spacious and well appointed, and include some that are
fully serviced. There is a tasteful bar plus a nice outdoor swimming pool. There
are wooden pods and a luxury lodge for hire. 6 acre site. 140 touring pitches.
100 hardstandings. Caravan pitches. Motorhome pitches. Tent pitches.
6 statics.

Open: Mar-Nov (rs Mar-May & Oct-Nov pool closed) **Last arrival:** 21.00hrs
Last departure: noon

Pitches: * ⌂ £19.50-£31.50 ⌂ £22.50-£31.50 Ⓐ £16.50-£26 ⌂ prices shown
below

Leisure: ⌂ **Facilities:** ⌂⌂⌂⌂⌂⌂⌂⌂⌂⌂⌂⌂⌂⌂⌂
Services: ⌂⌂⌂⌂⌂⌂⌂⌂⌂

Glamping: **Wooden Pods** 2, £75-£110 Min stay 2 nights En suite Own kitchen

Within 3 miles: ⌂⌂⌂⌂⌂⌂⌂

Notes: No groups, no dogs during spring half term & summer hols. Dogs must be kept
on leads.

AA Pubs & Restaurants nearby: The Little Angel, HENLEY-ON-THAMES, RG9 2LS,
01491 411008

Crooked Billet, STOKE ROW, RG9 5PU, 01491 681048

See advert on page 275

STANDLAKE
Map 5 SP30

Places to visit

Buscot Park, BUSCOT, SN7 8BU, 01367 240786 www.buscotpark.com

Harcourt Arboretum, OXFORD, OX44 9PX, 01865 343501
http://www.harcourt-arboretum.ox.ac.uk/

Great for kids: Cotswold Wildlife Park and Gardens, BURFORD, OX18 4JP,
01993 823006 www.cotswoldwildlifepark.co.uk

PREMIER PARK

Lincoln Farm Park Oxfordshire

▶▶▶▶▶ 96%

Best of British

tel: 01865 300239 **High St OX29 7RH**
email: info@lincolnfarmpark.co.uk **web:** www.lincolnfarmpark.co.uk
dir: *Exit A415 between Abingdon & Witney, 5m SE of Witney. Follow brown campsite
sign in Standlake.* **grid ref:** *SP395028*

This attractively landscaped family-run park, located in a quiet village near the
River Thames, offers a truly excellent camping or caravanning experience. There
are top class facilities throughout the park. It has excellent leisure facilities in
the Standlake Leisure Centre complete with two pools plus gym, sauna etc. This
is the perfect base for visiting the many attractions in Oxfordshire and the
Cotswolds. A warm welcome is assured from the friendly staff. 9 acre site. 90
touring pitches. 75 hardstandings. Caravan pitches. Motorhome pitches. Tent
pitches.

Open: Feb-Nov **Last arrival:** 20.00hrs **Last departure:** noon

Pitches: ⌂⌂Ⓐ

LEISURE: ⌂ Indoor pool ⌂ Outdoor pool ⌂ Children's playground ⌂ Kid's club ⌂ Tennis court ⌂ Games room ⌂ Golf course ⌂ Boat hire ⌂ Cycle hire
⌂ Cinema ⌂ Entertainment ⌂ Fishing ⌂ Mini golf ⌂ Pitch n putt ⌂ Watersports ⌂ Gym ⌂ Sports field ⌂ Stables **FACILITIES:** ⌂ Bath ⌂ Shower
⌂ Private washing cubicles ⌂ Electric shaver ⌂ Hairdryer ⌂ Ice Packs ⌂ Disabled facilities ⌂ Shop on site ⌂ Mobile shop ⌂ BBQ area ⌂ Picnic area
⌂ Wi-fi ⌂ Internet access ⌂ Recycling ⌂ Tourist info ⌂ Dog exercise area ⌂ Car hire can be arranged

Leisure: ≋ ⊕ ✎ Spa

Facilities: ⊙ ℱ ✲ ⅏ ⑤ ⤣ ⌐ WiFi ♻ ❸

Services: ⊞ ⑤ 🔒 ⌀ T ⛟ ⛽

Within 3 miles: ⌲ ⇶ ✐ ≋ ⑤ ↺

Notes: No gazebos, no noise after 23.00hrs. Dogs must be kept on leads. Putting green, outdoor chess.

AA Pubs & Restaurants nearby: Bear & Ragged Staff, CUMNOR, OX2 9QH, 01865 862329

The Vine Inn, CUMNOR, OX2 9QN, 01865 862567

RUTLAND

GREETHAM   Map 11 SK91

Places to visit

Rutland County Museum & Visitor Centre, OAKHAM, LE15 6HW, 01572 758440
www.rutland.gov.uk/museum

Great for kids: Oakham Castle, OAKHAM, LE15 6HW, 01572 757578
www.rutland.gov.uk/castle

PREMIER PARK

Rutland Caravan & Camping
► ► ► ► ► 85%

tel: 01572 813520 **Park Ln LE15 7FN**
email: info@rutlandcaravanandcamping.co.uk
dir: *From A1 onto B668 towards Greetham. Before Greetham turn right at x-roads, left to site.* **grid ref:** *SK925148*

This pretty caravan park, built to a high specification and surrounded by well-planted banks, continues to improve due to the enthusiasm and vision of its owner. The site has a swimming pool, luxury lodges and 40 fully serviced pitches. From the spacious reception and the innovative play area to the toilet block, everything is of a very high standard. The spacious grassy site is close to the Viking Way and other footpath networks, and well situated for visiting Rutland Water and the many picturesque villages in the area. 5 acre site. 130 touring pitches. 65 hardstandings. 20 seasonal pitches. Caravan pitches. Motorhome pitches. Tent pitches.

Open: all year **Last arrival:** 20.00hrs

Pitches: ⊞ ⇄ ▲

Leisure: ≋ ⌂ ✎

Facilities: ⌖ ⏚ P ⊙ ℱ ✲ ⅏ ⑤ ⤣ ⌐ WiFi ▦ ♻ ❸ ⇞

Services: ⊞ ⑤ 🔒 ⌀ T ◉ ⛟ ⛽

Within 3 miles: ⌲ ⇶ ✐ ◎ ≋ ⑤ ↺

Notes: No noise after 23.00hrs. Dogs must be kept on leads. Dog shower.

AA Pubs & Restaurants nearby: The Wheatsheaf, GREETHAM, LE15 7NP, 01572 812325

The Olive Branch, CLIPSHAM, LE15 7SH, 01780 410355

OAKHAM   Map 11 SK80

Places to visit

Oakham Castle, OAKHAM, LE15 6HW, 01572 757578 www.rutland.gov.uk/castle

Rutland County Museum & Visitor Centre, OAKHAM, LE15 6HW, 01572 758440 www.rutland.gov.uk/museum

Louisa-Alice Campsite
► ► ► 82%

tel: 01572 722984 & 07794 949568 **Ranksborough Hall Estates, Langham LE15 7JR**
dir: *Take A606 from Oakham towards Melton Mowbray, through Langham, left at Ranksborough Hall sign.* **grid ref:** *SK838110*

This small, intimate, tranquil touring park is situated in the grounds of Ranksborough Hall. It occupies a level, secluded and mature tree fringed area with clean, well-maintained toilets, and a high priority is given to security. Several attractive and historic market towns are a short drive away through rolling and unspoilt countryside, plus there are opportunities for walking, sailing and cycling at nearby Rutland Water. 1.5 acre site. 33 touring pitches. 33 hardstandings. 10 seasonal pitches. Caravan pitches. Motorhome pitches. Tent pitches.

Open: all year **Last arrival:** 19.00hrs **Last departure:** anytime

Pitches: ⊞ ⇄ ▲

Facilities: ⊙ ℱ ⌐ ♻ ❸

Services: ⊞ ⛟

Within 3 miles: ⌲ ✐ ≋ ⑤ ↺

Notes: ⊗ No cars by caravans or tents. Quiet time after 22.30hrs, BBQs must be off ground, no football games. Dogs must be kept on leads.

AA Pubs & Restaurants nearby: The Grainstore Brewery, OAKHAM, LE15 6RE, 01572 770065

The Fox & Hounds, KNOSSINGTON, LE15 8LY, 01664 452129

WING   Map 11 SK80

Places to visit

Lyddington Bede House, LYDDINGTON, LE15 9LZ, 01572 822438 www.english-heritage.org.uk/daysout/properties/lyddington-bede-house

Great for kids: Oakham Castle, OAKHAM, LE15 6HW, 01572 757578 www.rutland.gov.uk/castle

Wing Hall Caravan & Camping
► ► ► 71%

tel: 01572 737283 & 737090 **Wing Hall LE15 8RQ**
email: winghall1891@aol.com
dir: *From A1 take A47 towards Leicester, 14m, follow Morcott signs. In Morcott follow Wing signs. 2.5m, follow site signs.* **grid ref:** *SK892031*

A deeply tranquil and rural park set in the grounds of an old manor house. The four grassy fields with attractive borders of mixed, mature deciduous trees have exceptional views across the Rutland countryside and are within one mile of Rutland Water. There's a good farm shop which specialises in locally sourced produce, a licensed café, and there are high quality showers and a fully-equipped laundry. Children and tents are very welcome in what is a safe environment where

continued

PITCHES: ⊞ Caravans ⇄ Motorhomes ▲ Tents ⋒ Glamping accommodation **SERVICES:** ⊞ Electric hook up ⑤ Launderette ⌸ Licensed bar 🔒 Calor Gas ⌀ Camping Gaz T Toilet fluid ◉ Café/Restaurant ⏢ Fast Food/Takeaway ⛟ Battery charging ⛟ Baby care ⛽ Motorvan service point
ABBREVIATIONS: BHs – bank holidays Etr – Easter Spring BH – Spring Bank Holiday fr – from hrs – hours m – mile mdnt – midnight rdbt – roundabout rs – restricted service wk – week wknd – weekend x-roads – crossroads ⊗ No credit or debit cards ⊗ No dogs

WING *continued*

there is space to roam. 11 acre site. 250 touring pitches. 4 hardstandings. Caravan pitches. Motorhome pitches. Tent pitches.

Open: all year (rs Nov-Feb large motorhomes advised not to arrive if weather very wet) **Last arrival:** 21.00hrs **Last departure:** noon

Pitches: 🚐 🚌 ⛺

Facilities: 💨 ❄ 🛒 🐕 [WiFi] ♻ ℹ

Services: 🔌 🫧 🍺 🛢 🔥

Within 3 miles: ⛳ ⛵ 🎣 🏄 🛒 🫧 🐴

Notes: Dogs must be kept on leads. Coarse fishing.

AA Pubs & Restaurants nearby: King's Arms Inn, WING, LE15 8SE, 01572 737634

SHROPSHIRE

BRIDGNORTH — Map 10 SO79

Places to visit

Benthall Hall, BENTHALL, TF12 5RX, 01952 882159
www.nationaltrust.org.uk/main/w-benthallhall

Great for kids: Dudmaston Estate, QUATT, WV15 6QN, 01746 780866
www.nationaltrust.org.uk/dudmaston-estate

PREMIER PARK

Stanmore Hall Touring Park

►►►►► 88%

tel: 01746 761761 **Stourbridge Rd WV15 6DT**
email: stanmore@morris-leisure.co.uk
dir: *2m E of Bridgnorth on A458.* **grid ref:** *SO742923*

An excellent park in peaceful surroundings offering outstanding facilities. The pitches, many fully serviced (with Freeview TV), are arranged around the lake close to Stanmore Hall. Arboretum standard trees include some magnificent Californian Redwoods and an oak tree that is nearly 700 years old. The site is handy for visiting Ironbridge, the Severn Valley Railway and the attractive market town of Bridgnorth. 12.5 acre site. 129 touring pitches. 68 hardstandings. 12 seasonal pitches. Caravan pitches. Motorhome pitches. Tent pitches.

Open: all year **Last arrival:** 20.00hrs **Last departure:** noon

Pitches: * 🚐 £23.50-£29.30 🚌 £23.50-£29.30 ⛺ £23.50-£29.30

Leisure: 🛝 ⚽

Facilities: 🚿 ⊙ 💨 ❄ ♿ 🛒 🧺 🐕 [WiFi] ℹ

Services: 🔌 🫧 🛢 🔥 [T] 🍔 🚰

Within 3 miles: ⛳ ⛵ 🎬 🎣 🛒 🫧 🐴

Notes: Max 2 dogs per pitch. Dogs must be kept on leads.

AA Pubs & Restaurants nearby: Halfway House Inn, BRIDGNORTH, WV16 5LS, 01746 762670

CRAVEN ARMS — Map 9 SO48

Places to visit

Stokesay Castle, STOKESAY, SY7 9AH, 01588 672544
www.english-heritage.org.uk/daysout/properties/stokesay-castle

Great for kids: Ludlow Castle, LUDLOW, SY8 1AY, 01584 873355
www.ludlowcastle.com

Wayside Camping and Caravan Park

►►► 81%

tel: 01588 660218 **Aston on Clun SY7 8EF**
email: waysidecamping@hotmail.com
dir: *From Craven Arms on A49, W onto B4368 (Clun road) towards Clun Valley. Site approx 2m on right just before Aston on Clun.* **grid ref:** *SO399816*

A peaceful park with lovely views, close to excellent local walks and many places of interest. The modern toilet facilities provide a good level of comfort, and there are several electric hook-ups. You are assured of a warm welcome by the helpful owner. Out of season price reductions are available. Many places of interest are within easy reach including Stokesay Castle, Offa's Dyke and Ludlow. 2.5 acre site. 20 touring pitches. 13 hardstandings. Caravan pitches. Motorhome pitches. Tent pitches. 1 static.

Open: Apr-Oct

Pitches: * 🚐 £18-£20 🚌 £18-£20 ⛺ £10-£18

Facilities: ⊙ 💨 ❄ ♿ 🛒 🚚 ♻ ℹ

Services: 🔌 [T] 🍔 🚰

Within 3 miles: ⛳ ◎ 🛒 🫧

Notes: Adults only. ⊘ 1 dog per unit. Dogs must be kept on leads. Seasonal, organic vegetables for sale.

AA Pubs & Restaurants nearby: The Sun Inn, CRAVEN ARMS, SY7 9DF, 01584 861239

The Crown Country Inn, MUNSLOW, SY7 9ET, 01584 841205

LYNEAL (NEAR ELLESMERE) — Map 15 SJ43

Places to visit

Old Oswestry Hill Fort, OSWESTRY, 0370 333 1181
www.english-heritage.org.uk/daysout/properties/old-oswestry-hill-fort

Great for kids: Hawkstone Historic Park & Follies, WESTON-UNDER-REDCASTLE, SY4 5UY, 01948 841700 www.hawkstoneparkfollies.co.uk

Fernwood Caravan Park

►►►► 85%

tel: 01948 710221 **SY12 0QF**
email: enquiries@fernwoodpark.co.uk
dir: *From A495 in Welshampton take B5063, over canal bridge, turn right, follow signs.* **grid ref:** *SJ445346*

A peaceful park set in wooded countryside, with a screened, tree-lined touring area and coarse fishing lake. The approach to the site passes colourful flowerbeds, and the static area which is tastefully arranged around an attractive children's playing area. There is a small child-free touring area for those wanting complete relaxation, and the park has 40 acres of woodland where there are many walks to enjoy. 26

acre site. 60 touring pitches. 8 hardstandings. 30 seasonal pitches. Caravan pitches. Motorhome pitches. 165 statics.

Open: Mar-Nov (rs Mar & Nov shop closed) **Last arrival:** 21.00hrs **Last departure:** 17.00hrs

Pitches: 🚐 🚐

Leisure: 🎣 🖉

Facilities: 🔦 P️S ☉ 🖉 ✳ ♿ ⓢ 🎯 ♻ 🎯

Services: 🚐 🗑 ⓢ ⬛T ᶙ

Within 3 miles: ⅄ 🖉 ⓢ 🗑

Notes: No noise after 23.00hrs. Dogs must be kept on leads.

MINSTERLEY — Map 15 SJ30

Places to visit

Powis Castle & Garden, WELSHPOOL, SY21 8RF, 01938 551929 www.nationaltrust.org.uk

Great for kids: Shrewsbury Castle and Shropshire Regimental Museum, SHREWSBURY, SY1 2AT, 01743 358516 www.shropshireregimentalmuseum.co.uk

---

The Old School Caravan Park
▶▶▶86%

tel: 01588 650410 **Shelve SY5 0JQ**
dir: 6.5m SW of Minsterley on A488. Site on left, 2m after village sign for Hope.
grid ref: SO322977

Situated in the Shropshire Hills, an Area of Outstanding Natural Beauty, with many excellent walks starting directly from the site, and many cycle trails close by. Although a small site of just 1.5 acres, it is well equipped. It is a really beautiful park, often described as 'a gem', that has excellent facilities and offers all the requirements for a relaxing countryside holiday. The friendly owners, Terry and Jan, are always on hand to help out with anything. Nearby Snailbreach Mine offers guided tours on certain days. Please note that there is no laundry at this park. 1.5 acre site. 22 touring pitches. 10 hardstandings. 6 seasonal pitches. Caravan pitches. Motorhome pitches. Tent pitches.

Open: Mar-Jan **Last arrival:** 21.00hrs **Last departure:** 11.00hrs

Pitches: 🚐 🚐 🛆

Facilities: 🔦 P️S ☉ ✳ 🎯 ♻ 🎯

Services: 🚐

Within 3 miles: 🖉 ⓢ ∪

Notes: ⊘ No ball games or cycle riding. Dogs must be kept on leads.

AA Pubs & Restaurants nearby: The Sun Inn, MARTON, SY21 8JP, 01938 561211

The Lowfield Inn, MARTON, SY21 8JX, 01743 891313

SHREWSBURY

Places to visit

Attingham Park, ATCHAM, SY4 4TP, 01743 708123 www.nationaltrust.org.uk/attinghampark

Great for kids: Wroxeter Roman City, WROXETER, SY5 6PH, 01743 761330 www.english-heritage.org.uk/daysout/properties/wroxeter-roman-city

---

SHREWSBURY — Map 15 SJ41

PREMIER PARK

Beaconsfield Farm Caravan Park
▶▶▶▶▶91%

tel: 01939 210370 & 210399 **Battlefield SY4 4AA**
email: mail@beaconsfieldholidaypark.co.uk **web:** www.beaconsfieldholidaypark.co.uk
dir: At Hadnall, 1.5m NE of Shrewsbury. Follow sign for Astley from A49.
grid ref: SJ522189

A purpose-built, adults-only (21 years and over) family-run park on farmland in open countryside. This pleasant park offers quality in every area, including superior toilets, heated indoor swimming pool, luxury lodges for hire and attractive landscaping. Fly and coarse fishing are available from the park's own lake and The Bothy restaurant is excellent. Car hire is available directly from the site, and there's a steam room, plus free WiFi. 12 luxury lodges are available for hire or sale. 16 acre site. 60 touring pitches. 50 hardstandings. 10 seasonal pitches. Caravan pitches. Motorhome pitches. 35 statics.

Open: all year **Last arrival:** 19.00hrs **Last departure:** 11.00hrs

Pitches: ✳ 🚐 £22-£28 🚐 £25-£28 **Leisure:** 🖉 🖉 🎣

Facilities: 🖉 ✳ ♿ 🎯 WiFi 🖥 ♻ 🎯 🎣 **Services:** 🚐 🗑 ⬛ 🍴 ᶙ

Within 3 miles: 🖉 🗄 🖉 ◎ ⓢ 🗑

Notes: Adults only. Dogs must be kept on leads.

AA Pubs & Restaurants nearby: The Boat House, SHREWSBURY, SY3 8JQ, 01743 231658

The Prince of Wales, SHREWSBURY, SY3 7NZ, 01743 343301

Lion & Pheasant Hotel, SHREWSBURY, SY1 1XJ, 01743 770345

PITCHES: 🚐 Caravans 🚐 Motorhomes 🛆 Tents 🏠 Glamping accommodation **SERVICES:** 🚐 Electric hook up 🗑 Launderette 🍺 Licensed bar 🔋 Calor Gas 🖉 Camping Gaz ⬛T Toilet fluid 🍴 Café/Restaurant 🍔 Fast Food/Takeaway 🔋 Battery charging 🍼 Baby care ᶙ Motorvan service point **ABBREVIATIONS:** BHs – bank holidays Etr – Easter Spring BH – Spring Bank Holiday fr – from hrs – hours m – mile mdnt – midnight rdbt – roundabout rs – restricted service wk – week wknd – weekend x-roads – crossroads ⊘ No credit or debit cards ⊘ No dogs

SHREWSBURY *continued*

Oxon Hall Touring Park
▶▶▶▶▶88%

Best of British

tel: 01743 340868 **Welshpool Rd SY3 5FB**
email: oxon@morris-leisure.co.uk
dir: *Exit A5 (ring road) at junct with A458. Site shares entrance with Oxon Park & Ride.*
grid ref: *SJ455138*

A delightful park with quality facilities and a choice of grass and fully serviced pitches. A warm welcome is assured from the friendly staff. The adults-only section proves very popular, and there is an inviting patio area next to reception and the shop, overlooking a small lake. This site is ideally located for a visit to Shrewsbury and the surrounding countryside, and the site also benefits from the Oxon Park & Ride, a short walk through the park. 15 acre site. 105 touring pitches. 72 hardstandings. Caravan pitches. Motorhome pitches. Tent pitches. 60 statics.

Open: all year **Last arrival:** 20.00hrs **Last departure:** noon

Pitches: ⊕ ⊕ Å

Facilities: ♠ ℙ ⊙ ℱ ※ ⅙ ⑤ ♒ ⋒ ₩ℹ️ ▪ ♻ ❶

Services: ⊕ ⑤ 🛢 ⊘ Ⓣ ⬇️

Within 3 miles: ⅃ ₸ ℓ ⑤ ⑤ ∪

Notes: Max 2 dogs per pitch. Dogs must be kept on leads.

AA Pubs & Restaurants nearby: The Mytton & Mermaid Hotel, SHREWSBURY, SY5 6QG, 01743 761220

Albright Hussey Manor Hotel & Restaurant, SHREWSBURY, SY4 3AF, 01939 290571

Places to visit

Lilleshall Abbey, LILLESHALL, TF10 9HW, 0121 625 6820
www.english-heritage.org.uk/daysout/properties/lilleshall-abbey

Ironbridge Gorge Museums, IRONBRIDGE, TF8 7DQ, 01952 433424
www.ironbridge.org.uk

Severn Gorge Park
▶▶▶▶▶81%

tel: 01952 684789 **Bridgnorth Rd, Tweedale TF7 4JB**
email: info@severngorgepark.co.uk
dir: *S of Telford take A442 towards Bridgnorth. Onto A4169 signed Telford Town Centre. Right at Cuckoo Oak rdbt into Bridgenorth Rd (follow site signs). Site on right.*
grid ref: *SJ705051*

A very pleasant wooded site in the heart of Telford, that is well screened and well maintained. The sanitary facilities are fresh and immaculate, and landscaping of the grounds is carefully managed. Although the touring section is small, this is a really delightful park to stay at, and it is also well positioned for visiting nearby Ironbridge and its museums. The Telford bus stops at the end of the drive. 6 acre site. 12 touring pitches. 12 hardstandings. Caravan pitches. Motorhome pitches. 120 statics.

Open: all year **Last arrival:** 20.00hrs **Last departure:** noon

Pitches: ⊕ ⊕

Facilities: ♠ ℙ ⊙ ℱ ※ ⅙ ⋒ ♻ ❶

Services: ⊕ ⑤ 🛢 ⊘ ☲ ⬇️ **Within 3 miles:** ⅃ ₸ ℓ ◎ ⅃ ⑤ ⑤ ∪

Notes: Adults only. Well behaved dogs accepted only & must be kept on leads.

LEISURE: 🏊 Indoor pool 🏊 Outdoor pool 🛝 Children's playground 🤚 Kid's club 🎾 Tennis court 🎱 Games room ⛳ Golf course 🚣 Boat hire 🚲 Cycle hire ▤ Cinema 🎵 Entertainment 🎣 Fishing ◎ Mini golf ⛳ Pitch n putt 🏄 Watersports 🏋 Gym ♻ Sports field ∪ Stables **FACILITIES:** 🛁 Bath ♠ Shower ℙ Private washing cubicles ⊙ Electric shaver ℱ Hairdryer ※ Ice Packs ⅙ Disabled facilities ⑤ Shop on site 🏪 Mobile shop 🍖 BBQ area 🪵 Picnic area ₩ℹ️ Wi-fi ▪ Internet access ♻ Recycling ❶ Tourist info 🐕 Dog exercise area 🚗 Car hire can be arranged

WEM
Map 15 SJ52

Places to visit

Hawkstone Historic Park & Follies, WESTON-UNDER-REDCASTLE, SY4 5UY, 01948 841700 www.hawkstoneparkfollies.co.uk

Attingham Park, ATCHAM, SY4 4TP, 01743 708123 www.nationaltrust.org.uk/attinghampark

Great for kids: Shrewsbury Castle and Shropshire Regimental Museum, SHREWSBURY, SY1 2AT, 01743 358516 www.shropshireregimentalmuseum.co.uk

Lower Lacon Caravan Park
►►► 79%

tel: 01939 232376 **SY4 5RP**
email: info@llcp.co.uk **web:** www.llcp.co.uk
dir: A49 onto B5065. Site 3m on right. **grid ref:** SJ534304

A large, spacious park with lively club facilities and an entertainments' barn, set safely away from the main road. The park is particularly suited to families, with an outdoor swimming pool and many farm animals including alpacas and kune kune pigs. Family-size wooden pods are available for hire. 57 acre site. 270 touring pitches. 30 hardstandings. 100 seasonal pitches. Caravan pitches. Motorhome pitches. Tent pitches. 50 statics.

Open: all year (rs Winter entertainment barn & café closed) **Last arrival:** anytime **Last departure:** 16.00hrs

Pitches: 🚐 🚌 ▲ 🏠 prices shown below

Leisure: ⚲ ⚙ ⬆ ⚲

Facilities: 🚿 🏪 🅿 ⚙ 🌶 ❄ ⚙ 🔥 🛗 WiFi ♻ 🛈

Services: 🔌 🗑 🍴 🔋 ⚗ 🇹 🍴 🔋 🚼

Glamping. Wooden Pods 2, £42-£67 Min stay 2 nights Car by unit

Within 3 miles: 🦌 🎣 ⊚ 🛒 🛒

Notes: No skateboards, no commercial vehicles, no sign-written vehicles. Dogs must be kept on leads. Crazy golf.

WENTNOR
Map 15 SO39

Places to visit

Montgomery Castle, MONTGOMERY, 01443 336000 http://cadw.gov.wales/daysout/montgomerycastle

Great for kids: Shropshire Hills Discovery Centre, CRAVEN ARMS, SY7 9RS, 01588 676060 www.shropshirehillsdiscoverycentre.co.uk

The Green Caravan Park
►►► 81%

tel: 01588 650605 **SY9 5EF**
email: lin@greencaravanpark.co.uk
dir: 1m NE of Bishop's Castle on A489. Right at brown tourist sign. **grid ref:** SO380932

A pleasant site in a peaceful setting convenient for visiting Ludlow or Shrewsbury. Very family orientated, with good facilities. The grassy pitches are mainly level, and some hardstandings are available. 15 acre site. 140 touring pitches. 5 hardstandings. 42 seasonal pitches. Caravan pitches. Motorhome pitches. Tent pitches. 20 statics.

Open: Etr-Oct **Last arrival:** 21.00hrs **Last departure:** noon (fee charged for late departures)

Pitches: * 🚐 £16.50-£20 🚌 £16.50-£20 ▲ £16.50-£20

Leisure: 🎱 **Facilities:** 🚿 ⊙ 🅿 ⚙ 🌶 ❄ ⚙ 🔥 ♻ 🛈 ⚲

Services: 🔌 🗑 🍴 🔋 ⚗ 🇹 🍴 🚼 **Within 3 miles:** 🎣 🛒

Notes: No open fires, quiet from 22.00hrs-08.00 hrs. Dogs must be kept on leads.

AA Pubs & Restaurants nearby: The Crown Inn, WENTNOR, SY9 5EE, 01588 650613

WHEATHILL
Map 10 SO68

Places to visit

Ludlow Castle, LUDLOW, SY8 1AY, 01584 873355 www.ludlowcastle.com

PREMIER PARK

Wheathill Touring Park
►►►►► 82%

tel: 01584 823456 **WV16 6QT**
email: info@wheathillpark.co.uk
dir: On B4364 between Ludlow & Bridgnorth. (NB Sat Nav may give directions to exit B4364, this should be ignored). Site entrance well signed from B4364. Site entrance adjacent to Three Horseshoes pub. **grid ref:** SO603805

Ideally located in open countryside between the historic towns of Bridgnorth and Ludlow, this development, provides spacious, fully serviced pitches, most with stunning views and a top-notch amenities block with quality fittings and good privacy options. The park is situated adjacent to a pub serving a good range of ales and food. Please note that the on-site shop only sells caravan and camping spares but there's a licensed village shop within a 10-minute drive. 4 acre site. 25 touring pitches. 25 hardstandings. 5 seasonal pitches. Caravan pitches. Motorhome pitches.

Open: 15 Mar-15 Dec **Last arrival:** 19.00hrs **Last departure:** noon

Pitches: 🚐 🚌 **Facilities:** 🚿 🅿 ⊙ 🌶 ⚙ 🔥 🛗 WiFi 🖥 🛈

Services: 🔌 🗑 🔋 ⚗ 🇹 🚼 ⚙

Within 3 miles: 🎣 🛒 🛒 ⛳ **Notes:** Adults only. Dogs must be kept on leads.

PITCHES: 🚐 Caravans 🚌 Motorhomes ▲ Tents 🏠 Glamping accommodation **SERVICES:** 🔌 Electric hook up 🗑 Launderette 🍴 Licensed bar 🔋 Calor Gas ⚗ Camping Gaz 🇹 Toilet fluid 🍴 Café/Restaurant 🏪 Fast Food/Takeaway 🔋 Battery charging 🚼 Baby care ⚙ Motorvan service point
ABBREVIATIONS: BHs – bank holidays Etr – Easter Spring BH – Spring Bank Holiday fr – from hrs – hours m – mile mdnt – midnight rdbt – roundabout rs – restricted service wk – week wknd – weekend x-roads – crossroads ⊚ No credit or debit cards ⊗ No dogs

Somerset

Somerset means 'summer pastures' — appropriate given that so much of this county remains rural and unspoiled. Ever popular areas to visit are the limestone and red sandstone Mendips Hills rising to over 1,000 feet, and by complete contrast, to the south and southwest, the flat landscape of the Somerset Levels.

At the heart of Somerset lies the city of Wells, one of the smallest in the country and surely one of the finest. The jewel in the city's crown is its splendid cathedral, with a magnificent Gothic interior; adorned with sculptures, the West Front is a masterpiece of medieval craftsmanship. Nearby are Vicar's Close, a delightful street of 14th-century houses, and the Bishop's Palace, which is 13th century and moated.

Radiating from Wells are numerous paths and tracks, offering walkers the chance to escape the noise and bustle of the city and discover Somerset's rural delights. Deep within the county are the Mendip Hills, 25 miles long by 5 miles wide, that have a distinctive character and identity.

One of Somerset's more adventurous routes, and a long-term favourite with walkers, is the West Mendip Way, running for 50 miles between the coast and the town of Frome. The starting point at Uphill is spectacular – a ruined hilltop church overlooking the coast near the classic seaside resort of Weston-Super-Mare. The town's famous pier replaces a previous structure destroyed by fire in 2008. Weston and Minehead, which lie on the edge of Exmoor National Park, are two traditional, much-loved holiday destinations on this stretch of coastline.

From Uphill, the West Mendip Way makes for Cheddar Caves and Gorge where stunning geological formations attract countless visitors who are left with a lasting impression of unique natural beauty. For almost a mile the gorge's limestone cliffs rise vertically above the road, in places giving Cheddar a somewhat sinister and oppressive air. Beyond Cheddar the trail heads for Wells. The choice of walks in Somerset is impressive, as is the range of cycle routes.

Descend to the Somerset Levels, an evocative lowland landscape that was the setting for the Battle of Sedgemoor in 1685. In the depths of winter this is a desolate place and famously prone to extensive flooding. There is also a palpable sense of the distant past among these fields and scattered communities. It is claimed that Alfred the Great retreated here after his defeat by the Danes.

One of Somerset's most famous features is the ancient, enigmatic Glastonbury Tor. Steeped in early Christian and Arthurian legend, the Isle of Avalon is one of a number of 'islands' rising above the Somerset Levels. This was once the site of the largest and richest monastery in medieval England and it is claimed that in this setting, Joseph of Arimathea founded the first Christian church in the country. Today, near this spot, modern-day pilgrims come for worship of a very different kind – every summer Glastonbury's legendary festival attracts big names from the world of music and large crowds who brave the elements to support them.

Away from the flat country are the Quantocks, once the haunt of poets. Samuel Taylor Coleridge wrote *The Ancient Mariner* while living in the area and William Wordsworth and his sister Dorothy visited on occasion and often accompanied their friend Coleridge on his country rambles among these hills. The Quantocks are noted for their gentle slopes, heather covered moorland expanses and red deer. From the summit, the Bristol Channel is visible where it meets the Severn Estuary. So much of this hilly landscape has a timeless quality about it and large areas have hardly changed since Coleridge and William and Dorothy Wordsworth explored it on foot around the end of the 18th century.

◁ Cheddar Gorge

SOMERSET

BATH
Map 4 ST76

See also Bishop Sutton

Bath Mill Lodge Retreat
NEW HOLIDAY HOME PARK 93%

tel: 01225 333909 **Newton Rd BA2 9JF**
email: reception@bathmill.co.uk
dir: *From A36 from Bath towards Bristol at rdbt into Pennyquick road signed Newton St Loe (Globe Inn on right). 1m, left into Newton Rd. 1st left to park.* **grid ref:** ST716648

Bath Mill offers very high quality lodge accommodation in a beautifully landscaped park close to Bath. The lodges are fully equipped to a very high standard and are available with two, three or four bedrooms, plus there are 'Studio Lodges' suitable for a couple with king-size bed, sofa, an excellent bathroom and kitchen. There is an excellent bar and bistro and a well-equipped gym. It's a peaceful location that makes a perfect base for visiting Bath, Bristol and the Mendip Hills.

Open: all year   **Statics:** 15 Sleeps 2 Bedrms 1 Elec inc Gas inc

Lodges: 48 Sleeps 8 Bedrms 2-4 Elec inc Gas inc

Children: Cots (cot linen charged) Highchair **Dogs:** 2 on leads   **Leisure:**

BISHOP SUTTON
Map 4 ST55

Places to visit
Wookey Hole Caves & Papermill, WOOKEY HOLE, BA5 1BB, 01749 672243
www.wookey.co.uk

Roman Baths & Pump Room, BATH, BA1 1LZ, 01225 477785
www.romanbaths.co.uk

PREMIER PARK

Bath Chew Valley Caravan Park
▶▶▶▶▶ 96%

Best of British
GOLD

tel: 01275 332127 **Ham Ln BS39 5TZ**
email: enquiries@bathchewvalley.co.uk
dir: *From A4 towards Bath take A39 towards Weston-Super-Mare. Right onto A368. 6m, right opposite The Red Lion in Ham Ln, site 250mtrs on left.* **grid ref:** ST586598

This peaceful adults-only park can be described as 'a park in a garden', with caravan pitches set amidst lawns, shrubs and trees. There are excellent private facilities – rooms with showers, wash basins and toilets – all are spotlessly clean and well maintained. There is a good woodland walk on the park, and a new stylish fully-equipped lodge is available for hire. WiFi is available throughout the site and there is a free internet workstation. This site is well situated for visiting Bath, Bristol, Wells, Cheddar and Wookey Hole, and for walking in the Mendip Hills. Chew Valley Lake, noted for its top quality fishing, is close by. 4.5 acre site. 45 touring pitches. 4 seasonal pitches. Caravan pitches. Motorhome pitches. Tent pitches.

Open: all year **Last arrival:** 19.00hrs **Last departure:** 11.00hrs

Pitches: 🚐 🚏 ▲ **Facilities:** ⬆🅿⊙🏴✕⚒♿⑤📮📶💧🍴❂🛈❢

Services: 🔌⑤🛢🚽⊘🚰🍴⬆ **Within 3 miles:** 🎣⚓🚲⑤

Notes: Adults only. No cars by caravans or tents. Dogs must be kept on leads. Lending library. Shop & pub & restaurant 200mtrs from site.

BREAN
Map 4 ST25

Places to visit
King John's Hunting Lodge, AXBRIDGE, BS26 2AP, 01934 732012
www.kingjohnshuntinglodge.co.uk

Weston-Super-Mare Museum, WESTON-SUPER-MARE, BS23 1PR, 01934 621028
www.westonmuseum.org

Great for kids: The Helicopter Museum, WESTON-SUPER-MARE, BS24 8PP, 01934 635227 www.helicoptermuseum.co.uk

Warren Farm Holiday Centre
HOLIDAY CENTRE 93%

tel: 01278 751227 **Brean Sands TA8 2RP**
email: enquiries@warren-farm.co.uk **web:** www.warren-farm.co.uk
dir: *M5 junct 22 , B3140 through Burnham-on-Sea to Berrow & Brean. Site 1.5m past Brean Leisure Park.* **grid ref:** ST297564

A large family-run holiday park just a short walk from the beach and divided up into several fields, each with its own designated facilities. The pitches are spacious and level and hardstandings are available; there are good panoramic views of the Mendip Hills and Brean Down. The park has its own Beachcomber Inn with bar, restaurant and entertainment area. The site is perfect for families and has an indoor play barn. Lake fishing is available on site and there is also a fishing tackle and bait shop. 100 acre site. 575 touring pitches. 95 hardstandings. 400 seasonal pitches. Caravan pitches. Motorhome pitches. Tent pitches. 400 statics.

Open: Apr-Oct **Last arrival:** 20.00hrs **Last departure:** 11.00hrs

Pitches: * 🚐 £9.50-£19.50 🚏 £9.50-£19.50 ▲ £9.50-£19.50

LEISURE: 🏊 Indoor pool 🏖 Outdoor pool 🎢 Children's playground 🧒 Kid's club 🎾 Tennis court 🎱 Games room ⛳ Golf course ⛵ Boat hire 🚲 Cycle hire 🎬 Cinema 🎵 Entertainment 🎣 Fishing ⛳ Mini golf Pitch n putt 🏄 Watersports 🏋 Gym ⚽ Sports field ♘ Stables **FACILITIES:** 🛁 Bath 🚿 Shower 🅿 Private washing cubicles ⊙ Electric shaver ⚞ Hairdryer ❄ Ice Packs ♿ Disabled facilities ⑤ Shop on site 🚐 Mobile shop 🍴 BBQ area ⛱ Picnic area 📶 Wi-fi 💻 Internet access ♻ Recycling 🛈 Tourist info 🐕 Dog exercise area 🚗 Car hire can be arranged

Leisure:

Facilities:

Services:

Within 3 miles:

Notes: No commercial vehicles. Dogs must be kept on leads.

See advert below

Holiday Resort Unity
HOLIDAY CENTRE 92%

tel: 01278 751235 **Coast Rd, Brean Sands TA8 2RB**
email: admin@hru.co.uk
dir: *M5 junct 22, B3140 through Burnham-on-Sea, through Berrow to Brean. Site on left just before Brean Leisure Park.* **grid ref:** *ST294539*

This is an excellent, family-run holiday park offering very good touring facilities plus a wide range of family oriented activities, including bowling, RJ's entertainment club plus good eating outlets etc. Brean Splash Waterpark is situated directly opposite this touring park — a discounted entry price is available.

Wooden camping pods and ready-erected, fully-equipped safari tents are also available for hire. The park also holds 'themed' weekends and rallies are also welcome. 200 acre site. 453 touring pitches. 158 hardstandings. 168 seasonal pitches. Caravan pitches. Motorhome pitches. Tent pitches. 650 statics.

Open: Feb-Nov **Last arrival:** 21.00hrs **Last departure:** 10.00hrs (late departures available - charges apply)

Pitches:

Leisure:

Facilities:

Services:

Glamping: **Safari tents** 8, Car by unit **Wooden Pods** 3, Car by unit

Within 3 miles:

Notes: Family parties of 3 or more must be over 21yrs (young persons' policy applies). Dogs must be kept on leads. Arcade.

AA Pubs & Restaurants nearby: Crossways Inn, WEST HUNTSPILL, TA9 3RA, 01278 783756

PITCHES: Caravans Motorhomes Tents Glamping accommodation **SERVICES:** Electric hook up Launderette Licensed bar Calor Gas Camping Gaz Toilet fluid Café/Restaurant Fast Food/Takeaway Battery charging Baby care Motorvan service point **ABBREVIATIONS:** BHs – bank holidays Etr – Easter Spring BH – Spring Bank Holiday fr – from hrs – hours m – mile mdnt – midnight rdbt – roundabout rs – restricted service wk – week wknd – weekend x-roads – crossroads No credit or debit cards No dogs

BREAN *continued*

Northam Farm Caravan & Touring Park

▶ ▶ ▶ ▶ 94%

tel: 01278 751244 **TA8 2SE**
email: stay@northamfarm.co.uk **web:** www.northamfarm.co.uk
dir: *M5 junct 22, B3140 to Burnham-on-Sea & Brean. Park on right 0.5m past Brean Leisure Park.* **grid ref:** *ST299556*

An attractive site that's just a short walk from the sea and a long sandy beach. This quality park also has lots of children's play areas, and also owns the Seagull Inn about 600 yards away, which includes a restaurant and entertainment. There is a top quality fishing lake on site, which is very popular and has been featured on TV. The facilities on this park are excellent. A DVD of the site is available on request, free of charge. The park has a main caravan dealership plus full workshop and repair facility. 30 acre site. 350 touring pitches. 260 hardstandings. Caravan pitches. Motorhome pitches. Tent pitches.

Open: Mar-Oct (rs Mar & Oct - shop, café, takeaway limited hours)
Last arrival: 20.00hrs **Last departure:** 10.30hrs
Pitches: * 🚐 £13.75-£28 🚍 £13.75-£28 ▲ £12.25-£23.75
Leisure: ⚲ ✿ ✐
Facilities: 🛏 🏮 🅿 ☉ ☂ ✳ ♿ 🏠 🚿 🛗 🆆🅸🅵🅸 ♻ ❶
Services: 🔌 🔟 🔋 🚿 🕛 🎛 🍴 🛗 🛒 ↧
Within 3 miles: ↨ 🎡 ✐ ☉ 🛍 🐎 ∪
Notes: Families & couples only, no commercial vehicles. Dogs must be kept on leads.

BRIDGETOWN   Map 3 SS93

Places to visit

Dunster Castle, DUNSTER, TA24 6SL, 01643 821314
www.nationaltrust.org.uk/dunstercastle

Cleeve Abbey, WASHFORD, TA23 0PS, 01984 640377
www.english-heritage.org.uk/daysout/properties/cleeve-abbey

PREMIER PARK

Exe Valley Caravan Site

▶ ▶ ▶ ▶ ▶ 82%

tel: 01643 851432 **Mill House TA22 9JR**
email: info@exevalleycamping.co.uk **web:** www.exevalleycamping.co.uk
dir: *From S: M5 junct 27, A361 signed Tiverton. 7m, right at rdbt signed Bampton. Left at Exeter Inn rdbt, 2m, take A396. Through Exebridge to Bridgetown, left after Badgers Holt Inn, site on right. (NB for Sat Nav use TA22 9JN).* **grid ref:** *SS923333*

Set in the Exmoor National Park, this adults-only park occupies an enchanting, peaceful spot in a wooded valley alongside the River Exe. There is free fly-fishing, an abundance of wildlife and excellent walks leading directly from the park. The site has good, spotlessly clean facilities. The inn opposite serves meals at lunchtime and in the evening. 4 acre site. 48 touring pitches. 13 hardstandings. Caravan pitches. Motorhome pitches. Tent pitches.

Open: 17 Mar-16 Oct **Last arrival:** 22.00hrs **Last departure:** 11.00hrs
Pitches: * 🚐 £13-£20 🚍 £13-£20 ▲ £13-£23
Leisure: ✐ 🎡
Facilities: 🏮 🅿 ☉ ☂ ✳ ♿ 🏠 🚿 🛗 🆆🅸🅵🅸 ♻ ❶
Services: 🔌 🔟 🔋 🚿 🎛 🛒 ↧
Within 3 miles: ♨ ✐ 🛍 🐎 ∪
Notes: Adults only. 🐕 17th-century mill, TV sockets & cables.

LEISURE: 🏊 Indoor pool 🏊 Outdoor pool ⚲ Children's playground 🖐 Kid's club ♨ Tennis court 🎱 Games room ⛳ Golf course 🚣 Boat hire 🚴 Cycle hire 🎭 Cinema 🎵 Entertainment 🎣 Fishing ⛳ Mini golf 🏌 Pitch n putt 🏄 Watersports 🏋 Gym 🏟 Sports field ∪ Stables **FACILITIES:** 🛁 Bath 🚿 Shower 🅿 Private washing cubicles 🔌 Electric shaver ✂ Hairdryer ✳ Ice Packs ♿ Disabled facilities 🛍 Shop on site 🚐 Mobile shop 🍴 BBQ area 🏠 Picnic area 🆆🅸🅵🅸 Wi-fi 🖥 Internet access ♻ Recycling ❶ Tourist info 🐕 Dog exercise area 🚗 Car hire can be arranged

BRIDGWATER
Map 4 ST23

Places to visit

Hestercombe Gardens, TAUNTON, TA2 8LG, 01823 413923 www.hestercombe.com

Coleridge Cottage, NETHER STOWEY, TA5 1NQ, 01278 732662 www.nationaltrust.org.uk/coleridgecottage

Great for kids: Tropiquaria Animal and Adventure Park, WASHFORD, TA23 0QB, 01984 640688 www.tropiquaria.co.uk

Mill Farm Caravan & Camping Park
HOLIDAY CENTRE 85%

tel: 01278 732286 **Fiddington TA5 1JQ**
web: www.millfarm.biz
dir: From Bridgwater take A39 W, left at Cannington rdbt, 2m, right just beyond Apple Tree Inn towards Fiddington. Follow camping signs. **grid ref:** ST219410

A large holiday park with plenty to interest all the family, including indoor and outdoor pools, a boating lake, a gym, horse riding and a BMX track. There is also a clubhouse with bar, and a full entertainment programme in the main season. Although lively and busy in the main season, the park also offers a much quieter environment at other times; out of season, some activities and entertainment may not be available. 6 acre site. 275 touring pitches. 10 hardstandings. 40 seasonal pitches. Caravan pitches. Motorhome pitches. Tent pitches.

Open: Mar-1 Dec **Last arrival:** 23.00hrs **Last departure:** 10.00hrs

Pitches: * 🚐 £12.50-£29 🚍 £12.50-£29 ⛺ £12.50-£29

Leisure: 🏊 ⚽ 🎱 🎣 ♨ 🎵

Facilities: 🚽 🚿 💧 🔧 ⚒ ❄ 🚻 🧺 🛒 🛗 🐕 WiFi ♻ ℹ

Services: 🔌 📶 🍴 🛢 🌀 T 🍽 🚲

Within 3 miles: ⚓ 🏌 ◎ 🎣 🎯 ↺

Notes: No noise after 23.00hrs. Dogs must be kept on leads. Canoeing, pool table, trampolines, fitness classes, saunas.

AA Pubs & Restaurants nearby: The Hood Arms, KILVE, TA5 1EA, 01278 741210

See advert on page 288

BURNHAM-ON-SEA
Map 4 ST34

Places to visit

The Helicopter Museum, WESTON-SUPER-MARE, BS24 8PP, 01934 635227 www.helicoptermuseum.co.uk

King John's Hunting Lodge, AXBRIDGE, BS26 2AP, 01934 732012 www.kingjohnshuntinglodge.co.uk

Burnham-on-Sea Holiday Village
HOLIDAY CENTRE 89%

GOLD

tel: 01278 783391 **Marine Dr TA8 1LA**
email: burnhamonsea@haven.com **web:** www.haven.com/burnhamonsea
dir: M5 junct 22, A38 towards Highbridge. Over mini rdbt, right onto B3139 to Burnham. After petrol station, left into Marine Drive. Park 400yds on left. **grid ref:** ST305485

A large, family-orientated holiday village complex with a separate touring park containing 43 super pitches. There is a wide range of activities, including excellent indoor and outdoor pools, plus bars, restaurants and entertainment for all the family – there is plenty to do for all ages without even leaving the park. The coarse fishing lake is very popular, and the seafront at Burnham is only half a mile away. A wide range of well laid out holiday homes is available for hire and there's a Safari Village with fully-equipped safari tents for hire. 94 acre site. 75 touring pitches. 46 hardstandings. Caravan pitches. Motorhome pitches. Tent pitches. 700 statics.

continued

PITCHES: 🚐 Caravans 🚍 Motorhomes ⛺ Tents 🏕 Glamping accommodation **SERVICES:** 🔌 Electric hook up 🔲 Launderette 🍷 Licensed bar 🛢 Calor Gas 🌀 Camping Gaz T Toilet fluid 🍽 Café/Restaurant 🎏 Fast Food/Takeaway 🔋 Battery charging 🍼 Baby care 🚐 Motorvan service point **ABBREVIATIONS:** BHs – bank holidays Etr – Easter Spring BH – Spring Bank Holiday fr – from hrs – hours m – mile mdnt – midnight rdbt – roundabout rs – restricted service wk – week wknd – weekend x-roads – crossroads 🚫 No credit or debit cards 🚫 No dogs

BURNHAM-ON-SEA *continued*

Burnham-on-Sea Holiday Village

Open: mid Mar-end Oct (rs mid Mar-May & Sep-Oct facilities may be reduced)
Last arrival: anytime **Last departure:** 10.00hrs

Pitches: 🚐 🚙 ▲ 🏠 **Leisure:** 🌊 ⛵ 🏊 ⚽ 🎣 🎵 **Facilities:** 🚿 ✳ ♿ 🚽 WiFi

Services: 🔌 🚽 🍴 🧺 🍽 🛒 **Glamping:** Safari tents 8

Within 3 miles: 🏌 🏇 🎣 ◎ 🛒 🛒 U

Notes: No pets, no commercial vehicles, no bookings by persons under 21yrs unless a family booking.

AA Pubs & Restaurants nearby: Crossways Inn, WEST HUNTSPILL, TA9 3RA, 01278 783756

See advert on opposite page

Cheddar Woods Holiday Park
HOLIDAY HOME PARK 95%

tel: 01934 742610 **Axbridge Rd BS27 3DB**
email: enquiries@cheddarwoods.co.uk
dir: *From M5 junct 22 follow signs to Cheddar Gorge & Caves (8m). Site midway between Cheddar & Axbridge on A371.* **grid ref:** *ST448547*

Situated in the beatiful Mendip Hills, Cheddar Woods is the perfect place to relax and unwind. This state-of-the-art park is an ideal location for family holidays. Both large and smaller lodges are available for hire, all offering top quality accommodation. There are excellent leisure facilities including a gym, spa and swimming pool plus a 'Go Active' programme. In addition, there is a very tasteful bar and quality restaurant. The park is just outside the village of Cheddar with its

famous caves and is well positioned for visiting Wells, Weston-Super-Mare and many other attractions of the area. It should be noted this is a lodge-only park.

Open: all year (rs Xmas & New Year)

Changeover day: Mon, Fri, Sun

Arrival and departure times: Please contact the site

Lodges: 79 Sleeps 8 Bedrms 4 Bathrms 2 (inc en suite) Toilets 2 Dishwasher Wash Machine T/drier Freezer TV Sky/FTV DVD Modem/Wi-fi Linen inc Towels inc Elec inc Gas inc Grass area Garden/patio furniture Low season £355-£745 High season £909-£1745 Weekly price £600

Children: 🛉 Cots (cot linen charged) Highchair **Dogs:** 2 on leads

Leisure: 🖥 Spa 🏊 🛝 �

Within 3 miles: 🖥 Spa ∪ 🏌

COWSLIP GREEN Map 4 ST46

Brook Lodge Farm Camping & Caravan Park (Bristol)
►►► 87%

tel: 01934 862311 **BS40 5RB**
email: info@brooklodgefarm.com
dir: *M5 junct 22, A38 to Churchill. Site 4m on right opposite Holiday Inn. Or M5 junct 18, follow Bristol Airport signs. From A38 towards Bridgwater (airport on right). Site 3m on left at bottom of hill.* **grid ref:** *ST486620*

A naturally sheltered country touring park sitting in a valley of the Mendip Hills, surrounded by trees and a historic walled garden. A friendly welcome is always assured by the family owners who are particularly keen on preserving the site's environment and have won a green tourism award. This park is particularly well placed for visiting the Bristol Balloon Festival, held in August, plus the many country walks in the area. 4.5 acre site. 29 touring pitches. 3 hardstandings. Caravan pitches. Motorhome pitches. Tent pitches.

Open: Mar-Oct **Last arrival:** 21.00hrs **Last departure:** 11.45hrs

Pitches: 🚐 🚍 ▲ **Facilities:** ⊙ 🏴 ⚒ 🛒 🖳 🔌 📶 ♻ 𝒾

Services: 🔌 🗑 🛒 **Within 3 miles:** 🎣 🏌 🛒 ∪

Notes: Dogs by prior arrangement only. Dogs must be kept on leads. Cycle loan, walking maps available, fire pits. Bell tents are available for hire (contact site for more information).

AA Pubs & Restaurants nearby: The Langford Inn, LOWER LANGFORD, BS40 5BL, 01934 863059

CREWKERNE

See Drimpton (Dorset)

PITCHES: 🚐 Caravans 🚍 Motorhomes ▲ Tents 🏕 Glamping accommodation **SERVICES:** 🔌 Electric hook up 🗑 Launderette 🍺 Licensed bar 🛒 Calor Gas 🔥 Camping Gaz 🇹 Toilet fluid 🍴 Café/Restaurant 🍔 Fast Food/Takeaway 🔋 Battery charging 🍼 Baby care 🚐 Motorvan service point **ABBREVIATIONS:** BHs – bank holidays Etr – Easter Spring BH – Spring Bank Holiday fr – from hrs – hours m – mile mdnt – midnight rdbt – roundabout rs – restricted service wk – week wknd – weekend x-roads – crossroads ⊘ No credit or debit cards ⊗ No dogs

CROWCOMBE
Map 3 ST13

Places to visit

Cleeve Abbey, WASHFORD, TA23 0PS, 01984 640377
www.english-heritage.org.uk/daysout/properties/cleeve-abbey

Great for kids: Dunster Castle, DUNSTER, TA24 6SL, 01643 821314
www.nationaltrust.org.uk/dunstercastle

PREMIER PARK

Quantock Orchard Caravan Park
►►►►► 82%

tel: 01984 618618 Flaxpool TA4 4AW
email: member@flaxpool.freeserve.co.uk web: www.quantock-orchard.co.uk
dir: Take A358 from Taunton, follow Minehead & Williton signs. In 8m left just past Flaxpool Garage. Site immediately on left. grid ref: ST138357

This small family-run park is set at the foot of the beautiful Quantock Hills and makes an ideal base for touring Somerset, Exmoor and north Devon. It is also close to the West Somerset Railway. It has excellent facilities and there is a lovely heated outdoor swimming pool, plus gym and fitness centre; bike hire is also available. There are static homes for hire. 3.5 acre site. 60 touring pitches. 30 hardstandings. Caravan pitches. Motorhome pitches. Tent pitches. 15 statics.

Open: all year (rs 10 Sep-20 May swimming pool closed) **Last arrival:** 22.00hrs **Last departure:** noon

Pitches: * 🚐 £16-£27.50 🚆 £16-£27.50 ▲ £16-£27.50

Leisure: 🏊 🏸 ⚙ ⛱ Spa ⛳

Facilities: 🚿 🅿 ⊙ 🖤 ✳ ♿ 🛗 🛏 WiFi 💻 ♻ ❶

Services: 🚽 🔋 🗑 🕳 T 🍽 ⚗

Within 3 miles: 🏇 🎣 🛍 🏪 🗙 ♨

Notes: Dogs must be kept on leads. Off licence.

AA Pubs & Restaurants nearby: The White Horse, STOGUMBER, TA4 3TA, 01984 656277

The Blue Ball Inn, TRISCOMBE, TA4 3HE, 01984 618242

The Rising Sun Inn, WEST BAGBOROUGH, TA4 3EF, 01823 432575

DULVERTON
Map 3 SS92

Places to visit

Knightshayes, KNIGHTSHAYES, EX16 7RQ, 01884 254665
www.nationaltrust.org.uk/knightshayes

Great for kids: Tiverton Castle, TIVERTON, EX16 6RP, 01884 253200
www.tivertoncastle.com

Wimbleball Lake

►►► 81%

tel: 01398 371460 & 371116 Brompton Regis TA22 9NU
email: wimbleball@swlakestrust.org.uk
dir: From A396 (Tiverton to Minehead road) take B3222 signed Dulverton Services, follow signs to Wimbleball Lake. Ignore 1st entry (fishing) & take 2nd entry for tea room & camping. (NB care needed due to narrow roads). grid ref: SS960300

A grassy site overlooking Wimbleball Lake, set high up on Exmoor National Park. The camping area is adjacent to the visitor centre and café, which also includes the camping toilets and showers. The camping field, with 14 electric hook-ups and two hardstandings, is in a quiet and peaceful setting with good views of the lake, which is nationally renowned for its trout fishing; boats can be hired with advance notice. There are two camping pods for hire. 1.25 acre site. 30 touring pitches. 2 hardstandings. Caravan pitches. Motorhome pitches. Tent pitches.

Open: Mar-Oct **Last arrival:** 22.00hrs **Last departure:** 11.00hrs

Pitches: * 🚐 £14-£26 🚆 £14-£26 ▲ £14-£20 🏠 prices shown below

Leisure: ⚽ ⛱

Facilities: 🚿 ⊙ 🅿 ♿ 🛗 🛏 📷 🍴 💻 ♻ ❶

Services: 🚽 🔋 🍽

Glamping: Wooden Pods 2, £30-£40 Min stay 1 night Car by unit

Within 3 miles: ⛱ 🎣 🛍 🏪 🗙 ♨

Notes: No open fires, off-ground BBQs only, no swimming in lake, dogs not permitted in lake. Dogs must be kept on leads. Watersports & activity centre, bird watching, cycling, lakeside walks & bushcraft.

AA Pubs & Restaurants nearby: The Masons Arms, KNOWSTONE, EX36 4RY, 01398 341231

Who has won England Campsite of the Year?
See page 14

EMBOROUGH
Map 4 ST65

Places to visit

Glastonbury Abbey, GLASTONBURY, BA6 9EL, 01458 832267
www.glastonburyabbey.com

King John's Hunting Lodge, AXBRIDGE, BS26 2AP, 01934 732012
www.kingjohnshuntinglodge.co.uk

Wells Cathedral, WELLS, BA5 2UE, 01749 674483
www.wellscathedral.org.uk

Great for kids: East Somerset Railway, CRANMORE, BA4 4QP, 01749 880417
www.eastsomersetrailway.com

Old Down Touring Park
►►► 83%

tel: 01761 232355 **Old Down House BA3 4SA**
email: jsmallparkhomes@aol.com
dir: *A37 from Farrington Gurney through Ston Easton. In 2m left onto B3139 to Radstock.
Site opposite Old Down Inn.* **grid ref:** *ST628513*

A small family-run site set in open parkland, surrounded by well-established trees.
The good toilet facilities are well maintained as is every other aspect of the park.
Children are welcome. 4 acre site. 30 touring pitches. 15 hardstandings. 6 seasonal
pitches. Caravan pitches. Motorhome pitches. Tent pitches.

Open: all year **Last arrival:** 20.00hrs **Last departure:** noon

Pitches: 🚐 🚐 🛆

Facilities: ⊙ ☝ ☀ ☖ 🗄 ⟲ ❼

Services: 🔌 🔒 ∅ T ♨

Within 3 miles: ☝ ♨ ∅ 🖀 🖥 ∪

Notes: Dogs must be kept on leads.

AA Pubs & Restaurants nearby: The Oakhill Inn, OAKHILL, BA3 5HU, 01749 840442

The Holcombe Inn, HOLCOMBE, BA3 5EB, 01761 232478

EXFORD

Places to visit

Dunster Castle, DUNSTER, TA24 6SL, 01643 821314
www.nationaltrust.org.uk/dunstercastle

West Somerset Railway, MINEHEAD, TA24 5BG, 01643 704996
www.west-somerset-railway.co.uk

Tarr Steps Woodland National Nature Reserve, Near WITHYPOOL
www.exmoor-nationalpark.gov.uk

Great for kids: Exmoor Zoological Park, BLACKMOOR GATE, EX31 4SG,
01598 763352 www.exmoorzoo.co.uk

EXFORD

Westermill Farm
►► 87%

tel: 01643 831238 & 07970
email: info@westermill.com
dir: *In Exford follow Porlock si...*
(NB this is the only recommend...

An idyllic site for peace and qu...
which has won awards for cons...
camping. There are four waymar...
there's two miles of shallow wate...
fishing). Self-catering accommoda...
should only be approached from Ex... ...acre
site. 60 touring pitches. Caravan pi... ...ent pitches.

Open: all year (rs Nov-May larger toilet ...& shop closed)

Pitches: 🚐 £15.50-£18 🚐 £15.50-£18 🛆 £15.50-£18

Facilities: ⚡ 🅿 ⊙ ☝ ☀ ☖ 🗄 🚻 WiFi 🖥 ⟲ ❼

Services: 🗄 🔒 ∅ ♨

Within 3 miles: ∅ 🖀 🖥

Notes: No noise after 23.00hrs. Well behaved dogs accepted & must be kept on leads.

AA Pubs & Restaurants nearby: Crown Hotel, EXFORD, TA24 7PP, 01643 831554

FROME
Map 4 ST74

Places to visit

Stourhead, STOURHEAD, BA12 6QD, 01747 841152
www.nationaltrust.org.uk/stourhead

Nunney Castle, NUNNEY, 0370 333 1181
www.english-heritage.org.uk/daysout/properties/nunney-castle

Great for kids: Longleat, LONGLEAT, BA12 7NW, 01985 844400
www.longleat.co.uk

Seven Acres Caravan & Camping Site
►►► 85%

tel: 01373 464222 **Seven Acres, West Woodlands BA11 5EQ**
dir: *From rdbt on A361 (Frome bypass) onto B3092 towards Maiden Bradley , 0.75m to
site.* **grid ref:** *ST777444*

A level meadowland site beside the shallow River Frome, with a bridge across to an
adjacent field, and plenty of scope for families. The facilities are spotless. Set on
the edge of the Longleat Estate with its stately home, wildlife safari park, and many
other attractions. 3 acre site. 16 touring pitches. 16 hardstandings. Caravan
pitches. Motorhome pitches. Tent pitches.

Open: Mar-Oct **Pitches:** 🚐 🚐 🛆

Facilities: ⚡ ⊙ 🅿 ☀ 🖀 🚻 ⟲

Services: 🔌 **Within 3 miles:** ☝ 🖀 ∅ 🖥 🖀 ∪

Notes: 🚫 Dogs must be kept on leads.

AA Pubs & Restaurants nearby: The George at Nunney, NUNNEY, BA11 4LW,
01373 836458

Vobster Inn, LOWER VOBSTER, BA3 5RJ, 01373 812920

PITCHES: 🚐 Caravans 🚐 Motorhomes 🛆 Tents 🏕 Glamping accommodation **SERVICES:** 🔌 Electric hook up 🗄 Launderette 🍷 Licensed bar
🔒 Calor Gas ∅ Camping Gaz T Toilet fluid 🍽 Café/Restaurant 🍔 Fast Food/Takeaway ♨ Battery charging 🍼 Baby care ⚓ Motorvan service point
ABBREVIATIONS: BHs – bank holidays Etr – Easter Spring BH – Spring Bank Holiday fr – from hrs – hours m – mile mdnt – midnight
rdbt – roundabout rs – restricted service wk – week wknd – weekend x-roads – crossroads 🚫 No credit or debit cards 🚫 No dogs

Map 4 ST53

...ON, TA11 7HU, 01458 224471

...rg.uk/lytes-cary-manor

...museum, YEOVILTON, BA22 8HT, 01935 840565

...airarm.com

...eat for kids: Haynes International Motor Museum, SPARKFORD, BA22 7LH, 01963 440804 www.haynesmotormuseum.com

PREMIER PARK

The Old Oaks Touring Park
► ► ► ► ► 98%

tel: 01458 831437 **Wick Farm, Wick BA6 8JS**
email: info@theoldoaks.co.uk
dir: *M5 junct 23, A39 to Glastonbury. After Street take A39 towards Wells. At 3rd rdbt follow Wick & Brindham signs. Site 1.5m on right. (NB it is advisable not to use Sat Nav for last part of journey).* **grid ref:** ST521394

An exceptional adults-only park offering larger than average landscaped pitches (premier pitches have satellite HD TV), impeccably maintained grounds and wonderful views. The perfect 'get away from it all' spot where you can enjoy walking, cycling, fishing and touring or simply relaxing amid the abundant wildlife. The top class facilities include a well-stocked shop selling locally-sourced produce and home-baked cakes, a smart shower block with excellent wet rooms, WiFi, free walking and cycling maps, a half-acre fishing lake, a daily mini bus service to nearby towns and even a hot doggy shower! Six 2-person, heated wooden 'camping cabins' with their own covered decking are available for hire. 10 acre site. 98 touring pitches. 98 hardstandings. Caravan pitches. Motorhome pitches. Tent pitches.

Open: Mar-mid Nov (rs Mar & Oct-Nov reduced shop & reception hours)
Last arrival: 20.00hrs **Last departure:** noon

Pitches: ⊕ £20-£39 ⊖ £20-£39 ▲ £15-£25 ⋔ prices shown below

Leisure: 〽

Facilities: ⋔ P ⊙ P ✳ ⅁ ⌖ ⌨ WiFi ▭ ♻ 𝓲

Services: ⊕ ⓢ ⋔ ⊘ T ⇲ 🖤 ⇲

Glamping: **Wooden Pods** 6, £48-£64 Min stay 2 nights Car by unit

Within 3 miles: P ⅁ ⓢ

Notes: Adults only. No groups, no noise after 22.30hrs. Dogs must be kept on leads. Off licence, local produce boxes, caravan cleaning, dog owners' information pack, fish & chip nights, minibus.

AA Pubs & Restaurants nearby: Ring O'Bells, ASHCOTT, TA7 9PZ, 01458 210232

Middlewick Farm
► ► ► ► ► 83%

tel: 01458 832351 **Wick Ln BA6 8JW**
email: hello@themiddlewick.co.uk
dir: *From Glastonbury take A361 towards Frome. After Millfied Prep School (on right) take next left signed Wick. Site on left in 1.5m.* **grid ref:** ST520396

A short walk past the cottages on this camping site brings you to the glamping area where there are three stylish E-den wooden camping cabins with good privacy and views of the Tor. Each has a double bed, small fridge, heater, cutlery and clothes storage, plus a porch and deck area with table, chairs and BBQ. In addition each unit has a separate, spacious cabin with high quality toilet, washbasin and shower. There is also a shepherd's hut that accommodates additional guests. The site offers a peaceful glamping environment but is well located for visiting nearby Wells, Clarks Village or Weston-Super-Mare, all just a short drive away. 16 acre site.

Open: all year **Last arrival:** 20.00hrs **Last departure:** 10.00hrs

Glamping: **Wooden Pods** 2 **Shepherd's Huts** 1

AA Pubs & Restaurants nearby: The Two Brewers, STREET, BA16 0HB, 01458 442421
The Sheppey, LOWER GODNEY, BA5 1RZ, 01458 831594

Isle of Avalon Touring Caravan Park
► ► ► ► 86%

tel: 01458 833618 **Godney Rd BA6 9AF**
email: candicehatwell@hotmail.co.uk
dir: *M5 junct 23, A39 to outskirts of Glastonbury, 2nd exit signed Wells at B&Q rdbt, straight over next rdbt, 1st exit at 3rd rdbt (B3151), site 200yds on right.*
grid ref: ST494397

A popular site, on the south side of this historic town, and within easy walking distance of the centre. It is a level park, with a separate tent field, that offers a quiet environment. It makes an ideal spot from which to explore the many local attractions that include Glastonbury Tor, Wells, Wookey Hole and Clarks Village. Approved caravan storage is available. 8 acre site. 120 touring pitches. 70 hardstandings. Caravan pitches. Motorhome pitches. Tent pitches.

Open: all year **Last arrival:** 21.00hrs **Last departure:** 11.00hrs

Pitches: ⊕ ⊖ ▲

Facilities: ⊙ P ✳ ⅁ ⓢ ⌖ ⌨ WiFi ▭ ♻ 𝓲

Services: ⊕ ⓢ ⋔ ⊘ T ⇲ 🖤 ⇲

Within 3 miles: ⧠ P ⅁ ⓢ ⌣

AA Pubs & Restaurants nearby: Ring O'Bells, ASHCOTT, TA7 9PZ, 01458 210232

LEISURE: 🏊 Indoor pool 🏊 Outdoor pool ⛰ Children's playground 👋 Kid's club 🎾 Tennis court 🎱 Games room ⛳ Golf course ⛵ Boat hire 🚲 Cycle hire ⧠ Cinema 🎵 Entertainment ⌒ Fishing ◉ Mini golf ⚑ Pitch n putt 🏄 Watersports 🏋 Gym ⚽ Sports field ⌣ Stables **FACILITIES:** 🛁 Bath 🚿 Shower P Private washing cubicles ⊙ Electric shaver P Hairdryer ✳ Ice Packs ⅁ Disabled facilities ⓢ Shop on site 🏪 Mobile shop 🍖 BBQ area 🪑 Picnic area WiFi Wi-fi ▭ Internet access ♻ Recycling 𝓲 Tourist info ⌖ Dog exercise area ⚗ Car hire can be arranged

HIGHBRIDGE — Map 4 ST34

Greenacre Place Touring Caravan Park
NEW ►►► 84%

tel: 01278 785227 & 07717 822852 **Bristol Rd, Edithmead TA9 4HA**
email: info@greenacreplace.com
dir: *M5 junct 22, A38 signed Weston-Super-Mare & Burnham-on-Sea. At rdbt take A38 signed Highbridge & Bridgwater. Site on right.* **grid ref:** ST331484

An excellent small adults-only park, very well located near to the M5 junction 22, making it great for visiting the Somerset Levels, Burnham-on-Sea, Brean, Cheddar or Clarks Village. It also makes an excellent stopover when travelling to and from the West Country. All 10 pitches have electric hook-ups and the small facility block is very well appointed and clean. There is free WiFi and also a two-bedroom cottage available for hire where children are accepted. The park is also well placed for anyone visiting the Somerset Carnivals held in November. Dogs are welcome. 0.5 acre site. 10 touring pitches. Caravan pitches. Motorhome pitches.

Open: Mar-Nov **Last arrival:** 22.00hrs **Last departure:** 11.00hrs

Pitches: * 🚐 £13-£18 🚐 £13-£18

Facilities: 🔌 📶 ⊙ 🚿 📶 ♻ 𝒊

Services: 🔌

Within 3 miles: 🎣 ⚓ 🏇 🏌 ◎ 🚣 🛒 🎬 ↻

Notes: Adults only. Breathable groundsheets only, no ball games. Dogs must be kept on leads.

LANGPORT — Map 4 ST42

Places to visit
Montacute House, MONTACUTE, TA15 6XP, 01935 823289
www.nationaltrust.org.uk

Lytes Cary Manor, KINGSDON, TA11 7HU, 01458 224471
www.nationaltrust.org.uk/lytes-cary-manor

Great for kids: Fleet Air Arm Museum, YEOVILTON, BA22 8HT, 01935 840565
www.fleetairarm.com

Thorney Lakes Caravan Park
►►► 85%

GOLD

tel: 01458 250811 & 07803 005042 **Thorney Lakes, Muchelney TA10 0DW**
email: info@thorneylakes.co.uk
dir: *From A303 at Podimore rdbt take A372 to Langport. At Huish Episcopi Church turn left for Muchelney. In 100yds left (signed Muchelney & Crewkerne). Site 300yds after John Leach Pottery.* **grid ref:** ST430237

A small, peaceful site set in a cider apple orchard in the heart of the Somerset Levels. There are excellent coarse fishing lakes just a short stroll away from the campsite, and the good walks in the area include the Parrett Trail which is just 100 metres from the site. There are good toilet facilities with excellent family rooms. Although in a peaceful setting the site is well located for visiting Glastonbury, Taunton and the Fleet Air Arm Museum at Yeovilton. 6 acre site. 36 touring pitches. Caravan pitches. Motorhome pitches. Tent pitches.

Open: Etr-Oct

Pitches: 🚐 £15-£20 🚐 £15-£20 ⛺ £15-£20

Leisure: 🎣

Facilities: 🔌 ⊙ 🚿 🎣 🏇 ♻ 𝒊

Services: 🔌

Within 3 miles: 🎣 🏇 🛒

Notes: Dogs must be kept on leads. Electric vehicle charging point.

AA Pubs & Restaurants nearby: Rose & Crown (Eli's), HUISH EPISCOPI, TA10 9QT, 01458 250494

The Devonshire Arms, LONG SUTTON, TA10 9LP, 01458 241271

The Halfway House, PITNEY, TA10 9AB, 01458 252513

MARTOCK — Map 4 ST41

Places to visit
Montacute House, MONTACUTE, TA15 6XP, 01935 823289
www.nationaltrust.org.uk

Great for kids: Fleet Air Arm Museum, YEOVILTON, BA22 8HT, 01935 840565
www.fleetairarm.com

Southfork Caravan Park
►►►► 85%

BRONZE

tel: 01935 825661 **Parrett Works TA12 6AE**
email: info@southforkcaravans.co.uk
dir: *From E: approx 2m after Cargate rdbt exit A303, signed Crewkerne. At T-junct right onto A356 signed Martock. Through Bower Hinton, left signed South Petherton. Site approx 1m. From W: at Hayes End rdbt left signed South Petherton. Through South Petherton, follow Martock signs. Site on left.* **grid ref:** ST448188

A neat, level mainly grass park in a quiet rural area, just outside the pretty village of Martock. Some excellent spacious hardstandings are available. The facilities are always spotless and the whole site is well cared for by the friendly owners, who will ensure your stay is a happy one, a fact borne out by the many repeat customers. The park is unique in that it also has a fully-approved caravan repair and servicing centre with accessory shop. There are also static caravans and a camping pod available for hire. Caravan storage also available. 2 acre site. 27 touring pitches. 2 hardstandings. Caravan pitches. Motorhome pitches. Tent pitches. 3 statics.

Open: all year **Last arrival:** 22.30hrs **Last departure:** noon

Pitches: 🚐 🚐 ⛺ 🏕

Leisure: 🏕

Facilities: 🔌 📶 ⊙ 🎣 🚿 🛒 🏇 📶 ♻ 𝒊

Services: 🔌 🖲 🔋 🍼 📋 ⛽

Glamping: Wooden Pods 1

Within 3 miles: 🎣 🏇 🛒

Notes: Dogs must be kept on leads.

AA Pubs & Restaurants nearby: The Nag's Head Inn, MARTOCK, TA12 6NF, 01935 823432

Ilchester Arms, ILCHESTER, BA22 8LN, 01935 840220

PITCHES: 🚐 Caravans 🚐 Motorhomes ⛺ Tents 🏕 Glamping accommodation **SERVICES:** 🔌 Electric hook up 🖲 Launderette 🍺 Licensed bar 🔋 Calor Gas ⚗ Camping Gaz 📋 Toilet fluid 🍽 Café/Restaurant 🍟 Fast Food/Takeaway 🔋 Battery charging 🍼 Baby care ⛽ Motorvan service point
ABBREVIATIONS: BHs – bank holidays Etr – Easter Spring BH – Spring Bank Holiday fr – from hrs – hours m – mile mdnt – midnight rdbt – roundabout rs – restricted service wk – week wknd – weekend x-roads – crossroads 🚫 No credit or debit cards 🚫 No dogs

MINEHEAD
Map 3 SS94

Places to visit

West Somerset Railway, MINEHEAD, TA24 5BG, 01643 704996
www.west-somerset-railway.co.uk

Dunster Castle, DUNSTER, TA24 6SL, 01643 821314
www.nationaltrust.org.uk/dunstercastle

Great for kids: Tropiquaria Animal and Adventure Park, WASHFORD, TA23 0QB, 01984 640688 www.tropiquaria.co.uk

Minehead & Exmoor Caravan & Camping Park
►►► 78%

tel: 01643 703074 **Porlock Rd TA24 8SW**
email: enquiries@mineheadandexmoorcamping.co.uk
dir: 1m W of Minehead town centre, take A39 towards Porlock. Site on right.
grid ref: SS950457

A small terraced park, on the edge of Exmoor, spread over five small paddocks and screened by the mature trees that surround it. The level pitches provide a comfortable space for each unit on this family-run park. The site is very conveniently placed for visiting Minehead and the Exmoor National Park. 3 acre site. 50 touring pitches. 9 hardstandings. 10 seasonal pitches. Caravan pitches. Motorhome pitches. Tent pitches.

Open: Mar-Oct (rs Nov-Feb open certain weeks - phone site for details)
Last arrival: 21.00hrs **Last departure:** noon

Pitches: * ⊞ £12-£20 ⊞ £12-£20 ▲ £12-£20

Leisure: ⚑

Facilities: ⌕◉₧✱ᴇ🔧♻♻❄❂

Services: ☎🔒🗑🚿🚰

Within 3 miles: ⌖日₧◎⛷🏪🎣

Notes: 🐾 PayPal accepted. No open fires or loud music. Tumble dryer available.

AA Pubs & Restaurants nearby: The Luttrell Arms Hotel, DUNSTER, TA24 6SG, 01643 821555

The Stags Head Inn, DUNSTER, TA24 6SN, 01643 821229

PORLOCK
Map 3 SS84

Places to visit

West Somerset Railway, MINEHEAD, TA24 5BG, 01643 704996
www.west-somerset-railway.co.uk

Dunster Castle, DUNSTER, TA24 6SL, 01643 821314
www.nationaltrust.org.uk/dunstercastle

Great for kids: Tropiquaria Animal and Adventure Park, WASHFORD, TA23 0QB, 01984 640688 www.tropiquaria.co.uk

PREMIER PARK

Porlock Caravan Park
►►►►► 87%

tel: 01643 862269 **TA24 8ND**
email: info@porlockcaravanpark.co.uk **web:** www.porlockcaravanpark.co.uk
dir: From A39 in Porlock follow Porlock Weir & Harbour signs, site on right.
grid ref: SS882469

A sheltered touring park attractively laid out in the centre of lovely countryside on the edge of Porlock. The famous Porlock Hill, a few hundred yards from the site, leads to some spectacular areas of Exmoor and stunning views. Hardstanding pitches are available and the toilet facilities are superb; there is a dish-washing room and kitchen with microwave and freezer. Rallies can be catered for in a separate rally field (without electricity) but with superb views over the coast. Holiday homes are available for hire. 3 acre site. 40 touring pitches. 14 hardstandings. Caravan pitches. Motorhome pitches. Tent pitches. 55 statics.

Open: 15 Mar-Oct **Last arrival:** 20.00hrs **Last departure:** 11.00hrs

Pitches: * ⊞ £15-£19 ⊞ £19.50-£23.50 ▲ £15-£19

Facilities: ⌕🅿◉₧✱ᴇ🐕[WiFi]❂

Services: ☎🔒🗑🚰⛽

Within 3 miles: ⛷₧🏪⛵

Notes: No fires, rollerblades or scooters. Dogs must be kept on leads.

AA Pubs & Restaurants nearby: The Ship Inn, PORLOCK, TA24 8QD, 01643 862507

The Bottom Ship, PORLOCK, TA24 8PB, 01643 863288

Burrowhayes Farm Caravan & Camping Site & Riding Stables

▶▶▶▶ 92%

tel: 01643 862463 **West Luccombe TA24 8HT**
email: info@burrowhayes.co.uk **web:** www.burrowhayes.co.uk
dir: *A39 from Minehead towards Porlock for 5m. Left at Red Post to Horner & West Luccombe, site 0.25m on right, immediately before humpback bridge.* **grid ref:** *SS897460*

A delightful site on the edge of Exmoor that slopes gently down to Horner Water. The farm buildings have been converted into riding stables from where escorted rides onto the moors can be taken; the excellent toilet facilities are housed in timber-clad buildings. Hardstandings are available – some are fully serviced and many of the hook-ups have TV points. There is a popular, well-stocked shop and many countryside walks can be accessed directly from the site. 8 acre site. 120 touring pitches. 10 hardstandings. Caravan pitches. Motorhome pitches. Tent pitches. 19 statics.

Open: 15 Mar-Oct (rs before Etr - caravan hire & riding not available)
Last arrival: 22.00hrs **Last departure:** 11.00hrs

Pitches: * 🚐 £18.50-£23.50 🚐 £18.50-£23.50 ▲ £15-£21
Facilities: 🏌️☉🍴✳️♿🚿♨️ 📶💻♻️❗
Services: 🔌🗑️🛢️⊘🚽🚰🔧
Within 3 miles: ⬇️⛳️🎣♨️🗑️🔄U
Notes: Dogs must be kept on leads.
AA Pubs & Restaurants nearby: The Ship Inn, PORLOCK, TA24 8QD, 01643 862507
The Bottom Ship, PORLOCK, TA24 8PB, 01643 863288

PRIDDY

Places to visit

Glastonbury Abbey, GLASTONBURY, BA6 9EL, 01458 832267
www.glastonburyabbey.com

The Helicopter Museum, WESTON-SUPER-MARE, BS24 8PP, 01934 635227
www.helicoptermuseum.co.uk

Great for kids: Wookey Hole Caves & Papermill, WOOKEY HOLE, BA5 1BB, 01749 672243 www.wookey.co.uk

PRIDDY Map 4 ST55

Cheddar Mendip Heights Camping & Caravanning Club Site

▶▶▶▶ 88%

tel: 01749 870241 & 07392 006949 **Townsend BA5 3BP**
email: cheddar.site@thecampingandcaravanningclub.co.uk
dir: *From A39 take B3135 to Cheddar. Left in 4.5m. Site 200yds on right, signed.* **grid ref:** *ST522519*

A gently sloping site set high on the Mendip Hills and surrounded by trees. This excellent campsite offers really good facilities, including top notch family rooms and private cubicles which are spotlessly maintained. Fresh bread is baked daily and, along with pastries, can be ordered each morning from the well-stocked shop. The site is well positioned for visiting local attractions such as Cheddar, Wookey Hole, Wells and Glastonbury, and is popular with walkers. Self-catering caravans are now available for hire. 4.5 acre site. 90 touring pitches. 37 hardstandings. Caravan pitches. Motorhome pitches. Tent pitches. 2 statics.

Open: 15 Mar-5 Nov **Last arrival:** 20.00hrs **Last departure:** noon **Pitches:** 🚐 🚐 ▲
Leisure: 🎱 **Facilities:** 🏌️📵☉🍴✳️♿🚿♨️ 📶♻️❗🚰
Services: 🔌🗑️🛢️⊘🚽🔧 **Within 3 miles:** ⬇️♨️U
Notes: Site gates closed 23.00hrs-07.00hrs. Dogs must be kept on leads.
AA Pubs & Restaurants nearby: Wookey Hole Inn, WOOKEY HOLE, BA5 1BP, 01749 676677
The Burcott Inn, WOOKEY, BA5 1NJ, 01749 673874

SHEPTON MALLET Map 4 ST64

Places to visit

East Somerset Railway, CRANMORE, BA4 4QP, 01749 880417
www.eastsomersetrailway.com

The Bishop's Palace, WELLS, BA5 2PD, 01749 988111 www.bishopspalace.org.uk

Great for kids: Wookey Hole Caves & Papermill, WOOKEY HOLE, BA5 1BB, 01749 672243 www.wookey.co.uk

Greenacres Camping

▶▶ 96%

tel: 01749 890497 **Barrow Ln, North Wootton BA4 4HL**
email: stay@greenacres-camping.co.uk
dir: *Approx halfway between Glastonbury & Shepton Mallet on A361 turn at Steanbow Farm signed North Wootton. Or from A39 between Upper Coxley & Wells turn at Brownes Garden Centre into Woodford Ln. Follow North Wootton & site signs.* **grid ref:** *ST553417*

An immaculately maintained site peacefully set within sight of Glastonbury Tor. It is mainly family orientated and there is plenty of space for children to play games in a very safe environment; many thoughtful extra facilities are provided such as play houses and a children's entertainment team in the high season. There is even a 'glow worm safari' at certain times of the year. Facilities are exceptionally clean and cycle hire is available. Please note, caravans and large motorhomes are not accepted. 4.5 acre site. 40 touring pitches. Motorhome pitches. Tent pitches.

Open: Apr-Sep **Last arrival:** 21.00hrs **Last departure:** 11.00hrs
Pitches: * 🚐 £18 ▲ £18 **Leisure:** 🎱🎯🚲 **Facilities:** ☉🍴✳️♨️🍴 📶♻️❗🚰
Services: 🔌🛢️⊘🔧 **Within 3 miles:** ⬇️🎯🎣⛳️♨️🗑️U
Notes: 🚭 Fire pits, camp fires, free use of fridges & freezers, book library.
AA Pubs & Restaurants nearby: The Crown at Wells, WELLS, BA5 2RP, 01749 673457
The George Inn, CROSCOMBE, BA5 3QH, 01749 342306

PITCHES: 🚐 Caravans 🚐 Motorhomes ▲ Tents 🏠 Glamping accommodation **SERVICES:** 🔌 Electric hook up 🗑️ Launderette 🍺 Licensed bar 🛢️ Calor Gas ⊘ Camping Gaz 🚽 Toilet fluid 🍴 Café/Restaurant 🍔 Fast Food/Takeaway 🔋 Battery charging 👶 Baby care 🔧 Motorvan service point **ABBREVIATIONS:** BHs – bank holidays Etr – Easter Spring BH – Spring Bank Holiday fr – from hrs – hours m – mile mdnt – midnight rdbt – roundabout rs – restricted service wk – week wknd – weekend x-roads – crossroads No credit or debit cards No dogs

SPARKFORD Map 4 ST62

Places to visit

Lytes Cary Manor, KINGSDON, TA11 7HU, 01458 224471
www.nationaltrust.org.uk/lytes-cary-manor

Haynes International Motor Museum, SPARKFORD, BA22 7LH, 01963 440804
www.haynesmotormuseum.com

Long Hazel Park

►►►► 85%

tel: 01963 440002 **High St BA22 7JH**
email: longhazelpark@hotmail.com
dir: *Exit A303 at Hazlegrove rdbt, follow signs for Sparkford. Site 400yds on left.*
grid ref: *ST602262*

A very neat, adults-only park next to the village inn in the high street. This attractive park is run by friendly owners to a very good standard. Many of the spacious pitches have hardstandings. There are also luxury lodges on site for hire or purchase. The site is close to the Haynes International Motor Museum and the Yeovilton Air Museum. 3.5 acre site. 50 touring pitches. 30 hardstandings. 21 seasonal pitches. Caravan pitches. Motorhome pitches. Tent pitches. 2 statics.

Open: all year **Last arrival:** 21.00hrs **Last departure:** 11.00hrs

Pitches: * 🚐 £20-£25 🚌 £20-£25 ⛺ £20-£25

Facilities: 🚿 [P] ⊙ 💨 ❄ ♿ 🧺 [WiFi] ♻ ℹ

Services: 🔌 🗄 ■ ⌀ [T] 🍴 ⬇

Within 3 miles: ⛳ 🎣 [$]

Notes: Adults only. 🚫 PayPal accepted. No open fires or fire pits, no noise after 22.00hrs. Dogs must be kept on leads & exercised off site. Picnic tables available, camping spares.

AA Pubs & Restaurants nearby: The Walnut Tree, WEST CAMEL, BA22 7QW, 01935 851292

The Queens Arms, CORTON DENHAM, DT9 4LR, 01963 220317

TAUNTON Map 4 ST22

Places to visit

Hestercombe Gardens, TAUNTON, TA2 8LG, 01823 413923 www.hestercombe.com

Barrington Court, BARRINGTON, TA19 0NQ, 01460 241938
www.nationaltrust.org.uk

Cornish Farm Touring Park

►►►► 86%

tel: 01823 327746 **Shoreditch TA3 7BS**
email: info@cornishfarm.com **web:** www.cornishfarm.com
dir: *M5 junct 25, A358 towards Taunton. Left at lights. 3rd left into Ilminster Rd (follow Corfe signs). Right at rdbt, left at next rdbt. Right at T-junct, left into Killams Dr, 2nd left into Killams Ave. Over motorway bridge. Site on left, access via 2nd entrance.*
grid ref: *ST235217*

This smart park provides really top quality facilities throughout. Although only two miles from Taunton, it is set in open countryside and is a very convenient base for visiting the many attractions of the area such as Clarks Village, Glastonbury and Cheddar Gorge. Also makes an excellent base for watching county cricket at the nearby Somerset County Ground. 3.5 acre site. 50 touring pitches. 25 hardstandings. Caravan pitches. Motorhome pitches. Tent pitches.

Open: all year **Last arrival:** anytime **Last departure:** 11.30hrs

Pitches: * 🚐 £17-£20 🚌 £17-£20 ⛺ £17-£20

Facilities: 🚿 ⊙ 💨 ♿ 🧺 [WiFi] 💻 ℹ

Services: 🔌 🗄 ■ [T] ⬇

Within 3 miles: ⛳ 🎬 🎣 ◎ [$] 🗄 ∪

Notes: Dogs must be kept on leads.

AA Pubs & Restaurants nearby: The Hatch Inn, TAUNTON, TA3 6SG, 01823 480245

The Willow Tree Restaurant, TAUNTON, TA1 4AR, 01823 352835

Ashe Farm Camping & Caravan Site
►►►►80%

tel: 01823 443764 & 07891 989482 **Thornfalcon TA3 5NW**
email: info@ashefarm.co.uk **web:** www.ashefarm.co.uk
dir: *M5 junct 25, A358 E for 2.5m. Right at Nags Head pub. Site 0.25m on right.*
grid ref: ST279229

A well-screened site surrounded by mature trees and shrubs, with two large touring fields. The modern, upgraded facilities block includes toilets and showers plus a separate laundry room. This site is not far from the bustling market town of Taunton, and handy for both south and north coasts. Also makes a good stopover for people travelling on the nearby M5. 7 acre site. 30 touring pitches. 11 hardstandings. Caravan pitches. Motorhome pitches. Tent pitches. 3 statics.

Open: Apr-Oct **Last arrival:** 22.00hrs **Last departure:** noon

Pitches: 🚐 🚐 🛖

Leisure: ⚠ ♨

Facilities: 🅿 🅿 ⊙ 🥖 ☀ ⚐ ⛽ ♻ ❶

Services: 🔌 🔘

Within 3 miles: ⬆ 🍴 🖉 ◎ 🔘 🔘 ∪

Notes: ⊘ No camp fires, no noise after 22.00hrs. Dogs must be kept on leads. Baby changing facilities.

AA Pubs & Restaurants nearby: The Hatch Inn, TAUNTON, TA3 6SG, 01823 480245

The Willow Tree Restaurant, TAUNTON, TA1 4AR, 01823 352835

WATCHET

Places to visit

West Somerset Railway, MINEHEAD, TA24 5BG, 01643 704996
www.west-somerset-railway.co.uk

Dunster Castle, DUNSTER, TA24 6SL, 01643 821314
www.nationaltrust.org.uk/dunstercastle

Great for kids: Tropiquaria Animal and Adventure Park, WASHFORD, TA23 0QB, 01984 640688 www.tropiquaria.co.uk

---

WATCHET **Map 3 ST04**

Home Farm Holiday Centre
►►►►81%

tel: 01984 632487 **St Audries Bay TA4 4DP**
email: dib@homefarmholidaycentre.co.uk
dir: *From Bridgwater take A39 to West Quantoxhead (approx 15m), after garage, right onto B3191 signed Doniford, 0.25m, 1st right.* **grid ref:** ST106432

In a hidden valley beneath the Quantock Hills, this park overlooks its own private beach. The atmosphere is friendly and quiet, and there are lovely sea views from the level pitches. Flowerbeds, woodland walks and the Koi carp pond all enhance this very attractive site, along with a lovely indoor swimming pool, an excellent children's play area, and a beer garden. 45 acre site. 40 touring pitches. 35 hardstandings. Caravan pitches. Motorhome pitches. Tent pitches. 230 statics.

Open: all year (rs Nov-1 Mar no touring caravans, motorhomes or tents, shop & bar closed) **Last arrival:** dusk **Last departure:** noon

Pitches: 🚐 £12-£27.50 🚐 £12-£27.50 🛖 £12-£27.50

Leisure: 🏊 ⚠ 🖉

Facilities: 🅿 ⊙ 🥖 ☀ ⚐ 🔘 ✂ 📶 ♻ ❶

Services: 🔌 🔘 🍴 🛢 🖉 🅣

Within 3 miles: 🖉 🔘 🔘

Notes: No cars by caravans or tents. No noise after 23.00hrs. Dogs must be kept on leads. Table tennis, sea fishing. Baguettes, croissants & pain au chocolat available.

AA Pubs & Restaurants nearby: The Hood Arms, KILVE, TA5 1EA, 01278 741210

Doniford Bay Holiday Park
HOLIDAY HOME PARK 90%

tel: 01984 632423 **TA23 0TJ**
email: donifordbay@haven.com **web:** www.haven.com/donifordbay
dir: *M5 junct 23, A38 towards Bridgwater, A39 towards Minehead. 15m, at West Quantoxhead, right after St Audries garage. Park 1m on right.* **grid ref:** ST093432

This well-appointed holiday park, situated adjacent to a shingle and sand beach, offers a wide range of activities for the whole family. The holiday homes are spacious and well-appointed and there is plenty to keep children (of all ages) interested, including great indoor and outdoor pools, a multi-sports centre, slides and archery. The park has good eating outlets including a nice café/restaurant. Being close to the Exmoor National Park, it offers visitors the chance to seek out some of the best scenery in the county.

Open: Mar-Oct

Changeover day: Mon, Fri, Sat

Arrival and departure times: Please contact the site

Statics: 143 Sleeps 6-8 Bedrms 2-3 Bathrms 1-2 Toilets 1-2 Microwave Freezer TV Sky/FTV Elec inc Gas inc Grass area

Children: 🛉 Cots Highchair **Dogs:** 2 on leads No dangerous dogs

Leisure: 🏊 🏊 Cycle hire 🖐 ⚠

WELLINGTON
Map 3 ST12

Places to visit
Hestercombe Gardens, TAUNTON, TA2 8LG, 01823 413923 www.hestercombe.com

Great for kids: Diggerland, CULLOMPTON, EX15 2PE, 0871 227 7007 *(Calls cost 10p per minute plus your phone company's access charge)* www.diggerland.com

Greenacres Touring Park
►►►► 88%

tel: 01823 652844 **Haywards Ln, Chelston TA21 9PH**
email: enquiries@wellington.co.uk
dir: *M5 junct 26, A38 signed Wellington. Approx 1.5m, at Chelston rdbt take 1st left into West Buckland Rd signed A38. Straight on at next rdbt. Next left, follow sign for site.*
grid ref: ST156001

This attractively landscaped adults-only park is situated close to the Somerset/Devon border in a peaceful setting with great views of the Blackdown and Quantock Hills. It is in a very convenient location for overnight stays, being just one and half miles from the M5. This park is also well positioned for visiting both the north and south coasts, and it is also close to a local bus route. It has excellent facilities, which are spotlessly clean and well maintained. 2.5 acre site. 40 touring pitches. 30 hardstandings. Caravan pitches. Motorhome pitches.

Open: Apr-end Sep **Last arrival:** 19.00hrs **Last departure:** 11.00hrs

Pitches: 🚐 🚉 **Facilities:** 🍴🅿☺🅿♿🚻📶♻🛈

Services: 🔌

Within 3 miles: 🛶🍴🎣🛍🐟∪

Notes: Adults only. No RVs. Dogs must be kept on leads.

AA Pubs & Restaurants nearby: The Globe, MILVERTON, TA4 1JX, 01823 400534

Gamlins Farm Caravan Park
►►► 81%

tel: 01823 672859 & 07814 742462 & 07967 683738
Meadow View, Greenham TA21 0JU
email: gamlinsfarmcaravanpark@hotmail.co.uk
dir: *M5 junct 26, A38 towards Tiverton & Exeter. 5m, right for Greenham, site 1m on right.*
grid ref: ST083195

This peaceful site (only two minutes from the A38) is set in a secluded valley with excellent views of the Quantock Hills; it is well placed for visiting both Devon and Somerset. The facilities are very good and spotlessly clean, and free coarse fishing is available. Static holiday homes for hire. 4 acre site. 30 touring pitches. 12 hardstandings. 6 seasonal pitches. Caravan pitches. Motorhome pitches. Tent pitches. 4 statics.

Open: Mar-Oct **Last arrival:** 20.00hrs **Last departure:** 11.00hrs (later arrivals & departures by prior arrangement)

Pitches: * 🚐 £15-£19 🚉 £15-£19 ▲ £12-£15

Leisure: 🎣 🎣

Facilities: 🍴🅿☺🅿✳♿🐾📶🖥♻🛈

Services: 🔌🛍🛒🏧

Within 3 miles: 🛶🎣🛍🐟∪

Notes: PayPal accepted. No loud noise after 22.00hrs. Dogs must be kept on leads & not left unattended.

WELLS
Map 4 ST54

Places to visit
Glastonbury Abbey, GLASTONBURY, BA6 9EL, 01458 832267 www.glastonburyabbey.com

The Bishop's Palace, WELLS, BA5 2PD, 01749 988111 www.bishopspalace.org.uk

Wells Touring Park
►►►►► 90%

tel: 01749 676869 **Haybridge BA5 1AJ**
email: jason@wellstouringpark.co.uk **web:** www.wellstouringpark.co.uk
dir: *A38 then follow signs for Axbridge, Cheddar & Wells.* **grid ref:** ST531459

This well established, adults-only holiday park has first-class toilet facilities and many hardstandings, some of which are fully serviced. It is a restful park set in countryside on the outskirts of Wells, and is within easy walking distance of the city centre, with its spectacular cathedral and Bishop's Palace. Cheddar Gorge, Bath, Bristol, Weston-Super-Mare, Wookey Hole and Glastonbury are all within easy driving distance. The site has a function room, lounge and patio as well as a beauty salon. Holiday cottages are available for hire and luxury lodges for sale. 7.5 acre site. 72 touring pitches. 54 hardstandings. 20 seasonal pitches. Caravan pitches. Motorhome pitches. Tent pitches. 12 statics.

Open: all year **Last arrival:** 20.00hrs **Last departure:** noon

Pitches: * 🚐 £18-£27 🚉 £18-£27 ▲ £15-£27

Facilities: 🍴🅿☺🅿✳♿🛍🏧🚻📶♻🛈🚗

Services: 🔌🛒🛍🧺🅃🛒🏧

Within 3 miles: 🛶🍴🎣◎🛍🐟∪

Notes: Adults only. Dogs must be kept on leads. Pétanque.

AA Pubs & Restaurants nearby: The Crown at Wells, WELLS, BA5 2RP, 01749 673457

The Fountain Inn, WELLS, BA5 2UU, 01749 672317

Goodfellows, WELLS, BA5 2RR, 01749 673866

LEISURE: 🏊 Indoor pool 🏊 Outdoor pool 🎢 Children's playground 🧒 Kid's club 🎾 Tennis court 🎱 Games room ⛳ Golf course 🚣 Boat hire 🚲 Cycle hire 🎬 Cinema 🎭 Entertainment 🎣 Fishing ◎ Mini golf ⛳ Pitch n putt 🏄 Watersports 🏋 Gym 🏟 Sports field 🐴 Stables **FACILITIES:** 🛁 Bath 🚿 Shower 🅿 Private washing cubicles ☺ Electric shaver 🖒 Hairdryer ✳ Ice Packs ♿ Disabled facilities 🛍 Shop on site 🚐 Mobile shop 🍖 BBQ area 🪑 Picnic area 📶 Wi-fi 🖥 Internet access ♻ Recycling 🛈 Tourist info 🐕 Dog exercise area 🚗 Car hire can be arranged

Homestead Park

►►84%

tel: 01749 673022 **Wookey Hole BA5 1BW**
email: homesteadpark@onetel.com
dir: *0.5m NW from A371 (Wells to Cheddar road).* grid ref: *ST532474*

This attractive, small site for tents only is set on a wooded hillside and meadowland with access to the river and nearby Wookey Hole. This park is for adults only and the statics are residential caravans. 2 acre site. 30 touring pitches. Tent pitches. 28 statics.

Open: Etr-Sep **Last arrival:** 20.00hrs **Last departure:** noon

Pitches: * ▲ £18.50-£23

Facilities: ⌂ ☉ 🏪 ☀ ✿

Services: 🛢 ⌀ 🔋

Within 3 miles: ↓ 🎠 ✎ ⅃ ⛳ 🎣 🎠 🛥 ∪

Notes: Adults only. 🐕 Dogs must be kept on leads.

AA Pubs & Restaurants nearby: The Crown at Wells, WELLS, BA5 2RP, 01749 673457

The Fountain Inn, WELLS, BA5 2UU, 01749 672317

Goodfellows, WELLS, BA5 2RR, 01749 673866

Country View Holiday Park

►►►►85%

tel: 01934 627595 **Sand Rd, Sand Bay BS22 9UJ**
email: info@cvhp.co.uk **web:** www.cvhp.co.uk
dir: *M5 junct 21, A370 towards Weston-Super-Mare. Immediately into left lane, follow Kewstoke & Sand Bay signs. Straight over 3 rdbts onto Lower Norton Ln. At Sand Bay right into Sand Rd, site on right.* grid ref: *ST335647*

A pleasant open site in a rural area a few hundred yards from Sandy Bay and the beach. The park is also well placed for energetic walks along the coast at either end of the beach and is only a short drive away from Weston-Super-Mare. There is a

touring section for tents, caravans and motorhomes with a toilet and shower block. There are 14 hardstanding pitches plus grass pitches all with electricity. The facilities are excellent and well maintained, including a nice outdoor swimming pool and small tasteful bar. 20 acre site. 190 touring pitches. 150 hardstandings. 90 seasonal pitches. Caravan pitches. Motorhome pitches. Tent pitches. 65 statics.

Open: Mar-Jan **Last arrival:** 20.00hrs **Last departure:** noon

Pitches: 🚐 🚍 ▲

Leisure: 🏊 ✦ ⚽ 🎵

Facilities: ⌂ 🅿 ☉ 🏪 ☀ ♿ 🎠 🐕 WiFi 🖥 ♻ ✿

Services: 🔌 ⌀ 🍴 Ⓣ

Within 3 miles: ↓ 🎠 🎠 ✎ ◎ 🛥 🎣 🎠 ∪

Notes: Dogs must be kept on leads.

AA Pubs & Restaurants nearby: The Cove, WESTON-SUPER-MARE, BS23 2BX, 01934 418217

West End Farm Caravan & Camping Park

►►►84%

tel: 01934 822529 **Locking BS24 8RH**
email: robin@westendfarm.org **web:** www.westendcaravan.com
dir: *M5 junct 21 onto A370. Follow International Helicopter Museum signs. Right at rdbt, follow signs to site.* grid ref: *ST354600*

A spacious and well laid out park bordered by hedges, with good landscaping, and well-kept facilities. Fully serviced pitches are available and a new facility block is planned for 2017. It is handily located next to a helicopter museum, and offers good access to Weston-Super-Mare and the Mendips. 10 acre site. 75 touring pitches. 10 hardstandings. 30 seasonal pitches. Caravan pitches. Motorhome pitches. Tent pitches. 11 statics.

Open: all year **Last arrival:** 21.00hrs (arrivals from 10.00hrs) **Last departure:** noon

Pitches: * 🚐 £18-£24 🚍 £18-£24 ▲ £16-£24

Leisure: ✦

Facilities: ⌂ ☉ ♿ 🐕 WiFi 🖥 ♻ ✿

Services: 🔌 ⌀ 🛢 ⌀ ⚡

Within 3 miles: ↓ 🎠 🎠 ✎ ◎ 🛥 🎣 🎠 ∪

Notes: No noise after 22.00hrs. Dogs must be kept on leads.

AA Pubs & Restaurants nearby: The Cove, WESTON-SUPER-MARE, BS23 2BX, 01934 418217

WINSFORD Map 3 SS93

Places to visit

Dunster Castle, DUNSTER, TA24 6SL, 01643 821314 www.nationaltrust.org.uk/dunstercastle

Cleeve Abbey, WASHFORD, TA23 0PS, 01984 640377 www.english-heritage.org.uk/daysout/properties/cleeve-abbey

Great for kids: Tropiquaria Animal and Adventure Park, WASHFORD, TA23 0QB, 01984 640688 www.tropiquaria.co.uk

Halse Farm Caravan & Camping Park

►►►► 81%

tel: 01643 851259 **TA24 7JL**
email: info@halsefarm.co.uk **web:** www.halsefarm.co.uk
dir: *Signed from A396 at Bridgetown. In Winsford turn left, bear left past pub. 1m up hill, entrance on left immediately after cattle grid.* **grid ref:** *SS894344*

A peaceful little site on Exmoor overlooking a wooded valley with glorious views. This moorland site is quite remote, but it provides good modern toilet facilities which are kept immaculately clean. This is a good base for exploring the Exmoor National Park, and Minehead, Porlock and Lynton are only a short drive away. 3 acre site. 44 touring pitches. Caravan pitches. Motorhome pitches. Tent pitches.

Open: 20 Mar-Oct **Last arrival:** 22.00hrs **Last departure:** noon

Pitches:

Leisure:

Facilities:

Services:

Within 3 miles:

Notes: Dogs must be kept on leads.

AA Pubs & Restaurants nearby: Crown Hotel, EXFORD, TA24 7PP, 01643 831554

The Royal Oak Exmoor, WINSFORD, TA24 7JE, 01643 851455

WIVELISCOMBE Map 3 ST02

Places to visit

Cleeve Abbey, WASHFORD, TA23 0PS, 01984 640377 www.english-heritage.org.uk/daysout/properties/cleeve-abbey

Hestercombe Gardens, TAUNTON, TA2 8LG, 01823 413923 www.hestercombe.com

PREMIER PARK

Waterrow Touring Park

►►►►► 89%

tel: 01984 623464 **TA4 2AZ**
email: info@waterrowpark.co.uk **web:** www.waterrowpark.co.uk
dir: *M5 junct 25, A358 signed Minehead (bypassing Taunton), B3227 through Wiveliscombe. Site in 3m at Waterrow, 0.25m past Rock Inn.* **grid ref:** *ST053251*

Under pro-active ownership, this really delightful park for adults has spotless facilities, plenty of spacious hardstandings, including fully serviced pitches and a motorhome service point. The River Tone runs along a valley beneath the park, accessed by steps to a nature area created by the owners, where fly-fishing is permitted. Watercolour painting workshops and other activities are available, and the local pub is a short walk away. There is also a bus stop just outside the site. 8 acre site. 44 touring pitches. 40 hardstandings. Caravan pitches. Motorhome pitches. Tent pitches.

Open: all year **Last arrival:** 19.00hrs **Last departure:** 11.30hrs

Pitches:

Facilities:

Services:

Within 3 miles:

Notes: Adults only. No gazebos. Max 3 dogs per unit. Dogs must be kept on leads. Caravan storage.

STAFFORDSHIRE

CHEADLE
Map 10 SK04

Places to visit

Churnet Valley Railway, CHEDDLETON, ST13 7EE, 01538 750755
www.churnetvalleyrailway.co.uk

The Potteries Museum & Art Gallery, STOKE-ON-TRENT, ST1 3DW, 01782 232323
www.stoke.gov.uk/museum

Great for kids: Alton Towers Resort, ALTON, ST10 4DB, 0871 222 3330
(Calls cost 10p per minute plus your phone company's access charge) www.altontowers.com

Etruria Industrial Museum, STOKE-ON-TRENT, ST4 7AF, 07900 267711
www.etruriamuseum.org.uk

Quarry Walk Park
▶▶▶ 75%

tel: 01538 723412 **Coppice Ln, Croxden Common, Freehay ST10 1RQ**
email: quarry@quarrywalkpark.co.uk
dir: *From A522 (Uttoxeter to Cheadle road) in Mobberley follow Freehay sign. In 1m at rdbt, 3rd exit signed Great Gate. 1.25m to site on right.* **grid ref:** *SK045405*

A pleasant park (for tents only), close to Alton Towers, that was developed in an old quarry; it has well-screened pitches, each with water and electricity, and surrounded by mature trees and shrubs which enhance the peaceful ambience of the park. There are seven glades of varying sizes dedicated exclusively to tents, one with 10 electric hook-ups. There are timber lodges for hire, each with its own hot tub. Please note, caravans and motorhomes are not accepted. 46 acre site. Tent pitches.

Open: all year **Last arrival:** 18.00hrs **Last departure:** 11.00hrs

Pitches: Å

Facilities: 🐾 ⚹ ⅙ 🛒 🛁 WiFi 🖥 ♻ 🅸

Services: 🔌 ⊡

Within 3 miles: 🍴 🏇 ◎ 🛒 ⊡ ∪

Notes: No cars by tents. No noise after 23.00hrs. Dogs must be kept on leads.

AA Pubs & Restaurants nearby: The Queens at Freehay, CHEADLE, ST10 1RF, 01538 722383

LONGNOR
Map 16 SK06

Places to visit

Poole's Cavern (Buxton Country Park), BUXTON, SK17 9DH, 01298 26978
www.poolescavern.co.uk

Haddon Hall, HADDON HALL, DE45 1LA, 01629 812855 www.haddonhall.co.uk

PREMIER PARK

Longnor Wood Holiday Park

▶▶▶▶▶ 92%

tel: 01298 83648 & 07866 016567 **Newtown SK17 0NG**
email: info@longnorwood.co.uk
dir: *From A53 follow Longnor sign. Site signed from village, 1.25m.* **grid ref:** *SK072640*

Enjoying a secluded and very peaceful setting in the heart of the Peak District National Park, this spacious adults-only park is a hidden gem, surrounded by beautiful rolling countryside and sheltered by woodland where there is a variety of wildlife to observe. Expect a warm welcome from the O'Neill family and excellent, well-maintained facilities, including spotlessly clean modern toilets, good hardstanding pitches, high levels of security, a putting green, badminton courts, a 4-acre dog walk (a dog wash is available too) and super walks from the park gate. The reception building includes a small shop. There are lodges of different sizes and three equipped ready-erected tents for hire. 10.5 acre site. 47 touring pitches. 47 hardstandings. 13 seasonal pitches. Caravan pitches. Motorhome pitches. Tent pitches.

Open: Mar-10 Jan **Last arrival:** 19.00hrs **Last departure:** noon

Pitches: * 🚐 £24-£28.50 🚎 £24-£28.50 Å £20-£22 🏠 prices shown below

Leisure: 🏸

Facilities: 🐾 🅿 ⊙ 🍴 ⚹ ⅙ 🛒 🛁 WiFi 🖥 ♻ 🅸

Services: 🔌 ⊡ 🛢 🖊 ⊤ 🔋 ⚐

Glamping: Erected Tents 3, £30-£40 Changeover day Any day Min stay 2 nights Own kitchen Car by unit

Within 3 miles: 🚴 ⊡ ∪

Notes: Adults only. No fires, no noise after 23.00hrs. Dogs must be kept on leads.

AA Pubs & Restaurants nearby: The Queen Anne Inn, GREAT HUCKLOW, SK17 8RF, 01298 871246

The George, ALSTONEFIELD, DE6 2FX, 01335 310205

PITCHES: 🚐 Caravans 🚎 Motorhomes Å Tents 🏠 Glamping accommodation **SERVICES:** 🔌 Electric hook up ⊡ Launderette 🍺 Licensed bar
🛢 Calor Gas ⊘ Camping Gaz ⊤ Toilet fluid 🍴 Café/Restaurant 🍔 Fast Food/Takeaway 🔋 Battery charging ⚐ Baby care ⚐ Motorvan service point
ABBREVIATIONS: BHs – bank holidays Etr – Easter Spring BH – Spring Bank Holiday fr – from hrs – hours m – mile mdnt – midnight
rdbt – roundabout rs – restricted service wk – week wknd – weekend x-roads – crossroads ⊘ No credit or debit cards ⊗ No dogs

Suffolk

Suffolk is Constable country, where the county's crumbling, time-ravaged coastline spreads itself under wide skies to convey a wonderful sense of remoteness and solitude. Highly evocative and atmospheric, this is where rivers wind lazily to the sea and notorious 18th-century smugglers hid from the excise men.

It was the artist John Constable who was responsible for raising the region's profile in the 18th century. Constable immortalised these expansive flatlands in his paintings and today the marketing brochures and websites usually refer to the area as Constable Country. Situated on the River Stour at Flatford, Constable's mill is now a major tourist attraction in the area but a close look at the surroundings confirms rural Suffolk is little changed since the family lived here. Constable himself maintained that the Suffolk countryside 'made me a painter and I am grateful.'

Facing the European mainland and with easy access by the various rivers, the county's open, often bleak, landscape made Suffolk vulnerable in early times to attack from waves of invaders. In the Middle Ages, however, it prospered under the wool merchants: it was their wealth that built the great churches which dominate the countryside.

Walking is one of Suffolk's most popular recreational activities. It may be flat but the county has much to discover on foot – not least the isolated Heritage Coast, which can be accessed via the Suffolk Coast Path. Running along the edge of the shore, between Felixstowe and Lowestoft, the trail is a fascinating blend of ecology and military history. Near its southerly start, the path passes close to one of the National Trust's most unusual acquisitions – Orford Ness. Acquired by the Trust in 1993, and officially opened in 1995, this spectacular stretch of coastline had previously been closed to the public since 1915 when the Royal Flying Corps chose Orford Ness as the setting for military research. These days, it is a Site of Special Scientific Interest, recognised in particular for its rare shingle habitats. Visitors to Orford Ness cross the River Ore by National Trust ferry from Orford Quay.

Beyond Orford, the Suffolk Coast Path parts company with the North Sea, albeit briefly, to visit Aldeburgh. Nearby are Snape Maltings, renowned internationally as the home of the Aldeburgh Festival that takes place in June. Benjamin Britten lived at Snape and wrote *Peter Grimes* here. The Suffolk coast is where both the sea and the natural landscape have influenced generations of writers, artists and musicians. An annual literary festival is staged at Aldeburgh on the first weekend in March.

Back on the Suffolk coast, the trail makes for Southwold, with its distinctive, white-walled lighthouse standing sentinel above the town and its colourful beach huts and attractive pier that feature on many a promotional brochure. The final section of the walk is one of the most spectacular, with low, sandy cliffs, several shallow Suffolk broads and the occasional church tower peeping through the trees. Much of Suffolk's coastal heathland is protected as a designated Area of Outstanding Natural Beauty and shelters several rare creatures including the adder, the heath butterfly and the nightjar.

In addition to walking, there is a good choice of cycling routes. There is the Heart of Suffolk Cycle Route, which extends for 78 miles, while the National Byway, a 4,000-mile cycle route around Britain takes in part of Suffolk and is a very enjoyable way to explore the county.

For something less demanding, visit some of Suffolk's best-known towns. Bury St Edmunds, Sudbury and Ipswich feature prominently on the tourist trail, while Lavenham, Kersey and Debenham are a reminder of the county's important role in the wool industry and the vast wealth it yielded the wool merchants. In these charming old towns look out for streets of handsome, period buildings and picturesque, timber-framed houses.

◁ Coast at Dunwich

SUFFOLK

BUNGAY
Map 13 TM38

Places to visit
Norfolk & Suffolk Aviation Museum, FLIXTON, NR35 1NZ, 01986 896644
www.aviationmuseum.net

Outney Meadow Caravan Park
►►► 77%

tel: 01986 892338 **Outney Meadow NR35 1HG**
email: c.r.hancy@ukgateway.net
dir: *In Bungay, site signed from rdbt junction of A143 & A144.* **grid ref:** *TM333905*

Three pleasant grassy areas beside the River Waveney, with screened pitches. The central toilet block offers good modern facilities, especially in the ladies' section, and is open at all times. The views from the site across the wide flood plain could be straight out of a Constable painting. Canoeing and boating, coarse fishing and cycling are all available here. 6 acre site. 65 touring pitches. 12 hardstandings. 10 seasonal pitches. Caravan pitches. Motorhome pitches. Tent pitches. 20 statics.

Open: Mar-Oct **Last arrival:** 21.00hrs **Last departure:** 16.00hrs

Pitches: * ⊞ £15-£19 ⊞ £15-£19 ▲ £15-£19

Facilities: 🅛⊙🄿✳🅢♨🏇🛁🔁➊

Services: 🕰🔋🔒🗑📶🍽

Within 3 miles: ↨⚓🖊⛵🏪🔋

Notes: Dogs must be kept on leads. Boat, canoe & cycle hire.

AA Pubs & Restaurants nearby: The Castle Inn, BUNGAY, NR35 1AF, 01986 892283

BURY ST EDMUNDS
Map 13 TL86

Places to visit
Moyse's Hall Museum, BURY ST EDMUNDS, IP33 1DX, 01284 757160
www.moyseshall.org

Ickworth House, Park & Gardens, HORRINGER, IP29 5QE, 01284 735270
www.nationaltrust.org.uk/ickworth

Great for kids: National Horseracing Museum and Tours, NEWMARKET, CB8 8JH, 01638 667333 www.nhrm.co.uk

Dell Touring Park
►►►► 87%

tel: 01359 270121 **Beyton Rd, Thurston IP31 3RB**
email: info@thedellcaravanpark.co.uk
dir: *A14 junct 46 follow Thurston signs & brown camping signs to site. From A143 in Great Barton at x-roads follow Thurston & brown camping signs.* **grid ref:** *TL928640*

A small site with enthusiastic owners that has been developed to a high specification. Set in a quiet spot with lots of mature trees, the quality purpose-built toilet facilities include family rooms, dishwashing and laundry. This is an ideal base for exploring this picturesque area. 4 acre site. 50 touring pitches. 14 hardstandings. Caravan pitches. Motorhome pitches. Tent pitches.

Open: Mar-Oct **Last arrival:** 20.00hrs **Last departure:** noon

Pitches: ⊞ £13-£21 ⊞ £13-£21 ▲ £13-£24

Facilities: 🅛⊙🄿✳🅢♨🏇🔁➊

Services: 🕰🔋🔒🗑

Within 3 miles: 🖊🔋🔋

Notes: No footballs, no noise after 23.00hrs. Dogs must be kept on leads.

AA Pubs & Restaurants nearby: The Old Cannon Brewery, BURY ST EDMUNDS, IP33 1JR, 01284 768769

Maison Bleue, BURY ST EDMUNDS, IP33 1RG, 01284 760623

The Leaping Hare Restaurant & Country Store, BURY ST EDMUNDS, IP31 2DW, 01359 250287

DUNWICH
Map 13 TM47

Places to visit
RSPB Nature Reserve Minsmere, WESTLETON, IP17 3BY, 01728 648281
www.rspb.org.uk/minsmere

AA MOST IMPROVED CAMPSITE OF THE YEAR 2017

Haw Wood Farm Caravan Park
►►►► 91%

GOLD

tel: 01502 359550 **Hinton IP17 3QT**
email: info@hawwoodfarm.co.uk **web:** www.hawwoodfarm.co.uk
dir: *Exit A12, 1.5m N of Darsham level crossing at Darsham Hamper. Site 0.5m on right.* **grid ref:** *TM421717*

An unpretentious family-orientated park set in two large fields surrounded by low hedges. The amenity block is appointed to a very high standard – it includes an excellent reception with café, a good play area and excellent toilet and shower facilities. For 2016 they resurfaced the roads, created a new motorhome service point and added new planted areas and a recycling area; there are plans to increase the number of hardstandings and electric hook-ups, and add fully serviced pitches for the 2017 season. Guests can expect excellent levels of customer service during their stay. 15 acre site. 60 touring pitches. 10 hardstandings. 30 seasonal pitches. Caravan pitches. Motorhome pitches. Tent pitches. 55 statics.

Open: Mar-14 Jan **Last arrival:** 21.00hrs **Last departure:** 11.00hrs

Pitches: * ⊞ £12-£22.50 ⊞ £12-£22.50 ▲ £9-£20

Leisure: 🅐⚽

Facilities: 🅛🄿⊙🄿✳🅢♨🏇🔁📶🖥🔁➊

Services: 🕰🔋🔒🗑📶🍽🛒🏇

Within 3 miles: ↨🖊🔋🔋⛵

LEISURE: 🏊 Indoor pool 🏊 Outdoor pool 🅐 Children's playground 🅦 Kid's club 🎾 Tennis court 🎱 Games room 🏌 Golf course ⚓ Boat hire 🚲 Cycle hire 🎬 Cinema 🎵 Entertainment 🎣 Fishing 🏌 Mini golf ⛳ Pitch n putt 🏄 Watersports 💪 Gym ⚽ Sports field ⛎ Stables **FACILITIES:** 🛁 Bath 🚿 Shower 🅟 Private washing cubicles 🔌 Electric shaver 💈 Hairdryer ✳ Ice Packs ♿ Disabled facilities 🅢 Shop on site 🚐 Mobile shop 🍖 BBQ area 🌲 Picnic area 📶 Wi-fi 🖧 Internet access ♻ Recycling ➊ Tourist info 🐕 Dog exercise area 🚗 Car hire can be arranged

Notes: No noise after 22.00hrs. Dogs must be kept on leads. Fresh bread & pastries, rainy day craft tent, nature trail, children's story time, books & board games.

AA Pubs & Restaurants nearby: The Westleton Crown, WESTLETON, IP17 3AD, 01728 648777

The Ship at Dunwich, DUNWICH, IP17 3DT, 01728 648219

FELIXSTOWE   Map 13 TM33

Places to visit

Ipswich Museum, IPSWICH, IP1 3QH, 01473 433550
www.cimuseums.org.uk/Ipswich-Museum

Christchurch Mansion, IPSWICH, IP4 2BE, 01473 433554
www.cimuseums.org.uk/Christchurch-Mansion

Peewit Caravan Park
▶▶▶ 85%

tel: 01394 284511 **Walton Av IP11 2HB**
email: peewitpark@aol.com
dir: A14 junct 62, follow sign for town centre. Site 100mtrs on left. **grid ref:** TM290338

A grass touring area fringed by trees, with well-maintained grounds and a colourful floral display. This handy urban site is not overlooked by houses, and the toilet and shower facilities are clean and tidy. A function room contains a TV and library. The beach is a few minutes away by car. 13 acre site. 45 touring pitches. 4 hardstandings. Caravan pitches. Motorhome pitches. Tent pitches. 200 statics.

Open: Apr (or Etr if earlier)-Oct **Last arrival:** 21.00hrs **Last departure:** 11.00hrs (late departures available)

Pitches: * 🚐 £15.50-£29 🚌 £15.50-£29 ▲ £15-£33

Leisure: ⚑

Facilities: 🅿 ⊙ ☂ ⚒ 🔌 WiFi ♻ ❶ ⛾

Services: 🔌 ▣ 🔒

Within 3 miles: ⌚ 🎣 ▤ ✎ ◎ ≋ ▣ ▤

Notes: 5mph speed restriction on site, only foam footballs permitted. Dogs must be kept on leads. Boules area, bowling green, adventure trail.

AA Pubs & Restaurants nearby: The Westleton Crown, WESTLETON, IP17 3AD, 01728 648777

HOLLESLEY   Map 13 TM34

Places to visit

Woodbridge Tide Mill, WOODBRIDGE, IP12 1BY, 01394 382815
www.woodbridgetidemill.org.uk

Sutton Hoo, WOODBRIDGE, IP12 3DJ, 01394 389700
www.nationaltrust.org.uk/suttonhoo

Great for kids: Orford Castle, ORFORD, IP12 2ND, 01394 450472
www.english-heritage.org.uk/daysout/properties/orford-castle

Run Cottage Touring Park
▶▶▶▶ 87%

tel: 01394 411309 **Alderton Rd IP12 3RQ**
email: info@runcottage.co.uk **web:** www.runcottage.co.uk
dir: From A12 (Ipswich to Saxmundham road) onto A1152 at Melton. 1.5m, right at rdbt onto B1083. 0.75m, left to Hollesley. In Hollesley right into The Street, through village, down hill, over bridge, site 100yds on left. **grid ref:** TM350440

Located in the peaceful village of Hollesley on the Suffolk coast, this landscaped park is set behind the owners' house. The generously-sized pitches are serviced by a well-appointed and immaculately maintained toilet block which includes two fully serviced cubicles. Another landscaped field offers 22 extra pitches, each with an electric hook-up and TV point, and seven hardstanding pitches. Two camping pods are available for hire. This site is handy for the National Trust's Sutton Hoo, and also by travelling a little further north, the coastal centre and beach at Dunwich Heath, and the RSPB bird reserve at Minsmere. 4.25 acre site. 45 touring pitches. 14 hardstandings. 6 seasonal pitches. Caravan pitches. Motorhome pitches. Tent pitches.

Open: all year **Last arrival:** 20.00hrs **Last departure:** 11.00hrs

Pitches: 🚐 fr £20 🚌 fr £20 ▲ fr £18 ⛺

Facilities: 🅿 🅿 ⊙ ☂ ⚒ 🔌 ♻ ❶

Services: 🔌 ▣ T ▤

Glamping: Wooden Pods 2, Min stay 1 night (2 nights May-Sep) Car by unit

Within 3 miles: ⌚ ✎ ≋ ▣ U

Notes: No groundsheets, ball games or cycles. Dogs must be kept on leads. Satellite TV point on some pitches.

AA Pubs & Restaurants nearby: The Crown at Woodbridge, WOODBRIDGE, IP12 1AD, 01394 384242

Seckford Hall Hotel, WOODBRIDGE, IP13 6NU, 01394 385678

PITCHES: 🚐 Caravans 🚌 Motorhomes ▲ Tents ⛺ Glamping accommodation **SERVICES:** 🔌 Electric hook up ▣ Launderette 🍺 Licensed bar 🔥 Calor Gas ⊘ Camping Gaz T Toilet fluid 🍽 Café/Restaurant 🍟 Fast Food/Takeaway ▤ Battery charging 🍼 Baby care ⛟ Motorvan service point
ABBREVIATIONS: BHs – bank holidays Etr – Easter Spring BH – Spring Bank Holiday fr – from hrs – hours m – mile mdnt – midnight rdbt – roundabout rs – restricted service wk – week wknd – weekend x-roads – crossroads Ⓝ No credit or debit cards Ⓝ No dogs

KESSINGLAND
Map 13 TM58

Places to visit

East Anglia Transport Museum, LOWESTOFT, NR33 8BL, 01502 518459
www.eatransportmuseum.co.uk

Maritime Museum, LOWESTOFT, NR32 1XG, 01502 569165
www.lowestoftmaritimemuseum.co.uk

Great for kids: Africa Alive!, LOWESTOFT, NR33 7TF, 01502 740291
www.africa-alive.co.uk

Heathland Beach Caravan Park
▶▶▶▶ 91%

GOLD

tel: 01502 740337 **London Rd NR33 7PJ**
email: reception@heathlandbeach.co.uk
dir: *From rdbt on A12 (1m N of Kessingland) take B1437 signed Kessingland (& brown camping signs). Site 1st left.* **grid ref:** *TM533877*

A well-run and maintained park offering superb toilet facilities. The park is set in meadowland, with level grass pitches, and mature trees and bushes. There is direct access to the sea and beach, and good provisions for families on site with a heated swimming pool and three play areas. There is a well-stocked fishing lake, and sea fishing is also possible. 5 acre site. 63 touring pitches. 7 hardstandings. Caravan pitches. Motorhome pitches. Tent pitches. 200 statics.

Open: Apr-Oct **Last arrival:** 21.00hrs **Last departure:** 11.00hrs

Pitches: ⌖ ⌖ ⛺

Leisure: ⚲ ⋀ ⌁ ⊙ ⌁ ⚐ ⚐

Facilities: ⌂ ⓟ ⊙ ⌁ ✳ ⌂ ⓢ ⌂ ⋈ ᴡɪꜰɪ ▄ ⌁ ⓘ

Services: ⌂ ⓢ ⌁ ⌂ ⌁ ⌁ ⊤ ⍟ ⌁

Within 3 miles: ⌁ ⌁ ⌁ ⌁ ◎ ⌁ ⓢ ⓢ ∪

Notes: Only 1 dog per unit during peak times. Dogs must be kept on leads.

LEISTON

Places to visit

Long Shop Museum, LEISTON, IP16 4ES, 01728 832189
www.longshopmuseum.co.uk

Leiston Abbey, LEISTON, IP16 4TD, 01728 831354
www.english-heritage.org.uk/daysout/properties/leiston-abbey

Great for kids: Easton Farm Park, EASTON, IP13 0EQ, 01728 746475
www.eastonfarmpark.co.uk

LEISTON
Map 13 TM46

Cakes & Ale
▶▶▶▶▶ 90%

tel: 01728 831655 **Abbey Ln, Theberton IP16 4TE**
email: reception@cakesandale.co.uk **web:** www.cakesandale.co.uk
dir: *From Saxmundham E on B1119. 3m, follow minor road over level crossing, turn right, in 0.5m straight on at x-roads, entrance 0.5m on left.* **grid ref:** *TM432637*

A large, well spread out and beautifully maintained site on a former World War II airfield that has many trees and bushes. The spacious touring area includes plenty of hardstandings and 55 super pitches, and there is a good bar. There is a high-quality, solar-powered toilet block containing four fully serviced family rooms, seven cubicled toilet and washbasin rooms, dishwashing facilities, laundry and underfloor heating. 45 acre site. 55 touring pitches. 55 hardstandings. Caravan pitches. Motorhome pitches. Tent pitches. 200 statics.

Open: Apr-Oct (rs Low season - club, shop & reception limited hours)
Last arrival: 19.00hrs **Last departure:** 13.00hrs

Pitches: ⌖ ⌖ ⛺   **Leisure:** ⊙ ⌁

Facilities: ⌂ ⓟ ⊙ ⌁ ✳ ⌂ ⓢ ⌂ ᴡɪꜰɪ ▄ ⌁ ⓘ

Services: ⌂ ⓢ ⌁ ⌂ ⌁ ⊤ ⌁   **Within 3 miles:** ⌁ ⌁ ⌁ ⌁ ⓢ ⓢ ∪

Notes: No group bookings, no noise between 21.00hrs-08.00hrs. Dogs must be kept on leads. Golf practice range, football pitch, boules.

AA Pubs & Restaurants nearby: The Parrot and Punchbowl Inn & Restaurant, ALDRINGHAM, IP16 4PY, 01728 830221

Regatta Restaurant, ALDEBURGH, IP15 5AN, 01728 452011

See advert on opposite page

LEISURE: ⚲ Indoor pool ⚲ Outdoor pool ⋀ Children's playground ⚑ Kid's club ⌁ Tennis court ⚲ Games room ⌁ Golf course ⌁ Boat hire ⚲ Cycle hire ⊟ Cinema ♫ Entertainment ⌁ Fishing ◎ Mini golf ⚐ Pitch n putt ⚲ Watersports ⚐ Gym ⊙ Sports field ∪ Stables **FACILITIES:** ⌂ Bath ⌂ Shower ⓟ Private washing cubicles ⊙ Electric shaver ⌁ Hairdryer ✳ Ice Packs ⌂ Disabled facilities ⓢ Shop on site ⚲ Mobile shop ▄ BBQ area ⌂ Picnic area ᴡɪꜰɪ Wi-fi ▄ Internet access ⌁ Recycling ⓘ Tourist info ⌂ Dog exercise area ⚲ Car hire can be arranged

LOWESTOFT

See Kessingland

SAXMUNDHAM   Map 13 TM36

Places to visit

Long Shop Museum, LEISTON, IP16 4ES, 01728 832189
www.longshopmuseum.co.uk

Leiston Abbey, LEISTON, IP16 4TD, 01728 831354
www.english-heritage.org.uk/daysout/properties/leiston-abbey

Great for kids: RSPB Nature Reserve Minsmere, WESTLETON, IP17 3BY,
01728 648281 www.rspb.org.uk/minsmere

Carlton Meres Country Park
▶▶▶▶81%

tel: 01728 603344 **Rendham Rd, Carlton IP17 2QP**
email: carltonmeres@lifestylelivinguk.com
dir: *From A12, W of Saxmundham, take B1119 towards Framlingham (site signed).*
grid ref: *TM372637*

With two large fishing lakes, a modern fitness suite, a beauty salon, sauna and steam rooms, tennis court, a bar, and a heated outdoor swimming pool, Carlton

Meres offers a wealth of leisure facilities, and all for the exclusive use for those staying on the site (holiday statics and lodges for hire). The reception building and the modern, heated toilet block are appointed to a high standard, and security on the park is excellent. This site is well-placed for all the Suffolk coast attractions. 52 acre site. 160 touring pitches. 56 hardstandings. 25 seasonal pitches. Caravan pitches. Motorhome pitches. Tent pitches.

Open: Etr-Oct **Last arrival:** 17.00hrs **Last departure:** 10.00hrs

Pitches: * ⌂ £25-£45 ⌂ £25-£45 ▲ £10-£25

Leisure: ⌂ ⌂ ⌂ ⌂ ⌂ ⌂ ⌂ ⌂ ⌂ Spa ⌂

Facilities: ⌂ ⌂ ⌂ ⌂ ⌂ ⌂ WiFi ⌂ ⌂ ⌂

Services: ⌂ ⌂ ⌂ ⌂ ⌂ ⌂ ⌂

Within 3 miles: ⌂ ⌂ ⌂ ⌂

Notes: Dogs must be kept on leads.

AA Pubs & Restaurants nearby: Sibton White Horse Inn, SIBTON, IP17 2JJ, 01728 660337
Regatta Restaurant, ALDEBURGH, IP15 5AN, 01728 452011

PITCHES: ⌂ Caravans ⌂ Motorhomes ▲ Tents ⌂ Glamping accommodation **SERVICES:** ⌂ Electric hook up ⌂ Launderette ⌂ Licensed bar ⌂ Calor Gas ⌂ Camping Gaz ⌂ Toilet fluid ⌂ Café/Restaurant ⌂ Fast Food/Takeaway ⌂ Battery charging ⌂ Baby care ⌂ Motorvan service point **ABBREVIATIONS:** BHs – bank holidays Etr – Easter Spring BH – Spring Bank Holiday fr – from hrs – hours m – mile mdnt – midnight rdbt – roundabout rs – restricted service wk – week wknd – weekend x-roads – crossroads ⌂ No credit or debit cards ⌂ No dogs

SAXMUNDHAM *continued*

Marsh Farm Caravan Site
▶▶ 90%

tel: 01728 602168 **Sternfield IP17 1HW**
dir: *A12 onto A1094 (Aldeburgh road), at Snape x-roads left signed Sternfield, follow signs to site.* **grid ref:** *TM385608*

A very pretty site overlooking reed-fringed lakes which offer excellent coarse fishing. The facilities are very well maintained and include a new basic but fully-equipped facility block. The park truly is a peaceful haven. 30 acre site. 45 touring pitches. Caravan pitches. Motorhome pitches. Tent pitches.

Open: all year **Last arrival:** 21.00hrs **Last departure:** 17.00hrs

Pitches: ⊞ ⇌ Å

Facilities: ⋔ ※ ⑤ ㅋ ⊶ ♻ ❼

Services: ⊕ ♒

Within 3 miles: ⅃ 日 ℯ ⑤ ∪

Notes: ⊛ Campers must report to reception on arrival. Site closed when freezing temperatures are forecast. Only 1 car per caravan on site. Dogs must be kept on leads.

AA Pubs & Restaurants nearby: The Parrot and Punchbowl Inn & Restaurant, ALDRINGHAM, IP16 4PY, 01728 830221

Regatta Restaurant, ALDEBURGH, IP15 5AN, 01728 452011

| **THEBERTON** | **Map 13 TM46** |

Places to visit

Leiston Abbey, LEISTON, IP16 4TD, 01728 831354
www.english-heritage.org.uk/daysout/properties/leiston-abbey

RSPB Nature Reserve Minsmere, WESTLETON, IP17 3BY, 01728 648281
www.rspb.org.uk/minsmere

Sycamore Park
▶▶▶ 79%

tel: 01728 635830 & 830665 **Rearoff Pump Cottages, Main Rd IP16 4RA**
email: enquiries@sycamorepark.co.uk
dir: *From A12 at Yoxford take B1122 towards Theberton.* **grid ref:** *TM435660*

Sycamore Park is a very peaceful site in the village of Theberton, within easy reach of Southwold and Aldeburgh, and only three miles from RSPB Minsmere. There are 20 electric hook-ups on grass pitches set out in a compact field surrounded by mature trees. The small, but high quality and very stylish, toilet block contains combined cubicled facilities and has underfloor heating. 2 acre site. 20 touring pitches. Caravan pitches. Motorhome pitches. Tent pitches.

Open: 3 Mar-28 Jan **Last departure:** noon **Pitches:** ⊞ ⇌ Å

Facilities: ⋔ ㅋ ㆄ ♻ ❼ **Services:** ⊕

Within 3 miles: ⅃ ≛ 日 ℯ ⑤ ⑥

Notes: Adults only. ⊛ Dogs must be kept on leads.

LEISURE: 🏊 Indoor pool 🏊 Outdoor pool Ⓐ Children's playground 🎣 Kid's club 🎾 Tennis court 🎱 Games room ⛳ Golf course ⛵ Boat hire 🚲 Cycle hire 🎬 Cinema 🎵 Entertainment 🎣 Fishing ⊙ Mini golf 🏌 Pitch n putt 🏄 Watersports 🏋 Gym ⊙ Sports field ∪ Stables **FACILITIES:** 🛁 Bath 🚿 Shower 🅿 Private washing cubicles ⊙ Electric shaver 🖐 Hairdryer ❄ Ice Packs ♿ Disabled facilities ⑤ Shop on site 🏪 Mobile shop 🍖 BBQ area 🍴 Picnic area 📶 Wi-fi 🖥 Internet access ♻ Recycling ❓ Tourist info 🐕 Dog exercise area 🚗 Car hire can be arranged

WOODBRIDGE
Map 13 TM24

Places to visit

Sutton Hoo, WOODBRIDGE, IP12 3DJ, 01394 389700
www.nationaltrust.org.uk/suttonhoo

Orford Castle, ORFORD, IP12 2ND, 01394 450472
www.english-heritage.org.uk/daysout/properties/orford-castle

Great for kids: Easton Farm Park, EASTON, IP13 0EQ, 01728 746475
www.eastonfarmpark.co.uk

PREMIER PARK

Moon & Sixpence
▶▶▶▶▶ 92%

tel: 01473 736650 **Newbourn Rd, Waldringfield IP12 4PP**
email: info@moonandsixpence.eu **web:** www.moonandsixpence.eu
dir: *From A12 rdbt, E of Ipswich, follow brown caravan & Moon & Sixpence signs (Waldringfield). 1.5m, left at x-roads, follow signs.* **grid ref:** *TM263454*

A well-planned site, with tourers occupying a sheltered valley position around an attractive boating lake with a sandy beach. Toilet facilities are housed in a smart Norwegian-style cabin, and there is a laundry and dish-washing area. Leisure facilities include two tennis courts, a bowling green, fishing, boating and a games room; there's also a lake, woodland trails, a cycle trail and 9-hole golf. The park has an adult-only area, and a strict 'no groups and no noise after 9pm' policy. Please note, tents are not accepted. 5 acre site. 50 touring pitches. 10 hardstandings. Caravan pitches. Motorhome pitches. 225 statics.

Open: Apr-Oct (rs Low season club, shop, reception open limited hours)
Last arrival: 20.00hrs **Last departure:** noon

Pitches: * 🚐 £20-£36 🚐 £20-£36
Leisure: 🪁 ⚽ 🎣 🎱 ♪
Facilities: ☺ ☔ ⚒ ⑤ 🚻 WiFi 🖥 ♻ 🛈
Services: 🔌 ⑤ 🍺 🛢 ⊘ 🍴 🔋 ⛟
Within 3 miles: ♨ 🏇 ⚐ ⚓ ⑤ 🛍

Notes: No tents. No group bookings or commercial vehicles, quiet 21.00hrs-08.00hrs. Dogs must be kept on leads. 10-acre sports area, 100-acre woods.

AA Pubs & Restaurants nearby: The Crown at Woodbridge, WOODBRIDGE, IP12 1AD, 01394 384242

Seckford Hall Hotel, WOODBRIDGE, IP13 6NU, 01394 385678

See advert on opposite page

Moat Barn Touring Caravan Park
▶▶▶ 85%

tel: 01473 737520 **Dallinghoo Rd, Bredfield IP13 6BD**
dir: *Exit A12 at Bredfield, 1st right at village pump. Through village, 1m site on left.* **grid ref:** *TM269530*

An attractive small park for adults only, set in idyllic Suffolk countryside, perfectly located for touring the heritage coastline and for visiting the National Trust's Sutton Hoo. The modern toilet block is well equipped and maintained. There are 10 tent pitches and the park is located on the popular Hull to Harwich cycle route; cycle hire is available. 2 acre site. 33 touring pitches. 10 seasonal pitches. Caravan pitches. Motorhome pitches. Tent pitches.

Open: Mar-15 Jan **Last arrival:** 22.00hrs **Last departure:** noon

Pitches: * 🚐 fr £20 🚐 fr £20 ⛺ fr £20
Leisure: 🎱
Facilities: 🪣 ☺ ☔ ⚒ WiFi ♻ 🛈
Services: 🔌 ⛟ ⛟
Within 3 miles: ♨ 🏇 ⚐ ◎ ⚓ ⑤ 🛍 ⛳

Notes: Adults only. ⊗ No ball games, only breathable groundsheets permitted. Dogs must be kept on leads.

AA Pubs & Restaurants nearby: The Crown at Woodbridge, WOODBRIDGE, IP12 1AD, 01394 384242

Seckford Hall Hotel, WOODBRIDGE, IP13 6NU, 01394 385678

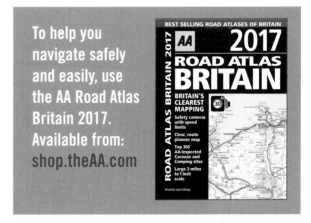

Sussex

East and West Sussex are adjoining counties packed with interest. This is a land of stately homes and castles, miles of breezy chalk cliffs overlooking the English Channel, pretty rivers, picturesque villages and links to our glorious past. In 2011, a large stretch of the two counties was designated a national park.

Mention Sussex to many people and images of the South Downs immediately spring to mind – 'vast, smooth, shaven, serene,' as the writer Virginia Woolf described them. She and her husband lived at Monk's House in the village of Rodmell, near Lewes, and today, her modest home is managed by the National Trust and open to the public.

Close by, on the downs, is Charleston Farmhouse where Woolf's sister, the artist Vanessa Bell, lived a bohemian life as part of the renowned Bloomsbury group, whose members were mainly notable writers, artists and thinkers. Rudyard Kipling resided at Bateman's, near Burwash, and described the house as 'a good and peaceable place,' after moving there in 1902. 'We have loved it ever since our first sight of it,' he wrote later. Bateman's is also in the care of the National Trust, as is Uppark House at South Harting, near Petersfield. The writer H. G. Wells stayed at Uppark as a boy while his mother was employed there as housekeeper. Away to the east, inland from Hastings, lies Great Dixter, an ancient house in a magical garden. This was the home of the pioneering gardening writer Christopher Lloyd and today both Great Dixter and its garden are open to visitors.

There are a great many historic landmarks within Sussex, but probably the most famous is the battlefield where William, Duke of Normandy defeated Harold and his Saxon army to become William the Conqueror of England. By visiting Battle, near Hastings, you can, with a little imagination, picture the bloody events that led to his defeat. Before the Battle of Hastings, William vowed that if God gave him victory that day, he would build an abbey on the site of the battle at Senlac Field. This he did, with the high altar set up on the spot where Harold died. The abbey was enlarged and improved over the years and today is maintained by English Heritage.

In terms of walking in Sussex, this county is spoilt for choice. Studying the map reveals a multitude of routes – many of them to be found within the boundaries of the South Downs National Park – and an assortment of scenic long-distance trails leading towards distant horizons; all of them offer a perfect way to get to the heart of 'Sussex by the sea,' as it has long been known. The Monarch's Way, one of the region's most popular trails, broadly follows Charles II's escape route in 1651, while the most famous of them, the South Downs Way, follows hill paths and cliff-top tracks all the way from Winchester to Eastbourne. As well as a good range of walks, Sussex offers exhilarating cycle rides through the High Weald, along the South Downs Way and via coastal routes between Worthing and Rye. There is also the Forest Way through East Grinstead to Groombridge. If you enjoy cycling with the salty tang of the sea for company, try the ride between Chichester and West Wittering. You can vary the return journey by taking the Itchenor ferry to Bosham.

Sussex is renowned for its many pretty towns, of course. There is Arundel, littered with period buildings and dominated by the castle, the family home of the Duke of Norfolk, that dates back nearly 1,000 years. Midhurst, Lewes, Rye and Uckfield also have their charms, while the cities of Chichester and Brighton offer countless museums and fascinating landmarks. Brighton's best-known and grandest feature is surely the Royal Pavilion, created as the seaside palace of the Prince Regent (later George IV). The town's genteel Regency terraces and graceful crescents reflect his influence on Brighton. Often referred to as 'London by the sea,' the city has long enjoyed a colourful reputation and has been used as a location in many high profile and highly successful films, including *Brighton Rock* and *Quadrophenia*.

Fulking Escarpment, South Downs Way ▷

EAST SUSSEX

BATTLE
Map 7 TQ71

Places to visit

1066 Battle of Hastings Abbey & Battlefield, BATTLE, TN33 0AD, 01424 773792
www.english-heritage.org.uk/daysout/properties/
1066-battle-of-hastings-abbey-and-battlefield

Yesterday's World - Battle, BATTLE, TN33 0AQ, 01424 777226
www.yesterdaysworld.co.uk

Great for kids: The Observatory Science Centre, HERSTMONCEUX, BN27 1RN,
01323 832731 www.the-observatory.org

Brakes Coppice Park
►►► 80%

tel: 01424 830322 **Forewood Ln TN33 9AB**
email: brakesco@btinternet.com
dir: *A2100 from Battle take A2100 towards Hastings. In 2m turn right signed Crowhurst.
Site 1m on left.* **grid ref:** *TQ765134*

A secluded farm site in a sunny meadow deep in woodland with a small stream and
a coarse fishing lake. The toilet block has quality fittings and there's a good fully-
serviced family/disabled room. Hardstanding pitches are neatly laid out on a
terrace, and tents are pitched on grass edged by woodland. The hands-on owners
offer high levels of customer care and this tucked-away gem proves a peaceful
base for exploring Battle and the south coast. 3 acre site. 60 touring pitches. 10
hardstandings. Caravan pitches. Motorhome pitches. Tent pitches. 1 static.

Open: Mar-Oct **Last arrival:** 21.00hrs **Last departure:** noon

Pitches: * 🚐 £18-£22 🚐 £18-£22 ▲ £15-£20

Facilities: 🐾 ⊙ 🏳 ☀ 🖈 👜 🛍 🚩 📶 💻 ♻ 🔧 ❼

Services: 🚚 🔧 🔒 ⚙ 🅃 🛎

Within 3 miles: ⅃ 🚴 🛍 ↺

Notes: No fires, footballs or kite flying. Dogs must be kept on leads.

AA Pubs & Restaurants nearby: Ash Tree Inn, ASHBURNHAM PLACE, TN33 9NX,
01424 892104

The Wild Mushroom Restaurant, WESTFIELD, TN35 4SB, 01424 751137

Senlac Wood
►►► 78%

tel: 01424 773969 **Catsfield Rd, Catsfield TN33 9LN**
email: senlacwood@xlninternet.co.uk **web:** www. senlacwood.co.uk
dir: *A271 from Battle onto B2204 signed Bexhill. Site on left.* **grid ref:** *TQ722153*

A woodland site with many secluded hardstanding bays and two peaceful grassy
glades for tents. The toilet block has been refurbished. The site is ideal for anyone
looking for seclusion and shade, and it is well placed for visiting nearby Battle and
the south coast beaches. 20 acre site. 35 touring pitches. 16 hardstandings.
Caravan pitches. Motorhome pitches. Tent pitches.

Open: Mar-Oct **Last arrival:** 22.00hrs **Last departure:** noon

Pitches: * 🚐 £15-£20.50 🚐 £15-£20.50 ▲ £15-£20.50

Leisure: 🔍

Facilities: ⊙ 🏳 ☀ 🖈 📶 ❼

Services: 🚚 🍴 🍽 🛎

Within 3 miles: ⅃ 🚴 🛍 ↺

Notes: No camp fires, no noise after 23.00hrs. Dogs must be kept on leads. Caravan
storage.

AA Pubs & Restaurants nearby: Ash Tree Inn, ASHBURNHAM PLACE, TN33 9NX,
01424 892104

The Wild Mushroom Restaurant, WESTFIELD, TN35 4SB, 01424 751137

LEISURE: 🏊 Indoor pool 🏊 Outdoor pool 🛝 Children's playground 👶 Kid's club 🎾 Tennis court 🔍 Games room ⛳ Golf course ⛵ Boat hire 🚲 Cycle hire 🎦 Cinema 🎵 Entertainment 🎣 Fishing ⊙ Mini golf ⛳ Pitch n putt 🏄 Watersports 🏋 Gym ⚽ Sports field ↺ Stables **FACILITIES:** 🛁 Bath 🚿 Shower P⁵ Private washing cubicles ⊙ Electric shaver 🏳 Hairdryer ☀ Ice Packs ♿ Disabled facilities 🛍 Shop on site 🚐 Mobile shop 🍖 BBQ area 🪑 Picnic area 📶 Wi-fi 💻 Internet access ♻ Recycling ❼ Tourist info 🐕 Dog exercise area 🚗 Car hire can be arranged

FURNER'S GREEN
Map 6 TQ42

Places to visit

Sheffield Park and Garden, SHEFFIELD PARK, TN22 3QX, 01825 790231
www.nationaltrust.org.uk/sheffieldpark

Nymans, HANDCROSS, RH17 6EB, 01444 405250
www.nationaltrust.org.uk/nymans

Great for kids: Bluebell Railway, SHEFFIELD PARK STATION, TN22 3QL,
01825 720800 www.bluebell-railway.co.uk

Heaven Farm
►►83%

tel: 01825 790226 **TN22 3RG**
email: heavenfarmleisure@btinternet.com
dir: On A275 between Lewes & East Grinstead, 1m N of Sheffield Park Garden.
grid ref: TQ403264

A delightful, small, rural site on a popular farm complex incorporating a farm
museum, craft shop, tea room and nature trail. The good, clean toilet facilities are
housed in well-converted outbuildings and chickens and ducks roam freely around
the site. Ashdown Forest, the Bluebell Railway and Sheffield Park Garden are
nearby. 1.5 acre site. 25 touring pitches. 2 hardstandings. Caravan pitches.
Motorhome pitches. Tent pitches. 3 statics.

Open: all year (rs Nov-Mar site may close due to bad weather) **Last arrival:** 21.00hrs
Last departure: noon

Pitches: * 🚐 fr £20 🚌 fr £20 ▲ fr £20

Leisure: 🎣

Facilities: 🐕🅿️☉⚒♿🛁🚻🎮📶❶

Services: 🔌🚰🍴🔋♻️

Within 3 miles: ♨️🎯🎣🛒⛳

Notes: Credit & debit cards accepted only in shop & café. Dogs must be kept on leads.
Fresh food shop every day.

AA Pubs & Restaurants nearby: The Coach and Horses, DANEHILL, RH17 7JF,
01825 740369

The Griffin Inn, FLETCHING, TN22 3SS, 01825 722890

HASTINGS
Map 7 TQ80

Places to visit

Shipwreck Museum, HASTINGS & ST LEONARDS, TN34 3DW, 01424 437452
www.shipwreckmuseum.co.uk

Great for kids: Blue Reef Aquarium, HASTINGS & ST LEONARDS, TN34 3DW,
01424 718776 www.bluereefaquarium.co.uk

Smugglers Adventure, HASTINGS & ST LEONARDS, TN34 3HY, 01424 422964
www.discoverhastings.co.uk

Hastings Touring Park
►►►82%

tel: 01424 423583 **Shearbarn Holiday Park, Barley Ln TN35 5DX**
email: touringwardens@shearbarn.co.uk
dir: On A259 at seafront in Hastings follow Folkestone (A259) signs. Right into Harold Rd
& follow Shearbarn Holiday Park signs . **grid ref:** TQ838105

This large, gently sloping site occupies a lofty position overlooking Hastings, and
has great views, instant access to downland walks and provides a peaceful base
for visiting this lovely area. The toilets are clean, tidy and well maintained; the two
older blocks are freshly painted each year and appointed with modern fixtures and
fittings, and the newer, bottom block offers privacy wash basins. There is an
excellent children's play area and guests at The Hastings Touring Park have access
to the bar, swimming pool, gym, shop and laundrette at the Shearbarn Holiday Park
which is opposite and under the same ownership. 150 touring pitches. 20
hardstandings. Caravan pitches. Motorhome pitches. Tent pitches.

Open: Mar-Oct **Last arrival:** 21.00hrs **Last departure:** 11.00hrs

Pitches: * 🚐 £20-£33 🚌 £20-£33 ▲ £16-£24

Leisure: 🏊🎯♠️🎱

Facilities: 🐕⚒♿🛁📷🚻🎮📶♻️❶

Services: 🔌🍴🔋🍴🔋♻️

Within 3 miles: 🚲🎣◎🛒🛍️

Notes: No fires, no commercial vehicles, no party groups, no noise after 23.00hrs. Dogs
must be kept on leads.

Combe Haven Holiday Park
HOLIDAY HOME PARK 87%

GOLD

tel: 01424 427891 **Harley Shute Rd, St Leonards-on-Sea TN38 8BZ**
email: combehaven@haven.com **web:** www.haven.com/combehaven
dir: A21 towards Hastings. In Hastings take A259 towards Bexhill. Park signed on right
grid ref: TQ779091

Close to a beach and the resort attractions of Hastings, this holiday park has been
designed with families in mind. Activities include a pirates' adventure playground,
heated swimming pools and a wealth of sports and outdoor activities.

Open: Mar-Oct

Changeover day: Mon, Fri, Sat

Arrival and departure times: Please contact the site

Statics: 296 Sleeps 6-8 Bedrms 2-3 Bathrms 1-2 Toilets 1-2 Microwave Freezer TV Sky/
FTV Elec inc Gas inc Grass area

Children: 👶 Cots Highchair **Dogs:** 2 on leads No dangerous dogs

Leisure: 🏊🚣 Cycle hire 🎣♠️

PEVENSEY BAY — Map 6 TQ60

Places to visit

"How We Lived Then" Museum of Shops & Social History, EASTBOURNE, BN21 4NS, 01323 737143 www.how-we-lived-then.co.uk

Alfriston Clergy House, ALFRISTON, BN26 5TL, 01323 871961 www.nationaltrust.org.uk/alfriston/

Great for kids: The Observatory Science Centre, HERSTMONCEUX, BN27 1RN, 01323 832731 www.the-observatory.org

Bay View Park
►►► 85%

tel: 01323 768688 Old Martello Rd BN24 6DX
email: holidays@bay-view.co.uk
dir: *Signed from A259 W of Pevensey Bay. On seaward side of A259 take private road towards beach.* **grid ref:** *TQ648028*

A pleasant well-run site just yards from the beach, in an area east of Eastbourne town centre known as 'The Crumbles'. The level grassy site is very well maintained and the toilet facilities feature fully-serviced cubicles. The seasonal tent field has marked pitches and toilet facilities with toilet and washbasins, and shower cubicles and washbasins. Adjacent there is a 9-hole par 4 golf course and clubhouse. 6 acre site. 94 touring pitches. 13 hardstandings. 33 seasonal pitches. Caravan pitches. Motorhome pitches. Tent pitches. 19 statics.

Open: Mar-Oct **Last arrival:** gates locked at 23.00hrs **Last departure:** noon

Pitches: * 🚐 £16.80-£26 🚛 £16.80-£26 ▲ £13.60-£22

Leisure: 🅰 ♪

Facilities: 🅁 🄿 ☉ ☝ ✳ ♿ 🅂 WiFi ♻ 🛈

Services: 🔌 🔥 🛢 🚿 T ⦿ 🚽

Within 3 miles: ⛳ 🎠 🛝 ☉ 🛥 🛒

Notes: Families & couples only, no commercial vehicles, no ball games, no noise after 23.00hrs. Dogs must be kept on leads. Fresh bread to order, newspaper order, Portuguese street food mobile catering (Fri-Sat).

WEST SUSSEX

ARUNDEL — Map 6 TQ00

Places to visit

Arundel Castle, ARUNDEL, BN18 9AB, 01903 882173 www.arundelcastle.org

Harbour Park, LITTLEHAMPTON, BN17 5LL, 01903 721200 www.harbourpark.com

Great for kids: Look & Sea! Visitor Centre, LITTLEHAMPTON, BN17 5AW, 01903 718984 www.lookandsea.co.uk

Ship & Anchor Marina
►► 79%

GOLD

tel: 01243 551262 Station Rd, Ford BN18 0BJ
email: enquiries@shipandanchormarina.co.uk
dir: *From A27 at Arundel take road S signed Ford. Site 2m on left after level crossing.* **grid ref:** *TQ002040*

Neatly maintained by the enthusiastic, hard working owner, this small, well located site has dated but spotlessly clean toilet facilities, a secluded tent area, and enjoys a pleasant position beside the Ship & Anchor pub and the tidal River Arun. There are good walks from the site to Arundel and the coast. River fishing is possible. 12 acre site. 120 touring pitches. 11 hardstandings. Caravan pitches. Motorhome pitches. Tent pitches.

Open: Mar-Oct **Last arrival:** 21.00hrs **Last departure:** noon

Pitches: * 🚐 £16-£23 🚛 £16-£23 ▲ £16-£23

Leisure: 🅰

Facilities: 🅁 ☉ 🄿 ✳ ♿ 🅂 🎠 ♻ 🛈

Services: 🔌 🍴 🛢 🚿 T ⦿ 🚮

Within 3 miles: ⛳ 🛝 🎣 ☉ 🛥 🛒 U

Notes: 🚫 No music audible to others. Dogs must be kept on leads.

AA Pubs & Restaurants nearby: The Town House, ARUNDEL, BN18 9AJ, 01903 883847

The George at Burpham, BURPHAM, BN18 9RR, 01903 883131

LEISURE: 🏊 Indoor pool 🏊 Outdoor pool 🅰 Children's playground 🙌 Kid's club 🎾 Tennis court 🎱 Games room ⛳ Golf course 🚣 Boat hire 🚲 Cycle hire 🎬 Cinema 🎵 Entertainment 🎣 Fishing ⛳ Mini golf 🏌 Pitch n putt 🏄 Watersports 🏋 Gym 🏟 Sports field U Stables **FACILITIES:** 🛁 Bath 🚿 Shower 🅟 Private washing cubicles ☉ Electric shaver 🄿 Hairdryer ✳ Ice Packs ♿ Disabled facilities 🅂 Shop on site 🏪 Mobile shop 🍖 BBQ area 🪑 Picnic area WiFi Wi-fi 💻 Internet access ♻ Recycling 🛈 Tourist info 🐕 Dog exercise area 🚗 Car hire can be arranged

BARNS GREEN
Map 6 TQ12

Places to visit

Parham House & Gardens, PULBOROUGH, RH20 4HS, 01903 742021
www.parhaminsussex.co.uk

Great for kids: Bignor Roman Villa & Museum, BIGNOR, RH20 1PH,
01798 869259 www.bignorromanvilla.co.uk

REGIONAL WINNER – SOUTH EAST ENGLAND
AA CAMPSITE OF THE YEAR 2017

Sumners Ponds Fishery & Campsite
▶▶▶▶ 88%

tel: 01403 732539 **Chapel Rd RH13 0PR**
email: bookings@sumnersponds.co.uk
dir: From A272 at Coolham x-roads, N towards Barns Green. In 1.5m take 1st left at small
x-roads. 1m, over level crossing. Site on left just after right bend. **grid ref:** TQ125268

Dedication to provide high quality camping continues at this working farm set in
attractive surroundings on the edge of the quiet village of Barns Green. There are
three touring areas; one continues to develop and includes camping pods and extra
hardstandings, and another, which has a stunning modern toilet block, has
excellent pitches on the banks of one of the well-stocked fishing lakes. For a
glamping holiday there are wooden pods, a stunning fully-equipped safari tent,
lodges and new shepherd's huts. There are many cycle paths on site and a
woodland walk has direct access to miles of footpaths. The Café by the Lake serves
meals from breakfast onwards. Horsham and Brighton are within easy reach. 40
acre site. 86 touring pitches. 45 hardstandings. Caravan pitches. Motorhome
pitches. Tent pitches.

Open: all year **Last arrival:** 20.00hrs **Last departure:** noon

Pitches: 🚐 🚍 Å ⋔

Leisure: ⌸ ✐

Facilities: 🔥 🅿 ⊙ 🗗 ✳ ⅙ 🗓 🛏 ⌆ 📶 ♻ ❶

Services: 🔌 🗓 🔋 ⌀ T ⍢ 🛒 ⚲

Glamping: **Safari tents** 1, £70-£130 Changeover day Mon, Fri **Wooden Pods** 6, £35-£57
Car by unit **Shepherd's Huts** 4, £60-£80 Changeover day Mon, Wed, Fri Car by unit

Within 3 miles: ⌿ ✐ ⛵ 🗓 🗓 ∪

Notes: 1 car per pitch. Only well behaved dogs accepted & must be kept on leads. Noise
curfew 22.30hrs. Easy access fishing platform.

AA Pubs & Restaurants nearby: The White Horse, MAPLEHURST, RH13 6LL, 01403 891208

BILLINGSHURST
Map 6 TQ02

Places to visit

Petworth House & Park, PETWORTH, GU28 0AE, 01798 342207
www.nationaltrust.org.uk/petworth

Petworth Cottage Museum, PETWORTH, GU28 0AU, 01798 342100
www.petworthcottagemuseum.co.uk

Limeburners Arms Camp Site

►► 74%

tel: 01403 782311 **Lordings Rd, Newbridge RH14 9JA**
email: chippy.sawyer@virgin.net
dir: A29 take A272 towards Petworth for 1m, left onto B2133. Site 300yds on left.
grid ref: TQ072255

A secluded site in rural West Sussex, at the rear of the Limeburners Arms public house, and surrounded by fields. It makes a pleasant base for touring the South Downs and the Arun Valley. The toilets are basic but very clean. 2.75 acre site. 40 touring pitches. Caravan pitches. Motorhome pitches. Tent pitches.

Open: Apr-Oct **Last arrival:** 22.00hrs **Last departure:** 14.00hrs

Pitches: ⌐⌐ ⌐⌐ Å

Facilities: ☺ ✳

Services: ▨ ▦ ▧ ⫶⫶ ▨ ⛏

Within 3 miles: ⌐ ⓢ ∪

Notes: Dogs must be kept on leads.

CHICHESTER
Map 5 SU80

Places to visit

Chichester Cathedral, CHICHESTER, PO19 1PX, 01243 782595
www.chichestercathedral.org.uk

Pallant House Gallery, CHICHESTER, PO19 1TJ, 01243 774557
www.pallant.org.uk

Concierge Camping

►►►►► 94%

Best of British

tel: 01243 573118 **Ratham Estate, Ratham Ln, West Ashling PO18 8DL**
email: service@conciergecamping.co.uk **web:** www.conciergecamping.co.uk
dir: From A27 onto A259 to Bosham. In Bosham at rdbt into Station Rd. Over railway line, over A27. At T-junct left onto B2146 signed West Ashling. 1st left into Ratham Lane. **grid ref:** SU811063

Developing this stunning park in a field adjoining their home has been a labour of love for Tracey and Guy. It is a first-class, small park for 15 units (the larger fully serviced pitches are suitable for American RVs and cars towing caravans), and the attention to detail throughout is very impressive. Everything is high spec, from very spacious pitches and the reception, complete with a shop that sells daily-delivered local produce, coffee, drinks, late-arrival and breakfast hampers, and smart alfresco tables and chairs for all to use, to the state-of-the-art amenities block. Here you'll find full-length mirrors, ultra-efficient rain showers, an air-blade hand-drier, stylish wash basins and showers with temperature controls, piped radio and Ratham Estate toiletries plus an excellent family/disabled room. 4 acre site. 15 touring pitches. 15 hardstandings. Caravan pitches. Motorhome pitches. Tent pitches.

LEISURE: 🏊 Indoor pool 🏊 Outdoor pool 🛝 Children's playground 🙌 Kid's club 🎾 Tennis court ⚫ Games room ⛳ Golf course 🚣 Boat hire 🚲 Cycle hire 🎬 Cinema 🎵 Entertainment 🎣 Fishing ⛳ Mini golf ⛳ Pitch n putt 🏄 Watersports 🏋 Gym ⚽ Sports field ∪ Stables **FACILITIES:** 🛁 Bath 🚿 Shower 🅿 Private washing cubicles ☺ Electric shaver 💈 Hairdryer ✳ Ice Packs ♿ Disabled facilities ⓢ Shop on site 🏪 Mobile shop 🍖 BBQ area 🎪 Picnic area 📶 Wi-fi 💻 Internet access ♻ Recycling ❶ Tourist info 🐕 Dog exercise area 🚗 Car hire can be arranged

Open: all year **Last arrival:** 18.00hrs **Last departure:** noon

Pitches: 🚐 £28-£65 🚑 £28-£65 ⛺ fr £45

Facilities: ➍🅿️☉ℓ♿🛁🚻 ♻WiFi🖥️❷

Services: ☎🗄️🍴Ⓣ🍽️↯

Within 3 miles: ↧♃🎡ℓ⛵🎣🎠🎢⟳

Notes: No cars by tents. No bookings accepted by under 18yrs. No noise after 23.00hrs. Late arrival times by prior arrangement. Dogs must be kept on leads. Fresh pastries available each morning.

See advert on page 315

Concierge Glamping
NEW ▷▷▷▷▷ 92%

tel: 01243 573118 **Ratham Estate, Ratham Ln, West Ashling PO18 8DL**
email: service@conciergecamping.co.uk **web:** www.conciergecamping.co.uk
dir: *From A27 onto A259 to Bosham. In Bosham at rdbt into Station Rd. Over railway line, over A27. At T-junct left onto B2146 signed West Ashling. 1st left into Ratham Lane.* **grid ref:** *SU811063*

Quality and attention to detail are very evident at Guy and Tracey Hodgkin's park near Chichester. They have now introduced four stunning safari tents, idyllically situated in an adjoining meadow to the main site (previous entry), beside a babbling chalk stream. These impressive 'lodges' are made from wood and top-quality canvas – they ooze style and comfort, with a range cooker, dishwasher, fridge-freezer, TV, underfloor heating and a Nespresso machine in the fully-fitted kitchen, a smart en suite shower room (with piped radio), and two good-size bedrooms; the twin-bedded room is situated at the top of a wooden staircase. Each tent has a large veranda, replete with stylish seating, picnic bench and barbecue, and they overlook a stream. 4 acre site.

Open: all year **Last arrival:** 20.00hrs **Last departure:** 10.00hrs

Facilities: 🚻

Glamping: Safari tents 4, £120-£180 Min stay 3 nights (packages available for Fri-Fri, Fri-Mon & Mon-Thu) En suite Own kitchen

Notes: Booking advisable. Dogs must be kept on leads.

See advert on page 315

Plush Tents Glamping
NEW ▷▷▷▷ 83%

tel: 07904 881005 **Chapel Ln, East Ashling PO18 9AW**
email: info@plushtentsglamping.co.uk
dir: *From A27 at Fishbourne rdbt, take Fishbourne exit. Right into Salthill Rd. Left onto B2178 towards East Ashling. Just after Oakwood School sign, right into Chapel Ln, pass St Mary Sennicotts Chapel, down track for 200yds to Plush Tents sign. Parking signed.* **grid ref:** *SU835074*

Situated at the end of a no-through lane in a 'rescued' wooded area on a peaceful farm at the foot of the South Downs, Plush Tents is a totally off-grid glamping experience offering yurts, a Lotus Belle tent, bell tents and a tipi dotted around a shaded glade and accessed by winding bark paths. All tents are very clean and tidy and well-equipped with hand-made wooden beds, quality linen and duvets; each has its own outside space with rustic tables and benches, a hammock, cooking station and barbecue (the charcoal supplied is made on the farm). The yurts and the Lotus Belle tent have wood-burning stoves. The simple toilets facilities include two compost toilets (the main cabin is due to be replaced for the 2017 season). A fire pit, charcoal-heated hot tub and communal kitchen area complete the picture at this friendly and well-run glamping site. It's not far from the coast and only five miles from the Goodwood Estate. 3.5 acre site.

Open: Apr-Oct **Last arrival:** 21.00hrs **Last departure:** 11.00hrs

Leisure: ⚛🎡♣🎯

Facilities: ➍🅿️♿🛁🚻♻WiFi♻❷🎯

Glamping: Bell tents 4, £57.50-£115 Lotus Belle tents 1, £64.50-£129 Tipis 1, £44.50-£89 Yurts 6, £79.50-£159

Within 3 miles: ♃🎡ℓ⛵🎣🎠⟳

Notes: PayPal accepted. No noise after 23.00hrs. Dogs must be kept on leads.

Ellscott Park
▷▷▷ 82%

tel: 01243 512003 **Sidlesham Ln, Birdham PO20 7QL**
email: camping@ellscottpark.co.uk
dir: *From Chichester take A286 towards West Wittering. In approx 4m left at Butterfly Farm sign, site 500yds right.* **grid ref:** *SU829995*

A well-kept park set in sheltered meadowland behind the owners' nursery and van storage area. The park, that attracts a peace-loving clientele, has spotless, well maintained toilet facilities, and is handy for the beach, Chichester, Goodwood House, the racing at Goodwood and walking on the South Downs. Home-grown produce is for sale. 6 acre site. 50 touring pitches. 26 seasonal pitches. Caravan pitches. Motorhome pitches. Tent pitches.

Open: Apr 2nd week Oct **Last arrival:** in daylight **Last departure:** variable

Pitches: * 🚐 £14-£20 🚑 £14-£20 ⛺ £11-£17

Leisure: ⚛♣

Facilities: ➍☉❄♿🛁🚻♻WiFi♻❷🎯

Services: ☎🗄️⊘Ⓣ🔋

Within 3 miles: ↧♃ℓ◎🎠🎢🎣⟳

Notes: 🚫 Site closed between 22.30hrs-07.00hrs. Dogs must be kept on leads.

AA Pubs & Restaurants nearby: The Crab & Lobster, SIDLESHAM, PO20 7NB, 01243 641233

PITCHES: 🚐 Caravans 🚑 Motorhomes ⛺ Tents 🏕️ Glamping accommodation **SERVICES:** ☎ Electric hook up 🗄️ Launderette 🍴 Licensed bar
🛢️ Calor Gas ⊘ Camping Gaz Ⓣ Toilet fluid 🍽️ Café/Restaurant 🏪 Fast Food/Takeaway 🔋 Battery charging 🍼 Baby care ↯ Motorvan service point
ABBREVIATIONS: BHs – bank holidays Etr – Easter Spring BH – Spring Bank Holiday fr – from hrs – hours m – mile mdnt – midnight
rdbt – roundabout rs – restricted service wk – week wknd – weekend x-roads – crossroads 🚫 No credit or debit cards 🚫 No dogs

---

DIAL POST
Map 6 TQ11

Places to visit

Parham House & Gardens, PULBOROUGH, RH20 4HS, 01903 742021
www.parhaminsussex.co.uk

RSPB Pulborough Brooks, PULBOROUGH, RH20 2EL, 01798 875851
www.rspb.org.uk/pulboroughbrooks

Honeybridge Park
►►►►85%

tel: 01403 710923 **Honeybridge Ln RH13 8NX**
email: enquiries@honeybridgepark.co.uk
dir: *10m S of Horsham. Take A24 towards Ashington. S of Dial Post left signed Ashurst. Site on right behind Old Barn Nursery.* **grid ref:** *TQ152183*

An attractive and very popular park on gently-sloping ground surrounded by hedgerows and mature trees. A comprehensive amenities building houses upmarket toilet facilities including luxury family and disabled rooms, as well as a laundry, shop and off-licence. There are plenty of hardstandings and electric hook-ups, a games room, and an excellent children's play area. 15 acre site. 130 touring pitches. 70 hardstandings. Caravan pitches. Motorhome pitches. Tent pitches. 50 statics.

Open: all year **Last arrival:** 19.00hrs **Last departure:** noon

Pitches: ⊞ ⊞ Å

Leisure: 🎱 🎣

Facilities: 🚿 🚻 P ⊙ ♒ ☀ ❄ 🚰 🗒 ➡ 🅿

Services: 🔌 🗑 🛒 🚮 T ♨ 🎪

Within 3 miles: 🎣 🏪 🏧

Notes: No open fires. Dogs must be kept on leads. Fridges available.

AA Pubs & Restaurants nearby: The Countryman Inn, SHIPLEY, RH13 8PZ, 01403 741383

The Crown Inn, DIAL POST, RH13 8NH, 01403 710902

The Queens Head, WEST CHILTINGTON, RH20 2JN, 01798 812244

HENFIELD
Map 6 TQ21

Places to visit

Bolney Wine Estate, BOLNEY, RH17 5NB, 01444 881575
www.bolneywineestate.com

Blacklands Farm Caravan & Camping
►►72%

tel: 01273 493528 & 07773 792577 **Wheatsheaf Rd BN5 9AT**
email: info@blacklandsfarm.co.uk
dir: *A23, B2118, B2116 towards Henfield. Site approx 4m on right.* **grid ref:** *TQ231180*

Tucked away off the B2116, east of Henfield, and well placed for visiting Brighton and exploring the South Downs National Park, this simple, grassy site has great potential, and the owners plan improvements that will not spoil the traditional feel of the campsite. There are spacious pitches down by fishing lakes and the basic portaloos are clean and tidy and have been smartly clad in wood, but future plans do include building a new toilet block. 5 acre site. 75 touring pitches. 10 hardstandings. Caravan pitches. Motorhome pitches. Tent pitches.

Open: Mar-Jan **Last arrival:** 20.00hrs **Last departure:** anytime

Pitches: ⊞ ⊞ Å

Leisure: 🎱 ⚽ 🎣 ⛳

Facilities: 🚻 P ♒ ☀ ❄ 🗒 ➡ WiFi ♻ 🛈

Services: 🔌 🚮 T

Within 3 miles: ⛳ 🎣 🏧 🏪 ♘

Notes: No commercial vehicles, no noise after 23.00hrs. Dogs must be kept on leads. Coffee machine.

AA Pubs & Restaurants nearby: The Fountain Inn, ASHURST, BN44 3AP, 01403 710219

Royal Oak, POYNINGS, BN45 7AQ, 01273 857389

LEISURE: 🏊 Indoor pool 🏊 Outdoor pool 🎠 Children's playground 👶 Kid's club 🎾 Tennis court 🎱 Games room ⛳ Golf course 🚣 Boat hire 🚲 Cycle hire 🎬 Cinema 🎵 Entertainment 🎣 Fishing ⛳ Mini golf 🏌 Pitch n putt 🏄 Watersports 🏋 Gym 🏟 Sports field ♘ Stables **FACILITIES:** 🛁 Bath 🚿 Shower P Private washing cubicles ⊙ Electric shaver 🪮 Hairdryer ❄ Ice Packs ♿ Disabled facilities 🏪 Shop on site 🏬 Mobile shop 🍖 BBQ area 🌲 Picnic area WiFi Wi-fi 💻 Internet access ♻ Recycling 🛈 Tourist info 🐕 Dog exercise area 🚗 Car hire can be arranged

HORSHAM

See Barns Green & Dial Post

PAGHAM

Map 6 SZ89

Places to visit

Chichester Cathedral, CHICHESTER, PO19 1PX, 01243 782595
www.chichestercathedral.org.uk

Pallant House Gallery, CHICHESTER, PO19 1TJ, 01243 774557
www.pallant.org.uk

Church Farm Holiday Park
HOLIDAY HOME PARK 90%

tel: 01243 262635 **Church Ln PO21 4NR**
email: churchfarm@haven.com **web:** www.haven.com/churchfarm
dir: *At rdbt on A27 (S of Chichester) take B2145 signed Hunston & Selsey. At mini rdbt take 1st left signed North Mundham, Pagham & Bognor Regis. Site in approx 3m.*
grid ref: *SZ885974*

Close to Portsmouth, Chichester and south coast beaches, this relaxing and fun-packed holiday park is located close to Pagham Harbour Nature Reserve. On-site activities include golf on the 9-hole course, tennis coaching, shopping, kids' play areas and evening entertainment. There are a range of holiday caravans and apartments.

Open: Mar-Oct

Changeover day: Mon, Fri, Sat

Arrival and departure times: Please contact the site

Statics: 189 Sleeps 6-8 Bedrms 2-3 Bathrms 1-2 Toilets 1-2 Microwave Freezer TV Sky/FTV Elec inc Gas inc Grass area

Children: ♦♦ Cots Highchair **Dogs:** 2 on leads No dangerous dogs

Leisure: 🏊 ⛱ 🎣 Cycle hire ✋ ⚙

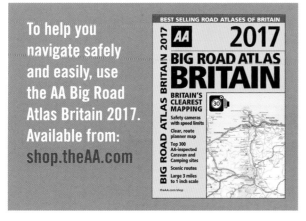
SELSEY

Map 5 SZ89

Places to visit

Chichester Cathedral, CHICHESTER, PO19 1PX, 01243 782595
www.chichestercathedral.org.uk

Pallant House Gallery, CHICHESTER, PO19 1TJ, 01243 774557
www.pallant.org.uk

Warner Farm
HOLIDAY CENTRE 82%

tel: 01243 604499 **Warner Ln, Selsey PO20 9EL**
email: touring@bunnleisure.co.uk **web:** www.warnerfarm.co.uk
dir: *From B2145 in Selsey turn right into School Lane & follow signs.* **grid ref:** *SZ845939*

A well-screened touring site that adjoins the three static parks under the same ownership. A courtesy bus runs around the complex to entertainment areas and supermarkets. The park backs onto open grassland, and the leisure facilities with bar, amusements and bowling alley, and swimming pool/sauna complex are also accessible to tourers. 10 acre site. 250 touring pitches. 60 hardstandings. 25 seasonal pitches. Caravan pitches. Motorhome pitches. Tent pitches.

Open: Mar-Jan **Last arrival:** 17.30hrs **Last departure:** 10.00hrs
Pitches: 🚐 £20-£65 🚍 £30-£65 ⛺ £20-£52.50 **Leisure:** 🏊 ⛱ 🎾 ✋ ⚙ 🎱 🎳 🎣 🎵
Facilities: 🔥 📶 ⊙ 📷 ✳ 🚿 🚽 🔥 🚐 📶 🛒 ♻ ⊘
Services: 🔌 ⊙ 🗑 📯 🚰 ⊘ T ⊙ 🚚 ⚙
Within 3 miles: ⛳ 🎿 ⌂ ◎ ⊙ 🚣 🎣 🛒 ∪ **Notes:** Dogs must be kept on leads.
AA Pubs & Restaurants nearby: The Crab & Lobster, SIDLESHAM, PO20 7NB, 01243 641233
See advert on opposite page

PITCHES: 🚐 Caravans 🚍 Motorhomes ⛺ Tents 🏕 Glamping accommodation **SERVICES:** 🔌 Electric hook up 🗑 Launderette 🍺 Licensed bar 🔥 Calor Gas 🔥 Camping Gaz T Toilet fluid 🍴 Café/Restaurant 🍔 Fast Food/Takeaway 🔋 Battery charging 👶 Baby care ⚙ Motorvan service point **ABBREVIATIONS:** BHs – bank holidays Etr – Easter Spring BH – Spring Bank Holiday fr – from hrs – hours m – mile mdnt – midnight rdbt – roundabout rs – restricted service wk – week wknd – weekend x-roads – crossroads ⊘ No credit or debit cards ⊗ No dogs

TYNE & WEAR

SOUTH SHIELDS
Map 21 NZ36

Places to visit

Arbeia Roman Fort & Museum, SOUTH SHIELDS, NE33 2BB, 0191 2771410
www.twmuseums.org.uk/arbeia

Souter Lighthouse & The Leas, WHITBURN, SR6 7NH, 0191 529 3161
www.nationaltrust.org.uk/souter

Great for kids: Blue Reef Aquarium, TYNEMOUTH, NE30 4JF, 0191 258 1031
www.bluereefaquarium.co.uk

Lizard Lane Caravan & Camping Site
►►►83%

tel: 0191 455 4455 & 455 1732 **Lizard Ln NE34 7AB**
email: info@littlehavenhotel.com
dir: *2m S of town centre on A183 (Sunderland road).* **grid ref:** *NZ399648*

This improving site is located in an elevated position with good sea views.
All touring pitches are fully serviced and the modern smart amenities block is
equipped with superb fixtures and fittings. A shop is also provided. 2 acre site.
47 touring pitches. Caravan pitches. Motorhome pitches. Tent pitches. 70 statics.

Open: Feb-28 Jan **Last arrival:** 18.00hrs **Last departure:** 11.00hrs

Pitches: * 🚐 £21-£36.50 🚐 £21-£36.50 ▲ £21-£36.50

Facilities: ☉ 🎋 ✳ ᵍᵉ ⟲ 🖩 🎢 ❋ ❶

Services: 🗨 ⬗ 🛒

Within 3 miles: ⌶ ⛸ 🍴 ≈ 🛒 🛍 ∪

Notes: Dogs must be kept on leads. 9-hole putting green.

WARWICKSHIRE

HARBURY
Map 11 SP35

Places to visit

Warwick Castle, WARWICK, CV34 4QU, 0871 265 2000 *(Calls cost 10p per minute plus
your phone company's access charge)* www.warwick-castle.com

Upton House & Gardens, UPTON HOUSE, OX15 6HT, 01295 670266
www.nationaltrust.org.uk/uptonhouse

Great for kids: British Motor Museum, GAYDON, CV35 0BJ, 01926 641188
www.heritage-motor-centre.co.uk

PREMIER PARK

Harbury Fields
►►►►►84%

tel: 01926 612457 **Harbury Fields Farm CV33 9JN**
email: rdavis@harburyfields.co.uk
dir: *M40 junct 12, B4451 (signed Kineton & Gaydon). 0.75m, right signed Lightborne.
4m, right at rdbt onto B4455 (signed Harbury). 3rd right by petrol station, site in
700yds by two cottages.* **grid ref:** *SP352604*

This developing park is in a peaceful farm setting with lovely countryside views.
All pitches are hardstanding and fully serviced, the reception is housed in an
attractive wooden chalet, and the facility block has fully serviced cubicles. The
park is well positioned for visiting Warwick and Royal Leamington Spa as well as
NEC Birmingham and Stoneleigh Park. Stratford is just 10 miles away, and
Upton House (NT) and Compton Valley Art Gallery are nearby. 6 acre site. 59
touring pitches. 59 hardstandings. Caravan pitches. Motorhome pitches.

Open: Feb-1 Dec **Last arrival:** 20.00hrs **Last departure:** noon

Pitches: 🚐 🚐

Facilities: ⋔ 🅿 ☉ ⅋ 🖩 🎢 📶 ⬛ ❶

Services: 🗨 🛍 ⬗

Within 3 miles: ⌶ 🍴 🛒

Notes: No traffic noise mdnt-07.30hrs. Dogs must be kept on leads.

AA Pubs & Restaurants nearby: The Dining Room at Mallory Court Hotel,
ROYAL LEAMINGTON SPA, CV33 9QB, 01926 330214

The Brasserie at Mallory Court, ROYAL LEAMINGTON SPA, CV33 9QB, 01926 453939

See which sites have been awarded Gold Pennants on pages 40-41

LEISURE: 🏊 Indoor pool 🏊 Outdoor pool 🛝 Children's playground ✋ Kid's club 🎾 Tennis court 🎱 Games room ⛳ Golf course ⛵ Boat hire 🚲 Cycle hire
🎬 Cinema 🎵 Entertainment 🎣 Fishing ◎ Mini golf ⛳ Pitch n putt 🏄 Watersports 💪 Gym ⚽ Sports field ∪ Stables **FACILITIES:** 🛁 Bath 🚿 Shower
🅿 Private washing cubicles ☉ Electric shaver 🎋 Hairdryer ✳ Ice Packs ♿ Disabled facilities 🛒 Shop on site 🛍 Mobile shop 🍴 BBQ area 🎢 Picnic area
📶 Wi-fi 🖥 Internet access ♻ Recycling ❶ Tourist info 🐕 Dog exercise area 🚗 Car hire can be arranged

KINGSBURY
Map 10 SP29

Places to visit

Drayton Manor Theme Park, TAMWORTH, B78 3TW, 0844 4721950 *(Calls cost 7p per minute plus your phone company's access charge)* www.draytonmanor.co.uk

Tamworth Castle, TAMWORTH, B79 7NA, 01827 709633 www.tamworthcastle.co.uk

Great for kids: Ash End House Children's Farm, MIDDLETON, B78 2BL, 0121 329 3240 www.childrensfarm.co.uk

Tame View Caravan Site
► 70%

tel: 01827 873853 **Cliff B78 2DR**
dir: *From A51 (Tamworth to Kingsbury road). Approx 1m N of Kingsbury into Cliff Hall Ln (opposite pub), 400yds to site.* **grid ref:** *SP209979*

A secluded spot overlooking the Tame Valley and river, sheltered by high hedges. Sanitary facilities are minimal but clean on this small park. The site is popular with many return visitors who like a peaceful, basic site. 5 acre site. Caravan pitches. Motorhome pitches. Tent pitches.

Open: all year **Last arrival:** 23.00hrs **Last departure:** 23.00hrs

Pitches: 🚐 🚐 Å **Facilities:** ☀ⓢ️🏕️♻️

Services: 🔌🛒 **Within 3 miles:** ↕️⛵🎣🎱⛽◎💤🎣🛒🎮∪

Notes: 🚭 No noise after mdnt. Dogs must be kept on leads. Fishing, takeaway food can be ordered for delivery.

WOLVEY
Map 11 SP48

Places to visit

Arbury Hall, NUNEATON, CV10 7PT, 024 7638 2804 www.arburyestate.co.uk

Lunt Roman Fort, COVENTRY, CV8 3AJ, 024 7678 6142 www.luntromanfort.org

Great for kids: Coventry Transport Museum, COVENTRY, CV1 1JD, 024 7623 4270 www.transport-museum.com

Wolvey Villa Farm Caravan & Camping Park
►►► 80%

tel: 01455 220493 **LE10 3HF**
dir: *M6 junct 2, B4065 follow Wolvey signs. Or M69 junct 1 & follow Wolvey signs.* **grid ref:** SP428869

A level grass site surrounded by trees and shrubs, on the border of Warwickshire and Leicestershire. This quiet country site has its own popular fishing lake, and is convenient for visiting Coventry and Leicester. 7 acre site. 110 touring pitches. 24 hardstandings. Caravan pitches. Motorhome pitches. Tent pitches.

Open: all year **Last arrival:** 22.00hrs **Last departure:** noon

Pitches: 🚐 🚐 Å **Leisure:** 🎮🎱🎣

Facilities: 🏕️◎⛵☀⛽ⓢ️🏕️🐶🎯 **Services:** 🔌🛒🏕️🧺⫯📋🛒

Within 3 miles: ↕️🎱⛵◎🎣🛒∪

Notes: 🚭 No twin axle vehicles. Dogs must be kept on leads. Putting green, off licence.

AA Pubs & Restaurants nearby: The Pheasant Eating House, WITHYBROOK, CV7 9LT, 01455 220480

WEST MIDLANDS

MERIDEN
Map 10 SP28

Places to visit

Blakesley Hall, BIRMINGHAM, B25 8RN, 0121 348 8120 www.bmag.org.uk/blakesley-hall

Packwood House, PACKWOOD HOUSE, B94 6AT, 01564 782024 www.nationaltrust.org.uk/main/w-packwoodhouse

Somers Wood Caravan Park
►►►► 92%

Best of British

tel: 01676 522978 **Somers Rd CV7 7PL**
email: enquiries@somerswood.co.uk
dir: *M42 junct 6, A45 signed Coventry. Keep left, do not take flyover. Right onto A452 signed Meriden & Leamington. At next rdbt left onto B4102 (Hampton Ln). Site in 0.5m on left.* **grid ref:** SP225824

A peaceful adults-only park set in the heart of England with spotless facilities. The park is well positioned for visiting the National Exhibition Centre (NEC), the NEC Arena and National Indoor Arena (NIA), and Birmingham is only 12 miles away. The park also makes an ideal touring base for Stratford-upon-Avon, Warwick and Coventry. Please note, tents are not accepted. 4 acre site. 48 touring pitches. 48 hardstandings. Caravan pitches. Motorhome pitches.

Open: all year **Last arrival:** variable **Last departure:** variable

Pitches: 🚐 🚐 **Facilities:** 🏕️ⓟ◎⛵☀⛽📶♻️🐶🎯

Services: 🔌ⓢ️🏕️⫯📋🧺🛒 **Within 3 miles:** ↕️⛵🛒🎮∪

Notes: Adults only. No noise 22.30hrs-08.00hrs. Dogs must be kept on leads.

AA Pubs & Restaurants nearby: The White Lion Inn, HAMPTON IN ARDEN, B92 0AA, 01675 442833

PITCHES: 🚐 Caravans 🚐 Motorhomes Å Tents 🏕️ Glamping accommodation **SERVICES:** 🔌 Electric hook up ⓢ️ Launderette 🍺 Licensed bar 🔋 Calor Gas 🛢️ Camping Gaz ⫯ Toilet fluid 🍴 Café/Restaurant 🧺 Fast Food/Takeaway 🔋 Battery charging 👶 Baby care ∪ Motorvan service point **ABBREVIATIONS:** BHs – bank holidays Etr – Easter Spring BH – Spring Bank Holiday fr – from hrs – hours m – mile mdnt – midnight rdbt – roundabout rs – restricted service wk – week wknd – weekend x-roads – crossroads 🚭 No credit or debit cards 🚫 No dogs

WILTSHIRE

AMESBURY
Map 5 SU14

Places to visit

Stonehenge, STONEHENGE, SP4 7DE, 0370 333 1181
www.english-heritage.org.uk/daysout/properties/stonehenge

Heale Gardens, MIDDLE WOODFORD, SP4 6NT, 01722 782504
www.healegarden.co.uk

Great for kids: Wilton House, WILTON (near Salisbury), SP2 0BJ, 01722 746714
www.wiltonhouse.com

Stonehenge Touring Park
►►►88%

tel: 01980 620304 **Orcheston SP3 4SH**
email: stay@stonehengetouringpark.com
dir: *From A360 towards Devizes turn right, follow lane, site at bottom of village on right.*
grid ref: *SU061456*

A quiet site adjacent to the small village of Orcheston near the centre of Salisbury Plain. There are modern and very clean facilities and an excellent on-site shop; some hardstandings are available. This is a well located site for visiting Stonehenge and nearby Salisbury plus it's less that an hour's drive from the heart of the New Forest National Park. 2 acre site. 30 touring pitches. 13 hardstandings. Caravan pitches. Motorhome pitches. Tent pitches.

Open: all year **Last arrival:** 19.00hrs **Last departure:** 11.00hrs

Pitches: * 🚐 £11.50-£17.50 🚕 £11.50-£17.50 ▲ £11.50-£27.50

Facilities: 🅿️⊙🎇☀️⑤WiFi♻️❶

Services: 🔌⑤🛢🧺T🚽⊎

Within 3 miles: ⑤⑤U

Notes: No noise after 23.00hrs. Dogs must be kept on leads.

AA Pubs & Restaurants nearby: The Boot Inn, BERWICK ST JAMES, SP3 4TN, 01722 790243

BERWICK ST JAMES

Places to visit

Stonehenge, STONEHENGE, SP4 7DE, 0370 333 1181
www.english-heritage.org.uk/daysout/properties/stonehenge

Heale Gardens, MIDDLE WOODFORD, SP4 6NT, 01722 782504
www.healegarden.co.uk

BERWICK ST JAMES
Map 5 SU03

Stonehenge Campsite & Glamping Pods
►►►87%

tel: 07786 734732 **SP3 4TQ**
email: stay@stonehengecampsite.co.uk
dir: *From Stonehenge Visitor Centre take A303 W, 2m. Through Winterbourne Stoke. Left onto B3083 towards Berwick St James. Site on left in 0.5m.* **grid ref:** *SU077405*

This small campsite is split into three areas and has good modern toilets and showers including a laundry facility. The lower end of the site has hardstandings for caravans and motorhomes plus five glamping pods, including the novel Festival Pod. The middle field is for tents, both for families and individuals, whilst the top area is for larger groups who can perhaps enjoy some of their holiday time sitting around open fires or fire pits. The site is close to Stonehenge and Longleat; there are plenty of excellent walks from the campsite and two good pubs nearby. 4 acre site. 35 touring pitches. 10 hardstandings. Caravan pitches. Motorhome pitches. Tent pitches.

Open: 10 Feb-Oct **Last arrival:** 20.30hrs **Last departure:** 10.45hrs

Pitches: 🚐🚕▲🏕

Facilities: 🅿️🅿️⊙🎇☀️🚿🛏WiFi♻️❶

Services: 🔌⑤🍴

Glamping: Wooden Pods 4, £45-£85 Min stay 2 nights (3 nights on BHs)
Cabins 1, £25-£45 Min stay 2 nights (3 nights on BHs)

Within 3 miles: 🎣⑤U

Notes: PayPal accepted. No noise 22.00-08.00hrs, no music at any time. Dogs must be kept on leads. Fire pit & mobile fire pits.

CALNE
Map 4 ST97

Places to visit

Avebury Manor & Garden, AVEBURY, SN8 1RF, 01672 539250
www.nationaltrust.org.uk/avebury

Bowood House & Gardens, CALNE, SN11 0LZ, 01249 812102 www.bowood.org

Great for kids: Alexander Keiller Museum, AVEBURY, SN8 1RF, 01672 539250
www.nationaltrust.org.uk/avebury

Blackland Lakes Holiday & Leisure Centre
►►►79%

tel: 01249 810943 **Stockley Ln SN11 0NQ**
email: enquiries@blacklandlakes.co.uk
dir: *From Calne take A4 E for 1.5m, right at camp sign. Site 1m on left.*
grid ref: *ST973687*

A rural site surrounded by the North and West Downs. The park is divided into several paddocks separated by hedges, trees and fences, and there are two well-stocked carp fisheries for the angling enthusiast. There are some excellent walks close by, and the interesting market town of Devizes is just a few miles away. 15 acre site. 180 touring pitches. 16 hardstandings. 25 seasonal pitches. Caravan pitches. Motorhome pitches. Tent pitches.

LEISURE: 🏊 Indoor pool 🏊 Outdoor pool ⑭ Children's playground 🖐 Kid's club ⚲ Tennis court 🎱 Games room ⛳ Golf course ⛵ Boat hire 🚲 Cycle hire 🎬 Cinema 🎵 Entertainment 🎣 Fishing ◎ Mini golf ⛳ Pitch n putt 🏄 Watersports 💪 Gym 🏟 Sports field U Stables **FACILITIES:** 🛁 Bath 🚿 Shower 🅿️ Private washing cubicles ⊙ Electric shaver 🎇 Hairdryer ❄️ Ice Packs ♿ Disabled facilities ⑤ Shop on site ⑤ Mobile shop 🍴 BBQ area 🍴 Picnic area WiFi Wi-fi 💻 Internet access ♻️ Recycling ❶ Tourist info 🐕 Dog exercise area 🚗 Car hire can be arranged

Open: all year (rs 30 Oct-1 Mar pre-paid bookings only) **Last arrival:** 22.00hrs **Last departure:** noon

Pitches: * 🚐 £16-£26.50 🚍 £16-£26.50 ⛺ £16-£17.50

Leisure: 🅰 ✎

Facilities: 🔦 ☉ ✳ ᵬ 🖊 🛒 ♻ ❢

Services: 🔌 🖅 🔋 ⊘ 🅣 ⚌ ⚡

Within 3 miles: ⚓ ✎ 🅟 🅢 🅢 ∪

Notes: No groups of under 25s. No noise after 22.30hrs, no loud music. Dogs must be on leads. Wildfowl sanctuary, cycle trail, nature trail, pygmy goats, licensed bar on BHs.

AA Pubs & Restaurants nearby: The White Horse, CALNE, SN11 8RG, 01249 813118

The Lansdowne, CALNE, SN11 0EH, 01249 812488

LACOCK
Map 4 ST96

Places to visit
Lacock Abbey, Fox Talbot Museum & Village, LACOCK, SN15 2LG, 01249 730459 www.nationaltrust.org.uk/lacock

Corsham Court, CORSHAM, SN13 0BZ, 01249 701610 www.corsham-court.co.uk

---

Piccadilly Caravan Park
▶▶▶▶84%

tel: 01249 730260 **Folly Lane West SN15 2LP**
email: info@piccadillylacock.co.uk **web:** www.piccadillylacock.co.uk
dir: *4m S of Chippenham just past Lacock. Exit A350 signed Gastard. Site 300yds on left.*
grid ref: ST913683

A peaceful, pleasant site, well established and beautifully laid-out, close to the village of Lacock and Lacock Abbey. Both the facilities and the grounds are immaculately maintained; there is very good screening. A section of the park has been developed to provide spacious pitches especially for tents, complete with its own toilet and shower block. 2.5 acre site. 41 touring pitches. 12 hardstandings. Caravan pitches. Motorhome pitches. Tent pitches.

Open: Etr & Apr-Oct **Last arrival:** 20.00hrs **Last departure:** noon

Pitches: * 🚐 £19-£21 🚍 £19-£21 ⛺ £19-£24.50

Leisure: 🅰 ✪

Facilities: 🔦 🅟 ☉ 🅟 ✳ 🖊 📶 ♻ ❢

Services: 🔌 🖅 🔋 ⊘ ⚌

Within 3 miles: ⚓ 🅗 ✎ 🅢 🅢 ∪

Notes: ⊗ Dogs must be kept on leads.

LANDFORD
Map 5 SU21

Places to visit
Furzey Gardens, MINSTEAD, SO43 7GL, 023 8081 2464 www.furzey-gardens.org

Mottisfont, MOTTISFONT, SO51 0LP, 01794 340757 www.nationaltrust.org.uk/mottisfont

Great for kids: Paultons Park, OWER, SO51 6AL, 023 8081 4442 www.paultonspark.co.uk

---

Greenhill Farm Caravan & Camping Park
▶▶▶▶▶86%

tel: 01794 324117 **Greenhill Farm, New Rd SP5 2AZ**
email: info@greenhillfarm.co.uk
dir: *M27 junct 2, A36 towards Salisbury. Approx 3m after Hampshire-Wiltshire border, pass Shoe Inn pub on right & BP garage on left, left into New Rd, signed Nomansland, 0.75m on left.* **grid ref:** SU266183

A tranquil, well-landscaped park hidden away in unspoilt countryside on the edge of the New Forest National Park. Pitches overlooking the fishing lake include hardstandings and are for adults only. The other section of the park is for families and includes a play area and games room. The site provides excellent toilet and shower blocks in both the family area and adults-only area. This site is also well placed for visiting Paultons Family Theme Park at Ower. 13 acre site. 160 touring pitches. 45 hardstandings. Caravan pitches. Motorhome pitches. Tent pitches.

Open: all year **Last arrival:** 21.30hrs **Last departure:** 11.00hrs

Pitches: * 🚐 £18-£28.50 🚍 £18-£28.50 ⛺ £16-£28.50

Leisure: 🅰 ✪ 🎣 ✎ 🚲

Facilities: 🔦 🅟 ☉ 🅟 ✳ ᵬ 🖊 🛒 ♻ ❢

Services: 🔌 🖅 🍺 🔋 ⊘ 🅣 ⚌ ⚡

Within 3 miles: ⚓ ✎ ☺ 🅢 🅢 ∪

Notes: No noise after 23.00hrs. Dogs must be kept on leads. Disposable BBQs, freshly baked bread available.

SALISBURY
Map 5 SU12

See also Amesbury

Places to visit

The Salisbury Museum, SALISBURY, SP1 2EN, 01722 332151
www.salisburymuseum.org.com

Salisbury Cathedral, SALISBURY, SP1 2EJ, 01722 555120
www.salisburycathedral.org.uk

Great for kids: Wilton House, WILTON (Near Salisbury), SP2 0BJ, 01722 746714
www.wiltonhouse.com

Coombe Touring Park
►►►► 91%

tel: 01722 328451 **Race Plain, Netherhampton SP2 8PN**
email: enquiries@coombecaravanpark.co.uk **web:** www.coombecaravanpark.co.uk
dir: *From Salisbury take A345 towards Blandford. Onto A3094 then follow Stratford Tony &
site signs. After racecourse turn left. 700yds to site on right. Or from A36 (W of Salisbury)
onto A3094 (signed Bournemouth), at Netherhampton Corner follow Stratford Tony &
racecourse signs. After racecourse turn left. 700yds to site on right.* **grid ref:** *SU099282*

A very neat and attractive site adjacent to the racecourse with views over the
downs. The park is well landscaped with shrubs and maturing trees, and the very
colourful beds are stocked from the owner's own greenhouse. This is a lovely quiet
and peaceful park to stay on with an excellent toilet and shower block, plus a
heated function room and campers' retreat. There are four static homes available
for hire. 3 acre site. 50 touring pitches. 6 hardstandings. Caravan pitches.
Motorhome pitches. Tent pitches. 6 statics.

Open: all year (rs Oct-Apr shop closed) **Last arrival:** 21.00hrs **Last departure:** noon
Pitches: 🚐 🚃 ▲
Leisure: 🎠
Facilities: 🕯 🅿 ⊙ 🖤 ⚡ ☀ ⛆ 🅂 🎞 ❼
Services: 🅀 🗒 🧺 🛒
Within 3 miles: �️ 🥅 🛒 🎣 ∪

Notes: 🐾 No disposable BBQs or fires, no mini motorbikes, no drones, no noise between
23.00hrs-07.00hrs. Dogs must be kept on leads. Table tennis, campers' kitchen,
children's bathroom.

AA Pubs & Restaurants nearby: The Wig and Quill, SALISBURY, SP1 2PH, 01722 335665

Alderbury Caravan & Camping Park
►►► 83%

tel: 01722 710125 **Southampton Rd, Whaddon SP5 3HB**
email: alderbury@aol.com
dir: *Follow Whaddon signs from A36, 3m from Salisbury. Site opposite The Three Crowns
pub.* **grid ref:** *SU197259*

A pleasant, attractive park set in the village of Whaddon not far from Salisbury. The
small site is well maintained by friendly owners, and is ideally positioned near the
A36 for overnight stops to and from the Southampton ferry terminals. 2 acre site.
39 touring pitches. 12 hardstandings. Caravan pitches. Motorhome pitches. Tent
pitches. 1 static.

Open: all year **Last arrival:** 21.00hrs **Last departure:** 12.30hrs
Pitches: 🚐 🚃 ▲
Facilities: ⊙ ☀ ⛆ 🚫 ❼
Services: 🅀 🗒 🧺 🛒
Within 3 miles: �️ 🥅 🛒 🎣 ∪

Notes: No open fires. Dogs must be kept on leads. Microwave & electric kettle available.

AA Pubs & Restaurants nearby: Salisbury Seafood & Steakhouse, SALISBURY, SP1 3TE,
01722 417411

The Cloisters, SALISBURY, SP1 2DH, 01722 338102

TROWBRIDGE
Map 4 ST85

Places to visit

Great Chalfield Manor and Garden, BRADFORD-ON-AVON, SN12 8NH,
01225 782239 www.nationaltrust.org.uk

The Courts Garden, HOLT, BA14 6RR, 01225 782875 www.nationaltrust.org.uk

Great for kids: Longleat, LONGLEAT, BA12 7NW, 01985 844400
www.longleat.co.uk

Stowford Manor Farm
►► 76%

tel: 01225 752253 **Stowford, Wingfield BA14 9LH**
email: stowford1@supanet.com
dir: *From Trowbridge take A366 W towards Radstock. Site on left in 3m.*
grid ref: *ST810577*

A very simple farm site set on the banks of the River Frome behind the farm
courtyard. The owners are friendly and relaxed and the park enjoys a similarly
comfortable ambience. Cream teas are available at the farmhouse. The unisex
facilities are kept clean and tidy. Farleigh & District Swimming Club, one of the few
remaining river swimming clubs, is just half a mile from the site. 1.5 acre site. 15
touring pitches. Caravan pitches. Motorhome pitches. Tent pitches.

Open: Etr-Oct **Last departure:** noon
Pitches: * 🚐 fr £16 🚃 fr £16 ▲ fr £16
Leisure: 🎣 **Facilities:** 🕯 ⊙ ☀ 🛒 📶 ♻
Services: 🅀 🍽 🛒 **Within 3 miles:** �️ 🥅 🛒 🎣 🛒 ∪

Notes: No open fires. Dogs must be kept on leads. Fishing, boating. Fire bowl hire.

AA Pubs & Restaurants nearby: Tuckers Grave, FAULKLAND, BA3 5XF, 01373 834230

LEISURE: 🏊 Indoor pool ⚓ Outdoor pool 🎠 Children's playground 👋 Kid's club 🎾 Tennis court 🎱 Games room ⛳ Golf course 🚣 Boat hire 🚴 Cycle hire 🎦 Cinema 🎵 Entertainment 🎣 Fishing ◉ Mini golf ⛳ Pitch n putt 🏄 Watersports 🏋 Gym ⚽ Sports field ∪ Stables **FACILITIES:** 🛁 Bath 🚿 Shower 🅿 Private washing cubicles ⊙ Electric shaver 🪮 Hairdryer ❄ Ice Packs ♿ Disabled facilities 🅂 Shop on site 📱 Mobile shop 🍖 BBQ area 🌳 Picnic area 📶 Wi-fi 💻 Internet access ♻ Recycling ❼ Tourist info 🐕 Dog exercise area 🚗 Car hire can be arranged

WESTBURY — Map 4 ST85

Places to visit

Great Chalfield Manor and Garden, BRADFORD-ON-AVON, SN12 8NH, 01225 782239 www.nationaltrust.org.uk

The Courts Garden, HOLT, BA14 6RR, 01225 782875 www.nationaltrust.org.uk

Brokerswood Country Park

►►►► 85%

DAVID BELLAMY CONSERVATION AWARD GOLD

tel: 01373 822238 **Brokerswood BA13 4EH**
email: info@brokerswoodcountrypark.co.uk **web:** www.brokerswoodcountrypark.co.uk
dir: *M4 junct 17, S on A350. Right at Yarnbrook to Rising Sun pub at North Bradley, left at rdbt. Left on bend approaching Southwick, 2.5m, site on right.* **grid ref:** *ST836523*

A popular site on the edge of an 80-acre woodland park with nature trails, fishing lakes and a good range of activities including archery, tree-top high rope course and kayaking. The adventure playground offers plenty of fun for all ages, and there is a miniature railway, an undercover play area and a breakfast bar. There are high quality toilet facilities. 5 acre site. 69 touring pitches. 21 hardstandings. Caravan pitches. Motorhome pitches. Tent pitches.

Open: Apr-4 Nov **Last arrival:** 21.30hrs **Last departure:** 11.00hrs

Pitches: 🚐 🚌 ⛺

Leisure: /A\ 🎣

Facilities: 🛁 🚿 [P] ⊙ 🚿 ✲ ♿ [$] 🪑 🐕 💻 ♻ ⓘ

Services: 🔌 🧺 🍷 🔥 🍃 [T] 🍴 ⬇

Within 3 miles: 🎣 [$]

Notes: Families only. Dogs must be kept on leads.

WORCESTERSHIRE

HONEYBOURNE — Map 10 SP14

Places to visit

Kiftsgate Court Garden, MICKLETON, GL55 6LN, 01386 438777 www.kiftsgate.co.uk

Hidcote Manor Garden, MICKLETON, GL55 6LR, 01386 438333 www.nationaltrust.org.uk/hidcote

Great for kids: Anne Hathaway's Cottage, SHOTTERY, CV37 9HH, 01789 338532 www.shakespeare.org.uk

PREMIER PARK

Ranch Caravan Park

►►►►► 86%

DAVID BELLAMY CONSERVATION AWARD GOLD

tel: 01386 830744 **Station Rd WR11 7PR**
email: enquiries@ranch.co.uk **web:** www.ranch.co.uk
dir: *From village x-roads towards Bidford, site 400mtrs on left.* **grid ref:** *SP113444*

An attractive and well-run park set amidst farmland in the Vale of Evesham and landscaped with trees and bushes. Tourers have their own excellent facilities in two locations, and the use of an outdoor heated swimming pool in peak season. There is also a licensed club serving meals. Please note that this site does not accept tents. 12 acre site. 120 touring pitches. 46 hardstandings. 23 seasonal pitches. Caravan pitches. Motorhome pitches. 218 statics.

Open: Mar-Nov (rs Mar-May & Sep-Nov swimming pool closed, shorter club hours) **Last arrival:** 20.00hrs **Last departure:** noon

Pitches: * 🚐 fr £25 🚌 fr £25

Leisure: 🏊 🍸 ⚽ 🔦 ♫

Facilities: 🚿 [P] ⊙ 🚿 ✲ ♿ [$] 🐕 💻 ♻ ⓘ 💷

Services: 🔌 🧺 🍷 🔥 🍃 [T] 🍴 🔋 🍔 ⬇

Within 3 miles: ⛳ 🎣 [$] 🧺 U

Notes: No unaccompanied minors. Dogs must be kept on leads.

AA Pubs & Restaurants nearby: The Fleece Inn, BRETFORTON, WR11 7JE, 01386 831173

The Ebrington Arms, EBRINGTON, GL55 6NH, 01386 593223

WORCESTER
Map 10 SO85

Places to visit

City Museum & Art Gallery, WORCESTER, WR1 1DT, 01905 25371
www.museumsworcestershire.org.uk

The Greyfriars' House and Garden, WORCESTER, WR1 2LZ, 01905 23571
www.nationaltrust.org.uk/greyfriars

Great for kids: West Midland Safari & Leisure Park, BEWDLEY, DY12 1LF,
01299 402114 www.wmsp.co.uk

Peachley Leisure Touring Park
►►► 87%

 GOLD

tel: 01905 641309 & 07764 540803 **Peachley Ln, Lower Broadheath WR2 6QX**
email: peachleyleisure@live.co.uk

dir: *M5 junct 7, A44 (Worcester ring road) towards Leominster. Exit at sign for Elgar's
Birthplace Museum. Pass museum, at x-roads turn right. In 0.75m at T-junct turn left.
Park signed on right.* **grid ref:** *SO807576*

The park is set in its own area in the grounds of Peachley Farm and has all
hardstanding and fully serviced pitches. The 25 super pitches have 16 amp
electricity, mains water and sewer. There are two fishing lakes, a really excellent
quad bike course and outdoor giant draughts, chess and jenga. The park proves to
be a peaceful haven, and is an excellent base from which to explore the area, which
includes The Elgar Birthplace Museum, Worcester Racecourse and the Worcester
Victorian Christmas Fayre (in late November); it is also convenient for Malvern's
Three Counties Showground. 8 acre site. 82 touring pitches. 82 hardstandings.
Caravan pitches. Motorhome pitches. Tent pitches.

Open: all year **Last arrival:** 21.30hrs **Last departure:** 15.00hrs

Pitches: 🚐 🚍 Å

Leisure: 🎾 ⚽

Facilities: 🔫 ☺ ✳ ♿ ⛱ 🐕 WiFi 🖥 ♻ ♻

Services: 🚰 🔋 🛒 ⚏

Within 3 miles: ⚓ ⛳ 🎱 🎣 ⛵ 🛒 🐎 ♻

Notes: No skateboards, no riding on motorbikes or scooters. Dogs must be kept on leads.
Table tennis.

AA Pubs & Restaurants nearby: The Talbot, KNIGHTWICK, WR6 5PH, 01886 821235

The Bear & Ragged Staff, BRANSFORD, WR6 5JH, 01886 833399

PITCHES: 🚐 Caravans 🚌 Motorhomes ⛺ Tents ⛺ Glamping accommodation **SERVICES:** 🔌 Electric hook up ⬚ Launderette 🍷 Licensed bar
🔋 Calor Gas ⊘ Camping Gaz Ⓣ Toilet fluid 🍽 Café/Restaurant ▦ Fast Food/Takeaway ⚡ Battery charging 🍼 Baby care ⬇ Motorvan service point
ABBREVIATIONS: BHs – bank holidays Etr – Easter Spring BH – Spring Bank Holiday fr – from hrs – hours m – mile mdnt – midnight
rdbt – roundabout rs – restricted service wk – week wknd – weekend x-roads – crossroads ⊘ No credit or debit cards ⊗ No dogs

Yorkshire

There is nowhere in the British Isles quite like Yorkshire. With such scenic and cultural diversity, it is almost a country within a country. For sheer scale, size and grandeur, there is nowhere to beat it. Much of it in the spectacular Pennines, Yorkshire is a land of glorious moors, gentle dales, ruined abbeys and picturesque market towns.

'My Yorkshire, a land of pure air, rocky streams and hidden waterfalls,' was how the celebrated vet Alf Wight described his adopted home. Wight was born in Sunderland but moved to the North Yorkshire market town of Thirsk soon after the outbreak of the Second World War. He fell in love with the place and in later years his affection for the beauty, spirit and character of this great county translated to the printed page when Wight, writing under the name of James Herriot, wrote eight best-selling volumes of memoirs about the life of a Yorkshire vet, which spawned two films and a long-running TV series. Today, thousands of visitors from near and far travel to the landscape he loved so dearly to see it all for themselves. His veterinary practice, and original home, in Thirsk is open to the public.

Not surprisingly, walking features prominently on the list of things to do in Yorkshire. There are countless footpaths and bridleways to explore and miles of long-distance trails across vast open moorland and through tranquil meandering valleys. The 81-mile Dales Way is a perfect way to discover the magnificent scenery of Wharfedale, Ribblesdale and Dentdale, while the Calderdale Way offers a fascinating insight into the Pennine heartland of industrial West Yorkshire. Most famous of all the region's longer routes is surely the Pennine Way, which opened over 50 years ago in April 1965. Its inception was the most important achievement in the history of the Ramblers' Association, marking Britain's first national long-distance footpath.

The Pennine Way was the brainchild of Tom Stephenson, one-time secretary of the Association but his vision for a trail for everyone was a long time in the planning. Landowners regularly thwarted his attempts to make the landscape accessible to walkers and there were countless prosecutions for trespassing 'I could never understand how anyone could own a mountain,' Stephenson wrote. 'Surely it was there for everybody.'

One of the more surprising features to be found on the route of the Pennine Way is the ruined house known as Top Withins. This is thought to be the inspiration for *Wuthering Heights*, the Earnshaw home in Emily Brontë's stirring novel of the same name. The Brontë sisters knew the area well, and their home, now the Brontë Parsonage Museum, lies just a few miles from the ruins in the village of Haworth. The parsonage draws thousands of visitors every year; its atmospheric setting amid bleak moorland and gritstone houses vividly captures the spirit of this uniquely talented trio of writers.

An easier, more comfortable way of exploring much of Yorkshire's scenic landscape is by train. A ride on the famous Settle to Carlisle railway represents one of the region's most memorable train journeys. For a while during the late 1980s the future of this line was in serious doubt, when it seemed British Rail might close it because of soaring maintenance costs. Thanks to Michael Portillo, a noted railway enthusiast who was Secretary of State for Transport at the time, the line was saved. Essentially, the Settle to Carlisle railway is a lifeline for commuters and the people of the more remote communities of the western Dales, but it is also an extremely popular tourist attraction. Carriages are regularly filled with summer visitors in search of stunning scenery and they are not disappointed. Elsewhere in Yorkshire, a very different train recalls a very different age. In the National Railway Museum at York you'll find countless locomotives, including a replica of Stephenson's Rocket and the much-loved *Flying Scotsman*.

EAST RIDING OF YORKSHIRE

BRANDESBURTON
Map 17 TA14

Places to visit

Beverley Guildhall, BEVERLEY, HU17 9AU, 01482 392783
www.eastriding.gov.uk/museums

Burton Constable Hall, SPROATLEY, HU11 4LN, 01964 562400
www.burtonconstable.com

Blue Rose Caravan Country Park
▶ ▶ ▶ ▶ 91%

tel: 01964 543366 & 07504 026899 **Star Carr Ln YO25 8RU**
email: info@bluerosepark.com
dir: *From A165 at rdbt into New Rd, signed Brandesburton, which becomes Star Carr Ln. Approx 1m, site on left.* **grid ref:** *TA110464*

A neat and well maintained adults-only site well placed for visiting Hornsea and the Yorkshire coastline. The park is within walking distance of Brandesburton and offers an idyllic stopover for caravanners wanting a peaceful break in the countryside. 12 acre site. 58 touring pitches. 58 hardstandings. 46 seasonal pitches. Caravan pitches. Motorhome pitches. 56 statics.

Open: all year **Last arrival:** 20.00hrs **Last departure:** noon

Pitches: 🚐 £20-£25 🚐 £20-£25

Facilities: ♠ 🅿 ⊙ 🅿 & 🚿 🚽 WiFi ♻ ❶

Services: 🚐 🖩 🚽 🔒 🗑 🅣

Within 3 miles: ↓ ✦ 🎣 ◎ ☆ 🛒 🎞 ∪

Notes: Adults only. Dogs must be kept on leads.

Dacre Lakeside Park
▶ ▶ ▶ 88%

tel: 0800 180 4556 & 01964 543704 **YO25 8RT**
email: dacrepark@btconnect.com
dir: *From A165 (bypass) midway between Beverley & Hornsea, follow Brandesburton & brown site sign.* **grid ref:** *TA118468*

A large lake popular with watersports enthusiasts is the focal point of this grassy site, which offers predominantly seasonal pitches – there are just three tent pitches and five caravan/motorhome pitches available. The clubhouse offers indoor activities; there's a fish and chip shop, a pub and a Chinese takeaway in the village, which is within walking distance. The six-acre lake is used for windsurfing, sailing, kayaking, canoeing and fishing. Camping pods are available for hire. 8 acre site. Touring pitches. 2 hardstandings. 107 seasonal pitches. Caravan pitches. Motorhome pitches. Tent pitches. 107 statics.

Open: Mar-Oct **Last arrival:** 21.00hrs **Last departure:** noon

Pitches: * 🚐 fr £19 🚐 fr £19 ▲ fr £17 🏠

Leisure: ⋀ ③ ✪ 🎯 ⚡ 🎣 🏌 ❀

Facilities: ♠ 🅿 ⊙ 🅿 ✳ & 🚿 WiFi 🖥 ❶

Services: 🚐 🖩 🚽 🔒 🅣 ◎ **Glamping:** Wooden Pods 3

Within 3 miles: ↓ ✦ 🎣 ☆ 🛒 🎞 ∪

Notes: No noise 23.00hrs-08.00hrs, no craft with engines permitted on lake. Dogs must be kept on leads.

BRIDLINGTON
Map 17 TA16

See also Rudston

Places to visit

Sewerby Hall & Gardens, BRIDLINGTON, YO15 1EA, 01262 673769
www.sewerbyhall.co.uk

RSPB Bempton Cliffs, BEMPTON, YO15 1JD, 01262 422212
www.rspb.org.uk/bemptoncliffs

Great for kids: Burton Agnes Hall, BURTON AGNES, YO25 4ND, 01262 490324
www.burtonagnes.com

Fir Tree Caravan Park
▶ ▶ ▶ ▶ 81%

tel: 01262 676442 **Jewison Ln, Sewerby YO16 6YG**
email: info@flowerofmay.com
dir: *1.5m from centre of Bridlington. Left onto B1255 at Marton Corner. Site 600yds on left.* **grid ref:** *TA195702*

Fir Tree Park is a large, mainly static park that has a well laid out touring area with its own facilities. It has an excellent swimming pool complex and the adjacent bar-cum-conservatory serves meals. There is also a family bar, games room and outdoor children's play area. Please note, this park only offers seasonal touring pitches. 22 acre site. 45 touring pitches. 45 hardstandings. 45 seasonal pitches. Caravan pitches. 400 statics.

Open: Mar-Oct (rs Early & late season bar & entertainment restrictions)

Pitches: 🚐

Leisure: 🏊 ⋀ 🎣 🎵

Facilities: ♠ 🅿 ⊙ ✳ & 🗑 🚿 WiFi ♻ ❶

Services: 🚐 🖩 🚽 🔒 🅣 ◎ 🖩 🛒

Within 3 miles: ↓ ✦ 🖺 🎣 ◎ ☆ 🛒 🎞 ∪

Notes: No noise after mdnt, dogs accepted by prior arrangement only. Dogs must be kept on leads.

AA Pubs & Restaurants nearby: The Seabirds Inn, FLAMBOROUGH, YO15 1PD, 01262 850242

KINGSTON UPON HULL

See Sproatley

RUDSTON
Map 17 TA06

Places to visit

Sewerby Hall & Gardens, BRIDLINGTON, YO15 1EA, 01262 673769
www.sewerbyhall.co.uk

Thorpe Hall Caravan & Camping Site
▶ ▶ ▶ ▶ 80%

tel: 01262 420393 & 420574 **Thorpe Hall YO25 4JE**
email: caravansite@thorpehall.co.uk
dir: *From Bridlington take B1253 W for 5m.* **grid ref:** *TA108677*

A delightful, peaceful small park within the walled gardens of Thorpe Hall yet within a few miles of the bustling seaside resort of Bridlington. The site offers a games field, its own coarse fishery, and a games and TV lounge. There are numerous walks locally. 4.5 acre site. 92 touring pitches. Caravan pitches. Motorhome pitches. Tent pitches.

Open: Mar-Oct **Last arrival:** 22.00hrs **Last departure:** noon

Pitches: 🚐 🚌 ▲ **Leisure:** 🎱 🎠 ⛾ 🎣 ℘

Facilities: ➤ ⋔ 🅿 🌐 ℘ ⚒ ⚲ ♿ 🚿 🎯 WiFi 🔄 🛁 🏧

Services: 🔌 🔆 🛢 🧴 🚽 🔋 **Within 3 miles:** ℘ 🛒 🔆 ∪

Notes: No ball games except on designated field, no noise 23.00hrs-08.00hrs. Shop/reception open 09.00hrs-11.30hrs & 16.30hrs-18.30hrs (longer hours when busy). Well behaved dogs only & must be kept on leads. 4.5-acre golf practice area/games field.

AA Pubs & Restaurants nearby: The Seabirds Inn, FLAMBOROUGH, YO15 1PD, 01262 850242

SKIPSEA

Places to visit

Hornsea Museum, HORNSEA, HU18 1AB, 01964 533443
www.hornseamuseum.com

Sewerby Hall & Gardens, BRIDLINGTON, YO15 1EA, 01262 673769
www.sewerbyhall.co.uk

SKIPSEA

Map 17 TA15

Skirlington Leisure Park
HOLIDAY CENTRE 89%

tel: 01262 468213 & 468466 **YO25 8SY**
email: info@skirlington.com
dir: *From M62 towards Beverley then Hornsea. Between Skipsea & Hornsea on B1242.*
grid ref: *TA188528*

A large, well-run seaside park set close to the beach in partly-sloping meadowland with young trees and shrubs. The site has five toilet blocks, a supermarket and an amusement arcade, plus occasional entertainment in the clubhouse. The wide range of family amenities includes an indoor heated swimming pool complex with sauna, steam room and gym. A 10-pin bowling alley and indoor soft play area for children are added attractions. 140 acre site. 280 touring pitches. 15 hardstandings. 180 seasonal pitches. Caravan pitches. Motorhome pitches. 650 statics.

Open: Mar-Oct (rs except school hols & BHs - diner & some facilities only open Fri-Sun) **Last arrival:** 20.00hrs **Last departure:** 11.00hrs

Pitches: 🚐 🚌 **Leisure:** 🏊 ⛾ 🎠 🎵 Spa

Facilities: 🌐 ℘ ♿ 🚿 🎯 WiFi 🔄 🛁 🏧

Services: 🔌 🔆 🍺 🛢 🧴 🍽 🔋 🏪 **Within 3 miles:** ⛵ 🔆 ℘ 🎣 🔆 🛒 🔆 ∪

Notes: No noise after 22.00hrs. Dogs must be kept on leads. Putting green, fishing lake, arcade, mini bowling alley, Sunday market.

PITCHES: 🚐 Caravans 🚌 Motorhomes ▲ Tents 🏕 Glamping accommodation **SERVICES:** 🔌 Electric hook up 🔆 Launderette 🍺 Licensed bar 🛢 Calor Gas 🧴 Camping Gaz 🅣 Toilet fluid 🍽 Café/Restaurant 🏪 Fast Food/Takeaway 🔋 Battery charging 🍼 Baby care 🚐 Motorvan service point
ABBREVIATIONS: BHs – bank holidays Etr – Easter Spring BH – Spring Bank Holiday fr – from hrs – hours m – mile mdnt – midnight rdbt – roundabout rs – restricted service wk – week wknd – weekend x-roads – crossroads 🚫 No credit or debit cards 🚫 No dogs

SPROATLEY
Map 17 TA13

Places to visit

Burton Constable Hall, SPROATLEY, HU11 4LN, 01964 562400
www.burtonconstable.com

Streetlife Museum Hull, KINGSTON UPON HULL, HU1 1PS, 01482 613902
www.hcandl.co.uk

Great for kids: The Deep, KINGSTON UPON HULL, HU1 4DP, 01482 381000
www.thedeep.co.uk

Burton Constable Holiday Park & Arboretum

▶▶▶▶ 90%

tel: 01964 562508 **Old Lodges HU11 4LJ**
email: info@burtonconstable.co.uk **web:** www.burtonconstable.co.uk
dir: A165 onto B1238 to Sproatley. Follow signs to site. **grid ref:** TA186357

Within the extensive estate of Constable Burton Hall, this large and secluded holiday destination provides a wide range of attractions including fishing and boating on the two 10-acre lakes, a snooker room, and a licensed bar with a designated family room. The grounds are immaculately maintained and generous pitch density offers good privacy. Wooden pods are available for hire. 90 acre site. 105 touring pitches. 10 hardstandings. 14 seasonal pitches. Caravan pitches. Motorhome pitches. Tent pitches. 388 statics.

Open: Mar-mid Feb (rs Nov-mid Feb no tourers or tents accepted) **Last arrival:** 22.00hrs **Last departure:** noon

Pitches: * 🚐 £18.50-£21.50 � £18.50-£21.50 ▲ £18.50-£31.50 🏠 prices shown below

Leisure: 🛝 ⊙ 🎱 🎵 🎣

Facilities: 🛁 🅿️ ⊙ 🧴 ⚡ 🛠 🛒 WiFi 📶 ♻ 🛈

Services: 🔌 🔦 🍳 💧 🚽 🚮 ⬇

Glamping: **Wooden Pods** 7, £35-£55 Changeover day Any day Min stay 2 nights Car by unit

Within 3 miles: 🎣 🏌️ 🛒 🛍 ♨

Notes: No skateboards or rollerblades. Dogs must be kept on leads. Snooker, table tennis.

TUNSTALL
Map 17 TA33

Sand le Mere Holiday Village

HOLIDAY CENTRE 88%

tel: 01964 670403 **Southfield Ln HU12 0JF**
email: info@sand-le-mere.co.uk **web:** www.sand-le-mere.co.uk
dir: From Hull A1033 signed Withernsea, B1362 (Hull Rd) signed Hedon. In Hedon continue on B3162 towards Withernsea. Turn left signed Roos. In Roos take B1242. Turn left at brown sign for site. In Tunstall right at T-junct, right into Seaside Ln to site.
grid ref: TA305318

Ideally located between Withernsea and Bridlington, this impressive development provides first-class indoor leisure facilities with swimming pool, entertainment and a kiddies' soft ball area. The touring pitches (10 with en suite bathroom pods) are level and surrounded by maturing trees and shrubs, and there are safari tents for hire. Please note, this site does not accept tents. 135 acre site. 72 touring pitches. 51 hardstandings. 24 seasonal pitches. Caravan pitches. Motorhome pitches. 14 statics.

Open: Mar-Nov **Last arrival:** 23.00hrs **Last departure:** 11.00hrs

Pitches: 🚐 � 🏠 **Leisure:** 🏊 🎾 🛝 ⚽ 🎱 🎵 Spa

Facilities: 🦱 ❄ ⚡ 🛒 WiFi 📶 ♻ 🛈

Services: 🔌 🔦 🍳 💧 🍽 🛍 🚮 ⬇

Glamping: **Safari tents** 3

Within 3 miles: 🎣 🏌️ ◎ 🛒 🛍

Notes: No noise after 23.00hrs, speed limits around site, no camp fires. Dogs must be kept on leads.

See advert on page 331

LEISURE: 🏊 Indoor pool 🏊 Outdoor pool ⛰ Children's playground 🛝 Kid's club 🎾 Tennis court 🎱 Games room 🏌️ Golf course ⛵ Boat hire 🚲 Cycle hire 🎬 Cinema 🎵 Entertainment 🎣 Fishing ◎ Mini golf ⛳ Pitch n putt 🏊 Watersports 💪 Gym 🏟 Sports field 🐴 Stables **FACILITIES:** 🛁 Bath 🚿 Shower 🅿️ Private washing cubicles ⊙ Electric shaver 🦱 Hairdryer ❄ Ice Packs ⚡ Disabled facilities 🛒 Shop on site 🛍 Mobile shop 🍳 BBQ area 🏕 Picnic area WiFi Wi-fi 📶 Internet access ♻ Recycling 🛈 Tourist info 🐕 Dog exercise area ⛽ Car hire can be arranged

NORTH YORKSHIRE

ACASTER MALBIS
Map 16 SE54

Places to visit

National Railway Museum, YORK, YO26 4XJ, 01904 621261 www.nrm.org.uk

York Minster, YORK, YO1 7HH, 01904 557200 www.yorkminster.org

Great for kids: Jorvik Viking Centre, YORK, YO1 9WT, 01904 615505 www.jorvik-viking-centre.com

Moor End Farm
▶▶76%

tel: 01904 706727 & 07860 405872 **YO23 2UQ**
email: moorendfarm@acaster99.fsnet.co.uk **web:** www.moor-end-farm.co.uk
dir: *At junct of A64 & A1237 at Copmanthorpe follow Acaster Malbis signs. In Copmanthorpe left into Station Rd signed Acaster Malbis. In approx 1.8m site on left.*
grid ref: SE589457

A very pleasant farm site with modernised facilities including a heated family/disabled shower room. A river boat pickup to York is 150 yards from the site entrance, and the village inn and restaurant are a short stroll away. A very convenient site for visiting York Racecourse. 1 acre site. 12 touring pitches. Caravan pitches. Motorhome pitches. Tent pitches. 7 statics.

Open: Etr or Apr-Oct **Last arrival:** 22.00hrs **Last departure:** noon

Pitches: * 🚐 £20-£24 🚚 £20-£24 ⛺ £16-£24

Facilities: ⊙ 🏳 ✳ ⅋ ♿ 🛒 WiFi ♻ 🅿

Services: 🔌 🔄 🔋

Within 3 miles: ⅃ 🎣 🔄

Notes: 💳 PayPal accepted. Dogs must be kept on leads. Fridge, freezer & microwave available.

AA Pubs & Restaurants nearby: Ye Old Sun Inn, COLTON, LS24 8EP, 01904 744261

ALLERSTON
Map 19 SE88

Places to visit

Scarborough Castle, SCARBOROUGH, YO11 1HY, 01723 372451 www.english-heritage.org.uk/daysout/properties/scarborough-castle

Pickering Castle, PICKERING, YO18 7AX, 01751 474989 www.english-heritage.org.uk/daysout/properties/pickering-castle

Great for kids: Flamingo Land Resort, KIRBY MISPERTON, YO17 6UX, 01653 668287 www.flamingoland.co.uk

---

ENGLAND & OVERALL WINNER OF THE AA CAMPSITE OF THE YEAR 2017

PREMIER PARK

Vale of Pickering Caravan Park
▶▶▶▶▶ 94%

tel: 01723 859280 **Carr House Farm YO18 7PQ**
email: tony@valeofpickering.co.uk **web:** www.valeofpickering.co.uk
dir: *On B1415, 1.75m from A170 (Pickering to Scarborough road).* **grid ref:** *SE879808*

A well-maintained, spacious family park with excellent facilities including a well-stocked shop and immaculate toilet facilities, and an interesting woodland walk. A beautifully designed extension to the toilet block houses five family bathrooms and a wet room for less able visitors. Younger children will enjoy the attractive play area, while the large ball sports area will appeal to older ones. The park is set in open countryside bounded by hedges, has manicured grassland and stunning seasonal floral displays, and is handy for the North Yorkshire Moors and the attractions of Scarborough. 13 acre site. 120 touring pitches. 100 hardstandings. 70 seasonal pitches. Caravan pitches. Motorhome pitches, Tent pitches.

Open: 6 Mar-3 Jan (rs Mar) **Last arrival:** 21.00hrs **Last departure:** 11.30hrs

Pitches: * 🚐 £18-£30 🚚 £18-£30 ⛺ £14-£30 **Leisure:** 🏀 ⚽

Facilities: 🚿 🏪 ▣ ⊙ 🏳 ✳ ⅋ ♿ 🛒 🚰 WiFi ♻ 🅿

Services: 🔌 🔄 🛢 🛒 T ⅃ **Within 3 miles:** ⅃ 🏌 🎣 🔄 U

Notes: No open fires or Chinese lanterns, no noise after 23.00hrs. Microwave available.

AA Pubs & Restaurants nearby: The New Inn, THORNTON LE DALE, YO18 7LF, 01751 474226

PITCHES: 🚐 Caravans 🚚 Motorhomes ⛺ Tents 🏕 Glamping accommodation **SERVICES:** 🔌 Electric hook up 🔄 Launderette 🍺 Licensed bar 🛢 Calor Gas 🔥 Camping Gaz T Toilet fluid 🍽 Café/Restaurant 🍔 Fast Food/Takeaway 🔋 Battery charging 🍼 Baby care ⅃ Motorvan service point
ABBREVIATIONS: BHs – bank holidays Etr – Easter Spring BH – Spring Bank Holiday fr – from hrs – hours m – mile mdnt – midnight rdbt – roundabout rs – restricted service wk – week wknd – weekend x-roads – crossroads 💳 No credit or debit cards 🚫 No dogs

ALNE
Map 19 SE46

Places to visit

Beningbrough Hall, Gallery & Gardens, BENINGBROUGH, YO30 1DD, 01904 472027 www.nationaltrust.org.uk/beningbrough

Sutton Park, SUTTON-ON-THE-FOREST, YO61 1DP, 01347 810249 www.statelyhome.co.uk

Great for kids: National Railway Museum, YORK, YO26 4XJ, 01904 621261 www.nrm.org.uk

PREMIER PARK

Alders Caravan Park
►►►►► 80%

tel: 01347 838722 Home Farm YO61 1RY
email: enquiries@homefarmalne.co.uk
dir: *From A19 exit at Alne sign, in 1.5m left at T-junct, 0.5m site on left in village centre.* grid ref: *SE497654*

A tastefully developed park on a working farm with screened pitches laid out in horseshoe-shaped areas. This well-designed park offers excellent toilet facilities including a bathroom and fully-serviced washing and toilet cubicles. A woodland area and a water meadow are pleasant places to walk. Wooden pods are located in a separate landscaped area. 12 acre site. 87 touring pitches. 6 hardstandings. 71 seasonal pitches. Caravan pitches. Motorhome pitches. Tent pitches.

Open: Mar-Oct Last arrival: 21.00hrs Last departure: 14.00hrs

Pitches: ⛺ 🚐 ♨ Ă ⛺

Facilities: ⚑ P ⊙ ↗ ✳ ⚲ 💈 ⌗ WiFi ♻ ⓘ

Services: 🔌 🗑 🛒 ⛽

Glamping: Wooden Pods 4, £40-£45 Min stay 1 night

Within 3 miles: ⚓ ↗ 🛒 🗑

Notes: Max 2 dogs per pitch. Dogs must be kept on leads. Summer house, farm produce for sale.

AA Pubs & Restaurants nearby: The Black Bull Inn, BOROUGHBRIDGE, YO51 9AR, 01423 322413

BISHOP MONKTON
Map 19 SE36

Places to visit

Newby Hall & Gardens, RIPON, HG4 5AE, 01423 322583 www.newbyhall.com

Fountains Abbey & Studley Royal, RIPON, HG4 3DY, 01765 608888 www.nationaltrust.org.uk/fountains-abbey

Great for kids: Lightwater Valley Theme Park, NORTH STAINLEY, HG4 3HT, 0871 720 0011 (*Calls cost 13p per minute plus your phone company's access charge*) www.lightwatervalley.co.uk

Church Farm Caravan Park
►►► 75%

tel: 01765 676578 & 07861 770164 Knaresborough Rd HG3 3QQ
email: churchfarmcaravan@btinternet.com
dir: *From A61 at x-roads follow Bishop Monkton signs. 1.25m to village. At x-roads right into Knaresborough Rd, site approx 500mtrs on right.* grid ref: *SE328660*

A very pleasant rural site on a working farm, on the edge of the attractive village of Bishop Monkton with its well-stocked shop and pubs. Whilst very much a place to relax, there are many attractions close by, including Fountains Abbey, Newby Hall, Ripon and Harrogate. 4 acre site. 45 touring pitches. 1 hardstanding. Caravan pitches. Motorhome pitches. Tent pitches. 3 statics.

Open: Mar-Oct Last arrival: 22.30hrs Last departure: 15.30hrs

Pitches: * ⛺ £16-£18 🚐 £16-£18 Ă £10-£18

Facilities: ⚑ P ⊙ ✳ ⚲ ♻ ⓘ

Services: 🔌 🛒 ⛽

Within 3 miles: ⚓ ↗ ◎ 💈 🗑 U

Notes: No ball games. Dogs must be kept on leads.

AA Pubs & Restaurants nearby: The Black Bull Inn, BOROUGHBRIDGE, YO51 9AR, 01423 322413

BOLTON ABBEY

Places to visit

National Park Centre, GRASSINGTON, BD23 5LB, 01756 751690 www.yorkshiredales.org.uk

Parcevall Hall Gardens, GRASSINGTON, BD23 6DE, 01756 720311 www.parcevallhallgardens.co.uk

Great for kids: Stump Cross Caverns, PATELEY BRIDGE, HG3 5JL, 01756 752780 www.stumpcrosscaverns.co.uk

LEISURE: 🏊 Indoor pool 🏊 Outdoor pool 🛝 Children's playground 🖐 Kid's club 🎾 Tennis court 🎱 Games room ⛳ Golf course 🚣 Boat hire 🚴 Cycle hire 🎬 Cinema 🎵 Entertainment 🎣 Fishing ◎ Mini golf ⛳ Pitch n putt 🏄 Watersports 🏋 Gym ⚽ Sports field U Stables FACILITIES: 🛁 Bath ⚑ Shower P Private washing cubicles ⊙ Electric shaver ⚲ Hairdryer ✳ Ice Packs ♿ Disabled facilities 💈 Shop on site 🚐 Mobile shop 🍴 BBQ area 🏕 Picnic area WiFi Wi-fi 🖥 Internet access ♻ Recycling ⓘ Tourist info 🐕 Dog exercise area 🚗 Car hire can be arranged

BOLTON ABBEY
Map 19 SE05

Howgill Lodge
►►►►80%

tel: 01756 720655 **Barden BD23 6DJ**
email: info@howgill-lodge.co.uk
dir: *From Bolton Abbey take B6160 signed Burnsall. In 3m at Barden Tower right signed Appletreewick. 1.5m, at phone box right into lane to site.* **grid ref:** *SE064592*

A beautifully-maintained and secluded site offering panoramic views of Wharfedale. The spacious hardstanding pitches are mainly terraced, and there is a separate tenting area with numerous picnic tables. There are three toilet facility blocks spread throughout the site, with the main block (including private, cubicled wash facilities) is appointed to a high standard. There is also a well-stocked shop. 4 acre site. 40 touring pitches. 20 hardstandings. Caravan pitches. Motorhome pitches. Tent pitches.

Open: mid Mar-Oct **Last arrival:** 20.00hrs **Last departure:** noon

Pitches: * ⬛ £21-£26 ⬛ £21-£26 ▲ £21-£26

Leisure: ⬤ **Facilities:** 🅿️⬤🝣⚒️🝣🚗♻🛈

Services: ⬤🛢📋🚽📦

Within 3 miles: ✐🛢🛢

Notes: Dogs must be kept on leads.

AA Pubs & Restaurants nearby: The Devonshire Brasserie & Bar, BOLTON ABBEY, BD23 6AJ, 01756 710710

CHOP GATE
Map 19 SE59

Lordstones Country Park
►►►►82%

tel: 01642 778482 & 778000 **Carlton Bank TS9 7JH**
email: info@lordstones.com
dir: *From A172 between Stokesley & Osmotherly follow signs to Carlton-in-Cleveland. Through Carlton-in-Cleveland to Lordstones entrance.* **grid ref:** *NZ524030*

Situated in the North York Moors National Park and commanding one of the highest spots in the county, Lordstones has glorious views that extend over 40 miles. It is a privately owned country park that has been developed to become a distinctive visitor venue. There is a first-class restaurant (The Belted Bull), a quality farm shop selling local produce and a small camping-cum-glamping park. There are 20 pitches, some with electricity, enclosed by woodland, and two fully-equipped bell tents, two bothy tents, and five luxury wooden pods, each with a wood-burning stove, kitchenette, toilet and outside decking with barbecue and seating. Yurts are the latest additions to choose from. There is a new purpose-built amenity building housing showers and toilet facilities. The Cleveland Way national trail passes close to the site. 150 acre site. 21 touring pitches. Tent pitches.

Open: all year **Last arrival:** 17.00hrs **Last departure:** 11.00hrs

Pitches: ▲ ⛺

Facilities: ⬤♿🛢🝣🚗♻🛈

Services: ⬤🍴🍽️🛒

Glamping: Bell tents 2, £55-£70 Changeover day Mon Min stay 2 nights Car by unit **Wooden Pods** 5, £55-£90 Changeover day Mon Min stay 2 nights **Yurts** 4 **Bothy tents** 2, £50-£60 Changeover day Mon Min stay 2 nights Car by unit

Within 3 miles: 🛢

Notes: Dogs must be kept on leads.

CONSTABLE BURTON
Map 19 SE19

Places to visit
Middleham Castle, MIDDLEHAM, DL8 4RJ, 01969 623899
www.english-heritage.org.uk/daysout/properties/middleham-castle

Great for kids: Bedale Museum, BEDALE, DL8 1AA, 01677 427516
www.bedalemuseum.org.uk

Constable Burton Hall Caravan Park
►►►►83%

tel: 01677 450428 **DL8 5LJ**
email: caravanpark@constableburton.com
dir: *From Leyburn on A684 towards Bedale, approx 3m site on left.* **grid ref:** *SE158907*

A pretty site in the former deer park of the adjoining Constable Burton Hall, screened from the road by the park walls and surrounded by mature trees in a quiet rural location. The laundry is housed in a converted 18th-century deer barn and there is a pub and restaurant opposite; seasonal pitches are available. Please note that this site does not accept tents. 10 acre site. 120 touring pitches. Caravan pitches. Motorhome pitches.

Open: Apr-Oct **Last arrival:** 20.00hrs **Last departure:** noon

Pitches: * ⬛ £20.50-£25.50 ⬛ £20.50-£25.50

Facilities: 🝣⬤🝣⚒️♿🚗📶♻🛈

Services: ⬤🛢📋📦

Within 3 miles: ⚓🛢

Notes: No commercial vehicles, no games. Dogs must be kept on leads. Family shower room.

AA Pubs & Restaurants nearby: Sandpiper Inn, LEYBURN, DL8 5AT, 01969 622206

The White Swan, MIDDLEHAM, DL8 4PE, 01969 622093

The Wensleydale Heifer, WEST WITTON, DL8 4LS, 01969 622322

EASINGWOLD
Map 19 SE56

Folly Garth Caravan Park
NEW ►► 75%

tel: 01347 821150 **Green Ln, Black Woods YO61 3ES**
dir: *From N: from A19 at rdbt follow Easingwold signs. In Easingwold follow Stillington signs. Approx 3m turn right into Green Ln, site on right. From S: from A19 at rdbt follow Easingwold signs. In Easingwold turn right signed Helmsley (B1363) & Stillington. Right into Green Ln, site on right.* **grid ref:** *SE554677*

A small country site tucked away at the end of a lane in a truly rural and tranquil setting, yet just 1.5 miles from the Georgian market town of Easingwold. Facilities include a well-equipped kitchen and a fully-carpeted lounge, with table and chairs, that opens onto a decking area. The toilets are appointed to a good standard. 3 acre site. 15 touring pitches. Caravan pitches. Motorhome pitches. Tent pitches. 6 statics.

Open: Feb-Dec

Pitches: ⬛ ⬛ ▲

PITCHES: ⬛ Caravans ⬛ Motorhomes ▲ Tents ⛺ Glamping accommodation **SERVICES:** ⬤ Electric hook up 🛢 Launderette 🍴 Licensed bar 🛢 Calor Gas ⊘ Camping Gaz 🚽 Toilet fluid 🍽️ Café/Restaurant 🛒 Fast Food/Takeaway 📦 Battery charging 🍼 Baby care ⚓ Motorvan service point **ABBREVIATIONS:** BHs – bank holidays Etr – Easter Spring BH – Spring Bank Holiday fr – from hrs – hours m – mile mdnt – midnight rdbt – roundabout rs – restricted service wk – week wknd – weekend x-roads – crossroads ⊗ No credit or debit cards ⊗ No dogs

FILEY — Map 17 TA18

Places to visit

Scarborough Castle, SCARBOROUGH, YO11 1HY, 01723 372451
www.english-heritage.org.uk/daysout/properties/scarborough-castle

Scarborough Sea Life Sanctuary, SCARBOROUGH, YO12 6RP, 01723 373414
www.sealife.co.uk

Flower of May Holiday Park
HOLIDAY CENTRE 91%

tel: 01723 584311 **Lebberston Cliff YO11 3NU**
email: info@flowerofmay.com **web:** www.flowerofmay.com
dir: Take A165 from Scarborough towards Filey. Site signed. **grid ref:** TA085835

A well-run, high quality family holiday park with top class facilities. This large landscaped park offers a full range of recreational activities, with plenty to occupy everyone. Grass and hard pitches are available — all are on level ground, and arranged in avenues screened by shrubs. Enjoy the 'Scarborough Fair' museum, with its collection of restored fairground attractions, including rides, organs and vintage cars. There are 4-berth and 5-berth wooden camping pods, each with a decking area. 13 acre site. 300 touring pitches. 250 hardstandings. 100 seasonal pitches. Caravan pitches. Motorhome pitches. Tent pitches. 193 statics.

Open: Etr-Oct (rs Early & late season restricted opening times in café, shop & bars)
Last arrival: dusk **Last departure:** noon

Pitches: * 🚐 £22-£28 🚐 £22-£28 ⛺ £22-£28 🏠 prices shown below
Leisure: ⛲ 🎠 🎯 🎣 🎵 🎱 **Facilities:** 🚿 ℗ ⊙ 🌡 ✳ ♿ ⓢ 🍴 🚻 WiFi ♻ ❓
Services: 🔌 🔋 🍴 🛢 🧴 ⓣ 🍴 🛒 ⛟

Glamping: Wooden Pods 10, £40-£50 Min stay 2 nights (3 nights in school hols & BHs) Car by unit

Within 3 miles: ↓ ✳ 🗓 ℗ ◎ 🌡 ⓢ 🛢 🌀 ∪

Notes: No noise after mdnt. 1 dog per pitch by prior arrangement only. Dogs must be kept on leads. Squash, bowling, basketball court, skate park, table tennis.

See advert on opposite page

Blue Dolphin Holiday Park
HOLIDAY CENTRE 82%

tel: 01723 515155 **Gristhorpe Bay YO14 9PU**
email: bluedolphin@haven.com **web:** www.haven.com/bluedolphin
dir: On A165, 2m N of Filey. **grid ref:** TA095829

There are great cliff-top views to be enjoyed from this fun-filled holiday centre with an extensive and separate touring area. The emphasis is on non-stop entertainment, with organised sports and clubs, all-weather leisure facilities, heated swimming pools (with multi-slide), and plenty of well-planned amusements. Pitches are mainly on level or gently-sloping grass plus there are some fully serviced hardstandings. The beach is just two miles away. 85 acre site. 210 touring pitches. 33 hardstandings. 20 seasonal pitches. Caravan pitches. Motorhome pitches. Tent pitches. 850 statics.

Open: mid Mar-end Oct (rs mid Mar-May & Sep-Oct some facilities may be reduced & outdoor pool closed) **Last arrival:** mdnt **Last departure:** 10.00hrs

Pitches: 🚐 🚐 ⛺ **Leisure:** ⛲ ⛲ 🎠 🎣 🎱 🎵 ∩ **Facilities:** 🚿 ⊙ ♿ ⓢ WiFi ♻ ❓
Services: 🔌 🔋 🍴 ♨ 🧴 ⓣ 🍴 🛒 ↯ **Within 3 miles:** ↓ ℗ ◎ ⓢ 🌡

Notes: No commercial vehicles, no bookings by persons under 21yrs unless a family booking. Max 2 dogs per booking, certain dog breeds banned. Dogs must be kept on leads.

See advert on page 339

Come touring or camping with us
and discover the gorgeous
Yorkshire coast and countryside...

FLOWER OF MAY
family holiday parks

SCARBOROUGH | YORK | PICKERING | RIPON
BOOK: FLOWEROFMAY.COM | 01723 584311

PITCHES: Caravans Motorhomes Tents Glamping accommodation SERVICES: Electric hook up Launderette Licensed bar
Calor Gas Camping Gaz Toilet fluid Café/Restaurant Fast Food/Takeaway Battery charging Baby care Motorvan service point
ABBREVIATIONS: BHs – bank holidays Etr – Easter Spring BH – Spring Bank Holiday fr – from hrs – hours m – mile mdnt – midnight
rdbt – roundabout rs – restricted service wk – week wknd – weekend x-roads – crossroads No credit or debit cards No dogs

FILEY *continued*

Primrose Valley Holiday Park
HOLIDAY CENTRE 81%

tel: 01723 513771 **YO14 9RF**
email: primrosevalley@haven.com **web:** www.haven.com/primrosevalley
dir: *Signed from A165 (Scarboroug to Bridlington road), 3m S of Filey.* **grid ref:** *TA123778*

A large all-action holiday centre with a wide range of sports and leisure activities to suit everyone from morning until late in the evening. The touring area is completely separate from the main park with its own high quality amenity block. All touring pitches are fully serviced hardstandings with grassed awning strips. The touring area has its own reception and designated warden. 160 acre site. 35 touring pitches. 35 hardstandings. Caravan pitches. Motorhome pitches. 1514 statics.

Open: mid Mar-end Oct **Last arrival:** anytime **Last departure:** 10.00hrs

Pitches: 🚐 🚚

Leisure: ⌒ ⌒ 🏊 ⚽ ♠ 🎵 🎣

Facilities: 🚿 🏠 ✂ ♿ 🛒 🍴 📶 🖥 ♻ ❶

Services: 🔌 🗑 🍴 🔒 🚿 🍴 🛒 🛗

Within 3 miles: 🎣 ⛳ 🏇 ◎ 🛒 🏇 🛒

Notes: No commercial vehicles, no bookings by persons under 21yrs unless a family booking. Max 2 dogs per booking, certain dog breeds banned. Dogs must be kept on leads.

See advert on opposite page

Reighton Sands Holiday Park
HOLIDAY CENTRE 79%

tel: 01723 890476 Reighton Gap YO14 9SH
email: reightonsands@haven.com **web:** www.haven.com/reightonsands
dir: *On A165, 5m S of Filey at Reighton Gap, signed.* **grid ref:** *TA142769*

A large, lively holiday centre with a wide range of entertainment and all-weather leisure facilities (including an indoor play area), located just a 10-minute walk from a long sandy beach. There are good all-weather pitches and a large tenting field. The site is particularly geared towards families with young children. 229 acre site. 147 touring pitches. 47 hardstandings. 5 seasonal pitches. Caravan pitches. Motorhome pitches. Tent pitches. 800 statics.

Open: mid Mar-end Oct (rs mid Mar-May & Sep-Oct some facilities may be reduced) **Last arrival:** 22.00hrs **Last departure:** 10.00hrs

Pitches: 🚐 🚚 ▲

Leisure: ⌒ ⌒ 🏊 ⚾ ♠ 🎵 🎣

Facilities: 🚿 ◎ 🏠 ✂ ♿ 🛒 🍴 📶 🖥 ♻ ❶

Services: 🔌 🗑 🍴 T 🍴 🛒 🛗

Within 3 miles: 🎣 🏛 ⛳ ◎ 🛒 🏇 U

Notes: No commercial vehicles, no bookings by persons under 21yrs unless a family booking. Max 2 dogs per booking, certain dog breeds banned. Dogs must be kept on leads.

See advert on opposite page

Blue Dolphin

Filey, Yorkshire

Save up to **50%*** on 2017 holidays

Our favourite bits

- Heated outdoor pool and indoor pool with multi-lane waterslide
- Indoor activities in our SportsDrome
- Family entertainment and kids' clubs
- 210 pitches on our grassy touring area
- Sandy beaches at Filey and Scarborough are both just a short drive away
- Large indoor soft play area for younger kids

For more information visit
haventouring.com/aabd or call 0333 202 1500 Quote: AABD
Calls to 0333 numbers are charged at standard UK rates and will be included in any inclusive minute bundles

Terms and conditions: *Save up to 50% discount is available on selected spring and autumn dates in 2017. Full booking terms and conditions apply. Haven Holidays is a trading name of Bourne Leisure Limited, registered in England and Wales, no 04011660. Registered office 1 Park Lane, Hemel Hempstead, Hertfordshire, HP2 4YL. 75561

Primrose Valley

Near Filey, Yorkshire

Save up to **50%*** on 2017 holidays

Our favourite bits

- Two indoor pools with thrilling slides and water features, plus an outdoor pool
- Family entertainment and kids' clubs
- Stunning sea views with access to the beach
- Nature Rockz activity programme
- Close by to the popular tourist destinations; Filey, Scarborough and Bridlington
- 35 pitches on our level hard-standing touring area

For more information visit
haventouring.com/aapv or call 0333 202 1500 Quote: AAPV
Calls to 0333 numbers are charged at standard UK rates and will be included in any inclusive minute bundles

Terms and conditions: *Save up to 50% discount is available on selected spring and autumn dates in 2017. Full booking terms and conditions apply. Haven Holidays is a trading name of Bourne Leisure Limited, registered in England and Wales, no 04011660. Registered office 1 Park Lane, Hemel Hempstead, Hertfordshire, HP2 4YL. 75561

Reighton Sands

Near Filey, North Yorkshire

Save up to **50%*** on 2017 holidays

Our favourite bits

- Indoor pool and outdoor Lazy River
- Family entertainment and kids' clubs
- Challenging 9-hole, par 34 golf course set in 140 acres with sea views
- Five miles of sandy beach below
- 147 hard-standing and 100 grassy gently sloping pitches

For more information visit
haventouring.com/aare or call 0333 202 1500 Quote: AARE
Calls to 0333 numbers are charged at standard UK rates and will be included in any inclusive minute bundles

Terms and conditions: *Save up to 50% discount is available on selected spring and autumn dates in 2017 Full booking terms and conditions apply. Haven Holidays is a trading name of Bourne Leisure Limited, registered in England and Wales, no 04011660. Registered office 1 Park Lane, Hemel Hempstead, Hertfordshire, HP2 4YL. 75561

PITCHES: 🚐 Caravans 🚍 Motorhomes ⛺ Tents ⛺ Glamping accommodation **SERVICES:** 🔌 Electric hook up 🧺 Launderette 🍺 Licensed bar
🔋 Calor Gas 🔥 Camping Gaz Ⓣ Toilet fluid 🍽 Café/Restaurant 🍔 Fast Food/Takeaway 🔋 Battery charging 🍼 Baby care 🚽 Motorvan service point
ABBREVIATIONS: BHs – bank holidays Etr – Easter Spring BH – Spring Bank Holiday fr – from hrs – hours m – mile mdnt – midnight
rdbt – roundabout rs – restricted service wk – week wknd – weekend x-roads – crossroads 🚫 No credit or debit cards 🚫 No dogs

FILEY *continued*

Lebberston Touring Park
▶▶▶▶ 91%

GOLD

tel: 01723 585723 **Filey Rd YO11 3PE**
email: info@lebberstontouring.co.uk
dir: *From A165 (Filey to Scarborough road) follow brown site signs.* **grid ref:** *TA077824*

A peaceful family park in a gently-sloping rural area, where the quality facilities are maintained to a high standard of cleanliness. The keen owners are friendly and helpful, and create a relaxing atmosphere. A natural area offers views of the surrounding countryside through the shrubbery. Additional land offers 25 hardstandings and a stunning toilet block. Please note, this park does not accept tents. 11 acre site. 125 touring pitches. 25 hardstandings. 84 seasonal pitches. Caravan pitches. Motorhome pitches.

Open: Mar-Oct **Last arrival:** 20.00hrs **Last departure:** 11.00hrs

Pitches: * ⊞ £15.50-£27 ⊞ £15.50-£27

Leisure: ⚽

Facilities: ⛺☕🅿️⊙🌳✳️🔥⛅🖐️ WiFi ♻️ ⓘ

Services: 🔌🔲🛒🧺🚽

Within 3 miles: 🏊‍♂️🚴🏇⊙♨️🏧🛒🛥️♻️

Notes: No noise after 22.00hrs. Dogs must be kept on leads.

Crows Nest Caravan Park
▶▶▶▶ 90%

tel: 01723 582206 **Gristhorpe YO14 9PS**
email: enquires@crowsnestcaravanpark.com **web:** www.crowsnestcaravanpark.com
dir: *5m S of Scarborough & 2m N of Filey. On seaward side of A165, signed from rdbt, near petrol station.* **grid ref:** *TA094826*

A beautifully situated park on the coast between Scarborough and Filey, with excellent panoramic views. This large and mainly static park offers lively entertainment, and two bars. A small touring area is close to the attractions, and the main touring and camping section is at the top of the park overlooking the sea; this area is equipped with some excellent fully serviced pitches and a superb amenities block. 20 acre site. 49 touring pitches. 49 hardstandings. Caravan pitches. Motorhome pitches. Tent pitches. 220 statics.

Crows Nest Caravan Park

Open: Mar-Oct **Last departure:** noon

Pitches: ⊞ ⊞ ▲ **Leisure:** 🏊‍♂️🎠⚽🎣🎵

Facilities: 🅿️⊙🌳✳️🔥⛅🖐️ WiFi ♻️ ⓘ

Services: 🔌🔲🛒🍽🧺🚽🛒 **Within 3 miles:** 🏊‍♂️🚴⊙♨️🏧🛒🛥️

Notes: Dogs must be kept on leads.

See advert on opposite page

Orchard Farm Holiday Village
▶▶▶▶ 82%

tel: 01723 891582 **Stonegate, Hunmanby YO14 0PU**
email: info@orchardfarmholidayvillage.co.uk **web:** www.orchardfarmholidayvillage.co.uk
dir: *A165 from Scarborough towards Bridlington. Turn right signed Hunmanby, site on right just after rail bridge.* **grid ref:** *TA105779*

Pitches are arranged around a large coarse fishing lake at this grassy park. The enthusiastic owners are friendly, and offer a wide range of amenities including an indoor heated swimming pool and a licensed bar. 14 acre site. 91 touring pitches. 34 hardstandings. Caravan pitches. Motorhome pitches. Tent pitches. 46 statics.

Open: Mar-Oct (rs Off peak - some facilities restricted) **Last arrival:** 23.00hrs **Last departure:** 11.00hrs

Pitches: ⊞ £18-£26 ⊞ £18-£26 ▲ £14-£26

Leisure: 🏊‍♂️🎠⚽🎵🎣 **Facilities:** 🅿️⊙🌳✳️🔥⛅🖐️

Services: 🔌🔲🍽🚽🛒

Within 3 miles: 🏊‍♂️🚴⊙♨️🛒

Notes: Dogs must be kept on leads. Miniature railway.

Centenary Way Camping & Caravan Park
▶▶▶ 83%

tel: 01723 516415 **Muston Grange YO14 0HU**
dir: *From A165 onto A1039 signed Filey. 1st right to site.* **grid ref:** *TA115798*

A well set-out family-owned park, with footpath access to the nearby beach. Close to the seaside resort of Filey, and caravan pitches enjoy views over open countryside. 3 acre site. 75 touring pitches. 25 hardstandings. Caravan pitches. Motorhome pitches. Tent pitches.

Open: Mar-Oct **Last arrival:** 21.00hrs **Last departure:** noon

Pitches: ＊ ⊡ £15-£26 ⊡ £15-£26 ⚊ £7-£26 **Leisure:** ⚲

Facilities: ⬧⬧⬧⬧⬧⬧⬧⬧ **Services:** ⬧⬧⬧⬧

Within 3 miles: ⬧⬧⬧⬧⬧⬧

Notes: ⊗ No group bookings in peak period, no 9-12 berth tents, no gazebos, no noise after 23.00hrs. Dogs must be kept on leads.

Filey Brigg Touring Caravan & Country Park
▶▶▶ 81%

tel: 01723 513852 **North Cliff YO14 9ET**
email: fileybrigg@scarborough.gov.uk
dir: *A165 from Scarborough to Filey. Left onto A1039, at rdbt into Church Cliff Dr, to site.* **grid ref:** *TA115812*

A municipal park overlooking Filey Brigg with splendid views along the coast, and set in a country park. The beach is just a short walk away, as is the resort of Filey. There is a good quality amenity block, and 50 all-weather pitches are available. An excellent children's adventure playground is adjacent to the touring areas. 9 acre site. 158 touring pitches. 82 hardstandings. Caravan pitches. Motorhome pitches. Tent pitches.

Open: end Feb-2 Jan **Last arrival:** 18.00hrs **Last departure:** noon

Pitches: ＊ ⊡ £16.30-£25.30 ⊡ £16.30-£25.30 ⚊ £13.30-£19.40 **Leisure:** ⚲⚘

Facilities: ⬧⬧⬧⬧⬧⬧⬧⬧⬧ **Services:** ⬧⬧⬧⬧⬧⬧

Within 3 miles: ⬧⬧⬧⬧⬧⬧

Notes: No ball games. Dogs must be kept on leads.

PREMIER PARK

Ripley Caravan Park
▶▶▶▶ 85%

tel: 01423 770050 **Knaresborough Rd, Ripley HG3 3AU**
email: ripleycaravanpark@talk21.com
dir: *3m N of Harrogate on A61. Right at rdbt onto B6165 signed Knaresborough. Site 300yds left.* **grid ref:** *SE289610*

A well-run rural site in attractive meadowland which has been landscaped with mature tree plantings. The resident owners lovingly maintain the facilities, and there is a heated swimming pool and sauna, a TV and games room, and a covered nursery playroom for small children. There is a bus every 15 minutes which gives easy access to Ripon and Leeds, and a cycleway/walkway leads from the site directly to Harrogate, a distance of approximately four miles. 24 acre site. 60 touring pitches. 60 hardstandings. 75 seasonal pitches. Caravan pitches. Motorhome pitches. Tent pitches. 75 statics.

Open: Etr-Oct **Last arrival:** 21.00hrs **Last departure:** noon **Pitches:** ⊡ ⊡ ⚊

Leisure: ⚲⚘⚘ **Facilities:** ⬧⬧⬧⬧⬧⬧⬧⬧⬧⬧⬧

Services: ⬧⬧⬧⬧⬧⬧⬧ **Within 3 miles:** ⬧⬧⬧⬧⬧⬧⬧

Notes: Family camping only, no open fires, off-ground BBQs only, no skateboards or rollerblades. Dogs must be kept on leads. Football, volleyball, table tennis, pool table.

AA Pubs & Restaurants nearby: The General Tarleton Inn, KNARESBOROUGH, HG5 0PZ, 01423 340284

PITCHES: ⊡ Caravans ⊡ Motorhomes ⚊ Tents ⌂ Glamping accommodation **SERVICES:** ⬧ Electric hook up ⬧ Launderette ⬧ Licensed bar ⬧ Calor Gas ⬧ Camping Gaz ⬧ Toilet fluid ⬧ Café/Restaurant ⬧ Fast Food/Takeaway ⬧ Battery charging ⬧ Baby care ⬧ Motorvan service point **ABBREVIATIONS:** BHs – bank holidays Etr – Easter Spring BH – Spring Bank Holiday fr – from hrs – hours m – mile mdnt – midnight rdbt – roundabout rs – restricted service wk – week wknd – weekend x-roads – crossroads ⊗ No credit or debit cards ⊗ No dogs

HARROGATE *continued*

Rudding Holiday Park
▶▶▶▶▶84%

tel: 01423 870439 **Follifoot HG3 1JH**
email: holiday-park@ruddingpark.com **web:** www.ruddingholidaypark.co.uk
dir: *From A1 take A59 to A658 signed Bradford. 4.5m, right & follow signs.*
grid ref: *SE333531*

A spacious park set in beautiful 200 acres of mature parkland and walled gardens of Rudding Park. The setting has been tastefully enhanced with terraced pitches and dry-stone walls. A separate area houses super pitches where all services are supplied including a picnic table and TV connection, and there are excellent toilets. An 18-hole golf course, a 6-hole short course, driving range, golf academy, heated outdoor swimming pool, the Deer House Family Pub, and a children's play area complete the amenities. 50 acre site. 86 touring pitches. 20 hardstandings. 50 seasonal pitches. Caravan pitches. Motorhome pitches. Tent pitches. 57 statics.

Open: Mar-Jan (rs Nov-Jan - shop & Deer House Pub limited opening times, outdoor swimming pool open summer only) **Last arrival:** 22.00hrs **Last departure:** 11.00hrs

Pitches: 🚐 🚍 ⛺

Leisure: ⛱ 🎢 ⊕ 🏐 ⛳ 🎣 🎵 Spa

Facilities: 🛁 🚿 🅿 ⊙ 🗝 ✳ ♿ 🚮 📷 WiFi 🖥 ♻ ⓘ

Services: 🚰 🖂 🍴 🛢 🧺 Ⓣ 🍽 🛒 🏧 ♻

Within 3 miles: 🚲 🍴 ✎ 🛍 🐎 ∪

Notes: Under 18s must be accompanied by an adult. Dogs must be kept on leads.

High Moor Farm Park
▶▶▶▶85%

tel: 01423 563637 & 564955 **Skipton Rd HG3 2LT**
email: highmoorfarmpark@btconnect.com **web:** www.highmoorfarmpark.co.uk
dir: *4m W of Harrogate on A59 towards Skipton.* **grid ref:** *SE242560*

An excellent site with very good facilities, set beside a small wood and surrounded by thorn hedges. The numerous touring pitches are located in meadowland fields, each area with its own toilet block. A large heated indoor swimming pool, games room, 9-hole golf course, full-sized crown bowling green, and a bar serving meals and snacks are all popular. Please note that this park does not accept tents. 15 acre site. 320 touring pitches. 51 hardstandings. 57 seasonal pitches. Caravan pitches. Motorhome pitches. 158 statics.

Open: Etr or Apr-Oct **Last arrival:** 23.30hrs **Last departure:** 15.00hrs

Pitches: 🚐 fr £25 🚍 fr £25

Leisure: 🏊 ⊕ 🏐 **Facilities:** ⊙ 🅿 ✳ ♿ 📷 🚮 WiFi ♻ ⓘ

Services: 🚰 🖂 🍴 🛢 🧺 Ⓣ 🍽 🛒 🏧 ♻

Within 3 miles: 🚲 🍴 ✎ 🛍 ∪

Notes: No noise after mdnt, no electric scooters. Dogs must be kept on leads. Coarse fishing.

AA Pubs & Restaurants nearby: The General Tarleton Inn, KNARESBOROUGH, HG5 0PZ, 01423 340284

Harrogate Caravan Park
▶▶▶ 90%

tel: 01423 546145 **Great Yorkshire Showground HG2 8NZ**
email: info@harrogatecaravanpark.co.uk
dir: *A1(M) junct 47, A59 to Harrogate. A658, then A661. At Sainsbury's lights turn left into Railway Rd.* **grid ref:** *SE329542*

Located on the perimeter of the Yorkshire Showground and owned by the Yorkshire Agricultural Society, this very peaceful park offers easy main road access and is popular at weekends and during the days of the shows. Investment has resulted in a high standard amenity block, extensive tree planting and smart, gravelled hardstanding pitches. This is a good base for visiting Harrogate and the Yorkshire Dales. 3.56 acre site. 66 touring pitches. 50 hardstandings. Caravan pitches. Motorhome pitches. Tent pitches.

Open: Mar-Nov **Last arrival:** 21.00hrs **Last departure:** 11.00hrs

Pitches: * 🚐 £19-£23 🚍 £19-£23 ⛺ £19-£23

Leisure: ⊕ **Facilities:** 🅿 ⊙ 🗝 ♿ 🚮 📷 WiFi 🖥 ♻ ⓘ

Services: 🔌🅾️🔋⚡

Within 3 miles: ♿🏌️🎯🎣◎🛒🛍️⛵

Notes: Dogs must be kept on leads. Shop & café adjacent, supermarket at end of road.

AA Pubs & Restaurants nearby: Hotel du Vin & Bistro Harrogate, HARROGATE, HG1 1LB, 01423 856800

Studley Hotel, HARROGATE, HG1 2SE, 01423 560425

The Fat Badger, HARROGATE, HG2 0NF, 01423 505681

Shaws Trailer Park
►►69%

tel: 01423 884432 **Knaresborough Rd HG2 7NE**
dir: On A59 1m from town centre. 0.5m SW of Starbeck railway crossing.
grid ref: SE325557

A long-established site just a mile from the centre of Harrogate. The all-weather pitches are arranged around a carefully kept grass area, and the toilets are basic but functional and clean. The entrance is on the bus route to Harrogate. 11 acre site. 60 touring pitches. 29 hardstandings. Caravan pitches. Motorhome pitches. Tent pitches. 146 statics.

Open: all year **Last arrival:** 20.00hrs **Last departure:** 14.00hrs

Pitches: * 🚐 £18-£20 🚐 £18-£20 ⛺

Facilities: 🚿🚰☉♿🏍

Services: 🔌🅾️🔒

Within 3 miles: ♿🏌️🎯🎣🛒🛍️

Notes: Adults only. 🐕 Dogs must be kept on leads.

AA Pubs & Restaurants nearby: The General Tarleton Inn, KNARESBOROUGH, HG5 0PZ, 01423 340284

| **HAWES** | Map 18 SD88 |

Places to visit
Dales Countryside Museum & National Park Centre, HAWES, DL8 3NT, 01969 666210 www.dalescountrysidemuseum.org.uk

Bainbridge Ings Caravan & Camping Site
►►80%

tel: 01969 667354 **DL8 3NU**
email: janet@bainbridge-ings.co.uk
dir: From Bainbridge towards Hawes on A684, left at Gayle sign, site 300yds on left.
grid ref: SD879895

A quiet, well-organised site in open countryside close to Hawes in the heart of Upper Wensleydale, popular with ramblers. Pitches are sited around the perimeter of several fields, each bounded by traditional stone walls. 5 acre site. 70 touring pitches. 8 hardstandings. Caravan pitches. Motorhome pitches. Tent pitches. 15 statics.

Open: Apr-Sep **Last arrival:** 20.00hrs **Last departure:** noon

Pitches: * 🚐 fr £19 🚐 fr £19 ⛺ fr £16

Facilities: 🏍☉🎣☀️📶♻️🏍

Services: 🔌🅾️🔒🚿🔋⚡

Within 3 miles: 🎣🛒🛍️

Notes: 🐕 No noise after 23.00hrs. Dogs must be kept on leads.

| **HELMSLEY** | Map 19 SE68 |

Places to visit
Duncombe Park, HELMSLEY, YO62 5EB, 01439 778625 www.duncombepark.com

Helmsley Castle, HELMSLEY, YO62 5AB, 01439 770442 www.english-heritage.org.uk/daysout/properties/helmsley-castle

Great for kids: Flamingo Land Resort, KIRBY MISPERTON, YO17 6UX, 01653 668287 www.flamingoland.co.uk

PREMIER PARK

Golden Square Caravan & Camping Park
►►►►88%

tel: 01439 788269 **Oswaldkirk YO62 5YQ**
email: reception@goldensquarecaravanpark.com
web: www.goldensquarecaravanpark.com
dir: From York take B1363 to Oswaldkirk. Left onto B1257, 2nd left onto unclassified road signed Ampleforth, site 0.5m on right. Or A19 from Thirsk towards York. Left, follow 'Caravan Route avoiding Sutton Bank' signs, through Ampleforth to site in 1m.
grid ref: SE604797

An excellent, popular and spacious site with very good facilities. This friendly, immaculately maintained park is set in a quiet rural situation with lovely views over the North York Moors. Terraced on three levels and surrounded by mature trees, it caters particularly for families, with excellent play areas and space for ball games. Country walks and mountain bike trails start here and an attractive holiday home area is also available. Please note that caravans are prohibited on the A170 at Sutton Bank between Thirsk and Helmsley. 12 acre site. 129 touring pitches. 10 hardstandings. 50 seasonal pitches. Caravan pitches. Motorhome pitches. Tent pitches. 21 statics.

Open: Mar-Oct **Last arrival:** 21.00hrs **Last departure:** noon

Pitches: 🚐 🚐 ⛺

Leisure: 🎱☉🏓🎣🎿

Facilities: 🚿🏍📸☉🎣☀️♿🛒🍴🚽📶🔋♻️🏍

Services: 🔌🅾️🔒🚿🚽🔋⚡

Within 3 miles: ♿🎯🎣◎🛒🛍️⛵

Notes: No skateboards or fires. Dogs must be kept on leads. Microwave available.

AA Pubs & Restaurants nearby: The Star Inn, HAROME, YO62 5JE, 01439 770397

Feversham Arms Hotel & Verbena Spa, HELMSLEY, YO62 5AG, 01439 770766

PITCHES: 🚐 Caravans 🚐 Motorhomes ⛺ Tents 🏕 Glamping accommodation **SERVICES:** 🔌 Electric hook up 🅾️ Launderette 🍺 Licensed bar 🔒 Calor Gas 🛢 Camping Gaz 🚽 Toilet fluid 🍴 Café/Restaurant 🍟 Fast Food/Takeaway 🔋 Battery charging 🚼 Baby care ⚡ Motorvan service point
ABBREVIATIONS: BHs – bank holidays Etr – Easter Spring BH – Spring Bank Holiday fr – from hrs – hours m – mile mdnt – midnight rdbt – roundabout rs – restricted service wk – week wknd – weekend x-roads – crossroads 🚫 No credit or debit cards 🚫 No dogs

HELMSLEY *continued*

Foxholme Caravan Park
►►► 81%

tel: 01439 771904 & 772336 **Harome YO62 5JG**
email: reservations@riccalvalecottages.co.uk
dir: *A170 from Helmsley towards Scarborough, right signed Harome, left at church, through village, follow signs.* **grid ref:** *SE658828*

A quiet park set in secluded wooded countryside, with well-shaded pitches in individual clearings divided by mature trees, although many were felled to open up the park and allow more sunlight to stream through. The facilities are well maintained, and the site is ideal as a touring base or a place to relax. Please note that caravans are prohibited on the A170 at Sutton Bank between Thirsk and Helmsley. 6 acre site. 60 touring pitches. 30 seasonal pitches. Caravan pitches. Motorhome pitches. Tent pitches.

Open: Etr-Oct **Last arrival:** 23.00hrs **Last departure:** noon

Pitches: ⊞ £20 ⊞ £20 ▲ £20

Facilities: ⇔ ⋔ P̄ ⊙ ⍟ ☆ 👶 🐕 ⓘ

Services: 🔧 🔄 🛢 🧺 T 🔌 ⛟

Within 3 miles: 🎣 🏕 🛍 🔄 ♲

Notes: Adults only. 🐕 Dogs must be kept on leads.

AA Pubs & Restaurants nearby: The Star Inn, HAROME, YO62 5JE, 01439 770397

Feversham Arms Hotel & Verbena Spa, HELMSLEY, YO62 5AG, 01439 770766

HIGH BENTHAM   **Map 18 SD66**

Places to visit

Great for kids: Yorkshire Dales Falconry & Wildlife Conservation Centre, SETTLE, LA2 8AS, 01729 822832 www.falconryandwildlife.co.uk

PREMIER PARK

Riverside Caravan Park
►►►►► 90%

tel: 015242 61272 **LA2 7FJ**
email: info@riversidecaravanpark.co.uk
dir: *M6 junct 34, A683 towards Kirkby Lonsdale, right onto B6480 signed Bentham, Site signed from High Bentham town centre.* **grid ref:** *SD665688*

A well-managed riverside park developed to a high standard, with level grass pitches set in avenues separated by trees, and there are excellent facilities for children, who are made to feel as important as the adults. It has an excellent, modern amenity block, including a family bathroom, and a well-stocked shop, laundry and information room. The superb games room and adventure playground are hugely popular, and the market town of High Bentham is close by. Please note that this site does not accept tents. Bentham Golf Club (within one mile) is also under same ownership with facilities available for Riverside customers. 12 acre site. 61 touring pitches. 27 hardstandings. 50 seasonal pitches. Caravan pitches. Motorhome pitches. 206 statics.

Open: Mar-2 Jan **Last arrival:** 20.00hrs **Last departure:** noon

Pitches: * ⊞ £21.75-£27.75 ⊞ £21.75-£27.75

Leisure: ⚠ 🎣 ✎

Facilities: ⋔ P̄ ⊙ ⍟ 👶 🛍 🐕 WiFi 🖥 ♲ ⓘ

Services: 🔧 🔄 🛢 🧺 T 🔌 ⛟

Within 3 miles: 🎣 ✎ 🛍 🔄 ♲

Notes: Dogs must be kept on leads. Chargeable permits for private fishing, discounted green fees at Bentham Golf Club.

AA Pubs & Restaurants nearby: The Traddock, AUSTWICK, LA2 8BY, 01524 251224

Lowther Hill Caravan Park
► 83%

tel: 015242 61657 & 07985 478750 **LA2 7AN**
dir: *A65 at Clapham onto B6480 signed Bentham. 3m to site on right. Or from M6 junct 34, A643 to Kirkby Lonsdale. In 6m turn right onto B6480 to Bentham. 9m, site on left between High Bentham & Clapham.* **grid ref:** *SD696695*

A simple site with stunning panoramic views from every pitch. Peace reigns on this little park, though the tourist villages of Ingleton, Clapham and Settle are not far away. All pitches have electricity, and there is a heated toilet/washroom and dishwashing facilities. 1 acre site. 9 touring pitches. 4 hardstandings. 7 seasonal pitches. Caravan pitches. Motorhome pitches. Tent pitches.

Open: all year **Last arrival:** 21.00hrs **Last departure:** 14.00hrs

Pitches: * ⊞ fr £16.50 ⊞ fr £16.50 ▲ £10

Facilities: ⋔ 👶 🐕 ♲   **Services:** 🔧

Within 3 miles: 🎣 ✎ 🛍 🔄

Notes: 🐕 Payment on arrival, no noise after mdnt. Dogs must be kept on leads.

AA Pubs & Restaurants nearby: The Traddock, AUSTWICK, LA2 8BY, 01524 251224

LEISURE: 🏊 Indoor pool ⛱ Outdoor pool ⚠ Children's playground 👋 Kid's club 🎾 Tennis court 🎯 Games room ⛳ Golf course ⛵ Boat hire 🚲 Cycle hire 🎬 Cinema 🎭 Entertainment 🎣 Fishing ◎ Mini golf ⛳ Pitch n putt 🏊 Watersports 🏋 Gym 🏉 Sports field ♻ Stables **FACILITIES:** ⇔ Bath ⋔ Shower P̄ Private washing cubicles ⊙ Electric shaver ⍟ Hairdryer ☆ Ice Packs 👶 Disabled facilities 🛍 Shop on site 🚚 Mobile shop 🍖 BBQ area ⛰ Picnic area WiFi Wi-fi 🖥 Internet access ♲ Recycling ⓘ Tourist info 🐕 Dog exercise area 🚗 Car hire can be arranged

HUTTON-LE-HOLE
Map 19 SE79

Places to visit

Nunnington Hall, NUNNINGTON, YO62 5UY, 01439 748283
www.nationaltrust.org.uk/nunnington-hall

Rievaulx Abbey, RIEVAULX, 01439 798228
www.english-heritage.org.uk/daysout/properties/rievaulx-abbey

Great for kids: Pickering Castle, PICKERING, YO18 7AX, 01751 474989
www.english-heritage.org.uk/daysout/properties/pickering-castle

---

Hutton-le-Hole Caravan Park
▶▶▶▶ 81%

tel: 01751 417261 **Westfield Lodge YO62 6UG**
email: huttonleholecaravanpark@hotmail.com
dir: *From A170 at Keldholme follow Hutton-le-Hole signs. Approx 2m, over cattle grid, left in 500yds into Park Drive, site signed.* **grid ref:** *SE705895*

A small, high quality park on a working farm in the North York Moors National Park. The purpose-built toilet block offers en suite family rooms, and there is a choice of hardstanding or grass pitches within a well-tended area surrounded by hedges and shrubs. The village facilities are a 10-minute walk away. Please note that caravans are prohibited from the A170 at Sutton Bank between Thirsk and Helmsley. 5 acre site. 42 touring pitches. 4 hardstandings. Caravan pitches. Motorhome pitches. Tent pitches.

Open: Etr-Oct **Last arrival:** 21.00hrs **Last departure:** noon

Pitches: ⊞ fr £19 ⊞ fr £19 ▲ fr £16

Facilities: ⬥ 🅿 ⊙ ℱ ※ ⅄ ㅈ ⛺ 🚿 ⚙ 🛈

Services: 🔌 🏴 Ⓣ **Within 3 miles:** ⅃ ⊚ 🏪 ∪

Notes: Boot, bike & dog washing area, farm walks.

AA Pubs & Restaurants nearby: Blacksmiths Arms, LASTINGHAM, YO62 6TN, 01751 417247

KETTLEWELL
Map 18 SD97

Kettlewell Camping
NEW ▶▶▶▶ 78%

tel: 07930 379079 & 01756 761684 **Conistone Ln BD23 5RE**
email: info@kettlewellcamping.co.uk
dir: *From rdbt on A65 (N of Skipton) take B6265 signed Grassington. Through Threshfield (do not turn right for Grassington). Road becomes B6160. In Kettlewell, right into Middle Ln signed 'Church'. Right into Conistone Ln signed Scargill House.* **grid ref:** *SD971721*

Created from former farm fields, this superb camping site has stunning countryside views and is enclosed by superb stone walling; it has the benefit of being just a few minutes' walk from the heritage village with its craft shops, pubs, tea rooms and a village shop. A top-notch amenities block, fed by a bio-mass boiler, has underfloor heating and modern quality fixtures and fittings, and includes a family room with shower, toilet and washbasin. Free WiFi is available, and two fully-equipped glamping bell tents are also offered. Please note, there is no laundry at this site. 0.6 acre site. 44 touring pitches. Tent pitches.

Open: Etr-Oct half term **Last arrival:** 20.30hrs **Last departure:** 11.00hrs

Pitches: ▲ 🏕
Facilities: ⬥ 🅿 ⊙ ℱ ※ ⅄ ㅈ ⛺ ⚙ 🛈
Services: 🔌
Glamping: Bell tents 2, £75-£105 Min stay 2 nights Car by unit
Within 3 miles: ℱ 🏪 🛍 ∪
Notes: Dogs must be kept on leads.
AA Pubs & Restaurants nearby: The Kings Head, KETTLEWELL, BD23 5RD, 01756 761600

KIRKLINGTON
Map 16 SE38

Camp Kátur
▶▶▶▶ 76%

tel: 01845 202100 **The Camphill Estate DL8 2LS**
email: info@campkatur.com
dir: *A1(M) junct 50, A6055 towards Bedale. Left at 1st rdbt, 1st right to Kirklington. Through Kirklington, approx 1.5m to site on left.* **grid ref:** *SE311825*

Located within The Camp Hill Estate, a popular centre for equestrian pursuits, quad biking, orienteering and corporate team building, Camp Kátur is a unique glamping destination with geo domes, safari tents, bell tents, hobbit pods (small wooden cabins) and tipis set in meadowland or wooded areas that comprise a wide variety of indigenous and imported trees. All the glamping units are spaced well apart ensuring optimum privacy, and all have the benefit of fire pits, barbecues and outside seating areas. The safari tents and geo domes have en suite facilities and other units are serviced by a communal shower, toilet and wash basin facility. There is a great focus on upcycling materials here with fire pits created from washing machine drums and galvanised buckets wash basins to name just two ideas. There's a campers' kitchen, a barbecue pod seating 16 around a central cooking area, and a rustic outdoor area ideal for gatherings such as a wedding reception or an anniversary or birthday celebration. The eco spa has a sauna and hot tub fuelled by wood-burning stoves. 20 acre site.

Open: Apr-Oct **Last arrival:** 22.00hrs **Last departure:** 11.00hrs

Leisure: ⋀ 🌀 🔍 Spa
Facilities: ⬥ ※ ⅄ 🚿 ㅈ ⛺ 🔋 ⚙ 🛈
Services: 🍴 ⚡

Glamping: Bell tents 2, £60-£90 Changeover day Mon, Wed, Fri, Sun Min stay 2 nights (1 night on Sun) Safari tents 3, £100-£160 Changeover day Mon, Wed, Fri, Sun Min stay 2 nights (1 night on Sun) En suite Own kitchen Tipis 1, £60-£95 Changeover day Mon, Wed, Fri, Sun Min stay 2 nights (1 night on Sun)
Cabins 4, £35-£55 Changeover day Mon, Wed, Fri, Sun Min stay 2 nights (1 night Sun) Geo domes 2, £80-£120 Changeover day Mon, Wed, Fri, Sun Min stay 2 nights (1 night on Sun) En suite Own kitchen Wooden unidomes 2, £70-£100 Changeover day Mon, Wed, Fri, Sun Min stay 2 nights (1 night on Sun)

Within 3 miles: ⅃ ℱ ⊚ 🏪 ∪
Notes: PayPal accepted. No noise after 22.00hrs, groups permitted only with management permission. Dogs must be kept on leads.

PITCHES: ⊞ Caravans ⊞ Motorhomes ▲ Tents 🏕 Glamping accommodation **SERVICES:** 🔌 Electric hook up 🧺 Launderette 🍺 Licensed bar 🔥 Calor Gas 🔥 Camping Gaz Ⓣ Toilet fluid 🍴 Café/Restaurant 🍟 Fast Food/Takeaway 🔋 Battery charging 👶 Baby care ⛟ Motorvan service point
ABBREVIATIONS: BHs – bank holidays Etr – Easter Spring BH – Spring Bank Holiday fr – from hrs – hours m – mile mdnt – midnight rdbt – roundabout rs – restricted service wk – week wknd – weekend x-roads – crossroads 🚫 No credit or debit cards 🚫 No dogs

KNARESBOROUGH
Map 19 SE35

Places to visit

RHS Garden Harlow Carr, HARROGATE, HG3 1QB, 0845 265 8070 *(Calls cost 5p per minute plus your phone company's access charge)* www.rhs.org.uk/harlowcarr

Aldborough Roman Site, ALDBOROUGH, YO51 9ES, 01423 322768 www.english-heritage.org.uk/daysout/properties/aldborough-roman-site

Kingfisher Caravan Park
▶▶▶80%

tel: 01423 869411 **Low Moor Ln, Farnham HG5 9JB**
email: enquiries@kingfisher-caravanpark.co.uk
dir: *From Knaresborough take A6055. Left in 1m towards Farnham, follow signs for Kingfisher. Park entrance on left.* **grid ref:** *SE343603*

A large grassy site with open spaces set in a wooded area in rural countryside. Whilst Harrogate, Fountains Abbey and York are within easy reach, anglers will want to take advantage of on-site coarse and fly fishing lakes. The park has a separate flat tenting field with electric hook-ups available. 14 acre site. 35 touring pitches. 30 seasonal pitches. Caravan pitches. Motorhome pitches. Tent pitches. 80 statics.

Open: Mar-Oct **Last arrival:** 21.00hrs **Last departure:** 16.00hrs

Pitches: 🚐 🚌 Å

Leisure: ⚲ ✐

Facilities: 🌂 ⊙ 🅟 ☀ ♿ 🛁 🅂 🎴 🐕 ❶

Services: 🚐 🔲 🛢 ⊘

Within 3 miles: ↓ ☕ 🎣 ✐ 🅂 🔲 ♉

Notes: ⊗ No football. Dogs must be kept on leads.

AA Pubs & Restaurants nearby: The General Tarleton Inn, KNARESBOROUGH, HG5 0PZ, 01423 340284

MARKINGTON
Map 19 SE26

Places to visit

Fountains Abbey & Studley Royal, RIPON, HG4 3DY, 01765 608888 www.nationaltrust.org.uk/fountains-abbey

Newby Hall & Gardens, RIPON, HG4 5AE, 01423 322583 www.newbyhall.com

Great for kids: Brimham Rocks, BRIMHAM, HG3 4DW, 01423 780688 www.nationaltrust.org.uk

Yorkshire Hussar Inn Holiday Caravan Park
▶▶▶85%

tel: 01765 677327 & 677715 **High St HG3 3NR**
email: yorkshirehussar@yahoo.co.uk
dir: *From A61 between Harrogate & Ripon at Wormald Green follow Markington signs, 1m, left past Post Office into High Street. Site signed on left behind The Yorkshire Hussar Inn.* **grid ref:** *SE288650*

A pleasant, terraced site behind the village inn with well-kept grass that offers spacious pitches (hardstanding and electric hook-up pitches are available) and a few holiday statics for hire. Although the Yorkshire Hussar Inn does not provide food, there is a pub within walking distance that does. 5 acre site. 20 touring pitches. 10 hardstandings. 12 seasonal pitches. Caravan pitches. Motorhome pitches. Tent pitches. 73 statics.

Open: Mar-Oct **Last arrival:** 19.00hrs **Last departure:** noon

Pitches: 🚐 🚌 Å **Leisure:** ⚲

Facilities: 🌂 🅿 ⊙ ☀ ♿ 🅂 📶 🔲 ♻ ❶

Services: 🚐 🔲 🛢 🛢 ⊙ 🔲 Å **Within 3 miles:** 🅂 🔲 ♉

Notes: PayPal accepted. Dogs must be kept on leads. Paddling pool.

LEISURE: 🏊 Indoor pool 🏊 Outdoor pool ⚲ Children's playground 🧒 Kid's club 🎾 Tennis court 🎱 Games room ⛳ Golf course 🚣 Boat hire 🚴 Cycle hire 🎦 Cinema 🎵 Entertainment 🎣 Fishing ⊙ Mini golf ⛳ Pitch n putt 🏄 Watersports 🏋 Gym 🏟 Sports field ♉ Stables **FACILITIES:** 🛁 Bath 🚿 Shower 🅟 Private washing cubicles ⊙ Electric shaver 🅟 Hairdryer ☀ Ice Packs ♿ Disabled facilities 🅂 Shop on site 🚐 Mobile shop 🔥 BBQ area 🎴 Picnic area 📶 Wi-fi 🔲 Internet access ♻ Recycling ❶ Tourist info 🐕 Dog exercise area 🚗 Car hire can be arranged

MASHAM Map 19 SE28

Places to visit

Theakston Brewery & Visitor Centre, MASHAM, HG4 4YD, 01765 680000 www.theakstons.co.uk

Norton Conyers, RIPON, HG4 5EQ, 01765 640333 www.nortonconyers.org.uk

Great for kids: Lightwater Valley Theme Park, NORTH STAINLEY, HG4 3HT, 0871 720 0011 *(Calls cost 13p per minute plus your phone company's access charge)* www.lightwatervalley.co.uk

Old Station Holiday Park

🛖

►►►► 78%

tel: 01765 689569 **Old Station Yard, Low Burton HG4 4DF**
email: oldstation@tiscali.co.uk
dir: *From S: A1(M) junct 50, B6267, left in 8m; From N: A1(M) junct 51, A684 to Bedale, then B6268, 4m to site.* **grid ref:** *SE232812*

An interesting site at a former station that still retains a railway theme. The enthusiastic and caring family owners have created a park with high quality facilities. The reception and café are situated in a carefully restored wagon shed and here a range of meals using local produce is offered. The small town of Masham, with its Theakston and Black Sheep Breweries, is within easy walking distance of the park. BBQ log cabins (large and small) are available for hire. 3.75 acre site. 50 touring pitches. 12 hardstandings. 16 seasonal pitches. Caravan pitches. Motorhome pitches. Tent pitches.

Open: Mar-Nov **Last arrival:** 20.00hrs **Last departure:** 11.00hrs

Pitches: 🚐 🚌 ⛺ 🛖

Facilities: ☺ 🚿 ✲ ♿ [S] 🪑 [WiFi] 💻 ♻ ℹ

Services: 🔌 🧺 🛢 [T] 🍴 🔋 🍔 ⬇

Glamping: Cabins 8

Within 3 miles: ⛳ 🎣 [S] 🧺 🐎

Notes: No cars by tents. No cycling on site, no campfires. Dogs must be kept on leads.

AA Pubs & Restaurants nearby: The Black Sheep Brewery, MASHAM, HG4 4EN, 01765 680101

Vennell's, MASHAM, HG4 4DX, 01765 689000

NABURN Map 16 SE54

Places to visit

Clifford's Tower, YORK, YO1 9SA, 01904 646940 www.english-heritage.org.uk/daysout/properties/cliffords-tower-york

Fairfax House, YORK, YO1 9RN, 01904 655543 www.fairfaxhouse.co.uk

Naburn Lock Caravan Park

►►►► 90%

tel: 01904 728697 **YO19 4RU**
email: petercatherine@naburnlock.co.uk
dir: *From A64 (York Designer Outlet) take A19 N, left signed Naburn onto B1222, site on right 0.5m.* **grid ref:** *SE596446*

A family park where the enthusiastic owners are steadily improving its quality. The mainly grass pitches are arranged in small groups separated by mature hedges. The park is close to the River Ouse, and the river towpath provides excellent walking and cycling opportunities. The river bus to nearby York leaves from a jetty beside the park. 7 acre site. 100 touring pitches. 50 hardstandings. Caravan pitches. Motorhome pitches. Tent pitches.

Open: Mar-Nov **Last arrival:** 20.00hrs **Last departure:** 12.30hrs

Pitches: 🚐 🚌 ⛺

Leisure: 🎣

Facilities: 🛁 ☺ 🚿 ✲ ♿ [S] 🐕 [WiFi] 💻 ♻ ℹ

Services: 🔌 🧺 🛢 🔥 [T] 🔋 ⬇

Within 3 miles: ⛵ 🎣 [S] 🧺 🐎

Notes: Adults-only section available, quiet 23.00hrs-07.00hrs. Debit cards accepted (no credit cards). Dogs must be kept on leads. River fishing.

AA Pubs & Restaurants nearby: Lamb & Lion Inn, YORK, YO1 7EH, 01904 612078

Blue Bell, YORK, YO1 9TF, 01904 654904

Lysander Arms, YORK, YO30 5TZ, 01904 640845

NORTHALLERTON Map 19 SE39

Places to visit

Mount Grace Priory, OSMOTHERLEY, DL6 3JG, 01609 883494 www.english-heritage.org.uk/daysout/properties/mount-grace-priory

Theakston Brewery & Visitor Centre, MASHAM, HG4 4YD, 01765 680000 www.theakstons.co.uk

Great for kids: Thirsk Birds of Prey Centre, THIRSK, YO7 4EU, 01845 587522 www.falconrycentre.co.uk

Otterington Park

🛖 DAVID BELLAMY CONSERVATION AWARD GOLD

►►►► 84%

tel: 01609 780656 **Station Farm, South Otterington DL7 9JB**
email: info@otteringtonpark.com
dir: *From A168 midway between Northallerton & Thirsk onto unclassified road signed South Otterington. Site on right just before South Otterington.* **grid ref:** *SE378882*

A high quality park on a working farm with open vistas across the Vale of York. It enjoys a peaceful location with a lovely nature walk and on-site fishing, which is very popular. Young children will enjoy the play area. The toilet facilities are very good. The attractions of Northallerton and Thirsk are a few minutes' drive away. Five wooden camping pods are available for hire. 6 acre site. 62 touring pitches. 62 hardstandings. Caravan pitches. Motorhome pitches.

Open: Mar-Oct **Last arrival:** 21.00hrs **Last departure:** 13.00hrs

Pitches: 🚐 🚌 🛖

Leisure: ⚽

Facilities: ☺ 🚿 ✲ ♿ [S] 🪑 🐕 [WiFi] ♻ ℹ

Services: 🔌 🧺 🛢 [T] 🔋

Glamping: Wooden Pods 5

Within 3 miles: ⛳ 🚣 🎣 🎯 [S] 🧺

Notes: Dogs must be kept on leads.

PITCHES: 🚐 Caravans 🚌 Motorhomes ⛺ Tents 🛖 Glamping accommodation **SERVICES:** 🔌 Electric hook up 🧺 Launderette 🍷 Licensed bar 🛢 Calor Gas 🔥 Camping Gaz [T] Toilet fluid 🍴 Café/Restaurant 🍔 Fast Food/Takeaway 🔋 Battery charging 🍼 Baby care ⬇ Motorvan service point
ABBREVIATIONS: BHs – bank holidays Etr – Easter Spring BH – Spring Bank Holiday fr – from hrs – hours m – mile mdnt – midnight rdbt – roundabout rs – restricted service wk – week wknd – weekend x-roads – crossroads 💳 No credit or debit cards 🚫 No dogs

NORTH STAINLEY

Map 19 SE27

Places to visit

Norton Conyers, RIPON, HG4 5EQ, 01765 640333 www.nortonconyers.org.uk

Theakston Brewery & Visitor Centre, MASHAM, HG4 4YD, 01765 680000 www.theakstons.co.uk

Great for kids: Lightwater Valley Theme Park, NORTH STAINLEY, HG4 3HT, 0871 720 0011 *(Calls cost 13p per minute plus your phone company's access charge)* www.lightwatervalley.co.uk

Sleningford Watermill Caravan Camping Park

►►►► 84%

GOLD

tel: 01765 635201 **HG4 3HQ**

email: sleningfordwatermill@gmail.com **web:** www.sleningfordwatermill.co.uk

dir: *Follow site sign on A6108 between North Stanley & West Tanfield.* **grid ref:** *SE280783*

The old watermill and the River Ure make an attractive setting for this touring park which is laid out in two areas. Pitches are placed in meadowland and close to mature woodland, and the park has two enthusiastic managers. This is a popular place with canoeists and seasonal fly fishing is possible. 14 acre site. 135 touring pitches. 8 hardstandings. 49 seasonal pitches. Caravan pitches. Motorhome pitches. Tent pitches.

Open: Etr & Apr-Oct **Last arrival:** 21.00hrs **Last departure:** 12.30hrs

Pitches: 🚐 🚉 ▲

Leisure: ⚽ ✏

Facilities: 🏪 🅿 ☉ ⌁ ✳ ⛽ Ⓢ 🚿 ♻ ⓘ

Services: 🔌 🔲 🚰 🚿 🅣 🍽

Within 3 miles: ⌁ ✏ 🎣 Ⓢ 🔲

Notes: No noise after 23.00hrs. Dogs must be kept on leads. Newspapers can be ordered.

AA Pubs & Restaurants nearby: The Bruce Arms, WEST TANFIELD, HG4 5JJ, 01677 470325

The Black Sheep Brewery, MASHAM, HG4 4EN, 01765 680101

Vennell's, MASHAM, HG4 4DX, 01765 689000

OSMOTHERLEY

Map 19 SE49

Places to visit

Mount Grace Priory, OSMOTHERLEY, DL6 3JG, 01609 883494 www.english-heritage.org.uk/daysout/properties/mount-grace-priory

Gisborough Priory, GUISBOROUGH, TS14 6HG, 01287 633801 www.english-heritage.org.uk/daysout/properties/gisborough-priory

Great for kids: Thirsk Birds of Prey Centre, THIRSK, YO7 4EU, 01845 587522 www.falconrycentre.co.uk

REGIONAL WINNER – NORTH EAST ENGLAND AA CAMPSITE OF THE YEAR 2017

PREMIER PARK

Cote Ghyll Caravan & Camping Park

►►►►► 89%

tel: 01609 883425 **DL6 3AH**

email: hills@coteghyll.com **web:** www.coteghyll.com

dir: *Exit A19 (dual carriageway) at A684 (Northallerton junct). Follow signs to Osmotherley. Left in village centre. Site entrance 0.5m on right.* **grid ref:** *SE459979*

A quiet, peaceful site in a pleasant valley on the edge of moorland, close to the village. The park is divided into terraces bordered by woodland, and the extra well-appointed amenity block is a welcome addition to this attractive park. Mature trees, shrubs and an abundance of seasonal floral displays create a relaxing and peaceful atmosphere and the whole park is immaculately maintained. There are pubs and shops nearby and holiday statics for hire. 7 acre site. 77 touring pitches. 22 hardstandings. 25 seasonal pitches. Caravan pitches. Motorhome pitches. Tent pitches. 18 statics.

Open: Mar-Oct **Last arrival:** 20.00hrs **Last departure:** noon

Pitches: * 🚐 £19-£26.50 🚉 £19-£26.50 ▲ £16-£23.50

Leisure: ⚠

Facilities: 🛁 🏪 🅿 ☉ ⌁ ✳ ⛽ Ⓢ 🚿 WiFi 💻 ♻ ⓘ

Services: 🔌 🔲 🚰 🚿 🅣 🍽 🛒 ⛽

Within 3 miles: ⌁ ✏ Ⓢ 🔲 ♨

Notes: Quiet after 22.00hrs, no camp fires. Dogs must be kept on leads. Freshly baked breakfast produce.

AA Pubs & Restaurants nearby: The Golden Lion, OSMOTHERLEY, DL6 3AA, 01609 883526

LEISURE: 🏊 Indoor pool 🏊 Outdoor pool ⚠ Children's playground 👶 Kid's club 🎾 Tennis court 🎱 Games room ⛳ Golf course 🚣 Boat hire 🚴 Cycle hire 🎬 Cinema 🎵 Entertainment 🎣 Fishing ⛳ Mini golf ⛳ Pitch n putt 🏄 Watersports 💪 Gym ♻ Sports field ♨ Stables **FACILITIES:** 🛁 Bath 🚿 Shower 🅿 Private washing cubicles ⊙ Electric shaver ⌁ Hairdryer ✳ Ice Packs ⛽ Disabled facilities Ⓢ Shop on site 📷 Mobile shop 🍖 BBQ area 🪑 Picnic area WiFi Wi-fi 💻 Internet access ♻ Recycling ⓘ Tourist info 🐕 Dog exercise area 🚗 Car hire can be arranged

PICKERING
Map 19 SE78

Places to visit

Pickering Castle, PICKERING, YO18 7AX, 01751 474989
www.english-heritage.org.uk/daysout/properties/pickering-castle

North Yorkshire Moors Railway, PICKERING, YO18 7AJ, 01751 472508
www.nymr.co.uk

Great for kids: Flamingo Land Resort, KIRBY MISPERTON, YO17 6UX,
01653 668287 www.flamingoland.co.uk

Wayside Holiday Park
►►►►78%

tel: 01751 472608 & 07940 938517 **Wrelton YO18 8PG**
email: wrelton@waysideholidaypark.co.uk
dir: 2.5m W of Pickering exit A170, follow signs at Wrelton. **grid ref:** SE764859

Located in the village of Wrelton, this well-maintained seasonal touring and holiday
home park is divided into small paddocks by mature hedging. The amenity block
has smart, modern facilities. The village pub and restaurant are within a few
minutes' walk of the park. Please note that this site has seasonal pitches only –
caravans, motorhomes and tents are not accepted. 20 acre site. 40 seasonal
pitches. 152 statics.

Open: Mar-Oct **Facilities:** ⊙ ℙ ♿ ♨ **🄯**
Services: 🔌🅟 **Within 3 miles:** ≛ 🎠 ℙ 🌭🛒 ∪

Notes: 🐕 Dogs must be kept on leads.

AA Pubs & Restaurants nearby: Fox & Hounds Country Inn, PICKERING, YO62 6SQ,
01751 431577

The White Swan Inn, PICKERING, YO18 7AA, 01751 472288

The Fox & Rabbit Inn, PICKERING, YO18 7NQ, 01751 460213

POCKLINGTON
Map 17 SE84

Places to visit

Burnby Hall Gardens & Museum, POCKLINGTON, YO42 2QF, 01759 307125
www.burnbyhallgardens.com

South Lea Caravan Park
NEW ►►►►84%

tel: 01759 303467 **The Balk YO42 2NX**
email: south.lea@btinternet.com
dir: From A1079 (York to Hull road) between Barmby Moor & Hayton follow Pocklington
(B1247) & brown tourist sign. Site 400yds on left. **grid ref:** SE808469

Located just off the main York road, South Lea Caravan Park is a tranquil, tidy and
level site – its entrance opens up onto 15 secluded acres. The five touring areas –
Sycamore, Birch, Ash, Oak and Willow – are serviced by a very well equipped and
spotlessly clean facilities block surrounded by colourful flower troughs; the
landscaping across the park is beautifully manicured. There's also a dog shower,
lush grass tent pitches, a football field and playground, good local walks, and a
bus service to local towns that stops at the front gate. 15 acre site. 70 touring
pitches. Caravan pitches. Motorhome pitches. Tent pitches. 27 statics.

Open: Mar-Oct **Last arrival:** 20.00hrs **Last departure:** 16.00hrs
Pitches: 🚐 £17-£24 🚍 £17-£24 ▲ £17-£24

Facilities: ⌐ ⊙ ℙ ✳ ♨ ♿ **🄯**
Services: 🔌 ♨ 🗑

Within 3 miles: ♨ ⚓ 🎠 ♨ 🛒 🐕 ∪

Notes: 🐕 Speed limit 5mph, no noise after 22.30hrs, no kites or drones, children must
be accompanied in toilet block. Dogs must be kept on leads.

RICHMOND
Map 19 NZ10

Places to visit

The Green Howards Museum, RICHMOND, DL10 4QN, 01748 826561
www.greenhowards.org.uk

Kiplin Hall, RICHMOND, DL10 6AT, 01748 818178 www.kiplinhall.co.uk

Great for kids: Richmond Castle, RICHMOND, DL10 4QW, 01748 822493
www.english-heritage.org.uk/daysout/properties/richmond-castle

Brompton Caravan Park
►►►►87%

tel: 01748 824629 **Brompton-on-Swale DL10 7EZ**
email: brompton.caravanpark@btconnect.com **web:** www.bromptoncaravanpark.co.uk
dir: Exit A1 signed Catterick. B6271 to Brompton-on-Swale, site 1m on left.
grid ref: NZ199002

An attractive and well-managed family park where pitches have an open outlook
across the River Swale. There is a good children's playground, an excellent family
recreation room, a takeaway food service, and fishing is available on the river. Three
river view camping pods and holiday apartments can also be hired. 14 acre site.
177 touring pitches. 25 hardstandings. 138 seasonal pitches. Caravan pitches.
Motorhome pitches. Tent pitches. 22 statics.

Open: mid Mar-Oct **Last arrival:** 21.00hrs **Last departure:** noon

Pitches: 🚐 🚍 ▲ 🏕 **Leisure:** 🎠 🎣 ℙ
Facilities: ⌐ ⊙ ℙ ✳ ♿ 🗑 ♨ ♨ **🄯** **Services:** 🔌 🗑 🅿 ♨ 🅣 🍴 ⚕
Glamping: **Wooden Pods** 3, £40-£150 Min stay 2 nights at wknds (3 nights on BHs)
Car by unit

Within 3 miles: ♨ ⚓ 🎠 ♨ 🛒 🐕 ∪

Notes: No group bookings. No motor, electric cars or scooters, no gazebos, no open fires
or woodburners, no electricity available for tents, quiet after mdnt. Dogs must be kept on
leads.

AA Pubs & Restaurants nearby: The Frenchgate Restaurant and Hotel, RICHMOND,
DL10 7AE, 01748 822087

PITCHES: 🚐 Caravans 🚍 Motorhomes ▲ Tents 🏕 Glamping accommodation SERVICES: 🔌 Electric hook up 🗑 Launderette 🍺 Licensed bar
🛢 Calor Gas 🗲 Camping Gaz 🅣 Toilet fluid 🍴 Café/Restaurant 🍟 Fast Food/Takeaway ⚡ Battery charging 👶 Baby care ⚕ Motorvan service point
ABBREVIATIONS: BHs – bank holidays Etr – Easter Spring BH – Spring Bank Holiday fr – from hrs – hours m – mile mdnt – midnight
rdbt – roundabout rs – restricted service wk – week wknd – weekend x-roads – crossroads 🚫 No credit or debit cards 🚫 No dogs

RIPON
Map 19 SE37

See also North Stainley

Places to visit

Fountains Abbey & Studley Royal, RIPON, HG4 3DY, 01765 608888
www.nationaltrust.org.uk/fountains-abbey

Norton Conyers, RIPON, HG4 5EQ, 01765 640333 www.nortonconyers.org.uk

Great for kids: Thirsk Birds of Prey Centre, THIRSK, YO7 4EU, 01845 587522
www.falconrycentre.co.uk

PREMIER PARK

Riverside Meadows Country Caravan Park
▶▶▶▶▶ 76%

tel: 01765 602964 **Ure Bank Top HG4 1JD**
email: info@flowerofmay.com **web:** www.flowerofmay.com
dir: From A61 rdbt (N of bridge) in Ripon follow A6108 Leyburn & Masham signs. At
next rdbt, 2nd exit into Ure Bank. Road becomes Ure Bank Top. Site at end of road.
grid ref: SE317726

This pleasant, well-maintained site stands on high ground overlooking the River
Ure, one mile from the town centre. The site has an excellent club with family
room and quiet lounge. There is no access to the river from the site. 28 acre site.
80 touring pitches. 40 hardstandings. 40 seasonal pitches. Caravan pitches.
Motorhome pitches. Tent pitches. 269 statics.

Open: Etr-Oct (rs Early & late season bar open wknds only) **Last arrival:** dusk
Last departure: noon

Pitches: * ⊡ £22-£28 ⊡ £22-£28 Å £22-£28

Leisure: ⚲ ⚲ ♫

Facilities: ⚡ ℙ ⊙ ℱ ✳ ⚑ ⑤ ⚘ ⊞ ▥ ☁ ❂ ❼

Services: ⊡ ⑤ ⚏ ▮ ⌀ ⊤ ⚒

Within 3 miles: ↨ ⚲ ⒣ ℱ ⚲ ⑤ ⑤ ∪

Notes: No noise after mdnt, dogs accepted by prior arrangement only. Dogs must be
kept on leads.

AA Pubs & Restaurants nearby: The Royal Oak, RIPON, HG4 1PB, 01765 602284

See advert on page 337

ROBIN HOOD'S BAY

See also Whitby

Places to visit

Whitby Abbey, WHITBY, YO22 4JT, 01947 603568
www.english-heritage.org.uk/daysout/properties/whitby-abbey

Scarborough Castle, SCARBOROUGH, YO11 1HY, 01723 372451
www.english-heritage.org.uk/daysout/properties/scarborough-castle

Great for kids: Scarborough Sea Life Sanctuary, SCARBOROUGH, YO12 6RP,
01723 373414 www.sealife.co.uk

ROBIN HOOD'S BAY
Map 19 NZ90

Grouse Hill Caravan Park
▶▶▶▶ 90%

tel: 01947 880543 & 880560 **Flask Bungalow Farm, Fylingdales YO22 4QH**
email: info@grousehill.co.uk **web:** www.grousehill.co.uk
dir: From A171 take loop road for Flask Inn (brown site sign). **grid ref:** NZ928002

A spacious family park on a south-facing slope with attractive, mostly level,
terraced pitches overlooking the North Yorkshire National Park. The site has quality,
solar-heated toilet blocks, a treatment plant to ensure excellent drinking water,
security barriers, play areas (including a woodland adventure play area), CCTV and
WiFi. Heated wooden wigwams are available for hire. Please note that there are no
hardstandings for tourers, only grass pitches, and this sloping site is not suitable
for disabled visitors (there are no disabled facilities). This is an ideal base for
walking and touring. 14 acre site. 175 touring pitches. 30 hardstandings. 20
seasonal pitches. Caravan pitches. Motorhome pitches. Tent pitches. 1 static.

Open: Mar-Oct (rs Etr-May shop & reception restricted) **Last arrival:** 20.30hrs
Last departure: noon

Pitches: ⊡ ⊡ Å ⚲

Leisure: ❂ **Facilities:** ⚘ ⚡ ℙ ⊙ ℱ ✳ ⚑ ⑤ ⚘ ▥ ☁ ❼

Services: ⊡ ⑤ ▮ ⌀ ⊤ ⚒ ⚑ **Within 3 miles:** ↨ ⑤ ⑤ ∪

Glamping: Wooden Wigwams 16, £30-£80 Min stay 2 nights at wknds, 3 nights at BHs
Car by unit 8 have en suite facilities

Notes: PayPal accepted. No noise after 22.30hrs. Dogs must be kept on leads.

AA Pubs & Restaurants nearby: The Magpie Café, WHITBY, YO21 3PU, 01947 602058

See advert on opposite page

LEISURE: ⚲ Indoor pool ⚲ Outdoor pool ⚲ Children's playground ⚲ Kid's club ⚲ Tennis court ⚲ Games room ⚲ Golf course ⚲ Boat hire ⚲ Cycle hire
⚲ Cinema ♫ Entertainment ℱ Fishing ⊙ Mini golf ⚑ Pitch n putt ⚲ Watersports ⚲ Gym ❂ Sports field ∪ Stables **FACILITIES:** ⚘ Bath ⚡ Shower
ℙ Private washing cubicles ⊙ Electric shaver ℱ Hairdryer ✳ Ice Packs ⑤ Disabled facilities ⑤ Shop on site ⚲ Mobile shop ▥ BBQ area ⚘ Picnic area
▥ Wi-fi ▤ Internet access ☁ Recycling ❼ Tourist info ⚑ Dog exercise area ⚒ Car hire can be arranged

Middlewood Farm Holiday Park

► ► ► ► 90%

tel: 01947 880414 **Middlewood Ln, Fylingthorpe YO22 4UF**
email: info@middlewoodfarm.com **web:** www.middlewoodfarm.com
dir: From A171 towards Robin Hood's Bay, into Fylingthorpe. Site signed from A171.
grid ref: NZ945045

A peaceful, friendly family park enjoying panoramic views of Robin Hood's Bay in a picturesque fishing village. The park has two toilet blocks with private facilities. The village pub is a five-minute walk away, and the beach can be reached via a path leading directly from the site, which is also accessible for wheelchair users. There are 14 wooden pods called Gypsy Cabins available for hire. 7 acre site. 100 touring pitches. 21 hardstandings. Caravan pitches. Motorhome pitches. Tent pitches. 30 statics.

Middlewood Farm Holiday Park

Open: 7 Feb-7 Jan (rs Nov-Etr no tents) **Last arrival:** 20.00hrs **Last departure:** 11.00hrs

Pitches: * 🚐 £19-£31 🚐 £19-£31 ▲ £14-£38 🏠 prices shown below

Leisure: 🎠

Facilities: 🍴 🐾 📮 ⊙ ℱ ❄ ♿ 🛏 🔔 Wifi ♻ ❶

Services: 🔌 🌀 🔋 ⊘ 🍴 📱 🛒 🚐 ♨

Glamping: Wooden Pods 14, £42-£57 Min stay 2 nights (longer minimum stays apply at peak times) Car by unit

Within 3 miles: ⌕ ⇞ ℘ 🎱 🛒 ∪

Notes: No radios or noise after 23.00hrs. No dangerous dog breeds accepted. Dogs must be kept on leads.

AA Pubs & Restaurants nearby: Laurel Inn, ROBIN HOOD'S BAY, YO22 4SE, 01947 880400
The Magpie Café, WHITBY, YO21 3PU, 01947 602058

See advert on page 352

PITCHES: 🚐 Caravans 🚐 Motorhomes ▲ Tents 🏠 Glamping accommodation **SERVICES:** 🔌 Electric hook up 🌀 Launderette 🍷 Licensed bar 🔋 Calor Gas ⊘ Camping Gaz 🔲 Toilet fluid 🍴 Café/Restaurant 🛒 Fast Food/Takeaway 📱 Battery charging 🚐 Baby care ♨ Motorvan service point **ABBREVIATIONS:** BHs – bank holidays Etr – Easter Spring BH – Spring Bank Holiday fr – from hrs – hours m – mile mdnt – midnight rdbt – roundabout rs – restricted service wk – week wknd – weekend x-roads – crossroads 🚫 No credit or debit cards 🚫 No dogs

ROSEDALE ABBEY
Map 19 SE79

Places to visit

Pickering Castle, PICKERING, YO18 7AX, 01751 474989
www.english-heritage.org.uk/daysout/properties/pickering-castle

North Yorkshire Moors Railway, PICKERING, YO18 7AJ, 01751 472508
www.nymr.co.uk

Great for kids: Flamingo Land Resort, KIRBY MISPERTON, YO17 6UX,
01653 668287 www.flamingoland.co.uk

Rosedale Caravan & Camping Park

► ► ► ► 88%

tel: 01751 417272 **YO18 8SA**
email: info@flowerofmay.com **web:** www.flowerofmay.com
dir: *From Pickering take A170 towards Sinnington for 2.25m. At Wrelton right onto
unclassified road signed Cropton & Rosedale, 7m. Site on left in village.*
grid ref: *SE725958*

Set in a sheltered valley in the centre of the North Yorkshire Moors National Park,
this popular park is close to the pretty village of Rosedale Abbey. It is divided into
separate areas for tents, tourers and statics. It has well-tended grounds, and
continues to be upgraded by the enthusiastic owners. Two toilet blocks offer private,
combined facilities. There are six camping pods (with or without electricity)
situated by the river. 10 acre site. 100 touring pitches. 20 seasonal pitches.
Caravan pitches. Motorhome pitches. Tent pitches. 35 statics.

Open: Mar-Oct **Last arrival:** dusk **Last departure:** noon

Pitches: * 🚐 £22-£28 🚐 £22-£28 ⛺ £22-£28 🏠 prices shown below

Leisure: 🅰

Facilities: 🐾 🄿ˢ ☉ ✳ ♿ 🔥 🖥 🚿 🕯 WiFi ❶

Services: 🔌 🔞 🛢 🚿 T 🛒 🚐

Glamping: Wooden Pods 6, £40 Min stay 2 nights (3 nights in school hols & BHs)
Car by unit

Within 3 miles: 👣 ☝ 🛒 🐎 ∪

Notes: No noise after mdnt, dogs accepted by prior arrangement only. Dogs must be kept
on leads. Freshly baked bread available.

AA Pubs & Restaurants nearby: Blacksmiths Arms, LASTINGHAM, YO62 6TN,
01751 417247

The New Inn, CROPTON, YO18 8HH, 01751 417330

See advert on page 337

SCARBOROUGH

See also Filey & Wykeham

Places to visit

Scarborough Castle, SCARBOROUGH, YO11 1HY, 01723 372451
www.english-heritage.org.uk/daysout/properties/scarborough-castle

Great for kids: Scarborough Sea Life Sanctuary, SCARBOROUGH, YO12 6RP,
01723 373414 www.sealife.co.uk

LEISURE: 🏊 Indoor pool 🏊 Outdoor pool 🅰 Children's playground 👦 Kid's club 🎾 Tennis court 🎱 Games room ⛳ Golf course ⛵ Boat hire 🚲 Cycle hire
🎬 Cinema 🎵 Entertainment 🎣 Fishing ◉ Mini golf ⛳ Pitch n putt 🏄 Watersports 🏋 Gym 🏟 Sports field ∪ Stables **FACILITIES:** 🛁 Bath 🚿 Shower
🄿ˢ Private washing cubicles ☉ Electric shaver 🦱 Hairdryer ✳ Ice Packs ♿ Disabled facilities 🔥 Shop on site 🏧 Mobile shop 🍖 BBQ area 🧺 Picnic area
WiFi Wi-fi 💻 Internet access ♻ Recycling ❶ Tourist info 🐕 Dog exercise area 🚗 Car hire can be arranged

SCARBOROUGH

Map 17 TA08

PREMIER PARK

Jacobs Mount Caravan Park
►►►►► 85%

tel: 01723 361178 **Jacobs Mount, Stepney Rd YO12 5NL**
email: jacobsmount@yahoo.co.uk **web:** www.jacobsmount.com
dir: *A170 towards Scarborough. Approx 2m after East Ayton turn right into site.*
grid ref: *TA021868*

An elevated family-run park surrounded by woodland and open countryside, yet only two miles from the beach. Touring pitches are terraced gravel stands with individual services. The Jacobs Tavern serves a wide range of appetising meals and snacks, and there is a separate well-equipped games room for teenagers. Four new pods were introduced for 2016 – two are family units that sleep a maximum of five. 18 acre site. 156 touring pitches. 131 hardstandings. Caravan pitches. Motorhome pitches. Tent pitches. 60 statics.

Open: Mar-Nov (rs Mar-May & Oct-Nov limited hours at shop & bar)
Last arrival: 22.00hrs **Last departure:** noon
Pitches: * ⊞ £13-£24 ⊞ £13-£24 ▲ £13-£24 ⋒ **Leisure:** ◣ ♫
Facilities: ⊙ ⌂ ⋇ ⅋ ⅋ ⅋ WiFi ▨ ♻ 𝒾 **Services:** ⊞ ⓢ ⍟ 🗎 ⊘ T ⍩ 🛒 ⌂
Glamping: Wooden Pods 4 **Within 3 miles:** ↓ ⋈ ⊞ ⌇ ◎ ⋈ ⓢⓢ ∪
Notes: Dogs must be kept on leads. Food preparation area.

Cayton Village Caravan Park
►►►► 90%

GOLD

tel: 01723 583171 **Mill Ln, Cayton Bay YO11 3NN**
email: info@caytontouring.co.uk
dir: *From Scarborough A64, B1261 signed Filey. In Cayton 2nd left after pedestrian crossing into Mill Ln. Site 150yds on left. Or from A165 from Scarborough towards Filey right at Cayton Bay rdbt into Mill Ln. Site 0.5m right. (NB it is advisable to follow these directions not Sat Nav).* **grid ref:** *TA063838*

A long established, quietly located holiday destination close to all the major coastal attractions. The immaculately maintained grounds provide excellent pitch density and many areas are hedge-screened to create privacy. The newest touring field, The Laurels, is equipped with fully serviced hardstanding pitches that include TV hook-up and free WiFi. 30 acre site. 310 touring pitches. 239 hardstandings. 180 seasonal pitches. Caravan pitches. Motorhome pitches. Tent pitches.

Open: Mar-Oct **Last arrival:** 18.00hrs **Last departure:** noon (late arrivals & departures available if pre-booked; charges may apply)

Pitches: * ⊞ £14-£36 ⊞ £16-£36 ▲ £14-£29 **Leisure:** ⋒ ☼
Facilities: ↤ ⌂ ⌿ ⊙ ⅋ ⋇ ⅋ ⓢ ⌢ ⊣ WiFi ♻ 𝒾
Services: ⊞ ⓢ 🗎 ⊘ T 🛒 **Within 3 miles:** ↓ ⋈ ⊞ ⌇ ◎ ⋈ ⓢⓢ
Notes: No noise after 23.00hrs, children must be supervised, no campfires. Dogs must be kept on leads. Dog walk, nature trail, maze.

AA Pubs & Restaurants nearby: Lanterna Ristorante, SCARBOROUGH, YO11 1HQ, 01723 363616

Scalby Close Park
►►►► 79%

tel: 01723 365908 **Burniston Rd YO13 0DA**
email: info@scalbyclosepark.co.uk
dir: *2m N of Scarborough on A615 (coast road), 1m from junct with A171.*
grid ref: *TA020925*

An attractive, well-landscaped park that is run by enthusiastic owners. The site has a shower block, laundry, fully serviced pitches and a motorhome service point. Just two miles from Scarborough, this makes an ideal base from which to explore both the coast and lovely countryside. 3 acre site. 42 touring pitches. 42 hardstandings. Caravan pitches. Motorhome pitches. 5 statics.

Open: Mar-Oct **Last arrival:** 22.00hrs **Last departure:** noon
Pitches: ⊞ ⊞ **Facilities:** ⊙ ⅋ ⋇ ⅋ ⓢ WiFi ▨
Services: ⊞ ⓢ ⊘ T 🛒 ⌂
Within 3 miles: ↓ ⋈ ⊞ ⌇ ⓢⓢ ∪
Notes: ⊗ Dogs must be kept on leads.
AA Pubs & Restaurants nearby: The Anvil Inn, SAWDON, YO13 9DY, 01723 859896
Lanterna Ristorante, SCARBOROUGH, YO11 1HQ, 01723 363616

Arosa Caravan & Camping Park
►►► 88%

tel: 01723 862166 & 07858 694077 **Ratten Row, Seamer YO12 4QB**
email: info@arosacamping.co.uk
dir: *A64 towards Scarborough onto B1261. On entering village 1st left at rdbt signed Seamer. From Pickering on A171 right at Seamer rdbt. Last right in village.*
grid ref: *TA014830*

A mature park in a secluded location, but with easy access to coastal attractions. Touring areas are hedge-screened to provide privacy, the toilet facilities are smart, and a well-stocked bar serving food is also available. Barbecues and hog roasts are a feature during the warmer months. 9 acre site. 118 touring pitches. 25 hardstandings. 40 seasonal pitches. Caravan pitches. Motorhome pitches. Tent pitches. 8 statics.

Open: Mar-4 Jan **Last arrival:** 21.00hrs **Last departure:** by arrangement
Pitches: ⊞ ⊞ ▲ **Leisure:** ⋒ ◣ ♫
Facilities: ⌂ ⊙ ⅋ ⋇ ⅋ ⓢ WiFi ▨ ♻ 𝒾
Services: ⊞ ⓢ ⍟ 🗎 ⊘ T ⍩ 🛒 ⌂
Within 3 miles: ↓ ⌇ ⓢⓢ ∪
Notes: No noise after 23.00hrs, no generators, no powered bikes or scooters. Dogs must be kept on leads.
AA Pubs & Restaurants nearby: Downe Arms Country Inn, SCARBOROUGH, YO13 9QB, 01723 862471

PITCHES: ⊞ Caravans ⊞ Motorhomes ▲ Tents ⋒ Glamping accommodation **SERVICES:** ⊞ Electric hook up ⓢ Launderette ⍟ Licensed bar
🗎 Calor Gas ⊘ Camping Gaz T Toilet fluid ⍩ Café/Restaurant 🛒 Fast Food/Takeaway ⌂ Battery charging ⌇ Baby care ⌂ Motorvan service point
ABBREVIATIONS: BHs – bank holidays Etr – Easter Spring BH – Spring Bank Holiday fr – from hrs – hours m – mile mdnt – midnight
rdbt – roundabout rs – restricted service wk – week wknd – weekend x-roads – crossroads ⊗ No credit or debit cards ⊗ No dogs

SCARBOROUGH *continued*

Killerby Old Hall
►►►80%

SILVER

tel: 01723 583799 **Killerby YO11 3TW**
email: killerbyhall@btconnect.com
dir: *From A165 between Scarborough & Filey, at Cayton Bay rdbt into Mill Lane towards Cayton. At T-junct left onto B1261 signed Filey. Site on left.* **grid ref:** *TA063829*

A small secluded park, well sheltered by mature trees and shrubs, located at the rear of the old hall. Use of the small indoor swimming pool is shared by visitors to the hall's holiday accommodation. There is a children's play area. 2 acre site. 20 touring pitches. 20 hardstandings. Caravan pitches. Motorhome pitches.

Open: 14 Feb-4 Jan **Last arrival:** 20.00hrs **Last departure:** noon

Pitches: * ⚐ £18.50-£26.50 ⚌ £18.50-£26.50

Leisure: 🏊 Ⓜ ☺ ◥

Facilities: �📷 ⊙ 🅿 🖵 🚿 WiFi ♻ 𝒊

Services: 🔌 🗑

Within 3 miles: 𝄞 ✐ ◎ 🎣 🛒 🗑 ∪

Notes: Dogs must be kept on leads.

AA Pubs & Restaurants nearby: The Anvil Inn, SAWDON, YO13 9DY, 01723 859896

Lanterna Ristorante, SCARBOROUGH, YO11 1HQ, 01723 363616

Scotch Corner Caravan Park
►►► 78%

tel: 01748 822530 & 07977 647722 **DL10 6NS**
email: marshallleisure@aol.com
dir: *From Scotch Corner junct of A1 & A66 take A6108 towards Richmond. 250mtrs, cross central reservation, return 200mtrs to site entrance.* **grid ref:** *NZ210054*

A well-maintained site with good facilities, ideally situated as a stopover, and an equally good location for touring. The Vintage Hotel, which serves food, can be accessed from the rear of the site. 7 acre site. 96 touring pitches. 4 hardstandings. Caravan pitches. Motorhome pitches. Tent pitches. 1 static.

Open: Etr or Apr-Oct **Last arrival:** 22.30hrs **Last departure:** noon

Pitches: * ⚐ fr £20 ⚌ fr £20 ▲ fr £14

Facilities: � 📷 ⊙ 🅿 ✳ 🛒 🗑 🖵 🚿 ♻ 𝒊

Services: 🔌 🗑 🍴 🛢 ⊘ T ⅃ 🍽 ⚒ ↓

Within 3 miles: 𝄞 🎿 ✐ 🛒 🗑 ∪

Notes: Dogs must be kept on leads. Recreation area for children, soft ball.

The Ranch Caravan Park
►►►► 86%

tel: 01757 638984 **Cliffe Common YO8 6PA**
email: contact@theranchcaravanpark.co.uk
dir: *Exit A63 at Cliffe signed Skipwith. Site 1m N on left.* **grid ref:** *SE664337*

A compact, sheltered park, set in seven acres in a peaceful area of Cliffe Common, that is run by enthusiastic and welcoming family owners. There is a smart wooden reception chalet close to the electronic gate at the park entrance. Of the 39 pitches, 14 are allocated to touring motorhomes and caravans and all are well spaced and neatly kept. Facilities include spotlessly clean toilets and showers, and Sean's Bar with its welcoming atmosphere. A wooden lodge development is part of the site. 7 acre site. 44 touring pitches. Caravan pitches. Motorhome pitches. Tent pitches.

Open: all year **Last arrival:** 21.00hrs **Last departure:** 13.00hrs

Pitches: * ⚐ £15-£25 ⚌ £18-£25 ▲

Notes: ⊗

LEISURE: 🏊 Indoor pool 🏊 Outdoor pool Ⓜ Children's playground 👋 Kid's club ♨ Tennis court ◥ Games room 𝄞 Golf course 🎿 Boat hire 🚲 Cycle hire Ⅱ Cinema ♫ Entertainment ✐ Fishing ◎ Mini golf ⛳ Pitch n putt 🏄 Watersports 🏋 Gym ♻ Sports field ∪ Stables **FACILITIES:** 🛁 Bath 🚿 Shower 🅿 Private washing cubicles ⊙ Electric shaver 𝄠 Hairdryer ✳ Ice Packs ♿ Disabled facilities 🛒 Shop on site 🏪 Mobile shop 🍴 BBQ area 🖵 Picnic area WiFi Wi-fi 🖥 Internet access ♻ Recycling 𝒊 Tourist info 🐕 Dog exercise area ⚒ Car hire can be arranged

SHERIFF HUTTON	Map 19 SE66

Places to visit

Kirkham Priory, KIRKHAM, YO60 7JS, 01653 618768
www.english-heritage.org.uk/daysout/properties/kirkham-priory

Sutton Park, SUTTON-ON-THE-FOREST, YO61 1DP, 01347 810249
www.statelyhome.co.uk

Great for kids: Castle Howard, MALTON, YO60 7DA, 01653 648333
www.castlehoward.co.uk

York Meadows Caravan Park
►►►►83%

tel: 01347 878508 & 01439 788269 **York Rd YO60 6QP**
email: reception@yorkmeadowscaravanpark.com
web: www.yorkmeadowscaravanpark.com
dir: *From York take A64 towards Scarborough. Left signed Flaxton & Sheriff Hutton. At West Lilling left signed Strensall. Site opposite junct.* **grid ref:** *SE644653*

Peacefully located in open countryside and surrounded by mature trees, shrubs and wildlife areas, this park provides all level pitches and a modern, well-equipped amenities block. Outdoor games such as draughts and snakes and ladders are available. 12 acre site. 45 touring pitches. 45 hardstandings. 10 seasonal pitches. Caravan pitches. Motorhome pitches. Tent pitches. 15 statics.

Open: Mar-Oct **Last arrival:** 21.00hrs **Last departure:** noon

Pitches: ⌂ ⌂ Å

Leisure: ⚲ ✧

Facilities: ⌂ ⌂ ⌂ ⊙ ⌂ ✲ ⌂ ⌂ ⌂ WiFi ✧ ⌂

Services: ⌂ ⌂ ⌂ ⌂ ⊤ ⌂

Within 3 miles: ⌂ ⌂ ⌂ ⌂ ⌂

Notes: No noise after 23.00hrs. Dogs must be kept on leads. Fresh bread available. Outdoor table tennis.

AA Pubs & Restaurants nearby: The Crown and Cushion, WELBURN, YO60 7DZ, 01653 618777

SLINGSBY	Map 19 SE67

Places to visit

Nunnington Hall, NUNNINGTON, YO62 5UY, 01439 748283
www.nationaltrust.org.uk/nunnington-hall

Castle Howard, MALTON, YO60 7DA, 01653 648333 www.castlehoward.co.uk

Robin Hood Caravan & Camping Park
►►►►88%

tel: 01653 628391 **Green Dyke Ln YO62 4AP**
email: info@robinhoodcaravanpark.co.uk **web:** www.robinhoodcaravanpark.co.uk
dir: *Access from B1257 (Malton to Helmsley road).* **grid ref:** *SE701748*

A pleasant, well-maintained, grassy park in a good location for touring North Yorkshire. Situated on the edge of the village of Slingsby, the park has hardstandings and electricity for every pitch; 12 super pitches are available. The site has a centrally heated toilet block, and there is a treasure trail and play area for children. 2 acre site. 32 touring pitches. 12 hardstandings. Caravan pitches. Motorhome pitches. Tent pitches. 34 statics.

Open: Mar-Oct **Last arrival:** 18.00hrs **Last departure:** noon

Pitches: ⌂ ⌂ Å **Facilities:** ⊙ ⌂ ✲ ⌂ ⌂ ⌂ WiFi ✧ ⌂

Services: ⌂ ⌂ ⌂ ⌂ ⊤ ⌂ ⌂ **Within 3 miles:** ⌂ ⌂ ⌂

Notes: No noise after 23.00hrs. Dogs must be kept on leads. Caravan hire, off licence.

AA Pubs & Restaurants nearby: The Malt Shovel, HOVINGHAM, YO62 4LF, 01653 628264

The Royal Oak Inn, NUNNINGTON, YO62 5US, 01439 748271

See advert on page 356

SNAINTON
Map 17 SE98

Places to visit

Scarborough Castle, SCARBOROUGH, YO11 1HY, 01723 372451
www.english-heritage.org.uk/daysout/properties/scarborough-castle

Pickering Castle, PICKERING, YO18 7AX, 01751 474989
www.english-heritage.org.uk/daysout/properties/pickering-castle

Great for kids: Scarborough Sea Life Sanctuary, SCARBOROUGH, YO12 6RP, 01723 373414 www.sealife.co.uk

PREMIER PARK

Jasmine Caravan Park
►►►►► 88%

tel: 01723 859240 **Cross Ln YO13 9BE**
email: enquiries@jasminepark.co.uk **web:** www.jasminepark.co.uk
dir: *Take A170 from Pickering towards Scarborough. In Snainton, right into Barker's Ln (follow brown site sign). 0.5m, at x-roads left into Cross Ln. Site on left.*
grid ref: *SE928813*

A peaceful and beautifully-presented park on the edge of a pretty village, and sheltered by high hedges. This picturesque park lies midway between Pickering and Scarborough on the southern edge of the North Yorkshire Moors. The toilet block with individual wash cubicles is maintained to a very high standard, and there is a licensed shop, a children's playground, and it is possible for larger units can be accommodated on hardstandings (please check when booking). Please note, there is no motorhome service point, but super pitches for motorhomes are available. 5 acre site. 68 touring pitches. 68 hardstandings. 42 seasonal pitches. Caravan pitches. Motorhome pitches. Tent pitches. 16 statics.

Open: Mar-Oct **Last arrival:** 20.00hrs **Last departure:** noon

Pitches: ⊞ ⇆ Å

Leisure: ⚽

Facilities: ℙⓈ ☉ ℙ ⚙ ♿ Ⓢ 🚰 WIFI 🖥 ♻ ✿ ❶

Services: 🚐 🗑 🛢 ⚙ Ⓣ

Within 3 miles: ↨ ℯ ◎ 🛢 🛢 ∪

Notes: No noise after 23.00hrs. Dogs must be kept on leads. Baby changing unit.

AA Pubs & Restaurants nearby: The Anvil Inn, SAWDON, YO13 9DY, 01723 859896
The New Inn, THORNTON LE DALE, YO18 7LF, 01751 474226

STAINFORTH — Map 18 SD86

Places to visit

Malham National Park Centre, MALHAM, BD23 4DA, 01729 833200 www.yorkshiredales.org.uk

Great for kids: Yorkshire Dales Falconry & Wildlife Conservation Centre, SETTLE, LA2 8AS, 01729 822832 www.falconryandwildlife.co.uk

Knight Stainforth Hall Caravan & Campsite

►►►► 91%

tel: 01729 822200 **BD24 0DP**
email: info@knightstainforth.co.uk
dir: *From W: A65 onto B6480 towards Settle, left before swimming pool signed Little Stainforth. From E: through Settle on B6480, over bridge, 1st right.* **grid ref:** *SD816672*

Located near Settle and the River Ribble in the Yorkshire Dales National Park, this well-maintained family site is sheltered by mature woodland. It is an ideal base for walking or touring the beautiful surrounding areas. The toilet block is appointed to a high standard and the lower part of the site benefits from the many trees that were planted a few years ago. A new building housing the reception and an excellent café and restaurant was completed for the 2016 season. There's also fishing on site. 6 acre site. 100 touring pitches. 30 hardstandings. Caravan pitches. Motorhome pitches. Tent pitches. 60 statics.

Open: Mar-Oct **Last arrival:** 22.00hrs **Last departure:** noon

Pitches: * 🚐 £17-£24 🚌 £17-£24 ⛺ £17-£24

Leisure: 🛝 ⚽ 🔍 🎣

Facilities: 🚿 [P] [⊙] 💨 ❄ ♿ [S] 🪑 🐕 [WiFi] 💻 ♻ ℹ

Services: 🔌 🧺 🍷 🛢 🔥 [T] 🍴 🔋 🚰

Within 3 miles: ⛳ 🎣 [S] 🧺

Notes: No groups of unaccompanied minors. Dogs must be kept on leads.

AA Pubs & Restaurants nearby: Black Horse Hotel, GIGGLESWICK, BD24 0BE, 01729 822506

The Traddock, AUSTWICK, LA2 8BY, 01524 251224

STILLINGFLEET — Map 16 SE54

Places to visit

Merchant Adventurers' Hall, YORK, YO1 9XD, 01904 654818 www.theyorkcompany.co.uk

Mansion House, YORK, YO1 9QN, 01904 613161 www.mansionhouseyork.com

Great for kids: National Railway Museum, YORK, YO26 4XJ, 01904 621261 www.nrm.org.uk

Home Farm Caravan & Camping

►► 75%

tel: 01904 728263 **Moreby YO19 6HN**
email: home_farm@hotmail.co.uk
dir: *6m from York on B1222, 1.5m N of Stillingfleet.* **grid ref:** *SE595427*

A traditional meadowland site on a working farm bordered by parkland on one side and the River Ouse on another. Facilities are in converted farm buildings, and the family owners extend a friendly welcome to tourers. An excellent site for relaxing and unwinding, yet only a short distance from the attractions of York. There are four log cabins for holiday hire. 5 acre site. 25 touring pitches. Caravan pitches. Motorhome pitches. Tent pitches.

Open: Feb-Dec **Last arrival:** 22.00hrs

Pitches: 🚐 🚌 ⛺

Facilities: 🚿 [⊙] 💨 ❄ 🐕 ♻ ℹ

Services: 🔌 🛢 🔥 [T] 🔋

Within 3 miles: ⛵ 🎣 🐎

Notes: 💳 Dogs must be kept on leads. Family washroom.

SUTTON-ON-THE-FOREST — Map 19 SE56

Places to visit

Sutton Park, SUTTON-ON-THE-FOREST, YO61 1DP, 01347 810249 www.statelyhome.co.uk

Treasurer's House, YORK, YO1 7JL, 01904 624247 www.nationaltrust.org.uk

Great for kids: Jorvik Viking Centre, YORK, YO1 9WT, 01904 615505 www.jorvik-viking-centre.com

PREMIER PARK

Goosewood Holiday Park

►►►►► 86%

tel: 01347 810829 **YO61 1ET**
email: enquiries@goosewood.co.uk **web:** www.flowerofmay.com
dir: *From A1237 take B1363. In 5m turn right. Right again in 0.5m, site on right.*
grid ref: *SE595636*

A relaxing and immaculately maintained park with its own lake and seasonal fishing. It is set in attractive woodland just six miles north of York. Mature shrubs and stunning seasonal floral displays at the entrance create an excellent first impression and the well-located toilet facilities are kept spotlessly clean. The generous patio pitches, providing optimum privacy, are randomly spaced throughout the site, and in addition to an excellent outdoor children's play area, you will find an indoor swimming pool, clubhouse, games room and bar and bistro. There are holiday homes for hire. 20 acre site. 100 touring pitches. 50 hardstandings. 50 seasonal pitches. Caravan pitches. Motorhome pitches. 45 statics.

Open: Mar-2 Jan (rs Low season - shop, bar & pool reduced hours) **Last arrival:** dusk **Last departure:** noon

Pitches: * 🚐 £22-£28 🚌 £22-£28

Leisure: 🏊 🛝 🔍 🎣

Facilities: 🚿 [P] [⊙] 💨 ❄ ♿ [S] 🪑 [WiFi] 💻 ♻ ℹ

Services: 🔌 🧺 🍷 🛢 🔥 [T] 🍴 🔋 👶 🚰

Within 3 miles: ⛳ [H] 🎣 [S] 🧺

Notes: No noise after mdnt, dogs accepted by prior arrangement only. Dogs must be kept on leads.

See advert on page 337

THIRSK
Map 19 SE48

Places to visit

Monk Park Farm Visitor Centre, THIRSK, YO7 2AG, 01845 597730
www.monkparkfarm.co.uk

Byland Abbey, COXWOLD, YO61 4BD, 01347 868614
www.english-heritage.org.uk/daysout/properties/byland-abbey

Great for kids: Thirsk Birds of Prey Centre, THIRSK, YO7 4EU, 01845 587522
www.falconrycentre.co.uk

Hillside Caravan Park
►►►► 89%

tel: 01845 537349 & 07711 643652 **Canvas Farm, Moor Rd, Knayton YO7 4BR**
email: info@hillsidecaravanpark.co.uk
dir: *From Thirsk take A19 N exit at Knayton sign. In 0.25m right (cross bridge over A19), through village. Site on left in approx 1.5m.* **grid ref:** *SE447889*

A high quality, spacious park with first-class facilities, set in open countryside. The striking sandstone amenity block houses the airy reception, shop and office, plus there's a kitchen and laundry, two excellent family rooms, a disabled room, a recreation room, two self-contained flats and two luxury camping pods for hire. This is an excellent base for walkers and for those wishing to explore the Thirsk area. Please note, the park does not accept tents. 9 acre site. 50 touring pitches. 50 hardstandings. Caravan pitches. Motorhome pitches.

Open: 4 Feb-4 Jan **Last arrival:** 21.00hrs **Last departure:** noon

Pitches: * 🚐 £23-£33 🚃 £23-£33 🏠 prices shown below

Leisure: 🎠 ✪

Facilities: ⛟ ➴ 𝖯 ⊙ 𝒫 ✳ ⅄ 🚻 🖐 ➶ WiFi 🖳 ♻ 𝒊

Services: 🚐 🔄 🛢 🚻 ⬆

Glamping: **Wooden Pods** 2, £40-£70 Min stay 2 nights at wknds En suite Own kitchen

Within 3 miles: 𝔏 🛢 ∪

Notes: Dogs must be kept on leads.

AA Pubs & Restaurants nearby: The Black Swan at Oldstead, OLDSTEAD, YO61 4BL, 01347 868387

Thirkleby Hall Caravan Park
►►► 75%

tel: 01845 501360 & 07799 641815 **Thirkleby YO7 3AR**
email: greenwood.parks@virgin.net **web:** www.greenwoodparks.com
dir: *3m S of Thirsk on A19. Turn left through arched gatehouse into site.*
grid ref: *SE472794*

A long-established site in the grounds of the old hall, with statics in wooded areas around a fishing lake and tourers based on slightly sloping grassy pitches. There is a quality amenities block and laundry. This well-screened park has superb views of the Hambledon Hills. 53 acre site. 50 touring pitches. 3 hardstandings. 20 seasonal pitches. Caravan pitches. Motorhome pitches. Tent pitches. 200 statics.

Open: Mar-Oct **Last arrival:** 17.30hrs **Last departure:** 14.30hrs

Pitches: 🚐 🚃 Å

Leisure: ✪

Facilities: ⊙ 𝒫 ✳ ⅄ 🚻 ➶ ♻ 𝒊

Services: 🚐 🔄 🍽 🛢 ⬆

Within 3 miles: 𝔏 🛢 𝒫 🛢 🔄

Notes: ⊗ No noise after 23.00hrs. Dogs must be kept on leads. Woodland walks.

AA Pubs & Restaurants nearby: The Black Swan at Oldstead, OLDSTEAD, YO61 4BL, 01347 868387

LEISURE: 🏊 Indoor pool 🏊 Outdoor pool 🎠 Children's playground 🖐 Kid's club 🎾 Tennis court 🎱 Games room ⛳ Golf course 🚣 Boat hire 🚲 Cycle hire 🎦 Cinema 🎵 Entertainment 🎣 Fishing ⊙ Mini golf ⚑ Pitch n putt 🏄 Watersports 🏋 Gym ✪ Sports field ∪ Stables **FACILITIES:** ⛟ Bath ➴ Shower 𝖯 Private washing cubicles ⊙ Electric shaver 𝒫 Hairdryer ✳ Ice Packs ⅄ Disabled facilities 🛒 Shop on site 🚚 Mobile shop 🍖 BBQ area 🪑 Picnic area WiFi Wi-fi 🖳 Internet access ♻ Recycling 𝒊 Tourist info 🐕 Dog exercise area 🚗 Car hire can be arranged

TOLLERTON Map 19 SE56

Places to visit

Beningbrough Hall, Gallery & Gardens, BENINGBROUGH, YO30 1DD, 01904 472027 www.nationaltrust.org.uk/beningbrough

Sutton Park, SUTTON-ON-THE-FOREST, YO61 1DP, 01347 810249 www.statelyhome.co.uk

Great for kids: Jorvik Viking Centre, YORK, YO1 9WT, 01904 615505 www.jorvik-viking-centre.com

Tollerton Holiday Park

►►►► 82%

tel: 01347 838313 **Station Rd YO61 1RD**
email: greenwood.parks@virgin.net **web:** www.greenwoodparks.com
dir: *From York take A19 towards Thirsk. At Cross Lanes left towards Tollerton. 1m to Chinese restaurant just before rail bridge. Site entrance through restaurant car park.*
grid ref: *SE513643*

Set in open countryside within a few minutes' walk of Tollerton and just a short drive from the Park & Ride for York, this is a small park. There's an amenities block of real quality, which includes a family bathroom and laundry. There is little disturbance from the East Coast mainline which passes nearby. 5 acre site. 50 touring pitches. 17 hardstandings. 25 seasonal pitches. Caravan pitches. Motorhome pitches. Tent pitches. 75 statics.

Open: Mar-Oct **Last arrival:** 20.00hrs **Last departure:** 15.00hrs

Pitches: 🚐 🚌 ⛺

Leisure: ⚽

Facilities: ⊙ 🚿 ✱ ♿ 🪑 🐕 ♻ [i]

Services: 🔌 🧺 🔥 🍴 🔋 🍔

Within 3 miles: ⛳ 🎣 [S] 🧺

Notes: 💳 No groups. Dogs must be kept on leads. Small fishing lake.

AA Pubs & Restaurants nearby: The Aldwark Arms, ALDWARK, YO61 1UB, 01347 838324

TOWTHORPE Map 19 SE65

Places to visit

Barley Hall, YORK, YO1 8AR, 01904 615505 www.barleyhall.co.uk

Great for kids: Jorvik Viking Centre, YORK, YO1 9WT, 01904 615505 www.jorvik-viking-centre.com

York Touring Caravan Site

►►►► 79%

tel: 01904 499275 **Greystones Farm, Towthorpe Moor Ln YO32 9ST**
email: info@yorkcaravansite.co.uk
dir: *From A64 follow Strensall & Haxby signs, site 1.5m on left.* **grid ref:** *SE648584*

This purpose-built golf complex and caravan park is situated just over five miles from York. There is a 9-hole golf course, crazy golf, driving range and golf shop with a coffee bar/café. The generously sized, level pitches are set within well-manicured grassland with a backdrop of trees and shrubs. 6 acre site. 44 touring pitches. 12 hardstandings. Caravan pitches. Motorhome pitches. Tent pitches.

Open: Mar-Oct **Last arrival:** 21.00hrs **Last departure:** noon

Pitches: 🚐 🚌 ⛺ **Leisure:** ⚽ ⛳ 🏌

Facilities: 🚿 [P] ⊙ 🚿 ✱ ♿ 🪑 🐕 [WiFi] ♻ [i] **Services:** 🔌 🧺 🔥 🍴 ⚓

Within 3 miles: ⛳ ◎ [S] 🧺

Notes: No noise after 23.00hrs, no commercial vehicles. Dogs must be kept on leads.

WEST KNAPTON Map 19 SE87

Places to visit

Pickering Castle, PICKERING, YO18 7AX, 01751 474989 www.english-heritage.org.uk/daysout/properties/pickering-castle

North Yorkshire Moors Railway, PICKERING, YO18 7AJ, 01751 472508 www.nymr.co.uk

Great for kids: Eden Camp Modern History Theme Museum, MALTON, YO17 6RT, 01653 697777 www.edencamp.co.uk

Wolds Way Caravan and Camping

►►►► 82%

tel: 01944 728463 & 728180 **West Farm YO17 8JE**
dir: *Signed between Rillington & West Heslerton on A64 (Malton to Scarborough road). Site 1.5m.* **grid ref:** *SE896743*

A park on a working farm in a peaceful, high position on the Yorkshire Wolds, with magnificent views over the Vale of Pickering. This is an excellent walking area, with the Wolds Way passing the entrance to the site. A pleasant one and a half mile path leads to a lavender farm, with its first-class coffee shop. 7.5 acre site. 70 touring pitches. 5 hardstandings. Caravan pitches. Motorhome pitches. Tent pitches.

Open: Mar-Oct **Last arrival:** 22.30hrs **Last departure:** 19.00hrs

Pitches: 🚐 🚌 ⛺

Facilities: ⊙ ✱ ♿ [S] 🪑 🐕 [WiFi] ♻ [i] **Services:** 🔌 🧺 🔥 [T] 🔋

Within 3 miles: 🎣 [S]

Notes: Free use of microwave, toaster & TV. Drinks machine, fridge & freezer.

AA Pubs & Restaurants nearby: The New Inn, THORNTON LE DALE, YO18 7LF, 01751 474226

WHITBY

Map 19 NZ81

See also Robin Hood's Bay

Places to visit

Whitby Abbey, WHITBY, YO22 4JT, 01947 603568
www.english-heritage.org.uk/daysout/properties/whitby-abbey

North Yorkshire Moors Railway, PICKERING, YO18 7AJ, 01751 472508
www.nymr.co.uk

Ladycross Plantation Caravan Park

92%

tel: 01947 895502 **Egton YO21 1UA**
email: enquiries@ladycrossplantation.co.uk **web:** www.ladycrossplantation.co.uk
dir: *From A171 (Whitby to Teesside road) onto unclassified road (site signed).*
grid ref: *NZ821080*

The unique forest setting creates an away-from-it-all feeling at this peaceful touring park set in 30 acres of woodland and run by enthusiastic owners. The pitches are sited in small groups in clearings around two smartly appointed amenity blocks which offer excellent facilities – underfloor heating, no-touch infra-red showers, cubicles, kitchen prep areas and laundry facilities. A 2016 development includes 26 hardstanding pitches and tarmac access roads. The site is well placed for visiting Whitby and exploring the North York Moors. Children will enjoy exploring the one-mile woodland and nature walks. Oak lodges are available for hire or sale. 30 acre site. 130 touring pitches. 77 hardstandings. 60 seasonal pitches. Caravan pitches. Motorhome pitches. Tent pitches.

Open: Mar-Nov **Last arrival:** 20.00hrs **Last departure:** noon

Pitches: 🚐 🚌 ⛺

Facilities: ⊙ 💨 ❄ ♿ [S] 🐕 [WiFi] ♻ ℹ

Services: 🔧 🧺 🔥 🍃 [T] 🚽 ⛽

Within 3 miles: ⛳ ⛵ 🎬 🎣 ◎ 🏄 [S]

Notes: No noise after 22.00hrs. Dogs must be kept on leads.

AA Pubs & Restaurants nearby: The Wheatsheaf Inn, EGTON, YO21 1TZ, 01947 895271

Horseshoe Hotel, EGTON BRIDGE, YO21 1XE, 01947 895245

The Magpie Café, WHITBY, YO21 3PU, 01947 602058

WYKEHAM

Map 17 SE98

Places to visit

Scarborough Castle, SCARBOROUGH, YO11 1HY, 01723 372451
www.english-heritage.org.uk/daysout/properties/scarborough-castle

Pickering Castle, PICKERING, YO18 7AX, 01751 474989
www.english-heritage.org.uk/daysout/properties/pickering-castle

Great for kids: Scarborough Sea Life Sanctuary, SCARBOROUGH, YO12 6RP, 01723 373414 www.sealife.co.uk

PREMIER PARK

St Helens Caravan Park

🛖

►►►►► 87%

tel: 01723 862771 **YO13 9QD**
email: caravans@wykeham.co.uk
dir: *On A170 in village, 150yds on left beyond Downe Arms Hotel towards Scarborough.*
grid ref: *SE967836*

Set on the edge of the North York Moors National Park, this delightfully landscaped park is immaculately maintained and thoughtfully laid out; the stunning floral displays around the park are impressive. There are top quality facilities and a high level of customer care can be expected. The site is divided into terraces with tree-screening that creates smaller areas including an adults' zone. There are 10 camping pods for hire (eight have electricity). A cycle route leads through to the surrounding Wykeham Estate and there is a short pathway to the adjoining Downe Arms Country Inn. 25 acre site. 250 touring pitches. 79 hardstandings. Caravan pitches. Motorhome pitches. Tent pitches.

Open: 16 Feb-15 Jan (rs Nov-Jan shop/laundry closed) **Last arrival:** 20.30hrs
Last departure: noon

Pitches: * 🚐 £18-£30.80 🚌 £18-£30.80 ⛺ £11.50-£23 🛖 prices shown below

Leisure: 🛝

Facilities: 🚿 [P] ⊙ 💨 ❄ ♿ [S] 🪑 🐕 [WiFi] 💻 ♻ ℹ

Services: 🔧 🧺 🔥 🍃 [T] 🍴 🚽 🥡 ⛽

Glamping: Wooden Pods 10, £16-£44 Min stay 2 nights Car by unit

Within 3 miles: ⛳ ⛵ 🎣 ◎ 🏄 [S] 🧺 🐴

Notes: No noise after 22.00hrs. Dogs must be kept on leads. Family & adult-only super pitches available, caravan storage.

AA Pubs & Restaurants nearby: Downe Arms Country Inn, SCARBOROUGH, YO13 9QB, 01723 862471

The New Inn, THORNTON LE DALE, YO18 7LF, 01751 474226

YORK
Map 16 SE65

See also Sheriff Hutton

Places to visit

York Minster, YORK, YO1 7HH, 01904 557200 www.yorkminster.org

National Railway Museum, YORK, YO26 4XJ, 01904 621261 www.nrm.org.uk

Rawcliffe Manor Caravan Park
▶▶▶▶ 79%

tel: 01904 640845 **Manor Ln, Shipton Rd YO30 5TZ**
email: christine@lysanderarms.co.uk
dir: *From rdbt junct of A1237 & A19, take A19 signed York, Clifton & Rawcliffe. 1st left into Manor Ln, follow brown camping signs.* grid ref: SE583550

A lovely little adults-only site tucked away behind the Lysander Arms and located only minutes from the centre of York. Each of the 13 generous-sized pitches is fully serviced with an individual chemical disposal point, and the central toilet block is very airy, modern and spotlessly clean. The grounds have been imaginatively landscaped. The pub offers good food and the York Park & Ride facility is a 10-minute walk away. 4.5 acre site. 13 touring pitches. 13 hardstandings. Caravan pitches. Motorhome pitches.

Open: all year **Last arrival:** 18.00hrs **Last departure:** 11.00hrs

Pitches: 🚐 🚐

Leisure: ⛳ 🏊 🎣 🎵 Spa

Facilities: 🌂 ⊙ ✳ ⚲ 🔥 WiFi ✿ 🄌

Services: 🔌 🔄 🍴 🔋 🍴 💷 🛒

Within 3 miles: 🏇 🎇 🌐 ⛳ 🎱 ∪

Notes: Adults only. No noise after 23.00hrs. Dogs must be kept on leads.

SOUTH YORKSHIRE

HATFIELD
Map 16 SE60

Places to visit

Doncaster Museum & Art Gallery, DONCASTER, DN1 2AE, 01302 734293 www.doncaster.gov.uk/museums

Hatfield Outdoor Activity Centre
▶▶ 73%

tel: 01302 841572 **Old Thorne Rd DN7 6EQ**
email: hatfield@dclt.co.uk
dir: *M180 junct 1, A18 towards Doncaster. Right to site.* grid ref: SE670100

Reached via a sweeping driveway, both the Activity Centre and campsite border a beautiful lake, the latter being set amongst mature trees with well-maintained grass pitches and a central toilet block. At the well-organised Activity Centre, campers can enjoy kayaking, sailing and windsurfing, learn to build a raft, or tackle the climbing wall. Buses for Doncaster stop at the entrance. Please note, there is no laundry. 11 acre site. 49 touring pitches. 1 hardstanding. Caravan pitches. Motorhome pitches. Tent pitches.

Open: Mar-Oct **Last arrival:** 16.30hrs **Last departure:** 11.00hrs

Pitches: 🚐 🚐 Å **Facilities:** ⊙ ⚲ 🔥 🄌 **Services:** 🔌

Within 3 miles: 🏇 🎇 🌐 ⛳ 🎱 🎲

Notes: Caravans or motorhomes are not accepted Sun night-Thu night. Dogs must be kept on leads.

WORSBROUGH
Map 16 SE30

Places to visit

Monk Bretton Priory, BARNSLEY, S71 5QD, 0370 333 1181 www.english-heritage.org.uk/daysout/properties/monk-bretton-priory

Millennium Gallery, SHEFFIELD, S1 2PP, 0114 278 2600 www.museums-sheffield.org.uk

Great for kids: Magna Science Adventure Centre, ROTHERHAM, S60 1DX, 01709 720002 www.visitmagna.co.uk

Greensprings Touring Park
▶▶▶ 75%

tel: 01226 288298 **Rockley Abbey Farm, Rockley Ln S75 3DS**
dir: *M1 junct 36, A61 to Barnsley. Left after 0.25m signed Pilley. Site 1m at bottom of hill.* grid ref: SE330020

A secluded and attractive farm site set amidst woods and farmland, with access to the river and several good local walks. There are two touring areas, one gently sloping. Although not far from the M1, there is almost no traffic noise, and this site is convenient for exploring the area's industrial heritage, as well as the Peak District. 4 acre site. 65 touring pitches. 30 hardstandings. 22 seasonal pitches. Caravan pitches. Motorhome pitches. Tent pitches.

Open: Apr-30 Oct **Last arrival:** 21.00hrs **Last departure:** noon

Pitches: * 🚐 fr £15 🚐 fr £15 Å fr £15 **Leisure:** ✿ **Facilities:** 🌂 ⊙ ✳ 🐾 🄌

Services: 🔌 🔋 **Within 3 miles:** 🏇 🎇 🌐 ⛳ 🎱 🎲 ∪

Notes: 🐕 Dogs must be kept on leads.

PITCHES: 🚐 Caravans 🚐 Motorhomes Å Tents 🏕 Glamping accommodation **SERVICES:** 🔌 Electric hook up 🔄 Launderette 🍺 Licensed bar 🔋 Calor Gas ⚗ Camping Gaz 🔳 Toilet fluid 🍴 Café/Restaurant 💷 Fast Food/Takeaway 🔋 Battery charging 🛒 Baby care 🛠 Motorvan service point **ABBREVIATIONS:** BHs – bank holidays Etr – Easter Spring BH – Spring Bank Holiday fr – from hrs – hours m – mile mdnt – midnight rdbt – roundabout rs – restricted service wk – week wknd – weekend x-roads – crossroads 🚫 No credit or debit cards 🚫 No dogs

WEST YORKSHIRE

BARDSEY — Map 16 SE34

Places to visit

Bramham Park, BRAMHAM, LS23 6ND, 01937 846000 www.bramhampark.co.uk

Thackray Medical Museum, LEEDS, LS9 7LN, 0113 244 4343 www.thackraymedicalmuseum.co.uk

Great for kids: Leeds Industrial Museum at Armley Mills, LEEDS, LS12 2QF, 0113 378 3173 www.leeds.gov.uk/armleymills

Glenfield Caravan Park

►►►► 83%

tel: 01937 574657 & 07761 710862 **Blackmoor Ln LS17 9DZ**
email: glenfieldcp@aol.com **web:** www.glenfieldcaravanpark.co.uk
dir: *3m from A1 junct 45. From A58 at Bardsey into Church Ln, past church, up hill. 0.5m, site on right.* **grid ref:** *SE351421*

A quiet family-owned rural site in a well-screened, tree-lined meadow. The site has an excellent toilet block complete with family room. A convenient touring base for Leeds and the surrounding area. Discounted fees and food are both available at the local golf club. 4 acre site. 30 touring pitches. 30 hardstandings. 10 seasonal pitches. Caravan pitches. Motorhome pitches. Tent pitches. 1 static.

Open: all year **Last arrival:** 21.00hrs **Last departure:** noon (later departures by prior arrangement)

Pitches: * 🚙 £18-£25 🚐 £18-£25 ⛺ £20-£25

Facilities: 🚿 ⊙ 💨 ❄ ♿ ⛱ 🐕 [WiFi] 💻 ♻ ℹ

Services: 🔧 🧺 🛢 🍃 🍳

Within 3 miles: ⛳ 🎬 🎣 ◎ 🏪 🧺 🐴

Notes: Children must be supervised. Dogs must be kept on leads. Walking maps available.

LEEDS — Map 19 SE23

Places to visit

Leeds Art Gallery, LEEDS, LS1 3AA, 0113 247 8256 www.leeds.gov.uk/artgallery

Temple Newsam Estate, LEEDS, LS15 0AE, 0113 336 7460 (House) www.leeds.gov.uk/templenewsamhouse

Moor Lodge Park

►►►► 88%

tel: 01937 572424 **Blackmoor Ln, Bardsey LS17 9DZ**
email: moorlodgecp@aol.com **web:** www.moorlodgecaravanpark.co.uk
dir: *From A1(M) take A659 (S of Wetherby) signed Otley. Left onto A58 towards Leeds for 5m. Right after New Inn pub (Ling Lane), right at x-roads, 1m. Site on right.*
grid ref: *SE352423*

A warm welcome is assured at this well-kept site set in a peaceful and beautiful setting, close to Harewood House and only 25 minutes' drive from York and the Dales; the centre of Leeds is just 15 minutes away. The touring area is for adults only. Please note, this site does not accept tents. 7 acre site. 12 touring pitches. Caravan pitches. Motorhome pitches. 60 statics.

Open: all year **Last arrival:** 20.00hrs **Last departure:** noon

Pitches: * 🚙 £17.50-£21 🚐 £17.50-£21

Facilities: 🚿 [P] ⊙ 💨 ❄ ⛱ 🐕 [WiFi] ♻ ℹ

Services: 🔧 🧺 🛢 🍃 🍳 ⤓

Within 3 miles: ⛳ 🎬 🎣 ◎ 🏪 🐴

Notes: Adults only. No large groups. Dogs must be kept on leads.

St Helena's Caravan Park
▶▶▶82%

tel: 0113 284 1142 **Otley Old Rd, Horsforth LS18 5HZ**
email: info@st-helenas.co.uk
dir: *From A658 follow signs for Leeds/Bradford Airport. Then follow site signs.*
grid ref: SE240421

A well-maintained parkland setting surrounded by woodland yet within easy reach of Leeds with its excellent shopping and cultural opportunities, Ilkley, and the attractive Wharfedale town of Otley. Some visitors may just want to relax in this adults-only park's spacious and pleasant surroundings. 25 acre site. 60 touring pitches. 31 hardstandings. 22 seasonal pitches. Caravan pitches. Motorhome pitches. Tent pitches. 40 statics.

Open: Apr-Oct **Last arrival:** 19.30hrs **Last departure:** 14.00hrs

Pitches: 🚐 🚍 ▲ **Facilities:** 🛒🐾⊙🅿✳🚿&🔥🐕♻🛈

Services: 🔌🖲 🚽 **Within 3 miles:** 🎣🚲🍴🛒🛒↺

Notes: Adults only.

CHANNEL ISLANDS
GUERNSEY

PREMIER PARK

Fauxquets Valley Campsite
▶▶▶▶▶85%

tel: 01481 255460 & 07781 413333 **GY5 7QL**
email: info@fauxquets.co.uk
dir: *From pier take 2nd exit at rdbt. At top of hill left into Queens Rd. 2m. Right into Candie Rd. Site opposite sign for German Occupation Museum.*

A beautiful, quiet farm site in a hidden valley close to the sea. The friendly and helpful owners, who understand campers' needs, offer good quality facilities and amenities, including spacious pitches and an outdoor swimming pool. There are sports areas, a nature trail, pigs, sheep and chickens for the children to visit, plus barbecue food and pizzas are available near the reception. There are fully serviced pitches and also four self-contained lodges for hire. Motorhomes up to 6.9 metres are allowed on Guernsey – contact the site for details and a permit. 3 acre site. 120 touring pitches. Motorhome pitches. Tent pitches.

Open: May-1 Sep **Pitches:** 🚍 ▲ **Leisure:** 🏊⚑⚽😊⚲
Facilities: 🛒🅿⊙🅿✳🚿&🔥🐕WiFi♻🛈
Services: 🔌🖲 🔋🚿🚽🍴🚚🍺 **Within 3 miles:** 🎣⚲🛒🍴◎↺🛒🛒↺
Notes: Dogs must be kept on leads. Birdwatching.
AA Pubs & Restaurants nearby: Fleur du Jardin, CASTEL, GY5 7JT, 01481 257996

Le Vaugrat Camp Site
▶▶▶ 90%

tel: 01481 257468 **Route de Vaugrat GY2 4TA**
email: enquiries@vaugratcampsite.com
dir: *From main coast road on NW of island, site signed at Port Grat Bay into Route de Vaugrat, near Peninsula Hotel.*

Overlooking the sea and set within the grounds of a lovely 17th-century house, this level grassy park is backed by woodland, and is close to the lovely sandy beaches of Port Grat and Grand Havre. It is run by a welcoming family who pride themselves on creating magnificent floral displays. The facilities here are excellent and there are 18 electric hook-ups, plus several fully equipped tents for hire. A 'round the island' bus stops very close to the site. Motorhomes up to 6.9 metres are allowed on Guernsey – contact the site for details and permit. 6 acre site. 150 touring pitches. Motorhome pitches. Tent pitches.

Open: May-mid Sep

Pitches: 🚍 ▲

Leisure: 🎠

Facilities: 🛒🅿⊙🅿✳🚿&🔥🔥WiFi♻🛈🎠

Services: 🔌🖲 🔋🚿🚚

Within 3 miles: 🎣🛒⚲◎↺🛒🛒↺

Notes: No pets.

AA Pubs & Restaurants nearby: The Pickled Pig, ST PETER PORT, GY1 2JP, 01481 721431

The Old Government House Hotel & Spa, ST PETER PORT, GY1 2NU, 01481 724921

The Absolute End, ST PETER PORT, GY1 2BG, 01481 723822

Mora Restaurant & Grill, ST PETER PORT, GY1 2LE, 01481 715053

PITCHES: 🚐 Caravans 🚍 Motorhomes ▲ Tents 🏕 Glamping accommodation **SERVICES:** 🔌 Electric hook up 🖲 Launderette 🍺 Licensed bar 🔋 Calor Gas 🕯 Camping Gaz 🚽 Toilet fluid 🍴 Café/Restaurant 🚚 Fast Food/Takeaway 🔋 Battery charging 🚼 Baby care ↯ Motorvan service point
ABBREVIATIONS: BHs – bank holidays Etr – Easter Spring BH – Spring Bank Holiday fr – from hrs – hours m – mile mdnt – midnight rdbt – roundabout rs – restricted service wk – week wknd – weekend x-roads – crossroads ⊘ No credit or debit cards ⊗ No dogs

VALE
Map 24

Places to visit

Guernsey Museum & Art Gallery, ST PETER PORT, GY1 1UG, 01481 726518
www.museums.gov.gg

Great for kids: Castle Cornet, ST PETER PORT, GY1 1AU, 01481 721657
www.museums.gov.gg

La Bailloterie Camping
▶▶▶▶ 84%

tel: 01481 243636 & 07781 103420 **Bailloterie Ln GY3 5HA**
email: info@campinginguernsey.com
dir: *3m N of St Peter Port into Vale Rd to Crossways, at x-roads right into Rue du Braye. Site 1st left at sign.*

A pretty rural site with one large touring field and a few small, well-screened paddocks. This delightful site has been privately run for over 50 years and offers good facilities in converted outbuildings. There are two, two-bedroom, well-equipped camping lodges, four top quality and very well-equipped safari tents (including a Cabanon tent) available for hire. The beaches and a supermarket are a short walk away. Motorhomes up to 6.9 metres are allowed on Guernsey — contact the site for detailed instructions. 10 acre site. 100 touring pitches. Motorhome pitches. Tent pitches.

Open: 15 May-15 Sep **Last arrival:** 23.00hrs **Last departure:** 11.00hrs

Pitches: 🚐 £20-£24 ▲ £20-£24 🏠 prices shown below

Leisure: 🎱 ⚫ 🎾 🚗

Facilities: 🔥 ⊙ 🅿 ✳ 👶 🚿 🛗 🚻 WiFi ♻ 🛈 🚗

Services: 🔌 🔋 🛢 🧺 🍽 🛒 🚰

Glamping: **Safari tents** 4, £25-£35 (prices per adult; family packages available) Changeover day Any day Min stay 2 nights Own kitchen Car by unit No dogs

Within 3 miles: 🎣 ⛳ 🎠 ◎ 🚲 🐎 ∪

Notes: Dogs by prior arrangement only, no dogs in log cabins or safari tents. Dogs must be kept on leads. Volleyball net, boules pitch.

AA Pubs & Restaurants nearby: The Pickled Pig, ST PETER PORT, GY1 2JP, 01481 721431

The Old Government House Hotel & Spa, ST PETER PORT, GY1 2NU, 01481 724921

The Absolute End, ST PETER PORT, GY1 2BG, 01481 723822

Mora Restaurant & Grill, ST PETER PORT, GY1 2LE, 01481 715053

Campsite cooking
See pages 24-31
for handy tips

LEISURE: 🏊 Indoor pool 🏊 Outdoor pool Ⓐ Children's playground 👋 Kid's club 🎾 Tennis court 🎱 Games room ⛳ Golf course 🚣 Boat hire 🚲 Cycle hire 🎬 Cinema 🎵 Entertainment 🎣 Fishing ◎ Mini golf 🚩 Pitch n putt 🏄 Watersports 🏋 Gym ♨ Sports field ∪ Stables **FACILITIES:** 🛁 Bath 🚿 Shower 🅿 Private washing cubicles 🔌 Electric shaver 🅿 Hairdryer ❄ Ice Packs ♿ Disabled facilities Ⓢ Shop on site 🏪 Mobile shop 🍖 BBQ area 🪑 Picnic area WiFi Wi-fi 💻 Internet access ♻ Recycling 🛈 Tourist info 🐕 Dog exercise area 🚗 Car hire can be arranged

JERSEY

ST MARTIN   Map 24

Places to visit

Mont Orgueil Castle, GOREY, JE3 6ET, 01534 853292 www.jerseyheritage.org

Maritime Museum & Occupation Tapestry Gallery, ST HELIER, JE2 3ND, 01534 811043 www.jerseyheritage.org

Great for kids: Elizabeth Castle, ST HELIER, JE3 3WU, 01534 723971 www.jerseyheritage.org

---

PREMIER PARK

Rozel Camping Park
►►►►►88%

tel: 01534 855200 **Summerville Farm JE3 6AX**
email: enquiries@rozelcamping.com
dir: *Take A6 from St Helier through Five Oaks to St Martins Church, turn right onto A38 towards Rozel, site on right.*

Customers can be sure of a warm welcome at this delightful family-run park. Set in the north-east of the island, it offers large spacious pitches, (many with electricity) for tents, caravans and motorhomes. Major improvements for 2016 included upgrading the swimming pool, adding new showers and creating more spacious pitches. The lovely Rozel Bay is just a short distance away and spectacular views of the French coast can be seen from one of the four fields on the park. Motorhomes and caravans will be met at the ferry and escorted to the park if requested when booking. Fully equipped, ready-erected tents available for hire. 4 acre site. 100 touring pitches. Caravan pitches. Motorhome pitches. Tent pitches. 20 statics.

Open: May-mid Sep **Last arrival:** 20.30hrs **Last departure:** noon
Pitches: * ⛟ £22-£23 ⛟ £22-£23 ▲ £22-£23 ⋔ prices shown below
Leisure: ⬟⛰⬙🔍 **Facilities:** 🐾🅿⊙🖋❄&🖺WIFI💻🛈
Services: ⊕🖸🛢⊘T🛒⬆
Glamping: Erected Tents 20, £56-£62 Min stay 5 nights Own kitchen Car by unit
Within 3 miles: ⌁⬚🖋◎⬙🖺🖸∪
Notes: No noise between 22.00hrs-07.30hrs. Dogs must be kept on leads. Free mini golf, table tennis. Freshly baked bread available.
AA Pubs & Restaurants nearby: Royal Hotel, ST MARTIN, JE3 6UG, 01534 856289

PREMIER PARK

Beuvelande Camp Site
►►►►►87%

tel: 01534 853575 **Beuvelande JE3 6EZ**
email: info@campingjersey.com
dir: *Take A6 from St Helier to St Martin & follow signs to site before St Martins Church.*

A well-established site with excellent toilet facilities, accessed via narrow lanes in peaceful countryside close to St Martin. An attractive bar and restaurant is the focal point of the park, especially in the evenings, and there is a small swimming pool and playground. Motorhomes and towed caravans will be met at the ferry and escorted to the site if requested when booking. There are now fully-equipped yurts and a safari tent located in a peaceful area, plus bell tents on decking and new Euro-style tents near the facilities and resturant. This site is popular with both families and couples. 6 acre site. 150 touring pitches. Caravan pitches. Motorhome pitches. Tent pitches. 75 statics.

Open: Apr-Sep (rs Apr-May & Sep pool & restaurant closed, shop hours limited)
Pitches: ⛟⛟▲⋔ **Leisure:** ⬟🔍🎵
Facilities: ⊙❄&🖺🐾WIFI💻🛈 **Services:** ⊕🖸🍴🛢⊘T🍽⬆⬆
Glamping: Bell tents 12 Safari tents 1 Erected Tents 20 Yurts 2
Within 3 miles: ⌁⬚🖋⬙🖺🖸∪
Notes: Dogs must be kept on leads.
AA Pubs & Restaurants nearby: Royal Hotel, ST MARTIN, JE3 6UG, 01534 856289

ST OUEN   Map 24

Places to visit

Judith Quérée's Garden, ST OUEN, JE3 2FE, 01534 482191 www.judithqueree.com

The Channel Islands Military Museum, ST OUEN, JE3 2FN, 01534 483205

Great for kids: The Living Legend, ST PETER, JE3 7ET, 01534 485496 www.jerseyslivinglegend.co.je

---

Daisy Cottage Campsite
►►►►88%

tel: 01534 481700 **Route de Vinchelez JE3 2DB**
email: hello@daisycottagecampsite.com
dir: *From St Helier harbour, at 2nd rdbt, 1st exit onto A2 (Victoria Ave) (becomes A1). At 'filter-in-turn' mini rdbt in Beaumont, right into La Route de Beaumont (signed St Ouen & A12). In St Ouen right into Route de Vinchelez. Site on right.*

The only campsite on the west side of the island. If you are looking for a peaceful site with spacious and well screened pitches and spotless facilities, Daisy Cottage would be the perfect choice. The whole emphasis is on having a peaceful and relaxing stay. The campsite also has a unique Retreat offering a wide range of therapies, an on-site chiropractor and also a secluded decking area where you can just unwind or take part in yoga or relaxation classes. The campsite is also very close to Greve de Lecq with its delightful beach. 2.5 acre site. 28 touring pitches. Caravan pitches. Motorhome pitches. Tent pitches.

Open: Apr-Oct
Pitches: * ⛟ £23-£36 ⛟ £23-£36 ▲ £20-£36 ⋔ prices shown below
Leisure: Spa
Facilities: 🐾❄🖺🍴WIFI💻🛈
Services: ⊕🖸🍴
Glamping: Shepherd's Huts 1, £65-£75 Min stay 3 nights Own kitchen Car by unit
Within 3 miles: ⬚🖋⬙🖺🖸
Notes: No noise after 22.00hrs.
AA Pubs & Restaurants nearby: St Mary's Country Inn, ST MARY, JE3 3DS, 01534 482897
Mark Jordan at the Beach, ST PETER, JE3 7YD, 01534 780180

PITCHES: ⛟ Caravans ⛟ Motorhomes ▲ Tents ⋔ Glamping accommodation   **SERVICES:** ⊕ Electric hook up 🖸 Launderette 🍴 Licensed bar 🛢 Calor Gas ⊘ Camping Gaz T Toilet fluid 🍽 Café/Restaurant 🏭 Fast Food/Takeaway ⬆ Battery charging 🛒 Baby care ⬆ Motorvan service point
ABBREVIATIONS: BHs – bank holidays   Etr – Easter   Spring BH – Spring Bank Holiday   fr – from   hrs – hours   m – mile   mdnt – midnight   rdbt – roundabout   rs – restricted service   wk – week   wknd – weekend   x-roads – crossroads   ⊛ No credit or debit cards   ⊗ No dogs

| **TRINITY** | **Map 24** |

AA GLAMPING SITE OF THE YEAR 2017

Durrell Wildlife Camp

▶ ▶ ▶ ▶ ▶ 93%

tel: 01534 860095 & 07797 832534 **Les Augres Manor, La Profonde Rue JE3 5BP**
email: ashley.mullins@durrell.org
dir: *From St Helier take A8 to Trinity. At T-junct right signed Rozel & Durrell Wildlife. Site on right.* **grid ref:** *SY161140*

Part of the Durrell Wildlife Park, the camp consists of 12 canvas geo pods set in a beautifully landscaped area. Each pod, named after different Lemur species, is sited in its own separate area offering good privacy. Inside is a king-size bed, two singles, a wood-burning stove and clothing storage space. Set on wooden decking, the pods have their own additional pod with high quality toilet, wash basin and shower plus a spacious fully-equipped kitchen. Table and chairs on the decking can be brought into the kitchen if the weather's not so good. Smaller tipis are available for extra children or guests. Guests have complimentary access to the Durrell Wildlife Zoo and have use of the zoo's excellent Café Firefly, which serves breakfasts, lunches and early evening meals, plus takeaway pizzas and Thai food.

Open: Mar-Oct **Last arrival:** 20.00hrs **Last departure:** 10.00hrs

Facilities: ✳ ❤ ♿ ⏚ ⏚ WiFi

Services: ⅋⊙

Glamping: Geo domes 12, £170–£210 En suite Own kitchen

Within 3 miles: ⚓ ⚑ ⚑ ⚑ U

Notes: No cars by geo domes. No pets. No noise after 23.00hrs. Free entry into Durrell Wildlife Park.

| **ISLE OF MAN** |

| **KIRK MICHAEL** | **Map 24 SC39** |

Places to visit

Peel Castle, PEEL, IM5 1TB, 01624 648000 www.manxnationalheritage.im

House of Manannan, PEEL, IM5 1TA, 01624 648000 www.manxnationalheritage.im

Great for kids: Curraghs Wildlife Park, BALLAUGH, IM7 5EA, 01624 897323 http://www.curraghswildlifepark.im/

Glen Wyllin Campsite

▶ ▶ ▶ 75%

tel: 01624 878231 & 878836 **IM6 1AL**
email: michaelcommissioners@manx.net
dir: *From Douglas take A1 to Ballacraine, right at lights onto A3 to Kirk Michael. Left onto A4 signed Peel. Site 100yds on right.* **grid ref:** *SC302901*

Set in a beautiful wooded glen with bridges over a pretty stream dividing the camping areas. A gently-sloping tarmac road gives direct access to a good beach. Hire tents are available. 9 acre site. 90 touring pitches. Caravan pitches. Motorhome pitches. Tent pitches. 18 statics.

Open: mid Apr-mid Sep **Last departure:** noon

Pitches: ⛺ ⛺ ▲

Facilities: ⊙ ⚑ ✳ ♿ ⏚ ⏚ ⏚ 🐕 WiFi ♻

Services: ⊟ ⓢ ⊙ ⌐ ⌐

Within 3 miles: ⚑ ⏚ ⏚ U

Notes: No excess noise after mdnt. Dogs must be kept on leads & under control

AA Pubs & Restaurants nearby: The Creek Inn, PEEL, IM5 1AT, 01624 842216

LEISURE: 🏊 Indoor pool 🏊 Outdoor pool 🎠 Children's playground 🧒 Kid's club ♟ Tennis court 🎱 Games room ⛳ Golf course 🚣 Boat hire 🚲 Cycle hire 🎬 Cinema 🎵 Entertainment 🎣 Fishing ◎ Mini golf ⛳ Pitch n putt 🏄 Watersports 🏋 Gym 🏉 Sports field U Stables **FACILITIES:** 🛁 Bath 🚿 Shower Ｐ Private washing cubicles ⊙ Electric shaver 🪮 Hairdryer ❄ Ice Packs ♿ Disabled facilities ⓢ Shop on site 🏪 Mobile shop 🍖 BBQ area 🪑 Picnic area WiFi Wi-fi 💻 Internet access ♻ Recycling ⓘ Tourist info 🐕 Dog exercise area 🚗 Car hire can be arranged

Scotland

Scotland

With its remarkable, timeless beauty, jagged coastline and long and eventful history, Scotland is a country with something very special to offer. Around half the size of England, but with barely one fifth of its population and nearly 800 islands, the statistics alone are enough to make you want to pack a suitcase and head north without hesitation.

The Scottish Borders region acts as a perfect introduction and is an obvious place to begin a tour of the country. The novelist and poet Sir Walter Scott was so moved by its remoteness and grandeur that he wrote: 'To my eye, these grey hills and all this wild border country have beauties peculiar to themselves. I like the very nakedness of the land; it has something bold and stern and solitary about it. If I did not see the heather at least once a year I think I should die.' Abbotsford, Scott's turreted mansion on the banks of the River Tweed near Melrose, was re-opened to the public in the summer of 2013 following a £12 million programme of major improvements.

Consisting of 1,800 square miles of dense forest, rolling green hills and the broad sweeps of heather that lifted Scott's spirits, this region is characterised by some of the country's most majestic landscapes. Adjacent to this region is Dumfries & Galloway, where, at Gretna Green on the border with England, eloping couples have tied the knot since Lord Hardwicke's Marriage Act came into force in 1754; it still can boast around 1,500 weddings a year. Travel north and you discover mile upon mile of open moorland and swathes of seemingly endless forest that stretch to the Ayrshire coast. At a crucial time in the country's history, it is fascinating to reflect on another momentous event in the story of Scotland when, following the signing of the Declaration of Arbroath in 1320, it became independent and was ruled by Robert the Bruce. Dumfries & Galloway is littered with the relics of his battles.

Not far from Dumfries is the cottage where Robert Burns, the Bard of Scotland, was born in 1759. This tiny white-washed dwelling, constructed of thatch and clay, was built by the poet's father two years earlier. In a 2009 poll, TV viewers voted Burns the 'Greatest ever Scot' and his song *Is there for Honest Poverty*

opened the new Scottish Parliament in 1999. The cottage at Alloway is one of Scotland's most popular tourist attractions with a new museum allowing the poet's collection of precious manuscripts, correspondence and artefacts to be housed in one building.

Scotland's two greatest cities, Glasgow and Edinburgh, include innumerable historic sites, popular landmarks and innovative visitor attractions. Edinburgh is home to the annual, internationally famous Military Tattoo; Glasgow, once the second city of the British Empire and yet synonymous with the dreadful slums and the grime of industry, has, in places, been transformed beyond recognition. The city hosted the Great Exhibitions of 1888 and 1901, was designated European City of Culture in 1990 and in 2014 became the setting for the highly successful Commonwealth Games.

To the north of Glasgow and Edinburgh lies a sublime landscape of tranquil lochs, fishing rivers, wooded glens and the fine cities of Perth and Dundee. There is also the superb scenery of The Trossachs, Loch Lomond and Stirling, which, with its handsome castle perched on a rocky crag, is Scotland's heritage capital. Sooner or later the might and majesty of the Cairngorms and the Grampians beckon, drawing you into a breathtakingly beautiful landscape of mountains and remote, rugged terrain. Scotland's isolated far north is further from many parts of England than a good many European destinations. Cape Wrath is Britain's most northerly outpost.

For many visitors, the Western Highlands is the place to go, evoking a truly unique and breathtaking sense of adventure. The list of island names seems endless – Skye, Mull, Iona, Jura, Islay – each with their own individual character and identity, and the reward of everlasting and treasured memories.

Sligachan, Isle of Skye ▷

ABERDEENSHIRE

ABOYNE | Map 23 NO59

Places to visit

Alford Valley Railway, ALFORD, AB33 8AD, 019755 63942
www.alfordvalleyrailway.org.uk

Crathes Castle Garden & Estate, CRATHES, AB31 5QJ, 01330 844525
www.nts.org.uk/Property/Crathes-Castle-Garden-and-Estate

Great for kids: Craigievar Castle, ALFORD, AB33 8JF, 01339 883635
www.nts.org.uk/Property/Craigievar-Castle

Aboyne Loch Caravan Park
►►► 76%

GOLD

tel: 01339 886244 & 882589 **AB34 5BR**
email: heatherreid24@yahoo.co.uk
dir: *On A93, 1m E of Aboyne.* **grid ref:** *NO538998*

Located on the outskirts of Aboyne on a small outcrop which is almost surrounded by Loch Aboyne, this is a mature site within scenic Royal Deeside. The facilities are well maintained, and pitches are set amongst mature trees with most having views over the loch. Boat hire is offered and fishing (coarse, and for pike) is available. There is a regular bus service from the site entrance. 6 acre site. 20 touring pitches. 25 hardstandings. Caravan pitches. Motorhome pitches. Tent pitches. 100 statics.

Open: 31 Mar-Oct **Last arrival:** 20.00hrs **Last departure:** noon
Pitches: * 🚐 £18-£25 🚍 £18-£25 ⛺ £13-£23
Leisure: 🎣 🛶
Facilities: 🏮 🅿 ⊙ 🍴 ✳ 🚿 WiFi 💻 ♻ 🅸 🐕 🚿
Services: 🔌 🔋 🛢 🚮 🚾 🔽
Within 3 miles: ⅃ 🎣 🛶 ◎ ⚓ 🏪 🛒 ♀
Notes: 🐕 Dogs must be kept on leads.

ALFORD | Map 23 NJ51

Places to visit

Alford Valley Railway, ALFORD, AB33 8AD, 019755 63942
www.alfordvalleyrailway.org.uk

Craigievar Castle, ALFORD, AB33 8JF, 01339 883635
www.nts.org.uk/Property/Craigievar-Castle

Haughton House Holiday Park
►►► 76%

tel: 01975 562107 **Montgarrie Rd AB33 8NA**
email: enquiries@haughtonhouse.co.uk
dir: *In Alford follow Haughton Country House signs.* **grid ref:** *NJ577168*

Located on the outskirts of Alford, this site is set within a large country park that has good countryside views. Now under the same ownership as Huntly Castle Caravan Park (Huntly), this park receives the same attention to detail to ensure facilities are of a high standard; the existing facilities are clean and well

maintained. The pitches are set amid mature trees and the tenting area is in the old walled garden. There is plenty to do on site and in the country park which has various activities for children, including a narrow gauge railway that runs to the Grampian Transport Museum in nearby Alford. 22 acre site. 71 touring pitches. 71 hardstandings. 20 seasonal pitches. Caravan pitches. Motorhome pitches. Tent pitches. 70 statics.

Open: Mar-mid/end Oct **Last arrival:** 21.00hrs **Last departure:** noon
Pitches: 🚐 🚍 ⛺
Leisure: ⚠
Facilities: 🏮 ⊙ 🅿 ✳ 🚿 🅶 🚿 🐕 WiFi ♻ 🅸
Services: 🔌 🔋 🛢 🚾 🔽 🔽
Within 3 miles: ⅃ 🎣 ◎ 🏪 🛒
Notes: No noise after 22.30hrs. Dogs must be kept on leads. Putting green, fishing permits.

BANFF | Map 23 NJ66

Places to visit

Banff Museum, BANFF, AB45 1AE, 01261 812941

Duff House, BANFF, AB45 3SX, 01261 818181 www.historic-scotland.gov.uk

Banff Links Caravan Park
►►►► 86%

tel: 01261 812228 **Inverboyndie AB45 2JJ**
email: banfflinkscaravanpark@btconnect.com
dir: *From W: A98 onto B9038 signed Whitehills. 2nd right signed Inverboyndie. 4th left to site. From E (Banff): A98, right at brown 'Banff Links Beach' sign.* **grid ref:** *NJ668644*

This delightful small park, where the family owners are keen that their visitors enjoy their stay, is set beside the award-winning sandy beach at Banff Links with magnificent views over the Moray coast. Set at sea level, there is direct access to the beach and also a large grass esplanade and play area for children. A pleasant walk on good level paths by the sea will take you to either Banff or the small village of Whitehill, which has a leisure boat harbour. It is ideally located to explore this lovely coastline. Six static caravans are for hire. 5.78 acre site. 55 touring pitches. 10 hardstandings. 10 seasonal pitches. Caravan pitches. Motorhome pitches. Tent pitches. 38 statics.

Open: Apr-Oct
Pitches: 🚐 🚍 ⛺
Facilities: 🅿 🅶 🅸 🚿 WiFi ♻ 🅸
Services: 🔌 🔋 🛢 🚾 🔽 🔽
Within 3 miles: ⅃ 🎣 ◎ 🏪 🛒 ♀
Notes: Dogs must be kept on leads.

LEISURE: 🏊 Indoor pool 🏊 Outdoor pool ⚠ Children's playground 👶 Kid's club 🎾 Tennis court 🎱 Games room ⛳ Golf course 🚣 Boat hire 🚲 Cycle hire 🎦 Cinema 🎵 Entertainment 🎣 Fishing ◎ Mini golf ⛳ Pitch n putt 🏄 Watersports 💪 Gym 🏟 Sports field ♀ Stables **FACILITIES:** 🛁 Bath 🚿 Shower 🅿 Private washing cubicles ⊙ Electric shaver 🅿 Hairdryer ✳ Ice Packs 🅶 Disabled facilities 🏪 Shop on site 🚚 Mobile shop 🍖 BBQ area 🌲 Picnic area WiFi Wi-fi 💻 Internet access ♻ Recycling 🅸 Tourist info 🐕 Dog exercise area 🚗 Car hire can be arranged

HUNTLY   Map 23 NJ53

Places to visit

Leith Hall, Garden & Estate, RHYNIE, AB54 4NQ, 01464 831 216
www.nts.org.uk/Property/Leith-Hall-Garden-and-Estate

Glenfiddich Distillery, DUFFTOWN, AB55 4DH, 01340 820373
www.glenfiddich.com

PREMIER PARK

Huntly Castle Caravan Park

▷▷▷▷▷ 90%

tel: 01466 794999 **The Meadow AB54 4UJ**
email: enquiries@huntlycastle.co.uk
dir: *From Aberdeen on A96 to Huntly. 0.75m after rdbt (on outskirts of Huntly) right towards town centre, left into Riverside Drive.* **grid ref:** *NJ525405*

A quality parkland site within striking distance of the Speyside Malt Whisky Trail, the beautiful Moray coast and the Cairngorm Mountains. The park provides exceptional toilet facilities, and there are some fully serviced pitches. The attractive town of Huntly is only a five-minute walk away, with its ruined castle plus a wide variety of restaurants and shops. 15 acre site. 90 touring pitches. 51 hardstandings. 10 seasonal pitches. Caravan pitches. Motorhome pitches. Tent pitches. 40 statics.

Open: Apr-Oct **Last arrival:** 20.00hrs **Last departure:** noon

Pitches: ⚏ ⛺ Ⓐ

Leisure: ⚐

Facilities: ⋔ 🅿 ⊙ ℱ ☀ ⅙ ⅋ 📶 ♻ ❂

Services: ⚡ ⓢ ⬛ Ⓣ 🛒 ⬇

Within 3 miles: ⌕ ⋰ ⬜ ⓢ

Notes: No noise after 23.00hrs. Dogs must be kept on leads.

KINTORE   Map 23 NJ71

Places to visit

Pitmedden Garden, PITMEDDEN, AB41 7PD, 01651 842352
www.nts.org.uk/Property/Pitmedden-Garden

Tolquhon Castle, PITMEDDEN, AB41 7LP, 01651 851286
www.historic-scotland.gov.uk

Great for kids: Castle Fraser, KEMNAY, AB51 7LD, 01330 833463
www.nts.org.uk/Property/Castle-Fraser-Garden-and-Estate

Hillhead Caravan Park

▶▶▶▶ 77%

tel: 01467 632809 **AB51 0YX**
email: enquiries@hillheadcaravan.com
dir: *From S: A96 at Broomhill Rdbt follow Kintore (& brown camping sign) onto B987. At mini rdbt 1st left, immediately left signed Kemnay. Over A96, straight on at next rdbt, Right signed Kintore. Site on right. From N: A96 at rdbt follow Kintore signs onto B987. 5th right into Forest Rd. Over A96, 1st left to site on left.* **grid ref:** *NJ777163*

An attractive, nicely landscaped site, located on the outskirts of Kintore in the valley of the River Dee with excellent access to forest walks and within easy reach of the many attractions in rural Aberdeenshire. The toilet facilities are of a high standard. There are good play facilities for smaller children plus a small café with TV and internet access. 1.5 acre site. 17 touring pitches. 17 hardstandings. 10 seasonal pitches. Caravan pitches. Motorhome pitches. Tent pitches. 40 statics.

Open: all year **Last arrival:** 21.00hrs **Last departure:** 13.00hrs

Pitches: ⚏ £17-£20 ⛺ £17-£20 Ⓐ £15-£17

Leisure: ⚲

Facilities: ⋔ ⊙ ℱ ☀ ⅙ ⓢ ⅋ 📶 🖥 ♻ ❂

Services: ⚡ ⓢ ⊘ Ⓣ 🍽 🛒 🖢

Within 3 miles: ⌕ ⋰ ⓢ

Notes: Dogs must be kept on leads. Caravan storage, accessories shop.

AA Pubs & Restaurants nearby: The Cock & Bull Bar & Restaurant, BALMEDIE, AB23 8XY, 01358 743249

Old Blackfriars, ABERDEEN, AB11 5BB, 01224 581922

The Adelphi Kitchen, ABERDEEN, AB11 5BL, 01224 211414

The Silver Darling, ABERDEEN, AB11 5DQ, 01224 576229

MACDUFF   Map 23 NJ76

Places to visit

Duff House, BANFF, AB45 3SX, 01261 818181 www.historic-scotland.gov.uk

Banff Museum, BANFF, AB45 1AE, 01261 812941

Wester Bonnyton Farm Site

▶▶ 68%

tel: 01261 832470 **Gamrie AB45 3EP**
email: westerbonnyton@fsmail.net
dir: *From A98 (1m S of Macduff) take B9031 signed Rosehearty. Site 1.25m on right.* **grid ref:** *NJ741638*

A spacious farm site, with level touring pitches, overlooking the Moray Firth. The small, picturesque fishing villages of Gardenstown and Crovie and the larger town of Macduff, which has a marine aquarium, are all within easy reach. All the touring pitches have good views of the coastline. Families with children are welcome, and there is a play area and play barn. 8 acre site. 8 touring pitches. 5 hardstandings. Caravan pitches. Motorhome pitches. Tent pitches. 67 statics.

Open: Mar-Oct

Pitches: * ⚏ £15-£20 ⛺ £15-£20 Ⓐ £10-£25

Leisure: ⚐ ⚲

Facilities: ⋔ ⊙ ℱ ⓢ ⅋ 📶 🖥 ♻ ❂

Services: ⚡ ⓢ ⬛

Within 3 miles: ⌕ ⚑ ⋰ ⬙ ⓢ

Notes: PayPal accepted. Dogs must be kept on leads.

PITCHES: ⚏ Caravans ⛺ Motorhomes Ⓐ Tents ⋔ Glamping accommodation   **SERVICES:** ⚡ Electric hook up ⓢ Launderette 🍸 Licensed bar
⬛ Calor Gas ⊘ Camping Gaz Ⓣ Toilet fluid 🍽 Café/Restaurant 🛒 Fast Food/Takeaway 🖢 Battery charging 🚼 Baby care 🖴 Motorvan service point
ABBREVIATIONS: BHs – bank holidays   Etr – Easter   Spring BH – Spring Bank Holiday   fr – from   hrs – hours   m – mile   mdnt – midnight
rdbt – roundabout   rs – restricted service   wk – week   wknd – weekend   x-roads – crossroads   ⊛ No credit or debit cards   ⊗ No dogs

MINTLAW
Map 23 NJ94

Places to visit

Aberdeenshire Farming Museum, MINTLAW, AB42 5FQ, 01771 624590
www.aberdeenshire.gov.uk/museums

Deer Abbey, OLD DEER, 01667 460232 www.historic-scotland.gov.uk

Aden Caravan and Camping Park
►►► 82%

tel: 01771 623460 **Aden Country Park AB42 5FQ**
email: info@adencaravanandcamping.co.uk
dir: *From Mintlaw take A950 signed New Pitsligo & Aden Country Park. Park on left.*
grid ref: *NJ981479*

Situated in the heart of Buchan in Aberdeenshire and within Aden Country Park, this is a small tranquil site offering excellent facilities. It is ideally located for visiting the many tourist attractions in this beautiful north-east coastal area, not least of which is the 230-acre country park itself. The site is only a short drive from the busy fishing towns of Fraserburgh and Peterhead, and as it is only an hour from Aberdeen's centre; this is an ideal spot for a short stay or a longer holiday, and there is one disabled-friendly static for hire. The country park plays host to numerous events throughout the year, including pipe band championships, horse events and various ranger-run activities. 11.1 acre site. 66 touring pitches. 31 hardstandings. 12 seasonal pitches. Caravan pitches. Motorhome pitches. Tent pitches. 17 statics.

Open: Apr-Oct **Last arrival:** 20.00hrs **Last departure:** 14.00hrs

Pitches: 🚐 🚙 Å

Leisure: ⋀ **Facilities:** 🌳 ⊙ ℙ & ⑤ ⌕ ⛺ ♻ 🛈

Services: 🔌 🔟 🛁 ⛽ **Within 3 miles:** 🎣 🏌 ⑤

Notes: PayPal accepted. Dogs must be kept on leads.

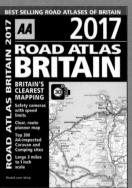

To help you navigate safely and easily, use the AA Road Atlas Britain 2017. Available from:
shop.theAA.com

NORTH WATER BRIDGE
Map 23 NO66

Places to visit

Edzell Castle and Garden, EDZELL, DD9 7UE, 01356 648631
www.historic-scotland.gov.uk

Dovecot Caravan Park
►►► 77%

tel: 01674 840630 **AB30 1QL**
email: adele@dovecotcaravanpark.co.uk
dir: *From Laurencekirk on A90, 5m, at Edzell Woods sign turn left. Site 500yds on left.*
grid ref: *NO648663*

A level grassy site in a country area close to the A90, with mature trees screening one side and the River North Esk on the other. The immaculate toilet facilities make this a handy overnight stop in a good touring area. 6 acre site. 25 touring pitches. 8 hardstandings. 8 seasonal pitches. Caravan pitches. Motorhome pitches. Tent pitches. 44 statics.

Open: Apr-Oct **Last arrival:** 20.00hrs **Last departure:** noon

Pitches: * 🚐 £16.50-£18.50 🚙 £16.50-£18.50 Å £13.50-£15.50

Leisure: 🔍

Facilities: 🌳 ⊙ ℙ ⌕ & ⛺ 🆆🅸🅵🅸 ♻ 🛈

Services: 🔌 🛁 🔟 ⛽

Notes: Dogs must be kept on leads.

PETERHEAD
Map 23 NK14

Places to visit

Arbuthnot Museum, PETERHEAD, AB42 1QD, 01771 622807
www.aberdeenshire.gov.uk/museums

Aberdeenshire Farming Museum, MINTLAW, AB42 5FQ, 01771 624590
www.aberdeenshire.gov.uk/museums

Lido Caravan Park
►►► 76%

tel: 01779 478950 & 473358 **South Rd AB42 2YP**
email: admin@peterheadprojects.co.uk
dir: *From A90 (Aberdeen to Peterhead road) at Invernetty rdbt take A982.*
grid ref: *NK123452*

This small site is located on The Lido with direct access to a small sandy beach with a nice play area and sand dunes. Each of the all-electric pitches has a view over Peterhead's busy harbour and there is always some boating activity taking place to keep you interested. The site is under the management of the local enterprise company Peterhead Projects Limited. The Martine Heritage Centre, a few minutes' walk from the site, has an excellent café. 2 acre site. 25 touring pitches. 5 seasonal pitches. Caravan pitches. Motorhome pitches. Tent pitches. 14 statics.

Open: Mar-Oct **Last departure:** noon

Pitches: * 🚐 £23 🚙 £23 Å £7.20-£26

Facilities: 🌳 ℙ ⊙ ℙ & ⛺ ♻

Services: 🔌 🔟 🛁

Within 3 miles: 🎣 ⛳ 🅷 🎣 🏌 ⑤ 🔟 ⛵

Notes: No ball games, no nuisance noise after 22.00hrs. Dogs must be kept on leads.

PORTSOY

Places to visit

Banff Museum, BANFF, AB45 1AE, 01261 812941

Duff House, BANFF, AB45 3SX, 01261 818181 www.historic-scotland.gov.uk

Great for kids: Macduff Marine Aquarium, MACDUFF, AB44 1SL, 01261 833369 www.macduff-aquarium.org.uk

PORTSOY   Map 23 NJ56

Portsoy Links Caravan Park
▶▶▶ 76%

tel: 01261 842695 **Links Rd, Portsoy AB45 2RQ**
email: contact@portsoylinks.co.uk
dir: At Portsoy from A98 into Church St. 2nd right into Institute St (follow brown camping sign). At T-junct right, down slope to site. **grid ref:** NJ591660

Taken into community ownership under the auspices of the Scottish Traditional Boats Festival, this is a lovely links-type site with stunning views across the bay. There is a large, safe fenced play area for smaller children and the toilet facilities are kept clean and well maintained. Portsoy is a typical small fishing port and has various eateries and shops; it is very convenient for visiting the other small fishing villages on the North East Scotland's Coastal Trail. 0.8 acre site. 51 touring pitches. 9 hardstandings. 7 seasonal pitches. Caravan pitches. Motorhome pitches. Tent pitches. 17 statics.

Open: 30 Mar-Oct **Last arrival:** 20.00hrs **Last departure:** noon

Pitches: * 🚐 £20.50-£22 🚐 £20.50-£22 ▲ £12-£19

Leisure: ⚑

Facilities: ⚒🅿🛁♿🗼WiFi🅓 **Services:** 🔌🔲🛢

Within 3 miles: 🚶🏇🛶🛥🏧

STRACHAN   Map 23 NO69

Places to visit

Banchory Museum, BANCHORY, AB31 5SX, 01771 622807 www.aberdeenshire.gov.uk/museums

Crathes Castle Garden & Estate, CRATHES, AB31 5QJ, 01330 844525 www.nts.org.uk/Property/Crathes-Castle-Garden-and-Estate

Great for kids: Go Ape Crathes Castle, CRATHES, AB31 5QJ, 0845 643 9215
(Calls cost 7p per minute plus your phone company's access charge)
www.goape.co.uk/crathes-castle

Feughside Caravan Park
▶▶▶▶ 82%

tel: 01330 850669 **AB31 6NT**
email: info@feughsidecaravanpark.co.uk **web:** www.feughsidecaravanpark.co.uk
dir: From Banchory take B974 to Strachan, 3m, take B976, 2m to Feughside Inn, follow site signs. **grid ref:** NO636913

A small, well maintained family-run site, set amongst mature trees and hedges and located five miles from Banchory and with stunning views of Clachnaben hill. The site is ideally suited to those wishing for a peaceful location that is within easy reach of scenic Royal Deeside. 5.5 acre site. 27 touring pitches. 10 hardstandings. 12 seasonal pitches. Caravan pitches. Motorhome pitches. Tent pitches. 54 statics.

Feughside Caravan Park

Open: Apr-Oct **Last arrival:** 22.00hrs **Last departure:** noon

Pitches: * 🚐 £20-£22 🚐 £20-£22 ▲ £10-£22

Leisure: ⚑

Facilities: ⚒🅿☺🗑♿🗼WiFi🖥♻🅓

Services: 🔌🔲🛢🚿🔋

Within 3 miles: 🚶🏇🛶🏧⛳

Notes: Quiet after 22.00hrs, no open fires. Dogs must be kept on leads & exercised off site.

TURRIFF   Map 23 NJ75

Places to visit

Fyvie Castle, TURRIFF, AB53 8JS, 01651 891266 www.nts.org.uk/Property/Fyvie-Castle

Turriff Caravan Park
▶▶▶ 77%

tel: 01888 562205 **Station Rd AB53 4ER**
email: turriffcaravanpark@btconnect.com
dir: On A947, S of Turriff. **grid ref:** NJ727492

Located on the outskirts of Turriff on the site of an old railway station, this site is owned by the local community. The pitches are level and the attractive landscaping is well maintained. The site also has a rally field. There is a large public park close to the site which has a boating pond and a large games park where the annual agricultural show is held. The town is only five minutes' walk through the park and has a good variety of shops. This is an ideal base for touring rural Aberdeenshire and the nearby Moray coastline with its traditional fishing villages. 5 acre site. 70 touring pitches. 4 hardstandings. Caravan pitches. Motorhome pitches. Tent pitches. 14 statics.

Open: Apr-Oct **Last arrival:** 18.00hrs **Last departure:** noon

Pitches: 🚐 🚐 ▲

Leisure: ⚑♻

Facilities: ⚒☺🗑♿🗼WiFi♻🅓 **Services:** 🔌🔲🛢🔋

Within 3 miles: 🚶🏇🛶◎⛳🏧⛳

Notes: Dogs must be kept on leads.

AA Pubs & Restaurants nearby: The Redgarth, OLDMELDRUM, AB51 0DJ, 01651 872353

PITCHES: 🚐 Caravans 🚐 Motorhomes ▲ Tents 🏕 Glamping accommodation **SERVICES:** 🔌 Electric hook up 🔲 Launderette 🍺 Licensed bar
🛢 Calor Gas 🗑 Camping Gaz 🅣 Toilet fluid 🍽 Café/Restaurant 🍔 Fast Food/Takeaway 🔋 Battery charging 🚼 Baby care ⛟ Motorvan service point
ABBREVIATIONS: BHs – bank holidays Etr – Easter Spring BH – Spring Bank Holiday fr – from hrs – hours m – mile mdnt – midnight
rdbt – roundabout rs – restricted service wk – week wknd – weekend x-roads – crossroads ⊗ No credit or debit cards ⊗ No dogs

ANGUS

MONIFIETH — Map 21 NO43

Places to visit

Barry Mill, BARRY, DD7 7RJ, 01241 856761 www.nts.org.uk/Property/Barry-Mill

HM Frigate Unicorn, DUNDEE, DD1 3BP, 01382 200900 www.frigateunicorn.org

Great for kids: Discovery Point & RRS Discovery, DUNDEE, DD1 4XA, 01382 309060 www.rrsdiscovery.com

Riverview Caravan Park

►►►► 82%

tel: 01382 535471 & 817979 **Marine Dr DD5 4NN**
email: info@riverview.co.uk
dir: *From Dundee on A930 follow signs to Monifieth, past supermarket, right signed golf course, left under rail bridge. Site signed on left.* **grid ref:** *NO502322*

A well-landscaped seaside site where the touring pitches are set in small areas; they are neatly divided by hedges and mature trees which are trimmed to allow light in; those on the beachfront enjoy excellent views. The site is a few minutes' walk from Monifieth and a pleasant stroll along the beachfront will take you to the nearby town of Broughty Ferry with its numerous boutique shops and other amenities. The site has good facilities, including a steam room and sauna and a gym. This is a good site for a traditional seaside holiday. The site has static homes, some of which are for hire. 5.5 acre site. 49 touring pitches. 45 hardstandings. Caravan pitches. Motorhome pitches. 46 statics.

Open: Mar-Oct **Last arrival:** 22.00hrs **Last departure:** 12.30hrs

Pitches: 🚐 🚌

Leisure: 🏋 ⚽ 🎱

Facilities: 🪒 💨 ♿ 🪑 🐕 [WiFi] 💻 ♻ ℹ

Services: 🔌 🫧 🛢 [T] 🍴 🚰

Within 3 miles: ⛳ 🎬 🎣 ◎ 🏄 [S] 🫧 🐎

Notes: Dogs must be kept on leads.

AA Pubs & Restaurants nearby: The Royal Arch Bar, BROUGHTY FERRY, DD5 2DS, 01382 779741

ARGYLL & BUTE

CARRADALE — Map 20 NR83

Carradale Bay Caravan Park

▷▷▷ 90%

tel: 01583 431665 **PA28 6QG**
email: info@carradalebay.com
dir: *A83 from Tarbert towards Campbeltown, left onto B842 (Carradale road), right onto B879. Site 0.5m.* **grid ref:** *NR815385*

A beautiful, natural site on the sea's edge with superb views over Kilbrannan Sound to the Isle of Arran. Pitches are landscaped into small bays broken up by shrubs and bushes, and backed by dunes close to the long sandy beach. The toilet facilities are appointed to a very high standard. An environmentally-aware site that requires the use of green toilet chemicals – available on the site. Lodges and static caravans for holiday hire. 8 acre site. 74 touring pitches. Caravan pitches. Motorhome pitches. Tent pitches. 15 statics.

Open: Apr-Sep **Last arrival:** 22.00hrs **Last departure:** noon

Pitches: 🚐 🚌 ⛺

Facilities: 🪒 💨 ❄ ♿ [S] 🪑 🐕 [WiFi] ♻ ℹ

Services: 🔌 🫧 [T]

Within 3 miles: ⛳ ⛵ 🎣 🏄 [S] 🫧 🐎

GLENDARUEL — Map 20 NR98

Places to visit

Benmore Botanic Garden, BENMORE, PA23 8QU, 01369 706261 www.rbge.org.uk

Glendaruel Caravan Park

►►► 82%

tel: 01369 820267 **PA22 3AB**
email: mail@glendaruelcaravanpark.com
dir: *A83 onto A815 to Strachur, 13m to site on A886. By ferry from Gourock to Dunoon take B836, then A886 for approx 4m N. (NB this route is not recommended for towing vehicles – 1:5 uphill gradient on B836).* **grid ref:** *NR005865*

Glendaruel Gardens, with an arboretum, is the peaceful setting for this pleasant, well established wooded site in a valley surrounded by mountains. It is set back from the main road and screened by trees so that a peaceful stay is ensured. It has level grass and hardstanding pitches. A regular local bus service and a ferry at Portavadie (where there are retail outlets and eateries) make a day trip to the Mull of Kintyre a possibility. The Cowal Way, a long distance path, and a national cycle path pass the site. Static caravans and a 'little' camping lodge are available for hire. 6 acre site. 27 touring pitches. 15 hardstandings. 12 seasonal pitches. Caravan pitches. Motorhome pitches. Tent pitches. 32 statics.

Open: Apr-Oct **Last arrival:** 22.00hrs **Last departure:** noon

Pitches: 🚐 🚌 ⛺

Leisure: ⚽ **Facilities:** 🪒 💨 ❄ [S] 🪑 🐕 [WiFi] ♻ ℹ

Services: 🔌 🫧 🛢 🔋 [T] 🍴 **Within 3 miles:** 🎣 [S] 🫧

Notes: Dogs must be kept on leads. Sea trout & salmon fishing, woodland walks, 24-hour emergency phone.

OBAN
Map 20 NM82

Places to visit

Dunstaffnage Castle and Chapel, OBAN, PA37 1PZ, 01631 562465
www.historic-scotland.gov.uk

Bonawe Historic Iron Furnace, TAYNUILT, PA35 1JQ, 01866 822432
www.historic-scotland.gov.uk

Oban Caravan & Camping Park
▶▶▶81%

tel: 01631 562425 **Gallanachmore Farm, Gallanach Rd PA34 4QH**
email: info@obancaravanpark.com
dir: *From Oban centre follow signs for Mull Ferry. After terminal follow Gallanach signs. 2m to site.* **grid ref:** *NM831277*

Situated two miles from Oban this is a lovely site, with pleasant terraced areas that are separated by large swathes of well maintained grass and natural landscaping. Many pitches overlook the busy ferry route between Oban and the Isle of Colonsay. The site is convenient for the ferry terminal in Oban, and the train and bus stations provide easy access for public transport, making this an ideal site for both main holidays or for shorter stays. The owners have invested in new washroom facilities and have plans to install family rooms together with a new washroom block in the near future. Well-equipped camping pods are located in an area that offers privacy. 15 acre site. 120 touring pitches. 35 hardstandings. 10 seasonal pitches. Caravan pitches. Motorhome pitches. Tent pitches. 17 statics.

Open: Etr & Apr-Oct (rs Etr-end May & Sep-Oct shop closed) **Last arrival:** 20.00hrs (later arrivals by prior arrangement) **Last departure:** noon

Pitches: * 🚐 £17-£20 🚍 £17-£20 ⛺ £16-£18 🏠 prices shown below

Leisure: 🎢 🎯

Facilities: 🏪 ⊙ 🗗 ⚹ 🗑 🚻 🚼 📶 ❶

Services: 🔌 🗄 💧 🗑 🚽 🚰 🛠

Glamping: Wooden Pods 6, £45-£65 Changeover day Any day Min stay 1 night (2 nights if a Saturday night is included) Own kitchen Car by unit

Within 3 miles: 🛥 ✎ 🗐 📎 ⛴ 🛒 🛍 ↻

Notes: No commercial vehicles, no noise after 23.00hrs. Dogs must be kept on leads. Indoor kitchen for tent campers, fresh bread available each morning.

AA Pubs & Restaurants nearby: Coast, OBAN, PA34 5NT, 01631 569900

SOUTH AYRSHIRE

AYR

Places to visit

Robert Burns Birthplace Museum, ALLOWAY, KA7 4PQ, 01292 443700
www.burnsmuseum.org.uk

Great for kids: Heads of Ayr Farm Park, ALLOWAY, KA7 4LD, 01292 441210
www.headsofayrfarmpark.co.uk

AYR
Map 20 NS32

Craig Tara Holiday Park
HOLIDAY CENTRE 87%

tel: 0800 975 7579 & 01292 265141 **KA7 4LB**
email: craigtara@haven.com **web:** www.haven.com/craigtara
dir: *A77 towards Stranraer, 2nd right after Bankfield rdbt. Follow signs for A719 & to park.* **grid ref:** *NS300184*

This lovely holiday centre on the outskirts of Ayr is set in a sheltered spot on the coast, with direct access to a small beach. The park has a great family atmosphere with welcoming staff and entertainment for all ages. The touring area is in a secluded area, with an amenity block and 40 fully serviced hardstanding pitches. At the heart of the holiday centre are various large complexes with show bars, restaurants, takeaways, computer games and slot machines. There are also good shops, a supermarket with a bakery, and a large soft play area. The pool complex facilities are excellent with flumes, slides, splash zones and overhead viewing walkways. There is a regular service bus to Ayr. 213 acre site. 44 touring pitches. 44 hardstandings. Caravan pitches. Motorhome pitches. 1100 statics.

Open: mid Mar-end Oct (rs mid Mar-May & Sep-Oct some facilities may be limited) **Last arrival:** 20.00hrs **Last departure:** 10.00hrs

Pitches: 🚐 🚍 **Leisure:** 🏊 🌊 🎯 🎵 🎶 **Facilities:** 🏪 ⊙ 🕹 🗑 🚻 📶 ♻ ❶

Services: 🔌 🗄 🍽 🛒 🍴 🍔 **Within 3 miles:** 🛥 🗐 📎 ◎ 🛒 🛍 ↻

Notes: No commercial vehicles, no bookings by persons under 21yrs unless a family booking. Max 2 dogs per booking, certain dog breeds banned. Dogs must be kept on leads.

AA Pubs & Restaurants nearby: Fairfield House Hotel, AYR, KA7 2AS, 01292 267461

See advert on page 378

PITCHES: 🚐 Caravans 🚍 Motorhomes ⛺ Tents 🏠 Glamping accommodation **SERVICES:** 🔌 Electric hook up 🗄 Launderette 🍽 Licensed bar 🔋 Calor Gas ⊘ Camping Gaz 🗑 Toilet fluid 🍴 Café/Restaurant 🍔 Fast Food/Takeaway 🛠 Battery charging 🚼 Baby care 🛠 Motorvan service point **ABBREVIATIONS:** BHs – bank holidays Etr – Easter Spring BH – Spring Bank Holiday fr – from hrs – hours m – mile mdnt – midnight rdbt – roundabout rs – restricted service wk – week wknd – weekend x-roads – crossroads ◎ No credit or debit cards ⊗ No dogs

BARRHILL
Map 20 NX28

Barrhill Holiday Park
►►►► 75%

tel: 01465 821355 **KA26 0PZ**
email: barrhillholidaypark@gmail.com
dir: *On A714 Newton Stewart to Girvan road. 1m N of Barrhill.* **grid ref:** *NX216835*

A small, friendly park in a tranquil rural location, screened from the A714 by trees. The park is terraced and well landscaped, and a high quality amenity block includes disabled facilities. The local bus to Girvan stops at the site entrance. 6 acre site. 30 touring pitches. 30 hardstandings. Caravan pitches. Motorhome pitches. Tent pitches. 49 statics.

Open: Mar-Jan **Last arrival:** 22.00hrs **Last departure:** 10.00hrs

Pitches: * 🚐 £15 🚐 £15 ⛺ £7-£15

Facilities: 📶 ⊙ 🍴 ✳ 👶 🚿 📮 🛒 ♻ ❗

Services: 🚐 🛢 🔒 🧺 🚽 🛒

Within 3 miles: 🚴 🏧

Notes: 😊 No noise after 23.00hrs. Dogs must be kept on leads.

GIRVAN
Map 20 NX19

Places to visit
Culzean Castle & Country Park, CULZEAN CASTLE, KA19 8LE, 01292 541940
www.nts.org.uk/Property/Culzean-Castle-and-Country-Park

Turnberry Holiday Park
HOLIDAY HOME PARK 79%

tel: 01655 331288 **KA26 9JW**
email: enquiries@turnberryholidaypark.co.uk **web:** www.turnberryholidaypark.co.uk
dir: *Site signed from A77 between Turnberry & Girvan. 250mtrs to site adjacent to Dowhill Farm.* **grid ref:** *NS203033*

Situated in beautiful South Ayrshire with views of the Firth of Clyde and the iconic Ailsa Craig, this 26-acre park is between the busy seaside town of Ayr and the fishing town of Girvan. The many tourist attractions in the area include Turnberry Golf Course, Maidens and Culzean Castle and Country Park. The park is set in open farmland and improvements are still ongoing. The Ailsa Bar provides family-centred entertainment as well as a café serving good food. There is a swimming pool, reception and sales office. There are 205 holiday homes, 9 statics, and a 3-bedroom chalet for hire.

Open: Mar-4 Jan

Changeover day: Mon, Fri & Sat

Arrival and departure times: Please contact the site

Statics: 15 Sleeps 8 Bedrms 2-3 Bathrms 1-2 (inc en suite) Toilets 1-2 Microwave Freezer TV Sky/FTV DVD Modem/Wi-fi Linen inc Elec inc Gas inc Grass area Low season £115-£398 High season £238-£573

Children: 🍼 Cots Highchair **Dogs:** 2 on leads

Leisure: 🚲 Cycle hire 🤚 🏔

Within 3 miles: Spa ⛎ 🚴

DUMFRIES & GALLOWAY

ANNAN   Map 21 NY16

Places to visit

Ruthwell Cross, RUTHWELL, 0131 550 7612 www.historic-scotland.gov.uk

Great for kids: Caerlaverock Castle, CAERLAVEROCK, DG1 4RU, 01387 770244 www.historic-scotland.gov.uk

Galabank Caravan & Camping Group
►►74%

tel: 01461 203539 & 07999 344520 **North St DG12 5DQ**
email: margaret.ramage@hotmail.com
dir: *Site access via North St.* **grid ref:** *NY192676*

A tidy, well-maintained grassy little park with spotless facilities close to the centre of town but with pleasant rural views, and skirted by the River Annan. 1 acre site. 30 touring pitches. Caravan pitches. Motorhome pitches. Tent pitches.

Open: Mar-Oct **Last departure:** noon

Pitches: ⊞ ⊞ ▲ **Facilities:** ⬤ ⊙ ⧽ ⚲

Services: ⊡ **Within 3 miles:** ↨ ⊟ ⧸ ⓢ ∪

Notes: ⊗ Dogs must be kept on leads. Washing machine & tumble dryer in ladies' block. Social club adjacent

AA Pubs & Restaurants nearby: Smiths at Gretna Green, GRETNA, DG16 5EA, 01461 337007

BRIGHOUSE BAY   Map 20 NX64

Places to visit

MacLellan's Castle, KIRKCUDBRIGHT, DG6 4JD, 01557 331856 www.historic-scotland.gov.uk

Broughton House & Garden, KIRKCUDBRIGHT, DG6 4JX, 01557 330437 www.nts.org.uk/Property/Broughton-House-and-Garden

Great for kids: Galloway Wildlife Conservation Park, KIRKCUDBRIGHT, DG6 4XX, 01557 331645 www.gallowaywildlife.co.uk

PREMIER PARK

Brighouse Bay Holiday Park
►►►►►88%

tel: 01557 870267 **DG6 4TS**
email: info@gillespie-leisure.co.uk
dir: *From Gatehouse of Fleet take A755 towards Kirkcudbright, onto B727 (signed Borgue). Or from Kirkcudbright take A755 onto B727. Site signed in 3m.*
grid ref: *NX628453*

This top class park has a country club feel and enjoys a marvellous coastal setting adjacent to the beach and has superb views. Pitches have been imaginatively sculpted into the meadowland, where stone walls and hedges blend in with the site's mature trees. These features, together with the large range of leisure activities, make this an excellent park for families who enjoy an active holiday. The site has an 18-hole golf course with its own PGA professional. Please note, many of the facilities are at an extra charge. Wooden pods and self-catering units are available for hire. 120 acre site. 190 touring pitches. 100 hardstandings. 50 seasonal pitches. Caravan pitches. Motorhome pitches. Tent pitches. 225 statics.

Open: all year (rs Outside school hols leisure club closed Mon-Wed inclusive)
Last arrival: 20.00hrs **Last departure:** 11.30hrs

Pitches: ⊞ ⊞ ▲ ⋔

Leisure: ⛱ ✦ ⛳ ♫ ♪ ⚘

Facilities: ⊙ ⧽ ✳ ⅋ ⓢ ⊞ ⚲ WiFi 🖥 ♻ ⓘ

Services: ⊡ ⓢ ⚭ 🛢 Ⓣ ⓘ⊙ 🛒 ↯

Glamping: Wooden Pods 3

Within 3 miles: ↨ ⧸ ⊚ ⓢ ⓢ

Notes: No noise after 22.30hrs, no jet skis, 10mph speed limit on site, restricted services in winter months. Dogs must be kept on leads. Mini golf, outdoor bowling green, jacuzzi, slipway, boating pond, coarse fishing, sea angling

AA Pubs & Restaurants nearby: Selkirk Arms Hotel, KIRKCUDBRIGHT, DG6 4JG, 01557 330402

PITCHES: ⊞ Caravans ⊞ Motorhomes ▲ Tents ⋔ Glamping accommodation **SERVICES:** ⊡ Electric hook up ⓢ Launderette ⚭ Licensed bar
🛢 Calor Gas ⧸ Camping Gaz Ⓣ Toilet fluid ⓘ⊙ Café/Restaurant 🛒 Fast Food/Takeaway 🔋 Battery charging 🛒 Baby care ↯ Motorvan service point
ABBREVIATIONS: BHs – bank holidays Etr – Easter Spring BH – Spring Bank Holiday fr – from hrs – hours m – mile mdnt – midnight
rdbt – roundabout rs – restricted service wk – week wknd – weekend x-roads – crossroads ⊗ No credit or debit cards ⊗ No dogs

| DALBEATTIE | Map 21 NX86 |

Places to visit

Threave Garden & Estate, CASTLE DOUGLAS, DG7 1RX, 01556 502575
www.nts.org.uk/Property/Threave-Estate

Orchardton Tower, PALNACKIE www.historic-scotland.gov.uk

Glenearly Caravan Park
►►►► 86%

tel: 01556 611393 **DG5 4NE**
email: glenearlycaravan@btconnect.com **web:** www.glenearlycaravanpark.co.uk
dir: *From Dumfries take A711 towards Dalbeattie. Site entrance after Edingham Farm on right (200yds before boundary sign).* **grid ref:** *NX838628*

An excellent small park set in open countryside with good views of Long Fell, Maidenpap and Dalbeattie Forest. The park is located in 84 acres of farmland which has been carefully managed over the years to provide a peaceful and secluded location for a tranquil holiday. The attention to detail is excellent with neatly kept grass, well tended borders and an excellent amenity block. There's a fishing lochan and woodland plus a wildlife walk. Dalbeattie is a leisurely 10-minute walk away and the local bus passes the end of the farm road. The beautiful Solway coast is just five minutes away by car with Rockcliffe, Colvend and Kippford interesting places to explore. For the more adventurous, the mountain bike trails are numerous. 10 acre site. 39 touring pitches. 33 hardstandings. 10 seasonal pitches. Caravan pitches. Motorhome pitches. Tent pitches. 74 statics.

Open: all year **Last arrival:** 19.00hrs **Last departure:** noon
Pitches: 🚐 £17-£19 🚙 £17-£19 ▲ £17-£19
Leisure: ⚠ ⚟ ⚲
Facilities: 🏠 🅿 ⊙ ☈ ✳ ⚹ 🐾 📶 ♻ ⓘ
Services: 🔌 🗑 🛁 🎇 ⛟
Within 3 miles: ⚓ ⚞ ⚲ ◎ ⚞ 🛒 🗑 U
Notes: No commercial vehicles. Dogs must be kept on leads. Table tennis, pool table.

| ECCLEFECHAN | Map 21 NY17 |

Places to visit

Robert Burns House, DUMFRIES, DG1 2PS, 01387 255297 www.dumgal.gov.uk

Old Bridge House Museum, DUMFRIES, DG2 7BE, 01387 256904
www.dumgal.gov.uk

Great for kids: Dumfries Museum & Camera Obscura, DUMFRIES, DG2 7SW, 01387 253374 www.dumgal.gov.uk/museums

| PREMIER PARK |

Hoddom Castle Caravan Park
►►►►► 82%

tel: 01576 300251 **Hoddom DG11 1AS**
email: enquiries@hoddomcastle.co.uk
dir: *M74 junct 19, B725 signed Ecclefechan. At next rdbt left onto B7076. Right at x-roads in Ecclefechan, follow site signs. Left at T-junct onto B723. Right onto B725 to site. Or from Annan on B721 take B723 signed Lockerbie & follow site signs.* **grid ref:** *NY154729*

A lovely, peaceful family park located close to Annan, with its large range of shops and eateries. There are three amenity blocks, one is adjacent to the reception in part of the old castle buildings. There are extensive grounds, with many walks including the Annan Way which borders the River Annan. The park is neatly divided into statics, seasonal tourers and touring pitches with a large area for tents, plus seven attractive wooden 'chill' pods and four Kelo huts for hire. Fishing, a nine-hole golf course and a large children's play area are available; the small restaurant and café are open daily. 28 acre site. 200 touring pitches. 63 hardstandings. 94 seasonal pitches. Caravan pitches. Motorhome pitches. Tent pitches. 54 statics.

Open: Etr or Apr-Oct **Last arrival:** 21.00hrs **Last departure:** 13.00hrs
Pitches: 🚐 🚙 ▲ 🏠
Leisure: ⚠ ⚟ 🎱 ⚲ ⚡
Facilities: 🚿 🏠 🅿 ⊙ ☈ ✳ ⚹ 🐾 📷 🛒 ⚞ ♻ ⓘ
Services: 🔌 🗑 🚽 🛁 T ◎ 🎇 ⛟
Glamping: **Wooden Pods** 7, £42-£52 Min stay 1 night (2 nights at wknds, 3 nights at BHs) Car by unit **Kelo huts** 4, £57-£67 Min stay 1 night (2 nights at wknds, 3 nights at BHs) Car by unit
Within 3 miles: ⚞ ⚲ ◎ 🛒 🗑
Notes: No electric scooters, no gazebos, no fires, no noise after mdnt. Cash only accepted in bar/restaurant. Dogs must be kept on leads.
AA Pubs & Restaurants nearby: Smiths at Gretna Green, GRETNA, DG16 5EA, 01461 337007

GATEHOUSE OF FLEET — Map 20 NX55

Places to visit

MacLellan's Castle, KIRKCUDBRIGHT, DG6 4JD, 01557 331856
www.historic-scotland.gov.uk

Great for kids: Galloway Wildlife Conservation Park, KIRKCUDBRIGHT, DG6 4XX,
01557 331645 www.gallowaywildlife.co.uk

Auchenlarie Holiday Park

HOLIDAY CENTRE 89%

tel: 01556 506200 & 206201 **DG7 2EX**
email: enquiries@auchenlarie.co.uk
dir: *Direct access from A75, 5m W of Gatehouse of Fleet.* **grid ref:** *NX536522*

A well-organised family park set on cliffs overlooking Wigtown Bay, with its own sandy beach. The tenting area, on sloping grassland surrounded by mature trees, has its own sanitary facilities, while the marked caravan pitches are in paddocks, with open views and the provision of high quality toilets. The leisure centre includes a swimming pool, gym, solarium and sports hall; there's an entertainment suite with live cabaret acts, and the Lavender Room offers beauty treatments and massages. There are static caravans and lodges to rent — five have hot tubs. 32 acre site. 49 touring pitches. 52 hardstandings. Caravan pitches. Motorhome pitches. Tent pitches. 400 statics.

Open: mid Feb-Oct **Last arrival:** 20.00hrs **Last departure:** noon
Pitches: * ⊞ £21-£26 ⊞ £21-£26 ▲ £21-£26 ⋔ prices shown below
Leisure:
Facilities:
Services:
Glamping: Swift S-Pods 2, £45-£55 En suite Own kitchen Car by unit
Within 3 miles:
Notes: Dogs must be kept on leads. Crazy golf, baby-changing facilities, children's entertainment.
AA Pubs & Restaurants nearby: Cally Palace Hotel, GATEHOUSE OF FLEET, DG7 2DL, 01557 814341

Anwoth Caravan Site

►►►► 80%

tel: 01557 814333 & 01556 506200 **DG7 2JU**
email: enquiries@auchenlarie.co.uk
dir: *From A75 into Gatehouse of Fleet, site on right towards Stranraer. Signed from town centre.* **grid ref:** *NX595563*

A very high quality park in a peaceful sheltered setting within easy walking distance of the village, ideally placed for exploring the scenic hills, valleys and coastline. Grass, hardstanding and fully serviced pitches are available and guests may use the leisure facilities at the sister site, Auchenlarie Holiday Park. 2 acre

site. 28 touring pitches. 13 hardstandings. Caravan pitches. Motorhome pitches. Tent pitches. 44 statics.

Open: Mar-Oct **Last arrival:** 20.00hrs **Last departure:** noon
Pitches: * ⊞ £16-£18.50 ⊞ £16-£18.50 ▲ £16-£18.50
Facilities:
Services:
Within 3 miles:
Notes: Dogs must be kept on leads.
AA Pubs & Restaurants nearby: Cally Palace Hotel, GATEHOUSE OF FLEET, DG7 2DL, 01557 814341

GRETNA — Map 21 NY36

Places to visit

Carlisle Cathedral, CARLISLE, CA3 8TZ, 01228 548071
www.carlislecathedral.org.uk

Tullie House Museum & Art Gallery Trust, CARLISLE, CA3 8TP, 01228 618718
www.tulliehouse.co.uk

Great for kids: Carlisle Castle, CARLISLE, CA3 8UR, 01228 591922
www.english-heritage.org.uk/daysout/properties/carlisle-castle

Braids Caravan Park

►►►► 78%

tel: 01461 337409 **Annan Rd DG16 5DQ**
email: enquiries@thebraidscaravanpark.co.uk
dir: *On B721, 0.5m from village on right, towards Annan.* **grid ref:** *NY313674*

A very well-maintained park conveniently located on the outskirts of Gretna village. Within walking distance is Gretna Gateway Outlet Village, and nearby is Gretna Green with the World Famous Old Blacksmith's Shop. It proves a convenient stop-over for anyone travelling to and from the north of Scotland or Northern Ireland (via the ferry at Stranraer). The park has first-class toilet facilities and generously-sized all-weather pitches. Please note that tents are not accepted. A rally field and a meeting room are available. 5 acre site. 50 touring pitches. 42 hardstandings. Caravan pitches. Motorhome pitches.

Open: all year **Last arrival:** 20.00hrs (19.00hrs in winter) **Last departure:** noon
Pitches: ⊞ ⊞
Facilities:
Services:
Within 3 miles:
Notes: Dogs must be kept on leads.
AA Pubs & Restaurants nearby: Smiths at Gretna Green, GRETNA, DG16 5EA, 01461 337007

GRETNA *continued*

King Robert the Bruce's Cave Caravan & Camping Park
▶▶▶▶ 76%

tel: 01461 800285 & 07779 138694 **Cove Estate, Kirkpatrick Fleming DG11 3AT**
email: enquiries@brucescave.co.uk **web:** www.brucescave.co.uk
dir: *Exit A74(M) junct 21, follow Kirkpatrick Fleming signs, N through village, pass Station Inn, left at Bruce's Court. Over rail crossing to site.* **grid ref:** *NY266705*

The lovely wooded grounds of an old castle and mansion are the setting for this pleasant park. The mature woodland is a haven for wildlife; there is a riverside walk to Robert the Bruce's Cave and on-site coarse fishing is available. A toilet block with en suite facilities is especially useful to families. The site is convenient for the M74 and there is a good local bus service available nearby; the site is on a National Cycle Route. 80 acre site. 75 touring pitches. 60 hardstandings. Caravan pitches. Motorhome pitches. Tent pitches. 35 statics.

Open: Apr-Nov (rs Nov shop closed, water restrictions) **Last arrival:** 22.00hrs **Last departure:** 16.00hrs

Pitches: 🚐 🚃 ▲

Leisure: ⚠ ⊙ 🔍 ♟ 🎣

Facilities: 🛁 🅿 ⊙ ℗ ✳ ⅏ ⓢ ⊞ ♨ WiFi 🖥 ♻ ❶

Services: 🔌 🗑 🔒 ⊘ Ⓣ 🛒 ⏚ ⬇

Within 3 miles: ℗ ⅏ ⓢ 🗑 ∪

Notes: No noise after 23.00hrs. Dogs must be kept on leads. BMX bike hire, first aid available.

AA Pubs & Restaurants nearby: Smiths at Gretna Green, GRETNA, DG16 5EA, 01461 337007

Places to visit
Orchardton Tower, PALNACKIE www.historic-scotland.gov.uk

Coastal Kippford
▶▶▶ 79%

GOLD

tel: 01556 620636 **DG5 4LF**
email: info@coastalkippford.com
dir: *From Dumfries take A711 to Dalbeattie, left onto A710 (Solway coast road) for 3.5m. Park 200yds beyond Kippford turn on right.* **grid ref:** *NX844564*

An attractively landscaped park set in hilly countryside close to the Urr Water estuary and a sand and shingle beach; there are spectacular views. The level touring pitches are on hardstands with private garden areas, and many are fully serviced; there are attractive lodges for hire. Doon Hill and woodland walks separate the park from the lovely village of Kippford. Red squirrels can be spotted in the woods, and opportunities to fish and to play golf are very close by. 18 acre site. 23 touring pitches. 14 hardstandings. 19 seasonal pitches. Caravan pitches. Motorhome pitches. Tent pitches. 157 statics.

Open: all year **Last arrival:** 21.30hrs **Last departure:** noon

Pitches: ✱ 🚐 £24-£29 🚃 £24-£29 ▲ £22-£27

Leisure: ⚠ ⊙

Facilities: 🅿 🅿 ⊙ ℗ ✳ ⅏ ⓢ ⊞ 🔧 WiFi 🖥 ♻ ❶

Services: 🔌 🗑 🔒 ⊘ Ⓣ ⏚ ⬇

Within 3 miles: ℗ ℗ ⊙ 🗑 🗑 ∪

Notes: No camp fires. Dogs must be kept on leads. Table tennis.

AA Pubs & Restaurants nearby: Balcary Bay Hotel, AUCHENCAIRN, DG7 1QZ, 01556 640217

KIRKCUDBRIGHT
Map 20 NX65

Places to visit

The Stewartry Museum, KIRKCUDBRIGHT, DG6 4AQ, 01557 331643
www.dumgal.gov.uk/museums

Tolbooth Art Centre, KIRKCUDBRIGHT, DG6 4JL, 01557 331556
www.dumgal.gov.uk/museums

Great for kids: Broughton House & Garden, KIRKCUDBRIGHT, DG6 4JX,
01557 330437 www.nts.org.uk/Property/Broughton-House-and-Garden

PREMIER PARK

Seaward Caravan Park
►►►►►84%

tel: 01557 870267 & 331079 **Dhoon Bay DG6 4TJ**
email: info@gillespie-leisure.co.uk
dir: 2m SW of Kirkcudbright take A755 W, then B727 signed Borgue.
grid ref: NX662492

An attractive park with outstanding views over Kirkcudbright Bay which forms part of the Dee Estuary. Access to a sandy cove with rock pools is just across the road. Facilities are well organised and neatly kept, and the park offers a very peaceful atmosphere. The leisure facilities at the other Gillespie Parks are available to visitors to Seaward Caravan Park. There are five static homes, three wooden pods and two mini lodges for hire. 23 acre site. 25 touring pitches. 20 hardstandings. 6 seasonal pitches. Caravan pitches. Motorhome pitches. Tent pitches. 54 statics.

Open: Mar-Oct (rs Mar-Spring BH & Sep-Oct swimming pool closed)
Last arrival: 20.00hrs **Last departure:** 11.30hrs

Pitches: 🚐 �" 🅰 ⛺

Leisure: 🏊 🎣

Facilities: ⊙ 🅿 ✳ ⚑ 🚿 🖽 🛎 ⓦⓘⓕⓘ ⓘ

Services: 🔌 🗑 🛢 🚿 Ⓣ

Glamping: Wooden Pods 3 Mini lodges 2

Within 3 miles: 🚵 🎣 ◎ 🛒 🗑

Notes: No noise after 22.30hrs, 10mph speed limit on site. Dogs must be kept on leads. Mini golf, sea angling.

AA Pubs & Restaurants nearby: Selkirk Arms Hotel, KIRKCUDBRIGHT, DG6 4JG, 01557 330402

LANGHOLM
Map 21 NY38

Places to visit

Hermitage Castle, HERMITAGE, TD9 0LU, 01387 376222
www.historic-scotland.gov.uk

Ewes Water Caravan & Camping Park
►►66%

tel: 013873 80386 **Milntown DG13 0BG**
dir: Accessed directly from A7, approx 0.5m N of Langholm. Site in Langholm Rugby Club.
grid ref: NY365855

On the banks of the River Esk, this attractive park lies in a sheltered wooded valley close to an unspoilt Borders' town. 2 acre site. 24 touring pitches. Caravan pitches. Motorhome pitches. Tent pitches.

Open: Apr-Sep **Last departure:** noon

Pitches: 🚐 �" 🅰

Facilities: ⊙ ✳ ⚑ 🚿 🛎 **Services:** 🔌 🛢 🚿 🛗

Within 3 miles: 🚵 🎣 🛒 **Notes:** 🚫 Large playing area.

LOCKERBIE

See Ecclefechan

PALNACKIE
Map 21 NX85

Places to visit

Orchardton Tower, PALNACKIE www.historic-scotland.gov.uk

Barlochan Caravan Park
►►►76%

tel: 01557 870267 **DG7 1PF**
email: info@gillespie-leisure.co.uk
dir: On A711. Site signed before Palnackie. **grid ref:** NX819572

This is a lovely small caravan site situated within a short drive of the county town of Dalbeattie. It is ideally situated for exploring this particularly attractive area. The site has a number of static homes set on level terraces, with mature planting, whilst the caravan and camping pitches are located on the lower area, near the outdoor heated pool. There are hardstanding pitches, grass pitches with electricty for tents and two wooden pods. The site is part of the Gillespie Group and customers can use the facilities of their other sites. 9 acre site. 20 touring pitches. 10 hardstandings. 2 seasonal pitches. Caravan pitches. Motorhome pitches. Tent pitches. 65 statics.

Open: Apr-Oct (rs Apr-Spring BH & Sep-Oct swimming pool closed) **Last arrival:** 20.00hrs
Last departure: 11.30hrs

Pitches: 🚐 �" 🅰 ⛺

Leisure: 🏊 ♟ 🎣 **Facilities:** 🅿 ✳ ⚑ 🚿 🖽 🛎 ⓦⓘⓕⓘ ♻ ⓘ

Services: 🔌 🗑 🛢 🚿 Ⓣ 🛗

Glamping: Wooden Pods 2

Within 3 miles: 🚵 🎣 ◎ 🛒 🗑

Notes: Dogs must be kept on leads.

AA Pubs & Restaurants nearby: Balcary Bay Hotel, AUCHENCAIRN, DG7 1QZ, 01556 640217

Who has won Campsite of the Year for Scotland?
See page 14

PITCHES: 🚐 Caravans �" Motorhomes 🅰 Tents ⛺ Glamping accommodation **SERVICES:** 🔌 Electric hook up 🗑 Launderette 🍺 Licensed bar 🛢 Calor Gas 🚿 Camping Gaz Ⓣ Toilet fluid 🍴 Café/Restaurant 🍟 Fast Food/Takeaway 🛗 Battery charging 🛒 Baby care 🚐 Motorvan service point **ABBREVIATIONS:** BHs – bank holidays Etr – Easter Spring BH – Spring Bank Holiday fr – from hrs – hours m – mile mdnt – midnight rdbt – roundabout rs – restricted service wk – week wknd – weekend x-roads – crossroads 🚫 No credit or debit cards 🚫 No dogs

PARTON
Map 20 NX67

Places to visit

Threave Garden & Estate, CASTLE DOUGLAS, DG7 1RX, 01556 502575
www.nts.org.uk/Property/Threave-Estate

Threave Castle, CASTLE DOUGLAS, DG7 1TJ, 07711 223101
www.historic-scotland.gov.uk

Loch Ken Holiday Park
►►►► 87%

GOLD

tel: 01644 470282 **DG7 3NE**
email: office@lochkenholidaypark.co.uk
dir: On A713, N of Parton. Site on main road (NB it is advisable not to use Sat Nav).
grid ref: NX687702

Run with energy, enthusiasm and commitment by the hands-on Bryson family, this busy and popular park, with a natural emphasis on water activities, is set on the eastern shores of Loch Ken. With superb views, it is in a peaceful and beautiful spot adjacent to the RSPB Ken Dee Marshes reserve, with direct access to the loch for fishing and boat launching. It is also on the Galloway Red Kite Trail. The park offers a variety of watersports (canoeing, sailing, water skiing) as well as farm visits and nature trails. 15 acre site. 40 touring pitches. 20 hardstandings. 15 seasonal pitches. Caravan pitches. Motorhome pitches. Tent pitches. 35 statics.

Open: Feb-mid Nov (rs Feb-Mar (except Etr) & Nov - reduced shop hours)
Last departure: noon

Pitches: ♥ ♥ ▲

Leisure: ♨ ⊙ ♫ ☂

Facilities: ⊙ ℱ ✻ ⅙ ⑤ ♒ ⊁ ☠ WiFi ♻ ❶

Services: ⊡ ⑤ ᵇ ⌀ Ⓣ ⌂

Within 3 miles: ⅙ ℱ ⌇ ⑤ ⑤

Notes: No noise after 22.00hrs. Dogs must be kept on leads. Boat & canoe hire.

AA Pubs & Restaurants nearby: Cross Keys Hotel, NEW GALLOWAY, DG7 3RN, 01644 420494

PORT WILLIAM
Map 20 NX34

Places to visit

Glenluce Abbey, GLENLUCE, DG8 0AF, 01581 300541
www.historic-scotland.gov.uk

Whithorn Priory and Museum, WHITHORN, DG8 8PY, 01988 500508
www.historic-scotland.gov.uk

Kings Green Caravan Site
►►► 79%

tel: 01988 700489 **South St DG8 9SG**
dir: Direct access from A747 at junct with B7085 towards Whithorn. **grid ref:** NX340430

Located on the edge of Port William, with beautiful views across Luce Bay as far as the Isle of Man, this is a community run site which offers good facilities and large grass pitches, with direct access to the pebble shore where otters have been seen. The road which runs along the coast is relatively traffic free so does not detract from the tranquillity of this small site. Two public boat launches are available. There are several good shops in the village and a local bus, with links to Whithorn,

Garlieston and Newton Stewart, runs past the site. 3 acre site. 30 touring pitches. Caravan pitches. Motorhome pitches. Tent pitches.

Open: mid Mar-Oct **Last arrival:** 20.00hrs **Last departure:** noon

Pitches: * ♥ £12-£15 ♥ £12-£15 ▲ £12-£15

Facilities: ↖ ⊙ ℱ ⅙ ⑤ ♒ ⊁ WiFi ❶

Services: ⊡ ⑤

Within 3 miles: ⅙ ℱ ⌇ ⑤

Notes: No golf, no fireworks. Dogs must be kept on leads. Free book lending.

AA Pubs & Restaurants nearby: The Steam Packet Inn, ISLE OF WHITHORN, DG8 8LL, 01988 500334

SANDHEAD
Map 20 NX04

Places to visit

Glenwhan Gardens, STRANRAER, DG9 8PH, 01581 400222
www.glenwhangardens.co.uk

Ardwell House Gardens, ARDWELL, DG9 9LY, 01776 860227

Great for kids: Castle Kennedy Gardens, STRANRAER, DG9 8SL, 01776 702024
www.castlekennedygardens.com

Sands of Luce Holiday Park
►►►► 88%

tel: 01776 830456 & 830296 **Sands of Luce DG9 9JN**
email: info@sandsofluceholidaypark.co.uk
dir: From S & E: left from A75 onto B7084 signed Drummore. Site signed at junct with A716. From N: A77 through Stranraer towards Portpatrick, 2m, follow A716 signed Drummore, site signed in 5m. **grid ref:** NX103510

This is a large, well-managed holiday park overlooking Luce Bay. It has a private boat launch and direct access to a wide sandy beach, which proves popular with kite surfers. The excellent, newly developed Lighthouse is a truly upmarket restaurant and bar with space for live entertainment. Attached to the Lighthouse is the new reception, and the staff at the bar can also handle arrivals and other enquiries; this arrangement significantly extends the checking in times. A wide range of entertainment, listed on daily planners, is on offer and includes kite flying, kite surfing, foraging and cooking, and entertainers for both adults and children. There is a regular bus that passes the park entrance, and Stranraer, the Mull of Galloway or Port Logan Botanical Gardens are not far away by car. 30 acre site. 80 touring pitches. 20 hardstandings. 50 seasonal pitches. Caravan pitches. Motorhome pitches. Tent pitches. 270 statics.

Open: Mar-Jan (rs Nov-Jan toilet block & shower closed) **Last arrival:** 20.00hrs
Last departure: noon

Pitches: ♥ ♥ ▲

Leisure: ⋀ ♻ ♣ ♫

Facilities: ⊙ ℱ ✻ ⅙ ⑤ ♒ ♒ ⊁ ☠ WiFi ▦ ♻ ❶

Services: ⊡ ⑤ ᵇ|| ⅏ ⌂ ⑊

Within 3 miles: ⅙ ⅙ ℱ ⌇ ⑤

Notes: No quad bikes, Dogs must be kept on leads & owners must clear up after their dogs. Boat launching & storage.

AA Pubs & Restaurants nearby: Tigh Na Mara Hotel, SANDHEAD, DG9 9JF, 01776 830210

Knockinaam Lodge, PORTPATRICK, DG9 9AD, 01776 810471

LEISURE: ⛱ Indoor pool ⛱ Outdoor pool ⋀ Children's playground ✋ Kid's club ☌ Tennis court ♣ Games room ⅙ Golf course ⌇ Boat hire ✇ Cycle hire ⬒ Cinema ♫ Entertainment ℱ Fishing ⊙ Mini golf ⌁ Pitch n putt ☰ Watersports ✦ Gym ♻ Sports field ☋ Stables **FACILITIES:** � Bath ↖ Shower ℙ Private washing cubicles ⊙ Electric shaver ℱ Hairdryer ✻ Ice Packs ⅙ Disabled facilities ⑤ Shop on site ℥ Mobile shop ▦ BBQ area ♒ Picnic area WiFi Wi-fi ▦ Internet access ♻ Recycling ⊙ Tourist info ♒ Dog exercise area ✇ Car hire can be arranged

SANDYHILLS
Map 21 NX85

Places to visit

Threave Garden & Estate, CASTLE DOUGLAS, DG7 1RX, 01556 502575
www.nts.org.uk/Property/Threave-Estate

Orchardton Tower, PALNACKIE www.historic-scotland.gov.uk

Great for kids: Threave Castle, CASTLE DOUGLAS, DG7 1TJ, 07711 223101
www.historic-scotland.gov.uk

Sandyhills Bay Leisure Park
►►►► 79%

tel: 01557 870267 **DG5 4NY**
email: info@gillespie-leisure.co.uk
dir: *On A710, 7m from Dalbeattie, 6.5m from Kirkbean.* grid ref: *NX892552*

A well maintained park in a superb location beside a beach, and close to many attractive villages. The level, grassy site is sheltered by woodland, and the south-facing Sandyhills Bay and beach, with their caves and rock pools provide endless entertainment for all the family. The leisure facilities at Brighouse Bay are available to visitors to Sandyhills Bay. Two new wooden pods have now joined the two wooden wigwams already offered – each has a TV, fridge, kettle and microwave. 15 acre site. 24 touring pitches. Caravan pitches. Motorhome pitches. Tent pitches. 32 statics.

Open: Apr-Oct **Last arrival:** 20.00hrs **Last departure:** 11.30hrs

Pitches: ⚏ ⚏ Å ⛺

Facilities: ⊙ 🏊 ☀ 🛁 🎋 🛗 WiFi 🅰

Services: 🔌 🔲 🔋 🚿 🚽 🔋 🛒 🚮

Glamping: Wooden Pods 2 Wooden Wigwams 2

Within 3 miles: ⚓ 🏌 🎣 🐎 U

Notes: No motorised scooters, jet skis or own quad bikes. Dogs must be kept on leads.

STRANRAER
Map 20 NX06

Places to visit

Glenwhan Gardens, STRANRAER, DG9 8PH, 01581 400222
www.glenwhangardens.co.uk

Great for kids: Castle Kennedy Gardens, STRANRAER, DG9 8SL, 01776 702024
www.castlekennedygardens.com

Aird Donald Caravan Park
►►►► 82%

tel: 01776 702025 **London Rd DG9 8RN**
email: enquiries@aird-donald.co.uk
dir: *From A75 left on entering Stranraer (signed). Opposite school, site 300yds.*
grid ref: *NX075605*

A spacious touring site set behind mature trees and within a five-minute walk of Stranraer town centre at the head of Loch Ryan. It is an ideal base for touring the 'Rhins of Galloway', to visit Port Logan Botanic Gardens (half an hour's drive) or the Mull of Galloway Lighthouse (a 45-minute drive). It provides a very convenient

stopover for the Cairnryan ferry to Ireland, but there's plenty to do in the area if staying longer. A 25-pitch rally field is available. 12 acre site. 50 touring pitches. 24 hardstandings. Caravan pitches. Motorhome pitches. Tent pitches.

Open: All year except 2 weeks at Xmas & New Year (rs Oct-Mar tents not accepted) **Last arrival:** 22.00hrs **Last departure:** 16.00hrs

Pitches: ⚏ ⚏ Å

Facilities: 🐕 📶 ⊙ 🏊 🛁 🎋 WiFi 🅰

Services: 🔌 🔲 🔋 🚿 🛒 🚮

Within 3 miles: ⚓ 🏊 🏌 🎣 🐎 🅿 U

Notes: 🐕 Dogs must be kept on leads.

AA Pubs & Restaurants nearby: Knockinaam Lodge, PORTPATRICK, DG9 9AD, 01776 810471

Corsewall Lighthouse Hotel, STRANRAER, DG9 0QG, 01776 853220

WIGTOWN
Map 20 NX45

Places to visit

RSPB Crook of Baldoon, WIGTOWN, 01988 402130 www.rspb.org.uk

AA SMALL CAMPSITE OF THE YEAR 2017

Drumroamin Farm Camping & Touring Site
►►► 90%

tel: 01988 840613 & 07752 471456 **1 South Balfern DG8 9DB**
email: enquiry@drumroamin.co.uk
dir: *A75 towards Newton Stewart, onto A714 for Wigtown. Left on B7005 through Bladnock, A746 through Kirkinner. Take B7004 signed Garlieston, 2nd left opposite Kilsture Forest, site 0.75m at end of lane.* grid ref: *NX444512*

Located near Wigtown and Newton Stewart, this is an easily accessible site for those wishing to stay in a rural location; it is an open and spacious site overlooking Wigtown Bay and the Galloway Hills. There is a large and separate tent field with a well-equipped day room, while the touring pitches can easily accommodate rally events. The toilet and other facilities are maintained in an exemplary manner. The sheltered camp kitchen proves very popular especially in adverse weather; a drive-through motorhome service point has also been added. The RSPB Crook of Baldoon reserve is a 10-minute walk away. There is a good bus service at the top of the road which goes to Newton Stewart, Wigtown and Whithorn. Two of the three statics on site are for hire. 5 acre site. 48 touring pitches. Caravan pitches. Motorhome pitches. Tent pitches. 3 statics.

Open: all year **Last arrival:** 21.00hrs **Last departure:** noon

Pitches: ⚏ ⚏ Å

Leisure: 🎲 🎣

Facilities: 🐕 ⊙ 🏊 ☀ 🛁 🎋 🛗 ♻ 🅰

Services: 🔌 🔲 🛒 🚮

Within 3 miles: ⚓ 🏌 🅿

Notes: No fires, no noise after 22.00hrs. Dogs must be kept on leads. Ball games area.

PITCHES: ⚏ Caravans ⚏ Motorhomes Å Tents ⛺ Glamping accommodation **SERVICES:** 🔌 Electric hook up 🔲 Launderette 🍺 Licensed bar
🔋 Calor Gas 🛢 Camping Gaz 🔲 Toilet fluid 🍽 Café/Restaurant 🛒 Fast Food/Takeaway 🔋 Battery charging 🚼 Baby care 🚮 Motorvan service point
ABBREVIATIONS: BHs – bank holidays Etr – Easter Spring BH – Spring Bank Holiday fr – from hrs – hours m – mile mdnt – midnight
rdbt – roundabout rs – restricted service wk – week wknd – weekend x-roads – crossroads 🚫 No credit or debit cards 🚫 No dogs

WEST DUNBARTONSHIRE

BALLOCH
Map 20 NS38

Places to visit

Loch Lomond Bird of Prey Centre, BALLOCH, G83 8QL, 01389 729239
www.llbopc.co.uk

The Tall Ship at Riverside, GLASGOW, G3 8RS, 0141 357 3699
www.thetallship.com

PREMIER PARK

Lomond Woods Holiday Park

▶▶▶▶▶ 82%

tel: 01389 755000 **Old Luss Rd G83 8QP**
email: lomondwoods@woodleisure.co.uk
dir: From A82, 17m N of Glasgow, take A811 (Stirling to Balloch road). Left at 1st rdbt, follow holiday park signs, 150yds on left. **grid ref:** NS383816

This site is ideally placed on the southern end of Loch Lomond, the UK's largest inland water and a designated National Park. This site has something to suit all tastes from the most energetic visitor to those who just wish to relax. Fully serviced pitches are available and there are three family rooms. There are loch cruises and boats to hire, plus retail outlets, superstores and eateries within easy walking distance. A drive or cycle ride along Loch Lomond reveals breathtaking views. There are two large boat storage areas. Please note that this site does not accept tents. Holiday caravans and lodges and three camping pods are available to let. 13 acre site. 115 touring pitches. 115 hardstandings. 55 seasonal pitches. Caravan pitches. Motorhome pitches. 35 statics.

Open: all year **Last arrival:** 20.00hrs **Last departure:** noon

Pitches: 🚐 🚏 🏕

Leisure: 🎠 🎣

Facilities: 🚿 🐾 🅿 ⊙ 🧴 👖 ✳ ♿ ⑤ 🛁 🛒 📶 🖥 ♻ ❶

Services: 🚗 ⑤ 🛋 🚽 🛒 ↯

Glamping: Wooden Pods 3, £45–£56 Min stay 1 night Car by unit

Within 3 miles: 🎯 ↯ 🏌 ⊙ ♨ ⑤ ⑤ ⛵

Notes: No jet skis, no commercial vehicles. Dogs must be kept on leads. Table tennis.

AA Pubs & Restaurants nearby: The Cameron Grill, BALLOCH, G83 8QZ, 01389 722582

FIFE

ST ANDREWS

Places to visit

St Andrews Castle, ST ANDREWS, KY16 9AR, 01334 477196
www.historic-scotland.gov.uk

British Golf Museum, ST ANDREWS, KY16 9AB, 01334 460046
www.britishgolfmuseum.co.uk

Great for kids: St Andrews Aquarium, ST ANDREWS, KY16 9AS, 01334 474786
www.standrewsaquarium.co.uk

ST ANDREWS
Map 21 NO51

PREMIER PARK

Cairnsmill Holiday Park

GOLD

▶▶▶▶▶ 94%

tel: 01334 473604 **Largo Rd KY16 8NN**
email: cairnsmill@aol.com **web:** www.cairnsmill.co.uk
dir: A915 from St Andrews towards Lathones. Approx 2m, site on right.
grid ref: NO502142

Hidden behind mature trees and hedging in open countryside on the outskirts of the historic university town of St Andrews, this top quality holiday park is ideally placed for visiting the nearby town and to explore further afield in Fife or across the Tay Bridge to the city of Dundee and beyond. The facilities on offer at this park are simply excellent and include a swimming pool complex, bar and café, games room, gym and a soft play area, in addition to the various play areas located throughout the park. There is a small fishing lochan with a walkway leading towards the town and the botanical gardens. The toilet facilities are first class with two blocks for the touring area and a separate block for the tent field. The six rooms in a bunkhouse means that extended family and friends can holiday together. The local bus service stops at the park entrance. 27 acre site. 62 touring pitches. 33 hardstandings. 24 seasonal pitches. Caravan pitches. Motorhome pitches. Tent pitches. 194 statics.

Open: all year (prior bookings only in winter) **Last arrival:** flexible
Last departure: 11.00hrs

Pitches: 🚐 🚏 🏕 **Leisure:** 🏊 🎣 🎵 Spa

Facilities: ⊙ 🅿 ✳ ♿ ⑤ 🛁 🛒 📶 🖥 ♻ ❶

Services: 🚗 ⑤ 🛋 🛁 📵 ⊘ 🛋 🅣 🍴 🛒 ↯ **Within 3 miles:** 🎯 ↯ 🎱 🏌 ⊙ ♨ ⑤ ⑤ ⛵

Notes: No noise after mdnt, 1 car per pitch. Dogs must be kept on leads.

LEISURE: 🏊 Indoor pool 🏊 Outdoor pool 🎠 Children's playground 👋 Kid's club 🎾 Tennis court 🎣 Games room ⛳ Golf course ⛵ Boat hire 🚲 Cycle hire 🎬 Cinema 🎵 Entertainment 🎣 Fishing ⊙ Mini golf 🏑 Pitch n putt 🏄 Watersports 💪 Gym ⚽ Sports field ⛵ Stables **FACILITIES:** 🚿 Bath 🐾 Shower 🅿 Private washing cubicles ⊙ Electric shaver 🅿 Hairdryer ✳ Ice Packs ♿ Disabled facilities ⑤ Shop on site 🏪 Mobile shop 🍖 BBQ area 🛒 Picnic area 📶 Wi-fi 🖥 Internet access ♻ Recycling ❶ Tourist info 🐕 Dog exercise area 🚗 Car hire can be arranged

Craigtoun Meadows Holiday Park

▶▶▶▶▶ 94%

tel: 01334 475959 **Mount Melville KY16 8PQ**
email: info@craigtounmeadows.co.uk **web:** www.craigtounmeadows.co.uk
dir: *M90 junct 8, A91 to St Andrews. Just after Guardbridge right for Strathkinness. At 2nd x-roads left for Craigtoun.* **grid ref:** *NO482150*

Craigtoun Meadows is only a short drive from the centre of St Andrews which has numerous tourist attractions – historic buildings, harbour aquarium and the wide, sandy beach where the running scene from *Chariots of Fire* was filmed. The site is set in part of the Craigtoun Estate and the holiday homes and touring area are separated by mature woodland and shrubs. The grounds are very well maintained and a large area of woodland has been set aside as a natural habitat for wildlife – deer and red squirrels are seen regularly. The well maintained amenity block is centrally located and provides private facilities, including spacious showers and baths. The pitches are very large, fully serviced and are exceptionally well spaced. Two wooden pods, in a lovely setting, are available for hire. St Andrews is 'the home of golf' so the numerous courses in the area are a challenge for any golfer. 32 acre site. 56 touring pitches. 56 hardstandings. 7 seasonal pitches. Caravan pitches. Motorhome pitches. Tent pitches. 199 statics.

Open: 15 Mar-Oct (rs Mar-Etr & Sep-Oct no shop, & restaurant opens shorter hours) **Last arrival:** 21.00hrs **Last departure:** 11.00hrs
Pitches: * 🚐 £23.50-£29 🚍 £23.50-£29 ▲ £20-£23.50 🏕 prices shown below
Leisure: 🅰 🔾 🍺
Facilities: ☺ 🔄 🌮 🐕 🏁 WiFi 🖥 ✪ 🔓
Services: 🔌 🔄 🍴 🎒 🏪 🔧
Glamping· Wooden Pods 2, £40-£45 Changeover day Sat Min stay 1 night Car by unit
Within 3 miles: 🚴 🚣 🏇 🎿 🏊 📷 🏪 🔓 ⛳

Notes: No groups of unaccompanied minors, no pets. Putting green, zip wire, all-weather football pitch.

AA Pubs & Restaurants nearby: Road Hole Restaurant, ST ANDREWS, KY16 9SP, 01334 474371

Resipole Farm Holiday Park
NEW ▶▶▶▶ 83%

tel: 01967 431235 **Resipole Farm PH36 4HX**
email: accounts@resipole.co.uk
dir: *From A82 between North Ballachulish & Fort William take ferry from Corran to Ardgour. Left onto A861 signed Strontian. Through Strontian towards Salen. Site in approx 8m on right.* **grid ref:** *NM725639*

Set within one of the most beautiful areas of Scotland, the views directly from the site over Loch Sunart to the remote West Highland mountains are truly stunning. The site is a perfect location for anyone who enjoys exploring mountains and lochs, seeing the amazing Scottish wildlife or just wants to relax and unwind in a truly tranquil place. The site has WiFi and a good mobile signal, a well-stocked shop and a slipway onto Loch Sunart. An art gallery adjoins the site. 8 acre site. 40 touring pitches. 20 hardstandings. 20 seasonal pitches. Caravan pitches. Motorhome pitches. Tent pitches. 32 statics.

Open: Etr-Oct **Last arrival:** 21.00hrs **Last departure:** noon
Pitches: 🚐 🚍 ▲ **Leisure:** 🅰 📷
Facilities: 🐾 🅿 ☺ 🌮 ✳ 🛁 🏁 WiFi ✪ 🔓
Services: 🔌 🔄 🔋 🏪 T 🎒 🔧 **Within 3 miles:** 🚴 📷 🏪 🔓

Notes: PayPal accepted. Dogs must be kept on leads.

Places to visit
Ben Wyvis National Nature Reserve, AVIEMORE, PH22 1QD, 01479 810477
www.nnr-scotland.org.uk/ben-wyvis

Aviemore Glamping
▶▶▶▶ 90%

tel: 01479 810717 **Eriskay, Craignagower Av PH22 1RW**
email: aviemoreglamping@outlook.com
dir: *From S: exit A9 onto B9152 signed Aviemore. Take 2nd exit at rdbt signed town centre. 2nd exit at next rdbt. 5th left into Craig Na Gower Ave (signed dental surgery). Site at end of lane.* **grid ref:** *NH894130*

Aviemore is a well known outdoor enthusiasts' hotspot attracting tourists throughout the year for hillwalking and climbing in the Cairngorms, watersports at Loch Morlich and Loch Insch and skiing in the winter. Aviemore Glamping is a bit of a hidden secret located in the landscaped grounds of the owner's home yet is only a short walk from the town centre. The four wooden eco-pods are beautifully built and luxuriously equipped with quality fittings and excellent en suite shower rooms; ideal for couples who are looking for something unique at a sensible price. The eco-pods are available all year and are heated to insulate against the chilly Scottish climate. 0.33 acre site.

Open: all year **Last arrival:** 18.00hrs **Last departure:** 10.00hrs
Facilities: 🐾 🅿 🌮 ✳ 🏁 WiFi 🖥 ✪
Glamping: Wooden Pods 4, £60-£80 Min stay 2 nights En suite
Within 3 miles: 🚴 🏇 📷 🏪 🔓 ⛳

Notes: 🚫 Breakfasts available.

PITCHES: 🚐 Caravans 🚍 Motorhomes ▲ Tents 🏕 Glamping accommodation **SERVICES:** 🔌 Electric hook up 🔄 Launderette 🍺 Licensed bar 🔋 Calor Gas 🔥 Camping Gaz T Toilet fluid 🍴 Café/Restaurant 🏪 Fast Food/Takeaway 🔋 Battery charging 🎒 Baby care 🔧 Motorvan service point
ABBREVIATIONS: BHs – bank holidays Etr – Easter Spring BH – Spring Bank Holiday fr – from hrs – hours m – mile mdnt – midnight rdbt – roundabout rs – restricted service wk – week wknd – weekend x-roads – crossroads 🚫 No credit or debit cards 🚫 No dogs

BALMACARA
Map 22 NG82

Places to visit

Balmacara Estate & Lochalsh Woodland Garden, BALMACARA, IV40 8DN, 01599 566325 www.nts.org.uk/Property/Balmacara-Estate-Woodland-Walks

Eilean Donan Castle, DORNIE, IV40 8DX, 01599 555202 www.eileandonancastle.com

---

Reraig Caravan Site
▶▶▶ 80%

tel: 01599 566215 **IV40 8DH**
email: warden@reraig.com
dir: On A87, 3.5m E of Kyle, 2m W of junct with A890. **grid ref:** NG815272

A lovely site, on the saltwater Sound of Sleet, set back from the main road amongst mature trees in a garden-type environment. It is located near the Skye Bridge and very handy for exploring the surrounding area including Plockton. There is a regular bus that stops at the site entrance. There is no need to pre-book for this site. 2 acre site. 40 touring pitches. 33 hardstandings. Caravan pitches. Motorhome pitches. Tent pitches.

Open: May-Sep **Last arrival:** 22.00hrs **Last departure:** noon
Pitches: * ⊕ £16.90-£17.40 ⊕ £16.90-£17.40 ▲ £14-£14.50
Facilities: ♠ ⊙ ℙ ♿ 🔥 WiFi ♻ ❶
Services: ⊕ ⬇
Within 3 miles: ⑤

Notes: Only small tents permitted. No awnings Jul & Aug. Dogs must be kept on leads. Charge for WiFi.

AA Pubs & Restaurants nearby: The Plockton Hotel, PLOCKTON, IV52 8TN, 01599 544274

Plockton Inn & Seafood Restaurant, PLOCKTON, IV52 8TW, 01599 544222

CORPACH
Map 22 NN07

Places to visit

West Highland Museum, FORT WILLIAM, PH33 6AJ, 01397 702169 www.westhighlandmuseum.org.uk

Great for kids: Inverlochy Castle, FORT WILLIAM, PH33 6SN, 01667 460232 www.historic-scotland.gov.uk

---

PREMIER PARK

Linnhe Lochside Holidays
▶▶▶▶▶ 87%

GOLD

tel: 01397 772376 **PH33 7NL**
email: relax@linnhe-lochside-holidays.co.uk
dir: On A830, 1m W of Corpach, 5m from Fort William. **grid ref:** NN074771

Set on the shores of Loch Eil, on the outskirts of Corpac, this site has views over Ben Nevis and Sunart and is only a few miles from Fort William, the Scottish outdoor enthusiasts' mecca. There is direct access from the site for kayaking and sailing and the steam train to Mallaig passes under the site access bridge (the drivers always seem to whistle to anyone on the bridge). The pitches are set in very well maintained landscaping with mature trees and shrubs and some have loch views. Tenters are well catered for in sheltered areas and there are

also some pitches directly on the lochside. The owners have worked hard over the years to provide a site where nature and campers can be in unison. This is a great site for relaxation or if you wish to be more active the choices are limitless. 5.5 acre site. 85 touring pitches. 63 hardstandings. 20 seasonal pitches. Caravan pitches. Motorhome pitches. Tent pitches. 20 statics.

Open: Dec-Oct (rs Dec-Etr shop closed) **Last arrival:** 21.00hrs
Last departure: 11.00hrs
Pitches: ⊕ ⊕ ▲
Facilities: ⊙ ℙ ※ ♿ 🔥 ⑤ ♠ 🏕 WiFi ♻ ❶
Services: ⊕ ⑤ 🔒 ⊘ Ⓣ 🛒 ⬇
Within 3 miles: ↓ ≋ ℙ ◎ ≋ ⑤ ⑤

Notes: No cars by tents. No large groups. Dogs must be kept on leads. Launching slipway, free fishing.

AA Pubs & Restaurants nearby: Inverlochy Castle Hotel, FORT WILLIAM, PH33 6SN, 01397 702177

Moorings Hotel, FORT WILLIAM, PH33 7LY, 01397 772797

DUROR
Map 22 NM95

Places to visit

Glencoe Folk Museum, GLENCOE, PH49 4HS, 01855 811664 www.glencoemuseum.com

Glencoe & Dalness Visitor Centre, GLENCOE, PH49 4LA, 01855 811307 www.nts.org.uk/Property/Glencoe-Dalness

---

Achindarroch Touring Park

▶▶▶ 78%

tel: 01631 740329 **PA38 4BS**
email: stay@achindarrochtp.co.uk
dir: A82 onto A828 at Ballachulish Bridge then towards Oban for 5.2m. In Duror, site on left, signed. **grid ref:** NM997554

A long established, well-laid out park which continues to be maintained to a high standard by an enthusiastic and friendly family team. There is a well-appointed heated toilet block and spacious all-weather pitches and there are also 2- and 4-person wooden camping pods for hire. The park is well placed for visits to Oban, Fort William and Glencoe. A wide variety of outdoor sports is available in the area. 5 acre site. 40 touring pitches. 21 hardstandings. 10 seasonal pitches. Caravan pitches. Motorhome pitches. Tent pitches.

Open: 24 Jan-16 Jan **Last departure:** 11.00hrs
Pitches: * ⊕ fr £20 ⊕ fr £20 ▲ fr £8 🏠 prices shown below
Facilities: ♠ ⊙ ℙ ※ ♿ 🔥 🏕 WiFi ♻ ❶
Services: ⊕ ⑤ 🔒 ⊘ 🛒 ⬇
Glamping: Wooden Pods 2, £40-£45 Min stay 2 nights (peak season & BHs)
Within 3 miles: ℙ ∪

Notes: Groups by prior arrangement only. Dogs must be kept on leads. Campers' kitchen with freezer, toaster, kettle, microwave & boot dryer.

AA Pubs & Restaurants nearby: Old Ferry Bar at Loch Leven Hotel, NORTH BALLACHULISH, PH33 6SA, 01855 821236

LEISURE: 🏊 Indoor pool 🏊 Outdoor pool 🎠 Children's playground 🎣 Kid's club 🎾 Tennis court 🎱 Games room ⛳ Golf course 🚤 Boat hire 🚴 Cycle hire 🎬 Cinema 🎵 Entertainment 🎣 Fishing ⛳ Mini golf 🏌 Pitch n putt 🏄 Watersports 🏋 Gym 🏟 Sports field ∪ Stables **FACILITIES:** 🛁 Bath 🚿 Shower ℙ Private washing cubicles ⊙ Electric shaver ✂ Hairdresser ❄ Ice Packs ♿ Disabled facilities ⑤ Shop on site 🚐 Mobile shop 🍖 BBQ area 🧺 Picnic area WiFi Wi-fi 🖥 Internet access ♻ Recycling ❶ Tourist info 🐕 Dog exercise area 🚗 Car hire can be arranged

FORT WILLIAM
Map 22 NN17

See also Corpach

Places to visit

West Highland Museum, FORT WILLIAM, PH33 6AJ, 01397 702169
www.westhighlandmuseum.org.uk

Great for kids: Inverlochy Castle, FORT WILLIAM, PH33 6SN, 01667 460232
www.historic-scotland.gov.uk

Glen Nevis Caravan & Camping Park
▷ ▷ ▷ ▷ 90%

tel: 01397 702191 **Glen Nevis PH33 6SX**
email: holidays@glen-nevis.co.uk **web:** www.glen-nevis.co.uk
dir: *From A82 (N outskirts of Fort William) follow Glen Nevis signs at mini rdbt. Site 2.5m on right.* **grid ref:** *NN124722*

This is a large and very well maintained park, situated in Glen Nevis with easy access to the main footpath leading to Ben Nevis. Located a few miles from Fort William, which has a gondola chairlift to the summit of Ben Nevis and Neptune's Staircase, and gives access to the Caledonian Canal and the Great Glen to Inverness. The site is divided into areas by beech hedges to give a sense of seclusion for caravan and motorhome users who have their own amenity blocks; tent campers have their own specific areas and large well-kept amenity blocks. To cater for those who are seeking a glamping experience, five luxury, wooden camping pods have been installed – all have unrivalled views towards Ben Nevis. The park has a restaurant and café. 30 acre site. 380 touring pitches. 150 hardstandings. Caravan pitches. Motorhome pitches. Tent pitches. 30 statics.

Glen Nevis Caravan & Camping Park

Open: 15 Mar-Oct (rs Mar & Oct limited restaurant facilities) **Last arrival:** 22.00hrs **Last departure:** noon

Pitches: * ⊞ fr £24 ⊞ fr £24 ▲ fr £20 ⋒ prices shown below

Facilities: ⋔ ⊙ ⍟ ⚒ ⚘ ⚐ 🛁 ⊟ ⊞ WiFi 🖥 ♻ 🅰

Services: 🔌 🗄 🍴 🔋 🚿 ⊤ 🍴 🛒 🖶 🖤

Glamping: Wooden Pods 5, £50-£60 dogs by prior arrangement only.

Within 3 miles: 🎣 ✎ 🛒 🗄

Notes: Quiet from 23.00hrs-08.00hrs.

See advert below

PITCHES: ⊞ Caravans ⊞ Motorhomes ▲ Tents ⋒ Glamping accommodation **SERVICES:** 🔌 Electric hook up 🗄 Launderette 🍴 Licensed bar 🔋 Calor Gas ⊘ Camping Gaz ⊤ Toilet fluid 🍴 Café/Restaurant 🖶 Fast Food/Takeaway 🔋 Battery charging 🚼 Baby care 🖤 Motorvan service point **ABBREVIATIONS:** BHs – bank holidays Etr – Easter Spring BH – Spring Bank Holiday fr – from hrs – hours m – mile mdnt – midnight rdbt – roundabout rs – restricted service wk – week wknd – weekend x-roads – crossroads 🚫 No credit or debit cards 🚫 No dogs

GAIRLOCH
Map 22 NG87

Places to visit

Gairloch Heritage Museum, GAIRLOCH, IV21 2BP, 01445 712287
www.gairlochheritagemuseum.org

Inverewe Garden, POOLEWE, IV22 2LG, 01445 712952
www.nts.org.uk/Property/Inverewe-Garden-and-Estate

Gairloch Caravan Park
►►► 79%

tel: 01445 712373 **Strath IV21 2BX**
email: info@gairlochcaravanpark.com
dir: From A832 take B8021 signed Melvaig towards Strath. In 0.5m turn right, just after Millcroft Hotel. Immediately right again. **grid ref:** NG798773

A clean, well-maintained site on flat coastal grassland close to Loch Gairloch. The owners and managers are hard working and well organised. The park offers hardstandings, good shrub and flower planting and a bunkhouse that provides accommodation for families. 6 acre site. 70 touring pitches. 13 hardstandings. 8 seasonal pitches. Caravan pitches. Motorhome pitches. Tent pitches.

Open: Apr-Oct **Last arrival:** 20.00hrs **Last departure:** noon

Pitches: * 🚐 £16-£21 🚗 £16-£21 ▲ £16-£19

Facilities: 🌂⊙🅿✳🛁️🖿 WIFI ♻ 🛈

Services: 🖾🛢🎍🧺⊤🔺✯

Within 3 miles: ↨≉🛈◎🖿️🛢

Notes: No noise after 23.00hrs. Dogs must be kept on leads.

AA Pubs & Restaurants nearby: The Old Inn, GAIRLOCH, IV21 2BD, 01445 712006

GLENCOE
Map 22 NN15

Places to visit

Glencoe & Dalness Visitor Centre, GLENCOE, PH49 4LA, 01855 811307
www.nts.org.uk/Property/Glencoe-Dalness

Great for kids: Glencoe Folk Museum, GLENCOE, PH49 4HS, 01855 811664
www.glencoemuseum.com

Invercoe Caravan & Camping Park
►►►► 85%

tel: 01855 811210 **PH49 4HP**
email: holidays@invercoe.co.uk **web:** www.invercoe.co.uk
dir: Exit A82 at Glencoe Hotel onto B863 for 0.25m. **grid ref:** NN098594

A level grass site set on the shore of Loch Leven, with excellent mountain views. The area is ideal for both walking and climbing, and also offers a choice of several freshwater and saltwater lochs. Convenient for the good shopping in Fort William. There are two 'micro lodge' wooden pods for hire. 5 acre site. 60 touring pitches. Caravan pitches. Motorhome pitches. Tent pitches. 4 statics.

Open: all year **Last departure:** noon   **Pitches:** 🚐🚗▲🏠
Facilities: ⊙🅿✳🛁🛢🖿️🖿 WIFI   **Services:** 🖾🛢🧺⊤🔺✯
Glamping: Wooden Pods 2, £45-£55 Min stay 1 night Car by unit
Within 3 miles: ↨≉🖿️🛢
Notes: No large group bookings.
AA Pubs & Restaurants nearby: Clachaig Inn, GLENCOE, PH49 4HX, 01855 811252

LEISURE: 🏊 Indoor pool 🏊 Outdoor pool 🅜 Children's playground 🖐 Kid's club ♋ Tennis court ♠ Games room ⛳ Golf course ⚓ Boat hire 🚲 Cycle hire 🎦 Cinema 🎵 Entertainment ♒ Fishing ◎ Mini golf ⛳ Pitch n putt 🏄 Watersports 🏋 Gym ⊕ Sports field ∪ Stables **FACILITIES:** 🛁 Bath 🚿 Shower 🅿 Private washing cubicles ⊙ Electric shaver 🖰 Hairdryer ✳ Ice Packs 🛁 Disabled facilities 🛢 Shop on site 🖿 Mobile shop 🍖 BBQ area 🪵 Picnic area WIFI Wi-fi 🖳 Internet access ♻ Recycling 🛈 Tourist info 🐕 Dog exercise area 🚗 Car hire can be arranged

JOHN O'GROATS
Map 23 ND37

Places to visit

The Castle & Gardens of Mey, THURSO, KW14 8XH, 01847 851473
www.castleofmey.org.uk

John O'Groats Caravan Site
►►►82%

tel: 01955 611329 & 07762 336359 **KW1 4YR**
email: info@johnogroatscampsite.co.uk
dir: At end of A99. **grid ref:** ND382733

An attractive site in an open position above the seashore and looking out towards the Orkney Islands. Nearby is the passenger ferry that makes day trips to the Orkneys, and there are grey seals to watch, and sea angling can be organised by the site owners. 4 acre site. 90 touring pitches. 30 hardstandings. Caravan pitches. Motorhome pitches. Tent pitches.

Open: Apr-Sep **Last arrival:** 22.00hrs **Last departure:** 11.00hrs

Pitches: 🚐 🚍 ▲ **Facilities:** 🏪 ⊙ 🅿 ✳ 🕭 🖈 📶 ♻ 𝟋

Services: 🔌 🗐 ⬗ 🚽 📶 **Within 3 miles:** 🖉 🗐 🗐

Notes: 🐾 No noise after 22.00hrs. Dogs must be kept on leads.

LAIDE
Map 22 NG89

Gruinard Bay Caravan Park
►►►71%

tel: 01445 731225 **IV22 2ND**
email: gruinard@ecosse.net
dir: From Inverness or Ullapool take A832 to Gairloch, follow signs to Laide. (NB on Inverness to Gairloch road – short stretch of single-track road with passing places just prior to Gairloch). **grid ref:** NG904919

With views across Gruinard Bay to the Summer Isles and the mountains, this is a lovely, small park in a particularly peaceful location. There is direct access to a small sandy beach and a small hotel nearby with a restaurant and free WiFi access; the small post office provides basic groceries, while larger shops can be found in Aultbuie, Poolewe, Gairloch and Ullapool, where there are ferries to the Outer Hebrides. Being beside a beach, the site has no hardstandings but the grass pitches are on well-compacted shingle. 3.5 acre site. 35 touring pitches. 2 seasonal pitches. Caravan pitches. Motorhome pitches. Tent pitches. 20 statics.

Open: Apr-Oct **Last arrival:** 22.00hrs **Last departure:** noon

Pitches: * 🚐 fr £17 🚍 fr £17 ▲ fr £15

Leisure: 🖉

Facilities: 🏪 🅿 ⊙ 🅿 ✳ 📶 ♻ 𝟋

Services: 🔌 🗐 🔋 🚽

Within 3 miles: 🖉 🗐 🗐

Notes: No noise after 22.00hrs. Dogs must be kept on leads.

LAIRG
Map 23 NC50

Loch Shin Wigwams
NEW ►►►►► 76%

tel: 01549 402936 & 07460 003301 **Forge Cottage, Achfrish, Shinness IV27 4DN**
email: traceyjcrosby@btinternet.com
dir: On A836 in Lairg (with loch on left) pass Pier Café on left. Approx 0.5m turn left onto A838. In approx 1.5m turn right signed Achfrish. Site (4th property) on left.
grid ref: NC559123

The views down the valley towards Loch Shin from this beautifully located glamping site are outstanding, and they can change dramatically depending on the time of year and the weather. The four self-contained wigwams are spotlessly clean and have excellent facilities. There are large picnic benches at each unit and two have their own wood-burners; a large stone broch provides an attractive and sheltered communal area for barbecues. There are many walking and cycling opportunities in the area. 1 acre site.

Open: 15 Mar-Oct **Last arrival:** 20.00hrs **Last departure:** 10.00hrs

Facilities: 🅿 🏪 🖈 ♻ 𝟋

Glamping: Wooden Wigwams 2, £65-£85 Changeover day Any day Min stay 2 nights En suite Own kitchen

Within 3 miles: 🖉

Notes: No noise after 22.00hrs. Dogs must be kept on leads. Stands for disposable BBQs & fire pits available.

Dunroamin Caravan and Camping Park
►►►74%

tel: 01549 402447 **Main St IV27 4AR**
email: enquiries@lairgcaravanpark.co.uk
dir: From A386 onto A839 towards Rogart, site 300mtrs from village centre on right.
grid ref: NC585062

An attractive little park with clean and functional facilities, adjacent to a licensed restaurant. The park is close to the lower end of Loch Shin and is the ideal spot for those seeking peace and quiet. 4 acre site. 20 touring pitches. 8 hardstandings. Caravan pitches. Motorhome pitches. Tent pitches. 9 statics.

Open: Apr-Oct **Last arrival:** 21.00hrs **Last departure:** noon

Pitches: 🚐 🚍 ▲

Facilities: ⊙ 🅿 ✳ ♻ 𝟋

Services: 🔌 🗐 🔋 ⬗ 🅣 🍽 🖴 🚽

Within 3 miles: ⅊ 🖉 ⬱ 🗐 🗐

Notes: No vehicles to be driven on site between 21.00hrs-07.00hrs. Dogs must be kept on leads.

PITCHES: 🚐 Caravans 🚍 Motorhomes ▲ Tents 🛖 Glamping accommodation **SERVICES:** 🔌 Electric hook up 🗐 Launderette 🍺 Licensed bar
🔋 Calor Gas ⬗ Camping Gaz 🅣 Toilet fluid 🍽 Café/Restaurant 🖴 Fast Food/Takeaway ⬱ Battery charging 🐣 Baby care 🚽 Motorvan service point
ABBREVIATIONS: BHs – bank holidays Etr – Easter Spring BH – Spring Bank Holiday fr – from hrs – hours m – mile mdnt – midnight
rdbt – roundabout rs – restricted service wk – week wknd – weekend x-roads – crossroads 🐾 No credit or debit cards 🚫 No dogs

LAIRG *continued*

Woodend Caravan & Camping Site
►►► 69%

tel: 01549 402248 **Achnairn IV27 4DN**
email: enquiries@woodendcampsite.co.uk
dir: *4m N of Lairg exit A836 onto A838, signed at Achnairn.* **grid ref:** *NC551127*

A clean, simple site set in hilly moors and woodland with access to Loch Shin. The area is popular with fishing and boating enthusiasts, and there is a choice of golf courses within a 30-mile radius. A spacious campers' kitchen is a useful amenity. There's also a holiday cottage to hire. 4 acre site. 55 touring pitches. 5 hardstandings. Caravan pitches. Motorhome pitches. Tent pitches.

Open: Apr-Sep **Last arrival:** 23.00hrs

Pitches: ⚏ ⚏ Å

Facilities: ⊙ ⌐ ※

Services: ⚏ ⑤

Within 3 miles: ⊰ ⌀ ⑤

Notes: ⊛ Dogs must be kept on leads.

Broomfield Holiday Park
►►► 78%

tel: 01854 612020 & 612664 **West Shore St IV26 2UT**
email: sross@broomfieldhp.com **web:** www.broomfieldhp.com
dir: *Into Ullapool on A893, 2nd right past harbour.* **grid ref:** *NH123939*

Set right on the water's edge of Loch Broom and the open sea, with lovely views of the Summer Isles. This clean, well maintained and managed park is close to the harbour and town centre with their restaurants, bars and shops. The Ullapool ferry allows easy access to the Hebridian islands for day trips or longer visits. 12 acre site. 140 touring pitches. Caravan pitches. Motorhome pitches. Tent pitches.

Open: Etr or Apr-Sep **Last departure:** noon

Pitches: ⚏ fr £20 ⚏ fr £19 Å £18-£20

Facilities: ⊙ ※ ⅙ ⚙ WIFI

Services: ⚏ ⑤ ⚏ ⌄

Within 3 miles: ⅃ ⊟ ⌀ ⑤ ⑤

Notes: No noise at night. Dogs must be kept on leads.

ABINGTON   Map 21 NS92

Places to visit
Museum of Lead Mining, WANLOCKHEAD, ML12 6UT, 01659 74387
www.leadminingmuseum.co.uk

Mount View Caravan Park
►►► 79%

tel: 01864 502808 **ML12 6RW**
email: info@mountviewcaravanpark.co.uk **web:** www.mountviewcaravanpark.co.uk
dir: *M74 junct 13, A702 S into Abington. Left into Station Rd, over river & railway. Site on right.* **grid ref:** *NS935235*

A delightfully maturing family park, surrounded by the Southern Uplands and handily located between Carlisle and Glasgow. It is an excellent stopover site for those travelling between Scotland and the south, and the West Coast Railway passes beside the park. 5.5 acre site. 42 touring pitches. 42 hardstandings. 18 seasonal pitches. Caravan pitches. Motorhome pitches. Tent pitches. 28 statics.

Open: Mar-Oct **Last arrival:** 20.45hrs **Last departure:** 11.30hrs

Pitches: ⚏ ⚏ Å

Leisure: ⚏

Facilities: ⚏ ⊙ ⌐ ⅙ ⚏ ❶

Services: ⚏ ⑤ ⚏

Within 3 miles: ⅃ ⌀ ⑤ ⑤

Notes: 5mph speed limit, Debit cards accepted (no credit cards). Dogs must be kept on leads & exercised off site. Emergency phone.

Find out about the AA's Pennant rating scheme on pages 10-11

LEISURE: 🏠 Indoor pool   🏊 Outdoor pool   ⋀ Children's playground   👋 Kid's club   🎾 Tennis court   🎱 Games room   ⛳ Golf course   🚣 Boat hire   🚴 Cycle hire   🎬 Cinema   🎵 Entertainment   🎣 Fishing   ◉ Mini golf   ⛳ Pitch n putt   🏊 Watersports   🏋 Gym   🏈 Sports field   ♘ Stables   **FACILITIES:** 🛁 Bath   🚿 Shower   P Private washing cubicles   ⊙ Electric shaver   ⌐ Hairdryer   ❄ Ice Packs   ⅙ Disabled facilities   ⑤ Shop on site   🚐 Mobile shop   🍖 BBQ area   ⌐ Picnic area   WIFI Wi-fi   💻 Internet access   ♻ Recycling   ❶ Tourist info   🐕 Dog exercise area   🚗 Car hire can be arranged

EAST LOTHIAN

DUNBAR
Map 21 NT67

Places to visit
Preston Mill & Phantassie Doocot, EAST LINTON, EH40 3DS, 01620 860426
www.nts.org.uk/Property/Preston-Mill-Phantassie-Doocot

Great for kids: Tantallon Castle, NORTH BERWICK, EH39 5PN, 01620 892727
www.historic-scotland.gov.uk

PREMIER PARK

Thurston Manor Leisure Park
▶▶▶▶▶ 90%

tel: 01368 840643 **Innerwick EH42 1SA**
email: holidays@thurstonmanor.co.uk
dir: *4m S of Dunbar, follow site signs from A1.* **grid ref:** *NT712745*

A pleasant park set in 250 acres of unspoilt countryside. The touring (no tents) and static areas of this large park are in separate areas. The main touring area occupies an open, level position, and the toilet facilities are modern and exceptionally well maintained. The park boasts a well-stocked fishing loch, a heated indoor swimming pool, steam room, sauna, jacuzzi, mini-gym and fitness room plus seasonal entertainment. There is a superb family toilet block. Fly fishing is available. 250 acre site. 120 touring pitches. 68 hardstandings. 60 seasonal pitches. Caravan pitches. Motorhome pitches. 570 statics.

Open: 13 Feb-Jan **Last arrival:** 23.00hrs **Last departure:** 10.00hrs

Pitches: ⊕ ⊕

Leisure: ≋ ᐅᐊᏔ ⛳ ⬟ ♫ Spa ✏

Facilities: ⋔ ⓅⒶⓄ♐✖⬥⓼Ⓗ⋔⋔ⅥⅣ🖥♻❶

Services: ⊖ 🔋 ♈️ 🔋⊘ⓉⓄ♈️⊶⇓

Within 3 miles: ✏ 🔋

Notes: Quiet after 23.00hrs. Dogs must be kept on leads.

AA Pubs & Restaurants nearby: Macdonald Marine Hotel & Spa, NORTH BERWICK, EH39 4LZ, 01620 897300

Belhaven Bay Caravan & Camping Park
▶▶▶ 77%

tel: 01368 865956 **Belhaven Bay EH42 1TS**
email: belhaven@meadowhead.co.uk
dir: *A1 onto A1087 towards Dunbar. 1m to site in John Muir Park.* **grid ref:** *NT661781*

Located on the outskirts of Dunbar, this is a sheltered park within walking distance of the beach. There is a regular bus service to Dunbar where there is an East Coast Main Line railway station. The site is also convenient for the A1 and well placed for visiting the area's many seaside towns and various visitor attractions. There is a large children's play area. Six static caravans and three wooden wigwam pods are available for hire. 40 acre site. 52 touring pitches. 11 hardstandings. Caravan pitches. Motorhome pitches. Tent pitches. 64 statics.

Open: Mar-13 Oct **Last arrival:** 20.00hrs **Last departure:** noon

Pitches: ⊕ ⊕ Ⓐ ⋔

Leisure: ⛳

Facilities: ⊙ ⓅⓄ✖⬥⓼Ⓗ⋔⋔ⅥⅣ🖥♻❶

Services: ⊖ 🔋 Ⓣ ⊶⇓

Glamping: Wooden Wigwams 3, £54.30-£92.60 Min stay 2 nights En suite Own kitchen

Within 3 miles: ↧✏Ⓞᐊ🔋🔋↺

Notes: No rollerblades or skateboards, no open fires, no noise 23.00hrs-07.00hrs. Dogs must be kept on leads.

AA Pubs & Restaurants nearby: Macdonald Marine Hotel & Spa, NORTH BERWICK, EH39 4LZ, 01620 897300

LONGNIDDRY
Map 21 NT47

Places to visit
Prestongrange Museum, PRESTONPANS, EH32 9RX, 0131 653 2904
www.prestongrange.org

Great for kids: Myreton Motor Museum, ABERLADY, EH32 0PZ, 01875 870288
www.myretonmotormuseum.co.uk

Seton Sands Holiday Village
HOLIDAY CENTRE 84%

tel: 01875 813333 **EH32 0QF**
email: setonsands@haven.com **web:** www.haven.com/setonsands
dir: *A1 to A198 exit, take B6371 to Cockenzie. Right onto B1348. Site 1m on right.*
grid ref: *NT420759*

A well-equipped holiday centre facing onto the Firth of Forth with mature landscaping. A dedicated entertainment team offers plenty of organised activities for children and there are pleasant bars, a show bar and a modern restaurant. It offers good sports and leisure facilities, including a multi-sports court, swimming pool, 9-hole golf course and a variety of play areas, so there's always plenty to do without leaving the park. The touring area offers fully-serviced pitches set in lovely landscaping with a dedicated on-site warden. There is a regular bus from the site entrance, which makes day trips to Edinburgh easy. 150 holiday homes are available for hire. Please note, this site does not accept tents. 1.75 acre site. 40 touring pitches. Caravan pitches. Motorhome pitches. 600 statics.

continued

PITCHES: ⊕ Caravans ⊕ Motorhomes Ⓐ Tents ⋔ Glamping accommodation **SERVICES:** ⊖ Electric hook up 🔋 Launderette ♈️ Licensed bar
🔋 Calor Gas ⊘ Camping Gaz Ⓣ Toilet fluid Ⓞ Café/Restaurant ⊶ Fast Food/Takeaway ⊶ Battery charging ⊶ Baby care ⇓ Motorvan service point
ABBREVIATIONS: BHs – bank holidays Etr – Easter Spring BH – Spring Bank Holiday fr – from hrs – hours m – mile mdnt – midnight
rdbt – roundabout rs – restricted service wk – week wknd – weekend x-roads – crossroads ⊛ No credit or debit cards ⊗ No dogs

LONGNIDORY *continued*

Seton Sands Holiday Village

Open: mid Mar-end Oct (rs mid Mar-May & Sep-Oct some facilities may be reduced) **Last arrival:** 22.00hrs **Last departure:** 10.00hrs

Pitches: 🚐 🚲

Leisure: 🏊 🛝 🎱 🎵 ♪

Facilities: 📶 🍴 ⚙ ♻ 🔧

Services: 🔌 📷 🚿 🛁 🍴 ♿

Within 3 miles: ⚽ 🎣 ♻

Notes: No commercial vehicles, no bookings by persons under 21yrs unless a family booking. Max 2 dogs per booking, certain dog breeds banned. Dogs must be kept on leads.

AA Pubs & Restaurants nearby: La Potinière, GULLANE, EH31 2AA, 01620 843214

The Longniddry Inn, LONGNIDDRY, EH32 0NF, 01875 852401

See advert below

See advert below

MUSSELBURGH   **Map 21 NT37**

Places to visit

National Museum of Flight Scotland, EAST FORTUNE, EH39 5LF, 0300 123 6789 www.nms.ac.uk/flight

Inveresk Lodge Garden, INVERESK, EH21 7TE, 0131 665 1855 www.nts.org.uk/Property/Inveresk-Lodge-Garden

Great for kids: Edinburgh Butterfly & Insect World, DALKEITH, EH18 1AZ, 0131 663 4932 www.edinburgh-butterfly-world.co.uk

Drum Mohr Caravan Park

►►►► 84%

tel: 0131 665 6867 **Levenhall EH21 8JS**
email: admin@drummohr.org
dir: *Exit A1 at A199 junct through Wallyford, at rdbt onto B1361 signed Prestonpans. 1st left, site 400yds.* **grid ref:** *NT373734*

This attractive park is carefully landscaped and sheltered by mature trees on all sides. It is divided into separate areas by mature hedging, trees and ornamental shrubs. The generously sized pitches include a number of fully serviced pitches, plus there are first-class amenities. The site is ideally located for exploring the East Lothian area with its numerous seaside towns, and the National Museum of Flight at East Fortune is just 15 miles away. It's an easy drive on the nearby A1 to Edinburgh or alternatively, there is a regular bus service which stops near the site. There are also camping pods (Hexilodges and Octolodges), bothys, and luxury lodges with hot tubs. 9 acre site. 120 touring pitches. 50 hardstandings. Caravan pitches. Motorhome pitches. Tent pitches. 12 statics.

Open: all year **Last arrival:** 18.00hrs (winter arrivals by prior arrangement)
Last departure: noon

Pitches: * 🚐 £20-£30 🚲 £20-£30 ⛺ £10-£30 🏠 prices shown below
Facilities: ☺ 🍴 ✳ ♿ ⚙ 🛏 🪑 📶 ♻ 🔧

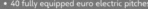

LEISURE: 🏊 Indoor pool 🏊 Outdoor pool 🛝 Children's playground 👋 Kid's club 🎾 Tennis court 🎱 Games room ⛳ Golf course 🚣 Boat hire 🚲 Cycle hire 🎬 Cinema ♪ Entertainment 🎣 Fishing 🏌 Mini golf ⛳ Pitch n putt 🏄 Watersports 💪 Gym 🏐 Sports field ⛺ Stables **FACILITIES:** 🛁 Bath 🚿 Shower 🅿 Private washing cubicles 🔌 Electric shaver 🍴 Hairdryer ✳ Ice Packs ♿ Disabled facilities 🏪 Shop on site 🏬 Mobile shop 🍴 BBQ area 🪑 Picnic area 📶 Wi-fi 💻 Internet access ♻ Recycling 🔧 Tourist info 🐕 Dog exercise area 🚗 Car hire can be arranged

Services: 🔌 🧺 🛢 🔥 [T] 🚰

Glamping: **Wooden Pods** 20, £40-£90 Changeover day Any day Min stay 1 night Own kitchen 8 pods have en suite toilet & basin Car by unit

Within 3 miles: ⛳ 🎣 [S] 🧺

Notes: Max 2 dogs per pitch. Dogs must be kept on leads. Freshly baked bread, croissants, tea & coffee in high season.

AA Pubs & Restaurants nearby: The Kitchin, EDINBURGH, EH6 6LX, 0131 555 1755

WEST LOTHIAN

EAST CALDER — Map 21 NT06

Places to visit

Almond Valley Heritage Trust, LIVINGSTON, EH54 7AR, 01506 414957 www.almondvalley.co.uk

Malleny Garden, BALERNO, EH14 7AF, 0131 449 2283 www.nts.org.uk/Property/Malleny-Garden

Linwater Caravan Park

►►►► 83%

🛖 DAVID BELLAMY CONSERVATION AWARD GOLD

tel: 0131 333 3326 **West Clifton EH53 0HT**
email: queries@linwater.co.uk
dir: *M9 junct 1, follow B7030 & Newbridge signs. Left after petrol station & Macdonalds onto B7030. 2m, after Edinburgh International Climbing Arena (EICA) right, follow site signs.* **grid ref:** *NT104696*

This is a farmland park in a peaceful rural area with access to good motorway and rail links enabling exploration of the heart of Scotland. The family who own the park are excellent hosts and offer a friendly service which is borne out by the many customers who return year after year. The grounds are very pleasant and the toilets are kept in an exemplary manner. It is a particularly popular park, especially with those wishing to visit the Royal Highland Show, the Edinburgh Festival and Military Tattoo. There are four wooden wigwams (known as timber tents), and a self-catering lodge in a half acre, for hire. 5 acre site. 60 touring pitches. 22 hardstandings. Caravan pitches. Motorhome pitches. Tent pitches.

Open: mid Mar-late Oct **Last arrival:** 21.00hrs **Last departure:** noon

Pitches: 🚐 £20-£26 🚌 £20-£26 ⛺ £18-£23 🛖 prices shown below

Facilities: 🚿 [P] ☺ 🧴 ❄ ♿ 🐕 [WiFi] ♻ ⓘ

Services: 🔌 🧺 🛢 🔥 [T] 🔋 🚰

Glamping: **Wooden Wigwams** 4, £34-£38 Changeover day Any day Min stay 1 night Car by unit

Within 3 miles: ⛳ 🎣 [S] 🧺

Notes: No noise after 23.00hrs. Dogs must be kept on leads. Takeaway food can be ordered for delivery, small shop sells basics only.

AA Pubs & Restaurants nearby: The Bridge Inn, RATHO, EH28 8RA, 0131 333 1320

LINLITHGOW — Map 21 NS97

Places to visit

Linlithgow Palace, LINLITHGOW, EH49 7AL, 01506 842896 www.historic-scotland.gov.uk

House of The Binns, LINLITHGOW, EH49 7NA, 01506 834255 www.nts.org.uk/Property/House-of-the-Binns

Great for kids: Blackness Castle, LINLITHGOW, EH49 7NH, 01506 834807 www.historic-scotland.gov.uk

Beecraigs Caravan & Camping Site

🛖

►►►► 90%

tel: 01506 844516 & 848943 **Beecraigs Country Park, The Visitor Centre EH49 6PL**
email: mail@beecraigs.com **web:** www.beecraigs.com
dir: *M9 junct 3 (from E) or junct 4 (from W), A803 to Linlithgow. From A803 into Preston Rd signed Beecraigs Country Park. Reception in visitor centre. (NB Preston Rd route is steep & winding).* **grid ref:** *NT006746*

Located on the hills above Linlithgow with unrivalled views towards the Forth Bridges, Beecraigs Country Park has an excellent caravan and camping site, with two modern washrooms, large hardstanding pitches and a secluded tenting area, together with 6- and 4-person cabins. There are extensive walks and cycle trails, a fishing loch, deer park, farm and a very large play area for children. There is a lovely visitor centre, shop and café at the site entrance and there are good road and train links nearby, making trips into Edinburgh an easy affair; for those who wish something simpler, boat trips are available. 6 acre site. 36 touring pitches. 36 hardstandings. Caravan pitches. Motorhome pitches. Tent pitches.

Open: all year (rs 25-26 Dec & 1-2 Jan no new arrivals) **Last arrival:** 20.00hrs
Last departure: noon

Pitches: * 🚐 £19.50-£24 🚌 £19.50-£24 ⛺ £16-£24 🛖 prices shown below

Leisure: 🛝 🎣

Facilities: 👶 🚿 [P] ☺ 🧴 ❄ ♿ 🪑 🐕 ♻ ⓘ

Services: 🔌 🧺 🛢 [T] 🚰

Glamping: **Cabins** 2, £40-£55 Min stay 1 night (additional fee applies), 2 nights if Fri-Sat or Sat-Sun Car by unit

Within 3 miles: ⛳ 🎣 🚤 [S] 🧺 🐎

Notes: No cars by tents. No ball games near caravans, no noise after 22.00hrs. Dogs must be kept on leads. Country park facilities including Ranger Service events. Children's bath available.

AA Pubs & Restaurants nearby: Champany Inn, LINLITHGOW, EH49 7LU, 01506 834532

MORAY

ABERLOUR
Map 23 NJ24

Places to visit

Balvenie Castle, DUFFTOWN, AB55 4DH, 01340 820121
www.historic-scotland.gov.uk

Glenfiddich Distillery, DUFFTOWN, AB55 4DH, 01340 820373
www.glenfiddich.com

Aberlour Gardens Caravan Park
▶▶▶ 80%

Best of British / GOLD

tel: 01340 871586 **AB38 9LD**
email: info@aberlourgardens.co.uk
dir: *Midway between Aberlour & Craigellachie on A95 turn onto unclassified road. Site signed. (NB vehicles over 10' 6" should use A941, Dufftown to Craigellachie road).*
grid ref: *NJ282434*

This attractive parkland site is set in the five-acre walled garden of the Victorian Aberlour House, surrounded by the spectacular scenery of the Cairngorm National Park, through pine tree glens, to the famous Moray coastline; the park is also well placed for taking the world renowned Speyside Malt Whisky Trail. It offers a small, well-appointed toilet block, laundry and small licensed shop. 5 acre site. 34 touring pitches. 16 hardstandings. 10 seasonal pitches. Caravan pitches. Motorhome pitches. Tent pitches. 32 statics.

Open: Mar-27 Dec (rs Winter - park opening dates weather dependant)
Last arrival: 19.00hrs **Last departure:** noon

Pitches: * 🚐 £20.65-£25.75 🚌 £20.65-£25.75 ▲ £16.30-£25.75

Leisure: 🎠 ⛹

Facilities: 🏪 🅿 ⊙ ☔ ✳ 🚿 🛁 🛡 WiFi ♻ ℹ

Services: 🚰 🚽 🛢 🚿 🗑 ⊤ ⬇

Within 3 miles: ⚲ 🎣 🛒

Notes: No ball games, max 5mph speed limit on site, no noise after 23.00hrs. Dogs must be kept on leads.

LEISURE: 🏊 Indoor pool 🏊 Outdoor pool 🎠 Children's playground 👶 Kid's club 🎾 Tennis court 🎱 Games room ⛳ Golf course 🚣 Boat hire 🚲 Cycle hire 🎬 Cinema 🎵 Entertainment 🎣 Fishing ⛳ Mini golf ⛳ Pitch n putt 🏄 Watersports 🏋 Gym ⚽ Sports field ♘ Stables **FACILITIES:** 🛁 Bath 🚿 Shower 🅿 Private washing cubicles ⊙ Electric shaver ☔ Hairdryer ✳ Ice Packs ♿ Disabled facilities 🛒 Shop on site 🚐 Mobile shop 🍖 BBQ area ⛱ Picnic area WiFi Wi-fi 💻 Internet access ♻ Recycling ℹ Tourist info 🐕 Dog exercise area 🚗 Car hire can be arranged

ELGIN
Map 23 NJ26

Places to visit
Elgin Cathedral, ELGIN, IV30 1HU, 01343 547171 www.historic-scotland.gov.uk

Elgin Museum, ELGIN, IV30 1EQ, 01343 543675 www.elginmuseum.org.uk

Woodlands Rest
NEW ►►►► 80%

tel: 0784 389 8930 **Aldroughty Woods**
email: reservations@aldroughtywoods.co.uk
dir: *Phone for directions.* **grid ref:** *NJ186624*

The traditional yurt and shepherd's hut at this glamping site blend seemingly into the private 25 acres of mature natural woodland, which forms part of Aldroughty Woods; both provide an ideal retreat for those looking for a peaceful and relaxing holiday. The units are far enough apart to ensure privacy but can be hired together; each has its own individual hut with cooking and toilet facilities. This site is totally off-grid and the owner has been very inventive in providing the power and water. The units are meticulously maintained and provide excellent facilities; the yurt has a large double bed and a set of bunk beds, table and seating, whilst the shepherd's hut has a double bed. Each has a wood-burner (wood and charcoal is provided), outdoor seating and fire pits. The customer service is excellent and the owner provides a friendly but unobtrusive daily service that includes making meals to your own requirements, from breakfast to full dinners. Woodlands Rest is a place to sit back and listen to birdsong, watch the red squirrels and spot roe deer as you walk through the beech woods. 25 acre site.

Open: all year **Last arrival:** 22.00hrs **Last departure:** 11.00hrs

Glamping: **Yurts** 1, £90 Changeover day Fri Min stay 1 night **Shepherd's Huts** 1, £90 Changeover day Fri Min stay 1 night

Notes: PayPal accepted.

LOSSIEMOUTH

Places to visit
Elgin Cathedral, ELGIN, IV30 1HU, 01343 547171 www.historic-scotland.gov.uk

Duffus Castle, DUFFUS, IV30 5RH, 01667 460232 www.historic-scotland.gov.uk

LOSSIEMOUTH
Map 23 NJ27

PREMIER PARK

Silver Sands Holiday Park
►►►►► 84%

tel: 01343 813262 **Covesea, West Beach IV31 6SP**
email: holidays@silver-sands.co.uk **web:** www.silver-sands.co.uk
dir: *Take B9040 from Lossiemouth, 2m to site.* **grid ref:** *NJ205710*

This is an ideal family park located on the Moray coast two miles from the busy seaside town of Lossiemouth. There is direct access to a sandy beach and the entertainment complex caters for both children and adults, with a pool, sauna, steam room and a large gym. There is a well-stocked shop, takeaway food and a small bistro-style café on site. With a golf course adjacent to the park and several others within easy driving distance (including the world famous Nairn Golf Course), this site makes a perfect base for golfers and those touring the area. There are fully serviced hardstandings and 15 static caravans for hire. 60 acre site. 140 touring pitches. 105 hardstandings. 35 seasonal pitches. Caravan pitches. Motorhome pitches. Tent pitches. 200 statics.

Open: 18 Mar-Oct **Last arrival:** 22.00hrs **Last departure:** noon
Pitches: 🚐 🚐 ⛺ **Leisure:** 🏊 🎯 ⚓ 🎱 🎣 🎵
Facilities: 🚿 🐾 ⊙ 🅿 ✳ 🔥 🛒 🛗 WiFi 🔌 ♻ ✆
Services: 🔌 🔋 🍺 🧺 T 🍴 🔋 🚰 🚮
Within 3 miles: 🚶 🎣 🏌 ⊚ 🎯 🚴 🔋 ∪
Notes: Dogs must be kept on leads.
See advert on opposite page

PERTH & KINROSS

BLAIR ATHOLL
Map 23 NN86

Places to visit

Blair Castle, BLAIR ATHOLL, PH18 5TL, 01796 481207 www.blair-castle.co.uk

Killiecrankie Visitor Centre, KILLIECRANKIE, PH16 5LG, 01796 473233 www.nts.org.uk/Property/Killiecrankie

AA CAMPSITE OF THE YEAR FOR SCOTLAND 2017

PREMIER PARK

Blair Castle Caravan Park
►►►►► 91%

tel: 01796 481263 **PH18 5SR**
email: mail@blaircastlecaravanpark.co.uk **web:** www.blaircastlecaravanpark.co.uk
dir: *From A9 onto B8079 at Aldclune, follow to Blair Atholl. Site on right after crossing bridge in village.* **grid ref:** *NN874656*

An attractive site set in impressive seclusion within the Atholl Estate, surrounded by mature woodland and the River Tilt. Although a large park, the various groups of pitches are located throughout the extensive grounds, and each has its own sanitary block with all-cubicled facilities of a very high standard. There is a choice of grass pitches, hardstandings and fully serviced pitches. This park is particularly suitable for the larger type of motorhome. There are now two wooden pods that each sleep two adults. 32 acre site. 226 touring pitches. 155 hardstandings. 68 seasonal pitches. Caravan pitches. Motorhome pitches. Tent pitches. 97 statics.

Open: Mar-Nov **Last arrival:** 21.30hrs **Last departure:** noon

Pitches: * ⛺ £23-£29 ⛺ £24-£33 ▲ £18-£23 ⛺ prices shown below

Leisure: ⚠ ⊙ ⚐ ✆ ⚬

Facilities: ⚑ ℙ⚲ ⊙ ⚐ ✳ ⚲ ⚑ ⚞ ⌂ WiFi 🖳 ♻ ❶

Services: ⚲⚬ ⚑ ❚ ⊤ ⚬ 🍽 🛒 🐕 ⚬

Glamping: Wooden Pods 2, £45-£60 Min stay 1 night

Within 3 miles: ⚬⚬ ⚬ ◎ ⑤⚬ ∪

Notes: Family park, no noise after 23.00hrs. Dogs must be kept on leads.

AA Pubs & Restaurants nearby: Killiecrankie Hotel, KILLIECRANKIE, PH16 5LG, 01796 473220

PREMIER PARK

River Tilt Caravan Park
►►►► 85%

tel: 01796 481467 **PH18 5TE**
email: stuart@rivertilt.co.uk
dir: *7m N of Pitlochry on A9, take B8079 to Blair Atholl. Site at rear of Tilt Hotel.*
grid ref: *NN875653*

An attractive park with magnificent views of the surrounding mountains, idyllically set in hilly woodland country on the banks of the River Tilt, adjacent to the golf course. There is also a leisure complex with heated indoor swimming pool, sun lounge area, spa pool and multi-gym, all available for an extra charge; outdoors there is a short tennis court. The toilet facilities are very good. 2 acre site. 30 touring pitches. Caravan pitches. Motorhome pitches. Tent pitches. 69 statics.

Open: 16 Mar-12 Nov **Last arrival:** 21.00hrs **Last departure:** noon

Pitches: * ⛺ £22 ⛺ £20-£22 ▲ £10-£18

Leisure: ⚑ ⚐ Spa

Facilities: ⊙ ⚐ ✳ ⚲ ⌂ ⚞ ⚑ WiFi 🖳 ♻ ❶

Services: ⚲⚬ ⚑ ❚ ⚬ 🍽 ⚬

Within 3 miles: ⚬⚬ ⚬ ◎ ⑤⚬ ∪

Notes: Dogs must be kept on leads. Sauna, solarium, steam room.

COMRIE
Map 21 NN72

Places to visit

Caithness Glass Visitor Centre, CRIEFF, PH7 4HQ, 01764 654014 www.caithnessglass.co.uk

Twenty Shilling Wood Caravan Park
NEW ►►► 77%

tel: 01764 670411 **PH6 2JY**
email: alowe20@aol.com
dir: *On A85, 0.5m W of Comrie towards St Fillans. Site opposite Tullybannocher café.*
grid ref: *NN749220*

Situated on the outskirts of Comrie, this is a tranquil and mature site that offers terraced pitches in a well maintained woodland setting which screens the site from the road. The site facilities are clean and well maintained and the family owners are very helpful. It is ideally located for exploring the Perthshire countryside – there are stunning drives to beautiful lochs and charming rural villages such as Comrie, which is a short walk away. There are various hiking and cycling trails, for all levels of ability, that can be accessed from the site. Please note, tents are not accepted. 10.5 acre site. 14 touring pitches. 14 hardstandings. 32 seasonal pitches. Caravan pitches. Motorhome pitches. 40 statics.

Open: 18 Mar-23 Oct **Last arrival:** 21.00hrs **Last departure:** 18.00hrs

Pitches: * ⛺ £23 ⛺ £23

Leisure: ⚠ ✆

Facilities: ⚑ ℙ⚲ ⊙ ⚐ ✳ ⚑ WiFi ♻ ❶

Services: ⚲⚬ ⚑ ⊤ ⚬

Notes: Booking advisable at all times, no noise after 23.00hrs. Max 2 dogs per pitch. Dogs must be kept on leads.

LEISURE: 🏊 Indoor pool 🏊 Outdoor pool ⚠ Children's playground 🖐 Kid's club 🎾 Tennis court 🎱 Games room ⚬ Golf course 🚣 Boat hire 🚲 Cycle hire 🎬 Cinema 🎵 Entertainment 🎣 Fishing ◎ Mini golf ⛳ Pitch n putt 🏄 Watersports 🏋 Gym ⚬ Sports field ∪ Stables **FACILITIES:** 🛁 Bath 🚿 Shower ℙ⚲ Private washing cubicles ⚬ Electric shaver ⚐ Hairdryer ✳ Ice Packs ⚞ Disabled facilities ⑤ Shop on site 🛒 Mobile shop 🍖 BBQ area 🍴 Picnic area WiFi Wi-fi 🖳 Internet access ♻ Recycling ❶ Tourist info 🐕 Dog exercise area 🚗 Car hire can be arranged

DUNKELD   Map 21 NO04

Places to visit

The Ell Shop & Little Houses, DUNKELD, PH8 0AN, 01350 728641
www.nts.org.uk/Property/Dunkeld

Loch of the Lowes Visitor Centre, DUNKELD, PH8 0HH, 01350 727337
www.swt.org.uk

Inver Mill Farm Caravan Park
▶▶▶▶ 80%

tel: 01350 727477 **Inver PH8 0JR**
email: invermill@talk21.com
dir: *A9 onto A822 then immediately right to Inver.* **grid ref:** *NO015422*

A peaceful park on level former farmland, located on the banks of the River Braan
and surrounded by mature trees and hills. The active resident owners keep the park
in very good condition. 5 acre site. 65 touring pitches. 3 hardstandings. Caravan
pitches. Motorhome pitches. Tent pitches.

Open: mid Mar-Oct **Last arrival:** 22.00hrs **Last departure:** noon

Pitches: 🚐 🚍 Å

Facilities: ☺ ℙ ⚒ ⚹ ⓦ ♻ 𝕴

Services: 🔌 🅧 🛢 ⌀ 🔋

Within 3 miles: ↓ ℐ 🅢 🅧

Notes: 🐾 Dogs must be kept on leads.

KINLOCH RANNOCH   Map 23 NN65

Kilvrecht Campsite
▶ 76%

tel: 0300 067638 **PH16 5QA**
email: tay.fd@forestry.gsi.gov.uk **web:** www.forestry.gov.uk
dir: *From north shore: on B846 to Kinloch Rannoch. Follow South Loch Rannoch sign. Over
river bridge, 1st right signed Kilvrecht. Approach via unclassified road along loch, with
Forestry Commission signs.* **grid ref:** *NN623567*

Set within a large forest clearing, approximately half a mile from the road to
Kinloch Rannoch which runs along the loch. This is a beautifully maintained site,
with good clean facilities, for those who wish for a peaceful break. It also makes an
ideal base for those who prefer the more active outdoor activities of hill walking
(Schiehallion is within easy reach) or mountain biking; it is a great spot to observe
the multitude of birds and wildlife in the area. Please note, the site has no

electricity. 17 acre site. 60 touring pitches. Caravan pitches. Motorhome pitches.
Tent pitches.

Open: Apr-Oct **Last arrival:** 22.00hrs **Last departure:** 10.00hrs

Pitches: * 🚐 £8 🚍 £8 Å £5-£8

Facilities: ℙ ⚒ ⓣ 𝕴

Within 3 miles: ↓ ℐ 🅢

Notes: 🐾 No fires. Dogs must be kept on leads.

PITLOCHRY   Map 23 NN95

Places to visit

Edradour Distillery, PITLOCHRY, PH16 5JP, 01796 472095 www.edradour.com

Milton of Fonab Caravan Park
▶▶▶▶ 90%

tel: 01796 472882 **Bridge Rd PH16 5NA**
email: info@fonab.co.uk **web:** www.fonab.co.uk
dir: *From S: on A924, pass petrol station on left, next left opposite Bell's Distillery into
Bridge Rd. Cross river, site on left. From N (& Pitlochry centre): on A924, under rail bridge,
turn right opposite Bell's Distillery into Bridge Rd.* **grid ref:** *NN945573*

This is a lovely, peaceful site set on the banks of the River Tummel on the outskirts
of Pitlochry. Getting here is easy as the A9 is nearby and there is a good bus service
and a mainline rail station in the town. The site is exceptionally well maintained,
with large pitches, good washrooms and a well-stocked shop, and it is an ideal
base for exploring this scenic part of Perthshire. The area is famous for the whisky
industry, and Bells distillery is a short walk from the site entrance as is the
Pitlochry Festival Theatre. 15 acre site. 154 touring pitches. Caravan pitches.
Motorhome pitches. Tent pitches. 34 statics.

Open: mid Mar-Oct **Last arrival:** 21.00hrs **Last departure:** 13.00hrs

Pitches: * 🚐 £20-£26 🚍 £20 £26 Å £20-£26

Leisure: ℐ

Facilities: 🚿 🎣 ℙ ☺ ℙ ⚒ ⚹ 🅢 🚻 ⓦ ♻ 𝕴

Services: 🔌 🅧 🛢 ⌀ 🛠 Ⓣ

Within 3 miles: ↓ ↯ ℐ ◎ 🅢 🅧

Notes: Couples & families only, no motorcycles. Dogs must be kept on leads.

AA Pubs & Restaurants nearby: Moulin Hotel, PITLOCHRY, PH16 5EH, 01796 472196

Killiecrankie Hotel, KILLIECRANKIE, PH16 5LG, 01796 473220

PITCHES: 🚐 Caravans 🚍 Motorhomes Å Tents 🎪 Glamping accommodation **SERVICES:** 🔌 Electric hook up 🅧 Launderette 🍷 Licensed bar
🛢 Calor Gas ⌀ Camping Gaz Ⓣ Toilet fluid 🍽 Café/Restaurant 🍔 Fast Food/Takeaway 🔋 Battery charging 🍼 Baby care 🛠 Motorvan service point
ABBREVIATIONS: BHs – bank holidays Etr – Easter Spring BH – Spring Bank Holiday fr – from hrs – hours m – mile mdnt – midnight
rdbt – roundabout rs – restricted service wk – week wknd – weekend x-roads – crossroads 🚫 No credit or debit cards 🚫 No dogs

PITLOCHRY *continued*

Faskally Caravan Park

►►►► 84%

tel: 01796 472007 **PH16 5LA**
email: info@faskally.co.uk
dir: *1.5m N of Pitlochry on B8019.* **grid ref:** *NN916603*

A large park near Pitlochry, which is divided into smaller areas by mature trees and set within well-tended grounds. This family-owned site has two large amenity blocks and an entertainment complex with a heated swimming pool, bar, restaurant and indoor games area. There are numerous walks from the site and it is ideal for either a longer stay to explore the area or as a convenient stopover. A regular bus service is available at the site entrance. 27 acre site. 300 touring pitches. 45 hardstandings. Caravan pitches. Motorhome pitches. Tent pitches. 130 statics.

Open: 15 Mar-Oct **Last arrival:** 23.00hrs **Last departure:** 11.00hrs

Pitches: * 🚐 £22-£26 🚌 £22-£26 ⛺ £22-£26

Leisure: 🏊 🎱 🎵 Spa

Facilities: 🪒 💨 ❄ ♿ 🛒 [WiFi] 💻 ♻ ℹ

Services: 🛠 🧺 🍷 ⛽ 🍃 [T] 🍽

Within 3 miles: ⛳ ⛵ 🎣 🛒 🧺 🐴

Notes: Dogs must be kept on leads.

AA Pubs & Restaurants nearby: Moulin Hotel, PITLOCHRY, PH16 5EH, 01796 472196

Killiecrankie Hotel, KILLIECRANKIE, PH16 5LG, 01796 473220

SCOTTISH BORDERS

LAUDER — Map 21 NT54

Thirlestane Castle Caravan & Camping Site

►►► 79%

tel: 01578 718884 & 07976 231032 **Thirlestane Castle TD2 6RU**
email: info@thirlestanecastlepark.co.uk
dir: *Signed from A68 & A697, just S of Lauder.* **grid ref:** *NT536473*

Located on the outskirts of Lauder, close to the A68 and within the grounds of Thirlestane Castle, this is an ideal site from which to explore the many attractions in the Scottish Borders. The amenity block is immaculately maintained and the pitches are behind the estate boundary wall that provides a secluded and peaceful location. There is a regular bus service near the site entrance. 5 acre site. 60 touring pitches. 22 hardstandings. 30 seasonal pitches. Caravan pitches. Motorhome pitches. Tent pitches. 31 statics.

Open: Apr-Oct **Last arrival:** 20.00hrs **Last departure:** noon

Pitches: * 🚐 £16-£21 🚌 £18-£21 ⛺ £8-£17

Leisure: 🛝 🎣

Facilities: 🚿 [P] 🪒 ❄ ♿ [WiFi] 💻 ♻ ℹ

Services: 🛠 🧺 ⤓

Within 3 miles: ⛳ 🎣 🛒 🧺

Notes: Dogs must be kept on leads. Tourer storage facilities, discounted access to castle & grounds during opening hours.

PAXTON — Map 21 NT95

Places to visit

Paxton House, Gallery & Country Park, BERWICK-UPON-TWEED, TD15 1SZ, 01289 386291 www.paxtonhouse.com

Paxton House Caravan Park

NEW ► 75%

tel: 01289 386291 & 07803 352706 **Paxton House TD15 1SZ**
email: info@paxtonhouse.com
dir: *From A1 (W of Berwick-upon-Tweed) take B6461 signed Paxton. Approx 5m, Paxton House entrance on left.* **grid ref:** *NT933525*

This site is situated within the walled garden of the glorious Paxton House just three miles from the attractions of Berwick-upon-Tweed. What this small basic site lacks in facilities, is more than made up for because of the free access for tourers, and for the beautiful gardens, woodland and river. In addition to woodland walks by the River Tweed, there are excellent, and adventurous, activities for children of all ages, lovely gardens to explore and home baking in the café to buy at a discount. For a small fee, a tour of the 18th-century, John Adams' designed Paxton House, is a must. 15 touring pitches. Caravan pitches. Motorhome pitches.

Open: all year **Last arrival:** 18.00hrs **Last departure:** 10.30hrs

Pitches: * 🚐 fr £12 🚌 fr £12

Facilities: 🐕 💻 ♻ **Services:** 🛠 🍽

Notes: Dogs must be kept on leads.

PEEBLES — Map 21 NT24

Places to visit

Kailzie Gardens, PEEBLES, EH45 9HT, 01721 720007 www.kailziegardens.com

Robert Smail's Printing Works, INNERLEITHEN, EH44 6HA, 01896 830206 www.nts.org.uk/Property/Robert-Smails-Printing-Works

Crossburn Caravan Park 🛖

►►►► 83%

tel: 01721 720501 **Edinburgh Rd EH45 8ED**
email: enquiries@crossburncaravans.co.uk
dir: *0.5m N of Peebles on A703.* **grid ref:** *NT248417*

A peaceful, family-run park, on the edge of Peebles and within easy driving distance for Edinburgh and the Scottish Borders. The park is divided by well-maintained landscaping and mature trees, and has good views over the countryside. There is a regular bus service at the site entrance and Peebles has a wide range of shops and attractions. The facilities are maintained to a high standard. Four-person wooden pods are available for hire. There is also a main caravan dealership on site, and a large stock of spares and accessories are available. 6 acre site. 45 touring pitches. 15 hardstandings. Caravan pitches. Motorhome pitches. Tent pitches. 85 statics.

Open: Apr-Oct **Last arrival:** 21.00hrs **Last departure:** 14.00hrs

Pitches: 🚐 🚌 ⛺ 🛖 **Facilities:** 🪒 💨 ♿ 🐕 [WiFi] ♻ ℹ

Services: 🛠 🧺 ⛽ 🍃 [T] 🍔 ⤓ **Glamping:** **Wooden Pods** 2

Within 3 miles: ⛳ 🎣 🛒 🐴

Notes: Dogs must be kept on leads.

STIRLING

ABERFOYLE
Map 20 NN50

Places to visit

Inchmahome Priory, PORT OF MENTEITH, FK8 3RA, 01877 385294
www.historic-scotland.gov.uk

PREMIER PARK

Trossachs Holiday Park
▶▶▶▶▶ 90%

GOLD

tel: 01877 382614 **FK8 3SA**
email: info@trossachsholidays.co.uk **web:** www.trossachsholidays.co.uk
dir: Access on E side of A81, 1m S of junct A821 & 3m S of Aberfoyle.
grid ref: NS544976

An attractively landscaped and peaceful park with outstanding views towards the hills, including the Munro of Ben Lomond. Set within the Loch Lomond National Park, boating, walking, cycling and beautiful drives over the Dukes Pass through the Trossachs are just some of the attractions within easy reach. Bikes can be hired from the reception and there is an internet café that sells home-baked items. There are lodges for hire. 40 acre site. 66 touring pitches. 46 hardstandings. 24 seasonal pitches. Caravan pitches. Motorhome pitches. Tent pitches. 84 statics.

Open: Mar-Oct **Last arrival:** 21.00hrs **Last departure:** noon
Pitches: * 🚐 £19-£25 🚌 £19-£25 ▲ £15-£21
Leisure: ◕ 🚴

Facilities: 🔧☉🗑️⚡☀️🛗🚿♨️🎣📶🖥️♻️⊘
Services: 🔌🗑️⚡Ⓣ🍽️🛒↯ **Within 3 miles:** ↓≿✎♨️🛒⛳↺
Notes: Groups by prior arrangement only.
AA Pubs & Restaurants nearby: The Clachan Inn, DRYMEN, G63 0BG, 01360 660824
See advert on page 402

BLAIRLOGIE
Map 21 NS89

Places to visit

Alloa Tower, ALLOA, FK10 1PP, 01259 211701
www.nts.org.uk/Property/Alloa-Tower

The National Wallace Monument, STIRLING, FK9 5LF, 01786 472140
www.nationalwallacemonument.com

Witches Craig Caravan & Camping Park
▶▶▶▶ 90%

GOLD

tel: 01786 474947 **FK9 5PX**
email: info@witchescraig.co.uk
dir: 3m NE of Stirling on A91 (Hillfoots to St Andrews road). **grid ref:** NS821968

In an attractive setting with direct access to the lower slopes of the dramatic Ochil Hills, this is a well-maintained family-run park. It is in the centre of 'Braveheart' country, with easy access to historical sites and many popular attractions. 5 acre site. 60 touring pitches. 60 hardstandings. 6 seasonal pitches. Caravan pitches. Motorhome pitches. Tent pitches.

Open: Apr-Oct **Last arrival:** 20.00hrs **Last departure:** noon
Pitches: * 🚐 £17.50-£24 🚌 £17.50-£24 ▲ £17-£22.75
Leisure: ⚂ **Facilities:** 🔧🖥️☉🗑️⚡☀️♿🎣🚿📶♻️⊘
Services: 🔌🗑️⚡∅Ⓣ🛒↯
Within 3 miles: ↓🎣✎◎🛒⛳↺
Notes: Dogs must be kept on leads. Food preparation area, cooking shelters, baby bath & changing area.

CALLANDER
Map 20 NN60

Places to visit

Doune Castle, DOUNE, FK16 6EA, 01786 841742 www.historic-scotland.gov.uk

Gart Caravan Park
▶▶▶▶ 87%

tel: 01877 330002 **The Gart FK17 8LE**
email: enquiries@theholidaypark.co.uk
dir: 1m E of Callander on A84. **grid ref:** NN643070

A very well appointed and spacious parkland site within easy walking distance of the tourist and outdoor activity-friendly town of Callander. The site is in an excellent location for touring the area; Loch Katrine (where there are trips on the SS *Sir Walter Scott*), The Trossachs and the Rob Roy Centre are only a few of the many nearby attractions. Free fishing is available on the River Teith which runs along the edge of the site. The static vans are in a separate area. Please note that tents are not accepted. 26 acre site. 128 touring pitches. 45 hardstandings. Caravan pitches. Motorhome pitches. 66 statics.

continued

PITCHES: 🚐 Caravans 🚌 Motorhomes ▲ Tents 🏕 Glamping accommodation **SERVICES:** 🔌 Electric hook up 🗑 Launderette 🍺 Licensed bar
🔋 Calor Gas ∅ Camping Gaz Ⓣ Toilet fluid 🍽️Café/Restaurant 🍟 Fast Food/Takeaway ⚡ Battery charging 👶 Baby care ↯ Motorvan service point
ABBREVIATIONS: BHs – bank holidays Etr – Easter Spring BH – Spring Bank Holiday fr – from hrs – hours m – mile mdnt – midnight
rdbt – roundabout rs – restricted service wk – week wknd – weekend x-roads – crossroads 🚫 No credit or debit cards ⊗ No dogs

CALLANDER *continued*

Open: Etr or Apr-15 Oct **Last arrival:** 22.00hrs **Last departure:** 18.00hrs

Pitches: 🚐 �caravan **Leisure:** ⚠ 🌀 ✎ **Facilities:** 🔥 ☉ ✳ ♿ 🐕 ✿ WiFi 🖥 ♻ ❢

Services: 🔌 🔟 🔋 T ⟲ **Within 3 miles:** ↥ ≱ ✎ ◎ ⚞ 💲 🛍 ↻

Notes: No commercial vehicles. Dogs must be kept on leads.

AA Pubs & Restaurants nearby: Roman Camp Country House Hotel, CALLANDER, FK17 8BG, 01877 330003

The Lade Inn, CALLANDER, FK17 8HD, 01877 330152

LUIB
Map 20 NN42

Glendochart Holiday Park
▶▶▶▶ 74%

tel: 01567 820637 **FK20 8QT**
email: info@glendochart-caravanpark.co.uk
dir: *On A85 (Oban to Stirling road) midway between Killin & Crianlarich.*
grid ref: *NN477278*

A small site located on the A85 some eight miles from Killin, with boating and fishing available on Loch Tay. It is also convenient for Oban, Fort William and Loch Lomond. Hill walkers have direct access to numerous walks to suit all levels of ability, including the nearby Munro of Ben More. There is a regular bus service at the site entrance, and nearby Crianlarich provides access to the West Highland Railway known as Britain's most scenic rail route, and also the West Highland Way. An ideal site as a stopover to the west coast or for a longer holiday. 15 acre site. 35 touring pitches. 28 hardstandings. Caravan pitches. Motorhome pitches. Tent pitches. 60 statics.

Open: Mar-Nov **Last arrival:** 21.00hrs **Last departure:** noon

Pitches: * 🚐 £18.50-£20 �caravan £18.50-£20 ▲ £12.50-£15

Facilities: ☉ ✎ ✳ ♿ 🔋 🐕 ❢ **Services:** 🔌 🔟 🔋 ♻ 🍴 **Within 3 miles:** ✎

Notes: Dogs must be kept on leads.

AA Pubs & Restaurants nearby: The Lade Inn, CALLANDER, FK17 8HD, 01877 330152

STIRLING

See Blairlogie

TYNDRUM
Map 20 NN33

Strathfillan Wigwam Village
▶▶▶▶▶ 80%

tel: 01838 400251 & 07817 483126 **Auchtertyre Farm FK20 8RU**
email: enquiries@wigwamholidays.com
dir: *From A82 (3m N of Crianarich) site on right. Follow signs for Strathfillan Wigwams & farm shop.* **grid ref:** *NN362273*

The hand-crafted wooden wigwams provide good accommodation, especially for walkers as this site is on the West Highland Way. Available all year, each unit is well insulated, has electric panel heaters and an external wood-burner (wood is available at the Trading Post shop). They are kept spotlessly clean and well maintained. The wigwams have been grouped in small clusters, some have outstanding mountain views and others benefit from the seclusion of a woodland setting. The lodges, with kitchen, shower and toilet, cater for up to eight, and a small yurt is also available for hire. The surrounding area offers many walking and mountain bike opportunities, and various eateries can be found in Tyndrum not far away. There is a local bus service at the end of the farm road. The site offers touring pitches as well. 6 acre site.

Open: all year **Last arrival:** 20.00hrs **Last departure:** 10.30hrs

Facilities: 🔥 P 🔋 ✎ 🔋 🐕 ✿ WiFi ♻ ❢

Services: 🔌 🔟 ⚞

Glamping: **Wooden Wigwams** 22, £40-£75 Min stay 1 night En suite Car by unit **Yurts** 1, £70-£80 Min stay 1 night Car by unit

Within 3 miles: ✎ 💲

Notes: No noise or music after 23.00hrs.

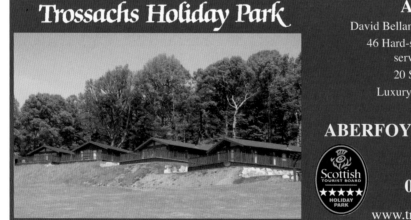
LEISURE: 🏊 Indoor pool ≋ Outdoor pool ⚠ Children's playground 🖐 Kid's club ⚲ Tennis court ⚫ Games room ⛳ Golf course ⚓ Boat hire 🚲 Cycle hire 🎦 Cinema 🎵 Entertainment ✎ Fishing ◎ Mini golf ⛳ Pitch n putt ≋ Watersports 🏋 Gym 🏐 Sports field ↻ Stables **FACILITIES:** 🛁 Bath 🔥 Shower P Private washing cubicles ☉ Electric shaver ✎ Hairdryer ✳ Ice Packs ♿ Disabled facilities 💲 Shop on site 🏪 Mobile shop 🍴 BBQ area 🌲 Picnic area WiFi Wi-fi 🖥 Internet access ♻ Recycling ❢ Tourist info 🐕 Dog exercise area ⚞ Car hire can be arranged

SCOTTISH ISLANDS

ISLE OF ARRAN

KILDONAN
Map 20 NS02

Places to visit

Brodick Castle, Garden & Country Park, BRODICK, KA27 8HY, 01770 302202
www.nts.org.uk/Property/Brodick-Castle-Garden-and-Country-Park

Isle of Arran Heritage Museum, BRODICK, KA27 8DP, 01770 302636
www.arranmuseum.co.uk

Sealshore Camping and Touring Site
►►►►84%

tel: 01770 820320 **KA27 8SE**
email: enquiries@campingarran.com
dir: *From ferry terminal in Brodick turn left, 12m, through Lamlash & Whiting Bay. Left to Kildonan, site on left.* **grid ref:** *NS024210*

On the south coast of Arran and only 12 miles from the ferry at Brodick, this is a peaceful, family-run site with direct access to a sandy beach. There are fabulous views across the water to Pladda Island and Ailsa Craig, and an abundance of wildlife. The site is suited for all types of touring vehicles but caters very well for non-motorised campers. The resident owner, also a registered fisherman, sells fresh lobster and crab, and on request will give fishing lessons on a small, privately owned lochan. There is an undercover barbecue, campers' kitchen and day room with TV. A bus, which stops on request, travels around the island. There are two wooden pods and two gypsy caravans for hire. 3 acre site. 43 touring pitches. 8 hardstandings. Caravan pitches. Motorhome pitches. Tent pitches.

Open: Mar-Oct **Last arrival:** 21.00hrs **Last departure:** noon

Pitches: * 🚐 £21-£22 🚐 £21-£22 ⛺ fr £8 🏕 prices shown below

Leisure: 🅰 🎣

Facilities: 🏛⊙🍴☀️🔥🛁🚻♨️🌀📶♻️☺🛈

Services: 🔌🗑🍺🛒🚰⛑🍴🍼♿

Glamping: **Wooden Pods** 2, £35 (1-2 persons; supplement for children over 6) Min stay 2 nights **Gypsy Vardos** 2, £45

Within 3 miles: ⛳🎣◉🛒🗑

Notes: No fires, no noise after 22.00hrs. Dogs must be kept on leads.

This symbol indicates that a site offers glamping accommodation

---

KILMORY
Map 20 NR92

Runach Arainn
NEW ►►►►►91%

tel: 01770 870515 **The Old Manse KA27 8PH**
email: runacharainn@gmail.com
dir: *From ferry at Brodick, turn right onto A481 signed South & Lamlash. Through Lamlash & Whiting Bay. Approx 9m to Kilmory. In Kilmory, 1st right, pass church to site.* **grid ref:** *NR964218*

Runach Arainn, Gaelic for 'Secret Arran', lives up to its name – hidden away in a quiet and beautiful part of the Isle of Arran, just a 15-minute walk from a lovely beach on the southern shore of the island. It offers superb 20ft-diameter yurts that were made in Scotland. The style of the interiors, together with private bathrooms for each yurt (in an amenity building), create a charming camping experience that includes many creature comforts for truly exceptional stay. Fire pits and outdoor cooking facilities are also available. 2 acre site.

Open: all year **Last arrival:** 22.00hrs **Last departure:** 10.00hrs

Facilities: 🏛P🅿️🛁🚻📶💻♨️☺🛈

Services: 🗑

Glamping: **Yurts** 3, £60-£110 Changeover day Any day Min stay 2 nights

Notes: No pets, no stag or hen parties.

ISLE OF MULL

CRAIGNURE
Map 20 NM73

Places to visit

Duart Castle, CRAIGNURE, PA64 6AP, 01680 812309 www.duartcastle.com

Shieling Holidays
►►►►86%

tel: 01680 812496 & 0131 556 0068 **PA65 6AY**
email: sales@shielingholidays.co.uk
dir: *From ferry left onto A849 to Iona. 400mtrs left at church, follow site signs towards sea.* **grid ref:** *NM724369*

A lovely site on the water's edge with spectacular views, and less than one mile from the ferry landing. Hardstandings and service points are provided for motorhomes, and there are astro-turf pitches for tents. The park also offers unique, en suite Shieling cottage tents for hire and bunkhouse accommodation for families. There is also a wildlife trail on site. 7 acre site. 90 touring pitches. 30 hardstandings. Caravan pitches. Motorhome pitches. Tent pitches.

Open: 6 Mar-2 Nov **Last arrival:** 22.00hrs **Last departure:** noon

Pitches: 🚐🚐⛺🏕

Leisure: 🎣

Facilities: ⊙🍴☀️🔥🛁🚻♨️📶♻️☺🛈

Services: 🔌🗑🛢️🚰⛑🛒♿

Glamping: **Shielings** (cottage tents) 16

Within 3 miles: ⛳🎣🛒🗑

Notes: Dogs must be kept on leads. Bikes available.

PITCHES: 🚐 Caravans 🚐 Motorhomes ⛺ Tents 🏕 Glamping accommodation **SERVICES:** 🔌 Electric hook up 🗑 Launderette 🍺 Licensed bar 🛢️ Calor Gas ⊘ Camping Gaz 🅃 Toilet fluid 🍴 Café/Restaurant 🍟 Fast Food/Takeaway 🔋 Battery charging 🍼 Baby care ♿ Motorvan service point
ABBREVIATIONS: BHs – bank holidays Etr – Easter Spring BH – Spring Bank Holiday fr – from hrs – hours m – mile mdnt – midnight rdbt – roundabout rs – restricted service wk – week wknd – weekend x-roads – crossroads Ⓝ No credit or debit cards Ⓧ No dogs

ISLE OF SKYE

EDINBANE
Map 22 NG35

Places to visit

Dunvegan Castle and Gardens, DUNVEGAN, IV55 8WF, 01470 521206
www.dunvegancastle.com

Skye Camping & Caravanning Club Site
▶▶▶▶ 92%

tel: 01470 582230 **Loch Greshornish, Borve, Arnisort IV51 9PS**
email: skye.site@thefriendlyclub.co.uk
dir: *Approx 12m from Portree on A850 (Dunvegan road). Site by loch shore.*
grid ref: *NG345527*

This campsite is memorable for its stunning waterside location and glorious views, the generous pitch density, the overall range of its facilities, and the impressive ongoing improvements made by the enthusiastic franchisee owners. The layout maximises the beauty of the scenery, and genuine customer care is very evident – an excellent tourist information room and campers' shelter being just two examples. The amenities block has smart, modern fittings, including excellent showers, a generously proportioned disabled room and a family bathroom. This is a 'green' site that uses only eco-friendly toilet fluids, which are available on site. There is a shop, and two camping pods for hire. Non-club members are very welcome too. 7.5 acre site. 105 touring pitches. 41 hardstandings. Caravan pitches. Motorhome pitches. Tent pitches.

Open: Apr-Oct **Last arrival:** 20.00hrs (earliest arrival 13.00hrs) **Last departure:** noon

Pitches: * 🚐 £19.35-£28.50 🚐 £19.35-£28.50 ▲ £19.35-£28.50 🏠 prices shown below

Leisure: 🎣

Facilities: 🐾 Ⓟ ⊙ 🅟 ☀ ⛄ ♿ Ⓢ 🍴 🚻 WiFi ♻ 🛈 🚗

Services: 🔌 🗑 🛢 🧺 Ⓣ 🛒 🔧

Glamping: Wooden Pods 2, £38 Changeover day Any day Min stay 2 nights Car by unit

Within 3 miles: 🎣 Ⓢ 🛍 Ⓤ

Notes: Barrier locked 23.00hrs-07.00hrs. Dogs must be kept on leads. Fresh fish van visits weekly.

AA Pubs & Restaurants nearby: Stein Inn, STEIN, IV55 8GA, 01470 592362

Loch Bay Restaurant, STEIN, IV55 8GA, 01470 592235

The Three Chimneys & The House Over-By, COLBOST, IV55 8ZT, 01470 511258

STAFFIN
Map 22 NG46

Staffin Camping & Caravanning
▶▶▶ 80%

tel: 01470 562213 **IV51 9JX**
email: staffincampsite@btinternet.com
dir: *On A855, 16m N of Portree. Turn right before 40mph signs.* **grid ref:** *NG492670*

This site provides an ideal base to rest and appreciate the peace and tranquillity of the north of Skye. It is a large sloping grassy site with level hardstandings for motorhomes and caravans. The site has older but good amenities. Nearby Staffin has a village store and a number of cafés. Sea and loch fishing are available nearby and the Totternish Ridge and surrounding area offer ample hill walking opportunities. It is a relatively short drive over the Quirang to reach the ferry terminal at Uig. 2.5 acre site. 50 touring pitches. 18 hardstandings. Caravan pitches. Motorhome pitches. Tent pitches.

Open: Apr-Oct **Last arrival:** 22.00hrs **Last departure:** 11.00hrs

Pitches: 🚐 🚐 ▲

Facilities: ⊙ 🅟 ☀ ♿ 🍴 🚻 WiFi ♻ 🛈

Services: 🔌 🗑 🛢 🧺 🛒

Within 3 miles: ⚓ 🎣 🛍 🛒

Notes: 🚫 No music after 22.00hrs. Dogs must be kept on leads. Picnic tables, kitchen area, campers' bothy.

AA Pubs & Restaurants nearby: Cuillin Hills Hotel, PORTREE, IV51 9QU, 01478 612003

PITCHES: 🚐 Caravans 🚐 Motorhomes ▲ Tents ⌂ Glamping accommodation **SERVICES:** ⊕ Electric hook up ⊚ Launderette 🍷 Licensed bar
🔒 Calor Gas ⌀ Camping Gaz Ⓣ Toilet fluid 🍽️ Café/Restaurant 🛒 Fast Food/Takeaway 🔋 Battery charging 🍼 Baby care ⛟ Motorvan service point
ABBREVIATIONS: BHs – bank holidays Etr – Easter Spring BH – Spring Bank Holiday fr – from hrs – hours m – mile mdnt – midnight
rdbt – roundabout rs – restricted service wk – week wknd – weekend x-roads – crossroads ⓔ No credit or debit cards ⊗ No dogs

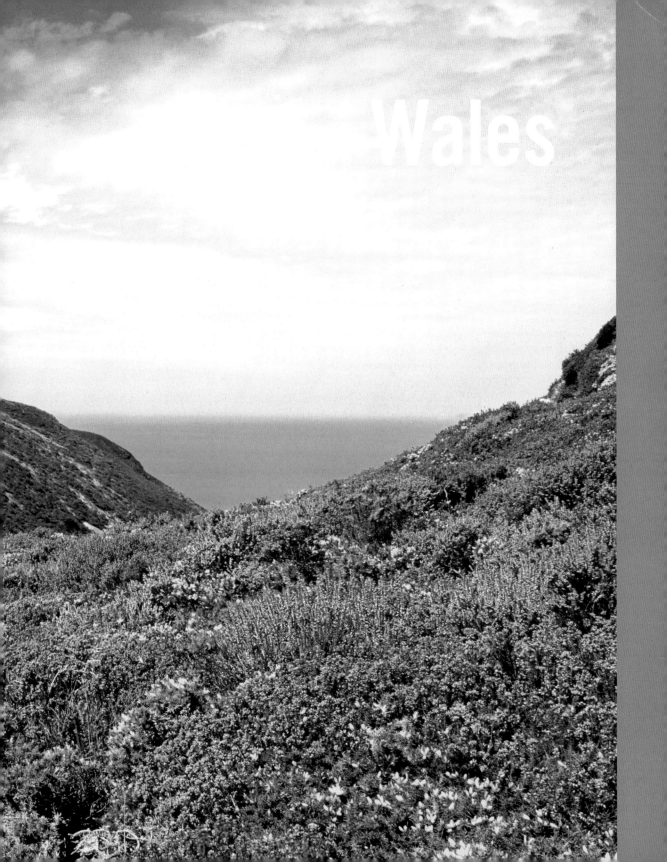

Wales

Wales

Wales — a place of myth and legend, a country loved passionately by actors and poets and male voice choirs, a land of rugged mountain grandeur and craggy, meandering coastline. Crossing the Severn Bridge, you sense at once you are entering a completely different country. The culture is different, so are the traditions and so are the physical characteristics. With its lush hills and dramatic headlands, it has echoes of other Celtic lands — most notably, Ireland and Scotland.

Wales's legacy of famous names from the world of the arts is truly impressive. Richard Burton hailed from the valleys in South Wales, Anthony Hopkins originates from Port Talbot and Dylan Thomas was born a century ago in a house on a hilltop street in Swansea. His birthplace in Cwmdonkin Drive can be hired for self-catering breaks and holidays and there is even the chance to sleep in the poet's tiny bedroom. Thomas described the house as 'a provincial villa…a small, not very well painted gateless house…very nice, very respective.'

Further west is the house where he lived in his final years. Thomas and his wife Caitlin moved to the Boat House at Laugharne, 40 miles from Swansea, in the spring of 1949. With its magnificent views across an expansive estuary, this was Dylan Thomas's perfect retreat and much of his creative writing was completed in the modest wooden shed on a bluff above the house. The Boat House is open to visitors and nearby Brown's Hotel, his favourite watering hole, offers the chance to relax and enjoy something to eat and drink.

On the Pembrokeshire coast, renowned for its beautiful beaches, is another, less familiar link with Dylan Thomas. The old fishing village of Lower Fishguard was home to a film unit of almost 100 people in the early months of 1971. Presided over by the film director Andrew Sinclair, filming of Thomas's classic play *Under Milk Wood* began, with Richard Burton and Peter O'Toole among the many film stars seen around the village. A young, virtually unknown David Jason, also appeared in the film. Sinclair and his team built false fronts on the dock cottages and created an undertaker's parlour – among other work. The National Eisteddfod in Llangollen is one of the most important events in the Welsh cultural calendar, celebrating the country's long heritage of storytelling, music and poetry.

Think of Wales and you often think of castles. The formidable Caernarfon Castle, the setting for the investure of the Prince of Wales in 1969, stands in the northwest corner of the country. Harlech Castle was built around 1283 by Edward I and from it are seen the peaks of Snowdonia. This glorious region of towering summits and crags, which has the highest range of mountains in England and Wales and is now a National Park, has long attracted walkers and climbers. Edmund Hillary and his team rehearsed here for the first successful assault on Everest in 1953. However, Snowdonia is not just about mountain peaks. There are plenty of gentler alternatives, including an extensive network of lowland routes, forest trails and waymarked walks. Below Snowdon lies the historic village of Llanberis, one of the region's most popular attractions and ideally placed for touring Snowdonia. Betws-y-Coed is another mountain resort with a range of delightful walks exploring picturesque river scenery and pretty, pastoral uplands.

For the buzz and vibrancy of the city, Swansea and Cardiff cannot be beaten, the latter boasting a lively café culture, docklands-style apartments, a science discovery centre that's fun for all the family, and the internationally renowned Wales Millennium Centre (Canolfan Mileniwm Cymru). However, in terms of Welsh scenery, there is so much waiting to be discovered and explored; the grand, immensely varied landscape of the Brecon Beacons, and the gentler, pastoral acres of the Welsh Borders – among a host of famed beauty spots throughout Wales.

◁ Elan Valley dam

ISLE OF ANGLESEY

BEAUMARIS — Map 14 SH67

Places to visit

Beaumaris Castle, BEAUMARIS, LL58 8AP, 01248 810361
http://cadw.gov.wales/daysout/beaumaris-castle/

Kingsbridge Caravan Park

►►►► 82%

DAVID BELLAMY CONSERVATION AWARD GOLD

tel: 01248 490636 & 07774 842199 **Camp Rd, Llanfaes LL58 8LR**
email: info@kingsbridgecaravanpark.co.uk **web:** www.kingsbridgecaravanpark.co.uk
dir: *From either Menai Bridge or Britannia Bridge follow signs for Beaumaris & A545. In Beaumaris (castle on left) take B5109 towards Llangoed, 2m to x-roads, turn left signed Kingsbridge.* **grid ref:** *SH605784*

Peacefully located two miles from historic Beaumaris, this long-established park has been transformed by its caring owners into a must-stay destination for lovers of walking and wildlife. The generously sized pitches are located in two separate touring areas – one for families and one for adults only – each has its own modern, well-equipped amenities block that are smartly presented with quality decor and fittings. Please note that a laundry is not provided but modern facilities are available in nearby Beaumaris. 14 acre site. 90 touring pitches. 21 hardstandings. 15 seasonal pitches. Caravan pitches. Motorhome pitches. Tent pitches. 29 statics.

Open: Mar-Oct **Last arrival:** 21.00hrs **Last departure:** noon

Pitches: * 🚐 £18-£24 🚌 £18-£24 ⛺ £18-£30

Leisure: 🛝 ⚽

Facilities: 🚿 🚪 ⊙ 💨 ❄ 🏪 📶 💻 ♻ ℹ

Services: 🔧 🔥 🔋 [T] ⚡ 🚽

Within 3 miles: ⛳ 🎣 🏄 🏪 🧺 🐴

Notes: No noise after 23.00hrs, no camp fires. Dogs must be kept on leads.

AA Pubs & Restaurants nearby: The Bull - Beaumaris, BEAUMARIS, LL58 8AP, 01248 810329

The Ship Inn, RED WHARF BAY, LL75 8RJ, 01248 852568

DULAS — Map 14 SH48

Places to visit

Din Lligwy Hut Group, LLANALLGO, 01443 336000
http://cadw.gov.wales/daysout/dinlligwyhutgroup/

PREMIER PARK

Tyddyn Isaf Caravan Park

►►►►► 92%

DAVID BELLAMY CONSERVATION AWARD GOLD

tel: 01248 410203 & 410667 **Lligwy Bay LL70 9PQ**
email: mail@tyddynisaf.co.uk **web:** www.tyddynisaf.co.uk
dir: *Take A5025 through Benllech to Moelfre rdbt, left towards Amlwch to Brynrefail. Turn right to Lligwy at phone box. Site 0.5m down lane on right.* **grid ref:** *SH486873*

A beautifully situated, and very spacious family park on rising ground adjacent to a sandy beach, with magnificent views overlooking Lligwy Bay. A private footpath leads directly to the beach and there is an excellent nature trail around the park. The site has very good toilet facilities, including a block with underfloor heating and excellent unisex privacy cubicles, a well-stocked shop, and bar/restaurant serving meals, which are best enjoyed on the terrace with its magnificent coast and sea views. Dogs are welcome in the two superb sea-view Mediterranean beach huts, located beside the terrace at the bar. 16 acre site. 80 touring pitches. 60 hardstandings. 50 seasonal pitches. Caravan pitches. Motorhome pitches. Tent pitches. 56 statics.

Open: Mar-Oct (rs Mar-Jul & Sep-Oct bar & shop opening limited)
Last arrival: 21.30hrs **Last departure:** 11.00hrs

Pitches: 🚐 🚌 ⛺

Facilities: 🚿 🚪 ⊙ 💨 ❄ ♿ 🏪 ⛱ 🐕 📶 💻 ♻ ℹ

Services: 🔧 🧺 🍷 🔥 🔋 [T] 🍴 ⚡ 🛒 🚽

Within 3 miles: ⛳ ⛵ 🎣 🏄 🏪 🧺 🐴

Notes: No groups, loud music or open fires, max 3 units can be booked together. Dogs must be kept on leads. Baby changing unit.

AA Pubs & Restaurants nearby: The Ship Inn, RED WHARF BAY, LL75 8RJ, 01248 852568

The Bull - Beaumaris, BEAUMARIS, LL58 8AP, 01248 810329

Bishopsgate House Hotel, BEAUMARIS, LL58 8BB, 01248 810302

MARIAN-GLAS
Map 14 SH58

Places to visit

Din Lligwy Hut Group, LLANALLGO, 01443 336000
http://cadw.gov.wales/daysout/dinlligwyhutgroup/

PREMIER PARK

Home Farm Caravan Park
▶▶▶▶▶ 94%

Best of British · GOLD

tel: 01248 410614 **LL73 8PH**
email: enq@homefarm-anglesey.co.uk **web:** www.homefarm-anglesey.co.uk
dir: On A5025, 2m N of Benllech. Site 300mtrs beyond church. **grid ref:** SH498850

A first-class park run with passion and enthusiasm, set in an elevated and secluded position sheltered by trees, and with good planting and landscaping. The peaceful rural setting affords views of farmland, the sea and the mountains of Snowdonia. The modern toilet blocks are spotlessly clean and well maintained, and there are excellent play facilities for children both indoors and out. Facilities also include a visitors' parking area and a smart reception and shop. The area is blessed with sandy beaches, and the local pubs and shops cater for everyday needs. 12 acre site. 102 touring pitches. 65 hardstandings. Caravan pitches. Motorhome pitches. Tent pitches. 84 statics.

Open: Apr-Oct **Last arrival:** 21.00hrs **Last departure:** noon
Pitches: * 🚐 £22-£36.50 🚍 £23.50-£36.50 Å £18-£30.50
Leisure: 🌳 😊 🎣
Facilities: ⊙ 🛒 ☀ ♿ ⓢ 🛒 📶 💻 ♻ ⓘ
Services: 🔌 🗑 ⌀ Ⓣ 🛒 ↻
Within 3 miles: ⅃ 🏌 ⚓ 🏪 ⌕ ∪
Notes: No roller blades, skateboards or scooters.
AA Pubs & Restaurants nearby: The Ship Inn, RED WHARF BAY, LL75 8RJ, 01248 852568

The Bull - Beaumaris, BEAUMARIS, LL58 8AP, 01248 810329

Bishopsgate House Hotel, BEAUMARIS, LL58 8BB, 01248 810302

RED WHARF BAY
Map 14 SH58

St David's Park
▶▶▶▶ 88%

tel: 01248 852341 & 852702 **LL75 8RJ**
email: info@stdavidspark.com
dir: A55 junct 8, A5025 towards Benllech. Approx 8m, right towards Red Wharf Bay, site 0.5m on left. **grid ref:** SH529811

In a stunning location with panoramic coastal and mountain views and direct access to a private sandy beach, this long-established holiday village provides touring pitches, 44 of which are allocated to seasonal customers. A haven for campers, the all-tent pitches have electric hook-up facilities and a stylish modern amenities block with hi-spec facilities. Spa treatments are available by appointment and the redesigned Tavern on the Bay offers 270° panoramic views of Benllech Bay and a wide range of drinks and imaginative food. 47 acre site. 45 touring pitches. 44 seasonal pitches. Caravan pitches. Motorhome pitches. Tent pitches. 180 statics.

Open: 15 Mar-end Sep **Last arrival:** 21.00hrs **Last departure:** noon
Pitches: 🚐 🚍 Å **Leisure:** 🌳 **Facilities:** 🛒 ☀ ♿ ⓢ 📶 ♻ ⓘ
Services: 🔌 🗑 🍴 🛒 🍽 **Within 3 miles:** ⅃ 🏌 ⚓ 🏪 ⌕ ∪
Notes: No group bookings, no jet skis, gazebos or disposable BBQs, no noise after 23.00hrs.
AA Pubs & Restaurants nearby: The Ship Inn, RED WHARF BAY, LL75 8RJ, 01248 852568

RHOS LLIGWY
Map 14 SH48

Places to visit

Din Lligwy Hut Group, LLANALLGO, 01443 336000
http://cadw.gov.wales/daysout/dinlligwyhutgroup/

Ty'n Rhos Caravan Park
▶▶▶ 68%

tel: 01248 852417 **Lligwy Bay, Moelfre LL72 8NL**
email: robert@bodafonpark.co.uk
dir: Take A5025 from Benllech to Moelfre rdbt, right to T-junct in Moelfre. Left, approx 2m, pass x-roads leading to beach, site 50mtrs on right. **grid ref:** SH495867

A family park close to the beautiful beach at Lligwy Bay, and cliff walks along the Heritage Coast. Historic Din Lligwy, and the shops at picturesque Moelfre are nearby. All the touring pitches have water, electric hook-up and TV connection. Please note that guests should register at Bodafon Caravan Park in Benllech where detailed directions will be given and pitches allocated. 10 acre site. 30 touring pitches. 4 hardstandings. 48 seasonal pitches. Caravan pitches. Motorhome pitches. Tent pitches. 80 statics.

Open: Mar-Oct **Last arrival:** 20.00hrs **Last departure:** 11.00hrs
Pitches: * 🚐 £23-£30 🚍 £23-£30 Å £20-£28
Facilities: 🛒 Ⓟ ⊙ ☀ ♿ 🛒 📶 💻 ♻ ⓘ
Services: 🔌 🗑 🔋 **Within 3 miles:** ⅃ 🏌 ⚓ 🏪 ∪
Notes: No campfires, no noise after 23.00hrs. Dogs must be kept on leads. Boat park.
AA Pubs & Restaurants nearby: The Ship Inn, RED WHARF BAY, LL75 8RJ, 01248 852568

The Bull - Beaumaris, BEAUMARIS, LL58 8AP, 01248 810329

Bishopsgate House Hotel, BEAUMARIS, LL58 8BB, 01248 810302

PITCHES: 🚐 Caravans 🚍 Motorhomes Å Tents 🏠 Glamping accommodation **SERVICES:** 🔌 Electric hook up 🗑 Launderette 🍴 Licensed bar 🔋 Calor Gas ⌀ Camping Gaz Ⓣ Toilet fluid 🍽 Café/Restaurant 🍔 Fast Food/Takeaway 🔋 Battery charging 🛒 Baby care ↻ Motorvan service point
ABBREVIATIONS: BHs – bank holidays Etr – Easter Spring BH – Spring Bank Holiday fr – from hrs – hours m – mile mdnt – midnight rdbt – roundabout rs – restricted service wk – week wknd – weekend x-roads – crossroads Ⓢ No credit or debit cards ⊗ No dogs

BRIDGEND

PORTHCAWL
Map 9 SS87

Places to visit

Newcastle, BRIDGEND, 01443 336000
http://cadw.gov.wales/daysout/newcastle/

Coity Castle, COITY, CF35 6BG, 01443 336000
http://cadw.gov.wales/daysout/coitycastle/

Brodawel Camping & Caravan Park
►►►►80%

tel: 01656 783231 **Moor Ln, Nottage CF36 3EJ**
email: info@brodawelcamping.co.uk
dir: *M4 junct 37, A4229 towards Porthcawl. After Grove Golf Club right into Moor Ln, follow site signs.* **grid ref:** *SS816789*

A lovely family park close to sea and other attractions, with a lush grass touring field that provides generously sized pitches; most have electric hook-up. There is a smart amenities block appointed to a high standard, with good privacy options, and a well-stocked shop and WiFi. 4 acre site. 100 touring pitches. 4 hardstandings. 40 seasonal pitches. Caravan pitches. Motorhome pitches. Tent pitches.

Open: Apr-mid Oct **Last arrival:** 19.00hrs **Last departure:** 11.00hrs
Pitches: * ⌂ £15-£21 ⌂ £15-£21 ▲ £15-£21
Leisure: ⌂ ⌂
Facilities: ⌂ ⌂ ⌂ ⌂ ⌂ ⌂ ⌂ ⌂ ⌂ ⌂ ⌂
Services: ⌂ ⌂ ⌂ ⌂ ⌂
Within 3 miles: ⌂ ⌂ ⌂ ⌂ ⌂ ⌂ ⌂ ⌂ ⌂

Notes: Dogs must be kept on leads. Free electrical sockets, undercover picnic area, baby changing facility.

AA Pubs & Restaurants nearby: Prince of Wales Inn, KENFIG, CF33 4PR, 01656 740356

CARMARTHENSHIRE

LAUGHARNE
Map 8 SN31

Places to visit

Laugharne Castle, LAUGHARNE, SA33 4SA, 01994 427906
http://cadw.gov.wales/daysout/laugharnecastle/

Dylan Thomas' Boat House, LAUGHARNE, SA33 4SD, 01994 427420
www.dylanthomasboathouse.com

Antshill Caravan & Camping Park
NEW ►►►► 84%

tel: 01994 427293 & 07977 110095 **Antshill SA33 4QN**
email: contact_us@antshill.co.uk
dir: *From E: on A40 at St Clears follow Laugharne & A4066 signs. At T-junct turn right onto A4066 (High St) signed Laugharne, in approx 3.5m, site on left. From W: at A40 & A477 rdbt follow Laugharne & A4066 signs. In St Clears at lights turn right signed Laugharne into High St. In approx 3.5m, site on left.* **grid ref:** *SN299117*

A long established family run holiday destination near the seafront and Dylan Thomas' Boathouse. It is especially family friendly with indoor and outdoor children's activities, a shielded, heated outside swimming pool and a clubhouse that provides entertainment and meals at weekends. All touring and camping areas are level and most have hardstandings. The stylish amenities block is equipped with modern fixtures and fittings and the showers are especially spacious. 8.4 acre site. 65 touring pitches. Caravan pitches. Motorhome pitches. Tent pitches. 61 statics.

Open: Mar-Oct **Last arrival:** 22.00hrs **Last departure:** noon
Pitches: * ⌂ £15-£25 ⌂ £15-£25 ▲ £15-£25
Leisure: ⌂ ⌂ ⌂ ⌂ ⌂
Facilities: ⌂ ⌂ ⌂ ⌂ ⌂ ⌂ ⌂ ⌂ ⌂ ⌂ ⌂ ⌂
Services: ⌂ ⌂ ⌂ ⌂ ⌂ ⌂ ⌂
Within 3 miles: ⌂ ⌂ ⌂ ⌂ ⌂ ⌂

Notes: Dogs must be kept on leads.

LLANDOVERY
Map 9 SN73

Places to visit

Dolaucothi Gold Mines, PUMSAINT, SA19 8US, 01558 650177
www.nationaltrust.org.uk/dolaucothi-gold-mines

PREMIER PARK

Erwlon Caravan & Camping Park
►►►►► 85%

Best of British

GOLD

tel: 01550 721021 & 720332 **Brecon Rd SA20 0RD**
email: peter@erwlon.co.uk
dir: *0.5m E of Llandovery on A40.* **grid ref:** *SN776343*

A long-established, family-run site set beside a brook in the Brecon Beacons foothills. The town of Llandovery and the hills overlooking the Towy Valley are a short walk away. The superb, Scandinavian-style facilities block has cubicled washrooms, family and disabled rooms. 8 acre site. 75 touring pitches. 15 hardstandings. Caravan pitches. Motorhome pitches. Tent pitches.

Open: all year **Last arrival:** anytime **Last departure:** noon
Pitches: * ⌂ £13-£17 ⌂ £13-£17 ▲ £5-£17
Leisure: ⌂ ⌂
Facilities: ⌂ ⌂ ⌂ ⌂ ⌂ ⌂ ⌂ ⌂ ⌂ ⌂ ⌂
Services: ⌂ ⌂ ⌂ ⌂ ⌂ ⌂
Within 3 miles: ⌂ ⌂ ⌂ ⌂ ⌂

Notes: Quiet after 22.30hrs, adult-only sections available. Dogs must be kept on leads. Fishing, cycle storage.

AA Pubs & Restaurants nearby: The Kings Head, LLANDOVERY, SA20 0AB, 01550 720393

LEISURE: ⌂ Indoor pool ⌂ Outdoor pool ⌂ Children's playground ⌂ Kid's club ⌂ Tennis court ⌂ Games room ⌂ Golf course ⌂ Boat hire ⌂ Cycle hire ⌂ Cinema ⌂ Entertainment ⌂ Fishing ⌂ Mini golf ⌂ Pitch n putt ⌂ Watersports ⌂ Gym ⌂ Sports field ⌂ Stables **FACILITIES:** ⌂ Bath ⌂ Shower ⌂ Private washing cubicles ⌂ Electric shaver ⌂ Hairdryer ⌂ Ice Packs ⌂ Disabled facilities ⌂ Shop on site ⌂ Mobile shop ⌂ BBQ area ⌂ Picnic area ⌂ Wi-fi ⌂ Internet access ⌂ Recycling ⌂ Tourist info ⌂ Dog exercise area ⌂ Car hire can be arranged

Llandovery Caravan Park

▶▶▶77%

tel: 01550 721065 & 07970 650606 **Church Bank SA20 0DT**
email: llandoverycaravanpark@gmail.com
dir: *A40 from Carmarthen, over rail crossing, past junct with A483 (Builth Wells). Turn right for Llangadog, past church, 1st right signed Rugby Club & Camping.*
grid ref: *SN762342*

Within easy walking distance of the town centre and adjacent to the notable Llandovery Dragons Rugby Club, this constantly improving park is an ideal base for touring the Brecon Beacons and many local attractions. Most pitches have both water and a hardstanding, and guests are welcome to use the popular on-site rugby club lounge bar. Please note, a laundry is not provided, but there is one in the town. 8 acre site. 20 touring pitches. 60 seasonal pitches. Caravan pitches. Tent pitches.

Open: all year **Last arrival:** 20.00hrs **Last departure:** 20.00hrs

Pitches: * ⊞ £15 ▲ £8-£15

Leisure: ⊛

Facilities: 🏕 ⊙ & ⊓ WiFi ♻ 𝟎

Services: ⊞ ⊐🍴 🔋

Within 3 miles: ↓🄷🖉📠🛒∪

Notes: 🐕 Dogs must be kept on leads.

AA Pubs & Restaurants nearby: The Kings Head, LLANDOVERY, SA20 0AB, 01550 720393

| LLANGENNECH | Map 8 SN50 |

Places to visit

WWT LLanelli Wetland Centre, LLANELLI, SA14 9SH, 01554 741087
www.wwt.org.uk/wetland-centres/llanelli/

South Wales Touring Park

▶▶▶ 91%

tel: 01554 820420 **Llwynifan Farm SA14 8AX**
email: info@southwalescaravanpark.com
dir: *M4 junct 48, A4138 signed Llanelli. In 11.5m right at rdbt. In 425yds left between bungalows into farm road.* **grid ref:** *SN554027*

This site is located in an elevated position close to Llanelli. The touring pitches, including 10 that are fully serviced, are on three terraced levels providing stunning countryside views. The grounds are immaculately maintained with a wide variety of trees, shrubs and pretty seasonal flowers, and a very well-equipped gym is also available. A same-day laundry service is provided too. Excellent customer care is assured; hands-on management from owners Cathrin and Hywel Davies means that visitors will have a memorable stay. 5 acre site. 27 touring pitches. 27 hardstandings. Caravan pitches. Motorhome pitches.

Open: Feb-Oct **Last arrival:** 19.00hrs **Last departure:** noon

Pitches: ⊞ ⊞

Leisure: 🏊 🚲 **Facilities:** 🏕 ⊙ 🅿 ☀ ⊓ WiFi ♻ 𝟎

Services: ⊞ 🔋 📠 🛒

Within 3 miles: ↓🄷🖉📠🛒

Notes: Adults only. No noise after 22.00hrs. Dogs must be kept on leads. Dog sitting service.

| NEWCASTLE EMLYN | Map 8 SN34 |

Places to visit

Cilgerran Castle, CILGERRAN, SA43 2SF, 01239 621339
http://cadw.gov.wales/daysout/cilgerran-castle/

Castell Henllys Iron Age Fort, CRYMYCH, SA41 3UT, 01239 891319
www.castellhenllys.com

PREMIER PARK

Cenarth Falls Holiday Park

▶▶▶▶▶88%

Best of British

tel: 01239 710345 **Cenarth SA38 9JS**
email: enquiries@cenarth-holipark.co.uk **web:** www.cenarth-holipark.co.uk
dir: *From Newcastle Emlyn on A484 towards Cardigan. Through Cenarth, site on right.*
grid ref: *SN265421*

Located close to the village of Cenarth where the River Teifi, famous for its salmon and trout fishing, cascades through the Cenarth Falls Gorge. With beautifully landscaped grounds and spotless amenities, the park also benefits from an indoor heated swimming pool, sauna, fitness suite and a restaurant with bar. 2 acre site. 30 touring pitches. 30 hardstandings. Caravan pitches. Motorhome pitches. Tent pitches. 89 statics.

Open: Mar-Nov (rs Off peak bar & meals restricted to wknds only)
Last arrival: 20.00hrs **Last departure:** 11.00hrs

Pitches: ⊞ £18.50-£28 ⊞ £18.50-£28 ▲ £18.50-£28

Leisure: 🏊 🚲 🏸 ⋔ 🎱 🎵

Facilities: ⊙ 🅿 ☀ & WiFi ♻ 𝟎

Services: ⊞ 🔋 📠 🔋 🛒 🍴 🔋 🛒

Within 3 miles: 🖉 🛒📠

Notes: No skateboards. Dogs must be kept on leads. Pool table.

PITCHES: ⊞ Caravans ⊞ Motorhomes ▲ Tents 🏕 Glamping accommodation **SERVICES:** ⊞ Electric hook up 🔋 Launderette 🍴 Licensed bar 🔋 Calor Gas 🔋 Camping Gaz 🅣 Toilet fluid 🍴 Café/Restaurant 🔋 Fast Food/Takeaway 🔋 Battery charging 🔋 Baby care 🛒 Motorvan service point
ABBREVIATIONS: BHs – bank holidays Etr – Easter Spring BH – Spring Bank Holiday fr – from hrs – hours m – mile mdnt – midnight rdbt – roundabout rs – restricted service wk – week wknd – weekend x-roads – crossroads 🚫 No credit or debit cards 🚫 No dogs

NEWCASTLE EMLYN *continued*

Moelfryn Caravan & Camping Park

►►►►86%

tel: 01559 371231 **Ty-Cefn, Pant-y-Bwlch SA38 9JE**
email: info@moelfryncaravanpark.co.uk
dir: *A484 from Carmarthen towards Cynwyl Elfed. Pass the shops on right, 200yds take left fork onto B4333 towards Hermon. In 7m follow brown sign on left. Turn left, site on right.* **grid ref:** *SN321370*

A small, beautifully maintained, family-run park in a glorious elevated location overlooking the valley of the River Teifi. Pitches are level and spacious, and well screened by hedging and mature trees. The centrally located amenities block has stylish decor, smart cladding, provision of good privacy options and excellent fixtures and fittings. 3 acre site. 25 touring pitches. 18 hardstandings. 12 seasonal pitches. Caravan pitches. Motorhome pitches. Tent pitches.

Open: Mar-10 Jan **Last arrival:** 22.00hrs **Last departure:** noon

Pitches: * ⊞ fr £14 ⊞ fr £14 Å fr £13

Facilities: ↖ ℙ ⊙ ℱ ✷ 🔥 📶 ♻ ❶

Services: 🔌 🔘 🥫 🍽 🛒

Within 3 miles: ⚓ 🎣 🎬 ℱ ⛵ 🛍 🛒 ∪

Notes: Games to be played in designated area only. Dogs must be kept on leads. Caravan storage.

AA Pubs & Restaurants nearby: Webley Waterfront Inn & Hotel, ST DOGMAELS, SA43 3LN, 01239 612085

Argoed Meadow Caravan and Camping Site

►►►►82%

tel: 01239 710690 **Argoed Farm SA38 9JL**
email: argoedfarm@btinternet.com **web:** www.cenarthcampsite.co.uk
dir: *From Newcastle Emlyn on A484 towards Cenarth, take B4332. Site 300yds on right.*
grid ref: *SN268415*

A warm welcome is assured at this attractive and immaculately maintained site, situated on the banks of the River Teifi and close to Cenarth Falls Gorge. The spotlessly clean amenities block provides very good privacy options for the less able visitors. 3 acre site. 30 touring pitches. 5 hardstandings. Caravan pitches. Motorhome pitches. Tent pitches. 5 statics.

Open: all year **Last arrival:** anytime **Last departure:** noon

Pitches: ⊞ ⊞ Å

Leisure: ✎

Facilities: ↖ ℙ ⊙ ℱ ✷ 🔥 🛍 ♻ ❶

Services: 🔌 🔘 🥫 🍽 🛒

Within 3 miles: 🎬 ℱ 🛍 🛒 ∪

Notes: No bikes or skateboards. Dogs must be kept on leads.

AA Pubs & Restaurants nearby: Webley Waterfront Inn & Hotel, ST DOGMAELS, SA43 3LN, 01239 612085

Afon Teifi Caravan & Camping Park

►►►►81%

tel: 01559 370532 **Pentrecagal SA38 9HT**
email: afonteifi@btinternet.com
dir: *Signed from A484, 2m E of Newcastle Emlyn.* **grid ref:** *SN338405*

Set on the banks of the River Teifi, a famous salmon and sea trout river, this secluded, family-owned and run park has good views. It is only two miles from the market town of Newcastle Emlyn. The smart amenities block is appointed to a high standard. 6 acre site. 110 touring pitches. 22 hardstandings. 25 seasonal pitches. Caravan pitches. Motorhome pitches. Tent pitches. 15 statics.

Open: Apr-Oct **Last arrival:** 23.00hrs

Pitches: ⊞ ⊞ Å

Leisure: ♻ 🔍 **Facilities:** ⊙ ℱ ✷ 🔥 🛍 🎣 ♻ ❶

Services: 🔌 🔘 🥫 🍽 🛒 **Within 3 miles:** ⚓ ℱ 🛍 🛒 ∪

Notes: No noise after mdnt, no bikes or scooters after dark. Dogs must be on leads.

AA Pubs & Restaurants nearby: Webley Waterfront Inn & Hotel, ST DOGMAELS, SA43 3LN, 01239 612085

LEISURE: 🏊 Indoor pool 🏊 Outdoor pool 🎢 Children's playground 👋 Kid's club ♨ Tennis court 🎱 Games room ⛳ Golf course 🚣 Boat hire 🚲 Cycle hire 🎬 Cinema 🎵 Entertainment 🎣 Fishing ⛳ Mini golf ⛳ Pitch n putt 🏄 Watersports 🏋 Gym ⚽ Sports field ∪ Stables **FACILITIES:** 🛁 Bath 🚿 Shower ℙ Private washing cubicles ⊙ Electric shaver ℱ Hairdryer ✷ Ice Packs 🔥 Disabled facilities 🛍 Shop on site 🚐 Mobile shop 🍽 BBQ area 🎪 Picnic area 📶 Wi-fi 💻 Internet access ♻ Recycling ❶ Tourist info 🐕 Dog exercise area 🚗 Car hire can be arranged

CEREDIGION

ABERAERON — Map 8 SN46

Places to visit

Llanerchaeron, ABERAERON, SA48 8DG, 01545 570200 www.nationaltrust.org.uk

Aeron Coast Caravan Park
▶▶▶ 92%

tel: 01545 570349 **North Rd SA46 0JF**
email: enquiries@aeroncoast.co.uk
dir: *From Aberaeron on A487 (coast road) towards Aberystwyth. Filling station on left at entrance.* **grid ref:** *SN460631*

A well-managed family holiday park on the edge of the attractive resort of Aberaeron, with direct access to the beach. The spacious pitches are all level. On-site facilities include an extensive outdoor pool complex, a multi-activity outdoor sports area, an indoor children's play area, a small lounge bar which serves food, a games room and an entertainment suite. 22 acre site. 100 touring pitches. 30 hardstandings. Caravan pitches. Motorhome pitches. Tent pitches. 200 statics.

Open: Mar-Oct **Last arrival:** 23.00hrs **Last departure:** 11.00hrs

Pitches: 🚐 🚎 ⛺

Leisure: 🏊 🏓 🎱 🎣

Facilities: 🚿

Services: 🔌

Within 3 miles:

Notes: Families only, no motorcycles. Dogs must be kept on leads.

AA Pubs & Restaurants nearby: The Harbourmaster, ABERAERON, SA46 0BT, 01545 570755

ABERYSTWYTH — Map 8 SN58

Places to visit

The National Library of Wales, ABERYSTWYTH, SY23 3BU, 01970 632565 www.llgc.org.uk

Vale of Rheidol Railway, ABERYSTWYTH, SY23 1PG, 01970 625819 www.rheidolrailway.co.uk

Ocean View Caravan Park
▶▶▶ 82%

tel: 01970 828425 **North Beach, Clarach Bay SY23 3DT**
email: enquiries@oceanviewholidays.com **web:** www.oceanviewholidays.com
dir: *In Bow Street village on A487 follow Clarach sign. In Llangorwen Clarach straight on at next x-roads. Site 2nd on right.* **grid ref:** *SN592842*

This site is in a sheltered valley on gently sloping ground, with wonderful views of both the sea and the countryside. The beach of Clarach Bay is just 200 yards away, and this welcoming park is ideal for all the family. There is a children's football field and dog walking area. Campers may use the pool, gym, restaurant and bar at Clarach Bay which is within walking distance of the site. 9 acre site. 24 touring pitches. 15 hardstandings. 20 seasonal pitches. Caravan pitches. Motorhome pitches. Tent pitches. 56 statics.

Ocean View Caravan Park

Open: Mar-Oct **Last arrival:** 20.00hrs **Last departure:** noon

Pitches: * 🚐 £17-£21 🚎 £17-£21 ⛺ £17-£21

Leisure: 🏊

Facilities: 🚿

Services: 🔌

Within 3 miles:

Notes: No noise 23.00hrs-08.00hrs, no games on park. Dogs must be kept on leads.

NEW QUAY — Map 8 SN35

Places to visit

Llanerchaeron, ABERAERON, SA48 8DG, 01545 570200 www.nationaltrust.org.uk

Quay West Holiday Park
HOLIDAY HOME PARK 86%

tel: 01545 560477 **SA45 9SE**
email: quaywest@haven.com **web:** www.haven.com/quaywest
dir: *From Cardigan on A487 left onto A486 into New Quay. Or from Aberystwyth on A487 right onto B4342 into New Quay.* **grid ref:** *SN397591*

This holiday park enjoys a stunning clifftop position overlooking picturesque New Quay and Cardigan Bay. It's an easy walk to a glorious sandy beach, and the all-action on-site activities include heated swimming pools, SplashZone, football, archery and fencing (with professional tuition), the Aqua Bar and terrace and a kiddies' Pic 'n' Paint room. There is a good range of holiday caravans.

Open: Mar-Oct

Changeover day: Mon, Fri, Sat

Arrival and departure times: Please contact the site

Statics: 125 Sleeps 6-8 Bedrms 2-3 Bathrms 1-2 Toilets 1-2 Microwave Freezer TV Sky/FTV Elec inc Gas inc Grass area

Children: Cots Highchair **Dogs:** 2 on leads No dangerous dogs

Leisure: Cycle hire

PITCHES: 🚐 Caravans 🚎 Motorhomes ⛺ Tents 🏕 Glamping accommodation **SERVICES:** 🔌 Electric hook up 🧺 Launderette 🍺 Licensed bar 🔋 Calor Gas 🔥 Camping Gaz 🚽 Toilet fluid 🍽 Café/Restaurant 🍟 Fast Food/Takeaway 🔋 Battery charging 👶 Baby care 🚐 Motorvan service point **ABBREVIATIONS:** BHs – bank holidays Etr – Easter Spring BH – Spring Bank Holiday fr – from hrs – hours m – mile mdnt – midnight rdbt – roundabout rs – restricted service wk – week wknd – weekend x-roads – crossroads No credit or debit cards No dogs

CONWY

BETWS-YN-RHOS
Map 14 SH97

Places to visit

Bodelwyddan Castle, BODELWYDDAN, LL18 5YA, 01745 584060
www.bodelwyddan-castle.co.uk

Bodnant Garden, TAL-Y-CAFN, LL28 5RE, 01492 650460
www.nationaltrust.org.uk/bodnant-garden

Plas Farm Caravan Park
►►►►86%

GOLD

tel: 01492 680254 & 07831 482176 **LL22 8AU**
email: info@plasfarmcaravanpark.co.uk **web:** www.plasfarmcaravanpark.co.uk
dir: *A55 junct 24, A547 through Abergele, straight on at 2 mini rdbts, follow Rhyd-Y-Foel signs, 3m. Left, follow signs.* **grid ref:** *SH897744*

Ideally located for exploring the many attractions of north Wales and within easy travelling distance of historic Chester, this beautifully landscaped park, adjacent to a 16th-century farmhouse, is certainly a popular choice. There are superb pitches, many fully serviced and on a terraced area; the camping area, sited in woodland, ensures tranquillity and relaxation, with only birdsong to disturb the peace. There are two modern amenities blocks, a good laundry and a well-equipped campers' kitchen. 10 acre site. 54 touring pitches. 54 hardstandings. Caravan pitches. Motorhome pitches. Tent pitches.

Open: Mar-Oct **Last arrival:** 19.00hrs **Last departure:** 11.00hrs

Pitches: 🚐 £19-£29 🚙 £19-£29 ▲ £10-£25

Leisure: ⚑

Facilities: 🚿 Ⓟ ⊙ ℘ ✳ ⚐ � 🎏 Wifi ♻ ❼

Services: 🔌 🗑 🚽 Ⓣ 🛒 ⬆

Within 3 miles: ⚓ 目 ℘ 🛶 ⛳ 🏵 🎱 U

Notes: Quiet after 23.00hrs, no campfires, no large groups. Dogs must be kept on leads. Woodland walk, shopping service.

AA Pubs & Restaurants nearby: The Kinmel Arms, ABERGELE, LL22 9BP, 01745 832207

Hunters Hamlet Caravan Park
►►►►85%

tel: 01745 832237 & 07721 552105 **Sirior Goch Farm LL22 8PL**
email: huntershamlet@aol.com
dir: *From A55 W'bound, A547 junct 24 into Abergele. At 2nd lights turn left by George & Dragon pub, onto A548. 2.75m right at x-roads onto B5381. Site 0.5m on left.*
grid ref: *SH928736*

A warm welcome is assured at this long established, family-run working farm park adjacent to the owners' Georgian farmhouse. Well-spaced pitches, including 15 with water, electricity and TV hook-up, are within two attractive hedge-screened grassy paddocks. The well-maintained amenities block, includes unisex bathrooms. Please note, this site does not accept tents. 2.5 acre site. 30 touring pitches. 30 hardstandings. Caravan pitches. Motorhome pitches.

Open: Mar-Oct **Last arrival:** 22.00hrs **Last departure:** noon

Pitches: 🚐 🚙

Leisure: ⚑

Facilities: 🚌 🚿 Ⓟ ⊙ ℘ ✳ ⚐ Wifi ♻ ❼

Services: 🔌 🗑 🛒 ⬆

Within 3 miles: ⚓ ℘ Ⓢ

Notes: No football. Dogs must be kept on leads & not be left unattended. Baby bath & changing facilities.

AA Pubs & Restaurants nearby: The Hawk & Buckle Inn, LLANNEFYDD, LL16 5ED, 01745 540249

The Kinmel Arms, ABERGELE, LL22 9BP, 01745 832207

LLANDDULAS
Map 14 SH97

Places to visit

Rhuddlan Castle, RHUDDLAN, LL18 5AD, 01745 590777
http://cadw.gov.wales/daysout/rhuddlancastle/

Bodelwyddan Castle, BODELWYDDAN, LL18 5YA, 01745 584060
www.bodelwyddan-castle.co.uk

PREMIER PARK

Bron-Y-Wendon Caravan Park
►►►►►87%

tel: 01492 512903 **Wern Rd LL22 8HG**
email: stay@northwales-holidays.co.uk
dir: *From A55 towards Llandudno turn right at Llanddulas & A547 junct 23 sign, sharp right. 200yds, under A55 bridge. Site on left.* **grid ref:** *SH903785*

A top quality site in a stunning location, with panoramic sea views from every pitch and excellent purpose-built toilet facilities including heated shower blocks. Pitch density is excellent, offering a high degree of privacy, and the grounds are beautifully landscaped and immaculately maintained. Super pitches are available. The staff are helpful and friendly, and everything from landscaping to maintenance has a stamp of excellence. An ideal seaside base for touring Snowdonia and visiting Colwyn Bay, Llandudno and Conwy. 8 acre site. 130 touring pitches. 110 hardstandings. Caravan pitches. Motorhome pitches.

Open: all year **Last arrival:** anytime **Last departure:** 11.00hrs

Pitches: * ⊞ £21-£28 ⊞ £21-£28

Leisure: ⚘

Facilities: ⬧ P ⊙ 𝒫 ☼ ⬧ ⬧ WiFi ⬛ ♻ ➋ 💧

Services: ⊞ 🗆 🔋 🚼 ⬧

Within 3 miles: ⬧ ⬧ 𝒫 ⬧ 🛒 🗆 ⟳

Notes: Dogs must be kept on leads.

AA Pubs & Restaurants nearby: Pen-y-Bryn, COLWYN BAY, LL29 6DD, 01492 533360

LLANRWST

Map 14 SH86

Places to visit

Gwydir Uchaf Chapel, LLANRWST, 01492 641687
http://cadw.gov.wales/daysout/gwydiruchafchapel/

Trefriw Woollen Mills, TREFRIW, LL27 0NQ, 01492 640462 www.t-w-m.co.uk

Great for kids: Conwy Valley Railway Museum, BETWS-Y-COED, LL24 0AL, 01690 710568 www.conwyrailwaymuseum.co.uk

---

PREMIER PARK

Bron Derw Touring Caravan Park
►►►►► 88%

tel: 01492 640494 **LL26 0YT**
email: bronderw@aol.com **web:** www.bronderw-wales.co.uk
dir: A55 onto A470 for Betws-y-Coed & Llanrwst. In Llanrwst left into Parry Rd signed Llanddoged. Left at T-junct, site signed at 1st farm entrance on right.
grid ref: SH798628

A previous AA campsite award winner, Bron Derw, once a dairy farm, is beautifully landscaped with stunning floral displays and surrounded by hills. The park has been built to a very high standard and is fully matured. All pitches are fully serviced, and there is a heated, stone-built toilet block with excellent and immaculately maintained facilities. The Parc Derwen adults-only field has 28 fully serviced pitches and its own designated amenities block. CCTV security cameras cover the whole park. 4.5 acre site. 48 touring pitches. 48 hardstandings. 17 seasonal pitches. Caravan pitches. Motorhome pitches.

Open: Mar-Oct **Last arrival:** 21.00hrs **Last departure:** 11.00hrs

Pitches: * ⊞ £22-£24 ⊞ £22-£24

Facilities: ⬧ ⊙ 𝒫 ⬧ ⬧ ⬧ WiFi ♻ ➋

Services: ⊞ 🗆 T 🔋 🚼 ⬧

Within 3 miles: 𝒫 🛒 🗆

Notes: Children must be supervised, no bikes, scooters or skateboards, no noise after 23.00hrs. Dogs must be kept on leads.

Bodnant Caravan Park
►►►► 85%

tel: 01492 640248 **Nebo Rd LL26 0SD**
email: ermin@bodnant-caravan-park.co.uk
dir: From A470 in Llanrwst at lights take B5427 signed Nebo (opposite garage). Immediately right signed Nebo. Site 300yds on right, opposite leisure centre.
grid ref: SH805609

This well maintained and stunningly attractive park is filled with flower beds, and the landscape includes shrubberies and trees. The statics are unobtrusively sited and the quality, spotlessly clean toilet blocks have fully serviced private cubicles. All caravan pitches are multi-service, and the tent pitches serviced. There is a separate playing field and rally field, and there are lots of farm animals on the park to keep children entertained. Victorian farming implements are on display around the touring fields. 5 acre site. 54 touring pitches. 20 hardstandings. Caravan pitches. Motorhome pitches. Tent pitches. 2 statics.

Open: Mar-end Oct **Last arrival:** 21.00hrs **Last departure:** 11.00hrs

Pitches: ⊞ ⊞ ▲

Facilities: ⬧ P ⊙ 𝒫 ⬧ ⬧ WiFi ⬛ ♻ ➋

Services: ⊞ 🔋 ⬧

Within 3 miles: ⬧ ⬧ 𝒫 🛒 🗆

Notes: No bikes, skateboards or camp fires, main gates locked 23.00hrs-08.00hrs, no noise after 23.00hrs. Dogs must be kept on leads.

PITCHES: ⊞ Caravans ⊞ Motorhomes ▲ Tents ⌂ Glamping accommodation **SERVICES:** ⊞ Electric hook up 🗆 Launderette 🍺 Licensed bar
🔋 Calor Gas ⬧ Camping Gaz T Toilet fluid 🍽 Café/Restaurant 🍔 Fast Food/Takeaway 🔋 Battery charging 🚼 Baby care ⬧ Motorvan service point
ABBREVIATIONS: BHs – bank holidays Etr – Easter Spring BH – Spring Bank Holiday fr – from hrs – hours m – mile mdnt – midnight
rdbt – roundabout rs – restricted service wk – week wknd – weekend x-roads – crossroads ⊗ No credit or debit cards ⊗ No dogs

DENBIGHSHIRE

PRESTATYN Map 15 SJ08

Places to visit

Basingwerk Abbey, HOLYWELL, CH8 7GH, 01443 336000
http://cadw.gov.wales/daysout/basingwerk-abbey/

Great for kids: Rhuddlan Castle, RHUDDLAN, LL18 5AD, 01745 590777
http://cadw.gov.wales/daysout/rhuddlancastle/

Presthaven Sands Holiday Park
HOLIDAY CENTRE 83%

GOLD

tel: 01745 856471 **Gronant LL19 9TT**
email: presthavensands@haven.com **web:** www.haven.com/presthavensands
dir: *A548 from Prestatyn towards Gronant. Site signed (NB for Sat Nav use LL19 9ST).*
grid ref: *SJ091842*

Set beside two miles of superb sandy beaches and dunes (with donkeys on site at weekends) this constantly improving holiday park provides a wide range of both indoor and outdoor attractions. The site can boast happy returning visitors. The small touring field at the park entrance offers good electric pitches — the majority are hardstandings and include five super pitches. The centrally located entertainment area includes two indoor swimming pools, excellent children's activities and a choice of eating outlets. 21 acre site. 50 touring pitches. 39 hardstandings. Caravan pitches. Motorhome pitches. 1052 statics.

Presthaven Sands Holiday Park

Open: mid Mar-end Oct (rs mid Mar-May & Sep-Oct facilities may be reduced)
Last arrival: 20.00hrs **Last departure:** 10.00hrs

Pitches: 🚐 🚌

Leisure: 🏊 🏊 🎣 🎵 🎶

Facilities: 🚿 ⊙ ♿ Ⓢ WIFI ♻ 🅗

Services: 🚽 🗑 🍴 🍽 🏪 ⚡

Within 3 miles: ⌃ 🏇 🚲 ⚓ ⊙ Ⓢ 🛍 ∪

Notes: No commercial vehicles, no bookings by persons under 21yrs unless a family booking. Max 2 dogs per booking, certain dog breeds banned. Dogs must be kept on leads.

See advert below

LEISURE: 🏊 Indoor pool 🏊 Outdoor pool Ⓐ Children's playground 👶 Kid's club 🎾 Tennis court 🎱 Games room ⛳ Golf course 🚤 Boat hire 🚲 Cycle hire 🎬 Cinema 🎵 Entertainment 🎣 Fishing ⛳ Mini golf 🏌 Pitch n putt 🏄 Watersports 🏋 Gym ⚽ Sports field ∪ Stables **FACILITIES:** 🛁 Bath 🚿 Shower Ⓟ Private washing cubicles ⊙ Electric shaver 💇 Hairdryer ❄ Ice Packs ♿ Disabled facilities Ⓢ Shop on site 🚐 Mobile shop 🍖 BBQ area 🍴 Picnic area WIFI Wi-fi 💻 Internet access ♻ Recycling ⊙ Tourist info 🐕 Dog exercise area 🚗 Car hire can be arranged

RHUALLT	Map 15 SJ07

Places to visit

Rhuddlan Castle, RHUDDLAN, LL18 5AD, 01745 590777
http://cadw.gov.wales/daysout/rhuddlancastle/

Bodelwyddan Castle, BODELWYDDAN, LL18 5YA, 01745 584060
www.bodelwyddan-castle.co.uk

Great for kids: Denbigh Castle, DENBIGH, LL16 3NB, 01745 813385
http://cadw.gov.wales/daysout/denbighcastle/

Penisar Mynydd Caravan Park
▷▷▷▷ 90%

tel: 01745 582227 & 07831 408017   **Caerwys Rd LL17 0TY**
email: contact@penisarmynydd.co.uk
dir: From A55 junct 29 follow Dyserth & brown caravan signs. Site 500yds on right.
grid ref: SJ093770

A very tranquil, attractively laid-out park set in three grassy paddocks with a superb facilities block including a disabled room and dishwashing area. The majority of pitches are super pitches. Immaculately maintained throughout, the park is within easy reach of historic Chester and the seaside resort of Rhyl. 6.6 acre site. 71 touring pitches. 71 hardstandings. 30 seasonal pitches. Caravan pitches. Motorhome pitches. Tent pitches.

Open: Mar-15 Jan **Last arrival:** 21.00hrs **Last departure:** 21.00hrs
Pitches: * 🚐 £15-£17 🚎 £15-£17 ⛺ £12-£16 **Leisure:** ⊗
Facilities: ⊙ ⚡ ⚻ 🚿 🔥 📶 💻 ♻ ❶ **Services:** 🔌 🔲 🔋 ⭐ ↯
Within 3 miles: ⚓ 🏛 ⌀ ◎ ⚓ 💲 🔲 ∪
Notes: No cycling, no fires. Dogs must be kept on leads. Rally area.
AA Pubs & Restaurants nearby: The Plough Inn, ST ASAPH, LL17 0LU, 01745 585080

GWYNEDD

ABERSOCH	Map 14 SH32

Places to visit

Plas-yn-Rhiw, PLAS YN RHIW, LL53 8AB, 01758 780219
www.nationaltrust.org.uk

Deucoch Touring & Camping Park
►►►► 85%

tel: 01758 713293 & 07740 281770   **Sarn Bach LL53 7LD**
email: info@deucoch.com
dir: From Abersoch take Sarn Bach road, at x-roads turn right, site on right in 800yds.
grid ref: SH301269

A colourful, sheltered site with stunning views of Cardigan Bay and the mountains, and situated just a mile from Abersoch and a long sandy beach. The friendly, enthusiastic, hands-on proprietors make year-on-year improvements to enhance their visitors' experience. Facilities include outside hot showers, a superb dishwashing facility, housed in an attractive log cabin, and caravan repairs. 5 acre site. 70 touring pitches. 10 hardstandings. Caravan pitches. Motorhome pitches. Tent pitches.

Open: Mar-Oct **Last arrival:** 18.00hrs **Last departure:** 11.00hrs

Pitches: 🚐 🚎 ⛺ **Leisure:** 🎱
Facilities: 🐕 ⊙ ⚡ 🚿 ♿ 📶 ♻ ❶
Services: 🔌 🔲 ↯ **Within 3 miles:** ⚓ ↟ ⌀ ⚓ 💲 ∪
Notes: ⊗ Families only. Dogs must be kept on leads.
AA Pubs & Restaurants nearby: Porth Tocyn Hotel, ABERSOCH, LL53 7BU, 01758 713303

Beach View Caravan Park
►►►► 83%

tel: 01758 712956 **Bwlchtocyn LL53 7BT**
email: enquiries@beachviewholidaypark.co.uk
dir: A499 to Abersoch. Through Abersoch & Sarn Bach. Straight on at x-roads, next left signed Porth Tocyn Hotel. Pass chapel. Left at next Porth Tocyn Hotel sign. Site on left.
grid ref: SH316262

A compact family park run by a very enthusiastic owner who makes continual improvements. Just a six-minute walk from the beach, the site's immaculately maintained grounds, good hardstanding pitches (mostly seasonal) and excellent facilities are matched by great sea and country views. 4 acre site. 47 touring pitches. 47 hardstandings. 40 seasonal pitches. Caravan pitches. Motorhome pitches. Tent pitches.

Open: mid Mar-mid Oct **Last arrival:** 19.00hrs **Last departure:** 11.00hrs
Pitches: 🚐 🚎 ⛺ **Facilities:** ⊙ ⚡ 🚿 🔥 ❶
Services: 🔌 🔲 🔋 ⌀ ⭐
Within 3 miles: ⚓ ↟ ⌀ ⚓ 💲 ∪
Notes: ⊗ Dogs must be kept on leads.
AA Pubs & Restaurants nearby: Porth Tocyn Hotel, ABERSOCH, LL53 7BU, 01758 713303

Tyn-y-Mur Touring & Camping
►►►► 83%

tel: 01758 712328 **Lon Garmon LL53 7UL**
email: info@tyn-y-mur.co.uk
dir: From Pwllheli into Abersoch on A499, sharp right at Land & Sea Garage. Site approx 0.5m on left. **grid ref:** SH304290

A family-only park in a glorious hill-top location overlooking a lush valley and with views extending across Abersoch to the mountains beyond Cardigan Bay. Good, clean, modern toilet facilities and spacious tent pitches in a level grassy field are on offer. A pretty shrub and flower display at the entrance surrounds a ship's anchor recovered from a Royal Navy frigate, which was lost in the bay in 1948. There is a pathway from the site to private river fishing, and the beach at Abersoch is just a short walk away. The park offers boat storage facilities and a new amenities block is planned for 2017. 22 acre site. 90 touring pitches. 49 hardstandings. 49 seasonal pitches. Caravan pitches. Motorhome pitches. Tent pitches.

Open: Apr-Oct **Last arrival:** 22.00hrs **Last departure:** 11.00hrs
Pitches: * 🚐 fr £27 🚎 fr £27 ⛺ £20-£30
Leisure: 🎱 ⊗ ⌀
Facilities: 🐕 ⊙ 🚿 ♿ 🔥 🔥 📶 ♻ ❶
Services: 🔌 🔲 🔋 ⌀ 🚽 ⭐ 🍴
Within 3 miles: ⚓ ↟ ⌀ ⚓ 💲 🔲 ∪
Notes: No open fires, no motorcycles, no noisy activity after 23.00hrs, 1 dog per unit. Dogs must be kept on leads. Boat park.
AA Pubs & Restaurants nearby: Porth Tocyn Hotel, ABERSOCH, LL53 7BU, 01758 713303

PITCHES: 🚐 Caravans 🚎 Motorhomes ⛺ Tents 🏠 Glamping accommodation **SERVICES:** 🔌 Electric hook up 🔲 Launderette 🍺 Licensed bar
🔋 Calor Gas ⌀ Camping Gaz Ⓣ Toilet fluid 🍴 Café/Restaurant 🍟 Fast Food/Takeaway ⭐ Battery charging 🚼 Baby care ↯ Motorvan service point
ABBREVIATIONS: BHs – bank holidays Etr – Easter Spring BH – Spring Bank Holiday fr – from hrs – hours m – mile mdnt – midnight
rdbt – roundabout rs – restricted service wk – week wknd – weekend x-roads – crossroads 💲 No credit or debit cards ⊗ No dogs

ABERSOCH *continued*

Rhydolion

►►►71%

tel: 01758 712342 **Llangian LL53 7LR**
email: enquiries@rhydolion.co.uk
dir: *From A499 take unclassified road to Llangian for 1m, left, through Llangian. Site 1.5m after road forks towards Hell's Mouth & Porth Neigwl.* **grid ref:** *SH283276*

A peaceful, small site with good views, on a working farm close to the long sandy surfers beach at Hell's Mouth. The simple toilet facilities are kept to a high standard by the friendly owners, and nearby Abersoch is a mecca for boat owners and water sports enthusiasts. 1.5 acre site. 28 touring pitches. Caravan pitches. Motorhome pitches. Tent pitches.

Open: Mar-Oct **Last arrival:** 22.00hrs **Last departure:** noon

Pitches: 🚐 🚌 ⛺ **Leisure:** ⚽

Facilities: ⊙ ✲ 🐕 ♻ ℹ

Services: 🔌 🧺 🛏

Within 3 miles: ⛳ ⛵ 🎣 ◎ 🌊 [$] 🧺 🐴

Notes: 🚫 Families & couples only. Dogs only accepted by prior arrangement & must be kept on leads. Fridge freezers & microwave available.

AA Pubs & Restaurants nearby: Porth Tocyn Hotel, ABERSOCH, LL53 7BU, 01758 713303

BANGOR **Map 14 SH57**

Places to visit

Penrhyn Castle, BANGOR, LL57 4HN, 01248 353084
www.nationaltrust.org.uk/penrhyncastle

Gwynedd Museum, BANGOR, LL57 1DT, 01248 353368
www.gwynedd.gov.uk/museums

Great for kids: GreenWood Forest Park, Y FELINHELI, LL56 4QN, 01248 671493
www.greenwoodforestpark.co.uk

Treborth Hall Farm Caravan Park

►►►74%

tel: 01248 364399 **The Old Barn, Treborth Hall Farm LL57 2RX**
email: enquiries@treborthleisure.co.uk
dir: *A55 junct 9, 1st left at rdbt, straight over 2nd rdbt, site approx 800yds on left.*
grid ref: *SH554707*

Set in eight acres of beautiful parkland with its own trout fishing lake and golf course, this park offers serviced pitches in a sheltered, walled orchard. Tents have a separate grass area, and there is a good clean toilet block. A static holiday caravan, with access for the less able, is available for hire. This is a useful base for families, with easy access to the Menai Straits, Anglesey beaches, Snowdon and the Lleyn peninsula. 8 acre site. 34 touring pitches. 34 hardstandings. Caravan pitches. Motorhome pitches. Tent pitches. 4 statics.

Open: Etr-end Oct **Last arrival:** 22.30hrs **Last departure:** 10.30hrs

Pitches: 🚐 £21-£27 🚌 £21-£27 ⛺

Leisure: ⛳ **Facilities:** 🪑 📶 ♻ ℹ

Services: 🔌

Within 3 miles: ⛳ 🎣 ◎ 🌊 [$] 🧺

Notes: Dogs must be kept on leads.

BARMOUTH **Map 14 SH61**

Places to visit

Harlech Castle, HARLECH, LL46 2YH, 01766 780552
http://cadw.gov.wales/daysout/harlechcastle/

Cymer Abbey, CYMER ABBEY, LL40 2HE, 01443 336000
http://cadw.gov.wales/daysout/cymer-abbey/

PREMIER PARK

Trawsdir Touring Caravans & Camping Park

Best of British

►►►►► 93%

tel: 01341 280999 **Llanaber LL42 1RR**
email: enquiries@barmouthholidays.co.uk
dir: *3m N of Barmouth on A496, just past Wayside pub on right.* **grid ref:** *SH596198*

Well run by the owners, this quality park enjoys spectacular views to the sea and hills, and is very accessible for motor traffic. The facilities are appointed to a very high standard, and include spacious cubicles containing showers and washbasins, individual showers, smart toilets with sensor-operated flush and underfloor heating. Tents and caravans have their own designated areas divided by dry-stone walls (both have spacious fully serviced pitches). The site is very convenient for large recreational vehicles, and there are camping pods for hire. There is an excellent children's play area, plus glorious seasonal floral displays and an illuminated dog walk that leads directly to the nearby pub! WiFi is available throughout the park. 15 acre site. 70 touring pitches. 70 hardstandings. 30 seasonal pitches. Caravan pitches. Motorhome pitches. Tent pitches.

Open: Mar-Jan **Last arrival:** 17.00hrs **Last departure:** 11.00hrs

Pitches: * 🚐 £18-£35 🚌 £18-£35 ⛺ £10-£30 🛖 prices shown below

Leisure: 🛝

Facilities: 🚿 ⊙ 💨 ✲ ♿ [$] 🪑 🐕 📶 ♻ ℹ

Services: 🔌 🧺 🔒 🍃 [T] 🛏 🛒 ⬇

Glamping: **Wooden Pods** 10, £30-£50 Min stay 2 nights Car by unit

Within 3 miles: 🎣 🌊 [$] 🧺

Notes: Families & couples only. Dogs must be kept on leads. Milk, bread etc available from reception, takeaway food can be delivered from sister site.

AA Pubs & Restaurants nearby: Victoria Inn, LLANBEDR, LL45 2LD, 01341 241213

LEISURE: 🏊 Indoor pool 🏊‍♂️ Outdoor pool 🛝 Children's playground ✋ Kid's club 🎾 Tennis court 🎱 Games room ⛳ Golf course ⛵ Boat hire 🚲 Cycle hire 🎬 Cinema 🎵 Entertainment 🎣 Fishing ◎ Mini golf 🏌 Pitch n putt 🌊 Watersports 💪 Gym ⚽ Sports field 🐴 Stables **FACILITIES:** 🛁 Bath 🚿 Shower [P] Private washing cubicles ⊙ Electric shaver 💨 Hairdryer ✲ Ice Packs ♿ Disabled facilities [$] Shop on site 🛍 Mobile shop 🍖 BBQ area 🪑 Picnic area 📶 Wi-fi 💻 Internet access ♻ Recycling ℹ Tourist info 🐕 Dog exercise area 🚗 Car hire can be arranged

PREMIER PARK

Hendre Mynach Touring Caravan & Camping Park
►►►►►86%

tel: 01341 280262 **Llanaber Rd LL42 1YR**
email: info@hendremynach.co.uk **web:** www.hendremynach.co.uk
dir: 0.75m N of Barmouth on A496. **grid ref:** SH605170

A constantly improving site where the enthusiastic owners invest year on year to enhance the customer experience. Although there is a steep decent to the arrivals' area, staff are always on hand to assist. The beautifully maintained touring areas benefit from attractive hedge screening around the large well-spaced pitches that are equipped with water and TV hook-ups. There is direct access to the seafront which leads to the town centre and its many attractions. 10 acre site. 240 touring pitches. 75 hardstandings. 23 seasonal pitches. Caravan pitches. Motorhome pitches. Tent pitches. 1 static.

Open: Mar-9 Jan (rs Winter months shop closed) **Last arrival:** 22.00hrs
Last departure: 11.30hrs

Pitches: ⊞ ⊞ Å

Facilities: ⊙ ⌲ ⚒ ☀ ㄥ ⓢ WiFi ▇ ♻ ✿ 𝟬

Services: ⊞ ⓢ 🛢 ⌀ T ➡ ⟱

Within 3 miles: ☷ ⌲ ⓢ ⓢ ∪

Notes: No open fires. Dogs must be kept on leads.

AA Pubs & Restaurants nearby: Victoria Inn, LLANBEDR, LL45 2LD, 01341 241213

BETWS GARMON **Map 14 SH55**

Places to visit
Snowdon Mountain Railway, LLANBERIS, LL55 4TY, 0844 493 8120
www.snowdonrailway.co.uk

Great for kids: Dolbadarn Castle, LLANBERIS, LL55 4UD, 01443 336000
http://cadw.gov.wales/daysout/dolbadarncastle/

Bryn Gloch Caravan & Camping Park
►►►►85%

tel: 01286 650216 **LL54 7YY**
email: eurig@bryngloch.co.uk **web:** www.campwales.co.uk
dir: On A4085, 5m SE of Caernarfon. **grid ref:** SH534574

An excellent family-run site with immaculate modern facilities, and all level pitches in beautiful surroundings. The park offers the best of two worlds, with its bustling holiday atmosphere and the peaceful natural surroundings; there are plenty of walks in the area. The 28 acres of level fields are separated by mature hedges and trees, guaranteeing sufficient space for families wishing to spread themselves out. There are some excellent fully serviced camping pitches and static holiday caravans for hire. 28 acre site. 160 touring pitches. 80 hardstandings. 80 seasonal pitches. Caravan pitches. Motorhome pitches. Tent pitches. 17 statics.

Open: all year (rs Nov-Feb shop & games room closed) **Last arrival:** 23.00hrs
Last departure: 17.00hrs

Pitches: * ⊞ £16-£31 ⊞ £16-£31 Å £16-£31

Leisure: ⚎ 🎣 ⌲

Facilities: ➡ ⌂ P ⊙ ⌲ ⚒ ☀ ㄥ ⓢ 🎅 ㅋ WiFi ▇ ♻ 𝟬

Services: ⊞ ⓢ 🛢 ⌀ T ➡ ⟱

Within 3 miles: ⌱ ≒ ⌲ ◎ ⓢ ⓢ ∪

Notes: PayPal accepted. No noise after 23.00hrs, no camp fires. Dogs must be kept on leads. Heated family bathroom, mother & baby room.

CAERNARFON
Map 14 SH46

See also Dinas Dinlle & Llandwrog

Places to visit

Welsh Highland Railway, CAERNARFON, LL55 2YD, 01766 516024
www.festrail.co.uk

Great for kids: Caernarfon Castle, CAERNARFON, LL55 2AY, 01286 677617
http://cadw.gov.wales/daysout/caernarfon-castle/

Riverside Camping
►►►► 88%

tel: 01286 678781 **Seiont Nurseries, Pont Rug LL55 2BB**
email: info@riversidecamping.co.uk
dir: 2m from Caernarfon on right of A4086 towards Llanberis, follow signs at entrance.
grid ref: SH505630

Set in the grounds of a former garden centre and enjoying a superb location along the River Seiont, this park is approached by an impressive tree-lined drive. Immaculately maintained by the owners, there is a mixture of riverside grassy pitches and fully serviced pitches for caravans and motorhomes. Hardstanding pitches have electric hook-up, water, drainage and TV connection (especially suitable for motorhomes). In addition to the smart amenities blocks, other facilities include an excellent café/restaurant, a volleyball court and boules pitch; river fishing permits are also available. The two superb chalets, each for six people, have wood-burning stoves, picnic gardens and Japanese hot tubs. This is a haven of peace close to Caernarfon, Snowdonia and some great walking opportunities. 5 acre site. 73 touring pitches. 16 hardstandings. 10 seasonal pitches. Caravan pitches. Motorhome pitches. Tent pitches.

Open: 14 Mar-Oct **Last arrival:** anytime **Last departure:** noon

Pitches: 🚐 🚍 Å

Facilities: ⊙ 🅿 ⚘ ✱ ⚷ 🔥 📶 💻 ♻ ❶

Services: 🔌 🛁 🏧 🍽 🚮 ⬇

Within 3 miles: ⚓ ✚ 🎡 🐟 ◎ 🛒 🏪 🛍 ᘛ

Notes: No fires, no loud music. Debit cards accepted (no credit cards). Dogs must be kept on leads. Family shower room, baby-changing facilities, undercover picnic area.

AA Pubs & Restaurants nearby: Seiont Manor Hotel, CAERNARFON, LL55 2AQ, 01286 673366

Llys Derwen Caravan & Camping Site
►►►► 86%

tel: 01286 673322 **Ffordd Bryngwyn, Llanrug LL55 4RD**
email: llysderwen@aol.com
dir: Exit A55 junct 11 (follow Bangor (A5) & Llanberis signs). At rdbt left signed Betws y Coed (A5) & Llanberis (A4244). At next rdbt right signed Llanberis. Right at T-junct signed Caernarfon onto A4086. Through Llanrug, left at Y Glyntwrog pub, site 500mtrs on right. **grid ref:** SH539629

On the outskirts of the village of Llanrug, three miles from Caernarfon on the way to Llanberis and Snowdon. A beautifully maintained site with enthusiastic owners who are constantly investing to improve the facilities. The amenities block is appointed to a high standard and the immaculately maintained grounds are planted with an abundance of colourful shrubs and seasonal flowers. 4 acre site. 20 touring pitches. Caravan pitches. Motorhome pitches. Tent pitches. 2 statics.

Open: Mar-Oct **Last arrival:** 22.00hrs **Last departure:** noon

Pitches: 🚐 🚍 Å

Facilities: 🐾 ⊙ 🅿 ✱ ⚷ 🔥 ♻ ❶

Services: 🔌 🛁 🏧 ⬇

Within 3 miles: ⚓ ✚ 🐟 🛒 🏪 ᘛ

Notes: 🐕 No open fires, no noise after 22.00hrs, no ball games. Dogs must be kept on leads.

AA Pubs & Restaurants nearby: Seiont Manor Hotel, CAERNARFON, LL55 2AQ, 01286 673366

Plas Gwyn Caravan & Camping Park
►►►► 81%

tel: 01286 672619 **Llanrug LL55 2AQ**
email: info@plasgwyn.co.uk
dir: A4086, 3m E of Caernarfon, site on right. Between River Seiont & Llanrug.
grid ref: SH520633

A secluded park in an ideal location for visiting the glorious nearby beaches, historic Caernarfon, the attractions of Snowdonia and for walking opportunities. The site is set within the grounds of Plas Gwyn House, a Georgian property with colonial additions; the friendly owners constantly improve the facilities. There is a 'breakfast butty' service and fresh tea and coffee is available for delivery to individual pitches. The all-electric pitches include hardstandings and five that are fully serviced. Three 'timber tents' (wooden pods) and five statics are available for hire. 3 acre site. 42 touring pitches. 8 hardstandings. 8 seasonal pitches. Caravan pitches. Motorhome pitches. Tent pitches. 18 statics.

Open: Mar-Oct **Last arrival:** 22.00hrs **Last departure:** 11.30hrs

Pitches: * 🚐 £18.50-£22 🚍 £18.50-£22 Å £11-£26 🏠 prices shown below

Facilities: 🐾 🅿 ⊙ 🅿 ✱ ⚷ 🛁 🔥 📶 ♻ ❶

Services: 🔌 🛁 🧺 🗑 Ⓣ 🏧 ⬇

Glamping: Wooden Pods 3, £31-£36 Car by unit

Within 3 miles: ⚓ ✚ 🐟 🛒 🏪 ᘛ

Notes: Minimum noise 22.00hrs-mdnt, complete quiet mdnt-08.00hrs.

AA Pubs & Restaurants nearby: Seiont Manor Hotel, CAERNARFON, LL55 2AQ, 01286 673366

Cwm Cadnant Valley
►►►80%

tel: 01286 673196 **Llanberis Rd LL55 2DF**
email: aa@cwmcadnant.co.uk **web:** www.cwmcadnant.co.uk
dir: On outskirts of Caernarfon on A4086 towards Llanberis, adjacent to fire station.
grid ref: SH487628

Set in an attractive wooded valley with a stream is this terraced site with secluded pitches, a good camping area for backpackers and clean, modern toilet facilities. It is located on the outskirts of Caernarfon in a rural location, close to the main Caernarfon-Llanberis road and just a 10-minute walk from the castle and town centre. 4.5 acre site. 60 touring pitches. 9 hardstandings. 5 seasonal pitches. Caravan pitches. Motorhome pitches. Tent pitches.

Open: 14 Mar-3 Nov **Last arrival:** 22.00hrs **Last departure:** 11.00hrs

Pitches: * 🚐 £16-£24 🚌 £16-£24 ▲ £12-£20

Facilities: 🅿️☉🅿️✳☆♿🎪 WiFi 💻♻🔌

Services: 🔌🗄🛢🖊Ⓣ🔋

Within 3 miles: ⬇🚴🎇♪🐎🏊🎱🎲⛳

Notes: No noise after 23.00hrs, no wood fires. Dogs must be kept on leads. Family room with baby-changing facilities.

AA Pubs & Restaurants nearby: Seiont Manor Hotel, CAERNARFON, LL55 2AQ, 01286 673366

CRICCIETH

Places to visit

Criccieth Castle, CRICCIETH, LL52 0DP, 01766 522227
http://cadw.gov.wales/daysout/criccieth-castle/

Portmeirion, PORTMEIRION, LL48 6FR, 01766 772306
www.portmeirion-village.com

Great for kids: Ffestiniog Railway, PORTHMADOG, LL49 9NF, 01766 516024
www.festrail.co.uk

Eisteddfa
►►►►87%

tel: 01766 522696 **Eisteddfa Lodge, Pentrefelin LL52 0PT**
email: info@eisteddfapark.co.uk
dir: From Porthmadog take A497 towards Criccieth. Approx 3.5m, through Pentrefelin, site signed 1st right after Plas Gwyn Nursing Home. **grid ref:** SH518394

A quiet, secluded park on elevated ground, sheltered by the Snowdonia Mountains and with lovely views of Cardigan Bay; Criccieth is nearby. The owners continue to steadily improve the park without diminishing its unspoilt beauty, and are keen to welcome families, who will appreciate the cubicled facilities. A superb new amenity block was introduced for the 2016 season. There's a field and play area, woodland walks, six superb slate-based hardstandings, a 'cocoon pod', two tipis and three static holiday caravans for hire, plus a three-acre coarse fishing lake adjacent to the park. Free WiFi is available across the park. 24 acre site. 100 touring pitches. 17 hardstandings. 20 seasonal pitches. Caravan pitches. Motorhome pitches. Tent pitches. 13 statics.

Open: Mar-Oct **Last arrival:** 22.30hrs **Last departure:** 11.00hrs

Pitches: * 🚐 £15.50-£19.50 🚌 £15.50-£19.50 ▲ £13.50-£19.50 🏠 prices shown below

Leisure: 🎱🎣 **Facilities:** 🅿️☉🅿️✳☆♿🎪♻🔌

Services: 🔌🗄🛢🖊🔋🔌

Glamping: Tipis 2, Min stay 2 nights Own kitchen Car by unit **Cabins** 1, £22.50-£28 Car by unit

Within 3 miles: ⬇🚴🎇♪🎇♪🏊🎱🎲⛳

Notes: No noise after 22.30hrs. Dogs must be kept on leads. Baby bath available.

AA Pubs & Restaurants nearby: Bron Eifion Country House Hotel, CRICCIETH, LL52 0SA, 01766 522385

Plas Bodegroes, PWLLHELI, LL53 5TH, 01758 612363

Llwyn-Bugeilydd Caravan & Camping Site
►►►82%

tel: 01766 522235 & 07752 784358 **LL52 0PN**
email: rroberts1948@icloud.com
dir: From Porthmadog on A497, 1m N of Criccieth on B4411. Site 1st on right. From A55 take A487 through Caernarfon. After Bryncir right onto B4411, site on left in 3.5m.
grid ref: SH498398

A quiet rural site, convenient for touring Snowdonia and coastal areas. It is set amid stunning scenery and has well-tended grass pitches enhanced by shrubs and seasonal flowers. The smartly presented amenities block was refurbished for the 2016 season. 6 acre site. 40 touring pitches. Caravan pitches. Motorhome pitches. Tent pitches.

Open: Mar-Oct **Last arrival:** anytime **Last departure:** 11.00hrs

Pitches: * 🚐 £18-£23 🚌 £18-£23 ▲ £12.15-£20

Leisure: 🎪🎱 **Facilities:** 🅿️🅿️☉✳🐾🎪 WiFi 💻♻🔌

Services: 🔌🗄🔋 **Within 3 miles:** ⬇🚴🎇♪🏊🎱🎲⛳

Notes: No skateboards, no noise between 22.30hrs-08.00hrs, caravan storage until evening of departure available if required. Dogs must be kept on leads.

AA Pubs & Restaurants nearby: Bron Eifion Country House Hotel, CRICCIETH, LL52 0SA, 01766 522385

Plas Bodegroes, PWLLHELI, LL53 5TH, 01758 612363

PITCHES: 🚐 Caravans 🚌 Motorhomes ▲ Tents 🏠 Glamping accommodation **SERVICES:** 🔌 Electric hook up 🗄 Launderette 🍷 Licensed bar 🛢 Calor Gas 🖊 Camping Gaz Ⓣ Toilet fluid 🍽 Café/Restaurant 🏪 Fast Food/Takeaway 🔋 Battery charging 🚼 Baby care ⛽ Motorvan service point **ABBREVIATIONS:** BHs – bank holidays Etr – Easter Spring BH – Spring Bank Holiday fr – from hrs – hours m – mile mdnt – midnight rdbt – roundabout rs – restricted service wk – week wknd – weekend x-roads – crossroads 🚫 No credit or debit cards 🚫 No dogs

DINAS DINLLE | Map 14 SH45

Places to visit

Caernarfon Airworld Museum, DINAS DINLLE, LL54 5TP, 01286 832154
www.airworldmuseum.com

Inigo Jones Slateworks, GROESLON, LL54 7UE, 01286 830242
www.inigojones.co.uk

Caernarfon Castle, CAERNARFON, LL55 2AY, 01286 677617
http://cadw.gov.wales/daysout/caernarfon-castle/

Great for kids: Welsh Highland Railway, CAERNARFON, LL55 2YD, 01766 516024
www.festrail.co.uk

PREMIER PARK

Dinlle Caravan Park
▶▶▶▶▶ 85%

tel: 01286 830324 **LL54 5TW**
email: enq@thornleyleisure.co.uk
dir: *From A487 at rdbt take A499 signed Pwllheli. Right at Caernarfon Airport & brown camping signs.* grid ref: *SH438568*

A very accessible, well-kept, grassy site adjacent to a sandy beach and with good views towards Snowdonia. The park, with a superb landscaped entrance, is situated on flat grassland that provides plenty of space for large groups. The man-made dunes offer campers additional protection from sea breezes. The lounge bar and family room are comfortable places in which to relax, and children will enjoy the exciting adventure playground. There are camping pods, with decking and barbecue areas, for hire. A golf club, a nature reserve and the Caernarfon Airworld Museum at the airport can all be accessed from the beach road. 20 acre site. 175 touring pitches. 20 hardstandings. Caravan pitches. Motorhome pitches. Tent pitches. 167 statics.

Open: Mar-Nov **Last arrival:** 23.00hrs **Last departure:** noon

Pitches: 🚐 🚃 ▲ 🏕

Leisure: 🏊 🎱 🎵

Facilities: ☉ 🚰 ✳ ᕦ WIFI 🛈

Services: 🔌 🗑 🍽 🛒 🛢 🧹

Glamping: Wooden Pods 7

Within 3 miles: 🎣 🛍 🏌

Notes: No skateboards. Dogs must be kept on leads.

DYFFRYN ARDUDWY

Places to visit

Cymer Abbey, CYMER ABBEY, LL40 2HE, 01443 336000
http://cadw.gov.wales/daysout/cymer-abbey/

Great for kids: Harlech Castle, HARLECH, LL46 2YH, 01766 780552
http://cadw.gov.wales/daysout/harlechcastle/

DYFFRYN ARDUDWY | Map 14 SH52

Murmur-yr-Afon Touring Park
▶▶▶ 81%

tel: 01341 247353 **LL44 2BE**
email: murmuryrafon1@btinternet.com
dir: *On A496, N of Dyffryn Ardudwy.* grid ref: *SH586236*

A pleasant family-run park alongside a wooded stream on the edge of the village, and handy for large sandy beaches. Expect good, clean facilities, and lovely views of rolling hills and mountains. 7.5 acre site. 78 touring pitches. 37 hardstandings. 30 seasonal pitches. Caravan pitches. Motorhome pitches. Tent pitches.

Open: Mar-Oct **Last arrival:** 22.00hrs **Last departure:** 11.00hrs

Pitches: 🚐 🚃 ▲

Leisure: 🏔

Facilities: 🌳 ☉ 🚰 ✳ ᕦ 🐾 🛈

Services: 🔌 🗑 🛢

Within 3 miles: 🎣 🚴 🏊 🛍 🏌

Notes: Dogs must be kept on leads.

AA Pubs & Restaurants nearby: Victoria Inn, LLANBEDR, LL45 2LD, 01341 241213

LLANDWROG | Map 14 SH45

Places to visit

Welsh Highland Railway, CAERNARFON, LL55 2YD, 01766 516024
www.festrail.co.uk

Great for kids: Caernarfon Castle, CAERNARFON, LL55 2AY, 01286 677617
http://cadw.gov.wales/daysout/caernarfon-castle/

White Tower Caravan Park
▶▶▶▶ 86%

tel: 01286 830649 & 07802 562785 **LL54 5UH**
email: whitetower@supanet.com
dir: *From Caernarfon take A487 Porthmadog road. 1st right into Pant Rd signed Llanfaglan & Saron. Site 3m on right.* grid ref: *SH453582*

There are lovely views of Snowdonia from this park located just two miles from the nearest beach at Dinas Dinlle. A well-maintained toilet block has key access, and the hardstanding pitches have water and electricity. Popular amenities include an outdoor heated swimming pool, a lounge bar with family room, and a games and TV room. 6 acre site. 52 touring pitches. 52 hardstandings. 50 seasonal pitches. Caravan pitches. Motorhome pitches. 74 statics.

Open: Mar-10 Jan (rs Mar-mid May & Sep-Nov bar closed weekdays)
Last arrival: 23.00hrs **Last departure:** noon

Pitches: * 🚐 £20-£30 🚃 £20-£30

Leisure: 🏊 🏔 🎱 🎵

Facilities: 🌳 🅿 ☉ 🚰 ᕦ WIFI 🖥 ♻ 🛈

Services: 🔌 🗑 🍽 🛢 🛒 🛢

Within 3 miles: 🎣 🚴 🏊 🛍 🏌

Notes: Dogs must be kept on leads.

AA Pubs & Restaurants nearby: Black Boy Inn, CAERNARFON, LL55 1RW, 01286 673604

LEISURE: 🏊 Indoor pool 🏊 Outdoor pool 🎢 Children's playground 🧒 Kid's club 🎾 Tennis court 🎱 Games room 🏌 Golf course 🚣 Boat hire 🚴 Cycle hire 🎬 Cinema 🎵 Entertainment 🎣 Fishing ◉ Mini golf 🏑 Pitch n putt 🏄 Watersports 💪 Gym ⚽ Sports field ♾ Stables **FACILITIES:** 🛁 Bath 🚿 Shower 🅿 Private washing cubicles ☉ Electric shaver 🚰 Hairdryer ✳ Ice Packs ᕦ Disabled facilities 🛍 Shop on site 🚚 Mobile shop 🍖 BBQ area 🪑 Picnic area WIFI Wi-fi 🖥 Internet access ♻ Recycling 🛈 Tourist info 🐾 Dog exercise area 🚗 Car hire can be arranged

PONT-RUG

See Caernarfon

PORTHMADOG

Map 14 SH53

Places to visit

Portmeirion, PORTMEIRION, LL48 6ER, 01766 772306
www.portmeirion-village.com

Great for kids: Ffestiniog Railway, PORTHMADOG, LL49 9NF, 01766 516024
www.festrail.co.uk

Greenacres Holiday Park
HOLIDAY CENTRE 87%

tel: 01766 512781 **Black Rock Sands, Morfa Bychan LL49 9YF**
email: greenacres@haven.com **web:** www.haven.com/greenacres
dir: *From Porthmadog High St follow Black Rock Sands signs between The Factory Shop & Post Office. Park 2m on left at end of Morfa Bychan.* **grid ref:** *SH539374*

A quality holiday park on level ground just a short walk from Black Rock Sands, and set against a backdrop of Snowdonia National Park. All touring pitches are on hardstandings surrounded by closely-mown grass, and near the entertainment complex. A full programme of entertainment, organised clubs, indoor and outdoor sports and leisure, pubs, shows and cabarets all add to a holiday experience here. The bowling alley and a large shop with bakery are useful amenities. The superb touring field has excellent fully serviced euro pitches, extensive, colourful planting and a smart, well-equipped amenities block. Six fully-equipped safari tents are also available for a glamping experience. 121 acre site. 39 touring pitches. 39 hardstandings. Caravan pitches. Motorhome pitches. 900 statics.

Greenacres Holiday Park

Open: mid Mar-end Oct (rs mid Mar-May & Sep-Oct some facilities may be reduced) **Last arrival:** anytime **Last departure:** 10.00hrs

Pitches: 🚐 🚍 ⛺ **Leisure:** 🏊 🎣 ⚽ 🎣 🎵

Facilities: 🛁 🚻 🚿 🔥 WiFi 🎠 🐕 **Services:** 🔌 🛒 🍽 🏧

Glamping: Safari tents 6, Changeover day Mon, Fri, Sat Min stay 3 nights Own kitchen

Within 3 miles: 🏌 🎯 🛒 🎣 U

Notes: No commercial vehicles, no bookings by persons under 21yrs unless a family booking, max 2 dogs per booking, certain dog breeds banned. Dogs must be kept on leads.

AA Pubs & Restaurants nearby: Royal Sportsman Hotel, PORTHMADOG, LL49 9HB, 01766 512015

The Hotel Portmeirion, PORTMEIRION, LL48 6ET, 01766 770000

See advert below

PITCHES: 🚐 Caravans 🚍 Motorhomes ⛺ Tents ⛺ Glamping accommodation **SERVICES:** 🔌 Electric hook up 🔲 Launderette 🍺 Licensed bar 🔋 Calor Gas 🔥 Camping Gaz 🔵 Toilet fluid 🍽 Café/Restaurant 🏧 Fast Food/Takeaway 🔋 Battery charging 👶 Baby care ⛽ Motorvan service point
ABBREVIATIONS: BHs – bank holidays Etr – Easter Spring BH – Spring Bank Holiday fr – from hrs – hours m – mile mdnt – midnight rdbt – roundabout rs – restricted service wk – week wknd – weekend x-roads – crossroads 🚫 No credit or debit cards 🚫 No dogs

PWLLHELI   Map 14 SH33

Places to visit

Lloyd George Museum, LLANYSTUMDWY, LL52 0SH, 01766 522071
www.gwynedd.gov.uk/museums

Great for kids: Criccieth Castle, CRICCIETH, LL52 0DP, 01766 522227
http://cadw.gov.wales/daysout/criccieth-castle/

Hafan y Môr Holiday Park
HOLIDAY CENTRE 89%

GOLD

tel: 01758 612112 **LL53 6HJ**
email: hafanymor@haven.com **web:** www.haven.com/hafanymor
dir: *From Caernarfon take A499 to Pwllheli. A497 to Porthmadog. Park on right, approx 3m from Pwllheli. Or from Telford, A5, A494 to Bala. Right for Porthmadog. Left at rdbt in Porthmadog signed Criccieth & Pwllheli. Park on left, 3m from Criccieth.*
grid ref: *SH431368*

Located between Pwllheli and Criccieth, and surrounded by mature trees that attract wildlife, this popular holiday centre provides a wide range of all-weather attractions. Activities include a sports hall, an ornamental boating lake, a large indoor swimming pool, a show bar and a high-ropes activity plus Segways are available. There are also great eating options – the Mash and Barrel bar and bistro, Traditional Fish and Chips, Burger King, Papa John's and a Starbucks coffeehouse. The touring area includes 75 fully serviced all-weather pitches and a top notch, air-conditioned amenities block. 500 acre site. 75 touring pitches. 75 hardstandings. Caravan pitches. Motorhome pitches. 800 statics.

Hafan y Môr Holiday Park

Open: mid Mar-end Oct (rs mid Mar-May & Sep-Oct reduced facilities)
Last arrival: 21.00hrs **Last departure:** 10.00hrs

Pitches: 🚐 🚃

Leisure: 🏊 💧 🎵 ⛳

Facilities: � 🍴 ⛃ 🛍 WiFi

Services: 🔌 💷 🚽 🔒 🍴 🏪

Within 3 miles: 🚣 ⛳ 🎣 ◎ 🛍 ⛵ ⛃ U

Notes: No commercial vehicles, no bookings by persons under 21yrs unless a family booking, max 2 dogs per booking, certain dog breeds banned. Dogs must be kept on leads.
See advert below

LEISURE: 🏊 Indoor pool 🏊 Outdoor pool 🎠 Children's playground 👶 Kid's club 🎾 Tennis court 🎱 Games room ⛳ Golf course 🚣 Boat hire 🚲 Cycle hire 🎬 Cinema 🎵 Entertainment 🎣 Fishing ⛳ Mini golf ⛳ Pitch n putt 🏄 Watersports 🏋 Gym ⚽ Sports field U Stables **FACILITIES:** 🛁 Bath 🚿 Shower 🅿 Private washing cubicles ⊙ Electric shaver 💇 Hairdryer ❄ Ice Packs ♿ Disabled facilities 🛍 Shop on site 🚐 Mobile shop 🍖 BBQ area 🪑 Picnic area WiFi Wi-fi 💻 Internet access ♻ Recycling ℹ Tourist info 🐕 Dog exercise area 🚗 Car hire can be arranged

Abererch Sands Holiday Centre

►►► 73%

tel: 01758 612327 **LL53 6PJ**
email: enquiries@abererch-sands.co.uk **web:** www.abererch-sands.co.uk
dir: *On A497 (Porthmadog to Pwllheli road), 1m from Pwllheli.* **grid ref:** *SH403359*

Glorious views of Snowdonia and Cardigan Bay can be enjoyed from this very secure, family-run site adjacent to a railway station and a four-mile stretch of sandy beach. A large heated indoor swimming pool, snooker room, pool room, fitness centre and children's play area make this an ideal holiday venue. 85 acre site. 70 touring pitches. 70 hardstandings. Caravan pitches. Motorhome pitches. Tent pitches. 90 statics.

Open: Mar-Oct **Last arrival:** 21.00hrs **Last departure:** 21.00hrs

Pitches: 🚐 🚍 Å

Leisure: 🏊 🎱

Facilities: ⊙ ✳ ♿ 🛁 ♻ WIFI ♻

Services: 🔌 🛒 🔒 🛢 ⌀ T 🛗 ⛟

Within 3 miles: ↓ 🎣 ⌴ 🅿 🚴 🛒 🛍 ∪

Notes: Dogs must be kept on leads.

AA Pubs & Restaurants nearby: Plas Bodegroes, PWLLHELI, LL53 5TH, 01758 612363

TAL-Y-BONT   Map 14 SH52

PREMIER PARK

Islawrffordd Caravan Park

►►►►► 91%

tel: 01341 247269 **LL43 2AQ**
email: info@islawrffordd.co.uk **web:** www.islawrffordd.co.uk
dir: *From A496 into Ffordd Glan-Mor towards sea, follow brown campsite sign. Over rail line, site on left.* **grid ref:** *SH584215*

Situated on the coast between Barmouth and Harlech and within the Snowdonia National Park. The site has clear views of Cardigan Bay, the Lleyn Peninsula and the Snowdonia and Cader Idris mountain ranges. This is an excellent, family-run and family-friendly park that has seen considerable investment over recent years. Fully matured, the touring area boasts fully-serviced pitches, a superb toilet block with underfloor heating and top-quality fittings; there is private access to miles of sandy beach. A superb restaurant and bar, 'Nineteen57', offers both formal and relaxed areas for enjoying locally-sourced food. 25 acre site. 105 touring pitches. 75 hardstandings. 50 seasonal pitches. Caravan pitches. Motorhome pitches. Tent pitches. 201 statics.

Open: 14 Feb-3 Jan **Last arrival:** 20.00hrs **Last departure:** noon

Pitches: 🚐 🚍 Å **Leisure:** 🏊 /\\ **Facilities:** 🐾 🅿 ⊙ 🎣 ✳ ♿ WIFI ♻ 🛈

Services: 🔌 🛒 🍴 🔒 🛢 ⌀ T 🍽 🛗 🛒 ⛟

Within 3 miles: 🅿 🚴 🛍

Notes: Strictly families & couples only. Dogs must be kept on leads.

AA Pubs & Restaurants nearby: Victoria Inn, LLANBEDR, LL45 2LD, 01341 241213

See advert on page 428

ISLAWRFFORDD CARAVAN PARK

A family owned park Est. 1957

TALYBONT, NR BARMOUTH, GWYNEDD, LL43 2AQ, NORTH WALES
01341 247269
Email: info@islawrffordd.co.uk   www.islawrffordd.co.uk

"AA CAMPSITE OF THE YEAR 2012"

Family owned and run since being established in 1957, Islawrffordd Caravan Park offers the very best in quality which you are immediately aware of when entering the award winning reception building.

Situated at the southern end of the magnificent Snowdonia National Park coastline in the village of Talybont, Islawrffordd offers 201 holiday home bases, 75 touring caravan/motorhome plots and 30 camping pitches all benefiting from the very best facilities, including a heated indoor swimming pool/sauna/jacuzzi. Islawrffordd boasts to owning one of the best Bar/Restaurants in the area. Benefiting from modern interior design, Nineteen57 offers bar food and fine dining of the highest quality.

Nigel Mansell, O.B.E., C.B.E. & 1992 Formula 1 World Champion & Indy Car World Champion 1993 has a Holiday Home association with Islawrffordd that stretches back from the present day to his childhood and his opinion of the Snowdonia Coastline area and our park is still the same "It's absolutely fantastic".

Choice of a Champion

LEISURE: 🏊 Indoor pool   🏊 Outdoor pool   🎢 Children's playground   🧒 Kid's club   🎾 Tennis court   🎱 Games room   ⛳ Golf course   🚤 Boat hire   🚲 Cycle hire   🎬 Cinema   🎵 Entertainment   🎣 Fishing   ⛳ Mini golf   ⛳ Pitch n putt   🏄 Watersports   🏋 Gym   🏟 Sports field   ♻ Stables   **FACILITIES:** 🛁 Bath   🚿 Shower   🅿 Private washing cubicles   ⚡ Electric shaver   💇 Hairdryer   ❄ Ice Packs   ♿ Disabled facilities   🅂 Shop on site   🛒 Mobile shop   🍖 BBQ area   🏕 Picnic area   📶 Wi-fi   💻 Internet access   ♻ Recycling   ℹ Tourist info   🐕 Dog exercise area   🚗 Car hire can be arranged

TYWYN
Map 14 SH50

Places to visit

Talyllyn Railway, TYWYN, LL36 9EY, 01654 710472 www.talyllyn.co.uk

Castell-y-Bere, LLANFIHANGEL-Y-PENNANT, 01443 336000
http://cadw.gov.wales/daysout/castell-y-bere/

Great for kids: King Arthur's Labyrinth, CORRIS, SY20 9RF, 01654 761584
www.kingarthurslabyrinth.co.uk

Ynysymaengwyn Caravan Park
▶▶▶▶ 81%

tel: 01654 710684 **LL36 9RY**
email: rita@ynysy.co.uk
dir: On A493, 1m N of Tywyn, towards Dolgellau. **grid ref:** SH602021

A lovely park set in the wooded grounds of a former manor house, with designated nature trails through 13 acres of wildlife-rich woodland, scenic river walks, fishing and a sandy beach nearby. The attractive stone amenity block is clean and well kept, and this smart municipal park is ideal for families. Free WiFi is available throughout park. 4 acre site. 80 touring pitches. Caravan pitches. Motorhome pitches. Tent pitches. 115 statics.

Open: Etr or Apr-Oct **Last arrival:** 23.00hrs **Last departure:** noon

Pitches: 🚐 🚍 🛆

Facilities: ⊙ 🅿 ⁂ ⅙ 🍴 🎢 🚾

Services: 🔌 🔲 🛢 🚼 🔋

Within 3 miles: 🚣 🏇 🖉 ◎ ⅛ 🛈 🛒 ∪

Notes: 🐾 Dogs must be kept on leads.

MONMOUTHSHIRE

ABERGAVENNY

Places to visit

Big Pit National Coal Museum, BLAENAVON, NP4 9XP, 029 20573650
www.museumwales.ac.uk

Hen Gwrt, LLANTILIO CROSSENNY, 01443 336000
http://cadw.gov.wales/daysout/hengwrtmoatedsite/

Great for kids: Raglan Castle, RAGLAN, NP15 2BT, 01291 690228
http://cadw.gov.wales/daysout/raglancastle/

ABERGAVENNY
Map 9 SO21

Wernddu Caravan Park
▶▶▶▶ 84%

tel: 01873 856223 **Old Ross Rd NP7 8NG**
email: info@wernddu-golf-club.co.uk
dir: From A465, N of Abergavenny, take B4521 signed Skenfrith. Site on right in 0.25m.
grid ref: SO321153

Located north of the town centre, this former fruit farm, adjacent to a golf club and driving range, is managed by three generations of the same family, and has been transformed into an ideal base for those visiting the many nearby attractions. The well-spaced touring pitches have water, electricity and waste water disposal, and the smart modern amenities block provides very good privacy options. Site guests are welcome to use the golf club bar which also serves meals during the busy months; they are also eligible for half-price green fees. There is no shop on site but a daily newspaper service is provided, and a mini-market is less than a mile away. 6 acre site. 70 touring pitches. 20 hardstandings. 30 seasonal pitches. Caravan pitches. Motorhome pitches. Tent pitches.

Open: Mar-Oct **Last arrival:** 21.00hrs **Last departure:** noon

Pitches: * 🚐 fr £20 🚍 fr £20 🛆 fr £15

Leisure: ⊰ ⌗ 🖉

Facilities: 🔦 🅿 ⁂ ⅙ 🎢 🚾 🛈

Services: 🔌 🔲 🚼 🍴 🏧 ⅏ ↯

Within 3 miles: 🚣 🏇 🖉 ◎ 🛈 🛒 ∪

Notes: Adults only. Dogs must be kept on leads. Driving range, bar with sports TV.

AA Pubs & Restaurants nearby: Walnut Tree Inn, ABERGAVENNY, NP7 8AW, 01873 852797

Angel Hotel, ABERGAVENNY, NP7 5EN, 01873 857121

Pyscodlyn Farm Caravan & Camping Site
▶▶▶▶ 81%

tel: 01873 853271 & 07816 447942 **Llanwenarth Citra NP7 7ER**
email: info@pyscodlyncaravanpark.com
dir: From Abergavenny take A40 (Brecon road), site 1.5m from entrance of Nevill Hall Hospital, on left 50yds past phone box. **grid ref:** SO266155

With its outstanding views of the mountains, this quiet park in the Brecon Beacons National Park makes a pleasant holiday venue for country lovers. The Sugarloaf Mountain and the River Usk are within easy walking distance and, despite being a working farm, dogs are welcome but must be under strict control of course. The separate ladies' and gents' amenities blocks are appointed to a high standard. Please note that credit and debit cards are not accepted at this site. 4.5 acre site. 60 touring pitches. Caravan pitches. Motorhome pitches. Tent pitches. 6 statics.

Open: Apr-Oct

Pitches: 🚐 🚍 🛆

Leisure: 🖉

Facilities: 🔦 🅿 ⊙ ⁂ ⅙ 🎢 ♻ 🛈 🛞

Services: 🔌 🔲 🛢 ⅏ ↯

Within 3 miles: 🚣 🏇 🖉 ◎ 🛈 ∪

Notes: 🐾 PayPal accepted. No noise after 23.00 hrs. Dogs must be kept on leads.

AA Pubs & Restaurants nearby: Angel Hotel, ABERGAVENNY, NP7 5EN, 01873 857121

Walnut Tree Inn, ABERGAVENNY, NP7 8AW, 01873 852797

PITCHES: 🚐 Caravans 🚍 Motorhomes 🛆 Tents 🏕 Glamping accommodation **SERVICES:** 🔌 Electric hook up 🔲 Launderette 🍴 Licensed bar 🛢 Calor Gas ⊘ Camping Gaz 🚽 Toilet fluid 🍴 Café/Restaurant 🏧 Fast Food/Takeaway 🔋 Battery charging 🚼 Baby care ↯ Motorvan service point **ABBREVIATIONS:** BHs – bank holidays Etr – Easter Spring BH – Spring Bank Holiday fr – from hrs – hours m – mile mdnt – midnight rdbt – roundabout rs – restricted service wk – week wknd – weekend x-roads – crossroads 🚫 No credit or debit cards 🚫 No dogs

DINGESTOW
Map 9 SO41

Places to visit

Raglan Castle, RAGLAN, NP15 2BT, 01291 690228
http://cadw.gov.wales/daysout/raglancastle/

Tintern Abbey, TINTERN PARVA, NP16 6SE, 01291 689251
http://cadw.gov.wales/daysout/tinternabbey/

Great for kids: The Nelson Museum & Local History Centre, MONMOUTH, NP25 3XA, 01600 710630

Bridge Caravan Park & Camping Site
►►► 85%

tel: 01600 740241 **Bridge Farm NP25 4DY**
email: info@bridgecaravanpark.co.uk
dir: M4 junct 24, A449 towards Monmouth. Left onto A40 towards Abergavenny. Turn right (across dual carriageway) signed Dinglestow (& brown caravan sign). **grid ref:** SO459104

The River Trothy runs along the edge of this quiet village park, which has been owned by the same family for many years. Touring pitches are both grass and hardstanding, and have a woodland backdrop. The quality facilities are enhanced by good laundry equipment. River fishing is available on site, and there is a dog walking area. The village shop is within 100 yards and a play field within 200 yards. 4 acre site. 94 touring pitches. 15 hardstandings. 50 seasonal pitches. Caravan pitches. Motorhome pitches. Tent pitches. 3 statics.

Open: Etr-Oct **Last arrival:** 22.00hrs **Last departure:** 16.00hrs
Pitches: * ⊞ £15-£18 ⊞ £15-£18 Å £15-£18
Leisure: ✏ **Facilities:** ⋔℗☉↗✳⅋👶💲⚥♻❂
Services: 🖲🗑🔒🧹Ⓣ📶⬇
Within 3 miles: ⅃⛳🎏℘💲⛲∪
Notes: 🐕 Dogs must be kept on leads.

LLANVAIR DISCOED
Map 9 ST49

Penhein Glamping
►►►►► 88%

tel: 01633 400581 **Penhein NP16 6RB**
email: enquiries@penhein.co.uk
dir: M48 junct 2, A446 towards Chepstow. 1st exit at rdbt onto A48 signed Caerwent. Approx 8m, through Caerwent, right signed Llanvair Discoed. 1st right at village sign, immediately left into private drive. Site 1.5m. **grid ref:** ST449932

Travel along a narrow lane and through two grazing fields to reach a small wood where there are large yurts (alachighs) and an Iranian communal yurt. The sumptuous yurt interiors have superb beds (a double, two truckle beds and a sofa bed for children), quality dining furniture, lanterns, a cold water sink, a large cool box and a wood-burning stove (wood provided), plus an en suite modern, low-level toilet. Outside each yurt there is a fire pit and carved tree-trunk seating. There are level bark pathways between the units, and a lean-to with kettle, microwave and freezer as there is no electricity in the yurts. The separate shower block has a drying room and unisex rooms with underfloor heating, monsoon showers and roll-top bath. The communal yurt has a wood-burning stove, bespoke oak tables, benches and electricity to power 13 amp sockets and lighting. On arrival visitors are provided with a welcome pack, and

there is a wild flower and hay meadow for archery, bike riding and orienteering. 11 acre site.

Open: Mar-Nov Xmas & New Year bookings possible.
Last arrival: 19.00hrs **Last departure:** 11.00hrs
Leisure: ❂🎏 **Facilities:** ⋔ℕ℗✳🚮♻❂
Services: 🛒
Glamping: Alachighs 6, £70-£191 Changeover day Mon, Wed, Fri Min stay 2 nights En suite Own kitchen
Within 3 miles: ⅃💲⛲
Notes: No pets.

USK
Map 9 SO30

Places to visit

Caerleon Roman Fortress and Baths, CAERLEON, NP18 1AE, 01663 422518
http://cadw.gov.wales/daysout/Caerleon-roman-fortress-baths/

Big Pit National Coal Museum, BLAENAVON, NP4 9XP, 029 20573650
www.museumwales.ac.uk

Great for kids: Greenmeadow Community Farm, CWMBRAN, NP44 5AJ, 01633 647662 www.greenmeadowcommunityfarm.org.uk

PREMIER PARK

Pont Kemys Caravan & Camping Park
►►►►► 86%

tel: 01873 880688 & 07976 960832 **Chainbridge NP7 9DS**
email: info@pontkemys.com **web:** www.pontkemys.com
dir: From Usk take B4598 towards Abergavenny. Approx 4m, over river bridge, bear right, 300yds to site. For other routes contact site for detailed directions.
grid ref: SO348058

A peaceful park next to the River Usk, offering an excellent standard of toilet facilities with family rooms. A section of the park has fully serviced pitches. The park is in a rural area with mature trees and country views, and attracts quiet visitors who enjoy the many attractions of this area. The local golf club is open during the day and serves breakfast and lunches. 8 acre site. 65 touring pitches. 29 hardstandings. 25 seasonal pitches. Caravan pitches. Motorhome pitches. Tent pitches.

Open: Mar-Oct **Last arrival:** 21.00hrs **Last departure:** noon

---

LEISURE: 🏊 Indoor pool 🏊 Outdoor pool 🛝 Children's playground 🧸 Kid's club 🎾 Tennis court 🎱 Games room ⛳ Golf course 🚣 Boat hire 🚲 Cycle hire 🎬 Cinema 🎵 Entertainment 🎣 Fishing ⛳ Mini golf ⛳ Pitch n putt 🏄 Watersports 🏋 Gym 🏟 Sports field ∪ Stables **FACILITIES:** 🛁 Bath 🚿 Shower ℗ Private washing cubicles ⊙ Electric shaver 🖫 Hairdryer ✳ Ice Packs ♿ Disabled facilities 💲 Shop on site 🚐 Mobile shop 🔥 BBQ area 🪑 Picnic area 📶 Wi-fi 💻 Internet access ♻ Recycling ❂ Tourist info 🐕 Dog exercise area 🚗 Car hire can be arranged

Pitches: * ⊡ £20-£24 ⊡ £20-£24 Å £20-£24

Leisure: ⊙ Facilities: ⫟⊙℘⁎⅋⊛Å🚽 🎏 ♻ 🛈

Services: 🔌🗑 🛢⌀T🔋🚼⌄

Within 3 miles: ⅛℘ⓢ

Notes: No music. Dogs must be kept on leads. Mother & baby room, kitchen facilities for groups.

AA Pubs & Restaurants nearby: The Nags Head Inn, USK, NP15 1BH, 01291 672820

The Raglan Arms, USK, NP15 1DL, 01291 690800

PEMBROKESHIRE

BROAD HAVEN — Map 8 SM81

Places to visit

Llawhaden Castle, LLAWHADEN, 01443 336000
http://cadw.gov.wales/daysout/llawhadencastle/

Great for kids: Scolton Manor Museum & Country Park, SCOLTON, SA62 5QL, 01437 731328 (Museum) www.pembrokeshirevirtualmuseum.co.uk

Creampots Touring Caravan & Camping Park
▶▶▶ 87%

tel: 01437 781776 **Broadway SA62 3TU**
email: creampots@btconnect.com
dir: *From Haverfordwest take B4341 to Broadway. Turn left, follow brown tourist signs to site.* grid ref: SM882131

Set just outside the Pembrokeshire National Park, this quiet site is just one and a half miles from a safe sandy beach at Broad Haven, and the coastal footpath. The park is well laid out and carefully maintained, and the toilet block offers a good standard of facilities. The owners welcome families. 8 acre site. 72 touring pitches. 45 hardstandings. Caravan pitches. Motorhome pitches. Tent pitches. 1 static.

Open: Mar-Nov Last arrival: 21.00hrs Last departure: 11.00hrs

Pitches: ⊡ ⊡ Å

Facilities: ⫟⊙℘⁎⅋⊛Å🎏 WiFi ♻ 🛈

Services: 🔌🗑 🛢⌀🚼

Within 3 miles: ⅛🗓℘≒ⓢ🗑⌣

Notes: Dogs must be kept on leads.

South Cockett Caravan & Camping Park
▶▶▶ 78%

tel: 01437 781296 & 781760 & 07774 782572 **South Cockett SA62 3TU**
email: esmejames@hotmail.co.uk
dir: *From Haverfordwest take B4341 to Broad Haven, at Broadway turn left, site 300yds.* grid ref: SM878136

A warm welcome is assured at this small site on a working farm. The touring areas are divided into neat paddocks by high, well-trimmed hedges, and there are good toilet facilities. The lovely beach at Broad Haven is only about two miles away. 6 acre site. 73 touring pitches. 25 seasonal pitches. Caravan pitches. Motorhome pitches. Tent pitches.

Open: Etr-Oct Last arrival: 22.30hrs

Pitches: ⊡ ⊡ Å

Leisure: ⊙ Facilities: ⫟⊙⁎⅋🎏 WiFi 🖥 ♻ 🛈

Services: 🔌🗑 🛢⌀🚼

Within 3 miles: ⅛℘≒ⓢ🗑⌣

Notes: 🐾 Dogs must be kept on leads.

FISHGUARD — Map 8 SM93

Places to visit

Pentre Ifan Burial Chamber, NEWPORT, 01443 336000
http://cadw.gov.wales/daysout/pentreifanburialchamber/

Great for kids: OceanLab, FISHGUARD, SA64 0DE, 01348 874737
www.ocean-lab.co.uk

Fishguard Bay Resort
▶▶▶ 92%

tel: 01348 811415 **Garn Gelli SA65 9ET**
email: enquiries@fishguardbay.com web: www.fishguardbay.com
dir: *Accessed from A487. Turn at park sign onto single track road. (NB if approaching Fishguard from Cardigan on A487 ignore Sat Nav to turn right).* grid ref: SM984383

Set high up on cliffs with outstanding views of Fishguard Bay, this site has the Pembrokeshire Coastal Path running right through its centre, so affording many opportunities for wonderful walks. The park is extremely well kept, with a good toilet block, a common room with TV, a lounge with library, laundry and a well-stocked shop. In addition to two camping pods which have superb sea views, the 'pamper pod' is a great place for a relaxing spa treatment. 7 acre site. 50 touring pitches. 6 hardstandings. Caravan pitches. Motorhome pitches. Tent pitches. 50 statics.

Open: Mar-9 Jan Last arrival: anytime Last departure: noon

Pitches: * ⊡ £15-£25 ⊡ £15-£25 Å £15-£25 ♨ prices shown below

Leisure: ⚠ 🔍

Facilities: ⫟🅿⊙℘⁎⊛Å🎏 WiFi 🖥 ♻ 🛈

Services: 🔌🗑 🛢⌀T🚼🍴

Glamping: Wooden Pods 2, £45-£65 Min stay 1 night Car by unit

Within 3 miles: ⅛🗓℘≒ⓢ🗑⌣

Notes: No commercial vehicles. Dogs must be kept on leads. Spa treatments. Freshly baked bread & pastries available.

AA Pubs & Restaurants nearby: The Sloop Inn, PORTHGAIN, SA62 5BN, 01348 831449

The Shed, PORTHGAIN, SA62 5BN, 01348 831518

Salutation Inn, NEWPORT, SA41 3UY, 01239 820564

PITCHES: ⊡ Caravans ⊡ Motorhomes Å Tents ♨ Glamping accommodation **SERVICES:** 🔌 Electric hook up 🗑 Launderette 🍺 Licensed bar 🛢 Calor Gas ⌀ Camping Gaz T Toilet fluid 🍴 Café/Restaurant 🍟 Fast Food/Takeaway 🔋 Battery charging 🚼 Baby care ⌄ Motorvan service point **ABBREVIATIONS:** BHs – bank holidays Etr – Easter Spring BH – Spring Bank Holiday fr – from hrs – hours m – mile mdnt – midnight rdbt – roundabout rs – restricted service wk – week wknd – weekend x-roads – crossroads 🚫 No credit or debit cards 🚫 No dogs

FISHGUARD *continued*

Gwaun Vale Touring Park
►►►80%

tel: 07530 381168 **Llanychaer SA65 9TA**
email: gwaunvale@hotmail.com
dir: *B4313 from Fishguard. Site 1.5m on right.* **grid ref:** *SM977356*

Located in the beautiful Gwaun Valley, this carefully landscaped park, with colourful, seasonal flowers, is set on the hillside with generously sized, tiered pitches on two levels that provide superb views of the surrounding countryside. 1.6 acre site. 29 touring pitches. 6 hardstandings. Caravan pitches. Motorhome pitches. Tent pitches. 1 static.

Open: Apr-Oct **Last arrival:** anytime **Last departure:** 11.00hrs

Pitches: * 🚐 £18-£21 🚐 £18-£21 ▲ £16-£23

Leisure: 🅰

Facilities: 🦮 🅿 ⊙ 🌡 ✳ 🛗 ♻ ❶

Services: 🔌 🗄

Within 3 miles: ⅌ 🍴 🗄 🐾 🅂 ⓤ

Notes: 🚫 No skateboards. Dogs must be kept on leads. Guidebooks available.

AA Pubs & Restaurants nearby: The Sloop Inn, PORTHGAIN, SA62 5BN, 01348 831449

The Shed, PORTHGAIN, SA62 5BN, 01348 831518

Salutation Inn, NEWPORT, SA41 3UY, 01239 820564

HASGUARD CROSS Map 8 SM80

Hasguard Cross Caravan Park
►►►85%

tel: 01437 781443 **SA62 3SL**
email: hasguard@aol.com
dir: *From Haverfordwest take B4327 towards Dale. In 7m right at x-roads. Site 1st right.* **grid ref:** *SM850108*

A very clean, efficient and well-run site in the Pembrokeshire National Park, just one and a half miles from the sea and beach at Little Haven, and with views of the surrounding hills. The toilet and shower facilities are immaculately clean, and there is a licensed bar (evenings only) serving a good choice of food. 4.5 acre site. 12 touring pitches. 3 hardstandings. Caravan pitches. Motorhome pitches. Tent pitches. 42 statics.

Open: all year (Aug - tent field available for 28 days) **Last arrival:** 21.00hrs
Last departure: 10.00hrs

Pitches: * 🚐 fr £15 🚐 fr £15 ▲ fr £15

Leisure: ⊙

Facilities: ⊙ 🅿 ✳ 🛗 🚿 🛗 ♻ ❶

Services: 🔌 🗄 🍴 📶 ⓘ 🛗 ⊔

Within 3 miles: ↓ ⅌ 🚴 🐾 🅂 ⓤ

Notes: PayPal accepted. No noise after 22.30hrs, no fires or open BBQs. Dogs must be kept on leads.

AA Pubs & Restaurants nearby: The Swan Inn, LITTLE HAVEN, SA62 3UL, 01437 781880

HAVERFORDWEST Map 8 SM91

Places to visit
Llawhaden Castle, LLAWHADEN, 01443 336000
http://cadw.gov.wales/daysout/llawhadencastle/

Great for kids: Oakwood Theme Park, NARBERTH, SA67 8DE, 01834 815170
www.oakwoodthemepark.co.uk

Nolton Cross Caravan Park
►►83%

tel: 01437 710701 & 07814 779020 **Nolton SA62 3NP**
email: info@noltoncross-holidays.co.uk
dir: *1m from A487 (Haverfordwest to St Davids road) at Simpson Cross, towards Nolton & Broadhaven.* **grid ref:** *SM879177*

High grassy banks surround the touring area of this park, adjacent to the owners' working farm. It is located on open ground above the sea and St Bride's Bay (within one and a half miles), and there is a coarse fishing lake close by — equipment for hire and reduced permit rates for campers are available. The site has a shepherd's hut for hire. WiFi is available. 4 acre site. 15 touring pitches. Caravan pitches. Motorhome pitches. Tent pitches. 30 statics.

Open: Mar-Dec **Last arrival:** 22.00hrs **Last departure:** noon

Pitches: * 🚐 £10-£17.50 🚐 £10-£17.50 ▲ £10-£17.50 🛖 prices shown below

Leisure: 🅰 ✐

Facilities: 🦮 ⊙ ✳ 🗄 🚿 📶 ♻ ❶

Services: 🔌 🗄 🛢 🅣 🛗 ⊔

Glamping: **Shepherd's Huts** 1, £40-£60 Changeover day Any day Min stay 2 nights Own kitchen

Within 3 miles: ✐ 🐾 🅂 ⓤ

Notes: No youth groups. Dogs must be kept on leads.

AA Pubs & Restaurants nearby: St Brides Inn, LITTLE HAVEN, SA62 3UN, 01437 781266

LITTLE HAVEN

See Hasguard Cross

ST DAVIDS

Places to visit
St Davids Bishop's Palace, ST DAVIDS, SA62 6PE, 01437 720517
http://cadw.gov.wales/daysout/stdavidsbishopspalace/

St Davids Cathedral, ST DAVID'S, SA62 6PE, 01437 720202
www.stdavidscathedral.org.uk

LEISURE: 🏊 Indoor pool 🏊 Outdoor pool 🅰 Children's playground 🖐 Kid's club 🎾 Tennis court 🎱 Games room ⛳ Golf course ⛵ Boat hire 🚲 Cycle hire
🎬 Cinema 🎵 Entertainment ✐ Fishing ⊙ Mini golf 🏌 Pitch n putt 🏄 Watersports 💪 Gym ⊙ Sports field ⓤ Stables **FACILITIES:** 🛁 Bath 🦮 Shower
🅿 Private washing cubicles ⊙ Electric shaver 🅿 Hairdryer ✳ Ice Packs ♿ Disabled facilities 🗄 Shop on site 🚚 Mobile shop 🛗 BBQ area 🚿 Picnic area
📶 Wi-fi 🖥 Internet access ♻ Recycling ❶ Tourist info 🐾 Dog exercise area 🚗 Car hire can be arranged

ST DAVIDS

Map 8 SM72

PREMIER PARK

Caerfai Bay Caravan & Tent Park
▶▶▶▶▶ 90%

tel: 01437 720274 **Caerfai Bay SA62 6QT**
email: info@caerfaibay.co.uk web: www.caerfaibay.co.uk
dir: *From E on A487 towards St Davids left into Caerfai Rd (Ffordd Caerfai) signed Caerfai & parking. Right at end of road.* grid ref: *SM759244*

Magnificent coastal scenery and an outlook over St Bride's Bay can be enjoyed from this delightful site, located just 300 yards from a bathing beach. The park offers good roadways, modern water points, solar-heated wet suit shower rooms and excellent toilet facilities, which include four family rooms. There is a very good farm shop (open May to September) just across the road. 10 acre site. 106 touring pitches. 26 hardstandings. Caravan pitches. Motorhome pitches. Tent pitches. 30 statics.

Open: Apr-mid Nov **Last arrival:** 21.00hrs **Last departure:** 11.00hrs

Pitches: 🚐 🚍 ▲

Facilities: 🌂 🅿 ⊙ 🌡 ✳ ⅄ 🚻 WiFi ⬛ ✿ ❶

Services: 🔌 🔟 🔋 🖊 🚽 🍼 ♻ ⚱

Within 3 miles: ⌁ ≑ ₰ ⛱ 🛒 🔟

Notes: No dogs in tent field mid Jul-Aug, no skateboards or rollerblades. Dogs must be kept on leads.

AA Pubs & Restaurants nearby: Cwtch, ST DAVIDS, SA62 6SD, 01437 720491
The Sloop Inn, PORTHGAIN, SA62 5BN, 01348 831449
The Shed, PORTHGAIN, SA62 5BN, 01348 831518

Tretio Caravan & Camping Park
▶▶▶ 82%

tel: 01437 781600 & 07814 588289 **SA62 6DE**
email: info@tretio.com
dir: *From St Davids take A487 towards Fishguard, left at Rugby Football Club, straight on for 3m. Site signed, right to site.* grid ref: *SM787292*

An attractive site in a very rural spot with distant country views, and close to beautiful beaches; the tiny cathedral city of St Davids is only three miles away. A mobile shop calls daily at peak periods, and orienteering advice and maps are available. 6.5 acre site. 40 touring pitches. 1 hardstanding. 8 seasonal pitches. Caravan pitches. Motorhome pitches. Tent pitches. 30 statics.

Open: Mar-Oct **Last arrival:** 20.00hrs **Last departure:** 10.00hrs

Pitches: * 🚐 £12-£30 🚍 £12-£30 ▲ £12-£30

Leisure: ⋀ ✿ ❧ ♨

Facilities: 🌂 🅿 ⊙ 🌡 ✳ ⅄ 🚻 ♻ ❶

Services: 🔌 🔟 🖊 🔟 ⚱

Within 3 miles: ⌁ ≑ ₰ ◎ 🛒 🔟

Notes: Dogs must be kept on leads. Climbing wall, play area.

AA Pubs & Restaurants nearby: Cwtch, ST DAVIDS, SA62 6SD, 01437 720491
The Sloop Inn, PORTHGAIN, SA62 5BN, 01348 831449
The Shed, PORTHGAIN, SA62 5BN, 01348 831518

Hendre Eynon Camping & Caravan Site
▶▶▶ 81%

tel: 01437 720474 **SA62 6DB**
email: hendreeynoninfo@gmail.com web: www.hendreeynon.co.uk
dir: *Take A487 from St Davids towards Fishguard. Left at rugby club signed Llanrhian. Site 2m on right (NB do no take turn to Whitesands).* grid ref: *SM771284*

A peaceful, level site on a working farm, with a modern toilet block including family rooms. Within easy reach of many lovely sandy beaches, and just two miles from the cathedral city of St Davids. The National Cycle Network's Celtic Trail (Route 4) passes the site. 7 acre site. 50 touring pitches. 20 seasonal pitches. Caravan pitches. Motorhome pitches. Tent pitches.

Open: Apr-Sep **Last arrival:** 21.00hrs **Last departure:** noon

Pitches: * 🚐 £10-£21 🚍 £10-£21 ▲ £10-£21

Facilities: 🌂 🅿 ⊙ ✳ 🚻 ❶

Services: 🔌 🔟 🔋 🖊 ⚱

Within 3 miles: ⌁ ≑ ₰ 🛒 🔟

Notes: 🐕 Max 2 dogs per pitch. Dogs must be kept on leads.

AA Pubs & Restaurants nearby: Cwtch, ST DAVIDS, SA62 6SD, 01437 720491
The Sloop Inn, PORTHGAIN, SA62 5BN, 01348 831449
The Shed, PORTHGAIN, SA62 5BN, 01348 831518

PITCHES: 🚐 Caravans 🚍 Motorhomes ▲ Tents 🏠 Glamping accommodation **SERVICES:** 🔌 Electric hook up 🔟 Launderette 🍺 Licensed bar
🔋 Calor Gas ⊘ Camping Gaz 🔟 Toilet fluid 🍴 Café/Restaurant 🍟 Fast Food/Takeaway ⚱ Battery charging 🍼 Baby care ⚑ Motorvan service point
ABBREVIATIONS: BHs – bank holidays Etr – Easter Spring BH – Spring Bank Holiday fr – from hrs – hours m – mile mdnt – midnight
rdbt – roundabout rs – restricted service wk – week wknd – weekend x-roads – crossroads Ⓢ No credit or debit cards Ⓧ No dogs

TENBY
Map 8 SN10

Places to visit

Tudor Merchant's House, TENBY, SA70 7BX, 01834 842279
www.nationaltrust.org.uk/tudormerchantshouse

Tenby Museum & Art Gallery, TENBY, SA70 7BP, 01834 842809
www.tenbymuseum.org.uk

Great for kids: Colby Woodland Garden, AMROTH, SA67 8PP, 01834 811885
www.nationaltrust.org.uk/main

Kiln Park Holiday Centre
HOLIDAY CENTRE 86%

GOLD

tel: 01834 844121 **Marsh Rd SA70 8RB**
email: kilnpark@haven.com **web:** www.haven.com/kilnpark
dir: Follow A477, A478 to Tenby for 6m. Then follow signs to Penally, site 0.5m on left.
grid ref: SN119002

A large holiday complex complete with leisure and sports facilities and lots of entertainment for all the family. There are bars and cafés, including the stylish

Harbwr Lights Bistro, and plenty of security. This touring, camping and static site is on the outskirts of town, and it's only a short walk through dunes to the sandy beach. The modern amenities block provides a stylish interior with underfloor heating and superb fixtures and fittings. 103 acre site. 146 touring pitches. 60 hardstandings. Caravan pitches. Motorhome pitches. Tent pitches. 703 statics.

Kiln Park Holiday Centre

Open: mid Mar-end Oct (rs mid Mar-May & Sep-Oct some facilities may be reduced) **Last arrival:** dusk **Last departure:** 10.00hrs
Pitches: 🚐 🚜 Å   **Leisure:** 🏊 🏊 ⚒ 🖐 ⚽ 🎵
Facilities: 🌳 🍴 🚿 🧴 WiFi ♻   **Services:** 🚾 🔌 🍳 🛢 🛒
Within 3 miles: ↓ 🎿 ⛳ ◎ 🚴 🚲 U

Notes: No commercial vehicles, no bookings by persons under 21yrs unless a family booking, max 2 dogs per booking, certain dog breeds banned. Dogs must be kept on leads. Entertainment complex, bowling & putting green.

AA Pubs & Restaurants nearby: Hope and Anchor, TENBY, SA70 7AX, 01834 842131
See advert below

LEISURE: 🏊 Indoor pool 🏊 Outdoor pool 🎪 Children's playground 🖐 Kid's club 🎾 Tennis court 🎱 Games room ⛳ Golf course 🚣 Boat hire 🚲 Cycle hire 🎬 Cinema 🎵 Entertainment 🎣 Fishing ⛳ Mini golf 🏏 Pitch n putt 🏄 Watersports 💪 Gym ⚽ Sports field U Stables **FACILITIES:** 🛁 Bath 🚿 Shower 🅿 Private washing cubicles ⊙ Electric shaver 💇 Hairdryer ❄ Ice Packs ♿ Disabled facilities 🅂 Shop on site 🚐 Mobile shop 🍖 BBQ area 🌲 Picnic area WiFi Wi-fi 💻 Internet access ♻ Recycling ❶ Tourist info 🐕 Dog exercise area 🚗 Car hire can be arranged

Trefalun Park

►►►►88%

tel: 01646 651514 **Devonshire Dr, St Florence SA70 8RD**
email: trefalun@aol.com **web:** www.trefalunpark.co.uk
dir: *1.5m NW of St Florence & 0.5m N of B4318.* **grid ref:** *SN093027*

Set within 12 acres of sheltered, well-kept grounds, this quiet country park offers well-maintained level grass pitches separated by bushes and trees, with plenty of space to relax in. Children can feed the park's friendly pets. Plenty of activities are available at the nearby Heatherton Country Sports Park, including go-karting, indoor bowls, golf and bumper boating. 12 acre site. 90 touring pitches. 90 hardstandings. 55 seasonal pitches. Caravan pitches. Motorhome pitches. Tent pitches. 10 statics.

Trefalun Park

Open: Etr-Oct **Last arrival:** 19.00hrs **Last departure:** noon

Pitches: 🚐 🚐 🛖

Leisure: ⚬

Facilities: 🐾 🅿 ☺ ☝ ✳ ♿ 🐕 WiFi ♻ ❶

Services: 🚐 🔲 🛢 🚿 T 🔋 ⚡

Within 3 miles: 🚴 🚣 🎯 ◉ ⛳ 🐕 🔲

Notes: No motorised scooters, no gazebos. Dogs must be kept on leads.

AA Pubs & Restaurants nearby: Hope and Anchor, TENBY, SA70 7AX, 01834 842131

See advert below

PITCHES: 🚐 Caravans 🚐 Motorhomes 🛖 Tents 🏕 Glamping accommodation **SERVICES:** 🚐 Electric hook up 🔲 Launderette 🍺 Licensed bar 🛢 Calor Gas ⚫ Camping Gaz T Toilet fluid 🍴 Café/Restaurant 🎗 Fast Food/Takeaway 🔋 Battery charging 🍼 Baby care ⚡ Motorvan service point **ABBREVIATIONS:** BHs – bank holidays Etr – Easter Spring BH – Spring Bank Holiday fr – from hrs – hours m – mile mdnt – midnight rdbt – roundabout rs – restricted service wk – week wknd – weekend x-roads – crossroads ⊘ No credit or debit cards ⊗ No dogs

TENBY *continued*

Well Park Caravan & Camping Site

▶▶▶▶82%

tel: 01834 842179 **SA70 8TL**
email: enquiries@wellparkcaravans.co.uk
dir: *A478 towards Tenby. At rdbt at Kilgetty follow Tenby & A478 signs. 3m to next rdbt, take 2nd exit, site 2nd right.* **grid ref:** *SN128028*

An attractive, well-maintained park with good landscaping from trees, ornamental shrubs and flower borders. The amenities include a launderette and indoor dishwashing, games room with table tennis, and an enclosed play area. The park is ideally situated between Tenby and Saundersfoot; Tenby just a 15-minute walk away, or the town can be reached via a traffic-free cycle track. 10 acre site. 100 touring pitches. 16 hardstandings. Caravan pitches. Motorhome pitches. Tent pitches. 42 statics.

Open: Mar-Oct (rs Mar-mid Jun & mid Sep-Oct bar may be closed) **Last arrival:** 22.00hrs **Last departure:** 11.00hrs

Pitches: * 🚐 £15-£28 🚐 £15-£28 ▲ £15-£20

Leisure: 🅰 🔍

Facilities: 🁢 🅿 ⊙ 🄲 ✳ 🕹 🎐 🀢 📶 ♻ 🛈

Services: 🔌 🔄 🍽 🁢 🚰 🛒

Within 3 miles: 🔱 🚣 🏌 ◎ 🏊 🛍 🕹 ∪

Notes: Family groups only. Dogs must be kept on leads. TV hook-ups.

AA Pubs & Restaurants nearby: Hope and Anchor, TENBY, SA70 7AX, 01834 842131

Wood Park Caravans

▶▶▶80%

tel: 01834 843414 **New Hedges SA70 8TL**
email: info@woodpark.co.uk
dir: *A477 from Carmarthen to St Clears. At rdbt onto A477 signed Pembroke Dock. At Kilgetty rdbt left onto A478 signed Tenby. At next rdbt take 2nd exit signed Tenby (ignore 1st exit signs for New Hedges & Saundersfoot). 2nd right to site (signed).* **grid ref:** *SN128025*

Situated in beautiful countryside between the popular seaside resorts of Tenby and Saundersfoot, and with Waterwynch Bay just a 15-minute walk away, this peaceful site provides a spacious and relaxing atmosphere for holidays. The slightly sloping touring area is divided by shrubs and hedge-screened paddocks, and a licensed bar and games room are also available. 10 acre site. 60 touring pitches. 40 hardstandings. 10 seasonal pitches. Caravan pitches. Motorhome pitches. Tent pitches. 90 statics.

Open: Spring BH-Sep (rs Sep - bar, laundrette & games room may be closed) **Last arrival:** 22.00hrs **Last departure:** 10.00hrs

Pitches: * 🚐 £16-£25 🚐 £16-£25 ▲ £15-£23

Leisure: 🅰 🔍

Facilities: 🁢 ⊙ 🄲 ✳ 📶 ♻ 🛈

Services: 🔌 🔄 🍽 🁢 🚰 📦

Within 3 miles: 🔱 🚣 🏌 ◎ 🏊 🛍 🕹

Notes: ⊘ No groups, 1 car per unit. Only small dogs accepted, no dogs Jul-Aug & BHs. Dogs must be kept on leads.

AA Pubs & Restaurants nearby: Hope and Anchor, TENBY, SA70 7AX, 01834 842131

POWYS

BRECON
Map 9 SO02

Places to visit
Regimental Museum of The Royal Welsh, BRECON, LD3 7EB, 01874 613310
www.royalwelsh.org.uk

Tretower Court & Castle, TRETOWER, NP8 1RD, 01874 730279
http://cadw.gov.wales/daysout/tretowercourtandcastle/

PREMIER PARK

Pencelli Castle Caravan & Camping Park

▶▶▶▶▶90%

tel: 01874 665451 **Pencelli LD3 7LX**
email: pencelli@tiscali.co.uk
dir: *Exit A40 2m E of Brecon onto B4558, follow signs to Pencelli.* **grid ref:** *SO096248*

Lying in the heart of the Brecon Beacons National Park, this charming park offers peace, beautiful scenery and high quality facilities. It is bordered by the Brecon and Monmouth Canal. The attention to detail is superb, and the well-equipped, heated toilets with en suite cubicles are matched by a drying room for clothes and boots, full laundry, and a shop. Regular buses stop just outside the gate and go to Brecon, Abergavenny and Swansea. 10 acre site. 80 touring pitches. 40 hardstandings. Caravan pitches. Motorhome pitches. Tent pitches.

Open: 15 Feb-Nov (rs mid Feb-Etr & 30 Oct-Nov shop closed) **Last arrival:** 22.00hrs **Last departure:** noon

Pitches: 🚐 🚐 ▲

Leisure: 🅰 ⊙ 🎐

Facilities: 🁢 🅿 ⊙ 🄲 ✳ 🕹 🛍 🀢 📶 ♻ 🛈

Services: 🔌 🔄 🁢 🚰 🔲 🛒

Within 3 miles: 🚣 🍴 🏌 🛍 🕹 ∪

Notes: Assistance dogs only. No radios, music or camp fires.

AA Pubs & Restaurants nearby: Star Inn, TALYBONT-ON-USK, LD3 7YX, 01874 676635
The Usk Inn, BRECON, LD3 7JE, 01874 676251

LEISURE: 🁢 Indoor pool 🁢 Outdoor pool 🅰 Children's playground 🖐 Kid's club 🁢 Tennis court 🔍 Games room 🏌 Golf course 🚣 Boat hire 🎐 Cycle hire 🁢 Cinema 🎵 Entertainment 🎣 Fishing ◎ Mini golf 🁢 Pitch n putt 🁢 Watersports 🁢 Gym ⊙ Sports field ∪ Stables **FACILITIES:** 🛁 Bath 🁢 Shower 🅿 Private washing cubicles ⊙ Electric shaver 🄲 Hairdryer ✳ Ice Packs 🕹 Disabled facilities 🛍 Shop on site 🀢 Mobile shop 🁢 BBQ area 🀢 Picnic area 📶 Wi-fi 🁢 Internet access ♻ Recycling 🛈 Tourist info 🁢 Dog exercise area 🎐 Car hire can be arranged

BRONLLYS
Map 9 SO13

Places to visit
Regimental Museum of The Royal Welsh, BRECON, LD3 7EB, 01874 613310
www.royalwelsh.org.uk

Anchorage Caravan Park
▶▶▶▶ 83%

tel: 01874 711246 & 711230 **LD3 0LD**
web: www.anchoragecp.co.uk
dir: *8m NE of Brecon in village centre.* **grid ref:** *SO142351*

A well-maintained site with a choice of south-facing, sloping grass pitches and superb views of the Black Mountains, or a more sheltered lower area with a number of excellent super pitches. The site is a short distance from the water sports centre at Llangorse Lake. 8 acre site. 110 touring pitches. 8 hardstandings. 60 seasonal pitches. Caravan pitches. Motorhome pitches. Tent pitches. 101 statics.

Open: all year (rs Nov-Mar TV room closed) **Last arrival:** 23.00hrs
Last departure: 18.00hrs

Pitches: 🚐 fr £13 🚍 fr £13 🛖 fr £13

Leisure: 🎱

Facilities: 🐕 ℗ ⊙ ℱ ✳ ♿ 🗑 🛒 ⊞ 🛜 ♻ ❻

Services: 🔌 🗒 🔋 ⊘ T 🔋📺

Within 3 miles: ℱ 🛒 🗒 ♻ ∪

Notes: Dogs must be kept on leads. Hairdresser.

AA Pubs & Restaurants nearby: The Harp Inn, GLASBURY, HR3 5NR, 01497 847373
The Old Black Lion, HAY-ON-WYE, HR3 5AD, 01497 820841

BUILTH WELLS
Map 9 SO05

PREMIER PARK

Fforest Fields Caravan & Camping Park
▶▶▶▶▶ 85%

tel: 01982 570406 **Hundred House LD1 5RT**
email: office@fforestfields.co.uk **web:** www.fforestfields.co.uk
dir: *From town centre follow New Radnor signs on A481. 4m to signed entrance on right, 0.5m before Hundred House village. (NB if using Sat Nav the entrance is not centred on post code).* **grid ref:** *SO100535*

This is a constantly improving, sheltered park surrounded by magnificent scenery and an abundance of wildlife. The spacious pitches are well laid out to create optimum privacy, and the superb eco-friendly amenities block is fuelled by a bio-mass boiler and solar panels. There are two bell tents, known as Betty and Harry, that have character shed kitchens; the licensed Fforest Café specialises in serving local produce. The historic town of Builth Wells and The Royal Welsh Showground are just four miles away. 15 acre site. 120 touring pitches. 30 hardstandings. 12 seasonal pitches. Caravan pitches. Motorhome pitches. Tent pitches.

Open: all year **Last arrival:** 21.00hrs **Last departure:** 18.00hrs

Pitches: * 🚐 £14-£21 🚍 £14-£21 🛖 £14-£21 🏠 prices shown below

Leisure: ✿

Facilities: ⊙ ℱ ✳ ♿ 🗑 🛒 🛜 🖥 ♻ ❻

Services: 🔌 🗒 🔋 ⊘ T 🍽 📺

Glamping: Bell tents 2, £70 per night (Mon-Fri), £90 (wknds) Own kitchen Car by unit

Within 3 miles: ⚓ ⛳ 🎏 ℱ ♻ 🛒 🗒

Notes: No loud music. Fridges, microwave, electric kettle & phone charging available.

AA Pubs & Restaurants nearby: The Laughing Dog, LLANDRINDOD WELLS, LD1 5PT, 01597 822406

PITCHES: 🚐 Caravans 🚍 Motorhomes 🛖 Tents 🏠 Glamping accommodation **SERVICES:** 🔌 Electric hook up 🗒 Launderette 🍺 Licensed bar 🔋 Calor Gas ⊘ Camping Gaz T Toilet fluid 🍽 Café/Restaurant 🍔 Fast Food/Takeaway 📺 Battery charging 🍼 Baby care 🚐 Motorvan service point
ABBREVIATIONS: BHs – bank holidays Etr – Easter Spring BH – Spring Bank Holiday fr – from hrs – hours m – mile mdnt – midnight rdbt – roundabout rs – restricted service wk – week wknd – weekend x-roads – crossroads 🚫 No credit or debit cards 🚫 No dogs

CHURCHSTOKE
Map 15 SO29

Places to visit
Montgomery Castle, MONTGOMERY, 01443 336000
http://cadw.gov.wales/daysout/montgomerycastle/

PREMIER PARK

Daisy Bank Caravan Park
▶▶▶▶▶ 84%

tel: 01588 620471 & 07918 680712 **Snead SY15 6EB**
email: enquiries@daisy-bank.co.uk
dir: *On A489, 2m E of Churchstoke.* **grid ref:** *SO309926*

Peacefully located between Craven Arms and Churchstoke and surrounded by rolling hills, this idyllic, adults-only park offers generously sized, fully serviced pitches; all are situated in attractive hedged areas, surrounded by lush grass and pretty seasonal flowers. The immaculately maintained amenity blocks provide smart, modern fittings and excellent privacy options. Camping pods, a pitch and putt course and free WiFi are also available. 7 acre site. 80 touring pitches. 75 hardstandings. 30 seasonal pitches. Caravan pitches. Motorhome pitches. Tent pitches. 5 statics.

Open: all year **Last arrival:** 20.00hrs **Last departure:** noon
Pitches: * 🚐 £20-£30 🚏 £20-£30 ▲ £20 🏠 prices shown below
Leisure: ⛳
Facilities: ⊙ 🌮 ✳ ♿ 🔊 🚻 WiFi 🖥 ♻ ❶ 🐾
Services: 🔌🔲 🛢 🗑 🧺 Ⓣ
Glamping: Wooden Pods 2, £34-£45 Changeover day Any day Min stay 1 night Car by unit
Within 3 miles: ◎ 🛒 🛍
Notes: Adults only. Dogs must be kept on leads. Caravan storage.
AA Pubs & Restaurants nearby: The Three Tuns Inn, BISHOP'S CASTLE, SY9 5BW, 01588 638797

CRICKHOWELL
Map 9 SO21

Places to visit
Tretower Court & Castle, TRETOWER, NP8 1RD, 01874 730279
http://cadw.gov.wales/daysout/tretowercourtandcastle/

Big Pit National Coal Museum, BLAENAVON, NP4 9XP, 029 20573650
www.museumwales.ac.uk

Riverside Caravan & Camping Park
▶▶▶ 81%

tel: 01873 810397 **New Rd NP8 1AY**
email: riversideccp@btopenworld.com
dir: *On A4077, well signed from A40.* **grid ref:** *SO215184*

A very well tended adults-only park in delightful countryside on the edge of the small country town of Crickhowell. The adjacent riverside park is an excellent facility for all, including dog-walkers. Crickhowell has numerous specialist shops including a first-class delicatessen. Within a few minutes' walk of the park are several friendly pubs with good restaurants. 3.5 acre site. 35 touring pitches. Caravan pitches. Motorhome pitches. Tent pitches. 20 statics.

Open: Mar-Oct **Last arrival:** 21.00hrs
Pitches: 🚐 🚏 ▲
Facilities: ⊙ 🌮 ✳ ❶
Services: 🔌🔲 🛢 🗑
Within 3 miles: 🖊 🚣 🛍 ∪
Notes: Adults only. 🚫 No hang gliders or paragliders. Dogs must be kept on leads. Large canopied area for cooking, drying clothes, etc.
AA Pubs & Restaurants nearby: The Bear, CRICKHOWELL, NP8 1BW, 01873 810408

LLANDRINDOD WELLS
Map 9 SO06

Disserth Caravan & Camping Park
▶▶▶▶ 83%

tel: 01597 860277 **Disserth, Howey LD1 6NL**
email: disserthcaravan@btconnect.com
dir: *1m from A483, between Newbridge-on-Wye & Howey, by church. Follow brown signs from A483 or A470.* **grid ref:** *SO035583*

By a 13th-century church, this is a delightfully secluded and predominantly adult park that sits in a beautiful valley on the banks of the River Ithon, a tributary of the River Wye. It has a small bar which is open at weekends and during busy periods. The amenities block and laundry are appointed to a high standard and provide good privacy options. The site offers a shepherd's hut and a wooden 'morphPod' for hire. 4 acre site. 30 touring pitches. 6 hardstandings. Caravan pitches. Motorhome pitches. Tent pitches. 25 statics.

Open: Mar-Oct **Last arrival:** sunset **Last departure:** noon
Pitches: * 🚐 £15-£20 🚏 £15-£20 ▲ £12-£25 🏠 prices shown below
Leisure: ✏
Facilities: 🚿 P̄ ⊙ 🌮 ✳ ♿ WiFi ♻ ❶
Services: 🔌🔲 🛢 🍴 🗑 🧺 Ⓣ 🛢
Glamping: Wooden Pods 1, Min stay 1 night Car by unit **Shepherd's Huts** 1, £30-£35 Min stay 1 night Car by unit
Within 3 miles: 🖊 🍴 ✏ 🛍 ∪
Notes: Quiet after 22.30hrs, max 2 pets. Dogs must be kept on leads. Private trout fishing.
AA Pubs & Restaurants nearby: The Laughing Dog, LLANDRINDOD WELLS, LD1 5PT, 01597 822406

Dalmore Camping & Caravanning Park
▶▶ 82%

tel: 01597 822483 **Howey LD1 5RG**
email: brianthorpe@tiscali.co.uk
dir: *From A483 between Llandrindod Wells & Builth Wells follow site signs at hill top. 3m from Llandrindod Wells & 4m from Builth Wells.* **grid ref:** *SO045569*

An intimate and well laid out adults-only park. Pitches are attractively terraced to ensure that all enjoy the wonderful views from this splendidly landscaped little park. 3 acre site. 20 touring pitches. 12 hardstandings. 6 seasonal pitches. Caravan pitches. Motorhome pitches. Tent pitches. 20 statics.

Open: Mar-Oct **Last arrival:** 22.00hrs **Last departure:** noon

LEISURE: 🏊 Indoor pool 🏊 Outdoor pool 🛝 Children's playground 🧒 Kid's club 🎾 Tennis court 🎱 Games room ⛳ Golf course 🚣 Boat hire 🚲 Cycle hire 🎬 Cinema 🎵 Entertainment 🎣 Fishing ⛳ Mini golf ⛳ Pitch n putt 🏄 Watersports 🏋 Gym 🏟 Sports field ∪ Stables **FACILITIES:** 🛁 Bath 🚿 Shower P̄ Private washing cubicles ⊙ Electric shaver ☝ Hairdryer ✳ Ice Packs ♿ Disabled facilities 🛍 Shop on site 🛒 Mobile shop 🍖 BBQ area 🍽 Picnic area WiFi Wi-fi 🖥 Internet access ♻ Recycling ❶ Tourist info 🐾 Dog exercise area 🚗 Car hire can be arranged

Pitches: * 🚐 £10-£13 � £10-£13 ▲ £10-£13

Facilities: 🅿️⊙🄿☀🄰𝟶

Services: 🄳🄰⊘🄱⛟

Within 3 miles: ⅃⌶🄿◎🄰🄰

Notes: Adults only. ⊛ Gates closed 23.00hrs-07.00hrs, no ball games. Dogs must be kept on leads. Separate male & female washing areas, no cubicles.

AA Pubs & Restaurants nearby: The Laughing Dog, LLANDRINDOD WELLS, LD1 5PT, 01597 822406

LLANGORS — Map 9 SO12

Places to visit

Regimental Museum of The Royal Welsh, BRECON, LD3 7EB, 01874 613310 www.royalwelsh.org.uk

Great for kids: Tretower Court & Castle, TRETOWER, NP8 1RD, 01874 730279 http://cadw.gov.wales/daysout/tretowercourtandcastle/

Lakeside Caravan Park
►►► 80%

tel: 01874 658226 **LD3 7TR**
email: reception@llangorselake.co.uk
dir: Exit A40 at Bwlch onto B4560 towards Llangorse. Site signed towards lake in Llangorse village. **grid ref:** SO128272

Surrounded by spectacular mountains and set alongside Llangorse Lake, with mooring and launching facilities, this is a must-do holiday destination for lovers of outdoor pursuits, from walking to watersports, and even pike fishing for which the lake is renowned. The hedge- or tree-screened touring areas provide generously sized pitches. There's a well-stocked shop, bar and café, with takeaway, under the same ownership. 2 acre site. 40 touring pitches. 8 hardstandings. Caravan pitches. Motorhome pitches. Tent pitches. 72 statics.

Open: Etr or Apr-Oct (rs Mar-May & Oct clubhouse, restaurant reduced hours)
Last arrival: 21.30hrs **Last departure:** 10.00hrs

Pitches: * 🚐 £17.75-£19.75 � £17.75-£19.75 ▲ £13.50-£15.50

Leisure: 🄰🅀🄿

Facilities: 🅿️⊙🄿☀🄰🄰🆆🄸🄰𝟶

Services: 🄳🄰🄾🄱⊘🅃◎⛟

Within 3 miles: ☡🄿⚓🄰🄰∪

Notes: No open fires, noise to be kept to a minimum after 23.00hrs. No dogs allowed in hire caravans. Dogs must be kept on leads. Boat hire in summer.

AA Pubs & Restaurants nearby: The Usk Inn, BRECON, LD3 7JE, 01874 676251

Star Inn, TALYBONT-ON-USK, LD3 7YX, 01874 676635

LLANIDLOES — Map 9 SN98

PREMIER PARK

Red Kite Touring Park
NEW ►►►►► 84%

Best of British

tel: 01686 412122 **Van Rd SY18 6NG**
email: info@redkitetouringpark.co.uk
dir: From rdbt on A470 at Llanidloes take B4518 signed Penffordd-las Staylittle. At next rdbt take 3rd exit signed Machynlleth. Over river. 1st left (B4518) signed Penffordd-las Staylittle. Pass Clywedog Riverside Holiday Home Park on left, site in approx 100yds. **grid ref:** SN944863

A new tourist destination for 2016, this stunningly located park has been created from undulating hills and fields, which include two lakes, one being a habitat for newts. All pitches are fully serviced to include a green chemical disposal point and TV hook-up, and the superb amenities block with underfloor heating provides excellent fixtures and fittings coupled with privacy provision for both men and women. Please not this is an adults-only park. 20 acre site. 66 touring pitches. Caravan pitches. Motorhome pitches.

Open: Mar-Oct **Last arrival:** 19.00hrs **Last departure:** 13.00hrs

Pitches: * 🚐 £24-£26 � £24-£26

Notes: Adults only.

MIDDLETOWN — Map 15 SJ31

Places to visit

Powis Castle & Garden, WELSHPOOL, SY21 8RF, 01938 551929 www.nationaltrust.org.uk

---

Bank Farm Caravan Park
►►► 81%

tel: 01938 570526 **SY21 8EJ**
email: bankfarmcaravans@yahoo.co.uk
dir: 13m W of Shrewsbury, 5m E of Welshpool on A458. **grid ref:** SJ293123

This is an attractive park on a small farm that's maintained to a high standard. There are two touring areas located on both sides of the A458; each has its own amenity block and direct access to the hills, mountains and woodland. The site has an excellent display of topiary, trimmed colourful shrubs, hedges and trees. A pub serving good food, and a large play area are nearby. 2 acre site. 40 touring pitches. Caravan pitches. Motorhome pitches. Tent pitches. 33 statics.

Open: Mar-Oct **Last arrival:** 20.00hrs

Pitches: * 🚐 fr £17 � fr £17 ▲ fr £14

Leisure: 🄰🅀🄿

Facilities: 🅿️⊙☀🄰🄰🆆🄸🄰𝟶

Services: 🄳🄰🄱🄰

Within 3 miles: 🄿

Notes: Dogs must be kept on leads. Coarse fishing, jacuzzi, snooker room.

AA Pubs & Restaurants nearby: The Old Hand and Diamond Inn, COEDWAY, SY5 9AR, 01743 884379

PITCHES: 🚐 Caravans � Motorhomes ▲ Tents 🏠 Glamping accommodation **SERVICES:** 🄳 Electric hook up 🄰 Launderette 🅃 Licensed bar 🄱 Calor Gas 🄰 Camping Gaz 🅃 Toilet fluid ◎ Café/Restaurant ⛟ Fast Food/Takeaway 🄰 Battery charging 🄱 Baby care ∪ Motorvan service point
ABBREVIATIONS: BHs — bank holidays Etr — Easter Spring BH — Spring Bank Holiday fr — from hrs — hours m — mile mdnt — midnight rdbt — roundabout rs — restricted service wk — week wknd — weekend x-roads — crossroads ⊛ No credit or debit cards ⊗ No dogs

SWANSEA

OLDWALLS
Map 8 SS49

Oldwalls Gower Glamping
▶▶▶▶ 84%

tel: 01792 391468 **SA3 1HA**
email: info@oldwallsgower.com
dir: M4 junct 42, A483 towards Swansea. At rdbt take A484 signed Llanelli & The Gower. In Gowerton follow B4295 signs. Through Llanrhidian to Oldwalls.
grid ref: SS488918

Head down the winding and well-maintained approach road, with rare breed sheep and llamas to admire on the way, to find this excellent glamping operation. It's a memorable destination – everything is immaculately presented with stone walling, lush neat grass, well-trimmed hedging and a stunning display of seasonal flowers. The glamping area is set beside an ornamental lake with abundant wild flowers; tarmac pathways lead to each of the 10 well-spaced bell tents. Each unit is on a level artificial grass hardstanding and the beautifully styled interiors have rattan flooring, oil-heated radiators, smart furnishings and quality double beds. Just a stroll away is a modern, bright centrally-heated amenities block that has five unisex shower, washbasin and toilet rooms.

Open: Apr-Oct **Last arrival:** 20.00hrs **Last departure:** 10.30hrs

Glamping: Bell tents 10

PONTARDDULAIS
Map 8 SN50

PREMIER PARK

River View Touring Park
NEW ▶▶▶▶▶ 85%

tel: 01635 844876 **The Dingle, Llanedi SA4 0FH**
email: info@riverviewtp.com
dir: M4 junct 49, A483 signed Llandeilo & Ammanford. 1st left after layby. Site in 300yds on left. (NB if approaching from N or W on A48 & using Sat Nav do not exit A48 before Port Abraham rdbt). **grid ref:** SN577086

Located in a peaceful valley surrounded by mature trees and with a river meandering through the lower touring areas, this long established holiday destination is constantly being improved by enthusiastic owners and wardens. A well-equipped amenities block is centrally located between upper and lower touring fields which are designated as 'family' and 'adults-only' respectively. There is one wooden pod that sleeps two adults and two children. 6 acre site. 60 touring pitches. 46 hardstandings. 16 seasonal pitches. Caravan pitches. Motorhome pitches. Tent pitches.

Open: Mar-Nov **Last arrival:** 20.30hrs **Last departure:** noon

Pitches: * 🚐 £17-£24 🚍 £17-£24 ▲ £17-£24 🏠 prices shown below

Leisure: 🎠 ☺ ✐

Facilities: 🚿 🅿 ☺ ✐ ✳ ⚅ 🖐 🛗 WiFi ♻ ✱

Services: 🔌 � 💧 🗑 T ♿

Glamping: Wooden Pods 1, £35-£45 Min stay 1 night Car by unit

Within 3 miles: ⌇ ✐ ◎ ⚓ 🛒 🛍 U

Notes: No commercial vehicles. Dogs must be kept on leads.

PORT EYNON
Map 8 SS48

Places to visit

Weobley Castle, LLANRHIDIAN, SA3 1HB, 01443 336000
http://cadw.gov.wales/daysout/weobleycastle/

Gower Heritage Centre, PARKMILL, SA3 2EH, 01792 371206
www.gowerheritagecentre.co.uk

Great for kids: Oxwich Castle, OXWICH, SA3 1ND, 01792 390359
http://cadw.gov.wales/daysout/oxwichcastle/

Carreglwyd Camping & Caravan Park
▶▶▶▶ 83%

tel: 01792 390795 **SA3 1NL**
email: booking@porteynon.com
dir: A4118 to Port Eynon, site adjacent to beach. **grid ref:** SS465863

Set in an unrivalled location alongside the safe sandy beach of Port Eynon on the Gower Peninsula, this popular park is an ideal family holiday spot; it is also close to an attractive village with pubs and shops. The sloping ground has been partly terraced and most pitches have sea views; the excellent toilet facilities include three superb family bathrooms. 12 acre site. 150 touring pitches. Caravan pitches. Motorhome pitches. Tent pitches.

Open: all year **Last arrival:** 22.00hrs **Last departure:** 15.00hrs

Pitches: 🚐 🚍 ▲

Facilities: ☺ ⚅ 🖐 🛗 WiFi ♻ ✱

Services: 🔌 � 💧 🗑 T ♿

Within 3 miles: ✐ 🛒 🛍 U

Notes: Dogs must be kept on leads.

AA Pubs & Restaurants nearby: Fairyhill, REYNOLDSTON, SA3 1BS, 01792 390139

King Arthur Hotel, REYNOLDSTON, SA3 1AD, 01792 390775

RHOSSILI

Places to visit

Weobley Castle, LLANRHIDIAN, SA3 1HB, 01443 336000
http://cadw.gov.wales/daysout/weobleycastle/

Gower Heritage Centre, PARKMILL, SA3 2EH, 01792 371206
www.gowerheritagecentre.co.uk

Great for kids: Oxwich Castle, OXWICH, SA3 1ND, 01792 390359
http://cadw.gov.wales/daysout/oxwichcastle/

LEISURE: 🏊 Indoor pool 🏊 Outdoor pool 🎠 Children's playground 🖐 Kid's club 🎾 Tennis court 🎱 Games room ⛳ Golf course 🚣 Boat hire 🚲 Cycle hire 🎬 Cinema 🎵 Entertainment ✐ Fishing ◎ Mini golf ⚑ Pitch n putt 🏄 Watersports 🏋 Gym ⚽ Sports field U Stables **FACILITIES:** 🛁 Bath 🚿 Shower 🅿 Private washing cubicles ☺ Electric shaver ✐ Hairdryer ✳ Ice Packs ⚅ Disabled facilities 🛒 Shop on site 🛍 Mobile shop 🍖 BBQ area 🪑 Picnic area WiFi Wi-fi 🖥 Internet access ♻ Recycling 🛈 Tourist info 🐕 Dog exercise area 🚗 Car hire can be arranged

RHOSSILI
Map 8 SS48

Pitton Cross Caravan & Camping Park

▶▶▶ 91%

tel: 01792 390593 **SA3 1PT**
email: admin@pittoncross.co.uk **web:** www.pittoncross.co.uk
dir: *2m W of Scurlage on B4247.* **grid ref:** *SS434877*

Surrounded by farmland close to sandy Mewslade Bay, which is within walking distance across fields, this grassy park is divided by hedging into paddocks, with hardstandings for motorhomes available; there are also shepherd's huts for hire. Some areas are deliberately left uncultivated, resulting in colourful displays of wild flowers including roses and orchids. Rhossili Beach, which is popular with surfers, and the Welsh Coastal Path are nearby. Both children's kites and power kites are sold on site, and instruction is available; geocaching and paragliding are possible too. 6 acre site. 100 touring pitches. 27 hardstandings. Caravan pitches. Motorhome pitches. Tent pitches.

Open: all year (rs Nov-Mar no bread, milk or newspapers) **Last arrival:** 20.00hrs
Last departure: 11.00hrs

Pitches: * ⚌ £20-£29 ⚌ £20-£29 ▲ £11-£35 ⋒

Facilities: 🅿️ ⊙ ✱ ⅍ 🖥 🚽 ♻ 𝟬

Services: 🔌 🔄 ⚋ 🚽

Glamping: Shepherd's Huts

Within 3 miles: ⅍ 🔄

Notes: Quiet at all times, charcoal BBQs must be off ground, no fire pits or log burning. Dogs must be kept on leads. Baby bath available.

AA Pubs & Restaurants nearby: Fairyhill, REYNOLDSTON, SA3 1BS, 01792 390139

King Arthur Hotel, REYNOLDSTON, SA3 1AD, 01792 390775

Kings Head, LLANGENNITH, SA3 1HX, 01792 386212

SWANSEA

Places to visit
Swansea Museum, SWANSEA, SA1 1SN, 01792 653763
www.swanseamuseum.co.uk

Great for kids: Plantasia, SWANSEA, SA1 2AL, 01792 474555 www.plantasia.org

SWANSEA
Map 9 SS69

Riverside Caravan Park
HOLIDAY CENTRE 78%

tel: 01792 775587 **Ynys Forgan Farm, Morriston SA6 6QL**
email: reception@riversideswansea.com
dir: *M4 junct 45 follow Swansea signs. Before joining A4067 turn left into private road signed to site.* **grid ref:** *SS679991*

A large and busy park close to the M4 but in a quiet location beside the River Taw. This friendly, family orientated site has a licensed club and bar with a full high-season entertainment programme. There is a choice of eating outlets – the clubhouse restaurant, takeaway and chip shop. The park has a good indoor pool. 5 acre site. 90 touring pitches. Caravan pitches. Motorhome pitches. Tent pitches. 256 statics.

Open: all year (rs Winter months pool & club closed) **Last arrival:** mdnt
Last departure: noon

Pitches: * ⚌ £16-£23.50 ⚌ £16-£23.50 ▲ £16-£23.50

Leisure: 🏊 ⋒ 🎣 ♪ 🎮 **Facilities:** 🅿️ ⊙ ✱ ⅍ 🖥 🚽 📶

Services: 🔌 🔄 🍴 🛢 ⚋ 🚽 🍔 **Within 3 miles:** ⅍ ✚ 🎣 🛍 🔄 ⛳

Notes: Dogs by prior arrangement only, no aggressive breeds permitted. Fishing on site by arrangement.

AA Pubs & Restaurants nearby: Hanson at the Chelsea Restaurant, SWANSEA, SA1 3LH, 01792 464068

WREXHAM

BRONINGTON
Map 15 SJ43

Places to visit
Erddig, WREXHAM, LL13 0YT, 01978 355314 www.nationaltrust.org.uk/erddig

The Little Yurt Meadow

▶▶▶▶ 86%

tel: 01948 780136 & 07984 400134 **Bay Tree Barns, Mill Rd SY13 3HJ**
email: info@thelittleyurtmeadow.co.uk
dir: *A525 from Whitchurch to Redbrook. In Redbrook left onto A495 (Oswestry). Right to Bronington. At staggered x-roads right into Mill Rd.* **grid ref:** *SJ483397*

Located in a former meadow on the Shropshire-Welsh border, this site has become a luxury glamping destination for those wishing to escape from the pressures of everyday life. Three spacious yurts with stylishly furnished interiors are equipped with sumptuous beds, two settees (one converts to a sofa bed), a wood-burning stove, mini-cooker and lots of quality extras. Each yurt has its own luxury shower room and there are areas for communal outdoor and indoor relaxation. 3 acre site.

Open: all year **Last arrival:** 23.00hrs **Last departure:** 11.00hrs

Leisure: ⚽ **Facilities:** 🎣 ✱ ⅍ 🖥 🚽 ♻ 𝟬 **Services:** 🔌 🔄

Glamping: Yurts 3, £140-£145 En suite Own kitchen Car by unit

Within 3 miles: ⅍ ✚ 🎣 🛍 🔄

Notes: 🅿 PayPal accepted. 🚫 No noise after 23.00hrs. Self-catering kitchen area, wet rooms.

PREMIER PARK

Plassey Holiday Park

▶▶▶▶▶ 94%

tel: 01978 780277 **The Plassey LL13 0SP**
email: enquiries@plassey.com **web:** www.plassey.com
dir: *From A483 at Bangor-on-Dee exit onto B5426 for 2.5m. Site entrance signed on left.* **grid ref:** *SJ353452*

A lovely park set in several hundred acres of quiet farm and meadowland in the Dee Valley. The superb toilet facilities include individual cubicles for total privacy and security, while the Edwardian farm buildings have been converted into a restaurant, coffee shop, beauty studio and various craft outlets. There is

plenty here to entertain the whole family, from scenic walks and a swimming pool to free fishing, and use of the 9-hole golf course. Wooden pods will be introduced for the 2017 season. 10 acre site. 90 touring pitches. 60 hardstandings. 60 seasonal pitches. Caravan pitches. Motorhome pitches. Tent pitches. 15 statics.

Plassey Holiday Park

Open: Feb-Nov **Last arrival:** 20.30hrs **Last departure:** noon

Pitches: * 🚐 £19.20-£32.40 🚐 £19.20-£32.40 ▲ £19.20-£32.40 🏕

Leisure: 🏊 🛝 ⛺ 🎯 🔍 ⛳ 🚣

Facilities: 🚿 📷 ⊙ 🦮 ✳ ♿ 🛁 🔥 📶 ♻ ℹ

Services: 🚐 🔌 🍴 🛒 🚰 🗑 🍴 🛒 🏧 🚗 🧺

Glamping: Wooden Pods 18

Within 3 miles: ⛳ 🎿 🏌 ◎ 🛍 🏇 ⛵

Notes: No footballs or skateboards, no noise after 23.00hrs. Dogs must be kept on leads. Sauna, badminton, table tennis, driving range.

AA Pubs & Restaurants nearby: The Boat Inn, ERBISTOCK, LL13 0DL, 01978 780666

See advert below

OVERTON
Map 15 SJ34

The Trotting Mare Caravan Park
▶▶▶▶83%

tel: 01978 711963 **LL13 0LE**
email: info@thetrottingmare.co.uk
dir: *From Oswestry towards Whitchurch take A495. In Ellesmere take A528 towards Overton. Site on left. Or from Wrexham take A525 signed Whitchurch. In Marchwiel turn right onto A528 towards Overton. Through Overton to Ellesmere A528, site on right.*
grid ref: *SJ374396*

Located between Overton-on-Dee and Ellesmere, this adults-only touring park is quietly located behind The Trotting Mare pub. The majority of pitches are fully serviced, and creative landscaping and a free coarse-fishing lake are additional benefits. A superb new amenities block opened in 2016. 4.2 acre site. 54 touring pitches. 43 hardstandings. Caravan pitches. Motorhome pitches. Tent pitches. 11 statics.

Open: all year **Last arrival:** 20.00hrs **Last departure:** noon

Pitches: 🚐 🚍 ⛺

Leisure: 🎣

Facilities: 🛒 🅿️ ☺ 🅿️ ❄ ♿ ♨ WiFi 🖥 ♻ ✱

Services: 🔌 🗑 🚰 T ♨ 🔋 🛗

Within 3 miles: 🚶 🎣 ◎ 🏪 🛒 ∪

Notes: Adults only. No commercial vehicles, no open fires, no gas bottles outside caravan or awning, no bikes, no ball games, no noise after 23.00 hrs. Dogs must be kept on leads.

RUABON
Map 15 SJ34

Places to visit

Plas Newydd, LLANGOLLEN, LL20 8AW, 01978 861314 www.denbighshire.gov.uk

Valle Crucis Abbey, LLANGOLLEN, LL20 8DD, 01978 860326 http://cadw.gov.wales/daysout/vallecrucisabbey/

Great for kids: Horse Drawn Boats Centre, LLANGOLLEN, LL20 8TA, 01978 860702 www.horsedrawnboats.co.uk

James' Caravan Park
▶▶▶75%

tel: 01978 820148 **LL14 6DW**
email: ray@carastay.demon.co.uk
dir: *From Oswestry on A483 take slip road signed Llangollen & A539. At rdbt left onto A539 towards Llangollen. Site 500yds on left. From Wrexham on A483 follow Llangollen & A539 signs. Right at rdbt onto A539, at next rdbt straight on, site on left.*
grid ref: *SJ300434*

A well-landscaped park on a former farm, with modern heated toilet facilities. Old farm buildings house a collection of restored original farm machinery, and the village shop, four pubs, takeaway and launderette are a 10-minute walk away. 6 acre site. 40 touring pitches. 4 hardstandings. Caravan pitches. Motorhome pitches.

Open: all year **Last arrival:** 21.00hrs **Last departure:** 11.00hrs

Pitches: 🚐 🚍

Facilities: ☺ 🅿️ ❄ ♿ ♨

Services: 🔌 🔥 🗑 🔋

Within 3 miles: 🚶 🏪 🛒

Notes: ⊗ No fires. Dogs must be kept on leads. Chest freezer available.

AA Pubs & Restaurants nearby: The Boat Inn, ERBISTOCK, LL13 0DL, 01978 780666

PITCHES: 🚐 Caravans 🚍 Motorhomes ⛺ Tents 🏠 Glamping accommodation **SERVICES:** 🔌 Electric hook up 🗑 Launderette 🍺 Licensed bar 🔥 Calor Gas ⊘ Camping Gaz T Toilet fluid 🍽 Café/Restaurant 🏬 Fast Food/Takeaway 🔋 Battery charging 🛗 Baby care ⛟ Motorvan service point
ABBREVIATIONS: BHs – bank holidays Etr – Easter Spring BH – Spring Bank Holiday fr – from hrs – hours m – mile mdnt – midnight rdbt – roundabout rs – restricted service wk – week wknd – weekend x-roads – crossroads ⊗ No credit or debit cards ⊗ No dogs

Ireland

NORTHERN IRELAND

COUNTY ANTRIM

ANTRIM	Map 1 D5

Places to visit

Antrim Round Tower, ANTRIM, BT41 1BJ, 028 9023 5000
www.discovernorthernireland.com/Antrim-Round-Tower-Antrim

Great for kids: Belfast Zoological Gardens, BELFAST, BT36 7PN, 028 9077 6277
www.belfastzoo.co.uk

Six Mile Water Caravan Park
►►►►81%

tel: 028 9446 4963 & 9446 3113 **Lough Rd BT41 4DG**
email: sixmilewater@antrimandnewtownabbey.gov.uk
dir: *From A6, Dublin road into Lough Rd signed Antrim Forum & Loughshore Park. Site at end of road on right.* **grid ref:** *J137870*

A pretty tree-lined site in a large municipal park, within walking distance of Antrim and the Antrim Forum leisure complex, yet very much in the countryside. The modern toilet block is well equipped, and other facilities include a laundry and electric hook-ups, and a new restaurant for the 2016 season. All the pitches are precisely set on generous plots. 9.61 acre site. 45 touring pitches. 37 hardstandings. Caravan pitches. Motorhome pitches. Tent pitches.

Open: Mar-Oct (Feb & Nov wknds only) **Last arrival:** 21.00hrs **Last departure:** noon
Pitches: 🚐 🚏 ▲ **Leisure:** 🔍
Facilities: 🏗️🅿️☺🖤🎨🚿🎸 WiFi 🍃🅾
Services: 🔌🗑️🍴🚽
Within 3 miles: ⚓🎈🏌️◎🎣🛒🖼️
Notes: Max stay 7 nights, no noise between 22.00hrs-08.00hrs. Dogs must be kept on leads. Watersports, angling stands.
AA Pubs & Restaurants nearby: Galgorm Resort & Spa, BALLYMENA, BT42 1EA, 028 2588 1001

BALLYCASTLE	Map 1 D6

Places to visit

Carrick-a-Rede Rope Bridge and Larrybane Visitor Centre, CARRICK-A-REDE, BT54 6LS, 028 2076 9839 www.nationaltrust.org.uk

Old Bushmills Distillery, BUSHMILLS, BT57 8XH, 028 2073 1521
www.bushmills.com

Watertop Farm
NEW ►►►►82%

tel: 028 2076 2576 **188 Cushendall Rd BT54 6RN**
email: watertopfarm@aol.com
dir: *From Ballycastle left at Margee bridge onto Cushendall Rd (A2). Through Ballyvoy. Site on left just before Ballypatrick Forest. Or from Cushendall take A2, pass Ballypatrick forest, site on right.* **grid ref:** *NW357953*

In an idyllic and peaceful location that's within easy reach of major attractions, this unique holiday destination provides very good standards for caravan, motorhome and camping customers. There are three strategically located areas that take full advantage of the surroundings – the lake, the farmland and woodlands. On-site attractions include lake boating, pony trekking, karting, and for indoor amusement there's a large multi-function games room and an animal barn with many domesticated breeds. 1 acre site. 26 touring pitches. 8 hardstandings. Caravan pitches. Motorhome pitches. Tent pitches.

Open: Etr-Oct (rs Outside peak season some activities restricted) **Last arrival:** Anytime
Last departure: 14.00hrs
Pitches: * 🚐 fr £25 🚏 fr £25 ▲ fr £15
Leisure: 🎢 🔍
Facilities: 🏗️🅿️◎🖤🚿🎸🚻🍃🅾
Services: 🔌🗑️🍴🚰🛒🚽
Within 3 miles: ⚓🎈🛶🛒🖼️U
Notes: PayPal accepted. No noise after 23.00hrs, no camp fires. Dogs must be kept on leads.

BALLYMONEY	Map 1 C6

Places to visit

Bonamargy Friary, BALLYCASTLE, 028 2076 2225
www.discovernorthernireland.com/Bonamargy-Friary-Ballycastle

Great for kids: Dunluce Castle, PORTBALLINTRAE, BT57 8UY, 028 2073 1938
www.discovernorthernireland.com/Dunluce-Castle

PREMIER PARK

Drumaheglis Marina & Caravan Park
►►►►►85%

tel: 028 2766 0280 & 7034 7034 **36 Glenstall Rd BT53 7QN**
email: drumaheglis@causewaycoastandglens.gov.uk
dir: *Signed from A26, approx 1.5m from Ballymoney towards Coleraine. Also accessed from B66, S of Ballymoney.* **grid ref:** *C901254*

An exceptionally well-designed and laid out park beside the Lower Bann River. It has very spacious pitches (all fully serviced), two quality toilet blocks, a stylish reception building, which also houses a games room, IT suite, and the Slipway Café serving fresh pastries and meals. There's table tennis, picnic and BBQ areas, a grass volleyball court and a nature walk. This makes an ideal base for watersport enthusiasts and for those touring County Antrim. Five camping pods, each sleeping a maximum of four people, are available too. 16 acre site. 54 touring pitches. 54 hardstandings. 20 seasonal pitches. Caravan pitches. Motorhome pitches. Tent pitches.

Open: 17 Mar-Oct **Last arrival:** 20.00hrs **Last departure:** noon
Pitches: * 🚐 £25-£26 🚏 £25-£26 ▲ £18-£21 🏠 prices shown below
Leisure: 🎢 🔍 🎣
Facilities: 🏗️🅿️◎🖤🚿🎨🚻🚻 WiFi 🍃🅾🎯
Services: 🔌🗑️🚰🍴🚽
Glamping: Wooden Pods 5, £30-£40 Min stay 1 night Car by unit
Within 3 miles: ⚓🎈🛶🛒🖼️
Notes: Dogs must be kept on leads. Marina berths, outdoor gym.

LEISURE: 🏊 Indoor pool 🏊 Outdoor pool 🎢 Children's playground 🙌 Kid's club 🎾 Tennis court 🔍 Games room 🏌️ Golf course 🛶 Boat hire 🚲 Cycle hire 🎬 Cinema 🎵 Entertainment 🎣 Fishing ◎ Mini golf 🏌️ Pitch n putt 🛶 Watersports 🏋️ Gym 🏐 Sports field U Stables **FACILITIES:** 🛁 Bath 🚿 Shower 🅿️ Private washing cubicles ☺ Electric shaver 🖤 Hairdryer ❄️ Ice Packs 🚻 Disabled facilities 🛒 Shop on site 🏪 Mobile shop 🍴 BBQ area 🪑 Picnic area WiFi Wi-fi 💻 Internet access ♻️ Recycling 🅾 Tourist info 🐕 Dog exercise area 🎯 Car hire can be arranged

BUSHMILLS — Map 1 C6

Places to visit

Old Bushmills Distillery, BUSHMILLS, BT57 8XH, 028 2073 1521
www.bushmills.com

PREMIER PARK

Ballyness Caravan Park
▶▶▶▶▶ 92%

GOLD

tel: 028 2073 2393 **40 Castlecatt Rd BT57 8TN**
email: info@ballynesscaravanpark.com
dir: 0.5m S of Bushmills on B66, follow signs. **grid ref:** C944397

A quality park with superb toilet and other facilities, on farmland beside St Columb's Rill, the stream that supplies the famous nearby Bushmills Distillery. The friendly owners created this park with the discerning camper in mind and continue to invest year on year to enhance the customer experience. There is a pleasant walk around several ponds, and the park is peacefully located close to the beautiful north Antrim coast. There is a spacious play barn and a holiday cottage to let. 16 acre site. 50 touring pitches. 50 hardstandings. Caravan pitches. Motorhome pitches. 65 statics.

Open: 17 Mar-Oct **Last arrival:** 21.00hrs **Last departure:** noon

Pitches: * 🚐 fr £25 🚐 fr £25

Leisure: 🄰 ⊛ ⚄

Facilities: 🖙 🅿 ⊙ 🌡 ☼ & ⑤ 🖕 📶 ♻ 𝒊

Services: 🔌 ⑤ 🗑 ⌀ 🅃 🔋 🜨

Within 3 miles: ⚓ 🧭 ⑤

Notes: No skateboards or rollerblades. Dogs must be kept on leads. Library.

AA Pubs & Restaurants nearby: Bushmills Inn Hotel, BUSHMILLS, BT57 8QG, 028 2073 3000

BELFAST

DUNDONALD

Places to visit

Mount Stewart, NEWTOWNARDS, BT22 2AD, 028 4278 8387
www.nationaltrust.org.uk/mount-stewart

Giant's Ring, BELFAST, 028 9023 5000
www.discovernorthernireland.com/Giants-Ring-Belfast

Great for kids: Belfast Zoological Gardens, BELFAST, BT36 7PN, 028 9077 6277
www.belfastzoo.co.uk

DUNDONALD — Map 1 D5

Dundonald Touring Caravan Park
▶▶▶▶ 80%

tel: 028 9080 9123 & 9080 9129 **111 Old Dundonald Rd BT16 1XT**
email: sales@castlereagh.gov.uk web: www.theicebowl.com
dir: From Belfast city centre follow M3 & A20 to City Airport. Then A20 to Newtownards, follow signs to Dundonald & Ulster Hospital. At hospital right at sign for Dundonald Ice Bowl. Follow to end, turn right, Ice Bowl on left. **grid ref:** J410731

A purpose-built park in a quiet corner of Dundonald Leisure Park on the outskirts of Belfast. This peaceful park is ideally located for touring County Down and exploring the capital. In the winter it offers an 'Aire de Service' for motorhomes. 1.5 acre site. 22 touring pitches. 22 hardstandings. Caravan pitches. Motorhome pitches. Tent pitches.

Open: 14 Mar-Oct (Nov-Mar Aire de Service restricted to motorhomes & caravans with own bathroom facilities) **Last arrival:** 23.00hrs **Last departure:** noon

Pitches: * 🚐 £8.50-£23.50 🚐 £8.50-£23.50 🛆 fr £15.50

Facilities: 🖙 🅿 ⊙ 🌡 ☼ & 🏠 📶 ♻ 𝒊

Services: 🔌 ⑤ 🜨 🜨

Within 3 miles: ⚓ 🍴 🧭 ◎ ⑤ ⑤ ∪

Notes: No commercial vehicles or vans permitted (including any on tow). Dogs must be kept on leads. Bowling, indoor play area, olympic-size ice rink (additional charges apply).

See advert on page 448

PITCHES: 🚐 Caravans 🚐 Motorhomes 🛆 Tents 🏕 Glamping accommodation **SERVICES:** 🔌 Electric hook up ⑤ Launderette 🍷 Licensed bar 🔋 Calor Gas ⌀ Camping Gaz 🅃 Toilet fluid 🍴 Café/Restaurant 🍟 Fast Food/Takeaway 🔋 Battery charging 🛒 Baby care 🜨 Motorvan service point
ABBREVIATIONS: BHs – bank holidays Etr – Easter Spring BH – Spring Bank Holiday fr – from hrs – hours m – mile mdnt – midnight rdbt – roundabout rs – restricted service wk – week wknd – weekend x-roads – crossroads ⊛ No credit or debit cards ⊗ No dogs

COUNTY FERMANAGH

BELCOO
Map 1 C5

Places to visit

Florence Court, ENNISKILLEN, BT92 1DB, 028 6634 8249
www.nationaltrust.org.uk

PREMIER PARK

Rushin House Caravan Park
►►►►► 85%

tel: 028 6638 6519 **Holywell BT93 5DY**
email: enquiries@rushinhousecaravanpark.com
dir: *From Enniskillen take A4 W for 13m to Belcoo. Right onto B52 towards Garrison for 1m. Site signed.* **grid ref:** *H835047*

This park occupies a scenic location overlooking Lough MacNean, close to the picturesque village of Belcoo, and is the product of meticulous planning and execution. There are 24 very generous, fully serviced pitches standing on a terrace overlooking the lough, with additional tenting pitches below; all are accessed via well-kept, wide tarmac roads. Facilities include a lovely, well-equipped play area and a hard surface, fenced five-a-side football pitch. There is a slipway providing boat access to the lough and, of course, fishing; there is an access path to the lake that is suitable for less able visitors to use. The excellent toilet facilities are purpose-built and include family rooms. 5 acre site. 38 touring pitches. 38 hardstandings. Caravan pitches. Motorhome pitches. Tent pitches.

Open: mid Mar-Oct (rs Nov-Mar Aire de Service facilities available)
Last arrival: 21.00hrs **Last departure:** 13.00hrs

Pitches: 🚐 🚙 ▲ **Leisure:** 🎣 ⚽ **Facilities:** ☺ ℙ ⚞ ⚐ 🚿 ⚘ WiFi ♻ ❶
Services: 🖪 ⬚ 🖊 🚽 ⬚ ⬆
Within 3 miles: ⚓ ⚞ ⛵ ⬚ ⬚

Notes: No cars by tents. Dogs must be kept on leads. Lakeside walk.

IRVINESTOWN
Map 1 C5

Places to visit

Castle Coole, ENNISKILLEN, BT74 6JY, 028 6632 2690 www.nationaltrust.org.uk

Great for kids: Castle Balfour, LISNASKEA, 028 9023 5000
www.discovernorthernireland.com/Castle-Balfour-Lisnaskea-Enniskillen

Castle Archdale Caravan Park & Camping Site
►►►► 83%

tel: 028 6862 1333 **Lisnarick BT94 1PP**
email: info@castlearchdale.com **web:** www.castlearchdale.com
dir: *From Irvinestown take B534 signed Lisnarick. Left onto B82 signed Enniskillen. Approx 1m right by church, signed.* **grid ref:** *H176588*

This park is located within the grounds of Castle Archdale Country Park on the shores of Lough Erne which boasts stunning scenery, forest walks and also war and wildlife museums. The site is ideal for watersport enthusiasts with its marina and launching facilities. Also on site there's a shop, licensed restaurant, takeaway and play park. There are 56 fully serviced, hardstanding pitches. 11 acre site. 158 touring pitches. 150 hardstandings. Caravan pitches. Motorhome pitches. Tent pitches. 164 statics.

Open: Apr-Oct (rs Apr-Jun & Sep-Oct shop & bar closed weekdays) **Last departure:** noon

Pitches: ❋ 🚐 £25-£30 🚙 £25-£30 ⛺ £10-£40

Leisure: 🎣

Facilities: 🌳 🅿️ ☉ ❋ ♿ 🛁 🚻 ➕ WiFi 🅿️ 🚰

Services: 🔌 🗄️ 🍴 📦 📶 T 🍽️ 🔋 ♨️ 🚽

Within 3 miles: ⅃ ≒ ⌂ ⚓ 🛥️ 🖈 🖈 ∪

Notes: No open fires, no noise after 23.00hrs. Dogs must be kept on leads.

AA Pubs & Restaurants nearby: Lough Erne Resort, ENNISKILLEN, BT93 7ED, 028 6632 3230

COUNTY TYRONE

DUNGANNON   Map 1 C5

Places to visit

The Argory, MOY, BT71 6NA, 028 8778 4753 www.nationaltrust.org.uk

U S Grant Ancestral Homestead, BALLYGAWLEY, BT70 1TW, 028 8555 7133 www.midulstercouncil.org

Great for kids: Mountjoy Castle, MOUNTJOY, 028 9023 5000 www.ehsni.gov.uk

Dungannon Park
▶▶▶▶85%

tel: 028 8772 8690 & 03000 132132 **Moy Rd BT71 6DY**
email: parks@midulstercouncil.org
dir: M1 junct 15, A29 towards Dungannon, left at 2nd lights. **grid ref:** H805612

A modern caravan park in a quiet area of a stunning public park with a fishing lake and excellent facilities, especially for disabled visitors. There are fully serviced pitches, a modern amenities block and a coffee shop. 4 acre site. 37 touring pitches. 24 hardstandings. Caravan pitches. Motorhome pitches. Tent pitches.

Open: Mar-Oct **Last arrival:** 20.00hrs **Last departure:** 14.00hrs

Pitches: ❋ 🚐 £16.50-£20.50 🚙 £16.50-£20.50 ⛺ £12.50-£20.50

Leisure: ⛰️ 🐾 ⚽ ⌂

Facilities: 🌳 🅿️ ☉ ⌂ ❋ ♿ 🛁 🚻 WiFi ♨️ 🅿️

Services: 🔌 🗄️ 🍽️ 🔋

Within 3 miles: ⅃ ≒ 🎯 ⌂ 🖈 🖈 ∪

Notes: No noise between 22.00hrs-08.00hrs, no generators, no commercial vehicles, speed limit 10mph, no dishwashing in toilet block. Dogs must be kept on leads.

Follow the AA on twitter @TheAA_Lifestyle

REPUBLIC OF IRELAND

COUNTY CORK

BALLINSPITTLE   Map 1 B2

Garrettstown House Holiday Park
▶▶▶▶80%

tel: 021 4778156 & 4775286
email: reception@garrettstownhouse.com
dir: 6m from Kinsale, through Ballinspittle, past school & football pitch on main road to beach. Beside stone estate entrance. **grid ref:** W588445

Elevated holiday park with tiered camping areas and superb panoramic views. Plenty of on-site amenities, and close to beach and forest park. 7 acre site. 60 touring pitches. 20 hardstandings. Caravan pitches. Motorhome pitches. Tent pitches. 80 statics.

Open: 4 May-9 Sep (rs Early season-1 Jun shop closed) **Last arrival:** 22.00hrs **Last departure:** noon

Pitches: 🚐 🚙 ⛺

Leisure: 🏸 🐾 🏊 🎱 🎵

Facilities: ☉ 🅿️ ❋ ♿ 🛁 🖈 WiFi ♨️ 🅿️

Services: 🔌 🗄️ 📦 📶 T 🔋 ♨️ 🚽

Within 3 miles: ⅃ ≒ ⌂ ☉ 🛥️ 🖈 🖈 ∪

Notes: 🐕 Dogs must be kept on leads. Crazy golf, video shows, snooker, adult reading lounge, tots' playroom.

BALLYLICKEY   Map 1 B2

Eagle Point Camping
▶▶▶▶85%

tel: 027 50630
email: info@eaglepointcamping.com
dir: From Cork: N71 to Bandon, R586 to Bantry, then N71, 4m to Glengarriff, opposite petrol station. From Killarney: N22 to Macroom, R584 to Ballickey Bridge, N71 to Glengarriff. **grid ref:** V995535

An immaculate park set in an idyllic position on a headland overlooking the rugged Bantry Bay and the mountains of West Cork. There are boat launching facilities, small and safe pebble beaches, a football field, tennis court, a small playground, and TV rooms for children and adults on the park. There is an internet café in the reception and a shop and petrol station across from the park entrance. Nearby are two golf courses, riding stables, a sailing centre and cycle hire facilities. 20 acre site. 125 touring pitches. 20 hardstandings, 60 seasonal pitches. Caravan pitches. Motorhome pitches. Tent pitches.

Open: 14 Apr-18 Sep **Last arrival:** 21.00hrs **Last departure:** noon

Pitches: 🚐 €26-€29 🚙 €26-€29 ⛺ €26-€29

Leisure: 🏊 ⚽ ⌂ 🎣

Facilities: 🌳 ☉ ❋ 🛁 WiFi ♨️ 🅿️

Services: 🔌 🗄️ 🚽

Within 3 miles: ⅃ 🖈 ⌂ 🖈 🖈

Notes: 🚫 No commercial vehicles, skates, scooters or jet skis. Children not permitted to ride bikes.

AA Pubs & Restaurants nearby: Seaview House Hotel, BALLYLICKEY, 027 50073

COUNTY DONEGAL

PORTNOO
Map 1 B5

Places to visit

Glebe House & Gallery, LETTERKENNY, 074 9137071
www.heritageireland.ie/en/glebehouseandgallery/

Tower Museum, LONDONDERRY, BT48 6LU, 028 7137 2411
www.derrycity.gov.uk/museums

Boyle's Caravan Park
►► 70%

tel: 074 9545131 & 086 8523131
email: pboylecaravans@gmail.com
dir: Exit N56 at Ardra onto R261, 6m. Follow signs for Santa Anna Drive.
grid ref: G702990

This open park sits among the sand dunes overlooking Narin Beach and close to a huge selection of water activities, including wind surfing, fishing, scuba diving and kayaking on a magnificent stretch of the Atlantic on the Donegal coast. There is an 18-hole golf links, and a café and shop at the entrance to the site. The park is very well maintained by the Boyle family. 1.5 acre site. 20 touring pitches. Caravan pitches. Motorhome pitches. Tent pitches. 80 statics.

Open: 18 Mar-Oct **Last arrival:** 23.00hrs **Last departure:** 11.00hrs

Pitches: * ⊞ €25-€30 ⊟ €25-€30 ▲ €25-€30

Leisure: ⚡ ♫ ⚓

Facilities: ⬆ P⬆ ⊙ ✳ ⬆ ⬆ ⬆ ⬆ WiFi ♻ ⬆ ☎

Services: ⬆ ⬆ ⬆ ⬆ ⬆ ⬆ ⬆

Within 3 miles: ⬆ ⬆ ⬆ ⬆ ⬆ ⬆ U

Notes: ⊘ No skateboards. Dogs must be kept on leads. 1.5m Blue Flag beach.

COUNTY DUBLIN

CLONDALKIN
Map 1 D4

Places to visit

Castletown, CELBRIDGE, 01 6288252 www.heritageireland.ie/en/castletown/

Irish Museum of Modern Art, DUBLIN, 01 6129900 www.imma.ie

Great for kids: Dublin Zoo, DUBLIN, 01 4748900 www.dublinzoo.ie

Camac Valley Tourist Caravan & Camping Park
►►►► 81%

tel: 01 4640644 **Naas Rd, Clondalkin**
email: info@camacvalley.com
dir: M50 junct 9, N7 (South), exit 2, follow signs for Corkagh Park. **grid ref:** O056300

A pleasant, lightly wooded park with good facilities, security and layout, situated within an hour's drive, or a bus ride, from the city centre. 15 acre site. 163 touring pitches. 113 hardstandings. Caravan pitches. Motorhome pitches. Tent pitches.

Open: all year **Last arrival:** 22.00hrs **Last departure:** noon

Pitches: ⊞ ⊟ ▲

Leisure: ⚓

Facilities: ⊙ P ✳ ⬆ ⬆ ⬆ WiFi ♻ ⬆

Services: ⬆ ⬆ ⬆ ⬆ T ⬆ ⬆

Within 3 miles: ⬆ ⬆ ⬆ ⬆ ⬆ ⬆ U

Notes: Lights must be out by 23.00hrs. Dogs must be kept on leads.

AA Pubs & Restaurants nearby: Ashling Hotel, Dublin, DUBLIN, 01 6772324

The AA on Social Media - follow us:
twitter: @TheAA_Lifestyle
facebook: www.facebook.com/TheAAUK

Find us on
Facebook

COUNTY MAYO

CASTLEBAR — Map 1 B4

Places to visit

Westport House, WESTPORT, 098 27766 www.westporthouse.ie

Lough Lannagh Caravan Park
►►►► 80%

tel: 094 9027111 **Old Westport Rd**
email: info@loughlannagh.ie **web:** www.loughlannagh.ie
dir: *N5, N60, N84 to Castlebar. At ring road follow signs for Westport. Signs for Lough Lannagh Village on all approach roads to Westport rdbt.* **grid ref:** *M140890*

This park is part of the Lough Lannagh Village which is situated in a wooded area a short walk from Castlebar. Leisure facilities include tennis courts, boules, children's play area and a café. 2.5 acre site. 20 touring pitches. 20 hardstandings. Caravan pitches. Motorhome pitches. Tent pitches.

Open: 14 Apr-Aug **Last arrival:** 18.00hrs **Last departure:** 10.00hrs

Pitches: ⚏ €25 ⚍ €25 ▲ €25

Leisure: ◈ ◐ ◌

Facilities: ⚏ ⋔ ☉ ⌀ ✳ ⅋ ⌂ WiFi ▤ ⚙ ❂ ❷ ⚗

Services: ⚐ ⊙ ⍩

Within 3 miles: ⌁ ⋇ ☶ ⌀ ◎ ⋛ ⑨ ⑤ U

Notes: No cars by tents. Pets accepted by prior arrangement only, no pets allowed Jun-Aug. Dogs must be kept on leads. Boating classes.

AA Pubs & Restaurants nearby: Knockranny House Hotel, WESTPORT, 098 28600

KNOCK — Map 1 B4

Knock Caravan and Camping Park
►►►► 76%

tel: 094 9388100 **Claremorris Rd**
email: caravanpark@knock-shrine.ie
dir: *From rdbt in Knock, through town. Site on left in 1km, opposite petrol station.*
grid ref: *M408828*

A pleasant, very well maintained camping park within the grounds of Knock Shrine, offering spacious terraced pitches and excellent facilities. 10 acre site. 88 touring pitches. 88 hardstandings. Caravan pitches. Motorhome pitches. Tent pitches. 8 statics.

Open: last Sun Mar-1st Sun Oct **Last arrival:** 22.00hrs **Last departure:** noon

Pitches: ⚏ ⚍ ▲

Leisure: ⚲

Facilities: ☉ ⌀ ✳ ⅋ ⌂ ⍩ WiFi ❂ ❷

Services: ⚐ ⊙ ⬛ ⌀ T ⍩ ⚌ ⌄

Within 3 miles: ⌁ ⌀ ⑤ ⑥ U

Notes: Dogs must be kept on leads.

COUNTY ROSCOMMON

BOYLE — Map 1 B4

Places to visit

King House - Georgian Mansion & Military Barracks, BOYLE, 071 9663242
www.kinghouse.ie

Lough Key Caravan & Camping Park
►►► 74%

tel: 071 9662212 **Lough Key Forest Park**
email: info@loughkey.ie
dir: *3km E of Boyle on N4. Follow Lough Key Forest Park signs, site within grounds. Approx 0.5km from entrance.* **grid ref:** *G846039*

Peaceful and very secluded site within the extensive grounds of a beautiful forest park. Lough Key offers boat trips and waterside walks, and there is a viewing tower. 15 acre site. 72 touring pitches. 52 hardstandings. Caravan pitches. Motorhome pitches. Tent pitches.

Open: Apr-20 Sep **Last arrival:** 18.00hrs **Last departure:** noon

Pitches: ⚏ ⚍ ▲

Facilities: ☉ ⌀ ⌂ ⍩

Services: ⚐ ⊙

Within 3 miles: ⌁ ⋇ ⌀ ⋛ ⑤ ⑥

Notes: No cars by tents.

PITCHES: ⚏ Caravans ⚍ Motorhomes ▲ Tents ⛺ Glamping accommodation **SERVICES:** ⚐ Electric hook up ⊙ Launderette ⍩ Licensed bar
⬛ Calor Gas ⌀ Camping Gaz T Toilet fluid ⍩ Café/Restaurant ⚌ Fast Food/Takeaway ⚌ Battery charging ⚏ Baby care ⌄ Motorvan service point
ABBREVIATIONS: BHs – bank holidays Etr – Easter Spring BH – Spring Bank Holiday fr – from hrs – hours m – mile mdnt – midnight
rdbt – roundabout rs – restricted service wk – week wknd – weekend x-roads – crossroads ⊘ No credit or debit cards ⊗ No dogs

COUNTY MAPS

England

1 Bedfordshire
2 Berkshire
3 Bristol
4 Buckinghamshire
5 Cambridgeshire
6 Greater Manchester
7 Herefordshire
8 Hertfordshire
9 Leicestershire
10 Northamptonshire
11 Nottinghamshire
12 Rutland
13 Staffordshire
14 Warwickshire
15 West Midlands
16 Worcestershire

Scotland

17 City of Glasgow
18 Clackmannanshire
19 East Ayrshire
20 East Dunbartonshire
21 East Renfrewshire
22 Perth & Kinross
23 Renfrewshire
24 South Lanarkshire
25 West Dunbartonshire

Wales

26 Blaenau Gwent
27 Bridgend
28 Caerphilly
29 Denbighshire
30 Flintshire
31 Merthyr Tydfil
32 Monmouthshire
33 Neath Port Talbot
34 Newport
35 Rhondda Cynon Taff
36 Torfaen
37 Vale of Glamorgan
38 Wrexham

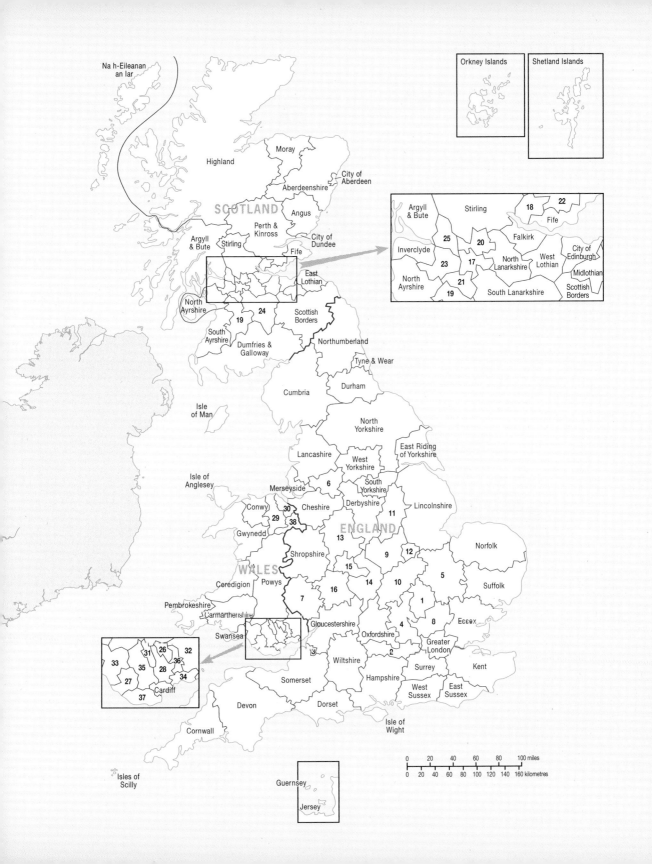

Na h-Eileanan
an Iar

Orkney Islands

Shetland Islands

Highland

Moray

City of Aberdeen

Aberdeenshire

SCOTLAND

Angus

Perth & Kinross

City of Dundee

Argyll & Bute

Stirling

Fife

East Lothian

Argyll & Bute

Stirling

18

22

Fife

25

20

Falkirk

Inverclyde

23

17

North Lanarkshire

West Lothian

City of Edinburgh

North Ayrshire

21

Midlothian

19

South Lanarkshire

Scottish Borders

North Ayrshire

19

24

Scottish Borders

South Ayrshire

Dumfries & Galloway

Northumberland

Tyne & Wear

Isle of Man

Cumbria

Durham

North Yorkshire

Lancashire

West Yorkshire

East Riding of Yorkshire

Isle of Anglesey

Merseyside

6

South Yorkshire

Lincolnshire

Conwy

30

Cheshire

Derbyshire

29

38

11

Gwynedd

13

Norfolk

ENGLAND

Shropshire

9

12

Ceredigion

Powys

15

14

10

5

Suffolk

WALES

16

7

1

Pembrokeshire

Carmarthenshire

Gloucestershire

4

8

Essex

Swansea

3

Oxdordshire

2

Greater London

31

26

32

Wiltshire

Surrey

Kent

33

35

28

36

34

Somerset

Hampshire

27

Cardiff

37

West Sussex

East Sussex

Devon

Dorset

Isle of Wight

Cornwall

Isles of Scilly

Guernsey

Jersey

0 20 40 60 80 100 miles

0 20 40 60 80 100 120 140 160 kilometres

KEY TO ATLAS

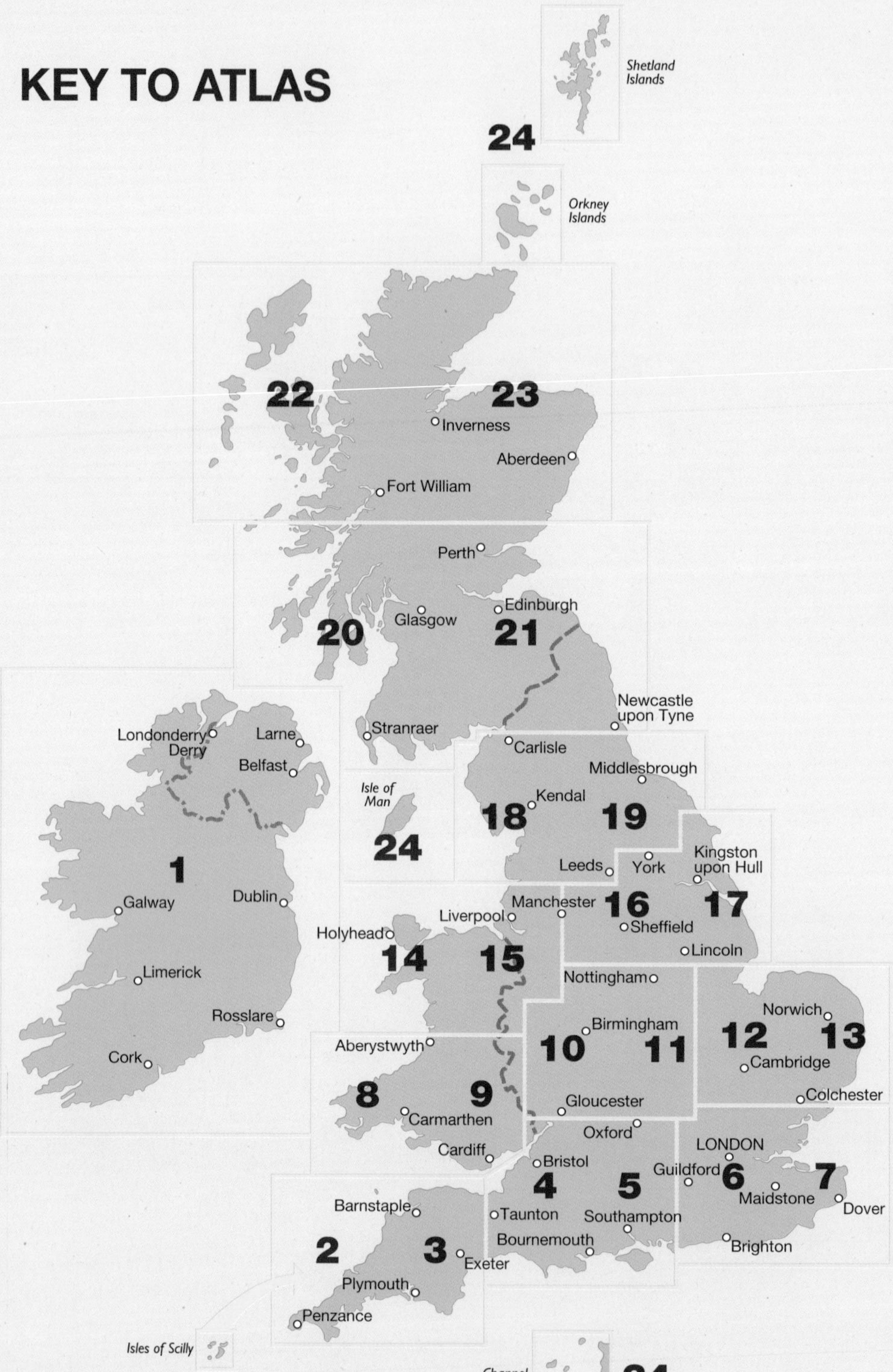

Shetland Islands

24

Orkney Islands

22

Inverness

23

Aberdeen

Fort William

Perth

20

Glasgow

Edinburgh

21

Stranraer

Newcastle upon Tyne

Londonderry Derry

Larne

Belfast

Carlisle

Middlesbrough

Isle of Man

Kendal

18

19

24

Leeds

York

Kingston upon Hull

1

Galway

Dublin

Holyhead

Liverpool

Manchester

16

17

Sheffield

Lincoln

Limerick

Nottingham

Rosslare

Aberystwyth

14

15

Birmingham

Norwich

Cork

8

9

10

11

12

13

Cambridge

Carmarthen

Gloucester

Colchester

Cardiff

Oxford

LONDON

Guildford

6

Bristol

5

7

Barnstaple

4

Taunton

Southampton

Maidstone

Dover

2

3

Bournemouth

Brighton

Exeter

Plymouth

Penzance

Isles of Scilly

Channel Islands

24

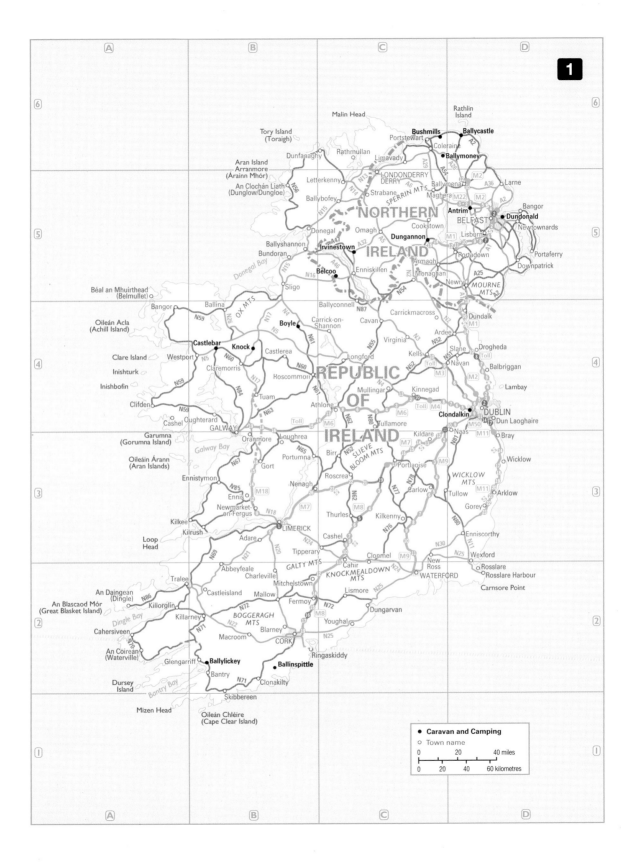

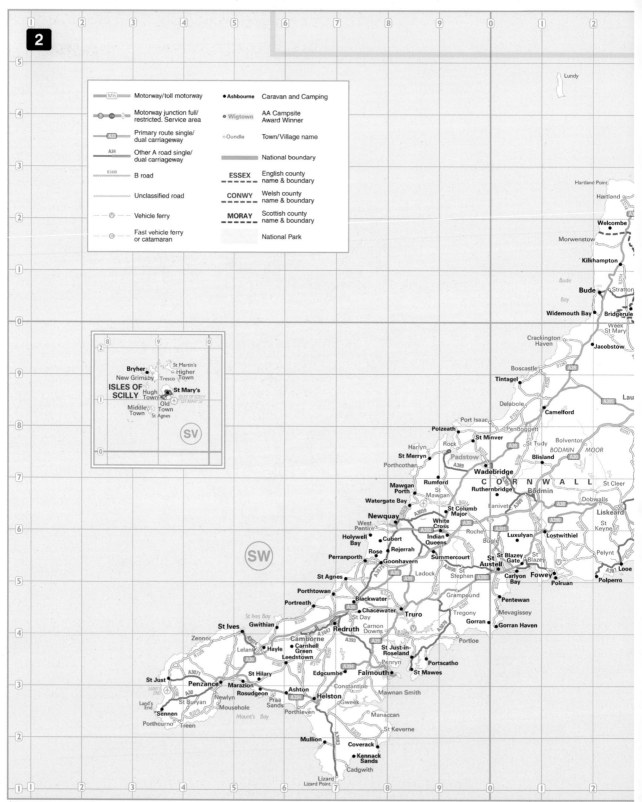

Motorway/toll motorway
Motorway junction full/ restricted. Service area
Primary route single/ dual carriageway
Other A road single/ dual carriageway
B road
Unclassified road
Vehicle ferry
Fast vehicle ferry or catamaran

• Ashbourne — Caravan and Camping
• Wigtown — AA Campsite Award Winner
○ Oundle — Town/Village name
National boundary
ESSEX — English county name & boundary
CONWY — Welsh county name & boundary
MORAY — Scottish county name & boundary
National Park

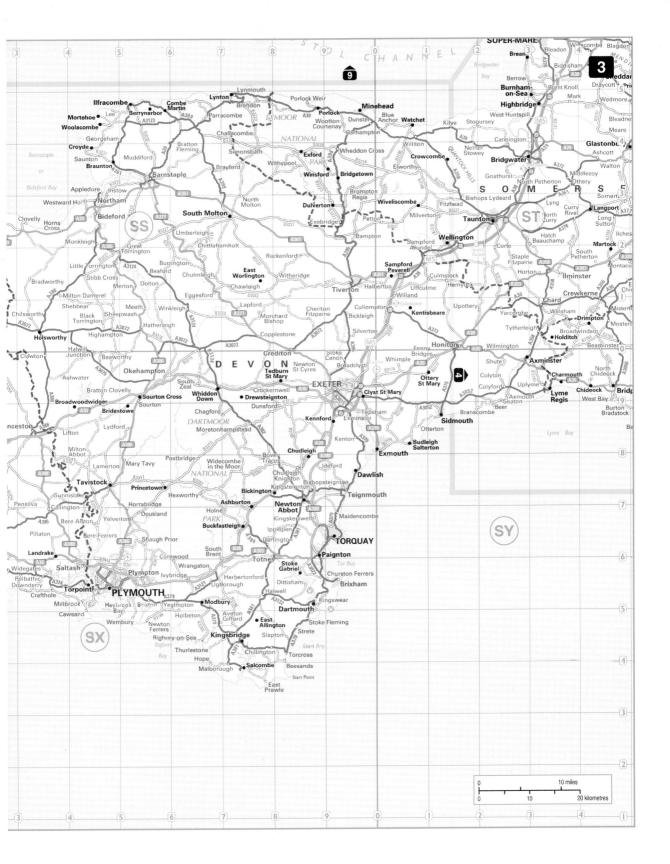

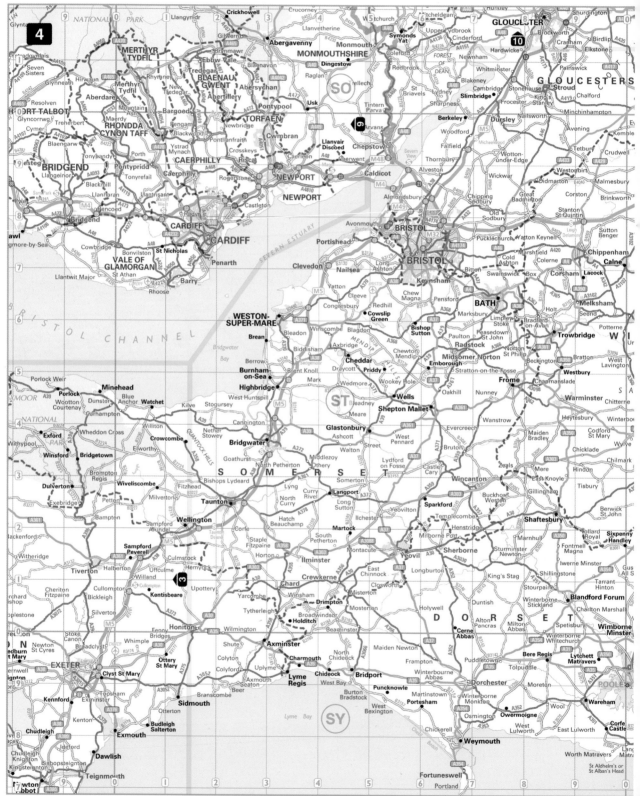

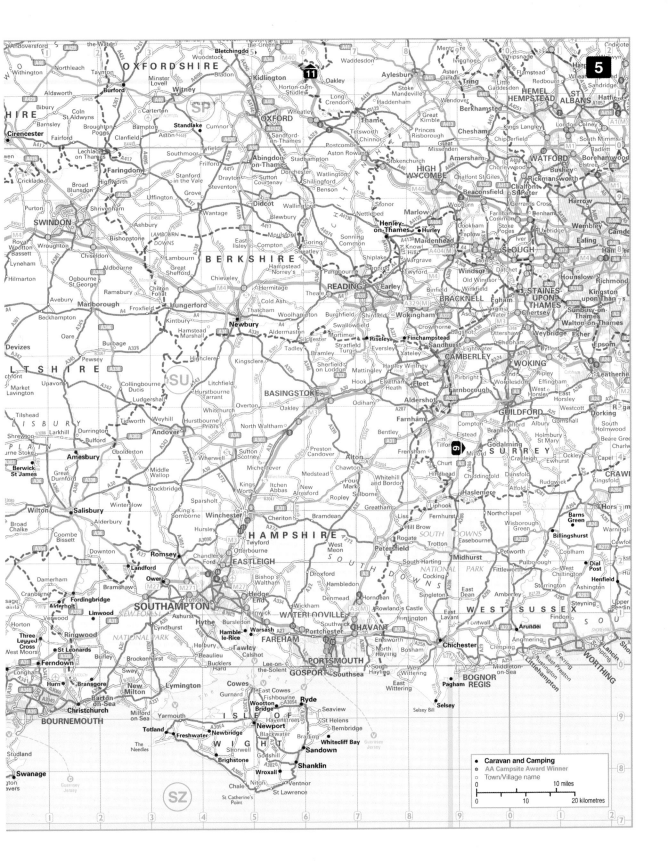

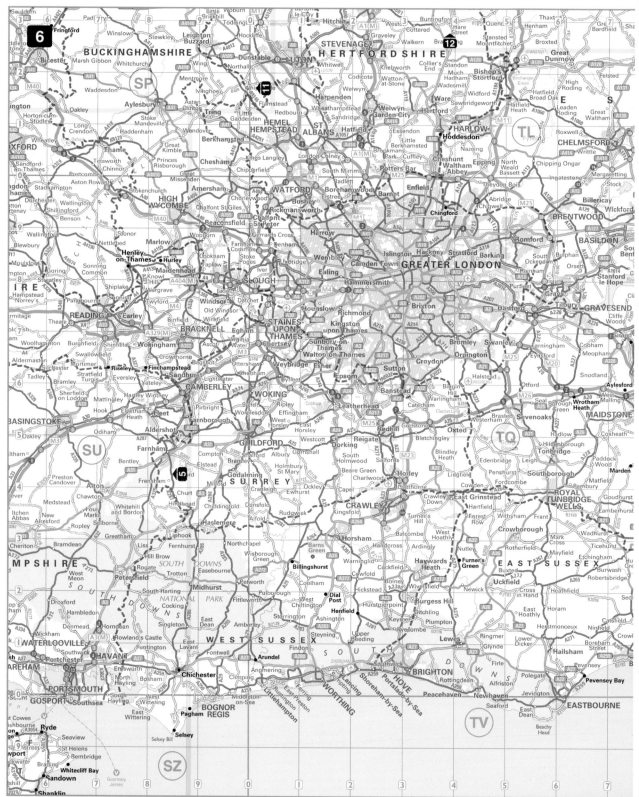

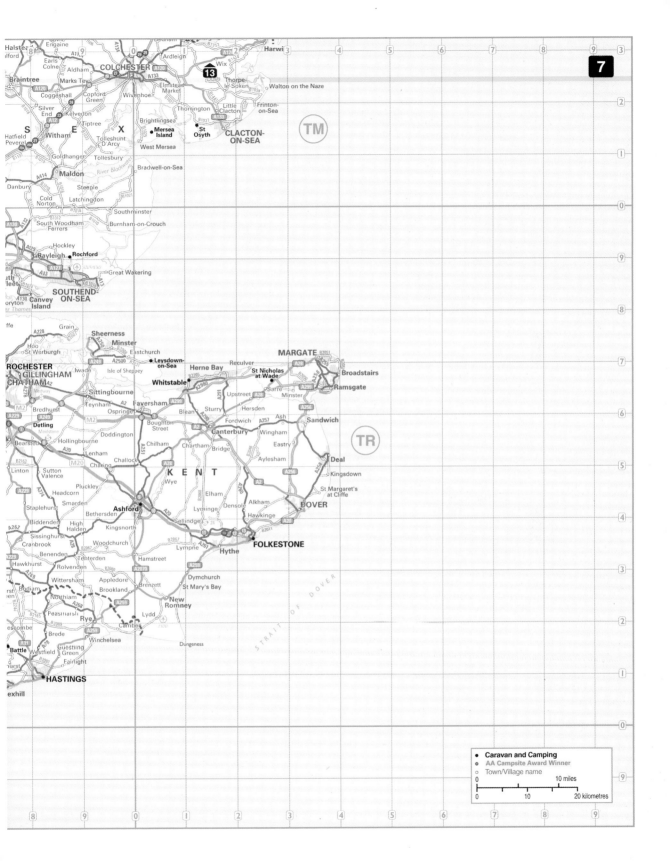

Aberdyfi

Borth

Llandre

Aberystwyth

Llanfarian

Llanrhystud

Llansantffraid

Aberarth

C E R E D

New
Quay **Aberaeron**

CARDIGAN

BAY

Liangranog

Aberporth Temple
Bar

Talgarreg Lampeter

St
Dogmaels **Cardigan** Blaenporth

Llechryd Rhydowen

SM

Nevern **Newcastle
Emlyn** Llandysul

Strumble Head Llangeler **SN**

Goodwick Newport Eglwyswrw Talley

Fishguard PEMBROKESHIRE COAST Cynwyl
NATIONAL PARK Elfed Brechfa

Letterston MYNYDD PRESELI

St David's
Head Wolf's
Castle

St Davids Solva **PEMBROKESHIRE** Llandissilio **C A R M A R T H E N S H I R E**

Newgale Roch Nantgaredig

St Brides
Bay Robeston
Wathen **Carmarthen** Llanarthne

PEMBROKESHIRE
COAST
NATIONAL PARK Narberth Whitland St Clears Llanddarog Cross Hands

**Broad
Haven** **Haverfordwest** Red
Roses **Laugharne** Llansteffan Pontyberem

Johnston Pontyates

Marloes **Hasguard
Cross** Kilgetty Amroth Carmarthen Kidwelly

Dale **Milford
Haven** Neyland Pendine Bay Pont Ab... **SWA**

Angle Pembroke
Dock Carew Saundersfoot Pembrey **Pontarddulais**

Castlemartin **Pembroke** St
Florence **Tenby** Pwll **M4**
Burry **Llangennech**
Port **Llanelli** **Gorseinon**

Manorbier Penally Gowerton

Bosherston Manorbier Dunvant **SWA**

Llanrhidian

Llangennith Oldwalls Reynoldston

Rhossili Bishopston

Worms
Head Oxwich

**Port
Einon**

SR **SS**

Lundy

Ilfracombe Combe
artin

● **Caravan and Camping**
◉ AA Campsite Award Winner
○ Town/Village name
0   10 miles
0   10   20 kilometres

Lee Berrynarbor

Mortehoe

For continuation pages refer to numbered arrows

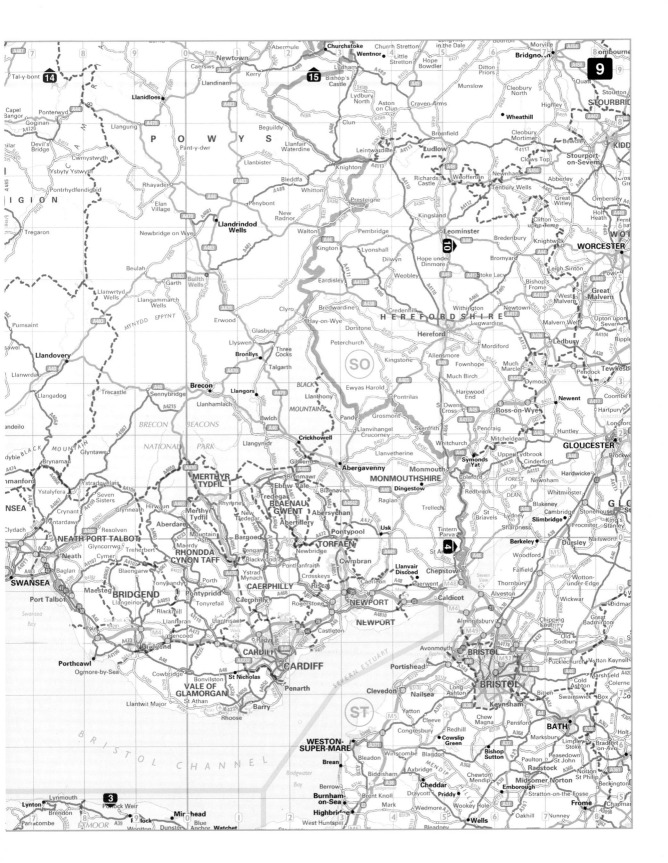

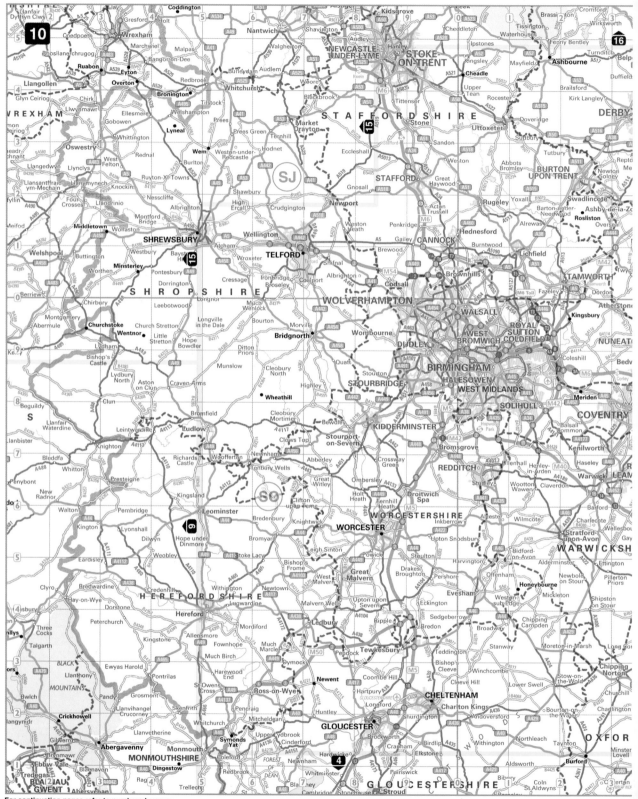

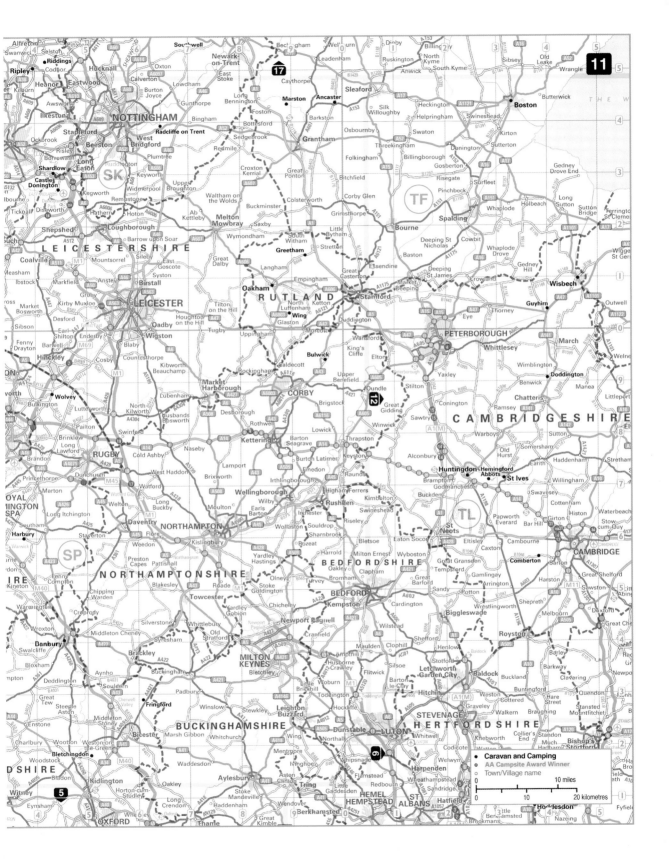

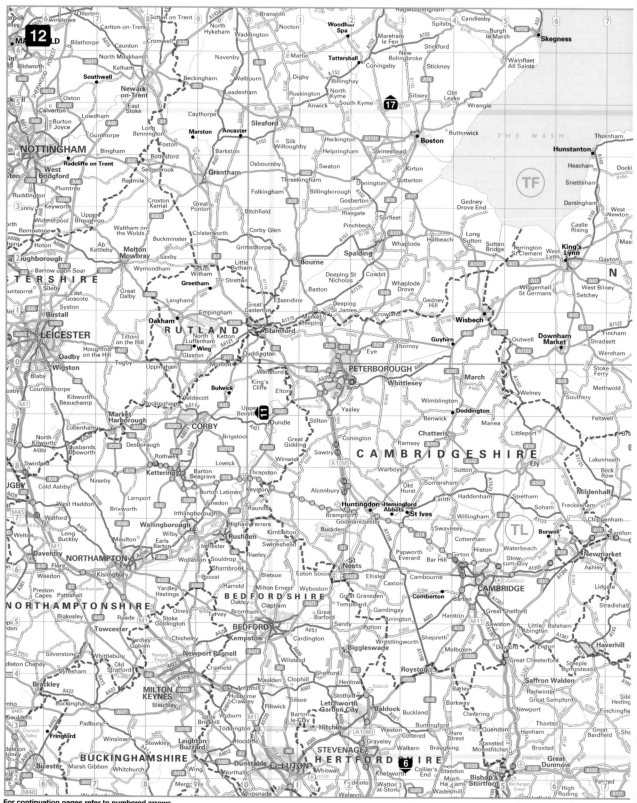

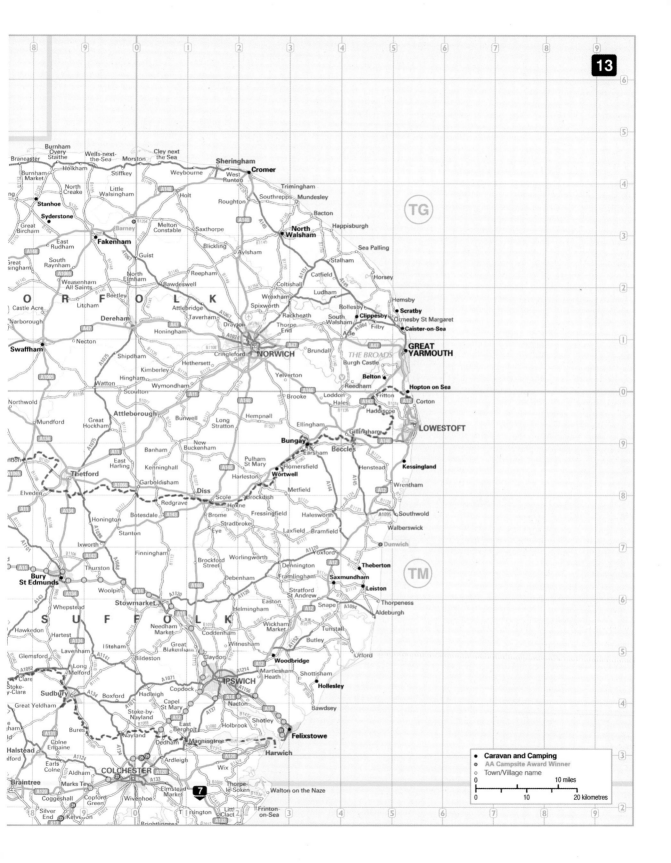

ISLE OF
ANGLESEY

Cemaes
Amlwch
Dulas
Rhôs Lligwy
Marian-Glas
Holyhead
Llanfachraeth
Llanerchymedd
Benllech
Red Wharf
Bay
Pentraeth
Trearddur Bay
Langefni
Llangoed
Holy
Island
Rhosneigr
Menai
Bridge
Bangor
Beaumaris
Llanfairfechan
Aberffraw
Llantair
P G
Llanllechid
Bethesda
Newborough
Y Felinheli
Llandudno
Deganwy
Rhôs-
on-Sea
Colwyn Bay
Rhyl
Conwy
Llanddulas
Abergele
Penmaenmawr
Llansanffraid
Glan Conwy
Betws-yn-Rhos
Llannefydd
Tal-y-Cafn
Tal-y-Bont
Trefriw
Llanrwst
Llanfair
Talhaiarn
Llansannan
Langernyw
Bylchau
CONWY
Caernarfon
Bontnewydd
Llanrug
Llanberis
Capel Curig
Llanwnda
Betws
Garmon
Llandwrog
Dinas Dinlle
Caernarfon
Bay
Penygroes
Rhyd Ddu
Betws-y-Coed
Dolwyddelan
Penmachno
Pentrefoelas
Cerrigydrudion
Clynnog-fawr
Beddgelert
Blaenau Ffestiniog
Y Maerdy
SH
Llanaelhaearn
Prenteg
Ffestiniog
Morfa Nefyn
Nefyn
PENINSULA
Tremadog
Maentwrog
Llandderfel
Bodfuan
Llanystumdwy
Porthmadog
Penrhyndeudraeth
Bala
LLEYN
Criccieth
Borth-y-Gest
Talsarnau
Trawsfynydd
SNOWDONIA
Sarn
Pwllheli
Harlech
GWYNEDD
NATIONAL
Llanbedrog
Llanuwchllyn
PARK
Aberdaron
Y Rhiw
Abersoch
Llanbedr
Ganllwyd
Llan
Bardsey
Island
Dyffryn Ardudwy
Tal-y-bont
Barmouth
Dolgellau
Dinas-Mawddwy
Fairbourne
Mallwyd
Llangadfan
Llwyngwril
Corris
Cemmaes
Road
Llanbrynmair
Bryncrug
Tywyn
Pennal
Machynlleth
Carno
Aberdyfi
SN
Borth
Tal-y-bont
Llandre
9
Llanidloes
Aberystwyth
Capel
Bangor
Ponterwyd

● Caravan and Camping
● AA Campsite Award Winner
○ Town/Village name
0   10 miles
0   10   20 kilometres

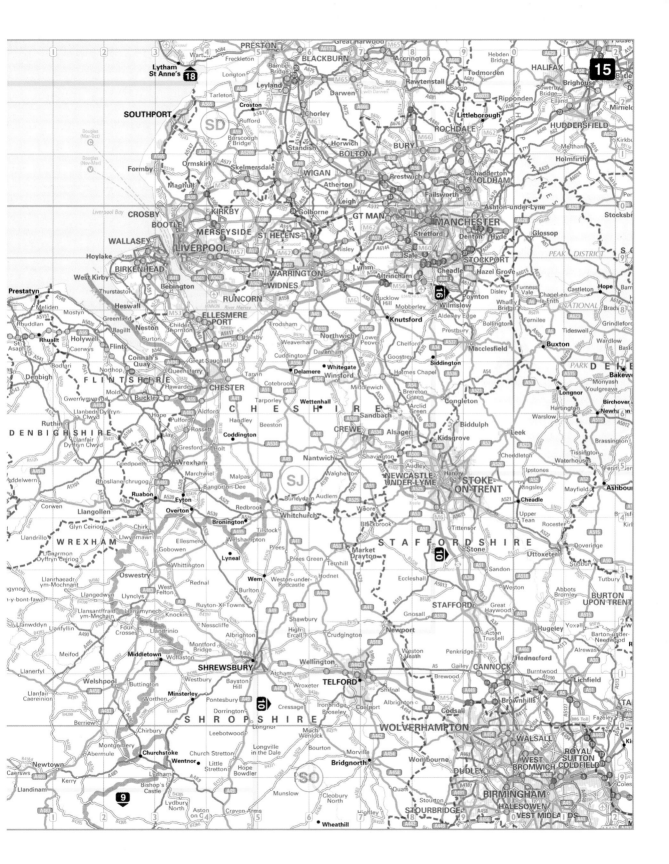

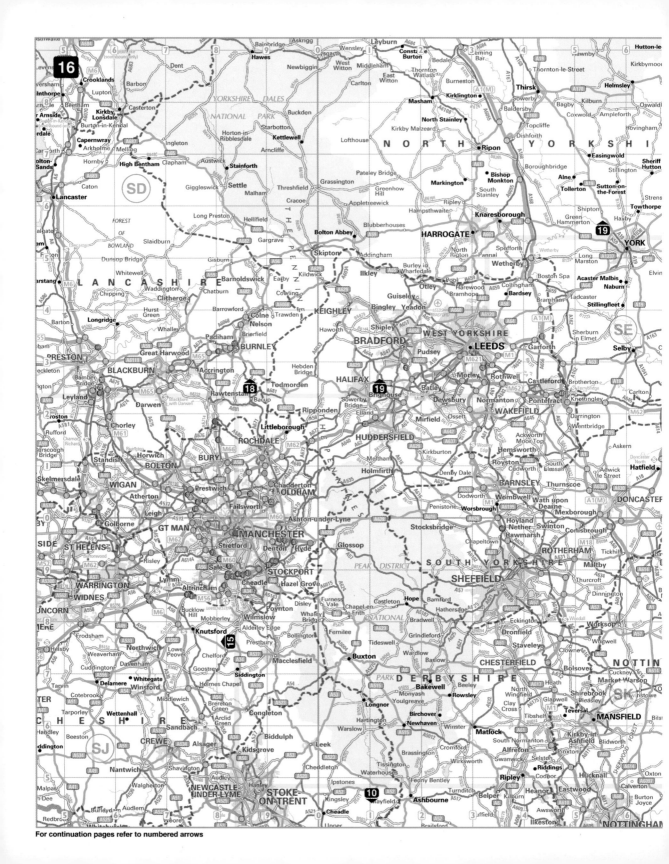

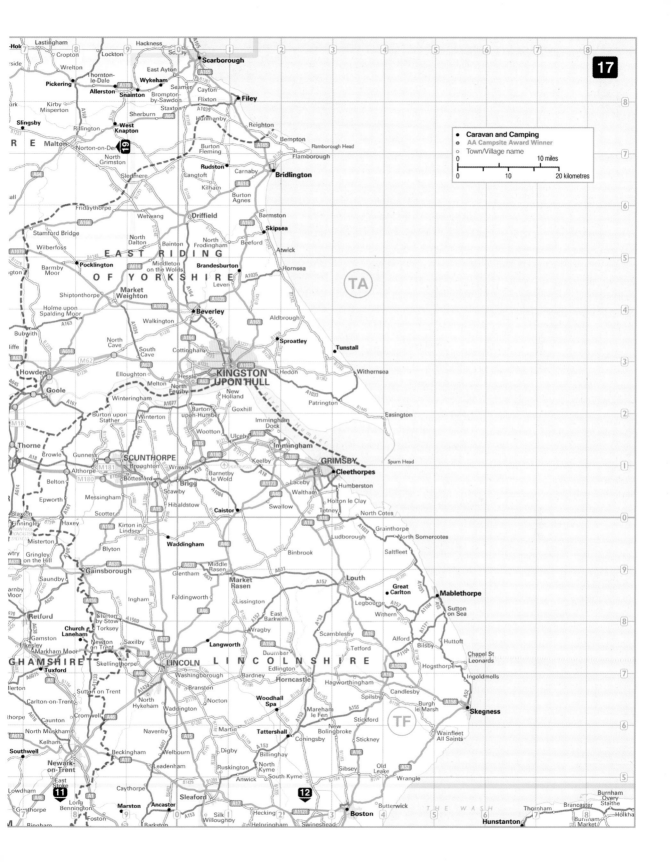

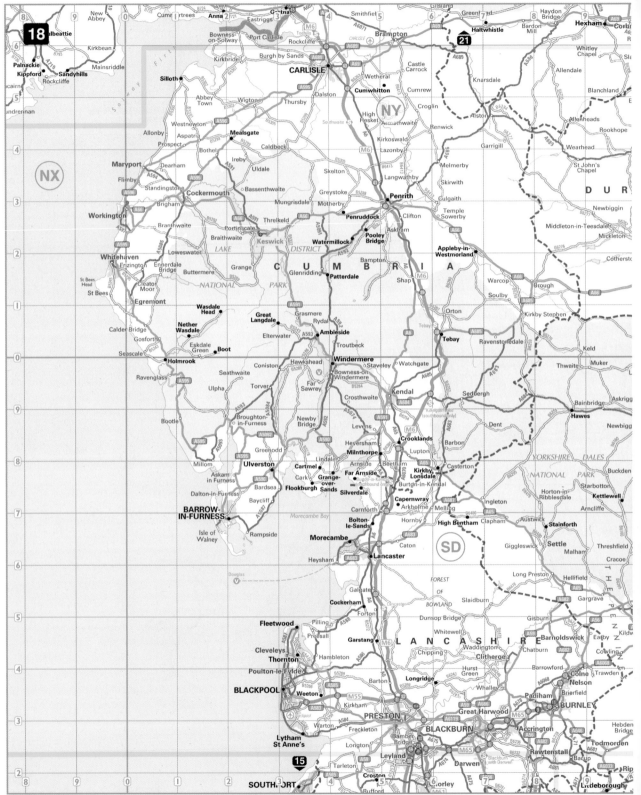

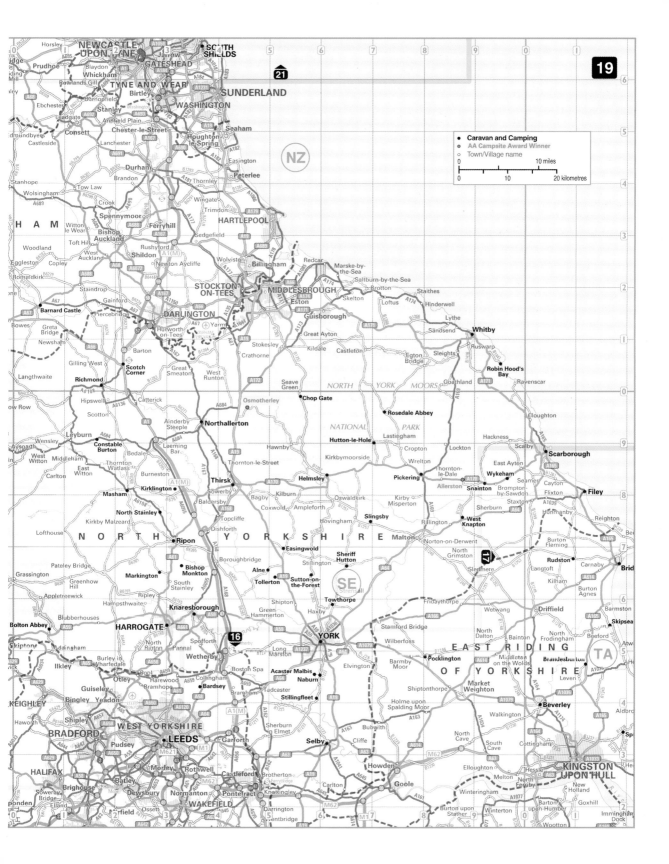

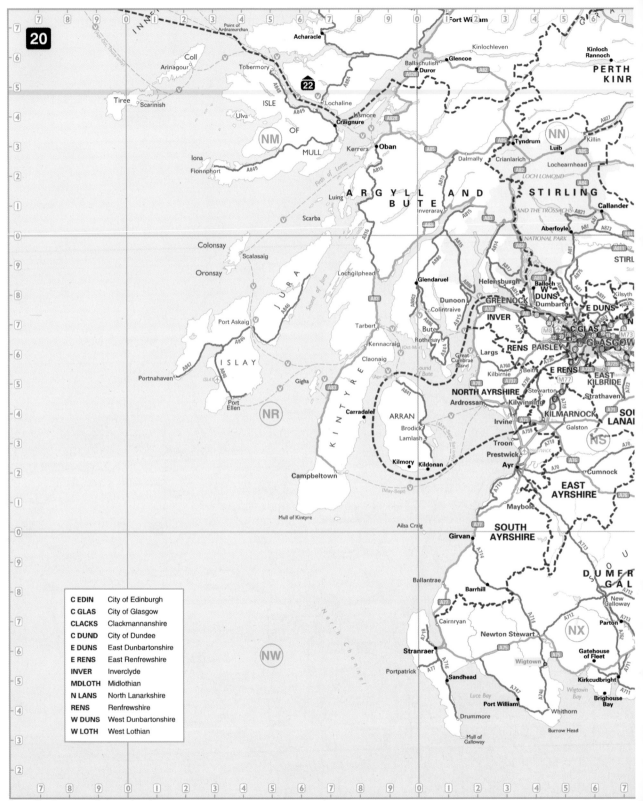

	C EDIN	City of Edinburgh
	C GLAS	City of Glasgow
	CLACKS	Clackmannanshire
	C DUND	City of Dundee
	E DUNS	East Dunbartonshire
	E RENS	East Renfrewshire
	INVER	Inverclyde
	MDLOTH	Midlothian
	N LANS	North Lanarkshire
	RENS	Renfrewshire
	W DUNS	West Dunbartonshire
	W LOTH	West Lothian

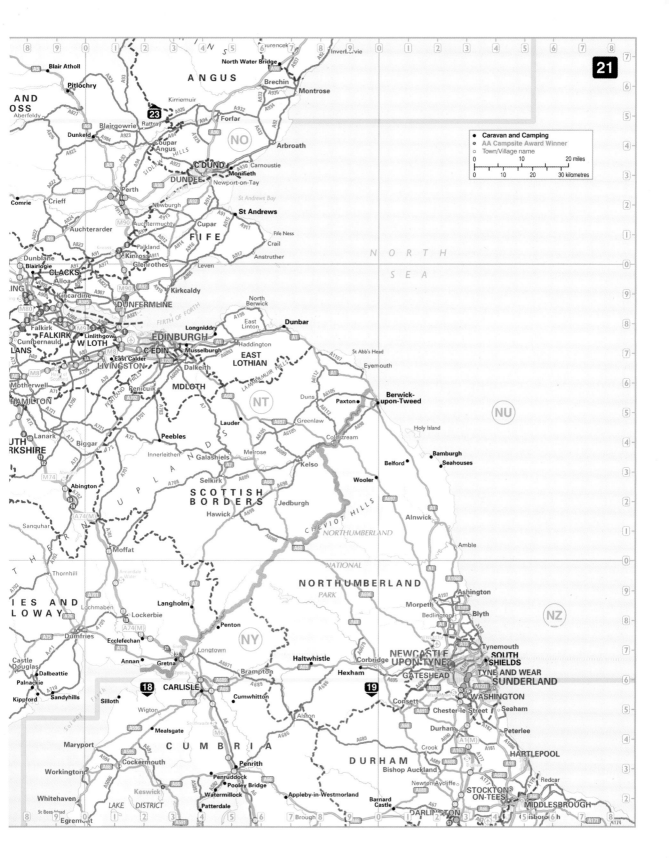

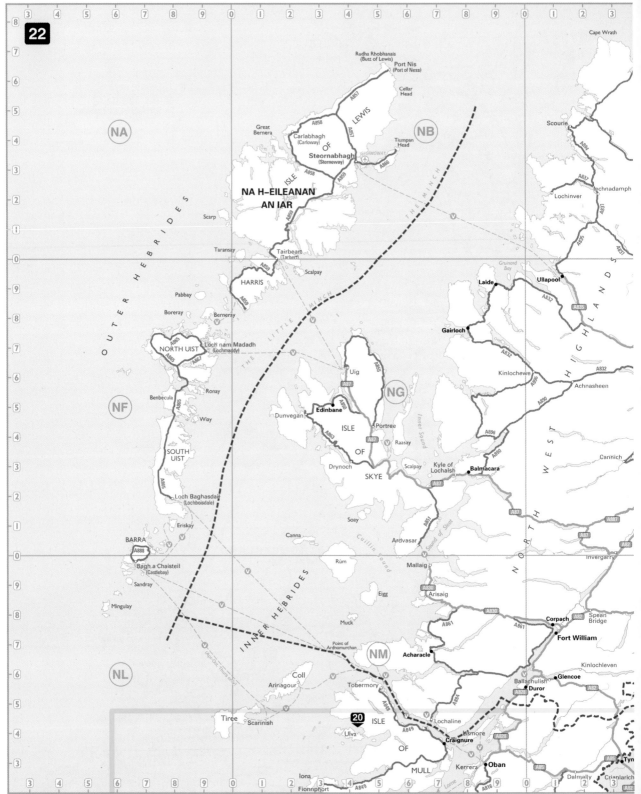

For continuation pages refer to numbered arrows

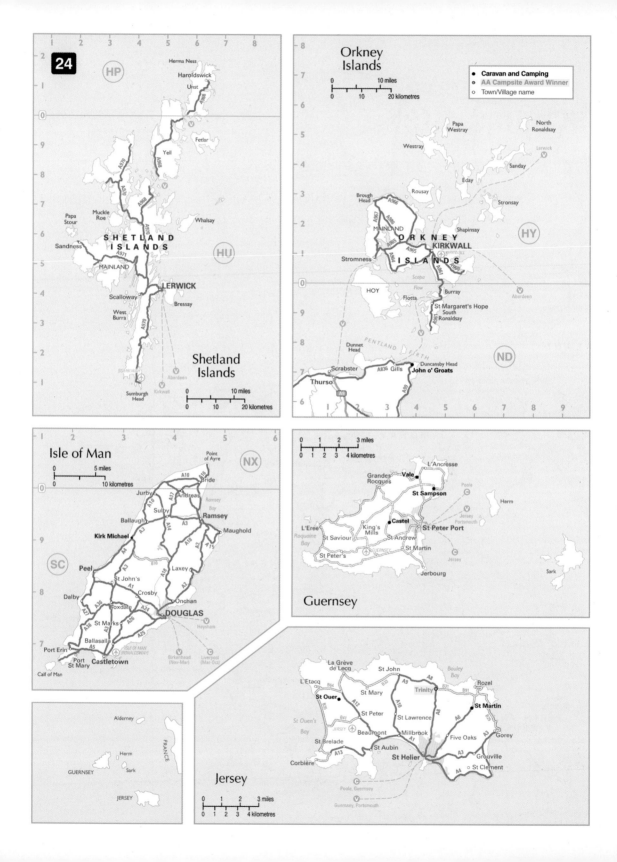

24

HP

Herma Ness
Haroldswick
Unst
A968
Fetlar
Yell
A970
A968
A968
Muckle
Roe
Papa
Stour
WHalsay
A970
A971
SHETLAND
ISLANDS
Sandness
MAINLAND
HU
Scalloway
LERWICK
Bressay
West
Burra
A970
SUMBURGH
Sumburgh
Head
Aberdeen
Kirkwall
Shetland
Islands
0   10 miles
0   10   20 kilometres

**Orkney
Islands**

● Caravan and Camping
◉ AA Campsite Award Winner
○ Town/Village name

0   10 miles
0   10   20 kilometres

Papa
Westray
North
Ronaldsay
Westray
Lerwick
Sanday
V
Rousay
Eday
Stronsay
Brough
Head
A966
Shapinsay
A967
A986
MAINLAND
ORKNEY
A965
KIRKWALL
A965
HY
A986
I S L A N D S
Stromness
A965
A960
A961
HOY
Scapa
Flow
Burray
Flotta
Aberdeen
V
St Margaret's Hope
South
Ronaldsay
A961
ND
Dunnet
Head
PENTLAND   FIRTH
Scrabster
A836   Gills
Duncansby Head
John o' Groats
Thurso
A9
A99

Isle of Man

Point
of Ayre
NX
0   5 miles
0   10 miles
Bride
A10
A16
Jurby
A10
Andreas
A17
Ramsey
Bay
Sulby
A18
A3
Ramsey
Ballaugh
A3
A14
Maughold
Kirk Michael
A4
A18
A2
A15
SC
B10
A1
Laxey
Peel
St John's
A18
Crosby
A2
Dalby
A36
Foxdale
A24
Onchan
A27
A5
DOUGLAS
St Marks
A26
A25
Ballasalla
A3
Heysham
Port Erin
A5
ISLE OF MAN
(DOUGLAS)
Birkenhead
(Nov-Mar)
Liverpool
(Mar-Oct)
Port
St Mary
Castletown
Calf of Man

0   1   2   3 miles
0 1 2 3 4 kilometres
L'Ancresse
Grandes
Rocques
Vale
St Sampson
Poole
C
Herm
Castel
L'Eree
King's
Mills
St Peter Port
Jersey
Portsmouth
Vazon
Bay
St Saviour
St Andrew
Jersey
St Peter's
St Martin
Sark
St Ouen's
Bay
Jerbourg
Guernsey

Alderney
FRANCE
Herm
Sark
GUERNSEY
JERSEY

La Grève
de Lecq
St John
Bouley
Bay
L'Etacq
B64
St Mary
B33
A9
A8
Rozel
B31
St Ouer
A12
St Peter
A10
Trinity
B91
B41
St Lawrence
A8
St Martin
St Ouen's
Bay
JERSEY
Beaumont
Millbrook
A8
A3
Five Oaks
St Brelade
A1
Gorey
St Aubin
A3
Grouville
St Helier
A4
St Clement
A13
Corbière
C
Poole, Guernsey
V
Guernsey, Portsmouth

Jersey
0   1   2   3 miles
0 1 2 3 4 kilometres

Glamping sites

These campsites offer one or more types of glamping accommodation, i.e. wooden pods, tipis, yurts, bell tents, safari tents, shepherd's huts, geo domes and vintage caravans.

ENGLAND

BERKSHIRE

FINCHAMPSTEAD
California Chalet & Touring Park

CAMBRIDGESHIRE

DODDINGTON
Fields End Water Caravan Park & Fishery

CORNWALL

BLISLAND
South Penquite Farm

BUDE
Widemouth Fields Caravan & Camping Park

CARLYON BAY
East Crinnis Camping & Caravan Park

CRANTOCK
Trevella Park

HAYLE
St Ives Bay Holiday Park

HELSTON
Poldown Caravan Park

HOLYWELL BAY
Trevornick

KILKHAMPTON
Upper Tamar Lake

LANDRAKE
Dolbeare Park Caravan and Camping

LOOE
Looe Country Park
Tregoad Park

NEWQUAY
Hendra Holiday Park
Porth Beach Holiday Park

PERRANPORTH
Perran Sands Holiday Park
Tollgate Farm Caravan & Camping Park

PORTREATH
Tehidy Holiday Park

RUTHERNBRIDGE
Ruthern Valley Holidays

ST AUSTELL
Meadow Lakes Holiday Park

ST MARY'S
Garrison Campsite

ST MINVER
Gunvenna Holiday Park

WADEBRIDGE
Lowarth Glamping
St Mabyn Holiday Park

CUMBRIA

AMBLESIDE
Low Wray National Trust Campsite

APPLEBY-IN-WESTMORLAND
Wild Rose Park

BOOT
Eskdale Camping & Caravanning Club Site

GREAT LANGDALE
Great Langdale National Trust Campsite

KESWICK
Castlerigg Hall Caravan & Camping Park

KIRKBY LONSDALE
Woodclose Caravan Park

MILNTHORPE
Hall More Caravan Park

NETHER WASDALE
Church Stile Farm & Holiday Park

PENRITH
Lowther Holiday Park

PENTON
Twin Willows

POOLEY BRIDGE
Waterfoot Caravan Park

SILLOTH
Stanwix Park Holiday Centre

WASDALE HEAD
Wasdale Head National Trust Campsite

WATERMILLOCK
The Quiet Site
Ullswater Holiday Park

WINDERMERE
Park Cliffe Camping & Caravan Estate

DERBYSHIRE

RIPLEY
Golden Valley Caravan & Camping Park

ROSLISTON
Beehive Woodland Lakes

DEVON

BERRYNARBOR
Mill Park Touring Caravan & Camping Park

CLYST ST MARY
Crealy Meadows Caravan and Camping Park

COMBE MARTIN
Newberry Valley Park

CROYDE
Bay View Farm Caravan & Camping Park

DAWLISH
Lady's Mile Holiday Park

ILFRACOMBE
Hele Valley Holiday Park

Glamping sites *continued*

KENTISBEARE
Forest Glade Holiday Park

OTTERY ST MARY
Cuckoo Down Farm Glamping

PAIGNTON
Whitehill Country Park

SIDMOUTH
Kings Down Tail Caravan & Camping Park
Oakdown Country Holiday Park

SOURTON CROSS
Bundu Camping & Caravan Park

TAVISTOCK
Harford Bridge Holiday Park
Langstone Manor Camping & Caravan Park
Woodovis Park

WELCOMBE
Koa Tree Camp

DORSET

ALDERHOLT
Hill Cottage Farm Camping and Caravan Park

BERE REGIS
Rowlands Wait Touring Park

BRIDPORT
Graston Copse Holiday Park
Highlands End Holiday Park

CHARMOUTH
Newlands Holidays

CHIDEOCK
Golden Cap Holiday Park

CORFE CASTLE
Woodyhyde Camp Site

FERNDOWN
St Leonards Farm Caravan & Camping Park

HOLDITCH
Crafty Camping

LYME REGIS
Shrubbery Touring Park

POOLE
South Lytchett Manor Caravan & Camping Park

ST LEONARDS
Back of Beyond Touring Park

SHAFTESBURY
Dorset Country Holidays

SWANAGE
Herston Caravan & Camping Park
Ulwell Cottage Caravan Park

THREE LEGGED CROSS
Woolsbridge Manor Farm Caravan Park

WEYMOUTH
Seaview Holiday Park

WIMBORNE MINSTER
Charris Camping & Caravan Park

HAMPSHIRE

FORDINGBRIDGE
Sandy Balls Holiday Village

HERTFORDSHIRE

HODDESDON
Lee Valley Caravan Park Dobbs Weir

ISLE OF WIGHT

BRIGHSTONE
Grange Farm

NEWPORT
Wight Glamping Holidays

RYDE
Roebeck Country Park

WHITECLIFF BAY
Whitecliff Bay Holiday Park

KENT

AYLESFORD
Kits Coty Glamping

MARDEN
Tanner Farm Touring Caravan & Camping Park

WHITSTABLE
Homing Park

LANCASHIRE

BOLTON LE SANDS
Bay View Holiday Park

CROSTON
Royal Umpire Caravan Park

FAR ARNSIDE
Hollins Farm Camping & Caravanning

SILVERDALE
Silverdale Caravan Park

THORNTON
Kneps Farm Holiday Park

LINCOLNSHIRE

LANGWORTH
Barlings Country Holiday Park

TATTERSHALL
Tattershall Lakes Country Park

WOODHALL SPA
Woodhall Country Park

LONDON

E4, CHINGFORD
Lee Valley Campsite

N9, EDMONTON
Lee Valley Camping & Caravan Park

NORFOLK

BELTON
Rose Farm Touring & Camping Park
Swallow Park Leisure
Wild Duck Holiday Park

GREAT YARMOUTH
Vauxhall Holiday Park

HUNSTANTON
Searles Leisure Resort

KING'S LYNN
King's Lynn Caravan and Camping Park

NORTHUMBERLAND

BAMBURGH
Waren Caravan & Camping Park

BELLINGHAM
Bellingham Camping & Caravanning Club Site

BERWICK-UPON-TWEED
Ord House Country Park

HALTWHISTLE
Herding Hill Farm, Glamping Site

WOOLER
Riverside Leisure Park

NOTTINGHAMSHIRE
TEVERSAL
Teversal Camping & Caravanning Club Site

OXFORDSHIRE
FRINGFORD
Glebe Leisure

HENLEY-ON-THAMES
Swiss Farm Touring & Camping

SHROPSHIRE
WEM
Lower Lacon Caravan Park

SOMERSET
BREAN
Holiday Resort Unity

BURNHAM-ON-SEA
Burnham-on-Sea Holiday Village

DULVERTON
Wimbleball Lake

GLASTONBURY
Middlewick Farm
The Old Oaks Touring Park

MARTOCK
Southfork Caravan Park

STAFFORDSHIRE
LONGNOR
Longnor Wood Holiday Park

SUFFOLK
HOLLESLEY
Run Cottage Touring Park

SUSSEX, WEST
BARNS GREEN
Sumners Ponds Fishery & Campsite

CHICHESTER
Concierge Glamping
Plush Tents Glamping

WILTSHIRE
BERWICK ST JAMES
Stonehenge Campsite & Glamping Pods

YORKSHIRE, EAST RIDING OF
BRANDESBURTON
Dacre Lakeside Park

SPROATLEY
Burton Constable Holiday Park & Arboretum

TUNSTALL
Sand le Mere Holiday Village

YORKSHIRE, NORTH
ALNE
Alders Caravan Park

CHOP GATE
Lordstones Country Park

FILEY
Flower of May Holiday Park

KETTLEWELL
Kettlewell Camping

KIRKLINGTON
Camp Kátur

MASHAM
Old Station Holiday Park

NORTHALLERTON
Otterington Park

RICHMOND
Brompton Caravan Park

ROBIN HOOD'S BAY
Grouse Hill Caravan Park
Middlewood Farm Holiday Park

ROSEDALE ABBEY
Rosedale Caravan & Camping Park

SCARBOROUGH
Jacobs Mount Caravan Park

THIRSK
Hillside Caravan Park

WYKEHAM
St Helens Caravan Park

CHANNEL ISLANDS

GUERNSEY
VALE
La Bailloterie Camping

JERSEY
ST MARTIN
Beuvelande Camp Site
Rozel Camping Park

ST OUEN
Daisy Cottage Campsite

TRINITY
Durrell Wildlife Camp

SCOTLAND

ARGYLL & BUTE
OBAN
Oban Caravan & Camping Park

DUMFRIES & GALLOWAY
BRIGHOUSE BAY
Brighouse Bay Holiday Park

ECCLEFECHAN
Hoddom Castle Caravan Park

GATEHOUSE OF FLEET
Auchenlarie Holiday Park

KIRKCUDBRIGHT
Seaward Caravan Park

Glamping sites *continued*

PALNACKIE
Barlochan Caravan Park

SANDYHILLS
Sandyhills Bay Leisure Park

DUNBARTONSHIRE, WEST
BALLOCH
Lomond Woods Holiday Park

FIFE
ST ANDREWS
Craigtoun Meadows Holiday Park

HIGHLAND
AVIEMORE
Aviemore Glamping

DUROR
Achindarroch Touring Park

FORT WILLIAM
Glen Nevis Caravan & Camping Park

GLENCOE
Invercoe Caravan & Camping Park

LAIRG
Loch Shin Wigwams

LOTHIAN, EAST
DUNBAR
Belhaven Bay Caravan & Camping Park

MUSSELBURGH
Drum Mohr Caravan Park

LOTHIAN, WEST
EAST CALDER
Linwater Caravan Park

LINLITHGOW
Beecraigs Caravan & Camping Site

MORAY
ELGIN
Woodlands Rest

PERTH & KINROSS
BLAIR ATHOLL
Blair Castle Caravan Park

SCOTTISH BORDERS
PEEBLES
Crossburn Caravan Park

STIRLING
TYNDRUM
Strathfillan Wigwam Village

SCOTTISH ISLANDS

ISLE OF ARRAN
KILDONAN
Sealshore Camping and Touring Site
KILMORY
Runach Arainn

ISLE OF MULL
CRAIGNURE
Shieling Holidays

ISLE OF SKYE
EDINBANE
Skye Camping & Caravanning Club Site

WALES

GWYNEDD
BARMOUTH
Trawsdir Touring Caravans & Camping Park

CAERNARFON
Plas Gwyn Caravan & Camping Park

CRICCIETH
Eisteddfa

DINAS DINLLE
Dinlle Caravan Park

PORTHMADOG
Greenacres Holiday Park

MONMOUTHSHIRE
LLANVAIR DISCOED
Penhein Glamping

PEMBROKESHIRE
FISHGUARD
Fishguard Bay Resort

HAVERFORDWEST
Nolton Cross Caravan Park

POWYS
BUILTH WELLS
Fforest Fields Caravan & Camping Park

CHURCHSTOKE
Daisy Bank Caravan Park

LLANDRINDOD WELLS
Disserth Caravan & Camping Park

SWANSEA
OLDWALLS
Oldwalls Gower Glamping

PONTARDDULAIS
River View Touring Park

RHOSSILI
Pitton Cross Caravan & Camping Park

WREXHAM
BRONINGTON
The Little Yurt Meadow

EYTON
Plassey Holiday Park

NORTHERN IRELAND

COUNTY ANTRIM
BALLYMONEY
Drumaheglis Marina & Caravan Park

Index

Entries are listed alphabetically by town name, then campsite name. The following abbreviations have been used: C&C – Caravan & Camping; HP – Holiday Park; CP – Caravan Park; C&C Club – Camping & Caravanning Club Site

Acknowledgments
AA Media would like to thank the following photographers, companies and picture libraries for their assistance in the preparation of this book.
Abbreviations for the picture credits are as follows – (t) top; (b) bottom; (c) centre; (l) left; (r) right; (b/g) background; (AA) AA World Travel Library.

Cover
Background Derek Croucher/Alamy.

Interior
3 AA/J Tims, 4 Rhys Llwyd/Alamy, 6 courtesy of Grouse Hill Caravan Park, 14–15b/g AA/A Burton, 14l courtesy of Vale of Pickering Caravan Park, 14r courtesy of Blair Castle Caravan Park, 15l courtesy of Fforest Fields Caravan & Camping Park, 15r courtesy of Padstow Touring Park, 16–17b/g AA/A Burton, 16l courtesy of Sumners Ponds Fishery & Campsite, 16r courtesy of The Old Brick Kilns, 17l courtesy of Castlerigg Hall Caravan & Camping, 17r courtesy of Cote Ghyll Caravan & Camping Park, 18–19b/g AA/A Burton, 18l courtesy of Rockley Park, 18r courtesy of Haw Wood Farm Caravan Park, 19l courtesy of Drumroamin Farm Camping & Touring, 19r courtesy of Durrell Wildlife Camp, 20 courtesy of Mike Ellis, 23tl courtesy of Mike Ellis, 23tr courtesy of Mike Ellis, 23bl courtesy of Mike Ellis, 23bm courtesy of Mike Ellis, 23br courtesy of Mike Ellis, 24 AA/J Tims, 26 AA/J Tims, 27 AA/J Tims, 29 AA/J Tims, 31tl AA/J Tims, 31tm AA/J Tims, 31tr AA/J Tims, 31ml AA/J Tims, 31mr AA/J Tims, 31br AA/J Tims, 32 AA/J Tims, 35 AA/J Tims, 43 courtesy of Rockley Park, 44 courtesy of Everland, 46 Stewart Smith/Alamy, 48–49 AA/A Burton, 60 AA/R Moss, 58–59 AA/J Welsh, 129 AA/Mockford & Bonetti, 150 AA/A Burton, 159 AA/N Hicks, 171 AA/N Hicks, 182 AA/C Jones, 183 AA/A Burton, 184 AA/A Newey, 199 AA/A Newey, 203 AA/A Burton, 221 AA/J Tims, 223 AA/S McBride, 232 AA/N Setchfield, 238 AA/D Clapp, 252 AA/D Clapp, 253 AA/S Day, 254 AA/T Souter, 280 AA/M Morris, 282 AA/James Tims, 302 AA/T Mackie, 310 AA/J Miller, 312 AA/L Noble, 314 AA/J Miller, 316 AA/J Miller, 320 AA/R Coulam, 326–327 AA/C Jones, 329 AA/J Tims, 344 AA/M Kipling, 346 AA/T Mackie, 354 AA/J Morrison, 364 AA/W Voysey, 367 AA/P Trenchard, 368–369 AA/S Day, 371 AA/J Henderson, 376 AA/S Anderson, 382 AA/S & O Matthews, 390 AA/P Sharpe, 405 AA/A J Hopkins, 406–407 AA/S Lewis, 408 AA/M Adelman, 414 AA/D Santillo, 443 AA/M Bauer, 444–445 AA/C Hill.

Every effort has been made to trace the copyright holders, and we apologise in advance for any unintentional omissions or errors. We would be pleased to apply any corrections in a following edition of this publication.